QUANTITATIVE METHODS FOR BUSINESS 7e

David R. Anderson
University of Cincinnati

Dennis J. Sweeney
University of Cincinnati

Thomas A. Williams
Rochester Institute of Technology

SOUTH-WESTERN College Publishing

An International Thomson Publishing Company

Sponsoring Editor: John R. Szilagyi
Developmental Editor: Alice C. Denny
Production Editor: Deanna Quinn
Production House: BookMasters, Inc.
Cover Designer: Michael H. Stratton
Cover Photo: Photonica
Internal Designer: Michael H. Stratton
Marketing Manager: Steve Scoble

LB60DA
© 1976, 1979, 1986, 1989, 1992, 1995
By West Pub Co., St. Paul MN
© 1998
By SOUTH-WESTERN COLLEGE PUBLISHING
Cincinnati, Ohio

3   4   5   7   8   9   WCBS   6   5   4   3   2   1   0   9   8
Printed in the United States of America

Library of Congress Cataloging-in-Publications Data:

Sweeney, Dennis J.
    Quantitative methods for business / Dennis Sweeney, David R.
  Anderson, Thomas A. Williams. — 7th ed.
     p. cm.
   Rev. ed. of: Quantitative methods for business / David R.
  Anderson, Dennis J Sweeney, Thomas A. Williams. 6th ed. ©1995.
   Includes index.
   ISBN 0-538-87601-8
   1. Management science.   I. Anderson, David Ray, 1941–
II. Williams, Thomas Arthur, 1944–   .   III. Anderson, David Ray,
1941–   Quantitative methods for business.   IV. Title.
T56.A63   1997
658.4′033—dc21   97-16589
                                                           CIP

International Thomson Publishing
South-Western is an ITP Company. The trademark ITP is used under license.

Dedicated to
Krista and Mark
Mark, Linda, Brad, Tim, Scott, and Lisa
Cathy, David, and Kristin

CONTENTS IN BRIEF

CONTENTS

Appendixes

PREFACE

The purpose of this seventh edition, as with previous editions, is to provide undergraduate and graduate students with a conceptual understanding of the role that quantitative methods play in the decision-making process. The text describes the many quantitative methods that have been developed over the years, explains how they work, and shows how the decision maker can apply and interpret them.

We have written this book with the nonmathematician in mind. It is applications oriented and uses the problem scenario approach. In each chapter a problem is described in conjunction with the quantitative procedure being introduced. The development of the quantitative technique or model includes applying it to the problem to generate a solution or recommendation. We have found that this approach helps to motivate the student by demonstrating not only how the procedure works, but also how it can contribute to the decision-making process.

The mathematical prerequisite for this text is a course in algebra. Two chapters on probability and probablility distributions have been included to provide the necessary background for the use of probability in subsequent chapters.

Throughout the text we utilize generally accepted notation for the topic being covered. In this regard students who pursue study beyond the level of this text will have little difficulty reading more advanced material. To assist in further study, a bibliography is included in the backmatter of this book.

Changes in the Seventh Edition

In preparing the seventh edition we were careful to maintain the overall format and approach of the previous editions. However, based on our own classroom experience and suggestions from users of previous editions, we made several significant changes to enhance the content, organization, and readability of the text.

● **Simulation**   Chapter 16 on simulation has been completely rewritten and modernized. The chapter begins with an application involving risk analysis and makes extensive use of spreadsheet output. An inventory simulation model and a waiting line simulation model are also covered. The use of spreadsheets has eliminated the dependence on using random number tables and performing simulation computations by hand. A chapter appendix shows how to use Microsoft Excel for simulation.

● **Markov Processes**   At the request of several users we have added a new Chapter 17 on Markov processes. We show how Markov process models can be used to analyze the effect of brand switching behavior on market share and we show how to compute and interpret steady state probabilities. A section is included on using Markov processes with absorbing states for accounts receivable analysis.

● **The Management Scientist Version 4.0**   The Management Scientist is a software package, developed by the authors, to solve most of the problems encountered in a quantitative methods course. Version 4.0 includes a graphical user interface and runs on Windows 95 and earlier versions of Windows. Easy to use dialog boxes and spreadsheets for data input make the system more user friendly.

● **More Emphasis on Applications and Managerial Interpretation**   We have increased our emphasis on applications and the use of quantitative methods to solve real problems. Several quantitative methods in action vignettes have been added, new case problems have been added in integer programming and simulation, and several new spreadsheet appendixes have been added. Spreadsheet appendixes are now included for 11 chapters. However, the chapters themselves are not dependent on knowledge of any particular computer software.

Other Changes

With this edition we have dropped the chapter on the simplex method and the sections on special purpose algorithms for the transportation and assignment problems. With the wide availability of problem solving software, instructors are now able to de-emphasize algorithms and focus on managerial issues.

Many other changes, suggested by users, have been made. For example, a new problem scenario is used to introduce integer linear programming in Chapter 11. A number of student annotations have been added and about 10 percent of the problems are new to this edition.

Supplementary Materials

As has always been the case, this new edition of *QUANTITATIVE METHODS FOR BUSINESS* has ancillaries that will increase the value of the text to both students and instructors.

● **Study Guide**   The *Study Guide* (ISBN: 0-538-87605-0) by John Loucks of St. Edward's University in Austin, Texas illustrates and reinforces the basic concepts of the text, and helps students organize text materials for review. Each chapter of the study guide includes illustrated problems that are worked out in full as well as problems for the student to do on his or her own. Answers are provided for these problems.

● **Solutions Manual**   The *Solutions Manual* (ISBN: 0-538-87602-6) prepared by the text authors, includes solutions for all textbook problems, and Quantitative Methods in Practice questions. At the request of the instructor, the Solutions Manual can be packaged with the text.

● **The Management Scientist™**   *The Management Scientist Version 4.0 for Windows™ and Windows® 95* (ISBN: 0-314-21646-4) provides 12 computer modules for working through the problems in the course. The software is class tested to run with little or no instructor supervision. Thorough documentation including examples of how to use the software on actual problems accompanies the IBM-compatible software. The software is available free to adopters as a site license; students may purchase the software packaged with the text for a small additional charge.

● **LINDO® 6.0 for Windows**   The new Windows version of LINDO has been completely redesigned to make it more intuitive and easier to use. It has the familiar Windows graphical interface with drop-down menus, dialog boxes and a tool bar for frequently used commands. An educational version of LINDO 6.0 software (ISBN: 0-538-87829-0) is sold at a discounted price when it is packaged with the text.

● **Instructor's Manual and Demonstration Problems**   The *Instructor's Manual* (ISBN: 0-538-87604-2), also prepared by the text authors, includes the topic for each end-of-chapter problem and the solutions to the case problems. Included with the manual are transparency masters for fully worked demonstration problems that parallel examples and end-of-chapter problems in the text.

● **PowerPoint Presentation Files**   Prepared by John Loucks of St. Edward's University, the PowerPoint presentation files (ISBN: 0-538-87607-7) contain a teaching outline that incorporates graphics to help professors create even more stimulating lectures. The Power Point 7.0 slides parallel the information provided in the Study Guide, and may be adapted using PowerPoint software to facilitate classroom use.

● **Test Bank and WESTEST™**   The *Test Bank* (ISBN: 0-538-87603-4) by Constance McLaren of Indiana State University includes multiple choice, true-false, short answer, and computational problems for each chapter. The WESTTEST (ISBN: 0-538-87608-5) computerized testing software allows instructors to create, edit, store and print exams.

Course Outline Flexibility

The text has been designed to give the instructor substantial flexibility in selecting topics to meet specific course needs. Although many variations are possible, the single-quarter and single-semester outlines that follow are illustrative of the options available.

● Possible One-Quarter Outline
Introduction (Chapter 1)
Decision Analysis (Chapters 4 and 5)
Linear Programming (Chapters 7, 8, and 9)
Transportation, Assignment, and Transshipment Problems (Chapter 10)
PERT/CPM (Chapter 12)
Waiting-Line Models (Chapter 15)
Simulation (Chapter 16)
● Possible One-Semester Outline
Introduction (Chapter 1)
Probability Concepts (Chapters 2 and 3)
Decision Analysis (Chapters 4 and 5)
Forecasting (Chapter 6)
Linear Programming (Chapters 7, 8, and 9)
Transportation, Assignment, and Transshipment Problems (Chapter 10)
Integer Linear Programming (Chapter 11)
PERT/CPM (Chapter 12)
Waiting-Line Models (Chapter 15)
Simulation (Chapter 16)

Many other possibilities exist for such a course, depending on course objectives and the student background.

Acknowledgments

We owe a debt to many of our colleagues and friends for their helpful comments and suggestions during the development of this and previous editions. Among these are Donald Adolphson, Shiv Kumar Aggarwah, E. Leonard Arnoff, Uttarayan Bagchi, Edward Baker, Norman Baker, Peter Barr, James Bartos, Stephen Becktold, Richard Beckwith, William Benoit, George Bohlen, Stanley Brooking, Randall Byers, Jeffrey Camm, Rodger D. Carlson, Thomas Case, Sohail Chaudhry, Dennis E. Drinka, John Eatman, Yar Ebadi, Ron Ebert, Margaret Eggers, Richard Ehrhardt, Candice Elliott, Peter Ellis, Lawrence Ettkin, Jim

Evans, Wade Ferguson, Edward Fox, John Flueck, Edward Fisher, Richard Flood, Robert Garfinkel, Roger Glaser, Fabienna Godlewski, Stephen Goodman, Jack Goodwin, Daniel Granor, Barry Griffin, Richard Gunther, Leland Gustafson, Ellie Hakak, Daniel G. Hotard, David Hott, Raymond Jackson, Edward Kao, Birsen Karpak, David Kelton, S. B. Khade, Rebecca Klemm, Bharat Kolluri, Andrew Lai, Darlene Lanier, John Lawrence, Jr., Charles Lienert, Constantine Loucopoulos, Phillip Lowery, Cynthia Ma, Barbara Mardis, T. Majtnay, Wiley Mangum, Prem Mann, R. Kipp Martin, Kamlesh Mathur, Joseph Mazzola, Richard McCready, Patrick McKeown, Constance McLaren, Edward Minieka, Alan Neebe, Susan Pariseau, Barnett Parker, David Pentico, Gary Pickett, Leonard Presby, Maurice Queyranne, Harold Rahmlow, B. Madhusudan Rao, Jeffrey L. Ringuest, Douglass Rippy, Richard Rosenthal, L. W. Shell, Wayland Smith, Jayavel Sounderpandian, Carol Stamm, Willban Terpening, Richard A. Toelle, Pitner Traughber, William Truscott, William Verdini, James Vigen, Leonard Volet, Craig Waring, Robert Winkler, Ed Winkofsky, Bruce Woodworth, M. Zafer Takin, Neba L'Abbe Wu, and Cathleen Zucco.

Our associates from organizations who supplied the Quantitative Methods in Practice applications made a major contribution to the text. These individuals are cited in a credit line on the first page of each application.

We are also indebted to our editors Alice Denny and John Szilagyi and others at South-Western College Publishing for their editorial counsel and support during the preparation of this text.

David R. Anderson
Dennis J. Sweeney
Thomas A. Williams

David R. Anderson.   David R. Anderson is Professor of Quantitative Analysis in the College of Business Administration at the University of Cincinnati. Born in Grand Forks, North Dakota, he earned his B.S., M.S., and Ph.D. degrees from Purdue University. Professor Anderson has served as Associate Dean of the College of Business Administration. In addition, he was the coordinator of the College's first Executive Program.

At the University of Cincinnati, Professor Anderson has taught introductory statistics for business students as well as graduate level courses in regression analysis, multivariate analysis, and management science. He has also taught statistical courses at the Department of Labor in Washington, D.C. He has been honored with nominations and awards for excellence in teaching and excellence in service to student organizations.

Professor Anderson has coauthored six textbooks in the areas of statistics, management science, linear programming, and production and operations management. He is an active consultant in the field of sampling and statistical methods.

Dennis J. Sweeney.   Dennis J. Sweeney is Professor of Quantitative Analysis at the University of Cincinnati. Born in Des Moines, Iowa, he earned a B.S.B.A. degree from Drake University, graduating summa cum laude. He received his M.B.A. and D.B.A. degrees from Indiana University where he was an NDEA Fellow. Since receiving his doctorate in 1971, Professor Sweeney has spent all but 2 years at the University of Cincinnati. During 1978–79, he spent a year working in the management science group at Procter & Gamble; during 1981–82, he was a visiting professor at Duke University. Professor Sweeney served 5 years as Head of the Department of Quantitative Analysis and 4 years as Associate Dean at the University of Cincinnati.

Professor Sweeney has published over 30 articles in the general area of management science. The National Science Foundation, IBM, Procter & Gamble, Federated Department Stores, and Cincinnati Gas & Electric have funded his research, which has been published in *Management Science, Operations Research, Mathematical Programming, Decision Sciences,* and other journals.

Professor Sweeney has coauthored six textbooks in the areas of statistics, management science, linear programming, and production and operations management.

Thomas A. Williams.   Thomas A. Williams is Professor of Management Science in the College of Business at Rochester Institute of Technology. Born in Elmira, New York, he earned his B.S. degree at Clarkson University. He did his graduate work at Rensselaer Polytechnic Institute, where he received his M.S. and Ph.D. degrees.

Before joining the College of Business at RIT, Professor Williams served for 7 years as a faculty member in the College of Business Administration at the University of Cincinnati, where he developed the undergraduate program in Information Systems and then served as its coordinator. At RIT he was the first chairman of the Decision Sciences Department. He teaches courses in management science and statistics, as well as more advanced courses in regression and decision analysis.

Professor Williams is the coauthor of seven textbooks in the areas of management science, statistics, production and operations management, and mathematics. He has been a consultant for numerous Fortune 500 companies and has worked on projects ranging from the use of elementary data analysis to the development of large-scale regression models. His current research focuses on the application of total quality management in an academic setting.

INTRODUCTION

This book is concerned with the use of quantitative methods to assist in decision making. The emphasis is not on the methods themselves, but rather on how they can contribute to better decisions. Our approach is to describe situations in which quantitative methods have been applied successfully and then show how a manager can use the methods to make better decisions. Brief descriptions of successful applications of quantitative methods are scattered throughout the book; these are entitled Q. M. in Action. Also at the end of most chapters is a write-up describing Quantitative Methods in Practice in some organizations.

Various names have been given to the body of knowledge involving quantitative approaches to decision making. The ones most commonly used are *management science* (MS), *operations research* (OR), and *decision science*. All are concerned with rational approaches to decision making based on the scientific method. The material described in this book is the core body of knowledge in these fields.

The scientific management revolution of the early 1900s, initiated by Frederic W. Taylor, provided the foundation for the use of quantitative methods in management. But modern usage of quantitative methods is generally considered to have originated during the World War II period, when teams were formed to deal with strategic and tactical problems faced by the military. These teams, which often consisted of people with diverse specialties (e.g., mathematicians, engineers, and behavioral scientists), were joined together to solve a common problem through the utilization of the scientific method. After the war, many of these team members continued their research on quantitative approaches to decision making.

Two developments that occurred during the post-World War II period led to the growth and use of quantitative methods in nonmilitary applications. First, continued research resulted in numerous methodological developments. Probably the most significant development was the discovery by George Dantzig, in 1947, of the simplex method for solving linear programming problems. Many more methodological developments followed, and in 1957 the first book on operations research was published by Churchman, Ackoff, and Arnoff.[1]

Concurrently with these methodological developments, a virtual explosion in computing power was made available through digital computers. Computers enabled practitioners to use the methodological advances to solve successfully a large variety of problems. The computer technology explosion continues; personal computers are now more powerful than the mainframe computers of the 1980s. Today, variants of the post-World War II methodological developments are being used on personal computers to solve problems larger than those solved on mainframe computers in the early 1990s.

1.1   PROBLEM SOLVING AND DECISION MAKING

Problem solving can be defined as the process of identifying a difference between the actual and the desired state of affairs and then taking action to resolve the difference. For problems important enough to justify the time and effort of careful analysis, the problem-solving process involves the following seven steps:

1. Identify and define the problem.
2. Determine the set of alternative solutions.
3. Determine the criterion or criteria that will be used to evaluate the alternatives.
4. Evaluate the alternatives.
5. Choose an alternative.
6. Implement the selected alternative (the decision).
7. Evaluate the results, and determine if a satisfactory solution has been obtained.

Decision making is the term generally associated with the first five steps of the problem-solving process. Thus, the first step of decision making is to identify and define the problem. Decision making ends with the choosing of an alternative, which is the act of making the decision.

Let us consider the following example of a decision-making process. For the moment assume that you will be graduating from college in the next few months, that you have completed the interviewing process, and that you have been lucky enough to receive job offers from four companies. You are currently unemployed and would like a position that will lead to a satisfying career.

Once the problem of obtaining a position that will lead to a satisfying career has been defined, the next step in the decision-making process is to identify the set of alternatives available. Suppose that you have job offers from companies located in Rochester, New York; Dallas, Texas; Greensboro, North Carolina; and Pittsburgh, Pennsylvania. Thus, the alternatives for your decision problem can be stated as follows:

1. Accept the position in Rochester, New York.
2. Accept the position in Dallas, Texas.

---

1. C. W. Churchman, R. L. Ackoff, and E. L. Arnoff, *Introduction to Operations Research* (New York: Wiley, 1957).

3. Accept the position in Greensboro, North Carolina.
4. Accept the position in Pittsburgh, Pennsylvania.

The next step of the decision-making process involves determining the criteria that will be used to evaluate the four alternatives. Obviously, the starting salary is going to be a factor of some importance. If this were the only criterion of importance to you, the alternative selected as "best" would be the one with the highest starting salary. Problems in which the objective is to find the best solution with respect to one criterion are referred to as **single-criterion decision problems.**

Suppose that you have also concluded that the potential for advancement and the location of the job are two other criteria of major importance. Thus, the three criteria in your decision problem are starting salary, potential for advancement, and location. Problems that involve more than one criterion are referred to as **multicriteria decision problems.**

The next step of the decision-making process is to evaluate each of the alternatives with respect to each criterion. For example, evaluating each alternative relative to the starting salary criterion is done simply by recording the starting salary for each job alternative. Evaluating each alternative with respect to the potential for advancement and the location of the job is more difficult to do, however, since these evaluations are based primarily on subjective factors that are often difficult to quantify. Suppose that for now you have decided to measure potential for advancement and job location by rating each of these criteria as poor, fair, average, good, or excellent and that the data you have compiled are shown in Table 1.1.

You are now ready to make a choice from the available alternatives. What makes this choice so difficult is that the criteria are probably not all equally important, and no one alternative is "best" with regard to all criteria. Although we will present a method for dealing with situations like this later in the text, for now let us suppose that after a careful evaluation of the data in Table 1.1, you have decided to select alternative 3 (Greensboro); alternative 3 is thus referred to as the **decision.**

At this point in time, the decision-making process is complete. In summary, we see that this process involved five steps:

1. Define the problem.
2. Identify the alternatives.
3. Determine the criteria.
4. Evaluate the alternatives.
5. Choose an alternative.

Note that missing from this list are the last two steps in the problem-solving process: implementing the selected alternative and evaluating the results to determine whether a satisfactory solution has been obtained. This omission is not meant to diminish the importance of each of these activities, but to emphasize the more limited scope of the term **decision**

Table 1.1	DATA FOR THE JOB EVALUATION DECISION-MAKING PROBLEM		
Alternative	Starting Salary	Potential Advancement	Job Location
Rochester	$28,500	Average	Average
Dallas	$26,000	Excellent	Good
Greensboro	$26,000	Good	Excellent
Pittsburgh	$27,000	Average	Good

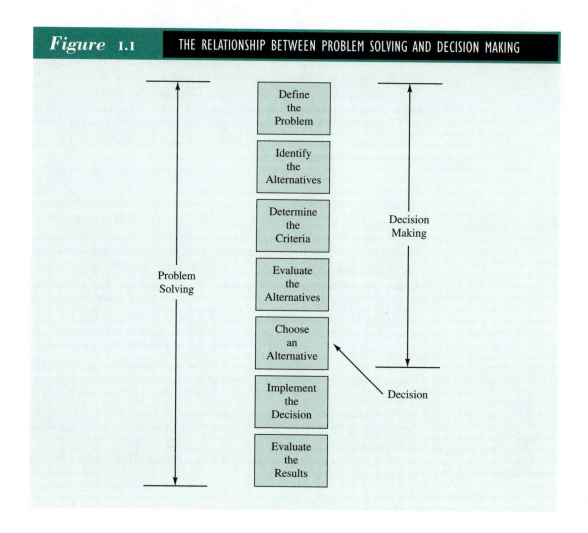

Figure 1.1   THE RELATIONSHIP BETWEEN PROBLEM SOLVING AND DECISION MAKING

making as compared to the term **problem solving.** Figure 1.1 summarizes the relationship between these two concepts.

1.2   QUANTITATIVE ANALYSIS AND DECISION MAKING

Consider the flowchart presented in Figure 1.2. Note that we have combined the first three steps of the decision-making process under the heading of "Structuring the Problem" and the latter two steps under the heading "Analyzing the Problem." Let us now consider in more detail how to carry out the set of activities that make up the decision-making process.

Figure 1.3 shows that the analysis phase of the decision-making process may take on two basic forms: qualitative and quantitative. Qualitative analysis is based primarily on the manager's judgment and experience; it includes the manager's intuitive "feel" for the problem and is more art than a science. If the manager has had experience with similar problems, or if the problem is relatively simple, heavy emphasis may be placed upon a qualitative analysis. However, if the manager has had little experience with similar prob-

Figure 1.2 AN ALTERNATE CLASSIFICATION OF THE DECISION-MAKING PROCESS

Figure 1.3 THE ROLE OF QUALITATIVE AND QUANTITATIVE ANALYSIS

lems, or if the problem is sufficiently complex, then a quantitative analysis of the problem can be an especially important consideration in the manager's final decision.

When using the quantitative approach, an analyst will concentrate on the quantitative facts or data associated with the problem and develop mathematical expressions that describe the objectives, constraints, and other relationships that exist in the problem. Then, by using one or more quantitative methods, the analyst will make a recommendation based on the quantitative aspects of the problem.

While skills in the qualitative approach are inherent in the manager and usually increase with experience, the skills of the quantitative approach can be learned only by studying and using quantitative methods. A manager can increase decision-making effectiveness by learning more about quantitative methodology and by better understanding its contribution to the decision-making process. The manager who is knowledgeable in quantitative decision-making procedures is in a much better position to compare and evaluate the qualitative and quantitative sources of recommendations and ultimately to combine the two sources in order to make the best possible decision.

Quantitative methods are especially helpful with large, complex problems. For example, in the coordination of the thousands of tasks associated with landing the Apollo 11 safely on the moon, quantitative techniques helped to ensure that over 300,000 pieces of work performed by over 400,000 people were integrated smoothly.

The box in Figure 1.3 entitled "Quantitative Analysis" encompasses most of the subject matter of this text. We will consider a managerial problem, introduce the appropriate quantitative methodology, and then develop the recommended decision.

In closing this section, let us briefly state some of the reasons that a quantitative approach might be used in the decision-making process:

You should understand why quantitative approaches might be needed in a particular problem. Try Problem 4.

1. The problem is complex, and the manager cannot develop a good solution without the aid of quantitative analysis.
2. The problem is very important (e.g., a great deal of money is involved), and the manager desires a thorough qualitative and quantitative analysis before attempting to make a decision.
3. The problem is new, and the manager has no previous experience from which to draw.
4. The problem is repetitive, and the manager saves time and effort by relying on computerized quantitative procedures to make routine decision recommendations.

1.3 QUANTITATIVE ANALYSIS

From Figure 1.3 we see that quantitative analysis begins once the problem has been structured. It usually takes imagination, teamwork, and considerable effort to transform a rather general problem description into a well-defined problem that can be approached via quantitative analysis. The more the analyst is involved in the process of structuring the problem, the more likely the ensuing quantitative analysis will make an important contribution to the decision process.

When both the manager and the quantitative analyst agree that the problem has been adequately structured, work can then begin on developing a model to represent the problem mathematically. Solution procedures can then be employed to find the best solution for the model. This best solution for the model then becomes a recommendation to the decision maker. The process of developing and solving models is the essence of the quantitative analysis process. Let's see how it works.

Model Development

Models are representations of real objects or situations. These models can be presented in various forms. For example, a scale model of an airplane is a representation of a real airplane. Similarly, a child's toy truck is a model of a real truck. The model airplane and toy truck are examples of models that are physical replicas of real objects. In modeling terminology, physical replicas are referred to as **iconic models.**

A second classification of models includes those that are physical in form but do not have the same physical appearance as the object being modeled. Such models are referred to as **analog models.** The speedometer of an automobile is an analog model; the position of the needle on the dial represents the speed of the automobile. A thermometer is another analog model representing temperature.

A third classification of models—the type we will primarily be studying—includes those that represent a problem by a system of symbols and mathematical relationships or expressions. Such models are referred to as **mathematical models** and are a critical part of any quantitative approach to decision making. For example, the total profit from the sale of a product can be determined by multiplying the profit per unit by the quantity sold. If we let x represent the number of units sold and P the total profit, then, with a profit of $10 per unit, the following mathematical model defines the total profit earned by selling x units:

$$P = 10x \qquad (1.1)$$

The purpose, or value, of any model is that it enables us to make inferences about the real situation by studying and analyzing the model. For example, an airplane designer might test an iconic model of a new airplane in a wind tunnel to learn about the potential flying characteristics of the full-size airplane. Similarly, a mathematical model may be used to make inferences about how much profit will be earned if a specified quantity of a particular product is sold. According to the mathematical model of equation (1.1), we would expect that selling three units of the product ($x = 3$) would provide a profit of $P = 10(3) = \$30$.

In general, experimenting with models requires less time and is less expensive than experimenting with a real object or situation. A model airplane is certainly quicker and less expensive to build and study than a full-size airplane. Similarly, the mathematical model in · equation (1.1) allows a quick identification of profit expectations without actually requiring the manager to produce and sell x units. Models also have the advantage of reducing the risk associated with experimenting with a real situation. In particular, bad designs or bad decisions that cause a model airplane to crash or a mathematical model to project a $10,000 loss can be avoided in a real situation.

The value of model-based conclusions and decisions is dependent on how well a model represents a real situation. The more closely a scale model represents a real airplane, the more accurate the conclusions and predictions will be. Similarly, the more closely a mathematical model represents a company's true profit–volume relationship, the more accurate the profit projections will be.

Since this text deals with quantitative analysis based on mathematical models, let us look more closely at the mathematical modeling process. When initially considering a managerial problem, we usually find that the problem structuring phase leads to a specific objective, such as maximization of profit or minimization of cost, and possibly a set of restrictions or **constraints,** such as production capacities. The success of the mathematical model and quantitative approach will depend heavily on how accurately the objective and constraints can be expressed in terms of mathematical equations or relationships.

A mathematical expression that describes the problem's objective is referred to as the **objective function.** For example, the profit equation $P = 10x$ would be an objective function for a firm attempting to maximize profit. A production capacity constraint would be necessary if, for instance, 5 hours are required to produce each unit and only 40 hours are available per week. Let x indicate the number of units produced each week. The production time constraint is given by

$$5x \le 40 \qquad (1.2)$$

The value of $5x$ is the total time required to produce x units; the symbol $\le$ indicates that the production time required must be less than or equal to the 40 hours available.

The decision problem or question is the following: How many units of the product should be scheduled each week to maximize profit? A complete mathematical model for this simple production problem is

Maximize $\quad P = 10x \quad$ objective function
subject to (s.t.)

$$\left. \begin{array}{c} 5x \le 40 \\ x \ge 0 \end{array} \right\} \text{constraints}$$

Herbert A. Simon, a Nobel prize winner in economics and an expert in decision making, said that a mathematical model does not have to be exact; it just has to be close enough to provide better results than can be obtained by common sense.

The $x \geq 0$ constraint requires the production quantity x to be greater than or equal to zero, which simply recognizes the fact that manufacturing a negative number of units is not possible. The optimal solution to this model can be easily calculated and is given by $x = 8$, with an associated profit of $80. This model is an example of a linear programming model. In subsequent chapters we will discuss more complicated mathematical models and learn how to solve them in situations where the answers are not nearly so obvious.

In the preceding mathematical model, the profit per unit ($10), the production time per unit (5 hours), and the production capacity (40 hours) are environmental factors that are not under the control of the manager or decision maker. Such environmental factors, which can affect both the objective function and the constraints, are referred to as **uncontrollable inputs** to the model. Inputs that are controlled or determined by the decision maker are referred to as **controllable inputs** to the model. In the example given, the production quantity x is the controllable input to the model. Controllable inputs are the decision alternatives specified by the manager and thus are also referred to as the **decision variables** of the model.

Once all controllable and uncontrollable inputs are specified, the objective function and constraints can be evaluated, and the output of the model determined. In this sense, the output of the model is simply the projection of what would happen if those particular environmental factors and decisions occurred in the real situation. A flowchart of how controllable and uncontrollable inputs are transformed by the mathematical model into output is shown in Figure 1.4. A similar flowchart showing the specific details of the production model is shown in Figure 1.5.

As stated earlier, the uncontrollable inputs are those the decision maker cannot influence. The specific controllable and uncontrollable inputs of a model depend on the particular problem or decision-making situation. In the production problem, the production time available (40), is an uncontrollable input. However, if it were possible to hire more employees or use overtime, the number of hours of production time would become a controllable input and therefore a decision variable in the model.

Uncontrollable inputs can either be known exactly or be uncertain and subject to variation. If all uncontrollable inputs to a model are known and cannot vary, the model is referred to as a **deterministic model.** Corporate income tax rates are not under the influence of the manager and thus constitute an uncontrollable input in many decision models. Since these rates are known and fixed (at least in the short run), a mathematical model with corporate income tax rates as the only uncontrollable input would be a deterministic model. The distinguishing feature of a deterministic model is that the uncontrollable input values are known in advance.

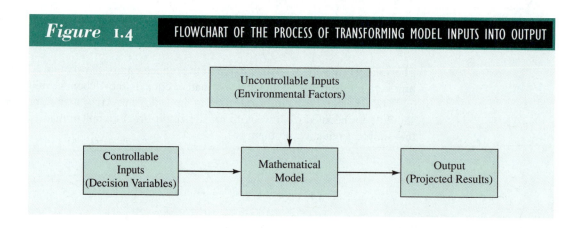

Figure 1.4   FLOWCHART OF THE PROCESS OF TRANSFORMING MODEL INPUTS INTO OUTPUT

Figure 1.5 — FLOWCHART FOR THE PRODUCTION MODEL

If any of the uncontrollable inputs are uncertain and subject to variation, the model is referred to as a **stochastic** or **probabilistic model.** An uncontrollable input to many production planning models is demand for the product. Since future demand may be any of a range of values, a mathematical model that treats demand with uncertainty would be called a *stochastic model.* In the production model, the number of hours of production time required per unit, the total hours available, and the unit profit were all uncontrollable inputs. Since the uncontrollable inputs were all known to take on fixed values, the model is deterministic. If, however, the number of hours of production time per unit could vary from 3 to 6 hours depending on the quality of the raw material, the model would be stochastic. The distinguishing feature of a stochastic model is that the value of the output cannot be determined even if the value of the controllable input is known because the specific values of the uncontrollable inputs are unknown. In this respect, stochastic models are often more difficult to analyze.

Data Preparation

Another step in the quantitative analysis of a problem is the preparation of the data required by the model. Data in this sense refer to the values of the uncontrollable inputs to the model. All uncontrollable inputs or data must be specified before we can analyze the model and recommend a decision.

In the production model, the values of the uncontrollable inputs or data were $10 per unit for profit, 5 hours per unit for production time, and 40 hours for production capacity. In the development of the model, these data values were known and incorporated into the model as it was being developed. If the model is relatively small and the uncontrollable input values or data required are few, the quantitative analyst will probably combine model development and data preparation into one step. That is, in these situations the data values are inserted as the equations of the mathematical model are developed.

However, in many mathematical modeling situations, the data or uncontrollable input values are not readily available. In these situations the quantitative analyst may know that the model will need profit per unit, production time, and production capacity data, but the values will not be known until the accounting, production, and engineering departments can be consulted. Rather than attempting to collect the required data as the model is being developed, the analyst will usually adopt a general notation for the model development step and then a separate data preparation step will be performed to obtain the uncontrollable input values required by the model.

Using the general notation

$$c = \text{profit per unit}$$
$$a = \text{production time in hours per unit}$$
$$b = \text{production capacity in hours}$$

the model development step of the production problem would result in the following general model:

$$\text{Max} \quad cx$$
$$\text{s.t.}$$
$$ax \leq b$$
$$x \geq 0$$

A separate data preparation step to identify the values for *c, a,* and *b* would then be necessary to complete the model.

Many inexperienced quantitative analysts assume that once the problem has been defined and a general model developed, the problem is essentially solved. These individuals tend to believe that data preparation is a trivial step in the process and can be easily handled by clerical staff. Actually, this assumption could not be farther from the truth, especially with large-scale models that have numerous data input values. For example, a moderate-size linear programming model with 50 decision variables and 25 constraints could have over 1300 data elements that must be identified in the data preparation step. The time required to prepare these data and the possibility of data collection errors will make the data preparation step a critical part of the quantitative analysis process. Because a fairly large database is needed to support a mathematical model, often information systems specialists also become involved in the data preparation step.

Model Solution

Once the model development and data preparation steps have been completed, we can proceed to the model solution step. In this step, the analyst will attempt to identify the values of the decision variables that provide the "best" output for the model. The specific decision-variable value or values providing the "best" output will be referred to as the **optimal solution** for the model. For the production problem, the model solution step involves finding the value of the production quantity decision variable *x* that maximizes profit while not causing a violation of the production capacity constraint.

One procedure that might be used in the model solution step involves a trial-and-error approach in which the model is used to test and evaluate various decision alternatives. In the production model, this would mean testing and evaluating the model under various production quantities or values of *x*. Referring to Figure 1.5, note that we could input trial values for *x* and check the corresponding output for projected profit and satisfaction of the production capacity constraint. If a particular decision alternative does not satisfy one or more of the model constraints, the decision alternative is rejected as being an **infeasible solution** regardless of the objective function value. If all constraints are satisfied, the decision alternative is a **feasible solution** and a candidate for the "best" solution or recommended decision. Through this trial-and-error process of evaluating selected decision alternatives, a decision maker can identify a good—and possibly the best—feasible solution to the problem. This solution would then be the recommended decision for the problem.

Table 1.2 shows the results of a trial-and-error approach to solving the production model of Figure 1.5. The recommended decision is a production quantity of 8 since the feasible solution with the highest projected profit occurs at $x = 8$.

While the trial-and-error solution process is often acceptable and can provide valuable information for the manager, it has the drawbacks of not necessarily providing the best solution and of being inefficient in terms of requiring numerous calculations if many decision alternatives are tried. Thus, quantitative analysts have developed special solution procedures for many models that are much more efficient than the trial-and-error approach. Throughout this text, you will be introduced to solution procedures that are applicable to the specific mathematical models that will be formulated. While some relatively small models or problems can be solved by hand computations, most practical applications require the use of a computer.

It is important to realize that the model development and model solution steps are not completely separable. While an analyst will want to develop an accurate model or representation of the actual problem situation, the analyst will also want to be able to find a solution to the model. If we approach the model development step by attempting to find the most accurate and realistic mathematical model, we may find the model so large and complex that it is impossible to obtain a solution. In this case, a simpler and perhaps more easily understood model with a readily available solution procedure is preferred even if the recommended solution is only a rough approximation of the best decision. As you learn more about quantitative solution procedures, you will have a better idea of the types of mathematical models that can be developed and solved.

After a model solution has been obtained, both the quantitative analyst and the manager will be interested in determining how good the solution really is. While the analyst has undoubtedly taken many precautions to develop a realistic model, often the goodness or accuracy of the model cannot be assessed until model solutions are generated. Model testing and validation are frequently conducted with relatively small "test" problems that have known or at least expected solutions. If the model generates the expected solutions, and if other output information appears correct, the go-ahead may be given to use the model on the full-scale problem. However, if the model test and validation identify potential problems or inaccuracies inherent in the model, corrective action, such as model modification

You should now understand the concept of a mathematical model and what is referred to as the optimal solution to the model. Try Problem 8.

Table 1.2	TRIAL-AND-ERROR SOLUTION FOR THE PRODUCTION MODEL OF FIGURE 1.5		
Decision Alternative (Production Quantity) x	**Projected Profit**	**Total Hours of Production**	**Feasible Solution? (capacity = 40)**
0	0	0	Yes
2	20	10	Yes
4	40	20	Yes
6	60	30	Yes
8	80	40	Yes
10	100	50	No
12	120	60	No

and/or collection of more accurate input data, may be taken. Whatever the corrective action, the model solution will not be used in practice until the model has satisfactorily passed testing and validation.

Report Generation

An important part of the quantitative analysis process is the preparation of managerial reports based on the model's solution. Referring to Figure 1.3, we see that the solution based on the quantitative analysis of a problem is one of the inputs the manager considers before making a final decision. Thus, it is essential that the results of the model appear in a managerial report that can be easily understood by the decision maker. The report should include the recommended decision and other pertinent information about the results that may be helpful to the decision maker.

A Note Regarding Implementation

As discussed in Section 1.2, the manager is responsible for integrating the quantitative solution with qualitative considerations in order to make the best possible decision. After doing this, the manager must oversee the implementation and follow-up evaluation of the decision. During the implementation and follow-up, the manager should continue to monitor the contribution of the model. At times, this process may lead to requests for model expansion or refinement that will cause the quantitative analyst to return to one of the earlier steps of the quantitative analysis process.

Successful implementation of results is of critical importance to the quantitative analyst as well as the manager. If the results of the quantitative analysis process are not correctly implemented, the entire effort may be of no value. It doesn't take too many unsuccessful implementations before the quantitative analyst is out of work. Because implementation often requires people to do things differently, it often meets with resistance. People want to know, "What's wrong with the way we've been doing it?" and so on. One of the most effective ways to ensure a successful implementation is to secure as much user involvement as possible throughout the modeling process. A user who feels involved in identifying the problem and developing the solution is much more likely to enthusiastically implement the results. The success rate for implementing the results of a quantitative analysis project is much greater for those projects in which there has been extensive user involvement.

1.4   MODELS OF COST, REVENUE, AND PROFIT

Some of the most basic quantitative models arising in business and economic applications are those involving the relationship between a volume variable—such as production volume or sales volume—and cost, revenue, and profit. Through the use of these models, a manager can determine the projected cost, revenue, and/or profit associated with an established production quantity or a forecasted sales volume. Financial planning, production planning, sales quotas, and other areas of decision making can benefit from such cost, revenue, and profit models.

Cost and Volume Models

The cost of manufacturing or producing a product is a function of the volume produced. This cost can usually be defined as a sum of two costs: fixed cost and variable cost. **Fixed**

cost is the portion of the total cost that does not depend on the production volume; this cost remains the same no matter how much is produced. **Variable cost,** on the other hand, is the portion of the total cost that is dependent on and varies with the production volume. For example, suppose that the setup cost for a production line is $3000. This is a fixed cost that is incurred regardless of the number of units eventually produced. In addition, suppose that variable labor and material costs are $2 for each unit produced. The cost-volume model for producing x units would be written as

$$C(x) = 3000 + 2x \qquad (1.3)$$

where

$$x = \text{production volume in units}$$
$$C(x) = \text{total cost of producing } x \text{ units}$$

Use of the model in equation (1.3) will determine the total production cost once the production volume is established. For example, a production volume of $x = 1200$ units would result in a total cost of $C(1200) = 3000 + 2(1200) = \$5400$.

Marginal cost is defined as the rate of change of the total cost with respect to volume. That is, it is the cost increase associated with a one-unit increase in the production volume. In the cost model of equation (1.3), we see that the total cost $C(x)$ will increase by $2 for each unit increase in the production volume. Thus, the marginal cost is $2. With more complex total cost models, marginal cost may depend on the production volume. In such cases, we could have marginal cost increasing or decreasing with the production volume x.

Revenue and Volume Models

A manager will also want information on the projected revenue associated with selling a specified number of units. Thus, a model of the relationship between revenue and volume is also needed. Suppose that the product in the preceding example sells for $5 per unit. The model for total revenue can be written as

$$R(x) = 5x \qquad (1.4)$$

where

$$x = \text{sales volume in units}$$
$$R(x) = \text{total revenue associated with selling } x \text{ units}$$

Marginal revenue is defined as the rate of change of total revenue with respect to sales volume. That is, it is the increase in total revenue resulting from a one-unit increase in sales volume. In the model of equation (1.4), we see that the marginal revenue is $5. In this case, marginal revenue is constant and does not vary with the sales volume. With more complex models, we may find that marginal revenue increases or decreases as the sales volume x increases.

Profit and Volume Models

One of the most important criteria for managerial decision making is profit. Managers need to be able to know the profit implications of their decisions. If we assume that we will only produce what can be sold, the production volume and sales volume will be equal. We can combine equations (1.3) and (1.4) to develop a profit-volume model that will determine profit associated with a specified production-sales volume. Since total profit is total revenue minus total cost, the following model provides the profit associated with producing and selling x units:

$$P(x) = R(x) - C(x) \tag{1.5}$$
$$= 5x - (3000 + 2x) = -3000 + 3x$$

Thus, the model for profit $P(x)$ can be derived from the models of the revenue-volume and cost-volume relationships.

Break-Even Analysis

Using equation (1.5), we can now determine the profit associated with any production volume x. For example, suppose a demand forecast indicates that 500 units of the product can be sold. The decision to produce and sell the 500 units results in a projected profit of

$$P(500) = -3000 + 3(500) = -1500$$

In other words, a loss of \$1500 is predicted. If sales are expected to be 500 units, the manager may decide against producing the product. However, a demand forecast of 1800 units would show a projected profit of

$$P(1800) = -3000 + 3(1800) = 2400$$

This profit may be enough to justify proceeding with the production and sale of the product.

We see that a volume of 500 units will yield a loss, whereas a volume of 1800 provides a profit. The volume that results in total revenue equaling total cost (providing \$0 profit) is called the **break-even point.** If the break-even point is known, a manager can quickly infer that a volume above the break-even point will result in a profit, while a volume below the break-even point will result in a loss. Thus, the break-even point for a product provides valuable information for a manager who must make a yes/no decision concerning production of the product.

Let us now return to the example and show how the profit model in equation (1.5) can be used to compute the break-even point. The break-even point can be found by setting the profit expression equal to zero and solving for the production volume. Using equation (1.5), we have

$$P(x) = -3000 + 3x = 0$$
$$3x = 3000$$
$$x = 1000$$

You should now be able to determine the break-even point for a quantitative model. Try Problem 15.

With this information, we know that production and sales of the product must be at least 1000 units before a profit can be expected. The graphs of the total cost model, the total revenue model, and the location of the break-even point are shown in Figure 1.6.

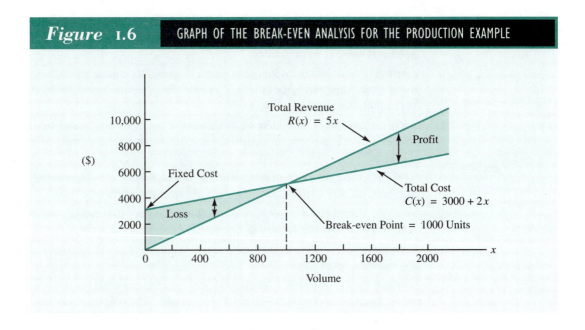

Figure 1.6 GRAPH OF THE BREAK-EVEN ANALYSIS FOR THE PRODUCTION EXAMPLE

1.5 QUANTITATIVE METHODS IN PRACTICE

In this section we present a brief overview of the quantitative methods covered in this text. We will then present the results of surveys that show which techniques have been used most frequently in practice and what needs to be done to enable you to successfully utilize quantitative approaches throughout your career.

Quantitative Methods

The following quantitative methods are covered in this text.

Linear Programming   Linear programming is a problem-solving approach that has been developed for situations involving maximizing or minimizing a linear function subject to linear constraints that limit the degree to which the objective can be pursued. The production model developed in Section 1.3 (see Figure 1.5) is an example of a simple linear programming model.

Integer Linear Programming   Integer linear programming is an approach used for problems that can be set up as linear programs with the additional requirement that some or all of the decision recommendations be integer values.

Project Scheduling: PERT/CPM   In many situations, managers are responsible for planning, scheduling, and controlling projects that consist of numerous separate jobs or tasks performed by a variety of departments, individuals, and so forth. The PERT (Program Evaluation and Review Technique) and CPM (Critical Path Method) techniques help managers carry out their project scheduling responsibilities.

Inventory Models   Inventory models are used by managers faced with the dual problems of maintaining sufficient inventories to meet demand for goods and, at the same time, incurring the lowest possible inventory holding costs.

Waiting-Line or Queueing Models   Waiting-line or queueing models have been developed to help managers understand and make better decisions concerning the operation of systems involving waiting lines.

Computer Simulation   Computer simulation is a technique used to model the operation of a system. This technique employs a computer program to model the operation and perform simulation computations.

Decision Analysis   Decision analysis can be used to determine optimal strategies in situations involving several decision alternatives and an uncertain or risk-filled pattern of events.

Goal Programming   Goal programming is a technique for solving multicriteria decision problems, usually within the framework of linear programming.

Analytic Hierarchy Process   This multicriteria decision-making technique permits the inclusion of subjective factors in arriving at a recommended decision.

Forecasting   Forecasting methods are techniques that can be used to predict future aspects of a business operation.

Markov-Process Models   Markov-process models are useful in studying the evolution of certain systems over repeated trials. For example, Markov processes have been used to describe the probability that a machine, functioning in one period, will function or break down in another period.

Methods Used Most Frequently

A study of surveys by Lane, Mansour, and Harpell indicated which quantitative methods practitioners and educators have found to be the most important and most useful.[2] The three methods that stand out as consistently being at the top of the list include statistical methods, linear programming, and simulation. The general preferences or ranking of quantitative methods are shown in Table 1.3. Multicriteria decision problems including goal programming and the analytic hierarchy process, forecasting and Markov-process models were not specifically mentioned in the Lane, Mansour, and Harpell study but are additional quantitative methods you will learn about in this text.

In a review of 12 company surveys and 3 practitioner surveys, Morgan provided further support for linear programming, simulation, and network models including PERT/CPM as being among the most frequently used quantitative methods.[3] More importantly, Morgan concluded that (1) any firm just beginning to use quantitative methods should locate analysts in functional areas, not in centralized units; (2) the initial use of quantitative methods should focus on the more frequently used and more useful methods; and (3) the barriers to the use of quantitative methods can best be removed by increasing the manager's understanding of quantitative methods. Furthermore, to gain the confidence and support of top management, quantitative analysts must learn to sell their approaches and solutions, with particular emphasis placed on improving communications with managers.

Helping to bridge the gap between the manager and the quantitative analyst is a major focus of this text. As authors and quantitative practitioners, we want to help develop an understanding of what quantitative methods are, how they are used, and, most importantly, how they can assist managers in making better decisions.

---

2. M. S. Lane, A. H. Mansour, and J. L. Harpell, "Operations Research Techniques," *Interfaces*, 23:2, March–April 1993, pp. 63–68.

3. C. L. Morgan, "A Survey of MS/OR Surveys," *Interfaces* 19:6, November–December, 1989, pp. 95–103.

Table 1.3	A RANKING OF THE IMPORTANCE AND USEFULNESS OF QUANTITATIVE METHODS

Methodology

Statistical Methods
Mathematical Programming Methods
   Linear Programming
   Integer Linear Programming
Simulation
Network Models (Including PERT/CPM)
Decision Analysis
Waiting Line Models
Inventory Models
Dynamic Programming

N O T E S and Comments

1. Operations research analyst is listed by the Bureau of Labor Statistics as one of the fastest growing occupations for careers requiring a bachelor's degree; they predict a growth from 57,000 jobs in 1990 to 100,000 jobs in 2005, an increase of 73%.

2. The Institute for Operations Research and the Management Sciences (INFORMS) and the Decision Sciences Institute (DSI) are two professional societies that publish journals and newsletters dealing with current research and applications of operations research and quantitative methods.

SUMMARY

This is a book about how quantitative methods may be used to help managers make better decisions. The focus of this text is on the decision-making process and on the role of quantitative methods in that process. We have discussed the problem orientation of this process and in an overview have shown how mathematical models can be used in this type of analysis.

The difference between the model and the situation or managerial problem it represents is an important point. Mathematical models are abstractions of real-world situations and, as such, cannot capture all the aspects of a real situation. However, if a model can capture the major relevant aspects of the problem and can then provide a solution recommendation, it can be a valuable aid to decision making.

One of the characteristics of quantitative analysis that will become increasingly apparent as we proceed through the text is the search for a best solution to the problem. In carrying out the quantitative analysis, we shall be attempting to develop procedures for finding the "best" or optimal solution.

GLOSSARY

Problem solving The process of identifying a difference between the actual and the desired state of affairs and then taking action to resolve the difference.

Decision making The process of defining the problem, identifying the alternatives, determining the criteria, evaluating the alternatives, and choosing an alternative.

Single-criterion decision problem A problem in which the objective is to find the "best" solution with respect to just one criterion.

Multicriteria decision problem A problem that involves more than one criterion; the objective is to find the "best" solution, taking into account all the criteria.

Decision The alternative selected.

Model A representation of a real object or situation.

Iconic model A physical replica, or representation, of a real object.

Analog model While physical in form, an analog model does not have a physical appearance similar to the real object or situation it represents.

Mathematical model Mathematical symbols and expressions used to represent a real situation.

Constraints Restrictions or limitations imposed on a problem.

Objective function A mathematical expression used to represent the criterion for evaluating solutions to a problem.

Controllable input The decision alternatives or inputs that can be specified by the decision maker.

Decision variable Another term for controllable input.

Uncontrollable input The environmental factors or inputs that cannot be controlled by the decision maker.

Deterministic model A model in which all uncontrollable inputs are known and cannot vary.

Stochastic model A model in which at least one uncontrollable input is uncertain and subject to variation; stochastic models are also referred to as probabilistic models.

Optimal solution The specific decision variable value or values that provide the "best" output for the model.

Feasible solution A decision alternative or solution that satisfies all constraints.

Infeasible solution A decision alternative or solution that violates one or more constraints.

Fixed cost The portion of the total cost that does not depend on the volume; this cost remains the same no matter how much is produced.

Variable cost The portion of the total cost that is dependent on and varies with the volume.

Marginal cost The rate of change of the total cost with respect to volume.

Marginal revenue The rate of change of total revenue with respect to volume.

Break-even point The volume at which total revenue equals total cost.

PROBLEMS

1. Define the terms management science and operations research.
2. Describe the major reasons for the growth in the use of quantitative methods since World War II.

3. Discuss the different roles played by the qualitative and quantitative approaches to managerial decision making. Why is having a good understanding of both of these approaches to decision making important for a manager or decision maker?

SELF TEST

4. A firm has just completed a new plant that will produce more than 500 different products, using more than 50 different production lines and machines. The production scheduling decisions are critical in that sales will be lost if customer demands are not met on time. If no individual in the firm has had experience with this production operation, and if new production schedules must be generated each week, why should the firm consider a quantitative approach to the production scheduling problem?

5. List and discuss the steps of the decision-making process.

6. Give an example of each of the three types of models discussed in this chapter: iconic, analog, and mathematical.

7. What are the advantages of analyzing and experimenting with a model as opposed to a real object or situation?

SELF TEST

8. Recall the production model from Section 1.3:

$$\text{Max} \quad 10x$$
$$\text{s.t.}$$
$$5x \leq 40$$
$$x \geq 0$$

Suppose the firm in this example considers a second product that has a unit profit of $5 and requires 2 hours for each unit produced. Use y as the number of units of product 2 produced.
   a. Show the mathematical model when both products are considered simultaneously.
   b. Identify the controllable and uncontrollable inputs for this model.
   c. Draw the flowchart of the input—output process for this model (see Figure 1.5).
   d. What are the optimal solution values of x and $y?$

9. Is the model developed in Problem 8 a deterministic or a stochastic model? Explain.

10. Suppose we modify the model in Section 1.3 to obtain the following mathematical model:

$$\text{Max} \quad 10x$$
$$\text{s.t.}$$
$$ax \leq 40$$
$$x \geq 0$$

where a is the number of hours required for each unit produced. With $a = 5$, the optimal solution is $x = 8$. If we have a stochastic model with $a = 3$, $a = 4$, $a = 5$, or $a = 6$ as the possible values for the number of hours required per unit, what is the optimal value for $x?$ What problems does this stochastic model cause?

11. A retail store in Des Moines, Iowa, receives shipments of a particular product from Kansas City and Minneapolis. Let

$$x = \text{units of product received from Kansas City}$$
$$y = \text{units of product received from Minneapolis}$$

   a. Write an expression for the total units of product received by the retail store in Des Moines.
   b. Shipments from Kansas City cost $0.20 per unit, and shipments from Minneapolis cost $0.25 per unit. Develop an objective function representing the total cost of shipments to Des Moines.
   c. Assuming that the monthly demand at the retail store is 5000 units, develop a constraint that requires 5000 units to be shipped to Des Moines.

d. No more than 4000 units can be shipped from Kansas City, and no more than 3000 units can be shipped from Minneapolis in a month. Develop constraints to model this situation.

e. Of course, negative amounts cannot be shipped. Combine the objective function and constraints developed to state a mathematical model for satisfying the demand at the Des Moines retail store at minimum cost.

12. Suppose you are going on a weekend trip to a city that is d miles away. Develop a model that determines your round-trip gasoline costs. What assumptions or approximations are necessary to treat this model as a deterministic model? Are these assumptions or approximations acceptable to you?

13. For most products, higher prices result in a decreased demand, whereas lower prices result in an increased demand. Let

$$d = \text{annual demand for a product in units}$$

$$p = \text{price per unit}$$

Assume that a firm accepts the following price-demand relationship as being realistic:

$$d = 800 - 10p$$

where p must be between $20 and $70.

a. How many units can the firm sell at the $20 per-unit price? At the $70 per-unit price?

b. Show the mathematical model for the total revenue (TR), which is the annual demand multiplied by the unit price.

c. Based on other considerations, the firm's management will only consider price alternatives of $30, $40, and $50. Use your model from part (b) to determine the price alternative that will maximize the total revenue.

d. What are the expected annual demand and the total revenue according to your recommended price?

14. Suppose that a manager has a choice between the following two mathematical models of a given situation: (a) a relatively simple model that is a reasonable approximation of the real situation and (b) a thorough and complex model that is the most accurate mathematical representation of the real situation possible. Why might the model described in part (a) be preferred by the manager?

SELF TEST

15. The O'Neill Shoe Manufacturing Company will produce a special-style shoe if the order size is large enough to provide a reasonable profit. For each special-style order, the company incurs a fixed cost of $1000 for the production setup. The variable cost is $30 per pair, and each pair sells for $40.

a. Let x indicate the number of pairs of shoes produced. Develop a mathematical model for the total cost of producing x pairs of shoes.

b. Let P indicate the total profit. Develop a mathematical model for the total profit realized from an order for x pairs of shoes.

c. How large must the shoe order be before O'Neill will break even?

16. Eastman Publishing Company is considering publishing a paperback textbook on spreadsheet applications for business. The fixed cost of manuscript preparation, textbook design, and production setup is estimated to be $80,000. Variable production and material costs are estimated to be $3 per book. Demand over the life of the book is estimated to be 4000 copies. The publisher plans to sell the text to college and university bookstores for $20 each.

a. What is the break-even point?

b. What profit or loss can be anticipated with a demand of 4000 copies?

c. With a demand of 4000 copies, what is the minimum price per copy that the publisher must charge to break even?

d. If the publisher believes that the price per copy could be increased to $25.95 and not affect the anticipated demand of 4000 copies, what action would you recommend? What profit or loss can be anticipated?

17. Preliminary plans are underway for the construction of a new stadium for a major league baseball team. City officials have questioned the number and profitability of the luxury corporate boxes planned for the upper deck of the stadium. Corporations and selected individuals may buy the boxes for $100,000 each. The fixed construction cost for the upper-deck area is estimated to be $1,500,000, with a variable cost of $50,000 for each box constructed.

   a. What is the break-even point for the number of luxury boxes in the new stadium?
   b. Preliminary drawings for the stadium show that space is available for the construction of up to 50 luxury boxes. Promoters indicate that buyers are available and that all 50 could be sold if constructed. What is your recommendation concerning the construction of luxury boxes? What profit is anticipated?

18. Financial Analysts, Inc., is an investment firm that manages stock portfolios for a number of clients. A new client has just requested that the firm handle an $80,000 portfolio. As an initial investment strategy, the client would like to restrict the portfolio to a mix of the following two stocks:

Stock	Price/ Share	Estimated Annual Return/Share	Maximum Possible Investment
Oil Alaska	$50	$6	$50,000
Southwest Petroleum	$30	$4	$45,000

   Let
   $$x = \text{number of shares of Oil Alaska}$$
   $$y = \text{number of shares of Southwest Petroleum}$$

   a. Develop the objective function, assuming that the client desires to maximize the total annual return.
   b. Show the mathematical expression for each of the following three constraints:
   (1) Total investment funds available are $80,000.
   (2) Maximum Oil Alaska investment is $50,000.
   (3) Maximum Southwest Petroleum investment is $45,000.
   Note: Adding the $x \geq 0$ and $y \geq 0$ constraints provides a linear programming model for the investment problem. A solution procedure for this model is discussed in Chapter 2.

19. Models of inventory systems frequently consider the relationships among a beginning inventory, a production quantity, a demand or sales, and an ending inventory. For a given production period j, let

   $$s_{j-1} = \text{ending inventory from the previous period (beginning inventory for period } j)$$
   $$x_j = \text{production quantity in period } j$$
   $$d_j = \text{demand in period } j$$
   $$s_j = \text{ending inventory for period } j$$

   a. Write the mathematical relationship or model that describes how these four variables are related.
   b. What constraint should be added if production capacity for period j is given by C_j?
   c. What constraint should be added if safety stock requirements for period j mandate an ending inventory of at least I_j?

..../ /............

APPENDIX 1.1   SPREADSHEETS FOR QUANTITATIVE METHODS

Spreadsheet software packages, such as Microsoft Excel and Lotus 1-2-3, have added capabilities that can be used in the application of many of the quantitative methods introduced in this text. Generally, the user enters data from a problem directly into the spreadsheet. Formulas appearing in other cells of the spreadsheet are based on the appropriate quantitative method. The formulas supplemented by built-in functions convert the input data into the desired decision-making information, which is displayed on the spreadsheet.

Spreadsheet applications of Microsoft Excel are presented in appendixes to many chapters in this text, but they are optional. For the interested reader, the appendixes show the development of each spreadsheet application along with one or more examples based on the types of problems encountered in the chapter. If you have access to Microsoft Excel, Lotus 1-2-3, or another spreadsheet package, the appendixes will guide you in developing your own spreadsheet applications of quantitative methods. In the following discussion, we introduce spreadsheets by showing how to use Microsoft Excel to conduct the cost, profit, and break-even analysis presented in Section 1.4.

We begin by showing a formula spreadsheet with the input data and the appropriate cell formulas clearly identified. Text information used for labels is screened, problem specific data is set in color type, and formulas all begin with an equal sign (=). See Figure 1.7. Two columns, labeled A and B, and 20 rows are used. As common to most spreadsheet applications, the cells in the spreadsheet are identified by a column letter and row number.

Figure 1.7   FORMULA SPREADSHEET FOR BREAK-EVEN ANALYSIS

	A	B
1	BREAK–EVEN ANALYSIS	
2		
3	SELLING PRICE/UNIT	5
4		
5	COST INFORMATION	
6	FIXED COST	3000
7	VARIABLE COST/UNIT	2
8		
9	VOLUME	500
10		
11		
12	PROFIT (LOSS) SUMMARY	
13		
14	TOTAL REVENUE	=B3*B9
15	TOTAL COST	=B6+B7*B9
16		
17	PROFIT (LOSS)	=B14-B15
18		
19		
20	BREAK–EVEN POINT	=B6/(B3-B7)

We first enter the selling price per unit, the fixed cost, the variable cost per unit, and the anticipated volume in cells **B3, B6, B7,** and **B9**, respectively. These inputs are shown in color. We then compute total revenue (**B14**), total cost (**B15**), profit or loss (**B17**), and the break-even point (**B20**), from the user input information. Note the appropriate cell formulas in those cells.

For example, we compute total revenue as the selling price per unit times the volume. Thus, **=B3*B9** is the formula for total revenue (see cell **B14**). The formula for total cost is simply the fixed cost plus the variable cost per unit times the volume. Thus, **=B6+B7*B9** is the formula for total cost (see cell **B15**). The profit or loss formula is **=B14−B15**, which is the total revenue minus the total cost (see cell **B17**). The general formula for the break-even point is the fixed cost cell (**B6**) divided by the profit contribution per unit (**B3−B7**), (see in cell **B20**).

Figure 1.8 shows the value spreadsheet for this example. In a value spreadsheet each formula is replaced by a computed value. Currency formats are included for the monetary values in column B where appropriate. The volume of 500 units projects a total revenue of $5(500) = $2,500 and a corresponding total cost of $3,000 + $2(500) = $4,000. These results combine to provide a projected loss of $2,500 − $4,000 = ($1,500). Thus a volume of 500 units will result in a loss for the firm. The break-even point shows that the product will not break even until 1000 units are sold.

One big advantage of spreadsheet applications of quantitative methods is that we can input changes to the original data and, in effect, ask "what if" questions to learn how the profit, loss, and/or break-even point are affected by the changes. We can try different volumes, selling prices, and/or costs with the spreadsheet, which quickly and easily indicates the impact of these changes on the profitability of the product.

Figure 1.8   VALUE SPREADSHEET FOR BREAK-EVEN ANALYSIS

	A	B
1	BREAK–EVEN ANALYSIS	
2		
3	SELLING PRICE/UNIT	$ 5
4		
5	COST INFORMATION	
6	FIXED COST	$ 3,000
7	VARIABLE COST/UNIT	$ 2
8		
9	VOLUME	500
10		
11		
12	PROFIT (LOSS) SUMMARY	
13		
14	TOTAL REVENUE	$ 2,500
15	TOTAL COST	$ 4,000
16		
17	PROFIT (LOSS)	$ (1,500)
18		
19		
20	BREAK–EVEN POINT	1000

APPENDIX 1.2   THE MANAGEMENT SCIENTIST SOFTWARE

Developments in computer technology have been a major factor in making quantitative methods available to decision makers. A software package called *The Management Scientist* has been prepared by the authors to accompany this text. Version 4.0 is now available for Windows and Windows 95 systems. This software can be used to solve problems in the text as well as small-scale problems encountered in practice. Using The Management Scientist will give you an understanding and appreciation of the role of the computer in applying quantitative methods to decision problems.

The Management Scientist contains twelve modules, or programs, that will enable you to solve problems in the following areas:

- Chapter 4   Decision analysis
- Chapter 6   Forecasting
- Chapter 7–9   Linear programming
- Chapter 10   Transportation and assignment
- Chapter 11   Integer linear programming
- Chapter 12   PERT/CPM
- Chapter 13   Inventory models
- Chapter 15   Waiting line models
- Chapter 17   Markov processes

Use of The Management Scientist with the text is optional. Occasionally, we insert a figure in the text that shows the output The Management Scientist provides for a problem. However, familiarity with the use of the software is not necessary to understand the figure and the text material. The remainder of this appendix provides an overview of the features and the use of the software.

Selecting a Module

After starting The Management Scientist, you will encounter the module selection screen as shown in Figure 1.9. The choices provide access to the 12 modules. Simply click the desired module and select OK to load the requested module into the computer's memory.

Figure 1.9   MODULE SELECTION SCREEN FOR THE MANAGEMENT SCIENTIST

Select A Module

- 1. Linear Programming
- 2. Transportation
- 3. Assignment
- 4. Integer Linear Programming
- 5. Shortest Route
- 6. Minimal Spanning Tree
- 7. PERT/CPM
- 8. Inventory
- 9. Waiting Lines
- 10. Decision Analysis
- 11. Forecasting
- 12. Markov Processes

OK

The File Menu

After a module is loaded, you will need to click the File menu to begin working with a problem. The File menu provides the following options.

New   Select this option to begin a new problem. Dialog boxes and input templates will guide you through the data input process.

Open   Select this option to retrieve a problem that has been previously saved. When the problem is selected it will be displayed on the screen so that you can verify the problem is the one you want to solve.

Save   Once a new problem has been entered, you may want to save it for future use or modification. The Save option will guide you through the naming and saving process. If you create a folder named Problems, the Open and Save options will take you automatically to the Problems folder.

Change Modules   This option returns control to the screen in Figure 1.9 and another module may be selected.

Exit   This option will exit The Management Scientist.

The Edit Menu

After a new problem has been solved, you may want to make one or more modifications to the problem before resolving. The Edit menu provides the option to display the problem and then make revisions in the problem before solving or saving. In the linear and integer programming modules, the Edit menu also has options to change the problem size by adding or deleting variables and adding or deleting constraints. Similar options to change the problem size are provided in the Edit menu of the transportation and assignment modules.

The Solution Menu

The Solution menu provides two options.

Solve   This option solves the current problem and displays the solution on the screen.

Print Solution   Once the solution is on the screen, the Solution menu has the Print Solution option, which sends the solution to a printer or to a text file. If the text file option is used, the file can be accessed later by a word processor so that the solution output may be displayed as part of a solution report.

Advice about Data Input

Any time a new problem is selected, the appropriate module will provide dialog boxes and forms for describing the features of the problem and for entering data. When using The Management Scientist, you may find the following data input suggestions helpful.

1. Do not enter commas (,) with your input data. For example, the value 104,000 should be entered with the six digits: 104000.
2. Do not enter the dollar sign ($) for profit or cost data. For example, a cost of $20.00 should be entered as 20.
3. Do not enter the percent sign (%) if percentage is requested. For example, 25% should be entered as 25, not 25% or .25.
4. Occasionally, a model may be formulated with fractional values such as 1/4, 2/3, 5/6, and so on. The data input for The Management Scientist must be in decimal form. The fraction 1/4 can be entered as .25. However, fractions such as 2/3 and 5/6

have repeating decimal forms. In these cases, we recommend the convention of rounding to five places such as .66667 and .83333.

5. Finally, we recommend that in general you attempt to scale extremely large input data so that smaller numbers may be input and processed by the computer. For example, costs such as $2,500,000 may be scaled to 2.5 with the understanding that the data used in the problem reflect millions of dollars.

QUANTITATIVE METHODS IN PRACTICE FEATURE

Quantitative Methods in Practice write-ups prepared by practitioners are presented at the end of 14 chapters. We feel these provide a meaningful extension to the text material. The purpose of these application write-ups is to provide the reader with a better appreciation for the types of companies that use quantitative analysis and the types of problems these companies are able to solve.

Each Quantitative Methods in Practice write-up begins with a description of the company involved and continues with a discussion of the areas where the company has successfully applied quantitative analysis. The remainder of the write-up deals with an application that is closely related to the preceding chapter and/or part of the book. An effort has been made to avoid unnecessary technical detail and to focus on the managerial aspects and the value of the results to the company.

Since Chapter 1 is designed to provide an introduction to quantitative analysis, we have not emphasized any particular solution methodology. Thus, we have placed the Mead Corporation write-up at the end of this first chapter because it provides an overview of several areas in which quantitative methods can be used effectively. It is evidence of the impact quantitative approaches to decision making are having at some companies.

MEAD CORPORATION*

DAYTON, OHIO

Mead is a major producer of papers for premium periodicals, books, commercial printing, and business forms, with special expertise in coating technologies. The company and its affiliates also produce pulp and lumber, a variety of specialty papers, and converted wood and paper products. Mead is a leader in the design and manufacture of packaging systems for beverage and other consumable markets. The company is a world leader in the production of coated board, and manufactures shipping containers and corrugating medium. Mead is a major manufacturer of paper-based school and office products, and operates a nationwide network of distribution centers for paper, packaging, and supplies.

Quantitative Methods at Mead Corporation

Quantitative analyses at Mead are developed and implemented by the company's Decision Analysis (DA) Department. The DA Department provides timely, efficient internal consulting services to the operating groups and corporate staff in the functional areas of operations, finance, marketing, and human resources. The department assists decision makers by providing them with quantitative tools as well as personal analysis and recommendations. Through conversations and observations, the department recognizes needs where quantitative methods are applicable, and it then recommends appropriate projects. In addition, the department provides a resource reservoir for information and assistance on quantitative methodology and assumes responsibility for keeping current in quantitative methods that could produce efficiencies at Mead. This charter results in a

variety of projects and applications that span the corporation. Four examples of quantitative methods at Mead are described here.

A Corporate Planning System

The DA Department built and maintains a corporate planning system. This system allows business units to create and evaluate their five-year plans in an interactive computer environment.

Once the individual business units have finished their planning, the system consolidates the information at a group level. The assumptions of the units and the group are evaluated and reconciled. The use of this computer model facilitates the process by ensuring uniformity of calculations and reporting by all the planning units. Ultimately, the information is consolidated and evaluated at a corporate level.

A Timberland Financing Model

Another example of quantitative methods involves the development of a timberland financing model. Working directly with financial management, analysts assisted in the creation of a deterministic model that considered the major factors in a timberland financing arrangement. The model was used to examine the liability and profitability of timberland acquisition under various assumptions concerning forest growth rates, the inflation rate, and other financial considerations. By using the model, management was able to examine fully the acquisition and modify the financial arrangement as operating conditions warranted. The model is currently operated and modified by financial management and is

*The authors are indebted to Dr. Edward P. Winkofsky, Mead Corporation, Dayton, Ohio, for providing this application.

considered a major tool in the examination of timberland financing.

Inventory Analysis

Inventory analysis is an area in which more sophisticated tools of quantitative analysis have been used. Simulation models have been used to describe the major factors (e.g., demand or usage rates, lead times, and production rates) in an inventory system. Typically, an inventory model includes purchase, storage, ordering, stockout, and degradation costs. The simulation model is used to evaluate reorder points, safety stocks, customer service levels, review periods, and the response time of the inventory system to extraordinary events.

Once developed and in place, the model can be updated as economic and operating conditions change. Thus, the model can be used by management to evaluate its inventory system on an ongoing basis and to ensure that it is operating in a cost-efficient manner. These inventory simulation models are user friendly and can be operated and maintained by management with little formal computer training.

A Timber Harvesting Model

Mead also uses models to assist with the long-range management of the company's timberland. Through the use of large-scale linear programs, timber harvesting plans have been developed to cover a substantial time horizon. These models consider wood market conditions, mill pulpwood requirements, harvesting capacities, and general forest management principles. Within these constraints, the model develops an optimal harvesting and purchasing schedule based on discounted cash flow. Alternative schedules are developed to reflect various assumptions concerning forest growth, wood availability, and general economic conditions.

Quantitative methods are also used in the development of the inputs for the linear programming models already described. Timber prices and supplies as well as mill requirements must be forecast over the time horizon. Advanced sampling techniques are used to evaluate land holdings and to project forest growth. The harvest schedule is developed through the use of a number of quantitative methods.

Summary

The applications briefly described here—although only a few of the many quantitative analyses at Mead—convey the breadth of the activities currently in use within the company. The quantitative analyst at Mead must be able to work in a number of different environments and be proficient in a wide range of quantitative methods. In addition, the analyst must possess exceptional oral and written communication skills. Only with this background will the analyst be able to achieve the major objective of quantitative analysis at Mead—the development and implementation of user-friendly quantitative models that will support and enhance management decision making throughout the organization.

Questions

1. Which methods listed in Table 1.3 are being used in the four applications described at the Mead Corporation?
2. Which of the Mead applications use a deterministic model, and which use a stochastic model? What conditions in the applications indicate a stochastic model is necessary?
3. Discuss how quantitative analysis described in Section 1.3 occurs in Mead's inventory analysis application.
4. Discuss the benefits associated with the quantitative applications at Mead.

2

INTRODUCTION TO PROBABILITY

Business decisions are often based on an analysis of uncertainties such as the following:

1. What are the chances that sales will decrease if we increase prices?
2. What is the "likelihood" that a new assembly method will increase productivity?
3. How "likely" is it that the project will be completed on time?
4. What are the "odds" in favor of a new investment being profitable?

Probability provides a better description of uncertainty than verbal expressions such as chances are "pretty good," chances are "fair," and so on.

Probability is a numerical measure of the likelihood that an event will occur. Thus, probabilities could be used as measures of the degree of uncertainty associated with the four events previously listed. If probabilities were available, we could determine the likelihood of each event occurring.

Probability values are always assigned on a scale from 0 to 1. A probability near 0 indicates that an event is very unlikely to occur; a probability near 1 indicates that an event is almost certain to occur. Other probabilities between 0 and 1 represent varying degrees of likelihood that an event will occur. Figure 2.1 depicts this view of probability.

Probability is important in decision making because it provides a way to measure, express, and analyze the uncertainties associated with future events. The Q. M. in Action: Airline Overbooking describes the role that probability plays in airline overbooking decisions.

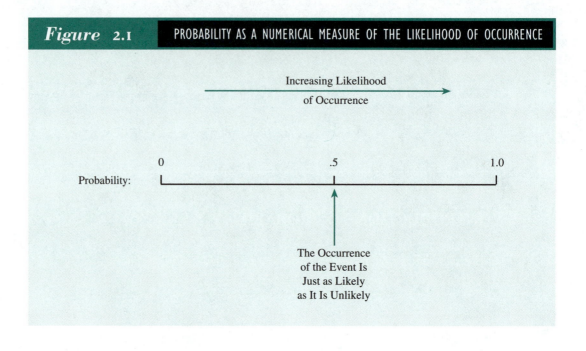

Figure **2.1**   PROBABILITY AS A NUMERICAL MEASURE OF THE LIKELIHOOD OF OCCURRENCE

2.1   EXPERIMENTS AND THE SAMPLE SPACE

In discussing probability, we define an **experiment** to be any process that generates well-defined outcomes. On any single repetition of an experiment *one and only one* of the possible experimental outcomes will occur. Several examples of experiments and their associated outcomes are as follows:

Experiment	Experimental Outcomes
Toss a coin	Head, tail
Select a part for inspection	Defective, nondefective
Conduct a sales call	Purchase, no purchase
Roll a die	1, 2, 3, 4, 5, 6
Play a football game	Win, lose, tie

The first step in analyzing a particular experiment is to define carefully the experimental outcomes. When we have defined *all* possible experimental outcomes, we have identified the **sample space** for the experiment. That is, the sample space is the set of all possible experimental outcomes. Any one particular experimental outcome is referred to as a **sample point** and is an element of the sample space.

Consider the experiment of tossing a coin. The experimental outcomes are defined by the upward face of the coin—a head or a tail. If we let S denote the sample space, we can use the following notation to describe the sample space and sample points for the coin-tossing experiment:

$$S = \{\text{Head, Tail}\}$$

Q.M. IN ACTION

AIRLINE OVERBOOKING*

Overbooking in the airline industry is the practice of selling more seats for a flight than the airplane's capacity. American Airlines estimates that, without overbooking, about 15% of seats would be unused at departure. As part of its yield management program, American uses quantitative decision tools to determine the optimal level of overbooking. Management attempts to maximize overbooking profitability by explicitly taking into account various probabilities and the revenue and cost implications of the decision.

Perhaps the primary consideration in determining the optimal level of overbooking is in assessing the relevant probabilities. Three probabilities are needed:

1. the probability that a passenger will cancel;
2. the probability that a passenger with an active reservation will not show up on the departure day; and

3. the probability that a passenger who is turned away will choose another American flight (recapture probability).

These probabilities together with the costs of overbooking and underbooking are the key determinants of American Airlines' overbooking policy. Thus, considerable effort is spent in obtaining good estimates of the probabilities. American Airlines expects an annual revenue contribution of more than $500 million from this and other aspects of its yield management program.

*Based on Smith, B. C., J. F. Leimkuhler, and R. M. Darrow, "Yield Management at American Airlines." *Interfaces,* Vol. 22, No. 3, pp. 8–31, 1992.

Using this notation for the second experiment in the table above, selecting a part for inspection, provides a sample space with sample points as follows:

$$S = \{\text{Defective, Nondefective}\}$$

Finally, suppose that we consider the fourth experiment in the table above, rolling a die. The experimental outcomes are defined as the number of dots appearing on the upward face of the die. In this experiment, the numerical values 1, 2, 3, 4, 5, and 6 represent the possible experimental outcomes or sample points. Thus the sample space is denoted

Try Problem 1 for practice in listing the experimental outcomes (sample points) for an experiment.

$$S = \{1, 2, 3, 4, 5, 6\}$$

N O T E S
and Comments

In probability, the notion of an experiment is somewhat different than in the laboratory sciences. In the laboratory sciences, the researcher assumes that each time an experiment is repeated in exactly the same way, the same outcome will occur. For the type of experiment we study in probability, the outcome is determined by chance. Even though the experiment might be repeated in exactly the same way, a different outcome may occur. Because of this difference, the experiments we study in probability are sometimes called random experiments.

2.2 ASSIGNING PROBABILITIES TO EXPERIMENTAL OUTCOMES

With an understanding of an experiment and the sample space, let us now see how probabilities for the experimental outcomes can be determined. The probability of an experimental outcome is a numerical measure of the likelihood that the experimental outcome will occur. In assigning probabilities to experimental outcomes, two **basic requirements of probability** must be satisfied.

1. The probability values assigned to each experimental outcome (sample point) must be between 0 and 1. That is, if we let E_i indicate the ith experimental outcome and $P(E_i)$ indicate the probability of this experimental outcome, we must have

$$0 \leq P(E_i) \leq 1 \qquad \text{for all } i \qquad (2.1)$$

2. The sum of *all* of the experimental outcome probabilities must be 1. For example, if a sample space has k experimental outcomes, we must have

$$P(E_1) + P(E_2) + \cdots + P(E_k) = 1 \qquad (2.2)$$

Any method of assigning probability values to the experimental outcomes that satisfies these two requirements and results in reasonable numerical measures of the likelihood of the outcomes is acceptable. In practice, the classical method, the relative frequency method, or the subjective method are often used.

Classical Method

To illustrate the classical method of assigning probabilities, let us again consider the experiment of flipping a coin. On any one flip, we will observe one of two experimental outcomes: head or tail. A reasonable assumption is that the two possible outcomes are equally likely. Therefore, as one of the two equally likely outcomes is a head, we logically should conclude that the probability of observing a head is ½, or 0.50. Similarly, the probability of observing a tail is 0.50. When the assumption of equally likely outcomes is used as a basis for assigning probabilities, the approach is referred to as the **classical method.** If an experiment has n possible outcomes, the classical method would assign a probability of $1/n$ to each experimental outcome.

As another illustration of the classical method, consider again the experiment of rolling a die. In Section 2.1 we described the sample space and sample points for this experiment with the notation

$$S = \{1, 2, 3, 4, 5, 6\}$$

A reasonable conclusion is that the six experimental outcomes are equally likely, and hence each outcome is assigned a probability of ⅙. Thus, if $P(1)$ denotes the probability that one dot appears on the upward face of the die, then $P(1) = ⅙$. Similarly, $P(2) = ⅙$, $P(3) = ⅙$, $P(4) = ⅙$, $P(5) = ⅙$, and $P(6) = ⅙$. Note that this probability assignment satisfies the two basic requirements for assigning probabilities. In fact, requirements (2.1) and (2.2) are automatically satisfied when the classical method is used, since each of the n sample points is assigned a probability of $1/n$.

The classical method was developed originally to analyze gambling problems, where the assumption of equally likely outcomes often is reasonable. In many business problems, however, this assumption is not valid. Hence, alternative methods of assigning probabilities are required.

Relative Frequency Method

Consider a firm that is preparing to market a new product. In order to estimate the probability that a customer will purchase the product, a test market evaluation has been set up wherein salespeople will call on potential customers. For each sales call conducted, there are two possible outcomes: The customer purchases the product, or the customer does not purchase the product. There is no reason to assume that the two experimental outcomes are equally likely, so the classical method of assigning probabilities is inappropriate.

Suppose that, in the test market evaluation of the product, 400 potential customers were contacted; 100 actually purchased the product, but 300 did not. In effect, then, we have repeated the experiment of contacting a customer 400 times and have found that the product was purchased 100 times. Thus, we might decide to use the relative frequency of the number of customers that purchased the product as an estimate of the probability of a customer making a purchase. We could assign a probability of 100/400 = 0.25 to the experimental outcome of purchasing the product. Similarly, 300/400 = 0.75 could be assigned to the experimental outcome of not purchasing the product. This approach to assigning probabilities is referred to as the **relative frequency method.**

Try Problem 2 for practice in assigning probabilities to experimental outcomes.

Subjective Method

The classical and relative frequency methods cannot be applied to all situations where probability assignments are desired. In some situations the experimental outcomes are not equally likely and relative frequency data are not available. For example, what is the probability that the Pittsburgh Steelers will win their next football game? The experimental outcomes of a win, a loss, or a tie are not necessarily equally likely. Also, the teams involved have not played several times previously this year, so no relative frequency data relevant to this upcoming game are available. Thus, if we want an estimate of the probability that the Steelers will win, we must use a subjective opinion of its value.

The classical method and relative frequency methods of assigning probabilities are objective. For the same experiment and data, we should agree on the probability assignments. However, the subjective method involves a personal "degree of belief." Different individuals looking at the same experiment can provide equally good but different subjective probabilities.

With the subjective method of assigning probabilities to the experimental outcomes, we may use any data available along with our experience and intuition. However, after we consider all available information, we must specify a probability value that expresses our *degree of belief* that the experimental outcome will occur. This method of assigning probability is referred to as the **subjective method.** Because subjective probability expresses a person's "degree of belief," it is personal. Different people can be expected to assign different probabilities to the same event. Care must be taken when using the subjective method to ensure that requirements (2.1) and (2.2) are satisfied. That is, regardless of a person's "degree of belief," the probability value assigned to each experimental outcome must be between 0 and 1, and the sum of all the experimental outcome probabilities must equal 1.

Even in situations where either the classical or relative frequency approach can be applied, management may want to provide subjective probability estimates. In such cases, the best probability estimates often are obtained by combining estimates from the classical or relative frequency approaches with subjective probability estimates.

2.3   EVENTS AND THEIR PROBABILITIES

An **event** is a collection of sample points (experimental outcomes). For example, in the experiment of rolling a die, the sample space has six sample points and is denoted $S = \{1, 2, 3, 4, 5, 6\}$. Now consider the event that the number of dots shown on the upward face of the die is an even number. There are three sample points in this event: 2, 4, and 6. Using the letter A to denote this event, we write A as a collection of sample points:

$$A = \{2, 4, 6\}$$

Thus, if the experimental outcome or sample point were 2, 4, or 6, we would say that the event A has occurred.

Much of the focus of probability analysis is involved with computing probabilities for various events that are of interest to a decision maker. If the probabilities of the sample points are defined, the *probability of an event* is equal to the sum of the probabilities of the sample points in the event.

Returning to the experiment of rolling a die, we used the classical method to conclude that the probability associated with each sample point is $\frac{1}{6}$. Thus, the probability of rolling a 2 is $\frac{1}{6}$, the probability of rolling a 4 is $\frac{1}{6}$, and the probability of rolling a 6 is $\frac{1}{6}$. The probability of event A—an even number of dots on the upward face of the die—is

$$P(A) = P(2) + P(4) + P(6)$$
$$= \frac{1}{6} + \frac{1}{6} + \frac{1}{6} = \frac{3}{6} = \frac{1}{2}$$

Try Problem 6 for practice in assigning probabilities to events.

Any time that we can identify all the sample points of an experiment and assign the corresponding sample point probabilities, we can use the above approach to compute the probability of an event. However, in many experiments the number of sample points is large and the identification of the sample points, as well as determining their associated probabilities, becomes extremely cumbersome if not impossible. In the remainder of this chapter we present some basic probability relationships that can be used to compute the probability of an event without knowing sample point probabilities. These probability relationships require a knowledge of the probabilities for some events in the experiment. Probabilities of other events are then computed from these known probabilities using one or more of the probability relationships.

N O T E S
and Comments

1. The sample space, S, is itself an event. It contains all the experimental outcomes, so it has a probability of 1; that is, $P(S) = 1$.

2. When the classical method is used to assign probabilities, the assumption is that the experimental outcomes are equally likely. In such cases, the probability of an event can be computed by counting the number of experimental outcomes in the event and dividing the result by the total number of experimental outcomes.

2.4   SOME BASIC RELATIONSHIPS OF PROBABILITY

In this section we present several relationships that will be helpful in computing probabilities. The relationships are the complement of an event, the addition law, conditional probability, and the multiplication law.

Complement of an Event

For an event A, the **complement of event A** is the event consisting of all sample points that are *not* in A. The complement of A is denoted by A^c. Figure 2.2 provides a diagram, known as a **Venn diagram,** that illustrates the concept of a complement. The rectangular area represents the sample space for the experiment and as such contains all possible sample points. The circle represents event A and contains only the sample points that belong to A. The remainder of the rectangle contains all sample points not in event A, which by definition is the complement of A.

In any probability application, event A and its complement A^c must satisfy the condition

$$P(A) + P(A^c) = 1$$

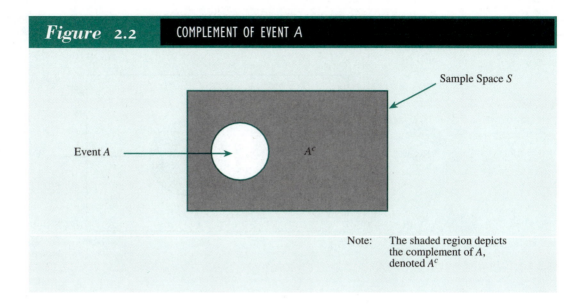

Figure 2.2   COMPLEMENT OF EVENT *A*

Sample Space *S*

Event *A*

A^c

Note: The shaded region depicts
the complement of *A*,
denoted A^c

Solving for $P(A)$, we have

$$P(A) = 1 - P(A^c) \tag{2.3}$$

Equation (2.3) shows that the probability of an event *A* can be computed easily if the probability of its complement, $P(A^c)$, is known.

Consider the case of a sales manager who, after reviewing sales reports, states that 80% of new customer contacts result in no sale. By letting *A* denote the event of a sale and A^c denote the event of no sale, the manager is stating that $P(A^c) = 0.80$. Using equation (2.3), we see that

$$P(A) = 1 - P(A^c) = 1 - 0.80 = 0.20$$

which shows that there is a 0.20 probability that a sale will be made on a new customer contact.

In another case, a purchasing agent states that there is a 0.90 probability that a supplier will send a shipment that is free of defective parts. Using the complement, we can conclude that there is a $1 - 0.90 = 0.10$ probability that the shipment will contain some defective parts.

Addition Law

The addition law is a useful relationship when we have two events and are interested in knowing the probability that at least one of the events occurs. That is, with events *A* and *B*, we are interested in knowing the probability that event *A* or event *B* or both will occur. Before we present the addition law, we need to discuss two concepts concerning the combination of events: the *union* of events and the *intersection* of events.

Key words for the union of events ($A \cup B$) are "either *A* or *B* occurs" or "at least one of the two events occurs."

For two events *A* and *B*, the **union of events A and B** is the event containing all sample points belonging to *A or B or both*. The union is denoted $A \cup B$. The Venn diagram shown in Figure 2.3 depicts the union of events *A* and *B;* the shaded region contains all the sample points in event *A*, as well as all the sample points in event *B*. The fact that the circles overlap indicates that some sample points are contained in both *A* and *B*.

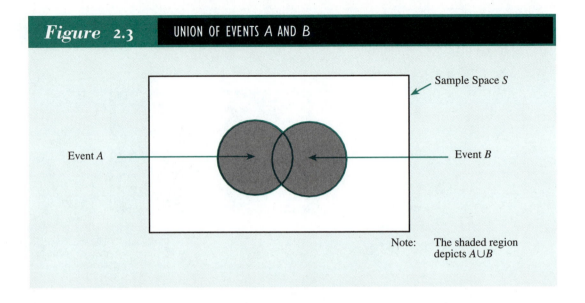

Figure 2.3   UNION OF EVENTS *A* AND *B*

Sample Space *S*

Event *A*   Event *B*

Note: The shaded region
depicts *A∪B*

Key words for the
intersection of events
(*A* ∩ *B*) are "both *A* and *B*
occur."

For two events *A* and *B,* the **intersection of events A and B** is the event containing the sample points belonging to *both A and B.* The intersection is denoted by *A* ∩ B. The Venn diagram depicting the intersection of the two events is shown in Figure 2.4. The area where the two circles overlap is the intersection; it contains the sample points that are in both *A* and *B.*

The addition law provides a way to compute the probability of event *A* or *B* or both occurring. In other words, the addition law is used to compute the probability of the union of two events, *A* ∪ *B.* The **addition law** is formally stated as follows:

$$P(A \cup B) = P(A) + P(B) - P(A \cap B) \qquad (2.4)$$

To obtain an intuitive understanding of the addition law, note that the first two terms in the addition law, $P(A) + P(B)$, account for all the sample points in *A* ∪ *B.* However, as the

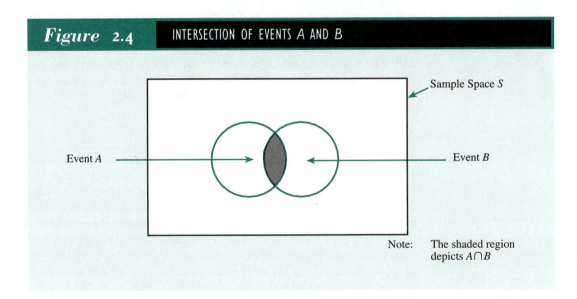

Figure 2.4   INTERSECTION OF EVENTS *A* AND *B*

Sample Space *S*

Event *A*   Event *B*

Note: The shaded region
depicts *A∩B*

sample points in the intersection $A \cap B$ are in both A and B, when we compute $P(A) + P(B)$ we in effect are counting each of the sample points in $A \cap B$ twice. We correct for this double counting by subtracting $P(A \cap B)$.

To apply the addition law, let us consider the following situations in a college course in quantitative methods for decision making. Of 200 students taking the course, 160 passed the mid-term examination and 140 passed the final examination; 124 students passed both exams. Let

$$A = \text{event of passing the mid-term exam}$$
$$B = \text{event of passing the final exam}$$

This relative frequency information leads to the following probabilities:

$$P(A) = \frac{160}{200} = 0.80$$

$$P(B) = \frac{140}{200} = 0.70$$

$$P(A \cap B) = \frac{124}{200} = 0.62$$

After reviewing the grades, the instructor decided to give a passing grade to any student who passed at least one of the two exams. That is, any student who passed the mid-term, any student who passed the final, and any student who passed both exams would receive a passing grade. What is the probability of a student receiving a passing grade in this course?

Your first reaction may be to try to count how many of the 200 students passed at least one exam, but note that the probability question is about the union of the events A and B. That is, we want to know the probability that a student passed the mid-term (A), passed the final (B), or passed both. Thus we want to know $P(A \cup B)$. Using the addition law (2.4) for the events A and B, we have

$$P(A \cup B) = P(A) + P(B) - P(A \cap B)$$

Knowing the three probabilities on the right-hand side of this expression, we obtain

$$P(A \cup B) = 0.80 + 0.70 - 0.62 = 0.88$$

This result tells us that there is an 88% chance of a student passing the course because there is a 0.88 probability of passing at least one of the exams.

Now consider a study involving the television viewing habits of married couples. It was reported that 30% of the husbands and 20% of the wives were regular viewers of a particular Friday evening program. For 12% of the couples in the study, both husband and wife were regular viewers of the program. What is the probability that at least one member of a married couple is a regular viewer of the program?

Let

$$H = \text{husband is a regular viewer}$$
$$W = \text{wife is a regular viewer}$$

We have $P(H) = 0.30$, $P(W) = 0.20$, and $P(H \cap W) = 0.12$; thus, the addition law yields

$$P(H \cup W) = P(H) + P(W) - P(H \cap W) = 0.30 + 0.20 - 0.12 = 0.38$$

This result shows that there is a 0.38 probability that at least one member of a married couple is a regular viewer of the program.

Before going on, let us see how the addition law is applied to **mutually exclusive events.** Two or more events are said to be mutually exclusive if the events do not have any sample points in common—that is, there are no sample points in the intersection of the events. For two events A and B to be mutually exclusive, $P(A \cap B) = 0$. Figure 2.5 provides a Venn diagram depicting two mutually exclusive events. Since $P(A \cap B) = 0$ for the *special case of mutually exclusive events,* the addition law becomes

> An event and its complement are mutually exclusive and their union is the entire sample space.

$$P(A \cup B) = P(A) + P(B) \tag{2.5}$$

> You should be able to solve Problem 7 at this point.

To compute the probability of the union of two mutually exclusive events, we simply add the corresponding probabilities.

Conditional Probability

In many probability situations, being able to determine the probability of one event when another event is known to have occurred is important. Suppose that we have an event A with probability $P(A)$ and that we obtain new information or learn that another event, denoted B, has occurred. If A is related to B, we will want to take advantage of this information in computing a new or revised probability for event A.

This new probability of event A is written $P(A \mid B)$. The "|" denotes the fact that we are considering the probability of event A *given the condition that event B has occurred.* Thus, the notation $P(A \mid B)$ is read "the probability of A *given B."*

Figure **2.5**   MUTUALLY EXCLUSIVE EVENTS

Event A Event B

In conditional probability such as $P(A \mid B) = 0.25$, the probability value of 0.25 refers only to the probability of event A. The conditional probability provides the probability of event A assuming that event B has occurred. There is no information about the probability of event B.

With two events A and B, the general definitions of **conditional probability** for A given B and for B given A are as follows:

$$P(A \mid B) = \frac{P(A \cap B)}{P(B)} \tag{2.6}$$

$$P(B \mid A) = \frac{P(A \cap B)}{P(A)} \tag{2.7}$$

Note that for these expressions to have meaning, $P(B)$ cannot equal 0 in equation (2.6) and $P(A)$ cannot equal 0 in equation (2.7).

To obtain an intuitive understanding of the use of equation (2.6), consider the Venn diagram in Figure 2.6. The lightly shaded region denotes that event B has occurred; the heavily shaded region denotes that the event $(A \cap B)$ has occurred. We know that once B has occurred, the only way that we can also observe event A is for event $(A \cap B)$ to occur. Thus, the ratio $P(A \cap B)/P(B)$ provides the probability that we will observe event A when event B has already occurred.

Figure 2.6   CONDITIONAL PROBABILITY

Event $A \cap B$

Event A

Event B

Note: The shaded region denotes that event B has occurred; heavily shaded region denotes $A \cap B$

Once Event B has occurred:

Event B with probability $P(B)$

Event $A \cap B$ with probability $P(A \cap B)$

Thus $P(A|B) = \dfrac{P(A \cap B)}{P(B)}$

Try Problem 12 for
practice computing
conditional probabilities.

We can apply conditional probability to the promotional status of male and female officers of a major metropolitan police force. It consists of 1200 officers: 960 men and 240 women. Over the past 2 years, 324 officers have been promoted. Table 2.1 shows the specific breakdown of promotions for male and female officers. Such a table is often called a *contingency table* or a *cross tabulation*.

After reviewing the promotional record, a committee of female officers filed a discrimination case on the basis that only 36 female officers had received promotions during the past 2 years. The police administration argued that the relatively low number of promotions for female officers is due not to discrimination but to the fact that few female officers are on the force. We use conditional probability to evaluate the discrimination charge.

Let

$$M = \text{event an officer is a man}$$
$$W = \text{event an officer is a woman}$$
$$B = \text{event an officer is promoted}$$

Dividing the data values in Table 2.1 by the total of 1200 officers permits us to summarize the available information as follows:

$$P(M \cap B) = \frac{288}{1200} = 0.24 \qquad \text{probability that an officer is a man } and \text{ is promoted}$$

$$P(M \cap B^c) = \frac{672}{1200} = 0.56 \qquad \text{probability that an officer is a man } and \text{ is not promoted}$$

$$P(W \cap B) = \frac{36}{1200} = 0.03 \qquad \text{probability that an officer is a woman } and \text{ is promoted}$$

$$P(W \cap B^c) = \frac{204}{1200} = 0.17 \qquad \text{probability that an officer is a woman } and \text{ is not promoted}$$

Because each of these values gives the probability of the intersection of two events, these probabilities are called **joint probabilities.** Table 2.2, which provides a summary of the probability information for the police officer promotion situation, is referred to as a **joint probability table.**

The values in the margins of the joint probability table provide the probabilities of each event separately. That is, $P(M) = 0.80$, $P(W) = 0.20$, $P(B) = 0.27$, and $P(B^c) = 0.73$. That is, 80% of the force is male, 20% of the force is female, 27% of all officers received

Table 2.1	CONTINGENCY TABLE FOR PROMOTIONAL STATUS OF POLICE OFFICERS DURING THE PAST 2 YEARS

	Promoted	Not Promoted	Total
Men	288	672	960
Women	36	204	240
Total	324	876	1200

| Table 2.2 | JOINT PROBABILITY TABLE FOR POLICE OFFICER PROMOTIONS |

	Promoted	Not Promoted	Total
Men	0.24	0.56	0.80
Women	0.03	0.17	0.20
Total	0.27	0.73	1.00

Joint probabilities
appear in the body
of the table

Marginal probabilities
appear in the margins
of the table

promotions, and 73% were not promoted. These probabilities are referred to as **marginal probabilities** because of their location in the margins of the joint probability table. Returning to the issue of discrimination against the female officers, we see that the probability of promotion of an officer is $P(B) = 0.27$ (regardless of whether that officer is male or female). However, the critical issue in the discrimination case involves the two conditional probabilities $P(B \mid M)$ and $P(B \mid W)$. That is, what is the probability of a promotion *given* that the officer is a man and what is the probability of a promotion *given* that the officer is a woman? If these two probabilities are equal, the discrimination case has no basis because the chances of a promotion are the same for male and female officers. However, different conditional probabilities will support the position that male and female officers are treated differently in terms of promotion.

Using equation (2.7), the conditional probability relationship, we obtain

$$P(B \mid M) = \frac{P(M \cap B)}{P(M)} = \frac{0.24}{0.80} = 0.30$$

$$P(B \mid W) = \frac{P(W \cap B)}{P(W)} = \frac{0.03}{0.20} = 0.15$$

What conclusions do you draw? The probability of a promotion for a male officer is 0.30. That is twice the 0.15 probability of a promotion for a female officer. Although the use of conditional probability does not in itself prove that discrimination exists in this case, the conditional probability values strongly support the argument presented by the female officers.

In this illustration $P(B) = 0.27$, $P(B \mid M) = 0.30$, and $P(B \mid W) = 0.15$. These probabilities show clearly that promotion (event B) is influenced by whether the officer is male or female. In particular, as $P(B \mid M) \neq P(B)$, events B and M are **dependent events.** That is, the probability of event B (promotion) is altered or affected by knowing whether M (the officer is male) occurs. Similarly, with $P(B \mid W) \neq P(B)$, events B and W are dependent events. But, if the probability of event B was not changed by the existence of event M, that is, $P(B \mid M) = P(B)$, events B and M would be **independent events.** That is, two events A and B are *independent* if

$$P(B \mid A) = P(B)$$

or

$$P(A \mid B) = P(A)$$

You should be able to solve
Problem 13 at this point.

Otherwise, the events are *dependent*.

Multiplication Law

The **multiplication law** can be used to find the probability of an intersection of two events. The multiplication law is derived from the definition of conditional probability. Using equations (2.6) and (2.7) and solving for $P(A \cap B)$, we obtain the multiplication law:

$$P(A \cap B) = P(A \mid B)P(B) \qquad (2.8)$$
$$P(A \cap B) = P(B \mid A)P(A) \qquad (2.9)$$

The multiplication law is useful in situations where probabilities such as $P(A)$, $P(B)$, $P(A \mid B)$, and/or $P(B \mid A)$ are known but where $P(A \cap B)$ is not. For example, suppose that a newspaper circulation department knows that 84% of its customers subscribe to the daily edition of the paper. Let D denote the event that a customer subscribes to the daily edition; hence, $P(D) = 0.84$. In addition, the department knows that the conditional probability that a customer who already holds a daily subscription also subscribes to the Sunday edition (event S) is 0.75; that is, $P(S \mid D) = 0.75$. What is the probability that a customer subscribes to both the daily and Sunday editions of the newspaper? Using equation (2.9), we compute $P(D \cap S)$:

$$P(D \cap S) = P(S \mid D)P(D) = 0.75(0.84) = 0.63$$

This result tells us that 63% of the newspaper's customers take both the daily and Sunday editions.

Before concluding this section, let us consider the special case of the multiplication law when the events involved are independent. Recall that independent events exist whenever $P(B \mid A) = P(B)$ or $P(A \mid B) = P(A)$. Returning to the multiplication law, equations (2.8) and (2.9), we can substitute $P(A)$ for $P(A \mid B)$ and $P(B)$ for $P(B \mid A)$. Hence, for the *special case of independent events,* the multiplication law becomes

$$P(A \cap B) = P(A)P(B) \qquad (2.10)$$

Thus, to compute the probability of the intersection of two independent events, we simply multiply the corresponding probabilities. For example, a service station manager knows from past experience that 40% of her customers use a credit card when purchasing gasoline. What is the probability that the next two customers purchasing gasoline will both use a credit card? If we let

A = event that the first customer uses a credit card

B = event that the second customer uses a credit card

the event of interest is $A \cap B$. With no other information, a reasonable assumption is that A and B are independent events. Thus

$$P(A \cap B) = P(A)P(B) = (0.40)(0.40) = 0.16$$

Do not confuse mutually exclusive events with independent events. Two events with nonzero probabilities cannot be both mutually exclusive and independent. If one mutually exclusive event is known to occur, the probability of the other occurring is reduced to zero. Thus, they cannot be independent.

2.5   BAYES' THEOREM

In the discussion of conditional probability, we indicated that revising probabilities when new information is obtained is an important phase of probability analysis. Often, we begin an analysis with initial or **prior probability** estimates for specific events of interest. Then, from sources such as a sample, a special report, or a product test, we obtain some additional information about the events. With this new information, we update the prior probability values by calculating revised probabilities, referred to as **posterior probabilities. Bayes' theorem** provides a means for making these probability calculations. The steps in this probability revision process are shown in Figure 2.7.

We can apply Bayes' theorem to a manufacturing firm that receives shipments of parts from two different suppliers. Let A_1 denote the event that a part is from supplier 1 and A_2 denote the event that a part is from supplier 2. Currently, 65% of the parts purchased by the company are from supplier 1, and the remaining 35% are from supplier 2. Thus, if a part is selected at random, we would assign the prior probabilities $P(A_1) = 0.65$ and $P(A_2) = 0.35$.

The quality of the purchased parts varies with the source of supply. Based on historical data, the conditional probabilities of receiving good and bad parts from the two suppliers are shown in Table 2.3. Thus, if we let G denote the event that a part is good and B denote the event that a part is bad, the information in Table 2.3 provides the following conditional probability values:

Figure 2.7   PROBABILITY REVISION USING BAYES' THEOREM

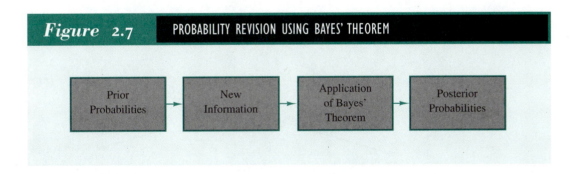

Table 2.3   CONDITIONAL PROBABILITIES OF RECEIVING GOOD AND BAD PARTS FROM TWO SUPPLIERS

	Good Parts	Bad Parts	
Supplier 1	0.98	0.02 ←	$P(B \mid A_1)$
Supplier 2	0.95	0.05	

$$P(G \mid A_1) = 0.98 \qquad P(B \mid A_1) = 0.02$$
$$P(G \mid A_2) = 0.95 \qquad P(B \mid A_2) = 0.05$$

The tree diagram shown in Figure 2.8 depicts the process of the firm receiving a part from one of the two suppliers and then discovering that the part is good or bad as a two-step experiment. There are four experimental outcomes; two correspond to the part being good, and two correspond to the part being bad.

Each of the experimental outcomes is the intersection of two events, so we can use the multiplication rule to compute the probabilities. For instance,

$$P(A_1 \cap G) = P(A_1)P(G \mid A_1)$$

The process of computing these joint probabilities can be depicted in what is sometimes called a *probability tree,* as shown in Figure 2.9. From left to right in the tree, the probabilities for each of the branches at step 1 are the prior probabilities, and the probabilities for each branch at step 2 are conditional probabilities. To find the probabilities of each experimental outcome, we simply multiply the probabilities on the branches leading to the outcome. Each of these joint probabilities is shown in Figure 2.9, along with the known probabilities for each branch. Note that the probabilities of the four experimental outcomes sum to 1.

Now suppose that the parts from the two suppliers are used in the firm's manufacturing process and that a bad part causes a machine to break down. What is the probability that the bad part came from supplier 1 and what is the probability that it came from supplier 2? With the information in the probability tree (Figure 2.9), we can use Bayes' theorem to answer these questions.

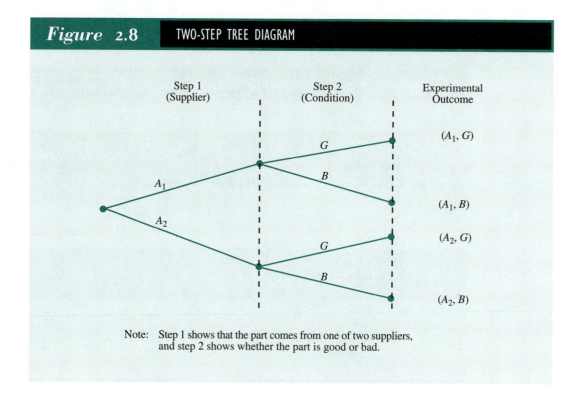

Figure 2.8   TWO-STEP TREE DIAGRAM

Note: Step 1 shows that the part comes from one of two suppliers, and step 2 shows whether the part is good or bad.

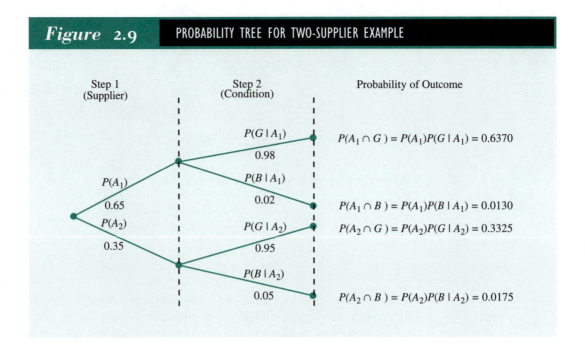

Figure 2.9 PROBABILITY TREE FOR TWO-SUPPLIER EXAMPLE

Step 1
(Supplier)

Step 2
(Condition)

Probability of Outcome

$P(G \mid A_1)$
0.98

$P(A_1 \cap G) = P(A_1)P(G \mid A_1) = 0.6370$

$P(A_1)$
0.65

$P(B \mid A_1)$
0.02

$P(A_1 \cap B) = P(A_1)P(B \mid A_1) = 0.0130$

$P(A_2)$
0.35

$P(G \mid A_2)$
0.95

$P(A_2 \cap G) = P(A_2)P(G \mid A_2) = 0.3325$

$P(B \mid A_2)$
0.05

$P(A_2 \cap B) = P(A_2)P(B \mid A_2) = 0.0175$

Letting B denote the event the part is bad, we are looking for the posterior probabilities $P(A_1 \mid B)$ and $P(A_2 \mid B)$. From the definition of conditional probability, we know that

$$P(A_1 \mid B) = \frac{P(A_1 \cap B)}{P(B)} \tag{2.11}$$

Referring to the probability tree, we see that

$$P(A_1 \cap B) = P(A_1)P(B \mid A_1) \tag{2.12}$$

To find $P(B)$, we note that event B can occur in only two ways: $(A_1 \cap B)$ and $(A_2 \cap B)$. Therefore, we have

$$\begin{aligned} P(B) &= P(A_1 \cap B) + P(A_2 \cap B) \\ &= P(A_1)P(B \mid A_1) + P(A_2)P(B \mid A_2) \end{aligned} \tag{2.13}$$

Substituting from equations (2.12) and (2.13) into equation (2.11) and writing a similar result for $P(A_2 \mid B)$, we obtain Bayes' theorem for the case of two events.

The Reverend Thomas Bayes (1702–1761), a Presbyterian minister, is credited with the original work leading to the version of Bayes' theorem in use today.

$$P(A_1 \mid B) = \frac{P(A_1)P(B \mid A_1)}{P(A_1)P(B \mid A_1) + P(A_2)P(B \mid A_2)} \tag{2.14}$$

$$P(A_2 \mid B) = \frac{P(A_2)P(B \mid A_2)}{P(A_1)P(B \mid A_1) + P(A_2)P(B \mid A_2)} \tag{2.15}$$

Using equation (2.14) and the probability values provided in our example, we have

$$P(A_1 \mid B) = \frac{P(A_1)P(B \mid A_1)}{P(A_1)P(B \mid A_1) + P(A_2)P(B \mid A_2)}$$

$$= \frac{(0.65)(0.02)}{(0.65)(0.02) + (0.35)(0.05)} = \frac{0.0130}{0.0130 + 0.0175}$$

$$= \frac{0.0130}{0.0305} = 0.4262$$

In addition, using equation (2.15), we obtain $P(A_2 \mid B)$:

$$P(A_2 \mid B) = \frac{(0.35)(0.05)}{(0.65)(0.02) + (0.35)(0.05)}$$

$$= \frac{0.0175}{0.0130 + 0.0175} = \frac{0.0175}{0.0305} = 0.5738$$

Note that in this application we initially started with a probability of 0.65 that a part selected at random was from supplier 1. However, given information that the part is bad, we determine the probability that the part is from supplier 1 drops to 0.4262. In fact, if the part is bad, there is a better than 50-50 chance that the part came from supplier 2; that is, $P(A_2 \mid B) = 0.5738$.

Bayes' theorem is applicable when the events for which we want to compute posterior probabilities are mutually exclusive and their union is the entire sample space.[1] Bayes' theorem can be extended to the case of n mutually exclusive events $A_1, A_2, \ldots, A_n$, whose union is the entire sample space. In such a case Bayes' theorem for the computation of any posterior probability $P(A_i \mid B)$ becomes

$$P(A_i \mid B) = \frac{P(A_i)P(B \mid A_i)}{P(A_1)P(B \mid A_1) + P(A_2)P(B \mid A_2) + \cdots + P(A_n)P(B \mid A_n)} \quad (2.16)$$

Try Problem 20 for practice using Bayes' theorem to compute posterior probabilities.

With prior probabilities $P(A_1)$, $P(A_2)$, ..., $P(A_n)$ and the appropriate conditional probabilities $P(B \mid A_1)$, $P(B \mid A_2)$, ..., $P(B \mid A_n)$, equation (2.16) can be used to compute the posterior probability of the events $A_1, A_2, \ldots, A_n$.

The Tabular Approach

The tabular approach is helpful in conducting the Bayes' theorem calculations simultaneously for all events A_i. Such an approach is shown in Table 2.4. The computations shown there involve the following steps.

Step 1. Prepare three columns:
    Column 1—The mutually exclusive events for which posterior probabilities are desired.
    Column 2—The prior probabilities for the events.
    Column 3—The conditional probabilities of the new information *given* each event.

---

1. If the union of events is the entire sample space, the events are often called *collectively exhaustive*.

Table 2.4	SUMMARY OF BAYES' THEOREM CALCULATIONS FOR THE TWO-SUPPLIER PROBLEM			
(1) Events A_i	**(2)** Prior Probabilities $P(A_i)$	**(3)** Conditional Probabilities $P(B \mid A_i)$	**(4)** Joint Probabilities $P(A_i \cap B)$	**(5)** Posterior Probabilities $P(A_i \mid B)$
A_1	0.65	0.02	0.0130	0.0130/0.0305 = 0.4262
A_2	0.35	0.05	0.0175	0.0175/0.0305 = 0.5738
	1.00		$P(B) = 0.0305$	1.0000

Step 2. In column 4, compute the joint probabilities for each event and the new information B by using the multiplication law. To get these joint probabilities, multiply the prior probabilities in column 2 by the corresponding conditional probabilities in column 3—that is, $P(A_i \cap B) = P(A_i)P(B \mid A_i)$.

Step 3. Sum the joint probabilities in column 4 to obtain the probability of the new information, $P(B)$. In the example there is a 0.0130 probability that a part is from supplier 1 and is bad and a 0.0175 probability that a part is from supplier 2 and is bad. These are the only two ways by which a bad part can be obtained, so the sum 0.0130 + 0.0175 shows an overall probability of 0.0305 of finding a bad part from the combined shipments of both suppliers.

Step 4. In column 5, compute the posterior probabilities by using the basic relationship of conditional probability

$$P(A_i \mid B) = \frac{P(A_i \cap B)}{P(B)}$$

Try Problem 25 for an application of Bayes' theorem involving the tabular approach.

Note that the joint probabilities $P(A_i \cap B)$ appear in column 4, whereas P(B) is the sum of the column 4 values.

N O T E S
and Comments

1. Bayes' theorem is used in decision analysis (see Chapter 4). The prior probabilities often are subjective estimates provided by a decision maker. Sample information is obtained and posterior probabilities are computed for use in developing a decision strategy.

2. An event and its complement are mutually exclusive, and their union is the entire sample space. Thus, Bayes' theorem is always applicable for computing posterior probabilities of an event and its complement.

SUMMARY

In this chapter we introduced basic probability concepts and illustrated how probability analysis can provide helpful decision-making information. We described how probability can be interpreted as a numerical measure of the likelihood that an event will occur. In addition, we showed that the probability of an event can be computed either by summing the probabilities of the experimental outcomes (sample points) comprising the event or by using the basic relationships of probability. When additional information becomes available, we showed how conditional probability and Bayes' theorem can be used to obtain revised or posterior probabilities.

The probability concepts covered will be helpful in future chapters when we describe quantitative methods based on the use of probability information. Specific chapters and quantitative methods that make use of probability are

- Chapter 3   Probability distributions
- Chapter 4   Decision analysis
- Chapter 5   Utility and decision making
- Chapter 12   Project scheduling: PERT/CPM
- Chapter 14   Inventory management: Independent demand
- Chapter 15   Waiting line models
- Chapter 16   Simulation

GLOSSARY

Probability A numerical measure of the likelihood that an event will occur.

Experiment Any process that generates well-defined outcomes.

Sample space The set of all possible sample points (experimental outcomes).

Sample point The individual outcome of an experiment.

Basic requirements of probability Two principles or requirements that restrict the manner in which probability assignments can be made:

1. For each experimental outcome E_i, $0 \leq P(E_i) \leq 1$; and
2. $P(E_1) + P(E_2) + \cdots + P(E_n) = 1$.

Classical method A method of assigning probabilities that is based on the assumption that the experimental outcomes are equally likely.

Relative frequency method A method of assigning probabilities based on experimentation or historical data.

Subjective method A method of assigning probabilities based on judgment.

Event A collection of sample points or experimental outcomes.

Complement of event A The event containing all sample points that are not in A.

Venn diagram A graphical device for representing the sample space and operations involving events.

Union of events A and B The event containing all sample points that are in A, in B, or in both.

Intersection of events A and B The event containing all sample points that are in both A and B.

Addition law A probability law used to compute the probability of a union: $P(A \cup B) = P(A) + P(B) - P(A \cap B)$. For mutually exclusive events, $P(A \cap B) = 0$, and it reduces to $P(A \cup B) = P(A) + P(B)$.

Mutually exclusive events Events that have no sample points in common; that is, $A \cap B$ is empty and $P(A \cap B) = 0$.

Conditional probability The probability of an event given another event has occurred. The conditional probability of A given B is $P(A \mid B) = P(A \cap B)/P(B)$.

Joint probability The probability of the intersection of two events.

Joint probability table A table used to display joint and marginal probabilities.

Marginal probabilities The values in the margins of the joint probability table, which provide the probability of each event separately.

Dependent events Two events A and B, where $P(A \mid B) \neq P(A)$ or $P(B \mid A) \neq P(B)$; that is, the probability of one event is altered or affected by knowing whether the other event occurs.

Independent events Two events A and B, where $P(A \mid B) = P(A)$ and $P(B \mid A) = P(B)$; that is, the events have no influence on each other.

Multiplication law A probability law used to compute the probability of an intersection: $P(A \cap B) = P(A)P(B \mid A)$ or $P(A \cap B) = P(B)P(A \mid B)$. For independent events, it reduces to $P(A \cap B) = P(A)P(B)$.

Prior probabilities Initial probabilities of events.

Posterior probabilities Revised probabilities of events based on additional information.

Bayes' theorem A method used to compute posterior probabilities.

PROBLEMS

SELF TEST

1. In a quality control process an inspector selects a completed part for inspection. The inspector then determines whether the part has a major defect, a minor defect, or no defect. Consider the selection and classification of the part as an experiment. List the sample points for the experiment.

2. An experiment with three outcomes has been repeated 50 times, and E_1 occurred 20 times, E_2 occurred 13 times, and E_3 occurred 17 times. Assign probabilities to the outcomes. What method did you use? Why?

SELF TEST

3. The manager of a large apartment complex provides the following subjective probability estimate about the number of vacancies that will exist next month.

Vacancies	Probability
0	0.05
1	0.15
2	0.35
3	0.25
4	0.10
5	0.10

List the sample points in each of the following events and provide the probability of
a. no vacancies.
b. at least four vacancies.
c. two or fewer vacancies.

4. In a survey of new matriculants to MBA programs, the following data were obtained on the marital status of the students.

Marital Status	Frequency
Never married	1106
Married	826
Other (separated, widowed, divorced)	106
Total	2038

a. What method would you recommend for assigning probabilities to the marital status of a new MBA student?

b. Show your probability assignments.

5. Strom Construction has made a bid on two contracts. The owner has identified the possible outcomes and subjectively assigned the following probabilities.

Experimental Outcome	Obtain Contract 1	Obtain Contract 2	Probability
1	Yes	Yes	0.15
2	Yes	No	0.15
3	No	Yes	0.30
4	No	No	0.25

a. Are these valid probability assignments? Why or why not?

b. What would have to be done to make the probability assignments valid?

SELF TEST

6. A sample of 100 customers of Montana Gas and Electric resulted in the following frequency distribution of monthly charges.

Amount ($)	Number
0–49	13
50–99	22
100–149	34
150–199	26
200–249	5

a. Let A be the event that monthly charges are $150 or more. Find $P(A)$.

b. **Let** B be the event that monthly charges are less than $150. Find $P(B)$.

7. Suppose that a sample space has five equally likely experimental outcomes: E_1, E_2, E_3, E_4, E_5. Let

$$A = \{E_1, E_2\}$$
$$B = \{E_3, E_4\}$$
$$C = \{E_2, E_3, E_5\}$$

a. Find $P(A)$, $P(B)$, and $P(C)$.

b. Find $P(A \cup B)$. Are A and B mutually exclusive?

c. Find A^c, C^c, $P(A^c)$, and $P(C^c)$.

    d. Find $A \cup B^c$ and $P(A \cup B^c)$.

    e. Find $P(B \cup C)$.

8. Let

$$A = \text{the event that a person runs 5 miles or more per week}$$
$$B = \text{the event that a person dies of heart disease}$$
$$C = \text{the event that a person dies of cancer}$$

    Further, suppose that $P(A) = 0.01$, $P(B) = 0.25$, and $P(C) = 0.20$.

    a. Are events A and B mutually exclusive? Can you find $P(A \cap B)$?

    b. Are events B and C mutually exclusive? Find the probability that a person dies of heart disease or cancer.

    c. Find the probability that a person dies from causes other than cancer.

9. A pharmaceutical company conducted a study to evaluate the effect of an allergy relief medicine; 250 patients with symptoms that included itchy eyes and a skin rash received the new drug. The results of the study are as follows: 90 of the patients treated experienced eye relief, 135 had their skin rash clear up, and 45 experienced both relief from itchy eyes and the skin rash. What is the probability that a patient who takes the drug will experience relief for at least one of the two symptoms?

10. A study of 100 students who had been awarded university scholarships showed that 40 had part-time jobs, 25 had made the dean's list the previous semester, and 15 had both a part-time job and had made the dean's list. What was the probability that a student had a part-time job or was on the dean's list?

11. Let A be an event that a person's primary method of transportation to and from work is an automobile and B be an event that a person's primary method of transportation to and from work is a bus. Suppose that in a large city $P(A) = 0.45$ and $P(B) = 0.35$.

    a. Are events A and B mutually exclusive? What is the probability that a person uses an automobile or a bus in going to and from work?

    b. Find the probability that a person's primary method of transportation is some means other than a bus.

SELF TEST

12. For two events A and B, $P(A) = 0.5$, $P(B) = 0.60$ and $P(A \cap B) = 0.40$.

    a. Find $P(A \mid B)$.

    b. Find $P(B \mid A)$.

    c. Are A and B independent? Why or why not?

SELF TEST

13. In a survey of MBA students, the following data were obtained on "Students' first reason for application to the school in which they matriculated."

		Reason for Application			
		School Quality	School Cost or Convenience	Other	Totals
Enrollment Status	**Full time**	421	393	76	890
	Part time	400	593	46	1039
	Totals	821	986	122	1929

    a. Develop a joint probability table using these data.

    b. Use the marginal probabilities of school quality, school cost or convenience, and other to comment on the most important reason for choosing a school.

c. If a student goes full time, what is the probability that school quality will be the first reason for choosing a school?

d. If a student goes part time, what is the probability that school quality will be the first reason for choosing a school?

e. Let A be the event that a student is full time and let B be the event that the student lists school quality as the first reason for applying. Are events A and B independent? Justify your answer.

14. A survey of automobile ownership was conducted for 200 families in Houston. The results of the study showing ownership of automobiles of U.S. and foreign manufacture were

		Do You Own a U.S. Car?		
		Yes	No	Totals
Do you own a foreign car?	Yes	30	10	40
	No	150	10	160
	Totals	180	20	200

a. Show the joint probability table for these data.

b. Use the marginal probabilities to compare U.S. and foreign car ownership.

c. What is the probability that a family will own both a U.S. car and a foreign car?

d. What is the probability that a family owns a car, U.S. or foreign?

e If a family owns a U.S. car, what is the probability that it also owns a foreign car?

f. If a family owns a foreign car, what is the probability that it also owns a U.S. car?

g. Are U.S. and foreign car ownership independent events? Explain.

15. The Texas Oil Company provides a limited partnership arrangement whereby small investors can pool resources to invest in large-scale oil exploration programs. In the exploratory drilling phase, the selection of locations for new wells is based on the geologic structure of the proposed drilling sites. Experience shows that the probability of a type A structure at the site of a productive well is 0.40. The company also knows that 50% of all wells are drilled in locations with type A structure. Finally, 30% of all wells drilled are productive.

a. What is the probability of a well being drilled in a type A structure *and* being productive?

b. If the drilling process begins in a location with a type A structure, what is the probability of having a productive well at that location?

c. Is finding a productive well independent of the type A geologic structure? Explain.

16. A purchasing agent has placed a rush order for a particular raw material with two different suppliers, A and B. If neither order arrives in 4 days the production process must be shut down until at least one of the orders arrives. The probability that supplier A can deliver the material in 4 days is 0.55. The probability that supplier B can deliver the material in 4 days is 0.35.

a. What is the probability that both suppliers deliver the material in 4 days? Since two separate suppliers are involved, assume independence.

b. What is the probability that at least one supplier delivers the material in 4 days?

c. What is the probability the production process is shut down in 4 days because of a shortage in raw material (that is, both orders are late)?

17. A market survey of 800 people revealed the following facts about the ability to recall a television commercial for a particular product and the actual purchase of the product.

	Could Recall Television Commercial	Could Not Recall Television Commercial	Totals
Purchased the Product	160	80	240
Had Not Purchased the Product	240	320	560
Totals	400	400	800

Let T be the event of the person recalling the television commercial and B the event of buying or purchasing the product.

a. Find $P(T)$, $P(B)$, and $P(T \cap B)$.

b. Are T and B mutually exclusive events? Use probability values to explain.

c. What is the probability that a person who could recall seeing the television commercial had actually purchased the product?

d. Are T and B independent events? Use probability values to explain.

e. Comment on the value of the commercial in terms of its relationship to purchases of the product.

18. In the evaluation of a sales training program, a firm discovered that of 50 salespeople receiving a bonus last year, 20 had attended a special sales training program. The firm has 200 salespeople. Let B = the event that a salesperson makes a bonus and S = the event that a salesperson attends the sales training program.

a. Find $P(B)$, $P(S \mid B)$, and $P(S \cap B)$.

b. Assume that 40% of the salespeople have attended the training program. What is the probability that a salesperson makes a bonus given that the salesperson attended the sales training program, $P(B \mid S)$?

c. If the firm evaluates the training program in terms of its effect on the probability of a salesperson's receiving a bonus, what is your evaluation of the training program? Comment on whether B and S are dependent or independent events.

19. A company has studied the number of lost-time accidents occurring at its Brownsville, Texas, plant. Historical records show that 6% of the employees had lost-time accidents last year. Management believes that a special safety program will reduce the accidents to 5% during the current year. In addition, it estimates that 15% of those employees having had lost-time accidents last year will have a lost-time accident during the current year.

a. What percentage of the employees will have lost-time accidents in both years?

b. What percentage of the employees will have at least one lost-time accident over the 2-year period?

SELF TEST

20. The prior probabilities for events A_1, A_2, and A_3 are $P(A_1) = 0.20$, $P(A_2) = 0.50$, and $P(A_3) = 0.30$. The conditional probabilities of event B given A_1, A_2, and A_3 are $P(B \mid A_1) = 0.50$, $P(B \mid A_2) = 0.40$, and $P(B \mid A_3) = 0.30$.

a. Compute $P(B \cap A_1)$, $P(B \cap A_2)$, and $P(B \cap A_3)$.

b. Apply Bayes' theorem, equation (2.16), to compute the posterior probability $P(A_2 \mid B)$.

c. Use the tabular approach to applying Bayes' theorem to compute $P(A_1 \mid B)$, $P(A_2 \mid B)$, and $P(A_3 \mid B)$.

21. A consulting firm has submitted a bid for a large research project. The firm's management initially felt there was a 50–50 chance of getting the bid. However, the agency to which the bid was submitted has subsequently requested additional information on the bid. Experience indicates that on 75% of the successful bids and 40% of the unsuccessful bids the agency requested additional information.

    a. What is your prior probability the bid will be successful (i.e., prior to receiving the request for additional information)?

    b. What is the conditional probability of a request for additional information given that the bid will ultimately be successful?

    c. Compute a posterior probability that the bid will be successful given that a request for additional information has been received.

22. A local bank is reviewing its credit card policy with a view toward recalling some of its credit cards. In the past approximately 5% of cardholders have defaulted, and the bank has been unable to collect the outstanding balance. Thus, management has established a prior probability of 0.05 that any particular cardholder will default. The bank has further found that the probability of missing one or more monthly payments for those customers who do not default is 0.20. Of course, the probability of missing one or more payments for those who default is 1.

    a. For a customer who has missed a monthly payment, compute the posterior probability that the customer will default.

    b. The bank would like to recall its card if the probability that a customer will default is greater than 0.20. Should the bank recall its card if the customer misses a monthly payment? Why or why not?

23. An oil company has purchased an option on land in Alaska. Preliminary geologic studies have assigned the following prior probabilities.

$$P(\text{high-quality oil}) \quad\quad = 0.50$$
$$P(\text{medium-quality oil}) = 0.20$$
$$P(\text{no oil}) \quad\quad\quad\quad\quad = 0.30$$

    a. What is the probability of finding oil?

    b. After 200 feet of drilling on the first well, a soil test is made. The probabilities of finding the particular type of soil identified by the test are

$$P(\text{soil} \mid \text{high-quality oil}) \quad\quad = 0.20$$
$$P(\text{soil} \mid \text{medium-quality oil}) = 0.80$$
$$P(\text{soil} \mid \text{no oil}) \quad\quad\quad\quad\quad = 0.20$$

How should the firm interpret the soil test? What are the revised probabilities, and what is the new probability of finding oil?

SELF TEST

25. The Wayne Manufacturing Company purchases a certain part from suppliers A, B, and C. Supplier A supplies 60% of the parts, B 30%, and C 10%. The quality of parts varies among the suppliers, with A, B, and C parts having 0.25%, 1%, and 2% defective rates, respectively. The parts are used in one of the company's major products.

    a. What is the probability that the company's major product is assembled with a defective part? Use the tabular approach to Bayes' theorem to solve.

    b. When a defective part is found, which supplier is the likely source?

26. *M.D. Computing* (Vol. 8, No. 5, 1991) describes the use of Bayes' theorem and conditional probability in medical diagnosis. Prior probabilities of diseases are based on the physician's assessment of factors such as geographic location, seasonal influence, and occurrence of epidemics. Assume that a patient is believed to have one of two diseases, denoted D_1 and D_2, with $P(D_1) = 0.60$ and $P(D_2) = 0.40$ and that medical research has shown a probability associated with each symptom that may accompany the diseases. Suppose that, given diseases D_1 and D_2, the probabilities a patient will have symptoms S_1, S_2, or S_3 are as follows:

		Symptoms			
		S_1	S_2	S_3	
Disease	D_1	0.15	0.10	0.15 ←	$P(S_3 \mid D_1)$
	D_2	0.80	0.15	0.03	

After finding that a certain symptom is present, the medical diagnosis may be aided by finding the revised probabilities the patient has each particular disease. Compute the posterior probabilities of each disease for the following medical findings.

a. The patient has symptom S_1.

b. The patient has symptom S_2.

c. The patient has symptom S_3

d. For the patient with symptom S_1 in part (a), suppose that symptom S_2 also is present? What are the revised probabilities of D_1 and D_2?

MORTON INTERNATIONAL*

CHICAGO, ILLINOIS

Morton International is a company with strong businesses in salt and household products, rocket motors, and specialty chemicals. Carstab Corporation, a subsidiary of Morton, produces a variety of specialty chemical products designed to meet the unique specifications of its customers. One such product, an expensive catalyst used in chemical processing, met the customer's exact specifications in only some, but not all, of the lots produced by Carstab.

Carstab's customer agreed to test each lot as it was received to determine whether the catalyst would perform the desired function. If the catalyst did not pass the test, the lot would be returned to Carstab. The problem was that only 60% of the lots sent to the customer were passing the test. This problem meant that, although the product was still good and usable by other customers, an unacceptably high percentage (40%) of the shipments to this particular customer were being returned.

Carstab explored the possibility of duplicating the customer's test, but equipment cost made this infeasible. Therefore, to improve customer service, Carstab's chemists designed a new test that was believed to indicate whether the lot would eventually pass the customer's test. The question was, "Would the Carstab test increase the probability that a lot shipped to the customer would then pass the customer's test?"

A sample of lots was tested under both the customer's procedure and Carstab's proposed procedure. Results were that 55% of the lots passed Carstab's test,

and 50% of the lots passed both the customer's and Carstab's test. In probability notation, we have

A = the event the lot passes the customer's test

B = the event the lot passes Carstab's test

where

$$P(B) = 0.55 \quad \text{and} \quad P(A \cap B) = 0.50$$

The probability information sought was the conditional probability $P(A \mid B)$ given by

$$P(A \mid B) = \frac{P(A \cap B)}{P(B)} = \frac{0.50}{0.55} = 0.909$$

Prior to Carstab's new test the probability a lot would pass the customer's test was 0.60. However, the new results showed that given a lot passed Carstab's new test it had a 0.909 probability of passing the customer's test. This result was good supporting evidence for the use of the test prior to shipment. Based on this probability analysis, the preshipment testing procedure was implemented at the company. Immediate results showed an improved level of customer service. A few lots were still being returned; however, the percentage was greatly reduced. The customer was more satisfied and return shipping costs were reduced.

Probability did not make the decision for the manager. However, some basic probability considerations provided important decision-making information and were a significant factor in the decision to implement the

*The authors are indebted to Michael Haskell of Morton International for providing this Quantitative Methods in Practice.

new testing procedure which resulted in improved service to the customer.

Questions

1. Why didn't Carstab produce a product that would meet customer specifications 100% of the time?

2. What probability information was helpful to Carstab in identifying its ability to produce a product that would meet the customer's specifications?

3. For the testing procedure described in this application, how would the results have changed if $P(B) = 0.40$ and $P(A \cap B) = 0.30$? Explain.

3

PROBABILITY DISTRIBUTIONS

In this chapter we continue the study of probability by introducing the concepts of random variables and probability distributions. We consider the probability distributions of both discrete and continuous random variables. The Q. M. in Action: Probability Distributions and a Treasure Hunt describes how the development and use of a probability distribution helped find a sunken ship. Of particular interest are five special probability distributions: the binomial, the Poisson, the uniform, the normal, and the exponential. These probability distributions are important because they are used extensively in practice.

Q.M. IN ACTION

PROBABILITY DISTRIBUTIONS AND A TREASURE HUNT*

The use of probability distributions played a key role in the location of a sunken ship. In 1857, while carrying passengers and gold from California to New York, the *SS Central America* sank in a hurricane, taking gold bars and coins worth an estimated $400 million to the ocean bottom. Central to the creation of the search plan was the development of a probability distribution for the position of the sunken ship.

Work began on developing the probability distribution in the summer of 1985. It involved combining information from various sources: Captain Herndon's last reported position, sightings by other ships, the drift of survivors, estimates of wind speed and ocean currents, and the like. Based on the information available, three separate probability distributions were developed and then merged into one, with subjective weights being assigned by the analysts. A search plan was based on these probabilities, and the actual search began during the summer of 1986.

Not until the summer of 1988 was the wreck finally discovered. In the summer of 1989, one ton of gold bars and gold coins was recovered from the wreck. The search team concluded that the sunken ship probably would not have been found without the use of the probability distribution for its location.

*Based on Stone, Lawrence D., "Search for the *SS Central America*: Mathematical Treasure Hunting." *Interfaces*, Vol. 22, No. 3, pp. 32–54, 1992.

3.1   RANDOM VARIABLES

Recall that in Chapter 2 we defined an experiment as any process that generates well-defined outcomes. We now want to concentrate on the process of assigning *numerical values* to outcomes. To do so we introduce the notion of a random variable.

For any particular experiment a random variable can be defined so that each possible experimental outcome generates exactly one numerical value for the random variable. For example, if we consider the experiment of selling automobiles for one day at a particular dealership, we could describe the experimental outcomes in terms of the *number* of cars sold. In this case, if x = number of cars sold, x is called a random variable. The particular numerical value that the random variable takes on depends on the outcome of the experiment. That is, we will not know the specific value of the random variable until we have observed the experimental outcome. For example, if on a given day three cars are sold, the value of the random variable is 3; if on another day (a repeat of the experiment) four cars are sold, the value is 4. We define a random variable as follows:

A **random variable** is a numerical description of the outcome of an experiment.

Some additional examples of experiments and their associated random variables are given in Table 3.1. Although many experiments have experimental outcomes that lend themselves quite naturally to numerical values, others do not. For example, for the experiment of tossing a coin one time, the experimental outcome will be either a head or a tail, neither of which has a natural numerical value. However, we still may want to express the outcomes in terms of a random variable. Thus, we need a rule that can be used to assign a numerical value to each of the experimental outcomes. One possibility is to let the random variable $x = 1$ if the experimental outcome is a head and $x = 0$ if the experimental outcome is a tail. Although the numerical values for x are arbitrary, x is a random variable because it describes the experimental outcomes numerically.

A random variable may be classified as either discrete or continuous, depending on the numerical values it can have. A random variable that may take on only a finite or an infi-

Table 3.1	EXAMPLES OF RANDOM VARIABLES	
Experiment	**Random Variable (x)**	**Possible Values for the Random Variable**
Make 100 sales calls	Total number of sales	0, 1, 2, ..., 100
Inspect a shipment of 70 radios	Number of defective radios	0, 1, 2, ..., 70
Build a new library	Percentage of project completed after 6 months	$0 \le x \le 100$
Operate a restaurant	Number of customers entering in one day	0, 1, 2, ...

nite sequence (e.g., 1, 2, 3, . . .) of values is a **discrete random variable.** The number of units sold, the number of defects observed, the number of customers that enter a bank during one day of operation, and so on, are examples of discrete random variables. The first two and the last random variables in Table 3.1 are discrete. Random variables such as weight, time, and temperature that may take on any value in a certain interval or collection of intervals are **continuous random variables.** For instance, the third random variable in Table 3.1 is a continuous random variable because it may take on any value in the interval from 0 to 100 (for example, 56.33, or 64.22).

Try Problem I for practice in identifying discrete and continuous random variables.

N O T E S	One way to determine whether a random variable is discrete or continuous is to think of the values of
and Comments	the random variable as points on a line. If the entire line segment between any two of these points also represents possible values for the random variable, the random variable is continuous.

3.2   DISCRETE RANDOM VARIABLES

We can demonstrate the use of a discrete random variable by considering the sales of automobiles at DiCarlo Motors, Inc., in Saratoga, New York. The owner of DiCarlo Motors is interested in the daily sales volume for automobiles. Suppose that we let x be a random variable denoting the number of cars sold on a given day. Sales records show that 5 is the maximum number of cars that DiCarlo has ever sold during one day. The owner believes that the previous history of sales adequately represents what will occur in the future, so we would expect the random variable x to take on one of the numerical values 0, 1, 2, 3, 4, or 5. The possible values of the random variable are finite; thus we would classify x as a discrete random variable.

The Probability Distribution of a Discrete Random Variable

Suppose that in checking DiCarlo's sales records we find that over the past year the firm has been open for business 300 days. The sales volumes generated and the frequency of their occurrence are summarized in Table 3.2. With these historical data available, the owner of DiCarlo Motors believes that the relative frequency method will provide a reasonable means of assessing the probabilities for the random variable x. The **probability function,** denoted $f(x)$, provides the probability that the random variable x takes on a specific value. Because on 54 of the 300 days of historical data DiCarlo Motors did not sell any cars and because no sales corresponds to $x = 0$, we assign to $f(0)$ the value $54/300 = 0.18$.

Similarly, $f(1)$ denotes the probability that x takes on the value 1, so we assign to $f(1)$ the value $117/300 = 0.39$. After computing the relative frequencies for the other possible values of x, we can develop a table of x and $f(x)$ values. Table 3.3 shows one way of representing the *probability distribution* of the random variable x.

We can also represent the probability distribution of x graphically. In Figure 3.1 the values of the random variable x are shown on the horizontal axis. The probability that x takes on these values is shown on the vertical axis. For many discrete random variables the probability distribution also can be represented as a formula that provides $f(x)$ for every possible value of x. We illustrate this approach in the next section.

In the development of a **discrete probability distribution,** two conditions must always be satisfied:

In Section 2.2 we defined the two basic requirements of all probability assignments as $0 \leq P(E_i) \leq 1$ and $\Sigma P(E_i) = 1$. Equations (3.1) and (3.2) are the analogs of these basic requirements.

$$f(x) \geq 0 \qquad\qquad (3.1)$$
$$\Sigma f(x) = 1 \qquad\qquad (3.2)$$

Condition (3.1) is the requirement that the probabilities associated with each value of x must be greater than or equal to zero, whereas condition (3.2) indicates that the sum of the probabilities for all values of the random variable x must be equal to 1. Table 3.3 shows that conditions (3.1) and (3.2) are satisfied. Thus, the probability distribution developed for DiCarlo Motors is a valid discrete probability distribution.

After establishing a random variable and its probability distribution, we can develop a variety of additional probability information, depending on the needs and interests of the

Table 3.2	CARS SOLD PER DAY AT DICARLO MOTORS

Sales Volume	Number of Days
No sales	54
Exactly one car	117
Exactly two cars	72
Exactly three cars	42
Exactly four cars	12
Exactly five cars	3
Total	300

Table 3.3	PROBABILITY DISTRIBUTION FOR THE NUMBER OF CARS SOLD PER DAY

x	$f(x)$
0	0.18
1	0.39
2	0.24
3	0.14
4	0.04
5	0.01
Total	1.00

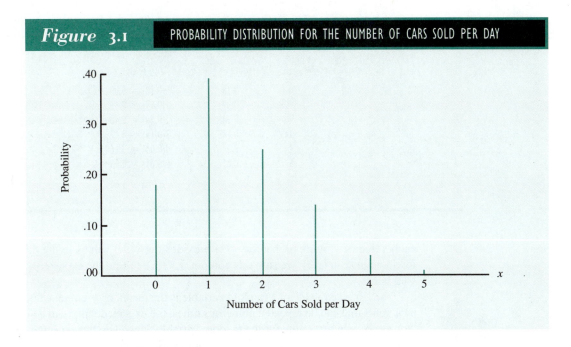

Figure 3.1 PROBABILITY DISTRIBUTION FOR THE NUMBER OF CARS SOLD PER DAY

decision maker. For example, in the DiCarlo Motors problem the probability distribution shown in Table 3.3 can be used to provide the following information.

1. There is a 0.18 probability that no cars will be sold during a day.
2. The most probable sales volume is 1, with $f(1) = 0.39$.
3. There is a 0.05 probability of an outstanding sales day with four or five cars being sold.

You should now be able to construct a discrete probability distribution. Try Problem 3.

Using probability information such as that just given, DiCarlo's management can understand better the uncertainties associated with the car sales operation. Perhaps this improved understanding can serve as the basis for a new policy or decision that will increase the effectiveness of the firm.

Expected Value

After constructing the probability distribution for a random variable, we often want to compute the mean or expected value of the random variable. The **expected value** of a discrete random variable is a weighted average of all possible values of the random variable, where the weights are the probabilities associated with the values. The mathematical formula for computing the expected value of a discrete random variable x is

$$E(x) = \mu = \Sigma \, xf(x) \tag{3.3}$$

As equation (3.3) shows, both the notations $E(x)$ and μ are used to refer to the expected value of a random variable.

To compute the expected value of a discrete random variable, we must multiply each value of the random variable by its corresponding probability and then add the resulting terms. Calculation of the expected value of the random variable (number of daily sales) for DiCarlo Motors is shown in Table 3.4. The first column contains the values of the random variable x, and the second column contains their associated probabilities $f(x)$. Multiplying

Table 3.4	EXPECTED VALUE CALCULATION	

x	$f(x)$	$xf(x)$
0	0.18	$0(0.18) = 0.00$
1	0.39	$1(0.39) = 0.39$
2	0.24	$2(0.24) = 0.48$
3	0.14	$3(0.14) = 0.42$
4	0.04	$4(0.04) = 0.16$
5	0.01	$5(0.01) = \underline{0.05}$
		$E(x) = 1.50$

each value of x by its probability $f(x)$ provides the $xf(x)$ values in the third column. Following equation (3.3), we sum this column, $\Sigma xf(x)$, to find the expected value of 1.50 cars sold per day.

The expected value of a random variable is the mean, or average, value. That is, for experiments that can be repeated numerous times, the expected value can be interpreted as the "long-run" average value for the random variable. However, the expected value is not necessarily the number that we think the random variable will assume the next time the experiment is conducted. In fact, it is impossible for DiCarlo to sell exactly 1.50 cars on any day. However, if we envision selling cars at DiCarlo Motors for many days into the future, the expected value of 1.50 cars provides the mean, or average, daily sales volume.

The expected value can be important to the manager from both the planning and decision-making points of view. For example, suppose that DiCarlo Motors will be open 60 days during the next 3 months. How many cars will be sold during this time? Although we can't specify the exact sales for any given day, the expected value of 1.50 cars per day provides an expected or average sales estimate of $60(1.50) = 90$ cars for the next 3-month period. In terms of setting sales quotas and/or planning orders, the expected value may provide helpful decision-making information.

Variance

The expected value gives us an idea of the average or central value for the random variable, but we often want a measure of the dispersion, or variability, of the possible values of the random variable. For example, if the values of the random variable range from quite large to quite small, we would expect a large value for the measure of variability. If the values of the random variable show only modest variation, we would expect a relatively small value. The variance is a measure commonly used to summarize the variability in the values of a random variable. The mathematical expression for the *variance* of a discrete random variable is

An alternative formula for the variance of a discrete random variable is $\text{Var}(x) = \Sigma x^2 f(x) - \mu^2$.

$$\text{Var}(x) = \sigma^2 = \Sigma (x - \mu)^2 f(x) \qquad (3.4)$$

As equation (3.4) shows, an essential part of the variance formula is a *deviation*, $x - \mu$, which measures how far a particular value of the random variable is from the expected value or mean, μ. In computing the variance of a discrete random variable, we square the deviations and then weight them by the corresponding probability. The sum of these weighted squared deviations for all values of the random variable is the **variance.** In other words, the variance is a weighted average of the squared deviations.

The calculation of the variance for the number of daily sales in the DiCarlo Motors problem is summarized in Table 3.5. We see that the variance for the number of cars sold per day is 1.25. A related measure of variability is the **standard deviation,** σ, which is defined as the positive square root of the variance. For DiCarlo Motors, the standard deviation of the number of cars sold per day is

$$\sigma = \sqrt{1.25} = 1.118$$

Try Problem 4 to be sure you can compute the expected value, variance, and standard deviation.

For the purpose of easier managerial interpretation, the standard deviation may be preferred over the variance because it is measured in the same units as the random variable ($\sigma = 1.118$ cars sold per day). The variance (σ^2) is measured in squared units and is thus more difficult for a manager to interpret.

At this point our interpretation of the variance and the standard deviation is limited to comparisons of the variability of different random variables. For example, if the daily sales data from a second DiCarlo dealership in Albany, New York, provided $\sigma^2 = 2.56$ and $\sigma = 1.6$, we can conclude that the number of cars sold per day at this dealership exhibits more variability than at the first DiCarlo dealership, where $\sigma^2 = 1.25$ and $\sigma = 1.118$. Later in this chapter we discuss the normal distribution. For that probability distribution, we show that the variance and the standard deviation of the random variable are essential for making probability calculations.

Table 3.5	VARIANCE CALCULATION			
x	$x - \mu$	$(x - \mu)^2$	$f(x)$	$(x - \mu)^2 f(x)$
0	$0 - 1.50 = -1.50$	2.25	0.18	$2.25(0.18) = 0.4050$
1	$1 - 1.50 = -0.50$	0.25	0.39	$0.25(0.39) = 0.0975$
2	$2 - 1.50 = 0.50$	0.25	0.24	$0.25(0.24) = 0.0600$
3	$3 - 1.50 = 1.50$	2.25	0.14	$2.25(0.14) = 0.3150$
4	$4 - 1.50 = 2.50$	6.25	0.04	$6.25(0.04) = 0.2500$
5	$5 - 1.50 = 3.50$	12.25	0.01	$12.25(0.01) = 0.1225$
				$\sigma^2 = 1.2500$

3.3 THE BINOMIAL DISTRIBUTION

In this section we consider a class of experiments that meet the following conditions.

1. The overall experiment can be described in terms of a sequence of n identical experiments called *trials.*
2. Two outcomes are possible on each trial. We refer to one outcome as a *success* and the other as a *failure.*
3. The probabilities of the two outcomes do not change from one trial to the next.
4. The trials are independent (i.e., the outcome of one trial does not affect the outcome of any other trial).

Experiments that satisfy conditions 2, 3, and 4 are said to be generated by a *Bernoulli process*. In addition, if condition 1 is satisfied (there are *n* identical trials), we have a *binomial experiment*. An important discrete random variable associated with the binomial experiment is the number of successful outcomes in the *n* trials. If we let *x* denote the value of this random variable, then *x* can have a value of 0, 1, 2, 3, . . . , *n*, depending on the number of successes observed in the *n* trials. The probability distribution associated with this random variable is called the **binomial probability distribution.**

In cases where the binomial distribution is applicable, the mathematical formula for computing the probability of any value for the random variable is the binomial probability function

Try Problem 9 (parts a–d) for practice computing binomial probabilities.

$$f(x) = \frac{n!}{x!(n - x)!} p^x(1 - p)^{n-x} \qquad x = 0, 1, \ldots, n \qquad (3.5)$$

where

$$n = \text{number of trials}$$
$$p = \text{probability of success on one trial}$$
$$x = \text{number of successes in } n \text{ trials}$$
$$f(x) = \text{probability of } x \text{ successes in } n \text{ trials}$$

The term *n*! in the above expression is referred to as *n factorial* and is defined as

$$n! = n(n - 1)(n - 2) \cdots (2)(1)$$

For example, 4! = (4)(3)(2)(1) = 24. Also, by definition, the special case of zero factorial is 0! = 1.

The Nastke Clothing Store Problem

To illustrate the binomial probability distribution, let us consider the experiment of customers entering the Nastke Clothing Store. To keep the problem relatively small, we restrict the experiment to the next three customers. If, based on experience, the store manager estimates that the probability of one customer making a purchase is 0.30, what is the probability that exactly two of the next three customers make a purchase?

We first want to demonstrate that three customers entering the clothing store and deciding whether to make a purchase can be viewed as a binomial experiment. Checking the four requirements for a binomial experiment, we note the following.

1. The experiment can be described as a sequence of three identical trials, one trial for each of the three customers who will enter the store.
2. Two outcomes—the customer makes a purchase (success) or the customer does not make a purchase (failure)—are possible for each trial.
3. The probabilities of the purchase (0.30) and no purchase (0.70) outcomes are assumed to be the same for all customers.
4. The purchase decision of each customer is independent of the purchase decision of the other customers.

Thus, if we define the random variable *x* as the number of customers making a purchase (i.e., the number of successes in the three trials), we satisfy the requirements of the binomial probability distribution.

With $n = 3$ trials and the probability of a purchase $p = 0.30$ for each customer, we use equation (3.5) to compute the probability of two customers making a purchase. This probability, denoted $f(2)$, is

$$f(2) = \frac{3!}{2!1!} (0.30)^2 (0.70)^1$$

$$= \frac{3 \times 2 \times 1}{2 \times 1 \times 1} (0.30)^2 (0.70)^1 = 0.189$$

Try Problem 12 for an application of the binomial distribution.

Similarly, the probability of no customers making a purchase, denoted $f(0)$, is

$$f(0) = \frac{3!}{0!3!} (0.30)^0 (0.70)^3$$

$$= \frac{3 \times 2 \times 1}{1 \times 3 \times 2 \times 1} (0.30)^0 (0.70)^3 = 0.343$$

Similarly, equation (3.5) can be used to show that the probabilities of one and three purchases are $f(1) = 0.441$ and $f(3) = 0.027$. Table 3.6 and Figure 3.2 summarize the binomial probability distribution for the Nastke Clothing Store problem.

If we consider any variation of the Nastke problem, such as 10 customers rather than 3 customers entering the store, the binomial probability function given by equation (3.5) still applies. For example, the probability that 4 of the 10 customers make a purchase is

$$f(4) = \frac{10!}{4!6!} (0.30)^4 (0.70)^6 = 0.2001$$

In this binomial experiment, $n = 10$, $x = 4$, and $p = 0.30$.

With the use of equation (3.5), tables have been developed that provide the probability of x successes in n trials for a binomial experiment. Such a table of binomial probability values is provided in Appendix A. We have included a portion of this table in Table 3.7. In order to use this table, specify the values of n, p, and x for the binomial experiment of interest. Check the use of this table by employing it to verify the probability of four successes in ten trials for the Nastke Clothing Store problem. Note that the value of $f(4) = 0.2001$ can be read directly from the table of binomial probabilities, making it unnecessary to perform the calculations required by equation (3.5).

Table 3.6	PROBABILITY DISTRIBUTION FOR THE NUMBER OF CUSTOMERS MAKING A PURCHASE

x	$f(x)$
0	0.343
1	0.441
2	0.189
3	0.027
Total	1.000

| **Figure 3.2** | PROBABILITY DISTRIBUTION FOR THE NASTKE CLOTHING STORE PROBLEM |

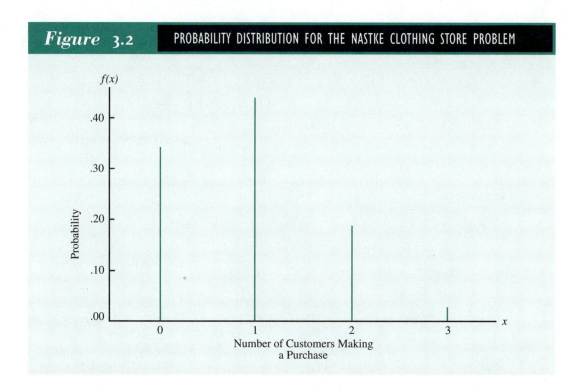

The Expected Value and Variance for the Binomial Distribution

From the probability distribution in Table 3.6, we can use equation (3.3) to compute the expected value or expected number of customers making a purchase:

$$\mu = \Sigma\, xf(x) = 0(0.343) + 1(0.441) + 2(0.189) + 3(0.027) = 0.9$$

Note that we could have obtained this same expected value simply by multiplying n (the number of trials) by p (the probability of success on any one trial):

$$np = 3(0.30) = 0.9$$

For the special case of a binomial probability distribution, the expected value of the random variable is given by

$$\mu = np \qquad\qquad (3.6)$$

Thus, if you know that the probability distribution is binomial, you do not have to make the detailed calculations required by equation (3.3) to compute the expected value.

Suppose that during the next month Nastke's Clothing Store expects 1000 customers to enter the store. What is the expected number of customers who will make a purchase? Using equation (3.6) the answer is $\mu = np = (1000)(0.3) = 300$. To increase the expected number of sales, Nastke's must induce more customers to enter the store and/or somehow increase the probability that any individual customer will make a purchase after entering.

Table 3.7		SELECTED VALUES FROM THE BINOMIAL PROBABILITY TABLES EXAMPLE: $n = 10, x = 4$, $p = 0.30; f(4) = 0.2001$								

n	x					p					
		0.05	0.10	0.15	0.20	0.25	0.30	0.35	0.40	0.45	0.50
9	0	0.6302	0.3874	0.2316	0.1342	0.0751	0.0404	0.0207	0.0101	0.0046	0.0020
	1	0.2985	0.3874	0.3679	0.3020	0.2253	0.1556	0.1004	0.0605	0.0339	0.0176
	2	0.0629	0.1722	0.2597	0.3020	0.3003	0.2668	0.2162	0.1612	0.1110	0.0703
	3	0.0077	0.0446	0.1069	0.1762	0.2336	0.2668	0.2716	0.2508	0.2119	0.1641
	4	0.0006	0.0074	0.0283	0.0661	0.1168	0.1715	0.2194	0.2508	0.2600	0.2461
	5	0.0000	0.0008	0.0050	0.0165	0.0389	0.0735	0.1181	0.1672	0.2128	0.2461
	6	0.0000	0.0001	0.0006	0.0028	0.0087	0.0210	0.0424	0.0743	0.1160	0.1641
	7	0.0000	0.0000	0.0000	0.0003	0.0012	0.0039	0.0098	0.0212	0.0407	0.0703
	8	0.0000	0.0000	0.0000	0.0000	0.0001	0.0004	0.0013	0.0035	0.0083	0.0176
	9	0.0000	0.0000	0.0000	0.0000	0.0000	0.0000	0.0001	0.0003	0.0008	0.0020
10	0	0.5987	0.3487	0.1969	0.1074	0.0563	0.0282	0.0135	0.0060	0.0025	0.0010
	1	0.3151	0.3874	0.3474	0.2684	0.1877	0.1211	0.0725	0.0403	0.0207	0.0098
	2	0.0746	0.1937	0.2759	0.3020	0.2816	0.2335	0.1757	0.1209	0.0763	0.0439
	3	0.0105	0.0574	0.1298	0.2013	0.2503	0.2668	0.2522	0.2150	0.1665	0.1172
	4	0.0010	0.0112	0.0401	0.0881	0.1460	**0.2001**	0.2377	0.2508	0.2384	0.2051
	5	0.0001	0.0015	0.0085	0.0264	0.0584	0.1029	0.1536	0.2007	0.2340	0.2461
	6	0.0000	0.0001	0.0012	0.0055	0.0162	0.0368	0.0689	0.1115	0.1596	0.2051
	7	0.0000	0.0000	0.0001	0.0008	0.0031	0.0090	0.0212	0.0425	0.0746	0.1172
	8	0.0000	0.0000	0.0000	0.0001	0.0004	0.0014	0.0043	0.0106	0.0229	0.0439
	9	0.0000	0.0000	0.0000	0.0000	0.0000	0.0001	0.0005	0.0016	0.0042	0.0098
	10	0.0000	0.0000	0.0000	0.0000	0.0000	0.0000	0.0000	0.0001	0.0003	0.0010
11	0	0.5688	0.3138	0.1673	0.0859	0.0422	0.0198	0.0088	0.0036	0.0014	0.0005
	1	0.3293	0.3835	0.3248	0.2362	0.1549	0.0932	0.0518	0.0266	0.0125	0.0054
	2	0.0867	0.2131	0.2866	0.2953	0.2581	0.1998	0.1395	0.0887	0.0531	0.0269
	3	0.0137	0.0710	0.1517	0.2215	0.2581	0.2568	0.2254	0.1774	0.1259	0.0806
	4	0.0014	0.0158	0.0536	0.1107	0.1721	0.2201	0.2428	0.2365	0.2060	0.1611
	5	0.0001	0.0025	0.0132	0.0388	0.0803	0.1321	0.1830	0.2207	0.2360	0.2256
	6	0.0000	0.0003	0.0023	0.0097	0.0268	0.0566	0.0985	0.1471	0.1931	0.2256
	7	0.0000	0.0000	0.0003	0.0017	0.0064	0.0173	0.0379	0.0701	0.1128	0.1611
	8	0.0000	0.0000	0.0000	0.0002	0.0011	0.0037	0.0102	0.0234	0.0462	0.0806
	9	0.0000	0.0000	0.0000	0.0000	0.0001	0.0005	0.0018	0.0052	0.0126	0.0269
	10	0.0000	0.0000	0.0000	0.0000	0.0000	0.0000	0.0002	0.0007	0.0021	0.0054
	11	0.0000	0.0000	0.0000	0.0000	0.0000	0.0000	0.0000	0.0000	0.0002	0.0005

For the special case of a binomial distribution the variance of the random variable is

$$\sigma^2 = np(1 - p) \qquad (3.7)$$

Try Problem 9 part e for practice computing the expected value, variance, and standard deviation.

For the Nastke Clothing Store problem with three customers, the variance and standard deviation for the number of customers making a purchase are

$$\sigma^2 = np(1 - p) = 3(0.3)(0.7) = 0.63$$
$$\sigma = \sqrt{0.63} = 0.79$$

··/ /············

3.4   THE POISSON DISTRIBUTION

In this section we will consider a discrete random variable that often is useful when we are dealing with the number of occurrences of an event over a specified interval of time or space. For example, the random variable of interest might be the number of arrivals at a car wash in 1 hour, the number of repairs needed in 10 miles of highway, or the number of leaks in 100 miles of pipeline. If the following two assumptions are satisfied, the **Poisson probability distribution** is applicable.

1. The probability of an occurrence of the event is the same for any two intervals of equal length.
2. The occurrence or nonoccurrence of the event in any interval is independent of the occurrence or nonoccurrence in any other interval. The probability function of the Poisson random variable is given by equation (3.8):

$$f(x) = \frac{\lambda^x e^{-\lambda}}{x!} \qquad \text{for } x = 0, 1, 2, \ldots \tag{3.8}$$

where

λ = mean or average number of occurrences in an interval

e = 2.71828

x = number of occurrences in the interval

$f(x)$ = probability of x occurrences in the interval

Note that equation (3.8) shows that there is no upper limit to the number of possible values that a Poisson random variable can take on. That is, although x is still a discrete random variable with an infinite sequence of values ($x = 0, 1, 2, \ldots$), the Poisson random variable has no specific upper limit.

An Example Involving Time Invervals

Suppose that we are interested in the number of arrivals at the drive-in teller window of a bank during a 15-minute period on weekday mornings. If we assume that the probability of a car arriving is the same for any two time periods of equal length and that the arrival or nonarrival of a car in any time period is independent of the arrival or nonarrival in any other time period, the Poisson probability function is applicable. Then if we assume that an analysis of historical data shows that the average number of cars arriving during a 15-minute interval of time is 10, the Poisson probability function with $\lambda = 10$ applies,

$$f(x) = \frac{\lambda^x e^{-\lambda}}{x!} = \frac{10^x e^{-10}}{x!} \qquad \text{for } x = 0, 1, 2, \ldots$$

If we wanted to know the probability of five arrivals in 15 minutes, we would set $x = 5$ and obtain[1]

---

1. Values of $e^{-\lambda}$ are available in Appendix D.

$$f(5) = \frac{10^5 e^{-10}}{5!} = 0.0378$$

Although we determined this probability by evaluating the probability function with $\lambda = 10$ and $x = 5$, the use of Poisson probability distribution tables often is easier. These tables provide probabilities for specific values of x and λ. We included such a table as Appendix B. For convenience we reproduced a portion of it as Table 3.8. To use the table of Poisson probabilities, you need know only the values of x and λ. Thus, from Table 3.8, the probability of five arrivals in a 15-minute period is the value in the row corresponding to $x = 5$ and the column corresponding to $\lambda = 10$. Hence, $f(5) = 0.0378$.

Try Problem 14 for practice computing Poisson probabilities.

An Example Involving Length or Distance Intervals

Suppose that we are concerned with the occurrence of major defects in a section of highway one month after resurfacing. We assume that the probability of a defect is the same for any two intervals of equal length, and that the occurrence or nonoccurrence of a defect in any one interval is independent of the occurrence or nonoccurrence in any other interval. Thus, the Poisson probability distribution applies.

| *Table* 3.8 | SELECTED VALUES FROM THE POISSON PROBABILITY TABLES EXAMPLE: $\lambda = 10, x = 5; f(5) = 0.0378$ |

λ

x	9.1	9.2	9.3	9.4	9.5	9.6	9.7	9.8	9.9	10
0	0.0001	0.0001	0.0001	0.0001	0.0001	0.0001	0.0001	0.0001	0.0001	0.0000
1	0.0010	0.0009	0.0009	0.0008	0.0007	0.0007	0.0006	0.0005	0.0005	0.0005
2	0.0046	0.0043	0.0040	0.0037	0.0034	0.0031	0.0029	0.0027	0.0025	0.0023
3	0.0140	0.0131	0.0123	0.0115	0.0107	0.0100	0.0093	0.0087	0.0081	0.0076
4	0.0319	0.0302	0.0285	0.0269	0.0254	0.0240	0.0226	0.0213	0.0201	0.0189
5	0.0581	0.0555	0.0530	0.0506	0.0483	0.0460	0.0439	0.0418	0.0398	**0.0378**
6	0.0881	0.0851	0.0822	0.0793	0.0764	0.0736	0.0709	0.0682	0.0656	0.0631
7	0.1145	0.1118	0.1091	0.1064	0.1037	0.1010	0.0982	0.0955	0.0928	0.0901
8	0.1302	0.1286	0.1269	0.1251	0.1232	0.1212	0.1191	0.1170	0.1148	0.1126
9	0.1317	0.1315	0.1311	0.1306	0.1300	0.1293	0.1284	0.1274	0.1263	0.1251
10	0.1198	0.1210	0.1219	0.1228	0.1235	0.1241	0.1245	0.1249	0.1250	0.1251
11	0.0991	0.1012	0.1031	0.1049	0.1067	0.1083	0.1098	0.1112	0.1125	0.1137
12	0.0752	0.0776	0.0799	0.0822	0.0844	0.0866	0.0888	0.0908	0.0928	0.0948
13	0.0526	0.0549	0.0572	0.0594	0.0617	0.0640	0.0662	0.0685	0.0707	0.0729
14	0.0342	0.0361	0.0380	0.0399	0.0419	0.0439	0.0459	0.0479	0.0500	0.0521
15	0.0208	0.0221	0.0235	0.0250	0.0265	0.0281	0.0297	0.0313	0.0330	0.0347
16	0.0118	0.0127	0.0137	0.0147	0.0157	0.0168	0.0180	0.0192	0.0204	0.0217
17	0.0063	0.0069	0.0075	0.0081	0.0088	0.0095	0.0103	0.0111	0.0119	0.0128
18	0.0032	0.0035	0.0039	0.0042	0.0046	0.0051	0.0055	0.0060	0.0065	0.0071
19	0.0015	0.0017	0.0019	0.0021	0.0023	0.0026	0.0028	0.0031	0.0034	0.0037
20	0.0007	0.0008	0.0009	0.0010	0.0011	0.0012	0.0014	0.0015	0.0017	0.0019
21	0.0003	0.0003	0.0004	0.0004	0.0005	0.0006	0.0006	0.0007	0.0008	0.0009
22	0.0001	0.0001	0.0002	0.0002	0.0002	0.0002	0.0003	0.0003	0.0004	0.0004
23	0.0000	0.0001	0.0001	0.0001	0.0001	0.0001	0.0001	0.0001	0.0002	0.0002
24	0.0000	0.0000	0.0000	0.0000	0.0000	0.0000	0.0000	0.0001	0.0001	0.0001

Suppose that major defects occur at the average rate of two per mile. We want to find the probability that no major defects will occur in a particular 3-mile section of the highway. The interval length is 3 miles, so λ = (2 defects/mile)(3 miles) = 6 represents the expected number of major defects over the 3-mile section of highway. Thus, by using equation (3.8) or Appendix B with λ = 6 and x = 0, we obtain the probability of no major defects of 0.0025. Thus, finding no major defects in the 3-mile section is very unlikely. In fact, there is a $1 - 0.0025 = 0.9975$ probability of at least one major defect in that section of highway.

N O T E S
and Comments

When working with the Poisson probability distribution, you need to be sure that λ is the mean number of occurrences for the desired interval. For instance, suppose that you know that 30 calls come into a switchboard every 15 minutes. To compute Poisson probabilities for the number of calls coming in over a 5-minute period, you would use λ = 10; to compute probabilities for the number of calls coming in over a 1-minute period, you would use λ = 2.

3.5   CONTINUOUS RANDOM VARIABLES

In this section we introduce probability distributions for continuous random variables. Recall from Section 3.1 that random variables that can take on any value in a certain interval or collection of intervals are said to be *continuous*. Examples of continuous random variables are

1. the *number of ounces* of soup placed in a can labeled "8 ounces";
2. the *flight time* of an airplane traveling from Chicago to New York;
3. the *lifetime* of the picture tube in a new television set; and
4. the *drilling depth* required to reach oil in an offshore drilling operation.

To understand the nature of continuous random variables more fully, suppose that, in the first example, one can of soup has 8.2 ounces and another 8.3 ounces. Other cans could weigh 8.25 ounces, 8.225 ounces, and so on. In fact, the actual weight can be any numerical value from 0 ounces for an empty can to, say, 8.5 ounces for a can filled to capacity. Because this interval contains infinitely many values, we can no longer list each value of the random variable and then identify its associated probability. In fact, for continuous random variables we need a new method for computing the probabilities associated with the values of the random variable.

Applying the Uniform Distribution

Let x denote the flight time of an airplane traveling from Chicago to New York. Assume that the minimum time is 2 hours and that the maximum time is 2 hours 20 minutes. Thus, in terms of minutes, the flight time can be any value in the interval from 120 minutes to 140 minutes (e.g., 124 minutes, 125.48 minutes, etc.). As the random variable x can take on any value from 120 to 140 minutes, x is a continuous rather than a discrete random variable. Assume that sufficient actual flight data are available to conclude that the probability of a flight time between 120 and 121 minutes is the same as the probability of a flight time within any other 1-minute interval up to and including 140 minutes. With every 1-minute interval being equally likely, the random variable x has a **uniform probability distribution.** The following **probability density function** describes the uniform probability distribution for the flight time random variable:

$$f(x) = \begin{cases} \dfrac{1}{20} & \text{for } 120 \leq x \leq 140 \\[2mm] 0 & \text{elsewhere} \end{cases} \tag{3.9}$$

Figure 3.3 shows a graph of this probability density function. In general, the uniform probability density function for a random variable x is

$$f(x) = \begin{cases} \dfrac{1}{b-a} & \text{for } a \leq x \leq b \\[2mm] 0 & \text{elsewhere} \end{cases} \tag{3.10}$$

In the flight time example, $a = 120$ and $b = 140$.

In the graph of a probability density function, $f(x)$ shows the height or value of the function at any particular value of x. Because the probability density function for flight time is *uniform,* the height or value of the function is the same for each value of x between 120 and 140. That is, $f(x) = \frac{1}{20}$ for all values of x between 120 and 140. The probability density function $f(x)$, unlike the probability function for a discrete random variable, represents the height of the function at any particular value of x and *not* probability. Recall that, for each value of a discrete random variable (say, $x = 2$), the probability function yielded the probability of x having *exactly* that value [for example, $f(2)$]. However, a continuous random variable has infinitely many values, so we can no longer identify the probability for each specific value of x. Rather, we must consider probability in terms of the likelihood that a random variable takes on a value within a *specified interval.* For example, in the flight time example an acceptable probability question is: What is the probability that the flight time is between 120 and 130 minutes? That is, what is $P(120 \leq x \leq 130)$? As the flight time must be between 120 and 140 minutes and as the probability is uniformly distributed over this interval, we feel comfortable saying that $P(120 \leq x \leq 130) = 0.50$. Indeed, as we will show, this is correct.

Figure 3.3   UUNFORM PROBABILITY DENSITY FUNCTION FOR FLIGHT TIME

Area as a Measure of Probability

Refer to Figure 3.4 and consider the *area under the graph of* $f(x)$ over the interval from 120 to 130. Note that the region is rectangular in shape and that the area of a rectangle is simply the width times the height. With the width of the interval equal to $130 - 120 = 10$ and the height of the graph $f(x) = \frac{1}{20}$, the area = width × height = $10(\frac{1}{20}) = \frac{10}{20} = 0.50$.

What observation can you make about the area under the graph of $f(x)$ and probability? They are identical! Indeed, that is true for all continuous random variables. In other words, once you have identified a probability density function $f(x)$ for a continuous random variable, you can obtain the probability that x takes on a value between some lower value a and some higher value b by computing the *area* under the graph of $f(x)$ over the interval a to b.

With the appropriate probability distribution and the interpretation of area as probability, we can answer any number of probability questions. For example, what is the probability of a flight time between 128 and 136 minutes? The width of the interval is $136 - 128 = 8$. With the uniform height of $\frac{1}{20}$, $P(128 \le x \le 136) = \frac{8}{20} = 0.40$.

Note that $P(120 \le x \le 140) = 20(\frac{1}{20}) = 1$. That is, the total area under the $f(x)$ graph is equal to 1. This property holds for all continuous probability distributions and is the analog of the condition that the sum of the probabilities has to equal 1 for a discrete probability distribution. A continuous probability distribution also requires that $f(x) \ge 0$ for all values of x. This is the analog of the requirement that $f(x) \ge 0$ for discrete probability distributions.

Two principal differences between continuous random variables and probability distributions and their discrete counterparts stand out.

1. We no longer talk about the probability of the random variable taking on a particular value. Instead we talk about the probability of the random variable taking on a value within some given interval.

2. The probability of the random variable taking on a value within some given interval is defined to be the area under the graph of the probability density function over the interval. This definition implies that the probability that a continuous random variable takes on any particular value is zero because the area under the graph of $f(x)$ at a single point is zero.

You should now be able to compute probabilities using the uniform probability distribution. Try Problem 18.

Figure 3.4   AREA PROVIDES PROBABILITY OF FLIGHT TIME

$P(120 \le x \le 130) = \text{Area} = 1/20(10) = 10/20 = .50$

$f(x)$

$\frac{1}{20}$

10

0   120   125   130   135   140 x

Flight Time in Minutes

NOTES and Comments	**1.** For any continuous random variable the probability of any particular value is zero, so $P(a \le x \le b) = P(a < x < b)$. Thus, the probability of a random variable assuming a value in any interval is the same whether the endpoints are included or not.

2. To see more clearly why the height of a probability density function is not a probability, think about a random variable with a uniform probability distribution of

$$f(x) = \begin{cases} 2 & \text{for } 0 \le x \le 0.5 \\ 0 & \text{elsewhere} \end{cases}$$

The height of the probability density function is 2 for values of x between 0 and 0.5. But, we know that probabilities can never be greater than 1.

3.6 THE NORMAL DISTRIBUTION

Perhaps the most important probability distribution used to describe a continuous random variable is the **normal probability distribution.** It is applicable in a great many practical problem situations, and its probability density function has the form of the bell-shaped curve shown in Figure 3.5.

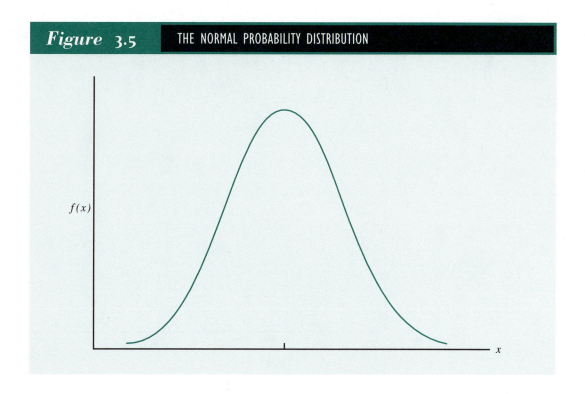

Figure 3.5   THE NORMAL PROBABILITY DISTRIBUTION

The normal distribution
was first observed by
Abraham deMoivre, a
French mathematician, in
the early 1700s. deMoivre's
work was motivated by the
study of probability
associated with gambling
and games of chance.

The mathematical form of the probability density function for the uniform distribution was fairly simple: $f(x) = 1/(b-a)$ for $a \leq x \leq b$. The nathematical function that provides the bell-shaped curve of the normal probability density function is more complex:

$$f(x) = \frac{1}{\sigma\sqrt{2\pi}}\, e^{-(x-\mu)^2/2\sigma^2} \qquad \text{for } -\infty < x < \infty \qquad (3.11)$$

where

μ = mean or expected value of the random variable x

σ^2 = variance of the random variable x

σ = standard deviation of the random variable x

π = 3.14159

e = 2.71828

Recall from the previous discussion of continuous random variables that $f(x)$ is the height of the curve at a particular value of x. Thus, once we specify the mean (μ) and either the standard deviation (σ) or variance (σ^2), we can use equation (3.11) to determine the graph for the corresponding normal distribution. Figure 3.6 shows two normal distributions, one with $\mu = 50$ and $\sigma = 15$ and another with $\mu = 50$ and $\sigma = 7.5$. Note in particular the effect that the standard deviation σ has on the general shape of the normal curve. A larger standard deviation tends to flatten and broaden the curve because larger values of σ indicate greater variability in the values of the random variable.

Fortunately, whenever we use the normal distribution to answer probability questions, we do not have to use the probability density function of equation (3.11). In fact, when we use the normal distribution, we will have tables of probability values [areas under the $f(x)$

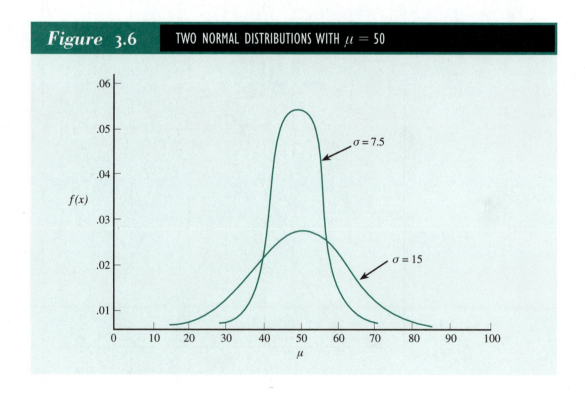

Figure 3.6   TWO NORMAL DISTRIBUTIONS WITH $\mu = 50$

curve] that can provide the desired probability information. To show how to use the tables of areas or probabilities for the normal distribution, we must first introduce the standard normal distribution.

The Standard Normal Distribution

A random variable that has a normal distribution with a mean of 0 and a standard deviation of 1 is said to have a **standard normal distribution.** We use the letter z to designate this particular normal random variable. Figure 3.7 shows the graph of the standard normal distribution. Note that it has the same general appearance as other normal distributions, but with the special properties of $\mu = 0$ and $\sigma = 1$. The units on the horizontal axis (z) measure the number of standard deviations from the mean.

Recall the procedure for finding probabilities associated with a continuous random variable. We want to determine the probability of the random variable having a value in a specified interval from a to b. Thus we have to find the area under the curve in the interval from a to b. In the preceding section we showed that finding probabilities, or areas under the curve, for a uniform distribution was relatively easy. All we had to do was multiply the width of the interval by the height of the graph. However, finding areas under the normal distribution curve appears at first glance to be much more difficult because the height of the curve varies. The mathematical technique for obtaining these areas is beyond the scope of the text, but fortunately tables are available that provide the areas or probability values for the standard normal distribution. Table 3.9 is such a table of areas. This table is also available as Appendix C.

To use Table 3.9 to find probabilities, first note that values of z appear in the left-hand column, with the second decimal value of z appearing in the top row. For example, for a z

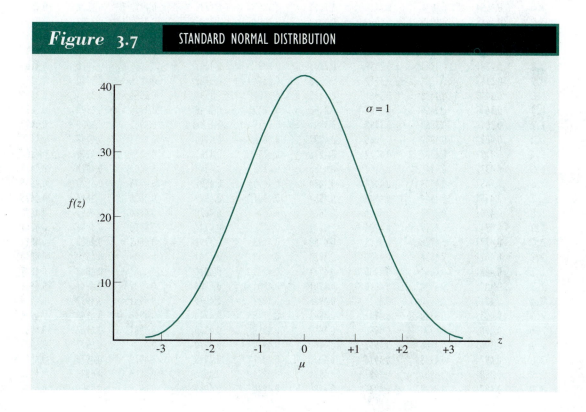

Figure 3.7 STANDARD NORMAL DISTRIBUTION

Table 3.9   AREAS OR PROBABILITIES FOR THE STANDARD NORMAL DISTRIBUTION

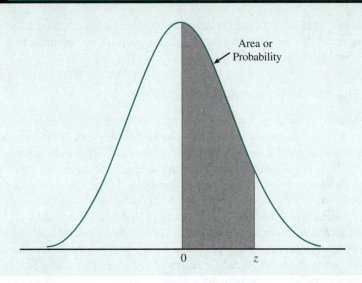

Entries in the table give the area under the curve between the mean and z standard deviations above the mean. For example, for $z = 1.25$, the area under the curve between the mean and z is 0.3944.

z	0.00	0.01	0.02	0.03	0.04	0.05	0.06	0.07	0.08	0.09
0.0	0.0000	0.0040	0.0080	0.0120	0.0160	0.0199	0.0239	0.0279	0.0319	0.0359
0.1	0.0398	0.0438	0.0478	0.0517	0.0557	0.0596	0.0636	0.0675	0.0714	0.0753
0.2	0.0793	0.0832	0.0871	0.0910	0.0948	0.0987	0.1026	0.1064	0.1103	0.1141
0.3	0.1179	0.1217	0.1255	0.1293	0.1331	0.1368	0.1406	0.1443	0.1480	0.1517
0.4	0.1554	0.1591	0.1628	0.1664	0.1700	0.1736	0.1772	0.1808	0.1844	0.1879
0.5	0.1915	0.1950	0.1985	0.2019	0.2054	0.2088	0.2123	0.2157	0.2190	0.2224
0.6	0.2257	0.2291	0.2324	0.2357	0.2389	0.2422	0.2454	0.2486	0.2518	0.2549
0.7	0.2580	0.2612	0.2642	0.2673	0.2704	0.2734	0.2764	0.2794	0.2823	0.2852
0.8	0.2881	0.2910	0.2939	0.2967	0.2995	0.3023	0.3051	0.3078	0.3106	0.3133
0.9	0.3159	0.3186	0.3212	0.3238	0.3264	0.3289	0.3315	0.3340	0.3365	0.3389
1.0	0.3413	0.3438	0.3461	0.3485	0.3508	0.3531	0.3554	0.3577	0.3599	0.3621
1.1	0.3643	0.3665	0.3686	0.3708	0.3729	0.3749	0.3770	0.3790	0.3810	0.3830
1.2	0.3849	0.3869	0.3888	0.3907	0.3925	**0.3944**	0.3962	0.3980	0.3997	0.4015
1.3	0.4032	0.4049	0.4066	0.4082	0.4099	0.4115	0.4131	0.4147	0.4162	0.4177
1.4	0.4192	0.4207	0.4222	0.4236	0.4251	0.4265	0.4279	0.4292	0.4306	0.4319
1.5	0.4332	0.4345	0.4357	0.4370	0.4382	0.4394	0.4406	0.4418	0.4429	0.4441
1.6	0.4452	0.4463	0.4474	0.4484	0.4495	0.4505	0.4515	0.4525	0.4535	0.4545
1.7	0.4554	0.4564	0.4573	0.4582	0.4591	0.4599	0.4608	0.4616	0.4625	0.4633
1.8	0.4641	0.4649	0.4656	0.4664	0.4671	0.4678	0.4686	0.4693	0.4699	0.4706
1.9	0.4713	0.4719	0.4726	0.4732	0.4738	0.4744	0.4750	0.4756	0.4761	0.4767
2.0	0.4772	0.4778	0.4783	0.4788	0.4793	0.4798	0.4803	0.4808	0.4812	0.4817
2.1	0.4821	0.4826	0.4830	0.4834	0.4838	0.4842	0.4846	0.4850	0.4854	0.4857
2.2	0.4861	0.4864	0.4868	0.4871	0.4875	0.4878	0.4881	0.4884	0.4887	0.4890
2.3	0.4893	0.4896	0.4898	0.4901	0.4904	0.4906	0.4909	0.4911	0.4913	0.4916
2.4	0.4918	0.4920	0.4922	0.4925	0.4927	0.4929	0.4931	0.4932	0.4934	0.4936
2.5	0.4938	0.4940	0.4941	0.4943	0.4945	0.4946	0.4948	0.4949	0.4951	0.4952
2.6	0.4953	0.4955	0.4956	0.4957	0.4959	0.4960	0.4961	0.4962	0.4963	0.4964
2.7	0.4965	0.4966	0.4967	0.4968	0.4969	0.4970	0.4971	0.4972	0.4973	0.4974
2.8	0.4974	0.4975	0.4976	0.4977	0.4977	0.4978	0.4979	0.4979	0.4980	0.4981
2.9	0.4981	0.4982	0.4982	0.4983	0.4984	0.4984	0.4985	0.4985	0.4986	0.4986
3.0	0.4986	0.4987	0.4987	0.4988	0.4988	0.4989	0.4989	0.4989	0.4990	0.4990

value of 1.00 we find the 1.0 in the left-hand column and 0.00 in the top row. Then by looking in the body of the table, we find that 0.3413 corresponds to the 1.00 value for z. The value of 0.3413 is the area under the curve between the mean ($z = 0.00$) and $z = 1.00$, shown graphically in Figure 3.8.

Thus, the values in Table 3.9 provide *the area under the curve between the mean ($z = 0.00$) and any specified positive value of z.* For another example, we can use the table to find that the area or probability of a z value in the interval $z = 0.00$ to $z = 1.25$ is 0.3944.

Suppose that we want the probability of obtaining a z value between $z = -1.00$ and $z = 1.00$. We already have used Table 3.9 to find that the probability of a z value between $z = 0.00$ and $z = 1.00$ is 0.3413. Note now that the normal distribution is symmetric. That is, the shape of the curve to the left of the mean is the mirror image of the shape of the curve to the right of the mean. Thus, the probability of a z value between $z = 0.00$ and $z = -1.00$ is the same as the probability of a z value between $z = 0.00$ and $z = 1.00$, or 0.3413. Hence, the probability of a z value between $z = -1.00$ and $z = 1.00$ is $0.3413 + 0.3413 = 0.6826$, shown graphically in Figure 3.9.

Similarly, we can find that the probability of a z value between -2.00 and $+2.00$ is $0.4772 + 0.4772 = 0.9544$ and that the probability of a z value between -3.00 and $+3.00$ is $0.4986 + 0.4986 = 0.9972$. We know that the total probability or total area under the curve for any continuous random variable must be 1.0000, so the probability of 0.9972 tells us the value of z almost always will fall between -3.00 and $+3.00$. Note that the figures depicting the standard normal distribution show this condition graphically.

We now consider two final examples of computing areas for the standard normal distribution. First let us find the probability that z is greater than 2.00. From Table 3.9 the area between $z = 0.00$ and $z = 2.00$ is 0.4772. As 0.5000 is the total area above the mean, the area above $z = 2.00$ must be $0.5000 - 0.4772 = 0.0228$, shown graphically in Figure 3.10.

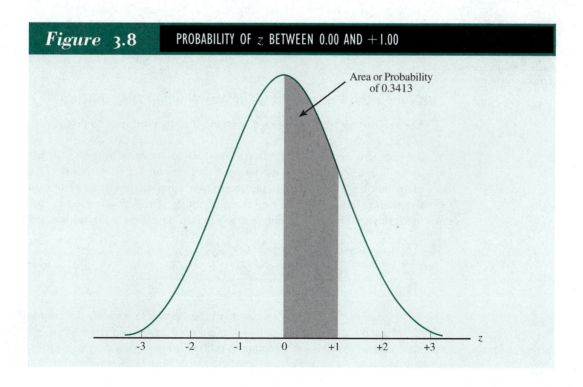

Figure 3.8   PROBABILITY OF z BETWEEN 0.00 AND $+1.00$

Area or Probability
of 0.3413

Figure 3.9   PROBABILITY OF z BETWEEN -1.00 AND $+1.00$

Area = 0.3413

Area = 0.3413

Total Area = 0.3413 + 0.3413
= 0.6826

Again, because the normal distribution is symmetric, the probability of obtaining a value of z less than $z = -2.00$ is also 0.0228.

Now let us find the probability that z is between 1.00 and 2.00. We first note that the area between the mean $z = 0.00$ and $z = 2.00$ is 0.4772. The area between the mean $z = 0.00$ and $z = 1.00$ is 0.3413. Thus the area between $z = 1.00$ and $z = 2.00$ must be $0.4772 - 0.3413 = 0.1359$, shown graphically in Figure 3.11.

Try Problem 21 for practice computing probabilities with the standard normal probability distribution.

Computing Probabilities for Any Normal Distribution

The reason that we have been discussing the standard normal distribution so extensively is that we can compute probabilities for any normal distribution by first converting to the standard normal distribution. Thus, when we have a normal distribution with any mean μ and any standard deviation σ, we can answer probability questions about this distribution by converting to the standard normal distribution. We then use Table 3.9 and the appropriate z values to find the probability. The formula used to convert any normal random variable x with mean μ and standard deviation σ to the standard normal distribution is

$$z = \frac{x - \mu}{\sigma} \tag{3.12}$$

When used in this way, z is a measure of the number of standard deviations that x is from μ.

We can most easily show how the conversion to the z value allows us to use the standard normal distribution to compute probabilities for any normal distribution with an example. Suppose that we have a normal distribution with $\mu = 10$ and $\sigma = 2$, as shown

Figure 3.10   PROBABILITY OF z GREATER THAN 2.00

0.5000 Is the Total Area Below 0

0.5000 Is the Total Area Above 0

0.4772 Is the Area Between 0 and 2

Area of z Greater Than 2 is 0.5000 − 0.4772 = 0.0228

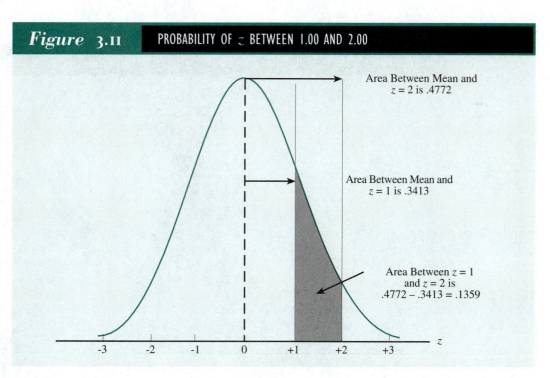

Figure 3.11   PROBABILITY OF z BETWEEN 1.00 AND 2.00

Area Between Mean and z = 2 is .4772

Area Between Mean and z = 1 is .3413

Area Between z = 1 and z = 2 is .4772 − .3413 = .1359

graphically in Figure 3.12. Note that, in addition to the values of the random variable shown on the x axis, we have included a second axis (the z axis) to show that for each value of x there is a corresponding value of z. For example, when $x = 10$ the corresponding z value (the number of standard deviations away from the mean) is $z = (x - \mu)/\sigma = (10 - 10)/2 = 0$. Similarly, for $x = 14$ we have $z = (x - \mu)/\sigma = (14 - 10)/2 = 2$.

Now suppose that we want to know the probability that the random variable x is between 10 and 14—that is, $P(10 \leq x \leq 14)$. We do not have tables that provide this probability directly. However, note that in Figure 3.12 the area under the curve (probability) for x between 10 and 14 is the *same* as the area under the curve for z between 0 and 2. Using $z = 2.00$ and Table 3.9, we find that the area or probability of z being between 0 and 2 is 0.4772. Thus, we conclude that the probability of x being between 10 and 14 also is 0.4772.

This procedure applies to any normal distribution problem. That is, for any x value a corresponding z value is given by equation (3.12). To find the probability that x is in a specified interval, simply convert the x interval to its corresponding z interval. Then use the table for the standard normal distribution to answer the probability question.

The Grear Tire Company Problem

Suppose that the Grear Tire Company has just developed a new steel-belted radial tire that will be sold through a national chain of discount stores. Because the tire is a new product, Grear's management believes that the mileage guarantee offered with the tire will be an important factor in the consumer acceptance of the product. Before finalizing the tire mileage

Figure 3.12   NORMAL DISTRIBUTION WITH $\mu = 10$ AND $\sigma = 2$

guarantee policy, Grear's management wants some probability information concerning the number of miles the tires will last.

From actual road tests with the tires, Grear's engineering group estimates the mean tire mileage at $\mu = 36{,}500$ miles and the standard deviation at $\sigma = 5000$ miles. In addition, the data collected indicate that a normal distribution is a reasonable assumption.

What percentage of the tires, then, can be expected to last more than 40,000 miles? In other words, what is the probability that the tire mileage will exceed 40,000? To compute this probability, we need to find the area of the shaded region in Figure 3.13.

At $x = 40{,}000$ we have

$$z = \frac{x - \mu}{\sigma} = \frac{40{,}000 - 36{,}500}{5{,}000} = \frac{3{,}500}{5{,}000} = 0.70$$

Thus the probability that the normal distribution for tire mileage will have an x value greater than 40,000 is the same as the probability that the standard normal distribution will have a z value greater than 0.70. Using Table 3.9, we find that the area corresponding to $z = 0.70$ is 0.2580. However, remember that the table always provides the area between the mean and the z value. Thus, we know that there is a 0.2580 area between the mean and $z = 0.70$. As the total area above the mean is 0.5000, we must have $0.5000 - 0.2580 = 0.2420$ as the area above $z = 0.70$. In terms of the tire mileage x, we can conclude that there is a 0.2420 probability that x will be above 40,000. Thus, about 24.2% of the tires manufactured by Grear can be expected to last more than 40,000 miles.

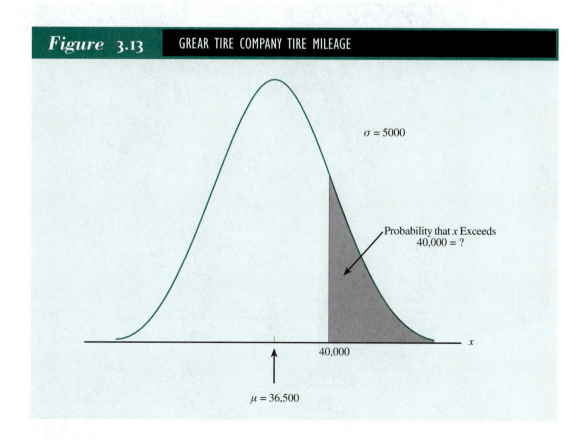

Figure 3.13   GREAR TIRE COMPANY TIRE MILEAGE

Let us now assume that Grear is considering a guarantee that will provide a discount on a new set of tires if the mileage on the original tires doesn't exceed the mileage stated on the guarantee. What should the guarantee mileage be if Grear wants no more than 10% of the tires to be eligible for the discount? This question is interpreted graphically in Figure 3.14. Note that 10% of the area is below the unknown guarantee mileage, so we know that 40% of the area must be between the mean and the unknown guarantee mileage. The question is, how many standard deviations (z value) do we have to be *below* the mean to find 40% of the area? If we look up 0.4000 in the *body* of Table 3.9, we see that a 0.4000 area occurs at approximately $z = 1.28$. The area is below the mean, so we know that the z value of interest must be -1.28. Hence, we must be 1.28 standard deviations less than the mean to find the desired guarantee mileage. This mileage then is

$$\text{Guarantee mileage} = \mu - 1.28\sigma$$
$$= 36,500 - 1.28(5,000) = 30,100$$

Therefore a guarantee of 30,100 miles will meet the requirement that approximately 10% of the tires will be eligible for the discount. With this information the firm might confidently set its tire mileage guarantee at 30,000 miles.

Try Problem 23 for practice finding a z value that cuts off a particular probability.

Again we see the important role that probability distributions play in providing decision-making information. Once a probability distribution is established for a particular problem, it can be used rather quickly and easily to provide probability information about the problem. Although this information does not make a decision recommendation

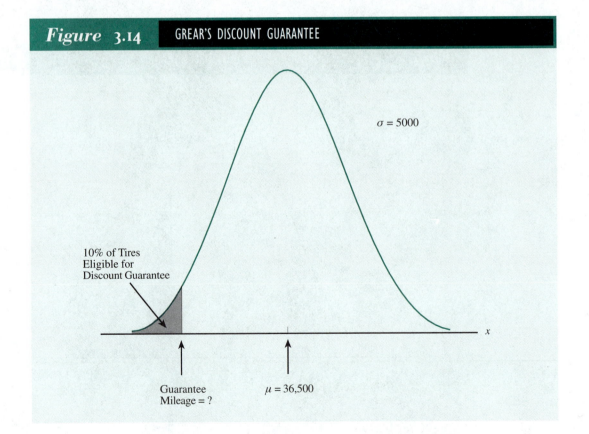

Figure 3.14 **GREAR'S DISCOUNT GUARANTEE**

directly, it does provide information that helps the decision maker understand the problem better. Ultimately, this information may assist the decision maker in reaching a good decision.

3.7   THE EXPONENTIAL DISTRIBUTION

A continuous probability distribution that is often useful in describing the time needed to complete a task is the **exponential probability distribution.** The exponential random variable can be used to describe the time between arrivals at a car wash, the time required to load a truck, the distance between major defects in a highway, and so on. The exponential probability density function is

$$f(x) = \frac{1}{\mu} e^{-x/\mu} \qquad \text{for } x \ge 0, \mu > 0 \qquad (3.13)$$

To provide an example of the exponential probability distribution, suppose that the time required to load a truck at the Schips loading dock follows an exponential probability distribution. If the mean, or average, time to load a truck is 15 minutes ($\mu = 15$), the appropriate probability density function is

$$f(x) = \frac{1}{15} e^{-x/15}$$

Figure 3.15 shows the graph of this density function.

Computing Probabilities for the Exponential Distribution

As with any continuous probability distribution, the area under the curve corresponding to some interval provides the probability that the random variable takes on a value in that interval. For example, for the Schips loading dock example the probability that 6 *minutes or less* ($x \le 6$) is needed to load a truck is defined to be the area under the curve from $x = 0$ to $x = 6$. Similarly, the probability that a truck is loaded in 18 *minutes or less* ($x \le 18$) is the area under the curve from $x = 0$ to $x = 18$. Note also that the probability of loading a truck in between 6 and 18 minutes ($6 \le x \le 18$) is the area under the curve from $x = 6$ to $x = 18$.

To compute exponential probabilities such as those described above, the following formula provides the probability of obtaining a value for the exponential random variable of less than or equal to some specific value of x, denoted by x_0:

$$P(x \le x_0) = 1 - e^{-x_0/\mu} \qquad (3.14)$$

Thus, for the Schips loading dock example, equation (3.14) becomes

$$P(\text{loading time} \le x_0) = 1 - e^{-x_0/15}$$

Hence, the probability that 6 minutes or less ($x \le 6$) are needed to load a truck is

$$P(\text{loading time} \le 6) = 1 - e^{-6/15} = 0.3297$$

Figure 3.15   EXPONENTIAL DISTRIBUTION FOR THE SCHIPS LOADING DOCK EXAMPLE

Note also the probability that 18 minutes or less ($x \le 18$) are needed to load a truck is

$$P(\text{loading time} \le 18) = 1 - e^{-18/15} = 0.6988$$

Try Problem 29 for
practice finding
probabilities with the
exponential probability
distribution.

Thus, the probability that 6 to 18 minutes are required to load a truck is $0.6988 - 0.3297 = 0.3691$. Probabilities for any other interval can be computed in a similar manner.

Relationship Between the Poisson and Exponential Distributions

In Section 3.4 we introduced the Poisson distribution as a discrete probability distribution that often is useful when we are dealing with the number of occurrences over a specified interval of time or space. Recall that the Poisson probability function is

The Poisson and
exponential probability
distributions are used in
the chapter on waiting line
models (Chapter 15). In
these models the Poisson
distribution is used as the
probability distribution for
the number of arrivals
while the exponential
probability distribution is
used as the probability
distribution for the service
time.

$$f(x) = \frac{\lambda^x e^{-\lambda}}{x!}$$

where

λ = expected value or mean number of occurrences in an interval

The continuous exponential probability distribution is related to the discrete Poisson distribution: The Poisson distribution provides an appropriate description of the number of occurrences per interval, the exponential distribution provides a description of the length of the interval between occurrences.

To illustrate this relationship, let us suppose that the number of cars that arrive at a car wash during 1 hour is described by a Poisson probability distribution with a mean of 10 cars per hour. Thus the Poisson probability function that provides the probability of x arrivals per hour is

$$f(x) = \frac{10^x e^{-10}}{x!}$$

The average number of arrivals is 10 cars per hour, so the average time between cars arriving is

$$\frac{1 \text{ hour}}{10 \text{ cars}} = 0.1 \text{ hour/car}$$

Try Problem 30 for an application of the exponential probability distribution.

Thus, the corresponding exponential distribution that describes the time between the arrival of cars has a mean of $\mu = 0.1$ hours per car. The appropriate exponential probability density function is

$$f(x) = \frac{1}{0.1} e^{-x/0.1} = 10e^{-10x}$$

··/ /············

SUMMARY

In this chapter we continued the discussion of probability by introducing the important concepts of random variables and probability distributions. Random variables provide numerical descriptions of the outcomes of experiments. When random variables are used, computations of the expected value, variance, and standard deviation can help the decision maker understand characteristics of the problem under study. We discussed the probability distributions for both discrete and continuous random variables.

Of particular interest are special probability distributions such as the binomial, Poisson, uniform, normal, and exponential distributions. These distributions are important because they have wide applicability and because special formulas and/or tables make the probability information easily available.

Through a variety of problems and applications we illustrated the role that probability distributions play in providing decision-making information. Although the probability values generated by the techniques and methods of this chapter do not by themselves make decision recommendations, they do provide assistance to the decision maker in terms of understanding the uncertainties inherent in the problem. Ultimately, this better understanding may lead to new and better decisions.

··/ /············

GLOSSARY

Random variable A numerical description of the outcome of an experiment.

Discrete random variable A random variable that can take on only a finite or infinite sequence of values.

Continuous random variable A random variable that may take on any value in an interval or collection of intervals.

Probability function A function, denoted $f(x)$, that provides the probability that a discrete random variable x takes on some specific value.

Discrete probability distribution A table, graph, or equation describing the values of the random variable and the associated probabilities.

Expected value A weighted average of the values of the random variable, for which the probability function provides the weights. If an experiment can be repeated a large number of times, the expected value can be interpreted as the "long-run average."

Variance A measure of the dispersion or variability in the random variable. It is a weighted average of the squared deviations from the mean, μ.

Standard deviation The positive square root of the variance.

Binomial probability distribution The probability distribution for a discrete random variable. It is used to compute the probability of x successes in n trials.

Poisson probability distribution The probability distribution for a discrete random variable. It is used to compute the probability of x occurrences over a specified interval.

Uniform probability distribution A continuous probability distribution in which the probability that the random variable will assume a value in any interval of equal length is the same for each interval.

Probability density function The function that describes the probability distribution of a continuous random variable.

Normal probability distribution A continuous probability distribution. Its probability density function is bell-shaped and determined by the mean, μ, and standard deviation, σ.

Standard normal distribution A normal distribution with a mean of 0 and a standard deviation of 1.

Exponential probability distribution A continuous probability distribution that is useful in describing the time to complete a task or the time between occurrences of an event.

PROBLEMS

SELF TEST

1. The following are examples of experiments and associated random variables. In each case identify the values that the random variable can take on and state whether the random variable is discrete or continuous.

Experiment	Random Variable (x)
a. Take a 20-question examination	Number of questions answered correctly
b. Observe cars arriving at a tollbooth for 1 hour	Number of cars arriving at the tollbooth
c. Audit 50 tax returns	Number of returns containing errors
d. Observe an employee's work for 8 hours	Number of nonproductive hours
e. Weigh a shipment of goods	Number of pounds

2. The following table shows a partial probability distribution for the MRA Company's projected profits (in thousands of dollars) for the first year of operation (the negative value denotes a loss).

x	$f(x)$
−100	0.10
0	0.20
50	0.30
100	0.25
150	0.10
200	

a. Find the missing value of $f(200)$. What is your interpretation of this value?
b. What is the probability that MRA will be profitable?
c. What is the probability that MRA will make at least $100,000?

SELF TEST

3. Data were collected on the number of operating rooms in use at Tampa General Hospital over a 20-day period. On 3 of the days only 1 operating room was used; on 5 days, 2 were used; on 8 days, 3 were used; and on 4 days all 4 rooms were used.
a. Use the relative frequency approach to construct a probability distribution for the number of operating rooms in use on any given day.
b. Draw a graph of the probability distribution.
c. Show that your probability distribution satisfies the required conditions for a valid discrete probability distribution.

SELF TEST

4. Shown is a probability distribution for the random variable x.

x	$f(x)$
3	0.25
6	0.50
9	0.25
Total	1.00

a. Compute $E(x)$, the expected value of x.
b. Compute σ^2, the variance of x.
c. Compute σ, the standard deviation of x.

5. A roulette wheel at a Las Vegas casino has 18 red numbers, 18 black numbers, and 2 green numbers. Assume that a $5 bet is placed on the black numbers. If a black number comes up, the player wins $5; otherwise, the player loses $5.
a. Let x be a random variable indicating the player's net winnings on one bet. Thus, $x = 5$ if the player wins and $x = -5$ if the player loses. Show the probability distribution of x.
b. What is the expected amount won on a bet? What is your interpretation of this value?
c. What is the variance in the amount won on a bet? What is the standard deviation?
d. If a player places 100 bets of $5 each, what are the expected winnings? Comment on why casinos like a high volume of betting.

6. The probability distribution for damage claims paid by the Newton Automobile Insurance Company on collision insurance is

Payment ($)	Probability
0	0.90
400	0.04
1000	0.03
2000	0.01
4000	0.01
6000	0.01

a. Use the expected collision payment to determine the collision insurance premium that would allow the company to break even.

b. The insurance company charges an annual rate of $260 for the collision coverage. What is the expected value of the collision policy for the policyholder? (Hint: It is the expected payments from the company minus the cost of coverage.) Why does the policyholder purchase a collision policy with this expected value?

7. The demand for a product of Carolina Industries varies greatly from month to month. Based on the past 2 years of data, the following probability distribution shows the company's monthly demand.

Unit demand	Probability
300	0.20
400	0.30
500	0.35
600	0.15

a. If the company places monthly orders equal to the expected value of the monthly demand, what should Carolina's monthly order quantity be for this product?

b. Assume that each unit demanded generates $70 in revenue and that each unit ordered costs $50. How much will the company gain or lose in a month if it places an order based on your answer to part a and the actual demand for the item is 300 units?

c. What are the variance and the standard deviation for the number of units demanded?

8. The J. R. Ryland Computer Company is considering a plant expansion that will enable the company to begin production of a new computer product. The company's president must determine whether to make the expansion a medium- or large-scale project. An uncertainty involves the demand for the new product, which for planning purposes may be low demand, medium demand, or high demand. The probability estimates for the demands are 0.20, 0.50 and 0.30, respectively. Letting x indicate the annual profit in $1000s, the firm's planners have developed profit forecasts for the medium- and large-scale expansion projects.

		Medium-Scale Expansion Profits		Large-Scale Expansion Profits	
		x	$f(x)$	y	$f(y)$
Demand	Low	50	0.20	0	0.20
	Medium	150	0.50	100	0.50
	High	200	0.30	300	0.30

a. Compute the expected value for the profit associated with the two expansion alternatives. Which decision is preferred for the objective of maximizing the expected profit?

b. Compute the variance for the profit associated with the two expansion alternatives. Which decision is preferred for the objective of minimizing the risk or uncertainty?

SELF TEST

9. Consider a binomial experiment with 2 trials and $p = 0.4$.
   a. Compute the probability of 1 success, $f(1)$.
   b. Compute $f(0)$.
   c. Compute $f(2)$.
   d. Find the probability of at least 1 success.
   e. Find the expected value, variance, and standard deviation.

10. Consider a binomial experiment with $n = 10$ and $p = 0.10$. Use the binomial tables (Appendix A) to answer parts (a)–(d).
   a. Find $f(0)$.
   b. Find $f(2)$.
   c. Find $P(x \le 2)$.
   d. Find $P(x \ge 1)$.
   e. Find $E(x)$.
   f. Find $\text{Var}(x)$ and σ.

11. The greatest number of complaints by owners of two-year-old automobiles is in the area of electrical system performance (*Consumer Reports 1992 Buyers Guide*). In an annual questionnaire of owners of over 300 makes and models of automobiles, *Consumer Reports* found that 10% of the owners of two-year-old automobiles experienced trouble with the electrical system that included the starter, alternator, battery, switch controls, instruments, wiring, lights, and radio.
   a. What is the probability that a sample of 12 owners of two-year-old automobiles will reveal 2 owners with electrical system problems?
   b. What is the probability that a sample of 12 owners of two-year-old automobiles will reveal at least 2 owners with electrical system problems?
   c. What is the probability that a sample of 20 owners of two-year-old automobiles will reveal at least one electrical system problem?

SELF TEST

12. When a new machine is functioning properly, only 3% of the items produced are defective. Assume that we will randomly select two parts produced on the machine and that we are interested in the number of defective parts found.
   a. Describe the conditions under which this situation would be a binomial experiment.
   b. How many experimental outcomes yield 1 defect?
   c. Compute the probabilities associated with finding no defects, 1 defect, and 2 defects.

13. Military radar and missile detection systems are designed to warn a country against enemy attacks. A reliability question deals with the ability of the detection system to identify an attack and issue the warning. Assume that a particular detection system has a 0.90 probability of detecting a missile attack. Answer the following questions using the binomial probability distribution.
   a. What is the probability that 1 detection system will detect an attack?
   b. If 2 detection systems are installed in the same area and operate independently, what is the probability that at least 1 of the systems will detect the attack?
   c. If 3 systems are installed, what is the probability that at least one of the systems will detect the attack?
   d. Would you recommend that multiple detection systems be operated? Explain.

14. Consider a Poisson probability distribution with an average number of occurrences per time period of 2.
   a. Write the appropriate Poisson probability function.
   b. What is the average number of occurrences in 3 time periods?
   c. Write the appropriate Poisson probability function to determine the probability of x occurrences in 3 time periods.
   d. Find the probability of 2 occurrences in 1 time period.
   e. Find the probability of 6 occurrences in 3 time periods.
   f. Find the probability of 5 occurrences in 2 time periods.

15. Telephone calls arrive at the rate of 48 per hour at the reservation desk for Regional Airways.
   a. Find the probability of receiving 3 calls in a 5-minute interval.
   b. Find the probability of receiving 10 calls in 15 minutes.

c. Suppose that no calls are currently on hold. If the agent takes 5 minutes to complete processing the current call, how many callers do you expect to be waiting by that time? What is the probability that none will be waiting?

d. If no calls are currently being processed, what is the probability the agent can take 3 minutes for personal time without being interrupted?

16. During rush hours, accidents occur in a particular metropolitan area at the rate of two per hour. The morning rush period lasts for 1 hour 30 minutes, and the evening rush period lasts for 2 hours.

a. On a particular day what is the probability of no accidents during the morning rush period?

b. What is the probability of 2 accidents during the evening rush period?

c. What is the probability of 4 or more accidents during the morning rush period?

d. On a particular day what is the probability of no accidents during both the morning and evening rush periods?

17. Airline passengers arrive randomly and independently at the passenger screening facility at a major international airport. The mean arrival rate is 10 passengers per minute.

a. What is the probability of no arrivals in a 1-minute period?

b. What is the probability of 3 or fewer arrivals in a 1-minute period?

c. What is the probability of no arrivals in a 15-second period?

d. What is the probability of at least 1 arrival in a 15-second period?

18. A random variable x is uniformly distributed between 1.0 and 1.5.

a. Show the graph of the probability density function.

b. Find $P(x = 1.25)$.

c. Find $P(1.0 \leq x \leq 1.25)$.

d. Find $P(1.20 < x < 1.5)$.

19. Delta Airlines quotes a flight time of 1 hour 52 minutes for its flights from Cincinnati to Tampa. Suppose that actual flight times are uniformly distributed between the quoted time and 2 hours 10 minutes.

a. Show the graph of the probability density function for flight times.

b. What is the probability the flight will be no more than 5 minutes late?

c. What is the probability the flight will be more than 10 minutes late?

20. Most computer languages have a function that can be used to generate random numbers. In Microsoft's Excel, the RAND function can be used to generate random numbers between 0 and 1. If we let x denote the random number generated, then x is a continuous random variable with the probability density function:

$$f(x) = \begin{cases} 1 & \text{for } 0 \leq x \leq 1 \\ 0 & \text{elsewhere} \end{cases}$$

a. Graph the probability density function.

b. What is the probability of generating a random number between 0.25 and 0.75?

c. What is the probability of generating a random number with a value less than or equal to 0.30?

d. What is the probability of generating a random number with a value greater than 0.60?

21. For the standard normal random variable z, compute the following probabilities.

a. $P(0 \leq z \leq 0.83)$

b. $P(-1.57 \leq z \leq 0)$

c. $P(z > 0.44)$

d. $P(z \geq -0.23)$

e. $P(z < 1.20)$

f. $P(z \leq -0.71)$

22. For the standard normal random variable z, find z for each situation.

a. The area between 0 and z is 0.4750.

b. The area between 0 and z is 0.2291.

c. The area to the right of z is 0.1314.

d. The area to the left of z is 0.6700.

23. For the standard normal random variable z, find z for each situation.

a. The area to the left of z is 0.2119.

b. The area between $-z$ and z is 0.9030.

c. The area between $-z$ and z is 0.2052.

d. The area to the left of z is 0.9948.

e. The area to the right of z is 0.6915.

24. The demand for a new product is estimated to be normally distributed with $\mu = 200$ and $\sigma = 40$. Let x be the number of units demanded and find the following probabilities.

a. $P(180 \leq x \leq 220)$

b. $P(x \geq 250)$

c. $P(x \leq 100)$

d. $P(225 \leq x \leq 250)$

25. The mean cost for employee alcohol rehabilitation programs involving hospitalization is $10,000 (*USA Today,* September 12, 1991). Assume that rehabilitation program cost has a normal probability distribution with a standard deviation of $2200.

a. What is the probability that a rehabilitation program will cost at least $12,000?

b. What is the probability that a rehabilitation program will cost at least $6000?

c. What is the cost range for the 10% most expensive rehabilitation programs?

26. General Hospital's patient account division has compiled data on the age of accounts receivables. The data collected indicate that the age of the accounts follows a normal distribution with $\mu = 28$ days and $\sigma = 8$ days.

a. What portion of the accounts are between 20 and 40 days old—that is, $P(20 \leq x \leq 40)$?

b. The hospital administrator is interested in sending reminder letters to the oldest 15% of accounts. How many days old should an account be before a reminder letter is sent?

c. The hospital administrator wants to give a discount to those accounts that pay their balance by the 21st day. What percentage of the accounts will receive the discount?

27. The Webster National Bank is reviewing its service charges and interest-paying policies on checking accounts. The average daily balance on personal checking accounts is $550, with a standard deviation of $150. In addition, the average daily balances are normally distributed.

a. What percentage of personal checking account customers carry average daily balances in excess of $800?

b. What percentage carry average daily balances below $200?

c. What percentage carry average daily balances between $300 and $700?

d. The bank is considering paying interest to customers carrying average daily balances in excess of a certain amount. If the bank does not want to pay interest to more than 5% of its customers, what is the minimum average daily balance it should be willing to pay interest on?

28. A machine fills containers with a particular product. The standard deviation of filling weights computed from past data is 0.6 ounces. If only 2% of the containers hold less than 18 ounces, what is the mean filling weight for the machine? That is, what must μ equal? Assume that the filling weights have a normal distribution.

29. Consider the exponential probability density function:

$$f(x) = \frac{1}{3} e^{-x/3} \qquad \text{for } x \geq 0$$

a. Write the formula for $P(x \leq x_0)$.   **b.** Find $P(x \leq 2)$.

c. Find $P(x \geq 3)$.   **d.** Find $P(x \leq 5)$.

e. Find $P(2 \leq x \leq 5)$.

30. There were 34 traffic fatalities in Clermont County, Ohio, during 1987 (The *Cincinnati Enquirer*, December 8, 1988). Assume that, for an average of 34 fatalities per year, an exponential distribution accurately describes the time between fatalities.
    a. What is the probability the time between fatalities is 1 month or less?
    b. What is the probability the time between fatalities is 1 week or more?

31. The time between arrivals of vehicles at a particular intersection follows an exponential probability distribution with a mean of 12 seconds.
    a. Sketch this exponential probability distribution.
    b. What is the probability the arrival time between vehicles is 12 seconds or less?
    c. What is the probability the arrival time between vehicles is 6 seconds or less?
    d. What is the probability there will be 30 or more seconds between arriving vehicles?

32. The lifetime (hours) of an electronic device is a random variable with the exponential probability density function:

$$f(x) = \frac{1}{50} e^{-x/50} \qquad \text{for } x \geq 0$$

    a. What is the mean lifetime of the device?
    b. What is the probability the device fails in the first 25 hours of operation?
    c. What is the probability the device operates 100 or more hours before failure?

33. The time (in minutes) between telephone calls at an insurance claims office has the exponential probability distribution:

$$f(x) = 0.50e^{-0.50x} \qquad \text{for } x \geq 0$$

    a. What is the mean time between telephone calls?
    b. What is the probability of 30 seconds or less between telephone calls?
    c. What is the probability of 1 minute or less between telephone calls?
    d. What is the probability of 5 or more minutes without a telephone call?

34. The time (in minutes) that a checkout lane is idle between customers at a supermarket follows an exponential probability distribution with a mean of 1.2 minutes.
    a. Show the probability density function for this distribution.
    b. What is the probability the next customer arrives between 0.5 to 1.0 minutes after a customer is served?
    c. What is the probability of the checkout lane being idle for more than 1.0 minute between customers?

Appendix 3.1   SPREADSHEETS FOR EXPECTED VALUE AND VARIANCE

Spreadsheets can be helpful in relieving the computational burden of computing probabilities, expected values, and variances. In this appendix we show how to use an Excel spreadsheet to compute the expected value and variance for a discrete probability distribution.

Refer to Tables 3.4 and 3.5, which show the computations involved in computing the expected value and variance for the number of cars sold per day at DiCarlo Motors. Figure 3.16 shows the formula spreadsheet for making these same calculations. Cells **A2** through **A7** contain the values of the random variable, and cells **B2** through **B7** contain the corresponding probabilities. Cells **C2** through **C7** contain the formulas for multiplying the values of the random variable by the corresponding probabilities. The formula in cell **C8** sums these values to compute the mean. The formulas in cells **D2** through **D7** multiply the

Figure 3.16	FORMULA SPREADSHEET FOR COMPUTING EXPECTED VALUE AND VARIANCE

	A	B	C	D
1	x	f(x)	xf(x)	$(x-mu)^2 f(x)$
2	0	0.18	=A2*B2	=(A2-C$8)^2*B2
3	1	0.39	=A3*B3	=(A3-C$8)^2*B3
4	2	0.24	=A4*B4	=(A4-C$8)^2*B4
5	3	0.14	=A5*B5	=(A5-C$8)^2*B5
6	4	0.04	=A6*B6	=(A6-C$8)^2*B6
7	5	0.01	=A7*B7	=(A7-C$8)^2*B7
8			=SUM(C2:C7)	=SUM(D2:D7)

squared deviations by the corresponding probabilities. The formula in cell **D8** sums these values to compute the variance.

Figure 3.17 is a value spreadsheet showing the results of those computations. The formulas are replaced with their values. Note that the results are the same as those shown in Tables 3.4 and 3.5.

For probability distributions, such as the binomial, the expected value and variance are given by a formula [e.g., $E(x) = np$ and $Var(x) = np(1 - p)$]. In such cases, spreadsheets are not necessary for computing the expected value and variance. But for discrete distributions that are not described by formulas, spreadsheets can be helpful in relieving the burden of computing the expected value and variance.

Figure 3.17	VALUE SPREADSHEET FOR COMPUTING EXPECTED VALUE AND VARIANCE

	A	B	C	D
1	x	f(x)	xf(x)	$(x-mu)^2 f(x)$
2	0	0.18	0.00	0.4050
3	1	0.39	0.39	0.0975
4	2	0.24	0.48	0.0600
5	3	0.14	0.42	0.3150
6	4	0.04	0.16	0.2500
7	5	0.01	0.05	0.1225
8			1.50	1.2500

QUANTITATIVE METHODS IN PRACTICE

XEROX CORPORATION*

STAMFORD, CONNECTICUT

Xerox Corporation is in the information products and systems business worldwide. Everyone is familiar with the Xerox copy machines, but the company is involved in many other businesses as well. Xerox's Multinational Documentation & Training Services (MD&TS) provides customers with timely, cost-effective, and high-quality communication services. The four basic services of MD&TS are documentation, training, translation, and publishing.

The professional writers and translators working for MD&TS use an online computerized publication system. For this system, management was interested in determining the effect of different system configurations on performance. Specifically, for a given system configuration, management was interested in determining the following:

1. The probability of a user being refused access by the system because of an excess number of users.
2. The probability of any specific number of users being on the system simultaneously.

A computer simulation model was developed for the purpose of determining these probabilities. In order to build the simulation model, it was necessary to identify the probability distribution for two key random variables:

1. The On Time per session (the length of time a user is on the system).
2. The Idle Time per session (the length of time between sessions).

Based on a survey of users, the probability distribution of on time per session was approximated as shown in the table below. Another probability distribution was developed for the random variable indicating idle time per session. These two probability distributions were key inputs to the simulation model. The results from the simulation study helped MD&TS determine a system configuration that ensured a near-zero probability that a user would be refused access to the system.

x	$f(x)$
10	0.05
20	0.06
30	0.08
40	0.20
50	0.25
60	0.20
70	0.08
80	0.06
90	0.02

The actual probability distribution used in the simulation study has been modified to protect proprietary information and to simplify the discussion.

Questions

1. What is the expected value of the on time per session based on the probability distribution shown in the table? What is your interpretation of this expected value?
2. What is the variance of the on time per session based on the probability distribution shown in the table?

*The authors are indebted to Soterios M. Flouris for providing this Quantitative Methods in Practice.

3. What is the probability the on time per session would be between 35 and 65 minutes?

4. Another simulation model might choose to represent the on time per session with a normal probability distribution. Use a normal probability distribution with the expected value of question 1 and the variance of question 2 to answer question 3.

4

DECISION ANALYSIS

Decision analysis can be used to determine optimal strategies when a decision maker is faced with several decision alternatives and an uncertain or risk-filled pattern of future events. For example, a manufacturer of a new line of seasonal clothing would like to manufacture large quantities if consumer acceptance and consequent demand for the product will be high. However, the manufacturer would like to produce much smaller quantities if consumer acceptance and demand for the product will be low. Unfortunately, seasonal clothing items require the manufacturer to make a production–volume decision before the demand is known. Actual consumer acceptance of the product will not be determined until the items have been placed into stores and buyers have had the opportunity to purchase them. Selection of the best production–volume decision from among several alternatives when the decision maker is faced with the uncertainty of future demand is a problem suited for decision analysis.

We begin the study of decision analysis by considering problems having reasonably few decision alternatives and reasonably few possible future events. We introduce the concepts of a payoff table and a decision tree to provide a structure for this type of decision situation and illustrate the fundamentals of decision analysis. We then extend the discussion to show how additional information obtained through experimentation can be combined with the decision maker's preliminary information to develop an optimal decision strategy.

..../ /.............

4.1   STRUCTURING THE DECISION PROBLEM

Pittsburgh Development Corporation (PDC) has purchased land for a luxury, riverfront condominium complex. The site provides a spectacular view of downtown Pittsburgh and the Golden Triangle where the Allegheny and Monongahela rivers meet to form the Ohio River. The individual units will be priced from $300,000 to $1,200,000, depending on the floor the unit is located on, the square footage of the unit, and optional features such as fireplaces and large balconies.

The company has had preliminary architectural drawings developed for three different project sizes: 6 floors with 30 units, 12 floors with 60 units, and 18 floors with 90 units. The financial success of the project will depend heavily on the decision that PDC makes regarding the size of the condominium project. Let us consider how decision analysis can help PDC determine which size project to develop.

The first step in the decision analysis approach is to identify the decision alternatives that are being considered. For PDC, there are three:

d_1 = a small condominium complex with 6 floors and 30 units

d_2 = a medium condominium complex with 12 floors and 60 units

d_3 = a large condominium complex with 18 floors and 90 units

A key factor in selecting one of these decision alternatives involves management's assessment of the demand for the condominiums.

When asked about possible market acceptance of the condominium project, management viewed the possible acceptance of the project as an all-or-nothing situation. That is, management believes that the market acceptance will be one of two possibilities: high market acceptance of the project and hence a substantial demand for the condominiums, or low market acceptance of the project and hence a limited demand for the condominiums. Although management can exercise some influence over market acceptance with advertising, the high prices for the units mean that demand will likely depend on a variety of other factors over which PDC will have no control.

In decision analysis, events that may occur but which the decision maker cannot control are referred to as **states of nature.** The list of possible states of nature includes everything that can happen, and individual states of nature are defined so that only one will actually occur. For the PDC condominium project, the two states of nature are

s_1 = high market acceptance and hence a substantial demand for the units

s_2 = low market acceptance and hence a limited demand for the units

Payoff Tables

Given the three decision alternatives and the two states of nature, which condominium size should PDC select? To answer this question, PDC will need information on the profit associated with each combination of a decision alternative and a state of nature. For example, what profit would PDC realize if it constructs a large condominium complex (d_3) and market acceptance turns out to be high (s_1)? But what would happen to the profit if PDC constructs a large condominium complex (d_3) and market acceptance turns out to be low (s_2)? In decision analysis, we refer to the outcome that results from a specific decision alternative and the occurrence of a particular state of nature as a **payoff.** A table showing the payoffs for all combinations of the decision alternatives and states of nature is a **payoff table.**

Using the best information available, management has estimated the payoffs, or profits, for the PDC condominium project. These estimates, with profits expressed in millions of dollars, are presented in Table 4.1. In general, entries in a payoff table can be stated in terms of profit, cost, time, distance, or any other measure of output that may be appropriate for the situation being analyzed. We will refer to the payoff associated with decision alternative i and state of nature j as V_{ij}. For example, Table 4.1 shows that $V_{31} = 20$, indicating that a $20 million profit is anticipated if the large complex is constructed (d_3) and a high market acceptance (s_1) occurs. However, $V_{32} = -9$ shows an anticipated loss of $9 million if the large complex is constructed (d_3) and a low market acceptance (s_2) occurs.

Decision Trees

A **decision tree** provides a graphical representation of the decision-making process. Figure 4.1 presents a decision tree for the PDC problem. Note that the decision tree shows the natural or logical progression that will occur over time. First, PDC must make a decision regarding the size of the condominium complex (d_1, d_2, or d_3). Then, after the decision is implemented, either state of nature s_1 or s_2 will occur. The number at each end point of the tree indicates the payoff associated with a particular sequence. For example the topmost payoff of 8 indicates that an $8 million profit is anticipated if PDC constructs a small condominium complex (d_1) and market acceptance turns out to be high (s_1). The next payoff of 7 indicates an anticipated profit of $7 million if PDC constructs a small condominium complex (d_1) and market acceptance turns out to be low (s_2). Thus, the decision tree shows graphically the sequences of decision alternatives and states of nature that provide the six possible outcomes and payoffs for PDC.

We refer to an intersection or junction point of the decision tree as a **node** and the arc or connector between nodes as a **branch.** Figure 4.1 shows the PDC decision tree with the nodes numbered 1–4. When the branches *leaving* a node are decision branches, we refer to the node as a *decision node* and represent it by a square. Similarly, when the branches leaving a node are state-of-nature branches, we refer to the node as a *state-of-nature node* and represent it by a circle. Hence, node 1 is a decision node, whereas nodes 2, 3, and 4 are state-of-nature nodes.

The identification of the decision alternatives, the states of nature, and the payoff associated with each decision alternative and state-of-nature combination are the first three steps in the decision analysis process. We now turn to this question: How can the decision maker best utilize the information presented in the payoff table or the decision tree to arrive at a decision? Several approaches may be used.

If you have a payoff table, you should be able to develop a decision tree. Try Problem 1(a).

Table 4.1	PAYOFF TABLE FOR THE PDC CONDOMINIUM PROJECT (PAYOFFS IN $ MILLION)	
Decision Alternative	**State of Nature**	
	High Acceptance s_1	Low Acceptance s_2
Small complex, d_1	8	7
Medium complex, d_2	14	5
Large complex, d_3	20	−9

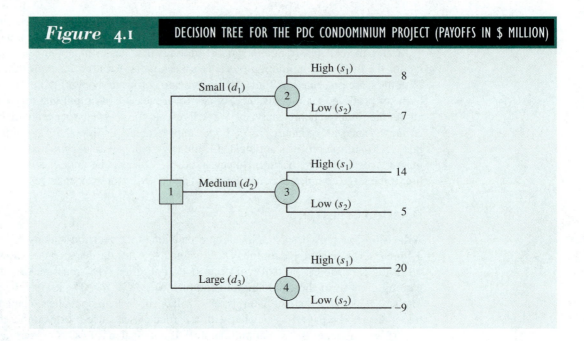

Figure 4.1 DECISION TREE FOR THE PDC CONDOMINIUM PROJECT (PAYOFFS IN $ MILLION)

1. Experts in problem solving agree that the first step in solving a complex problem is to decompose it into a series of smaller subproblems. Decision trees provide a useful way to show how the problem can be decomposed and the sequential nature of the decision process.

2. People often view the same problem from different perspectives. Thus, the discussion regarding the development of a decision tree may provide additional insight about the problem.

4.2 DECISION MAKING WITHOUT PROBABILITIES

Many people think of a good decision as one in which the outcome is good. However, in some instances, a good, well-thought-out decision may still lead to a bad or undesirable outcome.

In this section we consider approaches to decision making that do not require knowledge of the probabilities of the states of nature. These approaches are appropriate in situations in which the decision maker has little confidence in his or her ability to assess the probabilities of the various states of nature, or in which considering best and worst case analyses that are independent of state-of-nature probabilities is desirable. Because different approaches sometimes lead to different decision recommendations, the decision maker needs to understand the approaches available and then select the specific approach that, according to the decision maker's judgment, is the most appropriate.

Optimistic Approach

The **optimistic approach** evaluates each decision alternative in terms of the *best* payoff that can occur. The decision alternative that is recommended is the one that provides the best possible payoff. For a problem in which maximum profit is desired, as in the PDC problem, the optimistic approach would lead the decision maker to choose the alternative corresponding to the largest profit. For problems involving minimization, this approach leads to choosing the alternative with the smallest payoff.

For a maximization problem, the optimistic approach often is referred to as the *maximax approach;* for a minimization problem, the corresponding terminology is *minimim.*

To illustrate the optimistic approach, we will use it to develop a recommendation for the PDC problem. First, we determine the maximum payoff for each of the decision alternatives; then we select the decision alternative that provides the overall maximum payoff. These steps systematically identify the decision alternative that provides the largest possible profit. Table 4.2 illustrates these steps.

Table 4.2	MAXIMUM PAYOFF FOR EACH PDC DECISION ALTERNATIVE	
Decision Alternative	**Maximum Payoff**	
Small complex, d_1	8	
Medium complex, d_2	14	
Large complex, d_3	20	← Maximum of the maximum payoff values

Since 20, corresponding to d_3, is the largest payoff, the decision to construct the large condominium complex is the recommended decision alternative using the optimistic approach.

Conservative Approach

For a maximization problem, the conservative approach is often referred to as the *maximin approach;* for a minimization problem, the corresponding terminology is *minimax.*

The **conservative approach** evaluates each decision alternative in terms of the *worst* payoff that can occur. The decision alternative recommended is the one that provides the best of the worst possible payoffs. For a problem in which the output measure is profit, as in the PDC problem, the conservative approach would lead the decision maker to choose the alternative that maximizes the minimum possible profit that could be obtained. For problems involving minimization, this approach identifies the alternative that will minimize the maximum payoff.

To illustrate the conservative approach, we use it to develop a recommendation for the PDC problem. First, we identify the minimum payoff for each of the decision alternatives; then we select the decision alternative that maximizes the minimum payoff. Table 4.3 illustrates these steps for the PDC problem.

Because 7, corresponding to d_1, yields the maximum of the minimum payoffs, the decision alternative of a small condominium complex is recommended. This decision approach is considered conservative because it identifies the worst possible payoffs and then recommends the decision alternative that avoids the possibility of extremely "bad" payoffs. In the conservative approach, PDC is guaranteed a profit of at least $7 million. Although PDC may make more, it *cannot* make less than $7 million.

Table 4.3	MINIMUM PAYOFF FOR EACH PDC DECISION ALTERNATIVE	
Decision Alternative	**Minimum Payoff**	
Small complex, d_1	7	← Maximum of the minimum payoff values
Medium complex, d_2	5	
Large complex, d_3	−9	

Minimax Regret Approach

Minimax regret is an approach to decision making that is neither purely optimistic nor purely conservative. Let us illustrate the minimax regret approach by showing how it can be used to select a decision alternative for the PDC problem.

Suppose that the PDC constructs a small condominium complex (d_1) and market acceptance turns out to be high (s_1). Table 4.1 shows that the resulting profit for PDC would be $8 million. However, we now know that the high acceptance state of nature (s_1) has occurred, so we realize that the decision to construct a large condominium complex (d_3), yielding a profit of $20 million, would have been the best decision. The difference between the payoff for the best decision alternative ($20 million) and the payoff for the decision to construct a small condominium complex ($8 million) is the **opportunity loss,** or **regret,** associated with decision alternative d_1 when state of nature s_1 occurs; thus, for this case, the opportunity loss or regret is $20 million $-$ $8 million = $12 million. Similarly, if PDC makes the decision to construct a medium condominium complex (d_2) and the high acceptance state of nature (s_1) occurs, the opportunity loss, or regret, associated with d_2 would be $20 million $-$ $14 million = $6 million.

In general the following expression represents the opportunity loss, or regret.

$$R_{ij} = \left| V_j^* - V_{ij} \right| \tag{4.1}$$

where

R_{ij} = the regret associated with decision alternative d_i and state of nature s_j

V_j^* = the payoff value[1] corresponding to the best decision for the state of nature s_j

V_{ij} = the payoff corresponding to decision alternative d_i and state of nature s_j

Note the role of the absolute value in equation (4.1). That is, for minimization problems, the best payoff, V_j^*, is the smallest entry in column j. Because this value always is less than or equal to V_{ij}, the absolute value of the difference between V_j^* and V_{ij} ensures that the regret is always the magnitude of the difference.

Using equation (4.1) and the payoffs in Table 4.1, we can compute the regret associated with each combination of decision alternative d_i and state of nature s_j. Since the PDC problem is a maximization problem, V_j^* will be the largest entry in column j of the payoff table. Thus, to compute the regret, we simply subtract each entry in a column from the largest entry in the column. Table 4.4 shows the opportunity loss, or regret, table for the PDC problem.

The next step in applying the minimax regret approach is to list the maximum regret for each decision alternative; Table 4.5 shows the results for the PDC problem. Selecting the decision alternative with the *minimum* of the *maximum* regret values—hence, the name *minimax regret*—yields the minimax regret decision. For the PDC problem, the alternative to construct the medium condominium complex, with a corresponding maximum regret of $6 million, is the recommended minimax regret decision.

Note that the three approaches discussed in this section provide different recommendations, which in itself isn't bad. It simply reflects the difference in decision-making philosophies that underlie the various approaches. Ultimately, the decision maker will have

You should be able to develop a decision recommendation using the optimistic, conservative, and minimax regret approaches. Try Problem 1(b).

_____

1. In maximization problems, V_j^* will be the largest entry in column j of the payoff table. In minimization problems, V_j^* will be the smallest entry in column j of the payoff table.

Table 4.4	OPPORTUNITY LOSS, OR REGRET, TABLE FOR THE PDC CONDOMINIUM PROJECT ($ MILLION)

Decision Alternative	State of Nature	
	High Acceptance s_1	Low Acceptance s_2
Small complex, d_1	12	0
Medium complex, d_2	6	2
Large complex, d_3	0	16

to choose the most appropriate approach and then make the final decision accordingly. The main criticism of the approaches discussed in this section is that they do not consider any information about the probabilities of the various states of nature. In the next section we discuss an approach that utilizes probability information in selecting a decision alternative.

4.3 DECISION MAKING WITH PROBABILITIES

In many decision-making situations, we can obtain probability estimates for each of the states of nature. When such probabilities are available, we can use the **expected value approach** to identify the best decision alternative. Let us first define the expected value of a decision alternative and then apply it to the PDC problem.

Let

$$N = \text{the number of states of nature}$$
$$P(s_j) = \text{the probability of state of nature } s_j$$

Since one and only one of the N states of nature can occur, the probabilities must satisfy two conditions:

$$P(s_j) \geq 0 \qquad \text{for all states of nature} \tag{4.2}$$

$$\sum_{j=1}^{N} P(s_j) = P(s_1) + P(s_2) + \cdots + P(s_N) = 1 \tag{4.3}$$

Table 4.5	MAXIMUM REGRET FOR EACH PDC DECISION ALTERNATIVE

Decision Alternative	Maximum Regret	
Small complex, d_1	12	
Medium complex, d_2	6	← Minimum of the maximum regret
Large complex, d_3	16	

The **expected value (EV)** of decision alternative d_i is defined as follows.

$$EV(d_i) = \sum_{j=1}^{N} P(s_j)V_{ij} \tag{4.4}$$

In words, the expected value of a decision alternative is the sum of weighted payoffs for the decision alternative. The weight for a payoff is the probability of the associated state of nature and therefore the probability that the payoff will occur. Let us return to the PDC problem to see how the expected value approach can be applied.

PDC is optimistic about the potential for the luxury high-rise condominium complex. Suppose that this optimism provides an initial subjective probability assessment of 0.8 that market acceptance will be high (s_1) and a corresponding probability of 0.2 that market acceptance will be low (s_2). Thus, $P(s_1) = 0.8$ and $P(s_2) = 0.2$. Using the payoff values in Table 4.1 and equation (4.4), we compute the expected value for each of the three decision alternatives as follows:

$$EV(d_1) = 0.8(8) + 0.2(7) = 7.8$$
$$EV(d_2) = 0.8(14) + 0.2(5) = 12.2$$
$$EV(d_3) = 0.8(20) + 0.2(-9) = 14.2$$

Thus, using the expected value approach, we find that the large condominium complex, with an expected value of $14.2 million, is the recommended decision.

You should now be able to use the expected value approach to develop a decision recommendation. Try Problem 5.

The calculations required to identify the decision alternative with the best expected value can be conveniently carried out on a decision tree. Figure 4.2 shows the decision tree for the PDC problem with state-of-nature branch probabilities. Working backward through the decision tree, we first compute the expected value at each state-of-nature node. That is, at each state-of-nature node, we weight each possible payoff by its chance of occurrence. By doing so, we obtain the expected values for nodes 2, 3, and 4, as shown in Figure 4.3.

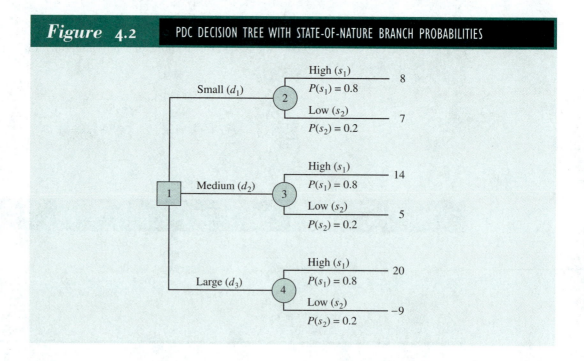

Figure **4.2**   PDC DECISION TREE WITH STATE-OF-NATURE BRANCH PROBABILITIES

Figure 4.3 APPLYING THE EXPECTED VALUE APPROACH USING DECISION TREES

Since the decision maker controls the branch leaving decision node 1 and since we are trying to maximize the expected profit, the best decision branch at node 1 is d_3. Thus, the decision tree analysis leads to a recommendation of d_3 with an expected value of $14.2 million. Note that this is the same recommendation obtained with the expected value approach in conjunction with the payoff table.

Other decision problems may be substantially more complex than the PDC problem, but if there are a reasonable number of decision alternatives and states of nature, you can use the decision tree approach outlined here. First, draw a decision tree consisting of decision and state-of-nature nodes and branches that describe the sequential nature of the problem. If you use the expected value approach, the next step is to determine the probabilities for each of the state-of-nature branches and compute the expected value at each state-of-nature node. Then select the decision branch leading to the state-of-nature node with the best expected value. The decision alternative associated with this branch is the recommended decision. The Q. M. in Action article on decision analysis and the selection of home mortgages describes how the decision analysis approach can be used to help home buyers select the best type of mortgage.

4.4 SENSITIVITY ANALYSIS

In this section we consider how changes in the probability estimates for the states of nature affect or alter the recommended decision alternative. The study of the effect of such changes is referred to as **sensitivity analysis.**

One approach to sensitivity analysis is to consider different probabilities for the states of nature and recompute the expected value for each decision alternative. Repeating this computation for several different probabilities, we can begin to learn how changes in the probabilities for the states of nature affect the recommended decision. For example, in the PDC problem, suppose that the probability of high acceptance is reduced to 0.2 and that the probability of low acceptance is increased to 0.8. Using $P(s_1) = 0.2$, $P(s_2) = 0.8$, and equation (4.4), we obtain the expected value for each decision alternative:

Q.M. IN ACTION

DECISION ANALYSIS AND THE SELECTION OF HOME MORTGAGES*

Purchasing a new home can be a stressful experience, especially when it may commit the new owners to a mortgage contract for the next 20 to 30 years. The decision is further complicated by the fact that mortgages have varying interest rates that range from traditional fixed-rate mortgages (FRM) to adjustable-rate mortgages (ARM) with a wide variety of special features.

A decision analysis approach to selecting the best type of mortgage involves the development of a decision tree that includes one branch for each of the mortgage alternatives available. For example, if the buyer is considering three different mortgage contracts—fixed rate, variable rate with a 3-year adjustment, and variable rate with a 5-year adjustment—the decision tree begins with three decision alternative branches.

The future events that indicate what can happen to interest rates over time are the states of nature branches for the decision tree. For instance, variable-rate mortgage branches have state-of-nature branches that indicate possible interest rate increases and decreases. The complete decision tree shows the outcomes for each mortgage alternative and its associated cost.

Using decision analysis criteria reflecting a conservative or an optimistic perspective, a prospective home buyer can select a recommended mortgage alternative. If probability estimates are available for the future mortgage rates, the expected value approach will use the probability information to recommend the best mortgage alternative.

*Luna, Robert E., and Richard A. Reid, "Mortgage Selection Using a Decision Tree Approach." *Interfaces,* vol. 16, no. 3, May–June 1986, pp. 73–81.

$$EV(d_1) = 0.2(8) + 0.8(7) = 7.2$$
$$EV(d_2) = 0.2(14) + 0.8(5) = 6.8$$
$$EV(d_3) = 0.2(20) + 0.8(-9) = -3.2$$

Thus, with these probabilities the recommended decision alternative is to construct a small condominium complex (d_1), with an expected value of $7.2 million. The probability of high acceptance is only 0.2, so constructing the large condominium complex (d_3) is the least preferred alternative, with an expected value or loss of $3.2 million.

Thus, when the probability of high acceptance is large, PDC should build the large complex; when the probability of high acceptance is small, PDC should build the small complex. Obviously, we could continue to modify the probabilities of the states of nature and learn even more about how changes in the probabilities affect the recommended decision alternative. The only drawback to this approach is the numerous calculations required to evaluate the effect of several possible changes in the state-of-nature probabilities.

For the special case of two states of nature, a graphical procedure substantially eases the sensitivity analysis computations. To demonstrate this procedure, we let p denote the probability of state of nature s_1; that is, $P(s_1) = p$. With only two states of nature in the PDC problem, the probability of state of nature s_2 is

$$P(s_2) = 1 - P(s_1) = 1 - p$$

Using equation (4.4) and the payoff values in Table 4.1, we determine the expected value for decision alternative d_1 as follows:

$$\begin{aligned}
EV(d_1) &= P(s_1)(8) + P(s_2)(7) \\
&= p(8) + (1-p)(7) \\
&= 8p + 7 - 7p = p + 7
\end{aligned}$$

(4.5)

Repeating the expected value computations for decision alternatives d_2 and d_3, we obtain expressions for the expected value of each decision alternative as a function of p:

$$EV(d_2) = 9p + 5 \qquad (4.6)$$

$$EV(d_3) = 29p - 9 \qquad (4.7)$$

Thus, we have developed three equations that show the expected value of the three decision alternatives as a function of the probability of state of nature s_1.

We continue by developing a graph with values of p on the horizontal axis and the associated EVs on the vertical axis. Because equations (4.5), (4.6), and (4.7) are linear equations, the graph of each equation is a straight line. For each equation, then, we can obtain the line by identifying two points that satisfy the equation and drawing a line through the points. For instance, if we let $p = 0$ in equation (4.5), $EV(d_1) = 7$. Then, letting $p = 1$, $EV(d_1) = 8$. Connecting these two points, (0, 7) and (1, 8), provides the line labeled $EV(d_1)$ in Figure 4.4. Similarly, we obtain the lines labeled $EV(d_2)$ and $EV(d_3)$; these lines are the graphs of equations (4.6) and (4.7), respectively.

Figure 4.4 shows how the recommended decision changes as p, the probability of the high acceptance state of nature (s_1), changes. Note that for small values of p, decision

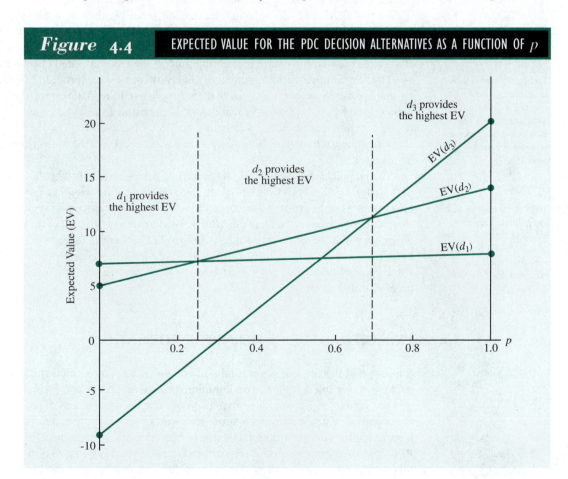

Figure 4.4 EXPECTED VALUE FOR THE PDC DECISION ALTERNATIVES AS A FUNCTION OF p

alternative d_1 (small complex) provides the largest expected value and is thus the recommended decision. When the value of p increases to a certain point, decision alternative d_2 (medium complex) provides the largest expected value and is the recommended decision. Finally, for large values of p, decision alternative d_3 (large complex) becomes the recommended decision.

The value of p for which the expected values of d_1 and d_2 are equal is the value of p corresponding to the intersection of the $EV(d_1)$ and the $EV(d_2)$ lines. To determine this value, we set $EV(d_1) = EV(d_2)$ and solve for the value of p:

$$p + 7 = 9p + 5$$
$$8p = 2$$
$$p = \frac{2}{8} = 0.25$$

Hence, whenever $p = 0.25$, decision alternatives d_1 and d_2 provide the same expected value. Repeating this calculation for the value of p corresponding to the intersection of the $EV(d_2)$ and $EV(d_3)$ lines we obtain $p = 0.70$.

Using Figure 4.4, we can conclude that decision alternative d_1 provides the largest expected value for $p < 0.25$, decision alternative d_2 provides the largest expected value for $0.25 < p < 0.70$, and decision alternative d_3 provides the largest expected value for $p > 0.70$. Since p is simply the probability of state of nature s_1 and $(1-p)$ is the probability of state of nature s_2, we now have the sensitivity analysis information that tells us how changes in the state-of-nature probabilities affect the recommended decision alternative.

Sensitivity analysis can assist management in deciding if they should invest more time and money to obtain more accurate probability estimates.

The benefit of performing sensitivity analysis is that it can provide a better perspective on management's original judgment regarding the state-of-nature probabilities. Management originally estimated the probability of high customer acceptance as $P(s_1) = 0.8$. As a result, decision alternative d_3 was recommended. After carrying out the sensitivity analysis, we can now tell management that as long as $P(s_1) > 0.70$, the d_3 decision alternative remains optimal.

You should now be able to use graphical sensitivity analysis to determine how changes in the probability estimates affect the recommended decision. Try Problem 8.

The graphical sensitivity analysis procedure just described for the PDC problem applies only to decision analysis problems with two states of nature. However, sensitivity analysis also is important in problems with more than two states of nature. In these cases, a spreadsheet or computer software package can be used to assist with the computations. Basically, we return to the approach of testing a variety of likely changes for the state-of-nature probabilities. A spreadsheet or software package is helpful in making the necessary expected value computations and providing the decision alternative recommendations with a minimum of time and effort.

4.5   EXPECTED VALUE OF PERFECT INFORMATION

Suppose that PDC has the opportunity to conduct a market research study that would help evaluate buyer interest in the condominium project and provide information that management could use to improve the probability assessments for the states of nature. To determine the potential value of this information, we begin by assuming that the study could provide *perfect information* regarding the states of nature; that is, we assume for the moment that PDC could determine with certainty which state of nature is going to occur. To make use of this perfect information, we will develop a decision strategy that PDC should follow once it knows which state of nature will occur. As we show, a decision strategy is simply a decision rule that specifies the decision alternative to be selected after the new information becomes available.

To help determine the decision strategy for PDC, we have reproduced PDC's payoff table as Table 4.6. Note that, if PDC knew for sure that state of nature s_1 would occur, the best decision alternative would be d_3, with a payoff of $20 million. Similarly, if PDC knew for sure that state of nature s_2 would occur, the best decision alternative would be d_1, with a payoff of $7 million. Thus, we can state PDC's optimal decision strategy based on perfect information as follows:

$$\text{If } s_1, \text{ select } d_3.$$
$$\text{If } s_2, \text{ select } d_1.$$

What is the expected value for this decision strategy? To compute the expected value with perfect information, we return to the original probability estimates for the states of nature: $P(s_1) = 0.8$, and $P(s_2) = 0.2$. Based on these probabilities, there is a 0.8 probability that the perfect information will indicate state of nature s_1. In this case, the resulting decision alternative d_3 will provide a $20 million profit. Similarly, with a 0.2 probability for state of nature s_2, the resulting decision alternative d_1 will provide a $7 million profit. Thus, from equation (4.4), the expected value of the decision strategy that uses perfect information is

$$0.8(20) + 0.2(7) = 17.4$$

We refer to the expected value of $17.4 million as the *expected value with perfect information* (EVwPI).

Recall from Section 4.3 that the recommended decision using the expected value approach is decision alternative d_3, with an expected value of $14.2 million. Because this decision recommendation and expected value computation were made without the benefit of perfect information, $14.2 million is referred to as the *expected value without perfect information* (EVwoPI).

The expected value with perfect information is $17.4 million, and the expected value without perfect information is $14.2; therefore, the expected value of the perfect information (EVPI) is $17.4 − $14.2 = $3.2 million. In other words, $3.2 million represents the additional expected value that can be obtained if perfect information were available about the states of nature. Figure 4.5 provides a summary of the computation of EVPI for the PDC problem.

Table 4.6	PAYOFF TABLE FOR THE PDC CONDOMINIUM PROJECT ($ MILLION)	
Decision Alternative	**State of Nature**	
	High Acceptance s_1	Low Acceptance s_2
Small complex, d_1	8	7
Medium complex, d_2	14	5
Large complex, d_3	20	−9

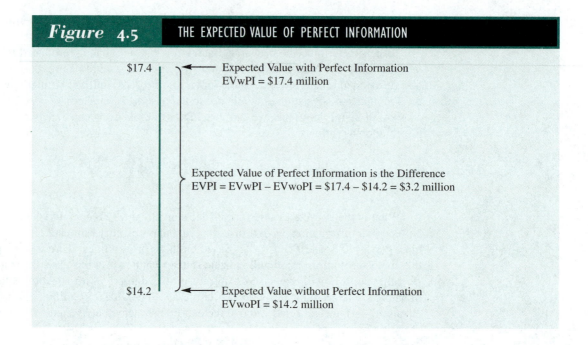

Figure 4.5   THE EXPECTED VALUE OF PERFECT INFORMATION

$17.4 — Expected Value with Perfect Information
EVwPI = $17.4 million

Expected Value of Perfect Information is the Difference
EVPI = EVwPI – EVwoPI = $17.4 – $14.2 = $3.2 million

$14.2 — Expected Value without Perfect Information
EVwoPI = $14.2 million

You should be able to determine the expected value of perfect information. Try Problem 12(d).

    Generally speaking, a market research study will not provide "perfect" information; however, if the market research study is a good one, the information gathered might be worth a sizable portion of the $3.2 million. Given the EVPI of $3.2 million, PDC should seriously consider the market survey as a way to obtain more information about the states of nature.

    In general, the expected value of perfect information is computed as follows.

$$\text{EVPI} = |\,\text{EVwPI} - \text{EVwoPI}\,| \tag{4.8}$$

where

$$\text{EVPI} = \text{expected value of perfect information}$$
$$\text{EVwPI} = \text{expected value } with \text{ perfect information about the states of nature}$$
$$\text{EVwoPI} = \text{expected value } without \text{ perfect information about the states of nature}$$

Note the role of the absolute value in equation (4.8). That is, for minimization problems the expected value with perfect information is always less than or equal to the expected value without perfect information. In this case, EVPI is the magnitude of the difference between EVwPI and EVwoPI, or the absolute value of the difference as shown in equation (4.8).

4.6   DECISION ANALYSIS WITH SAMPLE INFORMATION

In applying the expected value approach, we have shown how probability information about the states of nature affects the expected value calculations and thus the decision recommendation. Frequently, decision makers have preliminary or prior probability estimates for the states of nature that are the best probability values available. However, to make the best possible decision, the decision maker may want to seek additional information about the states of nature. This new information can be used to revise or update the prior proba-

We restate the *opportunity loss,* or *regret,* table for the PDC problem (see Table 4.4) as follows.

Decision Alternative	State of Nature	
	High Acceptance	Low Acceptance
	s_1	s_2
Small complex, d_1	12	0
Medium complex, d_2	6	2
Large complex, d_3	0	16

Using $P(s_1)$, $P(s_2)$, and the opportunity loss values, we can compute the *expected opportunity loss* (EOL) for each decision alternative. With $P(s_1) = 0.8$ and $P(s_2) = 0.2$, the expected opportunity loss for each of the three decision alternatives is

$$EOL(d_1) = 0.8(12) + 0.2(0) = 9.6$$
$$EOL(d_2) = 0.8(6) + 0.2(2) = 5.2$$
$$EOL(d_3) = 0.8(0) + 0.2(16) = 3.2$$

Regardless of whether the decision analysis involves maximization or minimization, the *minimum* expected opportunity loss always provides the best decision alternative. Thus, with $EOL(d_3) = 3.2$, d_3 is the recommended decision. In addition, the minimum expected opportunity loss always is *equal to the expected value of perfect information.* That is, EOL(best decision) = EVPI; for the PDC problem, this value is $3.2 million.

bilities so that the final decision is based on more accurate probability estimates for the states of nature.

Most often, additional information is obtained through experiments designed to provide sample information about the states of nature. Raw material sampling, product testing, and market research studies are examples of experiments that may enable management to revise or update the state-of-nature probabilities. In the following discussion, we reconsider the PDC problem and show how to use sample information to revise the state-of-nature probabilities. We then show how to use the revised probabilities to develop an optimal decision strategy for PDC.

Recall that PDC's management provided initial subjective probability estimates of 0.8 for high market acceptance and 0.2 for low market acceptance. Since $P(s_1) = 0.8$ and $P(s_2) = 0.2$ were estimates developed prior to the collection of any sample information, they are referred to as the **prior probabilities** for the states of nature. Recall that, using these prior probabilities, we determined that d_3, the decision to construct the large condominium complex, was optimal, yielding an expected value of $14.2 million. Calculation of the expected value of perfect information showed that new information about the states of nature could potentially be worth as much as $3.2 million.

Suppose that PDC considers undertaking a six-month market research study designed to evaluate market acceptance and ultimately buyer interest in purchasing the condominium units. The market research will provide new information that can be combined with the prior probabilities through a **Bayesian revision** procedure to obtain updated or revised probability estimates for the states of nature. These *revised* probabilities are called **posterior probabilities.** Figure 4.6 depicts the process of revising probabilities.

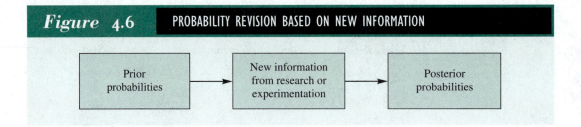

Figure 4.6   PROBABILITY REVISION BASED ON NEW INFORMATION

We refer to the new information obtained through research or experimentation as **sample information.** The sample information outcomes for the PDC market research study are as follows.

F = favorable market research report (i.e., the individuals contacted express interest in purchasing a PDC condominium)

U = unfavorable market research report (i.e., the individuals contacted express little interest in purchasing a PDC condominium)

To make effective use of the sample information, we must know something about the probability relationships between the sample information outcomes and the states of nature. For example, in the PDC problem, given that the state of nature ultimately turns out to be high acceptance, what is the probability that the market research study will result in a favorable report? In this case, we are asking about the conditional probability of F given state of nature s_1, written $P(F \mid s_1)$. To carry out the analysis, we will need conditional probabilities for all sample outcomes given all states of nature, that is, $P(F \mid s_1)$, $P(F \mid s_2)$, $P(U \mid s_1)$, and $P(U \mid s_2)$.

In the PDC problem, we assume that the following estimates are available for the conditional probabilities.

State of Nature	Market Research	
	Favorable, F	Unfavorable, U
High acceptance, s_1	$P(F \mid s_1) = 0.90$	$P(U \mid s_1) = 0.10$
Low acceptance, s_2	$P(F \mid s_2) = 0.25$	$P(U \mid s_2) = 0.75$

Note that these probability estimates provide a reasonable degree of confidence in the market research study. If the true state of nature is s_1, the probability of a favorable market research report is 0.90 and the probability of an unfavorable market research report is 0.10. If the true state of nature is s_2, the probability of a favorable market research report is 0.25 and the probability of an unfavorable market research report is 0.75. The reason for a 0.25 probability of a potentially misleading favorable market research report for state of nature s_2 is that when some potential buyers first hear about the new condominium project, their enthusiasm may lead them to overstate their real interest in it. A potential buyer's initial favorable response can change quickly to a "no thank you" when later faced with the reality of signing a purchase contract and making a down payment.

4.7   DEVELOPING A DECISION STRATEGY

The analysis performed to develop an optimal decision strategy is done before actually collecting the sample information. This analysis helps decide whether to seek the sample information and what to do if the information is obtained.

A decision strategy is a rule that is to be followed by the decision maker. In the PDC problem, a decision strategy is a rule that recommends a particular decision based on whether the market research report is favorable or unfavorable. We use a decision tree analysis to find the optimal decision strategy for PDC.

Figure 4.7 shows the decision tree for the PDC problem if a market research study is conducted. Note that, from left to right, the tree shows the natural or logical order that

Figure 4.7   PDC DECISION TREE INCORPORATING THE RESULTS OF THE MARKET RESEARCH STUDY (PAYOFFS IN $ MILLION)

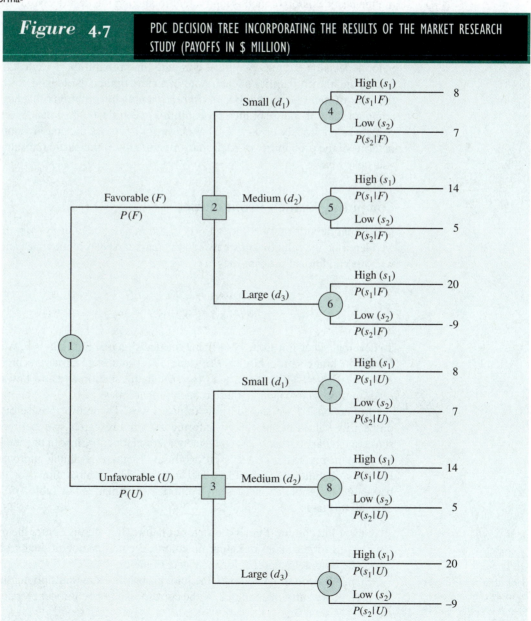

will occur in the decision-making process. First, PDC will obtain the market research outcome (F or U); then a decision (d_1, d_2, or d_3) will be made; finally, the state of nature (s_1 or s_2) will occur. The decision and the state of nature combine to provide the final profit or payoff.

Using decision tree terminology, we have now introduced a *sample information node*, node 1, and branches, F and U. Since the branches emanating from this node are not under the control of the decision maker, but are determined by chance, this node is represented by a circle as we did for the state-of-nature nodes. Nodes 2 and 3 are decision nodes, whereas nodes 4, 5, 6, 7, 8, and 9 are state-of-nature nodes. For decision nodes, the decision maker must select the specific branch d_1, d_2, or d_3 that will be taken. Selecting the best decision branch is equivalent to making the best decision. However, because the sample information and state-of-nature branches are not controlled by the decision maker, the specific branch leaving these nodes will depend on the probability associated with the branch. Thus, before we can carry out an analysis of the decision tree and develop a decision strategy, we must compute the probability of each sample information branch and the probability of each state-of-nature branch. Note from the decision tree that the state-of-nature branches occur *after* the sample information branches. Thus, when we compute state-of-nature branch probabilities, we will need to consider which sample outcome was previously observed. That is, we will express the state-of-nature probabilities in terms of the probability of each state of nature *given* the particular sample outcome that was observed.

Computing Branch Probabilities

Recall that the prior probabilities for PDC are $P(s_1) = 0.8$ and $P(s_2) = 0.2$. In Section 4.6 we identified the relationships between the market research outcomes and states of nature with the conditional probabilities

$$P(F \mid s_1) = 0.90 \qquad P(U \mid s_1) = 0.10$$
$$P(F \mid s_2) = 0.25 \qquad P(U \mid s_2) = 0.75$$

To develop a decision strategy utilizing the decision tree in Figure 4.7, we need sample information branch probabilities $P(F)$ and $P(U)$ and state-of-nature branch probabilities $P(s_1 \mid F)$, $P(s_2 \mid F)$, $P(s_1 \mid U)$, and $P(s_2 \mid U)$. In this section we show how to use a *Bayesian revision* process to calculate these branch probabilities.

In Section 2.5 we showed how to use Bayes' Theorem to revise or update the prior probability values based on new information from research or experimentation. We presented a tabular approach as a convenient method for carrying out the computations needed to obtain the revised or posterior probabilities. We use this tabular approach to compute the branch probabilities for the PDC decision tree. The computations for the PDC problem based on a favorable market research report are summarized in Table 4.7. The steps used to develop this table are as follows.

Step 1. In column 1 enter the states of nature. In column 2 enter the prior probabilities for the states of nature. In column 3 enter the conditional probabilities of a favorable report F for each state of nature.

Step 2. In column 4 compute the joint probabilities by multiplying the prior probability entry in column 2 by the corresponding conditional probability entry in column 3.

Spreadsheets can be used to easily compute the branch probabilities. See Appendix 4.1.

Table 4.7	BRANCH PROBABILITIES FOR THE PDC CONDOMINIUM PROJECT BASED ON A FAVORABLE MARKET RESEARCH REPORT			
States of Nature s_j	Prior Probabilities $P(s_j)$	Conditional Probabilities $P(F \mid s_j)$	Joint Probabilities $P(F \cap s_j)$	Posterior Probabilities $P(s_j \mid F)$
s_1	0.8	0.90	0.72	0.9351
s_2	0.2	0.25	0.05	0.0649
			$P(F) = 0.77$	

Step 3. Sum the joint probabilities in column 4 to obtain $P(F)$, the probability of a favorable market research report.

Step 4. Compute the posterior probabilities in column 5 by dividing each joint probability entry in column 4 by $P(F) = 0.77$.

Table 4.7 shows that the probability of obtaining a favorable market research report is $P(F) = 0.77$. In addition, $P(s_1 \mid F) = 0.9351$ and $P(s_2 \mid F) = 0.0649$ show the posterior probabilities of the states of nature based on a favorable market report. In particular, note that if the market report is favorable, there is a 0.9351 probability of a high market acceptance (s_1) for the condominium project. A favorable market research report will encourage PDC to go ahead with plans to build the large condominium complex.

The tabular procedure must be repeated for each possible sample information outcome. Table 4.8 shows the computations of the branch probabilities for the PDC problem based on an unfavorable market research report. Note that the probability of obtaining an unfavorable market research report is $P(U) = 0.23$. If an unfavorable report is obtained, the posterior probability of a high market acceptance (s_1) is 0.3478 and of a low market acceptance (s_2) is 0.6522. The branch probabilities from Table 4.7 and 4.8 are shown on the PDC decision tree in Figure 4.8.

You should now be able to compute revised or posterior probabilities. Try Problem 14.

An Optimal Decision Strategy

After we have computed the branch probabilities, we can use the expected value approach to determine the optimal decision strategy. Working *backward* through the decision tree in Figure 4.8, we first compute the expected value at each state-of-nature node. That is, at each

Table 4.8	BRANCH PROBABILITIES FOR THE PDC CONDOMINIUM PROJECT BASED ON AN UNFAVORABLE MARKET RESEARCH REPORT			
States of Nature s_j	Prior Probabilities $P(s_j)$	Conditional Probabilities $P(U \mid s_j)$	Joint Probabilities $P(U \cap s_j)$	Posterior Probabilities $P(s_j \mid U)$
s_1	0.8	0.10	0.08	0.3478
s_2	0.2	0.75	0.15	0.6522
			$P(U) = 0.23$	

Figure 4.8   DECISION TREE WITH BRANCH PROBABILITIES

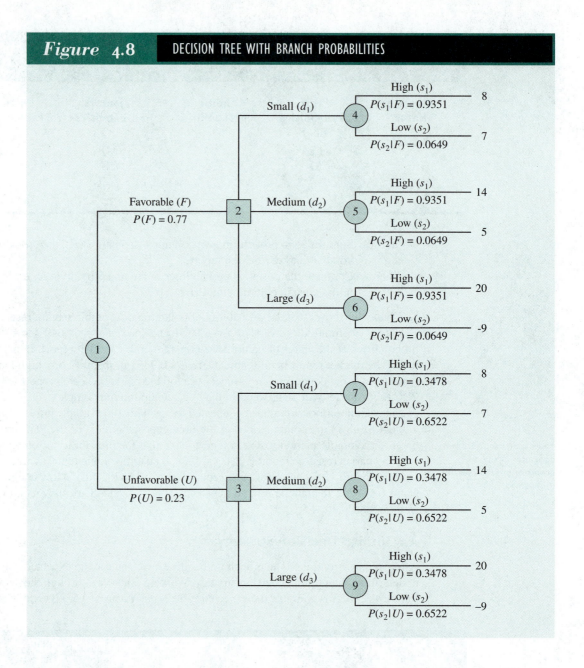

state-of-nature node, we weight the possible payoffs by their chance of occurring. Thus, the expected values for nodes 4–9 are

$$EV(\text{node } 4) = 0.9351(8) \ \ + 0.0649(7) \ \ = 7.935$$
$$EV(\text{node } 5) = 0.9351(14) + 0.0649(5) \ \ = 13.416$$
$$EV(\text{node } 6) = 0.9351(20) + 0.0649(-9) = 18.118$$
$$EV(\text{node } 7) = 0.3478(8) \ \ + 0.6522(7) \ \ = 7.348$$
$$EV(\text{node } 8) = 0.3478(14) + 0.6522(5) \ \ = 8.130$$
$$EV(\text{node } 9) = 0.3478(20) + 0.6522(-9) = 1.086$$

Figure 4.9 shows these calculations on the decision tree. Since the decision maker controls the branch leaving a decision node and is trying to maximize expected profit, the optimal decision at node 2 is d_3, with an expected value of 18.118. Thus, we write EV(node 2) as 18.118. A similar analysis at node 3 shows that the optimal decision branch is d_2, with an expected value of 8.130. Thus, EV(node 3) = 8.130.

We continue working backward in order to determine the expected value of node 1. Node 1 has two probability branches leaving it, corresponding to sample information outcomes F and U. We must use the branch probabilities, $P(F)$ and $P(U)$, to compute the overall expected value:

$$\text{EV(node 1)} = (0.77)\text{EV(node 2)} + (0.23)\text{EV(node 3)}$$
$$= (0.77)(18.118) + (0.23)(8.130) = 15.82$$

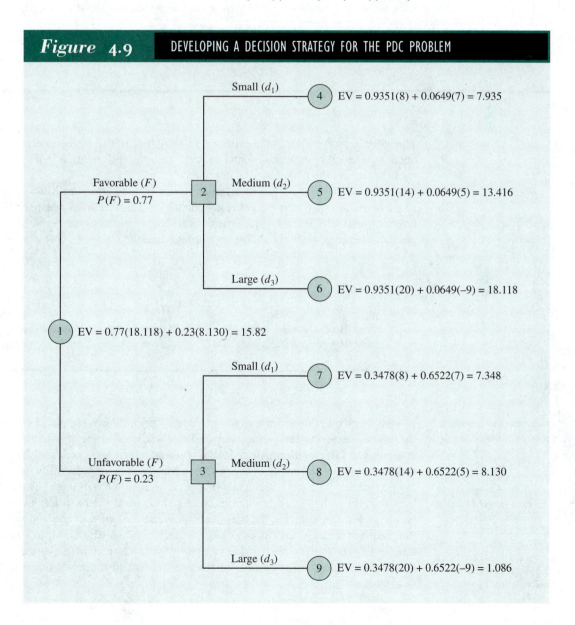

Figure 4.9   DEVELOPING A DECISION STRATEGY FOR THE PDC PROBLEM

Q.M. IN ACTION

DECISION ANALYSIS AND DRUG TESTING FOR STUDENT ATHLETES*

The athletic governing board of Santa Clara University considered whether to implement a drug-testing program for the university's intercollegiate athletes. The decision analysis framework contains two decision alternatives: implement a drug-testing program and do not implement a drug-testing program. Each student athlete is either a drug user or not a drug user, so these two possibilities are considered to be the states of nature for the problem.

If the drug-testing program is implemented, student athletes will be required to take a drug-screening test. Results of the test will be either positive (test indicates a potential drug user) or negative (test does not indicate a potential drug user). The test outcomes are considered to be the sample information in the decision problem. If the test result is negative, no follow-up action will be taken. However, if the test result is positive, follow-up action will be taken to determine whether the student athlete actually is a drug user. The payoffs include the cost of not identifying a drug user and the cost of falsely identifying a nonuser.

Decision analysis showed that if the test result is positive, there is still a reasonably high probability that the student athlete is not a drug user. The cost and other problems associated with this type of misleading test result were considered significant. Consequently, the athletic governing board decided not to implement the drug-testing program.

*Feinstein, Charles D., "Deciding Whether to Test Student Athletes for Drug Use." *Interfaces*, vol. 20, no. 3, May–June 1990, pp. 80–87.

The value $15.82 million is the expected value of the optimal decision strategy if PDC conducts the market research study and uses the resulting information to determine a recommended size for the condominium complex.

Note that PDC has not yet determined the size for the complex. Management will need to know the results of the market research study before deciding whether to construct the large complex (d_3) or the medium complex (d_2). The results of the decision analysis at this point, however, provide the following optimal decision strategy.

If	Then
Market research report is favorable (F),	Construct the large condominium complex (d_3).
Market research report is unfavorable (U),	Construct the medium condominium complex (d_2).

A decision tree provides a good visual description for small and relatively simple problems because it shows the overall structure of the problem. However, the tree size expands multiplicatively as additional stages are added. Thus, for large problems, representing the complete tree in one figure or on one computer screen becomes impossible.

Although other decision analysis problems may not be as simple as the PDC problem, the optimal decision strategy approach outlined is still applicable. First, draw a decision tree consisting of sample information, decision, and state-of-nature nodes and branches that describes the sequential nature of the problem. Make posterior probability calculations to establish sample outcome and state-of-nature branch probabilities. Then, by working backward through the tree, computing expected values at sample information and state-of-nature nodes, and selecting the best decision branch at decision nodes, determine an optimal decision strategy and its associated expected value. The Q. M. in Action article on drug testing for student athletes describes how Santa Clara University used decision analysis to make a decision regarding whether to implement a drug-testing program for student athletes.

..../ /.............

4.8   EXPECTED VALUE OF SAMPLE INFORMATION

The optimal decision strategy developed in the preceding section shows that if the market research report is favorable, PDC should construct the large condominium complex. However, if the market research report is unfavorable, PDC should construct the medium condominium complex. The expected value of this optimal decision strategy, $15.82 million, is the *expected value with sample information* (EVwSI).

In Section 4.3 we used the expected value approach to recommend a decision alternative based on PDC's original probability estimates of $P(s_1) = 0.8$ and $P(s_2) = 0.2$. That analysis showed that d_3, with an expected value of $14.2 million, is the best decision. However, that recommendation lacked the benefit of sample information, so the $14.2 million result is the *expected value without sample information* (EVwoSI).

Since the expected value with sample information is $15.82 million and the expected value without sample information is $14.2 million, the **expected value of sample information (EVSI)** is $15.82 − $14.2 = $1.62 million. In other words, $1.62 million is the increase in the expected value based on the sample information. In general, the expected value of sample information is computed as follows.

$$EVSI = |\ EVwSI - EVwoSI\ | \tag{4.9}$$

where

$$EVSI = \text{expected value of sample information}$$
$$EVwSI = \text{expected value } with \text{ sample information about the states of nature}$$
$$EVwoSI = \text{expected value } without \text{ sample information about the states of nature}$$

Note the role of the absolute value in equation (4.9). That is, for minimization problems the expected value with sample information always is less than or equal to the expected value without sample information. In this case, EVSI is the magnitude of the difference between EVwSI and EVwoSI; thus, by taking the absolute value of the difference as shown in equation (4.9), we can handle both the maximization and minimization cases with one equation.

Efficiency of Sample Information

In Section 4.5 we showed that the expected value of perfect information (EVPI) for the PDC problem is $3.2 million. We never anticipated that the market research report would obtain perfect information, but we can use an **efficiency** measure to express the value of the market research information. With perfect information having an efficiency rating of 100%, the efficiency rating E for sample information is computed as follows.

$$E = \frac{EVSI}{EVPI} \times 100 \tag{4.10}$$

For the PDC problem,

$$E = \frac{1.62}{3.2} \times 100 = 50.6\%$$

In other words, the information from the market research study is 50.6% as efficient as perfect information.

Low efficiency ratings for sample information might lead the decision maker to look for other types of information. However, high efficiency ratings indicate that the sample information is almost as good as perfect information and that additional sources of information would not yield significantly better results.

N O T E S and Comments

1. The use of computer software for decision analysis is becoming commonplace. The ARBORIST, available from Texas Instruments, allows the user to develop a graph of the decision tree on the screen; the program will then perform all the decision analysis calculations. Another product, SUPERTREE, from SDG Decision Systems, requires the user to specify the tree in a manner similar to that used in PERT/CPM problems; that is, the user provides the system with the nodes and their immediate predecessors, and the software develops the resulting decision tree. Although software such as the ARBORIST and SUPERTREE are not needed for problems as small as those introduced in this chapter, computer support is necessary for larger decision problems.

2. The expected value without perfect information (EVwoPI) defined in Section 4.5 and the expected value without sample information (EVwoSI) defined in Section 4.8 are the same. This value simply represents the expected value of the best decision based on prior probabilities.

SUMMARY

In this chapter we showed how decision analysis can be used to solve problems with a reasonable number of decision alternatives and a reasonable number of states of nature. The goal of decision analysis is to identify the best decision alternative in the face of uncertain or risk-filled future events (i.e., states of nature).

We presented three approaches to decision making without probabilities and discussed the use of the expected value approach for decision making with probabilities. Then we showed how to use additional information about the states of nature to revise or update the probability estimates and develop an optimal decision strategy. We utilized the concepts of expected value of sample information, expected value of perfect information, and efficiency of information to evaluate the contribution of the sample information.

GLOSSARY

States of nature Uncontrollable future events that affect the payoff associated with a decision alternative.

Payoff An outcome measure such as profit, cost, or time. Each combination of a decision alternative and a state of nature has an associated payoff.

Payoff table A tabular representation of the payoffs for a decision problem.

Decision tree A graphical representation of the decision problem that shows the sequential nature of the decision-making situation.

Node An intersection or junction point of a decision tree.

Branch A line or arc connecting nodes of a decision tree.

Optimistic approach An approach to choosing a decision alternative without using probabilities. For a maximization problem, it leads to choosing the decision alternative corresponding to the largest payoff; for a minimization problem, it leads to choosing the decision alternative corresponding to the smallest payoff.

Conservative approach An approach to choosing a decision alternative without using probabilities. For a maximization problem, it leads to choosing the decision alternative that maximizes the minimum payoff; for a minimization problem, it leads to choosing the decision alternative that minimizes the maximum payoff.

Minimax regret approach An approach to choosing a decision alternative without using probabilities. For each alternative, the maximum regret is computed. This approach leads to choosing the decision alternative that minimizes the maximum regret.

Opportunity loss, or regret The amount of loss (lower profit or higher cost) from not making the best decision for each state of nature.

Expected value approach An approach to choosing a decision alternative that is based on the expected value of each decision alternative. The recommended decision alternative is the one that provides the best expected value.

Expected value (EV) For a decision alternative, it is the weighted average of the payoffs. The weights are the state-of-nature probabilities.

Sensitivity analysis The study of how changes in the probability estimates for the states of nature affect the recommended decision alternative.

Expected value of perfect information (EVPI) The expected value of information that would tell the decision maker exactly which state of nature is going to occur (i.e., perfect information).

Prior probabilities The probabilities of the states of nature prior to obtaining sample information.

Posterior (revised) probabilities The probabilities of the states of nature after revising the prior probabilities based on given indicator information.

Sample information New information obtained through research or experimentation that enables an updating or revision of the state of nature probabilities.

Bayesian revision The process of revising prior probabilities to create the posterior probabilities based on sample information.

Expected value of sample information (EVSI) The difference between the expected value of an optimal strategy based on sample information and the "best" expected value without any sample information.

Efficiency The ratio of EVSI to EVPI; perfect information is 100% efficient.

PROBLEMS

SELF TEST

1. The following payoff table shows profit for a decision analysis problem with two decisions and three states of nature.
   a. Construct a decision tree for this problem.
   b. If the decision maker knows nothing about the probabilities of the three states of nature, what is the recommended decision using the optimistic, conservative, and minimax regret approaches?

Decision Alternative	State of Nature		
	s_1	s_2	s_3
d_1	250	100	25
d_2	100	100	75

2. Suppose that a decision maker faced with four decision alternatives and four states of nature develops the following profit payoff table.

Decision Alternative	State of Nature			
	s_1	s_2	s_3	s_4
d_1	14	9	10	5
d_2	11	10	8	7
d_3	9	10	10	11
d_4	8	10	11	13

a. If the decision maker knows nothing about the probabilities of the four states of nature, what is the recommended decision using the optimistic, conservative, and minimax regret approaches?

b. Which approach do you prefer? Explain. Is establishing the most appropriate approach before analyzing the problem important for the decision maker? Explain.

c. Assume that the payoff table provides *cost* rather than profit payoffs. What is the recommended decision using the optimistic, conservative, and minimax regret approaches?

3. Southland Corporation's decision to produce a new line of recreational products has resulted in the need to construct either a small plant or a large plant. The selection of plant size depends on how the marketplace reacts to the new product line. To conduct an analysis, marketing management has decided to view the possible long-run demand as either low, medium, or high. The following payoff table shows the projected profit in millions of dollars:

Decision Alternative	Long-Run Demand		
	Low	Medium	High
Small plant	150	200	200
Large plant	50	200	500

a. Construct a decision tree for this problem.

b. Recommend a decision based on the use of the optimistic, conservative, and minimax regret approaches.

4. Investment Advisors, Inc., has three investment strategies under consideration. Profits from the strategies will depend on what happens to the prime interest rate over the next three months. Payoffs (in thousand of dollars) are shown.

Decision Alternative	State of Nature		
	Rate Decrease, s_1	No Change, s_2	Rate Increase, s_3
Strategy, d_1	50	70	40
Strategy, d_2	55	35	80
Strategy, d_3	15	60	70

What investment strategy would you recommend based on the use of the optimistic, pessimistic, and minimax regret approaches?

SELF TEST

5. The profit payoff table presented in Problem 1 is repeated here.
   Suppose that the decision maker has obtained the following probability estimates: $P(s_1) = 0.65$, $P(s_2) = 0.15$, and $P(s_3) = 0.20$. Use the expected value approach to determine the optimal decision.

Decision Alternative	State of Nature		
	s_1	s_2	s_3
d_1	250	100	25
d_2	100	100	75

6. The profit payoff table presented in Problem 2 is repeated here.

Decision Alternative	State of Nature			
	s_1	s_2	s_3	s_4
d_1	14	9	10	5
d_2	11	10	8	7
d_3	9	10	10	11
d_4	8	10	11	13

Suppose that the decision maker obtains information that enables the following probability estimates to be made: $P(s_1) = 0.5$, $P(s_2) = 0.2$, $P(s_3) = 0.2$, and $P(s_4) = 0.1$.
   a. Use the expected value approach to determine the optimal decision.
   b. Now assume that the entries in the payoff table are costs; use the expected value approach to determine the optimal decision.

7. A firm is considering three options for managing its data processing operation: continuing with its own staff, hiring an outside vendor to do the managing (referred to as *outsourcing*), or a combination of its own staff and outside vendor. The cost of the operation depends on future demand. The annual cost of each decision alternative and state of nature (in thousands of dollars) is as follows.

Decision Alternative	State of Nature		
	High Demand s_1	Medium Demand s_2	Low Demand s_3
Own staff, d_1	650	650	600
Vendor, d_2	900	600	300
Combination, d_3	800	650	500

If the demand probabilities are 0.2, 0.5, and 0.3, which decision alternative will minimize the expected cost of the data processing operation? What is the expected annual cost associated with that recommendation?

8. The following payoff table shows the profit for a decision problem with two states of nature and two decision alternatives.

Decision Alternative	State of Nature	
	s_1	s_2
d_1	10	1
d_2	4	3

Use graphical sensitivity analysis to determine the probability of state of nature s_1 for which each of the decision alternatives has the largest expected value.

9. The following payoff table shows the profit for a decision problem with two states of nature and three decision alternatives.

Decision Alternative	State of Nature	
	s_1	s_2
d_1	80	50
d_2	65	85
d_3	30	100

Use graphical sensitivity analysis to determine the values of the probability of state of nature s_1 for which each of the decision alternatives has the largest expected value.

10. Political Systems, Inc., is a new firm specializing in information services such as surveys and data analysis for individuals running for political office. The firm is opening its headquarters in Chicago and is considering three office locations that differ in cost due to square footage and office equipment requirements. The profit projections shown (in thousands of dollars) for each location were based on both high demand and low demand states of nature.

Decision Alternative	State of Nature	
	High Demand s_1	Low Demand s_2
Location A	200	−20
Location B	120	10
Location C	100	60

a. Initially, management is uncomfortable stating probabilities for the states of nature. Let p denote the probability of the high demand state of nature. What does graphical sensitivity analysis tell management about location preferences? Can any location be dropped from consideration? Why or why not?

b. After further review, management estimated the probability of a high demand at 0.65. Based on the results in part (a), which location should be selected? What is the expected value associated with that decision?

11. Six months ago, Doug Reynolds paid $25,000 for an option to purchase a tract of land that he is considering developing. Another investor has offered to purchase Doug's option for $275,000. If Doug does not accept the investor's offer, he will purchase the property, clear the land, and prepare the site for building. He believes that once the site is prepared he can sell the land to a home builder. However, the success of the investment depends on the real estate market at the time he sells the property. If the real estate market is down, Doug believes that he will lose $1.5 million. If market conditions stay at their current level, he estimates that his profit will be $1 million; if market conditions are up at the time he sells, he estimates a profit of $4 million. Because of other commitments Doug does not consider it feasible to hold the land once he has developed it; thus, the only two alternatives are to sell the option or to develop the land. Suppose that the probabilities of the real estate market being down, at the current level, or up are 0.6, 0.3, and 0.1, respectively.

   a. What decision should Doug make using the expected value approach?
   b. Suppose that the probabilities of the real estate market being down, at the current level, or up are 0.5, 0.3, and 0.2, respectively. What decision should Doug make based on the expected value approach? What if the probabilities are 0.4, 0.4, and 0.2? What do the results suggest regarding the proposed investment?
   c. Suppose that, after further consideration, Doug concludes that 0.1 is a good estimate of the probability of the real estate market being up. However, he is unable to reach any definite conclusions regarding the probabilities for the other two states of nature. What would the probability of the market being down have to be for the expected value approach to recommend that he should sell his option for $275,000? Would this information help Doug make a decision regarding whether to sell the option or develop the site? Explain.

SELF TEST

12. The profit payoff table presented in Problems 1 and 5 is repeated below.

Decision Alternative	State of Nature		
	s_1	s_2	s_3
d_1	250	100	25
d_2	100	100	75

   The probabilities for the states of nature are: $P(s_1) = 0.65$, $P(s_2) = 0.15$, and $P(s_3) = 0.20$.
   a. What is the optimal decision strategy if perfect information were available?
   b. What is the expected value for the decision strategy developed in part (a)?
   c. Using the expected value approach, what is the recommended decision? What is its expected value?
   d. What is the expected value of perfect information?

13. The profit payoff table presented in Problems 2 and 6 is repeated below. The probabilities are $P(s_1) = 0.5$, $P(s_2) = 0.2$, $P(s_3) = 0.2$, and $P(s_4) = 0.1$.
   a. What is the optimal decision strategy if perfect information were available?
   b. What is the expected value for the decision strategy developed in part (a)?
   c. Using the expected value approach, what is the recommended decision? What is its expected value? What is the value of perfect information?

Decision Alternative	State of Nature			
	s_1	s_2	s_3	s_4
d_1	14	9	10	5
d_2	11	10	8	7
d_3	9	10	10	11
d_4	8	10	11	13

14. Suppose that you are given a decision situation with three possible states of nature: s_1, s_2, and s_3. The prior probabilities are $P(s_1) = 0.2$, $P(s_2) = 0.5$, and $P(s_3) = 0.3$. With sample information I, $P(I \mid s_1) = 0.1$, $P(I \mid s_2) = 0.05$, and $P(I \mid s_3) = 0.2$. Compute the revised or posterior probabilities: $P(s_1 \mid I)$, $P(s_2 \mid I)$, and $P(s_3 \mid I)$.

15. In the following profit payoff table for a decision problem with two states of nature and three decision alternatives, the prior probabilities for s_1 and s_2 are $P(s_1) = 0.8$ and $P(s_2) = 0.2$.

Decision Alternatives	State of Nature	
	s_1	s_2
d_1	15	10
d_2	10	12
d_3	8	20

 a. Use only the prior probabilities and the expected value approach to find the optimal decision.
 b. Use graphical sensitivity analysis to determine the values of the probability of state of nature s_1 for which each of the decision alternatives has the largest expected value.
 c. Find the EVPI.
 d. Suppose sample information I is obtained, with $P(I \mid s_1) = 0.2$ and $P(I \mid s_2) = 0.75$. Find the posterior probabilities $P(s_1 \mid I)$ and $P(s_2 \mid I)$. Recommend a decision alternative based on these probabilities.

16. Consider the following decision tree representation of a decision analysis problem with two sample information outcomes I_1 and I_2, two decision alternatives d_1 and d_2, and two states of nature s_1 and s_2.

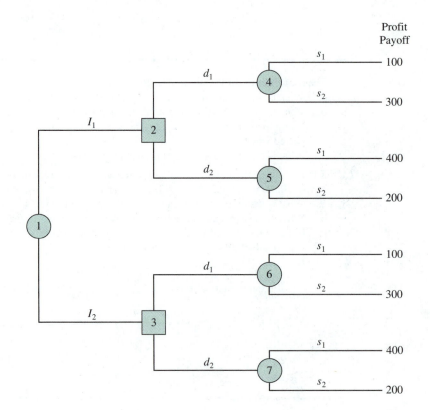

The probabilities are

$$P(s_1) = 0.4 \qquad P(I_1 \mid s_1) = 0.8 \qquad P(I_2 \mid s_1) = 0.2$$
$$P(s_2) = 0.6 \qquad P(I_1 \mid s_2) = 0.4 \qquad P(I_2 \mid s_2) = 0.6$$

a. What are the values for $P(I_1)$ and $P(I_2)$?
b. What are the values of $P(s_1 \mid I_1)$, $P(s_2 \mid I_1)$, $P(s_1 \mid I_2)$, and $P(s_2 \mid I_2)$?
c. Using the decision tree approach, determine the optimal decision strategy and its expected value.

17. A real estate investor has the opportunity to purchase land that is currently zoned residential. If the county board approves a request to rezone the property as commercial within the next year, the investor will be able to lease the land to a large discount firm that wants to open a new store on the property. However, if the zoning change is not approved, the investor will have to sell the property at a loss. Profits (in thousands of dollars) are shown in the following payoff table.

Decision Alternative	State of Nature	
	Rezoning Approved s_1	Rezoning Not Approved s_2
Purchase, d_1	600	−200
Do not purchase, d_2	0	0

a. If the probability that the rezoning will be approved is 0.5, what decision is recommended? What is the expected profit?
b. The investor can purchase an option to buy the land. Under the option, the investor maintains the rights to purchase the land anytime during the next 3 months while learning more about possible resistance to the rezoning proposal from area residents. Historical probabilities about such resistance by area residents for each state of nature are as follows.

	High Resistance H	Low Resistance L
Rezoning approved, s_1	0.2	0.8
Rezoning not approved, s_2	0.9	0.1

What is the optimal decision strategy if the investor uses the option period to learn more about the resistance from area residents before making the purchase decision?
c. If the option will cost the investor an additional $10,000, should the investor purchase the option? Why or why not? What is the maximum that the investor should be willing to pay for the option?

18. McHuffter Condominiums, Inc., of Pensacola, Florida, recently purchased land near the Gulf of Mexico and is attempting to determine the size of the condominium development it should build. It is considering three sizes of developments: small, d_1; medium, d_2; and large, d_3. At the same time, an uncertain economy makes ascertaining the demand for the new condominiums difficult. McHuffter's management realizes that a large development followed by low demand could be very costly to the company. However, if McHuffter makes a conservative small-development decision and then finds a high demand, the firm's profits will be lower than they might have been. With the three levels of demand—low, medium, and high—McHuffter's management has prepared the following profit (in thousands of dollars) payoff table.

Decision Alternative	Demand		
	Low s_1	Medium s_2	High s_3
Small, d_1	400	400	400
Medium, d_2	100	600	600
Large, d_3	−300	300	900

a. Construct a decision tree for this problem.
b. If nothing is known about the demand probabilities, what are the recommended decisions using the optimistic, conservative, and minimax regret approaches?
c. If $P(\text{low}) = 0.20$, $P(\text{medium}) = 0.35$, and $P(\text{high}) = 0.45$, what is the recommended decision using the expected value approach?
d. What is the expected value of perfect information?

Suppose that McHuffter Condominiums conducts a survey to help evaluate the demand for the new condominium development. The survey reports on three indicators of demand: weak (W), average (A), or strong (S). The conditional probabilities are shown here:

W	A	S
$P(W \mid s_1) = 0.6$	$P(A \mid s_1) = 0.3$	$P(S \mid s_1) = 0.1$
$P(W \mid s_2) = 0.4$	$P(A \mid s_2) = 0.4$	$P(S \mid s_2) = 0.2$
$P(W \mid s_3) = 0.1$	$P(A \mid s_3) = 0.4$	$P(S \mid s_3) = 0.5$

e. What is McHuffter's optimal strategy?
f. What is the value of the survey information?
g. What are the EVPI and the efficiency of the survey information?

19. Hale's TV Productions is considering producing a pilot for a comedy series for a major television network. The network may reject the pilot and the series, but it may also purchase the program for 1 or 2 years. Hale may decide to produce the pilot or transfer the rights for the series to a competitor for $100,000. Hale's profits are summarized in the following profit (in thousands of dollars) payoff table.

Decision Alternative	State of Nature		
	Reject s_1	1 Year s_2	2 Years s_3
Produce pilot, d_1	−100	50	150
Sell to competitor, d_2	100	100	100

a. If the probability estimates for the states of nature are $P(\text{reject}) = 0.2$, $P(1 \text{ year}) = 0.3$, and $P(2 \text{ years}) = 0.5$, what should the company do?
b. What is the maximum that Hale should be willing to pay for inside information on what the network will do?

For a consulting fee of $2500, an agency will review the plans for the comedy series and indicate the overall chances of a favorable network reaction to the series. If the special agency review results in a favorable (F) or an unfavorable (U) evaluation, what should Hale's decision strategy be? Assume that Hale believes that the following conditional probabilities are realistic appraisals of the agency's evaluation accuracy.

$$P(F \mid s_1) = 0.3 \qquad P(U \mid s_1) = 0.7$$
$$P(F \mid s_2) = 0.6 \qquad P(U \mid s_2) = 0.4$$
$$P(F \mid s_3) = 0.9 \qquad P(U \mid s_3) = 0.1$$

c. Show the decision tree for this problem.

d. What is the recommended decision strategy and the expected value, assuming that the agency information is obtained?

e. What is the EVSI? Is the agency's information worth the $2500 consulting fee? What is the maximum that Hale should be willing to pay for the information?

20. Martin's Service Station is considering investing in a heavy-duty snowplow this fall. Martin has analyzed the situation carefully and believes that it would be a profitable investment if the snowfall is heavy. Martin could still make a small profit if the snowfall is moderate, but he would lose money if the snowfall is light. Specifically, Martin forecasts a profit of $7000 if the snowfall is heavy, $2000 if it is moderate, and a $9000 loss if the snowfall is light. Based on the weather bureau's long-range forecast, Martin estimates that $P(\text{heavy snowfall}) = 0.4$, $P(\text{moderate snowfall}) = 0.3$, and $P(\text{light snowfall}) = 0.3$.

a. Prepare a decision tree for Martin's problem.

b. What is the expected value at each state-of-nature node?

c. Would the expected value approach recommend that Martin invest in a snowplow?

Suppose that Martin can purchase a blade to attach to his service truck that can also be used to plow driveways and parking lots. This truck must also be available to start cars, so Martin will not be able to generate as much revenue plowing snow if he chooses this alternative. But his loss will be smaller if the snowfall is light. Under this alternative, Martin forecasts a profit of $3500 if the snowfall is heavy, $1000 if it is moderate, and a $1500 loss if the snowfall is light.

d. Prepare a new decision tree showing all three alternatives.

e. What is the optimal decision using the expected value approach?

f. What is the expected value of perfect information?

Suppose that Martin decides to wait to check the September temperature pattern before making a final decision. Estimates of the probabilities associated with an unseasonably cold September (U) are $P(U|s_1) = 0.30$, $P(U|s_2) = 0.20$, and $P(U|s_3) = 0.05$.

g. If Martin observes an unseasonably cold September, what is the recommended decision?

h. If Martin does not observe an unseasonably cold September, what is the recommended decision?

21. Joseph Software, Inc. (JSI), has been investigating the possibility of developing a grammar-and-style checker for use on microcomputers. Based on its experience with other software projects, JSI estimates that the total cost to develop a prototype is $200,000. If the performance of the prototype is somewhat better than existing software, referred to as a *moderate success,* JSI believes that it could sell the rights to the software to a larger software developer for $600,000. If the performance of the prototype is significantly better than existing software, referred to as a *major success,* JSI believes that it can sell the software for $1.2 million. However, if the performance of the prototype does not exceed the performance of existing software, referred to as a *failure,* JSI will not be able to sell the software and hence will lose all its development costs.

a. Prepare a decision tree for JSI.

b. If the best estimates of the states of nature are $P(\text{failure}) = 0.70$, $P(\text{moderate success}) = 0.20$, and $P(\text{major success}) = 0.10$, what should JSI do if it uses the expected value approach?

Suppose that JSI can hire an independent consultant to review its ideas for the new software. For a fee of $5000, the consultant will make a recommendation as to whether JSI should develop a prototype. Based on previous experience with this consultant, JSI has assigned conditional probabilities:

$$P(D \mid s_1) = 0.2$$
$$P(D \mid s_2) = 0.6$$
$$P(D \mid s_3) = 0.9$$

where

$$D = \text{recommendation to develop a prototype}$$
$$s_1 = \text{failure}$$
$$s_2 = \text{moderate success}$$
$$s_3 = \text{major success}$$

    c.   Should JSI hire the consultant? Explain.

22. Milford Trucking Company of Chicago has requests to haul two shipments, one to St. Louis and one to Detroit. Because of a scheduling problem, Milford will be able to accept only one of these assignments. The St. Louis customer has guaranteed a return shipment, but the Detroit customer has not. Thus, if Milford accepts the Detroit shipment and cannot find a Detroit–Chicago return shipment, the truck will return to Chicago empty. The payoff table showing profit is as follows.

Shipment	Return Shipment from Detroit s_1	No Return Shipment from Detroit s_2
St. Louis, d_1	2000	2000
Detroit, d_2	2500	1000

    a.   If the probability of a Detroit return shipment is 0.4, what should Milford do?
    b.   Use graphical sensitivity analysis to determine the values of the probability of state of nature s_1 for which d_1 has the largest expected value.
    c.   What is the expected value of perfect information that would tell Milford Trucking whether Detroit has a return shipment?

Milford can telephone a Detroit truck dispatch center and determine whether the general Detroit shipping activity is busy (B) or slow (S). If shipping activity is busy, the chances of obtaining a return shipment will increase. Suppose that the conditional probabilities are

$$P(B \mid s_1) = 0.6 \qquad P(S \mid s_1) = 0.4$$
$$P(B \mid s_2) = 0.3 \qquad P(S \mid s_2) = 0.7$$

    d.   What should Milford do?
    e.   If the general Detroit shipping activity is busy, what is the probability that Milford will obtain a return shipment if it makes the trip to Detroit?
    f.   What is the efficiency of the telephone information?

23. Lawson's Department Store faces a buying decision for a seasonal product for which demand can be high, medium, and low. The purchaser for Lawson's can order 1, 2, or 3 lots of the product before the season begins but cannot reorder later. Profit projections (in thousands of dollars) are shown.

    a.   If the prior probabilities for the three states of nature are 0.3, 0.3, and 0.4, respectively, what is the recommended order quantity?

Decision Alternative	State of Nature		
	High Demand	Medium Demand	Low Demand
	s_1	s_2	s_3
Order 1 lot, d_1	60	60	50
Order 2 lots, d_2	80	80	30
Order 3 lots, d_3	100	70	10

b. At each preseason sales meeting, the vice president of sales provides his personal opinion regarding potential demand for this product. Because of his enthusiasm and optimistic nature, his predictions of market conditions have always been either "excellent" (E) or "very good" (V). Conditional probabilities for each state of nature are as follows.

State of Nature	Prediction	
	Excellent E	Very Good V
High demand, s_1	0.80	0.20
Medium demand, s_2	0.75	0.25
Low demand, s_3	0.60	0.40

What are the revised probabilities of each state of nature for each of the vice president's predictions?

c. What is the optimal decision strategy for the vice president's predictions?

d. Use the efficiency of sample information and discuss whether the firm should consider a consulting expert who could provide independent forecasts of market conditions for the product.

24. To save on gasoline expenses, Rona and Jerry agreed to form a carpool for traveling to and from work. After limiting the travel routes to two alternatives, they couldn't agree on the best way to travel to work. Jerry preferred the expressway because it usually was the fastest; however, Rona pointed out that traffic jams on the expressway sometimes led to long delays. Rona preferred the somewhat longer but more consistent Queen City Avenue. Although Jerry preferred the expressway, he agreed with Rona that they should take Queen City Avenue if the expressway had a traffic jam. Unfortunately, they do not know the state of the expressway ahead of time. The following payoff table provides the one-way time estimates in minutes for traveling to or from work.

Route	State of Nature	
	Expressway Open s_1	Expressway Jammed s_2
Expressway, d_1	25	45
Queen City Avenue, d_2	30	30

a. After driving to work on the expressway for one month (20 days), they found the expressway jammed three times. Assuming that these days are representative of future days, should they continue to use the expressway for traveling to work? Explain.

b. Use graphical sensitivity analysis to determine the values of the probability of state of nature s_1 for which d_1 has the best expected value.

c. Would not using the expected value approach for this particular problem make sense? Explain.

After a period of time, Rona and Jerry noted that the weather seemed to affect traffic conditions on the expressway. They identified three weather conditions (indicators) and gave them conditional probabilities:

$$C = \text{clear} \qquad O = \text{overcast} \qquad R = \text{rain}$$
$$P(C \mid s_1) = 0.8 \qquad P(O \mid s_1) = 0.2 \qquad P(R \mid s_1) = 0$$
$$P(C \mid s_2) = 0.1 \qquad P(O \mid s_2) = 0.3 \qquad P(R \mid s_2) = 0.6$$

d. Show the decision tree for the problem of traveling to work.

e. What are the optimal decision strategy and the expected travel time?

f. What is the efficiency of the weather information?

25. The Gorman Manufacturing Company must decide whether to purchase a component from a supplier or manufacture the component at its Milan, Michigan, plant. If demand is high, Gorman could profitably manufacture the component. However, if demand is low, Gorman's unit manufacturing cost would be high due to underutilization of equipment. The following table shows the projected profit (in thousands of dollars) for Gorman's make-or-buy decision.

Decision Alternative	Demand		
	Low s_1	Medium s_2	High s_3
Manufacture component, d_1	−20	40	100
Purchase component, d_2	10	45	70

The states of nature probabilities are $P(\text{low}) = 0.35$, $P(\text{medium}) = 0.35$, and $P(\text{high}) = 0.30$.

a. Use a decision tree to recommend a decision.

b. Use EVPI to determine whether Gorman should attempt to obtain a better estimate of demand. A test market study of the potential demand for the product is expected to report either a favorable (F) or unfavorable (U) condition. The relevant conditional probabilities are as follows:

$$P(F \mid s_1) = 0.10 \qquad P(U \mid s_1) = 0.90$$
$$P(F \mid s_2) = 0.40 \qquad P(U \mid s_2) = 0.60$$
$$P(F \mid s_3) = 0.60 \qquad P(U \mid s_3) = 0.40$$

c. What is the probability that the market research report will be favorable?

d. What is Gorman's optimal decision strategy?

e. What is the expected value of the market research information?

f. What is the efficiency of the information?

26. A quality control procedure involves 100% inspection of parts received from a supplier. Historical records indicate the defective rates shown at the top of page 135. The cost to inspect 100% of the parts received is $250 for each shipment of 500 parts. If the shipment is not 100% inspected, defective parts will cause rework problems later in the production process. The rework cost is $25 for each defective part.

Percent Defective	Probability
0	0.15
1	0.25
2	0.40
3	0.20

a. Complete the following payoff table, where the entries represent the total cost of inspection and reworking.

Inspection	Percent Defective			
	$0, s_1$	$1, s_2$	$2, s_3$	$3, s_4$
100% inspection, d_1	$250	$250	$250	$250
No inspection, d_2				

b. The plant manager is considering eliminating the inspection process to save the $250 inspection cost per shipment. Do you support this action? Use expected value to justify your answer.

c. Show the decision tree for this problem.

d. Suppose that a sample of five parts is selected from the shipment and that one defect is found. Let $I = 1$ defect in a sample of 5. Use the binomial probability distribution to compute $P(I \mid s_1)$, $P(I \mid s_2)$, $P(I \mid s_3)$, and $P(I \mid s_4)$. The binomial probability function is as follows:

$$f(x) = \frac{n!}{x!(n - x)!} p^x(1 - p)^{n - x}$$

where

n = the sample size

x = the number of defects

p = the proportion defective

In this problem, $n = 5$, $x = 1$, and $p = 0, 0.01, 0.02$, and 0.03.

e. If I occurs, what are the revised probabilities for the states of nature?

f. Should the entire shipment be 100% inspected whenever 1 defect is found in a sample of size 5?

g. What is the cost savings associated with the sample information?

Case Problem   PROPERTY PURCHASE STRATEGY

Glenn Foreman, president of Oceanview Development Corporation, is considering submitting a bid to purchase property that will be sold by sealed bid at a county tax foreclosure. Glenn's initial judgment is to submit a bid of $5 million. Based on his experience, Glenn estimates that a bid of $5 million will have a 0.2 probability of being the highest bid and securing the property for Oceanview. The current date is June 1. Sealed bids for the property must be submitted by August 15. The winning bid will be announced on September 1.

If Oceanview submits the highest bid and obtains the property, the firm plans to build and sell a complex of luxury condominiums. However, a complicating factor is that the property is currently zoned for single-family residences only. Glenn believes that a referendum could be placed on the voting ballot in time for the November election. Passage of the referendum would change the zoning of the property and permit construction of the condominiums.

The sealed-bid procedure requires the bid to be submitted with a certified check for 10% of the amount bid. If the bid is rejected, the deposit is refunded. If the bid is accepted, the deposit is the down payment for the property. However, if the bid is accepted and the bidder does not follow through with the purchase and meet the remainder of the financial obligation within six months, the deposit will be forfeited. In this case, the county will offer the property to the next highest bidder.

To determine whether Oceanview should submit the $5 million bid, Glenn has done some preliminary analysis. This preliminary work provided an estimate of 0.3 for the probability that the referendum for a zoning change will be approved and resulted in the following estimates of the costs and revenues that will be incurred if the condominiums are built.

Cost and Revenue Estimates

Revenue from condominium sales	$15,000,000
Cost	
Property	$5,000,000
Construction expenses	$8,000,000

If Oceanview obtains the property and the zoning change is not approved in November, Glenn believes that the best option would be for the firm not to complete the purchase of the property. In this case, Oceanview would forfeit the 10% deposit that accompanied the bid.

Because the likelihood that the zoning referendum will be approved is such an important factor in the decision process, Glenn has suggested that the firm hire a market research service to conduct a survey of voters. The survey would provide a better estimate of the likelihood that the referendum for a zoning change would be approved. The market research firm that Oceanview Development has worked with in the past has agreed to do the study for $15,000. The results of the study will be available August 1, so that Oceanview will have this information before the August 15 bid deadline. The results of the survey will be either a prediction that the zoning change will be approved or a prediction that the zoning change will not be approved. After considering the record of the market research service in previous studies conducted for Oceanview, Glenn has developed the following probability estimates concerning the accuracy of the market research information.

$$P(A \mid s_1) = 0.9 \qquad P(N \mid s_1) = 0.1$$
$$P(A \mid s_2) = 0.2 \qquad P(N \mid s_2) = 0.8$$

where

A = prediction that the zoning change will be approved
N = prediction that the zoning change will not be approved
s_1 = the zoning change is approved by the voters
s_2 = the zoning change is not approved by the voters

Managerial Report

Perform an analysis of the problem facing the Oceanview Development Corporation, and prepare a report that summarizes your findings and recommendations. Include the following items in your report:

1. A decision tree that shows the logical sequence of the decision problem
2. A recommendation regarding what Oceanview should do if the market research information is not available
3. A decision strategy that Oceanview should follow if the market research is conducted
4. A recommendation as to whether Oceanview should employ the market research firm, along with the value of the information provided by the market research firm. Include the details of your analysis as an appendix to your report.

Appendix 4.1 DECISION ANALYSIS AND SPREADSHEETS

A spreadsheet provides a convenient way to perform basic decision analysis computations. A spreadsheet may be designed for any of the decision analysis approaches described in this chapter. We will demonstrate use of the spreadsheet in decision analysis by solving the PDC condominium problem using the expected value approach.

Figure 4.10 shows the formula spreadsheet for the PDC problem. The values in color are the payoffs and the state of nature probabilities that the user must enter directly into the spreadsheet. In the EXPECTED VALUE column, we show the cell formulas used in the spreadsheet computations. For example, the expected value for decision alternative 1 is provided by the cell formula = $B$11*B7 + $C$11*C7.

In addition to making the expected value computation for all three decision alternatives, the cell D14 formula = MAX (D7:D9) indicates that this cell will contain the maximum of

Figure 4.10 FORMULA SPREADSHEET FOR THE EXPECTED VALUE OF THE PDC DECISION PROBLEM

	A	B	C	D
1	PDC DECISION PROBLEM			
2				
3				
4		STATE		EXPECTED
5		HIGH	LOW	VALUE
6				
7	SMALL	8	7	=$B$11*B7+$C$11*C7
8	MEDIUM	14	5	=$B$11*B8+$C$11*C8
9	LARGE	20	−9	=$B$11*B9+$C$11*C9
10				
11	PROBABILITY	0.8	0.2	
12				
13				
14	MAXIMUM EXPECTED VALUE			=MAX (D7:D9)
15				
16	EV OF PERFECT INFORMATION			=B11*MAX (B7:B9) +C11*MAX (C7:C9) −D14

the computed expected values. This computation indicates the expected value under the best decision alternative. Finally, the cell D16 formula provides the computation of expected value of perfect information, EVPI. Probabilities $P(s_1)$ and $P(s_2)$ are multiplied by the best payoff in column 1, MAX(B7:B9), and the best payoff column 2, MAX(C7:C9), to obtain the expected value with perfect information. Subtracting the value in cell D14 provides the EVPI.

Figure 4.11 shows the value spreadsheet for the PDC decision problem. The recommended decision alternative is the large complex with a maximum expected value of $14.2 million. The EVPI is $3.2 million, as computed previously in Section 4.5.

One advantage of the spreadsheet is its use in sensitivity analysis. For example, Figure 4.12 shows the solution under the assumption that the probabilities of the states of nature are changed to $P(s_1) = 0.2$ and $P(s_2) = 0.8$. Making these two data modifications provides the results shown. In this situation, the small complex is the recommended decision, with the maximum expected value reduced to $7.2 million. Similarly, further sensitivity analysis of other states of nature and/or modified payoff values can be quickly and easily considered.

Figure 4.13 shows the formula spreadsheet for the computation of the decision tree branch probabilities based on Bayes' Theorem. With this spreadsheet design, we input only the prior probabilities and the conditional probabilities, as shown in color. Branch probabilities are provided by P(F), P(U), and four posterior probabilities (POSTERIOR PROBS). Note that the prior probabilities have to be entered only once because the cell formulas of =B6 and =B8 in the PRIOR PROBS column for UNFAVORABLE show that the same prior probabilities of 0.8 and 0.2 will be used for the UNFAVORABLE probability revision process. Figure 4.14 shows the value spreadsheet. Determine whether you can follow the logic of the formula spreadsheet and verify that the results shown in Figure 4.14 are identical to the hand computation of the branch probabilities, as presented in Section 4.7.

Figure 4.11   VALUE SPREADSHEET FOR THE EXPECTED VALUE OF THE PDC DECISION PROBLEM

	A	B	C	D
1	PDC DECISION PROBLEM			
2				
3				
4		STATE		EXPECTED
5		HIGH	LOW	VALUE
6				
7	SMALL	8	7	7.8
8	MEDIUM	14	5	12.2
9	LARGE	20	−9	14.2
10				
11	PROBABILITY	0.8	0.2	
12				
13				
14	MAXIMUM EXPECTED VALUE			14.2
15				
16	EV OF PERFECT INFORMATION			3.2

Figure 4.12 VALUE SPREADSHEET FOR THE PDC DECISION PROBLEM WITH $P(s_1) = 0.2$ AND $P(s_2) = 0.8$

	A	B	C	D
1	PDC DECISION PROBLEM			
2				
3				
4		STATE		EXPECTED
5		HIGH	LOW	VALUE
6				
7	SMALL	8	7	7.2
8	MEDIUM	14	5	6.8
9	LARGE	20	−9	−3.2
10				
11	PROBABILITY	0.2	0.8	
12				
13				
14	MAXIMUM EXPECTED VALUE			7.2
15				
16	EV OF PERFECT INFORMATION			2.4

Figure 4.13 FORMULA SPREADSHEET FOR COMPUTING BRANCH PROBABILITIES FOR THE PDC DECISION PROBLEM

	A	B	C	D	E
1	FAVORABLE				
2					
3	STATES OF	PRIOR	COND	JOINT	POSTERIOR
4	NATURE	PROBS	PROBS	PROBS	PROBS
5					
6	S1	0.8	0.9	=B6*C6	=D6/D10
7					
8	S2	0.2	0.25	=B8*C8	=D8/D10
9					
10			P(F) =	=SUM (D6 : D8)	
11					
12					
13	UNFAVORABLE				
14					
15	STATES OF	PRIOR	COND	JOINT	POSTERIOR
16	NATURE	PROBS	PROBS	PROBS	PROBS
17					
18	S1	=B6	0.1	=B18*C18	=D18/D22
19					
20	S2	=B8	0.75	=B20*C20	=D20/D22
21					
22			P(U) =	=SUM (D18 : D20)	

Figure 4.14   VALUE SPREADSHEET OF BRANCH PROBABILITIES FOR THE PDC DECISION PROBLEM

	A	B	C	D	E
1	FAVORABLE				
2					
3	STATES OF	PRIOR	COND	JOINT	POSTERIOR
4	NATURE	PROBS	PROBS	PROBS	PROBS
5					
6	S1	0.8	0.90	0.72	0.9351
7					
8	S2	0.2	0.25	0.05	0.0649
9					
10			P(F) =	0.77	
11					
12	UNFAVORABLE				
13					
14					
15	STATES OF	PRIOR	COND	JOINT	POSTERIOR
16	NATURE	PROBS	PROBS	PROBS	PROBS
17					
18	S1	0.8	0.10	0.08	0.3478
19					
20	S2	0.2	0.75	0.15	0.6522
21					
22			P(U) =	0.23	

OHIO EDISON COMPANY*

AKRON, OHIO

Ohio Edison Company is an investor-owned electric utility headquartered in northeastern Ohio. Ohio Edison and a Pennsylvania subsidiary provide electrical service to more than two million people. Most of this electricity is generated by coal-fired power plants. To meet evolving air-quality standards, Ohio Edison replaced existing particulate control equipment at most of its generating plants with more efficient equipment. The combination of this program to upgrade air-quality control equipment with the continuing need to construct new generating plants to meet future power requirements resulted in a large capital investment program.

Quantitative Methods activities at Ohio Edison are distributed throughout the company rather than centralized in a specific department, and are more or less evenly divided among the following areas: fossil and nuclear fuel planning, environmental studies, capacity planning, large equipment evaluation, and corporate planning. Applications include decision analysis, optimal ordering strategies, computer modeling, and simulation.

A Decision Analysis Application

The flue gas emitted by coal-fired power plants contains small ash particles and sulfur dioxide (SO_2). Federal and state regulatory agencies have established emission limits for both particulates and sulfur dioxide. In the late 1970s, Ohio Edison developed a plan to comply with new air-quality standards at one of its largest power plants. This plant, which consists of seven coal-fired units (most of which were constructed in the 1960s), constitutes about one-third of the generating capacity of Ohio Edison and

*The authors are indebted to Thomas J. Madden and M. S. Hyrnick of Ohio Edison Company, Akron, Ohio, for providing this application.

its subsidiary company. Although all the units were initially constructed with particulate emission control equipment, that equipment was no longer capable of meeting new particulate emission requirements.

A decision had already been made to burn low-sulfur coal in four of the smaller units (units 1–4) at the plant in order to meet SO_2 emission standards. Fabric filters were to be installed on these units to control particulate emissions. Fabric filters, also known as baghouses, use thousands of fabric bags to filter out the particulates; they function in much the same way as a household vacuum cleaner.

It was considered likely, although not certain, that the three larger units (units 5–7) at this plant would burn medium- to high-sulfur coal. A method of controlling particulate emissions at these units had not yet been selected. Preliminary studies narrowed the particulate control equipment choice to a decision between fabric filters and electrostatic precipitators (which remove particulates suspended in the flue gas by passing the flue gas through a strong electric field). This decision was affected by a number of uncertainties, including the following:

- Uncertainty in the way some air-quality laws and regulations might be interpreted
- Potential requirements that either low-sulfur coal or high-sulfur Ohio coal (or neither) be burned in units 5–7
- Potential future changes to air quality laws and regulations
- An overall plant reliability improvement program already under way at this plant
- The outcome of this program itself, which would affect the operating costs of whichever pollution control technology was installed in these units

- Uncertain construction costs of the equipment, particularly since limited space at the plant site made it necessary to install the equipment on a massive bridge deck over a four-lane highway immediately adjacent to the power plant
- Uncertain costs associated with replacing the electrical power required to operate the particulate control equipment
- Various other factors, including potential accidents and chronic operating problems that could increase the costs of operating the generating units (the degree to which each of these factors could affect operating costs varied with the choice of technology and with the sulfur content of the coal).

Particulate Control Decision

The air-quality program involved a choice between two types of particulate control equipment (fabric filters and electrostatic precipitators) for units 5–7. Because of the complexity of the problem, the high degree of uncertainty associated with factors affecting the decision, and the importance (because of potential reliability and cost impact on Ohio Edison) of the choice, decision analysis was used in the selection process.

The decision measure used to evaluate the outcomes of the particulate technology decision analysis was the annual revenue requirements for the three large units over their remaining lifetime. Revenue requirements are the monies that would have to be collected from the utility customers to recover costs resulting from the decision. They include not only direct costs but also the cost of capital and return on investment.

A decision tree was constructed to represent the particulate control decision and its uncertainties and costs. A simplified version of this decision tree is shown in Figure 4.15. The decision and state-of-nature nodes are indicated. Note that to conserve space, a type of shorthand notation is used. The coal sulfur content state-of-nature node should actually be located at the end of each branch of the capital cost state-of-nature node, as the dashed lines indicate. Each of the state-of-nature nodes actually represents several probabilistic cost models or submodels. The total revenue requirements are the sum of the revenue requirements for capital and operating costs. Costs associated with these models were obtained from engineering calculations or estimates. Probabilities were obtained from existing

data or the subjective assessments of knowledgeable persons.

Results

A decision tree similar to that shown in Figure 4.15 was used to generate cumulative probability distributions for the annual revenue requirements outcomes calculated for each of the two particulate control alternatives. Careful study of these results led to the following conclusions:

- The expected value of annual revenue requirements for the electrostatic precipitator technology was approximately $1 million lower than that for the fabric filters.
- The fabric filter alternative had a higher upside risk—that is, a higher probability of high revenue requirements—than did the precipitator alternative.
- The precipitator technology had nearly an 80% probability of lower annual revenue requirements than the fabric filters.
- Although the capital cost of the fabric filter equipment (the cost of installing the equipment) was lower than for the precipitator, this cost was more than offset by the higher operating costs associated with the fabric filter.

These results led Ohio Edison to select the electrostatic precipitator technology for the generating units in question. Had the decision analysis not been performed, the particulate control decision might have been based chiefly on capital cost, a decision measure that would have favored the fabric filter equipment. Decision analysis offers a means for effectively analyzing the uncertainties involved in a decision. Because of this analysis, the use of decision analysis methodology in this application resulted in a decision that yielded both lower expected revenue requirements and lower risk.

Questions

1. Why was decision analysis used in the selection of particulate control equipment for units 5, 6, and 7?
2. List the decision alternatives for the decision analysis problem developed by Ohio Edison.
3. What were the benefits of using decision analysis in this application?

Figure 4.15   SIMPLIFIED PARTICULATE CONTROL EQUIPMENT DECISION TREE

5

UTILITY AND DECISION MAKING

In the preceding chapter we frequently expressed payoffs in terms of monetary values. When probability information was available about the states of nature, we recommended selecting the decision alternative with the best expected monetary value. However, in some situations, the decision alternative with the best expected monetary value is not necessarily the most desirable decision.

By the most desirable decision we mean the one that is preferred by the decision maker, taking into account not only monetary value but also many other factors such as the possibility of making a very large profit and/or incurring a very large loss. Examples of situations in which selecting the decision alternative with the best expected monetary value may not lead to the selection of the most preferred decision are numerous. One such example is the decision made by most people to buy insurance. Clearly, the decision to buy insurance for a house does not provide a higher expected monetary value than not buying such insurance. Otherwise insurance companies could not pay expenses and make a profit. Similarly, many people buy tickets for state lotteries even though the expected monetary value of such a decision is negative.

Should we conclude that people or businesses that buy insurance or participate in lotteries do so because they are unable to determine which decision alternative leads to the best expected monetary value? On the contrary, we take the view that in these cases monetary value is not the sole measure of the true worth of the outcome to the decision maker. When the expected monetary value approach does not lead to the most preferred decision alternative, expressing the value (or worth) of an outcome in terms of its *utility* will permit the use of *expected utility* to identify the most desirable decision.

..../ /............

5.1   THE MEANING OF UTILITY

Until 1944, when Von Neumann and Morgenstern published the book *Theory of Games and Economic Behavior*, the literature on decisions involving risk consisted primarily of applications involving the use of probability in gambling.

Utility is a measure of the total worth of a particular outcome; it reflects the decision maker's attitude toward a collection of factors such as profit, loss, and risk. Researchers have found that as long as the monetary value of payoffs stay within a range that the decision maker considers reasonable, selecting the decision alternative with the best expected monetary value usually leads to selection of the most preferred decision. However, when the payoffs become extreme, most decision makers are not satisfied with the decision that simply provides the best expected monetary value.

As an example of a situation in which utility can help in selecting the best decision alternative, let us consider the problem faced by Swofford, Inc., a relatively small real estate investment firm located in Atlanta, Georgia. Swofford currently has two investment opportunities that require approximately the same cash outlay. The cash requirements necessary prohibit Swofford from making more than one investment at this time. Consequently, three possible decision alternatives may be considered.

The three decision alternatives, denoted d_1, d_2, and d_3, are

$$d_1 = \text{make investment } A$$
$$d_2 = \text{make investment } B$$
$$d_3 = \text{do not invest}$$

The monetary payoffs associated with the investment opportunities depend largely on what happens to the real estate market during the next 6 months. Real estate prices will go up, remain stable, or go down. Thus the Swofford states of nature, denoted by s_1, s_2, and s_3, are

$$s_1 = \text{real estate prices go up}$$
$$s_2 = \text{real estate prices remain stable}$$
$$s_3 = \text{real estate prices go down}$$

Using the best information available, Swofford estimates the profits, or payoffs, associated with each decision alternative and state-of-nature combination. The resulting payoff table is shown in Table 5.1.

The best estimate of the probability that real estate prices will go up is 0.30; the best estimate of the probability that prices will remain stable is 0.50; and the best estimate of the probability that prices will go down is 0.20. Thus the expected values for the three decision alternatives are

$$EV(d_1) = 0.3(30,000) + 0.5(20,000) \quad + 0.2(-50,000) = 9,000$$
$$EV(d_2) = 0.3(50,000) + 0.5(-20,000) + 0.2(-30,000) = -1,000$$
$$EV(d_3) = 0.3(0) \qquad + 0.5(0) \qquad + 0.2(0) \qquad = 0$$

Under the expected value approach, the optimal decision is to select investment A with an expected monetary value of $9000. Is this really the best decision alternative? Let us consider some other relevant factors that relate to Swofford's capability for absorbing the loss of $50,000 if investment A is made and prices actually go down.

Table 5.1	PAYOFF TABLE FOR SWOFFORD, INC.		
Decision Alternative	**State of Nature**		
	Prices Up s_1	Prices Stable s_2	Prices Down s_3
Investment A, d_1	$30,000	$20,000	−$50,000
Investment B, d_2	$50,000	−$20,000	−$30,000
Do not invest, d_3	0	0	0

Actually, Swofford's current financial position is weak. This condition is partly reflected in Swofford's ability to make only one investment currently. More important, however, the firm's president believes that, if the next investment results in substantial losses, Swofford's future will be in jeopardy. Although the expected value approach leads to a recommendation for d_1, do you think this is the decision that the firm's president would prefer? We suspect that the president would select d_2 or d_3 to avoid the possibility of incurring a $50,000 loss. In fact, a reasonable conclusion is that, if a loss of even $30,000 could drive Swofford out of business, the president would select d_3, believing that both investments A and B are too risky for Swofford's current financial position.

The way to resolve Swofford's dilemma is first to determine Swofford's utility for the various monetary outcomes. Recall that the utility of any outcome is the total worth of that outcome, taking into account the risks and payoffs involved. If the utilities for the various outcomes are assessed correctly, the decision alternative with the highest expected utility is the most preferred, or best, alternative. In the next section we show how to determine the utility of the monetary outcomes so that the alternative with the highest expected utility is most preferred.

5.2 DEVELOPING UTILITIES FOR MONETARY PAYOFFS

Utility values of 0 and 1 could have been selected here; we selected 0 and 10 in order to avoid any possible confusion between the utility value for a payoff and the probability p.

The procedure we use to establish utility values for the payoffs in Swofford's situation requires that we first assign a utility value to the best and worst possible payoffs. Any values will work as long as the utility assigned to the best payoff is greater than the utility assigned to the worst payoff. In this case, $50,000 is the best payoff and −$50,000 is the worst. Suppose, then, that we arbitrarily make assignments to these two payoffs as follows:

$$\text{Utility of } -\$50,000 = U(-50,000) = 0$$
$$\text{Utility of } \quad \$50,000 = U(50,000) \quad = 10$$

Let us now determine the utility associated with every other payoff.

Consider the process of establishing the utility of a payoff of $30,000. First we ask Swofford's president to state a preference between a guaranteed $30,000 payoff and an opportunity to engage in the following **lottery**, or bet:

Lottery: Swofford's obtains a payoff of $50,000 with probability p
and a payoff of −$50,000 with probability $(1 - p)$

p is often referred to as the indifference probability.

Obviously, if *p* is very close to 1, Swofford's president would prefer the lottery to the guaranteed payoff of $30,000 because the firm would virtually ensure itself a payoff of $50,000. But if *p* is very close to 0, Swofford's president would clearly prefer the guarantee of $30,000. In any event, as *p* changes continuously from 0 to 1, the preference for the guaranteed payoff of $30,000 will change at some point into a preference for the lottery. At this value of *p*, Swofford's president would have no greater preference for the guaranteed payoff of $30,000 than for the lottery. For example, let us assume that when $p = 0.95$, Swofford's president is indifferent between the guaranteed payoff of $30,000 and the lottery. For this value of *p,* we can compute the utility of a $30,000 payoff as follows:

$$U(30,000) = pU(50,000) + (1 - p)U(-50,000)$$
$$= 0.95(10) + (0.05)(0)$$
$$= 9.5$$

Obviously, if we had started with a different assignment of utilities for a payoff of $50,000 and −$50,000, the result would have been a different utility for $30,000. For example, if we had started with an assignment of 100 for $50,000 and 10 for −$50,000, the utility of a $30,000 payoff would be

$$U(30,000) = 0.95(100) + 0.05(10)$$
$$= 95 + 0.5$$
$$= 95.5$$

Hence, we must conclude that the utility assigned to each payoff is not unique but merely depends on the initial choice of utilities for the best and worst payoffs. We will discuss this further at the end of this section. For now, however, we will continue to use a value of 10 for the utility of $50,000 and a value of 0 for the utility of −$50,000.

Before computing the utility for the other payoffs, let us consider the significance of Swofford's president assigning a utility of 9.5 to a payoff of $30,000. Clearly, when $p = 0.95$, the expected value of the lottery is

$$EV(\text{lottery}) = 0.95(\$50,000) + 0.05(-\$50,000)$$
$$= \$47,500 - \$2,500$$
$$= \$45,000$$

The difference between the expected value of the lottery and the guaranteed payoff can be viewed as the risk premium the decision maker is willing to pay.

Although the expected value of the lottery when $p = 0.95$ is $45,000, Swofford's president would just as soon take a guaranteed payoff of $30,000. Thus, Swofford's president is taking a conservative, or risk-avoiding, viewpoint. The president would rather have $30,000 for certain than risk anything greater than a 5% chance of incurring a loss of $50,000. In other words the difference between the EV of $45,000 and the guaranteed payoff of $30,000 is the risk premium that Swofford's president would be willing to pay to avoid the 5% chance of losing $50,000.

To compute the utility associated with a payoff of −$20,000, we must ask Swofford's president to state a preference between a guaranteed −$20,000 payoff and an opportunity to engage again in the following lottery:

Lottery: Swofford's obtains a payoff of $50,000 with probability *p*
and a payoff of −$50,000 with probability $(1 - p)$

Note that this lottery is exactly the same as the one we used to establish the utility of a payoff of $30,000. In fact, we use this lottery to establish the utility for any monetary value in the Swofford payoff table. We need to determine the value of p that would make the president indifferent between a guaranteed payoff of $-\$20,000$ and the lottery. For example, we might begin by asking the president to choose between a certain loss of $20,000 and the lottery with a payoff of $50,000 with probability $p = 0.90$ and a payoff of $-\$50,000$ with probability $(1 - p) = 0.10$. What answer do you think we would get? Surely, with this high probability of obtaining a payoff of $50,000, the president would elect the lottery. Next, we might ask whether $p = 0.85$ would result in indifference between the loss of $20,000 for certain and the lottery. Again the president might prefer the lottery. Suppose that we continue until we get to $p = 0.55$, at which point the president is indifferent between the payoff of $-\$20,000$ and the lottery. That is, for any value of p less than 0.55, the president would rather take a loss of $20,000 for certain than risk the potential loss of $50,000 with the lottery; and for any value of p above 0.55, the president would choose the lottery. Thus, the utility assigned to a payoff of $-\$20,000$ is

$$U(-\$20,000) = pU(50,000) + (1 - p)U(-\$50,000)$$
$$= 0.55(10) + 0.45(0)$$
$$= 5.5$$

Again let us compare the significance of this assignment to the expected value approach. When $p = 0.55$, the expected value of the lottery is

$$EV(\text{lottery}) = 0.55(\$50,000) + 0.45(-\$50,000)$$
$$= \$27,500 - \$22,500$$
$$= \$5,000$$

Thus, Swofford's president would just as soon absorb a loss of $20,000 for certain as take the lottery, even though the expected value of the lottery is $5000. Once again this preference demonstrates the conservative, or risk-avoiding, point of view of Swofford's president.

In these two examples we computed the utility for the monetary payoffs of $30,000 and $-\$20,000$. We can determine the utility for any monetary payoff M in a similar fashion. First, we must find the probability p for which the decision maker is indifferent between a guaranteed payoff of M and a lottery with a payoff of $50,000 with probability p and $-\$50,000$ with probability $(1 - p)$. The utility of M is then computed as follows:

$$U(M) = pU(\$50,000) + (1 - p)U(-\$50,000)$$
$$= p(10) + (1 - p)0$$
$$= 10p$$

Using this procedure we developed utility values for the rest of the payoffs in Swofford's problem. The results are presented in Table 5.2.

Now that we have determined the utility value of each of the possible monetary values, we can write the original payoff table in terms of utility values. Table 5.3 shows the utility for the various outcomes in the Swofford problem. The notation we use for the entries in the utility table is U_{ij}, which denotes the utility associated with decision alternative d_i and state of nature s_j. Using this notation, we see that $U_{23} = 4.0$.

Table 5.2	UTILITY OF MONETARY PAYOFFS FOR THE SWOFFORD, INC., PROBLEM		
	Monetary Value	Indifference Value of p	Utility Value
	$ 50,000	Does not apply	10.0
	30,000	0.95	9.5
	20,000	0.90	9.0
	0	0.75	7.5
	−20,000	0.55	5.5
	−30,000	0.40	4.0
	−50,000	Does not apply	0

Table 5.3	UTILITY TABLE FOR SWOFFORD, INC.		
Decision Alternative	State of Nature		
	Prices Up s_1	Prices Stable s_2	Prices Down s_3
Investment A, d_1	9.5	9.0	0
Investment B, d_2	10.0	5.5	4.0
Do not invest, d_3	7.5	7.5	7.5

The Expected Utility Approach

We can now apply the expected value computations introduced in Chapter 4 to the utilities in Table 5.3 in order to select an optimal decision alternative for Swofford, Inc. However, because utility values represent such a special case of expected value, we will refer to the expected value when applied to utility values as the **expected utility** (EU). Thus, the expected utility approach requires the analyst to compute the expected utility for each decision alternative and then select the alternative yielding the highest expected utility. With N possible states of nature, the expected utility of a decision alternative d_i is given by

$$\text{EU}(d_i) = \sum_{j=1}^{N} P(s_j)U_{ij} \qquad (5.1)$$

The expected utility for each of the decision alternatives in the Swofford problem is

$$\text{EU}(d_1) = 0.3(9.5) + 0.5(9.0) + 0.2(0) \quad = 7.35$$
$$\text{EU}(d_2) = 0.3(10) \ + 0.5(5.5) + 0.2(4.0) = 6.55$$
$$\text{EU}(d_3) = 0.3(7.5) + 0.5(7.5) + 0.2(7.5) = 7.50$$

You should now be able to use the expected utility approach to determine the optimal decision. Try Problem 1.

Note that the optimal decision using the expected utility approach is d_3, do not invest. The ranking of alternatives according to the president's utility assignments and the associated monetary values are as follows.

Ranking of Decision Alternatives	Expected Utility	Expected Monetary Value
Do not invest	7.50	0
Investment A	7.35	9000
Investment B	6.55	−1000

Note that although investment A had the highest expected monetary value of $9000, the analysis indicates that Swofford should decline this investment. The rationale behind not selecting investment A is that the 0.20 probability of a $50,000 loss was considered to involve a very serious risk by Swofford's president. The seriousness of this risk and its associated impact on the company were not adequately reflected by the expected monetary value of investment A. We assessed the utility for each payoff to assess this risk adequately.

N O T E S and Comments

In the Swofford problem we have been using a utility of 10 for the best payoff and 0 for the worst. The choice of values could have been anything, and we might have chosen 1 for the utility of the best payoff and 0 for the utility of the worst. Had we made this choice, the utility for any monetary value M would have been the value of p at which the decision maker was indifferent between a guaranteed payoff of M and a lottery in which the best payoff is obtained with probability p and the worst payoff is obtained with probability $(1 - p)$. Thus, the utility for any monetary value would have been equal to the probability of earning the best payoff. Often this choice is made because of the ease in computation. We chose not to do so to emphasize the distinction between the utility values and the indifference probabilities for the lottery.

5.3 SUMMARY OF STEPS FOR DETERMINING THE UTILITY OF MONEY

Before considering other aspects of utility, let us summarize the steps involved in determining the utility for a monetary value and using it within the decision analysis framework. The following steps state in general terms the procedure used to solve the Swofford, Inc., investment problem.

Step 1. Develop a payoff table using monetary values.
Step 2. Identify the best and worst payoff values in the table and assign each a utility value, with U(best payoff) > U(worst payoff).
Step 3. For every other monetary value M in the original payoff table, do the following to determine its utility value.
   a. Define the lottery: The best payoff is obtained with probability p and the worst payoff is obtained with probability $(1 - p)$.

      b. Determine the value of p such that the decision maker is indifferent between a guaranteed payoff of M and the lottery defined in Step 3a.

      c. Calculate the utility of M as follows:

$$U(M) = pU(\text{best payoff}) + (1 - p)U(\text{worst payoff})$$

Step 4. Convert the payoff table from monetary values to utility values.

Step 5. Apply the expected utility approach to the utility table developed in Step 4 and select the decision alternative with the highest expected utility.

5.4   RISK AVOIDERS VERSUS RISK TAKERS

The financial position of Swofford, Inc., was such that the firm's president evaluated investment opportunities from a conservative, or risk-avoiding, point of view. However, if the firm had a surplus of cash and a stable future, Swofford's president might have been looking for investment alternatives that, although perhaps risky, contained a potential for substantial profit. That type of behavior would have made the president a **risk taker.** In this section we analyze the decision problem faced by Swofford from the point of view of a decision maker who would be classified as a risk taker. We then compare the conservative, or risk-avoiding, point of view of Swofford's president with the behavior of a decision maker who is a risk taker.

    For the decision problem facing Swofford, Inc., and using the general procedure for developing utilities as discussed in Section 5.3, a risk taker might express the utility for the various payoffs shown in Table 5.4. As before, $U(50{,}000) = 10$ and $U(-50{,}000) = 0$. Note the difference in behavior reflected in Table 5.4 and Table 5.2. That is, in determining the value of p at which the decision maker is indifferent between a guaranteed payoff of M and a lottery in which \$50,000 is obtained with probability p and $-\$50{,}000$ with probability $(1 - p)$, the risk taker is willing to accept a greater risk of incurring a loss of \$50,000 in order to gain the opportunity to realize a profit of \$50,000.

    To help develop the utility table for the risk taker, we have reproduced the Swofford, Inc., payoff table in Table 5.5. Using these payoffs and the risk taker's utility values given in Table 5.4, we can write the risk taker's utility table as shown in Table 5.6. Using the state-

| Table 5.4 | REVISED UTILITY VALUES FOR THE SWOFFORD, INC., PROBLEM ASSUMING A RISK TAKER |

Monetary Value	Indifference Value of p	Utility Value
$ 50,000	Does not apply	10.0
30,000	0.50	5.0
20,000	0.40	4.0
0	0.25	2.5
−20,000	0.15	1.5
−30,000	0.10	1.0
−50,000	Does not apply	0

Table 5.5	PAYOFF TABLE FOR SWOFFORD, INC.		

Decision Alternative	State of Nature		
	Prices Up s_1	Prices Stable s_2	Prices Down s_3
Investment A, d_1	$30,000	$20,000	−$50,000
Investment B, d_2	$50,000	−$20,000	−$30,000
Do not invest, d_3	0	0	0

of-nature probabilities $P(s_1) = 0.3$, $P(s_2) = 0.5$, and $P(s_3) = 0.2$, the expected utility for each decision alternative is

$$EU(d_1) = 0.3(5.0) + 0.5(4.0) + 0.2(0) \quad = 3.50$$
$$EU(d_2) = 0.3(10) + 0.5(1.5) + 0.2(1.0) = 3.95$$
$$EU(d_3) = 0.3(2.5) + 0.5(2.5) + 0.2(2.5) = 2.50$$

What is the recommended decision? Perhaps somewhat to your surprise, the analysis recommends investment B, with the highest expected utility of 3.95. Recall that this investment has a −$1000 expected monetary value. Why is it now the recommended decision? Remember that the decision maker in this revised problem is a risk taker. Thus, although the expected value of investment B is negative, utility analysis has shown that this decision maker is enough of a risk taker to prefer investment B and its potential for the $50,000 profit.

The expected utility values give the following order of preference of the decision alternatives for the risk taker and the associated expected monetary values.

Ranking of Decision Alternatives	Expected Utility	Expected Monetary Value
Investment B	3.95	−$1000
Investment A	3.50	$9000
Do not invest	2.50	0

Table 5.6	UTILITY TABLE OF A RISK TAKER FOR THE SWOFFORD, INC., PROBLEM		

Decision Alternative	State of Nature		
	Prices Up s_1	Prices Stable s_2	Prices Down s_3
Investment A, d_1	5.0	4.0	0
Investment B, d_2	10.0	1.5	1.0
Do not invest, d_3	2.5	2.5	2.5

Comparing the utility analysis for a risk taker with the more conservative, **risk-avoider** preferences of the president of Swofford, Inc., we see that, even with the same decision problem, different attitudes toward risk can lead to different recommended decisions. The utility values established by Swofford's president indicated that the firm should not invest at this time, whereas the utilities established by the risk taker showed a preference for investment B. Note that both of these decisions differ from the best expected monetary value decision, which was investment A.

We can obtain another perspective of the difference between behaviors of a risk avoider and a risk taker by developing a graph that depicts the relationship between monetary value and utility. We use the horizontal axis of the graph to represent monetary values and the vertical axis to represent the utility associated with each monetary value. Now, consider the data in Table 5.2, with a utility value corresponding to each monetary value for the original Swofford, Inc., problem. These values can be plotted on a graph such as that in Figure 5.1, and a curve can be drawn through the observed points. The resulting curve is the **utility function for money** for Swofford's president. Recall that these points reflected the con-

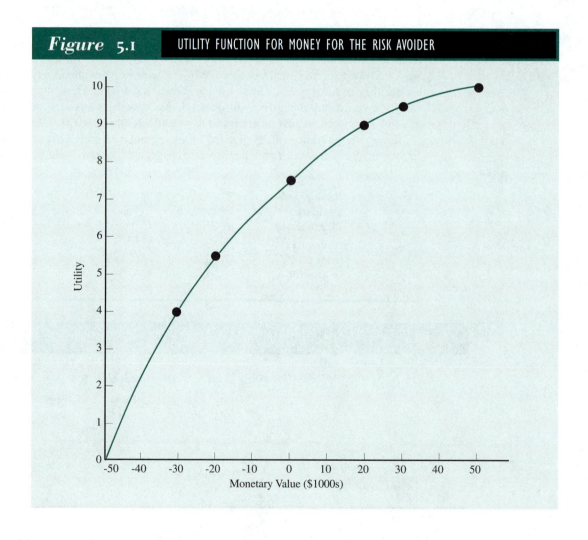

Figure 5.1   UTILITY FUNCTION FOR MONEY FOR THE RISK AVOIDER

servative, or risk-avoiding, nature of Swofford's president. Hence, we refer to the curve in Figure 5.1 as a utility function for a risk avoider. Using the data in Table 5.4, developed for a risk taker, we can plot these points on a graph such as that in Figure 5.2. The resulting curve depicts the utility function for a risk taker.

By looking at the utility functions of Figures 5.1 and 5.2, we can begin to generalize about the utility functions for risk avoiders and risk takers. Although the exact shape of the utility function will vary from one decision maker to another, we can see the general shape of these two types of utility functions. The utility function for a risk-avoider shows a diminishing marginal return for money. For example, the increase in utility going from a monetary value of $-\$30,000$ to $0 is $7.5 - 4.0 = 3.5$, whereas the increase in utility in going from $0 to $30,000 is only $9.5 - 7.5 = 2.0$. However, the utility function for a risk taker shows an increasing marginal return for money. For example, in Figure 5.2, the increase in utility in going from $-\$30,000$ to $0 is $2.5 - 1.0 = 1.5$, whereas the increase in utility in going from $0 to $30,000 is $5.0 - 2.5 = 2.5$. Note also that in either case the utility function is always increasing. That is, more money leads to more utility. All utility functions possess this property.

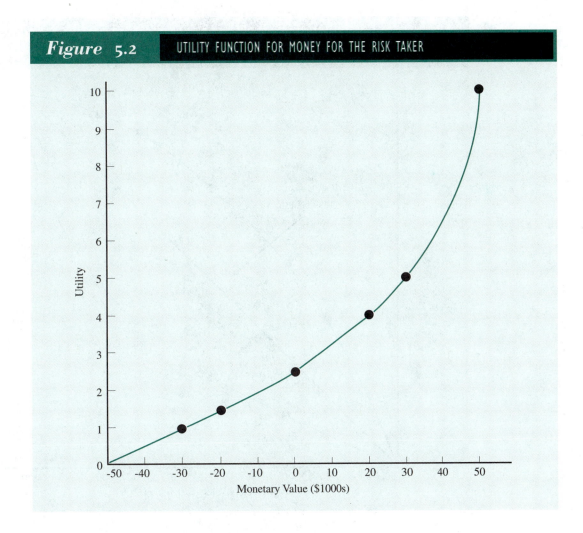

Figure 5.2   UTILITY FUNCTION FOR MONEY FOR THE RISK TAKER

We concluded that the utility function for a risk avoider shows a diminishing marginal return for money and that the utility function for a risk taker shows an increasing marginal return. When the marginal return for money is neither decreasing nor increasing but remains constant, the corresponding utility function describes the behavior of a decision maker who is neutral to risk. The following characteristics are associated with a **risk-neutral decision maker.**

1. The utility function can be drawn as a straight line connecting the "best" and the "worst" points.
2. The expected utility approach and the expected value approach applied to monetary payoffs result in the same action.

You should now be able to plot the utility function for risk-avoider, risk-taker, and risk-neutral decision makers. Try Problem 5.

Figure 5.3 depicts the utility function of a risk-neutral decision maker using the Swofford, Inc., problem data. For comparison purposes, we also show the utility functions for the cases where the decision maker is either a risk taker or a risk avoider.

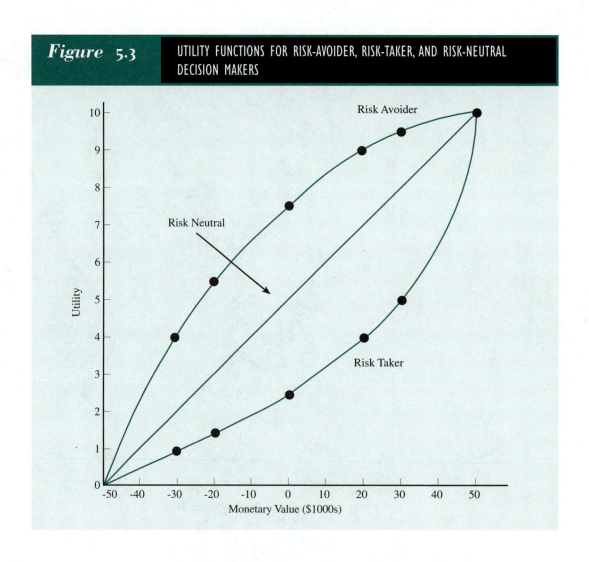

Figure 5.3 UTILITY FUNCTIONS FOR RISK-AVOIDER, RISK-TAKER, AND RISK-NEUTRAL DECISION MAKERS

..../ /...........

5.5   EXPECTED MONETARY VALUE VERSUS EXPECTED UTILITY AS AN APPROACH TO DECISION MAKING

In many decision-making problems, expected monetary value and expected utility will lead to identical recommendations. In fact, this result will always be true if the decision maker is risk neutral. In general, if the decision maker is almost risk neutral over the range of payoffs (from lowest to highest) for a particular decision problem, the decision alternative with the best expected monetary value leads to selection of the most preferred decision alternative. The trick lies in recognizing the range of monetary values over which a decision maker's utility function is risk neutral.

Generally, when the payoffs for a particular decision-making problem fall into a reasonable range—the best is not too good and the worst is not too bad—decision makers tend to express preferences in agreement with the expected monetary value approach. Thus, we suggest asking the decision maker to consider the best and worst possible payoffs for a problem and assess their reasonableness. If the decision maker believes that they are in the reasonable range, the decision alternative with the best expected monetary value can be used. However, if the payoffs appear unreasonably large or unreasonably small (for example, a huge loss) and if the decision maker believes that monetary values do not adequately reflect her or his true preferences for the payoffs, a utility analysis of the problem should be considered.

Unfortunately, determination of the appropriate utilities is not a trivial task. As we have shown, measuring utility requires a degree of subjectivity on the part of the decision maker, and different decision makers will have different utility functions. This aspect of utility often causes decision makers to feel uncomfortable about using the expected utility approach. However, if you encounter a decision situation in which you are convinced that monetary value is not the sole measure of performance, and if you agree that a quantitative analysis of the decision problem is desirable, you should recommend that utility analysis be considered.

..../ /...........

SUMMARY

In this chapter we suggested that expected utility be used in decision situations in which an analysis based on expected monetary value would not lead to the best decision. Unlike monetary value, utility is a measure of the total worth of an outcome resulting from the choice of a decision alternative and the occurrence of a state of nature. As such, utility takes into account the decision maker's attitude toward the profit, loss, and risk associated with an outcome. The examples showed how the use of utility analysis can lead to decision recommendations that differ from those based on expected monetary value.

Admittedly, a decision maker's utility can be difficult to measure. However, we presented a step-by-step procedure that can be used to determine a decision maker's utility for any payoff value. Using the decision maker's evaluation of a lottery involving only the best and worst payoffs, the procedure provides a method whereby each entry in the payoff table can be converted to a utility value. Then expected utility can be used to select the best decision alternative.

Even with utility as a measure of worth, we demonstrated how the analysis for a conservative, or risk-avoiding, decision maker could lead to different decision recommendations than for a risk taker. When the decision maker is risk neutral, we showed that the recommendations using expected utility are identical to the recommendations using expected monetary value.

..../ /..............

GLOSSARY

Utility A measure of the total worth of an outcome reflecting a decision maker's attitude toward considerations such as profit, loss, and risk.

Lottery A hypothetical investment alternative with a probability p of obtaining the best payoff and a probability of $(1 - p)$ of obtaining the worst payoff.

Expected utility (EU) The weighted average of the utilities associated with a decision alternative. The weights are the state-of-nature probabilities.

Risk taker A decision maker who tends to prefer decisions that, although risky, have a possibility for an extremely good payoff.

Risk avoider A decision maker who tends to avoid decisions that have the risk of an extremely bad payoff.

Utility function for money A curve that depicts the relationship between monetary value and utility.

Risk-neutral decision maker A decision maker who is neutral to risk. For this decision maker the decision alternative with the best expected monetary value is identical to the alternative with the highest expected utility.

..../ /..............

PROBLEMS

SELF TEST

1. A firm has three investment alternatives. Payoffs are in thousands of dollars.

Decision Alternative	Economic Conditions		
	Up s_1	Stable s_2	Down s_3
Investment A, d_1	100	25	0
Investment B, d_2	75	50	25
Investment C, d_3	50	50	50
Probabilities	0.40	0.30	0.30

a. Based on the expected value approach, which decision is preferred?
b. For the lottery having a payoff of $100,000 with probability p and $0 with probability $(1 - p)$, two decision makers expressed the indifference probabilities shown below. Find the most preferred decision for each decision maker using the expected utility approach.
c. Why don't decision makers A and B select the same decision alternative?

Profit	Indifference Probability (p)	
	Decision Maker A	Decision Maker B
$75,000	0.80	0.60
$50,000	0.60	0.30
$25,000	0.30	0.15

2. Alexander Industries is considering purchasing an insurance policy for its new office building in St. Louis, Missouri. The policy has an annual cost of $10,000. If Alexander Industries doesn't purchase the insurance and minor fire damage occurs, a cost of $100,000 is anticipated; the cost if major or total destruction occurs is $200,000. The costs, including the state-of-nature probabilities, are as follows.

Decision Alternative	Damage		
	None s_1	Minor s_2	Major s_3
Purchase insurance, d_1	10,000	10,000	10,000
Do not purchase insurance, d_2	0	100,000	200,000
Probabilities	0.96	0.03	0.01

a. Based on the expected value approach, what decision do you recommend?
b. What lottery would you use to assess utilities? (Note that, as the data are costs, the best payoff is $0.)
c. Assume that you found the following indifference probabilities for the lottery defined in part (b). What decision would you recommend?

Cost	Indifference Probability
10,000	$p = 0.99$
100,000	$p = 0.60$

d. Do you favor using expected value or expected utility for this decision problem? Why?

3. In a certain state lottery, a lottery ticket costs $2. In terms of the decision to purchase or not to purchase a lottery ticket, suppose that the following payoff table applies.

Decision Alternatives	State of Nature	
	Win s_1	Lose s_2
Purchase lottery ticket, d_1	300,000	−2
Do not purchase lottery ticket, d_2	0	0

a. A realistic estimate of the chances of winning are 1 in 250,000. Use the expected value approach to recommend a decision.
b. If a particular decision maker assigns an indifference probability of 0.000001 to the $0 payoff, would this individual purchase a lottery ticket? Use expected utility to justify your answer.

4. Two different routes may be used between two cities. Route A normally takes 60 minutes, and route B normally takes 45 minutes. If traffic problems are encountered on route A, the travel

time increases to 70 minutes; traffic problems on route B increase travel time to 90 minutes. The probability of the delay is 0.20 for route A and 0.30 for route B.

a. Using the expected value approach, what is the recommended route?

b. If utilities are to be assigned to the travel times, what is the appropriate lottery? Note that the smaller times should reflect higher utilities.

c. Use the lottery of part (b) and assume that the decision maker expresses indifference probabilities of

$$p = 0.80 \qquad \text{for 60 minutes}$$
$$p = 0.60 \qquad \text{for 70 minutes}$$

What route should this decision maker select? Is the decision maker a risk taker or a risk avoider?

SELF TEST

5. Three decision makers have assessed utilities for the following decision problem (payoff in dollars).

Decision Alternative	State of Nature		
	s_1	s_2	s_3
d_1	20	50	−20
d_2	80	100	−100

The indifference probabilities are as follows.

Payoff	Indifference Probability (p)		
	Decision Maker A	Decision Maker B	Decision Maker C
100	1.00	1.00	1.00
80	0.95	0.70	0.90
50	0.90	0.60	0.75
20	0.70	0.45	0.60
−20	0.50	0.25	0.40
−100	0.00	0.00	0.00

a. Plot the utility function for money for each decision maker.

b. Classify each decision maker as a risk avoider, a risk taker, or risk neutral.

c. For the payoff of 20, what is the premium that the risk avoider will pay to avoid risk? What is the premium that the risk taker will pay to have the opportunity of the high payoff?

6. In Problem 5, if $P(s_1) = 0.25$, $P(s_2) = 0.50$, and $P(s_3) = 0.25$, find a recommended decision for each of the three decision makers. Note that for the same decision problem, different utilities can lead to different decisions.

7. Suppose that the point spread for a particular sporting event is 10 points and that with this spread you are convinced you would have a 0.60 probability of winning a bet on your team. However, the local bookie will accept only a $1000 bet. Assuming that such bets are legal, would you bet on your team? (Disregard any commission charged by the bookie.) Remember that *you* must pay losses out of your own pocket. Your payoff table is as follows.

Decision Alternatives	State of Nature	
	You win s_1	You Lose s_2
Bet, d_1	1000	−1000
Don't bet, d_2	0	0

    a. What decision does the expected value approach recommend?

    b. What is *your* indifference probability for the $0 payoff? (Although this choice isn't easy, be as realistic as possible. It is required for an analysis that reflects your attitude toward risk.)

    c. What decision would you make based on the expected utility approach? In this case are you a risk taker or risk avoider?

    d. Would other individuals assess the same utility values you do? Explain.

    e. If your decision in part (c) was to place the bet, repeat the analysis assuming a minimum bet of $10,000.

8. A Las Vegas roulette wheel has 38 different numerical values. If an individual bets on one number and wins, the payoff is 35 to 1.

    a. Show a payoff table for a $10 bet on one number for decision alternatives of bet and do not bet.

    b. What is the recommended decision using the expected value approach?

    c. Do the Las Vegas casinos want risk-taking or risk-avoiding customers? Explain.

    d. What range of utility values would a decision maker have to assign to the $0 payoff in order to have expected utility justify a decision to place the $10 bet?

9. A new product has the following profit projections and associated probabilities.

Profit	Probability
$150,000	0.10
$100,000	0.25
$ 50,000	0.20
0	0.15
−$ 50,000	0.20
−$100,000	0.10

    a. Use the expected value approach to decide whether to market the new product.

    b. Because of the high dollar values involved, especially the possibility of a $100,000 loss, the marketing vice president has expressed some concern about the use of the expected value approach. As a consequence, if a utility analysis is performed, what is the appropriate lottery?

    c. Assume that the following indifference probabilities are assigned. Do the utilities reflect the behavior of a risk taker or a risk avoider?

Profit	Indifference Probability (p)
$100,000	0.95
$ 50,000	0.70
0	0.50
−$ 50,000	0.25

d.   Use expected utility to make a recommended decision.
e.   Should the decision maker feel comfortable with the final decision recommended by the analysis?

10.   A television network has been receiving low ratings for its programs. Currently, management is considering two alternatives for the Monday night 8:00 P.M.–9:00 P.M. time slot: a western with a well-known star, or a musical variety with a relatively unknown husband-and-wife team. The percentages of viewing audience estimates depend on the degree of program acceptance. The relevant data are as follows.

Program Acceptance	Percentage of Viewing Audience	
	Western	Musical Variety
High	30%	40%
Moderate	25%	20%
Poor	20%	15%

The probabilities associated with program acceptance levels are as follows.

Program Acceptance	Probability	
	Western	Musical Variety
High	0.30	0.30
Moderate	0.60	0.40
Poor	0.10	0.30

a.   Using the expected value approach, which program should the network choose?
b.   For a utility analysis, what is the appropriate lottery?
c.   Based on the lottery in part (b), assume that the network's program manager has assigned the following indifference probabilities. Based on the use of utility measures, which program would you recommend? Is the manager a risk taker or a risk avoider?

Percentage of Audience	Indifference Probability (p)
30%	0.40
25%	0.30
20%	0.10

6

FORECASTING

An essential aspect of managing any organization is planning for the future. Indeed, the long-run success of an organization is closely related to how well management is able to anticipate the future and develop appropriate strategies. Good judgment, intuition, and an awareness of the state of the economy may give a manager a rough idea or "feeling" of what is likely to happen in the future. However, converting this feeling into a number that can be used as next quarter's sales volume or next year's raw material cost per unit often is difficult. The purpose of this chapter is to introduce several **forecasting** methods.

Suppose that we have been asked to provide quarterly forecasts of the sales volume for a particular product during the coming year. Production schedules, raw material purchasing plans, inventory policies, and sales quotas will be affected by the quarterly forecasts that we provide. Consequently, poor forecasts may result in increased costs for the firm. How should we go about providing the quarterly sales volume forecasts?

We will certainly want to review the actual sales data for the product in previous periods. Using these historical data, we can identify the general level of sales and any trend such as an increase or decrease in sales volume over time. A further review of the data might reveal a seasonal pattern such as peak sales occurring in the third quarter of each year and sales volume bottoming out during the first quarter. By reviewing historical data, we can often develop a better understanding of the pattern of past sales, leading to better predictions of future sales for the product.

The historical sales data form a time series. A **time series** is a set of observations on a variable measured at successive points in time or over successive periods of time. In this chapter we introduce several procedures for analyzing time series. The objective of such analyses is to provide good **forecasts** or predictions of future values of the time series.

st
npanies can
ecast total
nand for all
ducts, as a
up, with
ors of less
n 5%.
wever,
ecasting
nand for
ividual
ducts may
ult in
nificantly
ner errors.

orecast is
ply a
diction of
at will
ppen in the
ure.
nagers must
n to accept
fact that,
ardless of
technique
d, they will
be able to
velop
fect
ecasts.

163

Forecasting methods can be classified as quantitative or qualitative. Quantitative forecasting methods can be used when (1) past information about the variable being forecast is available, (2) the information can be quantified, and (3) a reasonable assumption is that the pattern of the past will continue into the future. In such cases, a forecast can be developed using a time series method or a causal method.

If the historical data are restricted to past values of the variable that we are trying to forecast, the forecasting procedure is called a *time series method*. The objective of time series methods is to discover a pattern in the historical data and then extrapolate this pattern into the future; the forecast is based solely on past values of the variable that we are trying to forecast and/or on past forecast errors. In this chapter we discuss three time series methods: smoothing (moving averages, weighted moving averages, and exponential smoothing), trend projection, and trend projection adjusted for seasonal influence.

Causal forecasting methods are based on the assumption that the variable we are trying to forecast exhibits a cause–effect relationship with one or more other variables. In this chapter we discuss the use of regression analysis as a causal forecasting method. For instance, the sales volume for many products is influenced by advertising expenditures, so regression analysis may be used to develop an equation showing how these two variables are related. Then, once the advertising budget has been set for the next period, we could substitute this value into the equation to develop a prediction or forecast of the sales volume for that period. Note that if a time series method had been used to develop the forecast, advertising expenditures would not even have been considered; that is, a time series method would have based the forecast solely on past sales.

Qualitative methods generally involve the use of expert judgment to develop forecasts. For instance, a panel of experts might develop a consensus forecast of the prime rate for a year from now. An advantage of qualitative procedures is that they can be applied when the information on the variable being forecast cannot be quantified and when historical data either are not applicable or available. Figure 6.1 provides an overview of the types of forecasting methods.

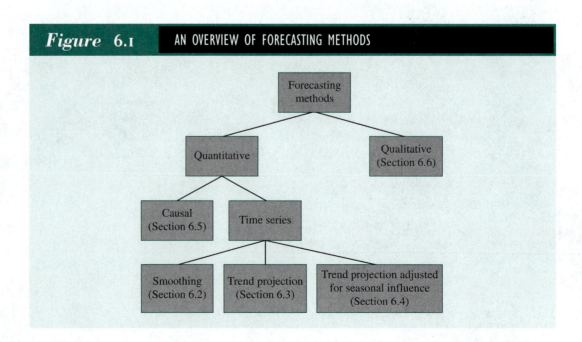

Figure 6.1　AN OVERVIEW OF FORECASTING METHODS

6.1 THE COMPONENTS OF A TIME SERIES

The pattern or behavior of the data in a time series has several components. The usual assumption is that four separate components—trend, cyclical, seasonal, and irregular—combine to provide specific values for the time series. Let us look more closely at each of these components.

Trend Component

In time series analysis, the measurements may be taken every hour, day, week, month, or year, or at any other regular interval. Although time series data generally exhibit random fluctuations, the time series may still show gradual shifts or movements to relatively higher or lower values over a longer period of time. The gradual shifting of the time series is referred to as the **trend** in the time series; this shifting or trend is usually the result of long-term factors such as changes in the population, demographic characteristics of the population, technology, and consumer preferences.

For example, a manufacturer of photographic equipment may observe substantial month-to-month variability in the number of cameras sold. However, in reviewing sales over the past 10 to 15 years, this manufacturer may note a gradual increase in the annual sales volume. Suppose that the sales volume was approximately 1700 cameras per month in 1987, 2300 cameras per month in 1992, and 2500 cameras per month in 1997. Although actual month-to-month sales volumes may vary substantially, this gradual growth in sales shows an upward trend for the time series. Figure 6.2 shows a straight line that may be a good approximation of the trend in camera sales. Although the trend for camera sales appears to be linear and increasing over time, sometimes the trend in a time series can be described better by some other pattern.

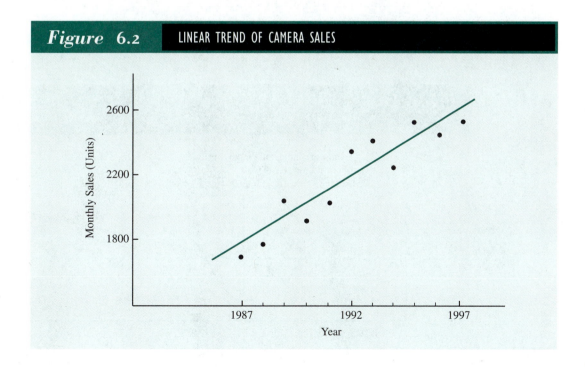

Figure **6.2** LINEAR TREND OF CAMERA SALES

Figure 6.3 shows some other possible time series trend patterns. Part (a) shows a non-linear trend; in this case, the time series shows little growth initially, then a period of rapid growth, and finally a leveling off. This trend pattern might be a good approximation of sales for a product from introduction through a growth period and into a period of market saturation. The linear decreasing trend in part (b) is useful for time series displaying a steady decline over time. The horizontal line in part (c) represents a time series that has no consistent increase or decrease over time and thus no trend.

Cyclical Component

Although a time series may exhibit a trend over long periods of time, all future values of the time series will not fall exactly on the trend line. In fact, time series often show alternating sequences of points below and above the trend line. Any recurring sequence of points above and below the trend line lasting more than one year can be attributed to the **cyclical component** of the time series. Figure 6.4 shows the graph of a time series with an obvious cyclical component. The observations are taken at intervals of one year.

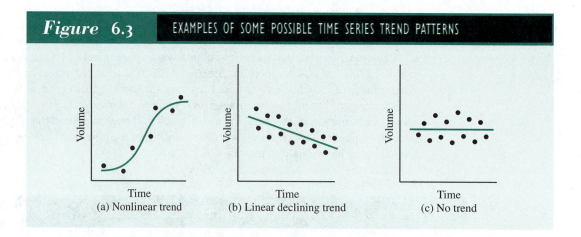

Figure 6.3   EXAMPLES OF SOME POSSIBLE TIME SERIES TREND PATTERNS

(a) Nonlinear trend   (b) Linear declining trend   (c) No trend

Figure 6.4   TREND AND CYCLICAL COMPONENTS OF A TIME SERIES (DATA POINTS ARE ONE YEAR APART)

Cycles are indicated by the runs of observations above and below the trend line

Trend line

Many time series exhibit cyclical behavior with regular runs of observations below and above the trend line. Generally, this component of the time series is due to multiyear cyclical movements in the economy. For example, periods of modest inflation followed by periods of rapid inflation can lead to many time series that alternate below and above a generally increasing trend line (e.g., a time series for housing costs). Many time series in the early 1980s displayed this type of behavior.

Seasonal Component

Whereas the trend and cyclical components of a time series are identified by analyzing multiyear movements in historical data, many time series show a regular pattern over one-year periods. For example, a manufacturer of swimming pools expects low sales activity in the fall and winter months, with peak sales occurring in the spring and summer months. Manufacturers of snow removal equipment and heavy clothing, however, expect just the opposite yearly pattern. Not surprisingly, the component of the time series that represents the variability in the data due to seasonal influences is called the **seasonal component.** Although we generally think of seasonal movement in a time series as occurring within one year, the seasonal component also may be used to represent any regularly repeating pattern that is less than one year in duration. For example, daily traffic volume data show within-the-day "seasonal" behavior, with peak levels during rush hours, moderate flow during the rest of the day, and light flow from midnight to early morning.

Irregular Component

The **irregular component** of the time series is the residual or "catchall" factor that accounts for the deviations of actual time series values from those expected given the effects of the trend, cyclical, and seasonal components. It accounts for the random variability in the time series. The irregular component is caused by the short-term, unanticipated, and nonrecurring factors that affect the time series. Because this component accounts for the random variability in the time series, it is unpredictable. We cannot attempt to predict its impact on the time series.

6.2 USING SMOOTHING METHODS IN FORECASTING

Many manufacturing environments require forecasts for thousands of items weekly or monthly. Thus, in choosing a forecasting technique, simplicity and ease of use are important criteria. The data requirements for the techniques in this section are minimal, and the techniques are easy to use and understand.

In this section we discuss three forecasting methods: moving averages, weighted moving averages, and exponential smoothing. Since the objective of each of these methods is to "smooth out" the random fluctuations caused by the irregular component of the time series, they are referred to as *smoothing methods*. Smoothing methods are appropriate for a stable time series—that is, one that exhibits no significant trend, cyclical, or seasonal effects—since they adapt well to changes in the level of the time series. However, without modification, they do not work as well when a significant trend and/or seasonal variation are present.

Smoothing methods are easy to use and generally provide a high level of accuracy for short-range forecasts such as a forecast for the next time period. One of the methods, exponential smoothing, has minimal data requirements and thus is a good method to use when forecasts are required for large numbers of items.

Moving Averages

The **moving averages** method uses the average of the *most recent n* data values in the time series as the forecast for the next period. Mathematically,

$$\text{Moving average} = \frac{\sum(\text{most recent } n \text{ data values})}{n} \tag{6.1}$$

The term *moving* indicates that, as a new observation becomes available for the time series, it replaces the oldest observation in equation (6.1), and a new average is computed. As a result, the average will change, or move, as new observations become available.

To illustrate the moving averages method, consider the 12 weeks of data presented in Table 6.1 and Figure 6.5. These data show the number of gallons of gasoline sold by a gasoline distributor in Bennington, Vermont, over the past 12 weeks. Figure 6.5 indicates that, although random variability is present, the time series appears to be stable over time. Thus, the smoothing methods of this section are applicable.

To use moving averages to forecast gasoline sales, we must first select the number of data values to be included in the moving average. For example, let us compute forecasts using a 3-week moving average. The moving average calculation for the first 3 weeks of the gasoline sales time series is

$$\text{Moving average (weeks } 1-3) = \frac{17 + 21 + 19}{3} = 19$$

We then use this moving average value as the forecast for week 4. The actual value observed in week 4 is 23, so the forecast error in week 4 is $23 - 19 = 4$. In general, the error associated with a forecast is the difference between the observed value of the time series and the forecast.

The calculation for the second 3-week moving average is

$$\text{Moving average (weeks } 2-4) = \frac{21 + 19 + 23}{3} = 21$$

You should now be able to use moving averages to compute a forecast. Try Problem 1.

Hence, the forecast for week 5 is 21, and the error associated with this forecast is $18 - 21 = -3$. Thus, the forecast error may be positive or negative, depending on

Table 6.1	GASOLINE SALES TIME SERIES DATA

Week	Sales (1000s of gallons)
1	17
2	21
3	19
4	23
5	18
6	16
7	20
8	18
9	22
10	20
11	15
12	22

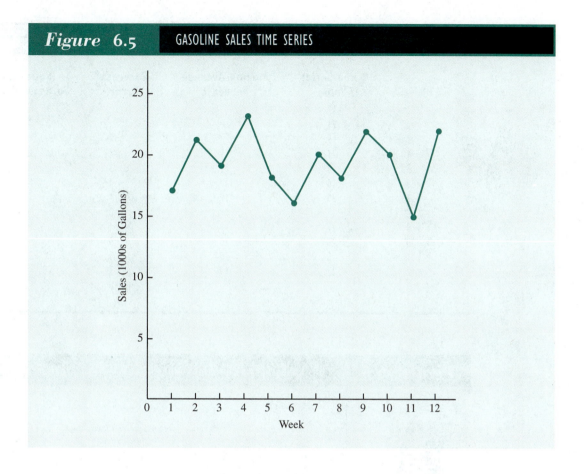

Figure 6.5   GASOLINE SALES TIME SERIES

whether the forecast is too low or too high. A complete summary of the 3-week moving average calculations for the gasoline sales time series is shown in Table 6.2 and Figure 6.6.

Forecast Accuracy   An important consideration in selecting a forecasting method is the accuracy of the forecast. Clearly, we want forecast errors to be small. The last two columns of Table 6.2, which contain the forecast errors and the forecast errors squared, can be used to develop measures of forecast accuracy.

For the gasoline sales time series, we can use the last column of Table 6.2 to compute the average of the sum of the squared errors. Doing so, we obtain

$$\text{Average of the sum of squared errors} = \frac{92}{9} = 10.22$$

This average of the sum of squared errors is commonly referred to as the **mean squared error** (MSE). The MSE is an often-used measure of the accuracy of a forecasting method and is the one we use in this chapter.

As we indicated previously, to use the moving averages method, we must first select the number of data values to be included in the moving average. Not surprisingly, for a particular time series, different lengths of moving averages will affect the accuracy of the forecast. One possible approach to choosing the number of values to be included is to use trial and error to identify the length that minimizes the MSE. Then, if we assume that the length that is best for the past will also be best for the future, we would forecast the next value in

You should now be able to use MSE as a measure of forecast accuracy. Try Problem 2.

Table 6.2		SUMMARY OF 3-WEEK MOVING AVERAGE CALCULATIONS		
Week	**Time Series Value**	**Moving Average Forecast**	**Forecast Error**	**Squared Forecast Error**
1	17			
2	21			
3	19			
4	23	19	4	16
5	18	21	− 3	9
6	16	20	− 4	16
7	20	19	1	1
8	18	18	0	0
9	22	18	4	16
10	20	20	0	0
11	15	20	− 5	25
12	22	19	3	9
			Totals 0	92

Figure 6.6	GASOLINE SALES TIME SERIES AND 3-WEEK MOVING AVERAGE FORECASTS

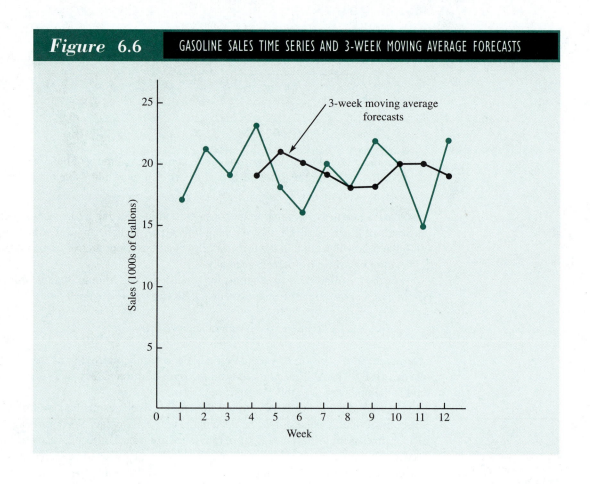

the time series using the number of data values that minimized the MSE for the historical time series.

Weighted Moving Averages

In the moving averages method, each observation in the calculation receives the same weight. One variation, known as **weighted moving averages,** involves selecting different weights for each data value and then computing a weighted average of the most recent n data values as the forecast. In most cases, the most recent observation receives the most weight, and the weight decreases for older data values. For example, we can use the gasoline sales time series to illustrate the computation of a weighted 3-week moving average, with the most recent observation receiving a weight three times as great as that given the oldest observation, and the next oldest observation receiving a weight twice as great as the oldest. For week 4 the computation is

$$\text{Weighted moving averages forecast for week 4} = \frac{3}{6}(19) + \frac{2}{6}(21) + \frac{1}{6}(17) = 19.33$$

Note that for the weighted moving average the sum of the weights is equal to 1. Actually, this condition was also true for the simple moving average: Each weight was ⅓. However, recall that the simple or unweighted moving average provided a forecast of 19.

Forecast Accuracy   To use the weighted moving averages method, we must first select the number of data values to be included in the weighted moving average and then choose weights for each of the data values. In general, if we believe that the recent past is a better predictor of the future than the distant past, larger weights should be given to the more recent observations. However, when the time series is highly variable, selecting approximately equal weights for each data value may be best. Note that the only requirement in selecting the weights is that their sum must equal 1. To determine whether one particular combination of number of data values and weights provides a more accurate forecast than another combination, we will continue to use the MSE criterion as the measure of forecast accuracy. That is, if we assume that the combination that is best for the past will also be best for the future, we would use the combination of number of data values and weights that minimized MSE for the historical time series to forecast the next value in the time series.

Exponential Smoothing

Exponential smoothing is simple and has few data requirements. Thus, it is an inexpensive, useful approach for firms that make many forecasts each period.

Exponential smoothing uses a weighted average of past time series values as the forecast; it is a special case of the weighted moving averages method in which we select only one weight—the weight for the most recent observation. The weights for the other data values are automatically computed and get smaller and smaller as the observations move farther into the past. The basic exponential smoothing model is:

$$F_{t+1} = \alpha Y_t + (1 - \alpha)F_t \tag{6.2}$$

where

$$F_{t+1} = \text{forecast of the time series for period } t + 1$$
$$Y_t = \text{actual value of the time series in period } t$$
$$F_t = \text{forecast of the time series for period } t$$
$$\alpha = \text{smoothing constant } (0 \leq \alpha \leq 1)$$

Equation (6.2) shows that the forecast for period $t + 1$ is a weighted average of the actual value in period t and the forecast for period t; note in particular that the weight given to the actual value in period t is α and that the weight given to the forecast in period t is $1 - \alpha$. We can demonstrate that the exponential smoothing forecast for any period also is a weighted average of *all the previous actual values* for the time series with a time series consisting of three periods of data: Y_1, Y_2, and Y_3. To start the calculations, we let F_1 equal the actual value of the time series in period 1; that is, $F_1 = Y_1$. Hence, the forecast for period 2

$$F_2 = \alpha Y_1 + (1 - \alpha)F_1$$
$$= \alpha Y_1 + (1 - \alpha)Y_1$$
$$= Y_1$$

Thus, the exponential smoothing forecast for period 2 is equal to the actual value of the time series in period 1.

The forecast for period 3 is

$$F_3 = \alpha Y_2 + (1 - \alpha)F_2 = \alpha Y_2 + (1 - \alpha)Y_1$$

Finally, substituting this expression for F_3 in the expression for F_4, we obtain

$$F_4 = \alpha Y_3 + (1 - \alpha)F_3$$
$$= \alpha Y_3 + (1 - \alpha)[\alpha Y_2 + (1 - \alpha)Y_1]$$
$$= \alpha Y_3 + \alpha(1 - \alpha)Y_2 + (1 - \alpha)^2 Y_1$$

Hence, F_4 is a weighted average of the first three time series values. The sum of the coefficients, or weights, for Y_1, Y_2, and Y_3 equals 1. A similar argument can be made to show that, in general, any forecast F_{t+1} is a weighted average of all the previous time series values.

Despite the fact that exponential smoothing provides a forecast that is a weighted average of all past observations, all the past data do not need to be saved in order to compute the forecast for the next period. In fact, once the **smoothing constant** α has been selected, only two pieces of information are required to compute the forecast. Equation (6.2) shows that with a given α we can compute the forecast for period $t + 1$ simply by knowing the actual and forecast time series values for period t—that is, Y_t and F_t.

To illustrate the exponential smoothing approach to forecasting, consider the gasoline sales time series presented previously in Table 6.1 and Figure 6.5. As indicated, the exponential smoothing forecast for period 2 is equal to the actual value of the time series in period 1. Thus, with $Y_1 = 17$, we set $F_2 = 17$ to get the exponential smoothing computations started. From the time series data in Table 6.1, we find an actual time series value in period 2 of $Y_2 = 21$. Thus, period 2 has a forecast error of $21 - 17 = 4$.

Continuing with the exponential smoothing computations, using a smoothing constant of $\alpha = 0.2$, provides the forecast for period 3:

$$F_3 = 0.2Y_2 + 0.8F_2 = 0.2(21) + 0.8(17) = 17.8$$

Once the actual time series value in period 3, $Y_3 = 19$, is known, we can generate a forecast for period 4:

$$F_4 = 0.2Y_3 + 0.8F_3 = 0.2(19) + 0.8(17.8) = 18.04$$

By continuing the exponential smoothing calculations, we can determine the weekly forecast values and the corresponding weekly forecast errors, as shown in Table 6.3. Note that we have not shown an exponential smoothing forecast or the forecast error for period 1 because no forecast was made. For week 12, we have $Y_{12} = 22$ and $F_{12} = 18.48$. Can we use this information to generate a forecast for week 13 before the actual value of week 13 becomes known? Using the exponential smoothing model, we have

$$F_{13} = 0.2Y_{12} + 0.8F_{12} = 0.2(22) + 0.8(18.48) = 19.18$$

You should now be able to use exponential smoothing to develop forecasts. Try Problem 4.

Thus, the exponential smoothing forecast of the amount sold in week 13 is 19.18, or 19,180 gallons of gasoline. With this forecast, the firm can make plans and decisions accordingly. The accuracy of the forecast will not be known until the end of week 13.

Figure 6.7 shows the plot of the actual and the forecast values from Table 6.3. Note in particular how the forecasts "smooth out" the irregular fluctuations in the time series.

Forecast Accuracy. In the preceding exponential smoothing calculations, we used a smoothing constant of $\alpha = 0.2$. Although any value of α between 0 and 1 is acceptable, some values will yield better forecasts than others. Insight into choosing a good value for α can be obtained by rewriting the basic exponential smoothing model as follows:

$$F_{t+1} = \alpha Y_t + (1 - \alpha)F_t \qquad (6.3)$$
$$= \alpha Y_t + F_t - \alpha F_t$$
$$= F_t + \alpha(Y_t - F_t)$$

Forecast in period t Forecast error in period t

Thus, the new forecast F_{t+1} is equal to the previous forecast F_t plus an adjustment, which is α times the most recent forecast error, $Y_t - F_t$. That is, the forecast in period $t + 1$ is obtained by adjusting the forecast in period t by a fraction of the forecast error. If the time

Table **6.3**	SUMMARY OF THE EXPONENTIAL SMOOTHING FORECASTS AND FORECAST ERRORS FOR GASOLINE SALES WITH SMOOTHING CONSTANT $\alpha = 0.2$		
Week (t)	**Time Series Value** (Y_t)	**Exponential Smoothing Forecast** (F_t)	**Forecast Error** ($Y_t - F_t$)
1	17		
2	21	17.00	4.00
3	19	17.80	1.20
4	23	18.04	4.96
5	18	19.03	−1.03
6	16	18.83	−2.83
7	20	18.26	1.74
8	18	18.61	−0.61
9	22	18.49	3.51
10	20	19.19	0.81
11	15	19.35	−4.35
12	22	18.48	3.52

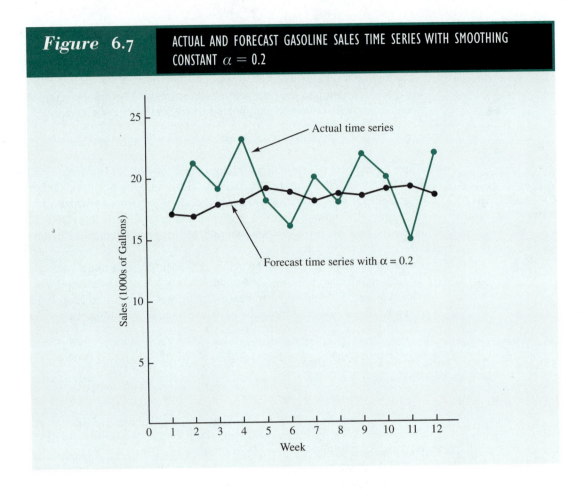

Figure 6.7   ACTUAL AND FORECAST GASOLINE SALES TIME SERIES WITH SMOOTHING CONSTANT $\alpha = 0.2$

series contains substantial random variability, a small value of the smoothing constant is preferred. The reason for this choice is that, because much of the forecast error is due to random variability, we do not want to overreact and adjust the forecasts too quickly. For a time series with relatively little random variability, larger values of the smoothing constant have the advantage of quickly adjusting the forecasts when forecasting errors occur and therefore allowing the forecast to react faster to changing conditions.

The criterion we use to determine a desirable value for the smoothing constant α is the same as the criterion we proposed earlier for determining the number of periods of data to include in the moving averages calculation. That is, we choose the value of α that minimizes the mean squared error. A summary of the MSE calculations for the exponential smoothing forecast of gasoline sales with $\alpha = 0.2$ is shown in Table 6.4. Note that there is one less squared error term than the number of periods of data because we had no past values with which to make a forecast for period 1. Would a different value of α have provided better results in terms of a lower MSE value? Perhaps the most straightforward way to answer this question is simply to try another value for α. We then compare its mean squared error with the MSE value of 8.98, obtained using a smoothing constant of $\alpha = 0.2$.

The exponential smoothing results with $\alpha = 0.3$ are shown in Table 6.5. With MSE = 9.35, a smoothing constant of $\alpha = 0.3$ results in less forecast accuracy than a smoothing constant of $\alpha = 0.2$. Thus, we would be inclined to use the original smooth-

For a given set of data, you should now be able to determine whether moving averages or exponential smoothing provides the best forecasts. Try Problem 5.

Table 6.4	MEAN SQUARED ERROR COMPUTATIONS FOR FORECASTING GASOLINE SALES WITH $\alpha = 0.2$

Week (t)	Time Series Value (Y_t)	Forecast (F_t)	Forecast Error $(Y_t - F_t)$	Squared Forecast Error $(Y_t - F_t)^2$
1	17			
2	21	17.00	4.00	16.00
3	19	17.80	1.20	1.44
4	23	18.04	4.96	24.60
5	18	19.03	−1.03	1.06
6	16	18.83	−2.83	8.01
7	20	18.26	1.74	3.03
8	18	18.61	−0.61	0.37
9	22	18.49	3.51	12.32
10	20	19.19	0.81	0.66
11	15	19.35	−4.35	18.92
12	22	18.48	3.52	12.39
			Total	98.80

$$MSE = 98.80/11 = 8.98$$

ing constant of 0.2. Using a trial-and-error calculation with other values of α, we can find a "good" value for the smoothing constant. This value can be used in the exponential smoothing model to provide forecasts for the future. At a later date, after new time series observations have been obtained, we analyze the newly collected time series data to determine whether the smoothing constant should be revised to provide better forecasting results.

NOTES and Comments

1. Another commonly used measure of forecast accuracy is the *mean absolute deviation* (**MAD**). This measure is simply the average of the absolute values of all the forecast errors. Using the errors given in Table 6.2, we obtain

$$MAD = \frac{4 + 3 + 4 + 1 + 0 + 4 + 0 + 5 + 3}{9} = 2.67$$

One major difference between the MSE and the MAD is that the MSE measure is influenced much more by large forecast errors than by small errors (for the MSE measure the errors are squared). The selection of the best measure of forecasting accuracy is not a simple matter. Indeed, forecasting experts often disagree as to which measure should be used. We use the MSE measure in this chapter.

2. Spreadsheet packages are an effective aid in choosing a good value of α for exponential smoothing and selecting weights for the weighted moving averages method. With the time series data and the forecasting formulas in the spreadsheets, you can experiment with different values of α (or moving average weights) and choose the value(s) providing the smallest MSE or MAD. In the chapter appendix, we show how this can be done.

Table 6.5	MEAN SQUARED ERROR COMPUTATIONS FOR FORECASTING GASOLINE SALES WITH $\alpha = 0.3$			
Week (t)	Time Series Value (Y_t)	Forecast (F_t)	Forecast Error $(Y_t - F_t)$	Squared Forecast Error $(Y_t - F_t)^2$
1	17			
2	21	17.00	4.00	16.00
3	19	18.20	0.80	0.64
4	23	18.44	4.56	20.79
5	18	19.81	-1.81	3.28
6	16	19.27	-3.27	10.69
7	20	18.29	1.71	2.92
8	18	18.80	-0.80	0.64
9	22	18.56	3.44	11.83
10	20	19.59	0.41	0.17
11	15	19.71	-4.71	22.18
12	22	18.30	3.70	13.69
			Total	102.83

$$\text{MSE} = 102.83/11 = 9.35$$

6.3 USING TREND PROJECTION IN FORECASTING

In this section we show how to forecast the values of a time series that exhibits a long-term linear trend. The type of time series for which the trend projection method is applicable shows a consistent increase or decrease over time; it is not stable so the smoothing methods described in the preceding section are not applicable.

Consider the time series for bicycle sales of a particular manufacturer over the past 10 years, as shown in Table 6.6 and Figure 6.8. Note that 21,600 bicycles were sold in year 1; 22,900 were sold in year 2; and so on. In year 10, the most recent year, 31,400 bicycles were sold. Although Figure 6.8 shows some up-and-down movement over the past 10 years, the time series for the number of bicycles sold seems to have an overall increasing or upward trend.

We do not want the trend component of a time series to follow each and every "up" and "down" movement. Rather, the trend component should reflect the gradual shifting—in this case, growth—of the time series values. After we view the time series data in Table 6.6 and the graph in Figure 6.8, we might agree that a linear trend as shown in Figure 6.9 provides a reasonable description of the long-run movement in the series.

We use the bicycle sales data to illustrate the calculations involved in applying regression analysis to identify a linear trend. For a linear trend, the estimated sales volume expressed as a function of time is

$$T_t = b_0 + b_1 t \tag{6.4}$$

Table 6.6	BICYCLE SALES DATA

Year (t)	Sales (1000s) (Y_t)
1	21.6
2	22.9
3	25.5
4	21.9
5	23.9
6	27.5
7	31.5
8	29.7
9	28.6
10	31.4

Figure 6.8	BICYCLE SALES TIME SERIES

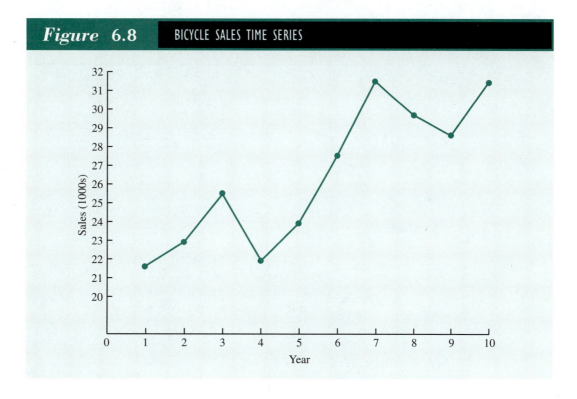

where

$$T_t = \text{trend value for bicycle sales in period } t$$
$$b_0 = \text{intercept of the trend line}$$
$$b_1 = \text{slope of the trend line}$$

Note that, for the time series on bicycle sales, $t = 1$ corresponds to the oldest time series value and $t = 10$ corresponds to the most recent time series value. Formulas for computing b_1 and b_0 are:

Figure 6.9   TREND REPRESENTED BY A LINEAR FUNCTION FOR BICYCLE SALES

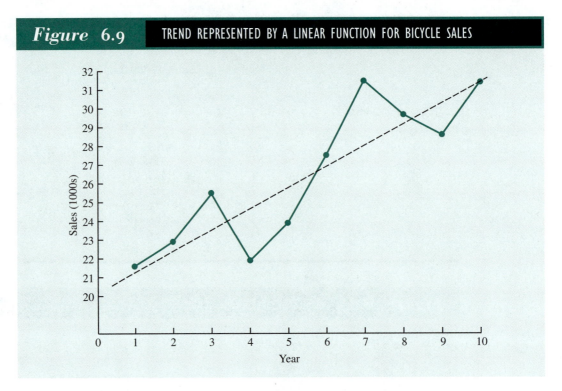

$$b_1 = \frac{\Sigma t Y_t - \left(\Sigma t \Sigma Y_t\right)/n}{\Sigma t^2 - \left(\Sigma t\right)^2/n} \tag{6.5}$$

$$b_0 = \overline{Y} - b_1 \overline{t} \tag{6.6}$$

where

Y_t = actual value of the time series in period t
n = number of periods
$\overline{Y}$ = average value of the time series; that is, $\overline{Y} = \Sigma Y_t / n$
$\overline{t}$ = average value of t; that is, $\overline{t} = \Sigma t / n$

	t	Y_t	tY_t	t^2
	1	21.6	21.6	1
	2	22.9	45.8	4
	3	25.5	76.5	9
	4	21.9	87.6	16
	5	23.9	119.5	25
	6	27.5	165.0	36
	7	31.5	220.5	49
	8	29.7	237.6	64
	9	28.6	257.4	81
	10	31.4	314.0	100
Totals	55	264.5	1545.5	385

Using these relationships for b_0 and b_1 and the bicycle sales data of Table 6.6, we obtain the following calculations.

$$\bar{t} = \frac{55}{10} = 5.5$$

$$\bar{Y} = \frac{264.5}{10} = 26.45$$

$$b_1 = \frac{1545.5 - (55)(264.5)/10}{385 - (55)^2/10} = 1.10$$

$$b_0 = 26.45 - 1.10(5.5) = 20.4$$

Therefore,

$$T_t = 20.4 + 1.1t \qquad (6.7)$$

is the equation for the linear trend component for the bicycle sales time series.

You should now be able to develop the equation for the linear trend component of a time series. Try Problem 14.

    The slope of 1.1 in the trend equation indicates that over the past 10 years the firm has experienced an average growth in sales of about 1100 units per year. If we assume that the past 10-year trend in sales is a good indicator of the future, we can use equation (6.7) to project the trend component of the time series. For example, substituting $t = 11$ into equation (6.7) yields next year's trend projection, T_{11}:

$$T_{11} = 20.4 + 1.1(11) = 32.5$$

Thus the trend component yields a sales forecast of 32,500 bicycles for next year.

    We can also use the trend line to forecast sales farther into the future. For instance, using equation (6.7), we develop forecasts for an additional 2 and 3 years into the future as follows:

$$T_{12} = 20.4 + 1.1(12) = 33.6$$
$$T_{13} = 20.4 + 1.1(13) = 34.7$$

    The use of a linear function to model the trend is common. However, as we discussed earlier, sometimes time series exhibit a curvilinear (nonlinear) trend similar to those shown in Figure 6.10. More advanced texts discuss how to develop models for these more complex relationships.

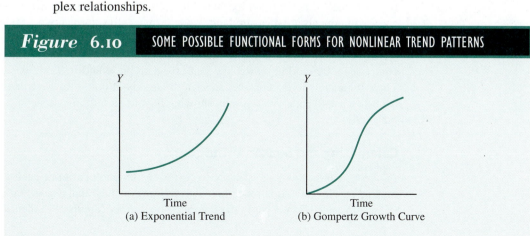

Figure **6.10**   SOME POSSIBLE FUNCTIONAL FORMS FOR NONLINEAR TREND PATTERNS

(a) Exponential Trend

(b) Gompertz Growth Curve

..../ /.............

6.4 USING TREND AND SEASONAL COMPONENTS IN FORECASTING

We have shown how to forecast the values of a time series that has a trend component. In this section we extend the discussion by showing how to forecast the values of a time series that has both trend and seasonal components.

Many situations in business and economics involve period-to-period comparisons. For instance, we might be interested to learn that unemployment is up 2% compared to last month, steel production is up 5% over last month, or that the production of electric power is down 3% from the previous month. Care must be exercised in using such information, however, because whenever a seasonal influence is present, such comparisons usually are not very meaningful. For instance, the fact that electric power consumption is down by 3% from August to September might be only the seasonal effect associated with a decrease in the use of air conditioning and not because of a long-term decline in the use of electric power. Indeed, after adjusting for the seasonal effect, we might even find that the use of electric power has increased.

Removing the seasonal effect from a time series is known as *deseasonalizing the time series*. After we do so, period-to-period comparisons are more meaningful and can help identify whether a trend exists. The approach we take in this section is appropriate in situations when only seasonal effects are present or in situations when both seasonal and trend components are present. The first step is to compute seasonal indexes and use them to deseasonalize the data. Then, if a trend is apparent in the deseasonalized data, we use regression analysis on the deseasonalized data to estimate the trend.

The Multiplicative Model

In addition to a trend component T and a seasonal component S, we assume that the time series also has an irregular component I. The irregular component accounts for the random effects in the time series that cannot be explained by the trend and seasonal components. Using T_t, S_t, and I_t to identify the trend, seasonal, and irregular components at time t, we assume that the actual time series value, denoted by Y_t, can be described by the **multiplicative time series model**

$$Y_t = T_t \times S_t \times I_t \tag{6.8}$$

In this model, T_t is the trend measured in units of the item being forecast. However, the S_t and I_t components are measured in relative terms, with values above 1.00 indicating effects above the trend, and values below 1.00 indicating effects below the trend.

We illustrate the use of the multiplicative model with trend, seasonal, and irregular components by working with the quarterly data presented in Table 6.7 and Figure 6.11. These data show television set sales (in thousands of units) for a particular manufacturer over the past 4 years. We begin by showing how to identify the seasonal component of the time series.

Calculating the Seasonal Indexes

Figure 6.11 indicates that sales are lowest in the second quarter of each year, followed by higher sales levels in quarters 3 and 4. Thus, we conclude that a seasonal pattern exists for television set sales. We begin the computational procedure used to identify each quarter's

Table 6.7 — QUARTERLY DATA FOR TELEVISION SET SALES

Year	Quarter	Sales (1000s)
1	1	4.8
	2	4.1
	3	6.0
	4	6.5
2	1	5.8
	2	5.2
	3	6.8
	4	7.4
3	1	6.0
	2	5.6
	3	7.5
	4	7.8
4	1	6.3
	2	5.9
	3	8.0
	4	8.4

Figure 6.11 — QUARTERLY TELEVISION SET SALES TIME SERIES

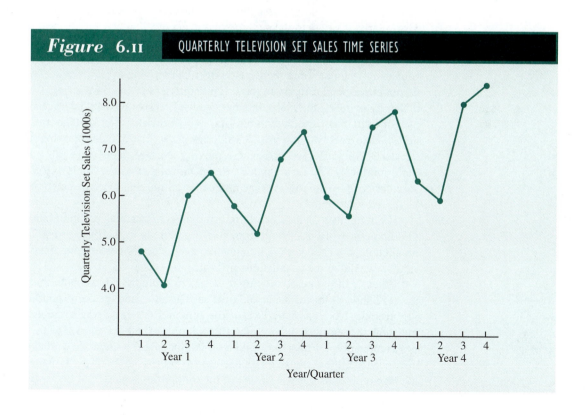

seasonal influence by computing a moving average to isolate the combined seasonal and irregular components, S_t and I_t.

To do so, we use 1 year of data in each calculation. Because we are working with a quarterly series, we use four data values in each moving average. The moving average calculation for the first 4 quarters of the television set sales data is

$$\text{First moving average} = \frac{4.8 + 4.1 + 6.0 + 6.5}{4} = \frac{21.4}{4} = 5.35$$

Note that the moving average calculation for the first 4 quarters yields the average quarterly sales over year 1 of the time series. Continuing the moving average calculation, we next add the 5.8 value for the first quarter of year 2 and drop the 4.8 for the first quarter of year 1. Thus, the second moving average is

$$\text{Second moving average} = \frac{4.1 + 6.0 + 6.5 + 5.8}{4} = \frac{22.4}{4} = 5.6$$

Similarly, the third moving average calculation is $(6.0 + 6.5 + 5.8 + 5.2)/4 = 5.875$.

Before we proceed with the moving average calculations for the entire time series, we return to the first moving average calculation, which resulted in a value of 5.35. The 5.35 value represents an average quarterly sales volume (across all seasons) for year 1. As we look back at the calculation of the 5.35 value, associating 5.35 with the "middle" quarter of the moving average group makes sense. Note, however, that we encounter some difficulty in identifying the middle quarter; with 4 quarters in the moving average, there is no middle quarter. The 5.35 value corresponds to the last half of quarter 2 and the first half of quarter 3. Similarly, if we go to the next moving average value of 5.60, the middle corresponds to the last half of quarter 3 and the first half of quarter 4.

Recall that the reason for computing moving averages is to isolate the combined seasonal and irregular components. However, the moving average values we have computed do not correspond directly to the original quarters of the time series. We can resolve this difficulty by using the midpoints between successive moving average values. For example, since 5.35 corresponds to the first half of quarter 3 and 5.60 corresponds to the last half of quarter 3, we can use $(5.35 + 5.60)/2 = 5.475$ as the moving average value for quarter 3. Similarly, we associate a moving average value of $(5.60 + 5.875)/2 = 5.738$ with quarter 4. The result is a *centered moving average*. Table 6.8 shows a complete summary of the moving average and centered moving average calculations for the television set sales data.

If the number of data points in a moving average calculation is an odd number, the middle point will correspond to one of the periods in the time series. In such cases, we would not have to center the moving average values to correspond to a particular time period, as we did in the calculations in Table 6.8.

What do the centered moving averages in Table 6.8 tell us about this time series? Figure 6.12 shows plots of the actual time series values and the corresponding centered moving average. Note particularly how the centered moving average values tend to "smooth out" both the seasonal and irregular fluctuations in the time series. The moving average values computed for 4 quarters of data do not include the fluctuations due to seasonal influences because the seasonal effect has been averaged out. Each point in the centered moving average represents what the value of the time series would be if there were no seasonal or irregular influence.

By dividing each time series observation by the corresponding centered moving average value, we can identify the seasonal–irregular effect in the time series. For example, the third quarter of year 1 shows $6.0/5.475 = 1.096$ as the combined seasonal–irregular com-

Table 6.8	MOVING AVERAGE AND CENTERED MOVING AVERAGE CALCULATIONS FOR THE TELEVISION SET SALES TIME SERIES

Year	Quarter	Sales (1000s)	4-Quarter Moving Average	Centered Moving Average
1	1	4.8		
	2	4.1		
			5.350	
	3	6.0		5.475
			5.600	
	4	6.5		5.738
			5.875	
2	1	5.8		5.975
			6.075	
	2	5.2		6.188
			6.300	
	3	6.8		6.325
			6.350	
	4	7.4		6.400
			6.450	
3	1	6.0		6.538
			6.625	
	2	5.6		6.675
			6.725	
	3	7.5		6.763
			6.800	
	4	7.8		6.838
			6.875	
4	1	6.3		6.938
			7.000	
	2	5.9		7.075
			7.150	
	3	8.0		
	4	8.4		

ponent. Table 6.9 summarizes the resulting seasonal–irregular values for the entire time series.

Consider the third quarter. The results from years 1, 2, and 3 show third-quarter values of 1.096, 1.075, and 1.109, respectively. Thus, in all cases the seasonal–irregular component appears to have an above average influence in the third quarter. The fluctuations over the 3 years can be attributed to the irregular component, so we can average the computed values to eliminate the irregular influence and obtain an estimate of the third-quarter seasonal influence:

$$\text{Seasonal effect of third quarter} = \frac{1.096 + 1.075 + 1.109}{3} = 1.09$$

We refer to 1.09 as the **seasonal index** for the third quarter. In Table 6.10 we summarize the calculations involved in computing the seasonal indexes for the television set sales time

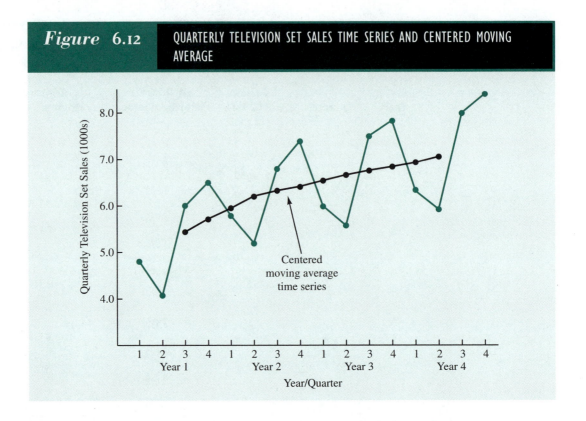

Figure 6.12   QUARTERLY TELEVISION SET SALES TIME SERIES AND CENTERED MOVING AVERAGE

Table 6.9   SEASONAL–IRREGULAR VALUES FOR THE TELEVISION SET SALES TIME SERIES

Year	Quarter	Sales (1000s)	Centered Moving Average	Seasonal–Irregular Value
1	1	4.8		
	2	4.1		
	3	6.0	5.475	1.096
	4	6.5	5.738	1.133
2	1	5.8	5.975	0.971
	2	5.2	6.188	0.840
	3	6.8	6.325	1.075
	4	7.4	6.400	1.156
3	1	6.0	6.538	0.918
	2	5.6	6.675	0.839
	3	7.5	6.763	1.109
	4	7.8	6.838	1.141
4	1	6.3	6.938	0.908
	2	5.9	7.075	0.834
	3	8.0		
	4	8.4		

series. Thus, the seasonal indexes for all 4 quarters are: quarter 1, 0.93; quarter 2, 0.84; quarter 3, 1.09; and quarter 4, 1.14.

Interpretation of the values in Table 6.10 provides some observations about the "seasonal" component in television set sales. The best sales quarter is the fourth quarter, with sales averaging 14% above the average quarterly value. The worst, or slowest, sales quarter is the second quarter, with its seasonal index at 0.84, showing the sales average 16% below the average quarterly sales. The seasonal component corresponds to the intuitive expectation that television viewing interest and thus television purchase patterns tend to peak in the fourth quarter, with its coming winter season and fewer outdoor activities. The low second-quarter sales reflect the reduced television interest resulting from the spring and presummer activities of the potential customers.

One final adjustment may be necessary in obtaining the seasonal indexes. The multiplicative model requires that the average seasonal index equal 1.00, so the sum of the four seasonal indexes in Table 6.10 must equal 4.00. In other words, the seasonal effects must even out over the year. The average of the seasonal indexes in our example is equal to 1.00, and hence, this type of adjustment is not necessary. In other cases, a slight adjustment may be necessary. To make the adjustment, multiply each seasonal index by the number of seasons divided by the sum of the unadjusted seasonal indexes. For instance, for quarterly data, multiply each seasonal index by 4/(sum of the unadjusted seasonal indexes). Some of the problems at the end of the chapter require this adjustment.

You should now be able to compute and interpret seasonal indexes for a time series. Try Problem 25.

Deseasonalizing the Time Series

With deseasonalized data, comparing sales in successive periods makes sense. With data that have not been deseasonalized, relevant comparisons can often be made between sales in the current period and sales in the same period one year ago.

The purpose of finding seasonal indexes is to remove the seasonal effects from a time series. This process is referred to as *deseasonalizing* the time series. Economic time series adjusted for seasonal variations (**deseasonalized time series**) are reported in the *Survey of Current Business, The Wall Street Journal* and *Business Week*. Using the notation of the multiplicative model, we have

$$Y_t = T_t \times S_t \times I_t$$

By dividing each time series observation by the corresponding seasonal index, we remove the effect of season from the time series. The deseasonalized time series for television set sales is summarized in Table 6.11. A graph of the deseasonalized television set sales time series is shown in Figure 6.13.

Table **6.10**	SEASONAL INDEX CALCULATIONS FOR THE TELEVISION SET SALES TIME SERIES	
Quarter	**Seasonal–Irregular Component Values** $(S_t I_t)$	**Seasonal Index** (S_t)
1	0.971, 0.918, 0.908	0.93
2	0.840, 0.839, 0.834	0.84
3	1.096, 1.075, 1.109	1.09
4	1.133, 1.156, 1.141	1.14

Table 6.11		DESEASONALIZED VALUES FOR THE TELEVISION SET SALES TIME SERIES		
Year	Quarter	Sales (1000s) (Y_t)	Seasonal Index (S_t)	Deseasonalized Sales $(Y_t/S_t = T_tI_t)$
1	1	4.8	0.93	5.16
	2	4.1	0.84	4.88
	3	6.0	1.09	5.50
	4	6.5	1.14	5.70
2	1	5.8	0.93	6.24
	2	5.2	0.84	6.19
	3	6.8	1.09	6.24
	4	7.4	1.14	6.49
3	1	6.0	0.93	6.45
	2	5.6	0.84	6.67
	3	7.5	1.09	6.88
	4	7.8	1.14	6.84
4	1	6.3	0.93	6.77
	2	5.9	0.84	7.02
	3	8.0	1.09	7.34
	4	8.4	1.14	7.37

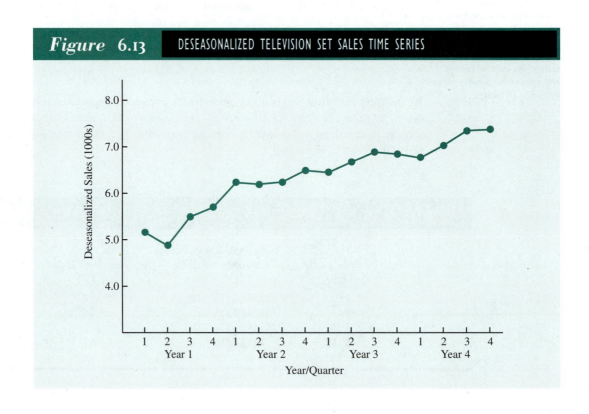

Figure 6.13   DESEASONALIZED TELEVISION SET SALES TIME SERIES

Using the Deseasonalized Time Series to Identify Trend

Although the graph in Figure 6.13 shows some up-and-down movement over the past 16 quarters, the time series seems to have an upward linear trend. To identify this trend, we use the same procedure as in the preceding section; in this case, the data used are quarterly deseasonalized sales values. Thus, for a linear trend, the estimated sales volume expressed as a function of time is

$$T_t = b_0 + b_1 t$$

where

T_t = trend value for television set sales in period t
b_0 = intercept of the trend line
b_0 = slope of the trend line

As before, $t = 1$ corresponds to the time of the first observation for the time series, $t = 2$ corresponds to the time of the second observation, and so on. Thus, for the deseasonalized television set sales time series, $t = 1$ corresponds to the first deseasonalized quarterly sales value and $t = 16$ corresponds to the most recent deseasonalized quarterly sales value. The formulas for computing the values of b_0 and b_1 again are

$$b_1 = \frac{\sum t Y_t - \left(\sum t \sum Y_t\right)/n}{\sum t^2 - \left(\sum t\right)^2/n} \quad \text{and} \quad b_0 = \bar{Y} - b_1 \bar{t}$$

Note, however, that Y_t now refers to the deseasonalized time series value at time t and not to the actual value of the time series. Using the given relationships for b_0 and b_1 and the deseasonalized sales data of Table 6.11, we make the following calculations.

t	Y_t (deseasonalized)	tY_t	t^2
1	5.16	5.16	1
2	4.88	9.76	4
3	5.50	16.50	9
4	5.70	22.80	16
5	6.24	31.20	25
6	6.19	37.14	36
7	6.24	43.68	49
8	6.49	51.92	64
9	6.45	58.05	81
10	6.67	66.70	100
11	6.88	75.68	121
12	6.84	82.08	144
13	6.77	88.01	169
14	7.02	98.28	196
15	7.34	110.10	225
16	7.37	117.92	256
Totals 136	101.74	914.98	1496

$$\bar{t} = \frac{136}{16} = 8.5$$

$$\bar{Y} = \frac{101.74}{16} = 6.359$$

$$b_1 = \frac{914.98 - (136)(101.74)/16}{1496 - (136)^2/16} = 0.148$$

$$b_0 = 6.359 - 0.148(8.5) = 5.101$$

Therefore,

$$T_t = 5.101 + 0.148t$$

is the equation for the linear trend component of the time series.

The slope of 0.148 indicates that over the past 16 quarters the firm has experienced an average deseasonalized growth in sales of about 148 sets per quarter. If we assume that the past 16-quarter trend in sales data is a reasonably good indicator of the future, we can use this equation to project the trend component of the time series for future quarters. For example, substituting $t = 17$ into the equation yields next quarter's trend projection, T_{17}:

$$T_{17} = 5.101 + 0.148(17) = 7.617$$

Thus, the trend component yields a sales forecast of 7617 television sets for the next quarter. Similarly, the trend component produces sales forecasts of 7765, 7913, and 8061 television sets in quarters 18, 19, and 20, respectively.

Seasonal Adjustments

The final step in developing the forecast when both trend and seasonal components are present is to use the seasonal index to adjust the trend projection. Returning to the television set sales example, we have a trend projection for the next 4 quarters. Now we must adjust the forecast for the seasonal effect. The seasonal index for the first quarter of year 5 ($t = 17$) is 0.93, so we obtain the quarterly forecast by multiplying the forecast based on trend ($T_{17} = 7617$) times the seasonal index (0.93). Thus, the forecast for the next quarter is 7617(0.93) = 7084. Table 6.12 shows the quarterly forecast for quarters 17–20. The forecasts show the high-volume fourth quarter with a 9190-unit forecast and the low-volume second quarter with a 6523-unit forecast.

Table 6.12	QUARTERLY FORECASTS FOR THE TELEVISION SET SALES TIME SERIES			
Year	Quarter	Trend Forecast	Seasonal Index (see Table 6.10)	Quarterly Forecast
5	1	7617	0.93	(7617)(0.93) = 7084
	2	7765	0.84	(7765)(0.84) = 6523
	3	7913	1.09	(7913)(1.09) = 8625
	4	8061	1.14	(8061)(1.14) = 9190

Models Based on Monthly Data

In the preceding television set sales example we used quarterly data to illustrate the computation of seasonal indexes. However, many businesses use monthly rather than quarterly forecasts. In such cases, the procedures introduced in this section can be applied with minor modifications. First, a 12-month moving average replaces the 4-quarter moving average; second, 12 monthly seasonal indexes, rather than the 4 quarterly indexes, must be computed. Other than these changes, the computational and forecasting procedures are identical.

Cyclical Component

Mathematically, the multiplicative model of equation (6.8) can be expanded to include a cyclical component as follows:

$$Y_t = T_t \times C_t \times S_t \times I_t \tag{6.9}$$

As with the seasonal component, the cyclical component is expressed as a multiple of trend. As mentioned in Section 6.1, this component is attributable to multiyear cycles in the time series. It is analogous to the seasonal component but over a longer period of time. However, because of the length of time involved, obtaining enough relevant data to estimate the cyclical component often is difficult. Another difficulty is that the length of cycles usually varies. We leave further discussion of the cyclical component to texts on forecasting methods.

6.5 USING REGRESSION ANALYSIS IN FORECASTING

Regression analysis is a statistical technique that can be used to develop a mathematical equation showing how variables are related. In regression terminology, the variable that is being predicted is called the *dependent* or *response* varible. The variable or variables that predict the value of the dependent variable are called the *independent* or *predictor* variables. Regression analysis involving one independent variable and one dependent variable for which the relationship between the variables is approximated by a straight line is called *simple linear regression*. Regression analysis involving two or more independent variables is called *multiple regression analysis*. In Section 6.3 we utilized simple linear regression to fit a linear trend to the bicycle sales time series. Recall that we developed a linear equation relating bicycle sales to the time period. The number of bicycles sold isn't actually causally related to time; instead, time is a surrogate for variables to which the number of bicycles sold is actually related but which are either unknown or too difficult or costly to measure. Thus, the use of regression analysis for trend projection is not a causal forecasting method because only past values of sales, the variable being forecast, were used.

When we use regression analysis to relate the variable that we want to forecast to other variables that are supposed to influence or explain that variable, it becomes a causal forecasting method. The Q. M. in Action: Spare Parts Forecasting at American Airlines explains why that company uses regression analysis as a causal forecasting method to estimate the demand for spare parts.

Using Regression Analysis when Time Series Data Are Not Available

Regression analysis also may be used to develop forecasts when time series data are not available. To illustrate how regression analysis is used in this context, we consider the sales

Q. M. IN ACTION

SPARE PARTS FORECASTING AT AMERICAN AIRLINES*

American Airlines developed the Rotables Allocation and Planning System (RAPS) to provide demand forecasts for spare parts, assist in allocating spare parts to airports, and calculate the availability level of each spare part. The demand forecasting module of RAPS provides monthly demand forecasts for more than 5000 parts, ranging from coffee makers to landing gears. The average price for parts covered by RAPS is approximately $5000.

Prior to RAPS, American Airlines used time series methodology to forecast spare parts demand. The time series methodology was slow to respond to external factors such as changes in aircraft utilization and major fleet expansions. To correct for these deficiencies, the forecasting component of RAPS involves the use of regression analysis "to establish a relationship between monthly part removals and various functions of monthly flying hours." The RAPS system generates the monthly demand forecasts in less than an hour.

Nearly all the parts covered by the RAPS system are essential to the operation of an aircraft. A part shortage can even result in cancellation of a flight, so the cost can be substantial. The materials management group at American Airlines estimated "that using RAPS has provided a one-time savings of $7 million and recurring annual savings of nearly $1 million."

Tedone, Mark J., "Repairable Part Management." *Interfaces*, Vol. 19, No. 4, July–August 1989, pp. 61–68.

---

forecasting problem faced by Armand, Inc. Armand, Inc., is a chain of Italian restaurants doing business in a five-state area. The most successful locations have been near college campuses. Before opening a new restaurant, management requires a forecast of yearly sales revenues. Such an estimate is used in planning restaurant capacity, making initial staffing decisions, and deciding whether the potential revenue justifies the cost of operation. No historical data are available on sales at a new store, so Armand cannot use time series data to develop the forecast.

Management believes that annual sales revenue is related to the size of the student population on the nearby campus. Intuitively, management believes that restaurants located near large campuses generate more revenue than those located near small campuses. If a relationship can be established between sales revenue and the size of the campus population, Armand can use the size of the campus population to predict revenues for the new restaurant. To evaluate the relationship between annual sales y and student population x, Armand collected data from a sample of 10 of its restaurants located near college campuses. These data are summarized in Table 6.13. For example, restaurant 1, with $y = 58$ and $x = 2$, had $58,000 in sales revenue and is located near a campus with 2000 students.

Figure 6.14 shows graphically the data presented in Table 6.13. The size of the student population is shown on the horizontal axis, with annual sales shown on the vertical axis. A graph such as this is called a *scatter diagram*. Usually the independent variable is plotted on the horizontal axis, and the dependent variable is plotted on the vertical axis. The advantage of a scatter diagram is that it provides an overview of the data and enables us to draw preliminary conclusions about a possible relationship between the variables.

What preliminary conclusions can we draw from Figure 6.14? Apparently, low sales volumes are associated with small student populations and higher sales volumes are associated with larger student populations. Also, it appears that the relationship between the two variables can be approximated by a straight line. In Figure 6.15 we have drawn a straight line through the data that appears to provide a good linear approximation of the relationship between the variables. Observe that the relationship isn't perfect. Indeed, few, if any, of the data fall exactly on the line. However, if we can develop the mathematical expression for this line, we may be able to use it to forecast the value of y corresponding to each possible value of x. The resulting equation of the line is the *estimated regression equation*.

Table 6.13	DATA ON ANNUAL SALES AND STUDENT POPULATION FOR 10 RESTAURANTS	
Restaurant	y = Annual Sales (1000s)	x = Student Population (1000s)
1	58	2
2	105	6
3	88	8
4	118	8
5	117	12
6	137	16
7	157	20
8	169	20
9	149	22
10	202	26

Figure 6.14   SCATTER DIAGRAM OF ANNUAL SALES VERSUS STUDENT POPULATION

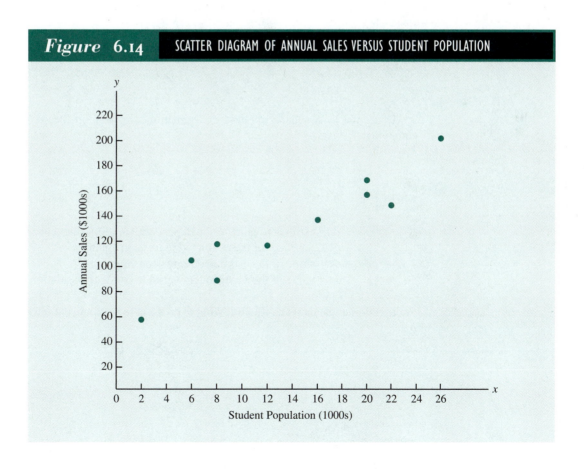

Figure 6.15   STRAIGHT-LINE APPROXIMATION FOR DATA ON ANNUAL SALES AND STUDENT POPULATION

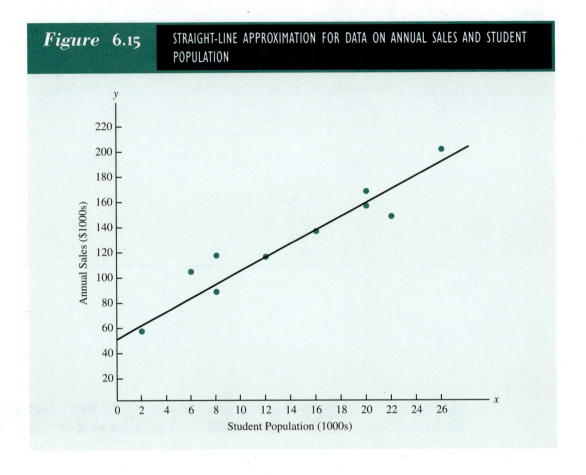

Using the least-squares method of estimation, we develop the estimated regression equation

$$\hat{y} = b_0 + b_1 x \qquad (6.10)$$

where

$\hat{y}$ = estimated value of the dependent variable (sales revenue)
b_0 = intercept of the estimated regression equation
b_1 = slope of the estimated regression equation
x = value of the independent variable (student population)

We use the sample data and the following expression to compute the intercept b_0 and slope b_1:

$$b_1 = \frac{\sum x_i y_i - \left(\sum x_i \sum y_i\right)/n}{\sum x_i^2 - \left(\sum x_i\right)^2/n} \qquad (6.11)$$

$$b_0 = \bar{y} - b_1 \bar{x} \qquad (6.12)$$

where

x_i = value of the independent variable for the ith observation
y_i = value of the dependent variable for the ith observation
$\bar{x}$ = mean value for the independent variable
$\bar{y}$ = mean value for the dependent variable
n = total number of observations

Some of the calculations necessary to develop the least-squares estimated regression equation for the data on student population and annual sales are shown in Table 6.14. Our example contains 10 restaurants or observations; hence $n = 10$. Using equations (6.11) and (6.12), we can now compute the slope and intercept of the estimated regression equation. We calculate the slope b_1 as follows:

$$b_1 = \frac{\sum x_i y_i - \left(\sum x_i \sum y_i\right)/n}{\sum x_i^2 - \left(\sum x_i\right)^2/n}$$

$$= \frac{21{,}040 - (140)(1300)/10}{2528 - (140)^2/10}$$

$$= \frac{2840}{568}$$

$$= 5$$

We then calculate the intercept b_0 as follows:

$$\bar{x} = \frac{\sum x_i}{n} = \frac{140}{10} = 14$$

$$\bar{y} = \frac{\sum y_i}{n} = \frac{1300}{10} = 130$$

$$b_0 = \bar{y} - b_1 \bar{x}$$

$$= 130 - 5(14)$$

$$= 60$$

Table **6.14**	CALCULATIONS NECESSARY TO DEVELOP THE LEAST-SQUARES ESTIMATED REGRESSION EQUATION FOR THE ARMAND DATA

Restaurant (i)	y_i	x_i	$x_i y_i$	x_i^2
1	58	2	116	4
2	105	6	630	36
3	88	8	704	64
4	118	8	944	64
5	117	12	1,404	144
6	137	16	2,192	256
7	157	20	3,140	400
8	169	20	3,380	400
9	149	22	3,278	484
10	202	26	5,252	676
Totals	1300	140	21,040	2528

Thus, the estimated regression equation found by using the method of least squares is

$$\hat{y} = 60 + 5x$$

We show the graph of this equation in Figure 6.16.

The slope of the estimated regression equation ($b_1 = 5$) is positive, implying that, as student population increases, annual sales increase. In fact, we can conclude (since sales are measured in thousands of dollars and student population in thousands) that an increase in the student population of 1000 is associated with an increase of $5000 in expected annual sales; that is, sales are expected to increase by $5 per student.

If we believe that the least-squares estimated regression equation adequately describes the relationship between x and y, using the estimated regression equation to forecast the value of y for a given value of x seems reasonable. For example, if we wanted to forecast annual sales for a new restaurant location near a campus with 16,000 students, we would compute

$$\hat{y} = 60 + 5(16)$$
$$= 140$$

You should now be able to use regression analysis to develop a forecast. Try Problem 33.

Hence, we would forecast sales of $140,000 per year.

The sales forecasting problem facing Armand, Inc., illustrates how simple linear regression analysis can be used to develop forecasts when time series data are not available. Multiple regression analysis also can be applied in these situations if additional data for other independent variables are available. For example, suppose that the management of

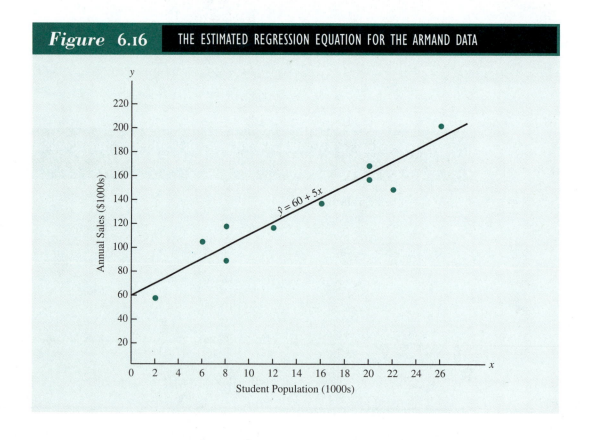

Figure 6.16   THE ESTIMATED REGRESSION EQUATION FOR THE ARMAND DATA

Armand, Inc., also believes that the number of competitors near the college campus is related to annual sales. Intuitively, management believes that restaurants located near campuses where there are fewer competitors generate more sales revenue than those located near campuses where there are more competitors. With additional data, multiple regression analysis could be used to develop an equation relating annual sales to the size of the student population and the number of competitors.

Using Regression Analysis with Time Series Data

In Section 6.3 we fit a linear trend to the bicycle sales time series to show how simple linear regression analysis can be used to forecast future values of a time series when past values of the time series are available. Recall that for this problem the annual sales in year t was treated as the dependent variable and the year t was treated as the independent variable. The inherent complexity of most real-world problems necessitates the consideration of more than one independent variable to predict the dependent variable. We now consider how multiple regression analysis is used to develop forecasts when time series data are available.

To use multiple regression analysis, we need a sample of observations for the dependent variable and all the independent variables. In time series analysis, the n periods of time series data provide a sample of n observations for each variable. To describe the wide variety of regression-based models that can be developed, we use the following notation:

$$Y_t = \text{actual value of the time series in period } t$$
$$x_{1t} = \text{value of independent variable 1 in period } t$$
$$x_{2t} = \text{value of independent variable 2 in period } t$$
$$.$$
$$.$$
$$.$$
$$x_{kt} = \text{value of independent variable } k \text{ in period } t$$

The n periods of data necessary to develop the estimated regression equation would appear as follows.

Period	Time Series Value (Y_t)	Value of Independent Variables					
		x_{1t}	x_{2t}	x_{3t}	· · ·		x_{kt}
1	Y_1	x_{11}	x_{21}	x_{31}	· · ·		x_{k1}
2	Y_2	x_{12}	x_{22}	x_{32}	· · ·		x_{k2}
.	.	.	.	.	· · · ·		.
.	.	.	.	.	· · · · ·		.
.	.	.	.	.	· · · · ·		.
n	Y_n	x_{1n}	x_{2n}	x_{3n}	· · ·		x_{kn}

As you might imagine, there are a number of choices for the independent variables in a forecasting model. One possible choice is simply time. We made this choice in Section 6.3 when we estimated the trend of the time series using a linear function of the independent variable time. Letting

$$x_{1t} = t$$

we obtain an estimated regression equation of the form

$$\hat{Y}_t = b_0 + b_1 t$$

where $\hat{Y}_t$ is the estimate of the time series value Y_t and where b_0 and b_1 are the estimated regression coefficients. In a more complex model, additional terms could be added corresponding to time raised to other powers. For example, if

$$x_{2t} = t^2 \quad \text{and} \quad x_{3t} = t^3$$

the estimated regression equation would become

$$\hat{Y}_t = b_0 + b_1 x_{1t} + b_2 x_{2t} + b_3 x_{3t}$$
$$= b_0 + b_1 t + b_2 t^2 + b_3 t^3$$

Note that this model provides a forecast of a time series with curvilinear characteristics over time.

Other regression-based forecasting models involve the use of a mixture of economic and demographic independent variables. For example, in forecasting the sale of refrigerators, we might select independent variables such as

x_{1t} = price in period t
x_{2t} = total industry sales in period $t - 1$
x_{3t} = number of building permits for new houses in period $t - 1$
x_{4t} = population forecast for period t
x_{5t} = advertising budget for period t

According to the usual multiple regression procedure, an estimated regression equation with five independent variables would be used to develop forecasts in this case.

Spyros Makridakis, a noted forecasting expert, has conducted research showing that simple techniques usually outperform more complex procedures for short-term forecasting. Using a more sophisticated and expensive procedure will not guarantee better forecasts.

Whether a regression approach provides a good forecast depends largely on how well we are able to identify and obtain data for independent variables that are closely related to the time series. Generally, during the development of an estimated regression equation, we will want to consider many possible sets of independent variables. Thus, part of the regression analysis procedure should focus on the selection of the set of independent variables that provides the best forecasting model.

In the chapter introduction we stated that **causal forecasting methods** utilized time series related to the one being forecast in an effort to explain better the cause of a time series' behavior. Regression analysis is the tool most often used in developing causal models. The related time series become the independent variables, and the time series being forecast is the dependent variable.

Another type of regression-based forecasting model occurs whenever all the independent variables are previous values of the *same* time series. For example, if the time series values are denoted $Y_1, Y_2, \ldots, Y_n$, we might try to find an estimated regression equation relating Y_t to the most recent time series values, Y_{t-1}, Y_{t-2}, and so on. For instance, if we use the actual values of the time series for the three most recent periods as independent variables, the estimated regression equation would be

$$\hat{Y}_t = b_0 + b_1 Y_{t-1} + b_2 Y_{t-2} + b_3 Y_{t-3}$$

Regression models such as this, where the independent variables are previous values of the time series, are referred to as **autoregressive models.**

Finally, another regression-based forecasting approach is one that incorporates a mixture of the independent variables previously discussed. For example, we might select a combination of time variables, some economic/demographic variables, and some previous values of the time series variable itself.

6.6 QUALITATIVE APPROACHES TO FORECASTING

In the preceding sections we discussed several types of quantitative forecasting methods. Most of these techniques require historical data on the variable of interest, so they cannot be applied when no historical data are available. Furthermore, even when such data are available, a significant change in environmental conditions affecting the time series may make the use of past data questionable in predicting future values of the time series. For example, a government-imposed gasoline rationing program would raise questions about the validity of a gasoline sales forecast based on historical data. Qualitative forecasting techniques offer an alternative in these and other cases.

If historical data are not available, managers may use a qualitative technique to develop forecasts. But the cost of using qualitative techniques can be high because of the time commitment required from the people involved.

Empirical evidence and theoretical arguments suggest that between 5 and 20 experts should be used in judgmental forecasting.

Delphi Method

One of the most commonly used qualitative forecasting techniques is the **Delphi method.** This technique, originally developed by a research group at the Rand Corporation, attempts to develop forecasts through "group consensus." In its usual application, the members of a panel of experts—all of whom are physically separated from and unknown to each other—are asked to respond to a series of questionnaires. The responses from the first questionnaire are tabulated and used to prepare a second questionnaire that contains information and opinions of the entire group. Each respondent is then asked to reconsider and possibly revise his or her previous response in light of the group information provided. This process continues until the coordinator feels that some degree of consensus has been reached. The goal of the Delphi method is not to produce a single answer as output, but instead to produce a relatively narrow spread of opinions within which the majority of experts concur.

Expert Judgment

Qualitative forecasts often are based on the judgment of a single expert or represent the consensus of a group of experts. For example, each year a group of experts at Merrill Lynch gather to forecast the level of the Dow Jones Industrial Average and the prime rate for the next year. In doing so, the experts individually consider information that they believe will

Q. M. IN ACTION

THE *BUSINESS WEEK* INDUSTRY OUTLOOK*

The *Business Week* industry outlook survey is a qualitative approach to forecasting based on expert judgment. It combines information from hundreds of interviews with industry leaders with the expertise of the magazine's editors who have followed the industries daily to provide a judgment on the prospects for the next year. Steven Schnaars and Iris Mohr conducted a study to evaluate the accuracy of the *Business Week* forecasts for five industries (autos, steel, chemicals, computers, and energy) over a nine-year period (1978–1986).

Schnaars and Mohr evaluated *Business Week's* approach in terms of its ability to predict correctly the general direction for the industry (getting better or getting worse) and the accuracy of specific forecasts

(e.g., sales and profit). They found that "nearly 80 percent of the outlooks correctly foresaw the overall direction in which the industry would move in the coming year." And, when comparing the *Business Week* forecast with a naive forecast of no change in the coming year, the *Business Week* forecast clearly was better. The authors conclude that judgmental forecasting can work well for forecasting the general direction of change.

*Schnaars, Steven P., and Iris Mohr, "The Accuracy of *Business Week's* Industry Outlook Survey." *Interfaces*, Vol. 18, No. 5, September–October 1988, pp. 31–38.

---

influence the stock market and interest rates; then, they combine their conclusions into a forecast. No formal model is used, and no two experts are likely to consider the same information in the same way.

Expert judgment is a forecasting method that is often recommended when conditions in the past are not likely to hold in the future. Even though no formal quantitative model is used, expert judgment has provided good forecasts in many situations. The Q. M. in Action: The *Business Week* Industry Outlook shows that the magazine provides a good one-year forecast of industry prospects.

Scenario Writing

The qualitative procedure referred to as **scenario writing** consists of developing a conceptual scenario of the future based on a well-defined set of assumptions. Different sets of assumptions lead to different scenarios. The job of the decision maker is to decide how likely each scenario is and then to make decisions accordingly.

Intuitive Approaches

Subjective, or *intuitive qualitative, approaches* are based on the ability of the human mind to process a variety of information that, in most cases, is difficult to quantify. These techniques are often used in group work, wherein a committee or panel seeks to develop new ideas or solve complex problems through a series of "brainstorming sessions." In such sessions, individuals are freed from the usual group restrictions of peer pressure and criticism because they can present any idea or opinion without regard to its relevancy and, even more importantly, without fear of criticism.

SUMMARY

In this chapter we discussed how forecasts can be developed to help management develop appropriate strategies for the future. We began by defining a time series as a set of observations on a variable measured at successive points in time or over successive periods of time. A time series may involve four separate components: trend, seasonal, irregular, and cyclical. By isolating these components and measuring their apparent effects, future values of the time series can be forecast.

Quantitative forecasting methods include time series methods and causal methods. A time series method is appropriate when the historical data are restricted to past values of the variable being forecast. The three time series methods discussed in the chapter are smoothing (moving averages, weighted moving averages, and exponential smoothing), trend projection, and trend projection adjusted for seasonal influence.

Smoothing methods are appropriate for a stable time series, that is, one that exhibits no significant trend, cyclical, or seasonal effects. The moving averages approach consists of computing an average of past values and then using this average as the forecast for the next period. The weighted moving averages method allows for the possibility of unequal weights for the data; thus, the moving averages method is a special case of the weighted moving averages method in which all the weights are equal. Exponential smoothing also is a special case of the weighted moving averages method involving only one parameter: the weight for the most recent observation.

When a time series consists of random fluctuations around a long-term trend line, a linear equation may be used to estimate the trend. When seasonal effects are present, seasonal indexes can be computed and used to deseasonalize the data and to develop forecasts. When both seasonal and long-term trend effects are present, a trend line is fitted to the deseasonalized data; the seasonal indexes are then used to adjust the trend projections.

Causal forecasting methods are based on the assumption that the variable being forecast exhibits a cause–effect relationship with one or more other variables. A causal forecasting method is one that relates the variable being forecast to other variables that are thought to influence or explain it. Regression analysis is a causal forecasting method that can be used to develop forecasts when time series data are not available.

Qualitative forecasting methods may be used when little or no historical data are available. Qualitative forecasting methods also are considered most appropriate when the historical pattern of the time series is not expected to continue into the future.

GLOSSARY

Time series A set of observations measured at successive points in time or over successive periods of time.

Forecast A projection or prediction of future values of a time series.

Trend The long-run increase or decrease in the time series observable over several periods of data.

Cyclical component The component of the time series model that results in periodic above-trend and below-trend behavior of the time series lasting more than one year.

Seasonal component The component of the time series model that shows a periodic pattern over one year or less.

Irregular component The component of the time series model that reflects the random variation of the actual time series values beyond what can be explained by the trend, cyclical, and seasonal components.

Moving averages A method of forecasting or smoothing a time series by averaging each successive group of data points. The moving averages method can also be used to isolate the seasonal component of the time series.

Mean squared error (MSE) One approach to measuring the accuracy of a forecasting model. This measure is the average of the sum of the squared differences between the actual time series values and the forecasted values.

Weighted moving averages A method of forecasting or smoothing a time series by computing a weighted average of past time series values. The sum of the weights must equal 1.

Exponential smoothing A forecasting technique that uses a weighted average of past time series values to arrive at smoothed time series values that can be used as forecasts.

Smoothing constant A parameter of the exponential smoothing model that provides the weight given to the most recent time series value in the calculation of the forecast.

Mean absolute deviation (MAD) A measure of forecast accuracy. The average of the absolute values of the forecast errors.

Multiplicative time series model A model that assumes that the separate components of the time series can be multiplied together to identify the actual time series value. When the four components of trend, cyclical, seasonal, and irregular are assumed present, we obtain $Y_t = T_t \times C_t \times S_t \times I_t$. When cyclical effects are not modeled, we obtain $Y_t = T_t \times S_t \times I_t$.

Seasonal index A measure of the seasonal effect on a time series. A seasonal index above 1 indicates a positive effect, a seasonal index of 1 indicates no seasonal effect, and a seasonal index less than 1 indicates a negative effect.

Deseasonalized time series A time series that has had the effect of season removed by dividing each original time series observation by the corresponding seasonal index.

Regression analysis A statistical technique that can be used to develop a mathematical equation showing how variables are related.

Causal forecasting methods Forecasting methods that relate a time series to other variables that are believed to explain or cause its behavior.

Autoregressive model A time series model that uses a regression relationship based on historical time series values to predict the future time series values.

Delphi method A qualitative forecasting method that obtains forecasts through group consensus.

Scenario writing A qualitative forecasting method that consists of developing a conceptual scenario of the future based on a well-defined set of assumptions.

PROBLEMS

SELF TEST

SELF TEST

1. Corporate Triple A Bond interest rates for 12 consecutive months are 9.5, 9.3, 9.4, 9.6, 9.8, 9.7, 9.8, 10.5, 9.9, 9.7, 9.6, and 9.6.
    a. Develop 3- and 4-month moving averages for this time series. Which moving average provides the better forecasts? Explain.
    b. What is the moving average forecast for the next month?
2. Refer to the gasoline sales time series data in Table 6.1.
    a. Compute 4- and 5-week moving averages for the time series.
    b. Compute the MSE for the 4- and 5-week moving average forecasts.

    c.   What appears to be the best number of weeks of past data to use in the moving average computation? Remember that the MSE for the 3-week moving average is 10.22.

3.   Refer again to the gasoline sales time series data in Table 6.1.

    a.   Use a weight of ½ for the most recent observation, ⅓ for the second most recent, and ⅙ for the third most recent to compute a 3-week weighted moving average for the time series.

    b.   Compute the MSE for the weighted moving average in part (a). Do you prefer this weighted moving average to the unweighted moving average? Remember that the MSE for the unweighted moving average is 10.22.

    c.   Suppose that you are allowed to choose any weights as long as they sum to 1. Could you always find a set of weights that would make the MSE smaller for a weighted moving average than for an unweighted moving average? Why or why not?

4.   Use the gasoline sales time series data from Table 6.1 to show the exponential smoothing forecasts using $\alpha = 0.1$. Using the mean squared error criterion, would you prefer a smoothing constant of $\alpha = 0.1$ or $\alpha = 0.2$?

5.   For the Hawkins Company, the monthly percentages of all shipments that were received on time over the past 12 months are 80, 82, 84, 83, 83, 84, 85, 84, 82, 83, 84, and 83.

    a.   Compare a 3-month moving average forecast with an exponential smoothing forecast for $\alpha = 0.2$. Which provides the better forecasts?

    b.   What is the forecast for next month?

6.   With a smoothing constant of $\alpha = 0.2$, equation (6.2) shows that the forecast for the 13th week of the gasoline sales data from Table 6.1 is given by $F_{13} = 0.2Y_{12} + 0.8F_{12}$. However, the forecast for week 12 is given by $F_{12} = 0.2Y_{11} + 0.8F_{11}$. Thus, we could combine these two results to write the forecast for the 13th week as

$$F_{13} = 0.2Y_{12} + 0.8(0.2Y_{11} + 0.8F_{11}) = 0.2Y_{12} + 0.16Y_{11} + 0.64F_{11}$$

    a.   Make use of the fact that $F_{11} = 0.2Y_{10} + 0.8F_{10}$ (and similarly for F_{10} and F_9) and continue to expand the expression for F_{13} until you have written it in terms of the past data values $Y_{12}, Y_{11}, Y_{10}, Y_9,$ and $Y_8,$ and the forecast for period 8.

    b.   Refer to the coefficients or weights for the past data values $Y_{12}, Y_{11}, Y_{10}, Y_9,$ and Y_8; what observation can you make about how exponential smoothing weights past data values in arriving at new forecasts? Compare this weighting pattern with the weighting pattern of the moving averages method.

7.   Alabama building contracts for a 12-month period (in millions of dollars) are 240, 350, 230, 260, 280, 320, 220, 310, 240, 310, 240, and 230.

    a.   Compare a 3-month moving average forecast with an exponential smoothing forecast using $\alpha = 0.2$. Which provides the better forecasts?

    b.   What is the forecast for the next month?

8.   Moving averages often are used in an effort to identify movements in stock prices. Approximate monthly closing prices (in dollars per share) for Toys of the Future for December 1996 through November 1997 are shown.

Month	Price	Month	Price
December 1996	40	June 1997	34
January 1997	38	July 1997	37
February 1997	39	August 1997	35
March 1997	41	September 1997	37
April 1997	36	October 1997	40
May 1997	41	November 1997	41

a. Use a 3-month moving average to smooth the time series. Forecast the closing price for December 1997.

b. Use a 3-month weighted moving average to smooth the time series. Use a weight of 0.4 for the most recent period, 0.4 for the next period back, and 0.2 for the third period back. Forecast the closing price for December 1997.

c. Use exponential smoothing with a smoothing constant of $\alpha = 0.35$ to smooth the time series. Forecast the closing price for December 1997.

d. Which of the three methods do you prefer? Why?

9. The following data represent 15 quarters of manufacturing capacity utilization (in percentages).

Quarter/Year	Utilization	Quarter/Year	Utilization
1/1994	82.5	1/1996	78.8
2/1994	81.3	2/1996	78.7
3/1994	81.3	3/1996	78.4
4/1994	79.0	4/1996	80.0
1/1995	76.6	1/1997	80.7
2/1995	78.0	2/1997	80.7
3/1995	78.4	3/1997	80.8
4/1995	78.0		

a. Compute 3- and 4-quarter moving averages for this time series. Which moving average provides the better forecast for the fourth quarter of 1997?

b. Use smoothing constants of $\alpha = 0.4$ and $\alpha = 0.5$ to develop forecasts for the fourth quarter of 1997. Which smoothing constant provides the better forecast?

c. Based on the analyses in parts (a) and (b), which method—moving averages or exponential smoothing—provides the better forecast? Explain.

10. The following time series shows the sales of a particular product over the past 12 months.

Month	Sales	Month	Sales
1	105	7	145
2	135	8	140
3	120	9	100
4	105	10	80
5	90	11	100
6	120	12	110

a. Use $\alpha = 0.3$ to compute the exponential smoothing values for the time series.

b. Use a smoothing constant of 0.5 to compute the exponential smoothing values. Does a smoothing constant of 0.3 or 0.5 appear to provide the better forecasts?

11. A chain of grocery stores experienced the following weekly demand (in cases) for a particular brand of automatic-dishwasher detergent.

Week	Demand	Week	Demand
1	22	6	24
2	18	7	20
3	23	8	19
4	21	9	18
5	17	10	21

Use exponential smoothing with $\alpha = 0.2$ to develop a forecast for week 11.

12. United Dairies, Inc., supplies milk to several independent grocers throughout Dade County, Florida. Management wants to develop a forecast of the number of half-gallons of milk sold per week. Sales data (in units) for the past 12 weeks are as follows.

Week	Sales	Week	Sales
1	2750	7	3300
2	3100	8	3100
3	3250	9	2950
4	2800	10	3000
5	2900	11	3200
6	3050	12	3150

Use exponential smoothing, with $\alpha = 0.4$, to develop a forecast of demand for week 13.

13. Ten weeks of data on the Commodity Futures Index are 7.35, 7.40, 7.55, 7.56, 7.60, 7.52, 7.52, 7.70, 7.62, and 7.55.
   a. Compute the exponential smoothing values for $\alpha = 0.2$.
   b. Compute the exponential smoothing values for $\alpha = 0.3$.
   c. Which exponential smoothing model provides the better forecasts? Forecast week 11.

14. The enrollment data (1000s) for a state college for the past 6 years are shown.

Year	1	2	3	4	5	6
Enrollment	20.5	20.2	19.5	19.0	19.1	18.8

Develop the equation for the linear trend component for this time series. Comment on what is happening to enrollment at this institution.

15. Automobile sales at B. J. Scott Motors, Inc., provided the following 10-year time series.

Year	Sales	Year	Sales
1	400	6	260
2	390	7	300
3	320	8	320
4	340	9	340
5	270	10	370

Plot the time series, and comment on the appropriateness of a linear trend. What type of functional form would be best for the trend pattern of this time series?

16. The president of a small manufacturing firm has been concerned about the continual growth in manufacturing costs over the past several years. The following is a time series of the cost per unit (in dollars) for the firm's leading product over the past 8 years.

Year	Cost Per Unit	Year	Cost Per Unit
1	20.00	5	26.60
2	24.50	6	30.00
3	28.20	7	31.00
4	27.50	8	36.00

    a. Graph this time series. Does a linear trend appear?
    b. Develop the equation for the linear trend component for the time series. What is the average cost increase per year?

17. Earnings per share (in dollars) for the Walgreen Company for a 10-year period are 0.84, 0.73, 0.94, 1.14, 1.33, 1.53, 1.67, 1.68, 2.10, and 2.50.
    a. Use a linear trend projection to forecast earnings per share for the coming year.
    b. What does this time series analysis tell you about the Walgreen Company? Do the historical data indicate the Walgreen Company is a good investment? Explain.

18. Gross revenues (in millions of dollars) for Delta Airlines for a 10-year period are shown.

Year	Revenue	Year	Revenue
1	2428	6	4264
2	2951	7	4738
3	3533	8	4460
4	3618	9	5318
5	3616	10	6915

    a. Develop a linear trend equation for this time series. What does it indicate about the gross revenue for Delta Airlines for the 10-year period?
    b. Forecast gross revenues for years 11 and 12.

19. The following data show the time series of the most recent quarterly capital expenditures (in billions of dollars) for the 1000 largest manufacturing firms: 24, 25, 23, 24, 22, 26, 28, 31, 29, 32, 37, and 42.
    a. Develop a linear trend equation for the time series.
    b. Graph the time series and the linear trend equation.
    c. What appears to be happening to capital expenditures? What is the forecast 1 year, or 4 quarters, into the future?

20. The Costello Music Company has been in business for 5 years. During that time, the sale of electric organs has grown from 12 units in the first year to 76 units in the most recent year. Fred Costello, the firm's owner, wants to develop a forecast of organ sales for the coming year based on the historical data shown.

Year	1	2	3	4	5
Sales	12	28	34	50	76

    a. Graph this time series. Does a linear trend appear?
    b. Develop the equation for the linear trend component for the time series. What is the average increase in sales per year for the firm?

21. Hudson Marine has been an authorized dealer for C&D marine radios for the past 7 years. The number of radios sold each year is shown.

Year	1	2	3	4	5	6	7
Number Sold	35	50	75	90	105	110	130

a. Graph this time series. Does a linear trend appear?

b. Develop the equation for the linear trend component for the time series.

c. Use the linear trend developed in part (b) to prepare a forecast for sales in year 8.

22. Aggregate personal income data (in billions of dollars) by month are as follows.

January	3.92	July	4.05
February	3.96	August	4.08
March	4.00	September	4.10
April	4.01	October	4.12
May	4.02	November	4.18
June	4.04	December	4.22

a. Develop a linear trend equation for the time series. What was happening to aggregate personal income during the year?

b. Provide estimates of aggregate personal income for the first 6 months of the coming year.

c. Assume that in June of the coming year the actual level of aggregate personal income turned out to be 4.41. Comment on the forecasting error based on your trend projection.

23. The Garden Avenue Seven sells tapes of its musical performances. The following data show sales for the past 18 months. The group's manager wants an accurate method for forecasting future sales.

Month	Sales	Month	Sales	Month	Sales
1	293	7	381	13	549
2	283	8	431	14	544
3	322	9	424	15	601
4	355	10	433	16	587
5	346	11	470	17	644
6	379	12	481	18	660

a. Use exponential smoothing, with $\alpha = 0.3$, 0.4, and 0.5. Which value of α provides the best forecasts?

b. Use trend projection to provide a forecast. What is the value of MSE?

c. Which method of forecasting would you recommend to the manager? Why?

24. The Mayfair Department Store in Davenport, Iowa, is trying to determine the amount of sales lost while it was shut down because of the summer 1993 floods. Sales data for January–June 1993 are shown.

Month	Sales ($1000s)
January	185.72
February	167.84
March	205.11
April	210.36
May	255.57
June	261.19

a. Use exponential smoothing, with $\alpha = 0.4$, to develop a forecast for July and August. (Hint: Use the forecast for July as the actual sales in July in developing the August forecast.) Comment on the use of exponential smoothing for forecasts more than one period into the future.
b. Use trend projection to forecast sales for July and August.
c. Mayfair's insurance company has proposed a settlement based on lost sales of $240,000 in July and August. Is this amount fair? If not, what amount would you counter with?

SELF TEST

25. The quarterly sales data (number of copies sold) for a college textbook over the past 3 years are as follows.

Quarter	Year 1	Year 2	Year 3
1	1690	1800	1850
2	940	900	1100
3	2625	2900	2930
4	2500	2360	2615

a. Show the 4-quarter moving average values for this time series. Plot both the original time series and the moving averages on the same graph.
b. Compute seasonal indexes for the 4 quarters.
c. When does the textbook publisher experience the largest seasonal index? Does this result appear to be reasonable? Explain.

26. Identify the monthly seasonal indexes for the following 3 years of expenses for a 6-unit apartment house in southern Florida. Use a 12-month moving average calculation.

Month	Year 1	Year 2	Year 3
January	170	180	195
February	180	205	210
March	205	215	230
April	230	245	280
May	240	265	290
June	315	330	390
July	360	400	420
August	290	335	330
September	240	260	290
October	240	270	295
November	230	255	280
December	195	220	250

27. Air pollution control specialists in southern California monitor the amount of ozone, carbon dioxide, and nitrogen dioxide in the air on an hourly basis. The hourly time series data exhibit seasonality, with the levels of pollutants showing similar patterns over the hours in the day. On July 15, 16, and 17, the observed levels of nitrogen dioxide in a city's downtown area for the 12 hours from 6:00 A.M. to 6:00 P.M. were as follows.

July 15	25	28	35	50	60	60	40	35	30	25	25	20
July 16	28	30	35	48	60	65	50	40	35	25	20	20
July 17	35	42	45	70	72	75	60	45	40	25	25	25

  a. Identify the hourly seasonal indexes for the 12-hourly daily readings.
  b. Based on the seasonal indexes in part (a), the trend equation developed for the deseasonalized data is $T_t = 32.983 + 0.3922t$. Use the trend component only to develop forecasts for the 12 hours for July 18.
  c. Use the seasonal indexes from part (a) to adjust the trend forecasts in part (b).

28. Refer to Problem 21. Suppose that the following are the quarterly sales data for the past 7 years.

Year	Quarter 1	Quarter 2	Quarter 3	Quarter 4	Total Sales
1	6	15	10	4	35
2	10	18	15	7	50
3	14	26	23	12	75
4	19	28	25	18	90
5	22	34	28	21	105
6	24	36	30	20	110
7	28	40	35	27	130

  a. Show the 4-quarter moving average values for this time series. Plot both the original time series and the moving averages on the same graph.
  b. Compute the seasonal indexes for the 4 quarters.
  c. When does Hudson Marine experience the largest seasonal effect? Does this result seem reasonable? Explain.

29. Consider the Costello Music Company scenario presented in Problem 20 and the following quarterly sales data.

Year	Quarter 1	Quarter 2	Quarter 3	Quarter 4	Total Yearly Sales
1	4	2	1	5	12
2	6	4	4	14	28
3	10	3	5	16	34
4	12	9	7	22	50
5	18	10	13	35	76

  a. Compute the seasonal indexes for the 4 quarters.
  b. When does Costello Music experience the largest seasonal effect? Does this result appear to be reasonable? Explain.

30. Refer to the Hudson Marine data in Problem 28.
    a. Deseasonalize the data, and use the deseasonalized time series to identify the trend.
    b. Use the results of part (a) to develop a quarterly forecast for next year based on trend.
    c. Use the seasonal indexes developed in Problem 28 to adjust the forecasts developed in part (b) to account for the effect of season.

31. Consider the Costello Music Company time series in Problem 29.
    a. Deseasonalize the data, and use the deseasonalized time series to identify the trend.
    b. Use the results of part (a) to develop a quarterly forecast for next year based on trend.
    c. Use the seasonal indexes developed in Problem 29 to adjust the forecasts developed in part (b) to account for seasonal effects.

32. Electric power consumption is measured in kilowatt-hours (kWh). The local utility company has an interrupt program, whereby commercial customers who participate receive favorable rates but must agree to cut back consumption if the utility requests them to do so. Timko Products cut back consumption at 12:00 noon Thursday. To assess the savings, the utility must estimate Timko's usage without the interrupt. The period of interrupted service was from noon to 8:00 P.M. Data on electric consumption for the past 72 hours is available.

Time Period	Monday	Tuesday	Wednesday	Thursday
12–4 A.M.	—	19,281	31,209	27,330
4–8 A.M.	—	33,195	37,014	32,715
8–12 noon	—	99,516	119,968	152,465
12–4 P.M.	124,299	123,666	156,033	
4–8 P.M.	113,545	111,717	128,889	
8–12 midnight	41,300	48,112	73,923	

    a. Is there a seasonal effect over the 24-hour period? Compute seasonal indexes for the six 4-hour periods.
    b. Use trend adjusted for seasonal factors to estimate Timko's normal usage over the period of interrupted service.

SELF TEST

33. Eddie's Restaurants collected the following data on the relationship between advertising and sales at a sample of five restaurants.

Advertising Expenditures ($1000s)	1.0	4.0	6.0	10.0	14.0
Sales ($1000s)	19.0	44.0	40.0	52.0	53.0

    a. Let x represent advertising expenditures and y represent sales. Use the method of least squares to develop a straight-line approximation of the relationship between the two variables.
    b. Use the equation developed in part (a) to forecast sales for an advertising expenditure of $8000.

34. The management of a chain of fast-food restaurants wants to investigate the relationship between the daily sales volume (in dollars) of a company restaurant and the number of competitor restaurants within a 1-mile radius. The following data have been collected.

Number of Competitors Within 1 Mile	Sales
1	3600
1	3300
2	3100
3	2900
3	2700
4	2500
5	2300
5	2000

a. Develop the least-squares estimated regression equation that relates daily sales volume to the number of competitor restaurants within a 1-mile radius.

b. Use the estimated regression equation developed in part (a) to forecast the daily sales volume for a particular company restaurant that has four competitors within a 1-mile radius.

35. The supervisor of a manufacturing process believed that assembly-line speed (in feet/minute) affected the number of defective parts found during on-line inspection. To test this theory, management had the same batch of parts inspected visually at a variety of line speeds. The following data were collected.

Line Speed	Number of Defective Parts Found
20	21
20	19
40	15
30	16
60	14
40	17

a. Develop the estimated regression equation that relates line speed to the number of defective parts found.

b. Use the equation developed in part (a) to forecast the number of defective parts found for a line speed of 50 feet per minute.

Case Problem   FORECASTING SALES

The Vintage Restaurant is located on Captiva Island, a resort community near Fort Meyers, Florida. The restaurant, which is owned and operated by Karen Payne, has just completed its third year of operation. During this time, Karen has sought to establish a reputation for the restaurant as a high-quality dining establishment that specializes in fresh seafood. The efforts made by Karen and her staff have proved successful, and her restaurant has become one of the best and fastest-growing restaurants on the island.

Karen has concluded that, to plan better for the growth of the restaurant in the future, she needs to develop a system that will enable her to forecast food and beverage sales by month for up to 1 year in advance. Karen has the following data on total food and beverage sales for the 3 years of operation.

Food and Beverage Sales for the Vintage Restaurant ($1000s)			
Month	First Year	Second Year	Third Year
January	242	263	282
February	235	238	255
March	232	247	265
April	178	193	205
May	184	193	210
June	140	149	160
July	145	157	166
August	152	161	174
September	110	122	126
October	130	130	148
November	152	167	173
December	206	230	235

Managerial Report

Perform an analysis of the sales data for the Vintage Restaurant. Prepare a report for Karen that summarizes your findings, forecasts, and recommendations. Include the following:

1. A graph of the time series.
2. An analysis of the seasonality of the data. Indicate the seasonal indexes for each month, and comment on the high seasonal and low seasonal sales months. Do the seasonal indexes make intuitive sense? Discuss.
3. Forecast sales for January through December of the fourth year.
4. Assume that January sales for the fourth year turned out to be $295,000. What was your forecast error? If this is a large error, Karen may be puzzled about the difference between your forecast and the actual sales value. What can you do to resolve her uncertainty in the forecasting procedure?
5. Recommendations as to when the system that you have developed should be updated to account for new sales data that will occur.
6. Include detailed calculations of your analysis in the appendix of your report.

Case Problem   FORECASTING LOST SALES

The Carlson Department Store suffered heavy damage when a hurricane struck on August 31, 1996. The store was closed for four months (September 1996 through December 1996), and Carlson is now involved in a dispute with its insurance company concerning the amount of lost sales during the time the store was closed. Two key issues must be resolved: (1) the amount of sales Carlson would have made if the hurricane had not struck; and (2) whether Carlson is entitled to any compensation for excess sales from increased business activity after the storm. More than $8 billion in federal disaster relief and insurance money came into the county, resulting in increased sales at department stores and numerous other businesses.

Table 6.15 shows the sales data for the 48 months preceding the storm. The U.S. Department of Commerce also has published total sales for the 48 months preceding the storm for all department stores in the county, as well as the total sales in the county for the 4 months the Carlson Department Store was closed. Table 6.16 shows these data. Management has asked you to analyze these data and develop estimates of the lost sales at the Carlson Department Store for the months of September through December 1996. Management also has asked you to determine whether a case can be made for excess storm-related sales during the same period. If such a case can be made, Carlson is entitled to compensation for excess sales it would have earned in addition to ordinary sales.

Table 6.15	SALES FOR CARLSON DEPARTMENT STORE, SEPTEMBER 1992 THROUGH AUGUST 1996				
Month	**1992**	**1993**	**1994**	**1995**	**1996**
Jan.		1.45	2.31	2.31	2.56
Feb.		1.80	1.89	1.99	2.28
Mar.		2.03	2.02	2.42	2.69
Apr.		1.99	2.23	2.45	2.48
May		2.32	2.39	2.57	2.73
June		2.20	2.14	2.42	2.37
July		2.13	2.27	2.40	2.31
Aug.		2.43	2.21	2.50	2.23
Sept.	1.71	1.90	1.89	2.09	
Oct.	1.90	2.13	2.29	2.54	
Nov.	2.74	2.56	2.83	2.97	
Dec.	4.20	4.16	4.04	4.35	

Table 6.16	DEPARTMENT STORE SALES FOR THE COUNTY, SEPTEMBER 1992 THROUGH DECEMBER 1996				
Month	**1992**	**1993**	**1994**	**1995**	**1996**
Jan.		46.8	46.8	43.8	48.0
Feb.		48.0	48.6	45.6	51.6
Mar.		60.0	59.4	57.6	57.6
Apr.		57.6	58.2	53.4	58.2
May		61.8	60.6	56.4	60.0
June		58.2	55.2	52.8	57.0
July		56.4	51.0	54.0	57.6
Aug.		63.0	58.8	60.6	61.8
Sept.	55.8	57.6	49.8	47.4	69.0
Oct.	56.4	53.4	54.6	54.6	75.0
Nov.	71.4	71.4	65.4	67.8	85.2
Dec.	117.6	114.0	102.0	100.2	121.8

Managerial Report

Prepare a report for the management of the Carlson Department store that summarizes your findings, forecasts, and recommendations. Include the following.

1. An estimate of sales had there been no hurricane.

2. An estimate of countywide department store sales had there been no hurricane.

3. Use the countywide actual department stores sales for September through December 1996 and the estimate in part (2) to make a case for or against excess storm-related sales.

4. An estimate of lost sales for the Carlson Department Store for September through December 1996.

Appendix 6.1   SPREADSHEETS FOR FORECASTING

Spreadsheets can be helpful in relieving the computational burden of using the forecasting methods described in this chapter. In this appendix, we show how an Excel spreadsheet can be used to compute moving averages, perform exponential smoothing, and find the least squares line when regression analysis is used for causal forecasting.

Moving Averages

To show how Excel can be used to develop forecasts using the moving averages method, we develop a forecast for the gasoline sales time series in Table 6.1 and Figure 6.5. We assume that the user has entered the sales data for the 12 weeks into worksheet rows 1 through 12 of column A. The following steps can be used to produce a 3-week moving average.

Step 1. Select the **Tools** pull-down menu
Step 2. Select the **Data Analysis** option
Step 3. When the Analysis Tools dialog box appears, choose **Moving Average**
Step 4. When the Moving Average dialog box appears:
  Enter A1:A12 in the **Input Range** box
  Enter 3 in the **Interval** box
  Enter B1 in the **Output Range** box
  Select **OK**

The 3-week moving average forecasts will appear in column B of the worksheet. Forecasts for periods of other length can be computed easily by entering the appropriate value in the Interval box.

Exponential Smoothing

We show how exponential smoothing can be applied to the gasoline sales time series in Table 6.1. We also show how an Exel spreadsheet can be used to choose a good value for the smoothing constant α.

Figure 6.17 shows the formula spreadsheet for exponential smoothing. Headings are highlighted; problem specific data and the value of α are shown in color. The gasoline sales data of Table 6.4, with $\alpha = 0.2$ is being used. To try a different value of α you must replace the value in cell B1. To solve a problem for a different time series, you must change the entries in cells A5:A16 and B5:B16. If the number of time periods is different, you must add

Figure 6.17 FORMULA SPREADSHEET FOR EXPONENTIAL SMOOTHING

	A	B	C	D	E
1	ALPHA =	0.2			
2					
3		ACTUAL			ERROR
4	PERIOD	DATA	FORECAST	ERROR	SQUARED
5	1	17	=$B$5		
6	2	21	=$B$1*B5+(1-$B$1)*C5	=B6-C6	=D6*D6
7	3	19	=$B$1*B6+(1-$B$1)*C6	=B7-C7	=D7*D7
8	4	23	=$B$1*B7+(1-$B$1)*C7	=B8-C8	=D8*D8
9	5	18	=$B$1*B8+(1-$B$1)*C8	=B9-C9	=D9*D9
10	6	16	=$B$1*B9+(1-$B$1)*C9	=B10-C10	=D10*D10
11	7	20	=$B$1*B10+(1-$B$1)*C10	=B11-C11	=D11*D11
12	8	18	=$B$1*B11+(1-$B$1)*C11	=B12-C12	=D12*D12
13	9	22	=$B$1*B12+(1-$B$1)*C12	=B13-C13	=D13*D13
14	10	20	=$B$1*B13+(1-$B$1)*C13	=B14-C14	=D14*D14
15	11	15	=$B$1*B14+(1-$B$1)*C14	=B15-C15	=D15*D15
16	12	22	=$B$1*B15+(1-$B$1)*C15	=B16-C16	=D16*D16
17					
18				MSE=	=AVERAGE(E6:E16)

or delete rows as appropriate. The formulas for using exponential smoothing to prepare a forecast are in cells **C5** to **C16**. Absolute references use the $ format; relative references do not.

Note in cell **C5** that the forecast value in period 1 is simply the actual data value for that period, **$B$5**. The formulas for computing the forecast error are in cells **D6:D16**, and they are squared in cells **E6:E16**. A forecast error is not computed for the first period because we set the forecast equal to the data value to start the method. Finally, the formula for computing the mean square error is in cell **E18**.

The result of using this spreadsheet for the gasoline sales data is shown in the value spreadsheet in Figure 6.18. Note that, allowing for rounding, it provides the same information as that in Table 6.4. Changing the value in cell **B1** allows you to experiment with different values for the smoothing constant.

Figure 6.19 shows how to extend the exponential smoothing spreadsheet to choose a good value for the smoothing constant. We use the data table capability of Excel. To set up the spreadsheet, we place the values of α we are interested in trying in cells **A20** to **A30**; they are evenly spaced over the interval from 0 to 1. The formula for computing the mean square errors is placed in cell **B19**. The boxed in area of Figure 6.19 shows where the mean square error for each value of the smoothing constant will be placed after invoking the data table commands. To generate these values, we first select the cells that represent the data table, **A19:B30**. We then choose **Table** from the **DATA** menu, specify cell **B1** as the **Column Input cell** and then choose **OK.** As shown in Figure 6.20, the system will then generate the mean square error in cells **B20** through **B30** for each value of α. We note that the smallest value of MSE is given with a value of $\alpha = .2$; MSE = 8.9822.

Figure 6.18 — VALUE SPREADSHEET FOR EXPONENTIAL SMOOTHING

	A	B	C	D	E
1	ALPHA =	0.2			
2					
3		ACTUAL			ERROR
4	PERIOD	DATA	FORECAST	ERROR	SQUARED
5	1	17	17.0000		
6	2	21	17.0000	4.0000	16.0000
7	3	19	17.8000	1.2000	1.4400
8	4	23	18.0400	4.9600	24.6016
9	5	18	19.0320	-1.0320	1.0650
10	6	16	18.8256	-2.8256	7.9840
11	7	20	18.2605	1.7395	3.0259
12	8	18	18.6084	-0.6084	0.3701
13	9	22	18.4867	3.5133	12.3432
14	10	20	19.1894	0.8106	0.6571
15	11	15	19.3515	-4.3515	18.9355
16	12	22	18.4812	3.5188	12.3820
17					
18				MSE=	8.9822

Figure 6.19 — DATA TABLE SETUP FOR CHOOSING EXPONENTIAL SMOOTHING CONSTANT

	A	B
18		
19		=AVERAGE(E6:E16)
20	0	
21	0.1	
22	0.2	
23	0.3	
24	0.4	
25	0.5	
26	0.6	
27	0.7	
28	0.8	
29	0.9	
30	1	

Figure 6.20	DATA TABLE OUTPUT FOR CHOOSING EXPONENTIAL SMOOTHING CONSTANT

	A	B
19		8.9822
20	0.0	11.9091
21	0.1	9.2528
22	0.2	8.9822
23	0.3	9.3509
24	0.4	9.9571
25	0.5	10.6985
26	0.6	11.5512
27	0.7	12.5178
28	0.8	13.6127
29	0.9	14.8568
30	1.0	16.2727

Regression Analysis

We illustrate the use of spreadsheets for regression analysis with the Armand's Pizza problem (the data are from Table 6.13). In the spreadsheet (see Figure 6.21), the data for the independent variable is placed in cells **B5:B14**. The data for the dependent variable are placed in cells **C5:C14**. After the data have been entered, the following steps will perform the regression analysis.

Step 1. Select the **Tools** pull-down menu
Step 2. Select **Data Analysis** option
Step 3. When the Analysis Tools dialog box appears, choose **Regression**
Step 4. When the **Regression** dialog box appears:
Enter C5:C14 in the **Input Y Range** box
Enter B5:B14 in the **Input X Range** box
Select **Output Range** and type A20 in the box
Select **OK**

The regression output is shown in rows 20–37 of Figure 6.21. The constant is the value found in cell **B36**; thus $b_0 = 60$. The coefficient of the independent variable, x, is the value in cell **B37** thus $b_1 = 5$. This provides an estimated regression equation of $y = 60 + 5x$.

The regression procedure just described can also be used to find a trend equation. Just let the period numbers be the values for the input variable.

Figure 6.21   SPREADSHEET FOR REGRESSION ANALYSIS

	A	B	C	D	E	F
1	FORECASTING WITH REGRESSION ANALYSIS					
2						
3		STUDENT	ANNUAL			
4	RESTAURANT	POPULATION	SALES			
5	1	2	58			
6	2	6	105			
7	3	8	88			
8	4	8	118			
9	5	12	117			
10	6	16	137			
11	7	20	157			
12	8	20	169			
13	9	22	149			
14	10	26	202			
15						
16						
17						
18						
19						
20	SUMMARY OUTPUT					
21						
22	*Regression Statistics*					
23	Multiple R	0.950122955				
24	R Square	0.90273363				
25	Adjusted R Square	0.89057334				
26	Standard Error	13.82931669				
27	Observations	10				
28						
29	ANOVA					
30		*df*	*SS*	*MS*	*F*	*Significance F*
31	Regression	1	14200	14200	74.24837	2.54887E-05
32	Residual	8	1530	191.25		
33	Total	9	15730			
34						
35		*Coefficients*	*Standard Error*	*t Stat*	*P-value*	
36	Intercept	60	9.22603481	6.50333553	0.000187	
37	X Variable 1	5	0.580265238	8.61674916	2.55E-05	

THE CINCINNATI GAS & ELECTRIC COMPANY*

CINCINNATI, OHIO

The Cincinnati Gas Light and Coke Company was chartered by the state of Ohio on April 3, 1837. Under this charter, the company manufactured gas by distillation of coal and sold it for lighting purposes. During the last quarter of the 19th century, the company successfully marketed gas for lighting, heating, and cooking and as fuel for gas engines.

In 1901 the Cincinnati Gas Light and Coke Company and the Cincinnati Electric Light Company merged to form The Cincinnati Gas & Electric Company (CG&E). This new company was able to shift from manufactured gas to natural gas and adopt the rapidly emerging technologies in generating and distributing electricity. CG&E operated as a subsidiary of the Columbia Gas Electric Company from 1909 until 1944.

In 1994, CG&E merged with Public Service of Indiana to form Cinergy Corporation. Today, CG&E is a subsidiary of Cinergy serving approximately 440,000 gas customers and 720,000 electric customers. The company's service area covers approximately 3000 square miles in and around the Greater Cincinnati area.

Forecasting at CG&E

As in any modern company, forecasting at CG&E is an integral part of operating and managing the business. Depending on the decision to be made, the forecasting techniques used range from judgment and graphical trend projections to sophisticated multiple regression models.

Forecasting in the utility industry offers some unique perspectives. Since there are no finished-goods or in-process inventories of electricity, this product must

be generated to meet the instantaneous requirements of the customers. Electrical shortages are not just lost sales, but "brownouts" or "blackouts." This situation places an unusual burden on the utility forecaster. On the positive side, the demand for energy and the sale of energy are more predictable than for many other products. Also, unlike the situation in a multiproduct firm, a great amount of forecasting effort and expertise can be concentrated on the two products: gas and electricity.

Forecasting Electric Energy and Peak Loads

The two types of forecasts discussed in this section are the long-range forecasts of electric peak load and electric energy. The largest observed electric demand for any given period, such as an hour, a day, a month, or a year, is defined as the peak load. The cumulative amount of energy generated and used over the period of an hour is referred to as electric energy.

Until the mid-1970s the seasonal patterns of both electric energy and electric peak load were very regular; the time series for both of these exhibited a fairly steady exponential growth. Business cycles had little noticeable effect on either. Perhaps the most serious shift in the behavior of these time series came from the increasing installation of air conditioning units in the Greater Cincinnati area, which caused an accelerated growth in the trend component and also in the relative magnitude of the summer peaks. Nevertheless, the two time series were very regular and generally quite predictable.

Trend projection was the most popular method used to forecast electric energy and electric peak load. The forecast accuracy was quite acceptable and even enviable

*The authors are indebted to Dr. Richard Evans, The Cincinnati Gas & Electric Company, Cincinnati, Ohio, for providing this application.

when compared to forecast errors experienced in other industries.

A New Era in Forecasting

In the mid-1970s a variety of actions by the government, the off-and-on energy shortages, and price signals to the consumer began to affect the consumption of electric energy. The behavior of the peak load and electric energy time series became less predictable, and a simple trend projection forecasting model was no longer adequate. As a result, a special forecasting model—referred to as an econometric model—was developed by CG&E to better account for the behavior of these time series.

The purpose of the econometric model is to forecast the annual energy consumption by residential, commercial, and industrial classes of service. These forecasts are then used to develop forecasts of summer and winter peak loads. First, energy consumption in the industrial and commercial classes is forecast. For an assumed level of economic activity, the projection of electric energy is made along with a forecast of employment in the area. The employment forecast is converted to a forecast of adult population through the use of unemployment rates and labor force participation rates. Household forecasts are then developed through the use of demographic statistics on the average number of persons per household. The resulting forecast of households is used as an indicator of residential customers.

At this point, a comparison is made with the demographic projections for the area population. The differences between the residential customers forecast and the population forecast are reconciled to produce the final forecast of residential customers. This forecast becomes the principal independent variable in forecasting residential electric energy.

Summer and winter peak loads are then forecast by applying class peak contribution factors to the energy forecasts. The contributions that each class makes toward the peak are summed to establish the peak forecast.

A number of economic and demographic time series are used in the construction of the above econometric model. Simply speaking, the entire forecasting system is a compilation of several statistically verified multiple regression equations.

Impact and Value of the Forecasts

The forecast of the annual electric peak load guides the timing decisions for constructing future generating units, and the financial impact of these decisions is great. For example, a large generating unit built by the company cost nearly $600 million, and the interest rate on a recent first mortgage bond was 16%. At this rate, annual interest costs would be nearly $100 million. Obviously, a timing decision that leads to having the unit available no sooner than necessary is crucial.

The energy forecasts are important in other ways also. For example, purchases of coal as fuel for the generating units are based on the forecast levels of energy needed. The revenue from the electric operations of the company is determined from forecasted sales, which in turn enters into the planning of rate changes and external financing. These planning and decision-making processes are among the most important management activities in the company. It is imperative that the decision makers have the best forecast information available to assist them in arriving at these decisions.

Questions

1. Describe some of the unique perspectives associated with forecasting in the utility industry as compared with other industries.
2. What type of forecasting procedure was used by CG&E into the mid-1970s? What necessitated a change?
3. Briefly describe CG&E's current approach to forecasting.
4. What are the benefits of accurate forecasts for CG&E?

7

LINEAR PROGRAMMING:
THE GRAPHICAL METHOD

Linear programming is a problem-solving approach that has been developed to help managers make decisions. The following are some typical applications of linear programming.

1. A manufacturer wants to develop a production schedule and an inventory policy that will satisfy sales demand in future periods. Ideally the schedule and policy will enable the company to satisfy demand and at the same time *minimize* the total production and inventory costs.
2. A financial analyst must select an investment portfolio from a variety of stock and bond investment alternatives. The analyst would like to establish the portfolio that *maximizes* the return on investment.
3. A marketing manager wants to determine how best to allocate a fixed advertising budget among alternative advertising media such as radio, television, newspaper, and magazines. The manager would like to determine the media mix that *maximizes* advertising effectiveness.
4. A company has warehouses in a number of locations throughout the United States. For a set of customer demands for its products, the company would like to determine how much each warehouse should ship to each customer so that the total transportation costs are *minimized*.

These are only a few examples of situations in which linear programming has been used successfully, but the examples illustrate the diversity of linear programming applications. A close scrutiny reveals one basic property that all of these examples have in common. In each example we were concerned with *maximizing* or *minimizing* some quantity. In example 1 the manufacturer wanted to minimize costs; in example 2 the financial analyst wanted to maximize return on investment; in example 3 the marketing manager wanted to maximize advertising effectiveness; and in example 4 the company wanted to minimize total transportation costs. *In all linear programming problems, the maximization or minimization of some quantity is the objective.*

All linear programming problems also have a second property: restrictions or **constraints** that limit the degree to which the objective can be pursued. In example 1 the manufacturer is restricted by constraints requiring product demand to be satisfied and by the constraints limiting production capacity. The financial analyst's portfolio problem is constrained by the total amount of investment funds available and the maximum amounts that can be invested in each stock or bond. The marketing manager's media selection decision is constrained by a fixed advertising budget and the availability of the various media. In the transportation problem, the minimum cost shipping schedule is constrained by the supply of product available at each warehouse. *Thus constraints are another general feature of every linear programming problem.*

7.1 A SIMPLE MAXIMIZATION PROBLEM

RMC, Inc., is a small firm that produces a variety of chemical-based products. In a particular production process, three raw materials are used to produce two products: a fuel additive and a solvent base. The fuel additive is sold to oil companies and is used in the production of gasoline and related fuels. The solvent base is sold to a variety of chemical firms and is used in both home and industrial cleaning products. The three raw materials are blended to form the fuel additive and solvent base as indicated in Table 7.1. It shows that a ton of fuel additive is a mixture of $2/5$ ton of material 1 and $3/5$ ton of material 3. A ton of solvent base is a mixture of $1/2$ ton of material 1, $1/5$ ton of material 2, and $3/10$ ton of material 3.

RMC's production is constrained by a limited availability of the three raw materials. For the current production period, RMC has available the following quantities of each raw material.

Material	Amount Available for Production
Material 1	20 tons
Material 2	5 tons
Material 3	21 tons

Table 7.1	MATERIAL REQUIREMENTS PER TON FOR THE RMC PROBLEM		
Product	**Material 1**	**Material 2**	**Material 3**
Fuel additive	2/5	0	3/5
Solvent base	1/2	1/5	3/10

1/2 ton of material 1 is used in each ton of solvent base.

Because of spoilage and the nature of the production process, any materials not used for current production are useless and must be discarded.

It is important to understand that we are maximizing profit contribution, not profit. Overhead and other shared costs must be deducted before arriving at a profit figure.

The accounting department has analyzed the production figures, assigned all relevant costs, and arrived at prices for both products that will result in a profit contribution[1] of $40 for every ton of fuel additive produced and $30 for every ton of solvent base produced. RMC's management, after an analysis of potential demand, has concluded that the prices established will ensure the sale of all the fuel additive and solvent base produced.

RMC's problem is to determine how many tons of each product should be produced in order to maximize total profit contribution. If you were in charge of production scheduling for RMC, Inc., what decision would you make? That is, how many tons of fuel additive and how many tons of solvent base would you produce for the current production period? Write your decision below. Later you can check and see how well you did.

Number of Tons of Fuel Additive	Number of Tons of Solvent Base	Total Profit Contribution

7.2 THE OBJECTIVE FUNCTION

As pointed out earlier, every linear programming problem has a maximization or minimization objective. For the RMC problem the objective is to maximize total profit contribution. We can write this objective in mathematical form with the introduction of some simple notation. Let

When formulating problems, it is especially important to correctly define the unit of measurement. For instance, in this problem, the variables are defined in tons, not pounds.

x_1 = the number of tons of fuel additive that RMC produces

x_2 = the number of tons of solvent base that RMC produces

RMC's profit contribution will come from two sources: (1) the profit contribution made by producing x_1 tons of fuel additive; and (2) the profit contribution made by producing x_2 tons of solvent base. Since RMC makes $40 for every ton of fuel additive produced, the company will make $40x_1$ if x_1 tons of fuel additive are produced. Also, since RMC makes $30 for every ton of solvent base produced, the company will make $30x_2$ if x_2 tons of solvent base are produced. Denoting the total profit contribution by z, and deleting the dollar sign, we have

$$\text{Total profit contribution} = z = 40x_1 + 30x_2 \qquad (7.1)$$

The optimal solution to RMC's problem is the production combination that will maximize total profit contribution. That is, RMC must determine the values of the variables x_1 and x_2

---

1. From an accounting perspective, profit contribution is more correctly described as the contribution margin per ton; overhead and other shared costs have not been allocated.

that will yield the highest possible value of z. In linear programming terminology, we refer to x_1 and x_2 as the *decision variables*. Since the objective—maximize total profit contribution—is a *function* of these decision variables, we refer to $40x_1 + 30x_2$ as the **objective function.** Using "Max" as an abbreviation for maximize, we write the objective as follows:

$$\text{Max } z = \text{Max } 40x_1 + 30x_2 \tag{7.2}$$

In the RMC problem, any particular production combination of fuel additive and solvent base is referred to as a **solution** to the problem. However, only those solutions that satisfy *all* the constraints are referred to as **feasible solutions.** The particular feasible production combination or feasible solution that results in the largest profit contribution is referred to as the *optimal* production combination or, equivalently, the **optimal solution.** At this point, however, we have no idea what the optimal solution will be. In fact, we have not even developed a procedure for identifying feasible solutions. The procedure for determining the feasible solutions requires us first to identify all the constraints of the problem.

7.3   THE CONSTRAINTS

With limited amounts of three raw materials available, we have three conditions that restrict the amount of fuel additive and solvent base RMC can produce. From the production information (see Table 7.1), we know that every ton of fuel additive will use ⅖ ton of material 1. Thus the total number of tons of material 1 used in the production of x_1 tons of fuel additive will be $\frac{2}{5}x_1$. In addition, every ton of solvent base will use ½ ton of material 1. As a result, x_2 tons of solvent base will use $\frac{1}{2}x_2$ tons of material 1. The total number of tons of material 1 required to produce x_1 tons of fuel additive and x_2 tons of solvent base is given by

$$\text{Total tons of material 1 required} = \tfrac{2}{5}x_1 + \tfrac{1}{2}x_2$$

The units of measurement on the left-hand side of the constraint must match the units of measurement on the right-hand side.

Because RMC has a maximum of 20 tons of material 1 available, the production combination we select must satisfy the requirement

$$\tfrac{2}{5}x_1 + \tfrac{1}{2}x_2 \leq 20 \tag{7.3}$$

Relationship (7.3) is referred to as an *inequality*. It states that the total number of tons of material 1 used in the production of x_1 tons of fuel additive and x_2 tons of solvent base must be less than or equal to the amount of material 1 that RMC has available.

Table 7.1 indicates that, although the fuel additive does not require material 2, every ton of solvent base produced requires ⅕ ton of material 2. Since there are 5 tons of material 2 available,

$$0x_1 + \tfrac{1}{5}x_2 \leq 5$$

or, simply,

$$\tfrac{1}{5}x_2 \leq 5 \tag{7.4}$$

Inequality (7.4) is the material 2 constraint for RMC. Verify for yourself that the material 3 constraint is

$$\tfrac{3}{5}x_1 + \tfrac{3}{10}x_2 \leq 21 \tag{7.5}$$

We now have specified the mathematical relationships for the constraints associated with the three materials. Have we forgotten any other constraints? Can RMC produce a negative number of tons of fuel additive or solvent base? Clearly, the answer is no. Thus, to prevent the decision variables from having negative values, two constraints,

$$x_1 \geq 0 \qquad \text{and} \qquad x_2 \geq 0 \tag{7.6}$$

must be added. These constraints ensure that the solution to the problem will contain non-negative values for the decision variables and are thus referred to as the **nonnegativity constraints.** Nonnegativity constraints are a general feature of all linear programming problems and may be written in the abbreviated form

$$x_1, x_2 \geq 0$$

..../ /............

7·4   THE MATHEMATICAL STATEMENT OF THE RMC PROBLEM

The mathematical statement, or mathematical formulation, of the RMC problem is now complete. We have translated the objective and constraints of the real-world problem into a set of mathematical relationships referred to as a **mathematical model.** The complete mathematical model for the RMC problem is

Max $\qquad 40x_1 + 30x_2$

subject to (s.t.)

$$\tfrac{2}{5}x_1 + \tfrac{1}{2}x_2 \leq 20 \quad \text{Material 1}$$
$$\tfrac{1}{5}x_2 \leq 5 \quad \text{Material 2}$$
$$\tfrac{3}{5}x_1 + \tfrac{3}{10}x_2 \leq 21 \quad \text{Material 3}$$
$$x_1, x_2 \geq 0$$

In the RMC problem the units of measurement in each constraint represented the number of tons of raw material used and available. If the decision variables had been defined in terms of pounds of fuel additive and solvent base, then the constraint right-hand sides would have had to be 40,000, 10,000, and 42,000, respectively.

Our job now is to find the product mix (i.e., the combination of x_1 and x_2) that satisfies all the constraints and, at the same time, yields a value for the objective function that is greater than or equal to the value given by any other feasible solution. In doing so, we will find the optimal solution to the problem.

This mathematical model of the RMC problem is a **linear program.** The problem has the objective function and constraints that we said earlier were common properties of all linear programs. But what is the special feature of this mathematical model that makes it a *linear* program? It is that the objective function and all **constraint functions** (the left-hand sides of the constraint inequalities) are linear functions of the decision variables.

Mathematical functions in which each variable appears in a separate term and is raised to the first power are called **linear functions.** The objective function $40x_1 + 30x_2$ is linear because each decision variable appears in a separate term and has an exponent of 1. If the objective function had appeared as $40x_1^2 + 30\sqrt{x_2}$, it would not have been a linear function, and we would not have had a linear program. The number of tons of material 1 required, $\tfrac{2}{5}x_1 + \tfrac{1}{2}x_2$, also is a linear function of the decision variables for the same reasons. Similarly, the functions on the left-hand side of all the constraint inequalities (the constraint functions) are linear functions. Thus the mathematical formulation of the RMC problem is referred to as a linear program.

Linear *programming* has nothing to do with computer programming. The use of the word *programming* here means "choosing a course of action." Linear programming involves choosing a course of action when the mathematical model of the problem contains only linear functions.

You should now be able to recognize the types of mathematical relationships that can be found in a linear program. Try Problem 1.

N O T E S and Comments

1. The three assumptions necessary for a linear programming model to be appropriate are proportionality, additivity, and divisibility. *Proportionality* means that the contribution to the objective function and the amount of resources used are proportional to the value of each decision variable. *Additivity* means that the value of the objective function and the total resources used can be found by summing the objective function contribution and the resources used for all decision variables. *Divisibility* means that the decision variables are continuous. The divisibility assumption plus the nonnegativity constraints means that decision variables can take on any value greater than or equal to zero.

2. Quantitative analysts formulate and solve a variety of mathematical models that contain an objective function and a set of constraints. Models of this type are referred to as *mathematical programming models*. Linear programming models are a special type of mathematical programming model in that the objective function and all constraint functions are linear.

7.5   GRAPHICAL SOLUTION

A linear programming problem involving only two decision variables can be solved graphically. We begin the graphical solution procedure by developing a graph that displays the possible solutions (x_1 and x_2 values) for the RMC problem. The graph (Figure 7.1) will have values of x_1 on the horizontal axis and values of x_2 on the vertical axis. Any point on the graph can be identified by the x_1 and x_2 values, which indicate the position of the point along the x_1 and x_2 axes, respectively. Every point (x_1, x_2) corresponds to a possible solution, so every point on the graph is called a *solution*. The solution where $x_1 = 0$ and $x_2 = 0$ is referred to as the *origin*.

The next step is to show which of the solutions correspond to feasible solutions for the linear program. Both x_1 and x_2 must be nonnegative, so we need only consider that portion of the graph where $x_1 \geq 0$ and $x_2 \geq 0$. In Figure 7.2 the arrows point to the portion of the solution region where these nonnegativity requirements are satisfied.

Earlier we determined that the inequality representing the material 1 constraint was

$$\tfrac{2}{5}x_1 + \tfrac{1}{2}x_2 \leq 20$$

To show all solution points that satisfy this relationship, we start by graphing the line corresponding to the equation

$$\tfrac{2}{5}x_1 + \tfrac{1}{2}x_2 = 20$$

We graph this equation by identifying two points and then drawing a line through the points. Setting $x_1 = 0$ and solving for x_2 gives $\tfrac{1}{2}x_2 = 20$ or $x_2 = 40$; hence the point ($x_1 = 0$,

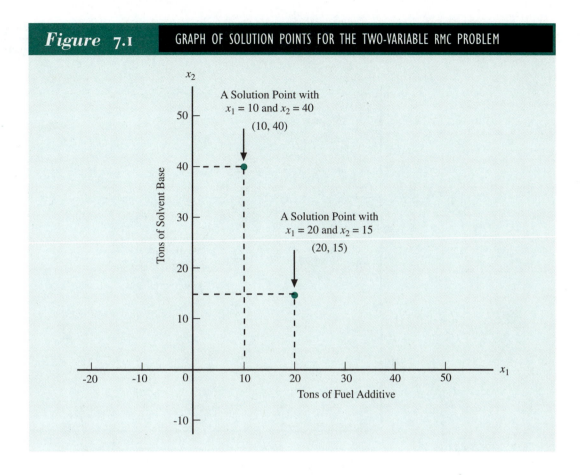

Figure 7.1 GRAPH OF SOLUTION POINTS FOR THE TWO-VARIABLE RMC PROBLEM

$x_2 = 40$) satisfies the preceding equation. To find a second point satisfying this equation, we set $x_2 = 0$ and solve for x_1. Doing so, we obtain $\frac{2}{5}x_1 = 20$, or $x_1 = 50$. Thus a second point satisfying the equation is ($x_1 = 50$, $x_2 = 0$). With these two points, we can now graph the line. This line, called the *material 1 constraint line,* is shown in Figure 7.3.

Recall that the inequality representing the material 1 constraint is

$$\tfrac{2}{5}x_1 + \tfrac{1}{2}x_2 \leq 20$$

Can you identify all the solutions that satisfy this constraint? First, note that any point on the line $\frac{2}{5}x_1 + \frac{1}{2}x_2 = 20$ must satisfy the constraint. But where are the solutions satisfying $\frac{2}{5}x_1 + \frac{1}{2}x_2 < 20$? Consider two solution points ($x_1 = 10$, $x_2 = 10$) and ($x_1 = 40$, $x_2 = 30$). Figure 7.3 shows that the first solution is below the constraint line and the second is above the constraint line. Which of these solutions satisfies the material 1 constraint? For the point ($x_1 = 10$, $x_2 = 10$) we have

$$\tfrac{2}{5}x_1 + \tfrac{1}{2}x_2 = \tfrac{2}{5}(10) + \tfrac{1}{2}(10) = 9$$

Since 9 tons is less than the 20 tons of material 1 available, the $x_1 = 10$, $x_2 = 10$ production combination, or solution, satisfies the constraint. For $x_1 = 40$ and $x_2 = 30$ we have

$$\tfrac{2}{5}x_1 + \tfrac{1}{2}x_2 = \tfrac{2}{5}(40) + \tfrac{1}{2}(30) = 31$$

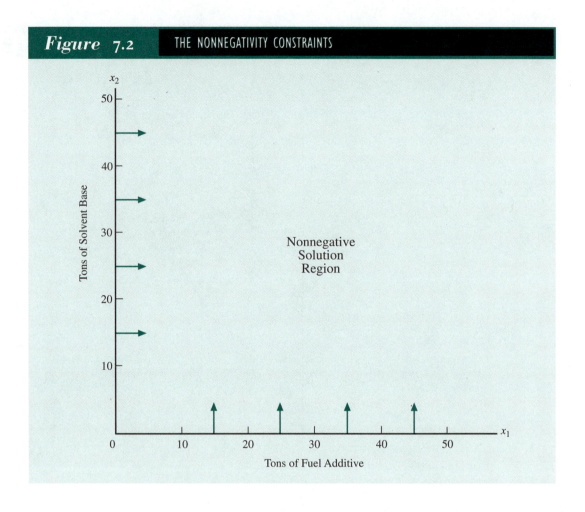

Figure 7.2   THE NONNEGATIVITY CONSTRAINTS

The 31 tons is greater than the 20 tons available, so the $x_1 = 40$, $x_2 = 30$ solution does not satisfy the constraint and thus is not feasible.

You should now be able to graph a constraint line and find the solution points that are feasible. Try Problem 2.

If a particular solution isn't feasible, all other solutions on the same side of the constraint line are not feasible. If a particular solution is feasible, all other solutions on the same side of the constraint line are feasible. Thus, you need to evaluate only one solution point to determine which side of a constraint line provides feasible solutions. In Figure 7.4 we show all the points that satisfy the material 1 constraint by shading the feasible area.

Next let us identify all solution points that satisfy the material 2 constraint:

$$\tfrac{1}{5}x_2 \le 5$$

We start by drawing the constraint line corresponding to the equation $\frac{1}{5}x_2 = 5$. Since this equation is equivalent to the equation $x_2 = 25$, we simply draw a line whose x_2 value is 25 for every value of x_1; this line is parallel to and 25 units above the horizontal axis. In Figure 7.5 we have drawn the line corresponding to the material 2 constraint. Following the approach we used for the material 1 constraint, we realize that only points on or below the line will satisfy the material 2 constraint. Thus, in Figure 7.5 the shaded region corresponds to all feasible production combinations or feasible solutions for the material 2 constraint.

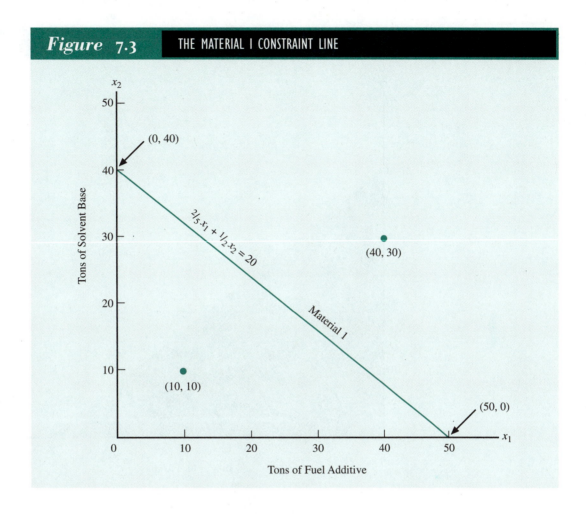

Figure 7.3 THE MATERIAL I CONSTRAINT LINE

Similarly, we can determine the set of all feasible solutions for the material 3 constraint. Figure 7.6 shows the result. For practice, try to graph the feasible region for the material 3 constraint and determine whether your result agrees with that shown in Figure 7.6.

We now have three separate graphs showing the feasible solutions for each of the three constraints. In a linear programming problem, we need to identify the solutions that satisfy *all* the constraints *simultaneously*. To find these solutions we can draw the three constraints on one graph and observe the region containing the points that do in fact satisfy all the constraints simultaneously.

You should now be able to find the feasible region given several constraints. Try Problem 7.

The graphs in Figures 7.4–7.6 can be superimposed to obtain one graph with all three constraints. Figure 7.7 shows this combined constraint graph. The shaded region in this figure includes every solution point that satisfies all the constraints simultaneously. Since solutions that satisfy all the constraints simultaneously are termed *feasible solutions,* the shaded region is called the *feasible solution region,* or simply the **feasible region.** Any point on the boundary of the feasible region, or within the feasible region, is a *feasible solution point.*

Now that we have identified the feasible region, we are ready to proceed with the graphical solution method and find the optimal solution to the RMC problem. Recall that the optimal solution for a linear programming problem is the feasible solution that provides

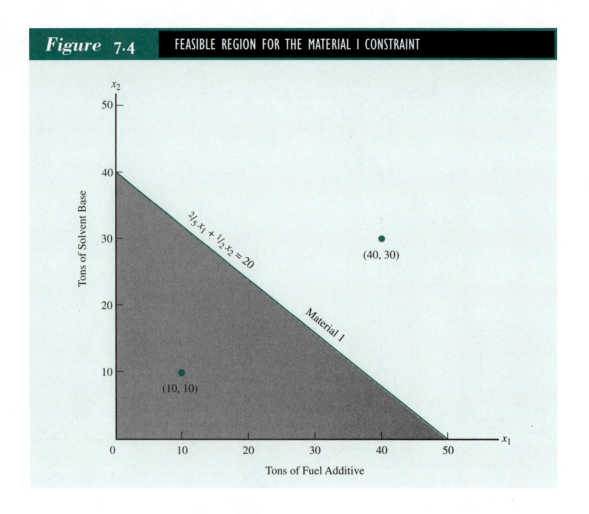

Figure 7.4   FEASIBLE REGION FOR THE MATERIAL 1 CONSTRAINT

the best possible value of the objective function. Let us start the optimizing step of the graphical solution procedure by redrawing the feasible region on a separate graph. Figure 7.8 shows the graph.

One approach to finding the optimal solution would be to evaluate the objective function for each feasible solution; the optimal solution would then be the one yielding the largest value. The difficulty with this approach is that there are too many feasible solutions (actually infinitely many); thus, evaluating all feasible solutions would not be possible. Hence, this trial-and-error procedure cannot be used to identify the optimal solution.

Rather than trying to compute the profit contribution for each feasible solution, we select an arbitrary value for profit contribution and identify all the feasible solutions (x_1, x_2) that yield the selected value. For example, what feasible solutions provide a profit contribution of $240? These solutions are given by the values of x_1 and x_2 in the feasible region that will make the objective function

$$40x_1 + 30x_2 = 240$$

This expression is simply the equation of a line. Thus all feasible solutions (x_1, x_2) yielding a profit contribution of $240 must be on the line. We learned earlier in this section how to graph a constraint line. The procedure for graphing the profit or objective function line is

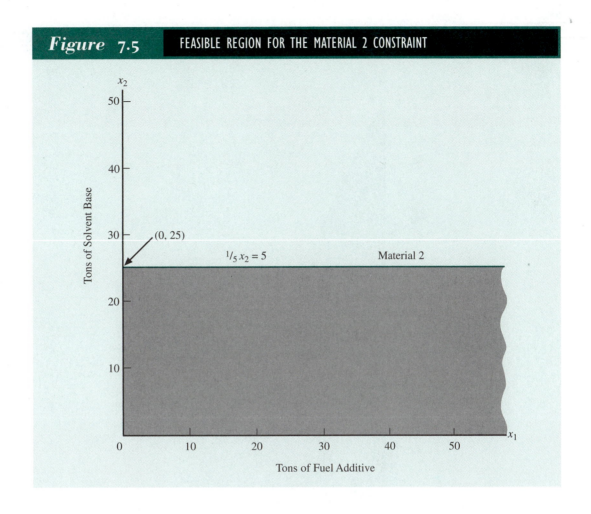

Figure 7.5   FEASIBLE REGION FOR THE MATERIAL 2 CONSTRAINT

the same. Letting $x_1 = 0$, we see that x_2 must be 8; thus the solution point ($x_1 = 0, x_2 = 8$) is on the line. Similarly, by letting $x_2 = 0$ we see that the solution point ($x_1 = 6, x_2 = 0$) is also on the line. Drawing the line through these two points identifies all the solutions that have a profit contribution of $240. A graph of this profit line is presented in Figure 7.9. It shows that an infinite number of feasible production combinations will provide a $240 profit contribution.

The objective is to find the feasible solution yielding the highest profit contribution, so we proceed by selecting higher profit contributions and finding the solutions that yield the stated values. For example, what solutions provide a profit contribution of $720? What solutions provide a profit contribution of $1200? To answer these questions we must find the x_1 and x_2 values that are on the profit lines

$$40x_1 + 30x_2 = 720 \quad \text{and} \quad 40x_1 + 30x_2 = 1200$$

Using the previous procedure for graphing profit and constraint lines, we graphed the $720 and $1200 profit lines presented in Figure 7.10. Not all solution points on the $1200 profit line are in the feasible region, but at least some points on the line are; thus, we can obtain a feasible solution that provides a $1200 profit contribution.

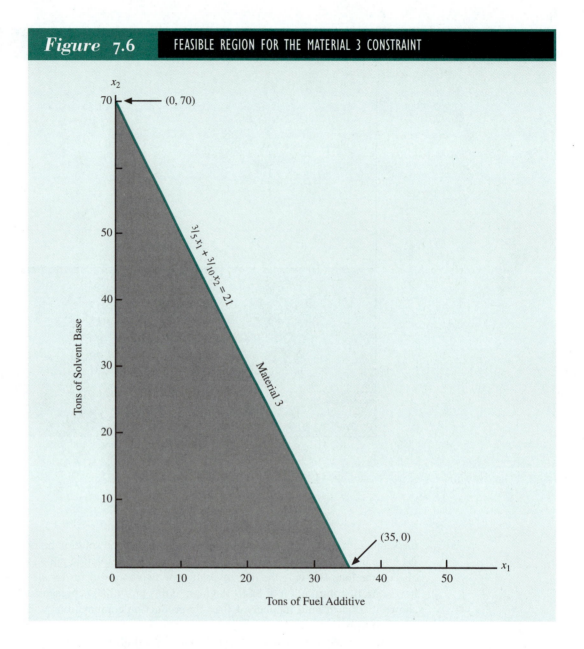

Figure 7.6   FEASIBLE REGION FOR THE MATERIAL 3 CONSTRAINT

Can we find a feasible solution yielding an even higher profit contribution? Look at Figure 7.10 and make some general observations about the profit lines. You should be able to identify the following properties: (1) the profit lines are *parallel* to each other; and (2) profit lines with higher profit contributions are farther from the origin. Algebraically, with z representing total profit contribution, the objective function is

$$z = 40x_1 + 30x_2$$

Solving for x_2 in terms of x_1 and z, we obtain

$$30x_2 = -40x_1 + z$$
$$x_2 = -\frac{40}{30}x_1 + \frac{1}{30}z$$

(7.7)

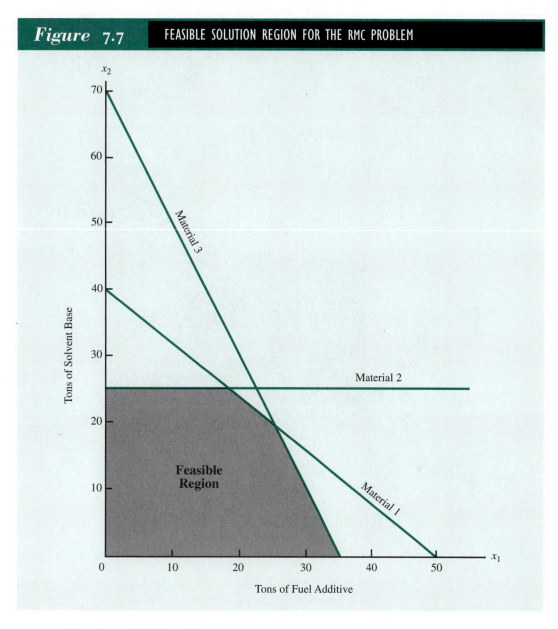

Figure 7.7   FEASIBLE SOLUTION REGION FOR THE RMC PROBLEM

Equation (7.7) is the *slope-intercept form* of the linear equation relating x_1 and x_2. The coefficient of x_1, $-40/30$, is the slope of the line, and the term $1/30z$ is the x_2 intercept (that is, the value of x_2 where the graph of equation (7.7) crosses the x_2 axis). Substituting the profit contributions of $z = 240$, $z = 720$, and $z = 1200$ into equation (7.7) yields the slope–intercept equations for the profit lines shown in Figure 7.10:

For $z = 240$,

$$x_2 = -\frac{40}{30}x_1 + 8$$

For $z = 720$,

$$x_2 = -\frac{40}{30}x_1 + 24$$

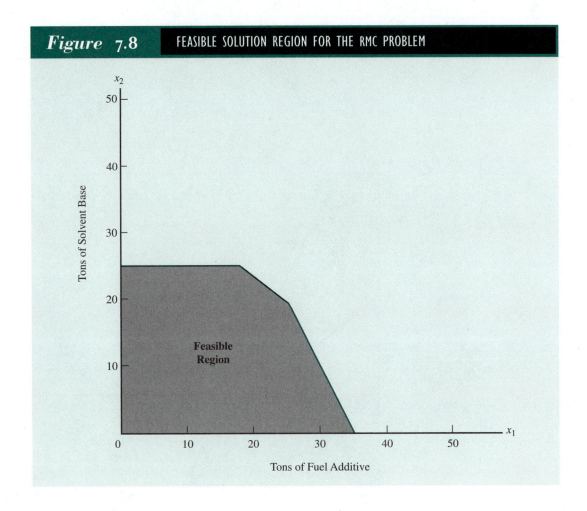

Figure 7.8   FEASIBLE SOLUTION REGION FOR THE RMC PROBLEM

For $z = 1200$,

$$x_2 = -\tfrac{40}{30}x_1 + 40$$

Since the slope ($-\tfrac{40}{30}$) is the same for each profit line, the profit lines are parallel. Moreover, the x_2 intercept increases with higher profit contributions. Thus, higher profit lines are farther from the origin.

Because the profit lines are parallel and higher profit lines are farther from the origin, we can obtain solutions that yield increasingly higher values for the objective function by continuing to move the profit line farther from the origin but keeping it parallel to the other profit lines. However, at some point any further outward movement will place the profit line entirely outside the feasible region. Since points outside the feasible region are unacceptable, the point in the feasible region that lies on the highest profit line is an optimal solution to the linear program.

You should now be able to identify the optimal solution point for the RMC problem. Use a ruler and move the profit line as far from the origin as you can. What is the last point in the feasible region? This point, which is the optimal solution, is shown graphically in Figure 7.11. The optimal values for the decision variables are the x_1 and x_2 values at this point.

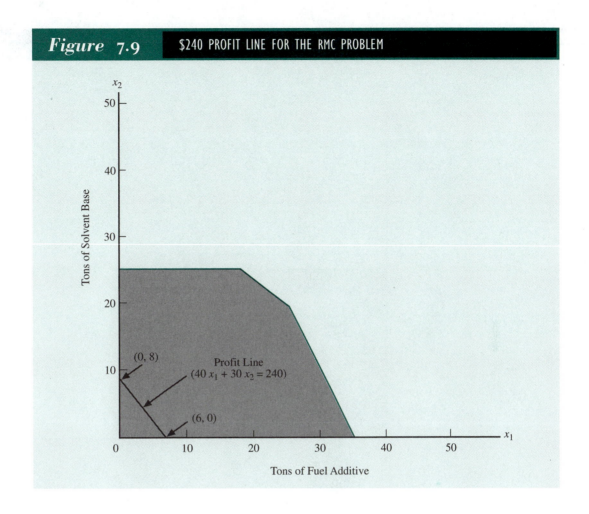

Figure 7.9 $240 PROFIT LINE FOR THE RMC PROBLEM

Depending on the accuracy of your graph, you may or may not be able to determine the exact optimal values of x_1 and x_2 directly from the graph. However, refer to Figure 7.7 and note that the optimal solution point for the RMC example is at the *intersection* of the material 1 and material 3 constraint lines. That is, the optimal solution is on both the material 1 constraint line,

$$\tfrac{2}{5}x_1 + \tfrac{1}{2}x_2 = 20 \tag{7.8}$$

and the material 3 constraint line,

$$\tfrac{3}{5}x_1 + \tfrac{3}{10}x_2 = 21 \tag{7.9}$$

Thus, the values of the decision variables x_1 and x_2 must satisfy both equations (7.8) and (7.9) simultaneously. Using (7.8) and solving for x_1 gives

$$\tfrac{2}{5}x_1 = 20 - \tfrac{1}{2}x_2$$

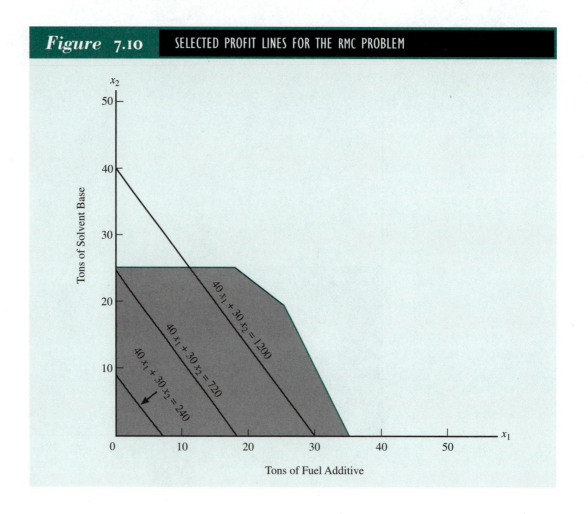

Figure 7.10   SELECTED PROFIT LINES FOR THE RMC PROBLEM

or

$$x_1 = 50 - \tfrac{5}{4}x_2 \tag{7.10}$$

Substituting this expression for x_1 into equation (7.9) and solving for x_2 yields

$$\tfrac{3}{5}(50 - \tfrac{5}{4}x_2) + \tfrac{3}{10}x_2 = 21$$
$$30 - \tfrac{3}{4}x_2 + \tfrac{3}{10}x_2 = 21$$
$$30 - \tfrac{30}{40}x_2 + \tfrac{12}{40}x_2 = 21$$
$$-\tfrac{18}{40}x_2 = -9$$
$$x_2 = \left(\tfrac{40}{18}\right)(9) = 20$$

Substituting $x_2 = 20$ in equation (7.10) and solving for x_1 provides

$$x_1 = 50 - \tfrac{5}{4}(20)$$
$$= 50 - 25 = 25$$

Although the optimal solution to the RMC problem consists of integer values for the decision variables, this will not always be the case.

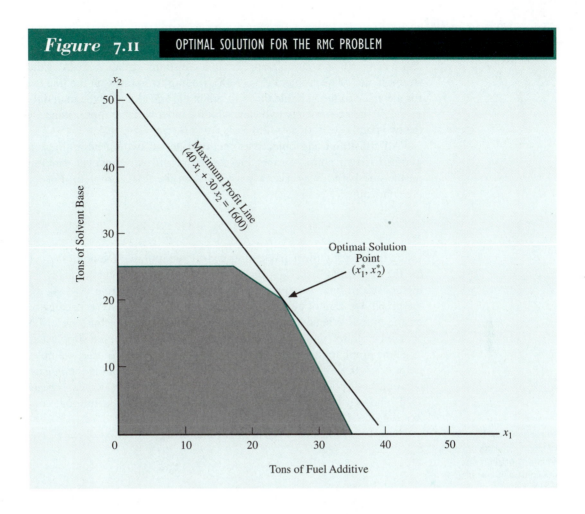

Figure 7.11 OPTIMAL SOLUTION FOR THE RMC PROBLEM

Thus, the exact location of the optimal solution point is $x_1 = 25$ and $x_2 = 20$. This solution point provides the optimal production quantities for RMC at 25 tons of fuel additive and 20 tons of solvent base and yields a profit contribution of $40(25) + 30(20) = \$1600$.

For a linear programming problem with two decision variables, you can determine the exact values of the decision variables at the optimal solution by first using the graphical procedure to identify the optimal solution point and then solving the two simultaneous equations associated with this point.

You should now be able to use the graphical solution procedure to identify the optimal solution and find the exact values of the decision variables at the optimal solution. Try Problem 11.

A Note on Graphing Lines

An important aspect of the graphical method is the ability to graph lines showing the constraints and the objective function of the linear program. The simplest procedure for graphing the equation of a line is to find any two points that satisfy the equation and then draw the line through the two points. For the material 1 constraint line of the RMC problem,

$$\tfrac{2}{5}x_1 + \tfrac{1}{2}x_2 = 20$$

this procedure identified the two points ($x_1 = 0$, $x_2 = 40$) and ($x_1 = 50$, $x_2 = 0$). We then graphed the material 1 constraint line by drawing a line through these two points.

When only one variable appears in a constraint equation, such as the material 2 constraint in the RMC problem ($\frac{1}{5}x_2 \leq 5$), finding two points on the line is easy. First, solve for the value of the variable that appears in the equation (for the material 2 constraint, it is $x_2 = 25$); then choose any two values for the other variable. For instance, you could choose the two points ($x_1 = 0$, $x_2 = 25$) and ($x_1 = 10$, $x_2 = 25$).

All constraint and objective function lines in two-variable linear programs can be graphed if two points on the line can be identified. However, finding the two points on the line isn't always as easy as it was in the RMC problem. For example, consider the constraint:

$$2x_1 - 1x_2 \leq 100$$

Using the equality form and setting $x_1 = 0$, we find that the point ($x_1 = 0$, $x_2 = -100$) is on the constraint line. Setting $x_2 = 0$, we find a second point ($x_1 = 50$, $x_2 = 0$) on the constraint line. If we have drawn only the nonnegative ($x_1 \geq 0$, $x_2 \geq 0$) portion of the graph, we cannot plot the first point ($x_1 = 0$, $x_2 = -100$) because $x_2 = -100$ is not on the graph. Whenever we have two points on the line but one or both of the points cannot be plotted in the nonnegative portion of the graph, the simplest approach is to enlarge the graph to include the negative x_1 and/or x_2 axes. In this example, we can plot the point ($x_1 = 0$, $x_2 = -100$) by extending the graph to include the negative x_2 axis. After locating both points that satisfy the constraint equation, we can draw the line. Figure 7.12 shows the constraint line and the feasible solutions for the constraint $2x_1 - 1x_2 \leq 100$.

Now let us consider a constraint of the form

$$1x_1 - 1x_2 \geq 0$$

To find all solutions satisfying the constraint as an equality, we first set $x_1 = 0$ and solve for x_2. This result shows that the origin ($x_1 = 0$, $x_2 = 0$) is on the constraint line. Setting $x_2 = 0$ and solving for x_1 provides the same point. However, we can obtain a second point on the line by setting x_2 equal to any value other than zero and then solving for x_1. For instance, setting $x_2 = 100$ and solving for x_1, we find that the point ($x_1 = 100$, $x_2 = 100$) is on the line. With the two points, ($x_1 = 0$, $x_2 = 0$) and ($x_1 = 100$, $x_2 = 100$), the constraint line $1x_1 - 1x_2 = 0$ can be plotted and the feasible solutions for $1x_1 - 1x_2 \geq 0$ can be determined as shown in Figure 7.13.

You should now be able to graph a constraint line when the origin is on the constraint line. Try Problem 5.

For practice in using the graphical solution procedure, try Problem 22(b)–(d).

Summary of the Graphical Solution Procedure for Maximization Problems

The graphical solution procedure is one method of solving two-variable linear programming problems, such as the RMC problem. The graphical solution procedure for a maximization problem involves the following steps.

1. Prepare a graph of the feasible solutions for each of the constraints.
2. Determine the feasible region by identifying the solutions that satisfy all the constraints simultaneously.
3. Draw an objective function line showing all values of the x_1 and x_2 variables that yield a specified value of the objective function.

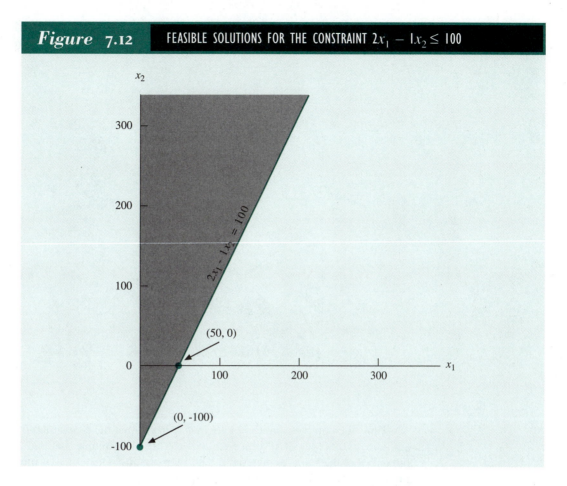

Figure 7.12 FEASIBLE SOLUTIONS FOR THE CONSTRAINT $2x_1 - 1x_2 \leq 100$

4. Move parallel objective function lines toward larger objective function values until further movement would take the line completely outside the feasible region.

5. Any feasible solution on the objective function line with the largest value is an optimal solution.

Slack Variables

In addition to the optimal solution and its associated profit contribution, the management of RMC will want information about the production requirements for the three materials. We can determine this information by substituting the optimal solution values ($x_1 = 25$, $x_2 = 20$) into the constraints of the linear program.

Constraint	Tons Required for $x_1 = 25, x_2 = 20$ Tons	Tons Available	Unused Tons
Material 1	$^2/_5(25) + \ ^1/_2(20) = 20$	20	0
Material 2	$0(25) + \ ^1/_5(20) = \ 4$	5	1
Material 3	$^3/_5(25) + \ ^3/_{10}(20) = 21$	21	0

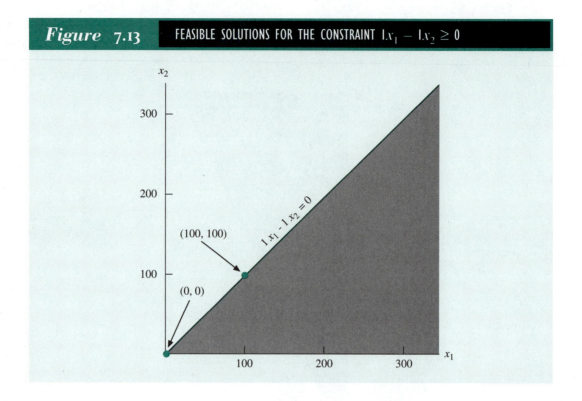

Figure 7.13   FEASIBLE SOLUTIONS FOR THE CONSTRAINT $1x_1 - 1x_2 \geq 0$

Thus, the complete solution tells management that the production of 25 tons of fuel additive and 20 tons of solvent base will require all available material 1 and material 3 but only 4 of the 5 tons of material 2. The 1 ton of unused material 2 is referred to as *slack*. In linear programming terminology, any unused or idle capacity for a $\leq$ constraint is referred to as the *slack associated with the constraint*. Thus, the material 2 constraint has a slack of 1 ton.

Often variables, called **slack variables,** are added to the formulation of a linear programming problem to represent the slack, or idle capacity. Unused capacity makes no contribution to profit, so slack variables have coefficients of zero in the objective function. More generally, slack variables represent the difference between the right-hand side and the left-hand side of a $\leq$ constraint. After the addition of slack variables to the mathematical statement of the RMC problem, the mathematical model becomes

Can you identify the slack associated with a constraint? Try Problem 22(e).

$$\text{Max} \quad 40x_1 + 30x_2 + 0s_1 + 0s_2 + 0s_3$$

$$\text{s.t.}$$

$$\frac{2}{5}x_1 + \frac{1}{2}x_2 + 1s_1 \qquad\qquad = 20$$

$$\frac{1}{5}x_2 \qquad + 1s_2 \qquad = 5$$

$$\frac{3}{5}x_1 + \frac{3}{10}x_2 \qquad\qquad + 1s_3 = 21$$

$$x_1, x_2, s_1, s_2, s_3 \geq 0$$

Whenever all the constraints in a linear program are expressed as equalities, it is said to be written in **standard form.**

Can you write a linear
program in standard form?
Try Problem 18.

Referring to the standard form of the RMC problem, we see that at the optimal solution ($x_1 = 25$, $x_2 = 20$) the values for the slack variables are

Constraint	Value of Slack Variable
Material 1	$s_1 = 0$
Material 2	$s_2 = 1$
Material 3	$s_3 = 0$

Could we have used the graphical analysis to provide some of the previous information? The answer is yes. By finding the optimal solution in Figure 7.7, we see that the material 1 constraint and the material 3 constraint restrict, or *bind*, the feasible region at this point. Thus, the optimal solution requires the use of all of these two resources. In other words, the graph shows that at the optimal solution material 1 and material 3 will have zero slack. But, since the material 2 constraint is not binding the feasible region at the optimal solution, we can expect some slack for this resource.

Recognizing redundant constraints is easy with the graphical solution method. In problems with more than two decision variables, however, redundant constraints usually will not be apparent.

Finally, some linear programs may have one or more constraints that do not affect the feasible region. That is, the feasible region remains the same whether or not the constraint is included in the problem. Since such a constraint does not affect the feasible region and thus cannot affect the optimal solution, it is called a **redundant constraint.** Redundant constraints can be dropped from the problem without having any effect on the optimal solution. However, in most linear programming problems redundant constraints are not discarded because they are not immediately recognizable as being redundant. The RMC problem had no redundant constraints because each constraint had an effect on the feasible region. Problem 13 at the end of the chapter concerns a linear program with a redundant constraint.

N O T E S
and Comments

1. In the standard form representation of a linear program, the objective function coefficients for slack variables are zero. This condition implies that slack variables, which represent unused resources, do not affect the value of the objective function. However, in some applications, some or all of the unused resources can be sold and contribute to profit. In such cases the corresponding slack variables become decision variables representing the amount of resources to be sold. For each of these variables, a nonzero coefficient in the objective function would reflect the profit associated with selling a unit of the corresponding resource.

2. Redundant constraints do not affect the feasible region; as a result they can be removed from a linear programming model without affecting the optimal solution. However, if the linear programming model is to be resolved later, changes in some of the data might change a previously redundant constraint into a binding constraint. Thus, we recommend keeping all constraints in the linear programming model even though one or more of the constraints may be redundant.

7.6 EXTREME POINTS AND THE OPTIMAL SOLUTION

Suppose that the profit contribution for 1 ton of solvent base increases from $30 to $60 while the profit contribution for 1 ton of fuel additive and all the constraints remain unchanged. The complete linear programming model of this new problem is identical to the mathematical model in Section 7.4, except for the revised objective function:

$$\text{Max} \quad 40x_1 + 60x_2$$

How does this change in the objective function affect the optimal solution to the RMC problem? Figure 7.14 shows the graphical solution of the RMC problem with the revised objective function. Note that since the constraints have not changed, the feasible region has not changed. However, the profit lines have been altered to reflect the new objective function.

By moving the profit line in a parallel manner away from the origin, we find the optimal solution as shown in Figure 7.14. The values of the decision variables at this point are $x_1 = 18.75$ and $x_2 = 25$. The increased profit for the solvent base has caused a change in the optimal solution. In fact, as you may have suspected, we are cutting back the production of the lower profit fuel additive and increasing the production of the higher profit solvent base.

What have you noticed about the location of the optimal solutions in the linear programming problems that we have solved thus far? Look closely at the graphical solu-

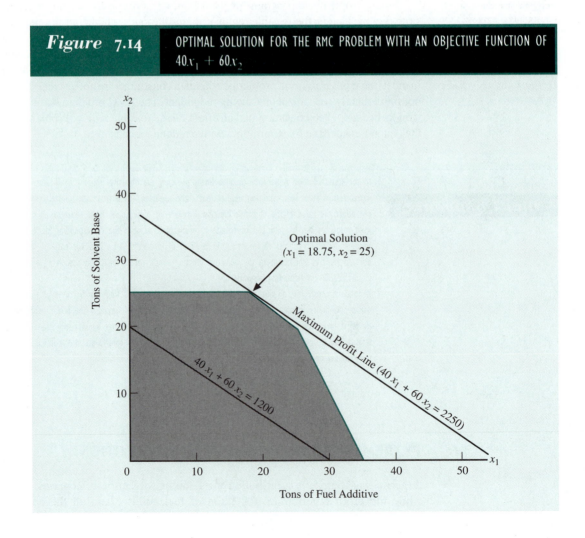

***Figure* 7.14** OPTIMAL SOLUTION FOR THE RMC PROBLEM WITH AN OBJECTIVE FUNCTION OF $40x_1 + 60x_2$

tions in Figures 7.11 and 7.14. An important observation that you should be able to make is that the optimal solutions occur at one of the vertices or "corners" of the feasible region. In linear programming terminology these vertices are referred to as the **extreme points** of the feasible region. Thus, the RMC has five vertices or five extreme points (Figure 7.15). We can now state our observation about the location of optimal solutions[2]:

The optimal solution to a linear programming problem can be found at an extreme point of the feasible region for the problem.

You should be able to identify the extreme points of the feasible region and determine the optimal solution by computing and comparing the objective function value at each extreme point. Try Problem 14.

This property means that, if you are looking for the optimal solution to a linear programming problem, you do not have to evaluate all feasible solution points. In fact, you have to consider *only* the feasible solutions that occur at the extreme points of the feasible region. Thus, for the RMC problem, instead of computing and comparing the profit for all feasible solutions, we can find the optimal solution by evaluating the five extreme-point

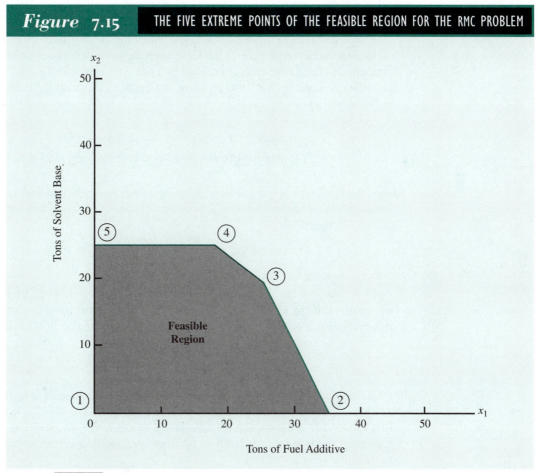

Figure 7.15 THE FIVE EXTREME POINTS OF THE FEASIBLE REGION FOR THE RMC PROBLEM

---

2. In Section 7.8 we show that two special cases (infeasibility and unboundedness) in linear programming have no optimal solution. The observation stated does not apply to these cases.

solutions and selecting the one that provides the highest profit. Actually, the graphical solution procedure is nothing more than a convenient way of identifying an optimal extreme point for two-variable problems.

7.7 A SIMPLE MINIMIZATION PROBLEM

Innis Investments manages funds for companies and wealthy clients. The investment strategy is tailored to each client's needs. For a new client, Innis has been authorized to invest up to $1.2 million in two investment funds: a stock fund and a money market fund. Each unit of the stock fund costs $50 and provides an annual rate of return of 10%; each unit of the money market fund costs $100 and provides an annual rate of return of 4%.

The client wants to minimize risk but earn an annual income from the investment of at least $60,000. According to Innis's risk measurement system, each unit purchased in the stock fund has a risk index of 8, and each unit purchased in the money market fund has a risk index of 3; the higher risk index associated with the stock fund simply indicates that it is the riskier investment. Innis's client also has specified that at least $300,000 be invested in the money market fund. How many units of each fund should Innis purchase for the client if the objective is to minimize the total risk index for the portfolio?

To find the best allocation of funds between the stock and money market funds, we will formulate the Innis Investments problem as a linear program. Following a procedure similar to the one used for the RMC problem, we begin by defining the decision variables for the problem. Let

$$x_1 = \text{number of units purchased in the stock fund}$$
$$x_2 = \text{number of units purchased in the money market fund}$$

Since the risk index is 8 for each unit purchased in the stock fund and 3 for each unit purchased in the money market fund, the objective function that will minimize the total risk index for the portfolio is

$$\text{Min} \quad 8x_1 + 3x_2$$

Next, consider the constraints associated with the problem. First, we recognize that Innis can invest up to $1,200,000. Since each unit of the stock fund costs $50 and each unit of the money market fund costs $100, the constraint needed on funds available is

$$50x_1 + 100x_2 \leq 1,200,000$$

In addition, the investment must result in an annual income of at least $60,000. With a 10% annual rate of return for the stock fund, each unit purchased in the stock fund will earn $0.10(\$50) = \$5$; similarly, the 4% annual rate of return for the money market fund results in earnings per unit of $0.04(\$100) = \$4$. Thus, the constraint required to ensure an annual income of at least $60,000 is

$$5x_1 + 4x_2 \geq 60,000$$

Finally, since each unit purchased in the money market fund costs $100, the requirement that at least $300,000 be invested in the money market fund means that at least 3000 units of the money market fund must be purchased; thus, we must add the constraint

$$x_2 \geq 3000$$

After adding the nonnegativity constraints ($x_1, x_2 \geq 0$), we obtain the linear programming model of the Innis Investments problem:

$$\text{Min} \quad 8x_1 + 3x_2$$

s.t.

$50x_1 + 100x_2 \leq$	1,200,000	Funds available
$5x_1 + 4x_2 \geq$	60,000	Annual income
$x_2 \geq$	3,000	Minimum units in money market

$$x_1, x_2 \geq 0$$

Because the linear programming model has only two decision variables, we can use the graphical solution procedure to find the optimal investment plan. The graphical method for this problem, as in the RMC problem, requires us first to graph the constraint lines to find the feasible region. By graphing each constraint line separately and then checking points on either side of the constraint line, we can identify the feasible solutions for each constraint. By combining the feasible solutions for each constraint on the same graph, we obtain the feasible region shown in Figure 7.16.

To find the optimal solution (the one that will minimize the total risk index for the portfolio), we now draw the objective function line corresponding to a particular value for the total risk index. For example, we might start by drawing the line $8x_1 + 3x_2 = 120,000$, as shown in Figure 7.17. Clearly, some points in the feasible region would provide a total risk index of 120,000. To find the values of x_1 and x_2 that provide a smaller total portfolio risk index, we move the objective function line down and to the left until, if we moved it any farther, it would be outside the feasible region. Note that the objective function line $8x_1 + 3x_2 = 62,000$ intersects the feasible region at the extreme point $x_1 = 4000$ and $x_2 = 10,000$. This extreme point provides the minimum portfolio risk index with an objective function value of 62,000. Figures 7.16 and 7.17 show that the funds available and the annual income constraints are binding.

Summary of the Graphical Solution Procedure for Minimization Problems

Can you use the graphical solution procedure to determine the optimal solution for a minimization problem? Try Problem 29.

The graphical solution procedure for a minimization problem involves the following steps.

1. Prepare a graph of the feasible solution region for each of the constraints.
2. Determine the feasible solution region by identifying the solutions that satisfy all the constraints simultaneously.
3. Draw an objective function line showing all values of the x_1 and x_2 variables that yield a specified value of the objective function.

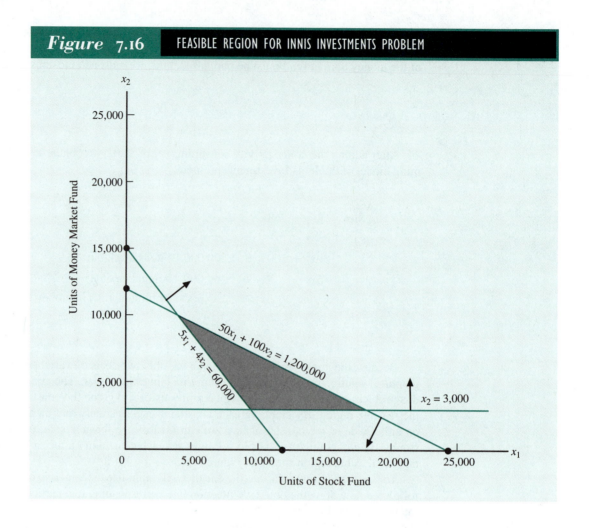

Figure 7.16   FEASIBLE REGION FOR INNIS INVESTMENTS PROBLEM

4. Move parallel objective function lines toward smaller objective function values until further movement would take the line completely outside the feasible region.
5. Any feasible solution on the objective function line with the smallest value is an optimal solution.

Surplus Variables

A complete analysis of the optimal solution to the Innis Investments problem shows that the total risk index for the optimal portfolio, $8x_1 + 3x_2 = 8(4,000) + 3(10,000) = 62,000$, is achieved by using all available funds. That is, $50x_1 + 100x_2 = 50(4,000) + 100(10,000) = 1,200,000$. The required annual income is achieved exactly, as $5(4,000) + 4(10,000) = 60,000$. Note, however, that the purchase of 10,000 units of the money market fund exceeds the minimum requirement of 3000 by 7000 units. In linear programming terminology, any such excess quantity corresponding to a $\geq$ constraint is referred to as *surplus*.

Recall that with a $\leq$ constraint a slack variable can be added to the left-hand side of the constraint in order to convert the constraint to equality form. With a $\geq$ constraint,

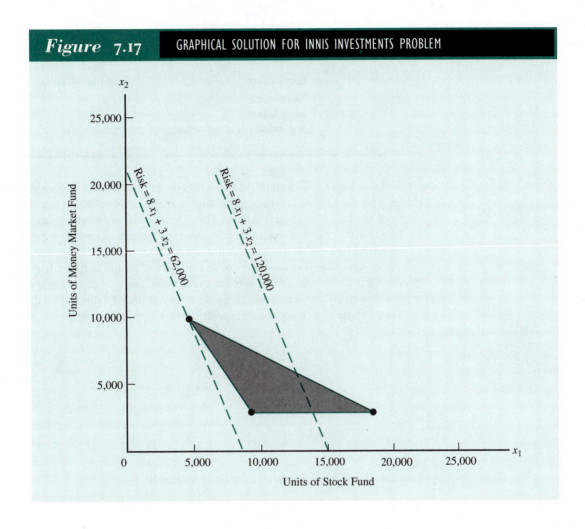

Figure 7.17   GRAPHICAL SOLUTION FOR INNIS INVESTMENTS PROBLEM

a **surplus variable** can be subtracted from the left-hand side to convert the constraint to equality form. As with slack variables, surplus variables are given a coefficient of zero in the objective function because they have no effect on its value. After including one slack variable for the $\leq$ constraint and two surplus variables for the $\geq$ constraints, the linear programming model of the Innis Investments problem becomes

$$\text{Min} \quad 8x_1 + 3x_2 + 0s_1 + 0s_2 + 0s_3$$
$$\text{s.t.}$$
$$50x_1 + 100x_2 + 1s_1 \qquad\qquad\qquad = 1{,}200{,}000$$
$$5x_1 + 4x_2 \qquad - 1s_2 \qquad\qquad = \quad 60{,}000$$
$$1x_2 \qquad\qquad\qquad - 1s_3 = \quad 3{,}000$$
$$x_1, x_2, s_1, s_2, s_3 \geq 0$$

You should now be able to use slack and surplus variables to write a linear program in standard form. Try Problem 33.

All the constraints are now equalities. Hence, the preceding formulation is the standard form representation of the Innis Investments problem. At the optimal solution, $x_1 = 4000$ and $x_2 = 10{,}000$, the values of the slack and surplus variables are

Constraint	Value of Slack or Surplus Variable
Funds available	$s_1 = 0$
Annual income	$s_2 = 0$
Minimum units in money market	$s_3 = 7000$

Refer to Figures 7.16 and 7.17. Note that the zero slack and surplus variables are associated with the constraints that are binding at the optimal solution; that is, the constraints on funds available and annual income. The surplus of 7000 units is associated with the nonbinding constraint on the minimum allowable investment in the money market fund.

Note that in the RMC problem all the constraints were of the $\leq$ type and that in the Innis Investments problem the constraints were a mixture of $\leq$ and $\geq$ types. In general, linear programming problems may have some $\leq$ constraints, some $\geq$ constraints, and some $=$ constraints. For an equality constraint, feasible solutions must lie directly on the constraint line.

An example of a linear program with all three constraint forms is

$$\text{Min} \quad 2x_1 + 2x_2$$
$$\text{s.t.}$$
$$1x_1 + 3x_2 \leq 12$$
$$3x_1 + 1x_2 \geq 13$$
$$1x_1 - 1x_2 = 3$$
$$x_1, x_2 \geq 0$$

The standard-form representation of this problem is

$$\text{Min} \quad 2x_1 + 2x_2 + 0s_1 + 0s_2$$
$$\text{s.t.}$$
$$1x_1 + 3x_2 + 1s_1 \qquad = 12$$
$$3x_1 + 1x_2 \qquad - 1s_2 = 13$$
$$1x_1 - 1x_2 \qquad\qquad = 3$$
$$x_1, x_2, s_1, s_2 \geq 0$$

The standard form requires a slack variable for the $\leq$ constraint and a surplus variable for the $\geq$ constraint. However, neither a slack nor a surplus variable is required for the third constraint because it is already in equality form.

When solving linear programs graphically, you don't have to rewrite the problem in its standard form. Nevertheless, you should be able to compute the values of the slack and surplus variables and understand what they mean. In Chapter 8 we demonstrate that the values of slack and surplus variables are included in the computer solution of linear programs.

A final point: The standard form of the linear programming problem is equivalent to the original formulation of the problem. That is, the optimal solution to any linear programming problem is the same as the optimal solution to the standard form of the problem. The standard form has not changed the basic problem; it has only changed how we write the constraints for the problem.

Try Problem 32 to practice solving a linear program with all three constraint forms.

7.8   SPECIAL CASES

In this section we discuss three special situations that can arise when we attempt to solve linear programming problems.

Alternative Optimal Solutions

From our discussion of the graphical solution procedure, we know that optimal solutions can be found at the extreme points of the feasible region. Now let us consider the special case where the optimal objective function line coincides with one of the binding constraint lines. It can lead to **alternative optimal solutions,** whereby more than one solution provides the optimal value for the objective function.

To illustrate the case of alternative optimal solutions, we return to the RMC, Inc., problem. However, let us assume that the profit contribution for the solvent base (x_2) has increased to \$50. The revised objective function is $40x_1 + 50x_2$. Figure 7.18 shows the graphical solution to this problem. Note that the optimal solution still occurs at an extreme

Figure 7.18 OPTIMAL SOLUTIONS FOR THE RMC PROBLEM WITH AN OBJECTIVE FUNCTION OF $40x_1 + 50x_2$

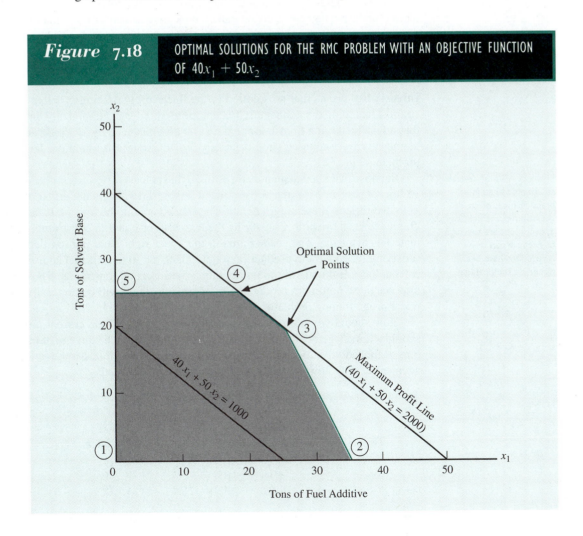

point. In fact, it occurs at two extreme points: extreme point ③ ($x_1 = 25$, $x_2 = 20$) and extreme point ④ ($x_1 = 18.75$, $x_2 = 25$).

The objective function values at these two extreme points are identical; that is,

$$40x_1 + 50x_2 = 40(25) + 50(20) = 2000$$

and

$$40x_1 + 50x_2 = 40(18.75) + 50(25) = 2000$$

Furthermore, any point on the line connecting the two optimal extreme points also provides an optimal solution. For example, the solution point ($x_1 = 21.875$, $x_2 = 22.5$), which is halfway between the two extreme points, also provides the optimal objective function value of

$$40x_1 + 50x_2 = 40(21.875) + 50(22.5) = 2000$$

A linear programming problem with alternative optimal solutions is generally a good situation for the manager or decision maker. It means that several combinations of the decision variables are optimal and that the manager can select the most desirable optimal solution.

Infeasibility

Infeasibility means that no solution to the linear programming problem satisfies all constraints, including the nonnegativity conditions x_1, $x_2 \geq 0$. Graphically, infeasibility means that a feasible region does not exist; that is, no points satisfy all constraint equations and nonnegativity conditions simultaneously. To illustrate this situation, let us return to the problem facing RMC.

Problems with no feasible solution do arise in practice. Most often it's because management's expectations are too high or because too many restrictions have been placed on the problem.

Suppose that management had specified that at least 30 tons of fuel additive and at least 15 tons of solvent base must be produced. Figure 7.19 shows the graph of the solution region that reflects these requirements. The shaded area in the lower left-hand portion of the graph depicts those points satisfying the less-than-or-equal-to constraints on the amount of materials available. The shaded area in the upper right-hand portion depicts those points satisfying the minimum production requirements of 30 tons of fuel additive and 15 tons of solvent base. But none of the points satisfy both sets of constraints. Thus, if management imposes these minimum production requirements, there will be no feasible solution to the linear programming problem.

How should we interpret this infeasibility in terms of the current problem? First, we should tell management that, for the available amounts of the three materials, producing 30 tons of fuel additive and 15 tons of solvent base isn't possible. Moreover, we can tell management exactly how much more of each material is needed.

Material	Minimum Tons Required for $x_1 = 30$, $x_2 = 15$	Tons Available	Additional Tons Required
Material 1	$2/5(30) + 1/2(15) = 19.5$	20	—
Material 2	$0(30) + 1/5(15) = 3$	5	—
Material 3	$3/5(30) + 3/10(15) = 22.5$	21	1.5

Figure 7.19	NO FEASIBLE REGION FOR THE RMC PROBLEM WITH MINIMUM PRODUCTION REQUIREMENTS

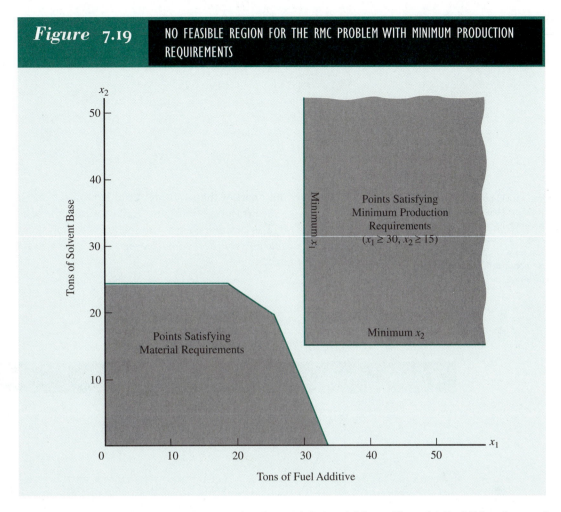

Thus, RMC has a sufficient supply of materials 1 and 2 but will need 1.5 additional tons of material 3 to meet management's production requirements of 30 tons of fuel additive and 15 tons of solvent base. If, after reviewing the above analysis, management still wants this level of production for the two products, RMC will somehow have to obtain the additional 1.5 tons of material 3.

Unbounded

The solution to a maximization linear programming problem is **unbounded** if the value of the solution may be made infinitely large without violating any of the constraints. For a minimization problem, the solution is unbounded if the value may be made infinitely small. This condition might be termed *managerial utopia*. For example, if this condition were to occur in a profit maximization problem, the manager could achieve unlimited profit.

However, in linear programming models of real-world problems, the occurrence of an unbounded solution means that the problem has been improperly formulated. We know that profits cannot increase indefinitely. Therefore, we must conclude that if a profit maximization problem results in an unbounded solution, the mathematical model doesn't represent the real-world problem sufficiently. Usually what has happened is that a constraint has been inadvertently omitted during problem formulation.

If a linear programming problem has an unbounded solution, the graph of the feasible region extends to infinity in some direction. For example, consider the following linear program:

$$\text{Max} \quad 2x_1 + 1x_2$$
$$\text{s.t.}$$
$$1x_1 \qquad \geq 2$$
$$1x_2 \leq 5$$
$$x_1, x_2 \geq 0$$

You should now be able to recognize whether a linear program involves alternative optimal solutions or infeasibility, or is unbounded. Try Problems 40 and 41.

Figure 7.20 can show only part of the resulting feasible region because it extends infinitely along the x_1 axis. The profit lines in Figure 7.20 show that the solution to this problem may be made as large as desired. That is, no matter what solution we choose, there will always be another feasible solution with a larger value. Thus, the solution to this linear program is unbounded.

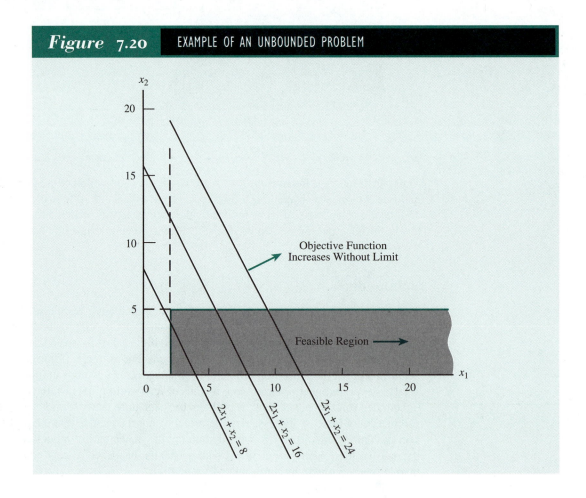

Figure 7.20   EXAMPLE OF AN UNBOUNDED PROBLEM

7.9   INTRODUCTION TO SENSITIVITY ANALYSIS

Sensitivity analysis is the study of how changes in the coefficients of a linear program affect the optimal solution. Using sensitivity analysis, we can answer questions such as the following.

1. How will a *change in a coefficient of the objective function* affect the optimal solution?
2. How will a *change in the right-hand-side value for a constraint* affect the optimal solution?

Since sensitivity analysis is concerned with how the above changes affect the optimal solution, the analysis does not begin until the optimal solution to the original linear programming problem has been obtained. For this reason, sensitivity analysis is often referred to as **postoptimality analysis.**

The primary reason that sensitivity analysis is important to decision makers is that real-world problems exist in a changing environment. Prices of raw materials change, product demand changes, companies purchase new machinery to replace old, stock prices fluctuate, employee turnover occurs, and so on. If a linear programming model has been used in such an environment, we can expect some of the coefficients to change over time. We will then want to determine how these changes affect the optimal solution to the original linear programming problem. Sensitivity analysis provides us with the information needed to respond to such changes without requiring the complete solution of a revised linear program.

Recall the RMC problem:

$$\text{Max} \quad 40x_1 + 30x_2$$

s.t.

$$\tfrac{2}{5}x_1 + \tfrac{1}{2}x_2 \le 20 \quad \text{Material 1}$$

$$\tfrac{1}{5}x_2 \le 5 \quad \text{Material 2}$$

$$\tfrac{3}{5}x_1 + \tfrac{3}{10}x_2 \le 21 \quad \text{Material 3}$$

$$x_1, x_2 \ge 0$$

The optimal solution, $x_1 = 25$ tons of fuel additive and $x_2 = 20$ tons of solvent base was based on profit contribution figures of \$40 per ton of fuel additive and \$30 per ton of solvent base. However, suppose that we later learn that a price reduction causes the profit contribution for the fuel additive to fall from $40 to $35 per ton. Sensitivity analysis can be used to determine whether the production schedule calling for 25 tons of fuel additive and 20 tons of solvent base is still best. If it is, there will be no need to solve a modified linear programming problem with $35x_1 + 30x_2$ as the new objective function.

Sensitivity analysis can also be used to determine which coefficients in a linear programming model are crucial. For example, suppose that management believes that the $30 per ton profit contribution for the solvent base is only a rough estimate of the profit contribution that will actually be obtained. If sensitivity analysis shows that 25 tons of fuel additive and 20 tons of solvent base will be the optimal solution as long as the profit contribution for the solvent base is between $20 and $40, management should feel comfortable with the $30 per ton estimate and the recommended production quantities. However, if sensitivity analysis shows that 25 tons of fuel additive and 20 tons of solvent base will be the optimal solution only if the profit contribution for the solvent base is between $29.90 and $32.00 per ton, management may want to review the accuracy of the $30 per ton estimate. Management would especially want to consider how the optimal production quantities should be revised if the profit contribution per ton for the solvent base were to drop.

Another aspect of sensitivity analysis concerns changes in the right-hand-side values of the constraints. Recall that in the RMC problem the optimal solution used all available material 1 and material 3. What would happen to the optimal solution and total profit contribution if RMC could obtain additional quantities of either of these resources? Sensitivity analysis can help determine how much each added ton of material is worth and how many tons can be added before diminishing returns set in.

7.10   GRAPHICAL SENSITIVITY ANALYSIS

For linear programming problems with two decision variables, graphical solution methods can be used to perform sensitivity analysis on the objective function coefficients and the right-hand-side values for the constraints.

Objective Function Coefficients

Let us consider how changes in the objective function coefficients might affect the optimal solution to the RMC problem. The current contribution to profit is $40 per ton of fuel additive and $30 per ton of solvent base. An increase in the profit contribution for one of the products might lead management to increase the production of that product and a decrease in the profit contribution for one of the products might lead management to decrease production of that product. But how much the profit contribution would have to change before management would want to change the production quantities is not obvious.

The current optimal solution to the RMC problem calls for producing 25 tons of fuel additive and 20 tons of solvent base. The **range of optimality** for each objective function coefficient provides the range of values for the coefficient over which the current solution will remain optimal. Managerial attention should be focused on those objective function coefficients that have a narrow range of optimality and coefficients near the endpoints of the range. A small change in these coefficients can necessitate modifying the optimal solution. Let us now compute the ranges of optimality for the RMC problem.

Figure 7.21 shows the graphical solution to the RMC problem. Careful inspection of this graph shows that, as long as the slope of the objective function is between the slope of line *A* (which coincides with the material 1 constraint line) and the slope of line *B* (which coincides with the material 3 constraint line), extreme point ③ with $x_1 = 25$ and $x_2 = 20$ will be optimal. Changing an objective function coefficient for x_1 or x_2 will cause the slope of the objective function to change. Figure 7.21 shows that such a change causes the objective function line to rotate about extreme point ③. However, as long as the objective function line stays within the shaded region, extreme point ③ will remain optimal.

The slope of the objective function line usually is negative; hence, rotating the objective function line clockwise makes the line steeper even though the slope is getting smaller (more negative).

Rotating the objective function line *counterclockwise* increases the slope. Thus when the objective function line has been rotated counterclockwise (slope increased) enough to coincide with line *A,* we obtain alternative optimal solutions between extreme points ③

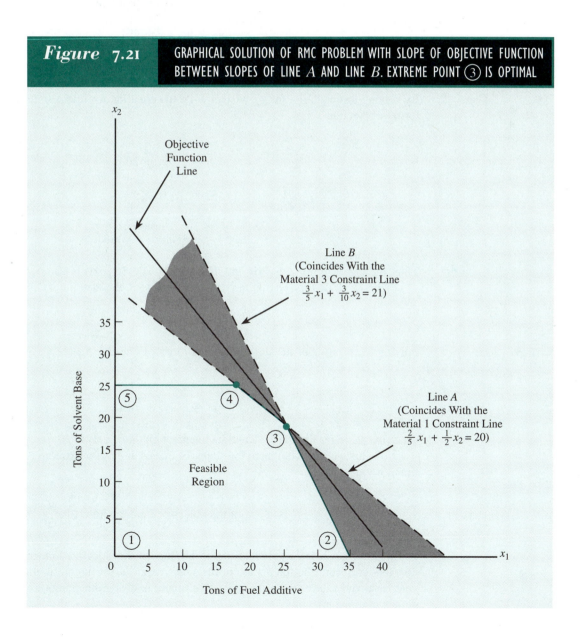

Figure 7.21 GRAPHICAL SOLUTION OF RMC PROBLEM WITH SLOPE OF OBJECTIVE FUNCTION BETWEEN SLOPES OF LINE *A* AND LINE *B.* EXTREME POINT ③ IS OPTIMAL

and ④. Any further counterclockwise rotation of the objective function line will cause extreme point ③ to be nonoptimal. Hence, the slope of line A provides an upper limit for the slope of the objective function line.

Rotating the objective function line *clockwise* decreases the slope. Thus, when the objective function line has been rotated clockwise (slope decreased and becoming more negative) enough to coincide with line B, we obtain alternative optimal solutions between extreme points ③ and ②. Any further clockwise rotation of the objective function line will cause extreme point ③ to be nonoptimal. Hence, the slope of line B provides a lower limit for the slope of the objective function line.

Thus, extreme point ③ will be the optimal solution as long as

Slope of line B ≤ slope of objective function line ≤ slope of line A

In Figure 7.21 the equation for line A, the material 1 constraint line, is

$$\frac{2}{5}x_1 + \frac{1}{2}x_2 = 20$$

By solving this equation for x_2, we can write the equation for line A in its slope–intercept form (see Section 7.5):

$$\frac{1}{2}x_2 = -\frac{2}{5}x_1 + 20$$

$$x_2 = -\frac{4}{5}x_1 + 40$$

Slope of line A ↗   ↑ Intercept of line A on x_2 axis

Thus, the slope for line A is −⅘ and its intercept on the x_2 axis is 40.

Figure 7.21 also shows that the equation for line B, the material 3 constraint line, is

$$\frac{3}{5}x_1 + \frac{3}{10}x_2 = 21$$

Solving for x_2 provides the slope–intercept form for line B:

$$\frac{3}{10}x_2 = -\frac{3}{5}x_1 + 21$$

$$x_2 = -2x_1 + 70$$

Thus, the slope for line B is −2 and its intercept on the x_2 axis is 70.

Now that we have computed the slopes of lines A and B, for extreme point ③ to be optimal, we must have

$$-2 \leq \text{slope of the objective function line} \leq -\frac{4}{5} \qquad (7.11)$$

We now consider the general form of the slope of the objective function line. Let c_1 denote the profit contribution per ton of fuel additive, c_2 the profit contribution per ton of solvent base, and z the value of the objective function. Using this notation, we can write the objective function as

$$z = c_1 x_1 + c_2 x_2$$

Solving for x_2 provides the slope–intercept form for the objective function line:

$$x_2 = -\left(\frac{c_1}{c_2}\right)x_1 + \frac{z}{c_2}$$

Thus, in general, the slope of the objective function line is $-c_1/c_2$. Substituting $-c_1/c_2$ into expression (7.11) shows that extreme point ③ will be optimal as long as

$$-2 \le -\frac{c_1}{c_2} \le -\frac{4}{5} \qquad\qquad (7.12)$$

To compute the range of optimality for c_1, the fuel additive coefficient, we hold c_2, the coefficient for the solvent base, at its initial value, $c_2 = 30$. Doing so, we obtain

$$-2 \le -\frac{c_1}{30} \le -\frac{4}{5}$$

From the left-hand inequality, we have

$$-2 \le -\frac{c_1}{30}$$

Thus,

$$-60 \le -c_1 \qquad \text{or} \qquad c_1 \le 60$$

From the right-hand inequality, we have

$$-\frac{c_1}{30} \le -\frac{4}{5}$$

Thus,

$$-c_1 \le -\frac{120}{5} = -24 \qquad \text{or} \qquad c_1 \ge 24$$

You should now be able to compute the range of optimality using the graphical solution procedure. Try Problem 52.

Combining these limits for c_1 provides the range of optimality for the fuel additive profit coefficient:

$$24 \le c_1 \le 60$$

In the original RMC problem, the fuel additive had a profit contribution of $40 per ton. The resulting optimal solution was 25 tons of fuel additive and 20 tons of solvent base. The range of optimality for c_1 tells RMC's management that, with other coefficients unchanged, the profit contribution for the fuel additive can be anywhere between $24 per ton and $60 per ton and the production quantities of 25 tons of fuel additive and 20 tons of solvent base will remain optimal. Note here that, although the production quantities will not change, the total profit contribution will vary because of the change in the profit contribution per ton of fuel additive.

We can repeat the preceding computations holding the profit contribution per ton of fuel additive constant at $c_1 = 40$. The range of optimality for c_2 can then be determined. Verify that this range is $20 \leq c_2 \leq 50$.

When rotation of the objective function line about an optimal extreme point causes the objective function line to become *vertical,* there will be either no upper limit or no lower limit for the slope as it appears in the form of expression (7.12). To show how this special situation can occur, we assume that the objective function for the RMC problem had been such that extreme point ② in Figure 7.22 provided the optimal solution. Rotating the

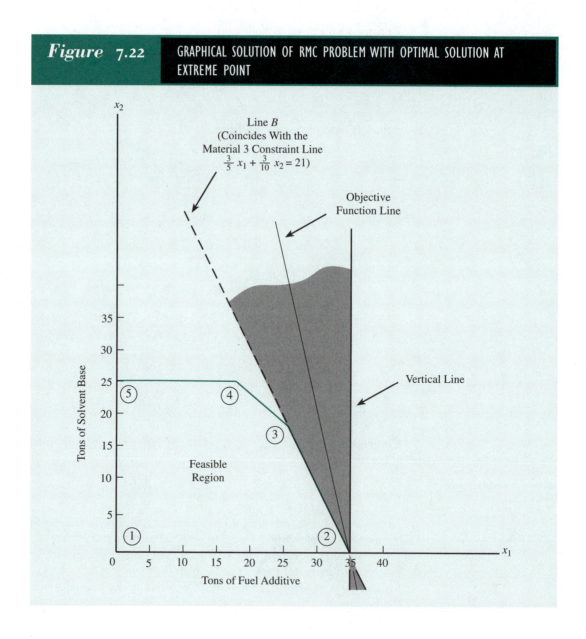

Figure 7.22   GRAPHICAL SOLUTION OF RMC PROBLEM WITH OPTIMAL SOLUTION AT EXTREME POINT

objective function line counterclockwise around extreme point ② provides an upper limit for the slope when the objective function line coincides with line B. Since we previously showed that the slope of line B is -2, the upper limit for the slope of the objective function line must be -2. However, rotating the objective function line clockwise causes the line to become vertical. In this case the slope becomes more and more negative, approaching a value of minus infinity, and hence there is no lower limit for the slope of the objective function. Using the upper limit of -2, we can write

$$-\frac{c_1}{c_2} \leq -2$$

Slope of the
objective function line

Following our previous procedure of holding c_2 constant at its original value, $c_2 = 30$, we have

$$-\frac{c_1}{30} \leq -2$$

Solving for c_1 yields

$$-c_1 \leq -60 \qquad \text{or} \qquad c_1 \geq 60$$

In Figure 7.22 note that extreme point ② remains optimal for all values of c_1 above 60.

Simultaneous Changes

The range of optimality for objective function coefficients is applicable only for changes made to one coefficient at a time. All other coefficients are assumed fixed at their initial values. If two or more objective function coefficients are changed simultaneously, further analysis is necessary to determine whether the optimal solution will change. However, when solving two-variable problems graphically, inequality (7.12) suggests an easy way to determine whether simultaneous changes in both objective function coefficients will cause a change in the optimal solution. Simply compute the slope of the objective function $(-c_1/c_2)$ for the new coefficient values. If this ratio is greater than or equal to the lower limit on the slope of the objective function and less than or equal to the upper limit, the changes made will not cause a change in the optimal solution.

Consider changes in both of the objective function coefficients for the RMC problem. Suppose that the profit contribution per ton of fuel additive is increased to $55 and that simultaneously the profit contribution per ton of solvent base is reduced to $25. Recall that the ranges of optimality for c_1 and c_2 (both computed in a one-at-a-time manner) are

$$24 \leq c_1 \leq 60 \tag{7.13}$$
$$20 \leq c_2 \leq 50 \tag{7.14}$$

For these ranges of optimality, we can conclude that changing either c_1 to $55 or c_2 to $25 (but not both) would not cause a change in the optimal solution of $x_1 = 25$ and $x_2 = 20$. But we cannot conclude that changing both coefficients simultaneously will not result in a change in the optimal solution.

In expression (7.12) we showed that extreme point ③ remains optimal as long as

$$-2 \leq -\frac{c_1}{c_2} \leq -\frac{4}{5}$$

If c_1 is changed to 55 and simultaneously c_2 is changed to 25, the new objective function slope becomes

$$-\frac{c_1}{c_2} = -\frac{55}{25} = -2.2$$

This value is less than the lower limit of -2, so the current solution of $x_1 = 25$ and $x_2 = 20$ will no longer be optimal. By resolving the problem with $c_1 = 55$ and $c_2 = 25$, we will find that extreme point ② is the new optimal solution.

Looking at the ranges of optimality, we concluded that changing either c_1 to \$55 or c_2 to \$25 (but not both) would not cause a change in the optimal solution. But in recomputing the slope of the objective function with simultaneous changes for both c_1 and c_2, we saw that the optimal solution did change. This result emphasizes that a range of optimality can be used only to draw a conclusion about changes made to one *objective function coefficient at a time*.

Right-Hand Sides

Let us now consider how a change in the right-hand-side value for a constraint may affect the feasible region and perhaps cause a change in the optimal solution to the problem. To illustrate this aspect of sensitivity analysis, we look at what happens if an additional 3 tons of material 3 become available. In this case, the right-hand side of the third constraint is changed from a 21 to 24, and the constraint is

$$\tfrac{3}{5}x_1 + \tfrac{3}{10}x_2 \leq 24$$

By obtaining an additional 3 tons of material 3, we have expanded the feasible region for the RMC problem; the new feasible region is shown in Figure 7.23. Since the feasible region has been enlarged, we now want to determine whether one of the new feasible solutions provides an improvement in the value of the objective function. Application of the graphical solution procedure to the problem with the enlarged feasible region shows that the extreme point with $x_1 = {}^{100}\!/_3$ and $x_2 = {}^{40}\!/_3$ now provides the optimal solution. The new value for the objective function is $40({}^{100}\!/_3) + 30({}^{40}\!/_3) = 1733.33$, providing an increase in profit of \$1733.33 − \$1600 = \$133.33. Thus, the increased profit occurs at a rate of \$133.33/3 = \$44.44 per ton of material 3 added.

Can you compute and interpret the dual price for a constraint? Try Problem 53.

The *improvement* in the value of the optimal solution per unit increase in the right-hand side of the constraint is called the **dual price.** Here, the dual price for the material 3 constraint is \$44.44 per ton; in other words, if we increase the right-hand side of the material 3 constraint by 1 ton, the value of the objective function will improve by \$44.44. Conversely, if we decrease the right-hand side of the material 3 constraint by 1 ton, the objective function will worsen by \$44.44. Generally, the dual price may be used to determine what will happen to the value of the objective function for a 1 unit change in the right-hand side of a constraint.

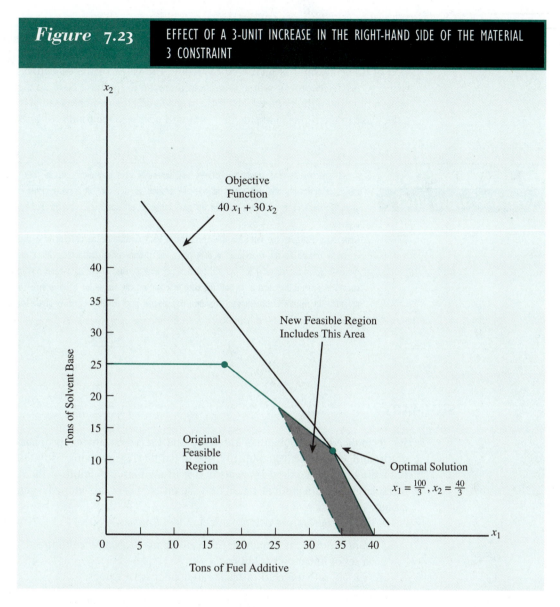

Figure 7.23 EFFECT OF A 3-UNIT INCREASE IN THE RIGHT-HAND SIDE OF THE MATERIAL 3 CONSTRAINT

However, the value of the dual price may be applicable only for small changes in the right-hand side. As more and more resources are obtained and the right-hand-side value continues to increase, other constraints will become binding and limit the change in the value of the objective function. For example, in the RMC problem we would eventually reach a point where more material 3 would be of no value. This result would occur when the material 3 constraint becomes nonbinding. Clearly, at that point the dual price would equal zero. In the next chapter we show how to determine the range of values for a right-hand side over which the dual price will accurately predict the change in the objective function. Finally, we note that the dual price for any nonbinding constraint will be zero because a change in the right-hand side of such a constraint will affect only the value of the slack or surplus variable for that constraint.

To illustrate the correct interpretation of dual prices for a minimization problem, suppose that we had solved a problem involving the minimization of total cost and that the value of the optimal solution was $100. Furthermore, suppose that the dual price for a particular constraint was −$10. The *negative dual price* tells us that the objective function *will not improve* if the value of the right-hand side is increased by 1 unit. Thus, if the right-hand side of this constraint is increased by 1 unit, the value of the objective function will get worse by $10. Becoming worse means an increase in the total cost, so the value of the objective function will become $110 if the right-hand side is increased by 1 unit. Conversely, a decrease in the right-hand side of 1 unit will decrease the total cost by $10.

N O T E S and Comments

1. If two objective function coefficients change simultaneously, both may move outside their respective ranges of optimality and not affect the optimal solution. For instance, in a two-variable linear program, the slope of the objective function will not change if both coefficients are changed by the same percentage.

2. Some texts associate the term *shadow price* with each constraint. The concept of a shadow price is closely related to the concept of a dual price. The shadow price associated with a constraint is the *change* in the value of the optimal solution per unit increase in the right-hand side of the constraint. In general, the dual price and the shadow price are the *same* for all *maximization* linear programs. In *minimization* linear programs, the shadow price is the *negative* of the corresponding dual price.

SUMMARY

We formulated two problems—the RMC and Innis Investments problems—as linear programs and solved them graphically. We noted that, if an optimal solution to a linear programming problem exists, it occurs at one of the extreme points of the feasible region. In formulating a mathematical model of these problems, we developed a general definition of a linear program.

A linear program is a mathematical model that has

1. a linear objective function that is to be maximized or minimized,
2. a set of linear constraints, and
3. variables that are all restricted to nonnegative values.

Slack variables may be used to write less-than-or-equal-to constraints in equality form, and surplus variables may be used to write greater-than-or-equal-to constraints in equality form. The value of a slack variable usually can be interpreted as the amount of unused resource, and the value of a surplus variable indicates the amount by which a minimum requirement is exceeded. When all constraints are written as equalities, the linear program is in its standard form. In the special cases of infeasibility and unboundedness, there is no optimal solution to the problem. In the case of infeasibility, there are no feasible solutions; whereas, in the case of unboundedness the objective function can be made infinitely large for a maximization problem or infinitely small for a minimization problem. In the case of alternative optimal solutions, these are two optimal extreme points, and all the points on the line segment connecting them also are optimal.

The chapter concluded with a discussion of sensitivity analysis, or how changes in the coefficients of a linear program affect the optimal solution. We showed how to use a graphical solution method to determine how a change in one of the objective function coefficients or a change in the right-hand-side value for a constraint will affect the optimal solution to the problem.

..../ /..............

GLOSSARY

Constraint An equation or inequality that restricts the values of the decision variables.

Constraint function The left-hand side of a constraint (i.e., the portion of the constraint containing the variables).

Objective function All linear programs have a linear objective function that is either to be maximized or minimized.

Solution Any set of values for the variables.

Optimal solution A feasible solution that maximizes or minimizes the value of the objective function.

Nonnegativity constraints A set of constraints that requires all variables to be nonnegative.

Mathematical model A representation of a problem where the objective function and all constraint conditions are described by mathematical expressions.

Linear program A mathematical model with a linear objective function, a set of linear constraints, and nonnegative variables.

Linear functions Mathematical expressions in which the variables appear in separate terms and are raised to the first power.

Feasible solution A solution that satisfies all the constraints.

Feasible region The set of solutions that satisfy all the constraints simultaneously.

Slack variable A variable added to the left-hand side of a less-than-or-equal-to constraint to convert the constraint into an equality.

Standard form A linear program in which all constraints are written as equalities. The optimal solution of the standard form of a linear program is the same as the optimal solution of the original formulation of the linear program.

Redundant constraint A constraint that does not affect the feasible region. If a constraint is redundant, it could be removed from the problem without affecting the feasible region.

Extreme points The feasible solution points occurring at the vertices or "corners" of the feasible region. With two variables, extreme points are determined by the intersection of the constraint lines.

Surplus variable A variable subtracted from the left-hand side of a greater-than-or-equal-to constraint to convert the constraint into an equality.

Alternative optimal solutions The situation in which a linear program has more than one solution that provides the optimal value for the objective function.

Infeasibility The situation in which there is no solution to the linear programming problem that satisfies all the constraints.

Unbounded A maximization linear programming problem in which the value of the solution may be made infinitely large without violating any of the constraints; or, a minimization problem in which the value of the solution may be made infinitely small.

Sensitivity analysis The study of how changes in the coefficients of a linear programming problem affect the optimal solution to the problem.

Postoptimality analysis Another name for sensitivity analysis, indicating that the analysis is performed after the optimal solution to the original linear programming problem has been obtained.

Range of optimality The range of values over which an objective function coefficient may vary without causing any change in the values of the decision variables in the optimal solution.

Dual price The improvement in the value of the optimal solution per unit increase in a constraint right-hand-side value.

PROBLEMS

SELF TEST

1. Which of the following mathematical relationships could be found in a linear programming model, and which could not? For the relationships that are unacceptable for linear programs, state the reason for your answer.
    a. $-1x_1 + 2x_2 - 1x_3 \le 70$
    b. $2x_1 - 2x_3 = 50$
    c. $1x_1 - 2x_2^2 + 4x_3 \le 10$
    d. $3\sqrt{x_1} + 2x_2 - 1x_3 \ge 15$
    e. $1x_1 + 1x_2 + 1x_3 = 6$
    f. $2x_1 + 5x_2 + 1x_1x_2 \le 25$

SELF TEST

2. Show a separate graph of the constraint lines and feasible solutions for each of the following constraints.
    a. $4x_1 + 2x_2 \le 16$
    b. $4x_1 + 2x_2 \ge 16$
    c. $4x_1 + 2x_2 = 16$

3. Show a separate graph of the constraint lines and feasible solutions for each of the following constraints.
    a. $3x_1 + 2x_2 \le 18$
    b. $12x_1 + 8x_2 \ge 480$
    c. $5x_1 + 10x_2 = 200$

4. Show a separate graph of the constraint lines and feasible solutions for each of the following constraints.
    a. $3x_1 - 4x_2 \ge 60$
    b. $-6x_1 + 5x_2 \le 60$
    c. $5x_1 - 2x_2 \le 0$

5. Show a separate graph of the constraint lines and feasible solutions for each of the following constraints.
    a. $x_1 \ge 0.25 (x_1 + x_2)$
    b. $x_2 \le 0.10 (x_1 + x_2)$
    c. $x_1 \le 0.50 (x_1 + x_2)$

SELF TEST

6. Three objective functions for linear programming problems are

$$z = 7x_1 + 10x_2$$

$$z = 6x_1 + 4x_2$$

$$z = -4x_1 + 7x_2$$

Determine the slope of each objective function. Show the graph of each for $z = 420$.

7. Identify the feasible region for the following set of constraints.

$$\tfrac{1}{2}x_1 + \tfrac{1}{4}x_2 \geq 30$$
$$1x_1 + 5x_2 \geq 250$$
$$\tfrac{1}{4}x_1 + \tfrac{1}{2}x_2 \leq 50$$
$$x_1, x_2 \geq 0$$

8. Identify the feasible region for the following set of constraints.

$$2x_1 - 1x_2 \leq 0$$
$$-1x_1 + 1.5x_2 \leq 200$$
$$x_1, x_2 \geq 0$$

9. Identify the feasible region for the following set of constraints.

$$3x_1 - 2x_2 \geq 0$$
$$2x_1 - 1x_2 \leq 200$$
$$1x_1 \leq 150$$
$$x_1, x_2 \geq 0$$

10. Solve the linear program:

$$\text{Max} \quad 5x_1 + 5x_2$$
$$\text{s.t.}$$
$$1x_1 \qquad\quad \leq 100$$
$$1x_2 \leq 80$$
$$2x_1 + 4x_2 \leq 400$$
$$x_1, x_2 \geq 0$$

11. For the linear program

$$\text{Max} \quad 2x_1 + 3x_2$$
$$\text{s.t.}$$
$$1x_1 + 2x_2 \leq 6$$
$$5x_1 + 3x_2 \leq 15$$
$$x_1, x_2 \geq 0$$

find the optimal solution. What is the value of the objective function at the optimal solution?

12. Consider the linear programming problem:

$$\text{Max} \quad 3x_1 + 3x_2$$
$$\text{s.t.}$$
$$2x_1 + 4x_2 \leq 12$$
$$6x_1 + 4x_2 \leq 24$$
$$x_1, x_2 \geq 0$$

    a. Find the optimal solution.

    b. If the objective function is changed to $2x_1 + 6x_2$, what will the optimal solution be?

    c. How many extreme points are there? What are the values of x_1 and x_2 at each extreme point?

13. Consider the linear programming problem:

$$\text{Max} \quad 3x_1 + 2x_2$$

s.t.

$$2x_1 + 2x_2 \le 8$$
$$3x_1 + 2x_2 \le 12$$
$$1x_1 + 0.5x_2 \le 3$$
$$x_1, x_2 \ge 0$$

    a. Find the optimal solution. What is the value of the objective function?

    b. Does this problem have a redundant constraint? If so, what is it? Does the solution change if the redundant constraint is removed from the problem? Explain.

SELF TEST

14. Consider the linear program:

$$\text{Max} \quad 1x_1 + 2x_2$$

s.t.

$$1x_1 \quad\quad\ \le 5$$
$$1x_2 \le 4$$
$$2x_1 + 2x_2 = 12$$
$$x_1, x_2 \ge 0$$

    a. Show the feasible region.

    b. What are the extreme points of the feasible region?

    c. Find the optimal solution using the graphical procedure.

15. Par, Inc., is a small manufacturer of golf equipment and supplies. Par has been convinced by its distributor that there is an existing market for both a medium-priced golf bag, referred to as a standard model, and a high-priced golf bag, referred to as a deluxe model. The distributor is so confident of the market that, if Par can make the bags at a competitive price, the distributor has agreed to purchase all the bags that Par can manufacture over the next three months. A careful analysis of the manufacturing requirements resulted in the following table, which shows the production time requirements for the four required manufacturing operations and the accounting department's estimate of the profit contribution per bag.

Product	Production Time (hours)				Profit per Bag
	Cutting and Dyeing	Sewing	Finishing	Inspection and Packaging	
Standard	7/10	1/2	1	1/10	$10
Deluxe	1	5/6	2/3	1/4	$ 9

The director of manufacturing estimates that 630 hours of cutting and dyeing time, 600 hours of sewing time, 708 hours of finishing time, and 135 hours of inspection and packaging time

will be available for the production of golf bags during the next 3 months.
- **a.** If the company wants to maximize total profit contribution, how many bags of each model should it manufacture?
- **b.** What profit contribution can Par earn on those production quantities?
- **c.** How many hours of production time will be scheduled for each operation?
- **d.** What is the slack time in each operation?

16. Suppose that Par's management (Problem 15) encounters the following situations.
- **a.** The accounting department revises its estimate of the profit contribution for the deluxe bag to $18 per bag.
- **b.** A new low-cost material is available for the standard bag, and the profit contribution per standard bag can be increased to $20 per bag. (Assume that the profit contribution of the deluxe bag is the original $9 value.)
- **c.** New sewing equipment is available that would increase the sewing operation capacity to 750 hours. (Assume that $10x_1 + 9x_2$ is the appropriate objective function.)

If each of these situations is encountered separately, what is the optimal solution and the total profit contribution.

17. Refer to the feasible region for the RMC problem in Figure 7.15.
- **a.** Develop an objective function that will make extreme point $(0,540)$ the optimal extreme point.
- **b.** What is the optimal solution for the objective function you selected in part (a)?
- **c.** What are the values of the slack variables associated with this solution?

SELF TEST

18. Write the following linear program in standard form.

$$\text{Max} \quad 5x_1 + 2x_2 + 8x_3$$

s.t.

$$1x_1 - 2x_2 + \tfrac{1}{2}x_3 \leq 420$$
$$2x_1 + 3x_2 - 1x_3 \leq 610$$
$$6x_1 - 1x_2 + 3x_3 \leq 125$$
$$x_1, x_2, x_3 \geq 0$$

19. For the linear program

$$\text{Max} \quad 4x_1 + 1x_2$$

s.t.

$$10x_1 + 2x_2 \leq 30$$
$$3x_1 + 2x_2 \leq 12$$
$$2x_1 + 2x_2 \leq 10$$
$$x_1, x_2 \geq 0$$

- **a.** Write the problem in standard form.
- **b.** Solve the problem.
- **c.** What are the values of the three slack variables at the optimal solution?

20. For the linear program

$$\text{Max} \quad 3x_1 + 4x_2$$

s.t.

$$-1x_1 + 2x_2 \leq 8$$
$$1x_1 + 2x_2 \leq 12$$
$$2x_1 + 1x_2 \leq 16$$
$$x_1, x_2 \geq 0$$

   a. Write the problem in standard form.
   b. Solve the problem.
   c. What are the values of the three slack variables at the optimal solution?

21. For the linear program

$$\text{Max} \quad 3x_1 + 2x_2$$

s.t.

$$x_1 + x_2 \geq 4$$
$$3x_1 + 4x_2 \leq 24$$
$$x_1 \qquad\;\; \geq 2$$
$$x_1 - x_2 \leq 0$$
$$x_1, x_2 \geq 0$$

   a. Write the problem in standard form.
   b. Solve the problem.
   c. What are the values of the slack and surplus variables at the optimal solution?

SELF TEST

22. Kelson Sporting Equipment, Inc., makes two different models of baseball gloves: a regular glove and a catcher's mitt. The firm has 900 hours of production time available in its cutting and sewing department, 300 hours available in its finishing department, and 100 hours available in its packaging and shipping department. The production time requirements and the profit contribution for each product are

Model	Production Time (hours)			Profit/Glove
	Cutting and Sewing	Finishing	Packaging and Shipping	
Regular glove	1	1/2	1/8	$5
Catcher's mitt	3/2	1/3	1/4	$8

Assume that the company is interested in maximizing the total profit contribution.
   a. What is the linear programming model for this problem?
   b. Find the optimal solution. How many gloves of each model should Kelson manufacture?
   c. What is the total profit contribution Kelson can earn with the above production quantities?
   d. How many hours of production time will be scheduled in each department?
   e. What is the slack time in each department?

23. George Johnson recently inherited a large sum of money; he wants to use a portion of this money to set up a trust fund for his two children. The trust fund has two investment options: (1) a bond fund and (2) a stock fund. The projected returns over the life of the investments are 6% for the bond fund and 10% for the stock fund. Whatever portion of the inheritance that he finally decides to commit to the trust fund, he wants to invest at least 30% of that amount in the bond fund. In addition, he wants to select a mix that will enable him to obtain a total return of at least 7.5%.
   a. Formulate a linear programming model that can be used to determine the percentage that should be allocated to each of the possible investment alternatives.
   b. Solve the problem using the graphical solution procedure.

24. The owner of the Sea Wharf Restaurant would like to determine the best way to allocate a monthly advertising budget of $1000 between newspaper advertising and radio advertising. Management has decided that at least 25% of the budget must be spent on each type of media, and that the amount of money spent on local newspaper advertising must be at least twice the amount spent on radio advertising. A marketing consultant has developed an index that measures audience exposure per dollar of advertising on a scale from 0 to 100, with higher values implying greater audience exposure. If the value of the index for local newspaper advertising is 50 and the value of the index for spot radio advertising is 80, how should management allocate the advertising budget to maximize the value of total audience exposure?

a. Formulate a linear programming model that can be used to determine how management should allocate the advertising budget to maximize the value of total audience exposure.

b. Solve the problem using graphical solution procedure.

25. Investment Advisors, Inc., is a brokerage firm that manages stock portfolios for clients. A new client has requested that the firm handle an $80,000 investment portfolio. As an initial investment strategy, the client wants to restrict the portfolio to a mix of the following stocks.

Stock	Price/Share	Estimated Annual Return/Share	Risk Index/Share
U.S. Oil	$25	$3	0.50
Hub Properties	$50	$5	0.25

The risk index for the stock is a rating of the relative risk of the two investment alternatives. For the data given, U.S. Oil is judged to be the riskier investment. By constraining the total risk for the portfolio, the investment firm avoids placing excessive amounts of the portfolio in potentially high-return, high-risk investments. For the current portfolio, an upper limit of 700 has been set for the total risk index of all investments. The firm also has set an upper limit of 1000 shares for the more risky U.S. Oil stock. How many shares of each stock should be purchased to maximize the total annual return?

26. Tom's Inc., produces various Mexican food products and sells them to Western Foods, a chain of grocery stores located in Texas and New Mexico. Tom's, Inc., makes two salsa products: Western Foods Salsa and Mexico City Salsa. Essentially, the two products have different blends of whole tomatoes, tomato sauce, and tomato paste. The Western Foods Salsa is a blend of 50% whole tomatoes, 30% tomato sauce, and 20% tomato paste. The Mexico City Salsa, which has a thicker and chunkier consistency, consists of 70% whole tomatoes, 10% tomato sauce, and 20% tomato paste. Each jar of salsa produced weighs 10 ounces. For the current production period Tom's, Inc., can purchase up to 280 pounds of whole tomatoes, 130 pounds of tomato sauce, and 100 pounds of tomato paste; the price per pound for these ingredients is $0.96, $0.64, and $0.56, respectively. The cost of the spices and the other ingredients is approximately $0.10 per jar. Tom's, Inc., buys empty glass jars for $0.02 each, and labeling and filling costs are estimated to be $0.03 for each jar of salsa produced. Tom's contract with Western Foods results in sales revenue of $1.64 for each jar of Western Foods Salsa and $1.93 for each jar of Mexico City Salsa.

a. Develop a linear programming model that will enable Tom's to determine the mix of salsa products that will maximize the total profit contribution.

b. Graph the feasible region.

c. Solve the appropriate simultaneous linear equations to determine the coordinates of each extreme point.

d. Find the optimal solution.

27. The production editor for Rayburn Publishing Company has 1800 pages of manuscript that must be copyedited. Because of the short time frame involved, only two copyeditors are available: Erhan Mergen and Sue Smith. Erhan has 10 days available, and Sue has 12 days available. Erhan can process 100 pages of manuscript per day, and Sue can process 150 pages of manuscript per day. Rayburn Publishing has developed an index used to measure the overall quality of a copyeditor on a scale from 1 (worst) to 10 (best). Erhan's quality rating is 9, and Sue's quality rating is 6. In addition, Erhan charges $3 per page of copyedited manuscript; Sue charges $2 per

page. If a budget of $4800 has been allocated for copyediting, how many pages should be assigned to each copyeditor to complete the project with the highest possible quality?

28. Car Phones, Inc., sells two models of car telephones: model X and model Y. Records show that 3 hours of sales time are used for each model X telephone that is sold and 5 hours of sales time for each model Y telephone. A total of 600 hours of sales time is available for the next 4-week period. In addition, management planning policies call for minimum sales goals of 25 units for both model X and model Y.
   a. Show the feasible region.
   b. If the company makes a $40 profit contribution for each model X sold and a $50 profit contribution for each model Y sold, what is the optimal sales goal for the company for the next 4-week period?
   c. Develop a constraint and show the feasible region if management adds the restriction that Car Phones must sell at least as many model Y telephones as model X telephones.
   d. What is the new optimal solution if the constraint in part (c) is added to the problem?

SELF TEST

29. Consider the following linear program:

$$\text{Min} \quad 3x_1 + 4x_2$$

s.t.

$$1x_1 + 3x_2 \geq 6$$
$$1x_1 + 1x_2 \geq 4$$
$$x_1, x_2 \geq 0$$

Identify the feasible region and find the optimal solution. What is the value of the objective function?

30. Identify the three extreme-point solutions for the Innis Investments problem (see Section 7.7). Identify the value of the objective function and the values of the slack and surplus variables at each extreme point.

31. Consider the linear program:

$$\text{Min} \quad x_1 + 2x_2$$

s.t.

$$x_1 + 4x_2 \leq 21$$
$$2x_1 + x_2 \geq 7$$
$$3x_1 + 1.5x_2 \leq 21$$
$$-2x_1 + 6x_2 \geq 0$$
$$x_1, x_2 \geq 0$$

   a. Find the optimal solution and the value of the objective function.
   b. Determine the amount of slack or surplus for each constraint.
   c. Suppose that the objective function is changed to max $5x_1 + 2x_2$. Find the optimal solution and the value of the objective function.

32. Consider the linear program:

$$\text{Min} \quad 2x_1 + 2x_2$$

s.t.

$$1x_1 + 3x_2 \leq 12$$
$$3x_1 + 1x_2 \geq 13$$
$$1x_1 - 1x_2 = 3$$
$$x_1, x_2 \geq 0$$

SELF TEST

a. Show the feasible region.
b. What are the extreme points of the feasible region?
c. Find the optimal solution using the graphical solution procedure.

SELF TEST

33. For the linear program

$$\text{Min} \quad 6x_1 + 4x_2$$

s.t.

$$2x_1 + 1x_2 \geq 12$$
$$1x_1 + 1x_2 \geq 10$$
$$1x_2 \leq 4$$
$$x_1, x_2 \geq 0$$

a. Write the problem in standard form.
b. Solve the problem using the graphical solution procedure.
c. What are the values of the slack and surplus variables?

34. Greentree Kennels, Inc., provides overnight lodging for pets. A particular feature at Greentree is the quality of care the pets receive, including excellent food. The kennel's dog food is made by mixing two brand-name dog food products to obtain what the kennel calls the "well-balanced dog diet." The data for the two dog foods are as follows.

Dog Food	Cost/ Ounce	Protein (%)	Fat (%)
Bark Bits	$.06	30	15
Canine Chow	$.05	20	30

If Greentree wants to be sure that the dogs receive at least 5 ounces of protein and at least 3 ounces of fat per day, what is the minimum cost mix of the two dog food products?

35. The New England Cheese Company produces two cheese spreads by blending mild cheddar cheese with sharp cheddar cheese. The cheese spreads are packaged in 12-ounce containers, which are then sold to distributors throughout the Northeast. The Regular blend contains 80% mild cheddar and 20% extra sharp, and the Zesty blend contains 60% mild cheddar and 40% extra sharp. This year, a local dairy cooperative has offered to provide up to 8100 pounds of mild cheddar cheese for $1.20 per pound and up to 3000 pounds of extra sharp cheddar cheese for $1.40 per pound. The cost to blend and package the cheese spreads, excluding the cost of the cheese, is $0.20 per container. If each container of Regular is sold for $1.95 and each container of Zesty is sold for $2.20, how many containers of Regular and Zesty should New England Cheese produce?

36. Healthtech Foods managers are considering developing a new low-fat snack food. It is to be a blend of two types of cereals, each of which has different fiber, fat, and protein characteristics. The following table shows these nutrition characteristics for one ounce of each type of cereal.

Cereal	Dietary Fiber (grams)	Fat (grams)	Protein (grams)
A	2	2	4
B	1.5	3	3

Note that each ounce of cereal A provides 2 grams of dietary fiber and that each ounce of cereal B provides 1.5 grams of dietary fiber. Thus, if Healthtech were to develop the new product using a mix consisting of 50% of cereal A and 50% cereal B, 1 ounce of the snack food would contain 1.75 grams of dietary fiber. Healthtech's nutrition requirements call for each ounce of the new food to have at least 1.7 grams of dietary fiber, no more than 2.8 grams of fat, and no more than 3.6 grams of protein. The cost of cereal A is $0.02 per ounce and the cost of cereal B is $0.025 per ounce. Healthtech wants to determine how much of each cereal is needed to produce 1 ounce of the new food product at the lowest possible cost.

   a. Formulate a linear programming model for this situation.

   b. Solve the problem using the graphical solution procedure.

   c. What are the values of the slack and surplus variables?

   d. If Healthtech markets the new snack food in an 8-ounce package, what is the cost per package?

37. M&D Chemicals produces two products that are sold as raw materials to companies manufacturing bath soaps, laundry detergents, and other soap products. Based on an analysis of current inventory levels and potential demand for the coming month, M&D's management has specified that the total production for products 1 and 2 combined must be at least 350 gallons. Also, a major customer's order for 125 gallons of product 1 must be satisfied. Product 1 requires 2 hours of processing time per gallon and product 2 requires 1 hour of processing time per gallon; for the coming month, 600 hours of processing time are available. Production costs are $2 per gallon for product 1 and $3 per gallon for product 2.

   a. Determine the production quantities that will satisfy the requirements specified at minimum cost.

   b. What is the total product cost?

   c. Identify the amount of any surplus production.

38. Photo Chemicals produces two types of photographic developing fluids. Both products cost Photo Chemicals $1 per gallon to produce. Based on an analysis of current inventory levels and outstanding orders for the next month, Photo Chemicals' management has specified that at least 30 gallons of product 1 and at least 20 gallons of product 2 must be produced during the next 2 weeks. Management also has stated that an existing inventory of highly perishable raw material required in the production of both fluids must be used within the next 2 weeks. The current inventory of the perishable raw material is 80 pounds. Although more of this raw material can be ordered if necessary, any of the current inventory that is not used within the next 2 weeks will spoil—hence, the management requirement that at least 80 pounds be used in the next 2 weeks. Furthermore, product 1 requires 1 pound of this perishable raw material per gallon and product 2 requires 2 pounds of the raw material per gallon. Since management's objective is to keep production costs at the minimum possible level, they are looking for a minimum-cost production plan that uses all the 80 pounds of perishable raw material and provides at least 30 gallons of product 1 and at least 20 gallons of product 2. What is the minimum-cost solution?

39. Bryant's Pizza, Inc., is a producer of frozen pizza products. The company makes a profit of $1.00 for each regular pizza it produces and $1.50 for each deluxe pizza produced. Each pizza includes a combination of dough mix and topping mix. The firm currently has 150 pounds of dough mix and 50 pounds of topping mix. Each regular pizza uses 1 pound of dough mix and 4 ounces of topping mix. Each deluxe pizza uses 1 pound of dough mix and 8 ounces of topping mix. Based on past demand, Bryant can sell at least 50 regular pizzas and at least 25 deluxe pizzas. How many regular and deluxe pizzas should the company make to maximize profits?

   a. What is the linear programming model for this problem?

   b. Write the linear program in standard form.

   c. Find the optimal solution.

   d. What are the values and interpretations of all slack and surplus variables?

   e. Which constraints are binding?

40. Does the following linear program involve infeasibility, unboundedness, and/or alternative optimal solutions? Explain.

SELF TEST

$$\text{Max} \quad 4x_1 + 8x_2$$

s.t.

$$2x_1 + 2x_2 \le 10$$
$$-1x_1 + 1x_2 \ge 8$$
$$x_1, x_2 \ge 0$$

41. Does the following linear program involve infeasibility, unboundedness, and/or alternative optimal solutions? Explain.

$$\text{Max} \quad 1x_1 + 1x_2$$

s.t.

$$8x_1 + 6x_2 \ge 24$$
$$4x_1 + 6x_2 \ge -12$$
$$2x_2 \ge 4$$
$$x_1, x_2 \ge 0$$

42. Consider the linear program:

$$\text{Max} \quad 1x_1 + 1x_2$$

s.t.

$$5x_1 + 3x_2 \le 15$$
$$3x_1 + 5x_2 \le 15$$
$$x_1, x_2 \ge 0$$

a. Find the optimal solution.
b. Suppose that the objective function is changed to $1x_1 + 2x_2$. Find the new optimal solution.
c. By adjusting the coefficient of x_2 in the objective function, develop a new objective function that will make the solutions found in parts (a) and (b) alternative optimal solutions.

43. Consider the linear program:

$$\text{Max} \quad 1x_1 - 2x_2$$

s.t.

$$-4x_1 + 3x_2 \le 3$$
$$1x_1 - 1x_2 \le 3$$
$$x_1, x_2 \ge 0$$

a. Graph the feasible region for the problem.
b. Is the feasible region unbounded? Explain.
c. Find the optimal solution.
d. Does an unbounded feasible region imply that the optimal solution to the linear program will be unbounded?

44. The manager of a small independent grocery store is trying to determine the best use of her shelf space for soft drinks. The store carries national and generic brands and currently has 200 square feet of shelf space available. The manager wants to allocate at least 60% of the space to the national brands and, regardless of the profitability, allocate at least 10% of the space to the generic brands. How many square feet of space should the manager allocate to the national brands and the generic brands if
a. the national brands are more profitable than the generic brands?
b. both brands are equally profitable?
c. the generic brand is more profitable than the national brand?

45. Discuss what happens to the Innis Investments problem (see Section 7.7) if the risk measure for the money market fund is increased to 6.4. What would you recommend? Explain.

46. Reconsider the Innis Investments problem in Section 7.7. Discuss what happens if the client requires an annual return on the investment of at least $100,000 and has specified that no more than $600,000 be invested in the stock fund.

47. Discuss what happens to the Par, Inc., situation in Problem 15 if the profit contribution for the standard model is $6.30. What would you recommend? Explain.

48. Reconsider the Par, Inc., situation in Problem 15. Suppose that management adds the requirements that at least 500 standard bags and at least 360 deluxe bags must be produced.
   a. Graph the constraints for this revised problem. What happens to the feasible region? Explain.
   b. If there are no feasible solutions, explain what is needed to produce 500 standard bags and 360 deluxe bags.

49. Reconsider the Kelson Sporting Equipment, Inc., production situation in Problem 22. Discuss the concepts of infeasibility, unboundedness, and alternative optimal solutions in parts (a) and (b).
   a. Management requests that the production of regular baseball gloves plus catcher's mitts be such that the total number produced is at least 750; that is, $1x_1 + 1x_2 \geq 750$.
   b. The original problem has to be solved again because the profit contribution for the regular glove is adjusted downward to $4 per glove.
   c. What would have to happen for this problem to be unbounded?

50. Recall the Par, Inc., situation in Problem 15. Letting

$$x_1 = \text{number of standard bags produced}$$
$$x_2 = \text{number of deluxe bags produced}$$

leads to the formulation

$$\text{Max} \quad 10x_1 + 9x_2$$
$$\text{s.t.}$$

$$\tfrac{7}{10}x_1 + 1x_2 \leq 630 \quad \text{Cutting and dyeing time}$$
$$\tfrac{1}{2}x_1 + \tfrac{5}{6}x_2 \leq 600 \quad \text{Sewing time}$$
$$1x_1 + \tfrac{2}{3}x_2 \leq 708 \quad \text{Finishing time}$$
$$\tfrac{1}{10}x_1 + \tfrac{1}{4}x_2 \leq 135 \quad \text{Inspection and packaging time}$$
$$x_1, x_2 \geq 0$$

Use the graphical sensitivity analysis approach to determine the range of optimality for the objective function coefficients.

51. For Problem 50 use the graphical sensitivity analysis approach to determine what happens if an additional 10 hours of cutting and dyeing time become available. What is the corresponding dual price for the constraint?

52. Consider the linear program

SELF TEST

$$\text{Max} \quad 2x_1 + 3x_2$$
$$\text{s.t.}$$
$$x_1 + x_2 \leq 10$$
$$2x_1 + x_2 \geq 4$$
$$x_1 + 3x_2 \leq 24$$
$$2x_1 + x_2 \leq 16$$
$$x_1, x_2 \geq 0$$

a. Solve this problem using the graphical solution procedure.
b. Compute the range of optimality for c_1.
c. Compute the range of optimality for c_2.
d. Suppose that c_1 is increased from 2 to 2.5. What is the new optimal solution?
e. Suppose that c_2 is decreased from 3 to 1. What is the new optimal solution?

53. For Problem 52 compute the dual prices for constraints 1 and 2 and interpret them.

SELF TEST

54. Consider the linear program:

$$\text{Min} \quad x_1 + x_2$$

$$\text{s.t.}$$

$$x_1 + 2x_2 \geq 7$$
$$2x_1 + x_2 \geq 5$$
$$x_1 + 6x_2 \geq 11$$
$$x_1, x_2 \geq 0$$

a. Solve this problem using the graphical solution procedure.
b. Compute the range of optimality for c_1.
c. Compute the range of optimality for c_2.
d. Suppose that c_1 is increased to 1.5. Find the new optimal solution.
e. Suppose that c_2 is decreased to ⅓. Find the new optimal solution.

55. For Problem 54 compute and interpret the dual prices for the constraints.

56. Consider the linear program:

$$\text{Max} \quad 5x_1 + 7x_2$$

$$\text{s.t.}$$

$$2x_1 + x_2 \geq 3$$
$$-x_1 + 5x_2 \geq 4$$
$$2x_1 - 3x_2 \leq 6$$
$$3x_1 + 2x_2 \leq 35$$
$$\tfrac{3}{7}x_1 + x_2 \leq 10$$
$$x_1, x_2 \geq 0$$

a. Solve this problem using the graphical solution procedure.
b. Compute the range of optimality for c_1.
c. Compute the range of optimality for c_2.
d. Suppose that c_1 is decreased to 2. What is the new optimal solution?
e. Suppose that c_2 is increased to 10. What is the new optimal solution?

57. Refer to Problem 56. Suppose that the objective function coefficient for c_2 is reduced to 3.
a. Resolve using the graphical solution procedure.
b. Compute the dual prices for constraints 2 and 3.

58. Refer again to Problem 52.
a. Suppose that c_1 is increased to 3 and c_2 is increased to 4. Find the new optimal solution.
b. Suppose that c_1 is increased to 3 and c_2 is decreased to 2. Find the new optimal solution.

59. Refer again to Problem 56.
a. Suppose that c_1 is decreased to 4 and c_2 is increased to 10. Find the new optimal solution.
b. Suppose that c_1 is decreased to 4 and c_2 is increased to 8. Find the new optimal solution.

60. Expedition Outfitters manufactures specialty clothing for hiking, skiing, and mountain climbing. Company management has decided to begin production on two new parkas designed for use in extremely cold weather; the names selected for the two models are the Mount Everest Parka and the Rocky Mountain Parka. The manufacturing plant has 120 hours of cutting time and 120 hours of sewing time available for producing these two parkas. Each Mount Everest Parka requires 30 minutes of cutting time and 45 minutes of sewing time, and each Rocky Mountain Parka requires 20 minutes of cutting time and 15 minutes of sewing time. The labor and material cost is $150 for each Mount Everest Parka and $50 for each Rocky Mountain Parka, and the retail prices through the firm's mail-order catalog are $250 for the Mount Everest Parka and $200 for the Rocky Mountain Parka. Because management believes that the Mount Everest Parka is a unique coat that will enhance the image of the firm, they have specified that at least 20% of the total production must consist of this model. Assuming that Expedition Outfitters can sell as many coats of each type as it can produce, how many units of each model should it manufacture to maximize the total profit contribution?

61. English Motors, Ltd, (EML), has developed a new all-wheel-drive sports utility vehicle. As part of the marketing campaign, EML has developed a videotape sales presentation that will be sent to both owners of current EML four-wheel-drive vehicles as well as to owners of four-wheel-drive sports utility vehicles offered by competitors; EML refers to these two target markets as the current customer market and the new customer market. Individuals who receive the new promotion video will also receive a coupon for a test drive of the new EML model for one weekend. A key factor in the success of the new promotion is the response rate, the percentage of individuals that receives the new promotion and test drives the new model, EML estimates that the response rate for the current customer market is 25%, and the response rate for the new customer market is 20%. The sales rate is the percentage of individuals that receives the new promotion, takes the test drive, and makes a purchase. Marketing research studies indicate that the sales rate is 12% for the current customer market and 20% for the new customer market. The cost for each promotion, excluding the test drive costs, are $5 for each promotion sent to the current customer market and $4 for each promotion sent to the new customer market. Management has also specified that a minimum of 30,000 current customers should be sent the new promotion and a minimum of 10,000 new customers should be sent the new promotion. In addition, the number of current customers that test drives the new vehicle must be at least twice the number of new customers that test drives the new vehicle. If the marketing budget, excluding test drive costs, is $1,200,000, how many promotions should be sent to each group of customers to maximize total sales?

62. Creative Sports Designs (CSD) manufactures a standard-size racket and an oversize racket. The firm's rackets are extremely light due to the use of a magnesium–graphite alloy that was invented by the firm's founder. Each standard-size racket uses 0.125 kilograms of the alloy and each oversize racket uses 0.4 kilograms; over the next 2-week production period only 80 kilograms of the alloy are available. Each standard-size racket uses 10 minutes of manufacturing time and each oversize racket uses 12 minutes. The profit contributions are $10 for each standard-size racket and $15 for each oversize racket, and 40 hours of manufacturing time are available each week. Management has specified that at least 20% of the total production must be the standard-size racket. How many rackets of each type should CSD manufacture over the next 2 weeks to maximize the total profit contribution? Assume that because of the unique nature of their products, CSD can sell as many rackets as it can produce.

63. Management of High Tech Services (HTS) wants to develop a model that will help allocate its technicians' time between service calls to regular contract customers and new customers. A maximum of 80 hours of technician time is available over the 2-week planning period. To satisfy cash flow requirements, at least $800 in revenue (per technician) must be generated during the 2-week period. Technician time for regular customers generates $25 per hour. However, technician time for new customers only generates an average of $8 per hour because in many cases a new customer contact does not provide billable services. To ensure that new customer contacts are being maintained, the technician time spent on new customer contacts must be at least 60% of the time spent on regular customer contacts. For the revenue and policy requirements stated, HTS would like to determine how to allocate technician time between regular cus-

tomers and new customers to maximize the total number of customers contacted during the 2-week period. Technicians require an average of 50 minutes for each regular customer contact and 1 hour for each new customer contact.

 a. Develop a linear programming model that will enable HTS to allocate technician time between regular customers and new customers.

 b. Graph the feasible region.

 c. Solve the appropriate simultaneous linear equations to determine the values of x_1 and x_2 at each extreme point of the feasible region.

 d. Find the optimal solution.

64. Jackson Hole Manufacturing is a small manufacturer of plastic products used in the automotive and computer industries. One major contract is with a large computer company and involves the production of plastic printer cases for the computer company's portable printers. The printer cases are produced on two injection molding machines. The M-100 machine has a production capacity of 20 printer cases per hour, and the M-200 machine has a production capacity of 40 cases per hour. Both machines use the same chemical material to produce the printer cases; the M-100 uses 40 pounds of the raw material per hour, and the M-200 uses 50 pounds per hour. The computer company has asked Jackson Hole to produce as many of the cases during the upcoming week as possible and has said that it will pay $18 for each case Jackson Hole can deliver. However, next week is a regularly scheduled vacation period for most of Jackson Hole's production employees; during this time, annual maintenance is performed for all equipment in the plant. Because of the downtime for maintenance, the M-100 will be available for no more than 15 hours, and the M-200 will be available for no more than 10 hours. However, because of the high setup cost involved with both machines, management has a requirement that, if production is scheduled on either machine, the machine must be operated for at least 5 hours. The supplier of the chemical material used in the production process has informed Jackson Hole that a maximum of 1000 pounds of the chemical material will be available for next week's production; the cost for this raw material is $6 per pound. In addition to the raw material cost, Jackson Hole estimates that the hourly cost of operating the M-100 and the M-200 are $50 and $75, respectively.

 a. Formulate a linear programming model that can be used to maximize the contribution to profit.

 b. Solve the problem using the graphical solution procedure.

..../ /..............

Case Problem   ADVERTISING STRATEGY

Midtown Motors, Inc., has hired a marketing services firm to develop an advertising strategy for promoting Midtown's used car sales. The marketing firm has recommended that Midtown use spot announcements on both television and radio as the advertising media for the proposed promotional campaign. Advertising strategy guidelines are expressed as follows:

 1. Use at least 30 announcements for combined television and radio coverage.

 2. Do not use more than 25 radio announcements.

 3. The number of radio announcements cannot be less than the number of television announcements.

  The television station has quoted a cost of $1200 per spot announcement, and the radio station has quoted a cost of $300 per spot announcement. Midtown's advertising budget has been set at $25,500. The marketing services firm has rated the various advertising media in terms of audience coverage and recall power of the advertisement. For Midtown's media alternatives, the television announcement is rated at 600 and the radio announcement is rated at 200. Midtown's president would like to know how many television and how many radio spot announcements should be used to maximize the overall rating of the advertising campaign.

Midtown's president believes that the television station will consider running the Midtown spot announcement on its highly rated evening news program (at the same cost) if Midtown will consider using additional television announcements.

Managerial Report

Perform an analysis of advertising strategy for Midtown Motors and prepare a report to Midtown's president presenting your findings and recommendations. Include (but do not limit your discussion to) a consideration of the following items.

a. The recommended number of television and radio spot announcements.
b. The relative merits of each advertising medium.
c. The rating that would be necessary for the news program before it would make sense to increase the number of television spots.
d. The number of television spots that should be purchased if the news program is rated highly enough to make increasing the number of television spots advisable.
e. The restrictions placed on the advertising strategy that Midtown might want to consider relaxing or altering.
f. The best use of any possible increase in the advertising budget.
g. Any other information that may help Midtown's president make the advertising strategy decision.

Include a copy of your linear programming model and graphical solution in an appendix to your report.

Case Problem   PRODUCTION STRATEGY

Better Fitness, Inc. (BFI) manufactures exercise equipment at its plant in Freeport, Long Island. It recently designed two universal weight machines for the home exercise market. Both machines use BFI-patented technology that provides the user with an extremely wide range of motion capability for each type of exercise performed. Until now, such capabilities have been available only on very expensive weight machines used primarily by physical therapists.

At a recent trade show, demonstrations of the machines resulted in significant dealer interest. In fact, the number of orders that BFI received at the trade show far exceeded its manufacturing capabilities for the current production period. As a result, management decided to begin production of the two machines. The two machines, which BFI has named the BodyPlus 100 and the BodyPlus 200, require different amounts of resources to produce.

The BodyPlus 100 consists of a frame unit, a press station, and a pec-dec station. Each frame produced uses 4 hours of machining and welding time and 2 hours of painting and finishing time. Each press station requires 2 hours of machining and welding time and 1 hour of painting and finishing time, and each pec-dec station uses 2 hours of machining and welding time and 2 hours of painting and finishing time. In addition, 2 hours are spent assembling, testing, and packaging each BodyPlus 100. The raw material costs are $450 for each frame, $300 for each press station, and $250 for each pec-dec station; packaging costs are estimated to be $50 per unit.

The BodyPlus 200 consists of a frame unit, a press station, a pec-dec station, and a leg-press station. Each frame produced uses 5 hours of machining and welding time and 4 hours of painting and finishing time. Each press station requires 3 hours of machining and welding time and 2 hours of painting and finishing time, each pec-dec station uses 2 hours of machining and welding time and 2 hours of painting and finishing time, and each leg-press station requires 2 hours of machining and welding time and 2 hours of painting and finishing time. In addition, 2 hours are spent assembling, testing, and packaging each BodyPlus 200. The raw material costs are $650 for each frame, $400 for each press station, $250 for each pec-dec station, and $200 for each leg-press station; packaging costs are estimated to be $75 per unit.

For the next production period, management estimates that 600 hours of machining and welding time, 450 hours of painting and finishing time, and 140 hours of assembly, testing, and packaging time will be available. Current labor costs are $20 per hour for machining and welding time, $15 per hour for painting and finishing time, and $12 per hour for assembly, testing, and packaging time. The market in which the two machines must compete suggests a retail price of $2400 for the BodyPlus 100 and $3500 for the BodyPlus 200, although some flexibility may be available to BFI because of the unique capabilities of the new machines. Authorized BFI dealers can purchase machines for 70% of the suggested retail price.

BFI's president believes that the unique capabilities of the BodyPlus 200 can help position BFI as one of the leaders in high-end exercise equipment. Consequently, he has stated that the number of units of the BodyPlus 200 produced must be at least 25% of the total production.

Managerial Report

Analyze Better Fitness, Inc.'s production problem and prepare a report to BFI's president presenting your findings and recommendations. Include (but do not limit your discussion to) a consideration of the following items.

1. The recommended number of BodyPlus 100 and BodyPlus 200 machines to produce.
2. The effect on profits of the requirement that the number of units of the BodyPlus 200 produced must be at least 25% of the total production.
3. Where efforts should be expended in order to increase profits.

Include a copy of your linear programming model and graphical solution in an appendix to your report.

8

LINEAR PROGRAMMING:

FORMULATION, COMPUTER

SOLUTION, AND INTERPRETATION

In this chapter we provide an introduction to the use of computers for solving linear programming problems. We begin by showing how to interpret computer output from The Management Scientist for the RMC and Innis Investments problems presented in Chapter 7. Then we extend the discussion by formulating and solving two slightly larger problems having three decision variables. In discussing the computer solution for each of these problems, we focus on the interpretation of the computer output, including both the optimal solution and sensitivity analysis information. The final section provides both general guidelines for problem formulation and further practice in the formulation, computer solution, and interpretation of computer output for a problem involving four decision variables and various types of constraints. Three appendixes provide details on using The Management Scientist, LINDO, and spreadsheets to solve linear programming problems.

..../ /..............

8.1   COMPUTER SOLUTION OF LINEAR PROGRAMS

In January 1952 the first successful computer solution of a linear programming problem was performed on the SEAC (Standards Eastern Automatic Computer). The SEAC, the first digital computer built by the National Bureau of Standards under U.S. Air Force sponsorship, had a 512-word memory and magnetic tape for external storage.

Computer programs designed to solve linear programming problems are now widely available. Most companies and universities have access to these computer programs. After a short period of familiarization with the specific features of the program, most users can solve linear programming problems with few difficulties. Problems involving thousands of variables and thousands of constraints are now routinely solved with computer packages. Most large linear programs can be solved with just a few minutes of computer time; small linear programs usually require only a few seconds.

Recently there has been a virtual explosion of software for personal computers. A large number of user-friendly computer programs that can solve linear programs are now available. These programs, developed by academicians and small software companies, are almost all easy to use. Most of these programs are designed to solve smaller linear programs (a few hundred variables). But some can be used to solve problems involving thousands of variables and constraints. Linear programming solvers are now part of many spreadsheet packages. In Appendix 8.3, we show how to use the solver available with Microsoft Excel.

The Management Scientist, a software package developed by the authors of this text, contains a linear programming module. Let us demonstrate its use by solving the RMC problem introduced in Chapter 7. Recall that the objective is to maximize total profit contribution from the production of x_1 tons of fuel additive and x_2 tons of solvent base. Because computer input must utilize decimal rather than fractional data values, we restate the linear program for the RMC problem with decimal coefficients:

$$\text{Max} \quad 40x_1 + 30x_2$$
$$\text{s.t.}$$
$$0.4x_1 + 0.5x_2 \leq 20 \quad \text{Material 1}$$
$$0.2x_2 \leq 5 \quad \text{Material 2}$$
$$0.6x_1 + 0.3x_2 \leq 21 \quad \text{Material 3}$$
$$x_1, x_2 \geq 0$$

The solution[1] generated by The Management Scientist is shown in Figure 8.1.

Interpretation of Computer Output

Let us look more closely at The Management Scientist output in Figure 8.1 and interpret the computer solution provided for the RMC problem. First, note that the number 1600.000, which appears to the right of objective function value, indicates that the optimal solution to this problem will provide a profit of $1600. Directly below the objective function value are the values of the decision variables at the optimal solution. Thus, we have $x_1 = 25$ tons of fuel additive and $x_2 = 20$ tons of solvent base as the optimal production quantities.

The information in the reduced costs column indicates how much the objective function coefficient of each decision variable would have to improve[2] before it would be possible for that variable to assume a positive value in the optimal solution. If a decision variable is already positive in the optimal solution, its reduced cost is zero. For the RMC

---

1. The steps required to generate this solution are described in Appendix 8.1
2. For a maximization problem, *improve* means get bigger; for a minimization problem, *improve* means get smaller.

Figure 8.1	THE MANAGEMENT SCIENTIST SOLUTION FOR THE RMC PROBLEM

Objective Function Value =   1600.000

Variable	Value	Reduced Costs
X1	25.000	0.000
X2	20.000	0.000

Constraint	Slack/Surplus	Dual Prices
1	0.000	33.333
2	1.000	0.000
3	0.000	44.444

OBJECTIVE COEFFICIENT RANGES

Variable	Lower Limit	Current Value	Upper Limit
X1	24.000	40.000	60.000
X2	20.000	30.000	50.000

RIGHT HAND SIDE RANGES

Constraint	Lower Limit	Current Value	Upper Limit
1	14.000	20.000	21.500
2	4.000	5.000	No Upper Limit
3	18.750	21.000	30.000

problem, the optimal solution is $x_1 = 25$ and $x_2 = 20$. Both variables already have positive values, so their corresponding reduced costs are zero. In Section 8.2 we interpret the reduced cost for a decision variable that does not have a positive value in the optimal solution.

Immediately following the optimal x_1 and x_2 values and the reduced cost information, the computer output provides information about the status of the constraints. Recall that the RMC problem had three less-than-or-equal-to constraints corresponding to the tons available for each of the three raw materials. The information shown in the slack/surplus column provides the value of the slack variable for each of the raw materials. This information is summarized as follows:

Constraint Number	Constraint Name	Slack
1	Material 1	0
2	Material 2	1
3	Material 3	0

From this information, we see that the binding constraints (the material 1 and material 3 constraints) have zero slack at the optimal solution. The material 2 constraint has 1 ton of slack, or unused capacity.

The dual prices column contains information about the value of each of the three resources at the optimal solution. In Chapter 7 we defined the dual price as follows:

The dual price associated with a constraint is the *improvement* in the value of the solution per-unit increase in the right-hand side of the constraint.

You should be able to use computer output to determine the optimal solution, and you should be able to interpret the values of the dual prices. Try Problem 1.

Thus, the nonzero dual prices of 33.333 for constraint 1 (material 1 constraint) and 44.444 for constraint 3 (material 3 constraint) tell us that an additional ton of material 1 improves (increases) the value of the optimal solution by \$33.33 and an additional ton of material 3 improves (increases) the value of the optimal solution by \$44.44. Thus, if the number of tons of material 1 were increased from 20 to 21 tons, with all other coefficients in the problem remaining the same, RMC's profit would be increased by \$33.33 from \$1600 to \$1600 + \$33.33 = \$1633.33. A similar interpretation for the material 3 constraint implies that an increase from 21 to 22 tons of material, with all other coefficients in the problem remaining the same, would increase RMC's profit to \$1600 + \$44.44 = \$1644.44. Since the material 2 constraint has slack or unused capacity available, the dual price of zero shows that additional hours of this resource will not improve the value of the objective function.

Referring again to the computer output in Figure 8.1, we see that after providing the constraint information on slack/surplus variables and dual prices, The Management Scientist prints the ranges on the objective function coefficients and the right-hand sides of the constraints.

The information provided under the computer output heading **OBJECTIVE COEFFICIENT RANGES** shows that variable x_1, which has a current profit coefficient of 40, has the following *range of optimality* for c_1:

$$24 \leq c_1 \leq 60$$

This range tells us that as long as the profit contribution associated with the fuel additive is between \$24 and \$60, the production of $x_1 = 25$ tons of fuel additive and $x_2 = 20$ tons of solvent base will remain the optimal solution. Note that this is the range of optimality that we obtained by performing graphical sensitivity analysis for c_1 in Section 7.10.

Using the objective function coefficient range information for the solvent base, The Management Scientist has computed the following range of optimality for c_2:

$$20 \leq c_2 \leq 50$$

This range tells us that as long as the profit contribution associated with the solvent base is between \$20 and \$50, the production of $x_1 = 25$ tons of fuel additive and $x_2 = 20$ tons of solvent base will remain the optimal solution.

The final section of the computer printout, **RIGHT HAND SIDE RANGES**, contains ranging information for the constraint right-hand sides. As long as the constraint right-hand side stays within this range, the associated dual price gives the improvement in the value of the optimal solution per-unit increase in the right-hand side. For example, let us consider the material 1 constraint with a current right-hand-side value of 20. Since the dual price for this constraint is \$33.33, we can conclude that additional tons of this material will increase the

You should now be able to use computer output to determine the ranges of optimality and the ranges of feasibility. Try Problem 2.

objective function by \$33.33 per ton. A reduction in the tons available will reduce the value of the objective function by \$33.33 per ton. From the range information given, we see that the dual price of \$33.33 is valid for increases up to 21.5 tons and decreases down to 14 tons. A similar interpretation for the material 3 constraint shows that the dual price of \$44.44 is applicable for increases up to 30 tons and decreases down to 18.75 tons.

As mentioned, the right-hand-side ranges provide limits within which the dual prices are applicable. For changes outside the range, the problem must be resolved to find the new optimal solution and the new dual price. We call the range over which the dual price is applicable the **range of feasibility.** The ranges of feasibility for the RMC problem are

Constraint	Min RHS	Max RHS
Material 1	14	21.5
Material 2	4	No upper limit
Material 3	18.75	30

As long as the values of the right-hand sides are within these ranges, the dual prices shown on the computer output will not change. Right-hand-side values outside these limits will result in changes in the dual price information.

Simultaneous Changes

The sensitivity analysis information in computer output is based on the assumption that only one coefficient changes and that all other coefficients will remain as originally stated. Thus, the ranges for the objective function coefficients and the constraint right-hand sides are applicable only for changes in a single coefficient. In many cases, however, we may be interested in what would happen if two or more coefficients are changed simultaneously. As we demonstrate, some analysis of simultaneous changes is possible with the help of the **100 percent rule.**[3] We begin by showing how the 100 percent rule applies to simultaneous changes in the objective function coefficients.

Suppose that in the RMC problem the accounting department concluded that the original profit contributions of \$40 and \$30 for the fuel additive and solvent base, respectively, were incorrectly computed; the correct values should have been \$44 and \$25. To determine what effect, if any, these simultaneous changes have on the optimal solution, we first need to define the terms "allowable increase" and "allowable decrease." For an objective function coefficient, the allowable increase is the maximum amount the coefficient may be increased without exceeding the upper limit of the range of optimality; the allowable decrease is the maximum amount the coefficient may be decreased without dropping below the lower limit of the range of optimality.

Figure 8.1 shows that the upper limit for the objective function coefficient of x_1 is 60; thus, the allowable increase is $60 - 40 = 20$. In terms of percentage change, the increase of \$4 in the objective function coefficient (from 40 to 44) for the fuel additive is $(4/20)(100) = 20\%$ of the allowable increase. For the lower limit of 20 for x_2, the allowable decrease for c_2 is $30 - 20 = 10$. In terms of percentage change, the decrease of \$5 in the objective function coefficient (from \$30 to \$25) for the solvent base is $(5/10)(100) = 50\%$ of the allowable

---

3. See Bradley, S. P., A. C. Hax, and T. L. Magnanti, *Applied Mathematical Programming* (Reading, Mass.: Addison-Wesley, 1977).

decrease. The sum of the percentage change of the allowable increase (20%) and the percentage change of the allowable decrease (50%) is 70%.

Let us now state the 100 percent rule as it applies to simultaneous changes in the objective function coefficients.

For all objective function coefficients that are changed, sum the percentages of the allowable increases and the allowable decreases represented by the changes. If the sum of the percentage changes does not exceed 100%, the optimal solution will not change.

Thus, since the sum of the two percentage changes in the objective function coefficients for the RMC problem is 70%, these simultaneous changes will not affect the optimal solution. Note, however, that although the optimal solution is still $x_1 = 25$ and $x_2 = 20$, the value of the optimal solution will change since the profit contribution for the fuel additive has increased to \$44, and the profit contribution for the solvent base has decreased to \$25.

However, the 100 percent rule does not say that the optimal solution will change if the sum of the percentage changes exceeds 100%. The optimal solution may not change even though the sum of the percentage changes exceeds 100%. When the 100 percent rule is not satisfied, we must resolve the problem to determine the effect such changes will have on the optimal solution.

A similar version of the 100 percent rule also applies to simultaneous changes in the constraint right-hand sides.

For all right-hand sides that are changed, sum the percentages of allowable increases and allowable decreases. If the sum of percentages does not exceed 100%, the dual prices will not change.

Let us illustrate the 100 percent rule for constraint right-hand sides by considering simultaneous changes in the right-hand sides for the RMC problem. Suppose that we could obtain 1 additional ton of material 1 and 2 additional tons of material 3. The allowable increase for material 1 is $21.5 - 20 = 1.5$, and the allowable increase for material 3 is $30 - 21 = 9$ (see Figure 8.1). The 1 additional ton of material 1 is $(1/1.5)(100) = 66.67\%$ of the allowable increase in the constraint's right-hand side. The 2 additional tons of material 3 are $(2/9)(100) = 22.22\%$ of the allowable increase in the material 3 constraint's right-hand side. The sum of the percentage changes is $66.67\% + 22.22\% = 88.89\%$. Since the sum of the percentage changes does not exceed 100%, we can conclude that the dual prices are applicable and that the objective function will improve by $(1)(33.33) + (2)(44.44) = 122.21$.

Interpretation of Computer Output—A Second Example

Recall the Innis Investments minimization problem introduced in Section 7.7. For a new client Innis has been authorized to invest up to \$1.2 million in two investment funds: a stock fund and a money market fund. The objective is to minimize the total risk index for the portfolio. The linear programming model for this problem is restated below, where x_1 = units purchased in the stock fund and x_2 = units purchased in the money market fund.

$$\text{Min} \quad 8x_1 + 3x_2$$

s.t.

$$50x_1 + 100x_2 \leq 1{,}200{,}000 \quad \text{Funds available}$$
$$5x_1 + 4x_2 \geq 60{,}000 \quad \text{Annual income}$$
$$x_2 \geq 3{,}000 \quad \text{Minimum units in money market}$$

$$x_1, x_2 \geq 0$$

The solution obtained using The Management Scientist is presented in Figure 8.2. The computer output shows that 4000 units of the stock fund ($x_1 = 4000$) and 10,000 units of the money market fund ($x_2 = 10{,}000$) provides the minimum total risk index portfolio.

The slack/surplus column shows that the $\geq$ constraint for the money market minimum (constraint corresponding to the minimum number of units purchased in the money market fund) has a surplus of 7000 units. Thus the number of units of the money market fund in the optimal solution exceeds the minimum requirement by 7000 units. The slack/surplus values are zero for the other two constraints, which indicates that these constraints are binding at the optimal solution.

The dual prices column again shows the improvement in the value of the optimal solution per-unit increase in the right-hand side of the constraint. Focusing first on the dual price of 0.057 for the funds available constraint (constraint 1), we see that if we can increase the funds available by $1, the objective function value will *improve* by 0.057 risk-index units. Since the objective is to minimize the total risk index, improvement in this case means a lowering of the total portfolio risk index. Thus, if $1 is available, the value of the optimal solution will improve (decrease) to 61,999.943. The right-hand side ranges section of the output shows that the upper limit for the funds available constraint (constraint 1) is 1,500,000. Thus, the dual price of $0.057 per unit would be applicable for every additional dollar up to a total of $1,500,000.

Let us again return to the dual prices section of the output and consider the dual price for the annual income constraint (constraint 2). The *negative dual price* tells us that the value of the optimal solution *will not improve* if the value of the right-hand side is increased by one unit. In fact, the dual price of -2.167 tells us that if the right-hand side of the annual income constraint is increased from $60,000 to $60,001 units, the value of the optimal solution will worsen by the amount of 2.167. Worsening means an increase in the total risk index, so the value of the optimal solution will become $62{,}000 + 2.167 = 62{,}002.167$ if the one-dollar increase in the annual income requirement is made.

Since the dual price refers to improvement in the value of the optimal solution per-unit increase in the right-hand side, a constraint with a negative dual price should not have its right-hand side increased. In fact, if the dual price is negative, efforts should be made to reduce the right-hand side of the constraint. If the right-hand side of the annual income constraint were decreased from $60,000 to $59,999, the dual price tells us that the total portfolio risk index could be lowered by 2.167 to $62{,}000 - 2.167 = 61{,}997.833$.

The dual price is the improvement in the value of the optimal solution per-unit increase in the right-hand side of a constraint. However, the interpretation of an *improvement* in the value of an objective function depends on whether we are solving a maximization or a minimization problem. The dual price for a $\leq$ constraint will always be greater than or equal to zero because increasing the right-hand side cannot make the value of the objective function worse. Similarly, the dual price for a $\geq$ constraint will always be less than or equal to zero because increasing the right-hand side cannot improve the value of the optimal solution.

```
Objective Function Value =                  62000.000

          Variable              Value            Reduced Costs
       --------------      ---------------      ------------------

            X1                 4000.000               0.000
            X2                10000.000               0.000


          Constraint         Slack/Surplus          Dual Prices
       --------------      ---------------      ------------------

             1                  0.000                 0.057
             2                  0.000                -2.167
             3               7000.000                 0.000

OBJECTIVE COEFFICIENT RANGES

     Variable       Lower Limit         Current Value      Upper Limit
   ------------   ---------------      ---------------   ---------------

       X1               3.750                8.000        No Upper Limit
       X2         No Lower Limit             3.000               6.400

RIGHT HAND SIDE RANGES

   Constraint       Lower Limit         Current Value      Upper Limit
   ------------   ---------------      ---------------   ---------------

       1             780000.000          1200000.000       1500000.000
       2              48000.000            60000.000        102000.000
       3          No Lower Limit            3000.000         10000.000
```

Finally, consider the right-hand-side ranges provided in Figure 8.2. The ranges of feasibility for the Innis Investments problem are

Constraint	Min RHS	Max RHS
Funds available	$780,000	$1,500,000
Annual income	$ 48,000	$ 102,000
Minimum money market	No lower limit	10,000

You should now be able to interpret the computer output for a minimization problem. Try Problem 6.

As long as the right-hand sides are within these ranges, the dual prices shown on the computer printout are applicable.

Cautionary Note on the Interpretation of Dual Prices

As stated previously, the dual price is the improvement in the value of the optimal solution per-unit increase in the right-hand side of a constraint. When the right-hand side of the constraint represents the amount of a resource available, the associated dual price often is interpreted as the maximum amount someone should be willing to pay for 1 additional unit of the resource. However, such an interpretation isn't always correct. To see why, we need to understand the difference between sunk and relevant costs. A **sunk cost** is one that is not affected by the decision made. It will be incurred regardless of the values the decision variables assume. A **relevant cost** is one that depends on the decision made. The amount of a relevant cost will vary, depending on the values of the decision variables.

Let us reconsider the RMC problem. The amount of material 1 available is 20 tons. The cost of material 1 is a sunk cost if it must be paid regardless of the number of tons of fuel additive and solvent base produced. It would be a relevant cost if RMC only had to pay for the number of tons of material 1 actually used to produce fuel additive and solvent base. All relevant costs should be reflected in the objective function of a linear program. Sunk costs should not be reflected in the objective function. For RMC, we have been assuming that the company has already paid for materials 1, 2, and 3. Therefore the cost of the raw materials for RMC is a sunk cost and has not been reflected in the objective function.

Only relevant costs should be included in the objective function.

When the cost of a resource is *sunk,* the dual price can be interpreted as the maximum amount the company should be willing to pay for 1 additional unit of the resource. When the cost of a resource used is relevant, the dual price can be interpreted as the amount by which the value of the resource exceeds its cost. Thus, when the resource cost is relevant, the dual price can be interpreted as the maximum premium over the normal cost that the company should be willing to pay for 1 additional unit of the resource.

N O T E S
and Comments

1. Computer software packages for solving linear programs are readily available. Most provide the optimal solution, dual price information, the range of optimality for the objective function coefficients, and the range of feasibility for the right-hand sides. The labels used for the ranges of optimality and feasibility may vary, but the meaning is the same as that used here.

2. Whenever one of the right-hand sides is at an end point of its range of feasibility, the dual prices provide only one-sided information. In this case, they only predict the change in the optimal value of the objective function for changes toward the interior of the range.

3. A condition called degeneracy can cause a subtle difference in how we interpret changes in the objective function coefficients beyond the end points of the range of optimality. Degeneracy occurs when the dual price equals zero for one of the binding constraints. Degeneracy does not affect the interpretation of changes toward the interior of the range of optimality. However, when degeneracy is present, changes beyond the end points of the range do not necessarily mean a different solution will be optimal. From a practical point of view, changes beyond the end points of the range of optimality necessitate resolving the problem.

4. The 100 percent rule permits an analysis of multiple changes in the right-hand sides or multiple changes in the objective function coefficients. But the 100 percent rule cannot be applied to changes in both objective function coefficients *and* right-hand sides at the same time. In order to consider simultaneous changes for *both* right-hand-side values and objective function coefficients, the problem must be resolved.

5. Managers are frequently called on to provide an economic justification for new technology. Often the new technology is developed, or purchased, in order to conserve resources. The dual price can be helpful in such cases because it can be used to determine the savings attributable to the new technology by showing the savings per unit of resource conserved.

..../ /............

8.2   LINEAR PROGRAMS WITH MORE THAN TWO DECISION VARIABLES

In this section we discuss the formulation of and computer solution for two linear programs with three decision variables. In doing so, we show how to interpret the reduced-cost portion of the computer output and also illustrate the interpretation of dual prices for constraints that involve percentages.

The Modified RMC Problem

In Section 8.1 we demonstrated the use of the linear programming module of The Management Scientist in solving the RMC problem. Again, we restate the original problem with decimal coefficients:

$$\text{Max}\quad 40x_1 + 30x_2$$

s.t.

$$0.4x_1 + 0.5x_2 \le 20 \quad \text{Material 1}$$
$$0.2x_2 \le 5 \quad \text{Material 2}$$
$$0.6x_1 + 0.3x_2 \le 21 \quad \text{Material 3}$$
$$x_1, x_2 \ge 0$$

Recall that x_1 is the number of tons of fuel additive produced and that x_2 is the number of tons of solvent base produced. Suppose that management also is considering producing a carpet cleaning fluid. Estimates are that each ton of carpet cleaning fluid will require 0.6 tons of material 1, 0.1 tons of material 2, and 0.3 tons of material 3. Because of the unique capabilities of the new product, RMC's management believes that the company will realize a profit contribution of $50 for each ton of carpet cleaning fluid produced during the current production period.

Let us consider the modifications in the original linear programming model that are needed to incorporate the effect of this additional decision variable. We let x_3 denote the number of tons of carpet cleaning fluid produced. After adding x_3 to the objective function and to each of the three constraints, we obtain the linear program for the modified problem:

$$\text{Max}\quad 40x_1 + 30x_2 + 50x_3$$

s.t.

$$0.4x_1 + 0.5x_2 + 0.6x_3 \le 20$$
$$0.2x_2 + 0.1x_3 \le 5$$
$$0.6x_1 + 0.3x_2 + 0.3x_3 \le 21$$
$$x_1, x_2, x_3 \ge 0$$

Figure 8.3 shows The Management Scientist solution to the modified RMC problem. The optimal solution calls for the production of 27.5 tons of fuel additive, 0 tons of solvent base, and 15 tons of carpet cleaning fluid. The value of the optimal solution is $1850.

Figure 8.3	THE MANAGEMENT SCIENTIST SOLUTION FOR THE MODIFIED RMC PROBLEM

Objective Function Value =   1850.000

Variable	Value	Reduced Costs
X1	27.500	0.000
X2	0.000	12.500
X3	15.000	0.000

Constraint	Slack/Surplus	Dual Prices
1	0.000	75.000
2	3.500	0.000
3	0.000	16.667

OBJECTIVE COEFFICIENT RANGES

Variable	Lower Limit	Current Value	Upper Limit
X1	33.333	40.000	100.000
X2	No Lower Limit	30.000	42.500
X3	33.333	50.000	60.000

RIGHT HAND SIDE RANGES

Constraint	Lower Limit	Current Value	Upper Limit
1	14.000	20.000	34.000
2	1.500	5.000	No Upper Limit
3	10.000	21.000	30.000

Note the information contained in the reduced costs column. Recall that the reduced costs indicate how much each objective function coefficient would have to improve before the corresponding decision variable could assume a positive value in the optimal solution. As the computer output shows, the reduced costs for x_1 and x_3 are zero because the corresponding decision variables already have positive values in the optimal solution. The reduced cost of 12.500 for variable x_2 tells us that the profit contribution for the solvent base would have to increase to at least $30 + $12.50 = $42.50 before x_2 *could* assume a positive value in the optimal solution.[4] In other words, unless the profit contribution for x_2 increases by at least $12.50 the value of x_2 will remain at zero in the optimal solution.

4. In the case of degeneracy, a variable may not assume a positive value in the optimal solution even when the improvement in the profit contribution exceeds the value of the reduced cost. Our definition of reduced costs, stated as "... *could* assume a positive value ...," provides for such special cases. More advanced texts on mathematical programming discuss these special types of situations.

Suppose that we increase the coefficient of x_2 by \$12.501 and then resolve the problem using The Management Scientist. Figure 8.4 shows the new solution. Although x_2 assumes a positive value in the new solution ($x_2 = 20.000$), the value of the optimal solution (\$1850.020) has only increased by two cents. Note that the difference of two cents is just 20, the number of units of x_2 produced in the new solution, times 0.001, the amount we increased the coefficient of x_2 beyond 12.50. In some computer software packages, increasing the objective function coefficient of x_2 by *exactly* \$12.50 will result in a solution in which x_2 assumes a positive value and the value of the objective function remains at 1850. In other words, increasing the profit contribution of x_2 by exactly the amount of the reduced cost will result in alternative optimal solutions. However, whenever the profit contribution of x_2 is increased by *more than* \$12.50, then x_2 will not remain at zero in the optimal solution.

Figure 8.3 also shows that the dual prices for constraints 1 and 3 are 75.000 and 16.667, respectively, indicating that these two constraints are binding in the optimal solution. Thus, each additional ton of material 1 would increase the value of the optimal solution by \$75 and each additional ton of material 3 would increase the value of the optimal solution by \$16.667.

Suppose that after reviewing the solution shown in Figure 8.3, management states that it will not consider any solution that doesn't include the production of some solvent base. Management then decides to add the requirement that the number of tons of solvent base produced must be at least 25% of the number of tons of fuel additive produced. Writing this requirement using the decision variables x_1 and x_2, we obtain

$$x_2 \geq 0.25x_1 \quad \text{or} \quad -0.25x_1 + x_2 \geq 0$$

Adding this new constraint to the modified RMC linear program and resolving the problem using The Management Scientist, we obtain the optimal solution shown in Figure 8.5.

Let us interpret the dual price for constraint 4, the requirement that the number of tons of solvent base produced must be at least 25% of the number of tons of fuel additive produced. The dual price of -12.121 indicates that a 1-unit increase in the right side of the constraint will lower profits by \$12.121. Thus, what the dual price of -12.121 is actually telling us is what will happen to the value of the optimal solution if the constraint is changed to

$$x_2 \geq 0.25x_1 + 1$$

The correct interpretation of the dual price of -12.121 can now be stated as follows: If we are forced to produce 1 ton of solvent base over and above the minimum 25% requirement, total profits will decrease by \$12.121. Conversely, if we relax the minimum 25% requirement by 1 ton ($x_2 \geq 0.25x_1 - 1$), total profits will increase by \$12.121.

The dual price for a percentage (or ratio) constraint such as this will not directly provide answers to questions concerning a percentage increase or decrease in the right-hand side of the constraint. For example, what would happen to the value of the optimal solution if the number of tons of solvent base produced has to be at least 26% of the number of standard bags? To answer such a question, we would resolve the problem using the constraint $-0.26x_1 + x_2 \geq 0$.

Because percentage (or ratio) constraints frequently occur in linear programming models, we need to consider another example. For instance, suppose that RMC's management states that the number of tons of carpet cleaning fluid produced may not exceed 20% of total production. Since total production is $x_1 + x_2 + x_3$, we can write this constraint as

Figure 8.4	THE MANAGEMENT SCIENTIST SOLUTION FOR THE MODIFIED RMC PROBLEM WITH THE COEFFICIENT OF x_2 INCREASED BY $12.50

Objective Function Value =   1850.020

Variable	Value	Reduced Costs
X1	25.000	0.000
X2	20.000	0.000
X3	0.000	0.001

Constraint	Slack/Surplus	Dual Prices
1	0.000	75.003
2	1.000	0.000
3	0.000	16.664

OBJECTIVE COEFFICIENT RANGES

Variable	Lower Limit	Current Value	Upper Limit
X1	34.001	40.000	40.008
X2	42.500	42.501	50.000
X3	No Lower Limit	50.000	50.001

RIGHT HAND SIDE RANGES

Constraint	Lower Limit	Current Value	Upper Limit
1	14.000	20.000	21.500
2	4.000	5.000	No Upper Limit
3	18.750	21.000	30.000

$$x_3 \leq 0.2(x_1 + x_2 + x_3)$$
$$x_3 \leq 0.2x_1 + 0.2x_2 + 0.2x_3$$
$$-0.2x_1 - 0.2x_2 + 0.8x_3 \leq 0$$

The solution obtained using The Management Scientist for the model that incorporates both the effects of this new percentage requirement and the previous requirement $(-0.25x_1 + x_2 \geq 0)$ is shown in Figure 8.6. After rounding, the dual price corresponding to the new constraint (constraint 5) is 16.13. Thus, every additional ton of carpet cleaning fluid that we are allowed to produce over the current 20% limit will increase the value of the

Figure 8.5	THE MANAGEMENT SCIENTIST SOLUTION FOR THE MODIFIED RMC PROBLEM WITH THE 25% SOLVENT BASE REQUIREMENT

Objective Function Value =   1766.667

Variable	Value	Reduced Costs
X1	26.667	0.000
X2	6.667	0.000
X3	10.000	0.000

Constraint	Slack/Surplus	Dual Prices
1	0.000	78.788
2	2.667	0.000
3	0.000	9.091
4	0.000	-12.121

OBJECTIVE COEFFICIENT RANGES

Variable	Lower Limit	Current Value	Upper Limit
X1	36.250	40.000	105.000
X2	15.000	30.000	42.500
X3	33.333	50.000	54.286

RIGHT HAND SIDE RANGES

Constraint	Lower Limit	Current Value	Upper Limit
1	16.333	20.000	32.571
2	2.333	5.000	No Upper Limit
3	10.000	21.000	25.714
4	-6.875	0.000	13.750

objective function by \$16.13; moreover, the right-hand-side range for this constraint shows that this interpretation is valid for increases of up to 1.333 tons.

The Bluegrass Farms Problem

To provide additional practice in formulating and interpreting the computer solution for linear programs involving more than two decision variables, we consider a minimization prob-

| Figure 8.6 | THE MANAGEMENT SCIENTIST SOLUTION FOR THE MODIFIED RMC PROBLEM WITH 25% SOLVENT BASE AND 20% CARPET CLEANING FLUID REQUIREMENTS |

```
Objective Function Value =                         1745.161

        Variable               Value            Reduced Costs
     --------------        --------------      ------------------

          X1                   26.452               0.000
          X2                    8.387               0.000
          X3                    8.710               0.000


       Constraint          Slack/Surplus           Dual Prices
     --------------        --------------      ------------------

           1                   0.000               38.710
           2                   2.452                0.000
           3                   0.000               46.237
           4                   1.774                0.000
           5                   0.000               16.129


OBJECTIVE COEFFICIENT RANGES

     Variable          Lower Limit        Current Value        Upper Limit
    ------------      --------------      --------------      --------------

        X1                23.462             40.000              64.000
        X2                16.667             30.000              42.500
        X3                33.333             50.000          No Upper Limit


RIGHT HAND SIDE RANGES

    Constaint          Lower Limit        Current Value        Upper Limit
   ------------      --------------      --------------      --------------

        1                19.463             20.000              24.000
        2                 2.548              5.000          No Upper Limit
        3                15.698             21.000              21.579
        4            No Lower Limit          0.000               1.774
        5                -9.000              0.000               1.333
```

lem involving three decision variables. Bluegrass Farms, located in Lexington, Kentucky, has been experimenting with a special diet for its racehorses. The feed components available for the diet are a standard horse feed product, a vitamin-enriched oat product, and a new vitamin and mineral feed additive. The nutritional values in units per pound and the costs for the three feed components are summarized in Table 8.1; for example, each pound of the standard feed component contains 0.8 unit of ingredient A, 1 unit of ingredient B, and

Table 8.1	NUTRITIONAL VALUE AND COST DATA FOR THE BLUEGRASS FARMS PROBLEM		
		Feed Component	
	Standard	Enriched Oat	Additive
Ingredient A	0.8	0.2	0.0
Ingredient B	1.0	1.5	3.0
Ingredient C	0.1	0.6	2.0
Cost per pound	$0.25	$0.50	$3.00

0.1 unit of ingredient C. The minimum daily diet requirements for each horse are three units of ingredient A, six units of ingredient B, and four units of ingredient C. In addition, to control the weight of the horses, the total daily feed for a horse should not exceed 6 pounds. Bluegrass Farms wants to determine the minimum-cost mix that will satisfy the daily diet requirements.

Formulation of the Bluegrass Farms Problem

To formulate a linear programming model for the Bluegrass Farms problem, we introduce three decision variables:

$$x_1 = \text{number of pounds of the standard horse feed product}$$
$$x_2 = \text{number of pounds of the enriched oat product}$$
$$x_3 = \text{number of pounds of the vitamin and mineral feed additive}$$

Using the data in Table 8.1, we write the objective function for minimizing the total cost associated with the daily feed as follows:

$$\text{Min}\quad 0.25x_1 + 0.50x_2 + 3x_3$$

For the minimum daily requirement for ingredient A of 3 units, we obtain the constraint

$$0.8x_1 + 0.2x_2 \geq 3$$

The constraint for ingredient B is

$$1.0x_1 + 1.5x_2 + 3.0x_3 \geq 6$$

and the constraint for ingredient C is

$$0.1x_1 + 0.6x_2 + 2.0x_3 \geq 4$$

Finally, the constraint that restricts the mix to no more than 6 pounds is

$$x_1 + x_2 + x_3 \leq 6$$

Combining all the constraints with the nonnegativity requirements enables us to write the complete linear programming model for the Bluegrass Farms problem as follows:

$$\text{Min} \quad 0.25x_1 + 0.50x_2 + 3x_3$$

s.t.

$$0.8x_1 + 0.2x_2 \qquad\qquad \geq 3 \quad \text{Ingredient A}$$
$$1.0x_1 + 1.5x_2 + 3.0x_3 \geq 6 \quad \text{Ingredient B}$$
$$0.1x_1 + 0.6x_2 + 2.0x_3 \geq 4 \quad \text{Ingredient C}$$
$$x_1 + \quad x_2 + \quad x_3 \leq 6 \quad \text{Weight}$$
$$x_1, x_2, x_3 \geq 0$$

Computer Solution and Interpretation for the Bluegrass Farms Problem

The output obtained using The Management Scientist to solve the Bluegrass Farms problem is shown in Figure 8.7. The optimal solution (after rounding) calls for a daily diet consisting of 3.51 pounds of the standard horse feed product, 0.95 pound of the enriched oat product, and 1.54 pounds of the vitamin and mineral feed additive. Thus, with feed component costs of $0.25, $0.50, and $3.00, the total cost of the optimal diet is

$$3.51 \text{ pounds @ \$0.25 per pound} = \$0.88$$
$$0.95 \text{ pound @ \$0.50 per pound} = 0.47$$
$$1.54 \text{ pounds @ \$3.00 per pound} = \underline{4.62}$$
$$\text{Total cost} = \$5.97$$

Note that, after rounding, this total is the same as the objective function value in the computer output (Figure 8.7).

Looking at the slack/surplus section of the computer output, we find a value of 3.554 for constraint 2. Since constraint 2 is a greater-than-or-equal-to constraint, 3.554 is the surplus; thus the optimal solution exceeds the minimum daily diet requirement for ingredient B (six units) by 3.554 units. Since the surplus values for constraints 1 and 3 are both zero, the optimal diet just meets the minimum requirements for ingredients A and C; moreover, a slack value of zero for constraint 4 shows that the optimal solution provides a total daily feed weight of 6 pounds.

The dual price (after rounding) for the ingredient A constraint (constraint 1) is -1.22. To interpret this value properly, we first look at the sign; it is negative, so we know that increasing the right-hand side of constraint 1 will cause the solution value to worsen. Because this is a minimization problem, "worsen" means that the total daily cost will increase; thus, a 1-unit increase in the right-hand side of constraint 1 will increase the total cost of the daily diet by $1.22. Conversely, a decrease of 1 unit in the right-hand side will decrease the total cost by $1.22. Looking at the right-hand-side ranges section of the computer output, we see that these interpretations are correct as long as the right-hand side is between 1.143 and 3.368.

Suppose that the Bluegrass management is willing to reconsider its position regarding the maximum weight of the daily diet. The dual price of 0.92 (after rounding) for constraint 4 shows that a 1-unit increase in the right-hand side of constraint 4 will reduce total cost by $0.92. The right-hand-side ranges section of the output shows that this interpretation is correct for increases in the right-hand-side up to a maximum of 8.478 pounds. Thus, the effect of increasing the right-hand side of constraint 4 from 6 to 8 pounds is a decrease in the

| Figure 8.7 | THE MANAGEMENT SCIENTIST SOLUTION FOR THE BLUEGRASS FARMS PROBLEM |

Objective Function Value =   5.973

Variable	Value	Reduced Costs
X1	3.514	0.000
X2	0.946	0.000
X3	1.541	0.000

Constraint	Slack/Surplus	Dual Prices
1	0.000	-1.216
2	3.554	0.000
3	0.000	-1.959
4	0.000	0.919

OBJECTIVE COEFFICIENT RANGES

Variable	Lower Limit	Current Value	Upper Limit
X1	-0.393	0.250	No Upper Limit
X2	No Lower Limit	0.500	0.925
X3	1.522	3.000	No Upper Limit

RIGHT HAND SIDE RANGES

Constraint	Lower Limit	Current Value	Upper Limit
1	1.143	3.000	3.368
2	No Lower Limit	6.000	9.554
3	2.100	4.000	4.875
4	5.563	6.000	8.478

total daily cost of 2 × $0.92 or $1.84. Keep in mind that if this change were made, the feasible region would change, and we would obtain a new optimal solution.

The objective coefficient ranges section of the computer output shows a lower limit of -0.393 for c_1. Clearly, in a real-world problem, the objective function coefficient of x_1 (the cost of the standard horse feed product) cannot take on a negative value. So, from a practical point of view, we can think of the lower limit for the objective function coefficient of x_1 as being zero. We can thus conclude that no matter how much the cost of the standard mix were to decrease, the optimal solution would not change. Even if Bluegrass Farms could obtain the standard horse feed product for free, the optimal solution would still specify a daily diet of 3.51 pounds of the standard horse feed product, 0.95 pound of the enriched oat product, and 1.54 pounds of the vitamin and mineral feed additive. However, any decrease in the per-unit cost of the standard feed would result in a decrease in the total cost for the optimal daily diet.

Note that the objective function coefficient values for x_1 and x_3 have no upper limit. Even if the cost of x_3 were to increase, for example, from \$3.00 to \$13.00 per pound, the optimal solution would not change; the total cost of the solution, however, would increase by \$10 (the amount of the increase) times 1.541 or \$15.41. The interpretations that we have made using the sensitivity analysis information in the computer output are appropriate only if all other coefficients in the problem do not change. To consider simultaneous changes you must use the 100 percent rule or resolve the problem after making the changes.

8.3   MODELING

As used in this text, problem formulation and modeling mean the same thing.

Modeling is the process of translating a verbal statement of a problem into a mathematical statement. In linear programming, the mathematical statement of the problem is a linear program. So far, the problems that we have considered have been small and not particularly difficult to model. But, as problems become larger and more complex, some general guidelines for model formulation are useful.

Guidelines for Model Formulation

The process of formulating linear programming models is an art that can be mastered only with practice and experience. Although every problem has *some* unique features, most problems also have common features. As a result, some general guidelines for model formulation can be helpful, especially for beginners.

1. **Understand the problem thoroughly.** Read the problem description thoroughly to get a feel for what is involved. Identify those items that you think should be included in the model. If the problem is especially complex, take notes; these notes will help you focus on the key ideas and facts.
2. **Write a verbal statement of the objective function and each constraint.** Later you will translate these verbal statements into mathematical statements. At this step, you might write the objective function as, for instance, maximize profit or minimize monthly operating costs. You might write a constraint limiting funds borrowed as follows: funds borrowed ≤ line of credit. Even experienced quantitative analysts find that they sometimes make mistakes when skipping this step.
3. **Define the decision variables.** Ask yourself what decisions the manager must make. What does she or he control? The decision variables should be chosen to represent these decisions. The decision variables also should be defined to facilitate writing a mathematical statement of the objective function and the left-hand side of the constraints.
4. **Write the objective function in terms of the decision variables.** Translate your verbal statement of the objective function developed in Step 2 into a mathematical statement; the mathematical statement must be a linear function of the decision variables.
5. **Write the constraints in terms of the decision variables.** Translate your verbal statement of each constraint developed in Step 2 into a mathematical statement; the left-hand side of the resulting equation or inequality must be a linear function of the decision variables.

Q.M. IN ACTION

AN OPTIMAL WOOD PROCUREMENT POLICY*

Wellborn Cabinet, Inc., operates an integrated sawmill and cabinet manufacturing system in Alabama. Its manufacturing facility consists of a sawmill, four dry kilns, and a wood cabinet assembly plant; the assembly plant includes a rough mill for producing cabinet components that are referred to as blanks. Because of the pressure to market quality products at competitive prices, a major concern for Wellborn Cabinet is to maintain consistency in product quality. A key factor in maintaining this quality depends on controlling the quality and costs of raw materials.

To produce blanks, Wellborn Cabinet purchases #1 and #2 grade hardwood logs, as well as #1 and #2 dry or green common grade lumber (note: higher numbers denote higher quality). During a typical five-day week of operation, the sawmill can process up to 1550 logs with a small-end diameter from 9 to 22 inches. Usually, the lumber is purchased in bundles containing random sizes. Both the logs processed by the sawmill and the green lumber purchased from outside suppliers are dried at the kilns to an average moisture content of 7%; the dried

material is then planed and converted into about 130 different sizes of blanks at the rough mill.

Wellborn developed a linear programming model of the blank production system. The objective was to determine a procurement plan that would minimize the total cost of producing blanks for a five-day work week. Constraints included capacities of the sawmill and dry kilns, the demand for blanks at the manufacturing plant, and the available supply of raw materials. The initial results indicate that the company can minimize the total cost of producing blanks by purchasing only #2 grade logs and #2 common green lumber; approximately 88% of the rough mill dry lumber requirements should come from #2 grade logs and the rest from purchased #2 common green lumber. The projected annual savings in raw material costs were $412,000.

*Based on Carino, H. F., and C. H. LeNoir, Jr., "Optimizing Wood Procurement in Cabinet Manufacturing." *Interfaces,* March–April 1988, pp. 10–19.

After carrying out these steps, you will have a linear programming model that represents the problem, or application, under study. Solution of the model will provide the optimal solution, the values of decision variables, the values of the slack/surplus variables, and a variety of information concerning the sensitivity analysis aspects of the problem. Proper interpretation of the solution can provide valuable decision-making information for the manager. The Q. M. in Action: An Optimal Wood Procurement Policy describes how Wellborn Cabinet, Inc., realized projected annual savings of $412,000 by using a linear programming model to determine an optimal wood procurement policy.

Next, we illustrate the modeling process for the Electronic Communications problem. After reading the written description of the problem, you should attempt to formulate a model based on the preceding guidelines. Then, solve the problem using a linear programming software package, and compare your solution with the one provided.

The Electronic Communications Problem

Electronic Communications manufactures portable radio systems that can be used for two-way communications. The company's new product, which has a range of up to 25 miles, is suitable for a variety of business and personal uses. The distribution channels for the new radio are

1. marine equipment distributors,
2. business equipment distributors,
3. national chain of retail stores, and
4. mail order.

Because of differing distribution and promotional costs, the profitability of the product will vary with the distribution channel. In addition, the advertising cost and the personal sales effort required will vary with the distribution channels. Table 8.2 summarizes the contribu-

Table 8.2	PROFIT, ADVERTISING COST, AND PERSONAL SALES TIME DATA FOR THE ELECTRONIC COMMUNICATIONS PROBLEM		
Distribution Channel	**Profit per Unit Sold**	**Advertising Cost per Unit Sold**	**Personal Sales Effort per Unit Sold**
Marine distributors	$90	$10	2 hours
Business distributors	$84	$ 8	3 hours
National retail stores	$70	$ 9	3 hours
Mail order	$60	$15	None

tion to profit, advertising cost, and personal sales effort data pertaining to the Electronic Communications problem. The firm has set the advertising budget at $5000, and a maximum of 1800 hours of sales force time is available for allocation to the sales effort. Management also decided to produce 600 units for the current production period. Finally, an ongoing contract with the national chain of retail stores requires that at least 150 units be distributed through this distribution channel.

Electronic Communications now faces the problem of establishing a distribution strategy for the radios that will maximize overall profitability of the new radio production. Decisions must be made about how many units should be allocated to each of the four distribution channels, as well as how to allocate the advertising budget and sales force effort to each of the four distribution channels.

Formulation of the Electronic Communications Problem

A written statement of the problem has been presented. Let us now attempt to write a verbal statement of the objective function and each constraint. For the objective function, we can write

Objective function: Maximize profit

Four constraints appear to be necessary for this problem because of (1) a limited advertising budget, (2) a limited sales force availability, (3) a production requirement, and (4) a retail stores distribution requirement.

Constraint 1: Advertising expenditures ≤ Budget

Constraint 2: Sales time used ≤ Time available

Constraint 3: Radios produced = Management requirement

Constraint 4: Retail distribution ≥ Contract requirement

With this verbal description of the objective function and the constraints, we are now ready to define the decision variables representing the decisions that the manager must make. For the Electronic Communications problem, we introduce four decision variables.

x_1 = the number of units produced for the marine equipment distribution channel
x_2 = the number of units produced for the business equipment distribution channel
x_3 = the number of units produced for the national retail chain distribution channel
x_4 = the number of units produced for the mail-order distribution channel

Using the data in Table 8.2, we write the objective function for maximizing the total contribution to profit associated with the radios as

$$\text{Max} \quad 90x_1 + 84x_2 + 70x_3 + 60x_4$$

We now develop a mathematical statement of the constraints for the problem. With an advertising budget of $5000, the constraint that limits the amount of advertising expenditure is

$$10x_1 + 8x_2 + 9x_3 + 15x_4 \leq 5000$$

Similarly, for the sales time limit of 1800 hours,

$$2x_1 + 3x_2 + 3x_3 \leq 1800$$

Management's decision to produce 600 units during the current production period yields

$$1x_1 + 1x_2 + 1x_3 + 1x_4 = 600$$

Finally, to account for the 150 or more units that must be distributed by the national chain of retail stores, we add the constraint

$$1x_3 \geq 150$$

Combining all the constraints with the nonnegativity requirements enables us to write the complete linear programming model for the Electronic Communications problem:

$$
\begin{aligned}
\text{Max} \quad & 90x_1 + 84x_2 + 70x_3 + 60x_4 \\
\text{s.t.} \quad & \\
& 10x_1 + 8x_2 + 9x_3 + 15x_4 \leq 5000 \quad \text{Advertising budget} \\
& 2x_1 + 3x_2 + 3x_3 \leq 1800 \quad \text{Sales force availability} \\
& 1x_1 + 1x_2 + 1x_3 + 1x_4 = 600 \quad \text{Production level} \\
& 1x_3 \geq 150 \quad \text{Retail stores requirement} \\
& x_1, x_2, x_3, x_4, \geq 0
\end{aligned}
$$

Computer Solution and Interpretation for the Electronic Communications Problem

A portion of the output obtained using The Management Scientist to solve the Electronic Communications problem is shown in Figure 8.8. The objective function value section shows that the optimal solution to the problem will provide a maximum profit of $48,450. The optimal values of the decision variables are given by $x_1 = 25$, $x_2 = 425$, $x_3 = 150$, and $x_4 = 0$. Thus, the optimal strategy for Electronic Communications is to concentrate on the business equipment distribution channel with $x_2 = 425$ units. In addition, the firm should allocate 25 units to the marine distribution channel ($x_1 = 25$) and meet its 150-unit commitment to the national retail chain store distribution channel ($x_3 = 150$). With $x_4 = 0$, the optimal solution indicates that the firm should not use the mail-order distribution channel.

Figure 8.8	A PORTION OF THE MANAGEMENT SCIENTIST COMPUTER OUTPUT FOR THE ELECTRONIC COMMUNICATIONS PROBLEM

```
Objective Function Value =            48450.000

        Variable            Value           Reduced Costs
        --------            -----           -------------
          X1              25.000               0.000
          X2             425.000               0.000
          X3             150.000               0.000
          X4               0.000              45.000


       Constraint      Slack/Surplus          Dual Prices
       ----------      -------------          -----------
           1               0.000                 3.000
           2              25.000                 0.000
           3               0.000                60.000
           4               0.000               -17.000
```

Now consider the information contained in the reduced costs column. Recall that the reduced costs indicate how much each objective function coefficient would have to improve before the corresponding decision variable could assume a positive value in the optimal solution. As the computer output shows, the first three reduced costs are zero because the corresponding decision variables already have positive values in the optimal solution. However, the reduced cost of 45.000 for variable x_4 tells us that the profit for the new radios distributed via the mail-order channel would have to increase from its current value of $60 per unit to at least $60 + $45 = $105 per unit before using the mail-order distribution channel would be profitable.

We restate the computer output information for the slack/surplus variables and the dual prices:

Constraint Number	Constraint	Type of Constraint	Slack or Surplus	Dual Price
1	Advertising budget	≤	0	3
2	Sales force availability	≤	25	0
3	Production level	=	0	60
4	Retail stores requirement	≥	0	− 17

The advertising budget constraint has a slack of zero, indicating that the entire budget of $5000 has been used. The corresponding dual price of 3 tells us that an additional dollar added to the advertising budget will improve the objective function (increase the profit) by $3. Thus, the possibility of increasing the advertising budget should be seriously considered by the firm. The slack of 25 hours for the sales force availability constraint shows that the allocated 1800 hours of sales time are adequate to distribute the radios produced and that 25 hours of sales time will remain unused. Since the production level constraint is an equality, the zero slack/surplus is expected. However, the dual price of 60 associated with this constraint shows that if the firm were to consider increasing the production level for the radios, the value of the objective function, or profit, would improve at the rate of $60 per unit produced. Finally, the surplus of zero associated with the retail store distribution channel commitment is a result of this constraint being binding. The negative dual price indicates that increasing the commitment from 150 to 151 units will actually decrease the profit by $17. Thus, Electronic Communications may want to consider reducing its commitment to the retail store distribution channel. A *decrease* in the commitment will actually improve profit at the rate of $17 per unit.

We now consider the additional sensitivity analysis information provided by the computer output shown in Figure 8.9. The ranges of optimality for the objective function coefficients are

> Reduced costs also are available from the objective coefficient ranges shown in Figure 8.9. For example, the reduced cost of $45 for x_4 is the difference between the upper limit of $105 and the current value of the objective function coefficient, $60.

$$84 \leq c_1 < \text{No upper limit}$$
$$50 \leq c_2 \leq 90$$
$$\text{No lower limit} < c_3 \leq 87$$
$$\text{No lower limit} < c_4 \leq 105$$

Note in particular the range of optimality associated with the mail-order distribution channel coefficient, c_4. This information is consistent with the earlier observation for the reduced costs portion of the output. In both instances, the profit per unit would have to increase to $105 before the mail-order distribution channel could be in the optimal solution with a positive value.

Figure 8.9 — OBJECTIVE COEFFICIENT AND RIGHT HAND SIDE RANGES PROVIDED BY THE MANAGEMENT SCIENTIST FOR THE ELECTRONIC COMMUNICATIONS PROBLEM

OBJECTIVE COEFFICIENT RANGES

Variable	Lower Limit	Current Value	Upper Limit
X1	84.000	90.000	No Upper Limit
X2	50.000	84.000	90.000
X3	No Lower Limit	70.000	87.000
X4	No Lower Limit	60.000	105.000

RIGHT HAND SIDE RANGES

Constraint	Lower Limit	Current Value	Upper Limit
1	4950.000	5000.000	5850.000
2	1775.000	1800.000	No Upper Limit
3	515.000	600.000	603.571
4	0.000	150.000	200.000

Finally, the sensitivity analysis information on right-hand side ranges provides the ranges of feasibility for the right-hand-side values.

Constraint	Min RHS	Current Value	Max RHS
Advertising budget	4950	5000	5850
Sales force availability	1775	1800	No upper limit
Production level	515	600	603.57
Retail stores requirement	0	150	200

Do you feel comfortable interpreting the computer output for problems involving more than two decision variables? Try Problems 8 and 9.

Several interpretations of these ranges are possible. In particular, recall that the dual price for the advertising budget constraint enabled us to conclude that each $1 increase in the budget would improve the profit by $3. The range for the advertising budget shows that this statement about the value of increasing the budget is appropriate up to $5850. Increases above this level would not necessarily be beneficial. Also note that the dual price of -17 for the retail stores requirement suggested the desirability of reducing this commitment. The range of feasibility for this constraint shows that the commitment could be reduced to zero and the value of the reduction would be at the rate of $17 per unit.

Again, the *sensitivity analysis* or *postoptimality analysis* provided by computer software packages for linear programming problems considers only *one change at a time,* with all other coefficients of the problem remaining as originally specified. As mentioned earlier, simultaneous changes can sometimes be analyzed without resolving the problem, provided that the cumulative changes are not large enough to violate the 100 percent rule.

Finally, recall that the complete solution to the Electronic Communications problem requested information not only on the number of units to be distributed over each channel, but also on the allocation of the advertising budget and the sales force effort to each distribution channel. Since the optimal solution is $x_1 = 25$, $x_2 = 425$, $x_3 = 150$, and $x_4 = 0$, we can simply evaluate each term in a given constraint to determine how much of the constraint resource is allocated to each distribution channel. For example, the advertising budget constraint of

$$10x_1 + 8x_2 + 9x_3 + 15x_4 \leq 5000$$

shows $10x_1 = 10(25) = \$250$, $8x_2 = 8(425) = \$3400$, $9x_3 = 9(150) = \$1350$, and $15x_4 = 15(0) = \$0$. Thus, the advertising budget allocations are, respectively, $250, $3400, $1350, and $0 for each of the four distribution channels. Making similar calculations for the sales force constraint results in the managerial summary of the Electronic Communications optimal solution shown in Table 8.3.

SUMMARY

In this chapter we showed how to use computer software packages to solve linear programming problems. Since the graphical method and graphical sensitivity analysis are limited to linear programs with two decision variables, we presented a computer solution procedure as a practical method of solving linear programming problems with more than two decision variables. Although many software packages are available for computer solution, we used The Management Scientist to illustrate linear programming solutions on a

| Table 8.3 | | PROFIT-MAXIMIZING STRATEGY FOR THE ELECTRONIC COMMUNICATIONS PROBLEM |

Distribution Channel	Volume	Advertising Allocation	Sales Force Allocation (hours)
Marine distributors	25	$ 250	50
Business distributors	425	3400	1275
National retail stores	150	1350	450
Mail order	0	0	0
Totals	600	$5000	1775

Projected total profit contribution = $48,450

personal computer. We showed the computer output for several example problems to demonstrate the use and interpretation of the results. In addition to the value of the objective function and the optimal values of the decision variables, the computer output provides a variety of additional information concerning slack, surplus, and dual prices, as well as objective function coefficient and right-hand-side ranges. In the final section of the chapter, we provided some general guidelines for model formulation and then applied them to a sample problem. In the chapter appendixes we show how The Management Scientist, LINDO, and spreadsheet packages are used to solve linear programs.

The Q.M. in Action: Using Linear Programming for Traffic Control provides another example of the widespread use of linear programming. It is being used all over the world for a wide variety of problems. In the next chapter we will see many more applications of linear programming.

GLOSSARY

Reduced cost The amount by which an objective function coefficient would have to improve (increase for a maximization problem, decrease for a minimization problem), before it would be possible for the corresponding variable to assume a positive value in the optimal solution.

Dual price The improvement in the value of the objective function per-unit increase in a constraint right-hand side.

Range of optimality The range of values over which an objective function coefficient may vary without causing any change in the values of the decision variables in the optimal solution.

Range of feasibility The range of values over which a right-hand side may vary without changing the value and interpretation of the dual price.

100 percent rule A rule indicating when simultaneous changes in two or more objective function coefficients will not cause a change in the optimal values for the decision variables. It can also be applied to indicate when two or more right-hand-side changes will not cause a change in any dual prices.

Sunk cost A cost that is not affected by the decision made. It will be incurred regardless of the values the decision variables assume.

Q.M. IN ACTION

USING LINEAR PROGRAMMING FOR TRAFFIC CONTROL*

The Hanshin Expressway was the first urban toll expressway in Osaka, Japan. Although in 1964 its length was only 2.3 kilometers, today it is a large-scale urban expressway network of 200 kilometers. The Hanshin Expressway provides service for the Hanshin (Osaka-Kobe) area, the second-most populated area in Japan. An average of 828,000 vehicles use the expressway each day, with daily traffic sometimes exceeding 1,000,000 vehicles. In 1970, the Hanshin Expressway Public Corporation started using an automated traffic-control system in order to maximize the number of vehicles flowing into the expressway network.

The automated traffic-control system relies on two control methods: (1) limiting the number of cars that enter the expressway at each entrance ramp; and (2) providing drivers with up-to-date and accurate traffic information, including expected travel times and information about accidents. The approach used to limit the number of vehicles depends upon whether the expressway is in a normal or steady state of operation, or whether some type of unusual event, such as an accident or a breakdown, has occurred.

In the first phase of the steady-state case, the Hanshin system uses a linear programming model to maximize the total number of vehicles entering the system, while preventing traffic congestion and adverse effects on surrounding road networks. The data that drives the linear programming model is collected from detectors installed every 500 meters along the expressway and at all entrance and exit ramps. Every five minutes the real-time data collected from the detectors is used to update the model coefficients and a new linear program computes the maximum number of vehicles the expressway can accommodate.

The automated traffic control system has been very successful. According to surveys, traffic control has decreased the length of congested portions of the expressway by 30 percent and the duration by 20 percent. It has been shown to be extremely cost effective, and drivers consider it an indispensable service.

*Based on Yoshino, T., T. Sasaki, and T. Hasegawa. "The Traffic-Control System on the Hanshin Expressway." *Interfaces*, January–February 1995, pp. 94–108.

Relevant cost A cost that depends upon the decision made. The amount of a relevant cost will vary depending on the values of the decision variables.

Modeling The process of translating a verbal statement of a problem into a mathematical statement.

PROBLEMS

SELF TEST

1. Recall the Kelson Sporting Equipment problem (Chapter 7, Problem 22). Letting

$$x_1 = \text{number of regular gloves}$$
$$x_2 = \text{number of catcher's mitts}$$

leads to the formulation:

Max $5x_1 + 8x_2$

s.t.

$$x_1 + \tfrac{3}{2}x_2 \leq 900 \quad \text{Cutting and sewing}$$
$$\tfrac{1}{2}x_1 + \tfrac{1}{3}x_2 \leq 300 \quad \text{Finishing}$$
$$\tfrac{1}{8}x_1 + \tfrac{1}{4}x_2 \leq 100 \quad \text{Packaging and shipping}$$
$$x_1, x_2 \geq 0$$

The computer solution obtained using The Management Scientist is shown in Figure 8.10.
   a.   What is the optimal solution and what is the value of the total profit contribution?
   b.   Which constraints are binding?
   c.   What are the dual prices for the resources? Interpret each.
   d.   If overtime can be scheduled in one of the departments, where would you recommend doing so?

2.   Refer to the computer solution of the Kelson Sporting Equipment problem shown in Figure 8.10 (see Problem 1).
   a.   What are the ranges of optimality for the objective function coefficients.
   b.   Interpret the ranges in part (a).
   c.   Interpret the range of feasibility for the right-hand sides.
   d.   How much will the value of the optimal solution improve if 20 extra hours of packaging and shipping time are made available?

SELF TEST

***Figure* 8.10**   THE MANAGEMENT SCIENTIST SOLUTION FOR THE KELSON SPORTING EQUIPMENT PROBLEM

```
Objective Function Value =          3700.00150

         Variable              Value              Reduced Costs
      --------------     ---------------       ------------------
            X1               500.00150                0.00000
            X2               149.99925                0.00000


        Constraint         Slack/Surplus            Dual Prices
      --------------     ---------------       ------------------
            1               174.99963                0.00000
            2                 0.00000                2.99999
            3                 0.00000               28.00006
```

OBJECTIVE COEFFICIENT RANGES

Variable	Lower Limit	Current Value	Upper Limit
X1	4.00000	5.00000	12.00012
X2	3.33330	8.00000	10.00000

RIGHT HAND SIDE RANGES

Constraint	Lower Limit	Current Value	Upper Limit
1	725.00037	900.00000	No Upper Limit
2	133.33200	300.00000	400.00000
3	75.00000	100.00000	134.99982

3. Recall the Investment Advisors problem (Chapter 7, Problem 25). Letting

$$x_1 = \text{shares of U.S. Oil}$$
$$x_2 = \text{shares of Hub Properties}$$

leads to the formulation:

Max $3x_1 + 5x_2$ Maximize total annual return

s.t.

$$25x_1 + 50x_2 \leq 80,000 \quad \text{Funds available}$$
$$0.50x_1 + 0.25x_2 \leq 700 \quad \text{Risk maximum}$$
$$1x_1 \leq 1000 \quad \text{U.S. Oil maximum}$$
$$x_1, x_2 \geq 0$$

The computer solution of this problem is shown in Figure 8.11.

a. What is the optimal solution and what is the value of the total estimated annual return?
b. Which constraints are binding? What is your interpretation of this condition in terms of the problem?
c. What are the dual prices for the constraints? Interpret each.
d. Would it be beneficial to relax the constraint on the amount invested in U.S. Oil? Why or why not?

4. Refer to Figure 8.11, which shows the computer solution of Problem 3.

a. How much would the estimated return per share for U.S. Oil have to increase before increasing the investment in this stock would be beneficial?
b. How much would the estimated return per share for Hub Properties have to decrease before reducing the investment in this stock would be beneficial?
c. How much would the total annual return be reduced if the U.S. Oil maximum were reduced to 900 shares?

5. Recall the M&D Chemicals problem (Chapter 7, Problem 37). Letting

$$x_1 = \text{gallons of product 1 produced}$$
$$x_2 = \text{gallons of product 2 produced}$$

leads to the formulation:

Min $2x_1 + 3x_2$

s.t.

$$1x_1 \geq 125 \quad \text{Demand for product 1}$$
$$1x_1 + 1x_2 \geq 350 \quad \text{Total production requirement}$$
$$2x_1 + 1x_2 \leq 600 \quad \text{Processing time limitation}$$
$$x_1, x_2 \geq 0$$

The Management Scientist solution is shown in Figure 8.12.

a. What is the optimal solution and what is the minimum production cost?
b. Specify the range of optimality for the objective function coefficients.
c. What are the dual prices for each constraint? Interpret each.
d. If the total production requirement were increased from 350 to 450 gallons, how would the value of the optimal solution change?
e. Identify the range of feasibility for the right-hand-side values.

Figure 8.11 — THE MANAGEMENT SCIENTIST SOLUTION FOR THE INVESTMENT ADVISORS PROBLEM

Objective Function Value =   8400.000

Variable	Value	Reduced Costs
X1	800.000	0.000
X2	1200.000	0.000

Constraint	Slack/Surplus	Dual Prices
1	0.000	0.093
2	0.000	1.333
3	200.000	0.000

OBJECTIVE COEFFICIENT RANGES

Variable	Lower Limit	Current Value	Upper Limit
X1	2.500	3.000	10.000
X2	1.500	5.000	6.000

RIGHT HAND SIDE RANGES

Constraint	Lower Limit	Current Value	Upper Limit
1	65000.000	80000.000	140000.000
2	400.000	700.000	775.000
3	800.000	1000.000	No Upper Limit

SELF TEST

6. Recall the Photo Chemicals problem (Chapter 7, Problem 38). Letting

$$x_1 = \text{gallons of product 1 produced}$$
$$x_2 = \text{gallons of product 2 produced}$$

leads to the formulation:

Min $1x_1 + 1x_2$ Minimize production cost

s.t.

$1x_1 + 2x_2 \geq 80$ Raw material

$1x_1 \qquad\;\; \geq 30$ Product 1 minimum

$\qquad\;\; 1x_2 \geq 20$ Product 2 minimum

$x_1, x_2 \geq 0$

Figure 8.12 THE MANAGEMENT SCIENTIST SOLUTION FOR THE M&D CHEMICALS PROBLEM

```
Objective Function Value =           800.000

        Variable            Value              Reduced Costs
       ------------        ------------        ------------------
          X1               250.000                 0.000
          X2               100.000                 0.000


        Constraint       Slack/Surplus            Dual Prices
       ------------        ------------        ------------------
          1                125.000                 0.000
          2                  0.000                -4.000
          3                  0.000                 1.000


OBJECTIVE COEFFICIENT RANGES

   Variable       Lower Limit       Current Value       Upper Limit
  ------------   ----------------   ----------------   ----------------
     X1          No Lower Limit         2.000               3.000
     X2               2.000             3.000          No Upper Limit


RIGHT HAND SIDE RANGES

Constraint        Lower Limit       Current Value       Upper Limit
------------     ----------------   ----------------   ----------------
     1           No Lower Limit         125.000             250.000
     2                300.000           350.000             475.000
     3                475.000           600.000             700.000
```

The Management Scientist solution is shown in Figure 8.13.
a. What is the optimal solution and what is minimum production cost?
b. Specify the range of optimality for the objective function coefficients.
c. What are the dual prices for each constraint? Interpret each.
d. If the amount of raw material to be processed were increased from 80 to 85 gallons, how would the optimal solution change?
e. Identify the range of feasibility for each of the right-hand-side values.

7. Recall the Tom's, Inc., problem (Chapter 7, Problem 26). Letting

$$x_1 = \text{jars of Western Foods Salsa produced}$$
$$x_2 = \text{jars of Mexico City Salsa produced}$$

leads to the formulation:

$$\text{Max} \quad 1x_1 + 1.25x_2$$

s.t.

$$5x_1 + 7x_2 \leq 4480 \quad \text{Whole tomatoes}$$
$$3x_1 + 1x_2 \leq 2080 \quad \text{Tomato sauce}$$
$$2x_1 + 2x_2 \leq 1600 \quad \text{Tomato paste}$$
$$x_1, x_2 \geq 0$$

| Figure 8.13 | THE MANAGEMENT SCIENTIST SOLUTION FOR THE PHOTO CHEMICALS PROBLEM |

Objective Function Value =   55.000

Variable	Value	Reduced Costs
X1	30.000	0.000
X2	25.000	0.000

Constraint	Slack/Surplus	Dual Prices
1	0.000	-0.500
2	0.000	-0.500
3	5.000	0.000

OBJECTIVE COEFFICIENT RANGES

Variable	Lower Limit	Current Value	Upper Limit
X1	0.500	1.000	No Upper Limit
X2	0.000	1.000	2.000

RIGHT HAND SIDE RANGES

Constraint	Lower Limit	Current Value	Upper Limit
1	70.000	80.000	No Upper Limit
2	0.000	30.000	40.000
3	No Lower Limit	20.000	25.000

The Management Scientist solution is shown in Figure 8.14.

a. What is the optimal solution and what are the optimal production quantities?
b. Specify the range of optimality for the objective function coefficients.
c. What are the dual prices for each constraint? Interpret each.
d. Identify the range of feasibility for each of the right-hand-side values.

SELF TEST

8. Suppose that in a product-mix problem x_1, x_2, x_3, and x_4 indicate the units of products 1, 2, 3, and 4, respectively, and the linear program is

Max $4x_1 + 6x_2 + 3x_3 + 1x_4$
s.t.

$$1.5x_1 + 2x_2 + 4x_3 + 3x_4 \leq 550 \quad \text{Machine A hours}$$
$$4x_1 + 1x_2 + 2x_3 + 1x_4 \leq 700 \quad \text{Machine B hours}$$
$$2x_1 + 3x_2 + 1x_3 + 2x_4 \leq 200 \quad \text{Machine C hours}$$
$$x_1, x_2, x_3, x_4 \geq 0$$

The computer solution developed using The Management Scientist is shown in Figure 8.15.

a. What is the optimal solution and what is the value of the objective function?
b. Which constraints are binding?

Figure 8.14   THE MANAGEMENT SCIENTIST SOLUTION FOR THE TOM'S, INC., PROBLEM

Objective Function Value =   860.000

Variable	Value	Reduced Costs
X1	560.000	0.000
X2	240.000	0.000

Constraint	Slack/Surplus	Dual Prices
1	0.000	0.125
2	160.000	0.000
3	0.000	0.187

OBJECTIVE COEFFICIENT RANGES

Variable	Lower Limit	Current Value	Upper Limit
X1	0.893	1.000	1.250
X2	1.000	1.250	1.400

RIGHT HAND SIDE RANGES

Constraint	Lower Limit	Current Value	Upper Limit
1	4320.000	4480.000	5600.000
2	1920.000	2080.000	No Upper Limit
3	1280.000	1600.000	1640.000

c. Which machines have excess capacity available? How much?

d. If the objective function coefficient of x_1 is increased by 0.50, will the optimal solution change?

SELF TEST

9. Refer to the computer solution of Problem 8 in Figure 8.15.

    a. Identify the range of optimality for each objective function coefficient.

    b. Suppose that the objective function coefficient for x_1 is decreased by 3, the objective function coefficient of x_2 is increased by 1.5, and the objective function coefficient for x_4 is increased by 1. What will the new optimal solution be?

    c. Identify the range of feasibility for the right-hand-side values.

    d. If the number of hours available on machine A is increased by 300, will the dual price for that constraint change?

10. Consider the following linear program and the computer solution shown in Figure 8.16.

$$\text{Min} \quad 15x_1 + 15x_2 + 16x_3$$

$$\text{s.t.}$$

$$1x_1 \qquad\quad + 1x_3 \le 30$$
$$0.5x_1 - 1x_2 + 6x_3 \ge 15$$
$$3x_1 + 4x_2 - 1x_3 \ge 20$$
$$x_1, x_2, x_3 \ge 0$$

Figure 8.15   THE MANAGEMENT SCIENTIST SOLUTION FOR PROBLEM 8

Objective Function Value =   525.000

Variable	Value	Reduced Costs
X1	0.000	0.050
X2	25.000	0.000
X3	125.000	0.000
X4	0.000	3.500

Constraint	Slack/Surplus	Dual Prices
1	0.000	0.300
2	425.000	0.000
3	0.000	1.800

OBJECTIVE COEFFICIENT RANGES

Variable	Lower Limit	Current Value	Upper Limit
X1	No Lower Limit	4.000	4.050
X2	5.923	6.000	9.000
X3	2.000	3.000	12.000
X4	No Lower Limit	1.000	4.500

RIGHT HAND SIDE RANGES

Constraint	Lower Limit	Current Value	Upper Limit
1	133.333	550.000	800.000
2	275.000	700.000	No Upper Limit
3	137.500	200.000	825.000

a. What is the optimal solution and what is the optimal value for the objective function?
b. Which constraints are binding?
c. What are the dual prices? Interpret each.
d. If you could change the right-hand side of one constraint by one unit, which one would you choose? What would be the new value of the right-hand side?

11. Refer to the computer solution of Problem 10 in Figure 8.16.
   a. Interpret the ranges of optimality for the objective function coefficients.
   b. Suppose that c_1 is increased by 0.25. What is the new optimal solution?
   c. Suppose that c_1 is increased by 0.25 and c_2 is decreased by 0.25. What is the new optimal solution?

Figure 8.16	THE MANAGEMENT SCIENTIST SOLUTION FOR PROBLEM 10

```
Objective Function Value =            139.730

        Variable            Value          Reduced Costs
     --------------     --------------     ------------------
          X1              7.297                0.000
          X2              0.000                0.676
          X3              1.892                0.000


       Constraint       Slack/Surplus        Dual Prices
     --------------     --------------     ------------------
          1              20.811                0.000
          2               0.000               -3.405
          3               0.000               -4.432


OBJECTIVE COEFFICIENT RANGES

     Variable      Lower Limit     Current Value     Upper Limit
   ------------    ------------    -------------    -------------
        X1             1.333          15.000             15.543
        X2            14.324          15.000        No Upper Limit
        X3            13.500          16.000            180.000


RIGHT HAND SIDE RANGES

    Constraint     Lower Limit     Current Value     Upper Limit
   ------------    ------------    -------------    -------------
        1              9.189          30.000        No Upper Limit
        2              3.333          15.000            111.250
        3             -2.500          20.000             90.000
```

12. Supersport Footballs, Inc., has to determine the best number of All-Pro (x_1), College (x_2), and High School (x_3) types of footballs to produce to maximize profits. Constraints include production capacity limitations (time available in minutes) in each of three departments (cutting and dyeing, sewing, and inspection and packaging) as well as a constraint that requires the production of at least 1000 All-Pro footballs. The linear programming model of Supersport's problem is

$$\text{Max} \quad 3x_1 + 5x_2 + 4x_3$$

s.t.

$$
\begin{aligned}
12x_1 + 10x_2 + 8x_3 &\le 18{,}000 \quad \text{Cutting and dyeing} \\
15x_1 + 15x_2 + 12x_3 &\le 18{,}000 \quad \text{Sewing} \\
3x_1 + 4x_2 + 2x_3 &\le 9{,}000 \quad \text{Inspection and packaging} \\
1x_1 \qquad\qquad\quad &\ge 1{,}000 \quad \text{All-Pro model} \\
x_1, x_2, x_3 &\ge 0
\end{aligned}
$$

The computer solution to the Supersport problem is shown in Figure 8.17.
  a. How many footballs of each type should Supersport produce to maximize the total profit contribution?
  b. Which constraints are binding?
  c. Interpret the slack and/or surplus in each constraint.
  d. Interpret the ranges of optimality for the profit contributions of the three types of football.

13. Refer to the computer solution of Problem 12 (see Figure 8.17).
  a. Overtime rates in the sewing department are $12 per hour. Would you recommend that the company consider using overtime in that department? Explain.
  b. What is the dual price for the fourth constraint? Interpret its value for management.
  c. Note that the reduced cost for x_3 is zero, but x_3 is not in the solution at a positive value. What is your interpretation?
  d. Suppose that the profit contribution of the College ball is increased by $1. How do you expect the solution to change?

Note: Problems 14–19 and the case problems require computer solution and interpretation of the results.

14. Better Products, Inc., manufactures three products on two machines. In a typical week, 40 hours are available on each machine. The profit contribution and production time in hours per unit are

Category	Product 1	Product 2	Product 3
Profit/unit	$30	$50	$20
Machine 1 hours/unit	0.5	2.0	0.75
Machine 2 hours/unit	1.0	1.0	0.5

Two operators are required for machine 1; thus, 2 hours of labor must be scheduled for each hour of machine 1 time. Only one operator is required for machine 2. A maximum of 100 labor hours is available for assignment to the machine during the coming week. Other production requirements are that product 1 cannot account for more than 50% of the units produced and that product 3 must account for at least 20% of the units produced.
  a. How many units of each product should be produced to maximize the total profit contribution? What is the projected weekly profit contribution associated with your solution?
  b. How many hours of production time will be scheduled on each machine?
  c. What is the value of an additional hour of labor?
  d. Assume that labor capacity can be increased to 120 hours. Would you be interested in using the additional 20 hours available for this resource? Develop the optimal product mix assuming that the extra hours are made available.

15. A manufacturer makes three components for sale to refrigeration companies. The components are processed on two machines: a shaper and a grinder. The times (in minutes) required on each machine are shown below.

Component	Machine Shaper	Grinder
1	6	4
2	4	5
3	4	2

Figure 8.17	THE MANAGEMENT SCIENTIST SOLUTION FOR THE SUPERSPORT FOOTBALLS PROBLEM

Objective Function Value =   4000.000

Variable	Value	Reduced Costs
X1	1000.000	0.000
X2	200.000	0.000
X3	0.000	0.000

Constraint	Slack/Surplus	Dual Prices
1	4000.000	0.000
2	0.000	0.333
3	5200.000	0.000
4	0.000	-2.000

OBJECTIVE COEFFICIENT RANGES

Variable	Lower Limit	Current Value	Upper Limit
X1	No Lower Limit	3.000	5.000
X2	5.000	5.000	No Upper Limit
X3	No Lower Limit	4.000	4.000

RIGHT HAND SIDE RANGES

Constraint	Lower Limit	Current Value	Upper Limit
1	14000.000	18000.000	No Upper Limit
2	15000.000	18000.000	24000.000
3	3800.000	9000.000	No Upper Limit
4	0.000	1000.000	1200.000

The shaper is available for 120 hours, and the grinder is available for 110 hours. No more than 200 units of component 3 can be sold, but up to 1000 units of each of the other components can be sold. In fact, the company already has orders for 600 units of component 1 that must be satisfied. The profit contributions for components 1, 2, and 3 are $8, $6, and $9, respectively.

   a. Formulate and solve for the recommended production quantities.
   b. What are the ranges of optimality for the profit contributions of the three components? Interpret these ranges for company management.
   c. What are the ranges of feasibility for the right-hand sides? Interpret these ranges for company management.
   d. If more time could be made available on the grinder, how much would it be worth?
   e. If more units of component 3 can be sold by reducing the sales price by $4, should the company reduce the price?

16. National Insurance Associates carries an investment portfolio of stocks, bonds, and other investment alternatives. Currently $200,000 of funds are available and must be considered for new investment opportunities. The four stock options National is considering and the relevant financial data are as follows:

Financial Data	Stock			
	A	B	C	D
Price per share	$100	$50	$80	$40
Annual rate of return	0.12	0.08	0.06	0.10
Risk measure per dollar invested	0.10	0.07	0.05	0.08

The risk measure indicates the relative uncertainty associated with the stock in terms of its realizing the projected annual return; higher values indicate greater risk. The risk measures are provided by the firm's top financial advisor.

National's top management has stipulated the following investment guidelines.

1. The annual rate of return for the portfolio must be at least 9%.
2. No one stock can account for more than 50% of the total dollar investment.
a. Use linear programming to develop an investment portfolio that minimizes risk.
b. If the firm ignores risk and uses a maximum return-on-investment strategy, what is the investment portfolio?
c. What is the dollar difference between the portfolios in parts (a) and (b)? Why might the company prefer the solution developed in part (a)?

17. The management of Carson Stapler Manufacturing Company forecasts a 5000-unit demand for its Sure-Hold model during the next quarter. This stapler is assembled from three major components: base, staple cartridge, and handle. Until now Carson has manufactured all three components. However, the forecast of 5000 units is a new high in sales volume, and the firm may not have sufficient production capacity to make all the components. Management is considering contracting with a local firm to produce at least some of the components. The production time requirements per unit are as follows:

Department	Production Time (hours)			Time Available (hours)
	Base	Cartridge	Handle	
A	0.03	0.02	0.05	400
B	0.04	0.02	0.04	400
C	0.02	0.03	0.01	400

Note that each component manufactured by Carson uses manufacturing time in each of three departments.

After considering the firm's overhead, material, and labor costs, the accounting department has determined the unit manufacturing cost for each component. These data, along with the purchase price quotations by the contracting firm, are as follows:

Component	Manufacturing Cost	Purchase Cost
Base	$0.75	$0.95
Cartridge	$0.40	$0.55
Handle	$1.10	$1.40

a. Determine the make-or-buy decision for Carson that will meet the 5000-unit demand at a minimum total cost. How many units of each component should be made and how many purchased?
b. Which departments are limiting the manufacturing volume? If overtime could be considered at the additional cost of $3 per hour, which department(s) should be allocated the overtime? Explain.
c. Suppose that up to 80 hours of overtime could be scheduled in department A. What would you recommend?

18. Golf Shafts, Inc. (GSI), produces graphite shafts for several manufacturers of golf clubs. Two GSI manufacturing facilities, one located in San Diego and the other in Tampa, have the capability to produce shafts in varying degrees of stiffness, ranging from regular models used primarily by average golfers to extra stiff models used primarily by low-handicap and professional golfers. GSI has just received a contract for the production of 200,000 regular shafts and 75,000 stiff shafts. Since both plants are currently producing shafts for previous orders, neither plant has sufficient capacity by itself to fill the new order. The San Diego plant can produce up to a total of 120,000 shafts, and the Tampa plant can produce up to a total of 180,000 shafts. Because of equipment differences at each of the plants and differing labor costs, the per-unit production costs vary as shown here:

	San Diego Cost	Tampa Cost
Regular Shaft	$5.25	$4.95
Stiff Shaft	$5.45	$5.70

a. Formulate a linear programming model to determine how GSI should schedule production for the new order in order to minimize the total production cost.
b. Use any linear programming code to solve the model that you developed in part (a).
c. Suppose that some of the previous orders at the Tampa plant could be rescheduled in order to free up additional capacity for the new order. Would this be worthwhile? Explain.
d. Suppose that the cost to produce a stiff shaft in Tampa had been incorrectly computed and that the correct cost is $5.30 per shaft. What effect, if any, would this have on the optimal solution developed in part (b)? What effect would this have on total production cost?

19. The Pfeiffer Company manages approximately $15 million for clients. For each client, Pfeiffer chooses a mix of three types of investments: a growth stock fund, an income fund, and a money market fund. Each client has different investment objectives and different tolerances for risk. To accommodate these differences, Pfeiffer places limits on the percentage of each portfolio that may be invested in the three funds and assigns a portfolio risk index to each client.
    Here's how the system works for Dennis Hartmann, one of Pfeiffer's clients. Based on an evaluation of Hartmann's risk tolerance, Pfeiffer has assigned Hartmann's portfolio a risk index of 0.05. Furthermore, to maintain diversity, the fraction of Hartmann's portfolio invested in the

growth and income funds must be at least 10% in each, and at least 20% must be invested in the money market fund.

The risk ratings for the growth, income, and money market funds are 0.10, 0.05, and 0.01, respectively. A portfolio risk index is computed as a weighted average of the risk ratings for the three funds where the weights are the fraction of the portfolio invested in each of the funds. Hartmann has given Pfeiffer $300,000 to manage. Pfeiffer is currently forecasting a yield of 20% on the growth fund, 10% on the income fund, and 6% on the money market fund.

a. Develop a linear programming model to select the best mix of investments for Hartmann's portfolio.
b. Solve the model you developed in part (a).
c. How much may the yields on the three funds vary before Pfeiffer has to modify Hartmann's portfolio?
d. If Hartmann were more risk tolerant, how much of a yield increase could he expect? For instance, what if his portfolio risk index is increased to 0.06?
e. If Pfeiffer revised its yield estimate for the growth fund downward to 0.10, how would you recommend modifying Hartmann's portfolio?
f. What information must Pfeiffer maintain on each client to use this system to manage client portfolios?
g. On a weekly basis Pfeiffer revises the yield estimates for the three funds. Suppose that Pfeiffer has 50 clients. Describe how Pfeiffer could make weekly modifications in each client's portfolio and allocate the total funds managed among the three investment funds.

20. La Jolla Beverage Products is considering producing a wine cooler that would be a blend of a white wine, a rosé wine, and fruit juice. To meet taste specifications, the wine cooler must consist of at least 50% white wine, at least 20% and no more than 30% rosé, and 20% fruit juice. La Jolla purchases the wine from local wineries and the fruit juice from a processing plant in San Francisco. For the current production period, 10,000 gallons of white wine and 8000 gallons of rosé wine can be purchased; there is no limit on the amount of fruit juice that can be ordered. The costs for the wine are $1.00 per gallon for the white and $1.50 per gallon for the rosé; the fruit juice can be purchased for $0.50 per gallon. La Jolla Beverage Products can sell all the wine cooler it can produce for $2.50 per gallon.

a. Is the cost of the wine and fruit juice a sunk cost or a relevant cost in this situation? Explain.
b. Formulate a linear program to determine the blend of the three ingredients that will maximize the total profit contribution. Solve the linear program to determine the number of gallons of each ingredient La Jolla should purchase and the total profit contribution they will realize from this blend.
c. If La Jolla could obtain additional amounts of the white wine, should they do so? If so, how much should they be willing to pay for each additional gallon, and how many additional gallons would they want to purchase?
d. If La Jolla Beverage Products could obtain additional amounts of the rosé wine, should they do so? If so, how much should they be willing to pay for each additional gallon, and how many additional gallons would they want to purchase?
e. Interpret the dual price for the constraint corresponding to the requirement that the wine cooler must contain at least 50% white wine. What is your advice to management given this dual price?
f. Interpret the dual price for the constraint corresponding to the requirement that the wine cooler must contain exactly 20% fruit juice. What is your advice to management given this dual price?

21. The program manager for Channel 10 wants to determine the best way to allocate the time for the 11:00–11:30 evening news broadcast. Specifically, she would like to determine the number of minutes of broadcast time to devote to local news, national news, weather, and sports. Over the 30-minute broadcast, 10 minutes are set aside for advertising. The station's broadcast policy states that at least 15% of the time available should be devoted to local news coverage; the time devoted to local news or national news must be at least 50% of the total broadcast time; the time devoted to the weather segment must be less than or equal to the time devoted to the

sports segment; the time devoted to the sports segment should be no longer than the total time spent on the local and national news; and at least 20% of the time should be devoted to the weather segment. The production costs per minute are $300 for local news, $200 for national news, $100 for weather, and $100 for sports.

a. Formulate and solve a linear program that can determine how the 20 available minutes should be used to minimize the total cost of producing the program.

b. Interpret the dual price for the constraint corresponding to the available time. What advice would you give the station manager given this dual price?

c. Interpret the dual price for the constraint corresponding to the requirement that at least 15% of the available time should be devoted to local coverage. What advice would you give the station manager given this dual price?

d. Interpret the dual price for the constraint corresponding to the requirement that the time devoted to the local and the national news must be at least 50% of the total broadcast time. What advice would you give the station manager given this dual price?

e. Interpret the dual price for the constraint corresponding to the requirement that the time devoted to the weather segment must be less than or equal to the time devoted to the sports segment. What advice would you give the station manager given this dual price?

22. Gulf Coast Electronics is ready to award contracts for printing its annual report. For the past several years, the four-color annual report has been printed by Johnson Printing and Lakeside Litho. A new firm, Benson Printing, has inquired into the possibility of doing a portion of the printing. The quality and service level provided by Lakeside Litho has been extremely high; in fact, only 0.5% of their reports have had to be discarded because of quality problems. Johnson Printing also has had a high quality level historically, producing an average of only 1% unacceptable reports. Since Gulf Coast Electronics has had no experience with Benson Printing, they have estimated its defective rate to be 10%. Gulf Coast would like to determine how many reports should be printed by each firm to obtain 75,000 reports of acceptable quality. To ensure that Benson Printing will receive some of the contract, management has specified that the number of reports awarded to Benson Printing must be at least 10% of the volume given to Johnson Printing. In addition, the total volume assigned to Benson Printing, Johnson Printing, and Lakeside Litho should not exceed 30,000, 50,000, and 50,000 copies, respectively. Because of the long-term relationship that has developed with Lakeside Litho, management also has specified that at least 30,000 reports should be awarded to Lakeside Litho. The cost per copy is $2.45 for Benson Printing, $2.50 for Johnson Printing, and $2.75 for Lakeside Litho.

a. Formulate and solve a linear program for determining how many copies should be assigned to each printing firm to minimize the total cost of obtaining 75,000 reports of acceptable quality.

b. Suppose that the quality level for Benson Printing is much better than estimated. What effect, if any, would this have?

c. Suppose that management is willing to reconsider its requirement that Lakeside Litho be awarded at least 30,000 reports. What effect, if any, would this have?

Case Problem   PRODUCT MIX

TJ's, Inc., makes three nut mixes for sale to grocery chains located in the Southeast. The three mixes, referred to as the Regular Mix, the Deluxe Mix, and the Holiday Mix, are made by mixing different percentages of five types of nuts.

In preparation for the fall season, TJ's has just purchased the following shipments of nuts (in pounds) at the prices shown.

Type of Nut	Shipment Amount	Cost per Shipment
Almond	6000	$7500
Brazil	7500	$7125
Filbert	7500	$6750
Pecan	6000	$7200
Walnut	7500	$7875

The Regular Mix consists of 15% almonds, 25% Brazil nuts, 25% filberts, 10% pecans, and 25% walnuts. The Deluxe Mix consists of 20% of each type of nut, and the Holiday Mix consists of 25% almonds, 15% Brazil nuts, 15% filberts, 25% pecans, and 20% walnuts.

TJ's accountant has analyzed the cost of packaging materials, sales price per pound, and other factors and has determined that the profit contribution per pound is $1.65 for the Regular Mix, $2.00 for the Deluxe Mix, and $2.25 for the Holiday Mix. These figures do not include the cost of specific types of nuts in the different mixes because that cost can vary greatly in the commodity markets.

Customer orders (in pounds) already received are summarized below:

Type of Mix	Orders
Regular	10,000
Deluxe	3,000
Holiday	5,000

Because demand is running high, TJ's expects to receive many more orders than it can satisfy.

TJ's is committed to using the available nuts to maximize total profit contribution over the fall season; nuts not used will be given to the Free Store. Even if it is not profitable to do so, TJ's president has indicated that the orders already received must be satisfied.

Managerial Report

Perform an analysis of TJ's product-mix problem, and prepare a report for TJ's president that summarizes your findings. Be sure to include information on and analysis of the following items.

1. The cost per pound of the nuts included in the Regular, Deluxe, and Holiday mixes.
2. The optimal product mix and the total profit contribution.
3. Recommendations regarding how the total profit contribution can be increased if additional quantities of nuts can be purchased.
4. A recommendation as to whether TJ's should purchase an additional 1000 pounds of almonds for $1000 from a supplier who overbought.
5. Recommendations on how profit contribution could be increased (if at all) if TJ's does not satisfy all existing orders.

Case Problem   TRUCK LEASING STRATEGY

Reep Construction has recently won a contract for the excavation and site preparation of a new rest area on the Pennsylvania turnpike. In preparing his bid for the job, Bob Reep, founder and president of Reep Construction, estimated that it would take 4 months to perform the work and that 10, 12, 14, and 8 trucks would be needed in months 1 through 4, respectively.

The firm currently has 20 trucks of the type needed to perform the work on the new project. These trucks were obtained last year when Bob signed a long-term lease with PennState Leasing. Although most of these trucks are currently being used on existing jobs, Bob estimates that one truck will be available for use on the new project in month 1, two trucks will be available in month 2, three trucks will be available in month 3, and one truck will be available in month 4. Thus, to complete the project, Bob will have to lease additional trucks.

The long-term leasing contract with PennState has a monthly cost of $600 per truck. Reep Construction pays its truck drivers $20 an hour, and daily fuel costs are approximately $100 per truck. All maintenance costs are paid by PennState Leasing. For planning purposes, Bob estimates that each truck used on the new project will be operating 8 hours a day, 5 days a week for approximately 4 weeks each month.

Bob does not believe that current business conditions justify committing the firm to additional long-term leases. In discussing the short-term leasing possibilities with PennState Leasing, Bob has learned that he can obtain short-term leases of 1–4 months. Short-term leases differ from long-term leases in that the short-term leasing plans include the cost of both a truck and a driver. Maintenance costs for short-term leases also are paid by PennState Leasing. The following costs for each of the 4 months cover the lease of a truck and driver.

Length of Lease	Cost per Month
1	$4000
2	$3700
3	$3225
4	$3040

Bob Reep would like to acquire a lease that would minimize the cost of meeting the monthly trucking requirements for his new project, but he also takes great pride in the fact that his company has never laid off employees. Bob is committed to maintaining his no-layoff policy; that is, he will use his own drivers even if costs are higher.

Managerial Report

Perform an analysis of Reep Construction's leasing problem and prepare a report for Bob Reep that summarizes your findings. Be sure to include information on and analysis of the following items

1. The optimal leasing plan.
2. The costs associated with the optimal leasing plan.
3. The cost for Reep Construction to maintain its current policy of no layoffs.

Appendix 8.1 SOLVING LINEAR PROGRAMS WITH THE MANAGEMENT SCIENTIST

In this appendix we describe how The Management Scientist software package can be used to solve the RMC linear programming problem (see Section 8.1). After starting the Management Scientist, execute the following steps.

Step 1. Select the **Linear Programming** module
Step 2. Choose **New** from the **File Menu**
Step 3. When the **Problem Features** dialog box appears:
    Enter 2 for **Number of Decision Variables**
    Enter 3 for **Number of Constraints**
    Select Maximize for **Optimization Type**
    Select **OK**
Step 4. When the data input worksheet appears (see Figure 8.18):
    Enter the objective function coefficients
    For each constraint:
        Enter the variable coefficients
        Enter the relation type ($<, =, >$)
        Enter the right-hand-side value
Step 5. Choose **Solve** from the **Solution menu**

The user entries in the data input worksheet are shown in color in Figure 8.18. The output from The Management Scientist is shown in Figure 8.1. In general, when entering the problem data, zero coefficients do not have to be entered. In addition, changes to the problem can be easily made by selecting the appropriate option from the Edit menu. Printed output can be obtained by selecting the Print Solution option from the Solution menu.

Appendix 8.2 SOLVING LINEAR PROGRAMS WITH LINDO®

LINDO (Linear, INteractive, and Discrete Optimizer) was developed by Linus E. Schrage at the University of Chicago; it is available in Command-line and Windows (Windows 3.1®, Windows NT®, or Windows 95®) versions. In this appendix we describe how to use the Windows version by entering and solving the RMC problem.

When you start LINDO, two windows are immediately displayed. The outer window labeled "LINDO" contains all the command menus and the command toolbar. The smaller window labeled "<untitled>" is the model window. This window is used to enter and edit the linear programming model that you want to solve. The first item you must enter into the model window is the objective function. Thus, for the RMC problem, type MAX 40X1 + 30X2. To indicate that the objective function has been completely entered and that the model constraints will follow, press the return key and type the words SUBJECT TO (or just the letters ST). Next, after pressing the return key to move to a new line, enter the first RMC constraint by typing

Figure 8.18   DATA INPUT WORKSHEET FOR THE RMC PROBLEM USING THE MANAGEMENT SCIENTIST

Optimization Type: Maximize				
Variable Names: [Change if Desired]	X1	X2		
Objective Function Coefficients	40	30		

	Coefficients			
Subject To:	X1	X2	Relation (<, =, >)	Right Hand Side
Constraint 1	0.4	0.5	<	20
Constraint 2	0	0.2	<	5
Constraint 3	0.6	0.3	<	21

0.4X1 + 0.5X2 < 20. Note that LINDO interprets the < symbol as ≤. Then, after pressing the return key, enter the second constraint by typing 0.2X2 < 5. Press the return key again and type the third and final constraint, 0.6X1 + 0.3X2 < 21. Finally, after pressing the return key, type END to signal LINDO that the model input is complete. The model window will now contain the following model:

$$\text{Max} \quad 40x_1 + 30x_2$$
$$\text{ST}$$
$$0.4x_1 + 0.5x_2 \leq 20$$
$$0.2x_2 \leq 5$$
$$0.6x_1 + 0.3x_2 \leq 21$$
$$\text{END}$$

If you make an error entering the model, you can correct it at any time by simply positioning the cursor where you made the error and typing the necessary corrections.

To solve the model that you have just entered, you must select the Solve command from the Solve menu, or press the Solve button on the LINDO toolbar. If LINDO does not find any errors in the model input, it will begin to solve the model. As part of the solution process, LINDO displays a Status Window that can be used to monitor the progress of the solver. When the solver is finished, LINDO will ask whether you want to do sensitivity and range analysis. If you select the "YES" button and close the Status Window, LINDO displays the complete solution to the RMC problem on a new window titled "Reports Window." The output that appears in the Reports Window is shown in Figure 8.19.

The first section of the output shown in Figure 8.19 is self-explanatory. For example, we see that the optimal solution is X1 = 25 and X2 = 20, and that the value of the objective function at the optimal solution is 1600. After printing the values of the slack variables and the dual prices, LINDO displays the ranges on the objective function coefficients and the right sides of the constraints.

Consider the information provided under the computer output heading **OBJ COEFFICIENT RANGES**. Variable x_1, with a current profit coefficient of 40, has an allowable increase of 20 and an allowable decrease of 16. Adding 20 to and subtracting 16 from the current coefficient of 40 provides the range of optimality for c_1:

$$24 \leq c_1 \leq 60$$

Similarly, the range of optimality for c_2 is

$$20 \leq c_2 \leq 50$$

The information under the heading **RIGHT HAND SIDE RANGES** permits computing the range of feasibility for each right-hand side. Simply subtract the allowable decrease from the current value to get the lower limit, and add the allowable increase to the current value to get the upper limit. Doing so, we obtain

Constraint	Min RHS	Max RHS
Material 1	14	21.5
Material 2	4	No upper limit
Material 3	18.75	30

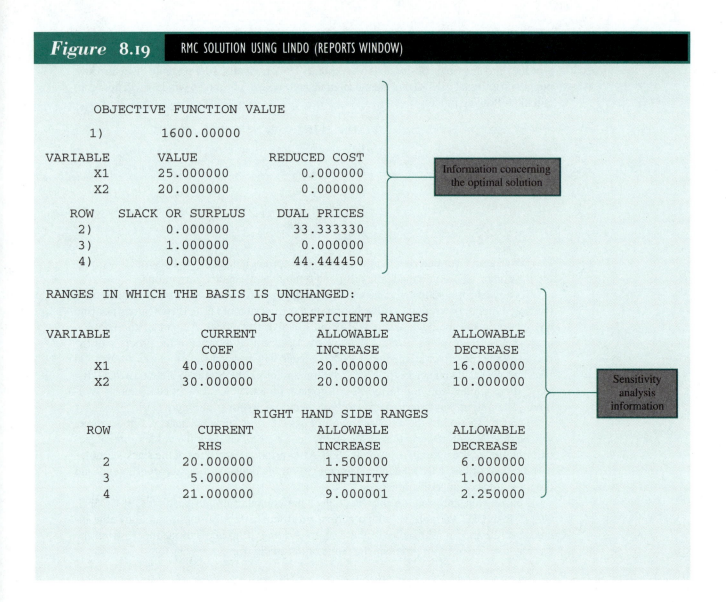

Figure 8.19   RMC SOLUTION USING LINDO (REPORTS WINDOW)

```
     OBJECTIVE FUNCTION VALUE

     1)        1600.00000

VARIABLE        VALUE           REDUCED COST
      X1      25.000000            0.000000
      X2      20.000000            0.000000

   ROW    SLACK OR SURPLUS      DUAL PRICES
    2)        0.000000           33.333330
    3)        1.000000            0.000000
    4)        0.000000           44.444450
```

Information concerning the optimal solution

RANGES IN WHICH THE BASIS IS UNCHANGED:

```
                      OBJ COEFFICIENT RANGES
VARIABLE          CURRENT         ALLOWABLE        ALLOWABLE
                  COEF            INCREASE         DECREASE
      X1       40.000000         20.000000        16.000000
      X2       30.000000         20.000000        10.000000

                      RIGHT HAND SIDE RANGES
   ROW           CURRENT         ALLOWABLE        ALLOWABLE
                 RHS             INCREASE         DECREASE
    2          20.000000          1.500000         6.000000
    3           5.000000          INFINITY         1.000000
    4          21.000000          9.000001         2.250000
```

Sensitivity analysis information

Appendix 8.3   SPREADSHEET SOLUTION OF LINEAR PROGRAMS

In this appendix we show how Excel can be used to solve the RMC linear programming problem. First, the data for the objective function coefficients, the constraint coefficients, and the right-hand sides must be entered into a spreadsheet. Second, cells must be identified for storing the values of the decision variables, the value for the objective function, and the values of the left-hand sides of the constraints. Figure 8.20 shows a spreadsheet for the RMC problem in which the cells in the upper portion of the spreadsheet are reserved for problem input data and the cells in the lower portion of the spreadsheet contains the following values:

Input Value	Cell Location
Objective function coefficients	B10:C10
Constraint coefficients	B6:C8
Right-hand sides	D6:D8

The Solution Output section of the spreadsheet contains the following optimal solution values:

Output Value	Cell Location
Decision variables	B17:C17
Objective function	D18
Tons used	B22:B24
Slack/Surplus	C22:C24

To solve the RMC problem we used Excel Solver, a general optimization and resource allocation tool. To use Solver, we must first write formulas that show how the values in the solution output section of the worksheet are related to the input data values. For instance, in the RMC problem, the profit contribution corresponding to the production of fuel additive is 40 times the number of tons of fuel additive produced, and the profit contribution from the production of solvent base is 30 times the number of tons of solvent base produced; thus, in cell **B18** we entered the formula = **B10*B17** (the contribution to profit from fuel additive) and in cell **C18** we entered the formula = **C10*C17** (the contribution to profit from solvent base). Since the total contribution to profit is the sum of these two values, in cell **D18** we entered the formula = **B18 + C18**.

The total number of tons used of material 1 is the product of the value in cell **B6** (0.4) times the value in cell **B17** (number of tons of fuel additive produced) plus the product of the value in cell **C6**(0.5) times the value in cell **C17** (number of tons of solvent base produced); thus, using the **SUMPRODUCT** function, we entered the following formula in cell **B22**;

$$= \text{SUMPRODUCT}(B6:C6,\$B\$17:\$C\$17)$$

After copying this formula to cells **B23** through **B24**, these cells will also contain the formulas for the number of tons used for each of the other two materials in the RMC problem.

Finally, to compute the slack/surplus value for each operation, we subtract the number of hours used from the number of hours available. Thus, in cell **C22** we entered the formula = **D6 − B22**. After copying this formula to cells **C23** through **C24**, these cells will contain the formulas for the slack/surplus values for each of the other two materials. Figure 8.21 shows the formula spreadsheet for the RMC problem.

We are now ready to use Solver to obtain an optimal solution to the problem. The following steps describe how to use Version 5.0 of Excel to obtain the optimal solution.

Step 1. Select the **Tools** pull-down menu
Step 2. Select the **Solver** option

Figure 8.20   SPREADSHEET FOR THE RMC PROBLEM

	A	B	C	D
1				
2	**Input Data**			
3		**Material Required**		
4		(tons required to produce one ton of product)		
5	**Material**	Fuel Additive	Solvent Base	Tons Available
6	Material 1	0.4	0.5	20
7	Material 2	0	0.2	5
8	Material 3	0.6	0.3	21
9				
10	**Profit Per Unit**	40	30	
11				
12				
13				
14	**Solution Output**			
15		**Decision Variables**		
16		Fuel Additive	Solvent Base	**Total Profit**
17	**Number of Tons**			
18	**Profit**			
19				
20				
21	**Material**	**Tons Used**	**Slack/Surplus**	
22	Material 1			
23	Material 2			
24	Material 3			

Step 3. When the **Solver Parameters** dialog box appears
Enter D18 in the **Set Target Cell** box
Select the **Max** option
Enter B17:C17 in the **By Changing Cells** box
Choose **Add**

Step 4. When the **Add Constraint** dialog box appears
Enter B22:B24 in the **Cell Reference** box
Select $<$ =
Enter D6:D8 in the **Constraint** box
Choose **Add**
Enter B17:C17 in the **Cell Reference** box
Select $>$ =
Enter 0 in the **Constraint** box
Select **OK**

Step 5. When the **Solver Parameters** dialog box appears
Choose **Options**

	A	B	C	D
1				
2	**Input Data**			
3		**Material Required**		
4		(tons required to produce one ton of product)		
5	**Material**	Fuel Additive	Solvent Base	Tons Available
6	Material 1	0.4	0.5	20
7	Material 2	0	0.2	5
8	Material 3	0.6	0.3	21
9				
10	**Profit Per Unit**	40	30	
11				
12				
13				
14	**Solution Output**			
15		**Decision Variables**		
16		Fuel Additive	Solvent Base	**Total Profit**
17	**Number of Tons**			
18	Profit	=B10*B17	=C10*C17	=B18+18
19				
20				
21	**Material**	**Tons Used**	**Sack/Surplus**	
22	Material 1	=SUMPRODUCT(B6:C6,$B$17:$C$17)	=D6-B22	
23	Material 2	=SUMPRODUCT(B7:C7,$B$17:$C$17)	=D7-B23	
24	Material 3	=SUMPRODUCT(B8:C8,$B$17:$C$17)	=D8-B24	

Figure 8.21   FORMULA SPREADSHEET FOR THE RMC PROBLEM

Step 6. When the **Solver Options** dialog box appears
Select **Assume Linear Model** box
Select **OK**

Step 7. When the **Solver Parameters** dialog box appears
Choose **Solve**

Step 8. When the **Solver Results** dialog box appears
Select **Keep Solver Solution**
Select **OK** to produce the optimal solution output

Figure 8.22 shows the optimal solution output. Note the optimal solution of 25 tons of fuel additive and 20 tons of solvent base is the same as we obtained using both the graphical solution procedure and The Management Scientist software package. In addition to the output information shown in Figure 8.22, Solver has an option to provide an answer report and sensitivity analysis information. Further, note that we could simply change selected input data entries in the spreadsheet and then resolve the problem using Solver to identify the effect the changes would have on the optimal solution.

Figure 8.22   SPREADSHEET SOLUTION FOR THE RMC PROBLEM

	A	B	C	D
1				
2	Input Data			
3		Material Required		
4		(tons required to produce one ton of product)		
5	Material	Fuel Additive	Solvent Base	Tons Available
6	Material 1	0.4	0.5	20
7	Material 2	0	0.2	5
8	Material 3	0.6	0.3	21
9				
10	Profit Per Unit	40	30	
11				
12				
13				
14	Solution Output			
15		Decision Variables		
16		Fuel Additive	Solvent Base	Total Profit
17	Number of Tons	25	20	
18	Profit	1000	600	1600
19				
20				
21	Material	Tons Used	Slack/Surplus	
22	Material 1	20	0	
23	Material 2	4	1	
24	Material 3	21	0	

EASTMAN KODAK*

ROCHESTER, NEW YORK

In 1880 entrepreneur/inventor George Eastman formed the Eastman Dry Plate Company with a vision that it would become a worldwide manufacturer and marketer of photographic goods. Today, Eastman Kodak has manufacturing operations on four continents, and customers in over 150 countries. Headquartered in Rochester, New York, Kodak's imaging products include amateur roll film, photographic paper, medical and industrial X-ray film, motion picture film, and graphic arts materials. In addition, Kodak is a manufacturer of imaging equipment and chemicals.

Quantitative Methods at Kodak

Applications involving quantitative methods at Kodak can be traced back to pioneering efforts in the 1950s. Since then, quantitative methods have been employed to solve a variety of problems involving most of the operational areas of the company. Today, the majority of the applications are conducted by the Management Services Division, while a small group called Distribution Operations Research focuses on applying quantitative analysis to worldwide logistics issues.

Assigning Products to Worldwide Facilities

The sensitizing operation is the heart of the manufacturing process for photographic paper and film. In this operation, a light-sensitive emulsion is coated on a base to produce a sensitized master roll. The sensitized master rolls are then sent to a finishing operation where they are cut into proper dimensions. The sensitizing operation, by virtue of its centrality to the overall process and the peculiarity of the manufacturing technologies required, receives a great deal of managerial attention, both at the operational and strategic levels.

One of Kodak's major planning issues involves the allocation of product to the various sensitizing facilities located throughout the world. The assignment of product to facilities is called the "world load." In determining the world load, Kodak is confronted with a number of interesting trade-offs. For instance, in terms of manufacturing costs, not all sensitizing facilities are equally efficient for all products. Some facilities tend to be more cost efficient over a broad range of products, but the margins by which they are better varies from product to product. However, many product–facility combinations are essentially impossible because of unique product specifications and machine capabilities. Nonetheless, there is a choice of facilities for practically every product.

The product–facility manufacturing costs are only part of the picture. The least expensive location to sensitize a particular product might, for example, be Australia. But, if most of the customers for that product are in Europe, then Australia becomes less favorable because of the high transportation costs involved. Transportation costs are therefore among the costs considered in determining the world load.

Another cost that must be considered involves the duties and duty drawbacks for the various countries throughout the world. Duty drawback is the "forgiving" of duty for a manufacturer who brings a semifinished product into a country, adds value to it, and then ships it out of that country. The effects of duty and duty drawback can significantly affect the allocation decision.

*The authors are indebted to Greg Sampson of Eastman Kodak for providing this application.

To assist in determining the world load, Kodak developed a linear programming model that accounts for the physical nature of the distribution problem and the various cost elements described above. More specifically, the program's objective is to minimize total cost (manufacturing, transportation, and duties) subject to "natural" constraints such as satisfying demand and capacity constraints for each facility.

Sensitivity Analysis and Interpretation

The linear programming model is a static representation of the problem situation, and the real world is always changing. Thus, Kodak cannot simply solve the linear program and implement the optimal solution; the static linear programming model must be used in a dynamic way. For instance, when demand expectations change, the model can be used to determine the effect the change will have on the world load. Or, suppose that country A and country B tear down duty barriers between them; what effect will this have on the world load? Suppose that the currency of country A rises compared to the currency of country B; how should the world load be modified? These examples show a few situations in which the world load must be reevaluated based on the impact of external stimuli.

In addition to using the linear programming model in a "how-to-react" mode, the model is useful in a more active mode by considering questions such as the following: Is it worthwhile for facility F to spend D dollars to lower the unit manufacturing cost of product P from X to Y? If such an investment is made, the effect may go well beyond the simple first-order impact at facility F. In fact, it is likely that the change at facility F will result in a reshuffling of the world load. The linear programming model helps evaluate the overall effect of possible changes at any facility.

Managerial Use

The world-load model gives excellent directional advice and integrates the complex interaction of many factors, but many aspects of the world-load problem do not fall neatly into the cost categories discussed previously. Although it might be possible to construct a model that would account for almost every aspect of the real-world situation, the time and cost needed to develop it would be prohibitive. Kodak has chosen to use a simpler world-load model; sensitivity analysis is then used to explore many of the questions that management may want to address. In the final analysis, managers recognize that they cannot use the model by simply turning it on, reading the results, and executing the solution. The model's recommendations combined with managerial judgment provide the final decisions and actions for world-load allocation.

Questions

1. What are some of the trade-offs associated with allocating the products to the various sensitizing facilities?
2. What costs are included in the objective function of the world-load model?
3. Briefly describe the role of sensitivity analysis in this application.
4. The world-load model does not account for all the various issues involved in assigning products to sensitizing facilities. What reason did Kodak have for not addressing *all* the issues, and what implications does this have for management?

9

LINEAR PROGRAMMING APPLICATIONS

In practice, linear programming has proven to be one of the most successful quantitative approaches to managerial decision making. Numerous applications have been reported in the chemical, airline, steel, paper, petroleum, and other industries. The problems that have been studied are diverse and have included production scheduling, media selection, financial planning, capital budgeting, transportation, plant location, product mix, staffing, blending, and many others.

As this variety of applications suggests, linear programming is a flexible problem-solving tool with applications in many disciplines. In this chapter we present several applications, including some from the areas of marketing, finance, and production management. Computer solutions obtained using The Management Scientist software package are presented for many of the examples.

..../ /............

9.1   MARKETING APPLICATIONS

Applications of linear programming in marketing are numerous. In this section we discuss applications in media selection and marketing research.

Media Selection

In Section 8.3 we provided some general guidelines for modeling more complex linear programming problems. You may want to review Section 8.3 before proceeding with the linear programming applications in this chapter.

Media selection applications of linear programming are designed to help marketing managers allocate a fixed advertising budget to various advertising media. Potential media include newspapers, magazines, radio, television, and direct mail. In these applications, the objective is to maximize reach, frequency, and quality of exposure. Restrictions on the allowable allocation usually arise during consideration of company policy, contract requirements, and media availability. In the application that follows, we illustrate how a media selection problem might be formulated and solved using a linear programming model.

Relax-and-Enjoy Lake Development Corporation is developing a lakeside community at a privately owned lake. The primary market for the lakeside lots and homes they hope to sell includes all middle- and upper-income families within approximately 100 miles of the development. Relax-and-Enjoy has employed the advertising firm of Boone, Phillips and Jackson (BP&J) to design the promotional campaign for the project.

After considering possible advertising media and the market to be covered, BP&J has recommended that the first month's advertising be restricted to five media. At the end of the month, BP&J will then reevaluate its strategy based on the month's results. BP&J has collected data on the number of potential customers reached, the cost per advertisement, the maximum number of times each is available, and the exposure quality rating for each of the five media. The quality rating is measured in terms of an exposure quality unit, a measure of the relative value of one advertisement in each of the media. This measure, based on BP&J's experience in the advertising business, takes into account factors such as audience demographics (age, income, and education of the audience reached), image presented, and quality of the advertisement. The information collected is presented in Table 9.1.

Relax-and-Enjoy provided BP&J with an advertising budget of $30,000 for the first month's campaign. In addition, Relax-and-Enjoy imposed the following restrictions on how BP&J may allocate these funds: At least 10 television commercials must be used, at least 50,000 potential customers must be reached, and no more than $18,000 may be spent on television advertisements. What advertising media selection plan should be recommended?

The decision to be made is how many times to use each medium. We begin by defining the decision variables:

$$DTV = \text{number of times daytime TV is used}$$
$$ETV = \text{number of times evening TV is used}$$
$$DN = \text{number of times daily newspaper is used}$$
$$SN = \text{number of times Sunday newspaper is used}$$
$$R = \text{number of times radio is used}$$

The data on quality of exposure in Table 9.1 show that each daytime TV (DTV) advertisement is rated at 65 exposure quality units. Thus, an advertising plan with DTV advertisements will provide a total of $65DTV$ exposure quality units. Continuing with the data in Table 9.1,

| Table 9.1 | ADVERTISING MEDIA ALTERNATIVES FOR THE RELAX-AND-ENJOY LAKE DEVELOPMENT CORPORATION |

Advertising Media	Number of Potential Customers Reached	Cost Per Advertisement	Maximum Times Available Per Month*	Exposure Quality Units
1. Daytime TV (1 min), station WKLA	1000	$1500	15	65
2. Evening TV (30 sec), station WKLA	2000	3000	10	90
3. Daily newspaper (full page), *The Morning Journal*	1500	400	25	40
4. Sunday newspaper magazine (¹/₂ page color), *The Sunday Press*	2500	1000	4	60
5. Radio, 8:00 A.M. or 5:00 P.M. news (30 sec), station KNOP	300	100	30	20

*The maximum number of times the medium is available is either the maximum number of times the advertising medium occurs (e.g., four Sundays for medium (4) or the maximum number of times BP&J recommends that the medium be used.

we find evening TV (ETV) rated at 90 exposure quality units, daily newspaper (DN) rated at 40 exposure quality units, Sunday newspaper (SN) rated at 60 exposure quality units, and radio (R) rated at 20 exposure quality units. With the objective of maximizing the total exposure quality units for the overall media selection plan, the objective function becomes

$$\text{Max} \quad 65DTV + 90ETV + 40DN + 60SN + 20R \quad \text{Exposure quality}$$

We now formulate the constraints for the model from the information given:

Care must be taken to ensure the linear programming formulation accurately reflects the problem being analyzed. You should review your formulation thoroughly before attempting to solve the problem.

$$
\begin{aligned}
DTV &\leq 15 \\
ETV &\leq 10 \\
DN &\leq 25 \\
SN &\leq 4 \\
R &\leq 30
\end{aligned}
\Bigg\} \text{Availability of media}
$$

$$1500DTV + 3000ETV + 400DN + 1000SN + 100R \leq 30{,}000 \quad \text{Budget}$$

$$
\begin{aligned}
DTV + ETV &\geq 10 \\
1500DTV + 3000ETV &\leq 18{,}000
\end{aligned}
\Bigg\} \text{Television restrictions}
$$

$$1000DTV + 2000ETV + 1500DN + 2500SN + 300R \geq 50{,}000 \quad \text{Customers reached}$$

$$DTV, ETV, DN, SN, R \geq 0$$

Problem 1 provides practice at formulating a similar media selection model.

The computer solution to this five-variable, nine-constraint linear programming model is shown in Figure 9.1; a summary is presented in Table 9.2.

The optimal solution calls for advertisements to be distributed among daytime TV, daily newspaper, Sunday newspaper, and radio. The maximum number of exposure quality units

THE MANAGEMENT SCIENTIST SOLUTION FOR THE RELAX-AND-ENJOY LAKE DEVELOPMENT CORPORATION PROBLEM

```
Objective Function Value =            2370.000

      Variable              Value              Reduced Costs
   --------------      ----------------      ------------------
        DTV                10.000                  0.000
        ETV                 0.000                 65.000
        DN                 25.000                  0.000
        SN                  2.000                  0.000
        R                  30.000                  0.000


     Constraint         Slack/Surplus           Dual Prices
   --------------      ----------------      ------------------
         1                 5.000                  0.000
         2                10.000                  0.000
         3                 0.000                 16.000
         4                 2.000                  0.000
         5                 0.000                 14.000
         6                 0.000                  0.060
         7                 0.000                -25.000
         8              3000.000                  0.000
         9             11500.003                  0.000
```

> Media Availability
> Budget
> Television Restrictions
> Audience Coverage

Table 9.2 ADVERTISING PLAN FOR THE RELAX-AND-ENJOY LAKE DEVELOPMENT CORPORATION

Media	Frequency	Budget
Daytime TV	10	$15,000
Daily newspaper	25	10,000
Sunday newspaper	2	2,000
Radio	30	3,000
		$30,000

Total customers reached = 61,500
Exposure quality units = 2,370

is 2370 and the total number of customers reached is 61,500. The reduced costs column in Figure 9.1 indicates that the number of exposure quality units for evening TV would have to increase by at least 65 before this media alternative could appear in the optimal solution. Note that the budget constraint (constraint 6) has a dual price of 0.060. That is, a $1.00 increase in the advertising budget will lead to an increase of 0.06 exposure quality units. The dual price of -25.000 for constraint 7 indicates that reducing the number of television commercials will increase the exposure quality of the advertising plan. Thus, Relax-and-Enjoy should consider reducing the requirement of having at least 10 television commercials.

A possible shortcoming of this model is that, even if the exposure quality measure were not subject to error, there is no guarantee that maximization of total exposure quality will lead to a maximization of profit or of sales (a common surrogate for profit). However, this issue is not a shortcoming of linear programming; rather, it is a shortcoming of the use of exposure quality as a criterion. If we were able to measure directly the effect of an advertisement on profit, we could use total profit as the objective to be maximized.

> More complex media selection models may include considerations such as the reduced exposure quality value for repeat media usage, cost discounts for repeat media usage, audience overlap by different media, and/or timing recommendations for the advertisements.

N O T E S and Comments

1. In previous chapters, we used the general notation x_1, x_2, and so on to denote the decision variables in a linear programming model. Practitioners often prefer using notation for the decision variables that is more descriptive and easier to interpret. For instance, in the Relax-and-Enjoy problem we used *DTV* for daytime TV, *ETV* for evening TV, *DN* for daily newspaper, *SN* for Sunday newspaper, and *R* for radio. The advantage of this notation is that it is easy to recall what each decision variable stands for when we review the computer output in Figure 9.1. We use descriptive notation for decision variables for several other linear programming applications presented in this chapter.

2. The media selection model required subjective evaluations of the exposure quality for the media alternatives. Marketing managers may have substantial data concerning exposure quality, but the final coefficients used in the objective function may also include considerations based primarily on managerial judgment. Judgment is an acceptable way of obtaining input for a linear programming model.

3. The media selection model presented in this section uses exposure quality as the objective function and places a constraint on the number of customers reached. An alternative formulation of this problem would be to use the number of customers reached as the objective function and add a constraint indicating the minimum total exposure quality required for the media plan.

Marketing Research

An organization conducts marketing research to learn about consumer characteristics, attitudes, and preferences. Marketing research firms that specialize in providing such information often do the actual research for client organizations. Typical services offered by a marketing research firm include designing the study, conducting market surveys, analyzing the data collected, and providing summary reports and recommendations for the client. In the research design phase, targets or quotas may be established for the number and types of respondents to be surveyed. The marketing research firm's objective is to conduct the survey so as to meet the client's needs at a minimum cost.

Market Survey, Inc. (MSI), specializes in evaluating consumer reaction to new products, services, and advertising campaigns. A client firm has requested MSI's assistance in ascertaining consumer reaction to a recently marketed household product. During meetings with the client, MSI agreed to conduct door-to-door personal interviews to obtain responses from households with children and households without children. In addition, MSI agreed to conduct both day and evening interviews. Specifically, the client's contract called for MSI to conduct 1000 interviews under the following quota guidelines.

1. At least 400 households with children would be interviewed.
2. At least 400 households without children would be interviewed.
3. The total number of households interviewed during the evening would be at least as great as the number of households interviewed during the day.
4. At least 40% of the interviews for households with children would be conducted during the evening.
5. At least 60% of the interviews for households without children would be conducted during the evening.

Because the interviews for households with children take additional interviewer time and because evening interviewers are paid more than daytime interviewers, the cost varies with the type of interview. Based on previous research studies, estimates of the interview costs are as follows:

| | | Interview Cost |
Household	Day	Evening
Children	$20	$25
No children	$18	$20

What is the household, time-of-day interview plan that will satisfy the contract requirements at a minimum total interviewing cost?

In formulating the linear programming model for the MSI problem, we utilize the following decision-variable notation:

DC = the number of daytime interviews of households with children

EC = the number of evening interviews of households with children

DNC = the number of daytime interviews of households without children

ENC = the number of evening interviews of households without children

We begin the linear programming model formulation by using the cost-per-interview data to develop the objective function:

$$\text{Min} \quad 20DC + 25EC + 18DNC + 20ENC$$

The constraint requiring a total of 1000 interviews is

$$DC + EC + DNC + ENC = 1000$$

The five specifications concerning the types of interviews are as follows.

Households with children:

$$DC + EC \geq 400$$

- Households without children:

$$DNC + ENC \geq 400$$

- At least as many evening interviews as day interviews:

$$EC + ENC \geq DC + DNC$$

The usual format for linear programming model formulation and computer input places all decision variables on the left side of the inequality and a constant (possibly zero) on the right side. Thus, we rewrite this constraint as

$$-DC + EC - DNC + ENC \geq 0$$

- At least 40% of interviews for households with children during the evening:

$$EC \geq 0.4(DC + EC) \quad \text{or} \quad -0.4DC + 0.6EC \geq 0$$

- At least 60% of interviews for households without children during the evening:

$$ENC \geq 0.6(DNC + ENC) \quad \text{or} \quad -0.6DNC + 0.4ENC \geq 0$$

When we add the nonnegativity requirements, the four-variable and six-constraint linear programming model becomes

$$\text{Min} \quad 20DC + 25EC + 18DNC + 20ENC$$

s.t.

$DC +$	$EC +$	$DNC +$	ENC	$=$	1000	Total interviews
$DC +$	EC			$\geq$	400	Households with children
		$DNC +$	ENC	$\geq$	400	Households without children
$-DC +$	$EC -$	$DNC +$	ENC	$\geq$	0	Evening interviews
$-0.4DC +$	$0.6EC$			$\geq$	0	Evening households with children
		$-0.6DNC +$	$0.4ENC$	$\geq$	0	Evening households without children

$$DC, EC, DNC, ENC \geq 0$$

The computer solution for this linear program is shown in Figure 9.2. The solution reveals that the minimum cost of $20,320 occurs with the following interview schedule.

	Number of Interviews		
Household	**Day**	**Evening**	**Totals**
Children	240	160	400
No children	240	360	600
Totals	480	520	1000

Figure 9.2 THE MANAGEMENT SCIENTIST SOLUTION FOR THE MARKET SURVEY PROBLEM

Objective Function Value =   20320.000

Variable	Value	Reduced Costs
DC	240.000	0.000
EC	160.000	0.000
DNC	240.000	0.000
ENC	360.000	0.000

Constraint	Slack/Surplus	Dual Prices
1	0.000	-19.200
2	0.000	-2.800
3	200.000	0.000
4	40.000	0.000
5	0.000	-5.000
6	0.000	-2.000

Hence, 480 interviews will be scheduled during the day and 520 during the evening. Households with children will be covered by 400 interviews, and households without children will be covered by 600 interviews.

Selected sensitivity analysis information from Figure 9.2 shows a dual price of -19.200 for constraint 1. In other words, the objective function will get worse (the total interviewing cost will increase) by \$19.20 if the number of interviews is increased from 1000 to 1001. Thus, \$19.20 is the incremental cost of obtaining additional interviews. It also is the savings that could be realized by reducing the number of interviews from 1000 to 999.

The surplus variable, with a value of 200.000, for constraint 3 shows that 200 more households without children will be interviewed than required. Similarly, the surplus variable, with a value of 40.000, for constraint 4 shows that the number of evening interviews exceeds the number of daytime interviews by 40. The zero values for the surplus variables in constraints 5 and 6 indicate that the more expensive evening interviews are being held at a minimum. Indeed, the dual price of -5.000 for constraint 5 indicates that if one more household (with children) than the minimum requirement must be interviewed during the evening, the total interviewing cost will go up by \$5.00. Similarly, constraint 6 shows that requiring one more household (without children) to be interviewed during the evening will increase costs by \$2.00.

9.2 FINANCIAL APPLICATIONS

In finance, linear programming has been applied in problem situations involving capital budgeting, make-or-buy decisions, asset allocation, portfolio selection, financial planning, and many more. In this section, we describe a portfolio selection problem and a problem involving funding of an early retirement program.

Portfolio Selection

Portfolio selection problems involve situations in which a financial manager must select specific investments—for example, stocks and bonds—from a variety of investment alternatives. Managers of mutual funds, credit unions, insurance companies, and banks frequently encounter this type of problem. The objective function for portfolio selection problems usually is maximization of expected return or minimization of risk. The constraints usually take the form of restrictions on the type of permissible investments, state laws, company policy, maximum permissible risk, and so on. Problems of this type have been formulated and solved using a variety of mathematical programming techniques. In this section we show how to formulate and solve a portfolio selection problem as a linear program.

Consider the case of Welte Mutual Funds, Inc., located in New York City. Welte has just obtained $100,000 by converting industrial bonds to cash and is now looking for other investment opportunities for these funds. Based on Welte's current investments, the firm's top financial analyst recommends that all new investments be made in the oil industry, steel industry, or in government bonds. Specifically, the analyst has identified five investment opportunities and projected their annual rates of return. The investments and rates of return are shown in Table 9.3.

Management of Welte has imposed the following investment guidelines.

1. Neither industry (oil or steel) should receive more than $50,000.
2. Government bonds should be at least 25% of the steel industry investments.
3. The investment in Pacific Oil, the high-return but high-risk investment, cannot be more than 60% of the total oil industry investment.

What portfolio recommendations—investments and amounts—should be made for the available $100,000? Given the objective of maximizing projected return subject to the budgetary and managerially imposed constraints, we answer this question by formulating a linear programming model of the problem. The solution will provide investment recommendations for the management of Welte Mutual Funds.

Let

$$A = \text{dollars invested in Atlantic Oil}$$
$$P = \text{dollars invested in Pacific Oil}$$
$$M = \text{dollars invested in Midwest Oil}$$
$$H = \text{dollars invested in Huber Steel}$$
$$G = \text{dollars invested in government bonds}$$

Table 9.3 **INVESTMENT OPPORTUNITIES FOR WELTE MUTUAL FUNDS**

Investment	Projected Rate of Return (%)
Atlantic Oil	7.3
Pacific Oil	10.3
Midwest Steel	6.4
Huber Steel	7.5
Government bonds	4.5

Using the projected rates of return shown in Table 9.3, we write the objective function for maximizing the total return for the portfolio as

$$\text{Max}\quad 0.073A + 0.103P + 0.064M + 0.075H + 0.045G$$

The constraint specifying investment of the available \$100,000 is

$$A + P + M + H + G = 100{,}000$$

The requirements that neither the oil nor the steel industry should receive more than \$50,000 are

$$A + P \le 50{,}000$$
$$M + H \le 50{,}000$$

The requirement that government bonds be at least 25% of the steel industry investment is expressed as

$$G \ge 0.25(M + H) \quad \text{or} \quad -0.25M - 0.25H + G \ge 0$$

Finally, the constraint that Pacific Oil cannot be more than 60% of the total oil industry investment is

$$P \le 0.60(A + P) \quad \text{or} \quad -0.60A + 0.40P \le 0$$

By adding the nonnegativity restrictions, we obtain the complete linear programming model for the Welte Mutual Fund investment problem:

Max $0.073A + 0.103P + 0.064M + 0.075H + 0.045G$

s.t.

$A +$	$P +$	$M +$	$H +$	G	$=$	$100{,}000$	Available funds
$A +$					$\le$	$50{,}000$	Oil industry maximum
		$M +$	H		$\le$	$50{,}000$	Steel industry maximum
	$-$	$0.25M -$	$0.25H +$	$G \ge$		0	Government bonds maximum
$-0.6A +$	$0.4P$				$\le$	0	Pacific Oil restriction

$A, P, M, H, G \ge 0$

We solved this problem using The Management Scientist; the output is shown in Figure 9.3. Table 9.4 shows how the funds are divided among the securities. Note that the optimal solution indicates that the portfolio should be diversified among all the investment opportunities except Midwest Steel. The projected annual return for this portfolio is \$8000, which is an overall return of 8%.

The computer printout shows the dual price for constraint 3 is zero. The reason is that the steel industry maximum isn't a binding constraint; increases in the steel industry limit of \$50,000 will not improve the value of the objective function. Indeed, the slack variable

Figure 9.3	THE MANAGEMENT SCIENTIST SOLUTION FOR THE WELTE MUTUAL FUNDS PROBLEM

```
Objective Function Value =            8000.000

        Variable            Value            Reduced Costs
    ---------------    ---------------    -------------------
           A              20000.000              0.000
           P              30000.000              0.000
           M                  0.000              0.011
           H              40000.000              0.000
           G              10000.000              0.000


        Constraint       Slack/Surplus          Dual Prices
    ---------------    ---------------    -------------------
           1                  0.000              0.069
           2                  0.000              0.022
           3              10000.000              0.000
           4                  0.000             -0.024
           5                  0.000              0.030
```

Table 9.4	OPTIMAL PORTFOLIO SELECTION FOR WELTE MUTUAL FUNDS

Investment	Amount	Expected Annual Return
Atlantic Oil	$ 20,000	$1,460
Pacific Oil	30,000	3,090
Huber Steel	40,000	3,000
Government bonds	10,000	450
Totals	$100,000	$8,000

Expected annual return of $8,000
Overall rate of return = 8%

for this constraint shows that the current steel industry investment is $10,000 below its limit of $50,000. The dual prices for the other constraints are nonzero, indicating that these constraints are binding.

The dual price of 0.069 for constraint 1 shows that the objective function can be increased by 0.069 if one more dollar can be made available for the portfolio investment. If more funds can be obtained at a cost of less than 6.9%, management should consider obtaining them. However, if a return in excess of 6.9% can be obtained by investing funds elsewhere (other than in these five securities), management should question the wisdom of investing the entire $100,000 in this portfolio.

The dual price for the available funds constraint provides information on the rate of return from additional investment funds.

Q.M. IN ACTION

USING LINEAR PROGRAMMING FOR OPTIMAL LEASE STRUCTURING*

GE Capital is a $70-billion subsidiary of General Electric. As one of the nation's largest and most diverse financial services companies, GE Capital arranges leases in both domestic and international markets, including leases for telecommunications; data processing; construction; and fleets of cars, trucks, and commercial aircraft. To help allocate and schedule the rental and debt payments of a leveraged lease, GE Capital analysts have developed an optimization model, which is available as an optional component of the company's lease analysis proprietary software.

Leveraged leases are designed to provide financing for assets with economic lives of at least five years, which require large capital outlays. A leveraged lease represents an agreement among the lessor (the owner of the asset), the lessee (the user of the asset), and the lender who provides a nonrecourse loan of 50% to 80% of the lessor's purchase price. In a nonrecourse loan, the lenders cannot turn to the lessor for repayment in the event of default. As the lessor in such arrangements, GE Capital is able to claim ownership and realize income tax benefits such as depreciation and interest deductions. These deductions usually produce tax losses during the early years of the lease, which reduces the total tax liability. Approximately 85% of all financial leases in the United States are leveraged leases.

In its simplest form, the leveraged lease structuring problem can be formulated as a linear program. The linear program models the after-tax cash flow for the lessor, taking into consideration rental receipts, borrowing and repaying of the loan, and income taxes. Constraints are formulated to ensure compliance with IRS guidelines and to enable customizing of leases to meet lessee and lessor requirements. The objective function can be entered in a custom fashion or selected from a predefined list. Typically, the objective is to minimize the lessee's cost, expressed as the net present value of rental payments, or to maximize the lessor's after-tax yield.

GE Capital developed an optimization approach that could be applied to single-investor lease structuring. In a study with the department most involved with these transactions, the optimization approach yielded substantial benefits. The approach has been used on a limited basis and has helped GE Capital win some single-investor transactions ranging in size from $1 million to $20 million.

*Based on Litty, C.J., "Optimal Lease Structuring at GE Capital." Interfaces, May–June, 1994, pp. 34–45.

Similar interpretations can be given to the other dual prices. Note that the dual price for constraint 4 is negative at −0.024. This result indicates that increasing the value on the right-hand side of the constraint by one unit can be expected to worsen the objective function by 0.024. That is, in terms of the optimal portfolio, if Welte invests one more dollar in government bonds (beyond the minimum requirement), the total return will decrease by $0.024. To see why this decrease occurs, note again from the dual price for constraint 1 that the marginal return on the funds invested in the portfolio is 6.9% (the average return is 8%). The rate of return on government bonds is 4.5%. Thus, the cost of investing one more dollar in government bonds is the difference between the marginal return on the portfolio and the marginal return on government bonds: 6.9% − 4.5% = 2.4%.

Practice formulating a variation of the Welte problem by working Problem 9.

Note that the optimal solution shows that Midwest Steel should not be included in the portfolio ($M = 0$). The associated reduced cost for M of 0.011 tells us that the objective function coefficient for Midwest Steel would have to increase by 0.011 before considering the Midwest Steel investment alternative would be advisable. With this increase the Midwest Steel return would be 0.064 + 0.011 = 0.075, making this investment just as desirable as the currently used Huber Steel investment alternative.

Finally, a simple modification of the Welte linear programming model permits determining the fraction of available funds invested in each security. That is, we divide each of the right-hand-side values by 100,000. Then the optimal values for the variables will give the fraction of funds that should be invested in each security for a portfolio of any size.

N O T E S
and Comments

1. The optimal solution to the Welte Mutual Funds problem indicates that $20,000 is to be spent on the Atlantic Oil stock. If Atlantic Oil sells for $75 per share, we would have to purchase exactly $266\,2/_3$ shares in order to spend exactly $20,000. The difficulty of purchasing fractional shares is usually handled by purchasing the largest possible integer number of shares with the allotted funds (e.g., 266 shares of Atlantic Oil). This approach guarantees that the budget constraint will not be violated. This approach, of course, introduces the possibility that the solution will no longer be optimal, but the danger is slight if a large number of securities are involved. In cases where the analyst believes that the decision variables *must* have integer values, the problem must be formulated as an integer linear programming model. Integer linear programming is the topic of Chapter 11.

2. Financial portfolio theory stresses obtaining a proper balance between risk and return. In the Welte problem, we explicitly considered return in the objective function. Risk is controlled by choosing constraints that ensure diversity among oil and steel stocks and a balance between government bonds and the steel industry investment.

Financial Planning

Linear programming has been used for a variety of financial planning applications. The Q.M. in Action: Using Linear Programming for Optimal Lease Structuring describes how GE Captial used linear programming to optimize the structure of a leveraged lease.

Hewlitt Corporation has established an early retirement program as part of its corporate restructuring. At the close of the voluntary sign-up period, 68 employees had elected early retirement. As a result of these early retirements, the company has incurred the following obligations over the next 8 years. Cash requirements (in thousands of dollars) are due at the beginning of each year.

Year	1	2	3	4	5	6	7	8
Cash Requirement	430	210	222	231	240	195	225	255

The corporate treasurer must determine how much money must be set aside today to meet the 8-year financial obligations as they come due. The financing plan for the retirement program includes investments in government bonds as well as savings. The investments in government bonds are limited to three choices:

Bond	Price	Rate	Years to Maturity
1	$1150	8.875	5
2	1000	5.500	6
3	1350	11.750	7

The government bonds have a par value of $1000, which means that even with different prices each bond pays $1000 at maturity. The rates shown are based on the par value. For purposes of planning, the treasurer has assumed that any funds not invested in bonds will be placed in savings and earn interest at an annual rate of 4%.

We define the decision variables as follows:

F = total dollars required to meet the retirement plan's 8-year obligation

B_1 = units of bond 1 purchased (par value $1000)

B_2 = units of bond 2 purchased (par value $1000)

B_3 = units of bond 3 purchased (par value $1000)

S_i = investment in savings at the beginning of the year i for $i = 1, \ldots, 8$

The objective function is to minimize the total dollars needed to meet the retirement plan's 8-year obligation, or

$$\text{Min} \quad F$$

A key feature of this type of financial planning problem is that there is a constraint for each year of the planning horizon. In general, each constraint takes the form:

$$\left(\begin{array}{c} \text{Funds avaliable at} \\ \text{the beginning of the year} \end{array} \right) - \left(\begin{array}{c} \text{Funds invested in bonds} \\ \text{and saved} \end{array} \right) = \left(\begin{array}{c} \text{Cash obligation for} \\ \text{the current year} \end{array} \right)$$

We defined F to be the funds available at the beginning of year 1. With a current price of $1150 for bond 1 and investments expressed in thousands of dollars, the total investment for B_1 units of bond 1 would be $1.15B_1$. Similarly, the total investment in bonds 2 and 3 would be $1B_2$ and $1.35B_3$, respectively. The investment in savings for year 1 is S_1. Using these results and the first-year obligation of 430, we obtain the constraint for year 1:

$$F - 1.15B_1 - 1B_2 - 1.35B_3 - S_1 = 430 \qquad \text{Year 1}$$

Investments in bonds can take place only in this first year, and the bonds will be held until maturity.

The funds available at the beginning of year 2 include the investment returns of 8.875% on the par value of bond 1, 5.5% on the par value of bond 2, 11.75% on the par value of bond 3, and 4% on savings. The new amount to be invested in savings for year 2 is S_2. With an obligation of 210, the constraint for year 2 is

$$0.08875B_1 + 0.055B_2 + 0.1175B_3 + 1.04S_1 - S_2 = 210 \quad \text{Year 2}$$

Similarly, the constraints for years 3 to 8 are

$$0.08875B_1 + 0.055B_2 + 0.1175B_3 + 1.04S_2 - S_3 = 222 \quad \text{Year 3}$$
$$0.08875B_1 + 0.055B_2 + 0.1175B_3 + 1.04S_3 - S_4 = 231 \quad \text{Year 4}$$
$$0.08875B_1 + 0.055B_2 + 0.1175B_3 + 1.04S_4 - S_5 = 240 \quad \text{Year 5}$$
$$1.08875B_1 + 0.055B_2 + 0.1175B_3 + 1.04S_5 - S_6 = 195 \quad \text{Year 6}$$
$$1.055B_2 + 0.1175B_3 + 1.04S_6 - S_7 = 225 \quad \text{Year 7}$$
$$1.1175B_3 + 1.04S_7 - S_8 = 255 \quad \text{Year 8}$$

Note that the constraint for year 6 shows that funds available from bond 1 are $1.08875B_1$. The coefficient of 1.08875 reflects the fact that bond 1 matures at the end of year 5. As a result, the par value plus the interest from bond 1 during year 5 is available at the beginning of year 6. Also, because bond 1 matures in year 5 and becomes available for use at the beginning of year 6, the variable B_1 does not appear in the constraints for years 7 and 8. Note the similar interpretation for bond 2, which matures at the end of year 6 and has the par value plus interest available at the beginning of year 7. In addition, bond 3 matures at the end of year 7 and has the par value plus interest available at the beginning of year 8.

Finally, note that a variable S_8 appears in the constraint for year 8. The retirement fund obligation will be completed at the beginning of year 8, so we anticipate that S_8 will be zero and no funds will be put into savings. However, the formulation includes S_8 in the event that the bond income plus interest from the savings in year 7 exceed the 255 cash requirement for year 8. Thus, S_8 is a surplus variable that shows any funds remaining after the 8-year cash requirements have been satisfied.

The solution to the 12 variable, 8 constraint linear program is shown in Figure 9.4. With an objective function value of 1728.79385, the total investment required to meet the retirement plan's 8-year obligation is $1,728,794. Using the current prices of $1150, $1000, and $1350 for each of the bonds respectively, we can summarize the initial investments in the three bonds as follows:

Bond	Decision Variable Value	Investment Amount
1	$B_1 = 144.988$	$1150(144.988) = $166,736
2	$B_2 = 187.856$	$1000(187.856) = $187,856
3	$B_3 = 228.188$	$1350(228.188) = $308,054

Figure 9.4	THE MANAGEMENT SCIENTIST SOLUTION FOR THE HEWLITT CORPORATION CASH REQUIREMENTS PROBLEM

```
Objective Function Value =            1728.79385

        Variable              Value            Reduced Costs
     --------------     ---------------     ------------------
           F              1728.79385             0.00000
          B1               144.98815             0.00000
          B2               187.85585             0.00000
          B3               228.18792             0.00000
          S1               636.14794             0.00000
          S2               501.60571             0.00000
          S3               349.68179             0.00000
          S4               182.68091             0.00000
          S5                 0.00000             0.06403
          S6                 0.00000             0.01261
          S7                 0.00000             0.02132
          S8                 0.00000             0.67084

      Constraint        Slack/Surplus          Dual Prices
     --------------     ---------------     ------------------
           1                 0.00000            -1.00000
           2                 0.00000            -0.96154
           3                 0.00000            -0.92456
           4                 0.00000            -0.88900
           5                 0.00000            -0.85480
           6                 0.00000            -0.76036
           7                 0.00000            -0.71899
           8                 0.00000            -0.67084
```

The solution also shows that $636,148 (see S_1) will be placed in savings at the beginning of the first year. By starting with $1,728,794, the company can make the specified bond and savings investments and have enough left over to meet the retirement program's first-year cash requirement of $430,000.

The optimal solution in Figure 9.4 shows that the decision variables S_1, S_2, S_3, and S_4 all are greater than zero, indicating investments in savings are required in each of the first four years. However, interest from the bonds plus the bond maturity incomes will be sufficient to cover the retirement program's cash requirements in years 6 through 8.

The dual prices have an interesting interpretation in this application. Each right-hand-side value corresponds to the payment that must be made in that year. Note that the dual prices are negative, indicating that reducing the payment in any year would be beneficial because the total funds required for the retirement program's obligation would be less. Also note that the dual prices show that reductions are more beneficial in the early years, with decreasing benefits in subsequent years. As a result, Hewlitt would benefit by reducing cash requirements in the early years even if it had to make equivalently larger cash payments in later years.

> In this application, the dual price can be thought of as the negative of the present value of each dollar in the cash requirement. For example, each dollar that must be paid in year 8 has a present value of $0.67084.

NOTES and Comments

1. The optimal solution for the Hewlitt Corporation problem shows fractional numbers of government bonds at 144.988, 187.856, and 228.188 units, respectively. However, fractional bond units usually are not available. If we were conservative and rounded up to 145, 188, and 229 units, respectively, the total funds required for the 8-year retirement program obligation would be approximately $1254 more than the total funds indicated by the objective function. Because of the magnitude of the funds involved, rounding up probably would provide a very workable solution. If an optimal integer solution were required, the methods of integer linear programming covered in Chapter 11 would have to be used.

2. We implicitly assumed that interest from the government bonds is paid annually. Investments such as treasury notes actually provide interest payments every 6 months. In such cases, the model can be reformulated with 6-month periods, with interest and/or cash payments occurring every 6 months.

9.3 PRODUCTION MANAGEMENT APPLICATIONS

Many linear programming applications have been developed for production and operations management, including scheduling, staffing, inventory control, and capacity planning. In this section we describe examples with make-or-buy decisions, production scheduling, and work-force assignments.

A Make-or-Buy Decision

We illustrate the use of a linear programming model to determine how much of each of several component parts a company should manufacture and how much it should purchase from an outside supplier. Such a decision is referred to as a make-or-buy decision.

The Janders Company markets various business and engineering products. Currently, Janders is preparing to introduce two new calculators: one for the business market called the Financial Manager and one for the engineering market called the Technician. Each calculator has three components: a base, an electronic cartridge, and a face plate or top. The same base is used for both calculators, but the cartridges and tops are different. All components can be manufactured by the company or purchased from outside suppliers. The manufacturing costs and purchase prices for the components are summarized in Table 9.5.

Janders' forecasters indicate that 3000 Financial Manager calculators and 2000 Technician calculators will be needed. However, manufacturing capacity is limited. The company has 200 hours of regular manufacturing time and 50 hours of overtime that can be scheduled for the calculators. Overtime involves a premium at the additional cost of $9 per hour. Table 9.6 shows manufacturing times (in minutes) for the components.

The problem for Janders is to determine how many units of each component to manufacture and how many units of each component to purchase. We define the decision variables as follows:

$$BM = \text{number of bases manufactured}$$
$$BP = \text{number of bases purchased}$$
$$FCM = \text{number of Financial cartidges manufactured}$$
$$FCP = \text{number of Financial cartridges purchased}$$
$$TCM = \text{number of Technician cartridges manufactured}$$
$$TCP = \text{number of Technician cartridges purchased}$$
$$FTM = \text{number of Financial tops manufactured}$$
$$FTP = \text{number of Financial tops purchased}$$
$$TTM = \text{number of Technician tops manufactured}$$
$$TTP = \text{number of Technician tops purchased}$$

Table 9.5 MANUFACTURING COSTS AND PURCHASE PRICES FOR JANDERS' CALCULATOR COMPONENTS

	Cost Per Unit	
Component	Manufacture (Regular Time)	Purchase
Base	$0.50	$0.60
Financial cartridge	3.75	4.00
Technician cartridge	3.30	3.90
Financial top	0.60	0.65
Technician top	0.75	0.78

Table 9.6 MANUFACTURING TIMES IN MINUTES PER UNIT FOR JANDERS' CALCULATOR COMPONENTS

Component	Manufacturing Time
Base	1.0
Financial cartridge	3.0
Technician cartridge	2.5
Financial top	1.0
Technician top	1.5

One additional decision variable is needed to determine the hours of overtime that must be scheduled:

$$OT = \text{number of hours of overtime to be scheduled}$$

The objective function is to minimize the total cost, including manufacturing costs, purchase costs and overtime costs. Using the cost per unit data in Table 9.5 and the overtime premium cost rate of $9 per hour, we write the objective function as

$$\text{Min} \quad 0.5BM + 0.6BP + 3.75FCM + 4FCP + 3.3TCM + 3.9TCP + 0.6FTM$$
$$+ 0.65FTP + 0.75TTM + 0.78TTP + 9OT$$

The first five constraints specify the number of each component that must be obtained to satisfy the demand for 3000 Financial Manager calculators and 2000 Technician calculators. A total of 5000 base components are needed, with the number of other components depending on the demand of the particular calculator. The five demand constraints are

$$
\begin{aligned}
BM + BP &= 5000 \quad &&\text{Bases} \\
FCM + FCP &= 3000 \quad &&\text{Financial cartridges} \\
TCM + TCP &= 2000 \quad &&\text{Technician cartridges} \\
FTM + FTP &= 3000 \quad &&\text{Financial tops} \\
TTM + TTP &= 2000 \quad &&\text{Technician tops}
\end{aligned}
$$

Two constraints are needed to guarantee that manufacturing capacities for regular time and overtime cannot be exceeded. The first constraint limits overtime capacity to 50 hours, or

$$OT \leq 50$$

The same units of measure must be used for both the left-hand side and right-hand side of the constraint. In this case, minutes are used.

The second constraint states that the total manufacturing time required for all components must be less than or equal to the total manufacturing capacity, including regular time plus overtime. The manufacturing times for the components are expressed in minutes so we state the total manufacturing capacity constraint in minutes, with the 200 hours of regular time capacity becoming $60(200) = 12{,}000$ minutes. The actual overtime required is unknown at this point, so we write the overtime as $60OT$ minutes. Using the manufacturing times from Table 9.6, we have

$$BM + 3FCM + 2.5TCM + FTM + 1.5TTM \leq 12{,}000 + 60OT$$

Moving the decision variable for overtime to the left-hand side of the constraint provides the manufacturing capacity constraint:

$$BM + 3FCM + 2.5TCM + FTM + 1.5TTM - 60OT \leq 12{,}000$$

The complete formulation of Janders' make-or-buy problem with all decision variables greater than or equal to zero is

$$\text{Min} \quad 0.5BM + 0.6BP + 3.75FCM + 4FCP + 3.3TCM + 3.9TCP$$
$$+ \ 0.6FTM + 0.65FTP + 0.75TTM + 0.78TTP + 9OT$$

s.t.

BM			$+$	$BP =$	5000	Bases
	FCM		$+$	$FCP =$	3000	Financial cartridges
		TCM	$+$	$TCP =$	2000	Technician cartridges
		FTM	$+$	$FTP =$	3000	Financial tops
		$TTM +$		$TTP =$	2000	Technician tops
				$OT \leq$	50	Overtime hours

$$BM + 3FCM + 2.5TCM + FTM + 1.5TTM - 60OT \leq 12{,}000 \quad \text{Manufacturing capacity}$$

The computer solution to this 11 variable, 7 constraint linear program is shown in Figure 9.5. The optimal solution indicates that all 5000 bases (BM), 667 Financial Manager cartridges (FCM), and 2000 Technician cartridges (TCM) should be manufactured. The remaining 2333 Financial Manager cartridges (FCP), all the Financial Manager tops (FTP), and all Technician tops (TTP) should be purchased. No overtime manufacturing is necessary, and the total cost associated with the optimal make-or-buy plan is $24,443.33.

Sensitivity analysis provides some additional information about the unused overtime capacity. The Reduced Costs column shows that the overtime (OT) premium would have to decrease by $4 per hour before overtime production should be considered. That is, if the overtime premium is $9 - $4 = $5 or less, Janders may want to replace some of the purchased components with components manufactured on overtime. Problem 12 at the end of the chapter asks you to reconsider the Janders problem with a lower overtime premium to show how the optimal make-or-buy solution changes.

Try Problem 12 for practice with a variation of the Janders make-or-buy problem.

The dual price for the manufacturing capacity constraint 7 is 0.083. This price indicates that an additional hour of manufacturing capacity is worth $0.083 per minute or ($0.083)(60) = $5 per hour. The range of feasibility for constraint 7 shows that this conclusion is valid until the amount of regular time increases to 19,000 minutes, or 316.7 hours.

Sensitivity analysis also indicates that a change in prices charged by the outside suppliers can affect the optimal solution. For instance, the range of optimality for the objective function coefficient for BP is 0.583 to no upper limit. If the purchase price for bases remains at $0.583 or more, the number of bases purchased (BP) will remain at zero. However, if the purchase price drops below $0.583, Janders should begin to purchase rather than manufacture the base component. Similar sensitivity analysis conclusions about the purchase price ranges can be drawn for the other components.

N O T E S *and Comments*

The proper interpretation of the dual price for manufacturing capacity (constraint 7) in the Janders problem is that an additional hour of manufacturing capacity is worth ($0.083)(60) = $5 per hour. Thus, the company should be willing to pay a premium of $5 per hour over and above the current regular time cost per hour, which is already included in the manufacturing cost of the product. Thus, if the regular time cost is $18 per hour, Janders should be willing to pay up to $18 + $5 = $23 per hour to obtain additional labor capacity.

Figure 9.5   THE MANAGEMENT SCIENTIST SOLUTION FOR THE JANDERS MAKE-OR-BUY PROBLEM

Objective Function Value =   24443.333

Variable	Value	Reduced Costs
BM	5000.000	0.000
BP	0.000	0.017
FCM	666.667	0.000
FCP	2333.333	0.000
TCM	2000.000	0.000
TCP	0.000	0.392
FTM	0.000	0.033
FTP	3000.000	0.000
TTM	0.000	0.095
TTP	2000.000	0.000
OT	0.000	4.000

Constraint	Slack/Surplus	Dual Prices
1	0.000	-0.583
2	0.000	-4.000
3	0.000	-3.508
4	0.000	-0.650
5	0.000	-0.780
6	50.000	0.000
7	0.000	0.083

OBJECTIVE COEFFICIENT RANGES

Variable	Lower Limit	Current Value	Upper Limit
BM	No Lower Limit	0.500	0.517
BP	0.583	0.600	No Upper Limit
FCM	3.700	3.750	3.850
FCP	3.900	4.000	4.050
TCM	No Lower Limit	3.300	3.692
TCP	3.508	3.900	No Upper Limit
FTM	0.567	0.600	No Upper Limit
FTP	No Lower Limit	0.650	0.683
TTM	0.655	0.750	No Upper Limit
TTP	No Lower Limit	0.780	0.875
OT	5.000	9.000	No Upper Limit

RIGHT HAND SIDE RANGES

Constraint	Lower Limit	Current Value	Upper Limit
1	0.000	5000.000	7000.000
2	666.667	3000.000	No Upper Limit
3	0.000	2000.000	2800.000
4	0.000	3000.000	No Upper Limit
5	0.000	2000.000	No Upper Limit
6	0.000	50.000	No Upper Limit
7	10000.000	12000.000	19000.000

Production Scheduling

One of the most important applications of linear programming deals with multiperiod planning such as production scheduling. The solution to a production scheduling problem enables the manager to establish an efficient low-cost production schedule for one or more products over several time periods (weeks or months). Essentially, a production scheduling problem can be viewed as a product-mix problem for each of several periods in the future. The manager must determine the production levels that will allow the company to meet product demand requirements, given limitations on production capacity, labor capacity, and storage space, while minimizing total production costs.

One advantage of using linear programming for production scheduling problems is that they recur. A production schedule must be established for the current month, then again for the next month, for the month after that, and so on. When looking at the problem each month, the production manager will find that, although demand for the products has changed, production times, production capacities, storage space limitations, and so on are roughly the same. Thus, the production manager is basically resolving the same problem handled in previous months, and a general linear programming model of the production scheduling procedure may be frequently applied. Once the model has been formulated, the manager can simply supply the data—demand, capacities, and so on—for the given production period and use the linear programming model repeatedly to develop the production schedule.

Let us consider the case of the Bollinger Electronics Company, which produces two different electronic components for a major airplane engine manufacturer. The airplane engine manufacturer notifies the Bollinger sales office each quarter of its monthly requirements for components for each of the next 3 months. The monthly requirements for the components may vary considerably, depending on the type of engine the airplane engine manufacturer is producing. The order shown in Table 9.7 has just been received for the next 3-month period.

After the order is processed, a demand statement is sent to the production control department. The production control department must then develop a 3-month production plan for the components. In arriving at the desired schedule, the production manager will want to identify

1. total production cost,
2. inventory holding cost, and
3. change-in-production-level costs.

In the remainder of this section, we show how to formulate a linear programming model of the production and inventory process for Bollinger Electronics to minimize the total cost.

To develop the model, we let x_{im} denote the production volume in units for product i in month m. Here $i = 1, 2$, and $m = 1, 2, 3$; $i = 1$ refers to component 322A, $i = 2$ refers to component 802B, $m = 1$ refers to April, $m = 2$ refers to May, and $m = 3$ refers to June. The purpose of the double subscript is to provide a more descriptive notation.

Table 9.7	THREE-MONTH DEMAND SCHEDULE FOR BOLLINGER ELECTRONICS COMPANY		
Component	**April**	**May**	**June**
322A	1000	3000	5000
802B	1000	500	3000

We could simply use x_6 to represent the number of units of product 2 produced in month 3, but x_{23} is more descriptive, identifying directly the product and month represented by the variable.

If component 322A costs \$20 per unit produced and component 802B costs \$10 per unit produced, the total production cost part of the objective function is

$$\text{Total production cost} = 20x_{11} + 20x_{12} + 20x_{13} + 10x_{21} + 10x_{22} + 10x_{23}$$

Since the production cost per unit is the same each month, we don't need to include the production costs in the objective function; that is, regardless of the production schedule selected, the total production cost will remain the same. In other words, production costs are not relevant costs for the production scheduling decision under consideration. In cases in which the production cost per unit is expected to change each month, the variable production costs per unit per month must be included in the objective function. Since the solution for the Bollinger Electronics problem will be the same whether these costs are included or not, we included them so that the value of the linear programming objective function will include all the costs associated with the problem.

To incorporate the relevant inventory holding costs into the model, we let s_{im} denote the inventory level for product i at the end of month m. Bollinger has determined that on a monthly basis inventory holding costs are 1.5% of the cost of the product; that is, $(0.015)(\$20) = \$0.30$ per unit for component 322A and $(0.015)(\$10) = \$0.15$ per unit for component 802B. A common assumption made in using the linear programming approach to production scheduling is that monthly ending inventories are an acceptable approximation to the average inventory levels throughout the month. Making this assumption, we write the inventory holding cost portion of the objective function as

$$\text{Inventory holding cost} = 0.30s_{11} + 0.30s_{12} + 0.30s_{13} + 0.15s_{21} + 0.15s_{22} + 0.15s_{23}$$

To incorporate the costs of fluctuations in production levels from month to month, we need to define two additional variables:

I_m = increase in the total production level necessary during month m

D_m = decrease in the total production level necessary during month m

After estimating the effects of employee layoffs, turnovers, reassignment training costs, and other costs associated with fluctuating production levels, Bollinger estimates that the cost associated with increasing the production level for any month is \$0.50 per unit increase. A similar cost associated with decreasing the production level for any month is \$0.20 per unit. Thus, we write the third portion of the objective function as

$$\text{Change-in-production-level costs} = 0.50I_1 + 0.50I_2 + 0.50I_3$$
$$+ 0.20D_1 + 0.20D_2 + 0.20D_3$$

Note that the cost associated with changes in production level is a function of the change in the total number of units produced in month m compared to the total number of units produced in month $m - 1$. In other production scheduling applications, fluctuations in production level might be measured in terms of machine hours or labor-hours required rather than in terms of the total number of units produced.

Combining all three costs, the complete objective function becomes

$$\begin{aligned}
\text{Min} \quad & 20x_{11} + 20x_{12} + 20x_{13} + 10x_{21} + 10x_{22} + 10x_{23} + 0.30s_{11} \\
& + 0.30s_{12} + 0.30s_{13} + 0.15s_{21} + 0.15s_{22} + 0.15s_{23} + 0.50I_1 \\
& + 0.50I_2 + 0.50I_3 + 0.20D_1 + 0.20D_2 + 0.20D_3
\end{aligned}$$

We now consider the constraints. First, we must guarantee that the schedule meets customer demand. Since the units shipped can come from the current month's production or from inventory carried over from previous months, the demand requirement takes the form

$$\begin{pmatrix} \text{Ending} \\ \text{inventory} \\ \text{from previous} \\ \text{month} \end{pmatrix} + \begin{pmatrix} \text{Current} \\ \text{production} \end{pmatrix} - \begin{pmatrix} \text{Ending} \\ \text{inventory} \\ \text{for this} \\ \text{month} \end{pmatrix} = \begin{pmatrix} \text{This month's} \\ \text{demand} \end{pmatrix}$$

Suppose that the inventories at the beginning of the 3-month scheduling period were 500 units for component 322A and 200 units for component 802B. The demand for both products in the first month (April) was 1000 units, so the constraints for meeting demand in the first month become

$$500 + x_{11} - s_{11} = 1000$$
$$200 + x_{21} - s_{21} = 1000$$

Moving the constants to the right-hand side, we have

$$x_{11} - s_{11} = 500$$
$$x_{21} - s_{21} = 800$$

Similarly, we need demand constraints for both products in the second and third months. We write them as follows.

Month 2

$$s_{11} + x_{12} - s_{12} = 3000$$
$$s_{21} + x_{22} - s_{22} = 500$$

Month 3

$$s_{12} + x_{13} - s_{13} = 5000$$
$$s_{22} + x_{23} - s_{23} = 3000$$

If the company specifies a minimum inventory level at the end of the 3-month period of at least 400 units of component 322A and at least 200 units of component 802B, we can add the constraints

$$s_{13} \geq 400$$
$$s_{23} \geq 200$$

Suppose that we have the additional information on machine, labor, and storage capacity shown in Table 9.8. Machine, labor, and storage space requirements are given in Table 9.9. To reflect these limitations, the following constraints are necessary.

Machine Capacity

$$0.10x_{11} + 0.08x_{21} \leq 400 \quad \text{Month 1}$$
$$0.10x_{12} + 0.08x_{22} \leq 500 \quad \text{Month 2}$$
$$0.10x_{13} + 0.08x_{23} \leq 600 \quad \text{Month 3}$$

Labor Capacity

$$0.05x_{11} + 0.07x_{21} \leq 300 \quad \text{Month 1}$$
$$0.05x_{12} + 0.07x_{22} \leq 300 \quad \text{Month 2}$$
$$0.05x_{13} + 0.07x_{23} \leq 300 \quad \text{Month 3}$$

Storage Capacity

$$2s_{11} + 3s_{21} \leq 10,000 \quad \text{Month 1}$$
$$2s_{12} + 3s_{22} \leq 10,000 \quad \text{Month 2}$$
$$2s_{13} + 3s_{23} \leq 10,000 \quad \text{Month 3}$$

One final set of constraints must be added to guarantee that I_m and D_m will reflect the increase or decrease in the total production level for month m. Suppose that the production levels for March, the month before the start of the current production scheduling period, had been 1500 units of component 322A and 1000 units of component 802B for a total pro-

Table 9.8	MACHINE, LABOR, AND STORAGE CAPACITIES FOR BOLLINGER ELECTRONICS		
Month	Machine Capacity (hours)	Labor Capacity (hours)	Storage Capacity (square feet)
April	400	300	10,000
May	500	300	10,000
June	600	300	10,000

Table 9.9	MACHINE, LABOR, AND STORAGE REQUIREMENTS FOR COMPONENTS 322A AND 802B		
Component	Machine (hours/unit)	Labor (hours/unit)	Storage (square feet/unit)
322A	0.10	0.05	2
802B	0.08	0.07	3

duction level of $1500 + 1000 = 2500$ units. We can find the amount of the change in production for April from the relationship

$$\text{April production} - \text{March production} = \text{change}$$

Using the April production variables, x_{11} and x_{21}, and the March production of 2500 units, we have

$$(x_{11} + x_{21}) - 2500 = \text{Change}$$

Note that the change can be positive or negative. A positive change reflects an increase in the total production level, and a negative change reflects a decrease in the total production level. We can use the increase in production for April, I_1, and the decrease in production for April, D_1, to specify the constraint for the change in total production for the month of April:

$$(x_{11} + x_{21}) - 2500 = I_1 - D_1$$

Of course, we cannot have an increase in production and a decrease in production during the same 1-month period; thus, either I_1 or D_1 will be zero. If April requires 3000 units of production, $I_1 = 500$ and $D_1 = 0$. If April requires 2200 units of production, $I_1 = 0$ and $D_1 = 300$. This approach of denoting the change in production level as the difference between two nonnegative variables, I_1 and D_1, permits both positive and negative changes in the total production level. If a single variable (say, c_m) had been used to represent the change in production level, only positive changes would be possible because of the nonnegativity requirement.

Using the same approach in May and June (always subtracting the previous month's total production from the current month's total production), we obtain the constraints for the second and third months of the production scheduling period:

$$(x_{12} + x_{22}) - (x_{11} + x_{21}) = I_2 - D_2$$
$$(x_{13} + x_{23}) - (x_{12} + x_{22}) = I_3 - D_3$$

Placing the variables on the left-hand side and the constants on the right-hand side yields the complete set of what are commonly referred to as production-smoothing constraints:

$$
\begin{aligned}
x_{11} + x_{21} \qquad\qquad\qquad\qquad\quad - I_1 + D_1 &= 2500 \\
-x_{11} - x_{21} + x_{12} + x_{22} \qquad\qquad - I_2 + D_2 &= 0 \\
- x_{12} - x_{22} + x_{13} + x_{23} - I_3 + D_3 &= 0
\end{aligned}
$$

The initially rather small, 2-product, 3-month scheduling problem has now developed into an 18-variable, 20-constraint linear programming problem. Note that in this problem we were concerned only with one type of machine process, one type of labor, and one type of storage area. Actual production scheduling problems usually involve several machine types, several labor grades, and/or several storage areas, requiring large-scale linear programs. For instance, a problem involving 100 products over a 12-month period could have over 1000 variables and constraints.

Problem 19 involves a production scheduling application with labor-smoothing constraints.

Figure 9.6 shows the computer solution to the Bollinger Electronics production scheduling problem. Table 9.10 contains a portion of the managerial report based on the computer solution.

Figure 9.6   THE MANAGEMENT SCIENTIST SOLUTION FOR THE BOLLINGER ELECTRONICS PROBLEM

Objective Function Value =   225295.000

Variable	Value	Reduced Costs
X11	500.000	0.000
X12	3200.000	0.000
X13	5200.000	0.000
X21	2500.000	0.000
X22	2000.000	0.000
X23	0.000	0.128
S11	0.000	0.172
S12	200.000	0.000
S13	400.000	0.000
S21	1700.000	0.000
S22	3200.000	0.000
S23	200.000	0.000
I1	500.000	0.000
I2	2200.000	0.000
I3	0.000	0.072
D1	0.000	0.700
D2	0.000	0.700
D3	0.000	0.628

Constraint	Slack/Surplus	Dual Prices
1	0.000	-20.000
2	0.000	-10.000
3	0.000	-20.128
4	0.000	-10.150
5	0.000	-20.428
6	0.000	-10.300
7	0.000	-20.728
8	0.000	-10.450
9	150.000	0.000
10	20.000	0.000
11	80.000	0.000
12	100.000	0.000
13	0.000	1.111
14	40.000	0.000
15	4900.000	0.000
16	0.000	0.000
17	8600.000	0.000
18	0.000	0.500
19	0.000	0.500
20	0.000	0.428

Table 9.10	MINIMUM-COST PRODUCTION SCHEDULE INFORMATION FOR THE BOLLINGER ELECTRONICS PROBLEM

Activity	April	May	June
Production			
Component 322A	500	3,200	5,200
Component 802B	2,500	2,000	0
Totals	3,000	5,200	5,200
Ending inventory			
Component 322A	0	200	400
Component 802B	1,700	3,200	200
Machine usage			
Scheduled hours	250	480	520
Slack capacity hours	150	20	80
Labor usage			
Scheduled hours	200	300	260
Slack capacity hours	100	0	40
Storage usage			
Scheduled storage	5,100	10,000	1,400
Slack capacity	4,900	0	8,600

Total production, inventory, and production-smoothing cost = $225,295

Linear programming models for production scheduling are often very large. Thousands of decision variables and constraints are necessary when the problem involves numerous products, machines, and time periods. Data collection for large-scale models can be more time-consuming than either the formulation of the model or the development of the computer solution.

Consider the monthly variation in the production and inventory schedule shown in Table 9.10. Recall that the inventory cost for component 802B is one-half the inventory cost for component 322A. Therefore, as might be expected, component 802B is produced heavily in the first month (April) and then held in inventory for the demand that will occur in future months. Component 322A tends to be produced when needed, and only small amounts are carried in inventory.

The costs of increasing and decreasing the total production volume tend to smooth the monthly variations. In fact, the minimum-cost schedule calls for a 500-unit increase in total production in April and a 2200-unit increase in total production in May. The May production level of 5200 units is then maintained during June.

The machine usage section of the report shows ample machine capacity in all 3 months. However, labor capacity is at full utilization (slack = 0 for constraint 13 in Figure 9.6) in the month of May. The dual price shows that an additional hour of labor capacity in May will improve the objective function (lower cost) by approximately $1.11.

A linear programming model of a 2-product, 3-month production system can provide valuable information in terms of identifying a minimum-cost production schedule. In larger production systems, where the number of variables and constraints is too large to track manually, linear programming models can provide a significant advantage in developing cost-saving production schedules. The Q.M. in Action: Libbey-Owens-Ford shows just how large linear programming models can be for applications involving production scheduling.

Work-Force Assignment

Work-force assignment problems frequently occur when production managers must make decisions involving staffing requirements for a given planning period. Work-force

Q.M. IN ACTION

LIBBEY-OWENS-FORD*

Libbey-Owens-Ford utilizes a large-scale linear programming model to achieve integrated production, distribution, and inventory planning for its flat glass products. The linear programming model is called FLAGPOL. Schedulers and planners in the flat-glass products group must coordinate production schedules for more than 200 different glass products. The products are made in 4 colors (clear, gray, bronze, and blue-green) and 26 thicknesses. Other options include 3 quality levels, 2 cutting classifications, 4 packaging modes, and various fabrication methods, including tempered glass and/or coated glass.

To integrate production, distribution, and inventory planning, company analysts developed a linear programming model that optimizes operations for all products over a 12-month planning horizon. The model is applied monthly, and its output helps planners react to unexpected changes in the operating environment and deal with strategic issues such as adding new plants and expanding capacity. A typical linear programming model has approximately 100,000 variables and 26,000 constraints. The computer solution for problems of this size can take 3 to 4 hours. The company estimates that the FLAGPOL model provides an annual savings of more than $2 million.

*Based on Martin, Clarence H., Denver C. Dent, and James C. Eckhart, "Integrated Production, Distribution and Inventory Planning at Libbey-Owens-Ford." *Interfaces*, May–June 1993, pp. 68–78.

---

assignments often have some flexibility, and at least some personnel can be assigned to more than one department or work center. Such is the case when employees have been cross-trained on two or more jobs or, for instance, when sales personnel can be transferred between stores. In the following application, we show how linear programming can be used to determine not only an optimal product mix, but also an optimal workforce assignment.

McCormick Manufacturing Company produces two products with contributions to profit per unit of $10 and $9, respectively. The labor requirements per unit produced and the total hours of labor available from personnel assigned to each of four departments are shown in Table 9.11. Assuming that the number of hours available in each department is fixed, we can formulate McCormick's problem as a standard product-mix linear program with the following decision variables:

$$P_1 = \text{units of product 1}$$
$$P_2 = \text{units of product 2}$$

Table 9.11	DEPARTMENTAL LABOR-HOURS PER UNIT AND TOTAL HOURS AVAILABLE FOR THE McCORMICK MANUFACTURING COMPANY

	Labor-Hours Per Unit		
Department	Product 1	Product 2	Total Hours Available
1	0.65	0.95	6500
2	0.45	0.85	6000
3	1.00	0.70	7000
4	0.15	0.30	1400

The linear program is

$$\text{Max} \quad 10P_1 + 9P_2$$

s.t.

$$0.65P_1 + 0.95P_2 \leq 6500$$
$$0.45P_1 + 0.85P_2 \leq 6000$$
$$1.00P_1 + 0.70P_2 \leq 7000$$
$$0.15P_1 + 0.30P_2 \leq 1400$$
$$P_1, P_2 \geq 0$$

The optimal solution to the linear programming model is shown in Figure 9.7. After rounding, it calls for 5744 units of product 1, 1795 units of product 2, and a total profit of $73,590. With this optimal solution, departments 3 and 4 are operating at capacity, and departments 1 and 2 have a slack of approximately 1062 and 1890 hours, respectively. We would anticipate that the product mix would change and that the total profit would increase if the work-force assignment could be revised so that the slack, or unused hours, in departments 1 and 2 could be transferred to the departments currently working at capacity. However, the production manager may be uncertain as to how the work force should be reallocated among the four departments. Let us expand the linear programming model to include decision variables that will help determine the optimal work-force assignment in addition to the profit-maximizing product mix.

The right-hand sides are now treated as decision variables.

Suppose that McCormick has a cross-training program that enables some employees to be transferred between departments. By taking advantage of the cross-training skills, a limited number of employees and labor-hours may be transferred from one department to another. For example, suppose that the cross-training permits transfers as shown in Table 9.12. Row 1 of this table shows that some employees assigned to department 1 have cross-training skills that permit them to be transferred to department 2 or 3. The right-hand

---

Figure 9.7 THE MANAGEMENT SCIENTIST SOLUTION FOR THE McCORMICK MANUFACTURING COMPANY PROBLEM WITH NO WORK-FORCE TRANSFERS PERMITTED

```
Objective Function Value =            73589.744

        Variable              Value           Reduced Costs
     ------------          ------------       --------------
           P1               5743.590               0.000
           P2               1794.872               0.000


       Constraint         Slack/Surplus          Dual Prices
     ------------          ------------       --------------
           1                1061.538               0.000
           2                1889.744               0.000
           3                   0.000               8.462
           4                   0.000              10.256
```

Table 9.12	CROSS-TRAINING ABILITY AND CAPACITY INFORMATION				
From Department	**Cross-Training Transfers Permitted to Department**				**Maximum Hours Transferable**
	1	**2**	**3**	**4**	
1	—	yes	yes	—	400
2	—	—	yes	yes	800
3	—	—	—	yes	100
4	yes	yes	—	—	200

column shows that, for the current production planning period, a maximum of 400 hours can be transferred from department 1. Similar cross-training transfer capabilities and capacities are shown for departments 2, 3, and 4.

When work-force assignments are flexible, we do not automatically know how many hours of labor should be assigned to or transferred from each department. We need to add decision variables to the linear programming model to account for such changes.

$$b_i = \text{the labor-hours allocated to department } i \text{ for } i = 1, 2, 3, \text{ and } 4$$

$$t_{ij} = \text{the labor-hours transferred from department } i \text{ to department } j$$

With the addition of decision variables b_1, b_2, b_3, and b_4, we write the capacity restrictions for the four departments as follows:

$$0.65P_1 + 0.95P_2 \leq b_1$$
$$0.45P_1 + 0.85P_2 \leq b_2$$
$$1.00P_1 + 0.70P_2 \leq b_3$$
$$0.15P_1 + 0.30P_2 \leq b_4$$

Since b_1, b_2, b_3, and b_4 are now decision variables, we follow the standard practice of placing these variables on the left side of the inequalities, and the first four constraints of the linear programming model become

$$0.65P_1 + 0.95P_2 - b_1 \qquad\qquad\qquad \leq 0$$
$$0.45P_1 + 0.85P_2 \qquad - b_2 \qquad\qquad \leq 0$$
$$1.00P_1 + 0.70P_2 \qquad\qquad - b_3 \qquad \leq 0$$
$$0.15P_1 + 0.30P_2 \qquad\qquad\qquad - b_4 \leq 0$$

The labor-hours ultimately allocated to each department must be determined by a series of labor balance equations, or constraints, that include the number of hours initially assigned to each department plus the number of hours transferred into the department minus the number of hours transferred out of the department. Using department 1 as an example, we determine the work-force allocation as follows:

$$b_1 = \left(\begin{array}{c} \text{Hours} \\ \text{initially in} \\ \text{department 1} \end{array} \right) + \left(\begin{array}{c} \text{Hours} \\ \text{transferred into} \\ \text{department 1} \end{array} \right) - \left(\begin{array}{c} \text{Hours} \\ \text{transferred out of} \\ \text{department 1} \end{array} \right)$$

Table 9.11 shows 6500 hours initially assigned to department 1. We use the transfer decision variables t_{i1} to denote transfers into department 1 and t_{1j} to denote transfers from department 1. Table 9.12 shows that the cross-training capabilities involving department 1 are restricted to transfers from department 4 (variable t_{41}) and transfers to either department 2 or department 3 (variables t_{12} and t_{13}). Thus, we can express the total work-force allocation for department 1 as

$$b_1 = 6500 + t_{41} - t_{12} - t_{13}$$

Moving the decision variables for the work-force transfers to the left-hand side, we have the labor balance equation or constraint

$$b_1 - t_{41} + t_{12} + t_{13} = 6500$$

This form of constraint will be needed for each of the four departments. Thus, the following labor balance constraints for departments 2, 3, and 4 would be added to the model.

$$b_2 - t_{12} - t_{42} + t_{23} + t_{24} = 6000$$
$$b_3 - t_{13} - t_{23} + t_{34} = 7000$$
$$b_4 - t_{24} - t_{34} + t_{41} + t_{42} = 1400$$

Finally, since Table 9.12 shows that the number of hours that may be transferred from each department is limited, a transfer capacity constraint must be added for each of the four departments. The additional constraints are

$$t_{12} + t_{13} \leq 400$$
$$t_{23} + t_{24} \leq 800$$
$$t_{34} \leq 100$$
$$t_{41} + t_{42} \leq 200$$

The complete linear programming model has 2 product decision variables (P_1 and P_2), 4 department work-force assignment variables (b_1, b_2, b_3, and b_4), 7 transfer variables (t_{12}, t_{13}, t_{23}, t_{24}, t_{34}, t_{41}, and t_{42}), and 12 constraints. Figure 9.8 shows the optimal solution to this linear program provided by The Management Scientist software package.

McCormick's profit can be increased by $10,421 to $84,011 by taking advantage of cross-training and work-force transfers. The optimal product mix of 6825 units of product 1 and 1751 units of product 2 can be achieved if $t_{13} = 400$ hours are transferred from department 1 to department 3; $t_{23} = 751$ hours are transferred from department 2 to department 3; and $t_{24} = 149$ hours are transferred from department 2 to department 4. The resulting work-force assignments for departments 1–4 would provide 6100, 5200, 8051, and 1549 hours, respectively.

If a manager has the flexibility to assign personnel to different departments, reduced work-force idle time, improved work-force utilization, and improved profit should result. The linear programming model in this section automatically assigns employees and labor-hours to the departments in the most profitable manner.

Variations in the work-force assignment model could be used in situations such as allocating raw material resources to products, allocating machine time to products, and allocating sales-force time to stores or sales territories.

| Figure 9.8 | THE MANAGEMENT SCIENTIST SOLUTION FOR THE McCORMICK MANUFACTURING COMPANY PROBLEM |

```
Objective Function Value =              84011.299

         Variable            Value            Reduced Costs
      --------------    ----------------    ------------------
           P1              6824.859               0.000
           P2              1751.412               0.000
           B1              6100.000               0.000
           B2              5200.000               0.000
           B3              8050.847               0.000
           B4              1549.153               0.000
          T41                 0.000               7.458
          T12                 0.000               8.249
          T13               400.000               0.000
          T42                 0.000               8.249
          T23               650.847               0.000
          T24               149.153               0.000
          T34                 0.000               0.000


        Constraint       Slack/Surplus          Dual Prices
      --------------    ----------------    ------------------
            1                 0.000               0.791
            2               640.113               0.000
            3                 0.000               8.249
            4                 0.000               8.249
            5                 0.000               0.791
            6                 0.000               0.000
            7                 0.000               8.249
            8                 0.000               8.249
            9                 0.000               7.458
           10                 0.000               8.249
           11               100.000               0.000
           12               200.000               0.000
```

9.4 BLENDING PROBLEMS

Blending problems arise whenever a manager must decide how to blend two or more resources to produce one or more products. In these situations, the resources contain one or more essential ingredients that must be blended into final products that will contain specific percentages of each. In most of these applications, then, management must decide how much of each resource to purchase to satisfy product specifications and product demands at minimum cost.

Blending problems occur frequently in the petroleum industry (e.g., blending crude oil to produce different-octane gasolines), chemical industry (e.g., blending chemicals to produce fertilizers and weed killers), and food industry (e.g., blending ingredients to produce soft drinks and soups). In this section we illustrate how to apply linear programming to a blending problem in the petroleum industry.

The Grand Strand Oil Company produces regular and premium gasoline for independent service stations in the southeastern United States. The Grand Strand refinery manufactures the gasoline products by blending three petroleum components. The gasolines are sold at different prices, and the petroleum components have different costs. The firm wants to determine how to mix or blend the three components into the two gasoline products and maximize profits.

Data available show that regular gasoline can be sold for $1.00 per gallon and premium gasoline for $1.08 per gallon. For the current production planning period, Grand Strand can obtain the three petroleum components at the cost per gallon and in the quantities shown in Table 9.13.

The product specifications for the regular and premium gasolines restrict the amounts of each component that can be used in each gasoline product. Table 9.14 lists the product specifications. Current commitments to distributors require Grand Strand to produce at least 10,000 gallons of regular gasoline.

The Grand Strand blending problem is to determine how many gallons of each component should be used in the regular gasoline blend and how many should be used in the premium gasoline blend. The optimal blending solution should maximize the firm's profit, subject to the constraints on the available petroleum supplies shown in Table 9.13, the product specifications shown in Table 9.14, and the required 10,000 gallons of regular gasoline.

Table 9.13	PETROLEUM COST AND SUPPLY FOR THE GRAND STRAND BLENDING PROBLEM

Petroleum Component	Cost/Gallon	Maximum Available
1	$0.50	5,000 gallons
2	$0.60	10,000 gallons
3	$0.84	10,000 gallons

Table 9.14	PRODUCT SPECIFICATIONS FOR THE GRAND STRAND BLENDING PROBLEM

Product	Specifications
Regular gasoline	At most 30% component 1
	At least 40% component 2
	At most 20% component 3
Premium gasoline	At least 25% component 1
	At most 40% component 2
	At least 30% component 3

We define the decision variables as

$$x_{ij} = \text{gallons of component } i \text{ used in gasoline } j,$$
$$\text{where } i = 1, 2, \text{ or } 3 \text{ for components } 1, 2, \text{ or } 3,$$
$$\text{and } j = r \text{ if regular or } j = p \text{ if premium}$$

The six decision variables are

$$x_{1r} = \text{gallons of component 1 in regular gasoline}$$
$$x_{2r} = \text{gallons of component 2 in regular gasoline}$$
$$x_{3r} = \text{gallons of component 3 in regular gasoline}$$
$$x_{1p} = \text{gallons of component 1 in premium gasoline}$$
$$x_{2p} = \text{gallons of component 2 in premium gasoline}$$
$$x_{3p} = \text{gallons of component 3 in premium gasoline}$$

The total number of gallons of each type of gasoline produced is the sum of the number of gallons produced using each of the three petroleum components.

Total Gallons Produced

$$\text{Regular gasoline} = x_{1r} + x_{2r} + x_{3r}$$
$$\text{Premium gasoline} = x_{1p} + x_{2p} + x_{3p}$$

The total gallons of each petroleum component are computed in a similar fashion.

Total Petroleum Component Use

$$\text{Component 1} = x_{1r} + x_{1p}$$
$$\text{Component 2} = x_{2r} + x_{2p}$$
$$\text{Component 3} = x_{3r} + x_{3p}$$

We develop the objective function of maximizing the profit contribution by identifying the difference between the total revenue from both gasolines and the total cost of the three petroleum components. By multiplying the $1.00 per gallon price by the total gallons of regular gasoline, the $1.08 per gallon price by the total gallons of premium gasoline, and the component cost per gallon figures in Table 9.13 by the total gallons of each component used, we obtain the objective function:

$$\text{Max} \quad 1.00(x_{1r} + x_{2r} + x_{3r}) + 1.08(x_{1p} + x_{2p} + x_{3p})$$
$$- 0.50(x_{1r} + x_{1p}) - 0.60(x_{2r} + x_{2p}) - 0.84(x_{3r} + x_{3p})$$

When we combine terms, the objective function becomes

$$\text{Max} \quad 0.50x_{1r} + 0.40x_{2r} + 0.16x_{3r} + 0.58x_{1p} + 0.48x_{2p} + 0.24x_{3p}$$

The limitations on the availability of the three petroleum components are

$$x_{1r} + x_{1p} \leq 5{,}000 \quad \text{Component 1}$$
$$x_{2r} + x_{2p} \leq 10{,}000 \quad \text{Component 2}$$
$$x_{3r} + x_{3p} \leq 10{,}000 \quad \text{Component 3}$$

Six constraints are now required to meet the product specifications stated in Table 9.14. The first specification states that component 1 can account for no more than 30% of the total gallons of regular gasoline produced. That is,

$$x_{1r} \leq 0.30(x_{1r} + x_{2r} + x_{3r})$$

Rewriting this constraint with the variables on the left-hand side and a constant on the right-hand side yields

$$0.70x_{1r} - 0.30x_{2r} - 0.30x_{3r} \leq 0$$

The second product specification listed in Table 9.14 becomes

$$x_{2r} \geq 0.40(x_{1r} + x_{2r} + x_{3r})$$

and thus,

$$-0.40x_{1r} + 0.60x_{2r} - 0.40x_{3r} \geq 0$$

Similarly, we write the four remaining blending specifications listed in Table 9.14 as

$$-0.20x_{1r} - 0.20x_{2r} + 0.80x_{3r} \leq 0$$
$$+0.75x_{1p} - 0.25x_{2p} - 0.25x_{3p} \geq 0$$
$$-0.40x_{1p} + 0.60x_{2p} - 0.40x_{3p} \leq 0$$
$$-0.30x_{1p} - 0.30x_{2p} + 0.70x_{3p} \geq 0$$

The constraint for at least 10,000 gallons of regular gasoline is

$$x_{1r} + x_{2r} + x_{3r} \geq 10,000$$

The complete linear programming model with 6 decision variables and 10 constraints is

Max $0.50x_{1r} + 0.40x_{2r} + 0.16x_{3r} + 0.58x_{1p} + 0.48x_{2p} + 0.24x_{3p}$

s.t.

$$
\begin{array}{llllllll}
x_{1r} & & & + & x_{1p} & & & \leq & 5{,}000 \\
& x_{2r} & & & + & x_{2p} & & \leq & 10{,}000 \\
& & x_{3r} & & & + & x_{3p} & \leq & 10{,}000 \\
0.70x_{1r} - 0.30x_{2r} - 0.30x_{3r} & & & & & & & \leq & 0 \\
-0.40x_{1r} + 0.60x_{2r} - 0.40x_{3r} & & & & & & & \geq & 0 \\
-0.20x_{1r} - 0.20x_{2r} + 0.80x_{3r} & & & & & & & \leq & 0 \\
& & & 0.75x_{1p} - 0.25x_{2p} - 0.25x_{3p} & & & & \geq & 0 \\
& & & -0.40x_{1p} + 0.60x_{2p} - 0.40x_{3p} & & & & \leq & 0 \\
& & & -0.30x_{1p} - 0.30x_{2p} + 0.70x_{3p} & & & & \geq & 0 \\
x_{1r} + x_{2r} + x_{3r} & & & & & & & \geq & 10{,}000 \\
\end{array}
$$

$$x_{1r}, x_{2r}, x_{3r}, x_{1p}, x_{2p}, x_{3p} \geq 0$$

Try Problem 15 as another example of a blending model.

The computer solution to the Grand Strand blending problem is shown in Figure 9.9. The optimal solution providing a profit of $9300 is summarized in Table 9.15. The optimal blending strategy shows that 10,000 gallons of regular gasoline should be produced. The regular gasoline will be manufactured as a blend of 8000 gallons of component 2 and 2000 gallons of component 3. The 15,000 gallons of premium gasoline will be manufactured as a blend of 5000 gallons of component 1, 2000 gallons of component 2, and 8000 gallons of component 3.

The interpretation of the slack and surplus variables associated with the product specification constraints (constraints 4–9) in Figure 9.9 needs some clarification. If the constraint is a ≤ constraint, the value of the slack variable can be interpreted as the gallons of compo-

Figure 9.9 THE MANAGEMENT SCIENTIST SOLUTION FOR THE GRAND STRAND BLENDING PROBLEM

```
Objective Function Value =          9300.000

      Variable            Value           Reduced Costs
      --------            -----           -------------
        X1R              0.000               0.000
        X2R           8000.000               0.000
        X3R           2000.000               0.000
        X1P           5000.000               0.000
        X2P           2000.000               0.000
        X3P           8000.000               0.000

     Constraint       Slack/Surplus         Dual Prices
     ----------       -------------         -----------
         1              0.000                 0.580
         2              0.000                 0.480
         3              0.000                 0.240
         4           3000.000                 0.000
         5           4000.000                 0.000
         6              0.000                 0.000
         7           1250.000                 0.000
         8           4000.000                 0.000
         9           3500.000                 0.000
        10              0.000                -0.080
```

Table 9.15 GRAND STRAND GASOLINE BLENDING SOLUTION

Gasoline	Gallons of Component (percentage)			Total
	Component 1	Component 2	Component 3	
Regular	0 (0%)	8000 (80%)	2000 (20%)	10,000
Premium	5000 (33 1/3%)	2000 (53 1/3%)	8000 (53 1/3%)	15,000

nent use below the maximum amount of the component use specified by the constraint. For example, the slack of 3000.000 for constraint 4 shows that component 1 use is 3000 gallons below the maximum amount of component 1 that could have been used in the production of 10,000 gallons of regular gasoline. If the product specification constraint is a $\geq$ constraint, a surplus variable shows the gallons of component use above the minimum amount of component use specified by the blending constraint. For example, the surplus of 4000.000 for constraint 5 shows that component 2 use is 4000 gallons above the minimum amount of component 2 that must be used in the production of 10,000 gallons of regular gasoline.

N O T E S
and Comments

A convenient way to define the decision variables in a blending problem is to use a matrix in which the rows correspond to the raw materials and the columns correspond to the final products. For example, in the Grand Strand blending problem, we could define the decision variables as follows:

		Final Products	
		Regular Gasoline	**Premium Gasoline**
Raw	Component 1	x_{1r}	x_{1p}
Materials	Component 2	x_{2r}	x_{2p}
	Component 3	x_{3r}	x_{3p}

This approach has two advantages: (1) it provides a systematic way to define the decision variables for any blending problem; and (2) it provides a visual image of the decision variables in terms of how they are related to the raw materials, products, and each other.

9.5 DATA ENVELOPMENT ANALYSIS

Data envelopment analysis (DEA) is an application of linear programming that has been used to measure the relative efficiency of operating units with the same goals and objectives. For example, DEA has been used within individual fast-food outlets in the same chain. In this case, the goal of DEA was to identify the inefficient outlets that should be targeted for further study and, if necessary, corrective action. Other applications of DEA have measured the relative efficiencies of hospitals, banks, courts, schools, and so on. In these applications, the performance of each institution or organization was measured relative to the performance of all operating units in the same system. The Q.M. in Action: Managing Bank Productivity describes how a large northeastern bank used DEA to determine which branches were operating inefficiently.

The operating units of most organizations have multiple inputs such as staff size, salaries, hours of operation, and advertising budget, as well as multiple outputs such as profit, market share, and growth rate. In these situations, it is often difficult for a manager to determine which operating units are inefficient in converting their multiple inputs into multiple outputs. This particular area is where data envelopment analysis has proven to be a helpful managerial tool. We illustrate the application of data envelopment analysis by evaluating the performance of a group of four hospitals.

Evaluating the Performance of Hospitals

The hospital administrators at General Hospital, University Hospital, County Hospital, and State Hospital have been meeting to discuss ways in which they can help one another

Q.M. IN ACTION

MANAGING BANK PRODUCTIVITY*

Management of a large northeastern bank wanted to expand its existing 33 branch system to cover a wider geographic region. To help finance the expansion, management wanted to identify ways in which they could streamline existing operations to obtain substantial savings, but at the same time avoid sacrificing quality of service. As the first step in reviewing productivity of the branches, data envelopment analysis (DEA) was used to indicate which branches were operating inefficiently.

The DEA model they developed compared the actual operating results of each branch with those of all other branches in order to identify the less-productive branches. A less-productive branch is one that requires more resources to produce the same output as the best-practice branches. The best-practice branches are identified by a DEA productivity rating of 100 percent ($E = 1.00$), and the inefficient or less-productive branches are identified by a productivity rating of less than 100 percent ($E < 1.00$).

Five key resources used by each branch were used, including the number of teller and manager personnel full-time equivalents (FTEs), branch operating expenses, and square feet of office space. In addition, 15 services that were performed by each branch were combined into five categories of service. For instance, the deposit, withdrawals, and checks cashed category was formed by treating each deposit, withdrawal, or check cashed as one transaction; for this service category, the output measure was the number of deposits, withdrawals, or checks cashed. Other service categories included measures of the number of bank checks, travelers checks, night deposits, and loans made by the branch.

For each branch, data were collected for these resources and service measures for the previous year.

The solution to the DEA linear programming model using these data showed that 10 of the 33 branches had a DEA productivity rating of 100 percent and that 23 branches had a rating of less than 100 percent. In other words, there were 23 less-productive branches. For instance, one branch had a DEA rating of 37 percent, indicating that it was using about 63 percent excess resources. Overall, the findings indicated that the bank could make substantial productivity improvements and realize significant cost reductions by improving performance at the 23 less-productive branches.

Focusing on the less-productive branches, the bank was able to identify ways in which these branches could significantly reduce their resource requirement without reducing quality of service and while maintaining or even increasing the volume of services provided. The total potential savings were determined to be approximately $9 million. However, some changes required square feet reductions at certain branches, something that could not be done in the short run. For the next year, management concluded and reported to the board of directors that savings of over $6 million of the $30 million operating costs for these less-productive branches could be realized.

*Based on Sherman, H. David, and George Ladino, "Managing Bank Productivity Using Data Envelopment Analysis (DEA)." *Interfaces*, March-April, 1995, pp. 60–73.

---

improve the performance at each of their hospitals. A consultant has suggested that they consider using DEA to measure the performance of each hospital relative to the performance of all four hospitals. In discussing how this could be done, the following three input measures and four output measures were identified:

Input Measures

1. The number of full-time equivalent (FTE) nonphysician personnel
2. The amount spent on supplies
3. The number of bed-days available

Output Measures

1. Patient-days of service under Medicare
2. Patient-days of service not under Medicare
3. Number of nurses trained
4. Number of interns trained

Problem 26 asks you to formulate and solve a linear program to assess the relative efficiency of General Hospital.

Summaries of the input and output measures for a one-year period at each of the four hospitals are shown in Tables 9.16 and 9.17. Let us show how DEA can use these data to identify relatively inefficient hospitals.

Table 9.16	ANNUAL RESOURCES CONSUMED (INPUTS) FOR THE FOUR HOSPITALS			
	Hospital			
Input Measure	**General**	**University**	**County**	**State**
Full-time equivalent nonphysicians	285.20	162.30	275.70	210.40
Supply expense ($1000s)	123.80	128.70	348.50	154.10
Bed-days available (1000s)	106.72	64.21	104.10	104.04

Table 9.17	ANNUAL SERVICES PROVIDED (OUTPUTS) FOR THE FOUR HOSPITALS			
	Hospital			
Output Measure	**General**	**University**	**County**	**State**
Medicare patient-days (1000s)	48.14	34.62	36.72	33.16
Non-Medicare patient-days (1000s)	43.10	27.11	45.98	56.46
Nurses trained	253	148	175	160
Interns trained	41	27	23	84

An Overview of the DEA Approach

In this application of DEA, a linear programming model will be developed for each hospital whose efficiency is to be evaluated. To illustrate the modeling process, we will formulate a linear program that can be used to determine the relative efficiency of County Hospital.

First, using a linear programming model, we construct a hypothetical composite hospital based on the outputs and inputs for all four hospitals. For each of the four output measures, the output for the composite hospital is determined by computing a weighted average of the corresponding outputs for all four hospitals. For each of the three input measures, the input for the composite hospital is determined by using the same weights to compute a weighted average of the corresponding inputs for all four hospitals. Constraints in the linear programming model require all outputs for the composite hospital to be *greater than or equal to* the outputs of County Hospital, the hospital being evaluated. If the inputs for the composite unit can be shown to be *less than* the inputs for County Hospital, the composite hospital is shown to have the same, or more, output for *less input*. In this case, the model shows that the composite hospital is more efficient than County Hospital. In other words, the hospital being evaluated is *less efficient* than the composite hospital. Because the composite hospital is based on all four hospitals, the hospital being evaluated can be judged *relatively inefficient* when compared to the other hospitals in the group.

The DEA Linear Programming Model

To determine the weight that each hospital will have in computing the outputs and inputs for the composite hospital, we use the following decision variables:

wg = weight applied to inputs and outputs for General Hospital

wu = weight applied to inputs and outputs for University Hospital

wc = weight applied to inputs and outputs for County Hospital

ws = weight applied to inputs and outputs for State Hospital

The DEA approach requires that the sum of these weights equal 1. Thus, the first constraint is

$$wg + wu + wc + ws = 1$$

In general, every DEA linear programming model will include a constraint that requires the weights for the operating units to sum to 1.

As we stated previously, for each output measure, the output for the composite hospital is determined by computing a weighted average of the corresponding outputs for all four hospitals. For instance, for output measure 1, the number of patient days of service under Medicare, the output for the composite hospital is

$$\begin{array}{l}\text{Medicare Patient-Days} \\ \text{for Composite Hospital}\end{array} = \left(\begin{array}{l}\text{Medicare Patient-Days} \\ \text{for General Hospital}\end{array}\right)wg + \left(\begin{array}{l}\text{Medicare Patient-Days} \\ \text{for University Hospital}\end{array}\right)wu$$

$$+ \left(\begin{array}{l}\text{Medicare Patient-Days} \\ \text{for County Hospital}\end{array}\right)wc + \left(\begin{array}{l}\text{Medicare Patient-Days} \\ \text{for State Hospital}\end{array}\right)ws$$

Substituting the number of medicare patient-days for each hospital as shown in Table 9.17, we obtain the following expression:

$$\begin{array}{l}\text{Medicare Patient-Days} \\ \text{for Composite Hospital}\end{array} = 48.14wg + 34.62wu + 36.72wc + 33.16ws$$

The other output measures for the composite hospital are computed in a similar fashion. Figure 9.10 provides a summary of the results.

For each of the four output measures, we need to write a constraint that requires the output for the composite hospital to be greater than or equal to the output for County Hospital. Thus, the general form of the output constraints is

$$\begin{array}{l}\text{Output for the} \\ \text{Composite Hospital}\end{array} \geq \begin{array}{l}\text{Output for} \\ \text{County Hospital}\end{array}$$

Since the number of medicare patient-days for County Hospital is 36.72, the output constraint corresponding to the number of medicare patient-days is

$$48.14wg + 34.62wu + 36.72wc + 33.16ws \geq 36.72$$

In a similar fashion, we formulated a constraint for each of the other three output measures, with the results as shown:

$$43.10wg + 27.11wu + 45.98wc + 56.46ws \geq 45.98 \quad \text{Non-Medicare}$$
$$253wg + 148wu + 175wc + 160ws \geq 175 \quad \text{Nurses}$$
$$41wg + 27wu + 23wc + 84ws \geq 23 \quad \text{Interns}$$

Figure 9.10 RELATIONSHIP BETWEEN THE OUTPUT MEASURES FOR THE FOUR HOSPITALS AND THE OUTPUT MEASURES FOR THE COMPOSITE HOSPITAL

wg General		wu University		wc County		ws State	
Medicare	48.14	Medicare	34.62	Medicare	36.72	Medicare	33.16
Non-Medicare	43.10	Non-Medicare	27.11	Non-Medicare	45.98	Non-Medicare	56.46
Nurses	253	Nurses	148	Nurses	175	Nurses	160
Interns	41	Interns	27	Interns	23	Interns	84

Composite	
Medicare	$48.14wg + 34.62wu + 36.72wc + 33.16ws$
Non-Medicare	$43.10wg + 27.11wu + 45.98wc + 56.46ws$
Nurses	$253wg + 148wu + 175wc + 160ws$
Interns	$41wg + 27wu + 23wc + 84ws$

The four output constraints require the linear programming solution to provide weights that will make each output measure for the composite hospital greater than or equal to the corresponding output measure for County Hospital. Thus, if a solution satisfying the output constraints can be found, the composite hospital will have produced at least as much of each output as County Hospital.

Next, we need to consider the constraints needed to model the relationship between the inputs for the composite hospital and the resources available to the composite hospital. A constraint is required for each of the three input measures. The general form for the input constraints is as follows:

$$\begin{array}{l} \text{Input for the} \\ \text{Composite Hospital} \end{array} \leq \begin{array}{l} \text{Resources Available to} \\ \text{the Composite Hospital} \end{array}$$

For each input measure, the input for the composite hospital is a weighted average of the corresponding input for each of the four hospitals. Thus, for input measure 1, the number of full-time equivalent nonphysicians, the input for the composite hospital is

$$\begin{array}{l} \text{FTE Nonphysicians} \\ \text{for Composite} \\ \text{Hospital} \end{array} = \left(\begin{array}{l} \text{FTE Nonphysicians} \\ \text{for General Hospital} \end{array} \right) wg + \left(\begin{array}{l} \text{FTE Nonphysicians} \\ \text{for University Hospital} \end{array} \right) wu$$

$$+ \left(\begin{array}{l} \text{FTE Nonphysicians} \\ \text{for County Hospital} \end{array} \right) wc + \left(\begin{array}{l} \text{FTE Nonphysicians} \\ \text{for State Hospital} \end{array} \right) ws$$

Substituting the values for the number of full-time equivalent nonphysicians for each hospital as shown in Table 9.16, we obtain the following expression for the number of full-time equivalent nonphysicians for the composite hospital:

$$285.20wg + 162.30wu + 275.70wc + 210.40ws$$

In a similar manner, we can write expressions for each of the other two input measures as shown in Figure 9.11.

To complete the formulation of the input constraints, we must write expressions for the right-hand-side values for each constraint. First, note that the right-hand side values are the resources available to the composite hospital. In the DEA approach, these right-hand-side values are a percentage of the input values for County Hospital. Thus, we must introduce the following decision variables:

E = the fraction of County Hospital's input available to the composite hospital

> The logic of a DEA model is to determine whether a composite facility can achieve the *same or more output* as the test facility *while requiring less input.* If more output with less input can be achieved, the test facility is judged to be relatively inefficient.

> The objective function in a DEA model is always Min E. The facility being analyzed (County Hospital in this example) can be judged relatively inefficient if the optimal solution provides E less than 1, indicating that the composite facility requires less input resources.

To illustrate the important role that E plays in the DEA approach, we show how to write the expression for the number of FTE nonphysicians available to the composite hospital. Table 9.16 shows that the number of FTE nonphysicians used by County Hospital was 275.70; thus, 275.70E is the number of FTE nonphysicians available to the composite hospital. If $E = 1$, the number of FTE nonphysicians available to the composite hospital is 275.70, the same as the number of FTE nonphysicians used by County Hospital. However, if E is greater than 1, the composite hospital would have available proportionally more FTE nonphysicians, while if E is less than 1, the composite hospital would have available proportionally fewer FTE nonphysicians. Because of the effect that E has in determining the resources available to the composite hospital, E is referred to as the *efficiency index.*

We can now write the input constraint corresponding to the number of FTE nonphysicians available to the composite hospital:

$$285.20wg + 162.30wu + 275.70wc + 210.40ws \leq 275.70E$$

In a similar manner, we can write the input constraints for the supplies and bed-days available to the composite hospital. First, using the data in Table 9.16, we note that for each of these resources, the amount that is available to the composite hospital is 348.50E and

---

Figure 9.11   RELATIONSHIP BETWEEN THE INPUT MEASURES FOR THE FOUR HOSPITALS AND THE INPUT MEASURES FOR THE COMPOSITE HOSPITAL

	wg		*wu*		*wc*		*ws*	
	General		**University**		**County**		**State**	
285.20	FTE nonphysicians	162.30	FTE nonphysicians	275.70	FTE nonphysicians	210.40	FTE nonphysicians
123.80	Supply expense	128.70	Supply expense	348.50	Supply expense	154.10	Supply expense
106.72	Bed-days	64.21	Bed-days	104.10	Bed-days	104.04	Bed-days

	Composite
$285.20wg + 162.30wu + 275.70wc + 210.40ws$	FTE nonphysicians
$123.80wg + 128.70wu + 348.50wc + 154.10ws$	Supply expense
$106.72wg + 64.21wu + 104.10wc + 104.04ws$	Bed-days

104.10E, respectively. Thus, the input constraints for the supplies and bed-days are written as follows:

$$123.80wg + 128.70wu + 348.50wc + 154.10ws \leq 348.50E \quad \text{Supplies}$$

$$106.72wg + 64.21wu + 104.10wc + 104.04ws \leq 104.10E \quad \text{Bed-days}$$

If a solution with $E < 1$ can be found, the composite hospital does not need as many resources as County Hospital needs to produce the same level of output.

The objective function for the DEA model is to minimize the value of E, which is equivalent to minimizing the input resources available to the composite hospital. Thus, the objective function is written as

$$\text{Min } E$$

The DEA efficiency conclusion is based on the optimal objective function value for E. The decision rule is as follows:

If $E = 1$, the composite hospital requires *as much input* as County Hospital does. There is no evidence that County Hospital is inefficient.

If $E < 1$, the composite hospital requires *less input* to obtain the output achieved by County Hospital. The composite hospital is more efficient; thus, County Hospital can be judged relatively inefficient.

The DEA linear programming model for the efficiency evaluation of County Hospital has five decision variables and eight constraints. The complete model is rewritten below:

Min $\qquad E$

s.t.

$$
\begin{aligned}
wg + wu + wc + ws &= 1 \\
48.14wg + 34.62wu + 36.72wc + 33.16ws &\geq 36.72 \\
43.10wg + 27.11wu + 45.98wc + 56.46ws &\geq 45.98 \\
253wg + 148wu + 175wc + 160ws &\geq 175 \\
41wg + 27wu + 23wc + 84ws &\geq 23 \\
-275.50E + 285.20wg + 162.30wu + 275.70wc + 210.40ws &\leq 0 \\
-348.50E + 123.80wg + 128.70wu + 348.50wc + 154.10ws &\leq 0 \\
-104.10E + 106.72wg + 64.21wu + 104.10wc + 104.04ws &\leq 0 \\
E, wg, wu, wc, ws &\geq 0
\end{aligned}
$$

Note that in this formulation of the model, we have moved the terms involving E to the left side of the three input constraints because E is a decision variable. This linear program was solved using The Management Scientist software package. The computer solution is shown in Figure 9.12.

We first note that the objective function shows that the efficiency score for County Hospital is 0.905. This score tells us that the composite hospital can obtain at least the level of each output that County Hospital obtains by having available no more than 90.5% of the input resources required by County Hospital. Thus, the composite hospital

Figure 9.12	THE MANAGEMENT SCIENTIST SOLUTION FOR THE DATA ENVELOPMENT ANALYSIS COUNTY HOSPITAL PROBLEM

```
Objective Function Value =              0.905

        Variable            Value           Reduced Costs
    --------------      ---------------     ------------------

           E                0.905               0.000
          WG                0.212               0.000
          WU                0.260               0.000
          WC                0.000               0.095
          WS                0.527               0.000


      Constraint        Slack/Surplus          Dual Prices
    --------------      ---------------     ------------------

           1               0.000                0.239
           2               0.000               -0.014
           3               0.000               -0.014
           4               1.615                0.000
           5              37.027                0.000
           6              35.643                0.000
           7             174.422                0.000
           8               0.000                0.010
```

is more efficient, and the DEA analysis has identified County Hospital as being relatively inefficient.

From the solution in Figure 9.12, we see that the composite hospital is formed from the weighted average of General Hospital ($wg = 0.212$), University Hospital ($wu = 0.260$), and State Hospital ($ws = 0.527$). Each input and output of the composite hospital is determined by the same weighted average of the inputs and outputs of these three hospitals.

The Slack/Surplus column provides some additional information about the efficiency of County Hospital compared to the composite hospital. Specifically, the composite hospital has at least as much of each output as County Hospital has (constraints 2–5) and provides 1.6 more nurses trained (surplus for constraint 4) and 37 more interns trained (surplus for constraint 5). The slack of zero from constraint 8 shows that the composite hospital uses approximately 90.5% of the bed-days used by County Hospital. The slack values for constraints 6 and 7 show that less than 90.5% of the FTE nonphysician and the supplies expense resources used at County Hospital are used by the composite hospital.

Clearly, the composite hospital is more efficient than County Hospital, and we are justified in concluding that County Hospital is relatively inefficient compared to the other hospitals in the group. Given the results of the DEA analysis, hospital administrators should examine operations to determine how County Hospital resources can be more effectively utilized.

Summary of the DEA Approach

To use data envelopment analysis to measure the relative efficiency of County Hospital, we used a linear programming model to construct a hypothetical composite hospital based on the outputs and inputs for the four hospitals in the problem. The approach to solving other types of problems using DEA is similar. That is, for each operating unit that we want to measure the efficiency of, we must formulate and solve a linear programming model similar to the linear program we solved to measure the relative efficiency of County Hospital. The following step-by-step procedure should help you in formulating a linear programming model for other types of DEA applications. Note that the operating unit that we want to measure the relative efficiency of is referred to as the jth operating unit.

Step 1. Define decision variables or weights (one for each operating unit) that can be used to determine the inputs and outputs for the composite operating unit.

Step 2. Write a constraint that requires the weights to sum to 1.

Step 3. For each output measure, write a constraint that requires the output for the composite operating unit to be greater than or equal to the corresponding output for the jth operating unit.

Step 4. Define a decision variable, E, which determines the fraction of the jth operating unit's input available to the composite hospital.

Step 5. For each input measure, write a constraint that requires the input for the composite operating unit to be less than or equal to the resources available to the composite operating unit.

Step 6. Write the objective function as Min E.

N O T E S	1. Remember that the goal of data envelopment analysis is to identify operating units that are relatively inefficient. The method *does not* necessarily identify the operating units that are *relatively efficient.* Just because the efficiency index is $E = 1$, we cannot conclude that the unit being analyzed is relatively efficient. Indeed, any unit that has the largest output on any one of the output measures cannot be judged relatively inefficient.
and Comments	2. It is possible for DEA to show all but one unit to be relatively inefficient. Such would be the case if a unit producing the most of every output also consumes the least of every input. Such cases are extremely rare in practice.
	3. In applying data envelopment analysis to problems involving a large group of operating units, practitioners have found that roughly 50% of the operating units can be identified as inefficient. Comparing each relatively inefficient unit to the units contributing to the composite unit may be helpful in understanding how the operation of each relatively inefficient unit can be improved.

SUMMARY

In this chapter we presented a broad range of applications that demonstrate how to use linear programming to assist in the decision-making process. We formulated and solved problems from marketing, finance, and production management, and illustrated how linear programming can be applied to blending problems and data envelopment analysis.

Many of the illustrations presented in this chapter are scaled-down versions of actual situations in which linear programming has been applied. In real-world applications, the problem may not be so concisely stated, the data for the problem may not be as readily available, and the problem most likely will involve numerous decision variables and/or constraints. However, a thorough study of the applications in this chapter is a good place to begin in applying linear programming to real problems.

..../ /...........

PROBLEMS

Note: The following problems have been designed to give you an understanding and appreciation of the broad range of problems that can be formulated as linear programs. You should be able to formulate a linear programming model for each of the problems. However, you will need access to a linear programming computer package to develop the solutions and make the requested interpretations.

SELF TEST

1. The Westchester Chamber of Commerce periodically sponsors public service seminars and programs. Currently, promotional plans are under way for this year's program. Advertising alternatives include television, radio, and newspaper. Audience estimates, costs, and maximum media usage limitations are as shown.

Constraint	Television	Radio	Newspaper
Audience per advertisement	100,000	18,000	40,000
Cost per advertisement	$2,000	$300	$600
Maximum media usage	10	20	10

To ensure a balanced use of advertising media, radio advertisements must not exceed 50% of the total number of advertisements authorized. In addition, television should account for at least 10% of the total number of advertisements authorized.

   a. If the promotional budget is limited to $18,200, how many commercial messages should be run on each medium to maximize total audience contact? What is the allocation of the budget among the three media, and what is the total audience reached?
   b. By how much would audience contact increase if an extra $100 were allocated to the promotional budget?

2. The management of Hartman Company is trying to determine the amount of each of two products to produce over the coming planning period. The following information concerns labor availability, labor utilization, and product profitability.

Department	Product (hours/unit) 1	Product (hours/unit) 2	Labor-Hours Available
A	1.00	0.35	100
B	0.30	0.20	36
C	0.20	0.50	50
Profit contribution/unit	$30.00	$15.00	

   a. Develop a linear programming model of the Hartman Company problem. Solve the model to determine the optimal production quantities of products 1 and 2.
   b. In computing the profit contribution per unit, management doesn't deduct labor costs because they are considered fixed for the upcoming planning period. However, suppose that

overtime can be scheduled in some of the departments. Which departments would you recommend scheduling for overtime? How much would you be willing to pay per hour of overtime in each department?

c. Suppose that 10, 6, and 8 hours of overtime may be scheduled in departments A, B, and C, respectively. The cost per hour of overtime is $18 in department A, $22.50 in department B, and $12 in department C. Formulate a linear programming model that can be used to determine the optimal production quantities if overtime is made available. What are the optimal production quantities and what is the revised total contribution to profit? How much overtime do you recommend using in each department? What is the increase in the total contribution to profit if overtime is used?

3. The employee credit union at State University is planning the allocation of funds for the coming year. The credit union makes four types of loans to its members. In addition, the credit union invests in risk-free securities to stabilize income. The various revenue-producing investments together with annual rates of return are as follows.

Type of Loan/Investment	Annual Rate of Return (%)
Automobile loans	8
Furniture loans	10
Other secured loans	11
Signature loans	12
Risk-free securities	9

The credit union will have $2,000,000 available for investment during the coming year. State laws and credit union policies impose the following restrictions on the composition of the loans and investments.

- Risk-free securities may not exceed 30% of the total funds available for investment.
- Signature loans may not exceed 10% of the funds invested in all loans (automobile, furniture, other secured, and signature loans).
- Furniture loans plus other secured loans may not exceed the automobile loans.
- Other secured loans plus signature loans may not exceed the funds invested in risk-free securities.

How should the $2,000,000 be allocated to each of the loan/investment alternatives to maximize total annual return? What is the projected total annual return?

4. Hilltop Coffee manufactures a coffee product by blending three types of coffee beans. The cost per pound and the available pounds of each bean are as follows.

Bean	Cost Per Pound	Available Pounds
1	$0.50	500
2	$0.70	600
3	$0.45	400

Consumer tests with coffee products were used to provide ratings on a scale of 0–100, with higher ratings indicating higher quality. Product quality standards for the blended coffee require a consumer rating for aroma to be at least 75 and a consumer rating for taste to be at least 80.

The individual ratings of the aroma and taste for coffee made from 100% of each bean are as follows.

Bean	Aroma Rating	Taste Rating
1	75	86
2	85	88
3	60	75

Assume that the aroma and taste attributes of the coffee blend will be a weighted average of the attributes of the beans used in the blend.
  a. What is the minimum-cost blend that will meet the quality standards and provide 1000 pounds of the blended coffee product?
  b. What is the cost per pound for the coffee blend?
  c. Determine the aroma and taste ratings for the coffee blend.
  d. If additional coffee were to be produced, what would be the expected cost per pound?

5. Ajax Fuels, Inc., is developing a new additive for airplane fuels. The additive is a mixture of three ingredients: A, B, and C. For proper performance, the total amount of additive (amount of A + amount of B + amount of C) must be at least 10 ounces per gallon of fuel. However, because of safety reasons, the amount of additive must not exceed 15 ounces per gallon of fuel. The mix or blend of the three ingredients is critical. At least 1 ounce of ingredient A must be used for every ounce of ingredient B. The amount of ingredient C must be greater than one-half the amount of ingredient A. If the costs per ounce for ingredients A, B, and C are $0.10, $0.03, and $0.09, respectively, find the minimum-cost mixture of A, B, and C for each gallon of airplane fuel.

6. G. Kunz and Sons, Inc., manufactures two products used in the heavy equipment industry. Both products require manufacturing operations in two departments. The following are the production time (in hours) and profit contribution figures for the two products.

		Labor-Hours	
Product	Profit Per Unit	Dept. A	Dept. B
1	$25	6	12
2	$20	8	10

For the coming production period, Kunz has available a total of 900 hours of labor that can be allocated to either of the two departments. Find the production plan and labor allocation (hours assigned in each department) that will maximize the total contribution to profit.

7. As part of the settlement for a class action lawsuit, Hoxworth Corporation must provide sufficient cash to make the following annual payments (in thousands of dollars).

Year	1	2	3	4	5	6
Payment	190	215	240	285	315	460

The annual payments must be made at the beginning of each year. The judge will approve an amount that, along with earnings on its investment, will cover the annual payments. Investment of the funds will be limited to savings (at 4% annually) and government securities, at prices and rates currently quoted in *The Wall Street Journal*.

Hoxworth wants to develop a plan for making the annual payments by investing in the following securities (par value = $1000). Funds not invested in these securities will be placed in savings.

Security	Current Price	Rate (%)	Years to Maturity
1	$1055	6.750	3
2	$1000	5.125	4

Assume that interest is paid annually. The plan will be submitted to the judge and, if approved, Hoxworth will be required to pay a trustee the amount that will be required to fund the plan.

a. Use linear programming to find the minimum cash settlement necessary to fund the annual payments.

b. Use the dual price to determine how much more Hoxworth should be willing to pay now to reduce the payment at the beginning of year 6 to $400,000.

c. Use the dual price to determine how much more Hoxworth should be willing to pay to reduce the year 1 payment to $150,000?

d. Suppose that the annual payments are to be made at the end of each year. Reformulate the model to accommodate this change. How much would Hoxworth save if this change could be negotiated?

8. The Clark County Sheriff's Department schedules police officers for 8-hour shifts. The beginning times for the shifts are 8:00 A.M., noon, 4:00 P.M., 8:00 P.M., midnight, and 4:00 A.M. An officer beginning a shift at one of the these times works for the next 8 hours. During normal weekday operations, the number of officers needed varies depending on the time of day. The department staffing guidelines require the following minimum number of officers on duty:

Time of Day	Minimum Officers on Duty
8:00 A.M.–noon	5
Noon–4:00 P.M.	6
4:00 P.M.–8:00 P.M.	10
8:00 P.M.–midnight	7
Midnight–4:00 A.M.	4
4:00 A.M.–8:00 A.M.	6

Determine the number of police officers that should be scheduled to begin the 8-hour shifts at each of the six times (8:00 A.M., noon, 4:00 P.M., 8:00 P.M., midnight, and 4:00 A.M.) to minimize the total number of officers required. (Hint: Let x_1 = the number of officers beginning work at 8:00 A.M., x_2 = the number of officers beginning work at noon, and so on.)

SELF TEST

9. Reconsider the Welte Mutual Funds problem from Section 9.2. Define your decision variables as the fraction of funds invested in each security. Also, modify the constraints limiting investments in the oil and steel industries as follows: No more than 50% of the total funds invested in stock (oil and steel) may be invested in the oil industry, and no more than 50% of the funds invested in stock (oil and steel) may be invested in the steel industry.

a. Solve the revised linear programming model. What fraction of the portfolio should be invested in each type of security?

b. How much should be invested in each type of security?

c. What are the total earnings for the portfolio?

d. What is the marginal rate of return on the portfolio? That is, how much more could be earned by investing one more dollar in the portfolio?

10. Lurix Electronics manufactures two products that can be produced on two different production lines. Both products have their lowest production costs when produced on the more modern of the two production lines. However, the modern production line does not have the capacity to handle the total production. As a result, some production will have to be routed to the older production line. The following data show total production requirements, production line capacities, and production costs.

Product	Production Cost/Unit		Minimum Production Requirements
	Modern Line	Old Line	
1	$ 3.00	$ 5.00	500 units
2	$ 2.50	$ 4.00	700 units
Production line capacities	800	600	

Formulate a linear programming model that can be used to make the production routing decision. What is the recommended decision and the total cost?

11. Edwards Manufacturing Company purchases two component parts from three different suppliers. The suppliers have limited capacity, and no one supplier can meet all the company's needs. In addition, the suppliers charge different prices for the components. Component price data (in price/unit) are as follows.

	Supplier		
Component	1	2	3
1	$12	$13	$14
2	$10	$11	$10

Each supplier has a limited capacity in terms of the total number of components it can supply. However, as long as Edwards provides sufficient advance orders, each supplier can devote its capacity to component 1, component 2, or any combination of the two components, if the total number of units ordered is within its capacity. Supplier capacities are as follows.

Supplier	1	2	3
Capacity	600	1000	800

If the Edwards production plan for the next period includes 1000 units of component 1 and 800 units of component 2, what purchases do you recommend? That is, how many units of each component should be ordered from each supplier? What is the total purchase cost for the components?

SELF TEST

12. Refer to the Janders application in Section 9.3. Consider each of the following variations of the original problem separately.

a. Suppose that Janders' supplier lowers the price for the bases to $0.55 per unit. What is the new optimal solution and its value?

b. Suppose that the supplier of the tops for the Technician calculator raises the unit price to $0.82. What is the new optimal solution and its value?

c. If Janders' employees were willing to work overtime for an overtime premium of only $2 per hour, should Janders schedule overtime? Why or why not? What is the new optimal solution and its value?

13. Reconsider the McCormick Manufacturing Company problem in Section 9.3. Each of the following parts presents a variation of the original problem. Consider each question separately.
   a. Suppose that no more than 600 hours can be transferred from department 2. Based on the dual price information, how does the value of the optimal solution change?
   b. Modify the linear programming model to reflect the change described in part (a). Use a computer solution of the revised formulation to verify your conclusion in part (a). What transfers are recommended?
   c. Suppose that the employees transferred from department 1 to department 3 are only 80% as productive in department 3 as the employees originally assigned to that department. Reformulate the original model in Section 9.3 accordingly and use a computer solution. What is the new optimal solution? (Hint: Modify the labor balance equation for department 3.)

14. The production manager for the Classic Boat Corporation must determine how many units of the Classic 21 model to produce over the next four quarters. The company has a beginning inventory of 100 Classic 21 boats, and demand for the four quarters is 2000 units in quarter 1, 4000 units in quarter 2, 3000 units in quarter 3, and 1500 units in quarter 4. The firm has limited production capacity in each quarter. That is, up to 4000 units can be produced in quarter 1, 3000 units in quarter 2, 2000 units in quarter 3, and 4000 units in quarter 4. Each boat held in inventory in quarters 1 and 2 incurs an inventory holding cost of $250 per unit; the holding cost for quarters 3 and 4 is $300 per unit. The production costs for the first quarter are $10,000 per unit; these costs are expected to increase by 10% each quarter because of increases in labor and material costs. Management has specified that the ending inventory for quarter 4 must be at least 500 boats.
   a. Formulate a linear programming model that can be used to determine the production schedule that will minimize the total cost of meeting demand in each quarter subject to the production capacities in each quarter and also to the required ending inventory in quarter 4.
   b. Solve the linear program formulated in part (a); then develop a table that will show for each quarter the number of units to manufacture, the ending inventory, and the costs incurred.
   c. Interpret each of the dual prices corresponding to the constraints developed to meet demand in each quarter. Based on these dual prices what advice would you give the production manager?
   d. Interpret each of the dual prices corresponding to the production capacity in each quarter. Based on each of these dual prices what advice would you give the production manager?

SELF TEST

15. Seastrand Oil Company produces two grades of gasoline: regular and high octane. Both gasolines are produced by blending two types of crude oil. Although both types of crude oil contain the two important ingredients required to produce both gasolines, the percentage of important ingredients in each type of crude oil differs, as does the cost per gallon. The percentage of ingredients A and B in each type of crude oil and the cost per gallon are shown.

Crude Oil	Cost	Ingredient A	Ingredient B	
1	$0.10	20%	60%	Crude oil 1 is 60% ingredient B
2	$0.15	50%	30%	

Each gallon of regular gasoline must contain at least 40% of ingredient A, whereas each gallon of high octane can contain at most 50% of ingredient B. Daily demand for regular and high-octane gasoline is 800,000 and 500,000 gallons, respectively. How many gallons of each type of crude oil should be used in the two gasolines to satisfy daily demand at a minimum cost?

16. The Ferguson Paper Company produces rolls of paper for use in adding machines, desk calculators, and cash registers. The rolls, which are 200 feet long, are produced in widths of 1½, 2½, and 3½ inches. The production process provides 200-foot rolls in 10-inch widths only. The firm must therefore cut the rolls to the desired final product sizes. The seven cutting alternatives and the amount of waste generated by each are as follows.

Cutting Alternative	Number of Rolls			Waste (inches)
	1½ in.	2½ in.	3½ in.	
1	6	0	0	1
2	0	4	0	0
3	2	0	2	0
4	0	1	2	½
5	1	3	0	1
6	1	2	1	0
7	4	0	1	½

The minimum requirements for the three products are

Roll Width (inches)	1½	2½	3½
Units	1000	2000	4000

a. If the company wants to minimize the number of 10-inch rolls that must be manufactured, how many 10-inch rolls will be processed on each cutting alternative? How many rolls are required, and what is the total waste (inches)?

b. If the company wants to minimize the waste generated, how many 10-inch units will be processed on each cutting alternative? How many rolls are required, and what is the total waste (inches)?

c. What are the differences in approaches (a) and (b) to this problem? In this case, which objective do you prefer? Explain. What types of situations would make the other objective more desirable?

17. Frandec Company manufactures, assembles, and rebuilds material handling equipment used in warehouses and distribution centers. One product, called a Liftmaster, is assembled from four components: a frame, a motor, two supports, and a metal strap. Frandec's production schedule calls for 5000 Liftmasters to be made next month. Frandec purchases the motors from an outside supplier, but the frames, supports, and straps may either be manufactured by the company or purchased from an outside supplier. Manufacturing and purchase costs per unit are shown.

Component	Manufacturing Cost	Purchase Cost
Frame	$38.00	$51.00
Support	11.50	15.00
Strap	6.50	7.50

Three departments are involved in the production of these components. The time (in minutes per unit) required to process each component in each department is given, along with the available capacity (in hours) for the three departments.

		Department	
Component	Cutting	Milling	Shaping
Frame	3.5	2.2	3.1
Support	1.3	1.7	2.6
Strap	0.8	—	1.7
Capacity (hours)	350	420	680

    a. Formulate and solve a linear programming model for this make-or-buy application. How many of each component should be manufactured and how many should be purchased?

    b. What is the total cost of the manufacturing and purchasing plan?

    c. How many hours of production time are used in each department?

    d. How much should Frandec be willing to pay for an additional hour of time in the shaping department?

    e. Another manufacturer has offered to sell frames to Frandec for $45 each. Could Frandec improve its position by pursuing this opportunity? Why or why not?

18. The Two-Rivers Oil Company near Pittsburgh transports gasoline to its distributors by truck. The company has recently contracted to supply gasoline distributors in southern Ohio, and it has $600,000 available to spend on the necessary expansion of its fleet of gasoline tank trucks. Three models of gasoline tank trucks are available.

Truck Model	Capacity (gallons)	Purchase Cost	Monthly Operating Cost, Including Depreciation
Super Tanker	5000	$67,000	$550
Regular Line	2500	$55,000	$425
Econo-Tanker	1000	$46,000	$350

The company estimates that the monthly demand for the region will be 550,000 gallons of gasoline. Because of the size and speed differences of the trucks, the number of deliveries or round trips possible per month for each truck model will vary. Trip capacities are estimated at 15 trips per month for the Super Tanker, 20 trips per month for the Regular Line, and 25 trips per month for the Econo-Tanker. Based on maintenance and driver availability, the firm does not want to add more than 15 new vehicles to its fleet. In addition, the company has decided to purchase at least three of the new Econo-Tankers for use on short-run, low-demand routes. As a final constraint, the company does not want more than half the new models to be Super Tankers.

    a. If the company wishes to satisfy the gasoline demand with a minimum monthly operating expense, how many models of each truck should be purchased?

    b. If the company did not require at least three Econo-Tankers and did not limit the number of Super Tankers to at most half the new models, how many models of each truck should be purchased?

SELF TEST

19. The Silver Star Bicycle Company will be manufacturing both men's and women's models for its Easy-Pedal 10-speed bicycles during the next 2 months. Management wants to develop a production schedule indicating how many bicycles of each model should be produced in each month. Current demand forecasts call for 150 men's and 125 women's models to be shipped during the first month and 200 men's and 150 women's models to be shipped during the second month. Additional data are shown.

Model	Production Costs	Labor Requirements (hours) Manufacturing	Assembly	Current Inventory
Men's	$120	2.0	1.5	20
Women's	$ 90	1.6	1.0	30

Last month the company used a total of 1000 hours of labor. The company's labor relations policy will not allow the combined total hours of labor (manufacturing plus assembly) to increase or decrease by more than 100 hours from month to month. In addition, the company charges monthly inventory at the rate of 2% of the production cost based on the inventory levels at the end of the month. The company would like to have at least 25 units of each model in inventory at the end of the 2 months.

a. Establish a production schedule that minimizes production and inventory costs and satisfies the labor-smoothing, demand, and inventory requirements. What inventories will be maintained and what are the monthly labor requirements?

b. If the company changed the constraints so that monthly labor increases and decreases could not exceed 50 hours, what would happen to the production schedule? How much will the cost increase? What would you recommend?

20. Filtron Corporation produces filtration containers used in water treatment systems. Although business has been growing, the demand each month varies considerably. As a result, the company utilizes a mix of part-time and full-time employees to meet production demands. Although this approach provides Filtron with great flexibility, it has resulted in increased costs and morale problems among employees. For instance, if Filtron needs to increase production from one month to the next, additional part-time employees have to be hired and trained, and costs go up. If Filtron has to decrease production, the work force has to be reduced and Filtron incurs additional costs in terms of unemployment benefits and decreased morale. Best estimates are that increasing the number of units produced from one month to the next will increase production costs by $1.25 per unit, and that decreasing the number of units produced will increase production costs by $1.00 per unit. In February Filtron produced 10,000 filtration containers but only sold 7500 units; 2500 units are currently in inventory. The sales forecasts for March, April, and May are for 12,000 units, 8,000 units, and 15,000 units, respectively. In addition, Filtron has the capacity to store up to 3000 filtration containers at the end of any month. Management would like to determine the number of units to be produced in March, April, and May that will minimize the total cost of the monthly production increases and decreases.

21. Greenville Cabinets has received a contract to produce speaker cabinets for a major speaker manufacturer. The contract calls for the production of 3300 bookshelf speakers and 4100 floor speakers over the next two months, with the following delivery schedule.

Model	Month 1	Month 2
Bookshelf	2100	1200
Floor	1500	2600

Greenville estimates that the production time for each bookshelf model is 0.7 hour and the production time for each floor model is 1 hour. The raw material costs are $10 for each bookshelf model and $12 for each floor model. Labor costs are $22 per hour using regular production time and $33 using overtime. Greenville has up to 2400 hours of regular production time available each month and up to 1000 additional hours of overtime available each month. If production for either cabinet exceeds demand in month 1, the cabinets can be stored at a cost of $5 per cabinet. For each product, determine the number of units that should be manufactured each month on regular time and on overtime to minimize total production and storage costs.

22. The Williams Calculator Company manufactures two kinds of calculators: the TW100 and the TW200. The assembly process requires three people. The assembly times are as follows.

	Calculator		Maximum Labor Available
Assembler	**TW100**	**TW200**	**(hours/day)**
1	4 min	3 min	8
2	2 min	4 min	8
3	3½ min	3 min	8

The company policy is to balance workloads on all assembly jobs. In fact, management wants to schedule work so that no assembler will have more than 30 minutes more work per day than other assemblers. That is, in a regular 8-hour shift, all assemblers will be assigned at least 7½ hours of work. If the firm makes a $2.50 profit for each TW100 and a $3.50 profit for each TW200, how many units of each calculator should be produced per day? How much time will each assembler be assigned per day?

23. Multiperiod production and inventory planning models determine a production schedule and an ending inventory schedule for each of several periods that will maximize profit or minimize cost. Considering selling price, regular production costs, overtime costs, inventory carrying costs, and lost sales costs, develop a three-period production and inventory planning model for Allen Manufacturing Company. Use the following relevant information.

Period	Selling Price Per Unit	Production Cost Per Unit	Demand	Ending Inventory Cost Per Unit
1	$5.00	$2.80	500	$0.50
2	$5.00	$2.90	300	$0.50
3	$5.50	$3.00	400	$0.55

	Production Capacity (units)	
Period	**Regular**	**Overtime**
1	250	100
2	300	100
3	300	125

The overtime cost per unit in each period is 20% greater than the production cost per unit shown. The lost sales cost, which is $4 per unit in any period, accounts for lost customer goodwill, but does not account for the cost associated with the lost revenue. The beginning inventory for period 1 is 100 units. In addition, the firm wants to have at least 50 units in ending inventory for period 3 to prepare for period 4.

To account for the multiperiod aspects of the problem, each period t will require balance equations or constraints based on two relationships:

$$\text{Lost sales } (t) = \text{demand } (t) - \text{sales } (t)$$

$$\text{Ending inventory } (t) = \text{beginning inventory } (t) + \text{production } (t) - \text{sales } (t)$$

Develop a linear program that can be used to determine the optimal production and inventory schedule for Allen Manufacturing. Determine the sales, regular production, overtime production, ending inventory, and lost sales for each of the three periods. What is the net profit associated with your solution?

24. The Morton Financial Institution must decide on the percentage of available funds to commit to each of two investments, referred to as A and B, over the next four periods. The following table shows the amount of new funds available for each of the four periods, as well as the cash expenditure required for each investment (negative values) or the cash income from the investment (positive values). The data shown (in thousands of dollars) reflect the amount of expenditure or income if 100% of the funds available in any period are invested in either A or B. For example, if Morton decides to invest 100% of the funds available in any period in investment A, it will incur cash expenditures of $1000 in period 1, $800 in period 2, $200 in period 3, and income of $200 in period 4. Note, however, if Morton made the decision to invest 80% in investment A, the cash expenditures or income would be 80% of the values shown.

Period	New Investment Funds Available	Investment	
		A	B
1	1500	−1000	−800
2	400	−800	−500
3	500	−200	−300
4	100	200	300

The amount of funds available in any period is the sum of the new investment funds for the period, the new loan funds, the savings from the previous period, the cash income from investment A, and the cash income from investment B. The funds available in any period can be used to pay the loan and interest from the previous period, placed in savings, used to pay the cash expenditures for investment A, or used to pay the cash expenditures for investment B.

Assume an interest rate of 10% per period for savings and an interest rate of 18% per period on borrowed funds. Let

$$S(t) = \text{the savings for period } t$$

$$L(t) = \text{the new loan funds for period } t$$

Then, in any period t, the savings income from the previous period is $1.1S(t-1)$ and the loan and interest expenditure from the previous period is $1.18L(t-1)$.

At the end of period 4, investment A is expected to have a cash value of $3200 (assuming a 100% investment in A), and investment B is expected to have a cash value of $2500 (assuming a 100% investment in B). Additional income and expenses at the end of period 4 will be income from savings in period 4 less the repayment of the period 4 loan plus interest.

Suppose that the decision variables are defined as

$$x_1 = \text{the proportion of investment A undertaken}$$

$$x_2 = \text{the proportion of investment B undertaken}$$

For example, if $x_1 = 0.5$, \$500 would be invested in investment A during the first period, and all remaining cash flows and ending investment A values would be multiplied by 0.5. The same holds for investment B. The model must include constraints $x_1 \leq 1$ and $x_2 \leq 1$ to make sure that no more than 100% of the investments can be undertaken.

If no more than \$200 can be borrowed in any period, determine the proportions of investments A and B and the amount of savings and borrowing in each period that will maximize the cash value for the firm at the end of the four periods.

25. Western Family Steakhouse offers a variety of low-cost meals and quick service. Other than management, the steakhouse operates with two full-time employees who work 8 hours per day. The rest of the employees are part-time employees who are scheduled for 4-hour shifts during peak meal times. On Saturdays the steakhouse is open from 11:00 A.M. to 10:00 P.M. Management wants to develop a schedule for part-time employees that will minimize labor costs and still provide excellent customer service. The average wage rate for the part-time employees is \$4.60 per hour. The total number of full-time and part-time employees needed varies with the time of day as shown as follows.

Time	Total Number of Employees Needed
11:00 A.M.–noon	9
Noon–1:00 P.M.	9
1:00 P.M.–2:00 P.M.	9
2:00 P.M.–3:00 P.M.	3
3:00 P.M.–4:00 P.M.	3
4:00 P.M.–5:00 P.M.	3
5:00 P.M.–6:00 P.M.	6
6:00 P.M.–7:00 P.M.	12
7:00 P.M.–8:00 P.M.	12
8:00 P.M.–9:00 P.M.	7
9:00 P.M.–10:00 P.M.	7

One full-time employee comes on duty at 11:00 A.M., works 4 hours, takes an hour off, and returns for another 4 hours. The other full-time employee comes to work at 1:00 P.M. and works the same 4-hours-on, 1-hour-off, 4-hours-on pattern.

a. Develop a minimum-cost schedule for part-time employees.

b. What is the total payroll for the part-time employees? How many part-time shifts are needed? Use the surplus variables to comment on the desirability of scheduling at least some of the part-time employees for 3-hour shifts.

c. Assume that part-time employees can be assigned either a 3-hour or 4-hour shift. Develop a minimum-cost schedule for the part-time employees. How many part-time shifts are needed and what is the cost savings compared to the previous schedule?

26. In Section 9.5 data envelopment analysis was used to evaluate the relative efficiencies of four hospitals. Data for three input measures and four output measures were provided in Tables 9.16 and 9.17.

a. Use these data to develop a linear programming model that could be used to evaluate the performance of General Hospital.

b. The computer solution obtained using The Management Scientist is shown below. Does the solution indicate that General Hospital is relatively inefficient?

```
Objective Function Value = 1.000000
            Variable     Value     Reduced Costs
               E         1.000         0.000
               WG        1.000         0.000
               WU        0.000         0.000
               WC        0.000         0.331
               WS        0.000         0.215
```

    c.   Which hospital or hospitals make up the composite unit used to evaluate General Hospital? State why this is true.

27.   Data envelopment analysis has been used to measure the relative efficiency of a group of hospitals (H. David Sherman, "Hospital Efficiency Measurement and Evaluation," *Medical Care,* October 1984). Sherman's study involved seven teaching hospitals; data on three input measures and four output measures are contained in the following tables.

	Input Measures		
Hospital	**Full-Time Equivalent Nonphysicians**	**Supply Expense ($1000s)**	**Bed-Days Available ($1000s)**
A	310.0	134.60	116.00
B	278.5	114.30	106.80
C	165.6	131.30	65.52
D	250.0	316.00	94.40
E	206.4	151.20	102.10
F	384.0	217.00	153.70
G	530.1	770.80	215.00

	Output Measures			
Hospital	**Patient-Days (65 or older) (1000s)**	**Patient-Days (under 65) (1000s)**	**Nurses Trained**	**Interns Trained**
A	55.31	49.52	291	47
B	37.64	55.63	156	3
C	32.91	25.77	141	26
D	33.53	41.99	160	21
E	32.48	55.30	157	82
F	48.78	81.92	285	92
G	58.41	119.70	111	89

    a.   Formulate a linear programming model so that data envelopment analysis can be used to evaluate the performance of hospital D.

    b.   Solve the model using a computer software package.

c. Is hospital D relatively inefficient? What is the interpretation of the value of the objective function?

d. How many patient-days of each type are produced by the composite hospital?

e. Which hospitals would you recommend hospital D consider emulating to improve the efficiency of its operation?

28. Refer again to the data presented in Problem 27.

a. Formulate a linear programming model that can be used to perform data envelopment analysis for hospital E.

b. Solve the model using a computer software package.

c. Is hospital E relatively inefficient? What is the interpretation of the value of the objective function?

d. Which hospitals are involved in making up the composite hospital? Can you make a general statement about which hospitals will make up the composite unit associated with a unit that is not inefficient?

29. The Ranch House, Inc., operates five fast-food restaurants. Input measures for the restaurants include weekly hours of operation, full-time equivalent staff, and weekly supply expenses. Output measures of performance include average weekly contribution to profit, market share, and annual growth rate. Data for the input and output measures are shown in the following tables.

	Input Measures		
Restaurant	Hours of Operation	FTE Staff	Supplies ($)
Bardstown	96	16	850
Clarksville	110	22	1400
Jeffersonville	100	18	1200
New Albany	125	25	1500
St. Matthews	120	24	1600

	Output Measures		
Restaurant	Weekly Profit	Market Share (%)	Growth Rate (%)
Bardstown	$3800	25	8.0
Clarksville	$4600	32	8.5
Jeffersonville	$4400	35	8.0
New Albany	$6500	30	10.0
St. Matthews	$6000	28	9.0

a. Develop a linear programming model that can be used to evaluate the performance of the Clarksville Ranch House restaurant.

b. Solve the model using a computer software package.

c. Is the Clarksville Ranch House restaurant relatively inefficient? Discuss.

d. Where does the composite restaurant have more output than the Clarksville restaurant? How much less of each input resource does the composite restaurant require when compared to the Clarksville restaurant?

e. What other restaurants should be studied to find suggested ways for the Clarksville restaurant to improve its efficiency?

Case Problem: ENVIRONMENTAL PROTECTION

Skillings Industrial Chemicals, Inc., operates a refinery in southwestern Ohio near the Ohio River. The company's primary product is manufactured from a chemical process that requires the use of two raw materials—material A and material B. The production of 1 pound of the primary product requires the use of 1 pound of material A and 2 pounds of material B. The output of the chemical process is 1 pound of the primary product, 1 pound of liquid waste material, and 1 pound of solid waste by-product. The solid waste by-product is given to a local fertilizer plant as payment for picking it up and disposing of it. The liquid waste material has no market value, so the refinery has been dumping it directly into the Ohio River. The company's manufacturing process is shown schematically in Figure 9.13.

Government pollution guidelines established by the Environmental Protection Agency will no longer permit disposal of the liquid waste directly into the river. The refinery's research group has developed the following set of alternative uses for the liquid waste material.

1. Produce a secondary product K by adding 1 pound of raw material A to every pound of liquid waste.
2. Produce a secondary product M by adding 1 pound of raw material B to every pound of liquid waste.
3. Specially treat the liquid waste so that it meets pollution standards before dumping it into the river.

These three alternatives are depicted in Figure 9.14.

The company's management knows that the secondary products will be low in quality and may not be very profitable. However, management also recognizes that the special treatment alternative will be a relatively expensive operation. The company's problem is to determine how to satisfy the pollution regulations and still maintain the highest possible profit. How should the liquid waste material be handled? Should Skillings produce product

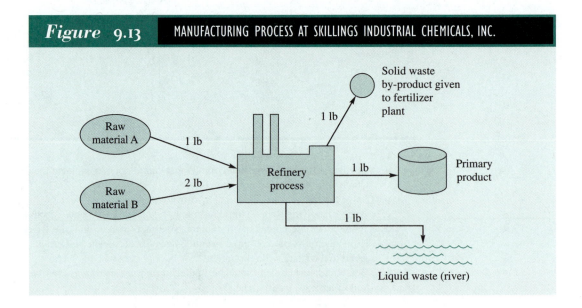

Figure 9.13   MANUFACTURING PROCESS AT SKILLINGS INDUSTRIAL CHEMICALS, INC.

Figure 9.14 ALTERNATIVES FOR HANDLING THE REFINERY LIQUID WASTE

K, produce product M, use the special treatment, or employ some combination of the three alternatives?

Last month 10,000 pounds of the company's primary product were produced. The accounting department has prepared a cost report showing the breakdown of fixed and variable expenses that were incurred during the month.

Cost Analysis for 10,000 Pounds of Primary Product

Fixed costs	
Administrative expenses	$12,000
Refinery overhead	4,000
Variable costs	
Raw material A	15,000
Raw material B	16,000
Direct labor	5,000
Total	$52,000

In this cost analysis, the fixed-cost portion of the expenses is the same every month regardless of production level. Direct labor costs are expected to run $0.20 per pound for product K and $0.10 per pound for product M.

The company's primary product sells for $5.70 per pound. Secondary products K and M sell for $0.85 and $0.65 per pound, respectively. The special treatment of the liquid waste will cost $0.25 per pound.

A company accountant believes that product K is too expensive to manufacture and cannot be sold at a price that recovers its material and labor cost. The accountant's recommendation is to eliminate product K as an alternative.

For the upcoming production period, 5000 pounds of raw material A and 7000 pounds of raw material B will be available.

Managerial Report

Develop an approach to the problem that will allow the company to determine how much primary product to produce, given the limitations on the amounts of the raw material available.

Include recommendations as to how the company should dispose of the liquid waste to satisfy the environmental protection guidelines. How many pounds of product K should be produced? How many pounds of product M should be produced? How many pounds of liquid waste should be specially treated and dumped into the river? Include a discussion and analysis of the following in your report:

1. A cost analysis showing the profit contribution per pound for the primary product, product K, and product M.
2. The optimal production quantities and waste disposal plan, including the projected profit.
3. A discussion of the value of additional pounds of each raw material.
4. A discussion of the sensitivity analysis of the objective function coefficients.
5. Comments on the accountant's recommendation to eliminate product K as an alternative. Does the recommendation appear reasonable? What is your reaction to the recommendation? How would the optimal solution change if product K were eliminated?

Case Problem: INVESTMENT STRATEGY

J. D. Williams, Inc., is an investment advisory firm that manages more than $120 million in funds for its numerous clients. The company uses an asset allocation model that recommends the portion of each client's portfolio to be invested in a growth stock fund, an income fund, and a money market fund. To maintain diversity in each client's portfolio, the firm places limits on the percentage of each portfolio that may be invested in each of the three funds. General guidelines indicate that the amount invested in the growth fund must be between 20% and 40% of the total portfolio value. Similar percentages for the other two funds stipulate that between 20% and 50% of the total portfolio value must be in the income fund and at least 30% of the total portfolio value must be in the money market fund.

In addition, the company attempts to assess the risk tolerance of each client and adjust the portfolio to meet the needs of the individual investor. For example, Williams has just contracted with a new client who has $800,000 to invest. Based on an evaluation of the client's risk tolerance, Williams has assigned a maximum risk index of 0.05 for the client. The firm's risk indicators show the risk of the growth fund at 0.10, the income fund at 0.07, and the money market fund at 0.01. An overall portfolio risk index is computed as a weighted average of the risk rating for the three funds where the weights are the fraction of the client's portfolio invested in each of the funds.

Additionally, Williams is currently forecasting annual yields of 18% for the growth fund, 12.5% for the income fund, and 7.5% for the money market fund. Based on the information provided, how should the new client be advised to allocate the $800,000 among the growth, income, and money market funds? Develop a linear programming model that will provide the maximum yield for the portfolio. Use your model to develop a managerial report as described next.

Managerial Report

1. Recommend how much of the $800,000 should be invested in each of the three funds. What is the annual yield you anticipate for the investment recommendation?
2. Assume that the client's risk index could be increased to 0.055. How much would the yield increase and how would the investment recommendation change?

3. Refer again to the original situation where the client's risk index was assessed to be 0.05. How would your investment recommendation change if the annual yield for the growth fund were revised downward to 16% or even to 14%?
4. Assume that the client has expressed some concern about having too much money in the growth fund. How would the original recommendation change if the amount invested in the growth fund is not allowed to exceed the amount invested in the income fund?
5. The asset allocation model you have developed may be useful in modifying the portfolios for all the firm's clients whenever the anticipated yields for the three funds are periodically revised. What is your recommendation as to whether this modification is possible?

Case Problem: TEXTILE MILL SCHEDULING

The Scottsville Textile Mill* produces five different fabrics. Each fabric can be woven on one or more of the mill's 38 looms. The sales department has forecast demand for the next month. The demand data are shown in Table 9.18, along with data on the selling price per yard, variable cost per yard, and purchase price per yard. The mill operates 24 hours a day and is scheduled for 30 days during the coming month.

The mill has two types of looms: dobbie and regular. The dobbie looms are more versatile and can be used for all five fabrics. The regular looms can produce only three of the fabrics. There are a total of 38 looms—8 dobbie and 30 regular. The rate of production for each fabric on each type of loom is given in Table 9.19. The time required to change over from producing one fabric to another is negligible and does not have to be considered.

The Scottsville Textile Mill satisfies all demand with either its own fabric or fabric purchased from another mill. That is, fabrics that cannot be woven at the Scottsville Mill because of limited loom capacity will be purchased from another mill. The purchase price of each fabric is also shown in Table 9.18.

Table 9.18 MONTHLY DEMAND, SELLING PRICE, VARIABLE COST, AND PURCHASE PRICE DATA FOR SCOTTSVILLE TEXTILE MILL FABRICS

Fabric	Demand (yards)	Selling Price ($/yard)	Variable Cost ($/yard)	Purchase Price ($/yard)
1	16,500	0.99	0.66	0.80
2	22,000	0.86	0.55	0.70
3	62,000	1.10	0.49	0.60
4	7,500	1.24	0.51	0.70
5	62,000	0.70	0.50	0.70

*This case is based on the Calhoun Textile Mill Case by Jeffrey D. Camm, P.M. Dearing, and Suresh K. Tadisnia, 1987.

Table 9.19	LOOM PRODUCTION RATES FOR THE SCOTTSVILLE TEXTILE MILL

	Loom Rate (yards/hour)	
Fabric	Dobbie	Regular
1	4.63	—
2	4.63	—
3	5.23	5.23
4	5.23	5.23
5	4.17	4.17

Note: Fabrics 1 and 2 can be manufactured only on the dobbie loom.

Managerial Report

Develop a model that can be used to schedule production for the Scottsville Textile Mill, and at the same time, determine how many yards of each fabric must be purchased from another mill. Include a discussion and analysis of the following items in your report.

1. The final production schedule and loom assignments for each fabric.
2. The projected total contribution to profit.
3. A discussion of the value of additional loom time. The mill is considering purchasing a ninth dobbie loom. What is your estimate of the monthly profit contribution of this additional loom?
4. A discussion of the ranges for the objective function coefficients.
5. A discussion of how the objective of minimizing total costs would provide a different model than the objective of maximizing total profit contribution. How would the interpretation of the ranges for the objective function coefficients differ for these two models?

Appendix 9.1 SPREADSHEET SOLUTION OF LINEAR PROGRAMS

In Appendix 8.3 we showed how Excel can be used to solve the RMC linear programming problem. To illustrate the use of Excel in solving a more complex linear programming problem, we show the solution to the Hewlitt Corporation financial planning problem presented in Section 9.2.

First, the data that represent the objective function and the constraints must be entered into a spreadsheet. Second, cells must be identified for storing the values of the decision variables, the value for the objective function, and the values of the left-hand sides of the constraints. Third, formulas must be written to show how the values for the left-hand sides of the constraints can be computed given the input data values and the values of the decision variables. Figure 9.15 shows the formula spreadsheet for the Hewlitt financial planning problem after completing these three steps. The decision variable values are stored in cells B5:M5, the value of the objective function is stored in cell B5, and cells N6:N13 show the formulas for the left-hand sides of the constraints

Figure 9.15 FORMULA SPREADSHEET FOR THE HEWLITT CORPORATION FINANCIAL PLANNING PROBLEM

	A	B	C	D	E	F	G	H	I	J	K	L	M	N	O
1		Funds	Gov't	Gov't	Gov't	Savings	Savings	Savings	Savings	Savings	Savings	Savings	Savings		
2		Required	Bond 1	Bond 2	Bond 3	Year 1	Year 2	Year 3	Year 4	Year 5	Year 6	Year 7	Year 8		
3		F	B1	B2	B3	S1	S2	S3	S4	S5	S6	S7	S8		
4															Cash
5														Cash Available	Req'd.
6	Year 1	1	-1.15	-1	-1.35	-1								=SUMPRODUCT(B$5:M$5,B6:M6)	430
7	Year 2		0.08875	0.055	0.1175	1.04	-1							=SUMPRODUCT(B$5:M$5,B7:M7)	210
8	Year 3		0.08875	0.055	0.1175		1.04	-1						=SUMPRODUCT(B$5:M$5,B8:M8)	222
9	Year 4		0.08875	0.055	0.1175			1.04	-1					=SUMPRODUCT(B$5:M$5,B9:M9)	231
10	Year 5		0.08875	0.055	0.1175				1.04	-1				=SUMPRODUCT(B$5:M$5,B10:M10)	240
11	Year 6		1.08875	0.055	0.1175					1.04	-1			=SUMPRODUCT(B$5:M$5,B11:M11)	195
12	Year 7			1.055	0.1175						1.04	-1		=SUMPRODUCT(B$5:M$5,B12:M12)	225
13	Year 8				1.1175							1.04	-1	=SUMPRODUCT(B$5:M$5,B13:M13)	255

The **SUMPRODUCT** function is used for cells **N6:N13**. For instance, cell **N6** contains the formula = SUMPRODUCT(B$5:M$5,B6:M6). This formula multiplies the values of the decision variables by the coefficients in the first constraint and adds them. Similar formula are used for cells **N7** through **N13**.

We are now ready to use the information in the spreadsheet to determine an optimal solution to the Hewlitt financial planning problem. The following steps describe how to use Excel Solver to obtain an optimal solution.

Step 1. Select the **Tools** pull-down menu

Step 2. Select the **Solver** option

Step 3. When the **Solver Parameters** dialog box appears
      Enter B5 in the **Set Target Cell** box
      Select the **Min** option
      Enter B5:M5 in the **By Changing Cells** box
      Choose **Add**

Step 4. When the **Add Constraint** dialog box appears
      Enter N6:N13 in the **Cell Reference** box
      Select =
      Enter O6:O13 in the **Constraint** box
      Choose **Add**
      Enter C5:M5 in the **Cell Reference** box
      Select > =
      Enter 0 in the **Constraint** box
      Select **OK**

Step 5. When the **Solver Parameters** dialog box appears
      Choose **Options**

Step 6. When the **Solver Options** dialog box appears
      Select **Assume Linear Model** box
      Select **OK**

Step 7. When the **Solver Parameters** dialog box appears
      Choose **Solve**

Step 8. When the **Solver Results** dialog box appears
      Select **Keep Solver Solution**
      Select **OK** to produce the optimal solution output

Figure 9.16 SPREADSHEET SOLUTION FOR THE HEWLITT CORPORATION FINANCIAL PLANNING PROBLEM

	A	B	C	D	E	F	G	H	I	J	K	L	M	N	O
1		Funds	Gov't	Gov't	Gov't	Savings	Savings	Savings	Savings	Savings	Savings	Savings	Savings		
2		Required	Bond 1	Bond 2	Bond 3	Year 1	Year 2	Year 3	Year 4	Year 5	Year 6	Year 7	Year 8		
3		F	G1	G2	G3	S1	S2	S3	S4	S5	S6	S7	S8		
4														Cash	Cash
5		1728.794	144.988	187.855	228.1879	636.1479	501.6057	349.6818	182.680	0	0	0	0	Available	Req'd.
6	Year 1	1	−1.15	−1	−1.35	−1								430	430
7	Year 2		0.08875	0.055	0.1175	1.04	−1							210	210
8	Year 3		0.08875	0.055	0.1175		1.04	−1						222	222
9	Year 4		0.08875	0.055	0.1175			1.04	−1					231	231
10	Year 5		0.08875	0.055	0.1175				1.04	−1				240	240
11	Year 6		1.08875	1.055	0.1175					1.04	−1			195	195
12	Year 7			1.055	0.1175						1.04	−1		225	225
13	Year 8				1.1175							1.04	−1	255	255

Figure 9.16 shows the optimal solution output. Except for some minor rounding differences, it is the same as the solution provided by The Management Scientist (see Figure 9.4). In addition to the solution shown in Figure 9.16, Excel Solver also provides options to obtain a variety of sensitivity analysis information. This information can be obtained by making appropriate selections from the Solver Results dialog box.

MARATHON OIL COMPANY*

FINDLAY, OHIO

Marathon Oil Company was founded in 1887 when 14 oilmen pooled their properties to organize an oil-producing company in the Trenton Rock oil fields of Ohio. In 1924 Marathon entered the refining and marketing phase of the petroleum industry. Today Marathon is a fully integrated oil company with significant international operations. In the United States the company markets petroleum products in 21 states, primarily in the Midwest and Southeast. Marathon is a unit of USX.

Quantitative Methods at Marathon Oil Company

Marathon Oil's Operations Research Department was formed in 1963 in order to aid problem solving and decision making in all areas of the company. Approximately 50% of the applications involve linear programming. Typical problems include refinery models, distribution models, gasoline and fuel oil blending models, and crude oil evaluation studies. Another 30% of the applications involve complex chemical engineering simulation models of process operations. The remaining applications involve solution techniques using nonlinear programming, network flow algorithms, and statistical techniques such as regression analysis.

A Marketing Planning Model

Marathon Oil Company has four refineries within the United States, operates 50 light products terminals, and has product demand at over 95 locations. The Supply and Transportation Division is faced with the problem of determining which refinery should supply which terminal and, at the same time, determining which products should be transported via which pipeline, barge, or tanker to minimize cost. Product demand must be satisfied, and the supply capability of each refinery must not be exceeded. To help solve this difficult problem, Marathon's Operations Research Department developed a marketing planning model for the Operations Planning Department.

The marketing planning model is a large-scale linear programming model that takes into account sales not only at Marathon product terminals but also at all exchange locations. An exchange contract is an agreement with other oil product marketers that involves exchanging or trading Marathon's products for theirs at different locations. Thus, some geographic imbalance between supply and demand can be reduced. Both sides of the exchanges are represented since this not only affects the net requirements at a demand location, but in addition has important financial implications. All pipelines, barges, and tankers within Marathon's marketing area are also represented in the linear programming model. The objective of the linear programming model is to minimize the cost of meeting a given demand structure, taking into account sales price, pipeline tariffs, exchange contract costs, product demand, terminal operating costs, refining costs, and product purchases.

The marketing planning model is used to solve a wide variety of planning problems. These vary from evaluating gasoline blending economics to analyzing the economics of a new terminal or pipeline. Although the types of problems that can be solved are almost unlimited, the model is most effective in handling the following:

*The authors are indebted to Robert W. Wernert of Marathon Oil Company, Findlay, Ohio, for providing this application.

1. Evaluating additional product demand locations, pipelines, and exchange contracts
2. Determining profitability of shifting sales from one product demand location to another
3. Determining the effects on supply and distribution when a pipeline increases its tariff
4. Optimizing production of the grades at the five refineries based on distribution

The linear programming model not only solves these problems, but also gives the financial impact of each solution.

Benefits

With daily sales of about 10 million gallons of refined light product, a savings of even one-thousandth of a cent per gallon can result in significant long-term savings. At the same time, what may appear to be a savings in one area, such as refining or transportation, may actually add to overall costs when the effects are fully realized throughout the system. The marketing planning model allows a simultaneous examination of this total effect.

Questions

1. What is the primary objective of Marathon's marketing planning model?
2. Describe the types of problems the marketing planning model is most effective in handling.
3. If daily savings using the model are one-tenth of a cent per gallon sold, what is the projected daily savings?

10

TRANSPORTATION, ASSIGNMENT, AND

TRANSSHIPMENT PROBLEMS

Transportation, assignment, and transshipment problems belong to a special class of linear programming problems called *network flow problems*. A separate chapter is devoted to these problems for two reasons. First, a wide variety of applications can be modeled as transportation, assignment, or transshipment problems. Second, these problems have a mathematical structure that has enabled management scientists to develop efficient specialized solution procedures for solving them; as a result, even large problems can be solved with just a few seconds of computer time.

We approach the network flow problems by illustrating each problem with a specific application. We first develop a graphical representation, called a **network**, of the problem and then show how each can be formulated and solved as a linear program.

··/ /············

10.1   THE TRANSPORTATION PROBLEM: THE NETWORK MODEL AND A LINEAR PROGRAMMING FORMULATION

The **transportation problem** arises frequently in planning for the distribution of goods and services from several supply locations to several demand locations. Typically, the quantity of goods available at each supply location (origin) is limited, and the quantity of goods needed at each of several demand locations (destinations) is known. The usual objective in a transportation problem is to minimize the cost of shipping goods from the origins to the destinations.

Let us illustrate by considering a transportation problem faced by Foster Generators. This problem involves the transportation of a product from three plants to four distribution centers. Foster Generators has plants in Cleveland, Ohio; Bedford, Indiana; and York, Pennsylvania. Production capacities over the next 3-month planning period for one particular type of generator are as follows:

Origin	Plant	3-Month Production Capacity (units)
1	Cleveland	5,000
2	Bedford	6,000
3	York	2,500
	Total	13,500

The firm distributes its generators through four regional distribution centers located in Boston, Chicago, St. Louis, and Lexington; the 3-month forecast of demand for the distribution centers is as follows:

Destination	Distribution Center	3-Month Demand Forecast (units)
1	Boston	6,000
2	Chicago	4,000
3	St. Louis	2,000
4	Lexington	1,500
	Total	13,500

Management would like to determine how much of its production should be shipped from each plant to each distribution center. Figure 10.1 shows graphically the 12 distribution routes Foster can use. Such a graph is called a *network;* the circles are referred to as **nodes** and the lines connecting the nodes as **arcs.** Each origin and destination is represented by a node, and each possible shipping route is represented by an arc. The amount of the supply is written next to each origin node, and the amount of the demand is written next to each destination node.

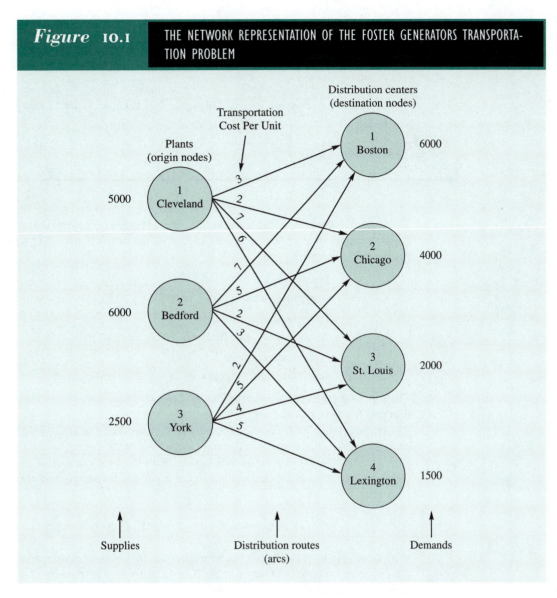

Figure 10.1　THE NETWORK REPRESENTATION OF THE FOSTER GENERATORS TRANSPORTATION PROBLEM

The goods shipped from the origins to the destinations represent the flow in the network. Note that the direction of flow (from origin to destination) is indicated by the arrows.

Try Problem 1 for practice in developing a network model of a transportation problem.

For Foster's transportation problem, the objective is to determine the routes to be used and the quantity to be shipped via each route that will provide the minimum total transportation cost. The cost for each unit shipped on each route is given in Table 10.1 and is shown on each arc in Figure 10.1.

The first subscript identifies the "from" node of the corresponding arc and the second subscript identifies the "to" node of the arc.

A linear programming model can be used to solve this transportation problem. We use double-subscripted decision variables, with x_{11} denoting the number of units shipped from origin 1 (Cleveland) to destination 1 (Boston), x_{12} denoting the number of units shipped from origin 1 (Cleveland) to destination 2 (Chicago), and so on. In general, the decision variables for a transportation problem having m origins and n destinations are written as follows:

$$x_{ij} = \text{number of units shipped from origin } i \text{ to destination } j$$
$$\text{where } i = 1, 2, \ldots, m \text{ and } j = 1, 2, \ldots, n$$

Table 10.1	TRANSPORTATION COST PER UNIT FOR THE FOSTER GENERATORS TRANSPORTATION PROBLEM

| | **Destination** | | | |
Origin	Boston	Chicago	St. Louis	Lexington
Cleveland	3	2	7	6
Bedford	7	5	2	3
York	2	5	4	5

Since the objective of the transportation problem is to minimize the total transportation cost, we can use the cost data in Table 10.1 or on the arcs in Figure 10.1 to develop the following cost expressions:

Transportation costs for
units shipped from Cleveland $= 3x_{11} + 2x_{12} + 7x_{13} + 6x_{14}$

Transportation costs for
units shipped from Bedford $= 7x_{21} + 5x_{22} + 2x_{23} + 3x_{24}$

Transportation costs for
units shipped from York $= 2x_{31} + 5x_{32} + 4x_{33} + 5x_{34}$

The sum of these expressions provides the objective function showing the total transportation cost for Foster Generators.

Transportation problems need constraints because each origin has a limited supply and each destination has a specific demand. We consider the supply constraints first. The capacity at the Cleveland plant is 5000 units. With the total number of units shipped from the Cleveland plant expressed as $x_{11} + x_{12} + x_{13} + x_{14}$, the supply constraint for the Cleveland plant is

$$x_{11} + x_{12} + x_{13} + x_{14} \leq 5000 \quad \text{Cleveland supply}$$

With three origins (plants), the Foster transportation problem has three supply constraints. Given the capacity of 6000 units at the Bedford plant and 2500 units at the York plant, the two additional supply constraints are

$$x_{21} + x_{22} + x_{23} + x_{24} \leq 6000 \quad \text{Bedford supply}$$
$$x_{31} + x_{32} + x_{33} + x_{34} \leq 2500 \quad \text{York supply}$$

With the four distribution centers as the destinations, four demand constraints are needed to ensure that destination demands will be satisfied:

$$x_{11} + x_{21} + x_{31} = 6000 \quad \text{Boston demand}$$
$$x_{12} + x_{22} + x_{32} = 4000 \quad \text{Chicago demand}$$
$$x_{13} + x_{23} + x_{33} = 2000 \quad \text{St. Louis demand}$$
$$x_{14} + x_{24} + x_{34} = 1500 \quad \text{Lexington demand}$$

Combining the objective function and constraints into one model provides a 12-variable, 7-constraint linear programming formulation of the Foster Generators transportation problem:

To obtain a feasible solution, the total supply must be greater than or equal to the total demand.

$$\text{Min} \quad 3x_{11} + 2x_{12} + 7x_{13} + 6x_{14} + 7x_{21} + 5x_{22} + 2x_{23} + 3x_{24} + 2x_{31} + 5x_{32} + 4x_{33} + 5x_{34}$$

s.t.

$$
\begin{array}{llllll}
x_{11} + x_{12} + x_{13} + x_{14} & & & \leq 5000 \\
& x_{21} + x_{22} + x_{23} + x_{24} & & \leq 6000 \\
& & x_{31} + x_{32} + x_{33} + x_{34} & \leq 2500 \\
x_{11} & + x_{21} & + x_{31} & = 6000 \\
\quad x_{12} & + x_{22} & + x_{32} & = 4000 \\
\quad\quad x_{13} & + x_{23} & + x_{33} & = 2000 \\
\quad\quad\quad x_{14} & + x_{24} & + x_{34} & = 1500 \\
\end{array}
$$

$$x_{ij} \geq 0 \quad \text{for } i = 1, 2, 3 \text{ and } j = 1, 2, 3, 4$$

You should now be able to use the computer to solve a linear programming model of a transportation problem. Try Problem 2.

Comparing the linear programming formulation to the network in Figure 10.1 leads to several observations. All the information needed for the linear programming formulation is on the network. Each node has one constraint, and each arc has one variable. The sum of the variables corresponding to arcs from an origin node must be less than or equal to the origin's supply, and the sum of the variables corresponding to the arcs into a destination node must be equal to the destination's demand.

We solved the Foster Generators problem with the linear programming module of The Management Scientist. The computer solution (see Figure 10.2) shows that the minimum total transportation cost is $39,500. The values for the decision variables show the optimal amounts to ship over each route. For example, with $x_{11} = 3500$, 3500 units should be shipped from Cleveland to Boston, and with $x_{12} = 1500$, 1500 units should be shipped from Cleveland to Chicago. Other values of the decision variables indicate the remaining shipping quantities and routes. Table 10.2 shows the minimum-cost transportation schedule and Figure 10.3 summarizes the optimal solution on the network.

Figure 10.2 THE MANAGEMENT SCIENTIST SOLUTION FOR THE FOSTER GENERATORS TRANSPORTATION PROBLEM

Objective Function Value =   39500.000

Variable	Value	Reduced Costs
X11	3500.000	0.000
X12	1500.000	0.000
X13	0.000	8.000
X14	0.000	6.000
X21	0.000	1.000
X22	2500.000	0.000
X23	2000.000	0.000
X24	1500.000	0.000
X31	2500.000	0.000
X32	0.000	4.000
X33	0.000	6.000
X34	0.000	6.000

Table 10.2		OPTIMAL SOLUTION TO THE FOSTER GENERATORS TRANSPORTATION PROBLEM		
Route		**Units**	**Cost**	**Total**
From	**To**	**Shipped**	**Per Unit**	**Cost**
Cleveland	Boston	3500	$3	$10,500
Cleveland	Chicago	1500	$2	3,000
Bedford	Chicago	2500	$5	12,500
Bedford	St. Louis	2000	$2	4,000
Bedford	Lexington	1500	$3	4,500
York	Boston	2500	$2	5,000
				$39,500

Figure 10.3   OPTIMAL SOLUTION TO THE FOSTER GENERATORS TRANSPORTATION PROBLEM

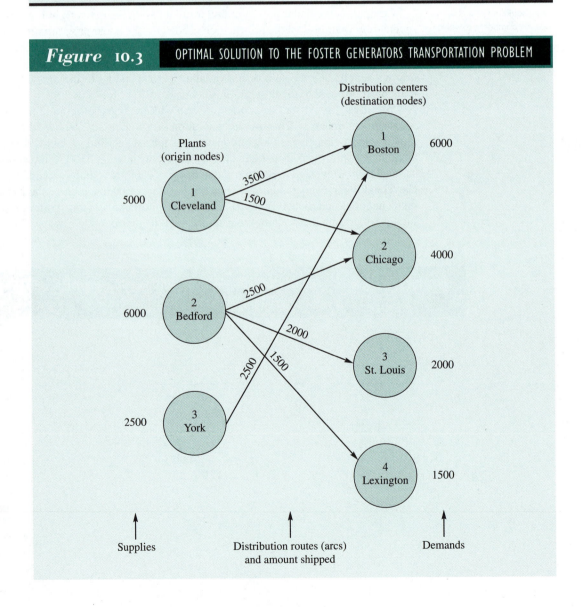

Problem Variations

The Foster Generators problem illustrates use of the basic transportation model. Variations of the basic transportation problem may involve one or more of the following situations:

1. total supply not equal to total demand
2. maximization objective function
3. route capacities or route minimums
4. unacceptable routes

With slight modifications in the linear programming model, you can easily accommodate these situations.

Total Supply Not Equal to Total Demand   Often *the total supply is not equal to the total demand*. If total supply exceeds total demand, no modification in the linear programming formulation is necessary. Excess supply will appear as slack in the linear programming solution. Slack for any particular origin can be interpreted as the unused supply or amount not shipped from the origin.

> Whenever total supply is less than total demand, the model does not determine how the unsatisfied demand is handled (e.g., backorders). The manager must handle this aspect of the problem.

If total supply is less than total demand, the linear programming model of a transportation problem will not have a feasible solution. In this case, we modify the network representation by adding a **dummy origin** with a supply equal to the difference between the total demand and the total supply. With the addition of the dummy origin, and an arc from the dummy origin to each destination, the linear programming model will have a feasible solution. A zero cost per unit is assigned to each arc leaving the dummy origin so that the value of the optimal solution for the revised problem will represent the shipping cost for the units actually shipped (no shipments actually will be made from the dummy origin). When the optimal solution is implemented, the destinations showing shipments being received from the dummy origin will be the destinations experiencing a shortfall or unsatisfied demand.

> Try Problem 8 to see whether you can handle a case where demand is greater than supply with a maximization objective.

Maximization Objective Function   In some transportation problems, the objective is to find a solution that maximizes profit or revenue. Using the values for profit or revenue per unit as coefficients in the objective function, we simply solve a maximization rather than a minimization linear program. This change does not affect the constraints.

Route Capacities and/or Route Minimums   The linear programming formulation of the transportation problem also can accommodate capacities and/or minimum quantities for one or more of the routes. For example, suppose that in the Foster Generators problem the York–Boston route (origin 3 to destination 1) had a capacity of 1000 units because of limited space availability on its normal mode of transportation. With x_{31} denoting the amount shipped from York to Boston, the route capacity constraint for the York–Boston route would be

$$x_{31} \leq 1000$$

Similarly, route minimums can be specified. For example,

$$x_{22} \geq 2000$$

would guarantee that a previously committed order for a Bedford–Chicago delivery of at least 2000 units would be maintained in the optimal solution.

Unacceptable Routes   Finally, establishing a route from every origin to every destination may not be possible. To handle this situation, we simply drop the corresponding arc from the network and remove the corresponding variable from the linear programming formulation. For example, if the Cleveland–St. Louis route were unacceptable or unusable, the arc from Cleveland to St. Louis could be dropped in Figure 10.1, and x_{13} could be removed from the linear programming formulation. Solving the resulting 11-variable, 7-constraint model would provide the optimal solution while guaranteeing that the Cleveland–St. Louis route is not used.

A General Linear Programming Model of the Transportation Problem

To show the general linear programming model of the transportation problem, we use the notation:

$$i = \text{index for origins, } i = 1, 2, \ldots, m$$
$$j = \text{index for destinations, } j = 1, 2, \ldots, n$$
$$x_{ij} = \text{number of units shipped from origin } i \text{ to destination } j$$
$$c_{ij} = \text{cost per unit of shipping from origin } i \text{ to destination } j$$
$$s_i = \text{supply or capacity in units at origin } i$$
$$d_j = \text{demand in units at destination } j$$

The general linear programming model of the m-origin, n-destination transportation problem is

$$\text{Min} \quad \sum_{i=1}^{m} \sum_{j=1}^{n} c_{ij} x_{ij}$$

s.t.

$$\sum_{j=1}^{n} x_{ij} \leq s_i \qquad i = 1, 2, \ldots, m \quad \text{Supply}$$

$$\sum_{i=1}^{m} x_{ij} = d_j \qquad j = 1, 2, \ldots, n \quad \text{Demand}$$

$$x_{ij} \geq 0 \qquad \text{for all } i \text{ and } j$$

As mentioned previously, we can add additional constraints of the form $x_{ij} \leq L_{ij}$ if the route from origin i to destination j has capacity L_{ij}. A transportation problem that includes constraints of this type is called a **capacitated transportation problem.** Similarly, we can add route minimum constraints of the form $x_{ij} \geq M_{ij}$ if the route from origin i to destination j must handle at least M_{ij} units.

<table>
<tr><td>

N O T E S
and Comments

</td><td>

1. Transportation problems encountered in practice usually lead to very large linear programs. Transportation problems with 100 origins and 100 destinations are not unusual. Such a problem would involve $(100)(100) = 10,000$ variables. For such a problem, special-purpose solution procedures are much more efficient than general-purpose linear programming codes. But if speed is not an issue, a general-purpose linear programming code that has the capability to solve large problems will solve most transportation problems.

2. To handle a situation in which some routes may be unacceptable, we stated that you could drop the corresponding arc from the network and remove the corresponding variable from the linear programming formulation. Another approach often used is to assign an extremely large objective function cost coefficient to any unacceptable arc. If the problem has already been formulated, another option is to add a constraint to the formulation that sets the variable you want to remove equal to zero.

3. The optimal solution to a transportation model will consist of integer values for the decision variables as long as all supply and demand values are integers. The reason is the special mathematical structure of the linear programming model. Each variable appears in exactly one supply and one demand constraint, and all coefficients in the constraint equations are 1 or 0.

4. Although many transportation problems involve minimizing the cost of transporting goods between locations, many other applications of the transportation model exist. The Q. M. in Action: Marine Corps Mobilization illustrates the use of a transportation model to send Marine Corps officers to billets.

</td></tr>
</table>

Q.M. IN ACTION

MARINE CORPS MOBILIZATION*

The U.S. Marine Corps has developed a network model for mobilizing its officers in the event of a world crisis or war. The problem is to send officers to billets (duty assignments) as quickly as possible. The model developed to solve this problem is a transportation model much like the ones discussed in this chapter, only much larger. The origins or supply nodes represent the officers available, and the destinations or demand nodes represent the billets. A realistic implementation might involve as many as 40,000 officers and 25,000 billets. If all officer-to-billets arc combinations are permitted, the transportation problem would have 1 billion arcs. To reduce the problem size, officers with similar qualifications are aggregated into the same supply node and similar duty assignments are aggregated into the same demand nodes. Using this approach and methods for eliminating infeasible arcs, the Marine Corps has solved problems involving 27,000 officers and 10,000 billets in 10 seconds on a personal computer.

Excellent results in sending officers of appropriate grade and job qualifications to the desired billets have been obtained. In a crisis, the availability and use of this system can make the difference between an appropriate response and disaster. The prior system required 2–4 days to produce a complete mobilization plan and provided a lower quality match between officer qualifications and billet needs. The Marine Corps is now using the mobilization model to enhance its peace-time capability.

*Based on Bausch, D. O., G. G. Brown, D. R. Hundley, S. H. Rapp, and R. E. Rosenthal, "Mobilizing Marine Corps Officers." *Interfaces,* July–August 1991, pp. 26–38.

10.2 THE ASSIGNMENT PROBLEM: THE NETWORK MODEL AND A LINEAR PROGRAMMING FORMULATION

The **assignment problem** arises in a variety of decision-making situations; typical assignment problems involve assigning jobs to machines, agents to tasks, sales personnel to sales territories, contracts to bidders, and so on. A distinguishing feature of the assignment problem is that *one* agent is assigned to *one and only one* task. Specifically, we look for the set of assignments that will optimize a stated objective, such as minimize cost, minimize time, or maximize profits.

To illustrate the assignment problem, let us consider the case of Fowle Marketing Research, which has just received requests for market research studies from three new clients. The company faces the task of assigning a project leader (agent) to each client (task). Currently, three individuals have no other commitments and are available for the project leader assignments. Fowle's management realizes, however, that the time required to complete each study will depend on the experience and ability of the project leader assigned. The three projects have approximately the same priority, and management wants to assign project leaders to minimize the total number of days required to complete all three projects. If a project leader is to be assigned to one client only, what assignments should be made?

To answer the assignment question, Fowle's management must first consider all possible project leader–client assignments and then estimate the corresponding project completion times. With three project leaders and three clients, nine assignment alternatives are possible. The alternatives and the estimated project completion times in days are summarized in Table 10.3.

Try part (a) of Problem 12 to see whether you can develop a network model for an assignment problem.

Figure 10.4 shows the network representation of Fowle's assignment problem. The nodes correspond to the project leaders and clients, and the arcs represent the possible assignments of project leaders to clients. The supply at each origin node and the demand at each destination node are 1; the cost of assigning a project leader to a client is the time it takes that project leader to complete the client's task. Note the similarity between the network models of the assignment problem (Figure 10.4) and the transportation problem (Figure 10.1). The assignment problem is a special case of the transportation problem in which all supply and demand values equal 1, and the amount shipped over each arc is either 0 or 1.

Since the assignment problem is a special case of the transportation problem, a linear programming formulation can be developed. Again, we need a constraint for each node and a variable for each arc. As in the transportation problem, we use double-subscripted decision variables, with x_{11} denoting the assignment of project leader 1 (Terry) to client 1, x_{12} denoting the assignment of project leader 1 (Terry) to client 2, and so on. Thus, we define the decision variables for Fowle's assignment problem as

$$x_{ij} = \begin{cases} 1 \text{ if project leader } i \text{ is assigned to client } j \\ 0 \text{ otherwise} \end{cases}$$

where $i = 1, 2, 3$, and $j = 1, 2, 3$

Table 10.3	ESTIMATED PROJECT COMPLETION TIMES (DAYS) FOR THE FOWLE MARKETING RESEARCH ASSIGNMENT PROBLEM		
		Client	
Project Leader	**1**	**2**	**3**
1. Terry	10	15	9
2. Carle	9	18	5
3. McClymonds	6	14	3

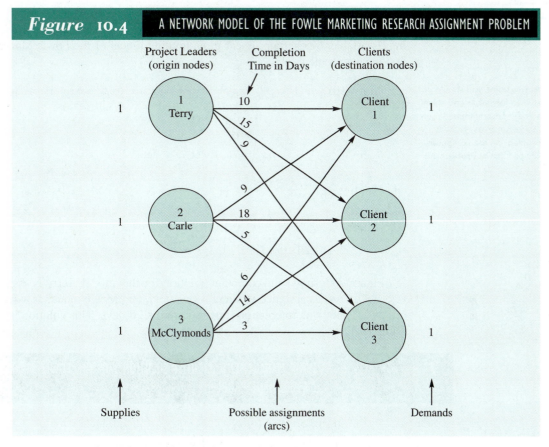

Figure 10.4 A NETWORK MODEL OF THE FOWLE MARKETING RESEARCH ASSIGNMENT PROBLEM

Using this notation and the completion time data in Table 10.3, we develop completion time expressions:

Days required for Terry's assignment $= 10x_{11} + 15x_{12} + 9x_{13}$
Days required for Carle's assignment $= 9x_{21} + 18x_{22} + 5x_{23}$
Days required for McClymonds's assignment $= 6x_{31} + 14x_{32} + 3x_{33}$

The sum of the completion times for the three project leaders will provide the total days required to complete the three assignments. Thus, the objective function is

$$\text{Min} \quad 10x_{11} + 15x_{12} + 9x_{13} + 9x_{21} + 18x_{22} + 5x_{23} + 6x_{31} + 14x_{32} + 3x_{33}$$

The constraints for the assignment problem reflect the conditions that each project leader can be assigned to at most one client and that each client must have one assigned project leader. These constraints are written as follows:

$$x_{11} + x_{12} + x_{13} \leq 1 \quad \text{Terry's assignment}$$
$$x_{21} + x_{22} + x_{23} \leq 1 \quad \text{Carle's assignment}$$
$$x_{31} + x_{32} + x_{33} \leq 1 \quad \text{McClymonds's assignment}$$
$$x_{11} + x_{21} + x_{31} = 1 \quad \text{Client 1}$$
$$x_{12} + x_{22} + x_{32} = 1 \quad \text{Client 2}$$
$$x_{13} + x_{23} + x_{33} = 1 \quad \text{Client 3}$$

Since the number of project leaders equals the number of clients, all the constraints could be written as equalites. But when the number of project leaders exceeds the number of clients, less-than-or-equal-to constraints must be used for the project leader constraints.

Note that there is one constraint for each node in Figure 10.4.

Combining the objective function and constraints into one model provides the following 9-variable, 6-constraint linear programming model of the Fowle Marketing Research assignment problem.

At this point, you should be able to formulate and solve a linear programming model for an assignment problem on the computer. Try part (b) of Problem 12.

$$\text{Min} \quad 10x_{11} + 15x_{12} + 9x_{13} + 9x_{21} + 18x_{22} + 5x_{23} + 6x_{31} + 14x_{32} + 3x_{33}$$

s.t.

$$
\begin{array}{rcl}
x_{11} + x_{12} + x_{13} & & \leq 1 \\
x_{21} + x_{22} + x_{23} & & \leq 1 \\
x_{31} + x_{32} + x_{33} & \leq 1 \\
x_{11} \quad\quad + x_{21} \quad\quad + x_{31} & & = 1 \\
x_{12} \quad\quad + x_{22} \quad\quad + x_{32} & & = 1 \\
x_{13} \quad\quad + x_{23} \quad\quad + x_{33} & = 1 \\
\end{array}
$$

$$x_{ij} \geq 0 \quad \text{for } i = 1, 2, 3; j = 1, 2, 3$$

Figure 10.5 shows the computer solution for this model. Terry is assigned to client 2 ($x_{12} = 1$), Carle is assigned to client 3 ($x_{23} = 1$), and McClymonds is assigned to client 1 ($x_{31} = 1$). The total completion time required is 26 days. This solution is summarized in Table 10.4.

Figure 10.5 THE MANAGEMENT SCIENTIST SOLUTION FOR THE FOWLE MARKETING RESEARCH ASSIGNMENT PROBLEM

```
Objective Function Value =              26.000

        Variable            Value              Reduced Costs
     --------------    ---------------     -------------------
          X11             0.000                  0.000
          X12             1.000                  0.000
          X13             0.000                  3.000
          X21             0.000                  0.000
          X22             0.000                  4.000
          X23             1.000                  0.000
          X31             1.000                  0.000
          X32             0.000                  3.000
          X33             0.000                  1.000
```

Table 10.4 OPTIMAL PROJECT LEADER ASSIGNMENTS FOR THE FOWLE MARKETING RESEARCH ASSIGNMENT PROBLEM

Project Leader	Assigned Client	Days
Terry	2	15
Carle	3	5
McClymonds	1	6
		Total 26

Problem Variations

Because the assignment problem can be viewed as a special case of the transportation problem, the problem variations that may arise in an assignment problem parallel those for the transportation problem. Specifically, we can handle

1. total number of agents (supply) not equal to the total number of tasks (demand)
2. a maximization objective function
3. unacceptable assignments

In the linear programming formulation of a problem with five clients and only three project leaders, we could get by with one dummy project leader by placing a 2 on the right-hand side of the constraint for the dummy project leader.

The situation in which the number of agents does not equal the number of tasks is analogous to total supply not equaling total demand in a transportation problem. If the number of agents exceeds the number of tasks, the extra agents simply remain unassigned in the linear programming model. If the number of tasks exceeds the number of agents, the linear programming model will not have a feasible solution. In this situation, a simple modification is to add enough dummy agents to equalize the number of agents and the number of tasks. For instance, in the Fowle problem we might have had five clients (tasks) and only three project leaders (agents). By adding two dummy project leaders, we can create a new assignment problem with the number of project leaders equal to the number of clients. The objective function coefficients for the assignment of dummy project leaders would be zero so that the value of the optimal solution would represent the total number of days required by the assignments actually made (no assignments will actually be made to the clients receiving dummy project leaders).

If the assignment alternatives are evaluated in terms of revenue or profit rather than time or cost, the linear programming formulation can be solved as a maximization rather than a minimization problem. In addition, if one or more assignments are unacceptable, the corresponding decision variable can be removed from the linear programming formulation. This situation could happen, for example, if an agent did not have the experience necessary for one or more of the tasks.

A General Linear Programming Model of the Assignment Problem

The general assignment problem involves m agents and n tasks. If we let $x_{ij} = 1$ or 0 according to whether agent i is assigned to task j or not, and if c_{ij} denotes the cost of assigning agent i to task j, we can write the general assignment model as

$$\text{Min} \quad \sum_{i=1}^{m} \sum_{j=1}^{n} c_{ij} x_{ij}$$

s.t.

$$\sum_{j=1}^{n} x_{ij} \leq 1 \qquad i = 1, 2, \ldots, m \qquad \text{Agents}$$

$$\sum_{i=1}^{m} x_{ij} = 1 \qquad j = 1, 2, \ldots, n \qquad \text{Tasks}$$

$$x_{ij} \geq 0 \qquad \text{for all } i \text{ and } j$$

Multiple Assignments

At the beginning of this section, we indicated that a distinguishing feature of the assignment problem is that *one* agent is assigned to *one and only one* task. In generalizations of the assignment problem where one agent can be assigned to two or more tasks, the linear programming formulation of the problem can be easily modified. For example, let us assume that in the Fowle Marketing Research problem Terry could be assigned up to two clients; in this case, the constraint representing Terry's assignment would be $x_{11} + x_{12} + x_{13} \leq 2$. In general, if a_i denotes the upper limit for the number of tasks to which agent i can be assigned, we write the agent constraints as

If some tasks require more than one agent, the linear programming formulation can also accommodate the situation. Use the number of agents required as the right-hand side of the appropriate task constraint.

$$\sum_{j=1}^{n} x_{ij} \leq a_i \qquad i = 1, 2, \ldots, m$$

Thus, we see that one advantage of formulating and solving assignment problems as linear programs is that special cases such as the situation involving multiple assignments can be easily handled.

N O T E S and Comments

1. As noted, the assignment model is a special case of the transportation model. We stated in the notes and comments at the end of the preceding section that the optimal solution to the transportation problem will consist of integer values for the decision variables as long as the supplies and demands are integers. For the assignment problem, all supplies and demands equal 1; thus, the optimal solution must be integer valued and the integer values must be 0 or 1.

2. Combining the method for handling multiple assignments with the notion of a dummy agent provides another means of dealing with situations when the number of tasks exceeds the number of agents. That is, we add one dummy agent, but provide the dummy agent with the capability to handle multiple tasks. The number of tasks the dummy agent can handle is equal to the difference between the number of tasks and the number of agents.

10.3 THE TRANSSHIPMENT PROBLEM: THE NETWORK MODEL AND A LINEAR PROGRAMMING FORMULATION

The **transshipment problem** is an extension of the transportation problem in which intermediate nodes, referred to as *transshipment nodes,* are added to account for locations such as warehouses. In this more general type of distribution problem, shipments may be made between any pair of the three general types of nodes: origin nodes, transshipment nodes, and destination nodes. For example, the transshipment problem permits shipments of goods from origins to transshipment nodes and on to destinations, from one origin to another origin, from one transshipment location to another, from one destination location to another, and directly from origins to destinations.

As was true for the transportation problem, the supply available at each origin is limited, and the demand at each destination is specified. The objective in the transshipment problem is to determine how many units should be shipped over each arc in the network so that all destination demands are satisfied with the minimum possible transportation cost.

Try part (a) of Problem 23 for practice in developing a network representation of a transshipment problem.

Let us consider the transshipment problem faced by Ryan Electronics. Ryan is an electronics company with production facilities in Denver and Atlanta. Components produced at either facility may be shipped to either of the firm's regional warehouses, which are located in Kansas City and Louisville. From the regional warehouses, the firm supplies retail outlets in Detroit, Miami, Dallas, and New Orleans. The key features of the problem are shown in the network model depicted in Figure 10.6. Note that the supply at each origin and demand at each destination are shown in the left and right margins, respectively. Nodes 1 and 2 are the origin nodes; nodes 3 and 4 are the transshipment nodes; and nodes 5, 6, 7, and 8 are the destination nodes. The transportation cost per unit for each distribution route is shown in Table 10.5 and on the arcs of the network model in Figure 10.6.

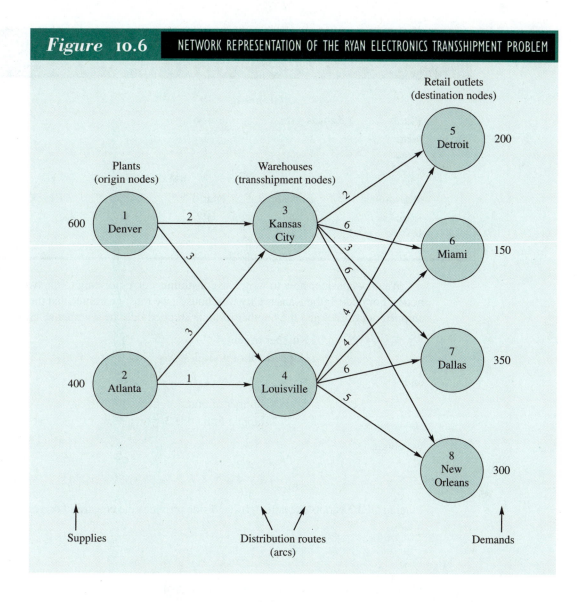

Figure 10.6   NETWORK REPRESENTATION OF THE RYAN ELECTRONICS TRANSSHIPMENT PROBLEM

Retail outlets
(destination nodes)

Plants
(origin nodes)

Warehouses
(transshipment nodes)

Supplies

Distribution routes
(arcs)

Demands

As with the transportation and assignment problems, we can formulate a linear programming model of the transshipment problem from a network representation. Again, we need a constraint for each node and a variable for each arc. Let x_{ij} denote the number of units shipped from node i to node j. For example, x_{13} denotes the number of units shipped from the Denver plant to the Kansas City warehouse, x_{14} denotes the number of units shipped from the Denver plant to the Louisville warehouse, and so on. Since the supply at the Denver plant is 600 units, the amount shipped from the Denver plant must be less than or equal to 600. Mathematically, we write this supply constraint as

$$x_{13} + x_{14} \leq 600$$

Similarly, for the Atlanta plant we have

$$x_{23} + x_{24} \leq 400$$

Table 10.5	TRANSPORTATION COSTS PER UNIT FOR THE RYAN ELECTRONICS TRANSSHIPMENT PROBLEM

	Warehouse	
Plant	**Kansas City**	**Louisville**
Denver	2	3
Atlanta	3	1

	Retail Outlet			
Warehouse	**Detroit**	**Miami**	**Dallas**	**New Orleans**
Kansas City	2	6	3	6
Louisville	4	4	6	5

We now consider how to write the constraints corresponding to the two transshipment nodes. For node 3 (the Kansas City warehouse), we must guarantee that the number of units shipped out must equal the number of units shipped into the warehouse. Since

$$\text{Number of units shipped out of node 3} = x_{35} + x_{36} + x_{37} + x_{38}$$

and

$$\text{Number of units shipped into node 3} = x_{13} + x_{23}$$

we obtain

$$x_{35} + x_{36} + x_{37} + x_{38} = x_{13} + x_{23}$$

Placing all the variables on the left-hand side provides the constraint corresponding to node 3 as

$$-x_{13} - x_{23} + x_{35} + x_{36} + x_{37} + x_{38} = 0$$

Similarly, the constraint corresponding to node 4 is

$$-x_{14} - x_{24} + x_{45} + x_{46} + x_{47} + x_{48} = 0$$

To develop the constraints associated with the destination nodes, we recognize that for each node the amount shipped to the destination must equal the demand. For example, to satisfy the demand for 200 units at node 5 (the Detroit retail outlet), we write

$$x_{35} + x_{45} = 200$$

Similarly, for nodes 6, 7, and 8, we have

$$x_{36} + x_{46} = 150$$
$$x_{37} + x_{47} = 350$$
$$x_{38} + x_{48} = 300$$

Try parts (b) and (c) of Problem 23 for practice in developing the linear programming model and in solving a transshipment problem on the computer.

As usual, the objective function reflects the total shipping cost over the 12 shipping routes. Combining the objective function and constraints leads to a 12-variable, 8-constraint linear programming model of the Ryan Electronics transshipment problem (see Figure 10.7). We used the linear programming module of The Management Scientist to obtain the optimal solution. Figure 10.8 shows the computer output, and Table 10.6 summarizes the optimal solution.

As mentioned at the beginning of this section, in the transshipment problem arcs may connect any pair of nodes. All such shipping patterns are possible in a transshipment problem. We still require only one constraint per node, but the constraint must include a variable for every arc entering or leaving the node. For origin nodes, the sum of the shipments out minus the sum of the shipments in must be less than or equal to the origin supply. For

---

Figure 10.7   LINEAR PROGRAMMING FORMULATION OF THE RYAN ELECTRONICS TRANSSHIPMENT PROBLEM

$$\text{Min} \quad 2x_{13} + 3x_{14} + 3x_{23} + 1x_{24} + 2x_{35} + 6x_{36} + 3x_{37} + 6x_{38} + 4x_{45} + 4x_{46} + 6x_{47} + 5x_{48}$$

s.t.

$$
\begin{array}{l}
x_{13} + x_{14} \leq 600 \\
x_{23} + x_{24} \leq 400 \\
-x_{13} - x_{23} + x_{35} + x_{36} + x_{37} + x_{38} = 0 \\
- x_{14} - x_{24} + x_{45} + x_{46} + x_{47} + x_{48} = 0 \\
x_{35} + x_{45} = 200 \\
x_{36} + x_{46} = 150 \\
x_{37} + x_{47} = 350 \\
x_{38} + x_{48} = 300
\end{array}
$$

Origin node constraints

Transshipment node constraints

Destination node constraints

$$x_{ij} \geq 0 \text{ for all } i \text{ and } j$$

Figure 10.8   THE MANAGEMENT SCIENTIST SOLUTION FOR THE RYAN ELECTRONICS TRANSSHIPMENT PROBLEM

```
Objective Function Value =          5200.000

          Variable              Value            Reduced Costs
        --------------     ----------------    ------------------
            X13              550.000                0.000
            X14               50.000                0.000
            X23                0.000                3.000
            X24              400.000                0.000
            X35              200.000                0.000
            X36                0.000                1.000
            X37              350.000                0.000
            X38                0.000                0.000
            X45                0.000                3.000
            X46              150.000                0.000
            X47                0.000                4.000
            X48              300.000                0.000
```

Table 10.6	OPTIMAL SOLUTION TO THE RYAN ELECTRONICS TRANSSHIPMENT PROBLEM			
Route			**Cost**	
From	**To**	**Units Shipped**	**Per Unit**	**Total Cost**
Denver	Kansas City	550	$2	$1100
Denver	Louisville	50	$3	150
Atlanta	Louisville	400	$1	400
Kansas City	Detroit	200	$2	400
Kansas City	Dallas	350	$3	1050
Louisville	Miami	150	$4	600
Louisville	New Orleans	300	$5	1500
				$5200

destination nodes, the sum of the shipments in minus the sum of the shipments out must equal demand. For transshipment nodes, the sum of the shipments out must equal the sum of the shipments in, as before.

For an illustration of this more general type of transshipment problem, let us modify the Ryan Electronics problem. Suppose that it is possible to ship directly from Atlanta to New Orleans at $4 per unit and from Dallas to New Orleans at $1 per unit. The network model corresponding to this modified Ryan Electronics problem is shown in Figure 10.9, the linear programming formulation is shown in Figure 10.10, and the computer solution is shown in Figure 10.11.

In Figure 10.9 we added two new arcs to the network model. Thus, two new variables are necessary in the linear programming formulation. Figure 10.10 shows that the new variables x_{28} and x_{78}, appear in the objective function and in the constraints corresponding to the nodes to which the new arcs are connected. Figure 10.11 shows that the value of the optimal solution has been reduced $600 by adding the two new shipping routes; $x_{28} = 250$ units are being shipped directly from Atlanta to New Orleans, and $x_{78} = 50$ units are being shipped from Dallas to New Orleans.

Try Problem 24 for practice working with transshipment problems with this more general structure.

Problem Variations

As with transportation and assignment problems, transshipment problems may be formulated with several variations, including

1. total supply not equal to total demand
2. maximization objective function
3. route capacities or route minimums
4. unacceptable routes

The linear programming model modifications required to accommodate these variations are identical to the modifications required for the transportation problem described in Section 10.1. When we add one or more constraints of the form $x_{ij} \leq L_{ij}$ to show that the route from node i to node j has capacity L_{ij}, we refer to the transshipment problem as a **capacitated transshipment problem.**

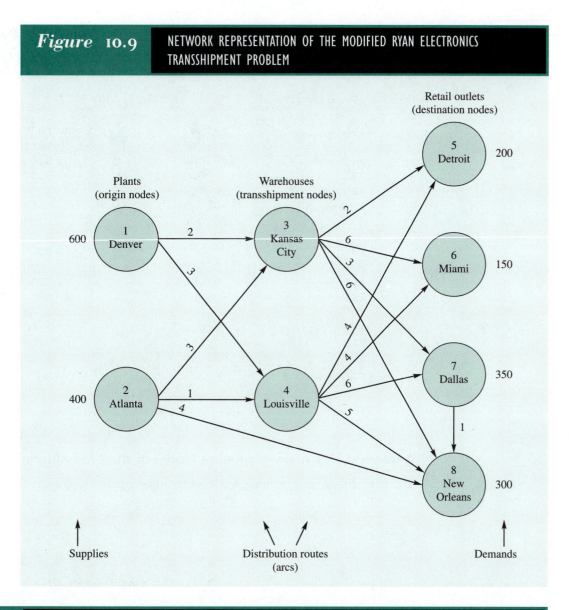

Figure 10.9 NETWORK REPRESENTATION OF THE MODIFIED RYAN ELECTRONICS TRANSSHIPMENT PROBLEM

Figure 10.10 LINEAR PROGRAMMING FORMULATION OF THE MODIFIED RYAN ELECTRONICS TRANSSHIPMENT PROBLEM

Min $2x_{13} + 3x_{14} + 3x_{23} + 1x_{24} + 2x_{35} + 6x_{36} + 3x_{37} + 6x_{38} + 4x_{45} + 4x_{46} + 6x_{47} + 5x_{48} + 4x_{28} + 1x_{78}$
s.t.

$$
\begin{array}{llll}
x_{13} + x_{14} & & \leq 600 & \left.\rule{0pt}{14pt}\right\} \text{Origin node constraints} \\
\quad\ x_{23} + x_{24} & \qquad\qquad\qquad + x_{28} & \leq 400 & \\
-x_{13} \quad\ - x_{23} \quad + x_{35} + x_{36} + x_{37} + x_{38} & & = 0 & \left.\rule{0pt}{14pt}\right\} \begin{array}{l}\text{Transshipment node} \\ \text{constraints}\end{array} \\
\quad - x_{14} \quad\ - x_{24} \qquad\qquad + x_{45} + x_{46} + x_{47} + x_{48} & & = 0 & \\
\qquad\qquad x_{35} \qquad\quad + x_{45} & & = 200 & \left.\rule{0pt}{28pt}\right\} \begin{array}{l}\text{Destination node} \\ \text{constraints}\end{array} \\
\qquad\qquad\quad x_{36} \qquad\qquad + x_{46} & & = 150 & \\
\qquad\qquad\qquad x_{37} \qquad\qquad\quad + x_{47} \quad - x_{78} & = 350 & \\
\qquad\qquad\qquad\quad x_{38} \qquad\qquad\qquad\quad + x_{48} + x_{28} + x_{78} & = 300 & \\
\end{array}
$$

$x_{ij} \geq 0$ for all i and j

Figure 10.11   THE MANAGEMENT SCIENTIST SOLUTION FOR THE MODIFIED RYAN ELECTRONICS TRANSSHIPMENT PROBLEM

```
Objective Function Value =           4600.000

        Variable              Value           Reduced Costs
      --------------      --------------      -----------------
          X13               600.000               0.000
          X14                 0.000               0.000
          X23                 0.000               3.000
          X24               150.000               0.000
          X35               200.000               0.000
          X36                 0.000               1.000
          X37               400.000               0.000
          X38                 0.000               2.000
          X45                 0.000               3.000
          X46               150.000               0.000
          X47                 0.000               4.000
          X48                 0.000               2.000
          X28               250.000               0.000
          X78                50.000               0.000
```

A General Linear Programming Model of the Transshipment Problem

The general linear programming model of the transshipment problem is

$$\text{Min} \quad \sum_{\text{all arcs}} c_{ij} x_{ij}$$

s.t.

$$\sum_{\text{arcs out}} x_{ij} - \sum_{\text{arcs in}} x_{ij} \leq s_i \quad \text{Origin nodes } i$$

$$\sum_{\text{arcs out}} x_{ij} - \sum_{\text{arcs in}} x_{ij} = 0 \quad \text{Transshipment nodes}$$

$$\sum_{\text{arcs in}} x_{ij} - \sum_{\text{arcs out}} x_{ij} = d_j \quad \text{Destination nodes } j$$

$$x_{ij} \geq 0 \text{ for all } i \text{ and } j$$

where

x_{ij} = number of units shipped from node i to node j

c_{ij} = cost per unit of shipping from node i to node j

s_i = supply at origin node i

d_j = demand at destination node j

N O T E S
and Comments

I. In more advanced treatments of linear programming and network flow problems, the capacitated transshipment problem is called the *pure network flow problem*. Efficient special-purpose solution procedures are available for network flow problems and their special cases.

2. In the general linear programming formulation of the transshipment problem, the constraints for the destination nodes are often written as

$$\sum_{\text{arcs out}} x_{ij} - \sum_{\text{arcs in}} x_{ij} = -d_j$$

The advantage of writing the constraints this way is that the left-hand side of each constraint then represents the flow out of the node minus the flow in. But such constraints would then have to be multiplied by −1 to obtain nonnegative right-hand sides before solving the problem by most linear programming codes.

10.4   A PRODUCTION AND INVENTORY APPLICATION

The introduction to the transportation and transshipment problems in Sections 10.1 and 10.3 involved applications for the shipment of goods from several supply locations or origins to several demand sites or destinations. Although the shipment of goods is the subject of many transportation and transshipment problems, transportation and/or transshipment models can be developed for applications that have nothing to do with the physical shipment of goods from origins to destinations. In this section we show how to use a transshipment model to solve a production scheduling and inventory problem.

Contois Carpets is a small manufacturer of carpeting for home and office installations. Production capacity, demand, production cost per square yard, and inventory holding cost per square yard for the next four quarters are shown in Table 10.7. Note that production capacity, demand, and production costs vary by quarter, whereas the cost of carrying inventory from one quarter to the next is constant at $0.25 per yard. Contois wants to determine how many yards of carpeting to manufacture each quarter to minimize the total production and inventory cost for the four-quarter period.

We begin by developing a network representation of the problem. First, we create four nodes corresponding to the production in each quarter and four nodes corresponding to the demand in each quarter. Each production node is connected by an outgoing arc to the demand node for the same period. The flow on the arc represents the number of square yards of carpet manufactured for the period. For each demand node, an outgoing arc represents

The fact that the network shows flows into and out of demand nodes is what makes the model a transshipment model.

Table 10.7	PRODUCTION, DEMAND, AND COST ESTIMATES FOR CONTOIS CARPETS			
Quarter	Production Capacity (square yards)	Demand (square yards)	Production Cost ($/square yard)	Inventory Cost ($/square yard)
I	600	400	2	0.25
2	300	500	5	0.25
3	500	400	3	0.25
4	400	400	3	0.25

the amount of inventory (square yards of carpet) carried over to the demand node for the next period. Figure 10.12 shows the network model. Note that nodes 1–4 represent the production for each quarter and that nodes 5–8 represent the demand for each quarter. The quarterly production capacities are shown in the left margin, and the quarterly demands are shown in the right margin.

The objective is to determine a production scheduling and inventory policy that will minimize the total production and inventory cost for the four quarters. Constraints involve production capacity and demand in each quarter. As usual, a linear programming model can be developed from the network by establishing a constraint for each node and a variable for each arc.

Let x_{15} denote the number of square yards of carpet manufactured in quarter 1. The capacity of the facility is 600 square yards in quarter 1, so the production capacity constraint is

$$x_{15} \leq 600$$

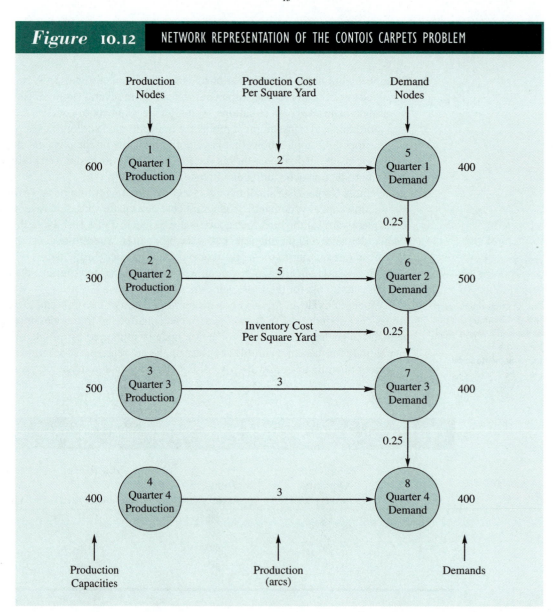

Figure 10.12   NETWORK REPRESENTATION OF THE CONTOIS CARPETS PROBLEM

Using similar decision variables, we obtain the production capacities for quarters 2–4:

$$x_{26} \leq 300$$
$$x_{37} \leq 500$$
$$x_{48} \leq 400$$

We now consider the development of the constraints for each of the demand nodes. For node 5, one arc enters the node, which represents the number of square yards of carpet produced in quarter 1, and one arc leaves the node, which represents the number of square yards of carpet that will not be sold in quarter 1 and will be carried over for possible sale in quarter 2. In general, for each quarter the beginning inventory plus the production minus the ending inventory must equal demand. However, for quarter 1 there is no beginning inventory; thus, the constraint for node 5 is

$$x_{15} - x_{56} = 400$$

The constraints associated with the demand nodes in quarters 2, 3, and 4 are

$$x_{56} + x_{26} - x_{67} = 500$$
$$x_{67} + x_{37} - x_{78} = 400$$
$$x_{78} + x_{48} = 400$$

Note that the constraint for node 8 (fourth-quarter demand) involves only two variables as there is no provision for holding inventory for a fifth quarter.

The objective is to minimize total production and inventory cost, so we write the objective function as

$$\text{Min} \quad 2x_{15} + 5x_{26} + 3x_{37} + 3x_{48} + 0.25x_{56} + 0.25x_{67} + 0.25x_{78}$$

The complete linear programming formulation of the Contois Carpets problem is

$$\text{Min} \quad 2x_{15} + 5x_{26} + 3x_{37} + 3x_{48} + 0.25x_{56} + 0.25x_{67} + 0.25x_{78}$$

s.t.

$$
\begin{aligned}
x_{15} &&&&&&&&&&&&& \leq 600 \\
& x_{26} &&&&&&&&&&&& \leq 300 \\
&& x_{37} &&&&&&&&&&& \leq 500 \\
&&& x_{48} &&&&&&&&&& \leq 400 \\
x_{15} &&&& - & x_{56} &&&&&&&& = 400 \\
& x_{26} &&&& + & x_{56} & - & x_{67} &&&&& = 500 \\
&& x_{37} &&&&&& + & x_{67} & - & x_{78} && = 400 \\
&&& x_{48} &&&&&&&& + & x_{78} & = 400 \\
\end{aligned}
$$

$$x_{ij} \geq 0 \quad \text{for all } i \text{ and } j$$

We used the linear programming module of The Management Scientist to solve the Contois Carpets problem. Figure 10.13 shows the results: Contois Carpets should manufacture 600 square yards of carpet in quarter 1, 300 square yards in quarter 2, 400 square yards in quarter 3, and 400 square yards in quarter 4. Note also that 200 square yards will be carried over from quarter 1 to quarter 2. The total production and inventory cost is $5150.

Figure 10.13	THE MANAGEMENT SCIENTIST SOLUTION FOR THE CONTOIS CARPETS PROBLEM

Objective Function Value =   5150.000

Variable	Value	Reduced Costs
X15	600.000	0.000
X26	300.000	0.000
X37	400.000	0.000
X48	400.000	0.000
X56	200.000	0.000
X67	0.000	2.250
X78	0.000	0.000

NOTES and Comments

1. Often the same problem can be modeled in different ways. In this section we modeled the Contois Carpets problem as a transshipment problem. It also can be modeled as a transportation problem.

2. In the network model we developed for the transshipment problem, the amount leaving the starting node for an arc is always equal to the amount entering the ending node for that arc. An extension of such a network model is the case where a gain or a loss occurs as an arc is traversed. The amount entering the destination node may be greater or smaller than the amount leaving the origin node. For instance, if cash is the commodity flowing across an arc, the cash earns interest from one period to the next. Thus, the amount of cash entering the next period is greater than the amount leaving the previous period by the amount of interest earned. Networks with gains or losses are treated in more advanced texts on network flow programming.

SUMMARY

In this chapter we introduced transportation, assignment, and transshipment problems. All three types of problems belong to the special category of linear programs called *network flow problems.* The network model of a transportation problem consists of nodes representing a set of origins and a set of destinations. In the basic model, an arc is used to represent the route from each origin to each destination. Each origin has a supply, and each destination has a demand. The problem is to determine the optimal amount to ship from each origin to each destination.

The assignment model is a special case of the transportation model in which all supply and all demand values are equal to 1. We represent each agent as an origin node and each task as a destination node. The transshipment model is an extension of the transportation model to distribution problems involving transfer points referred to as transshipment nodes. In this more general model, we allow arcs between any pair of nodes. A variation of the transshipment problem allows for placing capacities on the arcs. This variation, called the *capacitated transshipment problem,* is also known in the network flow literature as the *pure network problem.*

We showed how each of these network flow problems could be modeled as a linear program, and we solved each using a general-purpose linear programming computer package.

In network flow problems, the optimal solution will be integral as long as all supplies and demands are integral. Therefore, when solving any transportation, assignment, or transshipment problem in which the supplies and demands are integral, we can expect to obtain an integer-valued solution.

..../ /...............

GLOSSARY

Transportation problem A network flow problem that often involves minimizing the cost of shipping goods from a set of origins to a set of destinations; it can be formulated and solved as a linear program by including a variable for each arc and a constraint for each node.

Network A graphical representation of a problem consisting of numbered circles (nodes) interconnected by a series of lines (arcs); arrowheads on the arcs show the direction of flow. Transportation, assignment, and transshipment problems are network flow problems.

Nodes The intersection or junction points of a network.

Arcs The lines connecting the nodes in a network.

Capacitated transportation problem A variation of the basic transportation problem in which capacities are on some or all of the arcs.

Assignment problem A network flow problem that often involves the assignment of agents to tasks; it can be formulated as a linear program and is a special case of the transportation problem.

Transshipment problem An extension of the transportation problem to distribution problems involving transfer points and possible shipments between any pair of nodes.

Capacitated transshipment problem A variation of the transshipment problem in which capacities are on some or all of the arcs.

Dummy origin An origin added to a transportation problem to make the total supply equal to the total demand. The supply assigned to the dummy origin is the difference between the total demand and the total supply.

..../ /...............

PROBLEMS

Note: In many cases, we ask you to formulate and solve the problem as a linear program. Where the solution method is not specified, you may also use the transportation or assignment modules of The Management Scientist or some other software package.

SELF TEST

1. A company imports goods at two ports: Philadelphia and New Orleans. Shipments of one product are made to customers in Atlanta, Dallas, Columbus, and Boston. For the next planning period, the supplies at each port, customer demands, and shipping costs per case from each port to each customer are as follows:

Port	Atlanta	Dallas	Columbus	Boston	Port Supply
		Customers			**Port**
Philadelphia	2	6	6	2	5000
New Orleans	1	2	5	7	3000
Demand	1400	3200	2000	1400	

Develop a network representation of the distribution system (transportation problem).

2. Consider the following network representation of a transportation problem:

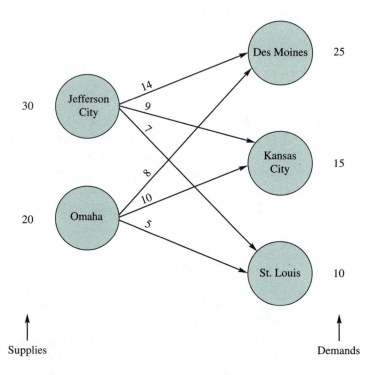

The supplies, demands, and transportation costs per unit are shown on the network.
   a. Develop a linear programming model for this problem; be sure to define the variables in your model.
   b. Solve the linear program to determine the optimal solution.

3. Reconsider the distribution system described in Problem 1.
   a. Develop a linear programming model that can be solved to minimize transportation cost.
   b. Solve the linear program to determine the minimum-cost shipping schedule.

4. A product is produced at three plants and shipped to three warehouses (the transportation costs per unit are shown in the following table).

Plant	Warehouse			Plant Capacity
	W_1	W_2	W_3	
P_1	20	16	24	300
P_2	10	10	8	500
P_3	12	18	10	100
Warehouse demand	200	400	300	

   a. Show a network representation of the problem.
   b. Develop a linear programming model for minimizing transportation costs; solve this model to determine the minimum-cost solution.
   c. Suppose that the entries in the table represent profit per unit produced at plant i and sold to warehouse j. How does the model formulation change from that in part (b)?

5. Tri-County Utilities, Inc., supplies natural gas to customers in a three-county area. The company purchases natural gas from two companies: Southern Gas and Northwest Gas. Demand forecasts for the coming winter season are Hamilton County, 400 units; Butler County, 200 units; and Clermont County, 300 units. Contracts to provide the following quantities have been written: Southern Gas, 500 units; and Northwest Gas, 400 units. Distribution costs for the counties vary, depending upon the location of the suppliers. The distribution costs per unit (in thousands of dollars) are as follows:

		To	
From	Hamilton	Butler	Clermont
Southern Gas	10	20	15
Northwest Gas	12	15	18

   a. Develop a network representation of this problem.
   b. Develop a linear programming model that can be used to determine the plan that will minimize total distribution costs.
   c. Describe the distribution plan and show the total distribution cost.
   d. Recent residential and industrial growth in Butler County has the potential for increasing demand by as much as 100 units. Which supplier should Tri-County contract with to supply the additional capacity?

6. Arnoff Enterprises manufactures the central processing unit (CPU) for a line of personal computers. The CPUs are manufactured in Seattle, Columbus, and New York and shipped to warehouses in Pittsburgh, Mobile, Denver, Los Angeles, and Washington, D.C. for further distribution. The following table shows the number of CPUs available at each plant, the number of CPUs required by each warehouse, and the shipping costs (dollars per unit).

			Warehouse			
Plant	Pittsburgh	Mobile	Denver	Los Angeles	Washington	CPUs Available
Seattle	10	20	5	9	10	9000
Columbus	2	10	8	30	6	4000
New York	1	20	7	10	4	8000
CPUs Required	3000	5000	4000	6000	3000	21,000

   a. Develop a network representation of this problem.
   b. Determine the amount that should be shipped from each plant to each warehouse to minimize the total shipping cost.
   c. The Pittsburgh warehouse has just increased its order by 1000 units, and Arnoff has authorized the Columbus plant to increase its production by 1000 units. Will this production increase lead to an increase or decrease in total shipping costs? Solve for the new optimal solution.

7. Premier Consulting has two consultants, Avery and Baker, who can be scheduled to work for clients up to a maximum of 160 hours each over the next four weeks. A third consultant, Campbell, has some administrative assignments already planned and is available for clients up to a maximum of 140 hours over the next four weeks. The company has four clients with projects in process. The estimated hourly requirements for each of the clients over the four-week period are

Client	Hours
A	180
B	75
C	100
D	85

Hourly rates vary for the consultant–client combination and are based on several factors, including project type and the consultant's experience. The rates (dollars per hour) for each consultant–client combination are

Consultant	Client A	Client B	Client C	Client D
Avery	100	125	115	100
Baker	120	135	115	120
Campbell	155	150	140	130

a. Develop a network representation of the problem.
b. Formulate the problem as a linear program, with the optimal solution providing the hours each consultant should be scheduled for each client to maximize the consulting firm's billings. What is the schedule and what is the total billing?
c. New information shows that Avery doesn't have the experience to be scheduled for client B. If this consulting assignment is not permitted, what impact does it have on total billings? What is the revised schedule?

8. Klein Chemicals, Inc., produces a special oil-base material that is currently in short supply. Four of Klein's customers have already placed orders that together exceed the combined capacity of Klein's two plants. Klein's management faces the problem of deciding how many units it should supply to each customer. Since the four customers are in different industries, different prices can be charged because of the various industry pricing structures. However, slightly different production costs at the two plants and varying transportation costs between the plants and customers make a "sell to the highest bidder" strategy unacceptable. After considering price, production costs, and transportation costs, Klein has established the following profit per unit for each plant–customer alternative.

SELF TEST

	Customer			
Plant	D_1	D_2	D_3	D_4
Clifton Springs	$32	$34	$32	$40
Danville	$34	$30	$28	$38

The plant capacities and customer orders are as follows:

Plant Capacity (units)		Distributor Orders (units)	
Clifton Springs	5000	D_1	2000
		D_2	5000
Danville	3000	D_3	3000
		D_4	2000

How many units should each plant produce for each customer to maximize profits? Which customer demands will not be met? Show your network model and linear programming formulation.

9. Sound Electronics, Inc., produces a battery-operated tape recorder at plants located in Martinsville, North Carolina; Plymouth, New York; and Franklin, Missouri. The unit transportation cost for shipments from the three plants to distribution centers in Chicago, Dallas, and New York are as follows:

	To		
From	**Chicago**	**Dallas**	**New York**
Martinsville	$1.45	$1.60	$1.40
Plymouth	$1.10	$2.25	$0.60
Franklin	$1.20	$1.20	$1.80

After considering transportation costs, management has decided that under no circumstances will it use the Plymouth–Dallas route. The plant capacities and distributor orders for the next month are as follows:

Plant	**Capacity (units)**
Martinsville	400
Plymouth	600
Franklin	300

Distributor	**Orders (units)**
Chicago	400
Dallas	400
New York	400

Because of different wage scales at the three plants, the unit production cost varies from plant to plant. Assuming the costs are $29.50 per unit at Martinsville, $31.20 per unit at Plymouth, and $30.35 per unit at Franklin, find the production and distribution plan that minimizes production and transportation costs.

10. The Ace Manufacturing Company has orders for three similar products:

Product	**Orders (units)**
A	2000
B	500
C	1200

Three machines are available for the manufacturing operations. All three machines can produce all the products at the same production rate. However, due to varying defect percentages of each product on each machine, the unit costs of the products vary depending on the machine used. Machine capacities for the next week, and the unit costs, are as follows:

Machine	Capacity (units)
1	1500
2	1500
3	1000

Machine	Product		
	A	B	C
1	$1.00	$1.20	$0.90
2	$1.30	$1.40	$1.20
3	$1.10	$1.00	$1.20

Use the transportation model to develop the minimum-cost production schedule for the products and machines. Show the linear programming formulation.

11. Forbelt Corporation has a one-year contract to supply motors for all refrigerators produced by the Ice Age Corporation. Ice Age manufactures the refrigerators at four locations around the country: Boston, Dallas, Los Angeles, and St. Paul. Plans call for the following number (in thousands) of refrigerators to be produced at each location.

Boston	50
Dallas	70
Los Angeles	60
St. Paul	80

Forbelt has three plants that are capable of producing the motors. The plants and production capacities (in thousands) are

Denver	100
Atlanta	100
Chicago	150

Because of varying production and transportation costs, the profit that Forbelt earns on each lot of 1000 units depends on which plant produced the lot and which destination it was shipped to. The following table gives the accounting department estimates of the profit per unit (shipments will be made in lots of 1000 units).

Produced At	Shipped To			
	Boston	Dallas	Los Angeles	St. Paul
Denver	7	11	8	13
Atlanta	20	17	12	10
Chicago	8	18	13	16

With profit maximization as a criterion, Forbelt's management wants to determine how many motors should be produced at each plant and how many motors should be shipped from each plant to each destination.

a. Develop a network representation of this problem.
b. Find the optimal solution.

SELF TEST

12. Scott and Associates, Inc., is an accounting firm that has three new clients. Project leaders will be assigned to the three clients. Based on the different backgrounds and experiences of the leaders, the various leader–client assignments differ in terms of projected completion times. The possible assignments and the estimated completion times in days are

Project Leader	Client		
	1	2	3
Jackson	10	16	32
Ellis	14	22	40
Smith	22	24	34

a. Develop a network representation of this problem.
b. Formulate the problem as a linear program, and solve. What is the total time required?

13. Assume that in Problem 12 an additional employee is available for possible assignment. The following table shows the assignment alternatives and the estimated completion times.

Project Leader	Client		
	1	2	3
Jackson	10	16	32
Ellis	14	22	40
Smith	22	24	34
Burton	14	18	36

a. What is the optimal assignment?
b. How did the assignment change compared to the best assignment possible in Problem 12? Was any savings associated with considering Burton as a possible project leader?
c. Which project leader remains unassigned?

14. Wilson Distributors, Inc., is opening two new sales territories in the western states. Three individuals currently selling in the Midwest and the East are being considered for promotion to regional sales manager positions in the new sales territories. Management has estimated total annual sales (in thousands of dollars) for the assignment of each individual to each sales territory. The management sales projections are as follows:

	Sales Region	
Regional Managers	Northwest	Southwest
Bostock	$100	$95
McMahon	$85	$80
Miller	$90	$75

a. Develop a network representation of the problem.
b. Formulate and solve a linear programming model to obtain the optimal solution to this problem.

15. Fowle Marketing Research has four project leaders available for assignment to three clients. Find the assignment of project leaders to clients that will minimize the total time to complete all projects. The estimated project completion times in days are as follows:

Project Leader	Client		
	1	2	3
Terry	10	15	9
Carle	9	18	5
McClymonds	6	14	3
Higley	8	16	6

16. In a job shop operation, four jobs may be performed on any of four machines. The numbers of hours required for each job on each machine are summarized in the following table. What is the minimum total time job–machine assignment?

Job	Machine			
	A	B	C	D
1	32	18	32	26
2	22	24	12	16
3	24	30	26	24
4	26	30	28	20

17. Mayfax Distributors, Inc., has four sales territories, each of which must be assigned a sales representative. From experience the firm's sales manager estimated the annual sales volume (in thousands of dollars) for each sales representative in each sales territory. Find the sales representative–territory assignments that will maximize sales.

Sales Representative	Sales Territory			
	A	B	C	D
Washington	44	80	52	60
Benson	60	56	40	72
Fredricks	36	60	48	48
Hodson	52	76	36	40

18. The department head of a quantitative methods department at a major midwestern university will be scheduling faculty to teach courses during the coming autumn term. Four core courses need to be covered. The four courses are at the UG, MBA, MS, and Ph.D. levels. Four professors will be assigned to the courses, with each professor receiving one of the courses. Student evaluations of professors are available from previous terms. Based on a rating scale of 4 (excellent), 3 (very good), 2 (average), 1 (fair), and 0 (poor), the average student evaluations for each professor are shown. Professor D does not have a Ph.D. and cannot be assigned to teach the Ph.D. level course. If the department head makes teaching assignments based on maximizing the student evaluation ratings over all four courses, what staffing assignments should be made?

		Course		
Professor	UG	MBA	MS	Ph.D.
A	2.8	2.2	3.3	3.0
B	3.2	3.0	3.6	3.6
C	3.3	3.2	3.5	3.5
D	3.2	2.8	2.5	—

19. A market research firm has three clients who have each requested that the firm conduct a sample survey. Four available statisticians can be assigned to these three projects; however, all four statisticians are busy, and therefore each can handle only one client. The following data show the number of hours required for each statistician to complete each job; the differences in time are based on experience and ability of the statisticians.

		Client	
Statistician	A	B	C
1	150	210	270
2	170	230	220
3	180	230	225
4	160	240	230

   a. Formulate and solve a linear programming model for this problem.
   b. Suppose that the time statistician 4 needs to complete the job for client A is increased from 160 to 165 hours. What effect will this change have on the solution?
   c. Suppose that the time statistician 4 needs to complete the job for client A is decreased to 140 hours. What effect will this change have on the solution?
   d. Suppose that the time statistician 3 needs to complete the job for client B increases to 250 hours. What effect will this change have on the solution?

20. Hatcher Enterprises uses a chemical called Rbase in production operations at five divisions. Only six suppliers of Rbase meet Hatcher's quality control standards. All six suppliers can produce Rbase in sufficient quantities to accommodate the needs of each division. The quantity of Rbase needed by each Hatcher division and the price per gallon charged by each supplier are as follows:

Division	Demand (1000s of gallons)	Supplier	Price Per Gallon ($)
1	40	1	12.60
2	45	2	14.00
3	50	3	10.20
4	35	4	14.20
5	45	5	12.00
		6	13.00

The cost per gallon ($) for shipping from each supplier to each division is provided in the following table.

	Supplier					
Division	1	2	3	4	5	6
1	2.75	2.50	3.15	2.80	2.75	2.75
2	0.80	0.20	5.40	1.20	3.40	1.00
3	4.70	2.60	5.30	2.80	6.00	5.60
4	2.60	1.80	4.40	2.40	5.00	2.80
5	3.40	0.40	5.00	1.20	2.60	3.60

Hatcher believes in spreading its business among suppliers so that the company will be less affected by supplier problems (e.g., labor strikes or resource availability). Company policy requires that each division have a separate supplier.

a. For each supplier–division combination, compute the total cost of supplying the division's demand.

b. Determine the optimal assignment of suppliers to divisions.

SELF TEST

21. The distribution system for the Herman Company consists of three plants, two warehouses, and four customers. Plant capacities and shipping costs (in $) from each plant to each warehouse are

	Warehouse		
Plant	1	2	Capacity
1	4	7	450
2	8	5	600
3	5	6	380

Customer demand and shipping costs per unit (in $) from each warehouse to each customer are

	Customer			
Warehouse	1	2	3	4
1	6	4	8	4
2	3	6	7	7
Demand	300	300	300	400

a. Develop a network representation of this problem.
b. Formulate a linear programming model of the problem.
c. Solve the linear program to determine the optimal shipping plan.

22. Refer to Problem 21. Suppose that shipments between the two warehouses are permitted at $2 per unit and that direct shipments can be made from plant 3 to customer 4 at a cost of $7 per unit.
a. Develop a network representation of this problem.
b. Formulate a linear programming model of this problem.
c. Solve the linear program to determine the optimal shipping plan.

23. A company has two plants (P_1 and P_2), one regional warehouse (W), and two retail outlets (R_1 and R_2). The plant capacities, retail outlet demands, and per-unit shipping costs are shown in the following network.

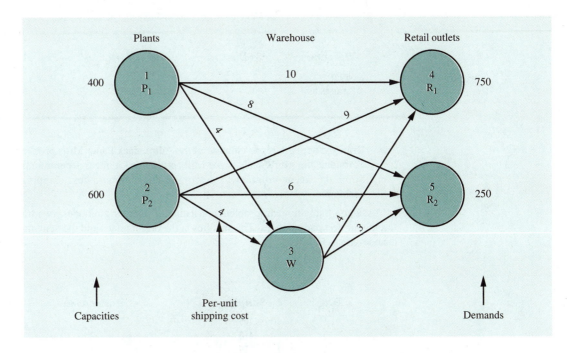

Plants   Warehouse   Retail outlets

Capacities   Per-unit shipping cost   Demands

a. Formulate a linear programming model to minimize shipping costs for this problem.
b. Solve the linear program to determine the optimal solution.
c. What change would have to be made in the linear programming model if the maximum amount of goods that can be shipped from W to R_1 is 500? How would this change the optimal solution?

24. Adirondack Paper Mills, Inc., has paper plants in Augusta, Maine, and Tupper Lake, New York. Warehouse facilities are located in Albany, New York, and Portsmouth, New Hampshire. Distributors are located in Boston, New York, and Philadelphia. The plant capacities and distributor demands for the next month are as follows:

Plant	Capacity (units)
Augusta	300
Tupper Lake	100

Distributor	Demand (units)
Boston	150
New York	100
Philadelphia	150

The unit transportation costs ($) for shipments from the two plants to the two warehouses and from the two warehouses to the three distributors are as follows:

	Warehouse	
Plant	Albany	Portsmouth
Augusta	7	5
Tupper Lake	3	4

		Distributor	
Warehouse	Boston	New York	Philadelphia
Albany	8	5	7
Portsmouth	5	6	10

a. Draw the network representation of the Adirondack Paper Mills problem.
b. Formulate the Adirondack Paper Mills problem as a linear programming problem.
c. Solve the linear program to determine the minimum-cost shipping schedule for the problem.

25. Consider a transshipment problem consisting of three origin nodes, two transshipment nodes, and four destination nodes. The supplies at the origin nodes and the demands at the destination nodes are as follows:

Origin	Supply
1	400
2	450
3	350

Destination	Demand
1	200
2	500
3	300
4	200

The shipping costs per unit ($) are provided in the following table.

			To					
From		Transshipment			Destination			
		1	2	1	2	3	4
Origin	1	6	8	—	—	—	—
	2	8	12	—	—	—	—
	3	10	5	—	—	—	—
Transshipment	1	—	—	9	7	6	10
	2	—	—	7	9	6	8

a. Draw the network representation of this problem.
b. Formulate this as a linear programming problem.
c. Solve for the optimal solution.

26. The Moore & Harman Company is in the business of buying and selling grain. An important aspect of the company's business is arranging for the purchased grain to be shipped to customers. If the company can keep freight costs low, profitability will be improved.

Currently, the company has purchased three rail cars of grain at Muncie, Indiana; six rail cars at Brazil, Indiana; and five rail cars at Xenia, Ohio. Twelve carloads of grain have been sold. The locations and the amount sold at each location are as follows:

Location	Number of Rail Car Loads
Macon, Ga.	2
Greenwood, S.C.	4
Concord, S.C.	3
Chatham, N.C.	3

All shipments must be routed through either Louisville or Cincinnati. Shown are the shipping costs per bushel (in cents) from the origins to Louisville and Cincinnati and the costs per bushel to ship from Louisville and Cincinnati to the destinations.

	To	
From	**Louisville**	**Cincinnati**
Muncie	8	6 ←———— Cost per bushel
Brazil	3	8 from Muncie to
Xenia	9	3 Cincinnati is 6¢

	To			
From	**Macon**	**Greenwood**	**Concord**	**Chatham**
Louisville	44	34	34	32
Cincinnati	57	35	28	24

Cost per bushel from
Cincinnati to Greenwood is 35¢

Determine a shipping schedule that will minimize the freight costs necessary to satisfy demand. Which (if any) rail cars of grain must be held at the origin until buyers can be found?

27. A rental car company has an imbalance of cars at seven of its locations. The following network shows the locations of concern (the nodes) and the cost to move a car between locations. A positive number by a node indicates an excess supply at the node, and a negative number indicates an excess demand.

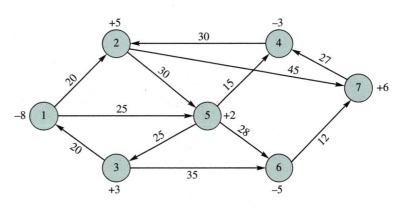

   a. Develop a linear programming model of this problem.

   b. Solve the model formulated in part (a) to determine how the cars should be redistributed among the locations.

28. The following linear programming formulation is for a transshipment problem.

$$\text{Min} \quad 11x_{13} + 12x_{14} + 10x_{21} + 8x_{34} + 10x_{35} + 11x_{42} + 9x_{45} + 12x_{52}$$

s.t.

$$
\begin{array}{rcl}
x_{13} + x_{14} - x_{21} & & \leq 5 \\
x_{21} - x_{42} - x_{52} & & \leq 3 \\
x_{13} - x_{34} - x_{35} & & = 6 \\
-x_{14} - x_{34} + x_{42} + x_{45} & & \leq 2 \\
x_{35} + x_{45} - x_{52} & & = 4
\end{array}
$$

$$x_{ij} \geq 0 \quad \text{for all } i, j$$

Show the network representation of this problem.

29. Refer to the Contois Carpets problem for which the network representation is shown in Figure 10.12. Suppose that Contois has a beginning inventory of 50 yards of carpet and requires an inventory of 100 yards at the end of quarter 4.

   a. Develop a network representation of this modified problem.

   b. Develop a linear programming model, and solve for the optimal solution.

30. Sanders Fishing Supply of Naples, Florida, manufactures a variety of fishing equipment, which it sells throughout the United States. For the next three months, Sanders estimates demand for a particular product at 150, 250, and 300 units, respectively. Sanders can supply this demand by producing on regular time or overtime. Because of other commitments and anticipated cost increases in month 3, the production capacities in units and the production costs per unit are as follows:

Production	Capacity (units)	Cost Per Unit
Month 1—Regular	275	$50
Month 1—Overtime	100	80
Month 2—Regular	200	50
Month 2—Overtime	50	80
Month 3—Regular	100	60
Month 3—Overtime	50	100

Inventory may be carried from one month to the next, but the cost is $20 per unit per month. For example, regular production from month 1 used to meet demand in month 2 would cost Sanders $50 + $20 = $70 per unit. This same month 1 production used to meet demand in month 3 would cost Sanders $50 + 2($20) = $90 per unit.

   a. Develop a network representation of this production scheduling problem as a transportation problem. (Hint: Use six origin nodes; the supply for origin node 1 is the maximum that can be produced in month 1 on regular time, and so on.)

   b. Develop a linear programming model that can be used to schedule regular and overtime production for each of the three months.

   c. What is the production schedule, how many units are carried in inventory each month, and what is the total cost?

   d. Is there any unused production capacity? If so, where?

..../ /.............

Case Problem   ASSIGNING UMPIRE CREWS*

The American Baseball League consists of 14 professional baseball teams organized into three divisions: the West Division with Seattle, Oakland, California, and Texas; the Central Division with Kansas City, Minnesota, Chicago, Milwaukee, and Cleveland; and the East Division with Detroit, Toronto, Baltimore, New York, and Boston.

In addition to the schedules for each team, the American League must determine the best way to assign the umpire crews to the various games played throughout the league. Umpire crews are assigned to specific home-team cities for the two-, three-, or four-game series in that city, but are not assigned on an individual-game basis. Since there are 14 American League teams, as many as seven games can be played at the same time (double-headers count as one game in assigning crews); hence, seven umpire crews must be assigned.

Several considerations are important in making the umpire crew assignments. Because of the amount of travel required, airline costs can be substantial. Thus, from a cost point of view, umpire crew assignments with minimum travel distances are desirable. However, a second consideration in the assignment of the umpire crews is that there should be a balance such that each crew works approximately the same number of games with each team and in each city. The considerations of minimizing travel distances and, at the same time, balancing the crew assignments among the teams and cities are in conflict.

In addition to these considerations, a number of requirements must be satisfied. The most important of these are

1. A crew cannot travel from city A to city B if the last game in city A is a night game and the first game in city B is an afternoon game on the next day.
2. A crew cannot travel from a West Coast location (Seattle, Oakland, or California) to Chicago, Milwaukee, Cleveland, or any East Division city without a day off.
3. Because of flight scheduling difficulties, a crew traveling into or out of Toronto must have a day off unless coming from or going to New York, Boston, Detroit, or Cleveland.
4. Any crew traveling from a night game in Seattle, Oakland, or California cannot be assigned to Kansas City or Texas for a game on the next day.
5. No crew should be assigned to the same team for more than two series in a row.

The umpire crews have already been scheduled for the first four series of the five-series schedule shown in Table 10.8. Table 10.9 summarizes the crew assignments for the first four series in the schedule and shows the pairings for the fifth series. The superscript next to each team identification indicates the umpire crew assigned for that pairing. For example, for the fourth series, crew 1 is assigned to the Boston–Toronto games, crew 2 is assigned to the Detroit–California games, and so on.

Table 10.10 shows the distances from the cities where the fourth series is being played to the cities where the fifth series is being played. There are some other issues league management would like considered in assigning crews to the next series. Over the past nine series, crew 4 has umpired three series with Kansas City and three series with Milwaukee. Also, crew 5 has not been assigned to any games with New York, Toronto, or Detroit over the past month.

---

*The authors are indebted to James R. Evans, consultant to the American League, New York, N.Y., for providing this case problem.

Managerial Report

Prepare a written recommendation to league management concerning the assignment of umpire crews to the fifth series that will minimize the distance traveled.

Table 10.8 — **SEGMENT OF THE AMERICAN LEAGUE SCHEDULE SHOWING FIVE SERIES**

Home Team

Series	Date	SEA	OAK	CAL	TEX	KC	MIN	CHI	MKE	DET	CLE	TOR	BAL	NY	BOS
1	Mon.		CAL*		BOS*		SEA		TOR*	NY*			CHI*		
	Tues.		CAL*		BOS*		SEA		TOR*	NY*	KC*		CHI*		
	Wed.		CAL		BOS*		SEA		TOR*	NY	KC*		CHI*		
2	Thurs.	DET*		MKE*	KC*						CHI*	TOR*			MIN*
	Fri.	DET*	NY*	MKE*	KC*						CHI*	TOR*			MIN*
	Sat.	DET*	NY	MKE*	KC*						CHI	TOR*			MIN*
	Sun.	DET	NY(2)	MKE	KC*						CHI	TOR			MIN*
3	Mon.	MKE*		NY*		BOS*							MIN*		
	Tues.	MKE*	DET*	NY*	CHI*	BOS*						CLE*	MIN*		
	Wed.	MKE*	DET*	NY*	CHI*	BOS*						CLE*	MIN*		
	Thurs.	MKE*	DET	NY*	CHI*							CLE*			
4	Fri.	NY*	MKE*	DET*	BAL*		CLE*	KC*				BOS*			
	Sat.	NY*	MKE	DET*	BAL*		CLE*	KC*				BOS			
	Sun.	NY*	MKE	DET	BAL*		CLE	KC				BOS			
5	Mon.				TEX*			CLE*				BOS*			
	Tues.				TEX*	BOS*	CLE*	CAL*	SEA*			BAL*		OAK*	
	Wed.				TEX*	BOS*	CLE*	CAL*	SEA*			BAL*		OAK*	
	Thurs.				TEX*	BOS		CAL	SEA*			BAL*		OAK*	

*Denotes night game or early-evening start. (2)Denotes doubleheader (two games in one day).

Table 10.9 — **UMPIRE CREW ASSIGNMENTS FOR THE FIRST FOUR SERIES ARE SHOWN AS SUPERSCRIPTS**

Home Team

Series	SEA	OAK	CAL	TEX	KC	MIN	CHI	MKE	DET	CLE	TOR	BAL	NY	BOS
1		CAL[5]		BOS[3]		SEA[7]		TOR[4]	NY[1]	KC[6]		CHI[2]		
2	DET[3]	NY[2]	MKE[7]	KC[5]						CHI[6]	TOR[4]			MIN[1]
3	MKE[2]	DET[7]	NY[3]	CHI[6]	BOS[5]						CLE[1]	MIN[4]		
4	NY[7]	MKE[3]	DET[2]	BAL[6]		CLE[5]	KC[4]				BOS[1]			
5				TEX	BOS	CLE	CAL	SEA			BAL		OAK	

For the fourth series, umpire crew 1 is assigned to the Boston at Toronto series

Table 10.10	DISTANCE COST MATRIX FOR UMPIRE CREW ASSIGNMENTS (SERIES 5)						
Crew From				**To**			
	KC	MIN	CHI	MKE	DET	TOR	NY
SEA(7)	1825	1399	2007	1694	1939	2124	2421
OAK(3)	1498	1589	2125	1845	2079	2286	2586
CAL(2)	1363	1536	2035	1756	1979	2175	2475
TEX(6)	506	853	798	843	982	1186	1383
MIN(5)	394	0	334	297	528	780	1028
CHI(4)	403	334	0	74	235	430	740
TOR(1)	968	897	497	583	206	0	366

Note: The numbers in parentheses reference umpire crews.

Case Problem   DISTRIBUTION SYSTEM DESIGN

The Darby Company manufactures and distributes meters used to measure electric power consumption. The company started with a small production plant in El Paso and gradually built a customer base throughout Texas. A distribution center was established in Ft. Worth, Texas, and later, as business expanded, a second distribution center was established in Santa Fe, New Mexico.

The El Paso plant was expanded when the company began marketing its meters in Arizona, California, Nevada, and Utah. With the growth of the West Coast business, the Darby Company opened a third distribution center in Las Vegas and just two years ago opened a second production plant in San Bernardino, California.

Manufacturing costs differ between the company's production plants. The cost of each meter produced at the El Paso plant is $10.50. The San Bernardino plant utilizes newer and more efficient equipment; as a result, manufacturing costs are $0.50 per meter less than at the El Paso plant.

Due to the company's rapid growth, not much attention had been paid to the efficiency of the distribution system, but Darby's management has decided that it is time to address this issue. The cost of shipping a meter from each of the two plants to each of the three distribution centers is shown in Table 10.11.

The quarterly production capacity is 30,000 meters at the older El Paso plant and 20,000 meters at the San Bernardino plant. Note that no shipments are allowed from the San Bernardino plant to the Ft. Worth distribution center.

The company serves nine customer zones from the three distribution centers. The forecast of the number of meters needed in each customer zone for the next quarter is shown in Table 10.12.

The cost per unit of shipping from each distribution center to each customer zone is given in Table 10.13; note that some distribution centers cannot serve certain customer zones.

In the current distribution system, demand at the Dallas, San Antonio, Wichita, and Kansas City customer zones is satisfied by shipments from the Ft. Worth distribution center. In a similar manner, the Denver, Salt Lake City, and Phoenix customer zones are served

Table 10.11	SHIPPING COST PER UNIT FROM PRODUCTION PLANTS TO DISTRIBUTION CENTERS (IN $)

| | Distribution Center | | |
Plant	Ft. Worth	Santa Fe	Las Vegas
El Paso	3.20	2.20	4.20
San Bernardino	—	3.90	1.20

Table 10.12	QUARTERLY DEMAND FORECAST

Customer Zone	Demand (meters)
Dallas	6300
San Antonio	4880
Wichita	2130
Kansas City	1210
Denver	6120
Salt Lake City	4830
Phoenix	2750
Los Angeles	8580
San Diego	4460

by the Santa Fe distribution center, and the Los Angeles and San Diego customer zones are served by the Las Vegas distribution center. To determine how many units to ship from each plant, the quarterly customer demand forecasts are aggregated at the distribution centers, and a transportation model is used to minimize the cost of shipping from the production plants to the distribution centers.

Managerial Report

You have been called in to make recommendations for improving the distribution system. Your report should address, but not be limited to, the following issues.

1. If the company does not change its current distribution strategy, what will its distribution costs be for the following quarter?
2. Suppose that the company is willing to consider dropping the distribution center limitations; that is, customers could be served by any of the distribution centers. Can costs be reduced? By how much?

Table 10.13	SHIPPING COST FROM THE DISTRIBUTION CENTERS TO THE CUSTOMER ZONES								

| Distribution Center | Customer Zone | | | | | | | | |
	Dallas	San Antonio	Wichita	Kansas City	Denver	Salt Lake City	Phoenix	Los Angeles	San Diego
Ft. Worth	0.3	2.1	3.1	4.4	6.0	—	—	—	—
Santa Fe	5.2	5.4	4.5	6.0	2.7	4.7	3.4	3.3	2.7
Las Vegas	—	—	—	—	5.4	3.3	2.4	2.1	2.5

3. The company wants to explore the possibility of satisfying some of the customer demand directly from the production plants. In particular, the shipping cost is $0.30 per unit from San Bernardino to Los Angeles and $0.70 from San Bernardino to San Diego. The cost for direct shipments from El Paso to San Antonio is $3.50 per unit. Can distribution costs be further reduced by considering these direct plant–customer shipments?

4. Over the next five years, Darby is anticipating moderate growth (5000 meters) to the North and West. Would you recommend that they consider plant expansion at this time?

··/ /·············

Appendix 10.1   SPREADSHEET SOLUTION OF TRANSPORTATION AND ASSIGNMENT PROBLEMS

In this appendix we show how Excel can be used to solve the Foster Generators transportation problem and the Fowle Marketing Research assignment problem. We begin by illustrating the solution for the transportation problem. First, the data for the transportation costs, the plant or origin capacities, and the distribution center or destination demands must be entered into a spreadsheet. Second, cells must be identified for storing the values of the decision variables x_{ij} (the number of units shipped from origin i to destination j), the value for the total transportation cost, the number of units shipped from each origin, and the number of units received at each destination. Figure 10.14 shows a spreadsheet for the Foster Generators problem in which the cells in the upper portion of the spreadsheet are reserved for problem input data, and the cells in the lower portion of the spreadsheet are reserved for the solution output. The Input Data section of the spreadsheet contains the following values:

Input Value	Cell Location
Transportation costs per unit	B4:E6
Plant capacities	F4:F6
Destination demands	B7:E7

The Solution Output section of the spreadsheet contains the following optimal solution values:

Output Value	Cell Location
Number of units shipped from origin i to destination j	B12:E14
Number of units shipped from each origin	F12:F14
Number of units received at each destination	B15:E15

To solve the Fosters Generator problem using Exel's solver, we must first write formulas that show how the values in the Solution Output section of the spreadsheet are related to the input data values. For instance, the total transportation cost in cell B17 is the sum of the products of the per unit shipping costs times the corresponding number of units shipped from each plant to each destination. Thus, the total cost is the sum of the products of the elements in cells B4:E6 times the corresponding elements in cells B12:E14. Using the SUMPRODUCT function, we entered the following formula in cell B17:

$$= \text{SUMPRODUCT (B4:E6,B12:E14)}$$

Since the number of units shipped from Cleveland is the sum of the values in cells B12:E12, in cell F12 we entered the formula = SUM(B12:E12). After copying this formula to cells F13 and F14, these cells will also contain the formulas for the number of units shipped from Bedford and York, respectively. Finally, note that the number of units received by Boston is the sum of the values in cells B12:B14; thus, in cell B15 we entered the formula = SUM(B12:B14). After copying this formula to cells C15:E15, these cells will also contain

Figure 10.14   SPREADSHEET FOR THE FOSTER GENERATORS TRANSPORTATION PROBLEM

	A	B	C	D	E	F
1	Input Data					
2			Destination			
3	Origin	Boston	Chicago	St. Louis	Lexington	Capacity
4	Cleveland	3	2	7	6	5000
5	Bedford	7	5	2	3	6000
6	York	2	5	4	5	2500
7	Demand	6000	4000	2000	1500	
8						
9	Solution Output					
10			Destination			
11	Origin	Boston	Chicago	St. Louis	Lexington	Units Shipped
12	Cleveland					
13	Bedford					
14	York					
15	Units Received					
16						
17	Total Cost					

the formulas for the number of units received at each of the other destinations. Figure 10.15 shows the formula spreadsheet for the Foster Generators problem.

We are now ready to use Solver to obtain an optimal solution to the problem. The following steps describe how to use Excel to obtain the optimal solution.

Step 1. Select the **Tools** pull-down menu
Step 2. Select the **Solver** option
Step 3. When the **Solver Parameters** dialog box appears
      Enter B17 in the **Set Target Cell** box
      Select the **Min** option
      Enter B12:E14 in the **By Changing Cells** box
      Choose **Add**
Step 4. When the **Add Constraint** dialog box appears
      Enter F12:F14 in the **Cell Reference** box
      Select < =
      Enter F4:F6 in the **Constraint** box
      Choose **Add**
      Enter B15:E15 in the **Cell Reference** box
      Select =
      Enter B7:E7 in the **Constraint** box
      Choose **Add**
      Enter B12:E14 in the **Cell Reference** box
      Select > =
      Enter 0 in the **Constraint** box
      Select **OK**
Step 5. When the **Solver Parameters** dialog box appears
      Choose **Options**

Figure 10.15 FORMULA SPREADSHEET FOR THE FOSTER GENERATORS TRANSPORTATION PROBLEM

	A	B	C	D	E	F
1	**Input Data**					
2				Destination		
3	**Origin**	Boston	Chicago	St. Louis	Lexington	Capacity
4	Cleveland	3	2	7	6	5000
5	Bedford	7	5	2	3	6000
6	York	2	5	4	5	2500
7	**Demand**	6000	4000	2000	1500	
8						
9	**Solution Output**					
10				Destination		
11	**Origin**	Boston	Chicago	St. Louis	Lexington	Units Shipped
12	Cleveland					=SUM(B12:E12)
13	Bedford					=SUM(B13:E13)
14	York					=SUM(B14:E14)
15	**Units Received**	=SUM(B12:B14)	=SUM(C12:C14)	=SUM(D12:D14)	=SUM(E12:E14)	
16						
17	**Total Cost**	=SUMPRODUCT(B4:E6,B12:E14)				

Step 6. When the **Solver Options** dialog box appears
Select **Assume Linear Model** box
Select **OK**
Step 7. When the **Solver Parameters** dialog box appears
Choose **Solve**
Step 8. When the **Solver Results** dialog box appears
Select **Keep Solver Solution**
Select **OK** to produce the optimal solution output

Figure 10.16 shows the optimal solution output. Note that the optimal solution is the same as we obtained using The Management Scientist software package.

Assignment problems such as the Fowle Marketing Research problem can also be solved in a similar fashion. That is, the assignment problem is a special case of the transportation problem in which all supply and demand values equal 1 and the amount shipped over each arc is either 0 or 1. Thus, to solve an assignment problem using the preceding approach, the per unit assignment costs simply replace the per unit transportation costs in the input data section of the spreadsheet, and the capacity and demand values are each set to a value of 1.

Figure 10.16   OPTIMAL SOLUTION FOR THE FOSTER GENERATORS TRANSPORTATION PROBLEM

	A	B	C	D	E	F
1	Input Data					
2		Destination				
3	Origin	Boston	Chicago	St. Louis	Lexington	Capacity
4	Cleveland	3	2	7	6	5000
5	Bedford	7	5	2	3	6000
6	York	2	5	4	5	2500
7	Demand	6000	4000	2000	1500	
8						
9	Solution Output					
10		Destination				
11	Origin	Boston	Chicago	St. Louis	Lexington	Units Shipped
12	Cleveland	3500	1500	0	0	5000
13	Bedford	0	2500	2000	1500	6000
14	York	2500	0	0	0	2500
15	Units Received	6000	4000	2000	1500	
16						
17	Total Cost	39500				

PROCTER & GAMBLE*

CINCINNATI, OHIO

Procter & Gamble (P&G) is in the consumer-products business worldwide. P&G produces and markets such products as detergents, disposable diapers, coffee, over-the-counter pharmaceuticals, dentifrices, bar soaps, mouthwashes, and paper towels. It has the leading brand in more categories than any other consumer-products company in the United States.

To maintain its leadership position in its many markets, P&G makes extensive use of quantitative methods. Some of the methodologies employed include probability and risk analysis, linear and integer programming, network flow analysis, and simulation. The individuals employing these methodologies are scattered throughout P&G's numerous divisions with perhaps the largest concentration being in the management systems division. P&G employs engineers, operations researchers, computer scientists, and businesspeople who are skilled in employing quantitative methodologies.

When P&G embarked on a major strategic planning initiative, the North American Product Sourcing Study, it was interested in consolidating its product sources and optimizing its distribution system design throughout North America. One of the decision support systems that proved to be a great aid in this project was called the Product Sourcing Heuristic (PSH). This heuristic was based on a transshipment model much like the ones described in this chapter.

In a preprocessing phase, all P&G products were aggregated into groups that shared the same technology and could be made at the same plant. The PSH was used by product strategy teams that had responsibility for de-

veloping product sourcing options for the separate product groups. The various plants that could produce the product group were source nodes, the company's regional distribution centers were the transshipment nodes, and P&G's customer zones were the destinations. Direct shipments to customer zones as well as shipments through distribution centers were employed.

The product strategy teams used the heuristic interactively to explore a variety of questions concerning product sourcing and distribution. For instance, the team might be interested in the impact of closing two plants and consolidating production in three remaining plants. The product sourcing heuristic would then delete the source nodes corresponding to the two closed plants, make any capacity modifications recommended to the sources corresponding to the remaining three plants, and resolve the transshipment problem. The product strategy team could then examine the new solution, make some more modifications, solve again, and so on.

The Product Sourcing Heuristic was viewed as a valuable decision support system by all who used it. Probably the most valuable feature was that the model permitted a rapid evaluation of a variety of strategic options. A feature that was viewed as a big plus by all who used it was that solutions provided by the PSH were displayed on a map of North America using a geographic information system. This map enabled strategic planners to review immediately the impact of their sourcing decisions across North America. The PSH has proven so successful that P&G is considering using it in other markets around the world.

*The authors are indebted to Mr. Franz Dill and Mr. Tom Chorman of Proctor & Gamble for providing this application.

11

INTEGER LINEAR PROGRAMMING

In this chapter we discuss a class of problems that are modeled as linear programs with the additional requirement that one or more of the variables must be integer. Such a linear program is called an **integer linear program.** If all variables must be integer, we have an **all-integer linear program.** If some, but not all, variables must be integer, we have a **mixed-integer linear program.** In many applications of integer linear programming, one or more integer variables are required to equal either 0 or 1. Such variables are called *0–1* or *binary variables.* If all integer variables are 0–1 variables, we have a **0–1 integer linear program.**

Integer variables—especially 0–1 variables—provide additional modeling flexibility. As a result, the number of applications that can be addressed with linear programming methodology is expanded. The cost of the added modeling flexibility is that problems involving integer variables are often much more difficult to solve. A linear programming problem with several thousand continuous variables can be solved with any of several commercial linear programming software packages. However, an all-integer linear programming problem with less than 100 variables can sometimes be extremely difficult to solve. Experienced quantitative analysts can help identify the types of integer linear programs that are easy, or at least reasonable, to solve. Commercial computer software packages, such as MPSX-MIP®, OSL®, CPLEX®, and LINDO®, have extensive capabilities for solving integer programming problems. The Management Scientist and spreadsheet packages, such as Excel, also have the capability for solving smaller integer linear programs.

The objective in this chapter is to provide an applications-oriented introduction to integer linear programming. First, we discuss the different types of integer linear programming models. Then we show the formulation, graphical solution, and computer

The modeling flexibility provided by the use of 0 –1 variables is a major contribution of integer programming.

solution of an all-integer linear program. In Section 11.3, we discuss four applications of integer linear programming that make use of 0–1 variables: capital budgeting, fixed-cost, distribution system design, and bank location problems. In Section 11.4, we provide additional illustrations of the modeling flexibility provided by 0–1 variables.

Some linear programming problems have special structures that guarantee the variables will take on integer values in the solution. The assignment, transportation, and transshipment problems of Chapter 10 have such structures. If the supply and demand values are all integer, the optimal linear programming solution of these problems will show integer amounts shipped over all routes. For the assignment problem, the optimal linear programming solution will consist of 0s and 1s. So, for these specially structured problems, using special integer programming capability to find integer solutions is unnecessary.

11.1   TYPES OF INTEGER LINEAR PROGRAMMING MODELS

The only difference between the problems studied in this chapter and the ones studied in earlier chapters on linear programming is that one or more of the variables are required to be integer. If all the variables are required to be integer, we have an all-integer linear program. The following is a two-variable, all-integer linear programming model.

$$\text{Max} \quad 2x_1 + 3x_2$$
$$\text{s.t.}$$
$$3x_1 + 3x_2 \leq 12$$
$$\tfrac{2}{3}x_1 + 1x_2 \leq 4$$
$$1x_1 + 2x_2 \leq 6$$
$$x_1, x_2 \geq 0 \text{ and integer}$$

Note that if we drop the phrase "and integer" from this model, we have the familiar two-variable linear program. The linear program that results from dropping the integer requirements is called the **LP** (linear programming) **Relaxation** of the integer linear program.

If some, but not all, of the variables are required to be integer, we have a mixed-integer linear program. The following is a two-variable, mixed-integer linear program.

$$\text{Max} \quad 3x_1 + 4x_2$$
$$\text{s.t.}$$
$$-1x_1 + 2x_2 \leq 8$$
$$1x_1 + 2x_2 \leq 12$$
$$2x_1 + 1x_2 \leq 16$$
$$x_1, x_2 \geq 0 \text{ and } x_2 \text{ integer}$$

We obtain the LP Relaxation of this mixed-integer linear program by dropping the requirement that x_2 be integer.

In many applications of integer programming, one or more integer variables are required to take on the values of 0 or 1. As we see later in the chapter, 0–1 variables add greatly to the ability to model real world applications. The Q.M. in Action: Planning the Size of

You should now be able to recognize the various types of integer programs and their LP Relaxations. Try Problem 1.

Q.M. IN ACTION

PLANNING THE SIZE OF KLM'S AIRCRAFT MAINTENANCE TEAMS*

KLM Royal Dutch Airlines has been the major Dutch carrier since 1919. Currently, KLM owns 90 aircraft of 8 different types and operates flights to 150 cities in 79 countries. To guarantee safety, KLM has a high-quality aircraft maintenance program with a workforce that includes 250 engineers and 150 nontechnical employees.

Preventive aircraft maintenance consists of both major inspections and minor inspections. Major inspections take from several hours to several months to complete. Minor inspections are conducted during the ground time between aircraft arrival and departure at the airport. Engineers from KLM's aircraft maintenance group are organized into teams that carry out the maintenance tasks required for a particular shift.

The engineers are highly skilled and well trained. A governmental rule specifies that maintenance engineers are allowed to carry out inspections on a specific aircraft type only if licensed for that aircraft type. KLM's internal safety rules further limit engineers to licenses on at most two aircraft types. When licensed for a particular aircraft, an individual engineer's skills are certified as being mechanical, electrical, or radio.

KLM's management strives to develop a good match between work load requirements and the abilities of the assigned workforce. Given a set of maintenance jobs, management trys to minimize the number of engineers with appropriate license and skill combinations necessary to complete the jobs. An integer linear programming model helps with this task. The objective function is to minimize the number of engineers required per maintenance team. Integer decision variables are required because the number of engineers with each license and skill combination cannot be fractional. In addition, 0–1 integer variables are included in the model to guarantee that each maintenance job is carried out exactly once. Another integer programming model is used to determine the maximum number of maintenance jobs that can be scheduled given the size and composition of the maintenance workforce.

KLM has found integer linear programming to be a valuable tool for solving problems that appear in personnel planning for aircraft maintenance.

*Based on Dijkstra, M. C., L. G. Kroon, M. Slomon, J. A. E. E. Van Nunen, and L. N. Van Wassenhove, "Planning the Size and Organization of KLM's Aircraft Maintenance Personnel," *Interfaces*, November–December 1994, pp. 47–58.

KLM's Aircraft Maintenance Teams describes how an integer linear programming model is used to determine the size of the engineering teams that perform maintenance on KLM's aircraft.

11.2   GRAPHICAL AND COMPUTER SOLUTION FOR AN ALL-INTEGER LINEAR PROGRAM

Eastborne Realty has $2,000,000 available for the purchase of new rental property. After an initial screening, Eastborne has reduced the investment alternatives to townhouses and apartment buildings. Each townhouse can be purchased for $282,000, but only five townhouses are available. Each apartment building contains six dwelling units and can be purchased for $400,000 per building. The developer has agreed to construct as many apartment buildings as Eastborne wants to purchase.

Eastborne's property manager can devote 140 hours a month to these new investments. Each townhouse will require 4 hours a month, and each apartment building will require 40 hours a month. The annual cash flow after deducting mortgage payments and operating expenses is estimated to be $10,000 per townhouse and $15,000 per apartment building. Eastborne's owner would like to determine the number of townhouses and the number of apartment buildings to purchase to maximize annual cash flow.

We begin by defining the decision variables as follows:

$$x_1 = \text{number of townhouses purchased}$$
$$x_2 = \text{number of apartment buildings purchased}$$

The objective function, measuring cash flow in thousands of dollars, is

$$\text{Max} \quad 10x_1 + 15x_2$$

Three constraints must be satisfied:

$282x_1 + 400x_2 \leq 2000$	Investment funds in thousands of dollars
$x_1 \qquad\quad \leq 5$	Townhouses available
$4x_1 + 40x_2 \leq 140$	Manager's time in hours

The variables x_1 and x_2 must be nonnegative. In addition, the purchase of a fractional number of townhouses and/or a fractional number of apartment buildings is unacceptable. Thus, x_1 and x_2 must be integer. The model for the Eastborne Realty problem is the following all-integer linear program.

$$\text{Max} \quad 10x_1 + 15x_2$$
$$\text{s.t.}$$
$$282x_1 + 400x_2 \leq 2000$$
$$x_1 \qquad\quad \leq 5$$
$$4x_1 + 40x_2 \leq 140$$
$$x_1, x_2 \geq 0 \text{ and integer}$$

Graphical Solution of the LP Relaxation

Let us drop the integer requirements for x_1 and x_2 and solve the LP Relaxation of the Eastborne Realty problem. Using the graphical solution procedure as presented in Chapter 7, the optimal solution is shown in Figure 11.1. It is $x_1 = 2.479$ townhouses and $x_2 = 3.252$ apartment buildings with an objective function value of 73.574 providing an annual cash flow of $73,574. The difficulty with this solution is that Eastborne cannot purchase fractional numbers of townhouses and apartment buildings. Further analysis is required.

Rounding to Obtain an Integer Solution

In many cases, a non-integer solution to a linear programming problem can be rounded to obtain an acceptable integer solution. For example, a linear programming solution for a breakfast cereal manufacturer might recommend the production of 15,132.4 cases of a particular cereal. The rounded integer solution of 15,132 cases would probably have minimal impact on the value of the objective function and the feasibility of the solution. In this situation, rounding to obtain an integer solution would be a very good and acceptable strategy. Indeed, whenever rounding has a minimal impact on the objective function and constraints, most managers find it acceptable. A near optimal solution is fine.

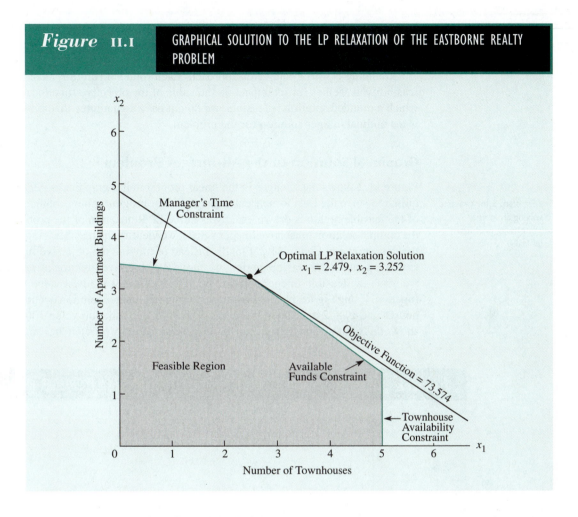

Figure 11.1 GRAPHICAL SOLUTION TO THE LP RELAXATION OF THE EASTBORNE REALTY PROBLEM

However, rounding to obtain an integer solution may not always be a good strategy. For example, suppose that a commercial airline company is considering expanding its fleet with the purchase of new multimillion dollar airplanes. If the linear programming solution calls for the purchase of 5.5 new airplanes, rounding to purchase either 5 or perhaps 6 airplanes may have a significant impact on both the value of the objective function and the feasibility of the solution. In this situation, rounding is not a good idea; one wants to be sure of obtaining the optimal integer solution.

Let us return to the LP Relaxation solution for the Eastborne Realty problem with $x_1 = 2.479$ townhouses and $x_2 = 3.252$ apartment buildings. Since each townhouse costs $282,000 and each apartment building costs $400,000, rounding to an integer solution can be expected to have a significant economic impact on the problem. Suppose that we round down to obtain the integer solution $x_1 = 2$ and $x_2 = 3$. This rounding provides a feasible integer solution with an objective function value of $10(2) + 15(3) = 65$ showing an annual cash flow of $65,000. This objective function value is not as good as the annual cash flow of $73,574 provided by the solution to the LP Relaxation. However, is this the optimal integer solution? Or would a different integer solution provide an annual cash flow better than $65,000? Exploring other rounding alternatives shows that the integer solution $x_1 = 3$ and $x_2 = 3$ is infeasible because the solution requires more funds than the $2,000,000 Eastborne has available for the new investments. The rounded integer solution of $x_1 = 2$ and $x_2 = 4$

If the problem has only less-than-or-equal-to constraints with positive coefficients for the variables, rounding down will always provide a feasible integer solution.

is also infeasible for the same reason. Thus, at this point, rounding to a feasible integer solution leaves us with two townhouses, three apartment buildings, and an annual cash flow of $65,000 as the best integer solution to the problem.

Rounding is a trial-and-error approach. Each rounded solution must be evaluated for feasibility as well as for its impact on the value of the objective function. Even in cases in which a rounded solution is feasible, we do not have a guarantee that the rounded solution is the optimal integer solution for the problem.

Graphical Solution to the All-Integer Problem

Try Problem 2 for practice in solving an integer programming problem graphically.

Figure 11.2 shows the changes in the linear programming graphical solution procedure required to solve the Eastborne Realty integer linear programming problem. First, the graph of the feasible region is drawn exactly as in the LP Relaxation of the problem. Then, since the optimal solution must have integer values, we identify the feasible integer solutions with the dots shown in Figure 11.2. Finally, instead of moving the objective function line to an extreme point of the feasible region, we move the objective function as far as we can until we reach the feasible integer solution point that provides the best value for the objective function. Using Figure 11.2, we see that this optimal integer solution occurs at $x_1 = 4$ townhouses and $x_2 = 2$ apartment buildings. The objective function value $10(4) + 15(2) = 70$ shows this optimal integer solution to the Eastborne Realty problem has an annual cash flow

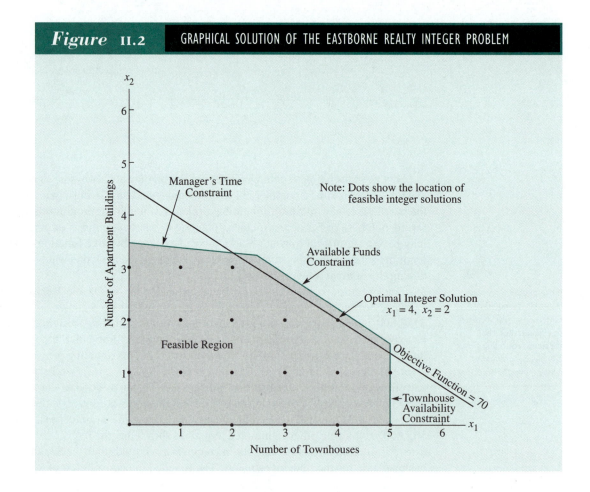

Figure 11.2 GRAPHICAL SOLUTION OF THE EASTBORNE REALTY INTEGER PROBLEM

Try Problem 5 and see if you can solve a mixed-integer program graphically.

of \$70,000. This solution is better than the best solution that we found by rounding $x_1 = 2$, $x_2 = 3$, with value = \$65,000.

A Note on the Use of the LP Relaxation Solution

An important observation can be made from the analysis of the Eastborne Realty problem. It has to do with the relationship between the value of the optimal integer solution and the value of the optimal LP Relaxation solution. This observation is stated as follows for maximization problems.[1]

The value of the optimal solution to any integer linear program involving maximization yields a value that is *less than or equal to* the value of the optimal solution to its LP Relaxation.

In the Eastborne Realty problem, the value of the optimal integer solution was \$70,000, which is less than the \$73,574 for the optimal solution to its LP Relaxation.

The above property tells us that if by chance the solution to the LP Relaxation problem turns out to be an integer solution, it must be the optimal solution to the integer linear programming problem. That is, nothing more needs to be done because the value of the optimal solution to an integer linear program must be less than or equal to the value of the optimal solution to its LP Relaxation. In practice, you can find an **upper bound** on the value of the objective function for any maximization integer programming problem by solving its LP Relaxation. Then, if you round the LP Relaxation solution to an integer solution that is feasible and that provides a value of the objective function that is *almost as good* as the value of the LP Relaxation solution, you know that you have a very good or near-optimal integer solution. When this occurs, you can avoid solving the integer linear programming problem directly.

Computer Solution

As mentioned earlier, commercial software packages that can solve integer linear programs are widely available. Generally, these packages are reliable for problems having up to approximately 100 integer variables and may be used to solve specially structured problems with several thousand integer variables.

The Management Scientist can be used to solve the integer linear programs in this chapter. To use The Management Scientist to solve the Eastborne Realty problem, the data input worksheet is completed in the same way as for any linear program (see Appendix 8.1). Then after instructing the computer to solve the problem, the user will be asked to indicate which of the variables are integer. Specifying both x_1 and x_2 as integer provides the optimal integer solution shown in Figure 11.3. The solution of $x_1 = 4$ townhouses and $x_2 = 2$ apartment buildings has a maximum annual cash flow of \$70,000. The values of the slack variables tell us that the optimal solution has \$72,000 of available funds unused, 1 of the available townhouses not purchased, and 44 hours of the manager's time still available.

---

1. For minimization problems, this observation would be stated with "greater than or equal to" substituted for "less than or equal to."

| Figure 11.3 | THE MANAGEMENT SCIENTIST SOLUTION FOR THE EASTBORNE REALTY PROBLEM |

Objective Function Value =   70.000

Variable	Value
X1	4.000
X2	2.000

Constraint	Slack/Surplus
1	72.000
2	1.000
3	44.000

11.3 APPLICATIONS INVOLVING 0–1 VARIABLES

Much of the modeling flexibility provided by integer linear programming is due to the use of 0–1 variables. In many applications, 0–1 variables provide selections or choices with the value of the variable equal to 1 if a corresponding activity is undertaken and equal to 0 if the corresponding activity is not undertaken. The capital budgeting, fixed cost, distribution system design, and bank location applications presented in this section make use of 0–1 variables.

Capital Budgeting

The Ice-Cold Refrigerator Company is considering investing in several projects that have varying capital requirements over the next four years. Faced with limited capital each year, management would like to select the most profitable projects for capital expenditures. The estimated net present value for each project,[2] the capital requirements, and the available capital over the four-year period are shown in Table 11.1.

We define four 0–1 decision variables as follows:

x_1 = 1 if the plant expansion project is accepted; 0 if rejected

x_2 = 1 if the warehouse expansion project is accepted; 0 if rejected

x_3 = 1 if the new machinery project is accepted; 0 if rejected

x_4 = 1 if the new product research project is accepted; 0 if rejected

The company's objective function is to maximize the net present value over all projects accepted. This problem has four constraints: one for the funds available in each of the next four years.

---

2. The estimated net present value is the net cash flow discounted back to the beginning of year 1.

| **Table 11.1** | PROJECT NET PRESENT VALUE, CAPITAL REQUIREMENTS, AND AVAILABLE CAPITAL FOR THE ICE-COLD REFRIGERATOR COMPANY |

	Project				
	Plant Expansion	**Warehouse Expansion**	**New Machinery**	**New Product Research**	
Estimated Net Present Value	$90,000	$40,000	$10,000	$37,000	Capital Available
Year 1 Capital	$15,000	$10,000	$10,000	$15,000	$40,000
Year 2 Capital	$20,000	$15,000		$10,000	$50,000
Year 3 Capital	$20,000	$20,000		$10,000	$40,000
Year 4 Capital	$15,000	$ 5,000	$4,000	$10,000	$35,000

The 0–1 integer linear programming model with dollars in thousands is as follows:

$$\text{Max} \quad 90x_1 + 40x_2 + 10x_3 + 37x_4$$

s.t.

$$15x_1 + 10x_2 + 10x_3 + 15x_4 \leq 40 \quad \text{(Year 1 capital available)}$$
$$20x_1 + 15x_2 \qquad\quad + 10x_4 \leq 50 \quad \text{(Year 2 capital available)}$$
$$20x_1 + 20x_2 \qquad\quad + 10x_4 \leq 40 \quad \text{(Year 3 capital available)}$$
$$15x_1 + 5x_2 + 4x_3 + 10x_4 \leq 35 \quad \text{(Year 4 capital available)}$$
$$x_1, x_2, x_3, x_4 = 0, 1$$

The integer programming solution from The Management Scientist is shown in Figure 11.4. The optimal solution is $x_1 = 1$, $x_2 = 1$, $x_3 = 1$, $x_4 = 0$, with a total estimated net present value of $140,000. Thus, the company should fund the plant expansion, the warehouse expansion, and the new machinery projects. The new product research project should be put on hold unless additional capital funds become available. The values of the slack variables (see Figure 11.4) show that the company will have $5,000 remaining in year 1, $15,000 remaining in year 2, and $11,000 remaining in year 4. Checking the capital requirements for the new product research project, we see that enough funds are available for this project in year 2 and year 4. However, the company would have to find additional capital funds of $10,000 in year 1 and $10,000 in year 3 to fund the new product research project.

Fixed Cost

In many applications, the cost of production has two components: a setup cost, which is a fixed charge not related to the production volume, and a variable cost, which is directly related to the production volume. The use of 0–1 variables makes possible including the fixed setup cost in a product mix or production scheduling problem.

For example, let us return to the RMC product mix problem as presented in Section 8.2. RMC is a small firm that produces a variety of chemical-based products. Let us assume RMC has expanded its product line to include three products: a fuel additive, a solvent base, and a carpet cleaning fluid. We define the decision variables as follows:

Figure II.4	THE MANAGEMENT SCIENTIST SOLUTION FOR THE ICE-COLD REFRIGERATOR COMPANY PROBLEM

```
Objective Function Value =                    140.000

         Variable                              Value
            X1                                 1.000

            X2                                 1.000

            X3                                 1.000

            X4                                 0.000


         Constraint                         Slack/Surplus
             1                                 5.000

             2                                15.000

             3                                 0.000

             4                                11.000
```

x_1 = tons of fuel additive produced

x_2 = tons of solvent base produced

x_3 = tons of carpet cleaning fluid produced

The profit contributions are $40 per ton for the fuel additive, $30 per ton for the solvent base, and $50 per ton for the carpet cleaning fluid. Each ton of fuel additive requires 0.4 tons of material 1 and 0.6 tons of material 3. Each ton of solvent base requires 0.5 tons of material 1, 0.2 tons of material 2, and 0.3 tons of material 3. Each ton of carpet cleaning fluid requires 0.6 tons of material 1, 0.1 tons of material 2, and 0.3 tons of material 3. For the upcoming production period, RMC has 20 tons of material 1, 5 tons of material 2, and 21 tons of material 3 available.

The linear programming model for the RMC problem is as follows:

$$\text{Max} \quad 40x_1 + 30x_2 + 50x_3$$

$$\text{s.t.}$$

$$0.4x_1 + 0.5x_2 + 0.6x_3 \leq 20 \quad \text{Material 1}$$

$$0.2x_2 + 0.1x_3 \leq 5 \quad \text{Material 2}$$

$$0.6x_1 + 0.3x_2 + 0.3x_3 \leq 21 \quad \text{Material 3}$$

$$x_1, x_2, x_3 \geq 0$$

This formulation does not include a fixed cost to set up for production of the products. Suppose that the following data are available concerning the setup cost and the maximum production quantity for each of the 3 products.

Product	Setup Cost	Maximum Production
Fuel additive	$200	50 tons
Solvent base	$ 50	25 tons
Carpet cleaning fluid	$400	40 tons

The modeling flexibility provided by 0–1 variables can now be used to incorporate the fixed setup costs into the production model. We define 0–1 variables as follows:

$y_1 = 1$ if the fuel additive is produced; 0 if it is not produced

$y_2 = 1$ if the solvent base is produced; 0 if it is not produced

$y_3 = 1$ if the carpet cleaning fluid is produced; 0 if it is not produced

Using these variables, the total setup cost is

$$200y_1 + 50y_2 + 400y_3$$

Thus, the objective function for the RMC problem including the setup cost is

$$\text{Max} \quad 40x_1 + 30x_2 + 50x_3 - 200y_1 - 50y_2 - 400y_3$$

Now we must write production capacity constraints so that if a setup variable equals 0, production is not permitted. When a setup variable equals 1, production is permitted up to the maximum quantity. For the fuel additive, we add the following constraint:

$$x_1 \leq 50y_1$$

Note that if $y_1 = 0$, production of the fuel additive is not permitted ($x_1 \leq 0$). However, if $y_1 = 1$, production of the fuel additive is permitted up to its maximum level ($x_1 \leq 50$). We can think of the setup variable as a switch. When it is off ($y_1 = 0$), production is not permitted; when it is on ($y_1 = 1$), production is permitted.

Similar production capacity constraints for the solvent base and carpet cleaning fluid products are

$$x_2 \leq 25y_2$$

and

$$x_3 \leq 40y_3$$

Moving all variables to the left-hand side of the constraints provides the following fixed charge model for the RMC problem.

$$\text{Max} \quad 40x_1 + 30x_2 + 50x_3 - 200y_1 - 50y_2 - 400y_3$$

s.t.

$$
\begin{array}{llll}
0.4x_1 + 0.5x_2 + 0.6x_3 & & \leq 20 & \text{Material 1} \\
 0.2x_2 + 0.1x_3 & & \leq 5 & \text{Material 2} \\
0.6x_1 + 0.3x_2 + 0.3x_3 & & \leq 21 & \text{Material 3} \\
x_1 & - 50y_1 & \leq 0 & \text{Maximum } x_1 \\
 x_2 & - 25y_2 & \leq 0 & \text{Maximum } x_2 \\
 x_3 & - 40y_3 \leq 0 & & \text{Maximum } x_3
\end{array}
$$

$$x_1, x_2, x_3 \geq 0; \ y_1, y_2, y_3 = 0, 1$$

Using the integer linear programming module of The Management Scientist, we obtain the optimal solution of 25 tons of fuel additive, 20 tons of solvent base, and 0 tons of carpet cleaning fluid. The objective function value including the setup costs is $1350. The setup cost for the fuel additive and the solvent base is $200 + $50 = $250. The more expensive $400 setup cost for the carpet cleaning fluid has been avoided by setting y_3 equal to 0.

The key to developing fixed charge models is the introduction of a 0–1 variable for each fixed charge and the specification of an upper bound for the corresponding production variable. A constraint of the form $x_i \leq M_i y_i$ can then be used to allow production when $y_i = 1$ and not to allow production when $y_i = 0$. The value of M_i should be large enough to allow for all reasonable levels of production, but not too large. Research has shown that choosing values of M_i too large will slow the solution procedure.

Distribution System Design

The Martin-Beck Company operates a plant in St. Louis with an annual capacity of 30,000 units. Product is shipped to regional distribution centers located in Boston, Atlanta, and Houston. Because of an anticipated increase in demand, Martin-Beck plans to increase capacity by constructing a new plant in one or more of the following cities: Detroit, Toledo, Denver, and/or Kansas City. The estimated annual fixed cost and the annual capacity for the four proposed plants are as follows:

Proposed Plant	Annual Fixed Cost	Annual Capacity
Detroit	$175,000	10,000
Toledo	$300,000	20,000
Denver	$375,000	30,000
Kansas City	$500,000	40,000

The company's long-range planning group has developed forecasts of the anticipated annual demand at the distribution centers as follows:

Distribution Center	Annual Demand
Boston	30,000
Atlanta	20,000
Houston	20,000

The shipping cost per unit from each plant to each distribution center is shown in Table 11.2. A network representation of the potential Martin-Beck distribution system is shown in Figure 11.5. Each potential plant location is shown; capacities and demands are shown in thousands of units. This network representation is for a transportation problem with a plant at all four proposed sites. However, the decision has not yet been made as to which new plant or plants will be constructed.

Let us show how 0–1 variables can be used to develop a model for choosing the best plant locations and for determining how much to ship from each plant to each distribution center. We can use the following 0–1 variables to represent the plant construction decision.

$$y_1 = 1 \text{ if a plant is constructed in Detroit; } 0 \text{ if not}$$
$$y_2 = 1 \text{ if a plant is constructed in Toledo; } 0 \text{ if not}$$
$$y_3 = 1 \text{ if a plant is constructed in Denver; } 0 \text{ if not}$$
$$y_4 = 1 \text{ if a plant is constructed in Kansas City; } 0 \text{ if not}$$

The variables representing the amount shipped from each potential plant site to each distribution center are defined just as for a transportation problem.

$$x_{ij} = \text{the units shipped in thousands from plant } i \text{ to distribution center } j$$
$$i = 1, 2, 3, 4, 5 \quad \text{and} \quad j = 1, 2, 3$$

Using the shipping cost data in Table 11.2, the annual transportation cost in thousand of dollars is written

$$5x_{11} + 2x_{12} + 3x_{13} + 4x_{21} + 3x_{22} + 4x_{23} + 9x_{31} + 7x_{32} + 5x_{33} + 10x_{41} + 4x_{42}$$
$$+ 2x_{43} + 8x_{51} + 4x_{52} + 3x_{53}$$

The annual fixed cost of operating the new plant or plants in thousand of dollars is written as

$$175y_1 + 300y_2 + 375y_3 + 500y_4$$

Note that the 0–1 variables are defined so that the above annual fixed cost of operating the new plants is only calculated for the plant or plants that are actually constructed (i.e., $y_i = 1$). If a plant is not constructed, $y_i = 0$ and the corresponding annual fixed cost is $0.

Table 11.2	SHIPPING COST PER UNIT FOR THE MARTIN-BECK DISTRIBUTION SYSTEM		
	Distribution Centers		
Plant Site	**Boston**	**Atlanta**	**Houston**
Detroit	5	2	3
Toledo	4	3	4
Denver	9	7	5
Kansas City	10	4	2
St. Louis	8	4	3

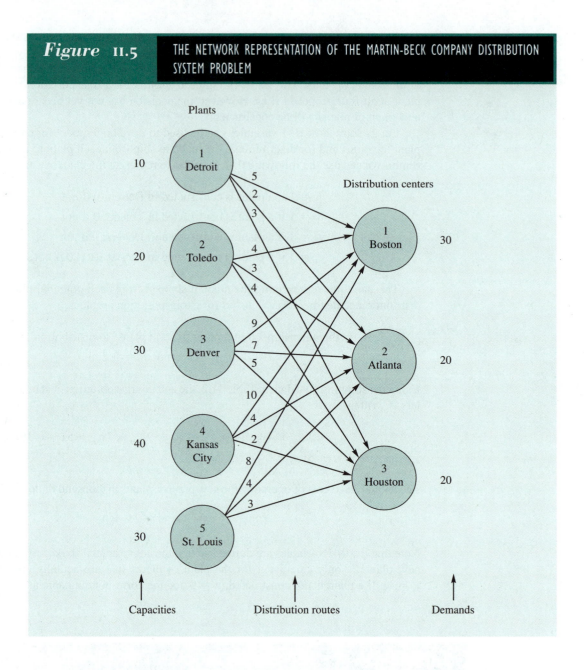

Figure 11.5   THE NETWORK REPRESENTATION OF THE MARTIN-BECK COMPANY DISTRIBUTION SYSTEM PROBLEM

The Martin-Beck objective function is the sum of the annual transportation cost plus the annual fixed cost of operating the newly constructed plants.

Now let us consider the capacity constraints at the four proposed plants. Using Detroit as an example, we write the following constraint:

$$x_{11} + x_{12} + x_{13} \leq 10y_1$$

If the Detroit plant is constructed, $y_1 = 1$ and the total amount shipped from Detroit to the three distribution centers must be less or equal to Detroit's 10,000-unit capacity. If the Detroit plant is not constructed, $y_1 = 0$ will result in a 0 capacity at Detroit. In this case, the variables corresponding to the shipments from Detroit must all equal zero: $x_{11} = 0$, $x_{12} = 0$, and $x_{13} = 0$. By placing all variables on the left-hand side of the constraints, we have the following Detroit capacity constraint:

$$x_{11} + x_{12} + x_{13} - 10y_1 \leq 0 \qquad \text{Detroit capacity}$$

In a similar fashion, the capacity constraint for the proposed plant in Toledo can be written

$$x_{21} + x_{22} + x_{23} - 20y_2 \leq 0 \qquad \text{Toledo capacity}$$

Similar constraints can be written for the proposed plants in Denver and Kansas City. Note that since the plant already exists in St. Louis, we do not define a 0–1 variable for this plant. Its capacity constraint can be written as follows:

$$x_{51} + x_{52} + x_{53} \leq 30 \qquad \text{St. Louis capacity}$$

Three demand constraints will be needed, one for each of the three distribution centers. The demand constraint for the Boston distribution center with units in thousands is written as

$$x_{11} + x_{21} + x_{31} + x_{41} + x_{51} = 30 \qquad \text{Boston demand}$$

Similar constraints appear for the Atlanta and Houston distribution centers.

The complete model for the Martin-Beck distribution system design problem is as follows:

$$\text{Min} \quad 5x_{11} + 2x_{12} + 3x_{13} + 4x_{21} + 3x_{22} + 4x_{23} + 9x_{31} + 7x_{32} + 5x_{33} + 10x_{41} + 4x_{42}$$
$$+ 2x_{43} + 8x_{51} + 4x_{52} + 3x_{53} + 175y_1 + 300y_2 + 375y_3 + 500y_4$$

s.t.

$$
\begin{aligned}
x_{11} + x_{12} + x_{13} \qquad\qquad - 10y_1 &\qquad\qquad\qquad \leq 0 \qquad \text{Detroit capacity}\\
x_{21} + x_{22} + x_{23} \qquad\qquad\quad - 20y_2 &\qquad\qquad\qquad \leq 0 \qquad \text{Toledo capacity}\\
x_{31} + x_{32} + x_{33} \qquad\qquad\qquad\quad - 30y_3 &\qquad\qquad \leq 0 \qquad \text{Denver capacity}\\
x_{41} + x_{42} + x_{43} \qquad\qquad\qquad\qquad\quad - 40y_4 &\leq 0 \qquad \text{Kansas City capacity}\\
x_{51} + x_{52} + x_{53} &\leq 30 \qquad \text{St. Louis capacity}\\
x_{11} + x_{21} + x_{31} + x_{41} + x_{51} &= 30 \qquad \text{Boston demand}\\
x_{12} + x_{22} + x_{32} + x_{42} + x_{52} &= 20 \qquad \text{Atlanta demand}\\
x_{13} + x_{23} + x_{33} + x_{43} + x_{53} &= 20 \qquad \text{Houston demand}
\end{aligned}
$$

$x_{ij} \geq 0$ for all i and j; $y_1, y_2, y_3, y_4 = 0, 1$

Using the integer linear programming module of The Management Scientist, we obtained the solution shown in Figure 11.6. The optimal solution calls for the construction of a plant in Kansas City ($y_4 = 1$); 20,000 units will be shipped from Kansas City to Atlanta ($x_{42} = 20$), 20,000 units will be shipped from Kansas City to Houston ($x_{43} = 20$), and 30,000 units will be shipped from St. Louis to Boston ($x_{51} = 30$). Note that the total cost of this solution including the fixed cost of $500,000 to construct the plant in Kansas City is $860,000.

Figure 11.6   THE MANAGEMENT SCIENTIST SOLUTION FOR THE MARTIN-BECK COMPANY DISTRIBUTION SYSTEM PROBLEM

```
OPTIMAL SOLUTION

Objective Function Value =                    860.000

        Variable                              Value
        _____                            _____
          X11                                 0.000
          X12                                 0.000
          X13                                 0.000
          X21                                 0.000
          X22                                 0.000
          X23                                 0.000
          X31                                 0.000
          X32                                 0.000
          X33                                 0.000
          X41                                 0.000
          X42                                20.000
          X43                                20.000
          X51                                30.000
          X52                                 0.000
          X53                                 0.000
           Y1                                 0.000
           Y2                                 0.000
           Y3                                 0.000
           Y4                                 1.000


       Constraint                        Slack/Surplus
       _____                        _____
           1                                 0.000
           2                                 0.000
           3                                 0.000
           4                                 0.000
           5                                 0.000
           6                                 0.000
           7                                 0.000
           8                                 0.000
```

This basic model can be expanded to accommodate distribution systems involving direct shipments from plants to warehouses, from plants to retail outlets, and of multiple products.[3] Using the special properties of 0–1 variables, the model can also be expanded to accommodate a variety of configuration constraints on the plant locations. For example, suppose in another problem, site 1 was in Dallas and site 2 was in Fort Worth. A company might not want to locate plants in both Dallas and Fort Worth because the cities are so close together. To prevent this result, the following constraint can be added to the model:

---

3. For computational reasons, it is usually preferable to replace the m plant capacity constraints with mn shipping route capacity constraints of the form $x_{ij} \leq \text{Min } \{s_i, d_j\} y_i$ for $i = 1, \ldots, m$ and $j = 1, \ldots, n$. The coefficient for y_i in each of these constraints is the smaller of the origin capacity (s_i) or the destination demand (d_j). These additional constraints often cause the solution of the LP Relaxation to be integer.

$$y_1 + y_2 \leq 1$$

This constraint allows either y_1 or y_2 to equal 1, but not both. If we had written the constraint as an equality, it would require that a plant be located in either Dallas or Fort Worth.

Problem 13, which is based on the Martin-Beck distribution system problem, provides additional practice involving 0–1 variables.

Bank Location

The long-range planning department for the Ohio Trust Company is considering expanding its operation into a 20-county region in northeastern Ohio (see Figure 11.7). Currently, Ohio Trust does not have a principal place of business in any of the 20 counties. According to the banking laws in Ohio, if a bank establishes a principal place of business (PPB) in any county, branch banks can be established in that county and in any adjacent county. However, to establish a new principal place of business, Ohio Trust must either obtain approval for a new bank from the state's superintendent of banks or purchase an existing bank.

Table 11.3 lists the 20 counties in the region and adjacent counties. For example, Ashtabula County is adjacent to Lake, Geauga, and Trumbull counties; Lake County is adjacent to Ashtabula, Cuyahoga, and Geauga counties; and so on.

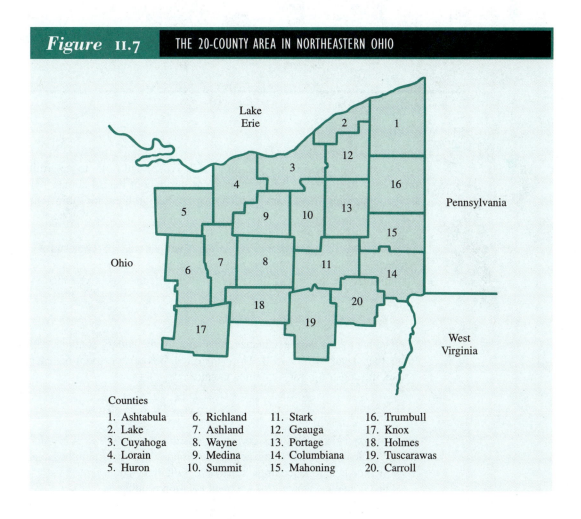

Figure **11.7**   THE 20-COUNTY AREA IN NORTHEASTERN OHIO

Counties

1. Ashtabula	6. Richland	11. Stark	16. Trumbull
2. Lake	7. Ashland	12. Geauga	17. Knox
3. Cuyahoga	8. Wayne	13. Portage	18. Holmes
4. Lorain	9. Medina	14. Columbiana	19. Tuscarawas
5. Huron	10. Summit	15. Mahoning	20. Carroll

Table 11.3	COUNTIES IN THE OHIO TRUST EXPANSION REGION

Counties Under Consideration	Adjacent Counties (by Number)
1. Ashtabula	2, 12, 16
2. Lake	1, 3, 12
3. Cuyahoga	2, 4, 9, 10, 12, 13
4. Lorain	3, 5, 7, 9
5. Huron	4, 6, 7
6. Richland	5, 7, 17
7. Ashland	4, 5, 6, 8, 9, 17, 18
8. Wayne	7, 9, 10, 11, 18
9. Medina	3, 4, 7, 8, 10
10. Summit	3, 8, 9, 11, 12, 13
11. Stark	8, 10, 13, 14, 15, 18, 19, 20
12. Geauga	1, 2, 3, 10, 13, 16
13. Portage	3, 10, 11, 12, 15, 16
14. Columbiana	11, 15, 20
15. Mahoning	11, 13, 14, 16
16. Trumbull	1, 12, 13, 15
17. Knox	6, 7, 18
18. Holmes	7, 8, 11, 17, 19
19. Tuscarawas	11, 18, 20
20. Carroll	11, 14, 19

As an initial step in its planning, Ohio Trust would like to determine the minimum number of PPBs necessary to do business throughout the 20-county region. A 0–1 integer programming model can be used to solve this problem for Ohio Trust. We define the variables as

$$x_i = 1 \text{ if a PPB is established in county } i; 0 \text{ otherwise}$$

To minimize the number of PPBs needed, we write the objective function as

$$\text{Min} \quad x_1 + x_2 + \cdots + x_{20}$$

The bank may locate branches in a county if the county contains a PPB or is adjacent to another county with a PPB. Thus, there will be one constraint for each county. For example, the constraint for Ashtabula County is

$$x_1 + x_2 + x_{12} + x_{16} \geq 1 \qquad \text{Ashtabula}$$

Note that satisfaction of this constraint ensures that a PPB will be placed in Ashtabula County *or* in one or more of the adjacent counties. This constraint thus guarantees that Ohio Trust will be able to place branch banks in Ashtabula County.

The complete statement of the bank location problem is

$$\text{Min} \quad x_1 + x_2 + \quad \cdots \quad + x_{20}$$

s.t.

$$x_1 + x_2 \quad + x_{12} + x_{16} \quad \geq 1 \quad \text{Ashtabula}$$

$$x_1 + x_2 + x_3 + x_{12} \quad \geq 1 \quad \text{Lake}$$

.   .

.   .

.   .

$$x_{11} + x_{14} + x_{19} + x_{20} \geq 1 \quad \text{Carroll}$$

$$x_i = 0, 1 \quad i = 1, 2, \ldots, 20$$

We used LINDO to solve this 20-variable, 20-constraint problem formulation. In Figure 11.8 we show a portion of the computer output. Note that the variable names correspond to the first four letters in the name of each county. Using the output, we see that the optimal solution calls for principal places of business in Ashland, Stark, and Geauga counties. With PPBs in these three counties, Ohio Trust can place branch banks in all 20

Figure 11.8 LINDO SOLUTION FOR THE BANK LOCATION PROBLEM

OBJECTIVE FUNCTION VALUE

1)   3.00000000

VARIABLE	VALUE	REDUCED COST
ASHT	.000000	.000000
LAKE	.000000	.000000
CUYA	.000000	.000000
LORA	.000000	.000000
HURO	.000000	.000000
RICH	.000000	1.000000
ASHL	1.000000	.000000
WAYN	.000000	.000000
MEDI	.000000	.000000
SUMM	.000000	.000000
STAR	1.000000	.000000
GEAU	1.000000	.000000
PORT	.000000	.000000
COLU	.000000	.000000
MAHO	.000000	.000000
TRUM	.000000	.000000
KNOX	.000000	1.000000
HOLM	.000000	.000000
TUSC	.000000	.000000
CARR	.000000	.000000

counties (see Figure 11.9). All other decision variables have an optimal value of zero, indicating that a PPB should not be placed in these counties. Clearly the integer programming model could be enlarged to allow for expansion into a larger area or throughout the entire state.[4]

N O T E S *and Comments*

1. Most practical applications of integer linear programming involve only 0–1 integer variables. Indeed, some mixed-integer computer codes are designed to handle only integer variables with binary values. However, if a clever mathematical trick is employed, these codes can still be used for problems involving general integer variables. The trick is called *binary expansion* and requires that an upper bound be established for each integer variable. More advanced texts on integer programming show how this can be done.

2. The Q. M. in Action: Analyzing Price Quotations Under Business Volume Discounts describes how 0–1 variables can be used in a model designed to take advantage of business volume discounts. Bellcore clients have saved millions of dollars by using a mixed-integer programming model.

3. General-purpose mixed-integer linear programming codes and some spreadsheet packages can be used for linear programming problems, all-integer problems, and problems involving some continuous and some integer variables. General-purpose codes are seldom the fastest for solving problems with special structure (such as the transportation, assignment, and transshipment problems); however, unless the problems are very large, speed is usually not a critical issue. Thus, most practitioners prefer to use one general-purpose computer package that can be used on a variety of problems rather than to maintain a variety of computer programs designed for special problems.

Q.M. IN ACTION

ANALYZING PRICE QUOTATIONS UNDER BUSINESS VOLUME DISCOUNTS*

Bellcore was formed in 1984 to provide various support services for the regional Bell operating telephone companies. To reduce the cost of buying goods and services, Bellcore client companies are increasingly requesting business volume discounts from suppliers in place of traditional quantity discounts. With traditional quantity discounts, the price of each item purchased is discounted on the basis of the amount of the item purchased. Business volume discounts differ from single-item quantity discounts in that the supplier discounts the price of each item by a percentage that is based on the total dollar volume of business over all items awarded to the supplier; whatever this percentage, it remains the same for each item. In general, a firm can realize lower overall purchasing costs with business volume discounts and a supplier can increase total revenues by obtaining a larger volume of that firm's business. However, business volume discounts greatly increase the complexity of the procurement process because the discount obtained depends on the purchase quantities and prices of all products purchased.

To assist Bellcore client companies in using business volume discounts, Bellcore developed the procurement decision support system (PDSS), a PC-based decision support program that uses a mixed-integer programming model to minimize the total cost of purchases. The model uses 0–1 integer variables to model the discount categories applicable to the problem and includes a variety of constraints involving factors such as supplier capacity and limits on the dollar amount awarded to a supplier. Since 1990, one Bellcore client company has reported two savings, one of $4.5 million and another of $15 million; these figures represent approximately 10% on the cost of purchases. Another client company has realized a reduction of approximately 80% in the cost of analyzing quotations, and users generally believe that PDSS is a useful tool in identifying opportunities in negotiations with suppliers.

*Based on Katz, P., A. Sadrian, and P. Tendick, "Telephone Companies Analyze Price Quotations with Bellcore's PDSS Software." *Interfaces*, January–February 1994, pp. 50–63.

---

4. A model of this type allowing for expansion throughout the state and some other variations is presented in Sweeney, D. J., L. Mairose, and R. Martin, "Strategic Planning in Bank Location," *Decision Sciences Proceedings*, November 1979.

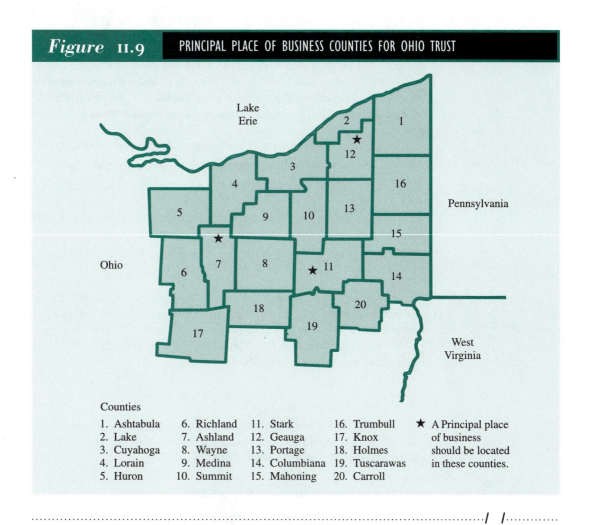

Figure 11.9 PRINCIPAL PLACE OF BUSINESS COUNTIES FOR OHIO TRUST

Lake Erie

Pennsylvania

Ohio

West Virginia

Counties

1. Ashtabula   6. Richland   11. Stark   16. Trumbull   ★ A Principal place
2. Lake   7. Ashland   12. Geauga   17. Knox   of business
3. Cuyahoga   8. Wayne   13. Portage   18. Holmes   should be located
4. Lorain   9. Medina   14. Columbiana   19. Tuscarawas   in these counties.
5. Huron   10. Summit   15. Mahoning   20. Carroll

11.4   MODELING FLEXIBILITY PROVIDED BY 0–1 INTEGER VARIABLES

In Section 11.3 we presented four applications involving 0–1 integer variables. In this section we continue the discussion of the use of 0–1 integer variables in modeling. First, we will show how 0–1 integer variables can be used to model multiple-choice and mutually exclusive constraints. Then, we show how 0–1 integer variables can be used to model situations in which exactly k of n projects must be selected, as well as situations in which the acceptance of one project is conditional on the acceptance of another. We close the section with a cautionary note on the role of sensitivity analysis in integer linear programming.

Multiple-Choice and Mutually Exclusive Constraints

Recall the Ice-Cold Refrigerator capital budgeting problem introduced in Section 11.3. We defined the decision variables for that problem as

$x_1 = 1$ if the plant expansion project is accepted; 0 if rejected

$x_2 = 1$ if the warehouse expansion project is accepted; 0 if rejected

$x_3 = 1$ if the new machinery project is accepted; 0 if rejected

$x_4 = 1$ if the new product research project is accepted; 0 if rejected

Suppose that, instead of one warehouse expansion project, the Ice-Cold Refrigerator Company actually has three warehouse expansion projects under consideration. One of the warehouses *must* be expanded because of increasing product demand, but new demand isn't sufficient to make expansion of more than one warehouse necessary. The following variable definitions and **multiple-choice constraint** could be incorporated into the previous 0–1 integer linear programming model to reflect this situation. Let

$x_2 = 1$ if the original warehouse expansion project is accepted; 0 if rejected
$x_5 = 1$ if the second warehouse expansion project is accepted; 0 if rejected
$x_6 = 1$ if the third warehouse expansion project is accepted; 0 if rejected

The multiple-choice constraint reflecting the requirement that exactly one of these projects must be selected is

$$x_2 + x_5 + x_6 = 1$$

You can easily see why this is called a multiple-choice constraint. Since x_2, x_5, and x_6 are allowed to assume only the values 0 or 1, one and only one of these projects must be selected from among the three choices.

If the requirement that one warehouse must be expanded did not exist, the multiple-choice constraint could be modified as follows:

$$x_2 + x_5 + x_6 \leq 1$$

This modification allows for the case of no warehouse expansion ($x_2 = x_5 = x_6 = 0$) but does not permit more than one warehouse to be expanded. This type of constraint is often called a **mutually exclusive constraint.**

k Out of n Alternatives Constraint

An extension of the notion of a multiple-choice constraint can be used to model situations in which *k out of a set of n* projects must be selected—a **k out of n alternatives constraint.** Suppose that x_2, x_5, x_6, x_7, and x_8 represent five potential warehouse expansion projects and that two of the five projects must be accepted. The constraint that satisfies this new requirement is

$$x_2 + x_5 + x_6 + x_7 + x_8 = 2$$

If no more than two of the projects are to be selected, we would use the following less-than-or-equal-to constraint:

$$x_2 + x_5 + x_6 + x_7 + x_8 \leq 2$$

Again, each of these variables must be restricted to 0–1 values.

Conditional and Corequisite Constraints

Sometimes the acceptance of one project is conditional on the acceptance of another. For example, suppose for the Ice-Cold Refrigerator Company that the warehouse expansion project was conditional on the plant expansion project. That is, management will not consider expanding the warehouse unless the plant is expanded. With x_1 representing plant expansion and x_2 representing warehouse expansion, a **conditional constraint** could be introduced to enforce this requirement:

$$x_2 \leq x_1$$

As both x_1 and x_2 must be 0 or 1, whenever x_1 is 0, x_2 will be forced to 0. When x_1 is 1, x_2 is also allowed to be 1; thus, both the plant and the warehouse can be expanded. However, we note that the preceding constraint does not force the warehouse expansion project (x_2) to be accepted if the plant expansion project (x_1) is accepted.

If the warehouse expansion project had to be accepted whenever the plant expansion project was, and vice versa, we would say that x_1 and x_2 represented **corequisite constraint** projects. To model such a situation, we simply write the preceding constraint as an equality:

$$x_2 = x_1$$

Try Problem 7 for practice with the modeling flexibility provided by 0–1 variables.

This constraint forces x_1 and x_2 to take on the same value.

A Cautionary Note about Sensitivity Analysis

Sensitivity analysis often is more crucial for integer linear programming problems than for linear programming problems. A very small change in one of the coefficients in the constraints can cause a relatively large change in the value of the optimal solution. To understand why, consider the following integer programming model of a simple capital budgeting problem involving four projects and a budgetary constraint for a single time period:

$$\text{Max} \quad 40x_1 + 60x_2 + 70x_3 + 160x_4$$
$$\text{s.t.}$$
$$16x_1 + 35x_2 + 45x_3 + 85x_4 \leq 100$$
$$x_1, x_2, x_3, x_4 = 0, 1$$

Dual prices cannot be used for sensitivity analysis as they are for linear programs. Multiple computer runs usually are necessary for sensitivity analysis of integer linear programs.

The optimal solution to this problem is $x_1 = 1$, $x_2 = 1$, $x_3 = 1$, and $x_4 = 0$, with an objective function value of $170. However, note that if the budget available is increased by $1 (from $100 to $101), the optimal solution changes to $x_1 = 1$, $x_2 = 0$, $x_3 = 0$, and $x_4 = 1$, with an objective function value of $200. That is, one additional dollar in the budget would lead to a $30 increase in the return. Surely management, when faced with such a situation, would increase the budget by $1. Because of the extreme sensitivity of the value of the optimal solution to the constraint coefficients, practitioners usually recommend resolving the integer linear program several times with slight variations in the coefficients before attempting to choose an optimal solution for implementation.

SUMMARY

In this chapter, we introduced the important extension of linear programming referred to as *integer linear programming*. The only difference between the integer linear programming problems discussed in this chapter and the linear programming problems studied in previous chapters is that one or more of the variables must be integer. If all variables must be integer, we have an all-integer linear program. If some, but not all, of the variables must be integer, we have a mixed-integer program. If all the variables are 0–1 or binary variables, we have a 0–1 integer linear program.

There are two major reasons for studying integer linear programming. First, integer linear programming may be helpful when fractional values for the variables are not permitted. Since rounding a linear programming solution may not provide an optimal integer solution, methods for finding optimal integer solutions are needed. A second reason for studying integer linear programming is the increased modeling flexibility provided through the use of 0–1 variables. We showed how 0–1 variables could be used to model important managerial considerations in capital budgeting, fixed cost, distribution system design, and bank location applications.

The number of applications of integer linear programming has been growing in recent years. This growth is due in part to the availability of commercial integer linear programming software packages. As researchers develop solution procedures capable of solving larger integer linear programs and as computer speed increases, a continuation of this growth of integer linear programming applications is expected.

GLOSSARY

Integer linear program   A linear program with the additional requirement that at least one of the variables must be integer.

All-integer linear program   An integer linear program in which all the variables are required to be integer.

0–1 integer linear program   An all-integer or mixed-integer linear program in which the integer variables are only permitted to assume the values 0 or 1.

Mixed-integer linear program   An integer linear program in which some, but not all, variables are required to be integer.

LP Relaxation   The linear program that results from dropping the integer requirements for the variables.

Upper bound   For a maximization problem, the value of the optimal solution to the LP Relaxation.

Continuous variable   A variable that may take on any real number as a value. The variables in a linear program are continuous.

Multiple-choice constraint   A constraint requiring that the sum of two or more 0–1 variables equal 1. Thus, any feasible solution makes a choice of one of these variables to set equal to 1.

Mutually exclusive constraint   A constraint requiring that the sum of two or more 0–1 variables be less than or equal to 1. Thus, if one of the variables equals 1, the others must equal 0. However, all variables could equal 0.

k out of n alternatives constraint   An extension of the multiple-choice constraint. This constraint requires that the sum of n 0–1 variables equal k.

Conditional constraints   A constraint involving 0–1 variables that does not allow certain variables to equal 1 unless certain other variables are equal to 1.

Corequisite constraint   A constraint requiring that two 0–1 variables be equal. Thus, they are both in or out of solution together.

PROBLEMS

1. Indicate which of the following is an all-integer linear program and which is a mixed-integer linear program. Write the LP Relaxation for the problem but do not attempt to solve.

   a. Max $30x_1 + 25x_2$

      s.t.

   $$3x_1 + 1.5x_2 \leq 400$$
   $$1.5x_1 + 2x_2 \leq 250$$
   $$1x_1 + 1x_2 \leq 150$$
   $$x_1, x_2 \geq 0 \text{ and } x_2 \text{ integer}$$

   b. Min $3x_1 + 4x_2$

      s.t.

   $$2x_1 + 4x_2 \geq 8$$
   $$2x_1 + 6x_2 \geq 12$$
   $$x_1, x_2 \geq 0 \text{ and integer}$$

SELF TEST

2. Consider the following all-integer linear program.

   $$\text{Max} \quad 5x_1 + 8x_2$$

   s.t.

   $$6x_1 + 5x_2 \leq 30$$
   $$9x_1 + 4x_2 \leq 36$$
   $$1x_1 + 2x_2 \leq 10$$
   $$x_1, x_2 \geq 0 \text{ and integer}$$

   a. Graph the constraints for this problem. Use dots to indicate all feasible integer solutions.
   b. Find the optimal solution to the LP Relaxation. Round down to find a feasible integer solution.
   c. Find the optimal integer solution. Is it the same as the solution obtained in part (b) by rounding down?

3. Consider the following all-integer linear program.

   $$\text{Max} \quad 1x_1 + 1x_2$$

   s.t.

   $$4x_1 + 6x_2 \leq 22$$
   $$1x_1 + 5x_2 \leq 15$$
   $$2x_1 + 1x_2 \leq 9$$
   $$x_1, x_2 \geq 0 \text{ and integer}$$

   a. Graph the constraints for this problem. Use dots to indicate all feasible integer solutions.
   b. Solve the LP Relaxation of this problem.
   c. Find the optimal integer solution.

4. Consider the following all-integer linear program.

$$\text{Max} \quad 10x_1 + 3x_2$$

s.t.

$$6x_1 + 7x_2 \leq 40$$
$$3x_1 + 1x_2 \leq 11$$
$$x_1, x_2 \geq 0 \text{ and integer}$$

a. Formulate and solve the LP Relaxation of the problem. Solve it graphically, and round down to find a feasible solution. Specify the upper bound on the value of the optimal solution.
b. Solve the integer linear program graphically. Compare the value of this solution with the solution obtained in part (a).
c. Suppose the objective function changes to Max $3x_1 + 6x_2$. Repeat parts (a) and (b).

5. Consider the following mixed-integer linear program.

$$\text{Max} \quad 2x_1 + 3x_2$$

s.t.

$$4x_1 + 9x_2 \leq 36$$
$$7x_1 + 5x_2 \leq 35$$
$$x_1, x_2 \geq 0 \text{ and } x_1 \text{ integer}$$

SELF TEST

a. Graph the constraints for this problem. Indicate on your graph all feasible mixed-integer solutions.
b. Find the optimal solution to the LP Relaxation. Round the value of x_1 down to find a feasible mixed-integer solution. Is this solution optimal? Why or why not?
c. Find the optimal solution for the mixed-integer linear program.

6. Consider the following mixed-integer linear program.

$$\text{Max} \quad 1x_1 + 1x_2$$

s.t.

$$7x_1 + 9x_2 \leq 63$$
$$9x_1 + 5x_2 \leq 45$$
$$3x_1 + 1x_2 \leq 12$$
$$x_1, x_2 \geq 0 \text{ and } x_2 \text{ integer}$$

a. Graph the constraints for this problem. Indicate on your graph all feasible mixed-integer solutions.
b. Find the optimal solution to the LP Relaxation. Round the value of x_2 down to find a feasible mixed-integer solution. Specify upper and lower bounds on the value of the optimal solution to the mixed-integer linear program.
c. Find the optimal solution to the mixed-integer linear program.

7. The following questions refer to a capital budgeting problem with six projects represented by 0–1 variables $x_1, x_2, x_3, x_4, x_5,$ and x_6.

SELF TEST

a. Write a constraint modeling a situation in which two of the projects 1, 3, 5, and 6 must be undertaken.
b. Write a constraint modeling a situation in which if projects 3 and 5 must be undertaken, they must be undertaken simultaneously.
c. Write a constraint modeling a situation in which project 1 or 4 must be undertaken, but not both.

    d. Write constraints modeling a situation where project 4 cannot be undertaken unless projects 1 and 3 also are undertaken.

    e. Revise the requirement in part (d) to accommodate the case in which, when projects 1 and 3 are undertaken, project 4 also must be undertaken.

8. Spencer Enterprises is attempting to choose among a series of new investment alternatives. The potential investment alternatives, the net present value of the future stream of returns, the capital requirements, and the available capital funds over the next 3 years are summarized as follows:

Alternative	Net Present Value ($)	Capital Requirements ($)		
		Year 1	Year 2	Year 3
Limited warehouse expansion	4,000	3,000	1,000	4,000
Extensive warehouse expansion	6,000	2,500	3,500	3,500
Test market new product	10,500	6,000	4,000	5,000
Advertising campaign	4,000	2,000	1,500	1,800
Basic research	8,000	5,000	1,000	4,000
Purchase new equipment	3,000	1,000	500	900
Capital funds available		10,500	7,000	8,750

    a. Develop and solve an integer programming model for maximizing the net present value.

    b. Assume that only one of the warehouse expansion projects can be implemented. Modify your model of part (a).

    c. Suppose that, if test marketing of the new product is carried out, the advertising campaign also must be conducted. Modify your formulation of part (b) to reflect this new situation.

9. Hawkins Manufacturing Company produces connecting rods for 4- and 6-cylinder automobile engines using the same production line. The cost required to set up the production line to produce the 4-cylinder connecting rods is $2000, and the cost required to set up the production line for the 6-cylinder connecting rods is $3500. Manufacturing costs are $15 for each 4-cylinder connecting rod and $18 for each 6-cylinder connecting rod. Hawkins makes a decision at the end of each week as to which product will be manufactured the following week. If there is a production changeover from one week to the next, the weekend is used to reconfigure the production line. Once the line has been set up, the weekly production capacities are 6000, 6-cylinder connecting rods and 8000, 4-cylinder connecting rods. Let

    x_4 = the number of 4-cylinder connecting rods produced next week

    x_6 = the number of 6-cylinder connecting rods produced next week

    s_4 = 1 if the production line is set up to produce the 4-cylinder connecting rods; 0 otherwise

    s_6 = 1 if the production line is set up to produce the 6-cylinder connecting rods; 0 otherwise

    a. Using the decision variables x_4 and s_4, write a constraint that limits next week's production of the 4-cylinder connecting rods to either 0 or 8000 units.

    b. Using the decision variables x_6 and s_6, write a constraint that limits next week's production of the 6-cylinder connecting rods to either 0 or 6000 units.

    c. Write 3 constraints that, taken together, limit the production of connecting rods for next week.

    d. Write an objective function for minimizing the cost of production for next week.

10. Grave City is considering the relocation of several police substations to obtain better enforcement in high-crime areas. The locations under consideration together with the areas that can be covered from these locations are given in the following table.

Potential Locations for Substations	Areas Covered
A	1, 5, 7
B	1, 2, 5, 7
C	1, 3, 5
D	2, 4, 5
E	3, 4, 6
F	4, 5, 6
G	1, 5, 6, 7

a. Formulate an integer programming model that could be used to find the minimum number of locations necessary to provide coverage to all areas.

b. Solve the problem in part (a).

11. Hart Manufacturing makes three products. Each product requires manufacturing operations in three departments: A, B, and C. The labor-hour requirements, by department, are

Department	Product 1	Product 2	Product 3
A	1.50	3.00	2.00
B	2.00	1.00	2.50
C	0.25	0.25	0.25

During the next production period, the labor-hours available are 450 in department A, 350 in department B, and 50 in department C. The profit contributions per unit are $25 for product 1, $28 for product 2, and $30 for product 3.

a. Formulate a linear programming model for maximizing total profit contribution.

b. Solve the linear program formulated in part (a). How much of each product should be produced and what is the projected total profit contribution?

c. After evaluating the solution obtained in part (b), one of the production supervisors noted that production setup costs had not been taken into account. She noted that setup costs are $400 for product 1, $550 for product 2, and $600 for product 3. If the solution developed in part (b) is to be used, what is the total profit contribution after taking into account the setup costs?

d. Management realized that the optimal product mix, taking setup costs into account, might be different from the one recommended in part (b). Formulate a mixed-integer linear program that takes setup costs into account.

e. Use a computer program to solve the mixed integer linear program formulated in part (d). How much of each product should be produced and what is the projected total profit contribution? Compare this profit contribution to that obtained in part (c).

12. Yates Company supplies road salt to county highway departments. The company has three trucks, and the dispatcher is trying to schedule tomorrow's deliveries to Polk, Dallas, and Jasper counties. Two trucks have 15-ton capacities, and the third truck has a 30-ton capacity. Based on these truck capacities, two counties will receive 15 tons and the third will receive 30 tons of road salt. The dispatcher wants to determine how much to ship to each county. Let

$$x_1 = \text{amount shipped to Polk County}$$
$$x_2 = \text{amount shipped to Dallas County}$$
$$x_3 = \text{amount shipped to Jasper County}$$

and

$$y_i = \begin{cases} 1 \text{ if the 30-ton truck is assigned to county } i \\ 0 \text{ otherwise} \end{cases}$$

a. Use these variable definitions and write constraints that appropriately restrict the amount shipped to each county.
b. The cost of assigning the 30-ton truck to the three counties is $100 to Polk, $85 to Dallas, and $50 to Jasper. Formulate and solve a mixed-integer linear program to determine how much to ship to each county.

SELF TEST

13. Recall the Martin-Beck Company distribution system problem in Section 11.3.
    a. Modify the formulation shown in Section 11.3 to account for the policy restriction that one plant, but not two, must be located either in Detroit or in Toledo.
    b. Modify the formulation shown in Section 11.3 to account for the policy restriction that no more than two plants can be located in Denver, Kansas City, and St. Louis.

14. An automobile manufacturer has five outdated plants: one each in Michigan, Ohio, and California and two in New York. Management is considering modernizing these plants to manufacture engine blocks and transmissions for a new model car. The cost to modernize each plant and the manufacturing capacity after modernization are as follows:

Plant	Cost ($ millions)	Engine Blocks (1000s)	Transmissions (1000s)
Michigan	25	500	300
New York	35	800	400
New York	35	400	800
Ohio	40	900	600
California	20	200	300

The projected needs are for total capacities of 900,000 engine blocks and 900,000 transmissions. Management wants to determine which plants to modernize to meet projected manufacturing needs and, at the same time, minimize the total cost of modernization.
    a. Develop a table that lists every possible option available to management. As part of your table, indicate the total engine block capacity and transmission capacity for each possible option, whether the option is feasible based on the projected needs, and the total modernization cost for each option.
    b. Based on your analysis in part (a), what recommendation would you provide management?
    c. Formulate a 0–1 integer programming model that could be used to determine the optimal solution to the modernization question facing management.
    d. Solve the model formulated in part (c) to provide a recommendation for management.

15. CHB, Inc., is a bank holding company that is evaluating the potential for expanding into a 13-county region in the southwestern part of the state. State law permits establishing branches in any county that is adjacent to a county in which a PPB (principal place of business) is located. The following map shows the 13-county region with the population of each county indicated.

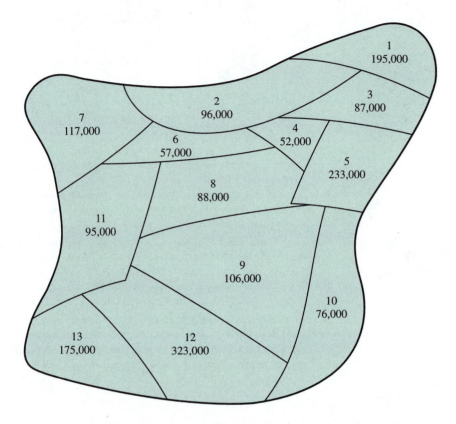

a. Assume that only one PPB can be established in the region. Where should it be located to maximize the population served? (Hint: Review the Ohio Trust formulation in Section 11.3. Consider minimizing the population not served, and introduce variable $y_i = 1$ if it is not possible to establish a branch in county i, and $y_i = 0$ otherwise.)

b. Suppose that two PPBs can be established in the region. Where should they be located to maximize the population served?

c. Management has learned that a bank located in county 5 is considering selling. If CHB purchases this bank, the requisite PPB will be established in county 5, and a base for beginning expansion in the region will also be established. What advice would you give the management of CHB?

16. The Northshore Bank is working to develop an efficient work schedule for full-time and part-time tellers. The schedule must provide for efficient operation of the bank including adequate customer service, employee breaks, and so on. On Fridays the bank is open from 9:00 A.M. to 7:00 P.M. The number of tellers necessary to provide adequate customer service during each hour of operation is summarized here.

Time	Number of Tellers	Time	Number of Tellers
9:00 A.M.–10:00 A.M.	6	2:00 P.M.–3:00 P.M.	6
10:00 A.M.–11:00 A.M.	4	3:00 P.M.–4:00 P.M.	4
11:00 A.M.–Noon	8	4:00 P.M.–5:00 P.M.	7
Noon–1:00 P.M.	10	5:00 P.M.–6:00 P.M.	6
1:00 P.M.–2:00 P.M.	9	6:00 P.M.–7:00 P.M.	6

Each full-time employee starts on the hour and works a four-hour shift, followed by one hour for lunch and then a three-hour shift. Part-time employees work one four-hour shift beginning on the hour. Considering salary and fringe benefits, full-time employees cost the bank $15 per hour ($105 a day), and part-time employees cost the bank $8 per hour ($32 a day).

   a. Formulate an integer programming model that can be used to develop a schedule that will satisfy customer service needs at a minimum employee cost. (Hint: Let x_i = number of full-time employees coming on duty at the beginning of hour i and y_i = number of part-time employees coming on duty at the beginning of hour i.)

   b. Solve the LP Relaxation of your model in part (a).

   c. Solve for the optimal schedule of tellers. Comment on the solution.

   d. After reviewing the solution to part (c), the bank manager has realized that some additional requirements must be specified. Specifically, she wants to ensure that one full-time employee is on duty at all times and that there is a staff of at least five full-time employees. Revise your model to incorporate these additional requirements and solve for the optimal solution.

17. Refer to the Ohio Trust bank location problem introduced in Section 11.3. Table 11.3 shows the counties under consideration and the adjacent counties.

   a. Write the complete integer programming model for expansion into the following counties only: Lorain, Huron, Richland, Ashland, Wayne, Medina, and Knox.

   b. Use trial and error to solve the problem in part (a).

   c. If you have a computer program for integer programs, use it to solve the problem.

18. Refer to Problem 14. Suppose that management determined that its cost estimates to modernize the New York plants were too low. Specifically, suppose that the actual cost is $40 million to modernize each plant.

   a. What changes in your previous 0–1 integer linear programming model are needed to incorporate these changes in costs?

   b. For these cost changes, what recommendations would you now provide management regarding the modernization plan?

   c. Reconsider the solution obtained using the revised cost figures. Suppose that management decides that closing two plants in the same state is not acceptable. How could this policy restriction be added to your 0–1 integer programming model?

   d. Based on the cost revisions and the policy restrictions presented in part (c), what recommendations would you now provide management regarding the modernization plan?

19. The Bayside Art Gallery is considering installing a video camera security system to reduce its insurance premiums. A diagram of the eight display rooms that Bayside uses for exhibitions is shown in Figure 11.10; the openings between the rooms are numbered 1–13. A security firm has proposed that two-way cameras be installed at some room openings. Each camera has the ability to monitor the two rooms between which the camera is located. For example, if a camera were located at opening number 4, rooms 1 and 4 would be covered; if a camera were located at opening 11, rooms 7 and 8 would be covered; and so on. Management has decided not to locate a camera system at the entrance to the display rooms. The objective is to provide security coverage for all eight rooms using the minimum number of two-way cameras.

   a. Formulate a 0–1 integer linear programming model that will enable Bayside's management to determine the locations for the camera systems.

   b. Solve the model formulated in part (a) to determine how many two-way systems to purchase and where they should be located.

   c. Suppose that management wants to provide additional security coverage for room 7. Specifically, management wants room 7 to be covered by two cameras. How would your model formulated in part (a) have to change to accommodate this policy restriction?

   d. With the policy restriction specified in part (c), determine how many two-way camera systems will need to be purchased and where they will be located.

20. The Delta Group is a management consulting firm specializing in the health care industry. A team is being formed to study possible new markets, and a linear programming model has been developed for selecting team members. However, one constraint the president has imposed is a

Figure 11.10   DIAGRAM OF DISPLAY ROOMS FOR PROBLEM 19

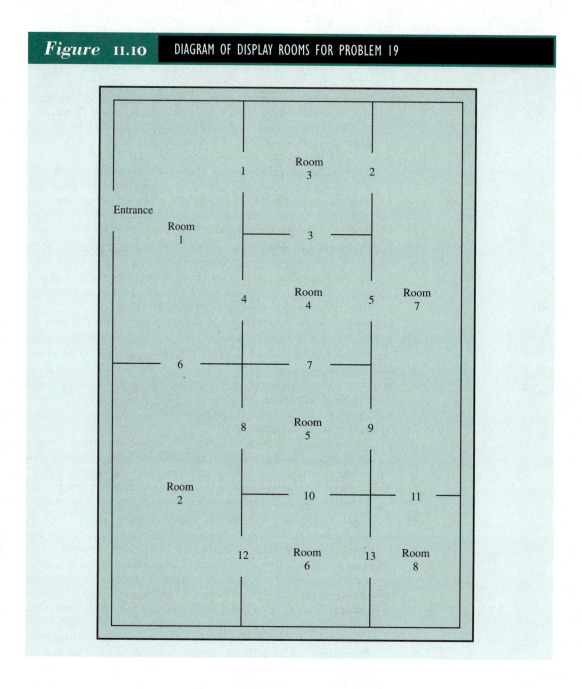

team size of three, five, or seven members. The staff can't figure out how to incorporate this requirement in the model. The current model requires that team members be selected from three departments and uses the following variable definitions.

x_1 = the number of employees selected from department 1

x_2 = the number of employees selected from department 2

x_3 = the number of employees selected from department 3

Show the staff how to write constraints that will ensure that the team will consist of three, five, or seven employees. The following integer variables should be helpful.

$$y_1 = \begin{cases} 1 & \text{if team size is 3} \\ 0 & \text{otherwise} \end{cases}$$

$$y_2 = \begin{cases} 1 & \text{if team size is 5} \\ 0 & \text{otherwise} \end{cases}$$

$$y_3 = \begin{cases} 1 & \text{if team size is 7} \\ 0 & \text{otherwise} \end{cases}$$

Case Problem   TEXTBOOK PUBLISHING

ASW Publishing, Inc., a small publisher of college textbooks, must make a decision regarding which books to publish next year. The books under consideration are listed in the following table, along with the projected three-year sales expected from each book.

Book Subject	Type of Book	Projected Sales (1000s)
Business calculus	New	20
Finite mathematics	Revision	30
General statistics	New	15
Mathematical statistics	New	10
Business statistics	Revision	25
Finance	New	18
Financial accounting	New	25
Managerial accounting	Revision	50
English literature	New	20
German	New	30

The books that are listed as revisions are texts that ASW already has under contract; these texts are being considered for publication as new editions. The books that are listed as new have been reviewed by the company, but contracts have not yet been signed.

The company has three individuals who can be assigned to these projects, all of whom have varying amounts of time available; John has 60 days available, and Susan and Monica both have 40 days available. The days required by each person to complete each project are shown in the following table. For instance, if the business calculus book is published, it will require 30 days of John's time and 40 days of Susan's time. An "X" indicates that the person will not be used on the project. Note that at least two staff members will be assigned to each project except the finance book.

Book Subject	John	Susan	Monica
Business calculus	30	40	X
Finite mathematics	16	24	X
General statistics	24	X	30
Mathematical statistics	20	X	24
Business statistics	10	X	16
Finance	X	X	14
Financial accounting	X	24	26
Managerial accounting	X	28	30
English literature	40	34	30
German	X	50	36

ASW will not publish more than two statistics books or more than one accounting text in a single year. In addition, management has decided that one of the mathematics books (business calculus or finite math) must be published, but not both.

Managerial Report

Prepare a report for the editorial director of ASW that describes your findings and recommendations regarding the best publication strategy for next year. In carrying out your analysis, assume that the fixed costs and the sales revenues per unit are approximately equal for all books; management is interested primarily in maximizing the total sales volume.

The editorial director has also asked that you include recommendations regarding the following possible changes.

1. If it would be advantageous to do so, Susan can be moved off another project to allow her to work 12 more days.
2. If it would be advantageous to do so, Monica can also be made available for another 10 days.
3. If one or more of the revisions could be postponed for another year, should they be? Clearly the company will risk losing market share by postponing a revision.

Include details of your analysis in an appendix to your report.

Case Problem   PRODUCTION SCHEDULING WITH CHANGEOVER COSTS

Buckeye Manufacturing produces heads for engines used in the manufacture of trucks. The production line is highly complex, and it measures 900 feet in length. Two types of engine heads are produced on this line: the P-Head and the H-Head. The P-Head is used in heavy-duty trucks, and the H-Head is used in smaller trucks. Because only one type of head can be produced at a time, the line is either set up to manufacture the P-Head or the H-Head, but not both. Changeovers are made over a weekend; costs are $1000 in going from a setup for the P-Head, to a setup for the H-Head, and vice-versa. When set up for the P-Head the maximum production rate is 1000 units per week and when set up for the H-Head, the maximum production rate is 800 units per week.

	Product Demand	
Week	P-Head	H-Head
1	550	380
2	550	380
3	440	300
4	0	0
5	450	480
6	450	480
7	360	580
8	350	570
9	350	580

Buckeye has just shut down for the week; the line has been producing the P-Head. The manager wants to plan production and changeovers for the next eight weeks. Currently, Buckeye has an inventory of 1247 P-Heads and 1430 H-Heads. Inventory carrying costs are charged at an annual rate of 19.5% of the value of inventory. The production cost for the P-Head is $225, and the production cost for the H-Head is $310. The objective in developing a production schedule is to minimize the sum of production cost, plus inventory carrying cost, plus changeover cost.

The demand for the P-Head and H-Head engines for the next nine weeks is shown at the bottom of page 480. Safety stock requirements are such that week-ending inventory must provide for at least 80% of the next week's demand.

Managerial Report

Prepare a report for Buckeye's management with a production and changeover schedule for the next eight weeks. Be sure to note how much of the total cost is due to production, how much is due to inventory, and how much is due to changeover.

Appendix 11.1   SPREADSHEET SOLUTION OF INTEGER LINEAR PROGRAMS

In this appendix we show how Excel can be used to solve the Eastborne Realty integer linear programming problem presented in Section 11.1. The spreadsheet process for solving integer programs is very similar to the procedure described for linear programming in Appendix 8.1. First, the data for the objective function coefficients, the constraint coefficients, and the values of the right-hand sides must be entered into a worksheet. Second, cells must be identified for storing the values of the decision variables, the value for the objective function, and the values of the left-hand sides of the constraints. Figure 11.11 shows a worksheet for the Eastborne problem in which the cells in rows 1 through 10 in the upper portion of the worksheet are reserved for problem input data and the cells in the lower portion of the worksheet are reserved for the solution output. The Input Data section of the worksheet contains the following values:

Input Value	Cell Location
Objective function coefficients	B10:C10
Constraint coefficients	B6:C8
Right-hand sides	D6:D8

The Solution Output section of the worksheet contains the following optimal solution values:

Output Value	Cell Location
Decision variables	B16:C16
Objective function	D17
Slack/Surplus	C21:C23

Figure II.II	EXCEL WORKSHEET FOR THE EASTBORNE REALTY PROBLEM

	A	B	C	D
1				
2	**Input Data**			
3				
4		**Constraint Coefficients**		
5	**Constraint**	Townhouses	Apartment Buildings	**Available**
6	Investment Funds	282	400	2000
7	Number of Townhouses	1		5
8	Manager's Time	4	40	140
9				
10	**Cash Flow per Unit**	10	15	
11				
12				
13	**Solution Output**			
14		**Decision Variables**		**Total Cash Flow**
15		Townhouses	Apartment Buildings	
16	**Number of Units**			
17	**Cash Flow**			
18				
19				
20	**Constraint**	**Usage**	**Slack/Surplus**	
21	Investment Funds			
22	Number of Townhouses			
23	Manager's Time			

To use the Excel Solver for the Eastborne integer linear programming problem, we must first enter formulas that show how the values in the solution output section of the worksheet are related to the input data values. For instance, the cash flow in thousands of dollars for the townhouses is 10 times the number of townhouses purchased, and the cash flow in thousands of dollars for the apartment buildings is 15 times the number of apartment buildings purchased. Thus, in cell **B17** we enter the formula = **B10*B16** (the cash flow from townhouses) and in cell **C17** we enter the formula = **C10*C16** (the cash flow from apartment buildings). Since the total cash flow is the sum of these two values, we enter the formula = **B17 + C17** in cell **D17**.

The total investment funds in thousands of dollars is the product of the value in cell **B6** (282) times the value in cell **B16** (the number of townhouses purchased) plus the product of the value in cell **C6** (400) times the value in cell **C16** (the number of apartment buildings purchased); thus using the **SUMPRODUCT** function, we enter the following formula in cell **B21**:

$$= \text{SUMPRODUCT(B6:C6,\$B\$16:\$C\$16)}$$

After copying this formula to cells **B22** and **B23**, these cells will contain the formulas for the townhouses available constraint and the manager's time constraint.

Finally, to compute the slack/surplus value for each constraint, we subtract the investment funds, townhouses, and manager's time required by the optimal solution from the total investment funds, townhouses, and manager's time available. Thus, in cell **C21**, we compute the slack/surplus for the investment funds by entering the formula = **D6 − B21**. Copying this cell to **C22** and **C23** will place the formula for the slack/surplus of townhouses

Figure II.12 EXCEL FORMULA WORKSHEET FOR THE EASTBORNE REALTY PROBLEM

	A	B	C	D
1				
2	**Input Data**			
3				
4		**Constraint Coefficients**		
5	**Constraint**	Townhouses	Apartment Buildings	**Available**
6	Investment Funds	282	400	2000
7	Number of Townhouses	1		5
8	Manager's Time	4	40	140
9				
10	**Cash Flow per Unit**	10	15	
11				
12				
13	**Solution Output**			
14		**Decision Variables**		
15		Townhouses	Apartment Buildings	**Total Cash Flow**
16	**Number of Units**			
17	**Cash Flow**	=B10*B16	=C10*C16	=B17+C17
18				
19				
20	**Constraint**	**Usage**	**Slack/Surplus**	
21	Investment Funds	=SUMPRODUCT(B6:C6,$B$16:$C$16)	=D6-B21	
22	Number of Townhouses	=SUMPRODUCT(B7:C7,$B$16:$C$16)	=D7-B22	
23	Manager's Time	=SUMPRODUCT(B8:C8,$B$16:$C$16)	=D8-B23	

in cell **C22** and the slack/surplus for the manager's time in cell **C23**. Figure 11.12 shows the formula worksheet for the Eastborne problem.

We are now ready to use Solver to obtain an optimal solution to the problem. The following steps describe how to use Excel to obtain the optimal integer solution.

Step 1. Select the **Tools** pull-down menu
Step 2. Select the **Solver** option
Step 3. When the **Solver Parameters** dialog box appears:
Enter D17 in the **Set Target Cell** box
Select the **Max** option
Enter B16:C16 in the **By Changing Cells** box
Choose **Add**
Step 4. When the **Add Constraint** dialog box appears:
Enter B21:B23 in the **Cell Reference** box
Select < =
Enter D6:D8 in the **Constraint** box
Choose **Add**
Enter B16:C16 in the **Cell Reference** box
Select > =
Enter 0 in the **Constraint** box
Choose **Add**
Enter B16:C16 in the **Cell Reference** box
Select **Int**
Select **OK**

Step 5.   When the **Solver Parameters** dialog box appears:
Choose **Options**
Step 6.   When the **Solver Options** dialog box appears:
Select **Assume Linear Model** box
Set **Tolerance** at 0%
Select **OK**
Step 7.   When the **Solver Parameters** dialog box appears:
Choose **Solve**
Step 8.   When the **Solver Results** dialog box appears:
Select **Keep Solver Solution**
Select **OK** to produce the optimal solution output

Figure 11.13 shows the optimal integer solution. The solution with four townhouses and two apartment buildings provided a maximum annual cash flow of $70,000. The amount of investment funds required is $1,928,000 leaving a slack of $72,000. The usage and slack for the number of townhouses constraint and the manager's time constraint are also shown. Note that this solution is the same integer solution as that provided by The Management Scientist software package (see Figure 11.3).

As a final note, refer to Step 6 where we set the tolerance at 0%. This tolerance forces solver to continue until the optimal integer solution has been reached. Since integer linear programs are often very difficult to solve, the tolerance default setting of 5% permits solver to stop when it is guaranteed to be within 5% of the optimal solution.

Figure 11.13   EXCEL SOLVER OUTPUT FOR THE EASTBORNE REALTY PROBLEM

	A	B	C	D
1				
2	**Input Data**			
3				
4		**Constraint Coefficients**		
5	**Constraint**	Townhouses	Apartment Buildings	**Available**
6	Investment Funds	282	400	2000
7	Number of Townhouses	1		5
8	Manager's Time	4	40	140
9				
10	**Cash Flow per Unit**	10	15	
11				
12				
13	**Solution Output**			
14		**Decision Variables**		
15		Townhouses	Apartment Buildings	**Total Cash Flow**
16	**Number of Units**	4	2	
17	**Cash Flow**	40	30	70
18				
19				
20	**Constraint**	**Usage**	**Slack/Surplus**	
21	Investment Funds	1928	72	
22	Number of Townhouses	4	1	
23	Manager's Time	96	44	

KETRON*

ARLINGTON, VIRGINIA

Ketron Division of The Bionetics Corporation is an operations research organization with offices throughout the United States. An important part of Ketron's business involves work for local, state, and national governmental agencies.

The Ketron Management Science group is responsible for the development, enhancement, marketing, and support of MPSIII, a proprietary mathematical programming system that runs on a wide range of computers—from PC to mainframes. Ketron Management Science provides consulting services for the design and implementation of mathematical programming applications. One such mixed-integer programming (MIP) application developed for a major sporting equipment company is outlined in the following sections.

A Customer Order Allocation Model

A major sporting equipment company satisfies demand for its products by making shipments from its factories and other locations around the country where inventories are maintained. The company markets approximately 300 products and has about 30 sources of supply (factory and warehouse locations). The problem of interest is to determine how best to allocate customer orders to the various sources of supply such that the total manufacturing cost is minimized. Although transportation cost is not directly considered, it can be accounted for indirectly by not including variables corresponding to shipments from distant locations. The following figure provides a graphical representation of this problem. Note in the figure that each customer can receive shipments from only a few of the various sources of supply.

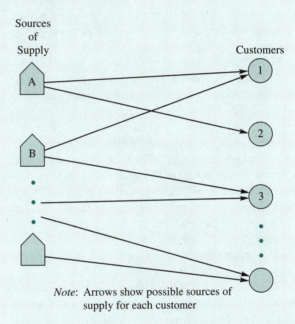

Note: Arrows show possible sources of supply for each customer

For example, we see that customer 1 may be supplied by source A or B, customer 2 may be supplied only by source A, and so on.

The customer order allocation problem is solved periodically. In a typical period, between 30 and 40 customers are to be supplied. Since most customers require several products, usually between 600 and 800 orders must be assigned to the sources of supply.

The sporting equipment company classifies each customer order as either a "guaranteed" or a "secondary"

---

*The authors are indebted to J. A. Tomlin for providing this application.

order. Guaranteed orders are single-source orders in that they must be filled by a single supplier to ensure that the complete order will be delivered to the customer at one time. This single-source requirement necessitates the use of integer variables in the model. Approximately 80% of the company's orders are guaranteed orders.

Secondary orders can be split among the various sources of supply. These orders are made by customers restocking inventory, and receiving partial shipments from different sources at different times is not a problem. The total of all secondary orders for a given product is treated as a goal or target in the model formulation. Deviations below the goal are permitted, but a penalty cost is associated with these deviations in the objective function. When deviations occur in the optimal solution, the secondary orders will not be completely satisfied; the shortfall is spread among customers in specified proportions.

Manufacturing considerations are such that raw material availability and the type of process used constrain the amount of production. In addition, groups of items that are similar may belong to a "model group" that must be jointly constrained at some factories. Several restrictions are also on international shipping. For various policy reasons, shipments between sources and customers in certain countries may not be made. This restriction reduces the number of variables in the model, but it necessitates extensive data checking to ensure that all guaranteed orders have a permissible source. If they do not, some means must be found to make the problem feasible before beginning to solve the mixed-integer programming model.

The primary objective of the model is to minimize the total manufacturing costs subject to the requirement that the guaranteed orders be met. As indicated previously, the deviations below the secondary demand goals are dealt with by defining variables that indicate the amount of any shortfall. The cost associated with these variables represents a penalty for not having the item in inventory when it is required.

A description of the constraints and the objective function for the model follows.

Constraints

- *Guaranteed orders:* Each customer's order for each product is assigned to a single supplier. (This is a multiple-choice constraint.)
- *Secondary orders:* For each product, the total amount of secondary demand assigned plus the shortfall must equal the total demand goal (target).
- *Raw material capacities:* The amount of each type of raw material used at a supply source cannot exceed the amount available.
- *Manufacturing capacities:* At each supply source, the capacity for each type of production process cannot be exceeded.
- *Individual product capacities:* The amount of product produced at a site cannot exceed that site's capacity for the product.
- *Group capacities:* The total production for a group of similar products at a site cannot exceed that site's capacity for the group of products.

Objective Function

The objective is to minimize the sum of (1) the manufacturing cost for guaranteed orders, (2) the manufacturing cost for secondary orders, and (3) the penalty cost for unsatisfied secondary demand.

Model Solution

It is unreasonable to expect to obtain an optimal solution for a problem of this complexity. Furthermore, the goal programming methodology for handling the secondary demand means that an "optimum" is of questionable interpretation. A "good" feasible mixed-integer solution is needed. If an integer solution is found whose value is within a few percent of the value of the LP Relaxation solution, the room for improvement is obviously small.

A fairly typical problem has about 800 constraints, 2000 0–1 assignment variables for the guaranteed orders, and 500 continuous variables associated with the secondary orders. This model is solved using Ketron's MPSIII system.

Implementation Notes

In large-scale applications such as this, considerable systems work is involved in generating the data for the model and the managerial reports. Special data processing languages are often available to ease the programming burden of these phases. The DATAFORM language facility of MPSIII is used to generate the data for this model and to prepare the reports.

In this application, making a completely separate preprocessing run is necessary to check for internal consistency and errors in the data. Only when the data appear logically error-free is the model generated and solved. Although tedious, this kind of preprocessing effort is critical for mixed-integer models since the cost of solving the wrong model can be significant. Furthermore, in some cases the data preprocessing step permits the size of the model to be reduced. Such a reduction is possible in this application when a demand for a product has only one legitimate source. The computational benefits of such reductions can be substantial.

Questions

1. Discuss the relationship between the method for handling secondary orders and feasibility.
2. Discuss what is meant by the statement, an "optimum" is of questionable interpretation. Does it mean that any feasible solution is acceptable?

12

PROJECT SCHEDULING: PERT/CPM

In many situations, managers are responsible for planning, scheduling, and controlling projects that consist of numerous separate jobs or tasks performed by a variety of departments and individuals. Often these projects are so large and/or complex that the manager cannot possibly remember all the information pertaining to the plan, schedule, and progress of the project. In these situations the **program evaluation and review technique (PERT)** and the **critical path method (CPM)** have proven to be extremely valuable.

PERT and CPM have been used to plan, schedule, and control a wide variety of projects, such as

1. research and development of new products and processes;
2. construction of plants, buildings, and highways;
3. maintenance of large and complex equipment; and
4. design and installation of new systems.

In projects such as these, project managers must schedule and coordinate the various jobs or activities so that the entire project is completed on time. A complicating factor in carrying out this task is the interdependence of the activities; for example, some activities depend on the completion of other activities before they can be started. Projects may have as many as several thousand activities, so project managers look for procedures that will help them answer questions such as the following.

1. What is the total time to complete the project?
2. What are the scheduled start and finish dates for each specific activity?
3. Which activities are "critical" and must be completed *exactly* as scheduled to keep the project on schedule?
4. How long can "noncritical" activities be delayed before they cause an increase in the total project completion time?

PERT and CPM can help answer these questions.

PERT (Navy) and CPM (Du Pont and Remmington Rand) differ because they were developed by different people working on different projects. Today, the best aspects of each have been combined to provide a valuable project scheduling technique.

Although PERT and CPM have the same general purpose and utilize much of the same terminology, the techniques were developed independently. PERT was developed in the late 1950s specifically for the Polaris missile project. Many activities associated with this project had never been attempted previously, so PERT was developed to handle uncertain activity times. CPM was developed primarily for industrial projects for which activity times generally were known. CPM offered the option of reducing activity times by adding more workers and/or resources, usually at an increased cost. Thus, a distinguishing feature of CPM was that it identified trade-offs between time and cost for various project activities.

Today's computerized versions of PERT and CPM have combined the best features of both approaches. Thus, the distinction between the two techniques is no longer necessary. As a result, we refer to the project scheduling procedures covered in this chapter as PERT/CPM. We begin the discussion of PERT/CPM by considering a project for the expansion of the Western Hills Shopping Center.

12.1 PROJECT SCHEDULING WITH KNOWN ACTIVITY TIMES

The owner of the Western Hills Shopping Center is planning to modernize and expand the current 32-business shopping center complex. The project is expected to provide room for 8 to 10 new businesses. Financing has been arranged through a private investor. All that remains is for the owner of the shopping center to plan, schedule, and complete the expansion project. Let us show how PERT/CPM can help.

The effort that goes into identifying activities, determining interrelationships among activities, and estimating activity times is crucial to the success of PERT/CPM. A significant amount of time may be needed to complete this initial phase of the project scheduling process.

The first step in the PERT/CPM scheduling process is to develop a list of the activities that make up the project. Table 12.1 shows the list of activities for the Western Hills Shopping Center expansion project. Nine activities are described and denoted A through I for later reference. Additional information in Table 12.1 includes immediate predecessor and activity times (in weeks). For a given activity, the **immediate predecessor** column identifies the activities that must be completed *immediately prior* to the start of that activity. Activities A and B do not have immediate predecessors and can be started as soon as the project begins; thus, a dash is written in the immediate predecessor column for these activities. The other entries in the immediate predecessor column show that ac-

Table 12.1	LIST OF ACTIVITIES FOR THE WESTERN HILLS SHOPPING CENTER PROJECT		
Activity	Activity Description	Immediate Predecessor	Activity Time
A	Prepare architectural drawings	—	5
B	Identify potential new tenants	—	6
C	Develop prospectus for tenants	A	4
D	Select contractor	A	3
E	Prepare building permits	A	1
F	Obtain approval for building permits	E	4
G	Perform construction	D, F	14
H	Finalize contracts with tenants	B, C	12
I	Tenants move in	G, H	2
			Total 51

Immediate predecessor information determines whether activities can be completed in parallel (worked on simultaneously) or in series (one completed before another begins). Generally, the more series relationships present in a project, the more time will be required to complete the project.

A project network is extremely helpful in visualizing the interrelationships among the activities. There are no rules for converting a list of activities and immediate predecessor information into a project network. The process of constructing a project network generally improves with practice and experience.

Try Problem 3. This problem provides the immediate predecessor information for a project with seven activities and asks you to develop the project network.

tivities C, D, and E cannot be started until activity A has been completed; activity F cannot be started until activity E has been completed; activity G cannot be started until both activities D and F have been completed; activity H cannot be started until both activities B and C have been completed; and, finally, activity I cannot be started until both activities G and H have been completed. The project is finished when activity I is completed.

The last column in Table 12.1 shows the number of weeks required to complete each activity. For example, activity A takes 5 weeks, activity B takes 6 weeks, and so on. The sum of activity times is 51. As a result, you may think that the total time required to complete the project is 51 weeks. However, as we show, two or more activities often may be scheduled concurrently, thus shortening the completion time for the project. Ultimately, PERT/CPM will provide a detailed activity schedule for completing the project in the shortest time possible.

Using the immediate predecessor information in Table 12.1, we can construct a graphical representation of the project, or the **project network.** Figure 12.1 depicts the project network for Western Hills Shopping Center. The activities correspond to the *nodes* of the network (drawn as rectangles) and the *arcs* (the lines with arrows) show the precedence relationships among the activities. In addition, nodes have been added to the network to denote the start and the finish of the project. A project network will help a manager visualize the activity relationships and provide a basis for carrying out the PERT/CPM computations.

Figure 12.1   PROJECT NETWORK FOR THE WESTERN HILLS SHOPPING CENTER

The Concept of a Critical Path

To facilitate the PERT/CPM computations, we modified the project network as shown in Figure 12.2. Note that the upper left-hand corner of each node contains the corresponding activity letter. The activity time appears immediately below the letter.

For convenience, we use the convention of referencing activities with letters. Generally, we assign the letters in approximate order as we move from left to right through the project network.

To determine the project completion time, we have to analyze the network and identify what is called the **critical path** for the network. However, before doing so, we need to define the concept of a path through the network. A **path** is a sequence of connected nodes that leads from the Start node to the Finish node. For instance, one path for the network in Figure 12.2 is defined by the sequence of nodes A–E–F–G–I. By inspection, we see that other paths are possible, such as A–D–G–I, A–C–H–I, and B–H–I. All paths in the network must be traversed in order to complete the project, so we will look for the path that requires the most time. Since all other paths are shorter in duration, this *longest* path determines the total time required to complete the project. If activities on the longest path are delayed, the entire project will be delayed. Thus, the longest path is the *critical path*. Activities on the critical path are referred to as the **critical activities** for the project. The following discussion presents a step-by-step algorithm for finding the critical path in a project network.

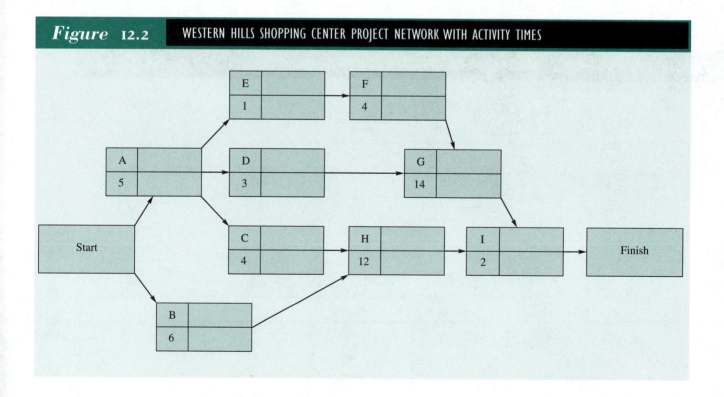

Figure 12.2   WESTERN HILLS SHOPPING CENTER PROJECT NETWORK WITH ACTIVITY TIMES

Determining the Critical Path

We begin by finding the **earliest start time** and a **latest start time** for all activities in the network. Let

$$ES = \text{earliest start time for an activity}$$
$$EF = \text{earliest finish time for an activity}$$
$$t = \text{activity time}$$

The **earliest finish time** for any activity is

$$EF = ES + t \qquad (12.1)$$

Activity A can start as soon as the project starts, so we set the earliest start time for activity A equal to 0. With an activity time of 5 weeks, the earliest finish time for activity A is $EF = ES + t = 0 + 5 = 5$.

We will write the earliest start and earliest finish times in the node to the right of the activity letter. Using activity A as an example, we have

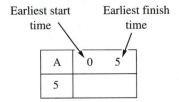

Since an activity cannot be started until *all* immediately preceding activities have been finished, the following rule can be used to determine the earliest start time for each activity.

The earliest start time for an activity is equal to the *largest* of the earliest finish times for all its immediate predecessors.

Let us apply the earliest start time rule to the portion of the network involving nodes A, B, C, and H, as shown in Figure 12.3. With an earliest start time of 0 and an activity time of 6 for activity B, we show $ES = 0$ and $EF = ES + t = 0 + 6 = 6$ in the node for activity B. Looking at node C, we note that activity A is the only immediate predecessor for activity C. The earliest finish time for activity A is 5, so the earliest start time for activity C must be $ES = 5$. Thus, with an activity time of 4, the earliest finish time for activity C is $EF = ES + t = 5 + 4 = 9$. Both the earliest starting time and the earliest finish time can be shown in the node for activity C (see Figure 12.4).

Continuing with Figure 12.4, we move on to activity H and apply the earliest start time rule for this activity. With both activities B and C as immediate predecessors, the earliest start time for activity H must be equal to the largest of the earliest finish times for activities B and C. Thus, with $EF = 6$ for activity B and $EF = 9$ for activity C, we select the largest value, 9,

Figure 12.3 A PORTION OF THE WESTERN HILLS SHOPPING CENTER PROJECT NETWORK, SHOWING ACTIVITIES A, B, C, AND H

Figure 12.4 DETERMINING THE EARLIEST START TIME FOR ACTIVITY H

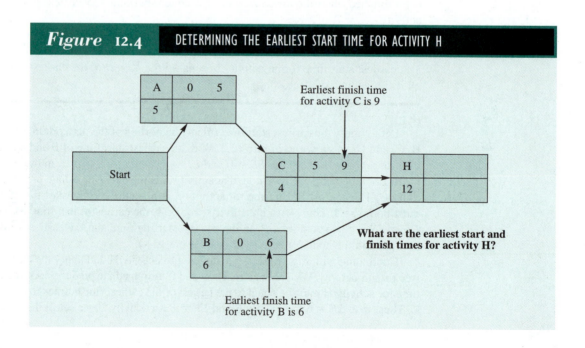

as the earliest start time for activity H ($ES = 9$). With an activity time of 12 as shown in the node for activity H, the earliest finish time is $EF = ES + t = 9 + 12 = 21$. The $ES = 9$ and $EF = 21$ values can now be entered in the node for activity H in Figure 12.4.

Continuing with this **forward pass** through the network, we can establish the earliest start times and the earliest finish times for all activities in the network. Figure 12.5 shows the Western Hills Shopping Center project network with the ES and EF values for each activity. Note that the earliest finish time for activity I, the last activity in the project, is 26 weeks. Therefore, we now know that the total completion time for the project is 26 weeks.

We now continue the algorithm for finding the critical path by making a **backward pass** through the network. Since the project can be completed in 26 weeks, we begin the backward pass with a **latest finish time** of 26 for activity I. Once the latest finish time for an activity is known, the *latest start time* for an activity can be computed as follows. Let

$$LS = \text{latest start time for an activity}$$
$$LF = \text{latest finish time for an activity}$$

then

$$LS = LF - t \qquad (12.2)$$

Beginning the backward pass with activity I, we know that the latest finish time is $LF = 26$ and that the activity time is $t = 2$. Thus, the latest start time for activity I is

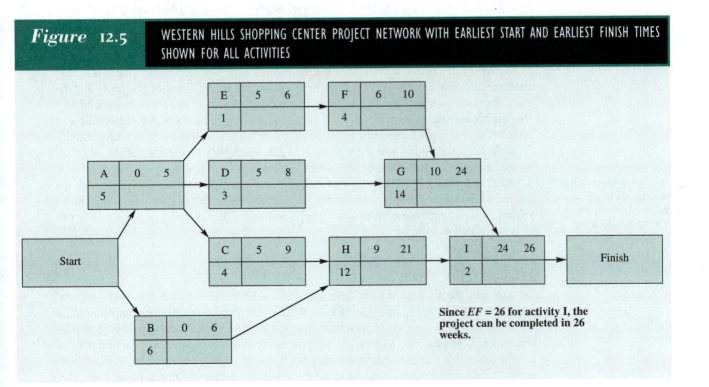

Figure 12.5 WESTERN HILLS SHOPPING CENTER PROJECT NETWORK WITH EARLIEST START AND EARLIEST FINISH TIMES SHOWN FOR ALL ACTIVITIES

Since $EF = 26$ for activity I, the project can be completed in 26 weeks.

$LS = LF - t = 26 - 2 = 24$. We will write the LS and LF values in the node directly below the earliest start (ES) and earliest finish (EF) times. Thus, for node I, we have

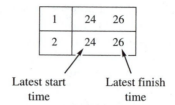

Latest start   Latest finish
time   time

The following rule can be used to determine the latest finish time for each activity in the network.

The latest finish time for an activity is the *smallest* of the latest start times for all activities that immediately follow the activity.

Logically, this rule states that the latest time an activity can be finished equals the earliest (smallest) value for the latest start time of following activities. Figure 12.6 shows the complete project network with the LS and LF backward pass results. We can use the latest finish time rule to verify the LS and LF values shown for activity H. The latest finish time for activity H must be the latest start time for activity I. Thus, we set $LF = 24$ for activity H. Using equation (12.2), we find that $LS = LF - t = 24 - 12 = 12$ as the latest start time for activity H. These values are shown in the node for activity H in Figure 12.6.

Activity A requires a more involved application of the latest start time rule. First, note that three activities (C, D, and E) immediately follow activity A. Figure 12.6 shows that the latest start times for activities C, D, and E are $LS = 8$, $LS = 7$, and $LS = 5$, respectively. The latest finish time rule for activity A states that the LF for activity A is the smallest of the latest start times for activities C, D, and E. With the smallest value being 5 for activity E, we set the latest finish time for activity A to $LF = 5$. Verify this result and the other latest start times and latest finish times shown in the nodes in Figure 12.6.

The slack for each activity indicates the length of time the activity can be delayed without increasing the project completion time.

After we have completed the forward and backward passes, we can determine the amount of slack associated with each activity. **Slack** is the length of time an activity can be delayed without increasing the project completion time. The amount of slack for an activity is computed as follows:

$$\text{Slack} = LS - ES = LF - EF \qquad (12.3)$$

For example, the slack associated with activity C is $LS - ES = 8 - 5 = 3$ weeks. Hence, activity C can be delayed up to 3 weeks, and the entire project can still be completed in 26 weeks. In this sense, activity C is not critical to the completion of the entire project in 26 weeks. Next, we consider activity E. Using the information in Figure 12.6, we find that the slack is $LS - ES = 5 - 5 = 0$. Thus, activity E has zero, or no, slack. Thus, this activity cannot be delayed without increasing the completion time for the entire project. In other

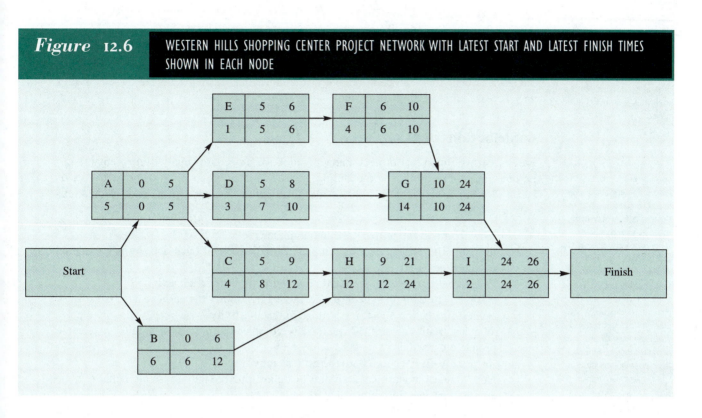

Figure 12.6 WESTERN HILLS SHOPPING CENTER PROJECT NETWORK WITH LATEST START AND LATEST FINISH TIMES SHOWN IN EACH NODE

One of the primary contributions of PERT/CPM is the identification of the critical activities. The project manager will want to monitor critical activities closely because a delay in any one of these activities will lengthen the project completion time.

words, completing activity E exactly as scheduled is critical in terms of keeping the project on schedule. Thus, activity E is a critical activity. In general, the *critical activities* are the activities with zero slack.

The start and finish times shown in Figure 12.6 can be used to develop a detailed start time and finish time schedule for all activities. Putting this information in tabular form provides the activity schedule shown in Table 12.2. Note that the slack column shows that

Table 12.2 ACTIVITY SCHEDULE FOR THE WESTERN HILLS SHOPPING CENTER PROJECT

Activity	Earliest Start (ES)	Latest Start (LS)	Earliest Finish (EF)	Latest Finish (LF)	Slack (LS − ES)	Critical Path?
A	0	0	5	5	0	Yes
B	0	6	6	12	6	
C	5	8	9	12	3	
D	5	7	8	10	2	
E	5	5	6	6	0	Yes
F	6	6	10	10	0	Yes
G	10	10	24	24	0	Yes
H	9	12	21	24	3	
I	24	24	26	26	0	Yes

activities A, E, F, G, and I have zero slack. Hence, these activities are the critical activities for the project. The path formed by nodes A–E–F–G–I is the *critical path* in the Western Hills Shopping Center project network. The detailed schedule shown in Table 12.2 indicates the slack or delay that can be tolerated for the noncritical activities before these activities will increase project completion time.

The critical path algorithm is essentially a longest path *algorithm. From the start node to the finish node, the critical path identifies the path that requires the most time.*

Contributions of PERT/CPM

Previously, we stated that project managers look for procedures that will help answer important questions regarding the planning, scheduling, and controlling of projects. Let us reconsider these questions in light of the information that the critical path calculations have given us.

1. How long will the project take to complete?
   Answer: The project can be completed in 26 weeks if each activity is completed on schedule.
2. What are the scheduled start and completion times for each activity?
   Answer: The activity schedule (see Table 12.2) shows the earliest start, latest start, earliest finish, and latest finish times for each activity.
3. Which activities are critical and must be completed *exactly* as scheduled to keep the project on schedule?
   Answer: A, E, F, G, and I are the critical activities.
4. How long can noncritical activities be delayed before they cause an increase in the completion time for the project?
   Answer: The activity schedule (see Table 12.2) shows the slack associated with each activity.

If the total time required to complete the project is too long, judgment about where and how to shorten the time of critical activities must be exercised. If any activity times are altered, the critical path calculations should be repeated to determine the impact on the activity schedule and the impact on total project completion time. In Section 12.3 we show how to use linear programming to find the least-cost way to shorten the project completion time.

Such information is valuable in managing any project. Although larger projects may increase substantially the time required to make the necessary calculations, the procedure and contributions of PERT/CPM to larger projects are identical to those for the shopping center expansion project. Furthermore, computer packages may be used to carry out the steps of the PERT/CPM procedure. Figure 12.7 shows the activity schedule for the shopping center expansion project developed by The Management Scientist software package. Input to the

Software packages such as The Management Scientist perform the critical path calculations quickly and efficiently. The project manager can modify any aspect of the project and quickly determine how the modification affects the activity schedule and the total time required to complete the project.

Q.M. IN ACTION

PROJECT MANAGEMENT ON THE PC*

More than 100 project management software packages are available for personal computers (PCs). A survey of users of well-known project management software packages for PCs identified applications such as the construction of a $20 million sawmill, the installation of a new software system in a hospital, the development of a communications satellite, the production of an electronic device, and the relocation of a facility. These projects ranged in size from 1000 activities for the sawmill construction project to 6500 activities for the facility relocation project.

At the low end of the market, packages generally cost less than $500. In this group, Harvard Total Project Manager®, Microsoft Project®, SuperProject Plus®, and Time Line® account for the majority of sales.

These packages have modest memory requirements, the ability to analyze projects with as many as 1000 activities, and can produce a wide range of reports. At the high end of the market, prices generally exceed $2000; this group includes packages such as OPEN®, PLAN®, PMS-II Professional®, Primavera Project Planner®, and PROMIS®. These more sophisticated systems are designed to handle projects with as many as 10,000 activities and have the ability to produce presentation-quality graphics.

*Based on Wasil, E., and A. A. Assad, "Project Management on the PC: Software, Applications, and Trends." *Interfaces*, March–April 1988, pp. 75–84.

program included the activities, their immediate predecessors, and the expected activity times. Only a few minutes were required to input the information and generate the critical path and activity schedule. The Q.M. in Action: Project Management on the PC describes the important role software packages play in the management of projects with 1000 or more activities.

Summary of the PERT/CPM Critical Path Procedure

Before leaving this section, let us summarize the PERT/CPM critical path procedure.

Step 1. Develop a list of the activities that make up the project.
Step 2. Determine the immediate predecessors for each activity in the project.
Step 3. Estimate the completion time for each activity.
Step 4. Draw a project network depicting the activities and immediate predecessors listed in steps 1 and 2.
Step 5. Use the project network and the activity time estimates to determine the earliest start and the earliest finish time for each activity by making a forward pass through the network. The earliest finish time for the last activity in the project identifies the total time required to complete the project.
Step 6. Use the project completion time identified in step 5 as the latest finish time for the last activity and make a backward pass through the network to identify the latest start and latest finish time for each activity.
Step 7. Use the difference between the latest start time and the earliest start time for each activity to determine the slack for the activity.
Step 8. Find the activities with zero slack; these are the critical activities.
Step 9. Use the information from steps 5 and 6 to develop the activity schedule for the project.

Figure 12.7 THE MANAGEMENT SCIENTIST ACTIVITY SCHEDULE FOR THE WESTERN HILLS SHOPPING CENTER PROJECT

```
            ***    ACTIVITY  SCHEDULE    ***

          EARLIEST  LATEST   EARLIEST  LATEST          CRITICAL
ACTIVITY   START    START    FINISH    FINISH  SLACK  ACTIVITY
-----------------------------------------------------------------
   A         0        0        5         5       0      YES
   B         0        6        6        12       6
   C         5        8        9        12       3
   D         5        7        8        10       2
   E         5        5        6         6       0      YES
   F         6        6       10        10       0      YES
   G        10       10       24        24       0      YES
   H         9       12       21        24       3
   I        24       24       26        26       0      YES
-----------------------------------------------------------------

     CRITICAL PATH:   A-E-F-G-I

     PROJECT COMPLETION TIME = 26
```

N O T E S
and Comments

If after analyzing a PERT/CPM network and finding that the project completion time is unacceptable (i.e., the project is going to take too long), a manager must take one or both of the following steps. First, review the original PERT/CPM network to see if the immediate predecessor relationships can be modified so that at least some of the critical path activities can be done simultaneously. Second, consider adding resources to critical path activities in an attempt to shorten the critical path; we discuss this alternative, referred to as **crashing**, in Section 12.3.

12.2 PROJECT SCHEDULING WITH UNCERTAIN ACTIVITY TIMES

In this section we consider the details of project scheduling for a problem involving new-product research and development. Because many of the activities in this project have never been attempted, the project manager wants to account for uncertainties in the activity times. Let us show how project scheduling can be conducted with uncertain activity times.

The Daugherty Porta-Vac Project

The H. S. Daugherty Company has manufactured industrial vacuum cleaning systems for many years. Recently, a member of the company's new-product research team submitted a report suggesting that the company consider manufacturing a cordless vacuum cleaner. The new product, referred to as a Porta-Vac, could contribute to Daugherty's expansion into the household market. Management hopes that it can be manufactured at a reasonable cost and that its portability and no-cord convenience will make it extremely attractive.

Daugherty's management wants to study the feasibility of manufacturing the Porta-Vac product. The feasibility study will recommend the action to be taken. To complete this study, information must be obtained from the firm's research and development (R&D), product testing, manufacturing, cost estimating, and market research groups. How long will this feasibility study take? In the following discussion, we show how to answer this question and provide an activity schedule for the project.

Again, the first step in the project scheduling process is to identify all activities that make up the project and then determine the immediate predecessors for each activity. Table 12.3 shows these data for the Porta-Vac project.

The Porta-Vac project network is shown in Figure 12.8. Verify that the network does in fact maintain the immediate predecessor relationships shown in Table 12.3.

Uncertain Activity Times

Accurate activity time estimates are important in the development of an activity schedule. When activity times are uncertain, the three time estimates—optimistic, most probable, and pessimistic—allow the project manager to take uncertainty into consideration in determining the critical path and the activity schedule. This approach was developed by the designers of PERT.

Once we have developed the project network, we will need information on the time required to complete each activity. This information is used in the calculation of the total time required to complete the project and in the scheduling of specific activities. For repeat projects, such as construction and maintenance projects, managers may have the experience and historical data necessary to provide accurate activity time estimates. However, for new or unique projects, estimating the time for each activity may be quite difficult. In fact, in many cases, activity times are uncertain and are best described by a range of possible values rather than by one specific time estimate. In these instances, the uncertain activity times are treated as random variables with associated probability distributions. As a result, probability statements will be provided about the ability to meet a specific project completion date.

To incorporate uncertain activity times into the analysis, we need to obtain three time estimates for each activity:

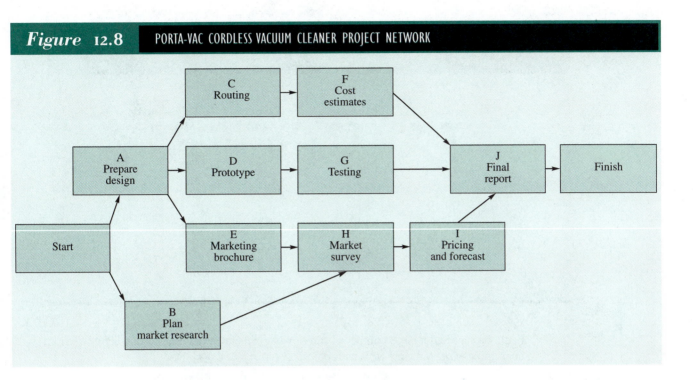

Figure 12.8   PORTA-VAC CORDLESS VACUUM CLEANER PROJECT NETWORK

Table 12.3   ACTIVITY LIST FOR THE PORTA-VAC PROJECT

Activity	Description	Immediate Predecessor
A	Develop product design	—
B	Plan market research	—
C	Prepare routing (manufacturing engineering)	A
D	Build prototype model	A
E	Prepare marketing brochure	A
F	Prepare cost estimates (industrial engineering)	C
G	Do preliminary product testing	D
H	Complete market survey	B, E
I	Prepare pricing and forecast report	H
J	Prepare final report	F, G, I

Optimistic time a = the minimum activity time if everything progresses ideally

Most probable time m = the most probable activity time under normal conditions

Pessimistic time b = the maximum activity time if significant delays are encountered

To illustrate the PERT/CPM procedure with uncertain activity times, let us consider the optimistic, most probable, and pessimistic time estimates for the Porta-Vac activities as presented in Table 12.4. Using activity A as an example, we see that the most probable time is 5 weeks with a range from 4 weeks (optimistic) to 12 weeks (pessimistic). If the activity

Table 12.4	OPTIMISTIC, MOST PROBABLE, AND PESSIMISTIC ACTIVITY TIME ESTIMATES (IN WEEKS) FOR THE PORTA-VAC PROJECT		
Activity	Optimistic (a)	Most Probable (m)	Pessimistic (b)
A	4	5	12
B	1	1.5	5
C	2	3	4
D	3	4	11
E	2	3	4
F	1.5	2	2.5
G	1.5	3	4.5
H	2.5	3.5	7.5
I	1.5	2	2.5
J	1	2	3

could be repeated a large number of times, what is the average time for the activity? This average or **expected time** (t) is as follows:

$$t = \frac{a + 4m + b}{6} \tag{12.4}$$

For activity A we have an average or expected time of

$$t_A = \frac{4 + 4(5) + 12}{6} = \frac{36}{6} = 6 \text{ weeks}$$

With uncertain activity times, we can use the **variance** to describe the dispersion or variation in the activity time values. The variance of the activity time is given by the formula[1]

$$\sigma^2 = \left(\frac{b - a}{6}\right)^2 \tag{12.5}$$

The difference between the pessimistic (b) and optimistic (a) time estimates greatly affects the value of the variance. Large differences in these two values reflect a high degree of uncertainty in the activity time. Using equation (12.5), we obtain the measure of uncertainty—that is, the variance—of activity A, denoted σ_A^2:

$$\sigma_A^2 = \left(\frac{12 - 4}{6}\right)^2 = \left(\frac{8}{6}\right)^2 = 1.78$$

Equations (12.4) and (12.5) are based on the assumption that the activity time distribution can be described by a **beta probability distribution.**[2] With this assumption, the probability distribution for the time to complete activity A is as shown in Figure 12.9. Using

---

1. The variance equation is based on the notion that a standard deviation is approximately $1/6$ of the difference between the extreme values of the distribution: ($b - a/6$). The variance is the square of the standard deviation.

2. The equations for t and σ^2 require additional assumptions about the parameters of the beta probability distribution. However, even when these additional assumptions are not made, the equations still provide very good approximations of t and σ^2.

Figure 12.9 ACTIVITY TIME DISTRIBUTION FOR PROJECT DESIGN ACTIVITY A OF THE PORTA-VAC PROJECT

equations (12.4) and (12.5) and the data in Table 12.4, we calculated the expected times and variances for all Porta-Vac activities; the results are summarized in Table 12.5. The Porta-Vac project network with expected activity times is shown in Figure 12.10.

The Critical Path

When we have the project network and the expected activity times, we are ready to proceed with the critical path calculations necessary to determine the expected time required to complete the project and determine the activity schedule. In these calculations, we treat the expected activity times (Table 12.5) as the **fixed length** or **known duration** of each

> When uncertain activity times are used, the critical path calculations will determine only the expected or average time to complete the project. The actual time required to complete the project may differ. However, for planning purposes, the expected time should be valuable information for the project manager.

Table 12.5 EXPECTED TIMES AND VARIANCES FOR THE PORTA-VAC PROJECT ACTIVITIES

Activity	Expected Time (weeks)	Variance
A	6	1.78
B	2	0.44
C	3	0.11
D	5	1.78
E	3	0.11
F	2	0.03
G	3	0.25
H	4	0.69
I	2	0.03
J	2	0.11
	Total 32	

Figure 12.10   PORTA-VAC PROJECT NETWORK WITH EXPECTED ACTIVITY TIMES

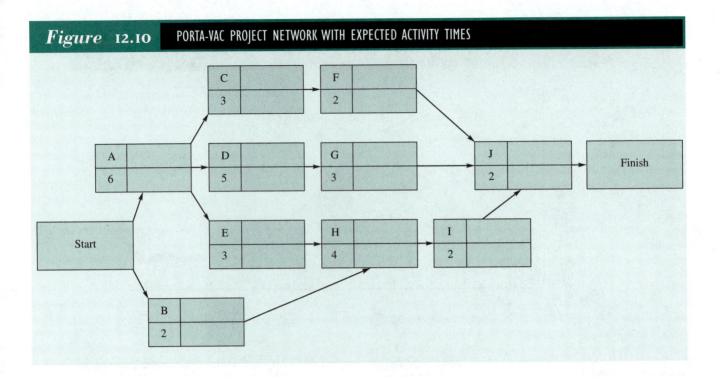

activity. As a result, we can use the PERT/CPM critical path procedure introduced in Section 12.1 to find the critical path for the Porta-Vac project. After the critical activities and the expected time to complete the project have been determined, we analyze the effect of the activity time variability.

Proceeding with a forward pass through the network shown in Figure 12.10, we can establish the earliest start (ES) and earliest finish (EF) times for each activity. Figure 12.11 shows the project network with the ES and EF values. Note that the earliest finish time for activity J, the last activity, is 17 weeks. Thus, the expected completion time for the project is 17 weeks. Next, we make a backward pass through the network. The backward pass provides the latest start (LS) and latest finish (LF) shown in Figure 12.12.

> Activities that have larger variances show a greater degree of uncertainty. The project manager should monitor the progress of any activity with a large variance even if the expected times do not identify the activity as a critical activity.

The activity schedule for the Porta-Vac project is shown in Table 12.6. Note that the slack time (LS − ES) is also shown for each activity. The activities with zero slack (A, E, H, I, and J) form the critical path for the Porta-Vac project network.

Variability in Project Completion Time

We know that for the Porta-Vac project the critical path of A–E–H–I–J resulted in an expected total project completion time of 17 weeks. However, variation in critical activities can cause variation in the project completion time. Variation in noncritical activities ordinarily has no effect on the project completion time because of the slack time associated with these activities. However, if a noncritical activity is delayed long enough to expend its slack time, it becomes part of a new critical path and may affect the project completion time. Variability leading to a longer-than-expected total time for the critical activities will always extend the project completion time, and conversely, variability that results in a shorter critical will produce a shorter-than-expected project completion time, unless other activities

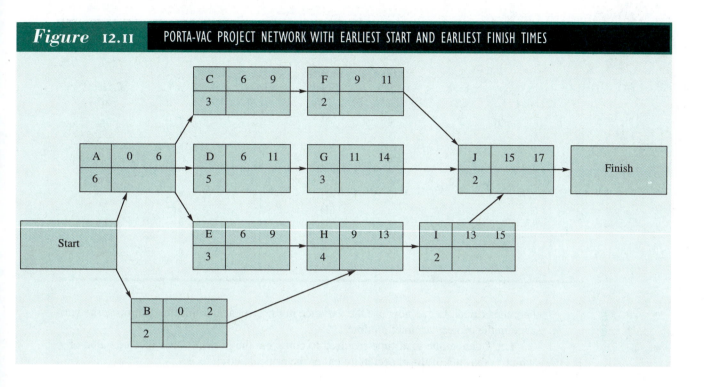

Figure 12.11 PORTA-VAC PROJECT NETWORK WITH EARLIEST START AND EARLIEST FINISH TIMES

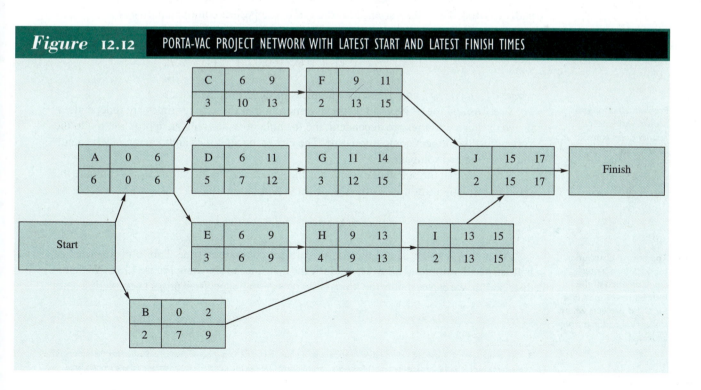

Figure 12.12 PORTA-VAC PROJECT NETWORK WITH LATEST START AND LATEST FINISH TIMES

	Table 12.6		ACTIVITY SCHEDULE FOR THE PORTA-VAC PROJECT				
Activity	**Earliest Start (ES)**	**Latest Start (LS)**	**Earlist Finish (EF)**	**Latest Finish (LF)**	**Slack (LS − ES)**	**Critical Path?**
A	0	0	6	6	0	Yes
B	0	7	2	9	7	
C	6	10	9	13	4	
D	6	7	11	12	1	
E	6	6	9	9	0	Yes
F	9	13	11	15	4	
G	11	12	14	15	1	
H	9	9	13	13	0	Yes
I	13	13	15	15	0	Yes
J	15	15	17	17	0	Yes

become critical. Let us now use the variance in the critical activities to determine the variance in the project completion time.

Let T denote the total time required to complete the project. The expected value of T, which is the sum of the expected times for the critical activities is

$$E(T) = t_A + t_E + t_H + t_I + t_J$$
$$= 6 + 3 + 4 + 2 + 2 = 17 \text{ weeks}$$

The variance in the project completion time is the sum of the variances of the critical path activities. Thus, the variance for the Porta-Vac project completion time is

$$\sigma^2 = \sigma_A^2 + \sigma_E^2 + \sigma_H^2 + \sigma_I^2 + \sigma_J^2$$
$$= 1.78 + 0.11 + 0.69 + 0.03 + 0.11 = 2.72$$

where σ_A^2, σ_E^2, σ_H^2, σ_I^2, and σ_J^2 are the variances of the critical activities.

Problem 10 involves a project with uncertain activity times and asks you to compute the expected completion time and the variance for the project.

The formula for σ^2 is based on the assumption that the activity times are independent. If two or more activities are dependent, the formula provides only an approximation to the variance of the project completion time. The closer the activities are to being independent, the better the approximation.

Knowing that the standard deviation is the square root of the variance, we compute the standard deviation σ for the Porta-Vac project completion time as

$$\sigma = \sqrt{\sigma^2} = \sqrt{2.72} = 1.65$$

The normal distribution tends to be a better approximation of the distribution of total time for larger projects where the critical path has many activities.

Assuming that the distribution of the project completion time T follows a normal or bell-shaped distribution[3] allows us to draw the distribution shown in Figure 12.13. With this distribution, we can compute the probability of meeting a specified project completion date.

---

3. Use of the normal distribution as an approximation is based on the central limit theorem, which indicates that the sum of independent random variables (activity times) follows a normal distribution as the number of random variables becomes large.

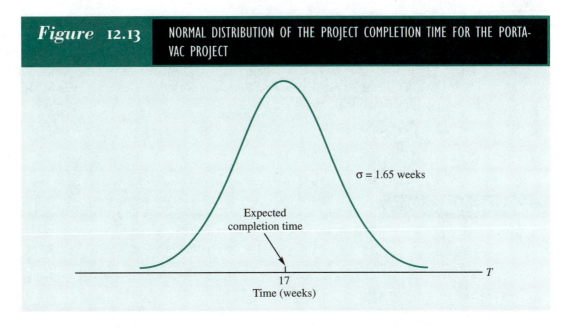

Figure 12.13 NORMAL DISTRIBUTION OF THE PROJECT COMPLETION TIME FOR THE PORTA-VAC PROJECT

For example, suppose that management has allotted 20 weeks for the Porta-Vac project. What is the probability that we will meet the 20-week deadline? Using the normal probability distribution shown in Figure 12.14, we are asking for the probability that $T \leq 20$; this probability is shown graphically as the shaded area in the figure. The z value for the normal probability distribution at $T = 20$ is

$$z = \frac{20 - 17}{1.65} = 1.82$$

Figure 12.14 PROBABILITY OF A PORTA-VAC PROJECT COMPLETION DATE PRIOR TO THE 20-WEEK DEADLINE

Using $z = 1.82$ and the table for the normal distribution (see Appendix C), we find that the probability of the project meeting the 20-week deadline is $0.4656 + 0.5000 = 0.9656$. Thus, even though activity time variability may cause the completion time to exceed 17 weeks, there is an excellent chance that the project will be completed before the 20-week deadline. Similar probability calculations can be made for other project deadline alternatives.

N O T E S
and Comments

For projects involving uncertain activity times, the probability that the project can be completed within a specified amount of time is helpful managerial information. However, remember that this probability estimate is based *only* on the critical activities. When uncertain activity times exist, longer-than-expected completion times for one or more noncritical activities may cause an original noncritical activity to become critical and hence increase the time required to complete the project. By frequently monitoring the progress of the project to make sure all activities are on schedule, the project manager will be better prepared to take corrective action if a noncritical activity begins to lengthen the duration of the project.

12.3   CONSIDERING TIME—COST TRADE-OFFS

The original developers of CPM provided the project manager with the option of adding resources to selected activities to reduce project completion time. Added resources (such as more workers, overtime, and so on) generally increase project costs, so the decision to reduce activity times must take into consideration the additional cost involved. In effect, the project manager has to make a decision that involves trading reduced activity time for additional project cost.

Using more resources to reduce activity times was proposed by the developers of CPM. The shortening of activity times is referred to as *crashing*.

Table 12.7 defines a two-machine maintenance project consisting of five activities. Since management has had substantial experience with similar projects, the times for maintenance activities are considered to be known; hence, a single time estimate is given for each activity. The project network is shown in Figure 12.15.

Table **12.7**   ACTIVITY LIST FOR THE TWO-MACHINE MAINTENANCE PROJECT

Activity	Description	Immediate Predecessor	Expected Time (days)
A	Overhaul machine I	—	7
B	Adjust machine I	A	3
C	Overhaul machine II	—	6
D	Adjust machine II	C	3
E	Test system	B, D	2

Figure 12.15 TWO-MACHINE MAINTENANCE PROJECT NETWORK

The procedure for making critical path calculations for the maintenance project network is the same one we used to find the critical path in the networks for both the Western Hills Shopping Center expansion project and the Porta-Vac project. Making the forward pass and backward pass calculations for the network in Figure 12.15, we obtained the activity schedule shown in Table 12.8. The zero slack times, and thus the critical path, are associated with activities A–B–E. The length of the critical path, and thus the total time required to complete the project, is 12 days.

Crashing Activity Times

Now suppose that current production levels make completing the maintenance project within 10 days imperative. By looking at the length of the critical path of the network (12 days), we realize that meeting the desired project completion time is impossible unless we can shorten selected activity times. This shortening of activity times, which usually can be achieved by adding resources, is referred to as **crashing.** However, the added resources associated with crashing activity times usually result in added project costs, so we will want to identify the activities that cost the least to crash and then crash those activities only the amount necessary to meet the desired project completion time.

Table 12.8 ACTIVITY SCHEDULE FOR THE TWO-MACHINE MAINTENANCE

Activity	Earliest Start (ES)	Latest Start (LS)	Earliest Finish (EF)	Latest Finish (LF)	Slack (LS − ES)	Critical Path?
A	0	0	7	7	0	Yes
B	7	7	10	10	0	Yes
C	0	1	6	7	1	
D	6	7	9	10	1	
E	10	10	12	12	0	Yes

To determine just where and how much to crash activity times, we need information on how much each activity can be crashed and how much the crashing process costs. Hence, we must ask for the following information:

1. Activity cost under the normal or expected activity time
2. Time to complete the activity under **maximum crashing** (i.e., the shortest possible activity time)
3. Activity cost under maximum crashing

Let

$$\tau_i = \text{expected time for activity } i$$

$$\tau'_i = \text{time for activity } j \text{ under maximum crashing}$$

$$M_i = \text{maximum possible reduction in time for activity } i \text{ due to crashing}$$

Given τ_i and τ'_i, we can compute M_i:

$$M_i = \tau_i - \tau'_i \tag{12.6}$$

Next, let C_i denote the cost for activity i under the normal or expected activity time and C'_i denote the cost for activity i under maximum crashing. Thus, per unit of time (e.g., per day), the crashing cost K_i for each activity is given by

$$K_i = \frac{C'_i - C_i}{M_i} \tag{12.7}$$

For example, if the normal or expected time for activity A is 7 days at a cost of $C_A = \$500$ and the time under maximum crashing is 4 days at a cost of $C'_A = \$800$, equations (12.6) and (12.7) show that the maximum possible reduction in time for activity A is

$$M_A = 7 - 4 = 3 \text{ days}$$

with a crashing cost of

$$K_A = \frac{C'_A - C_A}{M_A} = \frac{800 - 500}{3} = \frac{300}{3} = \$100 \text{ per day}$$

We make the assumption that any portion or fraction of the activity crash time can be achieved for a corresponding portion of the activity crashing cost. For example, if we decided to crash activity A by only 1½ days, the added cost would be 1½($100) = $150, which results in a total activity cost of $500 + $150 = $650. Figure 12.16 shows the graph of the time–cost relationship for activity A. The complete normal and crash activity data for the two-machine maintenance project are given in Table 12.9.

Which activities should be crashed—and by how much—to meet the 10-day project completion deadline at minimum cost? Your first reaction to this question may be to consider crashing the critical activities—A, B, or E. Activity A has the lowest crashing cost per day of the three, and crashing this activity by 2 days will reduce the A–B–E path to the desired 10 days. Keep in mind, however, that as you crash the current critical activities, other paths may become critical. Thus, you will need to check the critical path in the revised network and perhaps either identify additional activities to crash or modify your initial

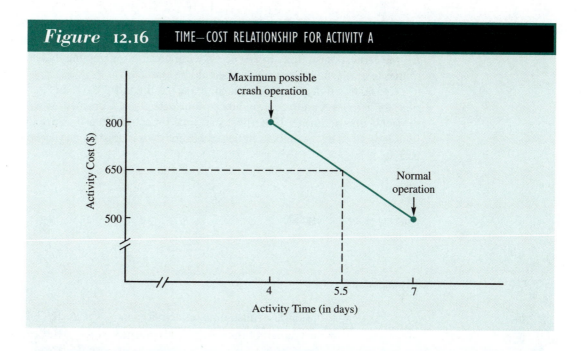

Figure 12.16   TIME–COST RELATIONSHIP FOR ACTIVITY A

Table 12.9   NORMAL AND CRASH ACTIVITY DATA FOR THE TWO-MACHINE MAINTENANCE PROJECT

Activity	Time (days) Normal	Time (days) Crash	Total Cost Normal (C_i)	Total Cost Crash (C_i')	Maximum Reduction in Time (M_i)	Crash Cost Per day $\left(K_i = \dfrac{C_i' - C_i}{M_i}\right)$
A	7	4	$ 500	$ 800	3	$100
B	3	2	200	350	1	150
C	6	4	500	900	2	200
D	3	1	200	500	2	150
E	2	1	300	550	1	250
			$1700	$3100		

crashing decision. For a small network, this trial-and-error approach can be used to make crashing decisions; in larger networks, however, a mathematical procedure is required to determine the optimal crashing decisions. The following discussion shows how linear programming can be used to solve the network crashing problem.

A Linear Programming Model for Crashing Decisions

In the PERT/CPM procedure, we used

$$EF = ES + t$$

to determine the earliest finish time for an activity. Note that if *ES,* the earliest start time for an activity, is known, the effect of crashing a particular activity will be to reduce *t* and hence *EF,* the earliest finish time. In essence, we use linear programming to determine which activities to crash and how much they should be crashed.

Consider activity A, which has an expected time of 7 days. Let x_A = earliest finish time for activity A and y_A = amount of time activity A is crashed. If we assume that the project begins at time 0, the earliest start time for activity A is 0. Since the time for activity A is reduced by the amount of time that activity A is crashed, the earliest finish time for activity A is

$$x_A \geq 0 + (7 - y_A)$$

Moving y_A to the left side,

$$x_A + y_A \geq 7$$

In general, let

$$x_i = \text{the earliest finish time for activity } i \qquad i = \text{A, B, C, D, E}$$
$$y_i = \text{the amount of time activity } i \text{ is crashed} \quad i = \text{A, B, C, D, E}$$

If we follow the same approach that we used for activity A, the constraint corresponding to the earliest finish time for activity C (expected time = 6 days) is

$$x_C \geq 0 + (6 - y_C) \quad \text{or} \quad x_C + y_C \geq 6$$

Continuing with the forward pass of the PERT/CPM procedure, we see that the earliest start time for activity B is x_A, the earliest finish time for activity A. Thus, the constraint corresponding to the earliest finish time for activity B is

$$x_B \geq x_A + (3 - y_B) \quad \text{or} \quad x_B + y_B - x_A \geq 3$$

Similarly, we obtain the constraint for the earliest finish time for activity D:

$$x_D \geq x_C + (3 - y_D) \quad \text{or} \quad x_D + y_D - x_C \geq 3$$

Finally, we consider activity E. The earliest start time for activity E equals the *largest* of the earliest finish times for activities B and D. Because the earliest finish times for both activities B and D will be determined by the crashing procedure, we must write two constraints for activity E, one based on the earliest finish time for activity B and one based upon the earliest finish time for activity D:

$$x_E + y_E - x_B \geq 2 \quad \text{and} \quad x_E + y_E - x_D \geq 2$$

Recall that current production levels made completing the maintenance project within 10 days imperative. Thus, the constraint for the earliest finish time for activity E is

$$x_E \leq 10$$

In addition, we must add the following five constraints corresponding to the maximum allowable crashing time for each activity:

$$y_A \leq 3, \quad y_B \leq 1, \quad y_C \leq 2, \quad y_D \leq 2, \quad \text{and} \quad y_E \leq 1$$

As with all linear programs, we add the usual nonnegativity requirements for the decision variables.

All that remains is to develop an objective function for the model. Since the total project cost for a normal completion time is fixed at $1700 (see Table 12.9), we can minimize the total project cost (normal cost plus crashing cost) by minimizing the total crashing costs. Thus, the linear programming objective function becomes

$$\text{Min} \quad 100y_A + 150y_B + 200y_C + 150y_D + 250y_E$$

Thus, to determine the optimal crashing for each of the activities, we must solve a 10-variable, 12-constraint linear programming model. The linear programming module of The Management Scientist provides the optimal solution of crashing activity A by 1 week and activity E by 1 week, with a total crashing cost of $350. We can now develop a detailed activity schedule by using $7 - 1 = 6$ as the revised time for activity A and $2 - 1 = 1$ day as the revised time for activity E.

N O T E S and Comments

Note that the two-machine maintenance project network for the crashing illustration (see Figure 12.15) has only one activity, activity E, leading directly to the Finish node. As a result, the project completion time is equal to the completion time for activity E. Thus, the linear programming constraint requiring the project completion in 10 days or less could be written $x_E \leq 10$.

If two or more activities lead directly to the Finish node of a project network, a slight modification is required in the linear programming model for crashing. Consider the following portion of a project network:

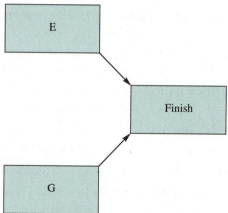

In this case, we suggest creating an additional variable, x_{FIN}, which indicates the finish or completion time for the entire project. The fact that the project cannot be finished until both activities E and G are completed can be modeled by the two constraints

$$x_{FIN} \geq x_E \quad \text{or} \quad x_{FIN} - x_E \geq 0$$

$$x_{FIN} \geq x_G \quad \text{or} \quad x_{FIN} - x_G \geq 0$$

The constraint that the project must be finished by time T can be added as $x_{FIN} \leq T$. Problem 22 gives you practice with this type of project network.

..../ /...........

SUMMARY

In this chapter we showed how PERT/CPM can be used to plan, schedule, and control a wide variety of projects. The key to this approach to project scheduling is the development of a PERT/CPM project network that depicts the activities and their precedence relationships. From this project network and activity time estimates, the critical path for the network and the associated critical activities can be identified. In the process, an activity schedule showing the earliest start and finish times, the latest start and finish times, and the slack for each activity can be identified.

We showed how we can include capabilities for handling variable or uncertain activity times and how to use this information to provide a probability statement about the chances the project can be completed in a specified period of time. We introduced crashing as a procedure for reducing activity times to meet project completion deadlines. A linear programming model can be used to determine the crashing decisions that will minimize the cost of reducing the project completion time.

..../ /...........

GLOSSARY

Program evaluation and review technique (PERT) A network-based project scheduling procedure.

Critical path method (CPM) A network-based project scheduling procedure.

Activities Specific jobs or tasks that are components of a project. They are represented by nodes in a project network.

Immediate predecessors The activities that must be completed immediately prior to the start of a given activity.

Project network A graphical representation of a project that depicts the activities and shows the predecessor relationships among the activities.

Critical path The longest path in a project network.

Path A sequence of connected nodes that leads from the Start node to the Finish node.

Critical activities The activities on the critical path.

Earliest start time The earliest time an activity may begin.

Earliest finish time The earliest time an activity may be completed.

Forward pass Part of the PERT/CPM procedure that involves moving forward through the project network to determine the earliest start and earliest finish times for each activity.

Latest start time The latest time an activity may begin without increasing the project completion time.

Latest finish time The latest time an activity may be completed without increasing the project completion time.

Backward pass Part of the PERT/CPM procedure that involves moving backward through the network to determine the latest start and latest finish times for each activity.

Optimistic time The minimum activity time if everything progresses ideally.

Most probable time The most probable activity time under normal conditions.

Pessimistic time The maximum activity time if significant delays are encountered.

Expected time The average activity time.

Beta probability distribution A probability distribution used to describe activity times.

Slack The length of time an activity can be delayed without affecting the project completion time.

Crashing The shortening of activity times by adding resources and hence usually increasing cost.

PROBLEMS

1. The Mohawk Discount Store is designing a management training program for individuals at its corporate headquarters. The company wants to design the program so that trainees can complete it as quickly as possible. Important precedence relationships must be maintained between assignments or activities in the program. For example, a trainee cannot serve as an assistant to the store manager until the trainee has obtained experience in the credit department and at least one sales department. The following activities are the assignments that must be completed by each trainee in the program. Construct a project network for this problem. Do not perform any further analysis.

Activity	A	B	C	D	E	F	G	H
Immediate Predecessor	—	—	A	A, B	A, B	C	D, F	E, G

2. Bridge City Developers is coordinating the construction of an office complex. As part of the planning process, the company generated the following activity list. Draw a project network that can be used to assist in the scheduling of the project activities.

Activity	A	B	C	D	E	F	G	H	I	J
Immediate Predecessor	—	—	—	A, B	A, B	D	E	C	C	F, G, H, I

SELF TEST

3. Construct a project network for the following project. The project is completed when activities F and G are both complete.

Activity	A	B	C	D	E	F	G
Immediate Predecessor	—	—	A	A	C, B	C, B	D, E

4. Assume that the project in Problem 3 has the following activity times (in months).

Activity	A	B	C	D	E	F	G
Time	4	6	2	6	3	3	5

  a. Find the critical path.
  b. The project must be completed in 1½ years. Do you anticipate difficulty in meeting the deadline? Explain.

5. Management Decision Systems (MDS) is a consulting company that specializes in the development of decision support systems. MDS has just obtained a contract to develop a computer system to assist the management of a large company in formulating its capital expenditure plan. The project leader has developed the following list of activities and immediate predecessors. Construct a project network for this problem.

Activity	A	B	C	D	E	F	G	H	I	J
Immediate Predecessor	—	—	—	B	A	B	C,D	B,E	F,G	H

6. Consider the following project network and activity times (in weeks).

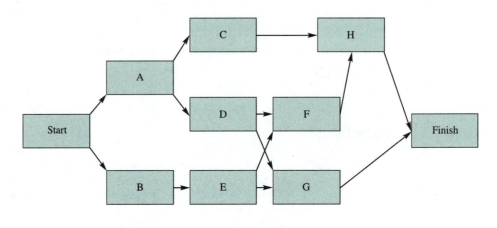

Activity	A	B	C	D	E	F	G	H
Activity Times	5	3	7	6	7	3	10	8

a. Identify the critical path.
b. How much time will be needed to complete this project?
c. Can activity D be delayed without delaying the entire project? If so, by how many weeks?
d. Can activity C be delayed without delaying the entire project? If so, by how many weeks?
e. What is the schedule for activity E?

7. A project involving the installation of a computer system comprises eight activities. The following table lists immediate predecessors and activity times (in weeks).

Activity	Immediate Predecessor	Time
A	—	3
B	—	6
C	A	2
D	B, C	5
E	D	4
F	E	3
G	B, C	9
H	F, G	3

a. Draw a project network.
b. What are the critical activities?
c. What is the expected project completion time?

8. Colonial State College is considering building a new multipurpose athletic complex on campus. The complex would provide a new gymnasium for intercollegiate basketball games, expanded office space, classrooms, and intramural facilities. The following activities would have to be undertaken before construction can begin.

Activity	Description	Immediate Predecessor	Time (weeks)
A	Survey building site	—	6
B	Develop initial design	—	8
C	Obtain board approval	A, B	12
D	Select architect	C	4
E	Establish budget	C	6
F	Finalize design	D, E	15
G	Obtain financing	E	12
H	Hire contractor	F, G	8

a. Draw a project network.
b. Identify the critical path.
c. Develop the activity schedule for the project.
d. Does it appear reasonable that construction of the athletic complex could begin one year after the decision to begin the project with the site survey and initial design plans? What is the expected completion time for the project?

9. Hamilton County Parks is planning to develop a new park and recreational area on a recently purchased 100-acre tract. Project development activities include clearing playground and picnic areas, constructing roads, constructing a shelter house, purchasing picnic equipment, and so on. The following network and activity times (in weeks) are being used in the planning, scheduling, and controlling of this project.

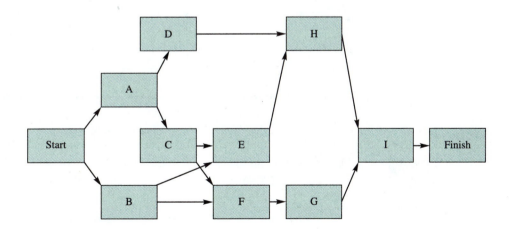

Activity	A	B	C	D	E	F	G	H	I
Activity Time	9	6	6	3	0	3	2	6	3

a. What is the critical path for this network?
b. Show the activity schedule for this project.
c. The park commissioner would like to open the park to the public within six months from the time the work on the project is started. Does this opening date appear to be feasible? Explain.

SELF TEST

10. The following estimates of activity times (in days) are available for a small project.

Activity	Optimistic	Most Probable	Pessimistic
A	4	5.0	6
B	8	9.0	10
C	7	7.5	11
D	7	9.0	10
E	6	7.0	9
F	5	6.0	7

   a. Compute the expected activity completion times and the variance for each activity.
   b. An analyst determined that the critical path consists of activities B–D–F. Compute the expected project completion time and the variance.

11. Building a backyard swimming pool consists of nine major activities. The activities and their immediate predecessors are shown. Develop the project network.

Activity	A	B	C	D	E	F	G	H	I
Immediate Predecessor	—	—	A, B	A, B	B	C	D	D, F	E, G, H

12. Assume that the activity time estimates (in days) for the swimming pool construction project in Problem 11 are

Activity	Optimistic	Most Probable	Pessimistic
A	3	5	6
B	2	4	6
C	5	6	7
D	7	9	10
E	2	4	6
F	1	2	3
G	5	8	10
H	6	8	10
I	3	4	5

   a. What are the critical activities?
   b. What is the expected time to complete the project?
   c. What is the probability that the project can be completed in 25 days or less?

13. Suppose that the following estimates of activity times (in weeks) were provided for the network shown in Problem 6.

SELF TEST

Activity	Optimistic	Most Probable	Pessimistic
A	4.0	5.0	6.0
B	2.5	3.0	3.5
C	6.0	7.0	8.0
D	5.0	5.5	9.0
E	5.0	7.0	9.0
F	2.0	3.0	4.0
G	8.0	10.0	12.0
H	6.0	7.0	14.0

What is the probability that the project will be completed
a. Within 21 weeks?
b. Within 22 weeks?
c. Within 25 weeks?

14. Consider the following project network.

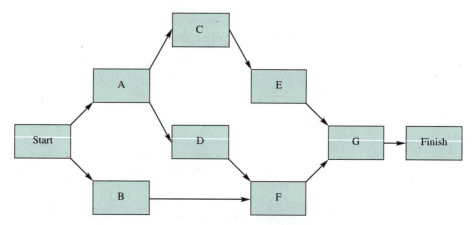

Estimates of the optimistic, most probable, and pessimistic times (in days) for the activities are

Activity	Optimistic	Most Probable	Pessimistic
A	5	6	7
B	5	12	13
C	6	8	10
D	4	10	10
E	5	6	13
F	7	7	10
G	4	7	10

a. Find the critical path.
b. How much slack time, if any, is in activity C?
c. Determine the expected project completion time and the variance.
d. Find the probability that the project will be completed in 30 days or less.

15. Doug Casey is in charge of planning and coordinating next spring's sales management training program for his company. Doug has listed the following activity information for this project.

Activity	Description	Immediate Predecessor	Optimistic	Time (weeks) Most Probable	Pessimistic
A	Plan topic	—	1.5	2.0	2.5
B	Obtain speakers	A	2.0	2.5	6.0
C	List meeting locations	—	1.0	2.0	3.0
D	Select location	C	1.5	2.0	2.5
E	Finalize speaker travel plans	B, D	0.5	1.0	1.5
F	Make final check with speakers	E	1.0	2.0	3.0
G	Prepare and mail brochure	B, D	3.0	3.5	7.0
H	Take reservations	G	3.0	4.0	5.0
I	Handle last-minute details	F, H	1.5	2.0	2.5

a. Draw a project network.
b. Prepare an activity schedule.
c. What are the critical activities and what is the expected project completion time?
d. If Doug wants a 0.99 probability of completing the project on time, how far ahead of the scheduled meeting date should he begin working on the project?

16. The Daugherty Porta-Vac project discussed in Section 12.2 had an expected project completion time of 17 weeks. The probability that the project could be completed in 20 weeks or less was 0.9656. The noncritical paths in the Porta-Vac project network are

A–D–G–J
A–C–F–J
B–H–I–J

a. Use the information in Table 12.5 to compute the expected time and variance for each path shown.
b. Compute the probability that each path will be completed in the desired 20-week period.
c. Why is the computation of the probability of completing a project on time based on the analysis of the critical path? In what case, if any, would making the probability computation for a noncritical path be desirable?

17. The Porsche Shop, founded in 1985 by Dale Jensen, specializes in the restoration of vintage Porsche automobiles. One of Jensen's regular customers asked him to prepare an estimate for the restoration of a 1964 model 356SC Porsche. To estimate the time and cost to perform such a restoration, Jensen broke the restoration process into four separate activities: disassembly and initial preparation work (A), body restoration (B), engine restoration (C), and final assembly (D). Once activity A has been completed, activities B and C can be performed independently of each other; however, activity D can be started only if both activities B and C have been completed. Based on his inspection of the car, Jensen believes that the following time estimates (in days) are applicable.

Activity	Optimistic	Most Probable	Pessimistic
A	3	4	8
B	5	8	11
C	2	4	6
D	4	5	12

Jensen estimates that the parts needed to restore the body will cost $3000 and that the parts needed to restore the engine will cost $5000. His current labor costs are $400 a day.
a. Develop a project network.
b. What is the expected project completion time?
c. Densen's business philosophy is based on making decisions using a best and worst case scenario. Develop cost estimates for completing the restoration based on both a best and worst case analysis. Assume that the total restoration cost is the sum of the labor cost plus the material cost.
d. If Jensen obtains the job with a bid that is based on the costs associated with an expected completion time, what is the probability that he will lose money on the job?
e. If Jensen obtains the job based on a bid of $16,800, what is the probability that he will lose money on the job?

18. The manager of the Oak Hills Swimming Club is planning the club's swimming team program. The first team practice is scheduled for May 1. The activities, their immediate predecessors, and the activity time estimates (in weeks) are as follows.

Activity	Description	Immediate Predecessor	Optimistic	Time (weeks) Most Probable	Pessimistic
A	Meet with board	—	1	1	2
B	Hire coaches	A	4	6	8
C	Reserve pool	A	2	4	6
D	Announce program	B, C	1	2	3
E	Meet with coaches	B	2	3	4
F	Order team suits	A	1	2	3
G	Register swimmers	D	1	2	3
H	Collect fees	G	1	2	3
I	Plan first practice	E, H, F	1	1	1

a. Draw a project network.
b. Develop an activity schedule.
c. What are the critical activities and what is the expected project completion time?
d. If the club manager plans to start the project on February 1, what is the probability the swimming program will be ready by the scheduled May 1 date (13 weeks)? Should the manager begin planning the swimming program before February 1?

19. The product development group at Landon Corporation has been working on a new computer software product that has the potential to capture a large market share. Through outside sources, Landon's management has learned that a competitor is working to introduce a similar product. As a result, Landon's top management has increased its pressure on the product development group. The group's leader has turned to PERT/CPM as an aid to scheduling the activities remaining before the new product can be brought to the market. The project network is as follows.

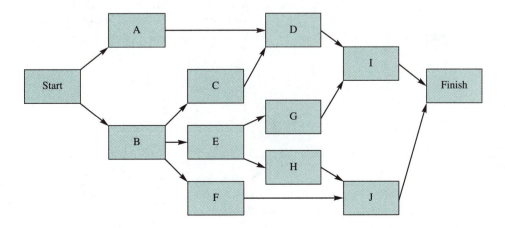

The activity time estimates (in weeks) are

Activity	Optimistic	Most Probable	Pessimistic
A	3.0	4.0	5.0
B	3.0	3.5	7.0
C	4.0	5.0	6.0
D	2.0	3.0	4.0
E	6.0	10.0	14.0
F	7.5	8.5	12.5
G	4.5	6.0	7.5
H	5.0	6.0	13.0
I	2.0	2.5	6.0
J	4.0	5.0	6.0

a. Develop an activity schedule for this project and identify the critical path activities.
b. What is the probability that the project will be completed so that Landon Corporation may introduce the new product within 25 weeks? Within 30 weeks?

20. Return to the computer installation project in Problem 7 and assume that the project has to be completed in 16 weeks. Crashing of the project is necessary. Use the following relevant information.

Activity	Time (weeks)		Cost ($)	
	Normal	Crash	Normal	Crash
A	3	1	900	1700
B	6	3	2000	4000
C	2	1	500	1000
D	5	3	1800	2400
E	4	3	1500	1850
F	3	1	3000	3900
G	9	4	8000	9800
H	3	2	1000	2000

a. Formulate a linear programming model that can be used to make the crashing decisions for this project.
b. Solve the linear programming model and make the minimum-cost crashing decisions. What is the added cost of meeting the 16-week completion time?
c. Develop a complete activity schedule based on the crashed activity times.

21. Consider the following project network and activity times (in days).

SELF TEST

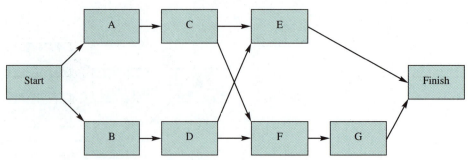

Activity	A	B	C	D	E	F	G
Activity Time	3	2	5	5	6	2	2

The crashing data for this project are as follows.

Activity	Time (days)		Total Cost ($)	
	Normal	Crash	Normal	Crash
A	3	2	800	1400
B	2	1	1200	1900
C	5	3	2000	2800
D	5	3	1500	2300
E	6	4	1800	2800
F	2	1	600	1000
G	2	1	500	1000

    a. Find the critical path and the expected project completion time.
    b. What is the total project cost using the normal times?

22. Refer to Problem 21. Assume that management desires a 12-day project completion time.
    a. Formulate a linear programming model that can be used to assist with the crashing decisions.
    b. What activities should be crashed?
    c. What is the total project cost for the 12-day completion time?

SELF TEST

23. Consider the following project network. Note that the normal or expected activity times are denoted τ_i, $i = A, B, \ldots, I$. Let $x_i =$ the earliest finish time for activity i. Formulate a linear programming model that can be used to determine the length of the critical path.

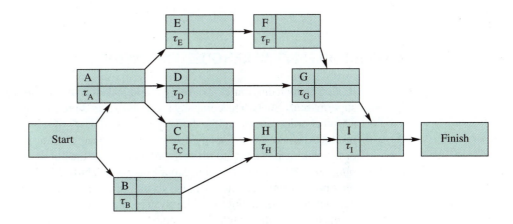

24. Office Automation, Inc., has developed a proposal for introducing a new computerized office system that will improve word processing and interoffice communications for a particular company. Contained in the proposal is a list of activities that must be accomplished to complete the new office system project. Use the following relevant information about the activities.

Activity	Description	Immediate Predecessor	Time (weeks)		Cost ($1000s)	
			Normal	Crash	Normal	Crash
A	Plan needs	—	10	8	30	70
B	Order equipment	A	8	6	120	150
C	Install equipment	B	10	7	100	160
D	Set up training lab	A	7	6	40	50
E	Conduct training course	D	10	8	50	75
F	Test system	C, E	3	3	60	—

a. Develop a project network.

b. Develop an activity schedule.

c. What are the critical activities and what is the expected project completion time?

d. Assume that the company wants to complete the project in 6 months or 26 weeks. What crashing decisions do you recommend to meet the desired completion time at the least possible cost? Work through the network and attempt to make the crashing decisions by inspection.

e. Develop an activity schedule for the crashed project.

f. What added project cost is required to meet the 6-month completion time?

25. Because Landon Corporation (see Problem 19) is being pressured to complete the product development project at the earliest possible date, the project leader has requested that the possibility of crashing the project be evaluated.

a. Formulate a linear programming model that could be used in making the crashing decisions.

b. What information would have to be provided before the linear programming model could be implemented?

..../ /.............

CASE PROBLEM   WAREHOUSE EXPANSION

R. C. Coleman distributes a variety of food products that are sold through grocery store and supermarket outlets. The company receives orders directly from the individual outlets, with a typical order requesting the delivery of several cases of anywhere from 20 to 50 different products. Under the company's current warehouse operation, warehouse clerks dispatch order-picking personnel to fill each order and have the goods moved to the warehouse shipping area. Because of the high labor costs and relatively low productivity of hand order-picking, management has decided to automate the warehouse operation by installing a computer-controlled order-picking system, along with a conveyor system for moving goods from storage to the warehouse shipping area.

R. C. Coleman's director of material management has been named the project manager in charge of the automated warehouse system. After consulting with members of the engineering staff and warehouse management personnel, the director has compiled a list of activities associated with the project. The optimistic, most probable, and pessimistic times (in weeks) have also been provided for each activity.

Activity	Description	Immediate Predecessor
A	Determine equipment needs	—
B	Obtain vendor proposals	—
C	Select vendor	A, B
D	Order system	C
E	Design new warehouse layout	C
F	Design warehouse	E
G	Design computer interface	C
H	Interface computer	D, F, G
I	Install system	D, F
J	Train system operators	H
K	Test system	I, J

Activity	Optimistic	Time Most Probable	Pessimistic
A	4	6	8
B	6	8	16
C	2	4	6
D	8	10	24
E	7	10	13
F	4	6	8
G	4	6	20
H	4	6	8
I	4	6	14
J	3	4	5
K	2	4	6

Managerial Report

Develop a report that presents the activity schedule and expected project completion time for the warehouse expansion project. Include a project network in the report. In addition, take into consideration the following issues.

1. R. C. Coleman's top management has established a required 40-week completion time for the project. Can this completion time be achieved? Include probability information in your discussion. What recommendations do you have if the 40-week completion time is required?

2. Suppose that management requests that activity times be shortened to provide an 80% chance of meeting the 40-week completion time. If the variance in the project completion time is the same as you found in part (a), how much should the expected project completion time be shortened to achieve the goal of an 80% chance of completion within 40 weeks?

3. Using the expected activity times as the normal times and the following crashing information, determine the activity crashing decisions and revised activity schedule for the warehouse expansion project.

Activity	Crashed Activity Time (weeks)	Cost ($) Normal	Cost ($) Crashed
A	4	1,000	1,900
B	7	1,000	1,800
C	2	1,500	2,700
D	8	2,000	3,200
E	7	5,000	8,000
F	4	3,000	4,100
G	5	8,000	10,250
H	4	5,000	6,400
I	4	10,000	12,400
J	3	4,000	4,400
K	3	5,000	5,500

SEASONGOOD & MAYER

CINCINNATI, OHIO

Seasongood & Mayer, established in 1887, is an investment securities firm that engages in the following areas of municipal finance:

1. Underwriting new issues of municipal bonds
2. Trading—for example, acting as a market maker for the buying and selling of previously issued bonds
3. Investment banking—that is, the process of obtaining money from the capital markets at the lowest possible cost

The major applications of quantitative methods at Seasongood & Mayer are in the investment banking area. One particular application involved the use of PERT/CPM in the introduction of a $31 million hospital revenue bond issue.

Scheduling the Introduction of a Bond Issue

In any major building project there are certain common steps:

1. Defining the project
2. Determining the cost of the project
3. Financing the project

The investment banker's role in building projects is to develop the method of financing that will result in the owner's receiving the necessary funds in a timely manner. In a hospital building project, the typical method of financing is tax-free hospital revenue bonds.

The construction cost for the building project is an important factor in determining the best approach to financing. Normally, the construction cost is based on a bid submitted by a contractor or a construction manager.

However, this cost is usually guaranteed only for a specified period of time such as 60–90 days. The major function of the hospital's investment banker is to arrange the timing of the financing in such a way that the proceeds of the bond issue can be made available within the time limit of the guaranteed-price construction bid. Since most hospitals must have the proceeds of their permanent long-term financing in hand prior to committing to major construction contracts, the investment banker's role is a significant one.

To arrange for the financing, the investment banker must coordinate the activities of hospital attorneys, the bond counsel, and so on. The cooperation of all parties and the coordination of project activities are best achieved if everyone recognizes the interdependency of the activities and the necessity of completing individual tasks in a timely manner. Seasongood & Mayer has found PERT/CPM to be useful in scheduling and coordinating such a project.

As managing underwriter for a $31,050,000 issue of Hospital Facilities Revenue Bonds for Providence Hospital in Hamilton County, Ohio, Seasongood & Mayer used the PERT/CPM critical path procedure to coordinate and schedule the project financing activities. Descriptions of the activities, times required, and immediate predecessors are given in Table 12.10. The project network is shown in Figure 12.17. The critical path activities K–L–M–N–P–Q–R–S–U–W resulted in a scheduled project completion time of 29.14 weeks. Specific schedules showing start and finish times for all activities were used to keep the entire project on track. The use of PERT/CPM was instrumental in helping Seasongood & Mayer obtain financing for this project within the time specified in the construction bid.

Questions

1. What is the role of the investment banker in building projects?

2. For the hospital project described, what is the primary objective of the investment banker?

3. Perform the critical path calculations for the project network shown in Figure 12.17. Is there more than one critical path? Discuss.

Figure 12.17   SEASONGOOD & MAYER PROJECT NETWORK

Table 12.10	ACTIVITIES FOR THE SEASONGOOD & MAYER PROJECT

Activity	Time Required (weeks)	Description of Activity	Immediate Predecessor
A	4	Drafting and distribution of legal documents	—
B	3	Preparation and distribution of unaudited financial statements of hospital	—
C	2	Drafting and distribution of hospital history, description of services, and existing facilities for Preliminary Official Statement (POS)	—
D	8	Drafting and distribution of demand portion of feasibility study	—
E	4	Review (additions/deletions) and approval as to form of legal documents	A
F	1	Review (additions/deletions) and approval of history, etc., for POS	C
G	4	Review (additions/deletions) and approval of demand portion of feasibility study	D
H	2	Drafting and distribution of financial portion (as to form) of feasibility study	E, G
I	2	Drafting and distribution of plan of financing and all pertinent facts relevant to the bond transaction for POS	E
J	0.5	Review and approval of unaudited financial statements	B
K	20	Receipt of firm price for project	—
L	1	Review (additions/deletions), approval, and completion of financial portion of feasibility study	H, K
M	1	Drafting of POS completed	F, I, J, L
N	0.14	Distribution of all material to bond rating services	M
O	0.28	Printing and distribution of POS to all interested parties	M
P	1	Presentation to bond rating services (Standard & Poor's, Moody's)	N
Q	1	Receipt of bond rating	P
R	2	Marketing of bonds	O, Q
S	0	Execution of Purchase Contract	R
T	0.14	Authorization and completion of Final Official Statement, completion of legal documents	S
U	3	Fulfillment of all terms and conditions of Purchase Contract	S
V	0	Bond proceeds available to hospital	T, U
W	0	Hospital able to sign construction contract	T, U

13

INVENTORY MANAGEMENT:

INDEPENDENT DEMAND

Inventory refers to idle goods or materials that are held by an organization for use sometime in the future. Items carried in inventory include raw materials, purchased parts, components, subassemblies, work-in-process, finished goods, and supplies. One reason organizations maintain inventory is that their managers can rarely predict sales levels, production times, demand, and usage needs exactly. Thus, inventory serves as a buffer against uncertain and fluctuating usage and keeps a supply of items available in case the items are needed by the organization or its customers. While inventory serves an important and essential role, the expense associated with financing and maintaining inventories is a substantial part of the cost of doing business. In large organizations, the cost associated with inventory can run into millions of dollars.

Independent demand does not depend on demand for other items produced by the firm. The topic of inventory management with dependent demand is discussed in Chapter 14.

In this chapter, we consider inventory models for items that have an **independent demand.** That is, the demand for an item is independent of the demand for other products or items. Most often independent demand is generated by customers placing orders for finished goods. **Dependent demand** is characterized by demand for items such as components and subassemblies that are directly related to the demand for other items produced by the firm. We discuss inventory management with dependent demand in Chapter 14.

In applications involving inventory management with independent demand, managers must answer two important questions.

1. *How much* should be ordered when the inventory for an item is replenished?
2. *When* should the inventory for an item be replenished?

The purpose of this chapter is to show how quantitative models can assist in making such decisions.

We will first consider **deterministic inventory models** that are applicable for a constant or nearly constant rate of demand for an item. Later we will consider **probabilistic inventory models** that are applicable when demand for an item can be described only in probabilistic terms.

··/ /············

13.1 ECONOMIC ORDER QUANTITY (EOQ) MODEL

The cost associated with developing and maintaining inventory is larger than many people think. Models such as the ones presented in this chapter can be used to develop cost-effective inventory management decisions.

The **economic order quantity (EOQ) model** is applicable when the demand for an item has a constant, or nearly constant, rate and when the entire quantity ordered arrives in inventory at one point in time. The **constant demand rate** assumption means that the same number of units is taken from inventory each period of time such as 5 units every day, 25 units every week, 100 units every 4-week period, and so on.

To illustrate the EOQ model, let us consider the situation faced by the R & B Beverage Company. R & B Beverage is a distributor of beer, wine, and soft drink products. From a main warehouse located in Columbus, Ohio, R & B supplies nearly 1000 retail stores with beverage products. The beer inventory, which constitutes about 40% of the company's total inventory, averages approximately 50,000 cases. With an average cost per case of approximately $8, R & B estimates the value of its beer inventory to be $400,000.

The warehouse manager has decided to do a detailed study of the inventory costs associated with Bub Beer, the number-one-selling R & B beer. The purpose of the study is to establish the *how-much*-to-order and the *when*-to-order decisions for Bub Beer that will result in the lowest possible total cost. As the first step in the study, the warehouse manager has obtained the following demand data for the past 10 weeks:

Week	Demand (cases)
1	2,000
2	2,025
3	1,950
4	2,000
5	2,100
6	2,050
7	2,000
8	1,975
9	1,900
10	2,000
Total cases	20,000
Average cases per week	2,000

One of the most criticized assumptions of the EOQ model is the constant demand rate. Obviously, the model would be inappropriate for items with widely fluctuating and variable demand rates. However, as this example attempts to show, the EOQ model can provide a realistic approximation of the optimal order quantity when demand is relatively stable and occurs at a nearly constant rate.

Strictly speaking, these weekly demand figures do not show a constant demand rate. However, given the relatively low variability exhibited by the weekly demand, inventory planning with a constant demand rate of 2000 cases per week appears acceptable. In practice, you will find that the actual inventory situation seldom, if ever, satisfies the assumptions of the model exactly. Thus, in any particular application, the manager must determine whether the model assumptions are close enough to reality for the model to be useful. In this situation, since demand varies from a low of 1900 cases to a high of 2100 cases, the assumption of constant demand of 2000 cases per week appears to be a reasonable approximation.

The how-much-to-order decision involves selecting an order quantity that draws a compromise between (1) keeping small inventories and ordering frequently and (2) keeping large inventories and ordering infrequently. The first alternative can result in undesirably high ordering costs, while the second alternative can result in undesirably high inventory holding costs. To find an optimal compromise between these conflicting alternatives, let us consider a mathematical model that shows the total cost as the sum of the holding cost and the ordering cost.[1]

As with other quantitative models, accurate estimates of cost parameters are critical. In the EOQ model, estimates of both the inventory holding cost and the ordering cost are needed. Also see footnote 1, which refers to *relevant* costs.

Holding costs are the costs associated with maintaining or carrying a given level of inventory; these costs depend on the size of the inventory. First, there is the cost of financing the inventory investment. When a firm borrows money, it incurs an interest charge. If the firm uses its own money, it experiences an opportunity cost associated with not being able to use the money for other investments. In either case, an interest cost exists for the capital tied up in inventory. This **cost of capital** is usually expressed as a percentage of the amount invested. R & B estimates its cost of capital at an annual rate of 18%.

A number of other holding costs such as insurance, taxes, breakage, pilferage, and warehouse overhead also depend on the value of the inventory. R & B estimates these other costs at an annual rate of approximately 7% of the value of its inventory. Thus, the total holding cost for the R & B beer inventory is 25% of the value of the inventory.

Assume that the cost of one case of Bub Beer is $8. Since R & B estimates its annual holding cost to be 25% of the value of its inventory, the cost of holding one case of Bub Beer in inventory for 1 year is 0.25($8) = $2.00. Note that defining the holding cost as a percentage of the value of the product is convenient because it is easily transferable to other products. For example, a case of Carle's Red Ribbon Beer, which costs $7.00 per case, would have an annual holding cost of 0.25($7.00) = $1.75 per case.

The next step in the inventory analysis is to determine the **ordering cost.** This cost, which is considered fixed regardless of the order quantity, covers the preparation of the voucher, the processing of the order including payment, postage, telephone, transportation, invoice verification, receiving, and so on. For R & B Beverage, the largest portion of the ordering cost involves the salaries of the purchasers. An analysis of the purchasing process showed that a purchaser spends approximately 45 minutes preparing and processing an order for Bub Beer. With a wage rate and fringe benefit cost for purchasers of $20 per hour, the labor portion of the ordering cost is $15. Making allowances for paper, postage, telephone, transportation, and receiving costs at $17 per order, the manager estimates that the ordering cost is $32 per order. That is, R & B is paying $32 per order regardless of the quantity requested in the order.

The holding cost, ordering cost, and demand information are the three data items that must be known prior to the use of the EOQ model. Since these data have now been developed for the R & B problem, let us see how they are used to develop a total-cost model. We begin by defining Q to be the order quantity. Thus, the how-much-to-order decision involves finding the value of Q that will minimize the sum of holding and ordering costs.

---

1. While quantitative analysts typically refer to "total-cost" models for inventory systems, often these models describe only the total *variable* or total *relevant* costs for the decision being considered. Costs that are not affected by the how-much-to-order decision are considered fixed or constant and are not included in the model.

The inventory level for Bub will have a maximum value of Q units when an order of size Q is received from the supplier. R & B will then satisfy customer demand from inventory until the inventory is depleted, at which time another shipment of Q units will be received. Suppose that R & B is open 5 days each week. Thus, assuming a constant demand rate of 2000 cases per week or 400 cases per day, the graph of the inventory level for Bub Beer is as shown in Figure 13.1. Note that the graph indicates an average inventory level of $\frac{1}{2}Q$ for the period in question. This level should appear reasonable since the maximum inventory level is Q, the minimum is zero, and the inventory level declines at a constant rate over the period.

Figure 13.1 shows the inventory pattern during one order cycle of length T. As time goes on, this pattern will repeat. The complete inventory pattern is shown in Figure 13.2. If the average inventory during each cycle is $\frac{1}{2}Q$, the average inventory level over any number of cycles is also $\frac{1}{2}Q$.

The holding cost can be calculated using the average inventory level. That is, we can calculate the holding cost by multiplying the average inventory level by the cost of carrying one unit in inventory for the stated period. The period selected for the model is up to you; it could be 1 week, 1 month, 1 year, or more. However, since the holding cost for many industries and businesses is expressed as an *annual* percentage, most inventory models are developed on an *annual cost* basis.

> Most inventory cost models use an *annual cost.* Thus, demand should be expressed in units per year and inventory holding cost should be based on an annual rate. The ordering cost should be expressed as a cost per order with the model providing the calculation of the total annual ordering cost.

Let

$$I = \text{annual holding cost rate}$$
$$C = \text{unit cost of the inventory item}$$
$$C_h = \text{annual cost of holding one unit in inventory}$$

The annual cost of holding one unit in inventory is

$$C_h = IC \qquad\qquad (13.1)$$

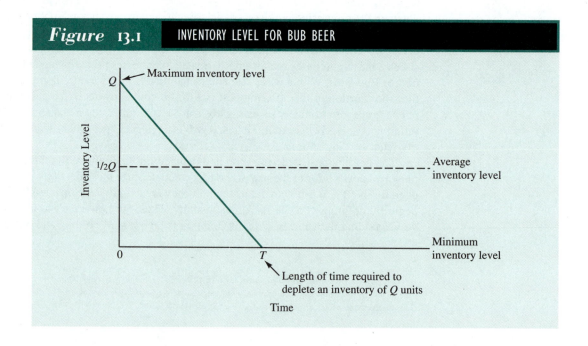

Figure 13.1   INVENTORY LEVEL FOR BUB BEER

Figure 13.2   INVENTORY PATTERN FOR THE EOQ INVENTORY MODEL

Inventory is used at the constant demand rate of 2000 units per week

Inventory Level

Q

$\frac{1}{2}Q$

Average inventory level

0

Time

C_h is the cost of holding one unit in inventory for one year. Since smaller order quantities Q will result in lower inventory levels, total annual holding cost can be reduced by using smaller order quantities.

The general equation for the annual holding cost for the average inventory of $\frac{1}{2}Q$ units is as follows:

$$\begin{pmatrix} \text{Annual} \\ \text{holding cost} \end{pmatrix} = \begin{pmatrix} \text{Average} \\ \text{inventory} \\ \text{level} \end{pmatrix} \begin{pmatrix} \text{Annual holding} \\ \text{cost} \\ \text{per unit} \end{pmatrix}$$

$$= \frac{1}{2}QC_h \tag{13.2}$$

To complete the total-cost model, we must now include the annual ordering cost. The goal is to express the annual ordering cost in terms of the order quantity Q. The first question is, How many orders will be placed during the year? Let D denote the annual demand for the product. For R & B Beverage, $D = (52 \text{ weeks})(2000 \text{ cases per week}) = 104{,}000$ cases per year. We know that by ordering Q units every time we order, we will have to place D/Q orders per year. If C_o is the cost of placing one order, the general equation for the annual ordering cost is as follows:

C_o the fixed cost per order, is independent of the amount ordered. For a given annual demand of D units, the total annual ordering cost can be reduced by using larger order quantities.

$$\begin{pmatrix} \text{Annual} \\ \text{ordering cost} \end{pmatrix} = \begin{pmatrix} \text{Number of} \\ \text{orders} \\ \text{per year} \end{pmatrix} \begin{pmatrix} \text{Cost} \\ \text{per} \\ \text{order} \end{pmatrix}$$

$$= \left(\frac{D}{Q}\right)C_o \tag{13.3}$$

Thus, the total annual cost, denoted TC, can be expressed as follows:

The cost of goods (DC) is not included in the total annual cost equation (13.4) because it is *not* a *relevant cost* for the EOQ model.

$$\begin{matrix} \text{Total} & \text{Annual} & \text{Annual} \\ \text{annual} & = \text{holding} & + \text{ordering} \\ \text{cost} & \text{cost} & \text{cost} \end{matrix}$$

$$TC = \frac{1}{2}QC_h + \frac{D}{Q}C_o \tag{13.4}$$

Using the Bub Beer data ($C_h = IC = (0.25)(\$8) = \$2$, $C_o = \$32$, and $D = 104{,}000$), the total annual cost model is

$$TC = \frac{1}{2}Q(\$2) + \frac{104,000}{Q}(\$32) = Q + \frac{3,328,000}{Q}$$

The development of the total-cost model has gone a long way toward solving the inventory problem. We now are able to express the total annual cost as a function of *how much* should be ordered. The development of a realistic total-cost model is perhaps the most important part of the application of quantitative methods to inventory decision making. Equation (13.4) is the general total-cost equation for inventory situations in which the assumptions of the economic order quantity model are valid.

The How-Much-to-Order Decision

The next step is to find the order quantity Q that will minimize the total annual cost for Bub Beer. Using a trial-and-error approach, we can compute the total annual cost for several possible order quantities. As a starting point, let us consider $Q = 8000$. The total annual cost for Bub Beer is

$$TC = Q + \frac{3,328,000}{Q}$$

$$= 8000 + \frac{3,328,000}{8000} = \$8416$$

A trial order quantity of 5000 gives

$$TC = 5000 + \frac{3,328,000}{5000} = \$5666$$

The results of several other trial order quantities are shown in Table 13.1. As can be seen, the lowest cost solution is around 2000 cases. Graphs of the annual holding and ordering costs, and total annual costs are shown in Figure 13.3.

The advantage of the trial-and-error approach is that it is rather easy to do and provides the total annual cost for a number of possible order quantity decisions. In this case, the minimum-cost order quantity appears to be approximately 2000 cases. The disadvantage of this approach, however, is that it does not provide the exact minimum-cost order quantity.

Table 13.1	ANNUAL HOLDING, ORDERING, AND TOTAL COSTS FOR VARIOUS ORDER QUANTITIES OF BUB BEER		
		Annual Cost	
Order Quantity	**Holding**	**Ordering**	**Total**
5000	$5000	$ 666	$5666
4000	4000	832	4832
3000	3000	1109	4109
2000	2000	1664	3664
1000	1000	3328	4328

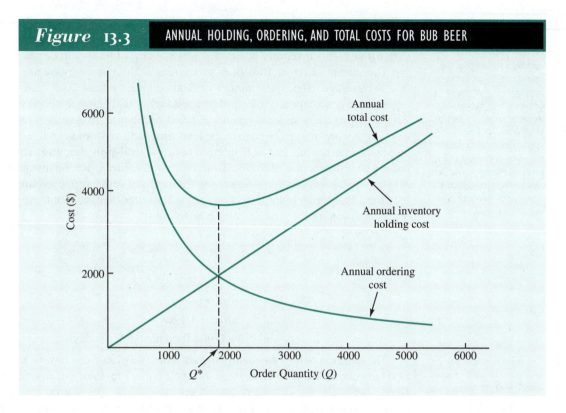

Figure 13.3   ANNUAL HOLDING, ORDERING, AND TOTAL COSTS FOR BUB BEER

The EOQ formula determines the optimal order quantity by balancing the annual holding cost and the annual ordering cost. Problem 2 at the end of the chapter will show that the optimal order quantity Q^* will provide an annual holding cost equal to the annual ordering cost.

In 1915 F. W. Harris derived the mathematical formula for the economic order quantity. This was the first application of quantitative methods to the area of inventory management.

Refer to Figure 13.3. The minimum total-cost order quantity is denoted by an order size of Q^*. By using differential calculus, it can be shown (see Appendix 13.2) that the value of Q^* that minimizes the total annual cost is given by the formula

$$Q^* = \sqrt{\frac{2DC_o}{C_h}} \qquad (13.5)$$

This formula is referred to as the *economic order quantity (EOQ) formula.*

Using equation (13.5), the minimum total-annual-cost order quantity for Bub Beer is

$$Q^* = \sqrt{\frac{2(104,000)32}{2}} = 1824 \text{ cases}$$

The use of an order quantity of 1824 in equation (13.4) shows that the minimum-cost inventory policy for Bub Beer has a total annual cost of $3649. Note that $Q^* = 1824$ has balanced the holding and ordering costs. Check for yourself to see that these costs are equal.[2] (Problem 2 at the end of the chapter asks you to show that equal holding and ordering costs is a property of the EOQ model.)

The When-to-Order Decision

Now that we know how much to order, we want to address the question of *when* to order. To answer this question, we need to introduce the concept of inventory position. The

---

2. Actually, Q^* from equation (13.5) is 1824.28, but since we cannot order fractional cases of beer, a Q^* of 1824 is shown. This value of Q^* may cause a few cents deviation between the two costs. If Q^* is used at its exact value, the holding and ordering costs will be exactly the same.

inventory position for an item is defined as the amount of inventory on hand plus the amount of inventory on order. The when-to-order decision is expressed in terms of a **reorder point**—the inventory position at which a new order should be placed.

The manufacturer of Bub Beer guarantees a 2-day delivery on any order placed by R & B Beverage. Hence, assuming a constant demand rate of 2000 cases per week or 400 cases per day, we expect (2 days)(400 cases/day) = 800 cases of Bub to be sold during the 2 days it takes a new order to reach the R & B warehouse. In inventory terminology, the 2-day delivery period is referred to as the **lead time** for a new order, and the 800-case demand anticipated during this period is referred to as the **lead-time demand.** Thus, R & B should order a new shipment of Bub Beer from the manufacturer when the inventory level reaches 800 cases. For inventory systems using the constant demand rate assumption and a fixed lead time, the reorder point is the same as the lead-time demand. For these systems, the general expression for the reorder point is as follows:

$$r = dm \qquad (13.6)$$

where

$$r = \text{reorder point}$$
$$d = \text{demand per pay}$$
$$m = \text{lead time for a new order in days}$$

The question of how frequently the order will be placed can now be answered. The period between orders is referred to as the **cycle time.** Previously in equation (13.2), we defined D/Q as the number of orders that will be placed in a year. Thus, $D/Q^* = 104{,}000/1824 = 57$ is the number of orders R & B Beverage will place for Bub Beer each year. If R & B places 57 orders over 250 working days, it will order approximately every $250/57 = 4.4$ working days. Thus, the cycle time is 4.4 working days. The general expression for a cycle time[3] of T days is given by

$$T = \frac{250}{D/Q^*} = \frac{250Q^*}{D} \qquad (13.7)$$

Sensitivity Analysis in the EOQ Model

Even though substantial time may have been spent in arriving at the cost per order ($32) and the holding cost rate (25%), we should realize that these figures are at best good estimates. Thus, we may want to consider how much the recommended order quantity would change if the estimated ordering and holding costs had been different. To determine this, we can calculate the recommended order quantity under several different cost conditions. Table 13.2 shows the minimum total-cost order quantity for several cost possibilities. As you can see from the table, the value of Q^* appears relatively stable, even with some variations in the cost estimates. Based on these results, the best order quantity for Bub Beer is somewhere around 1700–2000 cases. If operated properly, the total cost for the Bub Beer inventory system should be close to $3400–$3800 per year. We also note that very little risk is associated with implementing the calculated order quantity of 1824. For example, if hold-

3. This general expression for cycle time is based on 250 working days per year. If the firm operated 300 working days per year and wanted to express cycle time in terms of working days, the cycle time would be given by $T = 300Q^*/D$.

Table 13.2	OPTIMAL ORDER QUANTITIES FOR SEVERAL COST POSSIBILITIES			
Possible Inventory Holding Cost (%)	**Possible Cost Per Order**	**Optimal Order Quantity (Q^*)**	**Projected Total Annual Cost**	
			Using Q^*	**Using $Q = 1824$**
24	$30	1803	$3461	$3462
24	34	1919	3685	3690
26	30	1732	3603	3607
26	34	1844	3835	3836

ing cost rate = 24%, C_o = $34, and the true optimal order quantity Q^* = 1919, there is only a $5 increase in the total annual cost; that is, $3690 − $3685 = $5, with Q = 1824.

From the preceding analysis, we would say that this EOQ model is insensitive to small variations or errors in the cost estimates. This insensitivity is a property of EOQ models in general, which indicates that if we have at least reasonable estimates of ordering cost and holding cost, we can expect to obtain a good approximation of the true minimum-cost order quantity.

The Manager's Use of the EOQ Model

The EOQ model results in a recommended order quantity of 1824 units. Is this the final decision, or should the manager's judgment enter into the establishment of the final inventory policy? Although the model has provided a good order-quantity recommendation, it may not have taken into account all aspects of the inventory situation. As a result, the decision maker may want to modify the final order-quantity recommendation to meet the unique circumstances of the inventory situation. In this case, the warehouse manager felt that increasing the order quantity from 1824 cases to 2000 cases to have an order quantity equal to 5 working days' demand would be desirable. By doing so, R & B Beverage can maintain a weekly order cycle.

The total-cost curve in Figure 13.3 is relatively flat near the value of Q^*. Consequently, the inventory manager can adjust the EOQ slightly to a more convenient level without seriously affecting the total cost.

The warehouse manager also realized that the EOQ model was based on the constant demand rate assumption of 2000 cases per week. While this rate is a good approximation, we must also recognize that sometimes the demand exceeds 2000 cases per week. If a reorder point of 800 cases is used, we would be expecting an 800-case demand during the lead time and the new order to arrive exactly when the inventory level reached zero. Such close timing would have little room for error, and the scheduling of arrivals would be critical if stockouts (shortages) were to be avoided. To protect against shortages due to higher-than-expected demands or slightly delayed incoming orders, the warehouse manager recommended a 1200-case reorder point. Thus, under normal conditions, R & B Beverage will order 2000 cases of Bub whenever the current inventory reaches 1200 cases. During the expected 2-day lead time, 800 cases should be demanded, and 400 cases should be in inventory when an order arrives. The extra 400 cases serve as a safety precaution against a higher-than-expected demand or a delayed incoming order. In general, the amount by which the reorder point exceeds the expected lead-time demand is referred to as **safety stock.**

The decisions to adjust the order quantity and reorder point were purely judgment decisions and were not necessarily made with a minimum-cost objective in mind. However, they are examples of how managerial judgment might interface with the inventory decision model to arrive at a sound inventory policy. The final decision of $Q = 2000$ with a 400-case safety stock resulted in a total annual cost of $4464.[4]

How Has the EOQ Decision Model Helped?

The EOQ model has objectively included holding and ordering costs and, with the aid of some management judgment, has led to a low-cost inventory policy. In addition, the general optimal order-quantity model, equation (13.5), is potentially applicable to other R & B products. For example, Red Ribbon Beer ($7/case), which has an ordering cost of $32, a constant demand rate of 1200 cases per week (62,400 cases/year), and a 2-day lead-time period, has a recommended order quantity of

$$Q^* = \sqrt{\frac{2(62,400)(32)}{(0.25)(7)}} = 1511 \text{ cases}$$

Problem 1 provides practice in applying the EOQ model to another R & B product.

a cycle time of $T = [250(1511)]/62,400 = 6.05$ days, and a reorder point of $r = (240)(2) = 480$ cases.

A Summary of the EOQ Model Assumptions

To use the optimal order-quantity and reorder-point model described here, an analyst must make assumptions about how the inventory system operates. The EOQ model with its economic order quantity formula is based on some specific assumptions about the R & B inventory system. A summary of the assumptions for this model is provided in Table 13.3.

You should carefully review the assumptions of the inventory model before applying it in an actual situation. Several inventory models discussed later in this chapter alter one or more of the assumptions of the EOQ model.

Before using the EOQ formula, carefully review these assumptions to ensure that they are applicable to the inventory system being analyzed. If the assumptions are not reasonable, seek a different inventory model.

Various types of inventory systems are in practice, and the inventory models presented in the following sections alter one or more of the EOQ model assumptions shown in Table 13.3 to meet the needs of the different systems. When the assumptions change, a different inventory model with different optimal operating policies becomes necessary.

Table 13.3   SUMMARY OF THE EOQ MODEL ASSUMPTIONS

1. Demand D is deterministic and occurs at a constant rate.
2. The order quantity Q is the same for each order. The inventory level increases by Q units each time an order is received.
3. The cost per order, C_o, is constant and does not depend on the quantity ordered.
4. The purchase cost per unit, C, is constant and does not depend on the quantity ordered.
5. The inventory holding cost per unit per time period, C_h, is constant. The total inventory holding cost depends on both C_h and the size of the inventory.
6. Shortages such as stockouts or backorders are not permitted.
7. The lead time for an order is constant.
8. The inventory position is reviewed continuously. As a result, an order is placed as soon as the inventory position reaches the reorder point.

---

4. A Q of 2000 units resulted in a total cost of $3664 (see Table 13.1). The additional safety stock inventory of 400 units increases the average inventory by 400 units since it is on hand all year long. Thus, the inventory carrying charge is increased by 2(400) = $800, the total cost of the revised policy is $3664 + $800 = $4464.

N O T E S	With relatively long lead times, the lead-time demand and the resulting reorder point *r*, determined by
and Comments	equation (13.6), may exceed Q^*. If this condition occurs, at least one order will be outstanding when

a new order is placed. For example, assume that Bub Beer has a lead time of $m = 6$ days. With a daily demand of $d = 400$ cases, equation (13.6) shows that the reorder point would be $r = dm = 6 \times 400 = 2400$ cases. Thus, a new order for Bub Beer should be placed whenever the inventory position (the amount of inventory on hand plus the amount of inventory on order) reaches 2400. With an economic order quantity of $Q^* = 1824$ cases, the inventory position of 2400 cases occurs when one order of 1824 cases is outstanding and $2400 - 1824 = 576$ cases are on hand.

13.2 ECONOMIC PRODUCTION LOT-SIZE MODEL

The inventory model presented in this section is similar to the EOQ model in that we are attempting to determine *how much* we should order and *when* the order should be placed. We again assume a constant demand rate. However, instead of assuming that the goods arrive in a shipment of size Q^*, as in the EOQ model, we assume that units are supplied to inventory at a constant rate over several days or several weeks. The **constant supply rate** assumption implies that the same number of units is supplied to inventory each period of time (e.g., 10 units every day or 50 units every week). This model is designed for production situations in which, once an order is placed, production begins and a constant number of units is added to inventory each day until the production run has been completed.

The inventory model in this section alters assumption 2 of the EOQ model (see Table 13.3). The assumption concerning the arrival of Q units each time an order is received is changed to a constant production supply rate.

If we have a production system that produces 50 units per day and we decide to schedule 10 days of production, we have a $50(10) = 500$-unit production lot size. The **lot size** is the number of units in an order. In general, if we let Q indicate the production lot size, the approach to the inventory decisions is similar to the EOQ model; that is, we build a holding and ordering cost model that expresses the total cost as a function of the production lot size. Then we attempt to find the production lot size that minimizes the total cost.

One other condition that should be mentioned at this time is that the model only applies to situations where the production rate is greater than the demand rate; the production system must be able to satisfy demand. For instance, if the constant demand rate is 2000 units per week, the production rate must be at least 2000 units per week to satisfy demand.

During the production run, demand will be reducing the inventory while production will be adding to inventory. Since we have assumed that the production rate exceeds the demand rate, each day during a production run we will be producing more units than are demanded. Thus, the excess production will cause a gradual inventory buildup during the production period. When the production run is completed, the continuing demand will cause the inventory to gradually decline until a new production run is started. The inventory pattern for this system is shown in Figure 13.4.

This model differs from the EOQ model in that a setup cost replaces the ordering cost and the saw-tooth inventory pattern shown in Figure 13.4 differs from the inventory pattern shown in Figure 13.2.

As in the EOQ model, we are now dealing with two costs, the holding cost and the ordering cost. While the holding cost is identical to the definition in the EOQ model, the interpretation of the ordering cost is slightly different. In fact, in a production situation the ordering cost is more correctly referred to as the production **setup cost.** This cost, which includes labor, material, and lost production costs incurred while preparing the production system for operation, is a fixed cost that occurs for every production run regardless of the production lot size.

Figure 13.4   INVENTORY PATTERN FOR THE PRODUCTION LOT-SIZE INVENTORY MODEL

The Total-Cost Model

Let us begin building the production lot size model by writing the holding cost in terms of the production lot size Q. Again, the approach is to develop an expression for average inventory and then establish the holding costs associated with the average inventory level. We use a 1-year time period and an annual cost for the model.

In the EOQ model the average inventory is one-half the maximum inventory or $\frac{1}{2}Q$. Figure 13.4 shows that for a production lot-size model a constant inventory buildup rate occurs during the production run and a constant inventory depletion rate occurs during the nonproduction period; thus, the average inventory will be one-half the maximum inventory level. However, in this inventory system the production lot size Q does not go into inventory at one point in time, and thus the inventory level never reaches a level of Q units.

To show how we can compute the maximum inventory level, let

$$d = \text{daily demand rate for the product}$$
$$p = \text{daily production rate for the product}$$
$$t = \text{number of days for a production run}$$

At this point, the logic of the production lot-size model is easier to follow using a daily demand rate *d* and a daily production rate *p*. However, when the total annual cost model is eventually developed (see equation (13.15), we recommend that inputs to the model be expressed in terms of the annual demand rate *D* and the annual production rate *P*.

Since we are assuming that p will be larger than d, the daily inventory buildup rate during the production phase is $p - d$. If we run production for t days and place $p - d$ units in inventory each day, the inventory level at the end of the production run will be $(p - d)t$. From Figure 13.4 we can see that the inventory level at the end of the production run is also the maximum inventory level. Thus

$$\text{Maximum inventory level} = (p - d)t \tag{13.8}$$

If we know we are producing a production lot size of Q units at a daily production rate of p units, then $Q = pt$, and the length of the production run t must be

$$t = \frac{Q}{p} \text{ days} \tag{13.9}$$

Thus

$$\text{Maximum inventory level} = (p - d)t = (p - d)\left(\frac{Q}{p}\right)$$

$$= \left(1 - \frac{d}{p}\right)Q \tag{13.10}$$

The average inventory level, which is one-half the maximum inventory level, is given by

$$\text{Average inventory level} = \frac{1}{2}\left(1 - \frac{d}{p}\right)Q \tag{13.11}$$

With an annual per unit holding cost of C_h, the general equation for annual holding cost is as follows:

$$\begin{array}{c}\text{Annual}\\\text{holding cost}\end{array} = \left(\begin{array}{c}\text{Average}\\\text{inventory}\\\text{level}\end{array}\right)\left(\begin{array}{c}\text{Annual}\\\text{cost}\\\text{per unit}\end{array}\right)$$

$$= \frac{1}{2}\left(1 - \frac{d}{p}\right)QC_h \tag{13.12}$$

If D is the annual demand for the product and C_o is the setup cost for a production run, then the annual setup cost, which takes the place of the annual ordering cost in the EOQ model, is as follows:

$$\text{Annual setup cost} = \left(\begin{array}{c}\text{Number of production}\\\text{runs per year}\end{array}\right)\left(\begin{array}{c}\text{Setup cost}\\\text{per run}\end{array}\right)$$

$$= \frac{D}{Q}C_o \tag{13.13}$$

Thus, the total annual cost (TC) model is

$$TC = \frac{1}{2}\left(1 - \frac{d}{p}\right)QC_h + \frac{D}{Q}C_o \tag{13.14}$$

Suppose that a production facility operates 250 days per year; 115 days are idle due to weekends and holidays. Then we can write daily demand d in terms of annual demand D as follows:

$$d = \frac{D}{250}$$

Now let P denote the annual production for the product if the product were produced every day. Then

$$P = 250p \quad \text{and} \quad p = \frac{P}{250}$$

Thus[5]

$$\frac{d}{p} = \frac{D/250}{P/250} = \frac{D}{P}$$

---

5. The ratio $d/p = D/P$ regardless of the number of days of operation; 250 days is used here merely as an illustration.

Therefore, we can write the total annual cost model as follows:

$$TC = \frac{1}{2}\left(1 - \frac{D}{P}\right)QC_h + \frac{D}{Q}C_o \tag{13.15}$$

Equations (13.14) and (13.15) are equivalent. However, equation (13.15) may be used more frequently since an *annual* cost model tends to make the analyst think in terms of collecting *annual* demand data (D) and *annual* production data (P) rather than daily data.

Finding the Economic Production Lot Size

As the production rate P approaches infinity, D/P approaches zero. In this case, equation (13.16) is equivalent to the EOQ model in equation (13.5).

Given estimates of the holding cost (C_h), setup cost, (C_o), annual demand rate (D), and annual production rate (P), we could use a trial-and-error approach to compute the total annual cost for various production lot sizes (Q). However, this is not necessary; we can use the minimum-cost formula for Q^* that has been developed using differential calculus (see Appendix 13.3). The equation is as follows:

$$Q^* = \sqrt{\frac{2DC_o}{(1 - D/P)C_h}} \tag{13.16}$$

An Example   Beauty Bar Soap is produced on a production line that has an annual capacity of 60,000 cases. The annual demand is estimated at 26,000 cases, with the demand rate essentially constant throughout the year. The cleaning, preparation, and setup of the production line cost approximately \$135. The manufacturing cost per case is \$4.50, and the annual holding cost is figured at a 24% rate. Thus, $C_h = IC = 0.24(\$4.50) = \$1.08$. What is the recommended production lot size?

Using equation (13.16), we have

$$Q^* = \sqrt{\frac{2(26,000)(135)}{(1 - 26,000/60,000)(1.08)}} = 3387$$

The total annual cost using equation (13.15) and $Q^* = 3387$ is \$2073.

Work Problem 13 as an example of an economic production lot-size model.

Other relevant data include a 1-week lead time to schedule and set up a production run. Thus, the lead-time demand of $26,000/52 = 500$ cases is the reorder point. The cycle time is the time between production runs. Using equation (13.7), the cycle time is estimated to be $T = 250Q^*/D = [(250)(3387)]/26,000$, or about 33 working days. Thus, we should plan a production run of 3387 units about every 33 working days.

Certainly the manager will want to review the model recommendations. Adjusting the recommended $Q^* = 3387$ to a slightly different figure and/or adding safety stock may be desirable.

13.3 AN INVENTORY MODEL WITH PLANNED SHORTAGES

A shortage or stockout is a demand that cannot be supplied. In many situations, shortages are undesirable and should be avoided if at all possible. However, there are other cases in which it may be desirable—from an economic point of view—to plan for and allow shortages. In practice, these types of situations are most commonly found where the value of the inventory per unit is very high and hence the holding cost is high. An example of this type of situation is a new-car dealer's inventory. Often a specific car that a customer wants may not be in stock. However, if the customer is willing to wait a few weeks, the dealer is usually able to order it.

The assumptions of the EOQ model in Table 13.3 apply to this inventory model with the exception that shortages, referred to as *backorders,* are now permitted.

The model developed in this section takes into account a type of shortage known as a **backorder.** In a backorder situation, we assume that when a customer places an order and discovers that the supplier is out of stock, the customer waits until the new shipment arrives, and then the order is filled. Frequently, the waiting period in backordering situations is relatively short. Thus, by promising the customer top priority and immediate delivery when the goods become available, companies may be able to convince the customer to wait until the order arrives. In these cases, the backorder assumption is valid.

The backorder model that we develop is an extension of the EOQ model presented in Section 13.1. We use the EOQ model in which all goods arrive in inventory at one time and there is a constant demand rate (see Table 13.3 for a summary of the EOQ model assumptions). If we let S indicate the number of backorders that are accumulated when a new shipment of size Q is received, then the inventory system for the backorder case has the following characteristics:

- If S backorders exist when a new shipment of size Q arrives, the S backorders are shipped to the appropriate customers, and the remaining $Q - S$ units are placed in inventory. Therefore, $Q - S$ is the maximum inventory level.
- The inventory cycle of T days is divided into two distinct phases; t_1 days when inventory is on hand and orders are filled as they occur, and t_2 days when there are stockouts and all new orders are placed on backorder.

The inventory pattern for the inventory model with backorders, where negative inventory represents the number of backorders, is shown in Figure 13.5.

With the inventory pattern now defined, we can proceed with the basic step of all inventory models—namely, the development of a total-cost model. For the inventory model with backorders, we encounter the usual holding costs and ordering costs. We also incur a backorder cost in terms of the labor and special delivery costs directly associated with the handling of the backorders. Another portion of the backorder cost accounts for the loss of goodwill because some customers will have to wait for their orders. Since the **goodwill cost** depends on how long a customer has to wait, it is customary to adopt the convention of expressing backorder cost in terms of the cost of having a unit on backorder for a stated period of time. This method of costing backorders on a time basis is similar to the method used to compute the inventory holding cost, and we can use it to compute a total annual

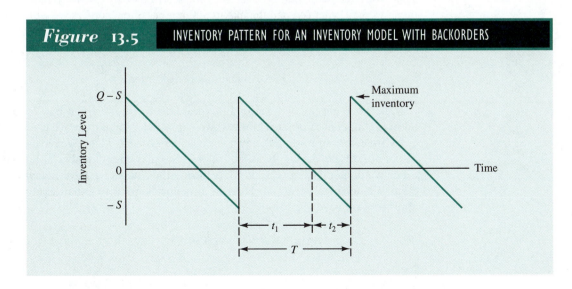

Figure 13.5   INVENTORY PATTERN FOR AN INVENTORY MODEL WITH BACKORDERS

cost of backorders once the average backorder level and the backorder cost per unit per period are known.

Let us begin the development of a total-cost model by calculating the inventory holding costs for a small hypothetical problem. If we have an average inventory of two units for 3 days and no inventory on the fourth day, what is the average inventory level over the 4-day period? It is

$$\frac{2 \text{ units (3 days) } + 0 \text{ units (1 day)}}{4 \text{ days}} = \frac{6}{4} = 1.5 \text{ units}$$

Refer to Figure 13.5. You can see that this situation is what happens in the backorder model. With a maximum inventory of $Q - S$ units, the t_1 days we have inventory on hand will have an average inventory of $(Q - S)/2$. No inventory is carried for the t_2 days in which we experience backorders. Thus, over the total cycle time of $T = t_1 + t_2$ days, we can compute the average inventory level as follows:

$$\text{Average inventory level} = \frac{\frac{1}{2}(Q - S)t_1 + 0t_2}{t_1 + t_2} = \frac{\frac{1}{2}(Q - S)t_1}{T} \tag{13.17}$$

Can we find other ways of expressing t_1 and T? Since we know that the maximum inventory is $Q - S$ and that d represents the constant daily demand, we have

$$t_1 = \frac{Q - S}{d} \text{ days} \tag{13.18}$$

That is, the maximum inventory level of $Q - S$ units will be used up in $(Q - S)/d$ days. Since Q units are ordered each cycle, we know the length of a cycle must be

$$T = \frac{Q}{d} \text{ days} \tag{13.19}$$

Combining equations (13.18) and (13.19) with equation (13.17), we can compute the average inventory level as follows:

$$\text{Average inventory level} = \frac{\frac{1}{2}(Q - S)[(Q - S)/d]}{Q/d} = \frac{(Q - S)^2}{2Q} \tag{13.20}$$

Thus, the average inventory level is expressed in terms of two inventory decisions: how much we will order (Q) and the maximum number of backorders we will allow (S).

The formula for the annual number of orders placed using this model is identical to that for the EOQ model. With D representing the annual demand, we have

$$\text{Annual number of orders} = \frac{D}{Q} \tag{13.21}$$

The next step is to develop an expression for the average backorder level. Since there is a maximum of S backorders, we can use the same logic we used to establish average inventory in finding the average number of backorders. We have an average number of backorders during the period t_2 of ½ the maximum number of backorders or ½S. Since we do not have any backorders during the t_1 days we have inventory, we can calculate the average backorder level in a manner similar to equation (13.17). Using this approach, we have

$$\text{Average backorder level} = \frac{0t_1 + (S/2)t_2}{T} = \frac{(S/2)t_2}{T} \tag{13.22}$$

Since we let the maximum number of backorders reach an amount S at a daily rate of d, the length of the backorder portion of the inventory cycle is

$$t_2 = \frac{S}{d} \tag{13.23}$$

Using equations (13.23) and (13.19) in equation (13.22), we have

$$\text{Average backorder level} = \frac{(S/2)(S/d)}{Q/d} = \frac{S^2}{2Q} \tag{13.24}$$

Let

$$C_h = \text{cost to maintain one unit in inventory for 1 year}$$
$$C_o = \text{cost per order}$$
$$C_b = \text{cost to maintain one unit on backorder for 1 year}$$

The backorder cost C_b is one of the most difficult costs to estimate in inventory models. The reason is that it attempts to measure the cost associated with the loss of goodwill when a customer must wait for an order. Expressing this cost on an annual basis adds to the difficulty.

The total annual cost (TC) for the inventory model with backorders becomes

$$TC = \frac{(Q - S)^2}{2Q} C_h + \frac{D}{Q} C_o + \frac{S^2}{2Q} C_b \tag{13.25}$$

Given the cost estimates C_h, C_o, and C_b and the annual demand D, the minimum-cost values for the order quantity Q^* and the planned backorders S^* are as follows (see Appendix 13.4):

$$Q^* = \sqrt{\frac{2DC_o}{C_h}\left(\frac{C_h + C_b}{C_b}\right)} \tag{13.26}$$

$$S^* = Q^*\left(\frac{C_h}{C_h + C_b}\right) \tag{13.27}$$

An Example   Suppose that the Higley Radio Components Company has a product for which the assumptions of the inventory model with backorders are valid. Information obtained by the company is as follows:

$$D = 2000 \text{ units per year}$$
$$I = 0.20$$
$$C = \$50 \text{ per unit}$$
$$C_h = IC = (0.20)(\$50) = \$10 \text{ per unit per year}$$
$$C_o = \$25 \text{ per order}$$

The company is considering the possibility of allowing some backorders to occur for the product. The annual backorder cost has been estimated to be \$30 per unit per year. Using equations (13.26) and (13.27), we have

$$Q^* = \sqrt{\frac{2(2000)(25)}{10}\left(\frac{10 + 30}{30}\right)} = 115$$

and

$$S^* = 115\left(\frac{10}{10 + 30}\right) = 29$$

An inventory situation that incorporates backorder costs is considered in Problem 15.

If this solution is implemented, the system will operate with the following properties:

$$\text{Maximum inventory} = Q - S = 115 - 29 = 86$$

$$\text{Cycle time} = T = \frac{Q}{D}(250) = \frac{115}{2000}(250) = 14.4 \text{ working days}$$

The total annual cost is

$$\text{Holding cost} = \frac{(86)^2}{2(115)}(10) = \$322$$

$$\text{Ordering cost} = \frac{2000}{115}(25) = \$435$$

If backorders can be tolerated, the total cost including the backordering cost will be less than the total cost of the EOQ model. Some people think the model with backordering will have a greater cost because it includes a backordering cost in addition to the usual inventory holding and ordering costs. You can point out the fallacy in this thinking by noting that the backorder model leads to lower inventory levels and hence lower inventory holding costs.

$$\text{Backorder cost} = \frac{(29)^2}{2(115)}(30) = \$110$$

$$\text{Total cost} = \$867$$

If the company had chosen to prohibit backorders and had adopted the regular EOQ model, the recommended inventory decision would have been

$$Q^* = \sqrt{\frac{2(2000)(25)}{10}} = \sqrt{10,000} = 100$$

This order quantity would have resulted in a holding cost and an ordering cost of $500 each or a total annual cost of $1000. Thus, in this problem, allowing backorders is projecting a $1000 − $867 = $133 or 13.3% savings in cost from the no-stockout EOQ model. The preceding comparison and conclusion are based on the assumption that the backorder model with an annual cost per backordered unit of $30 is a valid model for the actual inventory situation. If the company is concerned that stockouts might lead to lost sales, then the savings might not be enough to warrant switching to an inventory policy that allowed for planned shortages.

NOTES and Comments

Equation (13.27) shows that the optimal number of planned backorders S^* is proportional to the ratio $C_h/(C_h + C_b)$, where C_h is the annual holding cost per unit and C_b is the annual backorder cost per unit. Whenever C_h increases, this ratio becomes larger, and the number of planned backorders increases. This explains why items that have a high per-unit cost and a correspondingly high annual holding cost are more economically handled on a backorder basis. On the other hand, whenever the backorder cost C_b increases, the ratio becomes smaller, and the number of planned backorders decreases. Thus, the model provides the intuitive result that items with high backordering costs will be handled with few backorders. In fact, with high backorder costs, the backorder model and the EOQ model with no backordering allowed provide similar inventory policies.

..../ /............

13.4 QUANTITY DISCOUNTS FOR THE EOQ MODEL

In the quantity discount model, assumption 4 of the EOQ model in Table 13.3 is altered. The cost per unit varies depending on the quantity ordered.

Quantity discounts occur in numerous situations in which suppliers provide an incentive for large order quantities by offering a lower purchase cost when items are ordered in larger lots or quantities. In this section we show how the EOQ model can be used when quantity discounts are available.

Assume that we have a product in which the basic EOQ model (see Table 13.3) is applicable. Instead of a fixed unit cost, the supplier quotes the following discount schedule.

Discount Category	Order Size	Discount (%)	Unit Cost
1	0 to 999	0	$5.00
2	1000 to 2499	3	4.85
3	2500 and over	5	4.75

The 5% discount for the 2500-unit minimum order quantity looks tempting. However, realizing that higher order quantities result in higher inventory holding costs, we should prepare a thorough cost analysis before making a final ordering and inventory policy recommendation.

Suppose that the data and cost analyses show an annual holding cost rate of 20%, an ordering cost of $49 per order, and an annual demand of 5000 units; what order quantity should we select? The following three-step procedure shows the calculations necessary to make this decision. In the preliminary calculations, we use Q_1 to indicate the order quantity for discount category 1, Q_2 for discount category 2, and Q_3 for discount category 3.

Step 1. For each discount category, compute a Q^* using the EOQ formula based on the unit cost associated with the discount category.

Recall that the EOQ model provides $Q^* = \sqrt{2DC_o/C_h}$, where $C_h = IC = (0.20)C$. With three discount categories providing three different unit costs C, we obtain

$$Q_1^* = \sqrt{\frac{2(5000)49}{(0.20)(5.00)}} = 700$$

$$Q_2^* = \sqrt{\frac{2(5000)49}{(0.20)(4.85)}} = 711$$

$$Q_3^* = \sqrt{\frac{2(5000)49}{(0.20)(4.75)}} = 718$$

Since the only differences in the EOQ formulas are slight differences in the holding cost, the economic order quantities resulting from this step will be approximately the same. However, these order quantities will usually not all be of the size necessary to qualify for the discount price assumed. In the preceding case, both Q_2^* and Q_3^* are insufficient order quantities to obtain their assumed discounted costs of $4.85 and $4.75, respectively. For those order quantities for which the assumed price cannot be obtained, the following procedure must be used.

Step 2. For the $Q*$ that is too small to qualify for the assumed discount price, adjust the order quantity upward to the nearest order quantity that will allow the product to be purchased at the assumed price.

In our example, this adjustment causes us to set

$$Q_2^* = 1000$$

and

$$Q_3^* = 2500$$

If a calculated $Q*$ for a given discount price is large enough to qualify for a bigger discount, that value of $Q*$ cannot lead to an optimal solution. Although the reason may not be obvious, it does turn out to be a property of the EOQ quantity discount model. Problem 23 at the end of the chapter asks you to show that this property is true.

> In the EOQ model with quantity discounts, the annual purchase cost must be included because purchase cost depends on the order quantity. Thus, it is a relevant cost.

In the previous inventory models considered, the annual purchase cost of the item was not included because it was constant and never affected by the inventory-order policy decision. However, in the quantity discount model, the annual purchase cost depends on the order-quantity and the associated unit cost. Thus, annual purchase cost (annual demand $D \times$ unit cost C) is included in the equation for total cost as shown here.

$$TC = \frac{Q}{2} C_h + \frac{D}{Q} C_o + DC \qquad (13.28)$$

Using this total-cost equation, we can determine the optimal order quantity for the EOQ discount model in step 3.

Step 3. For each order quantity resulting from steps 1 and 2, compute the total annual cost using the unit price from the appropriate discount category and equation (13.28). The order quantity yielding the minimum total annual cost is the optimal order quantity.

> Problem 21 will give you practice in applying the EOQ model to situations with quantity discounts.

The step 3 calculations for the example problem are summarized in Table 13.4. As you can see, a decision to order 1000 units at the 3% discount rate yields the minimum-cost solution. While the 2500-unit order quantity would result in a 5% discount, its excessive holding cost makes it the second best solution. Figure 13.6 shows the total-cost curve for each of the three discount categories. Note that $Q* = 1000$ provides the minimum-cost order quantity.

Table 13.4 TOTAL ANNUAL COST CALCULATIONS FOR THE EOQ MODEL WITH QUANTITY DISCOUNTS

Discount Category	Unit Cost	Order Quantity	Annual Cost			
			Holding	Ordering	Purchase	Total
1	$5.00	700	$ 350	$350	$25,000	$25,700
2	4.85	1000	485	245	24,250	24,980
3	4.75	2500	1188	98	23,750	25,036

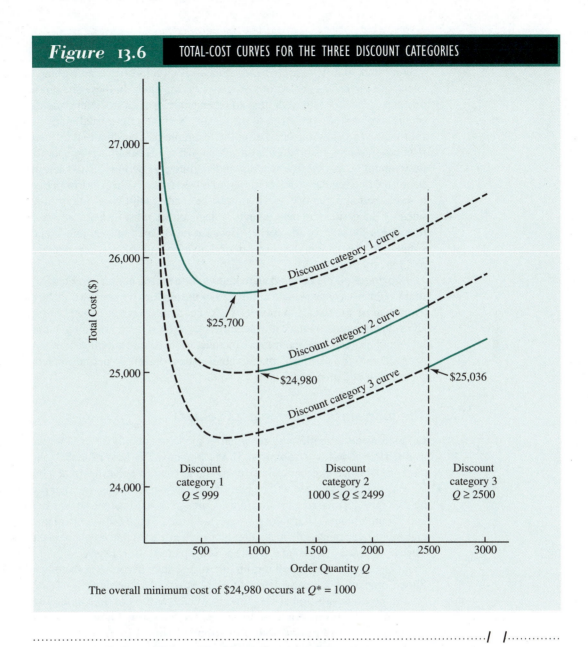

Figure 13.6   TOTAL-COST CURVES FOR THE THREE DISCOUNT CATEGORIES

The overall minimum cost of $24,980 occurs at $Q^* = 1000$

13.5   A SINGLE-PERIOD INVENTORY MODEL WITH PROBABILISTIC DEMAND

This inventory model is the first in the chapter that explicitly treats probabilistic demand. Unlike the EOQ model, it is for a single period with unused inventory not carried over to future periods.

The inventory models that we have discussed thus far have been based on the assumption that the demand rate is constant and *deterministic* throughout the year. We developed minimum-cost order quantity and reorder-point policies based on this assumption. In situations in which the demand rate is not deterministic, models have been developed that treat demand as *probabilistic* and best described by a probability distribution. In this section we consider a **single-period inventory model** with probabilistic demand.

The single-period inventory model refers to inventory situations in which *one* order is placed for the product; at the end of the period, the product has either sold out, or a surplus of unsold items will be sold for a salvage value. The single-period inventory model is applicable in situations involving seasonal or perishable items that cannot be carried in inventory and sold in future periods. Seasonal clothing (such as bathing suits and winter coats) are typically handled in a single-period manner. In these situations, a buyer places one preseason order for each item and then experiences a stockout or holds a clearance sale on the surplus stock at the end of the season. No items are carried in inventory and sold the following year. Newspapers are another example of a product that is ordered one time and is either sold or not sold during the single period. Although newspapers are ordered daily, they cannot be carried in inventory and sold in later periods. Thus, newspaper orders may be treated as a sequence of single-period models; that is, each day or period is separate, and a single-period inventory decision must be made each period (day). Since we order only once for the period, the only inventory decision we must make is *how much* of the product to order at the start of the period. Because newspaper sales is an excellent example of a single-period situation, the single-period inventory problem is sometimes referred to as the *newsboy problem.*

Obviously, if the demand were known for a single-period inventory situation, the solution would be easy; we would simply order the amount we knew would be demanded. However, in most single-period models, the exact demand is not known. In fact, forecasts may show that demand can have a wide variety of values. If we are going to analyze this type of inventory problem in a quantitative manner, we need information about the probabilities associated with the various demand values. Thus, the single-period model presented in this section is based on probabilistic demand.

The Johnson Shoe Company Problem

Let us consider a single-period inventory model that could be used to make a how-much-to-order decision for the Johnson Shoe Company. The buyer for the Johnson Shoe Company has decided to order a shoe for men that has just been shown at a buyers' meeting in New York City. The shoe will be part of the company's spring-summer promotion and will be sold through nine retail stores in the Chicago area. Since the shoe is designed for spring and summer months, it cannot be expected to sell in the fall. Johnson plans to hold a special August clearance sale in an attempt to sell all shoes that have not been sold by July 31. The shoes cost $40 a pair and retail for $60 a pair. At the sale price of $30 a pair, all surplus shoes can be expected to sell during the August sale. If you were the buyer for the Johnson Shoe Company, how many pairs of the shoes would you order?

An obvious question at this time is, What are the possible values of demand for the shoe? We need this information to answer the question of how much to order. Let us suppose that the uniform probability distribution shown in Figure 13.7 can be used to describe the demand for the size 10D shoes. In particular, note that the range of demand is from 350 to 650 pairs of shoes, with an average, or expected, demand of 500 pairs of shoes.

Incremental analysis is a method that can be used to determine the optimal order quantity for a single-period inventory model. Incremental analysis addresses the how-much-to-order question by comparing the cost or loss of *ordering one additional unit* with the cost or loss of *not ordering one additional unit.* The costs involved are defined as follows:

c_o = cost per unit of *overestimating* demand. This cost represents the loss of ordering one additional unit and finding that it cannot be sold.

c_u = cost per unit of *underestimating* demand. This cost represents the opportunity loss of not ordering one additional unit and finding that it could have been sold.

Figure 13.7 UNIFORM PROBABILITY DISTRIBUTION OF DEMAND FOR THE JOHNSON SHOE COMPANY PROBLEM

The cost of underestimating demand is usually harder to determine than the cost of overestimating demand. The reason is that the cost of underestimating demand includes a lost profit and may include a customer goodwill cost because the customer is unable to purchase the item when desired.

In the Johnson Shoe Company problem, the company will incur the cost of overestimating demand whenever it orders too much and has to sell the extra shoes during the August sale. Thus, the cost per unit of overestimating demand is equal to the purchase cost per unit minus the August sales price per unit; that is, $c_o = \$40 - \$30 = \$10$. Therefore, Johnson will lose \$10 for each pair of shoes that it orders over the quantity demanded. The cost of underestimating demand is the lost profit because a pair of shoes that could have been sold was not available in inventory. Thus, the per-unit cost of underestimating demand is the difference between the regular selling price per unit and the purchase cost per unit; that is, $c_u = \$60 - \$40 = \$20$.

Since the exact level of demand for the size 10D shoes is unknown, we have to consider the probability of demand and thus the probability of obtaining the associated costs or losses. For example, let us assume that Johnson Shoe Company management wishes to consider an order quantity equal to the average or expected demand for 500 pairs of shoes. In incremental analysis, we consider the possible losses associated with an order quantity of 501 (ordering one additional unit) and an order quantity of 500 (not ordering one additional unit). The order-quantity alternatives and the possible losses are summarized here.

Order-Quantity Alternatives	Loss Occurs If	Possible Loss	Probability Loss Occurs
$Q = 501$	Demand overestimated; the additional unit *cannot* be sold.	$c_o = \$10$	$P(\text{demand} \leq 500)$
$Q = 500$	Demand underestimated; an additional unit *could* have been sold.	$c_u = \$20$	$P(\text{demand} > 500)$

By looking at the demand probability distribution in Figure 13.7, we see that $P(\text{demand} \leq 500) = 0.50$ and that $P(\text{demand} > 500) = 0.50$. By multiplying the possible losses, $c_o = \$10$ and $c_u = \$20$, by the probability of obtaining the loss, we can compute the expected value of the loss, or simply the *expected loss* (EL), associated with the order-quantity alternatives. Thus

$$\text{EL}(Q = 501) = c_o P(\text{demand} \leq 500) = \$10(0.50) = \$5$$
$$\text{EL}(Q = 500) = c_u P(\text{demand} > 500) = \$20(0.50) = \$10$$

Based on these expected losses, do you prefer an order quantity of 501 or 500 pairs of shoes? Since the expected loss is greater for $Q = 500$, and since we want to avoid this higher cost or loss, we should make $Q = 501$ the preferred decision. We could now consider incrementing the order quantity one additional unit to $Q = 502$ and repeating the expected loss calculations.

Although we could continue this unit-by-unit analysis, it would be time-consuming and cumbersome. We would have to evaluate $Q = 502$, $Q = 503$, $Q = 504$, and so on, until we found the value of Q where the expected loss of ordering one incremental unit is equal to the expected loss of not ordering one incremental unit; that is, the optimal order quantity Q^* occurs when the incremental analysis shows that

$$\text{EL}(Q^* + 1) = \text{EL}(Q^*) \tag{13.29}$$

When this relationship holds, increasing the order quantity by one additional unit has no economic advantage. Using the logic with which we computed the expected losses for the order quantities of 501 and 500, the general expressions for $\text{EL}(Q^* + 1)$ and $\text{EL}(Q^*)$ can be written

$$\text{EL}(Q^* + 1) = c_o P(\text{demand} \leq Q^*) \tag{13.30}$$

$$\text{EL}(Q^*) = c_u P(\text{demand} > Q^*) \tag{13.31}$$

Since we know from basic probability that

$$P(\text{demand} \leq Q^*) + P(\text{demand} > Q^*) = 1 \tag{13.32}$$

we can write

$$P(\text{demand} > Q^*) = 1 - P(\text{demand} \leq Q^*) \tag{13.33}$$

Using this expression, equation (13.31) can be rewritten as

$$\text{EL}(Q^*) = c_u[1 - P(\text{demand} \leq Q^*)] \tag{13.34}$$

Equations (13.30) and (13.34) can be used to show that $\text{EL}(Q^* + 1) = \text{EL}(Q^*)$ whenever

$$c_o P(\text{demand} \leq Q^*) = c_u[1 - P(\text{demand} \leq Q^*)] \tag{13.35}$$

Solving for $P(\text{demand} \leq Q^*)$, we have

$$P(\text{demand} \leq Q^*) = \frac{c_u}{c_u + c_o} \tag{13.36}$$

This expression provides the general condition for the optimal order quantity Q^* in the single-period inventory model.

In the Johnson Shoe Company problem, $c_o = \$10$ and $c_u = \$20$. Thus, equation (13.36) shows that the optimal order size for Johnson shoes must satisfy the following condition:

$$P(\text{demand} \le Q^*) = \frac{c_u}{c_u + c_o} = \frac{20}{20 + 10} = \frac{20}{30} = \frac{2}{3}$$

We can find the optimal order quantity Q^* by referring to the assumed probability distribution shown in Figure 13.7 and finding the value of Q that will provide $P(\text{demand} \le Q^*) = \frac{2}{3}$. To do this, we note that in the uniform distribution the probability is evenly distributed over the entire range of 350–650 pairs of shoes. Thus, we can satisfy the expression for Q^* by moving two-thirds of the way from 350 to 650. Since this is a range of $650 - 350 = 300$, we move 200 units from 350 toward 650. Doing so provides the optimal order quantity of 550 pairs of size 10D shoes.

In summary, the key to establishing an optimal order quantity for single-period inventory models is to identify the probability distribution that describes the demand for the item and the costs of overestimation and underestimation. Then, using the information for the costs of overestimation and underestimation, equation (13.36) can be used to find the location of Q^* in the probability distribution.

The Kremer Chemical Company Problem

As another example of a single-period inventory model with probabilistic demand, consider the situation faced by the Kremer Chemical Company. Kremer has a contract with one of its customers to supply a unique liquid chemical product. Historically, the customer places orders approximately every 6 months. Since a 2-month aging condition exists for the product, Kremer will have to make its production quantity decision before the customer places an order. Kremer's inventory problem is to determine the number of pounds of the chemical to produce in anticipation of the customer's order.

Kremer's manufacturing costs for the chemical are $15 per pound, and the product sells at the fixed contract price of $20 per pound. If Kremer underproduces, it will be unable to satisfy the customer's demand. If this condition occurs, Kremer has agreed to absorb the added cost of filling the order by purchasing a higher quality substitute product from another chemical firm. The substitute product, including additional transportation expenses, will cost Kremer $19 per pound. If Kremer overproduces, it will have more product in inventory than the customer requires. Because of the spoilage potential for the product, Kremer cannot store excess production until the customer's next order. As a result, Kremer reprocesses the excess production and sells the surplus for $5 per pound.

Based on previous experience with the customer's orders, Kremer believes that the normal probability distribution shown in Figure 13.8 best describes the possible demand. Note that the normal distribution shows an average or expected demand of $\mu = 1000$ pounds with a standard deviation of $\sigma = 100$ pounds. Using Kremer's price and cost data as well as the probability distribution of demand shown in Figure 13.8, how much production should Kremer plan for in anticipation of the customer's order for the liquid chemical?

Let us compute the cost of underestimation, c_u, and the cost of overestimation, c_o, as required for equation (13.36). First, if Kremer underproduces, it will have to purchase a substitute product at a higher cost per unit to satisfy the customer's demand for the product. Since the substitute product costs $19 per pound and Kremer could have manufactured the product for $15 per pound, a cost of $c_u = \$19 - \$15 = \$4$ exists for every pound of underestimated demand. If Kremer overestimates demand, the company incurs a cost of $15 per pound to manufacture the product and then sells the reprocessed excess product for $5 per pound. Thus, Kremer has a per-unit cost of $c_o = \$15 - \$5 = \$10$ for overestimating demand.

Figure 13.8 NORMAL PROBABILITY DISTRIBUTION OF DEMAND FOR THE KREMER CHEMICAL COMPANY PROBLEM

Expected demand
$\mu = 1000$

$\sigma = 100$

1000
Demand in Pounds

Applying equation (13.36) indicates that the optimal order quantity must satisfy the following condition:

$$P(\text{demand} \leq Q^*) = \frac{c_u}{c_u + c_o} = \frac{4}{4 + 10} = 0.29$$

We can use the normal probability distribution for demand as shown in Figure 13.9 to find the order quantity that satisfies the condition that $P(\text{demand} \leq Q^*) = 0.29$. From Appendix C, we see that 0.29 of the area in the left tail of the curve of the normal probability distribution occurs at $z = 0.55$ standard deviations *below* the mean. Since the mean or expected demand is given by $\mu = 1000$ and the standard deviation is $\sigma = 100$, we have

$$Q^* = \mu - 0.55\sigma$$
$$= 1000 - 0.55(100) = 945$$

An example of a single-period inventory model with probabilistic demand described by a normal probability distribution is considered in Problem 25.

Thus, with the assumed normal probability distribution of demand, the Kremer Chemical Company should produce 945 pounds of the chemical in anticipation of the customer's or-

Figure 13.9 PROBABILITY DISTRIBUTION OF DEMAND FOR THE KREMER CHEMICAL COMPANY PROBLEM SHOWING THE LOCATION OF THE OPTIMAL ORDER QUANTITY Q^*

$P(\text{demand} \leq Q^*) = 0.29$

$\sigma = 100$

1000
$Q^* = 945$ Demand

der. Note that in this case the cost of underestimation is less than the cost of overestimation. Thus, Kremer is willing to risk a higher probability of underestimation and hence a higher probability of a stockout. In fact, Kremer's optimal order quantity has a 0.29 probability of having a surplus and a $1 - 0.29 = 0.71$ probability of a stockout.

N O T E S	**I.** In any probabilistic inventory model, the assumption about the probability distribution for demand is
and Comments	critical and can affect the recommended inventory decision. In the problems presented in this section, we used the uniform and the normal probability distributions to describe demand. In some situations, other probability distributions may be more appropriate. In using probabilistic inventory models, we must exercise care in selecting the probability distribution that most realistically describes demand.

2. In the single-period inventory model, the value of $c_u/(c_u + c_o)$ plays a critical role in selecting the order quantity [see equation (13.36)]. Whenever $c_u = c_o$, $c_u/(c_u + c_o)$ equals 0.50; in this case, we should select an order quantity corresponding to the median demand. With this choice, a stockout is just as likely as a surplus because the two costs are equal. However, whenever $c_u < c_o$, a smaller order quantity will be recommended. In this case, the smaller order quantity will provide a higher probability of a stockout; however, the more expensive cost of overestimating demand and having a surplus will tend to be avoided. Finally, whenever $c_u > c_o$, a larger order quantity will be recommended. In this case, the larger order quantity provides a lower probability of a stockout in an attempt to avoid the more expensive cost of underestimating demand and experiencing a stockout.

13.6 AN ORDER-QUANTITY, REORDER-POINT MODEL WITH PROBABILISTIC DEMAND

The inventory model in this section is based on the assumptions of the EOQ model shown in Table 13.3 with the exception that demand is probabilistic rather than deterministic. With probabilistic demand, occasional shortages may occur.

In the previous section we considered a single-period inventory model with probabilistic demand. In this section we extend our discussion to a multiperiod order-quantity, reorder-point inventory model with probabilistic demand. In the multiperiod model, the inventory system operates continuously with many repeating periods or cycles; inventory can be carried from one period to the next. Whenever the inventory position reaches the reorder point, an order for Q units is placed. Since demand is probabilistic, the time the reorder point will be reached, the time between orders, and the time the order of Q units will arrive in inventory cannot be determined in advance.

The inventory pattern for the order-quantity, reorder-point model with probabilistic demand will have the general appearance shown in Figure 13.10. Note that the increases or jumps in the inventory level occur whenever an order of Q units arrives. The inventory level decreases at a nonconstant rate based on the probabilistic demand. A new order is placed whenever the reorder point is reached. At times, the order quantity of Q units will arrive before inventory reaches zero. However, at other times, higher demand will cause a stockout before a new order is received. As with other order-quantity, reorder-point models, the manager must determine the order quantity Q and the reorder point r for the inventory system.

The exact mathematical formulation of an order-quantity, reorder-point inventory model with probabilistic demand is beyond the scope of this text. However, we present a procedure that can be used to obtain good, workable order-quantity and reorder-point inventory policies. The solution procedure can be expected to provide only an approximation of the optimal solution, but it can yield very good solutions in many practical situations.

Let us consider the inventory problem of Dabco Industrial Lighting Distributors. Dabco purchases a special high-intensity light bulb for industrial lighting systems from a

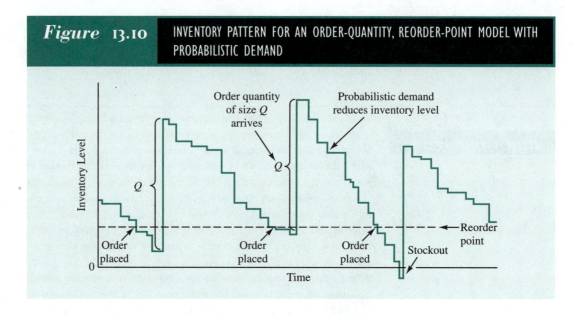

Figure 13.10   INVENTORY PATTERN FOR AN ORDER-QUANTITY, REORDER-POINT MODEL WITH PROBABILISTIC DEMAND

well-known light bulb manufacturer. Dabco would like a recommendation on how much to order and when to order so that a low-cost inventory policy can be maintained. Pertinent facts are that the ordering cost is $12 per order, one bulb costs $6, and Dabco uses a 20% annual holding cost rate for its inventory ($C_h = IC = 0.20 \times \$6 = \$1.20$). Dabco, which has over 1000 different customers, experiences a probabilistic demand; in fact, the number of units demanded varies considerably from day to day and from week to week. The lead time for a new order of light bulbs is 1 week. Historical sales data indicate that demand during a 1-week lead time can be described by a normal probability distribution with a mean of 154 light bulbs and a standard deviation of 25 light bulbs. The normal distribution of demand during the lead time is shown in Figure 13.11. Since the mean demand during 1-week is 154 units, Dabco can anticipate a mean or expected annual demand of 154 units per week × 52 weeks per year = 8008 units per year.

Figure 13.11   LEAD-TIME DEMAND PROBABILITY DISTRIBUTION FOR DABCO LIGHT BULBS

The How-Much-to-Order Decision

Although we are in a probabilistic demand situation, we have an estimate of the expected annual demand of 8008 units. We can apply the EOQ model from Section 13.1 as an approximation of the best order quantity, with the expected annual demand used for *D*. In Dabco's case

$$Q^* = \sqrt{\frac{2DC_o}{C_h}} = \sqrt{\frac{2(8008)(12)}{(1.20)}} = 400 \text{ units}$$

When we studied the sensitivity of the EOQ model, we learned that the total cost of operating an inventory system was relatively insensitive to order quantities that were in the neighborhood of *Q**. Using this knowledge, we expect 400 units per order to be a good approximation of the optimal order quantity. Even if annual demand were as low as 7000 units or as high as 9000 units, an order quantity of 400 units should be a relatively good low-cost order size. Thus, given our best estimate of annual demand at 8008 units, we will use *Q** = 400.

We have established the 400-unit order quantity by ignoring the fact that demand is probabilistic. Using *Q** = 400, Dabco can anticipate placing approximately *D/Q** = 8008/400 = 20 orders per year with an average of approximately 250/20 = 12.5 working days between orders.

The When-to-Order Decision

We now want to establish a when-to-order decision rule or reorder point that will trigger the ordering process. With a mean lead-time demand of 154 units, you might first suggest a 154-unit reorder point. However, considering the probability of demand now becomes extremely important. If 154 is the mean lead-time demand, and if demand is symmetrically distributed about 154, then the lead-time demand will be more than 154 units roughly 50% of the time. When the demand during the 1-week lead time exceeds 154 units, Dabco will experience a shortage or stockout. Thus, using a reorder point of 154 units, approximately 50% of the time (10 of the 20 orders a year) Dabco will be short of bulbs before the new supply arrives. This shortage rate would most likely be viewed as unacceptable.

Refer to the **lead-time demand distribution** shown in Figure 13.11. Given this distribution, we can now determine how the reorder point *r* affects the probability of a stockout. Since stockouts occur whenever the demand during the lead time exceeds the reorder point, we can find the probability of a stockout by using the lead-time demand distribution to compute the probability that demand will exceed *r*.

> The probability of a stockout during any one inventory cycle is easiest to estimate by first determining the number of orders that are expected during the year. The inventory manager can usually state a willingness to allow perhaps one, two, or three stockouts during the year. The allowable stockouts per year divided by the number of orders per year will provide the desired probability of a stockout.

We could now approach the when-to-order problem by defining a cost per stockout and then attempting to include this cost in a total-cost equation. Alternatively, we can ask management to specify the average number of stockouts that can be tolerated per year. If demand for a product is probabilistic, a manager who will never tolerate a stockout is being somewhat unrealistic because attempting to avoid stockouts completely will require high reorder points, high inventory levels, and an associated high holding cost.

Suppose in this case that Dabco management is willing to tolerate an average of one stockout per year. Since Dabco places 20 orders per year, this decision implies that management is willing to allow demand during lead time to exceed the reorder point one time in 20, or 5% of the time. The reorder point *r* can be found by using the lead-time demand distribution to find the value of *r* with a 5% chance of having a lead-time demand that will exceed it. This situation is shown graphically in Figure 13.12.

Figure 13.12   REORDER POINT r THAT ALLOWS A 5% CHANCE OF A STOCKOUT FOR DABCO LIGHT BULBS

From the standard normal probability distribution table in Appendix C, we see that the r value is 1.645 standard deviations above the mean. Therefore, for the assumed normal distribution for lead-time demand with $\mu = 154$ and $\sigma = 25$, the reorder point r is

$$r = 154 + 1.645(25) = 195$$

If a normal distribution is used for lead-time demand, the general equation for r is

$$r = \mu + z\sigma \qquad (13.37)$$

where z is the number of standard deviations necessary to obtain the acceptable stockout probability.

Thus, the recommended inventory decision is to order 400 units whenever the inventory level reaches the reorder point of 195. Since the mean or expected demand during the lead time is 154 units, the $195 - 154 = 41$ units serve as a safety stock, which absorbs higher-than-usual demand during the lead time. Roughly 95% of the time, the 195 units will be able to satisfy demand during the lead time. The anticipated annual cost for this system is as follows:

Ordering cost	$(D/Q)C_o = (8000/400)12 =$	$240.00
Holding cost, normal inventory	$(Q/2)C_h = (400/2)(1.20) =$	$240.00
Holding cost, safety stock	$(41)C_h = \quad 41(1.20) \quad =$	$\underline{\$\ 49.20}$
	Total	$529.20

Try Problem 29 as an example of an order-quantity, reorder-point model with probabilistic demand.

If Dabco could have assumed that a known, constant demand rate of 8008 units per year existed for the light bulbs, then $Q^* = 400$, $r = 154$, and a total annual cost of $240 + $240 = $480 would have been optimal. When demand is uncertain and can only be expressed in probabilistic terms, a larger total cost can be expected. The larger cost occurs in the form of larger holding costs because more inventory must be maintained to limit the number of stockouts. For Dabco, this additional inventory or safety stock was 41 units, with an additional annual holding cost of $49.20. The Q.M. in Action: Information from a Netherlands Supplier Lowers Inventory Cost describes how a warehouser in the Netherlands has implemented an order-quantity, reorder-point system with probabilistic demand.

Q.M. IN ACTION

INFORMATION FROM A NETHERLANDS SUPPLIER LOWERS INVENTORY COST*

In the Netherlands, companies such as Philips, Rank Xerox, and Fokker have followed the trend of developing closer relations between the firm and its suppliers. As teamwork, coordination, and information sharing improve, opportunities are available for better cost control in the operation of inventory systems.

One Dutch public warehouser has a contract with its supplier under which the supplier routinely provides information regarding the status and schedule of upcoming production runs. The warehouser's inventory system operates as an order-quantity, reorder-point system with probabalistic demand. When the order-quantity, Q, has been determined, the warehouser selects the desired reorder point for the product. The distribution of the lead-time demand is essential in determining the reorder point. Usually, the lead-time demand distribution is approx-

imated directly, taking into account both the probablilistic demand and the probabilistic length of the lead-time period.

The supplier's information concerning scheduled production runs provides the warehouser with a better understanding of the lead time involved for a product and the resulting lead-time demand distribution. With this information, the warehouse can modify the reorder point accordingly. Information sharing by the supplier thus enables the order-quantity, reorder-point system to operate with a lower inventory holding cost.

*Based on van der Duyn Schouten, F. A., M. J. G. van Eijs, and R. M. J. Heuts, "The Value of Supplier Information to Improve Management of a Retailer's Inventory." *Decision Sciences*, vol. 25, no. 1, January–February 1994, pp. 1–14.

NOTES
and Comments

The Dabco reorder point was based on a 5% probability of a stockout during the lead-time period. Thus, on 95% of all order cycles Dabco will be able to satisfy customer demand without experiencing a stockout. Defining **service level** as the percentage of all order cycles that do not experience a stockout, we would say that Dabco has a 95% service level. However, other definitions of service level may include the percentage of all customer demand that can be satisfied from inventory. Thus, when a inventory manager expresses a desired service level, clarify exactly what the manager means by the term "service level."

13.7 A PERIODIC-REVIEW MODEL WITH PROBABILISTIC DEMAND

The order-quantity, reorder-point inventory models previously discussed require a **continuous-review** inventory system. In a continuous-review inventory system, the inventory position is monitored continuously so that an order can be placed whenever the reorder point is reached. Computerized inventory systems can easily provide the continuous review required by the order-quantity, reorder-point models.

Up to this point, we have assumed that the inventory position is reviewed continuously so that an order can be placed as soon as the inventory position reaches the reorder point. The inventory model in this section assumes probabilistic demand and a periodic review of the inventory position.

An alternative to the continuous-review system is the **periodic-review inventory system.** With a periodic-review system, the inventory level is checked and reordering is done only at specified points in time. For example, inventory levels may be checked and orders placed on a weekly, biweekly, monthly, or some other periodic basis. When a firm or business handles multiple products, the periodic-review system has the advantage of requiring that orders for several items be placed at the same preset periodic-review time. With this type of inventory system, the shipping and receiving of orders for multiple products are easily coordinated. Under the previously discussed order-quantity, reorder-point systems, the reorder points for various products can be encountered at substantially different points in time, making the coordination of orders for multiple products more difficult.

To illustrate this system, let us consider Dollar Discounts, a firm with several retail stores that carry a wide variety of products for household use. The company operates its inventory system with a two-week periodic review. Under this system, a retail store manager may order any number of units of any product from the Dollar Discounts central warehouse every two weeks. Orders for all products going to a particular store are combined into one shipment. When making the order-quantity decision for each product at a given review period, the store manager knows that a reorder for the product cannot be made until the next review period.

Assuming that the lead time is less than the length of the review period, an order placed at a review period will be received prior to the next review period. In this case, the how-much-to-order decision at any review period is determined using the following:

$$Q = M - H \tag{13.38}$$

where

$$Q = \text{the order quantity}$$
$$M = \text{the replenishment level}$$
$$H = \text{the inventory on hand at the review period}$$

Since the demand is probabilistic, the inventory on hand at the review period, H, will vary. Thus, the order quantity that must be sufficient to bring the inventory position back to its maximum or replenishment level M can be expected to vary each period. For example, if the replenishment level for a particular product is 50 units, and the inventory on hand at the review period is $H = 12$ units, an order of $Q = M - H = 50 - 12 = 38$ units should be made. Thus, under the periodic-review model, enough units are ordered each review period to bring the inventory position back up to the replenishment level.

A typical inventory pattern for a periodic-review system with probabilistic demand is shown in Figure 13.13. Note that the time between periodic reviews is predetermined and fixed. The order quantity Q at each review period can vary and is shown to be the difference between the replenishment level and the inventory on hand. Finally, as with other probabilistic models, an unusually high demand can result in an occasional stockout.

The decision variable in the periodic-review model is the replenishment level M. To determine M, we could begin by developing a total-cost model, including holding, ordering, and stockout costs. Instead, we describe an approach that is often used in practice. In this approach, the objective is to determine a replenishment level that will meet a desired performance level, such as a reasonably low probability of stockout or a reasonably low number of stockouts per year.

In the Dollar Discounts problem, we assume that management's objective is to determine the replenishment level with only a 1% chance of a stockout. In the periodic-review model, the order quantity at each review period must be sufficient to cover demand for the *review period plus the demand for the following lead time.* That is, the order quantity that brings the inventory position up to the replenishment level M must last until the order made at the next review period is received in inventory. The length of this time is equal to the review period plus the lead time. Figure 13.14 shows the normal probability distribution of demand during the review period plus the lead-time period for one of the Dollar Discounts products. The mean demand is 250 units, and the standard deviation of demand is 45 units. Given this situation, the logic used to establish M is similar to the logic used to establish the reorder point in Section 13.6. Figure 13.15 shows the replenishment level M with a 1%

| Figure 13.13 | INVENTORY PATTERN FOR PERIODIC-REVIEW MODEL WITH PROBABILISTIC DEMAND |

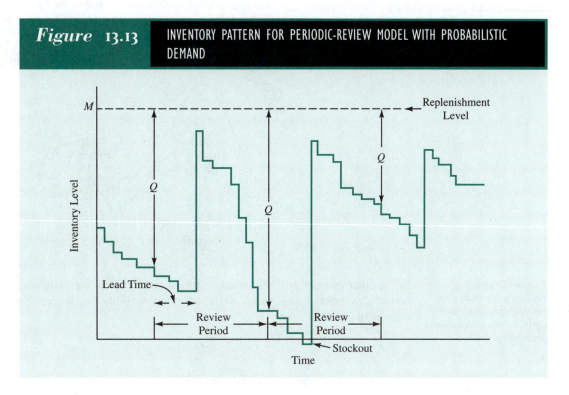

chance that demand will exceed that replenishment level. In other words, Figure 13.15 shows the replenishment level that allows a 1% chance of a stockout associated with the replenishment decision. Using the normal probability distribution table in Appendix C, we see that a value of M that is 2.33 standard deviations above the mean will allow stockouts with a 1% probability. Therefore, for the assumed normal probability distribution with $\mu = 250$ and $\sigma = 45$, the replenishment level is determined by

$$M = 250 + 2.33(45) = 355$$

| Figure 13.14 | PROBABILITY DISTRIBUTION OF DEMAND DURING THE REVIEW PERIOD AND LEAD TIME FOR THE DOLLAR DISCOUNTS PROBLEM |

Figure 13.15   REPLENISHMENT LEVEL M THAT ALLOWS A 1% CHANCE OF A STOCKOUT FOR THE DOLLAR DISCOUNTS PROBLEM

Problem 33 gives you practice in computing the replenishment level for a periodic-review model with probabilistic demand.

While other probability distributions can be used to express the demand during the review period plus the lead-time period, if the normal probability distribution is used, the general expression for M is

$$M = \mu + z\sigma \qquad (13.39)$$

where z is the number of standard deviations necessary to obtain the acceptable stockout probability.

Periodic-review systems provide advantages of coordinated orders for multiple items. However, periodic-review systems require larger safety stock levels than corresponding continuous-review systems.

If demand had been deterministic rather than probabilistic, the replenishment level would have been the demand during the review period plus the demand during the lead-time period. In this case, the replenishment level would have been 250 units, and no stockout would have occurred. However, with the probabilistic demand, we have seen that higher inventory levels are necessary to allow for uncertain demand and to control the probability of a stockout. In the Dollar Discounts problem, $355 - 250 = 105$ is the safety stock that is necessary to absorb any higher-than-usual demand during the review period plus the demand during the lead-time period. This safety stock limits the probability of a stockout to 1%. The Q.M. in Action: Inventory Model Helps Hewlett-Packard's Product Design for Worldwide Markets describes a periodic-review inventory system at Hewlett-Packard.

More Complex Periodic-Review Models

The periodic-review model that we have just discussed is one approach to determining a replenishment level for the periodic-review inventory system with probabilistic demand. More complex versions of the periodic-review model incorporate a reorder point as another decision variable. That is, instead of ordering at every periodic review, a reorder point is established. If the inventory on hand at the periodic review is at or below the reorder point, a decision is made to order up to the replenishment level. However, if the inventory on hand at the periodic review is greater than the reorder level, such an order is not placed, and the system continues until the next periodic review. In this case, the cost of ordering is a relevant cost and can be included in a cost model along with holding and stockout costs. Optimal policies can be reached based on minimizing the expected total cost. Situations with lead times longer than the review period add to the complexity of the model. The mathematical level required to treat these more extensive periodic-review models is beyond the scope of this text.

Q.M. IN ACTION

INVENTORY MODEL HELPS HEWLETT-PACKARD'S PRODUCT DESIGN FOR WORLDWIDE MARKETS*

Product design always affects the efficiency of manufacturing operations. At Hewlett-Packard's Vancouver, Washington, division, managers are also learning how product design affects product customization, distribution, and delivery to worldwide markets. In most cases, different markets require different product configurations because of language, environment, and/or government regulations. Should Hewlett-Packard design variations of each product to meet the unique requirements of each market, or should it design a more general product with product customization being completed in the local market area?

An inventory model was used to study the inventory levels and costs associated with the product design alternatives for the Hewlett-Packard Deskjet-Plus printer. Inventory levels for the printer are maintained on a periodic-review basis. Planners review the inventory position (on-hand inventory plus inventory in the pipeline) weekly. Orders are placed for quantities needed to return the inventory position to the target inventory level. Demand during the lead time is assumed to follow a normal probability distribution.

The inventory model projected the inventory cost associated with each product design alternative. As a result, Hewlett-Packard's Vancouver, Washington, division redesigned its products to support final customization of the product at the local distribution center level. The inventory model projected an 18% reduction in the total inventory investment, which saved millions of dollars.

*Based on Lee, H. L., C. Billington, and B. Carter, "Hewlett-Packard Gains Control of Inventory and Service through Design for Localization." *Interfaces*, vol. 23, no. 4, July–August 1993, pp. 1–11.

NOTES and Comments

1. The periodic-review model presented in this section is based on the assumption that the lead time for an order is less than the periodic-review period. Most periodic-review systems operate under this condition. However, the case in which the lead time is longer than the review period can be handled by defining H in equation (13.38) as the inventory position, where H includes the inventory on hand plus the inventory on order. In this case, the order quantity at any review period is the amount needed for the inventory on hand plus *all* outstanding orders needed to reach the replenishment level.

2. In the order-quantity, reorder-point model discussed in Section 13.6, a continuous review was used to initiate an order whenever the reorder point was reached. The safety stock for this model was based on the probabilistic demand during the lead time. The periodic-review model presented in this section also determined a recommended safety stock. However, since the inventory review was only periodic, the safety stock was based on the probabilistic demand during the *review period plus the lead-time period*. This longer period for the safety stock computation means that periodic-review systems tend to require a larger safety stock than do continuous-review systems.

SUMMARY

In this chapter we presented some of the approaches quantitative analysts use to assist managers in establishing low-cost inventory policies. We first considered cases where the demand rate for the product is constant. In analyzing these inventory systems, total-cost models were developed, which included ordering costs, holding costs, and, in some cases, backordering costs. Then minimum-cost formulas for the order quantity Q were presented. A reorder point r can be established by considering the lead-time demand for the item.

In addition, we discussed inventory models where a deterministic and constant rate could not be assumed, and thus, demand was described by a probability distribution. A critical issue with these probabilistic inventory models is obtaining a probability distribution that most realistically approximates the demand distribution for the item. We first described a single-period model where only one order is placed for the product and, at the end of the period, either the product has sold out or a surplus of unsold products will be sold for a salvage value. Solution procedures were then presented for multiperiod models based on either an order-quantity, reorder-point, continuous-review system or a replenishment-level, periodic-review system.

In closing this chapter, we reemphasize that inventory and inventory systems can be an expensive phase of a firm's operation. Because of the utmost economic importance, managers need to be aware of the cost of inventory systems and to make the best possible operating policy decisions for the inventory system. Inventory models, as presented in this chapter, can help managers develop good inventory policies.

GLOSSARY

Economic order quantity (EOQ) The order quantity that minimizes the annual holding cost plus the annual ordering cost.

Constant demand rate An assumption of many inventory models that states that the same number of units are taken from inventory each period of time.

Holding cost The cost associated with maintaining an inventory investment, including the cost of the capital investment in the inventory, insurance, taxes, warehouse overhead, and so on. This cost may be stated as a percentage of the inventory investment or as a cost per unit.

Cost of capital The cost a firm incurs to obtain capital for investment. It may be stated as an annual percentage rate, and it is part of the holding cost associated with maintaining inventory levels.

Ordering cost The fixed cost (salaries, paper, transportation, etc.) associated with placing an order for an item.

Setup cost The fixed cost (labor, materials, lost production) associated with preparing for a new production run.

Inventory position The inventory on hand plus the inventory on order.

Reorder point The inventory position at which a new order should be placed.

Lead time The time between the placing of an order and its receipt in the inventory system.

Lead-time demand The number of units demanded during the lead-time period.

Cycle time The length of time between the placing of two consecutive orders.

Safety stock Inventory maintained in order to reduce the number of stockouts resulting from higher-than-expected demand.

Constant supply rate A situation in which the inventory is built up at a constant rate over a period of time.

Backorder The receipt of an order for a product when no units are in inventory. These backorders become shortages, which are eventually satisfied when a new supply of the product becomes available.

Goodwill cost A cost associated with a backorder, a lost sale, or any form of stockout or unsatisfied demand. This cost may be used to reflect the loss of future profits because a customer experienced an unsatisfied demand.

Quantity discounts Discounts or lower unit costs offered by the manufacturer when a customer purchases larger quantities of the product.

Deterministic Inventory model A model where demand is considered known and not subject to uncertainty.

Probabilistic Inventory model A model where demand is not known exactly; probabilities must be associated with the possible values for demand.

Single-period inventory model An inventory model in which only one order is placed for the product, and at the end of the period either the item has sold out, or a surplus of unsold items will be sold for a salvage value.

Incremental analysis A method used to determine an optimal order quantity by comparing the cost of ordering an additional unit with the cost of not ordering an additional unit.

Lead-time demand distribution The distribution of demand that occurs during the lead-time period.

Continuous-review inventory system A system in which the inventory position is monitored or reviewed on a continuous basis so that a new order can be placed as soon as the reorder point is reached.

Periodic-review inventory system A system in which the inventory position is checked or reviewed at predetermined periodic points in time. Reorders are placed only at periodic-review points.

Independent demand Demand for an item that is independent of the demand for other products or items. Usually independent demand is generated by customers placing orders for finished goods.

Dependent demand Demand for a product, component, subassembly, or item that is dependent on the demand for another product or item.

PROBLEMS

SELF TEST

1. Suppose that the R & B Beverage Company has a soft-drink product that has a constant annual demand rate of 3600 cases. A case of the soft drink costs R & B $3. Ordering costs are $20 per order and holding costs are 25% of the value of the inventory. R & B has 250 working days per year, and the lead time is 5 days. Identify the following aspects of the inventory policy.
   a. Economic order quantity   c. Cycle time
   b. Reorder point   d. Total annual cost

2. A general property of the EOQ inventory model is that total inventory holding and total ordering costs are equal at the optimal solution. Use the data in Problem 1 to show that this result is true. Use equations (13.1), (13.2), and (13.3) to show that, in general, total holding costs and total ordering costs are equal whenever Q^* is used.

3. The reorder point [see equation (13.6)] is defined as the lead-time demand for an item. In cases of long lead times, the lead-time demand and thus the reorder point may exceed the economic order quantity Q^*. In such cases, the inventory position will not equal the inventory on hand when an order is placed, and the reorder point may be expressed in terms of either the inventory position or the inventory on hand. Consider the economic order quantity model with $D = 5000$, $C_o = \$32$, $C_h = \$2$, and 250 working days per year. Identify the reorder point in terms of the inventory position and in terms of the inventory on hand for each of the following lead times.

   a. 5 days   c. 25 days
   b. 15 days   d. 45 days

4. Westside Auto purchases a component used in the manufacture of automobile generators directly from the supplier. Westside's generator production operation, which is operated at a constant rate, will require 1000 components per month throughout the year (12,000 units annually). Assume that the ordering costs are $25 per order, the unit cost is $2.50 per component, and that annual holding costs are 20% of the value of the inventory. Westside has 250 working days per year, and the lead time is 5 days. Answer the following inventory policy questions.

   a. What is the EOQ for this component?
   b. What is the reorder point?
   c. What is the cycle time?
   d. What are the total annual holding and ordering costs associated with your recommended EOQ?

5. Suppose that Westside's management in Problem 4 likes the operational efficiency of ordering once each month and in quantities of 1000 units. How much more expensive would this policy be than your EOQ recommendation? Would you recommend in favor of the 1000-unit order quantity? Explain. What would the reorder point be if the 1000-unit quantity were acceptable?

6. Tele-Reco is a new specialty store that sells television sets, videotape recorders, video games, and other television-related products. A new Japanese-manufactured videotape recorder costs Tele-Reco $600 per unit. Tele-Reco's annual holding cost rate is 22%. Ordering costs are estimated to be $70 per order.

   a. If demand for the new videotape recorder is expected to be constant with a rate of 20 units per month, what is the recommended order quantity for the videotape recorder?
   b. What are the estimated annual inventory holding and ordering costs associated with this product?
   c. How many orders will be placed per year?
   d. With 250 working days per year, what is the cycle time for this product?

7. A large distributor of oil-well drilling equipment has operated over the past 2 years with EOQ policies based on an annual holding cost rate of 22%. Under the EOQ policy, a particular product has been ordered with a $Q^* = 80$. A recent evaluation of holding costs shows that because of an increase in the interest rate associated with bank loans, the annual holding cost rate should be 27%.

   a. What is the new economic order quantity for the product?
   b. Develop a general expression showing how the economic order quantity changes when the annual holding cost rate is changed from I to I'.

8. Nation-Wide Bus Lines is proud of its 6-week bus driver training program that it conducts for all new Nation-Wide drivers. As long as the class size remains less than or equal to 35, a 6-week training program costs Nation-Wide $22,000 for instructors, equipment, and so on. The Nation-Wide training program must provide the company with approximately five new drivers per month. After completing the training program, new drivers are paid $1600 per month but do not work until a full-time driver position is open. Nation-Wide views the $1600 per month paid to each idle new driver as a holding cost necessary to maintain a supply of newly trained drivers available for immediate service. Viewing new drivers as inventory-type units, how large should the training classes be to minimize Nation-Wide's total annual training and new driver idle-time

costs? How many training classes should the company hold each year? What is the total annual cost associated with your recommendation?

9. Cress Electronic Products manufactures components used in the automotive industry. Cress purchases parts for use in its manufacturing operation from a variety of different suppliers. One particular supplier provides a part where the assumptions of the EOQ model are realistic. The annual demand is 5000 units, the ordering cost is $80 per order, and the annual holding cost rate is 25%.
   a. If the cost of the part is $20 per unit, what is the economic order quantity?
   b. Assume 250 days of operation per year. If the lead time for an order is 12 days, what is the reorder point?
   c. If the lead time for the part is 7 weeks (35 days), what is the reorder point?
   d. What is the reorder point for part (c) if the reorder point is expressed in terms of the inventory on hand rather than the inventory position?

10. All-Star Bat Manufacturing, Inc., supplies baseball bats to major and minor league baseball teams. After an initial order in January, demand over the 6-month baseball season is approximately constant at 1000 bats per month. Assuming that the bat production process can handle up to 4000 bats per month, the bat production setup costs are $150 per setup, the production cost is $10 per bat, and that holding costs have a monthly rate of 2%, what production lot size would you recommend to meet the demand during the baseball season? If All-Star operates 20 days per month, how often will the production process operate, and what is the length of a production run?

11. Assume that a production line operates such that the production lot-size model of Section 13.2 is applicable. Given $D = 6400$ units per year, $C_o = \$100$, and $C_h = \$2$ per unit per year, compute the minimum-cost production lot size for each of the following production rates:
   a. 8000 units per year   c. 32,000 units per year
   b. 10,000 units per year   d. 100,000 units per year
   Compute the EOQ recommended lot size using equation (13.5). What two observations can you make about the relationship between the EOQ model and the production lot-size model?

12. Assume that you are reviewing the production lot-size decision associated with a production operation where $P = 8000$ units per year, $D = 2000$ units per year, $C_o = \$300$, and $C_h = \$1.60$ per unit per year. Also assume that current practice calls for production runs of 500 units every 3 months. Would you recommend changing the current production lot-size? Why or why not? How much could be saved by converting to your production lot-size recommendation?

SELF TEST

13. Wilson Publishing Company produces books for the retail market. Demand for a current book is expected to occur at a constant annual rate of 7200 copies. The cost of one copy of the book is $14.50. The holding cost is based on an 18% annual rate, and production setup costs are $150 per setup. The equipment on which the book is produced has an annual production volume of 25,000 copies. Wilson has 250 working days per year, and the lead time for a production run is 15 days. Use the production lot-size model to compute the following values:
   a. Minimum-cost production lot size   e. Maximum inventory level
   b. Number of production runs per year   f. Total annual cost
   c. Cycle time   g. Reorder point
   d. Length of a production run

14. A well-known manufacturer of several brands of toothpaste uses the production lot-size model to determine production quantities for its various products. The product known as Extra White is currently being produced in production lot sizes of 5000 units. The length of the production run for this quantity is 10 days. Because of a recent shortage of a particular raw material, the supplier of the material has announced a cost increase that will be passed along to the manufacturer of Extra White. Current estimates are that the new raw material cost will increase the manufacturing cost of the toothpaste products by 23% per unit. What will be the effect of this price increase on the production lot sizes for Extra White?

SELF TEST

15. Suppose that Westside Auto of Problem 4, with $D = 12{,}000$ units per year, $C_h = (2.50)(0.20) = \$0.50$, and $C_o = \$25$, decided to operate with a backorder inventory policy. Backorder costs are estimated to be \$5 per unit per year. Identify the following:

    a. Minimum-cost order quantity   **d.** Cycle time

    b. Maximum number of backorders   **e.** Total annual cost

    c. Maximum inventory level

16. Assuming 250 days of operation per year and a lead time of 5 days, what is the reorder point for Westside Auto in Problem 15? Show the general formula for the reorder point for the EOQ model with backorders. In general, is the reorder point when backorders are allowed greater than or less than the reorder point when backorders are not allowed? Explain.

17. A manager of an inventory system believes that inventory models are important decision-making aids. While often using an EOQ policy, the manager has never considered a backorder model because of the assumption that backorders were "bad" and should be avoided. However, with upper management's continued pressure for cost reduction, you have been asked to analyze the economics of a backordering policy for some products that can possibly be backordered. For a specific product with $D = 800$ units per year, $C_o = \$150$, $C_h = \$3$, and $C_b = \$20$, what is the difference in total annual cost between the EOQ model and the planned shortage or backorder model? If the manager adds constraints that no more than 25% of the units can be backordered and that no customer will have to wait more than 15 days for an order, should the backorder inventory policy be adopted? Assume 250 working days per year.

18. If the lead time for new orders is 20 days for the inventory system discussed in Problem 17, find the reorder point for both the EOQ and the backorder models.

19. The A&M Hobby Shop carries a line of radio-controlled model racing cars. Demand for the cars is assumed to be constant at a rate of 40 cars per month. The cars cost \$60 each, and ordering costs are approximately \$15 per order, regardless of the order size. The annual holding cost rate is 20%.

    a. Determine the economic order quantity and total annual cost under the assumption that no backorders are permitted.

    b. Using a \$45 per unit per year backorder cost, determine the minimum-cost inventory policy and total annual cost for the model racing cars.

    c. What is the maximum number of days a customer would have to wait for a backorder under the policy in part (b)? Assume that the Hobby Shop is open for business 300 days per year.

    d. Would you recommend a no-backorder or a backorder inventory policy for this product? Explain.

    e. If the lead time is 6 days, what is the reorder point for both the no-backorder and backorder inventory policies?

20. Assume that the following quantity discount schedule is appropriate. If annual demand is 120 units, ordering costs are \$20 per order, and the annual holding cost rate is 25%, what order quantity would you recommend?

Order Size	Discount (%)	Unit Cost
0 to 49	0	\$30.00
50 to 99	5	28.50
100 or more	10	27.00

SELF TEST

21. Apply the EOQ model to the following quantity discount situation in which $D = 500$ units per year, $C_o = \$40$, and the annual holding cost rate is 20%. What order quantity do you recommend?

Discount Category	Order Size	Discount (%)	Unit Cost
1	0 to 99	0	$10.00
2	100 or more	3	9.70

22. Keith Shoe Stores carries a basic black dress shoe for men that sells at an approximate constant rate of 500 pairs of shoes every 3 months. Keith's current buying policy is to order 500 pairs each time an order is placed. It costs Keith $30 to place an order. The annual holding cost rate is 20%. With the order quantity of 500, Keith obtains the shoes at the lowest possible unit cost of $28 per pair. Other quantity discounts offered by the manufacturer are as follows. What is the minimum-cost order quantity for the shoes? What are the annual savings of your inventory policy over the policy currently being used by Keith?

Order Quantity	Price Per Pair
0–99	$36
100–199	32
200–299	30
300 or more	28

23. In the EOQ model with quantity discounts, we stated that if the Q^* for a price category is larger than necessary to qualify for the category price, the category cannot be optimal. Use the two discount categories in Problem 21 to show that this statement is true. That is, plot the total-cost curves for the two categories and show that if the category 2 minimum cost Q is an acceptable solution, we do not have to consider category 1.

24. The J&B Card Shop sells calendars depicting a different Colonial scene each month. The once-a-year order for each year's calendar arrives in September. From past experience, the September-to-July demand for the calendars can be approximated by a normal probability distribution with $\mu = 500$ and $\sigma = 120$. The calendars cost $1.50 each, and J&B sells them for $3 each.
    a. If J&B throws out all unsold calendars at the end of July (i.e., salvage value is zero), how many calendars should be ordered?
    b. If J&B reduces the calendar price to $1 at the end of July and can sell all surplus calendars at this price, how many calendars should be ordered?

25. The Gilbert Air-Conditioning Company is considering the purchase of a special shipment of portable air conditioners manufactured in Japan. Each unit will cost Gilbert $80, and it will be sold for $125. Gilbert does not want to carry surplus air conditioners over until the following year. Thus, all surplus air conditioners will be sold to a wholesaler for $50 per unit. Assume that the air conditioner demand follows a normal probability distribution with $\mu = 20$ and $\sigma = 8$.
    a. What is the recommended order quantity?
    b. What is the probability that Gilbert will sell all units it orders?

SELF TEST

26. A popular newsstand is attempting to determine how many copies of the local newspaper it should purchase each day. Demand for the newspaper can be approximated by a normal probability distribution with $\mu = 450$ and $\sigma = 100$. The newspaper costs the newsstand 35¢ a copy and sells for 50¢ a copy. The newsstand does not receive any value from surplus papers and thus absorbs a 100% loss on all unsold papers.
    a. How many copies of the newspaper paper should be purchased each day?
    b. What is the probability that the newsstand will have a stockout?

c. The manager of the newsstand is concerned about the newsstand's image if the probability of stockout is high. Customers often purchase other items after coming to the newsstand. Frequent stockouts would cause customers to go to another newsstand. The manager agrees that a 50¢ goodwill cost should be assigned to any stockout. What is the new recommended order quantity and the new probability of a stockout?

27. A perishable dairy product is ordered daily at a particular supermarket. The product, which costs $1.19 per unit, sells for $1.65 per unit. If units are unsold at the end of the day, the supplier takes them back at a rebate of $1 per unit. Assume that daily demand is approximately normally distributed with $\mu = 150$ and $\sigma = 30$.

    a. What is your recommended daily order quantity for the supermarket?

    b. What is the probability that the supermarket will sell all the units it orders?

    c. In problems such as these, why would the supplier offer a rebate as high as $1? For example, why not offer a nominal rebate of, say, 25¢ per unit? What happens to the supermarket order quantity as the rebate is reduced?

28. A retail outlet sells a seasonal product for $10 per unit. The cost of the product is $8 per unit. All units not sold during the regular season are sold for half the retail price in an end-of-season clearance sale. Assume that demand for the product is uniformly distributed between 200 and 800.

    a. What is the recommended order quantity?

    b. What is the probability that at least some customers will ask to purchase the product after the outlet is sold out? That is, what is the probability of a stockout using your order quantity in part (a)?

    c. To keep customers happy and returning to the store later, the owner feels that stockouts should be avoided if at all possible. What is your recommended order quantity if the owner is willing to tolerate a 0.15 probability of a stockout?

    d. Using your answer to part (c), what is the goodwill cost you are assigning to a stockout?

SELF TEST

29. Floyd Distributors, Inc., provides a variety of auto parts to small local garages. Floyd purchases parts from manufacturers according to the EOQ model and then ships the parts from a regional warehouse direct to its customers. For a particular type of muffler, Floyd's EOQ analysis recommends orders with $Q^* = 25$ to satisfy an annual demand of 200 mufflers. Floyd's has 250 working days per year, and the lead time averages 15 days.

    a. What is the reorder point if Floyd assumes a constant demand rate?

    b. Suppose that an analysis of Floyd's muffler demand shows that the lead-time demand follows a normal probability distribution with $\mu = 12$ and $\sigma = 2.5$. If Floyd's management can tolerate one stockout per year, what is the revised reorder point?

    c. What is the safety stock for part (b)? If $C_h = \$5$/unit/year, what is the extra cost due to the uncertainty of demand?

30. For Floyd Distributors in Problem 29, we were given $Q^* = 25$, $D = 200$, $C_h = \$5$, and a normal lead-time demand distribution with $\mu = 12$ and $\sigma = 2.5$.

    a. What is Floyd's reorder point if the firm is willing to tolerate two stockouts during the year?

    b. What is Floyd's reorder point if the firm wants to restrict the probability of a stockout on any one cycle to at most 1%?

    c. What are the safety stock levels and the annual safety stock costs for the reorder points found in parts (a) and (b)?

31. A product with an annual demand of 1000 units has $C_o = \$25.50$ and $C_h = \$8$. The demand exhibits some variability such that the lead-time demand follows a normal probability distribution with $\mu = 25$ and $\sigma = 5$.

    a. What is the recommended order quantity?

    b. What are the reorder point and safety stock if the firm desires at most a 2% probability of stockout on any given order cycle?

    c. If a manager sets the reorder point at 30, what is the probability of a stockout on any given order cycle? How many times would you expect to stockout during the year if this reorder point were used?

32. The B&S Novelty and Craft Shop in Bennington, Vermont, sells a variety of quality handmade items to tourists. B&S will sell 300 hand-carved miniature replicas of a Colonial soldier each year, but the demand pattern during the year is uncertain. The replicas sell for $20 each, and B&S uses a 15% annual inventory holding cost rate. Ordering costs are $5 per order, and demand during the lead time follows a normal probability distribution with $\mu = 15$ and $\sigma = 6$.
    a. What is the recommended order quantity?
    b. If B&S is willing to accept a stockout roughly twice a year, what reorder point would you recommend? What is the probability that B&S will have a stockout in any one order cycle?
    c. What are the safety stock and annual safety stock costs for this product?

SELF TEST

33. A firm uses a 1-week periodic review inventory system. A 2-day lead time is needed for any order, and the firm is willing to tolerate an average of one stockout per year.
    a. Using the firm's service guideline, what is the probability of a stockout associated with each replenishment decision?
    b. What is the replenishment level if demand during the review period plus lead-time period is normally distributed with a mean of 60 units and a standard deviation of 12 units?
    c. What is the replenishment level if demand during the review period plus lead-time period is uniformly distributed between 35 and 85 units?

34. Foster Drugs, Inc., handles a variety of health and beauty aid products. A particular hair conditioner product costs Foster Drugs $2.95 per unit. The annual holding cost rate is 20%. An order-quantity, reorder-point inventory model recommends an order quantity of 300 units per order.
    a. Lead time is one week and the lead-time demand is normally distributed with a mean of 150 units and a standard deviation of 40 units. What is the reorder point if the firm is willing to tolerate a 1% chance of stockout on any one cycle?
    b. What safety stock and annual safety stock cost are associated with your recommendation in part (a)?
    c. The order-quantity, reorder-point model requires a continuous-review system. Management is considering making a transition to a periodic-review system in an attempt to coordinate ordering for many of its products. The demand during the proposed two-week review period and the one-week lead-time period is normally distributed with a mean of 450 units and a standard deviation of 70 units. What is the recommended replenishment level for this periodic-review system if the firm is willing to tolerate the same 1% chance of stockout associated with any replenishment decision?
    d. What safety stock and annual safety stock cost are associated with your recommendation in part (c)?
    e. Compare your answers to parts (b) and (d). The company is seriously considering the periodic-review system. Would you support this decision? Explain.
    f. Would you tend to favor the continuous-review system for more expensive items? For example, assume that the product in the above example sold for $295 per unit. Explain.

35. Statewide Auto Parts uses a 4-week periodic-review system to reorder parts for its inventory stock. A 1-week lead time is required to fill the order. Demand for one particular part during the 5-week replenishment period is normally distributed with a mean of 18 units and a standard deviation of 6 units.
    a. At a particular periodic review, 8 units are in inventory. The parts manager places an order for 16 units. What is the probability that this part will have a stockout before an order that is placed at the next 4-week review period arrives?
    b. Assume that the company is willing to tolerate a 2.5% chance of a stockout associated with a replenishment decision. How many parts should the manager have ordered in part (a)? What is the replenishment level for the 4-week periodic-review system?

36. Rose Office Supplies, Inc., which is open 6 days a week, uses a 2-week periodic review for its store inventory. On alternating Monday mornings, the store manager fills out an order sheet requiring a shipment of various items from the company's warehouse. A particular three-ring notebook sells at an average rate of 16 notebooks per week. The standard deviation in sales is 5

notebooks per week. The lead time for a new shipment is 3 days. The mean lead time demand is 8 notebooks with a standard deviation of 3.5.

a. What is the mean or expected demand during the review period plus the lead-time period?
b. Under the assumption of independent demand from week to week, the variances in demands are additive. Thus, the variance of the demand during the review period plus the lead-time period is equal to the variance of demand during the first week plus the variance of demand during the second week plus the variance of demand during the lead-time period. What is the variance of demand during the review period plus the lead-time period? What is the standard deviation of demand during the review period plus the lead-time period?
c. Assuming that demand has a normal probability distribution, what is the replenishment level that will provide an expected stockout rate of one per year?
d. On Monday, March 22, 18 notebooks remain in inventory at the store. How many notebooks should the store manager order?

Case Problem   A MAKE-OR-BUY ANALYSIS

Managers at Wagner Fabricating Company are reviewing the economic feasibility of manufacturing a part that it currently purchases from a supplier. Forecasted annual demand for the part is 3200 units. Wagner operates 250 days per year.

Wagner's financial analysts have established a cost of capital of 14% for the use of funds for investments within the company. In addition, over the past year $600,000 has been the average investment in the company's inventory. Accounting information shows that a total of $24,000 was spent on taxes and insurance related to the company's inventory. In addition, an estimated $9000 was lost due to inventory shrinkage, which included damaged goods as well as pilferage. A remaining $15,000 was spent on warehouse overhead, including utility expenses for heating and lighting.

An analysis of the purchasing operation shows that approximately 2 hours are required to process and coordinate an order for the part regardless of the quantity ordered. Purchasing salaries average $28 per hour, including employee benefits. In addition, a detailed analysis of 125 orders showed that $2375 was spent on telephone, paper, and postage directly related to the ordering process.

A 1-week lead time is required to obtain the part from the supplier. An analysis of demand during the lead time shows that lead-time demand is approximately normally distributed with a mean of 64 units and a standard deviation of 10 units. Service level guidelines indicate that one stockout per year is acceptable.

Currently, the company has a contract to purchase the part from a supplier at a cost of $18 per unit. However, over the past few months, the company's production capacity has been expanded. As a result, excess capacity is now available in certain production departments, and the company is considering the alternative of producing the parts itself.

Forecasted utilization of equipment shows that production capacity will be available for the part being considered. The production capacity is available at the rate of 1000 units per month, with up to 5 months of production time available. Management believes that with a 2-week lead time, schedules can be arranged so that the part can be produced whenever needed. The demand during the 2-week lead time is approximately normally distributed, with a mean of 128 units and a standard deviation of 20 units. Production costs are expected to be $17 per part.

A concern of management is that setup costs will be significant. The total cost of labor and lost production time is estimated to be $50 per hour, and a full 8-hour shift will be needed to set up the equipment for producing the part.

Managerial Report

Develop a report for management of Wagner Fabricating that will address the question of whether the company should continue to purchase the part from the supplier or begin to produce the part itself. Include the following factors in your report:

1. An analysis of the holding costs, including the appropriate annual holding cost rate.
2. An analysis of ordering costs, including the appropriate cost per order from the supplier.
3. An analysis of setup costs for the production operation.
4. A development of the inventory policy for the following two alternatives:
    a. Ordering a fixed quantity Q from the supplier
    b. Ordering a fixed quantity Q from in-plant production
5. Include the following in the policies of parts 4(a) and 4(b) above.
    a. Optimal quantity $Q*$
    b. Number of order or production runs per year
    c. Cycle time
    d. Reorder point
    e. Amount of safety stock
    f. Expected maximum inventory level
    g. Average inventory level
    h. Annual holding cost
    i. Annual ordering cost
    j. Annual cost of the units purchased or manufactured
    k. Total annual cost of the purchase policy and the total annual cost of the production policy
6. Make a recommendation as to whether the company should purchase or manufacture the part. What is the saving associated with your recommendation as compared with the other alternative?

Appendix 13.1   INVENTORY MODELS WITH SPREADSHEETS

In this appendix we demonstrate the use of spreadsheets to implement the economic order quantity inventory model. The approach demonstrated for the EOQ model can be modified to accommodate the other inventory models presented in this chapter.

Figure 13.16 shows the formula spreadsheet for the R&B Beverage Company EOQ model introduced in Section 13.1. The annual demand, cost per unit, inventory holding cost rate, cost per order, days per year, and lead time in days are placed in spreadsheet cells **B3–B8**. The values shown in color in Figure 13.16 correspond to the Bub Beer data. The economic order quantity, $Q*$, is computed by the formula in cell **B11**. Cell **B12** then uses the economic order quantity from cell **B11** to compute the total annual cost. The formula in cell **B14** assumes implementation of the recommended economic order quantity in cell **B11**. The remaining spreadsheet formulas provide additional information that will help the manager understand the inventory operation and determine the final order quantity to be used. In addition to the breakdown of the total annual cost into annual inventory and annual ordering costs, the results show inventory levels that can be anticipated, the reorder point, the number of orders per year, and the cycle time. The general equations for these aspects of the inventory operation are presented in Section 13.1. The corresponding spreadsheet formulas appear in cells **B16–B24**.

Figure 13.17 is the value spreadsheet for the Bub Beer EOQ problem. The economic order quantity of 1824.28 cases, with a minimum total annual cost of $3,648.56, is shown. The spreadsheet enables the user to view the economic order quantity and then evaluate alternative order quantities. For example, assume that the inventory manager believes that, operationally, an order quantity of 2000 cases would be easier to implement. The analyst simply enters 2000 cases as the requested order quantity in cell **B14**. The spreadsheet will

Figure 13.16   FORMULA SPREADSHEET FOR THE ECONOMIC ORDER QUANTITY MODEL

	A	B
1	ECONOMIC ORDER QUANTITY MODEL	
2		
3	ANNUAL DEMAND	104000
4	COST PER UNIT	8
5	HOLDING COST RATE %	25
6	COST PER ORDER	32
7	DAYS PER YEAR	250
8	LEAD TIME (DAYS)	2
9		
10		
11	MINIMUM COST EOQ	=SQRT(2*B3*B6/(B4*B5/100))
12	TOTAL ANNUAL COST	= (B11/2)*(B4*B5/100)+B3*B6/B11
13		
14	REQUESTED ORDER QUANTITY	=B11
15		
16	ANNUAL INVENTORY COST	= (B14/2)*(B4*B5/100)
17	ANNUAL ORDER COST	= (B3/B14)*B6
18	TOTAL ANNUAL COST	=B16+B17
19		
20	MAXIMUM INVENTORY	=B14
21	AVERAGE INVENTORY	=B20/2
22	REORDER POINT	= (B3/B7)*B8
23	NUMBER ORDERS PER YEAR	=B3/B14
24	CYCLE TIME (DAYS)	=B7/B23
25		
26	ANNUAL COST OVER EOQ	=B18-B12
27	PERCENTAGE	=B26/B12

Figure 13.17	VALUE SPREADSHEET FOR THE ECONOMIC ORDER QUANTITY MODEL

	A	B
1	ECONOMIC ORDER QUANTITY MODEL	
2		
3	ANNUAL DEMAND	104000
4	COST PER UNIT	8
5	HOLDING COST RATE %	25
6	COST PER ORDER	32
7	DAYS PER YEAR	250
8	LEAD TIME (DAYS)	2
9		
10		
11	MINIMUM COST EOQ	1824.28
12	TOTAL ANNUAL COST	$3,648.56
13		
14	REQUESTED ORDER QUANTITY	1824.28
15		
16	ANNUAL INVENTORY COST	$1,824.28
17	ANNUAL ORDER COST	$1,824.28
18	TOTAL ANNUAL COST	$3,648.56
19		
20	MAXIMUM INVENTORY	1824.28
21	AVERAGE INVENTORY	912.14
22	REORDER POINT	832.00
23	NUMBER ORDERS PER YEAR	57.01
24	CYCLE TIME (DAYS)	4.39
25		
26	ANNUAL COST OVER EOQ	$0.00
27	PERCENTAGE	0.00%

then automatically recompute the inventory system characteristics. Figure 13.18 shows the results based on the order quantity of 2000 cases. In particular note that the last two entries on the spreadsheet show that the added cost is only $15.44 per year, or a 0.42% increase. The manager may prefer the 2000-case order quantity with its slight cost increase over the EOQ model's solution.

Finally, as with most other spreadsheet applications, the manager may change or vary one or more of the model's inputs and quickly learn how the changes affect the inventory cost and optimal solution. For example, changing the inventory holding cost and/or ordering cost would show how sensitive the recommended EOQ and total annual cost are to these values.

Figure 13.18 VALUE SPREADSHEET FOR THE ECONOMIC ORDER QUANTITY MODEL WITH A REQUESTED QUANTITY OF 2000 CASES

	A	B
1	ECONOMIC ORDER QUANTITY MODEL	
2		
3	ANNUAL DEMAND	104000
4	COST PER UNIT	8
5	HOLDING COST RATE %	25
6	COST PER ORDER	32
7	DAYS PER YEAR	250
8	LEAD TIME (DAYS)	2
9		
10		
11	MINIMUM COST EOQ	1824.28
12	TOTAL ANNUAL COST	$3,648.56
13		
14	REQUESTED ORDER QUANTITY	2000.00
15		
16	ANNUAL INVENTORY COST	$2,000.00
17	ANNUAL ORDER COST	$1,664.00
18	TOTAL ANNUAL COST	$3,664.00
19		
20	MAXIMUM INVENTORY	2000.00
21	AVERAGE INVENTORY	1000.00
22	REORDER POINT	832.00
23	NUMBER ORDERS PER YEAR	52.00
24	CYCLE TIME (DAYS)	4.81
25		
26	ANNUAL COST OVER EOQ	$15.44
27	PERCENTAGE	0.42%

Appendix 13.2 DEVELOPMENT OF THE OPTIMAL ORDER-QUANTITY (Q) FORMULA FOR THE EOQ MODEL

Given equation (13.4) as the total annual cost for the EOQ model,

$$TC = \frac{1}{2} Q C_h + \frac{D}{Q} C_o \tag{13.4}$$

we can find the order quantity Q that minimizes the total cost by setting the derivative, dTC/dQ, equal to zero and solving for Q^*.

$$\frac{dTC}{dQ} = \frac{1}{2}\, C_h - \frac{D}{Q^2}\, C_o = 0$$

$$\frac{1}{2}\, C_h = \frac{D}{Q^2}\, C_o$$

$$C_h Q^2 = 2DC_o$$

$$Q^2 = \frac{2DC_o}{C_h}$$

Hence,

$$Q^* = \sqrt{\frac{2DC_o}{C_h}} \qquad (13.5)$$

The second derivative is

$$\frac{d^2TC}{dQ^2} = \frac{2D}{Q^3}\, C_o$$

Since the value of the second derivative is greater than zero for D, C_o, and Q greater than zero, Q^* from equation (13.5) is the minimum-cost solution.

Appendix 13.3 DEVELOPMENT OF THE OPTIMAL LOT-SIZE (Q^*) FORMULA FOR THE PRODUCTION LOT-SIZE MODEL

Given equation (13.15) as the total annual cost for the production lot-size model,

$$TC = \frac{1}{2}\left(1 - \frac{D}{P}\right)QC_h + \frac{D}{Q}\, C_o \qquad (13.15)$$

we can find the order quantity Q that minimizes the total cost by setting the derivative, dTC/dQ, equal to zero and solving for Q^*.

$$\frac{dTC}{dQ} = \frac{1}{2}\left(1 - \frac{D}{P}\right)C_h - \frac{D}{Q^2}\, C_o = 0$$

Solving for Q^*, we have

$$\frac{1}{2}\left(1 - \frac{D}{P}\right)C_h = \frac{D}{Q^2}\, C_o$$

$$\left(1 - \frac{D}{P}\right)C_h Q^2 = 2DC_o$$

$$Q^2 = \frac{2DC_o}{(1 - D/P)C_h}$$

Hence,

$$Q^* = \sqrt{\frac{2DC_o}{(1 - D/P)C_h}} \qquad (13.28)$$

The second derivative is

$$\frac{d^2TC}{dQ^2} = \frac{2DC_o}{Q^3}$$

Since the value of the second derivative is greater than zero for D, C_o, and Q greater than zero, Q^* from equation (13.16) is a minimum-cost solution.

..../ /.............

Appendix 13.4   DEVELOPMENT OF THE OPTIMAL ORDER-QUANTITY (Q^*) AND OPTIMAL BACKORDER (S^*) FORMULAS FOR THE PLANNED SHORTAGE MODEL

Given equation (13.25) as the total annual cost for the planned shortage model,

$$TC = \frac{(Q - S)^2}{2Q} C_h + \frac{D}{Q} C_o + \frac{S^2}{2Q} C_b \tag{13.25}$$

we have two inventory decision variables, Q and S. To find the Q and S values that minimize equation (13.25), we must set the two partial derivatives, $\partial TC/\partial Q$ and $\partial TC/\partial S$, equal to zero. First, let us rewrite equation (13.25) as follows:

$$TC = \left(\frac{Q^2 - 2QS + S^2}{2Q}\right)C_h + \frac{D}{Q} C_o + \frac{S^2}{2Q} C_b$$

$$= \frac{Q}{2} C_h - SC_h + \frac{C_h}{2Q}S^2 + \frac{DC_o}{Q} + \frac{C_b}{2Q} S^2$$

$$= \left(\frac{C_h + C_b}{2Q}\right)S^2 - SC_h + \frac{QC_h}{2} + \frac{DC_o}{Q}$$

Then, setting $\partial TC/\partial S = 0$, we obtain

$$\frac{\partial TC}{\partial S} = \left(\frac{C_h + C_b}{Q}\right)S - C_h = 0$$

Solving for S^*, we have

$$\left(\frac{C_h + C_b}{Q}\right)S = C_h$$

Thus

$$S^* = Q\left(\frac{C_h}{C_h + C_b}\right) \tag{13.27}$$

Setting $\partial TC/\partial Q = 0$, we obtain

$$\frac{\partial TC}{\partial Q} = \frac{-(C_h + C_b)S^2}{2Q^2} + \frac{C_h}{2} - \frac{DC_o}{Q^2} = 0$$

Substituting S^* of equation (13.27), we have

$$\frac{\partial TC}{\partial Q} = \frac{-(C_h + C_b)Q^2(C_h)^2/(C_h + C_b)^2}{2Q^2} + \frac{C_h}{2} - \frac{DC_o}{Q^2} = 0$$

We can solve for Q^* as follows:

$$\frac{-C_h^2}{2(C_h + C_b)} + \frac{C_h}{2} = \frac{DC_o}{Q^2}$$

$$\frac{-C_h^2 + C_h(C_h + C_b)}{2(C_h + C_b)} = \frac{DC_o}{Q^2}$$

$$Q^2 = \frac{2(C_h + C_b)DC_o}{C_h C_b}$$

$$Q^2 = \frac{2C_h DC_o}{C_h C_b} + \frac{2C_b DC_o}{C_h C_b}$$

$$Q^2 = \frac{2DC_o}{C_h}\left(\frac{C_h}{C_b} + \frac{C_b}{C_b}\right)$$

Hence

$$Q^* = \sqrt{\frac{2DC_o}{C_h}\left(\frac{C_h + C_b}{C_b}\right)} \qquad (13.26)$$

The second-order conditions will show that equations (13.26) and (13.27) are the minimum-cost solutions.

REVCO, INC.*

TWINSBURG, OHIO

Revco, Inc., is a chain of drugstores with locations in 15 states. The company operates a total of 345 stores that are part of Hook-SupeRx, Inc., which operates more than 1100 stores, primarily in the Midwest and Northeast. As in any retail business, the company's primary functions and concerns revolve around sales growth, profit margins, expense control, and inventory management.

Inventory management is undergoing a rapid transformation from an art to a science. No longer can any retail business expect to operate profitably without a sound inventory management program, and Revco has recognized this. A key consideration for the company is product movement information that in turn determines reorder quantities at both the store and warehouse levels. Seasonal fluctuations and advertising can affect product movement, and their effects must be measured using historical data rather than seat-of-the-pants guesswork.

General inventory management for Revco involves several product categories: basic products carried on an everyday basis, seasonal products carried only during certain times of the year (such as fruitcakes during holidays), and special items bought on an in-and-out basis throughout the year.

By far the most critical inventory issue is the replenishment of basic products. At Revco, as at most retail drug chains, this type of product is ordered under a periodic-review inventory system, with the review period being one week. The weekly review uses electronic ordering equipment that scans an order label affixed to the shelf. Such a label is located on the shelf directly below each item. Among other information on this label is the "order-to quantity." (*Note:* This is the replenishment

level referred to in the periodic-review inventory model of Section 13.7.) The store employee placing the order determines the quantity to order by subtracting the number of units of product on the shelf from the order-to quantity (OTQ). For example, if the OTQ is 6 and two units of product are on the shelf, the quantity ordered would be 4. The OTQ is the key factor in inventory control for basic products.

Several factors are considered in determining individual item OTQs. The most obvious is average weekly demand or movement. Revco uses movement figures from the warehouse to the stores. Suppose, for example, an item averages two units per week per store in warehouse deliveries. Setting the OTQ equal to 2 would not allow for sales fluctuations that exceeded the average of 2. To compensate for this, and to avoid stockouts, Revco sets the OTQ equal to a 3-week demand or movement. Thus, in our example, the OTQ would become 6.

Another factor to consider is whether an item can be ordered in units or cases. In some instances, delivering in anything less than case quantities is not feasible for the warehouse. An example would be candy bars. Stores must order a minimum of one case (36 units), no matter what the movement indicates. Thus, the OTQ is 36 or a multiple of 36 to accommodate the case order restriction. Merchandising esthetics must also be considered when determining an OTQ. If an item has four facings or open positions on the shelf, but the optimum OTQ determined by movement is 3, one space would be without product. This vacancy would create an out-of-stock impression to the customer, and, thus, the OTQ would be increased to at least 4. Seasonal fluctuations in move-

---

*The authors are indebted to Bob Carver of Revco, Inc. for providing this application.

ment must be considered when OTQs are determined. For example, the OTQ for a cough and cold item would be significantly higher in January than it would be in July. Adhesive bandages would be just the opposite, with higher usage in the summer than in the winter.

Revco is in the process of taking advantage of new technological breakthroughs in inventory management. Today, its OTQs are based on average company warehouse movement into the stores. Soon Revco will have a program in place to produce OTQs by item by individual store, based on that store's movement, rather than on the company movement. Once that is in place, Revco will be able to accommodate seasonal fluctuations by individual store as well.

The chain drug industry is well behind other retail industries (most notably the grocery industry) in the ability to capture point-of-sale information with the use of scanning registers. Revco is in the process of installing them, and once they are in place, the company will be able to use actual point-of-sale product information instead of warehouse movement. These scanning registers also have the ability to place an order to the warehouse automatically, based on what is actually sold that week, so the inventory movement management can only continue to improve.

Good inventory management does not occur in a vacuum, but must be interrelated with sales, gross margin, and expense control objectives. Revco is fortunate in that it has had planning software in place for some time. This system allows Revco merchandisers to act out "what if" scenarios relating to OTQs, product costs, retail sales prices, inventory carrying costs, sales, and other factors. As an example, optimum order-to quantities normally result in some percentage of missed sales because of individual item movement fluctuations. On the other hand, increasing the OTQs to maximize sales also increases inventory, decreases inventory turnover, and thus ties up capital that could otherwise be used for building new stores, remodeling existing locations, and so on. By using the new inventory management techniques, Revco can maximize both sales and inventory turnover. Rapidly becoming a necessity rather than a luxury, the use of this technology ensures the maximization of sales, profits, and inventory turnovers that ultimately determine the success or failure of a drug chain.

Questions

1. Does Revco use a continuous-review or a periodic-review inventory system? Why would this system be preferred for a retail business such as Revco?
2. What is the decision rule that Revco uses to provide a safety stock and minimize stockouts?
3. What is Revco doing to obtain information that will help continue to improve inventory management?

14

INVENTORY MANAGEMENT: DEPENDENT DEMAND

The inventory management techniques discussed in the previous chapter are most appropriate for managing **finished goods inventories.** In this chapter we focus on the management of **manufacturing inventories.** They consist of the raw materials, parts, and subassemblies that make up a finished good or product. Manufacturing inventories are converted into finished products, so the amount needed depends on the demand for the finished goods they will become part of. Once the demand for the finished good is known, the demand for the raw materials, parts, and subassemblies that comprise the item can be determined.

Because the demand for manufacturing inventories depends on the demand for the final product, the independent demand models of the preceding chapter should not be used to manage manufacturing inventories. Instead, techniques that apply to dependent demand should be used.

Material requirements planning (MRP) is a technique that can be used to translate a set of period-by-period requirements for finished products into a set of period-by-period requirements for the raw materials, parts, and subassemblies that make up the finished product. One of the goals of MRP is to minimize the investment in manufacturing inventories. Another goal is to ensure that all raw materials, parts, and subassemblies are available when needed and thereby prevent production delays from occurring.

The first book on material requirements planning, written by Joseph Orlicky, was published in 1975. In 1973, while preparing a study guide on material requirements planning for the American Production and Inventory Control Society (APICS), Joseph Orlicky found that the entire MRP literature consisted of only 26 items.

First, we discuss the difference between managing finished goods inventories and manufacturing inventories. Then, we discuss the inputs to an MRP system: the master production schedule, the bill of materials, and inventory records. Next, we show how to use these inputs to determine the net requirements for any component over the planning horizon. Then, we illustrate lot sizing and safety stock issues and the MRP time-phasing calculations that result in a period-by-period production schedule for all items. Finally, we present some issues involved in implementing an MRP system and provide a brief overview of just-in-time operations.

14.1   INDEPENDENT VERSUS DEPENDENT DEMAND

To illustrate the differences between managing finished goods inventories (independent demand) and managing manufacturing inventories (dependent demand), we consider an example involving the Clark Furniture Company. Clark manufactures a variety of Early American furniture at its New Bern, North Carolina, plant. To begin, we consider the factors involved in managing the finished kitchen chair inventory and the inventory of the seats used in the manufacture of these chairs. The seats are purchased from a supplier.

The top panel of Figure 14.1 shows the inventory level for the finished kitchen chairs. When the inventory level drops to the reorder point, R, a production order is issued. A lead time is needed for processing the paperwork and making the setup. Production begins at point A on the time axis. When production of the finished product is initiated, seats are withdrawn from inventory to support manufacturing needs. The inventory level for the seats is shown in the bottom panel of Figure 14.1. Note that it starts decreasing when production of the finished product begins at time A.

If we were using an independent demand inventory model to manage the seat inventory, an order for seats would be placed with the supplier whenever the inventory level falls below its reorder point. Depending on the lead time, the shipment of seats will be received at some time in the future; suppose that this is time B in Figure 14.1. However, the next production run for the chairs is not scheduled to begin until time C, so we have incurred an unnecessary holding cost for the seats that must be carried in inventory between their arrival time at B and use at time C.

We could have eliminated this unnecessary holding cost by delaying ordering the seats so that they will not arrive prior to time C. That is, we could "back up" from time C by the amount of the lead time and place the order then. Figure 14.2 shows the reduction in the seat inventory resulting from such an ordering policy. In Figure 14.2 the order policy takes into account the fact that the demand for the seat depends on the demand for the finished product (kitchen chair).

This simple example demonstrates that, in the management of manufacturing inventories, savings in inventory holding costs can be realized by taking into account the dependent nature of demand. An approach used to manage manufacturing inventories is called *material requirements planning (MRP)*. When implemented correctly, an MRP system can reduce the investment in inventory, improve work flow, reduce shortages of raw materials, parts, and subassemblies, and help achieve more reliable delivery schedules.

Figure 14.1 — FINISHED PRODUCT AND COMPONENT INVENTORY LEVELS USING AN INDEPENDENT DEMAND INVENTORY MODEL

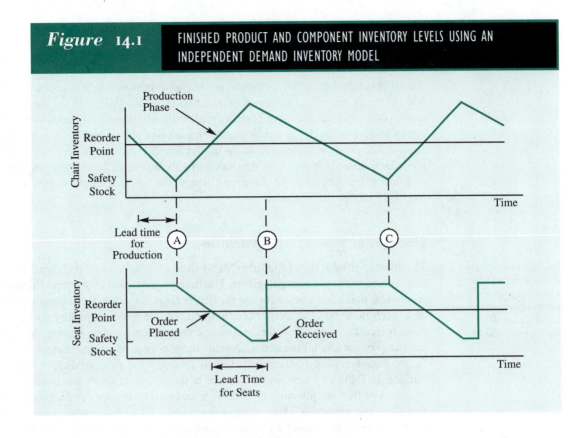

Figure 14.2 — FINISHED PRODUCT AND COMPONENT PART INVENTORY LEVELS WITH A TIME-PHASED ORDER POLICY

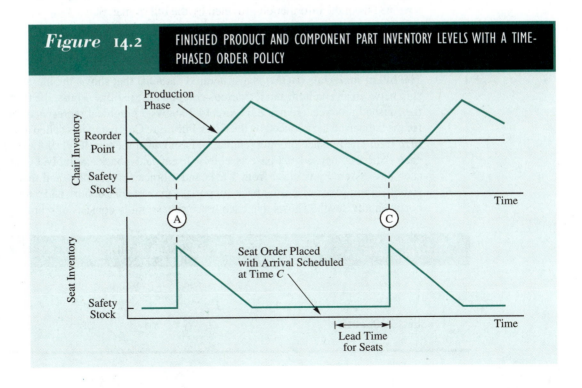

14.2   INPUTS TO MATERIAL REQUIREMENTS PLANNINGS

An MRP system has three key inputs: the master production schedule, the bill of materials, and inventory records. The master production schedule (MPS) shows the demand for finished goods over the planning horizon, which usually is several weeks into the future. The bill of materials (BOM) is a structured parts list that shows how raw materials, parts, and subassemblies are combined to make up the finished product. Finally, an MRP inventory record is prepared for each raw material, part, or subassembly that shows the inventory level and ordering policy over the planning horizon. Each of these inputs must be available before MRP can be implemented.

The Master Production Schedule

The master production
schedule should be a
statement of what can and
will be produced; it should
not represent a
management wish list.

The **master production schedule (MPS)** shows the number of end items needed in each time period of the **planning horizon.** The time periods, also called *time buckets,* may be of any length that makes sense for the particular firm; however, most firms use time buckets of 1 week duration. The master production schedule is developed by taking into account sales forecasts, customer orders, economic production lot sizes, production capacity, and the like. For the Clark Furniture Company the master production schedule would show the future manufacturing requirements for all products the firm produces over the planning horizon. In Table 14.1 we show the portion of the master production schedule for the kitchen chairs; note that the planning horizon is 6 weeks. The master production schedule shows that Clark must produce 700 kitchen chairs in week 1, 0 chairs in week 2, 600 chairs in week 3, and so on. After this schedule has been established, the number of components needed to produce the 700 kitchen chairs in week 1, the 600 chairs in week 3, and so on, can be determined from the information provided by the bill of materials.

The Bill of Materials

The **bill of materials (BOM)** is a structured parts list that shows the hierarchical relationship between an end item and its various components; in other words, the BOM shows how the finished products are made. Figure 14.3 shows a graphical representation of the BOM for the kitchen chair produced by the Clark Furniture Company; it is called a **product structure tree.** The finished product (end item) is shown at the top (level 0). Level 1 shows that each chair is composed of 1 base assembly, 1 seat, and 1 back assembly. Level 2 shows that each base assembly is made from 4 legs and 1 brace subassembly and that each back assembly is composed of 2 outer back supports, 1 upper back support, and 5 middle back supports. Finally, level 3 shows that each brace subassembly consists of 4 braces.

Table 14.1	MASTER PRODUCTION SCHEDULE FOR KITCHEN CHAIRS					
	Week					
	1	2	3	4	5	6
Production Quantity	700		600	600		700

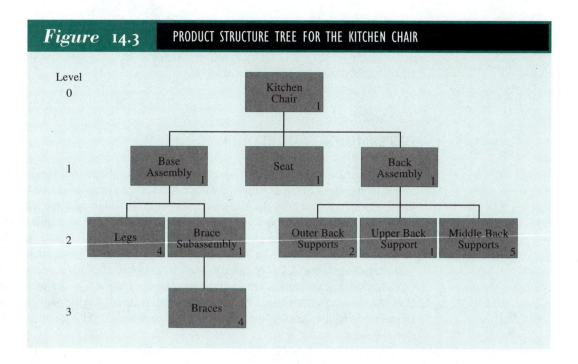

Figure 14.3   PRODUCT STRUCTURE TREE FOR THE KITCHEN CHAIR

The component parts or subassemblies shown at each level are said to be the *parents* of the parts or subassemblies directly below them. Each item in the BOM, except the top item, has a parent.

In general, the product structure tree shows how the final product is assembled from its components. Although in the Clark Furniture example we chose to show only the parts and subassemblies that make up the kitchen chair, any needed raw materials, such as wood or glue, could have been included. In practice, considerable thought must be given to the components that should be included in the BOM, and specialized reference books have been written to help manufacturers carry out this process.

The BOM clearly shows the dependent nature of demand for the components needed to produce the end item. Thus, using the BOM, we can determine exactly how many components are needed to produce the quantity of finished products stated in the master production schedule. For instance, the product structure tree shows that a demand for 700 kitchen chairs in week 1 creates a demand for 700 base assemblies, 700 seats, and 700 back assemblies. The demand for the 700 base assemblies in turn creates a demand for 2800 legs and 700 brace subassemblies. The demand for the 700 brace subassemblies in turn creates a demand for 2800 braces. Similarly, the demand for the 700 back assemblies creates a demand for 1400 outer back supports, 700 upper back supports, and 3500 middle back supports. Before showing how a production schedule is developed for these dependent demand components, we first discuss the concept of an MRP inventory record.

The MRP Inventory Record

Inventory status information such as how many units are in inventory must be maintained for each item in the BOM. In general, the information contained in the **inventory record** for each component can be classified as (1) inventory transaction information or (2) planning information. The inventory transaction information includes inventory events such as the receipt of goods from a supplier, the disbursement of items from inventory to satisfy production, the generation of scrap during manufacturing, and so on. The planning information includes the lead time required to obtain the item, the safety stock (if any), the lot sizing method used for the item, and so on.

14.3   DETERMINING NET REQUIREMENTS

To illustrate how an MRP system can be used to manage inventories for dependent demand items, let us return to the example involving the kitchen chairs produced by the Clark Furniture Company, and consider the seat component. In Table 14.1 we showed the master production schedule for the next 6-week planning period, and in Figure 14.3 we showed the BOM (as a product structure tree) for the kitchen chair. Suppose that the inventory record for the seat shows a balance of 300 seats in inventory, a lead time of 1 week, a lot size of 800 seats, and a safety stock of 0 units. Suppose also that a previous order of 800 units has been scheduled to arrive at the beginning of week 1 of the current planning period. We must now determine how many seats will be needed at the beginning of each week to meet the requirements of the master production schedule. This quantity is referred to as **net requirements.**

A primary function of material requirements planning is to convert gross requirements into net requirements. Once the net requirements are established, shop orders and purchase orders can be issued to cover the net requirements.

To compute net requirements, we use a worksheet referred to as the *MRP planning worksheet*. First, recall that the master production schedule provides **gross requirements** for each week. The gross requirements are the number of kitchen chairs needed to satisfy the MPS without taking into account the number of kitchen chairs currently in inventory. The BOM shows that one seat is needed for each kitchen chair we produce, so the gross requirements for the seats are the same as the gross requirements for the finished product. Table 14.2 shows the initial MRP planning worksheet for the kitchen seats, which contains the gross requirements data and the information from the inventory record for the seats.

To determine the net requirements in week 1, we first note that 800 seats are scheduled to arrive in week 1 **(scheduled receipts).** As is customary with MRP, we assume that these units arrive at the beginning of week 1. Thus, since there are 300 seats currently in inventory **(projected balance)** at the beginning of week 1, the number of seats available for use in this period is $800 + 300 = 1100$. As the gross requirements are 700 seats, the net requirements in period 1 are 0. We now enter 400 as the projected ending inventory balance for week 1 and 0 for the net requirements. The gross requirements are 0 in period 2, so the projected balance of 400 in week 1 is carried over to week 2. Table 14.3 shows the revised worksheet.

Table 14.2	MRP PLANNING WORKSHEET							
SEAT **Lot size: 800**	**Lead time: 1 wk** **Safety stock: 0**		**1**	**2**	**Week** **3**	**4**	**5**	**6**
Gross requirements			700	0	600	600	0	700
Scheduled receipts			800					
Projected balance		300						
Net requirements								
Planned order receipts								
Planned order releases								

Table 14.3	MRP PLANNING WORKSHEET AT WEEK 2							
SEAT Lot size: 800	**Lead time: 1 wk** Safety stock: 0		**1**	**2**	**Week** **3**	**4**	**5**	**6**
Gross requirements			700	0	600	600	0	700
Scheduled receipts			800					
Projected balance		300	400	400				
Net requirements			0					
Planned order receipts								
Planned order releases								

Looking forward to week 3, however, we see that the projected balance of 400 sets at the end of week 2 is insufficient to satisfy the gross requirements of 600 seats in week 3. Therefore, with a lead time of 1 week to obtain a seat from the supplier, we must release an order at the beginning of week 2 to provide sufficient inventory in week 3. Since this order is placed during the current planning period, we refer to its placement at the beginning of week 2 as a **planned order release,** and its arrival at the beginning of week 3 as a **planned order receipt.** Now, we are ready to determine the net requirements for week 3. With a projected balance for week 2 of 400 units and a planned order receipt of 800 units (the lot size) at the beginning of week 3, the number of seats available in week 3 is 1200. Since the gross requirements are 600, the projected balance at the end of week 3 is 600. Moreover, as we had a beginning balance of 400 seats, only 200 units of the planned order receipts are actually needed to cover the gross requirements for the period; thus, we refer to the 200 seats as the net requirements for week 3. The worksheet now appears as shown in Table 14.4.

We continue this process for week 4. With a projected balance at the end of week 3 of 600 and gross requirements in week 4 of 600, we have a projected balance of 0 at the end of week 4 and a net requirement of 0 in week 4. In week 5 the gross requirement is 0, and thus we have a projected balance, and a net requirement of 0. In week 6, however, the gross requirements are 700, so an order for 800 units is released in week 5. Table 14.5 shows the resulting MRP planning worksheet.

The MRP worksheet shows that, for an initial inventory of 300 seats and an order quantity (lot size) of 800 seats, we will need to release orders for 800 seats at the beginning of

Table 14.4	MRP PLANNING WORKSHEET AT WEEK 3							
SEAT Lot size: 800	**Lead time: 1 wk** Safety stock: 0		**1**	**2**	**Week** **3**	**4**	**5**	**6**
Gross requirements			700	0	600	600	0	700
Scheduled receipts			800					
Projected balance		300	400	400	600			
Net requirements			0	0	200			
Planned order receipts					800			
Planned order releases				800				

Table 14.5	FINAL MRP PLANNING WORKSHEET						

SEAT **Lot size: 800**	**Lead time: 1 wk** **Safety stock: 0**	**Week**					
		1	**2**	**3**	**4**	**5**	**6**
Gross requirements		700	0	600	600	0	700
Scheduled receipts		800					
Projected balance	300	400	400	600	0	0	100
Net requirements		0	0	200	0	0	700
Planned order receipts				800			800
Planned order releases			800			800	

weeks 2 and 5 to ensure that the required number of seats will be available each week. Before continuing our discussion of how MRP can be used to manage dependent demand inventories, let us briefly review some of the major concepts illustrated in this example.

1. The gross requirements indicate the number of components needed at the *beginning of each week* to meet the requirements stated in the MPS; the gross requirements do not take into account any beginning inventory or scheduled receipts.
2. Scheduled receipts, such as the 800 units in week 1, are items that were ordered prior to the beginning of the current planning horizon (weeks 1–6 in our example); these items are assumed to arrive at the *beginning of the week.*
3. The initial projected balance of 300 is the number of units available at the beginning of the current planning horizon. In weeks 1–6, the projected balance is the number of units that are available at the *end of the week.*
4. The net requirements tell us, once any scheduled receipts and/or projected balances have been accounted for, how many units are needed at the *beginning of each week.* A positive value for net requirements initiates a planned order release.
5. Planned order releases represent orders placed during the current planning horizon. Planned order receipts represent orders received as the result of planned order releases. Planned order releases and planned order receipts are assumed to occur at the *beginning of each week.*

You should now be able to complete an MRP worksheet. Try Problem 1.

N O T E S *and Comments*

A master production schedule usually consists of a combination of forecasts of customer orders and booked customer orders. Because forecasts are often wrong, the resulting incorrect entries in the master production schedule can lead to disastrous results. Obtaining accurate forecasts and establishing a system to deal with the inherent problems associated with forecasting (such as revising the MRP when forecasts are revised) is one of the biggest challenges facing manufacturers.

14.4   LOT SIZING AND SAFETY STOCK

To develop a production schedule using the MRP approach, we must know the lot size, the production or purchase lead time, and the amount of safety stock necessary for each component. Two commonly employed lot sizing rules are the *fixed order size* and the *lot-for-lot* rules. The **fixed order-size rule** calls for each order to be for the same number of items such as an economic order quantity. In the preceding section we used a fixed order-size rule in managing the kitchen chair seat inventory. Recall that each time a planned order release occurred, an order was placed for 800 seats; the MRP worksheet shown in Table 14.5 contains the results of using the fixed order size rule to manage the seat inventory. Orders will be placed at the beginning of weeks 2 and 5.

The fixed order-size rule is appropriate for purchased components when such a lot size is necessary to take advantage of quantity discounts or when an economic order quantity rule (see Chapter 13) is being used. The fixed order-size rule also is appropriate for manufactured items when batches must be of a certain size because of machine or equipment capacities.

Another commonly employed method for lot sizing is called the **lot-for-lot rule.** When this rule is used, the lot size equals the net requirement in the period the lot will become available. Table 14.6 shows a completed MRP worksheet for the seats based on the lot-for-lot rule.

The lot-sizing rule doesn't affect the gross requirements, so the first row of Table 14.6 is the same as the first row of Table 14.5. In Table 14.6 we assumed that the lot-for-lot rule also had been used in the prior planning horizon and that the projected balance at the beginning of the current planning horizon is 0. Note that the scheduled receipts in week 1, 700, are just enough to cover the gross requirements in week 1; thus, the projected balance at the end of week 1 is 0. Indeed, there is no projected balance (ending inventory) at the end of any week because all lot sizes are just large enough to cover gross requirements. The planned order releases in the last row indicate that the amount of each planned order release is the same as the gross requirements in the next period. Except for week 1, the gross requirements are equal to the net requirements.

In theory, when the lot-for-lot rule is used, the projected balance at the end of each week is 0, and the planned order release for each week equals the gross requirements in the next week. In practice, however, this situation often is not the case. For instance, suppose that, in the week prior to week 1 of the current planning horizon, the gross requirements for kitchen chairs turned out to be 100 units fewer than forecast in the master production schedule. In this case, the gross requirements for seats for that week would have been overstated by 100 units; thus, the projected balance at the beginning of the current planning horizon would be 100 and not 0. Table 14.7 shows the MRP worksheet based on the lot-for-lot rule with a projected balance of 100 seats at the beginning of the planning horizon. Note that in

Table 14.6 — MRP PLANNING WORKSHEET BASED ON THE LOT-FOR-LOT RULE

SEAT Lot-for-Lot	Lead time: 1 wk Safety stock: 0	1	2	3	4	5	6
Gross requirements		700	0	600	600	0	700
Scheduled receipts		700					
Projected balance	0	0	0	0	0	0	0
Net requirements		0	0	600	600	0	700
Planned order receipts				600	600		700
Planned order releases			600	600		700	

Table 14.7	MRP PLANNING WORKSHEET BASED ON THE LOT-FOR-LOT RULE WITH A BEGINNING PROJECTED BALANCE OF 100 SEATS

SEAT Lot-for-Lot	Lead time: 1 wk Safety stock: 0		1	2	3	4	5	6
Gross requirements			700	0	600	600	0	700
Scheduled receipts			700					
Projected balance		100	100	100	0	0	0	0
Net requirements			0	0	500	600	0	700
Planned order receipts					500	600		700
Planned order releases				500	600		700	

this case the projected balance isn't 0 each week. The planned order release for week 2 is not equal to the gross requirement for week 3; instead, the planned order release for week 2 is equal to the *net requirement* in week 3.

Try Problem 3 for practice in completing an MRP worksheet using the lot-for-lot rule.

The lot-for-lot rule is designed to minimize inventory investment. Orders are released in the smallest amount necessary to prevent shortages. As we pointed out previously, in theory, the lot-for-lot rule leads to a projected balance of zero at the end of each week in the planning horizon. However, we also demonstrated that projected balances of greater than 0 can occur in situations where the gross requirements have been overstated in any period.

A more serious situation can occur with the lot-for-lot rule if defective parts are discovered, materials are damaged, or other problems are encountered. In such cases, if there is no safety stock, the lot-for-lot rule will lead to stockouts that may result in production stoppages. Another potential difficulty with the lot-for-lot rule is that it may result in lot sizes that are too small to be economically justified. In these cases the usual procedure is to modify the lot-for-lot rule by establishing a minimum lot size.

Safety stock can buffer the production system against unexpected events such as uncertainty about gross requirements, uncertainty about lead times, defective parts produced in-house or purchased from suppliers, pilferage, and so on. As noted in the preceding chapter, safety stock increases inventory holding cost; as a result, no more safety stock than necessary should be used.

To illustrate how the use of safety stock for an item affects the development of the MRP worksheet, suppose that a safety stock of 20 units is utilized for the kitchen chair seat example in conjunction with a lot-for-lot order sizing rule. Table 14.8 shows how the safety stock affects the MRP worksheet; note that we assumed that in the prior planning horizon the lot-for-lot rule also had been used with a safety stock of 20 units. The projected balance of 20 seats, which represents the safety stock, remains at that level for the rest of the planning horizon. The safety stock of 20 units is available to buffer the production process against unexpected occurrences that would affect the inventory level. The cost of protecting the production process is the additional holding cost of the 20 units.

Try Problem 7 for practice in completing an MRP worksheet with safety stock.

The determination of the appropriate amount of safety stock to carry (if any) involves weighing the trade-off between inventory holding costs and production downtime. The determination of the best lot-sizing rule involves a trade-off between inventory holding cost and setup cost; larger lot sizes increase holding cost but decrease setup cost. More advanced books and research articles on manufacturing planning provide procedures for balancing these costs in determining optimal lot sizes and safety stocks.

Table 14.8	MRP PLANNING WORKSHEET BASED ON THE LOT-FOR-LOT RULE WITH A SAFETY STOCK OF 20 UNITS						
SEAT **Lot-for-Lot**	**Lead time: I wk** **Safety stock: 20**	**Week**					
		I	**2**	**3**	**4**	**5**	**6**
Gross requirements		700	0	600	600	0	700
Scheduled receipts		700					
Projected balance	20	20	20	20	20	20	20
Net requirements		0	0	600	600	0	700
Planned order receipts				600	600		700
Planned order releases			600	600		700	

14.5 MRP AND A TIME-PHASED PRODUCTION SCHEDULE

A schematic diagram of an MRP system is shown in Figure 14.4. As noted earlier, customer orders and forecasts are used to develop the master production schedule. The MPS, BOM, and current inventory files are the inputs needed to begin the MRP computations. The outputs from the MRP system are the net requirements for each item in the BOM, along with the dates each item is needed. This information is used to plan order releases for production and purchasing.

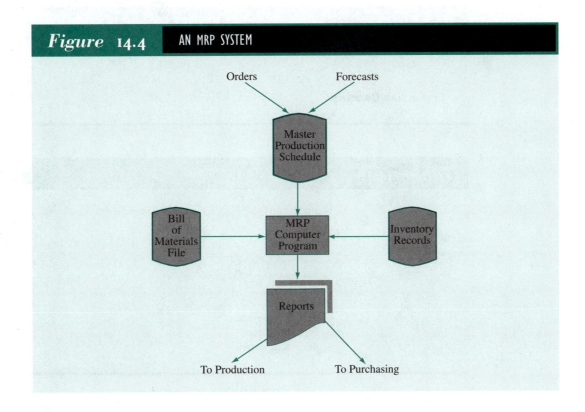

Figure 14.4 AN MRP SYSTEM

In this section we show how the MRP system uses the inputs in Figure 14.4 to develop a time-phased production schedule. To illustrate how MRP can result in the right component being available at exactly the right time, we develop the MRP worksheets for each item in the BOM for the kitchen chair produced by the Clark Furniture Company. To differentiate the computations in this section from those in the previous sections of this chapter, suppose that the current planning horizon corresponds to weeks 19–24. Table 14.9 shows the MPS for this planning horizon.

Suppose that the time required to assemble the three level-1 components (the base assembly, the seat, and the back assembly) into a finished chair is 1 week. Since the MPS calls for the final assembly of 400 chairs during week 19, 400 base assemblies, 400 seats, and 400 back assemblies must be available at the beginning of week 19. To determine when each of the remaining components must be available to meet the requirements of 400 chairs during week 19, we need to know the lead times associated with each of the components used to produce the kitchen chair. Table 14.10 shows this information, which would be contained in the inventory record for each item.

Using the lead times in Table 14.10, we can determine when production of each component must take place to permit the final assembly of 400 kitchen chairs during week 19. Figure 14.5 shows the result of these calculations: the time-phased requirement for each component. Figure 14.5 was developed by backscheduling from the time each item is required by the amount of its lead time.

The focus of an MRP system is on timing.

Figure 14.5 shows that to complete the final assembly of the kitchen chairs in week 19, production of the braces must start at the beginning of week 14. Thus, a 1-week lead time will ensure that the braces will be available at the beginning of week 15 so that production may begin on the brace subassembly. Note that with the 2-week lead time for the brace sub-

| Table 14.9 | MASTER PRODUCTION SCHEDULE FOR KITCHEN CHAIRS FOR WEEKS 19–24 |

	Week					
	19	20	21	22	23	24
Production Quantity	400	750	600	100	850	700

| Table 14.10 | LEAD TIMES FOR COMPONENTS OF KITCHEN CHAIR |

Component	Lead Time (weeks)
Base Assembly	2
Legs	1
Brace Subassembly	2
Braces	1
Seat	1
Back Assembly	3
Outer Back Supports	1
Upper Back Support	1
Middle Back Supports	1

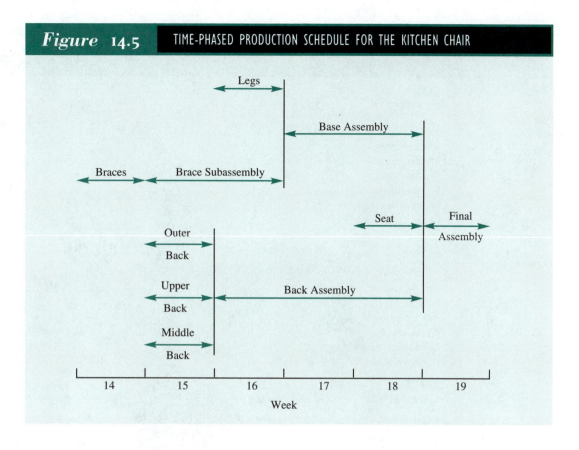

Figure 14.5   TIME-PHASED PRODUCTION SCHEDULE FOR THE KITCHEN CHAIR

assembly, the brace subassembly will be available for use in the base assembly at the beginning of week 17. The legs, which also are needed to produce the base assembly, have a 1-week lead time. Therefore, production of the legs must start at the beginning of week 16 so that they will be available at the beginning of week 17. An order is released to begin production of the base assembly at the beginning of week 17; with a 2-week lead time the base assemblies will be available for use in the final assembly during week 19.

The MPS calls for the final assembly of 400 chairs during week 19. The time-phased requirements shown in Figure 14.5 indicate that, to meet such a schedule, production of the components must begin sooner. Indeed, production of the braces must begin 5 weeks before the chairs are to be assembled. However, we still have not determined how many units of each component must be produced in each week. Thus, we now need to develop the MRP worksheets for each of the components to determine the net requirements for each item.

Table 14.11 shows the MRP planning worksheets needed to perform the time-phased calculations for each component. Note that there is one MRP worksheet for each part or subassembly shown in the bill of materials. The information shown in Table 14.11 was developed by backscheduling from the time each item is required by the amount of its lead time. In performing the calculations we assumed that the beginning inventory of each component is 0, lot sizes are determined by the lot-for-lot method, and there are no scheduled receipts.

We begin by looking at the MRP worksheets corresponding to the base assembly, the seat, and the back assembly. As we previously stated, to produce 400 chairs in week 19, we must have 400 base assemblies, 400 seats, and 400 back assemblies available at the beginning of week 19. Since each kitchen chair consists of 1 base assembly, 1 seat, and 1 back

Table 14.11	MRP WORKSHEETS SHOWING TIME-PHASED MATERIAL REQUIREMENTS TO SUPPORT PRODUCTION OF 400 CHAIRS IN WEEK 19

BASE ASSEMBLY

Lead time: 2 wks

Week

Lot-for-Lot — Safety stock: 0

		14	15	16	17	18	19
Gross requirements							400
Scheduled receipts							
Projected balance	0					0	
Net requirements							400
Planned order receipts							400
Planned order releases						(400)	

4 legs required

LEGS

Lead time: 1 wk

Week

Lot-for-Lot — Safety stock: 0

		14	15	16	17	18	19
Gross requirements					(1600)		
Scheduled receipts							
Projected balance	0				0		
Net requirements					1600		
Planned order receipts					1600		
Planned order releases				1600			

BRACE SUBASSEMBLY

Lead time: 2 wks

Week

Lot-for-Lot — Safety stock: 0

		14	15	16	17	18	19
Gross requirements					(400)		
Scheduled receipts							
Projected balance	0				0		
Net requirements					400		
Planned order receipts					400		
Planned order releases			(400)				

4 braces required

BRACES

Lead time: 1 wk

Week

Lot-for-Lot — Safety stock: 0

		14	15	16	17	18	19
Gross requirements			(1600)				
Scheduled receipts							
Projected balance	0	0					
Net requirements			1600				
Planned order receipts			1600				
Planned order releases		1600					

SEAT

Lead time: 1 wk

Week

Lot-for-Lot — Safety stock: 0

		14	15	16	17	18	19
Gross requirements							400
Scheduled receipts							
Projected balance	0					0	
Net requirements							400
Planned order receipts							400
Planned order releases						400	

Inventory Management: Dependent Demand

Table 14.11 (CONTINUED)

BACK ASSEMBLY

Lot-for-Lot	Lead time: 3 wks Safety stock: 0	14	15	Week 16	17	18	19
Gross requirements							400
Scheduled receipts							
Projected balance		0				0	
Net requirements							400
Planned order receipts							400
Planned order releases				(400)			

2 outer back supports required

OUTER BACK SUPPORT

Lot-for-Lot	Lead time: 1 wk Safety stock: 0	14	15	Week 16	17	18	19
Gross requirements				(800)			
Scheduled receipts							
Projected balance		0	0				
Net requirements				800			
Planned order receipts				800			
Planned order releases			800				

1 upper back support required

UPPER BACK SUPPORT

Lot-for-Lot	Lead time: 1 wk Safety stock: 0	14	15	Week 16	17	18	19
Gross requirements				(400)			
Scheduled receipts							
Projected balance		0	0				
Net requirements				400			
Planned order receipts				400			
Planned order releases			400				

5 middle back supports required

MIDDLE BACK

Lot-for-Lot	Lead time: 1 wk Safety stock: 0	14	15	Week 16	17	18	19
Gross requirements				(2000)			
Scheduled receipts							
Projected balance		0	0				
Net requirements				2000			
Planned order receipts				2000			
Planned order releases			2000				

assembly, the gross requirements for these components in week 19 are also 400. Since there are no units in inventory and no scheduled receipts, the net requirements are also 400.

Table 14.10 indicates that the lead time for the base assembly is 2 weeks. Thus, to satisfy the net requirement of 400 base assemblies at the beginning of week 19, an order for 400 base assemblies must be released at the beginning of week 17. Note that this planned order release shows up in week 19 as a planned order receipt. Recall that each base assembly consists of 4 legs and 1 brace subassembly; hence, at the beginning of week 17 we must have available $4(400) = 1600$ legs and $1(400) = 400$ brace subassemblies. The 1600 legs and the 400 brace subassemblies are entered as the gross requirements in week 17 for these two components. The legs have a lead time of 1 week, so we show a planned order release of 1600 legs at the beginning of week 16. Note that these 1600 legs also show up as a planned order receipt of 1600 at the beginning of week 17. The net requirements also are 1600 because no units were in inventory and there are no scheduled receipts.

The lead time for the brace subassembly is 2 weeks. Thus, to have 400 brace subassemblies available at the beginning of week 17, we must release an order for 400 brace subassemblies at the beginning of week 15. This planned order release then shows up as a planned order receipt of 400 units at the beginning of week 17.

Backtracking one step further, we see that each brace subassembly consists of 4 braces; thus, we will need to have available $4(400) = 1600$ braces at the beginning of week 15. The lead time for the braces is 1 week, so we will need to release an order for 1600 braces at the beginning of week 14. This planned order release shows up as planned order receipts of 1600 units in week 15.

Recall that the seat has no components below it in the product structure tree (Figure 14.3), so it doesn't generate requirements for any other items. Looking at the back assembly, the final level-1 component, we see that it has a lead time of 3 weeks and that an order for 400 back assemblies must be released at the beginning of week 16 to ensure that 400 units are available at the beginning of week 19. Each back assembly consists of 2 outer back supports, 1 upper back support, and 5 middle back supports, giving gross requirements in week 16 of $2(400) = 800$ outer back supports, $1(400) = 400$ upper back supports, and $5(400) = 2000$ middle back supports. These gross requirements lead to planned order releases of 800, 400, and 2000 units in week 15, and show up as planned order receipts in week 16.

The process of generating net requirements for components from the MPS for an end item is called a **BOM explosion.** Note also that the use of lead times to backschedule planned order releases allows the MRP system to generate a production schedule for all the items in the BOM.

When the projected balance for an item is not 0, as we assumed in our example, the gross requirements for each item are still computed as multiples of the planned order releases for its parent item. But, in these cases the net requirements will be less than the gross requirements by the amount of the projected balance at the end of the previous period and any scheduled receipts. In this case, the planned order receipts will be the same as the net requirements for the item.

When there are safety stock requirements for some, or possibly all, items, the planned order receipts must be adjusted by the amount of the safety stock requirements. That is, planned order sizes should be just large enough to leave a projected balance equal to the amount of safety stock required after the gross requirements have been satisfied.

In Table 14.12 we show part of the BOM explosion for the kitchen chair when there is a projected balance of 50 units in week 18 for the base assembly and a fixed lot size of 450. Table 14.12 also shows that the projected balance is 100 braces in week 14 and that there is a safety stock requirement of 500 braces. In this revised example we show MRP worksheets only for the base assembly and its descendant items.

Table 14.12	A PORTION OF THE MRP WORKSHEETS SHOWING TIME-PHASED MATERIAL REQUIREMENTS TO SUPPORT PRODUCTION OF 400 CHAIRS IN WEEK 19 (SHOWS EFFECT OF INVENTORIES, FIXED LOT SIZE, AND SAFETY STOCK)

BASE ASSEMBLY
Lot size: 450

	Lead time: 2 wks			Week			
	Safety stock: 0	14	15	16	17	18	19
Gross requirements							400
Scheduled receipts							
Projected balance						50	100
Net requirements							350
Planned order receipts							450
Planned order releases					450		

LEGS
Lot-for-Lot

	Lead time: 1 wk			Week			
	Safety stock: 0	14	15	16	17	18	19
Gross requirements					1800		
Scheduled receipts							
Projected balance				0			
Net requirements					1800		
Planned order receipts					1800		
Planned order releases				1800			

BRACE SUBASSEMBLY
Lot-for-Lot

	Lead time: 2 wks			Week			
	Safety stock: 0	14	15	16	17	18	19
Gross requirements					450		
Scheduled receipts							
Projected balance				0			
Net requirements					450		
Planned order receipts					450		
Planned order releases				450			

BRACES
Lot-for-Lot

	Lead time: 1 wk			Week			
	Safety stock: 500	14	15	16	17	18	19
Gross requirements			1800				
Scheduled receipts							
Projected balance		100	100	500			
Net requirements			1700				
Planned order receipts			2200				
Planned order releases		2200					

We look first at the MRP worksheet for the base assembly. The projected balance of 50 units at the beginning of week 18 means that there will be 50 base assemblies in inventory at the beginning of week 19. Thus, only 350 units are needed to satisfy the gross requirements of 400 base assemblies in week 19; hence, the net requirements for week 19 are 350. But, with a fixed lot size of 450 units, we must plan for an order release of 450 units at the beginning of week 17 and the receipt of those units at the beginning of week 19. Thus, the projected balance for the base assembly at the end of week 19 is 100.

As in Table 14.11, the planned order releases at one level of the BOM generates the gross requirements (the appropriate multiplier must be used) for the next level down. Thus, we have gross requirements for 1800 legs and 450 brace subassemblies in week 17. The planned order releases of 450 for the brace subassembly in week 15, in turn, generates gross requirements for 1800 braces in week 15.

Let us now look more closely at the MRP inventory record for the braces to see how the safety stock affects the situation. The gross requirements for 1800 braces could be satisfied by the projected beginning balance of 100 braces plus a lot of 1700 braces. But, such a lot size would cause the inventory level to be reduced to zero and thus the safety stock requirement of 500 would be violated. Therefore, a lot size of 2200 units must be scheduled; planned order releases of 2200 units are shown in week 14. When this lot is received at the beginning of week 15, the gross requirements can be satisfied with a safety stock of 500 units.

In this section we have shown how the MRP system links the production plans for all the items in a bill of materials for an end item (final product). The value of an MRP system should now be apparent. It ensures that materials are available when they are needed for production but not before. Thus, inventory investment is minimized and the flow of materials is smoothed.

Try Problem 10 for practice in developing a time-phased production schedule.

14.6   IMPLEMENTING AN MRP SYSTEM

Large amounts of data and records must be stored and processed during implementation of an MRP system. As a result, most MRP systems require a fairly sophisticated computer information system. Referring to Figure 14.4, we see that an MRP system must obtain information from the MPS, the BOM file, and the inventory records. The system prepares a variety of reports for production and purchasing and updates MRP inventory records. In other words, successful implementation of an MRP system depends on accurate records.

Inaccuracies in MPS, BOM, and/or inventory records will lead to inaccuracies in the output of the MRP system. Inaccuracies in these system inputs can wreak havoc with MRP because the dependent nature of component requirements can amplify any errors throughout the system. Such errors can result in the failure to order materials when needed and/or in the right amounts, can cause production shutdowns because of a lack of raw materials, parts, or subassemblies, and can lead to many other scheduling problems.

Accurate data and timely updating of records are essential to the proper functioning of an MRP system. When engineering makes a change in product design, the BOM must be updated. When changes are made in the MPS because of forecast errors or changes in customer orders, these updates must be entered in the MRP system. Finally, changes often are necessary in the inventory records because of damage to parts, the need to use some parts in quality control testing, and the like. Needless to say, any changes in MPS, BOM, or inventory records must be communicated to the MRP system as soon as possible.

Updating MRP Records

Until now, we have been concerned only with using MRP to develop period-by-period net requirements for components in response to the master production schedule needs of an end item. However, conditions change rapidly and the MRP system must be capable of responding to changes in forecasts, lead times, product design, and so on. We must be able to update MRP records in a timely fashion to adapt to such changes. Essentially, there are two issues to consider: How frequently should the records be updated and which records need to be updated.

Two approaches are used to update MRP records: regeneration and net change. In the **regeneration approach** the records for all items are updated periodically. For instance, we might choose to update completely all the records in the MRP system each week with current information. Thus, we would extend the MPS 1 week into the future, update BOM and inventory records to incorporate any changes, and then completely recalculate net requirements.

In the **net change approach,** the MRP system recalculates net requirements whenever changes make it necessary; however, only the records affected by the new or revised information are updated. Both approaches to updating records are used and are effective; in practice, the regeneration approach is used more often. The key differences between the approaches involve the frequency of updating and the cost of updating. Because more records are updated each time, the regeneration approach is more costly. But, the net change approach requires more frequent processing.

Capacity Requirements Planning

MRP generates a time-phased production schedule for all items in the BOM but doesn't take into account capacity limitations. The planned order releases may call for more production at a work center than labor or machine resources available. In such cases, the MPS may have to be modified, earlier production of an item may have to be scheduled, or overtime may have to be scheduled. But, if the MRP system calls for underutilization of a critical work center during one period, it may be necessary to modify the schedule to increase utilization of the work center.

Capacity requirements planning is the process of determining the time-phased labor and machine resources necessary to meet the MPS. The integration of capacity requirements with the MRP leads to what is often called a *closed-loop MRP system.* The MRP process has also been extended to encompass the financial plans necessary to support production and provide resources. Moreover, in some companies, MRP now has the capability to provide "what-if" analysis of companywide operations. This company-wide view of MRP is called **manufacturing resource planning (MRP II).**

The Q.M. in Action: Integrating Process Planning with MRP describes how process planning has been integrated with an MRP system to move a company closer to complete computer-integrated manufacturing.

N O T E S
and Comments

1. Inventory systems can be designed to determine what can be produced with a given capacity *or* to determine what must be produced to meet a given master production schedule. An MRP system is designed to the latter requirement.

2. The first continuous net change material requirements planning system was designed and installed in 1961 for the J. I. Case Tractor Company under the direction of Joseph Orlicky. The computer system used was an IBM 305 RAMAC with 15 million characters of disk file capacity. The development of the computer software for this system took a team of programmers 10 months and expended approximately 6 person-years in the programming effort.

Q.M. IN ACTION

INTEGRATING PROCESS PLANNING WITH MRP*

Computer-aided process planning (CAPP) was integrated with an existing MRP system at one of Turkey's largest manufacturers of domestic appliances, Arcelik A.S. The company installed a computerized MRP system in 1984 and later added the CAPP system. Process planning involves determining the operations necessary to manufacture a component, their sequence, the necessary machining and tooling, setup times, and material requirements. The CAPP system obviously needed to be integrated with the company's MRP system. A benefit of implementing the CAPP system was use of the information content of the process plans to improve the accuracy of the MRP system.

Arcelik has developed several application programs to make use of the integrated CAPP/MRP database. The integration of process planning and

MRP provides the foundation for a real-time, work-in-process tracking system and is viewed by the company as a major step toward complete computer-integrated manufacturing. The computer-aided process planning system has replaced manual systems completely at two Istanbul plants. The authors believe that the manufacturing database resulting from the CAPP and MRP systems provides the information base the company needs to apply quantitative methods to production planning and control.

*Based on Ulusoy, G., and R. Uzsoy, "Computer-Aided Process Planning and Material Requirements Planning: First Steps towards Computer-Integrated Manufacturing." *Interfaces*, March–April 1992, pp. 76–86.

14.7   JUST-IN-TIME

Just-in-time (JIT) is a philosophy of operations management that focuses on eliminating waste. The JIT approach strives for zero inventory, zero employee nonproductive time, zero defects, and so on. We provide a brief overview of some of the goals and objectives of JIT in this section, emphasizing the impact of JIT on inventory.

Inventory can be viewed as expensive waste because it represents idle resources and incurs a holding cost. Ideally, inventory would not be needed in a manufacturing system. Each part should be made available at the right time and at the right place; that is, "just in time" to be used. That would mean no inventory holding cost and small production lot sizes. Recall, however, that the optimal production lot size involves a trade-off between setup cost and inventory holding cost. Larger setup costs lead to larger lot sizes and more inventory. Thus, just-in-time systems strive to reduce setup time and cost so that production lot sizes may be smaller and production runs more frequent. A goal of JIT is continuous production at just the rate the product, or part, is being used (i.e., sold or used in downstream production).

With a just-in-time system, a defective part can halt production. Because no inventory is available, workers cannot discard a defective part and use another. Thus, just-in-time systems automatically focus workers' attention on minimizing defects and, when one is found, correcting it immediately. Each worker must be acutely aware of the quality of the product being produced and know how to correct defects.

One of the consequences of a JIT system is an integrated manufacturing process. With no, or small, inventories to provide a buffer between successive workstations, a production process must be integrated. A common approach to providing this integration is the *pull system of production*. With the pull system, items are not produced at an upstream workstation until they are needed by the downstream workstation using them. No manufacturing is done just to keep workers busy. With a push system, a workstation would produce parts according to its own schedule and "push" them on to the next station when finished, leading to a buildup of system inventories.

Q.M. IN ACTION

ECUADOR'S COMMUNITY HEALTH WORKERS USE JIT*

Just-in-time approaches are as valid in service industries as they are in manufacturing industries. A key JIT issue for the Ecuadorian Ministry of Public Health (MOH) was the economical and efficient distribution of medical supplies to the country's community health workers so that sufficient supplies were available at the right place at the right time. Community health workers provide primary health care to most of the nation's population; each worker is responsible for one or several communities.

Community health workers obtain medical supplies from MOH or mission pharmacies, private pharmacies, and other outlets. Various problems (e.g., availability of supplies, cost, and travel to the supply facility) made keeping adequate supplies in the hands of the workers difficult. With the objective of providing same-day replenishment at low cost, the

MOH decided to assign workers to decentralized facilities (centers and subcenters) for supply replenishment. The MOH used quantitative methods to determine the optimal number of facilities and assign workers to them. The approach ultimately chosen involved trade-offs between supply site operational costs and transportation costs for community health workers. Interestingly, transportation costs were not always proportional to distance because the mode of transportation varied from airplanes to buses to canoes to foot travel through dense jungle.

*Based on Smith, H. L., K. R. Mangelsdorf, J. C. Luna, and R. A. Reid, "Supplying Ecuador's Health Workers Just in Time." *Interfaces*, May–June, 1989, pp. 1–12.

The implementation of JIT systems has led to shorter cycle times and reductions in inventory cost, labor cost, space requirements, and material costs. Achieving these improvements requires a tightly integrated production system and the wholehearted involvement of both blue-collar and white-collar employees. JIT approaches also are being applied successfully in service industries. The Q.M. in Action: Ecuador's Community Health Workers use JIT describes how JIT principles have improved the health care delivery system in Ecuador.

SUMMARY

We began this chapter with a discussion of the differences involved in managing independent and dependent demand inventory systems. Dependent demand systems are common with manufactured goods; the key is that once the demand for the end item is known, the demand for each of its components is also known. We noted that the inventory models of Chapter 13 were inappropriate for managing manufacturing inventories. Material requirements planning (MRP) is the approach used by many companies to manage manufacturing inventories.

The objective of MRP is to have the right components available at the right time in order to minimize inventory holding costs and to ensure a smooth flow of materials. The three key inputs to the MRP system are the master production schedule (MPS), the bill of materials (BOM), and inventory records. The MPS shows the production schedule for end items, the BOM shows the product structure of the end item, and the inventory records contain information such as how many units of each item are in inventory at the beginning of the planning period. The MRP system takes into account item lead times, lot sizes, and components and develops a time-phased production schedule for each item in the BOM. We noted that two approaches to updating the MRP are used in practice: regeneration and net change.

Planned order releases, an output of the MRP system, can be used to compute the labor and machine capacities required to implement the MRP. In this sense, MRP facilitates capacity requirements planning. If sufficient capacity isn't available to implement the MRP, management must find ways to either expand capacity or modify the schedule.

With an increasing emphasis on lowering costs and improving productivity, the continued use of quantitative models for optimal inventory decisions, as well as the development of new methods of inventory management, can be expected. A development that evolved from the Japanese approach to material management and control is just-in-time (JIT). JIT is based on the goal of producing or delivering parts and materials only when and where they are needed. The JIT approach results in less inventory investment, reduces scrap, provides higher quality, and in general improves productivity. Although a full discussion of JIT is beyond the scope of this text, further information can be found in a variety of texts dealing with modern techniques of production and operations management.

MRP and JIT can be thought of as two sides of the same coin. MRP addresses the need for good planning and JIT addresses the need for good execution.

GLOSSARY

Manufacturing inventories Consist of the raw materials, parts, and subassemblies that make up a finished good or product.

Material requirements planning (MRP) A technique that is used to translate a set of period-by-period requirements for finished products (end items) into a set of period-by-period requirements for the raw materials, parts, and subassemblies that make up the finished products.

Dependent demand Demand for a component is dependent on demand for the product it is used in.

Planning horizon The number of periods into the future for which plans are developed.

Master production schedule (MPS) The schedule showing how many units of the finished product are to be produced for each period in the planning horizon.

Bill of materials (BOM) A structured parts list that shows the hierarchical relationship between an end item and its various components; the BOM shows how the finished product is made from each of its components.

Product structure tree A graphical representation of the bill of materials.

Inventory record A record containing information on the availability of each item in the bill of materials.

Net requirements The quantity that must be ordered or produced in a period; net requirements take into account the projected balance and any scheduled receipts.

Gross requirements The total number of units of an item that are needed in a period, excluding any projected balance or scheduled receipts.

Projected balance The amount of inventory available at the end of a period that can be used to satisfy gross requirements in future periods.

Scheduled receipts Items that were ordered prior to the current planning horizon. Scheduled receipts are assumed to be available at the beginning of the period in which they arrive.

Planned order release An order placed during the current planning horizon. Planned order releases are assumed to be placed at the beginning of the period.

Planned order receipt An item expected to be received at some period in the future as a result of planned order releases. Planned order receipts are assumed to arrive at the beginning of the period.

Lot size The number of units in an order. If the item is to be manufactured, it is the production lot size; if the item is purchased, it is the order quantity.

Fixed order-size rule A rule stating that the lot size must be the same each time an order is placed.

Lot-for-lot rule A rule for computing lot sizes. The lot size varies from order to order; it is chosen just large enough to satisfy the net requirements, taking into account the lead time and any required safety stock.

BOM explosion The process of translating the end item requirements into requirements for its components.

Regeneration approach An approach to updating the materials requirement plan at fixed intervals of time. All records are updated at once.

Net change approach An approach to updating the materials requirement plan whenever changes make it necessary. Only those records affected by the changes are updated.

Capacity requirements planning The process of determining time-phased labor and machine resources necessary to meet the MPS.

Manufacturing resource planning (MRP II) A broader view of MRP that encompasses companywide operations.

Just-in-time (JIT) An approach to operations management that focuses on minimizing waste. Its goals include zero inventories and zero defects.

PROBLEMS

SELF TEST

1. Table 14.13 contains a partially completed MRP worksheet for a wheel subassembly.
    a. Complete the worksheet by showing the appropriate entries in the remaining cells. (It is not necessary to show zero entries.)
    b. Suppose that the beginning projected balance is 180 (instead of 80). Complete the worksheet.
    c. Suppose that the beginning projected balance is 80 and that the lot size is 500. Complete the worksheet.

2. Refer to the partially completed worksheet for a wheel subassembly in Table 14.13.
    a. Complete the worksheet for a lead time of 1 week (instead of 2 weeks).
    b. Complete the worksheet for a lead time of 3 weeks.
    c. What effect, if any, do the different lead times have on the inventory level?

Table 14.13	PARTIAL MRP WORKSHEET FOR WHEEL SUBASSEMBLY							
WHEEL SUBASSEMBLY	**Lead time: 2 wks**				**Week**			
Lot size 400	**Safety stock: 0**	1	2	3	4	5	6	
Gross requirements			250		300		260	
Scheduled receipts			400					
Projected balance		80						
Net requirements								
Planned order receipts								
Planned order releases								

SELF TEST

3. Refer to the partially completed worksheet for a wheel subassembly in Table 14.13.
   a. Complete the worksheet using the lot-for-lot rule instead of a fixed lot size of 400.
   b. Suppose that the beginning projected balance is 180 (instead of 80). Complete the worksheet using the lot-for-lot rule.

4. One component used in manufacturing a dresser is a drawer subassembly. Table 14.14 contains a partially completed MRP worksheet for the drawer subassembly.
   a. Complete the worksheet by showing the appropriate entries in the remaining cells. (It is not necessary to show zero entries.)
   b. Suppose that the beginning projected balance is 120 (instead of 0). Complete the worksheet.
   c. Suppose that the beginning projected balance is 0, as in part (a). Change the lot size to 800 and complete the entries in the MRP worksheet.
   d. Would you expect the inventory holding cost to be higher using a lot size of 500 or a lot size of 800? Under what conditions would the lot size of 800 be preferable?

5. Refer to Table 14.14, which shows the partially completed MRP worksheet for a drawer subassembly. Complete the worksheet for a lead time of 2 weeks.

6. Refer to Table 14.14, which shows the partially completed MRP worksheet for a drawer subassembly.
   a. Complete the worksheet using the lot-for-lot rule for choosing a lot size.
   b. Suppose that the beginning projected balance is 120 (instead of 0). Complete the MRP worksheet using the lot-for-lot rule.
   c. What is the relationship between net requirements and planned order releases when the lot-for-lot rule is used?
   d. In Problem 4(b), a fixed lot size of 500 was used; in Problem 6(c) the lot-for-lot rule was used. In both cases the beginning projected balance, the gross requirements, and the scheduled receipts were the same. Which lot sizing rule results in the lower inventory holding cost?

SELF TEST

7. Refer to Table 14.14, which shows the partially completed MRP worksheet for a drawer subassembly.
   a. Complete the worksheet for a safety stock of 30. What effect does the safety stock have on inventory holding cost?
   b. Suppose that the beginning projected balance is 120 (instead of 0). Complete the worksheet using a safety stock of 100. What effect does the safety stock have on the inventory holding cost?

8. One component of a stapler is the base subassembly. A partially completed MRP worksheet for the base subassembly is shown in Table 14.15.
   a. Complete the worksheet by showing the appropriate entries in the remaining cells. Use a fixed lot size of 400.
   b. Complete the worksheet using the lot-for-lot rule.

Table 14.14	PARTIAL MRP WORKSHEET FOR DRAWER SUBASSEMBLY							

DRAWER SUBASSEMBLY Lot size 500	Lead time: 1 wk Safety stock: 0			Week				
		1	2	3	4	5	6	
Gross requirements		450		300	250		500	
Scheduled receipts		500						
Projected balance	0							
Net requirements								
Planned order receipts								
Planned order releases								

BASE SUBASSEMBLY	Lead time: I wk Safety stock: 0	Week					
		1	2	3	4	5	6
Gross requirements		200	250	200	200	150	200
Scheduled receipts		150					
Projected balance	150						
Net requirements							
Planned order receipts							
Planned order releases							

Table 14.15 — PARTIALLY COMPLETED MRP WORKSHEET FOR STAPLER BASE SUBASSEMBLY

   c. Compare the effect of the lot sizing rules in parts (a) and (b) on inventory holding cost. What are the conditions under which each rule would be preferable?

9. Refer to Table 14.15, which shows the partially completed MRP worksheet for the stapler base subassembly.

   a. Complete the worksheet for a safety stock of 100 and a fixed lot size of 400.

   b. Complete the worksheet for a safety stock of 100 and the lot-for-lot rule.

   c. What effect does safety stock have on inventory holding cost? Why would the company consider using safety stock?

SELF TEST

10. Figure 14.6 shows the product structure tree for an end item referred to as product E. A partially completed MRP worksheet for component B is shown in Table 14.16.

   a. Complete the worksheet for component B for weeks 21–26.

   b. Part D has a projected balance of 50 at the end of week 19 and a lead time of 1 week. Show the MRP worksheet for this part for weeks 20–23 using the lot-for-lot rule and no safety stock.

11. The product structure tree for product F is shown in Figure 14.7. A partially completed worksheet for subassembly E is shown in Table 14.17.

   a. Complete the MRP worksheet for subassembly E.

   b. Prepare an MRP worksheet for part B for weeks 11–15. Use a lead time of 2 weeks and a lot size of 400. The beginning projected balance is 400 and there are no scheduled receipts.

Figure 14.6 — PRODUCT STRUCTURE TREE FOR PRODUCT E

Table 14.16   PARTIALLY COMPLETED MRP WORKSHEET FOR PART B

PART B Lot size: 500	Lead time: 3 wks Safety stock: 0	Week					
		21	22	23	24	25	26
Gross requirements			450		600		400
Scheduled receipts			500				
Projected balance		150					
Net requirements							
Planned order receipts							
Planned order releases							

Figure 14.7   PRODUCT STRUCTURE TREE FOR PRODUCT F

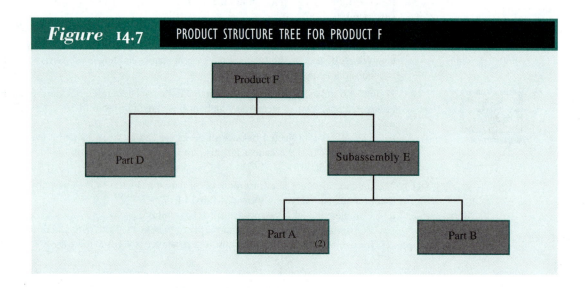

Table 14.17   PARTIALLY COMPLETED MRP WORKSHEET FOR SUBASSEMBLY E

SUBASSEMBLY E Lot size: 300	Lead time: 1 wk Safety stock: 0	Week					
		11	12	13	14	15	16
Gross requirements			250	200	280	250	230
Scheduled receipts		200					
Projected balance		80					
Net requirements							
Planned order receipts							
Planned order releases							

    c.   Prepare an MRP worksheet for part A for weeks 11–15. The beginning projected balance is 500, and the lead time is 1 week. Use the lot-for-lot rule. Note that 2 units of A are needed for each unit of E.

12.   The Spiecker Company manufactures a 14-inch snowblower. Figure 14.8 shows the product structure tree. The master production schedule for the snowblower results in a gross requirement of 1250 for the engine assembly during week 20. Lead times (in weeks) for the engine assembly and its components are

Component	Lead time
Engine assembly	4
Air cleaner subassembly	1
Filter housing	2

The inventory on hand of the engine assembly at the beginning of week 20 is 450. Assume that no inventory is on hand for the air cleaner subassembly and the filter housing.

    a.   Compute the net requirement for the engine assembly in week 20.

    b.   When must the order be released for the air cleaner subassemblies? How many air cleaner subassemblies must be ordered using the lot-for-lot rule?

    c.   When must the order be released for the filter housings? How many filter housings must be ordered using the lot-for-lot rule?

13.   Refer to Figure 14.8, the product structure tree for the 14-inch snowblower. Gross requirements for the wheel assembly during week 22 are 800. The projected balance at the end of week 21 is

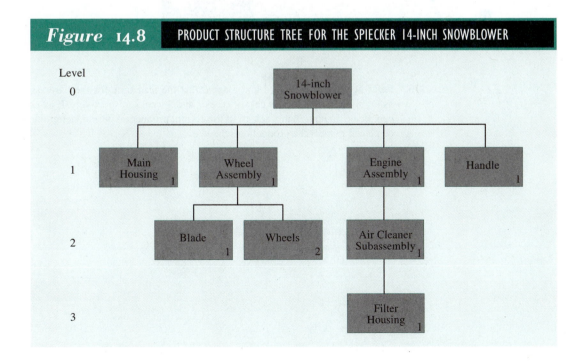

***Figure* 14.8**   PRODUCT STRUCTURE TREE FOR THE SPIECKER 14-INCH SNOWBLOWER

450. Lead times are 2 weeks for the wheel assembly, 2 weeks for the blade, and 1 week for the wheels. The lot-for-lot rule is being used for all three items.

    a.   When must the order be released for the wheel assemblies needed? How many wheel assemblies must be ordered?

    b.   When must the order be released for the wheels? How many wheels must be ordered? Assume that none are in inventory.

    c.   When must the order be released for the blade? How many blades must be ordered? Assume that there is a projected balance of 200 when the net requirements are computed.

14. C & D Lawn Products manufactures a rotary spreader for applying fertilizer. The following is a portion of the product structure tree. If 3000 lawn spreaders are needed to satisfy a customer's order, determine the net requirements for the base assembly, wheel subassembly, and tires (sets of 2). Assume that 1000 base assemblies, 1500 wheel subassemblies, and 800 tires are currently in inventory.

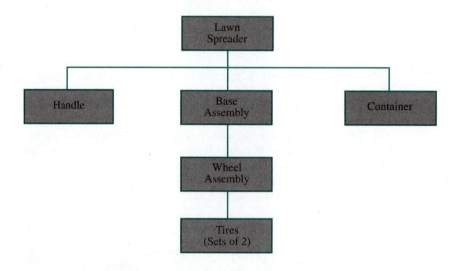

15. Refer again to Problem 14 and assume that the lead time for the base assembly, wheel subassembly, and tires are 2 weeks, 4 weeks, and 5 weeks, respectively. If all components must be completed no later than week 15 of the current production period, determine when orders must be placed to meet the production schedule.

15

WAITING LINE MODELS

Recall the last time that you had to wait at a supermarket checkout counter, for a teller at your local bank, or to be served at a fast-food restaurant. In these and many other waiting line situations, the time spent waiting is undesirable. Adding more checkout clerks, bank tellers, or servers is not always the most economical strategy for improving service, so businesses need to determine ways to keep waiting times within tolerable limits.

Models have been developed to help managers understand and make better decisions concerning the operation of waiting lines. In quantitative methods terminology, a waiting line is also known as a **queue,** and the body of knowledge dealing with waiting lines is known as **queuing theory.** In the early 1900s A. K. Erlang, a Danish telephone engineer, began a study of the congestion and waiting times occurring in the completion of telephone calls. Since then, queuing theory has grown far more sophisticated and has been applied to a wide variety of waiting line situations.

Waiting line models consist of mathematical formulas and relationships that can be used to determine the **operating characteristics** (performance measures) for a waiting line. Some of the operating characteristics of interest are

1. the probability that no units are in the system,
2. the average number of units in the waiting line,
3. the average number of units in the system (the number of units in the waiting line plus the number of units being served),
4. the average time a unit spends in the waiting line,
5. the average time a unit spends in the system (the waiting time plus the service time), and
6. the probability that an arriving unit has to wait for service.

Managers who have such information are better able to make decisions that balance desirable service levels against the cost of providing the service.

15.1   THE STRUCTURE OF A WAITING LINE SYSTEM

The study of waiting lines is referred to as **queuing theory.** The word *queuing* comes from the use of the word **queue,** which refers to a line of people waiting for service.

To illustrate the basic features of a waiting line model, we consider the waiting line at the Burger Dome fast-food restaurant. Burger Dome sells hamburgers, cheeseburgers, french fries, soft drinks, and milk shakes, as well as a limited number of specialty items and dessert selections. Although Burger Dome would like to serve each customer immediately, at times more customers arrive than can be handled by the Burger Dome food-service staff. Thus, customers wait in line to place and receive their orders.

Burger Dome is concerned that the methods they are currently using to serve customers are resulting in excessive waiting times. Management has asked that a waiting line study be performed to help determine the best approach to reducing waiting times and improving service.

The Single-Channel Waiting Line

In the current Burger Dome operation, a server takes a customer's order, determines the total cost of the order, takes the money from the customer, and then fills the order. Once the first customer's order is filled, the server takes the order of the next customer waiting for service. This operation is an example of a **single-channel waiting line.** By this, we mean that each customer entering the Burger Dome restaurant must pass through the *one* channel—one order-taking and order-filling station—to place an order, pay the bill, and receive the food. When more customers arrive than can be served immediately, they form a waiting line and wait for the order-taking and order-filling station to become available. A diagram of the Burger Dome single-channel waiting line is shown in Figure 15.1.

The Distribution of Arrivals

Defining the arrival process for a waiting line involves determining the probability distribution for the number of arrivals in a given period of time. For many waiting line situations, the arrivals occur *randomly and independently* of other arrivals, and we cannot predict when an arrival will occur. In such cases, quantitative analysts have found that the **Poisson probability distribution** provides a good description of the arrival pattern.

The Poisson probability function[1] defines the probability of x arrivals in a specific time period as

$$P(x) = \frac{\lambda^x e^{-\lambda}}{x!} \quad \text{for } x = 0, 1, 2, \ldots \tag{15.1}$$

where

x = the number of arrivals in the time period

λ = the average or mean number of arrivals per time period

e = 2.71828

---

1. The term $x!$, *x factorial,* is defined as $x! = x(x-1)(x-2)\ldots(2)(1)$. For example, $4! = (4)(3)(2)(1) = 24$. For the special case of $x = 0$, $0! = 1$ by definition.

| Figure 15.1 | THE BURGER DOME SINGLE-CHANNEL WAITING LINE |

Values of $e^{-\lambda}$ can be found by using a calculator or by using Appendix D.

Suppose that Burger Dome has analyzed data on customer arrivals and has concluded that the mean arrival rate is 45 customers per hour. For a 1-minute period, the mean number of arrivals would be $\lambda = 45/60 = 0.75$ arrivals per minute. Thus, we can use the following Poisson probability function to compute the probability of x arrivals during a 1-minute period:

$$P(x) = \frac{\lambda^x e^{-\lambda}}{x!} = \frac{0.75^x e^{-0.75}}{x!} \tag{15.2}$$

Thus, the probabilities of 0, 1, and 2 arrivals during a 1-minute period are

$$P(0) = \frac{(0.75)^0 e^{-0.75}}{0!} = e^{-0.75} = 0.4724$$

$$P(1) = \frac{(0.75)^1 e^{-0.75}}{1!} = 0.75e^{-0.75} = 0.75(0.4724) = 0.3543$$

$$P(2) = \frac{(0.75)^2 e^{-0.75}}{2!} = \frac{(0.75)^2 e^{-0.75}}{2!} = \frac{(0.5625)(0.4724)}{2} = 0.1329$$

The probability of no arrivals in a 1-minute period is 0.4724, the probability of 1 arrival in a 1-minute period is 0.3543, and the probability of 2 arrivals in a 1-minute period is 0.1329. Table 15.1 shows the Poisson probability distribution of arrivals during a 1-minute period.

The waiting line models presented in Sections 15.2 and 15.3 use the Poisson probability distribution to describe the customer arrivals at Burger Dome. In practice, you should record the actual number of arrivals per time period for several days or weeks and compare the frequency distribution of the observed number of arrivals to the Poisson probability distribution to determine whether the Poisson probability distribution provides a reasonable approximation of the arrival distribution.

The Distribution of Service Times

The service time is the time a customer spends at the service facility once the service has started. At Burger Dome, the service time starts when a customer begins to place the order with the food server and continues until the customer has received the order. Service times

Table 15.1	POISSON PROBABILITIES FOR THE NUMBER OF ARRIVALS AT A BURGER DOME RESTAURANT DURING A 1-MINUTE PERIOD ($\lambda = 0.75$)

Number of Arrivals	Probability
0	0.4724
1	0.3543
2	0.1329
3	0.0332
4	0.0062
5 or more	0.0010

are rarely constant. At Burger Dome, the number of items ordered and the mix of items ordered vary considerably from one customer to the next. Small orders can be handled in a matter of seconds, but larger orders may require more than 2 minutes to process.

Quantitative analysts have found that, if service times can be assumed to have an **exponential probability distribution,** formulas are available for providing useful information about the operation of the waiting line. If the probability distribution for the service times follows an exponential probability distribution, the probability that the service time will be less than or equal to a time of length t is

$$P(\text{service time} \leq t) = 1 - e^{-\mu t} \tag{15.3}$$

where

μ = the average or mean number of units that can be served per time period

A property of the exponential probability distribution is that there is a 0.6321 probability that the random variable takes on a value less than the mean. In waiting line applications, the exponential probability distribution indicates that approximately 63% of the service times are less than the mean service time and approximately 37% of the service times are greater than the mean service time.

Suppose that Burger Dome has studied the order-taking and order-filling process and has found that the single food server can process an average of 60 customer orders per hour. On a 1-minute basis, the average or mean service rate would be $\mu = 60/60 = 1$ customer per minute. For example, with $\mu = 1$, we can use equation (15.3) to compute probabilities such as the probability an order can be processed in ½ minute or less, 1 minute or less, and 2 minutes or less. These computations are

$$P(\text{service time} \leq 0.5 \text{ min.}) = 1 - e^{-1(0.5)} = 1 - 0.6065 = 0.3935$$
$$P(\text{service time} \leq 1.0 \text{ min.}) = 1 - e^{-1(1.0)} = 1 - 0.3679 = 0.6321$$
$$P(\text{service time} \leq 2.0 \text{ min.}) = 1 - e^{-1(2.0)} = 1 - 0.1353 = 0.8647$$

Thus, we would conclude that there is a 0.3935 probability that an order can be processed in ½ minute or less, a 0.6321 probability that it can be processed in 1 minute or less, and a 0.8647 probability that it can be processed in 2 minutes or less.

In several of the waiting line models presented in this chapter, we assume that the probability distributions for the service times follow an exponential probability distribution. In practice, you should collect data on actual service times to see whether the exponential probability distribution is a reasonable approximation of the service times for your application.

Queue Discipline

In describing a waiting line system, we must define the manner in which the waiting units are arranged for service. For the Burger Dome waiting line, and in general for most customer-oriented waiting lines, the units waiting for service are arranged on a **first-come, first-served** basis; this approach is referred to as an **FCFS** queue discipline. However, some situations call for different queue disciplines. For example, when people wait for an elevator, the last one on the elevator is usually the first one to complete service (i.e., the first to leave the elevator). Other types of queue disciplines assign priorities to the waiting units and then serve the unit with the highest priority first. In this chapter we consider only waiting lines based on a first-come, first-served queue discipline.

Steady-State Operation

When the Burger Dome restaurant opens in the morning, no customers are in the restaurant. Gradually, activity builds up to a normal or steady state. The beginning or start-up period is referred to as the **transient period.** The transient period ends when the system reaches the normal or **steady-state operation.** Waiting line models describe the steady-state operating characteristics of the waiting line.

15.2 THE SINGLE-CHANNEL WAITING LINE MODEL WITH POISSON ARRIVALS AND EXPONENTIAL SERVICE TIMES

In this section we present formulas that can be used to determine the steady-state operating characteristics for a single-channel waiting line. The formulas should be used only if the following assumptions are reasonable.

Waiting line models are often based on assumptions such as Poisson arrivals and exponential service times. When applying any waiting line model, data should be collected on the actual system to ensure that the assumptions of the model are reasonable.

1. The waiting line has a single channel.
2. The arrivals follow a Poisson probability distribution.
3. The service times follow an exponential probability distribution.
4. The queue discipline is first-come, first-served (FCFS).

As these assumptions apply to the Burger Dome waiting line problem introduced in Section 15.1, we show how formulas can be used to determine Burger Dome's operating characteristics and thus provide management with helpful decision-making information.

The mathematical methodology used to derive the formulas for the operating characteristics of waiting lines is rather complex. However, our purpose in this chapter is not to provide the theoretical development of waiting line models, but rather to show how the formulas that have been developed can provide information about operating characteristics of the waiting line. Readers interested in the mathematical development of the formulas can consult the specialized texts listed in the References and Bibliography section at the end of the text.

The Operating Characteristics

The following formulas can be used to develop the steady-state operating characteristics for a single-channel waiting line with Poisson arrivals and exponential service times, where

λ = the mean or average number of arrivals per time period (the mean arrival rate)

μ = the mean or average number of services per time period (the mean service rate)

Equations (15.4) through (15.10) show that waiting line models do not provide formulas for *optimal* conditions. Rather, these equations provide information about the steady-state operating characteristics of the system.

1. The probability that no units are in the system:

$$P_0 = 1 - \frac{\lambda}{\mu} \qquad (15.4)$$

2. The average number of units in the waiting line:

$$L_q = \frac{\lambda^2}{\mu(\mu - \lambda)} \qquad (15.5)$$

3. The average number of units in the system:

$$L = L_q + \frac{\lambda}{\mu} \qquad (15.6)$$

4. The average time a unit spends in the waiting line:

$$W_q = \frac{L_q}{\lambda} \qquad (15.7)$$

5. The average time a unit spends in the system:

$$W = W_q + \frac{1}{\mu} \qquad (15.8)$$

6. The probability that an arriving unit has to wait for service:

$$P_w = \frac{\lambda}{\mu} \qquad (15.9)$$

7. The probability of n units in the system:

$$P_n = \left(\frac{\lambda}{\mu}\right)^n P_0 \qquad (15.10)$$

The values of the **mean arrival rate** λ and the **mean service rate** μ are clearly important components in determining the operating characteristics. Equation (15.9) shows that the ratio of the mean arrival rate to the mean service rate, λ/μ, provides the probability that an arriving unit has to wait because the service facility is busy. Hence, λ/μ often is referred to as the *utilization factor* for the service facility.

The operating characteristics presented in equations (15.4) through (15.10) are applicable only when the mean service rate μ is *greater than* the mean arrival rate λ—in other words, when $\lambda/\mu < 1$. If this condition does not exist, the waiting line will continue to grow without limit because the service facility does not have sufficient capacity to handle the arriving units. Thus, in using equations (15.4) through (15.10), we must have $\mu > \lambda$.

Operating Characteristics for the Burger Dome Problem

Recall that for the Burger Dome problem we had a mean arrival rate of $\lambda = 0.75$ customers per minute and a mean service rate of $\mu = 1$ customer per minute. Thus, with $\mu > \lambda$, equations (15.4) through (15.10) can be used to provide operating characteristics for the Burger Dome single-channel waiting line:

$$P_0 = 1 - \frac{\lambda}{\mu} = 1 - \frac{0.75}{1} = 0.25$$

$$L_q = \frac{\lambda^2}{\mu(\mu - \lambda)} = \frac{0.75^2}{1(1 - 0.75)} = 2.25 \text{ customers}$$

$$L = L_q + \frac{\lambda}{\mu} = 2.25 + \frac{0.75}{1} = 3 \text{ customers}$$

$$W_q = \frac{L_q}{\lambda} = \frac{2.25}{0.75} = 3 \text{ minutes}$$

$$W = W_q + \frac{1}{\mu} = 3 + \frac{1}{1} = 4 \text{ minutes}$$

$$P_w = \frac{\lambda}{\mu} = \frac{0.75}{1} = 0.75$$

Problem 5 asks you to compute the operating characteristics for a single-channel waiting line application.

Equation (15.10) can be used to determine the probability of any number of customers in the system. Applying it provides the probability information summarized in Table 15.2.

The Manager's Use of Waiting Line Models

The results of the single-channel waiting line for Burger Dome show several important things about the operation of the waiting line. In particular, customers wait an average of 3 minutes before beginning to place an order, which appears somewhat long for a business based on fast service. In addition, the facts that the average number of customers waiting in line is 2.25 and that 75% of the arriving customers have to wait for service are indicators that something should be done to improve the waiting line operation. Table 15.2 shows a 0.1335 probability that seven or more customers are in the Burger Dome system at one time. This condition indicates a fairly high probability that Burger Dome will experience some long waiting lines if it continues to use the single-channel operation.

Waiting line models often indicate where improvements in operating characteristics are desirable. However, the decision of how to modify the waiting line configuration to improve the operating characteristics must be based on the insights and creativity of the analyst.

If the operating characteristics are unsatisfactory in terms of meeting company standards for service, Burger Dome's management should consider alternative designs or plans for improving the waiting line operation.

Improving the Waiting Line Operation

After reviewing the operating characteristics provided by the waiting line model, Burger Dome's management concluded that improvements designed to reduce waiting times are desirable. Improvements in the waiting line operation most often focus on ways to improve the service rate. Generally, service improvements are made by the following:

Table 15.2	THE PROBABILITY OF n CUSTOMERS IN THE SYSTEM FOR THE BURGER DOME WAITING LINE PROBLEM

Number of Customers	Probability
0	0.2500
1	0.1875
2	0.1406
3	0.1055
4	0.0791
5	0.0593
6	0.0445
7 or more	0.1335

1. Increase the mean service rate μ by making a creative design change or by using new technology.
2. Add service channels so that more units can be served simultaneously.

Assume that in considering alternative 1, Burger Dome's management decides to employ an order filler who will assist the order taker at the cash register. The customer begins the service process by placing the order with the order taker. As the order is placed, the order taker announces the order over an intercom system, and the order filler begins filling the order. When the order is completed, the order taker handles the money, while the order filler continues to fill the order. With this design, Burger Dome's management estimates the mean service rate can be increased from the current service rate of 60 customers per hour to 75 customers per hour. Thus, the mean service rate for the revised system is $\mu = 75/60 = 1.25$ customers per minute. For $\lambda = 0.75$ and $\mu = 1.25$, equations (15.4) through (15.10) provide the operating characteristics summarized in Table 15.3.

Table 15.3 indicates that all the operating characteristics have improved because of the increased service rate provided by the order filler. In particular, the average time in the system has been reduced from 4 to 2 minutes. Are other alternatives possible for increasing the service rate? If so—and if the mean service rate μ can be identified for these alternatives—equations (15.4) through (15.10) will provide the information needed to assess the amount of improvement for the proposed alternatives. The added cost of any proposed change can be compared to the corresponding service improvements to help the manager determine whether the proposed service improvements are worthwhile.

Problem 11 asks you to determine whether a change in the mean service rate will meet the company's service guideline for its customers.

As mentioned previously, another option that is usually available is to provide one or more additional service channels so that more than one customer may be served at the same time. The extension of the single-channel waiting line model to the multiple-channel waiting line model is the topic of the next section.

Table 15.3	OPERATING CHARACTERISTICS FOR THE BURGER DOME SYSTEM WITH THE MEAN SERVICE RATE INCREASED TO $\mu = 1.25$ CUSTOMERS PER MINUTE

Probability of no units in the system	0.400
Average number of units in the waiting line	0.900
Average number of units in the system	1.500
Average time in the waiting line	1.200 minutes
Average time in the system	2.000 minutes
Probability that an arriving unit has to wait	0.600
Probability that seven or more are in system	0.028

N O T E S
and Comments

1. The assumption that arrivals follow a Poisson probability distribution is equivalent to the assumption that the time between arrivals has an exponential probability distribution. For example, if the arrivals for a waiting line follow a Poisson probability distribution with a mean of 20 arrivals per hour, the time between arrivals will follow an exponential probability distribution, with a mean time between arrivals of $1/20$ or 0.05 hour.

2. Many individuals believe that whenever the mean service rate μ is greater than the mean arrival rate λ, the system should be able to handle or serve all arrivals. However, as the Burger Dome example shows, the variability of arrival times and service times may result in long waiting times even when the mean service rate exceeds the mean arrival rate. A contribution of waiting line models is that they can point out undesirable waiting line operating characteristics even when the $\mu > \lambda$ condition appears satisfactory.

15.3   THE MULTIPLE-CHANNEL WAITING LINE MODEL WITH POISSON ARRIVALS AND EXPONENTIAL SERVICE TIMES

A **multiple-channel waiting line** consists of two or more channels or service locations that are assumed to be identical in terms of service capability. In the multiple-channel system, arriving units wait in a single waiting line and then move to the first available channel to be served.

You may be familiar with multiple-channel systems that also have multiple waiting lines. The waiting line model in this section has multiple channels, but only a single waiting line. Operating characteristics for a multiple-channel system are better when a single waiting line, rather than multiple waiting lines, is used.

The single-channel Burger Dome operation could be expanded to a two-channel system by opening a second service channel. Figure 15.2 shows a diagram of the Burger Dome two-channel waiting line.

In this section we present formulas that can be used to determine the steady-state operating characteristics for a multiple-channel waiting line. These formulas are applicable if

1. the waiting line has two or more channels,
2. the arrivals follow a Poisson probability distribution,
3. the service time for each channel follows an exponential probability distribution,
4. the mean service rate μ is the same for each channel,
5. the arrivals wait in a single waiting line and then move to the first open channel for service, and
6. the queue discipline is first-come, first-served (FCFS).

The Operating Characteristics

The following formulas can be used to compute the steady-state operating characteristics for multiple-channel waiting lines, where

Figure 15.2   THE BURGER DOME TWO-CHANNEL WAITING LINE

λ = the mean arrival rate for the system

μ = the mean service rate for *each* channel

k = the number of channels

1. The probability no units are in the system:

$$P_0 = \frac{1}{\displaystyle\sum_{n=0}^{k-1} \frac{(\lambda/\mu)^n}{n!} + \frac{(\lambda/\mu)^k}{k!}\left(\frac{k\mu}{k\mu - \lambda}\right)} \qquad (15.11)$$

2. The average number of units in the waiting line:

$$L_q = \frac{(\lambda/\mu)^k \lambda \mu}{(k-1)!(k\mu - \lambda)^2} P_0 \qquad (15.12)$$

3. The average number of units in the system:

$$L = L_q + \frac{\lambda}{\mu} \qquad (15.13)$$

4. The average time a unit spends in the waiting line:

$$W_q = \frac{L_q}{\lambda} \qquad (15.14)$$

5. The average time a unit spends in the system:

$$W = W_q + \frac{1}{\mu} \qquad (15.15)$$

6. The probability that an arriving unit has to wait for service:

$$P_w = \frac{1}{k!}\left(\frac{\lambda}{\mu}\right)^k \left(\frac{k\mu}{k\mu - \lambda}\right) P_0 \qquad (15.16)$$

7. The probability of n units in the system:

$$P_n = \frac{(\lambda/\mu)^n}{n!} P_0 \quad \text{for } n \le k \qquad (15.17)$$

$$P_n = \frac{(\lambda/\mu)^n}{k!k^{(n-k)}} P_0 \quad \text{for } n > k \qquad (15.18)$$

Because μ is the mean service rate for each channel, $k\mu$ is the mean service rate for the multiple-channel system. As was true for the single-channel waiting line model, the formulas for the operating characteristics of multiple-channel waiting lines can be applied only in situations where the mean service rate for the system is greater than the mean arrival rate for the system; in other words, the formulas are applicable only if $k\mu$ is greater than λ.

Some of the expressions for the operating characteristics of multiple-channel waiting lines are more complex than their single-channel counterparts. However, equations (15.11) through (15.18) provide the same information as provided by the single-channel model. To help simplify the use of the multiple-channel equations, Table 15.4 contains values of P_0 for selected values of λ/μ and k. The values provided in the table correspond to cases where $k\mu > \lambda$, and hence the service rate is sufficient to process all arrivals.

Table 15.4	VALUES OF P_0 FOR MULTIPLE-CHANNEL WAITING LINES WITH POISSON ARRIVALS AND EXPONENTIAL SERVICE TIMES			

	Number of Channels (k)			
Ratio λ/μ	2	3	4	5
0.15	0.8605	0.8607	0.8607	0.8607
0.20	0.8182	0.8187	0.8187	0.8187
0.25	0.7778	0.7788	0.7788	0.7788
0.30	0.7391	0.7407	0.7408	0.7408
0.35	0.7021	0.7046	0.7047	0.7047
0.40	0.6667	0.6701	0.6703	0.6703
0.45	0.6327	0.6373	0.6376	0.6376
0.50	0.6000	0.6061	0.6065	0.6065
0.55	0.5686	0.5763	0.5769	0.5769
0.60	0.5385	0.5479	0.5487	0.5488
0.65	0.5094	0.5209	0.5219	0.5220
0.70	0.4815	0.4952	0.4965	0.4966
0.75	0.4545	0.4706	0.4722	0.4724
0.80	0.4286	0.4472	0.4491	0.4493
0.85	0.4035	0.4248	0.4271	0.4274
0.90	0.3793	0.4035	0.4062	0.4065
0.95	0.3559	0.3831	0.3863	0.3867
1.00	0.3333	0.3636	0.3673	0.3678
1.20	0.2500	0.2941	0.3002	0.3011
1.40	0.1765	0.2360	0.2449	0.2463
1.60	0.1111	0.1872	0.1993	0.2014
1.80	0.0526	0.1460	0.1616	0.1646
2.00		0.1111	0.1304	0.1343
2.20		0.0815	0.1046	0.1094
2.40		0.0562	0.0831	0.0889
2.60		0.0345	0.0651	0.0721
2.80		0.0160	0.0521	0.0581
3.00			0.0377	0.0466
3.20			0.0273	0.0372
3.40			0.0186	0.0293
3.60			0.0113	0.0228
3.80			0.0051	0.0174
4.00				0.0130
4.20				0.0093
4.40				0.0063
4.60				0.0038
4.80				0.0017

Operating Characteristics for the Burger Dome Problem

To illustrate the multiple-channel waiting line model, we return to the Burger Dome fast-food restaurant waiting line problem. Suppose that management wants to evaluate the desirability of opening a second order-processing station so that two customers can be served simultaneously. Assume that there will be a single waiting line with the next customer in line moving to the first available server, giving Burger Dome a two-channel waiting line. Let us evaluate the operating characteristics for this two-channel system.

We use equations (15.12) through (15.18) for the $k = 2$ channel system. For a mean arrival rate of $\lambda = 0.75$ customers per minute and mean service rate of $\mu = 1$ customer per minute for each channel, we obtain the operating characteristics:

$$P_0 = 0.4545 \quad \text{(from Table 15.4 with } \lambda/\mu = 0.75)$$

$$L_q = \frac{(0.75/1)^2(0.75)(1)}{(2-1)![2(1)-0.75]^2}(0.4545) = 0.1227 \text{ customer}$$

$$L = L_q + \frac{\lambda}{\mu} = 0.1227 + \frac{0.75}{1} = 0.8727 \text{ customer}$$

$$W_q = \frac{L_q}{\lambda} = \frac{0.1227}{0.75} = 0.16 \text{ minute}$$

$$W = W_q + \frac{1}{\mu} = 0.16 + \frac{1}{1} = 1.16 \text{ minutes}$$

$$P_w = \frac{1}{2!}\left(\frac{0.75}{1}\right)^2\left[\frac{2(1)}{2(1)-0.75}\right](0.4545) = 0.2045$$

Try Problem 19, which will give you practice in determining the operating characteristics for a two-channel waiting line.

Using equations (15.17) and (15.18), we can compute the probabilities of n customers in the system. The results from these computations are summarized in Table 15.5.

We can now compare the steady-state operating characteristics of the two-channel system to the operating characteristics of the original single-channel system discussed in Section 15.2.

1. The average time a customer spends in the system (waiting time plus service time) is reduced from $W = 4$ minutes to $W = 1.16$ minutes.
2. The average number of customers in the waiting line is reduced from $L_q = 2.25$ customers to $L_q = 0.1227$ customers.
3. The average time a customer spends in the waiting line is reduced from $W_q = 3$ minutes to $W_q = 0.16$ minutes.
4. The probability that a customer has to wait for service is reduced from $P_w = 0.75$ to $P_w = 0.2045$.

Table 15.5 THE PROBABILITY OF n CUSTOMERS IN THE SYSTEM FOR THE BURGER DOME TWO-CHANNEL WAITING LINE

Number of Customers	Probability
0	0.4545
1	0.3409
2	0.1278
3	0.0479
4	0.0180
5 or more	0.0109

Clearly the two-channel system will significantly improve the operating characteristics of the waiting line. However, adding an order filler at each service station would further increase the mean service rate and improve the operating characteristics. The final decision regarding the staffing policy at Burger Dome rests with the Burger Dome management. The waiting line study has simply provided the operating characteristics that can be anticipated under three configurations: a single-channel system with one employee, a single-channel system with two employees, and a two-channel system with an employee for each channel. After considering these results, what action would you recommend? In this case, Burger Dome adopted the following policy statement: For periods when customer arrivals are expected to average 45 customers per hour, Burger Dome will open two order-processing stations with one employee assigned to each station.

By changing the mean arrival rate λ to reflect arrival rates at different times of the day, and then computing the operating characteristics, Burger Dome's management can establish guidelines and policies that tell the store managers when they should schedule service operations with a single channel, two channels, or perhaps even three or more channels. The Q.M. in Action article for Lourdes Hospital shows how a multiple-channel waiting line model has been used to make hospital staffing decisions.

N O T E S *and Comments*

The multiple-channel waiting line model is based on a single waiting line. You may have also encountered situations where each of the k channels has its own waiting line. Quantitative analysts have shown that the operating characteristics of multiple-channel systems are better if a single waiting line is used. People like them better also; no one who comes in after you can be served ahead of you. Thus, when possible, banks, airline reservation counters, food-service establishments, and other businesses typically use a single waiting line for a multiple-channel system.

Q.M. IN ACTION

HOSPITAL STAFFING BASED ON A MULTIPLE-CHANNEL WAITING LINE MODEL*

Lourdes Hospital in Binghamton, New York, uses a centralized staff to schedule appointments for the hospital's outpatient, inpatient, and ambulance services. Physicians, their staffs, hospital personnel, and patients contact the centralized scheduling office by telephone to establish desired appointment times.

Efficiency of the scheduling process depends on the department's staff being able to process incoming telephone calls in a timely manner. Periodically, incoming requests for services overload the staff's ability to answer the telephone and process the appointments. As a result, users reported undesirable delays and lengthy waiting times. Management used a waiting line model to study the operation and suggest staffing changes that could improve the efficiency of the centralized scheduling process.

Data were collected on the number of telephone calls that arrived during each 15-minute period. The calls were random, not depending on the day of the week. A Poisson probability distribution was a good description of the random arrivals, with peak arrival times occurring between 9:00 A.M. and 11:30 A.M. and between 2:00 P.M. and 3:45 P.M. each

day. An investigation of service times found that, although service times were not exactly exponential, the exponential probability distribution provided a reasonable approximation.

In effect, the hospital's scheduling service was viewed as a multiple-channel waiting line with Poisson arrivals and exponential service times. The number of channels was simply the number of individuals on the scheduling staff. With the mean arrival rate adjusted for the different periods of the day, a waiting line model with k channels was used to estimate the probability that an arriving call would have to wait for service. The staff size was determined by selecting the number of channels that kept the steady state probability of waiting to no more than 10%. Staff schedules and work loads were adjusted, efficiency improved, and the number of complaints about waiting for service declined.

*Based on Agnihothri, S. R., and P. F. Taylor, "Staffing a Centralized Appointment Scheduling Department in Lourdes Hospital." *Interfaces,* vol. 21, no. 5, September–October 1991, pp. 1–11.

··/ /···········

15.4   SOME GENERAL RELATIONSHIPS FOR WAITING LINE MODELS

In Sections 15.2 and 15.3 we presented formulas for computing the operating characteristics for single-channel and multiple-channel waiting lines with Poisson arrivals and exponential service times. The operating characteristics of interest included

$$L_q = \text{the average number of units in the waiting line}$$
$$L = \text{the average number of units in the system}$$
$$W_q = \text{the average time a unit spends in the waiting line}$$
$$W = \text{the average time a unit spends in the system}$$

John D. C. Little showed that several relationships exist among these four characteristics and that these relationships apply to a variety of different waiting line systems. Two of the relationships, referred to as *Little's flow equations,* are

$$L = \lambda W \tag{15.19}$$

$$L_q = \lambda W_q \tag{15.20}$$

Equation (15.19) shows that the average number of units in the system, L, can be found by multiplying the mean arrival rate, λ, by the average time a unit spends in the system, W. Equation (15.20) shows that the same relationship holds between the average number of units in the waiting line, L_q, and the average time a unit spends in the waiting line, W_q.

Using equation (15.20) and solving for W_q, we obtain

$$W_q = \frac{L_q}{\lambda} \tag{15.21}$$

Equation (15.21) follows directly from Little's second flow equation. We used it for the single-channel waiting line model in Section 15.2 and the multiple-channel waiting line model in Section 15.3 [see equations (15.7) and (15.14)]. Once L_q is computed for either of these models, equation (15.21) can then be used to compute W_q.

Another general expression that applies to waiting line models is that the average time in the system, W, is equal to the average time in the waiting line, W_q, plus the average service time. For a system with a mean service rate μ, the average or mean service time is $1/\mu$. Thus, we have the general relationship

$$W = W_q + \frac{1}{\mu} \tag{15.22}$$

The advantage of Little's flow equations is that they show how operating characteristics L, L_q, W, and W_q are related in any waiting line system. Arrivals and service times do not have to follow specific probability distributions for the flow equations to be applicable.

Recall that we used equation (15.22) to provide the average time in the system for both the single- and multiple-channel waiting line models [see equations (15.8) and (15.15)].

The importance of Little's flow equations is that they apply to *any waiting line model* regardless of whether arrivals follow the Poisson probability distribution and regardless of whether service times follow the exponential probability distribution. For example, in a study of the grocery checkout counters at Murphy's Foodliner, an analyst concluded that arrivals follow the Poisson probability distribution with the mean arrival rate of 24 customers per hour or $\lambda = 24/60 = 0.40$ customers per minute. However, the analyst found that service times follow a normal probability distribution rather than an exponential probability distribution. The mean service rate was found to be 30 customers per hour or

$\mu = 30/60 = 0.50$ customers per minute. A time study of actual customer waiting times showed that, on average, a customer spends 4.5 minutes in the system (waiting time plus checkout time); that is, $W = 4.5$. Using the waiting line relationships discussed in this section, we can now compute other operating characteristics for this waiting line.

First, using equation (15.22) and solving for W_q, we have

$$W_q = W - \frac{1}{\mu} = 4.5 - \frac{1}{0.50} = 2.5 \text{ minutes}$$

With both W and W_q known, we can use Little's flow equations, (15.19) and (15.20), to compute

The application of Little's flow equations are demonstrated in Problem 25.

$$L = \lambda W = 0.40(4.5) = 1.8 \text{ customers}$$
$$L_q = \lambda W_q = 0.40(2.5) = 1 \text{ customer}$$

The manager of Murphy's Foodliner can now review these operating characteristics to see whether action should be taken to improve the service and to reduce the waiting time and the length of the waiting line.

N O T E S **and Comments**

In waiting line systems where the length of the waiting line is limited (e.g., a small waiting area), some of the arriving units will be blocked from joining the waiting line and will be lost. In this case, the blocked or lost arrivals will make the arrival rate in terms of units entering the system something less than the overall mean arrival rate. By defining λ as the mean arrival rate for units *joining the system*, rather than the overall mean arrival rate, the relationships used in this section can be used to determine W, L, W_q, and L_q.

15.5 ECONOMIC ANALYSIS OF WAITING LINES

Frequently, decisions involving the design of waiting lines will be based on a subjective evaluation of the operating characteristics of the waiting line. For example, a manager may decide that an average waiting time of one minute or less and an average of two customers or less in the system are reasonable goals. The waiting line models presented in the preceding sections can be used to determine the number of channels that will meet the manager's waiting line performance goals.

On the other hand, a manager may want to identify the cost of operating the waiting line system and then base the decision regarding system design on a minimum hourly or daily operating cost. Before an economic analysis of a waiting line can be conducted, a total-cost model, which includes the cost of waiting and the cost of service, must be developed.

To develop a total-cost model for a waiting line, we begin by defining the notation to be used:

Generally, c_s is easier to estimate than c_w. The reason is that the cost of customer waiting, c_w, is more subjective in that it often includes the cost of lost goodwill owing to customer waiting time. This difficulty is analogous to that of estimating backordering costs for an inventory model with planned shortages.

c_w = the waiting cost per time period for each unit

L = the average number of units in the system

c_s = the service cost per time period for each channel

k = the number of channels

TC = the total cost per time period

Note that waiting cost is based on average number of units in the system. Thus the waiting cost includes the time spent waiting in line plus the time spent waiting while being served.

The total cost is the sum of the waiting cost and the service cost; that is,

$$TC = c_w L + c_s k \qquad (15.23)$$

To conduct an economic analysis of a waiting line, we must obtain reasonable estimates of the waiting cost and the service cost. Of these two costs, the waiting cost is usually the more difficult to evaluate. In the Burger Dome restaurant problem, the waiting cost would be the cost per minute for a customer waiting for service. This cost is not a direct cost to Burger Dome. However, if Burger Dome ignores this cost and allows long waiting lines, customers ultimately will take their business elsewhere. Thus, Burger Dome will experience lost sales and, in effect, incur a cost.

The service cost is generally easier to determine. This cost is the relevant cost associated with operating each service channel. In the Burger Dome problem, this cost would include the server's wages, benefits, and any other direct costs associated with operating the service channel. At Burger Dome, this cost is estimated to be $7 per hour.

Adding more channels always improves the operating characteristics of the waiting line and reduces the waiting cost. However, additional channels increases the service cost. An economic analysis of waiting lines attempts to find the number of channels that will minimize total cost by balancing the waiting cost and the service cost.

To demonstrate the use of equation (15.23), we assume that Burger Dome is willing to assign a cost of $10 per hour for customer waiting time. We use the average number of units in the system, L, as computed in Sections 15.2 and 15.3 to obtain the total hourly cost for the single-channel and two-channel systems:

Single-channel system ($L = 3$ customers)

$$TC = c_w L + c_s k$$
$$TC = \$10(3) + \$7(1) = \$37.00 \text{ per hour}$$

Two-channel system ($L = 0.8727$ customer):

$$TC = c_w L + c_s k$$
$$= \$10(0.8727) + \$7(2) = \$22.73 \text{ per hour}$$

Thus, based on the cost data provided by Burger Dome, the two-channel system provides the most economical operation.

Working Problem 21 will give you the chance to test your ability to conduct an economic analysis of proposed single-channel and two-channel waiting line systems.

Figure 15.3 shows the general shapes of the cost curves in the economic analysis of waiting lines. The service cost increases as the number of channels is increased. However, with more channels, the service is better. As a result, waiting time and cost decrease as the number of channels is increased. The number of channels that will provide a good approximation of the minimum total-cost design can be found by evaluating the total cost for several design alternatives.

N O T E S and Comments

1. In dealing with government agencies and utility companies, customers may not be able to take their business elsewhere. In these situations, no lost business occurs when long waiting times are encountered. This condition is one of the reasons that service in such organizations may be poor, and that customers in such situations may experience long waiting times.

2. In some instances, the organization providing the service also employs the units waiting for the service. For example, consider the case of a company that owns and operates the trucks used to deliver goods to and from its manufacturing plant. In addition to the costs associated with the trucks waiting to be loaded or unloaded, the firm also pays the wages of the truck loaders and unloaders who operate the service channel. In this case, the cost of having the trucks wait and the cost of operating the service channel are direct expenses to the firm. An economic analysis of the waiting line system is highly recommended for these types of situations.

| Figure 15.3 | THE GENERAL SHAPE OF WAITING COST, SERVICE COST, AND TOTAL-COST CURVES IN WAITING LINE MODELS |

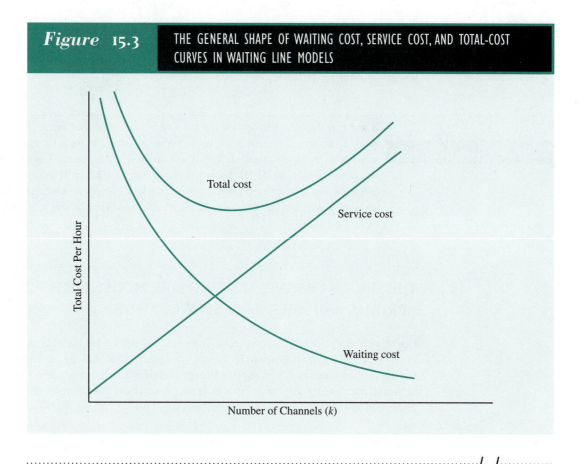

15.6 OTHER WAITING LINE MODELS

D. G. Kendall suggested a notation that is helpful in classifying the wide variety of different waiting line models that have been developed. The three-symbol Kendall notation is as follows:

$$A/B/k$$

where

A denotes the probability distribution for the arrivals

B denotes the probability distribution for the service time

k denotes the number of channels

Depending on the letter appearing in the A or B position, a wide variety of waiting line systems can be described. The letters that are commonly used are as follows:

M designates a Poisson probability distribution for the arrivals or an exponential probability distribution for service time

D designates that the arrivals or the service time is deterministic or constant

G designates that the arrivals or the service time has a general probability distribution with a known mean and variance

Using the Kendall notation, the single-channel waiting line model with Poisson arrivals and exponential service times is classified as an *M/M/*1 model. The 2-channel waiting line model with Poisson arrivals and exponential service times presented in Section 15.3 would be classified as an *M/M/*2 model.

N O T E S
and Comments

In some cases, the Kendall notation is extended to five symbols. The fourth symbol indicates the largest number of units that can be in the system, and the fifth symbol indicates the size of the input or calling population. The fourth symbol is used in situations where the waiting line can hold a finite or maximum number of units, and the fifth symbol is necessary when the population of arriving units or customers is finite. When the fourth and fifth symbols of the Kendall notation are omitted, the waiting line system is assumed to have infinite capacity, and the calling population is assumed to be infinite.

15.7   THE SINGLE-CHANNEL WAITING LINE MODEL WITH POISSON ARRIVALS AND ARBITRARY SERVICE TIMES

Let us return to the single-channel waiting line model where arrivals are described by a Poisson probability distribution. However, we now assume that the probability distribution for the service times is not an exponential probability distribution. Thus, using the Kendall notation, the waiting line model that is appropriate is an *M/G/*1 model, where *G* denotes a general or unspecified probability distribution.

Operating Characteristics for the *M/G/*1 Model

When providing input to the M/G/1 model, you should be consistent in terms of the time period. For example, if λ and μ are expressed in terms of the number of units per hour, the standard deviation of the service time should be expressed in hours. The example that follows uses minutes as the time period for the arrival and service data.

The notation used to describe the operating characteristics for the *M/G/*1 model is

$$\lambda = \text{the mean arrival rate}$$

$$\mu = \text{the mean service rate}$$

$$\frac{1}{\mu} = \text{the average or mean service time}$$

$$\sigma = \text{the standard deviation of the service time}$$

Some of the steady-state operating characteristics of the *M/G/*1 waiting line model are as follows:

1. The probability that no units are in the system:

$$P_0 = 1 - \frac{\lambda}{\mu} \tag{15.24}$$

2. The average number of units in the waiting line:

$$L_q = \frac{\lambda^2 \sigma^2 + (\lambda/\mu)^2}{2(1 - \lambda/\mu)} \tag{15.25}$$

3. The average number of units in the system:

$$L = L_q + \frac{\lambda}{\mu} \tag{15.26}$$

4. The average time a unit spends in the waiting line:

$$W_q = \frac{L_q}{\lambda} \tag{15.27}$$

5. The average time a unit spends in the system:

$$W = W_q + \frac{1}{\mu} \tag{15.28}$$

6. The probability that an arriving unit has to wait for service:

$$P_w = \frac{\lambda}{\mu} \tag{15.29}$$

Note that the relationships for L, W_q, and W are the same as the relationships used for the waiting line models in Sections 15.2 and 15.3. They also are based on Little's flow equations.

An Example   Retail sales at Hartlage's Seafood Supply are handled by one clerk. Customer arrivals are random, and the average arrival rate is 21 customers per hour or $\lambda = 21/60 = 0.35$ customers per minute. A study of the service process shows that the average or mean service time is 2 minutes per customer, with a standard deviation of $\sigma = 1.2$ minutes. The mean time of 2 minutes per customer shows that the clerk has a mean service rate of $\mu = \frac{1}{2} = 0.50$ customers per minute. The operating characteristics of this $M/G/1$ waiting line system are

Problem 27 provides another application of a single-channel waiting line with Poisson arrivals and arbitrary service times.

$$P_0 = 1 - \frac{\lambda}{\mu} = 1 - \frac{0.35}{0.50} = 0.30$$

$$L_q = \frac{(0.35)^2(1.2)^2 + (0.35/0.50)^2}{2(1 - 0.35/0.50)} = 1.11 \text{ customers}$$

$$L = L_q + \frac{\lambda}{\mu} = 1.11 + \frac{0.35}{0.50} = 1.81 \text{ customers}$$

$$W_q = \frac{L_q}{\lambda} = \frac{1.11}{0.35} = 3.17 \text{ minutes}$$

$$W = W_q + \frac{1}{\mu} = 3.17 + \frac{1}{0.50} = 5.17 \text{ minutes}$$

$$P_w = \frac{\lambda}{\mu} = \frac{0.35}{0.50} = 0.70$$

Hartlage's manager can review these operating characteristics to determine whether scheduling a second clerk appears to be worthwhile.

Constant Service Times

We want to comment briefly on the single-channel waiting line model that assumes random arrivals but constant service times. Such a waiting line can occur in production and manufacturing environments where machine-controlled service times are constant. This waiting line is described by the $M/D/1$ model, with the D referring to the deterministic service times. With the $M/D/1$ model, the average number of units in the waiting line, L_q, can be found by using equation (15.25) with the condition that the standard deviation of the constant service time is $\sigma = 0$. Thus, the expression for the average number of units in the waiting line for the $M/D/1$ waiting line becomes

$$L_q = \frac{(\lambda/\mu)^2}{2(1 - \lambda/\mu)} \tag{15.30}$$

The other expressions presented earlier in this section can be used to determine additional operating characteristics of the *M/D/*1 system.

Whenever the operating characteristics of a waiting line are unacceptable, managers often try to improve service by increasing the mean service rate μ. This decision is a good idea, but equation (15.25) shows that the variation in the service times also affects the operating characteristics of the waiting line. Because the standard deviation of service times, σ, appears in the numerator of equation (15.25), a larger variation in service times results in a larger average number of units in the waiting line. Hence, another alternative for improving the service capabilities of a waiting line is to reduce the variation in the service times. Thus, even when the mean service rate of the service facility cannot be increased, a reduction in σ will reduce the average number of units in the waiting line and improve the other operating characteristics of the system.

15.8 A MULTIPLE-CHANNEL MODEL WITH POISSON ARRIVALS, ARBITRARY SERVICE TIMES, AND NO WAITING LINE

An interesting variation of the waiting line models discussed so far involves a system in which no waiting is allowed. Arriving units or customers seek service from one of several service channels. If all the channels are busy, arriving units are denied access to the system. In waiting line terminology, arrivals occurring when the system is full are **blocked** and are cleared from the system. Such customers may be lost or may attempt a return to the system later.

The specific model considered in this section is based on the following assumptions.

1. The system has k channels.
2. The arrivals follow a Poisson probability distribution, with mean arrival rate λ.
3. The service times for each channel may have any probability distribution.
4. The mean service rate μ is the same for each channel.
5. The arrivals enter the system only if at least one of the k channels is available. Arrivals occurring when all channels are busy are blocked—that is, denied service and not allowed to enter the system.

With G denoting a general or unspecified probability distribution for service times, the appropriate model for this situation is referred to as an *M/G/k* model with "blocked customers cleared." The question addressed in this type of situation is, How many channels or servers should be used?

A primary application of this model involves the design of telephone and other communication systems where the arrivals are the calls and the channels are the number of telephone or communication lines available. In such a system, the calls are made to one telephone number, with each call automatically switched to an open channel if possible. When all channels are busy, additional calls receive a busy signal and are denied access to the system.

The Operating Characteristics for the *M/G/k* Model with Blocked Customers Cleared

We approach the problem of selecting the best number of channels by computing the steady-state probabilities that *j* of the *k* channels will be busy. These probabilities are

$$P_j = \frac{(\lambda/\mu)^j/j!}{\sum\limits_{i=0}^{k} (\lambda/\mu)^i/i!} \tag{15.31}$$

where

λ = the mean arrival rate

μ = the mean service rate for each channel

k = the number of channels

P_j = the probability that *j* of the *k* channels are busy

for $j = 0, 1, 2, \ldots, k$

The most important probability value is P_k, which is the probability that all *k* channels are busy. On a percentage basis, P_k indicates the percentage of arrivals that are blocked and denied access to the system.

Another operating characteristic of interest is the average number of units in the system; note that this is equivalent to the average number of channels in use. Letting *L* denote the average number of units in the system, we have

$$L = \frac{\lambda}{\mu}(1 - P_k) \tag{15.32}$$

An Example   Microdata Software, Inc., uses a telephone ordering system for its computer software products. Callers place orders with Microdata by using the company's 800 telephone number. Assume that calls to this telephone number arrive at an average rate of 12 per hour. The time required to process a telephone order varies considerably from order to order. However, each Microdata sales representative can be expected to handle an average of six calls per hour. Currently, the Microdata 800 telephone number has three internal lines or channels, each operated by a separate sales representative. Calls received on the 800 number are automatically transferred to one of the open lines or channels if available.

Whenever all three lines are busy, callers receive a busy signal. In the past, Microdata has assumed that callers receiving a busy signal will call back later. However, recent research on telephone ordering has shown that a substantial number of callers who are denied access do not call back later. These lost calls represent lost revenues for the firm, so Microdata's management has requested an analysis of the telephone ordering system. Specifically, management wants to know the percentage of callers who are getting busy signals and are being blocked from the system. If management's goal is to provide sufficient capacity to handle 90% of the callers, how many telephone lines and sales representatives should Microdata use?

We can demonstrate the use of equation (15.31) by computing P_3, the probability that all three of the currently available telephone lines will be in use and additional callers will be blocked:

$$P_3 = \frac{(\frac{12}{6})^3/3!}{(\frac{12}{6})^0/0! + (\frac{12}{6})^1/1! + (\frac{12}{6})^2/2! + (\frac{12}{6})^3/3!} = \frac{1.3333}{6.3333} = 0.2105$$

With $P_3 = 0.2105$, approximately 21% of the calls, or slightly more than one in five calls, are being blocked. Only 79% of the calls are being handled immediately by the 3-line system.

Let us assume Microdata expands to a 4-line system. Then, the probability that all four channels will be in use and that callers will be blocked is

$$P_4 = \frac{(\frac{12}{6})^4/4!}{(\frac{12}{6})^0/0! + (\frac{12}{6})^1/1! + (\frac{12}{6})^2/2! + (\frac{12}{6})^3/3! + (\frac{12}{6})^4/4!} = \frac{0.6667}{7} = 0.0952$$

Try Problem 30 to obtain practice in multiple-channel systems with no waiting line.

With only 9.52% of the callers blocked, 90.48% of the callers will reach the Microdata sales representatives. Thus, Microdata should expand its order-processing operation to 4 lines to meet management's goal of providing sufficient capacity to handle at least 90% of the callers. The average number of calls in the 4-line system and thus the average number of lines and sales representatives that will be busy is

$$L = \frac{\lambda}{\mu}(1 - P_4) = \frac{12}{6}(1 - 0.0952) = 1.81$$

Although an average of less than 2 lines will be busy, the 4-line system is necessary to provide the capacity to handle at least 90% of the callers. We used equation (15.31) to calculate the probability that 0, 1, 2, 3, or 4 lines will be busy. These probabilities are summarized in Table 15.6.

As we discussed in Section 15.5, an economic analysis of waiting lines can be used to guide system design decisions. In the Microdata system, the cost of the additional line and additional sales representative should be relatively easy to establish. This cost can be balanced against the cost of the blocked calls. With 9.52% of the calls blocked and $\lambda = 12$ calls per hour, an 8-hour day will have an average of $8(12)(0.0952) = 9.1$ blocked calls. If Microdata can estimate the cost of possible lost sales, the cost of these blocked calls can be established. The economic analysis based on the service cost and the blocked-call cost can assist in determining the optimal number of lines for the system.

Table 15.6	PROBABILITIES OF BUSY LINES FOR THE MICRODATA 4-LINE SYSTEM

Number of Busy Lines	Probability
0	0.1429
1	0.2857
2	0.2857
3	0.1905
4	0.0952

N O T E S
and Comments

Many of the operating characteristics we have considered in previous sections are not relevant for the $M/G/k$ model with blocked customers cleared. In particular, the average time in the waiting line, W_q, and the average number of units in the waiting line, L_q, are no longer considered because waiting is not permitted in this type of system.

·····/ /·····

15.9 WAITING LINE MODELS WITH FINITE CALLING POPULATIONS

For the waiting line models introduced so far, the population of units or customers arriving for service has been considered to be unlimited. In technical terms, when no limit is placed on how many units may seek service, the model is said to have an **infinite calling population.** Under this assumption, the mean arrival rate λ remains constant regardless of how many units are in the waiting line system. This assumption of an infinite calling population is made in most waiting line models.

In other cases, the maximum number of units or customers that may seek service is assumed to be finite. In this situation, the mean arrival rate for the system changes, depending on the number of units in the waiting line, and the waiting line model is said to have a **finite calling population.** The formulas for the operating characteristics of the previous waiting line models must be modified to account for the effect of the finite calling population.

The finite calling population model discussed in this section is based on the following assumptions.

1. The waiting line has a single channel.
2. The population of units that may seek service is finite.
3. The arrivals for *each unit* follow a Poisson probability distribution, with mean arrival rate λ.
4. The service times follow an exponential probability distribution, with mean service rate μ.
5. The queue discipline is first-come, first-served (FCFS).

The waiting line model that is appropriate in such cases is referred to as an *M/M/*1 model with a finite calling population.

The mean arrival rate for the *M/M/*1 model with a finite calling population is defined in terms of how often *each unit* arrives or seeks service. This situation differs from that for previous waiting line models in which λ denoted the mean arrival rate for the system. With a finite calling population, the mean arrival rate for the system varies, depending on the number of units in the system. Instead of adjusting for the changing system arrival rate, in the finite calling population model λ indicates the mean arrival rate for each unit.

> In previous waiting line models, the arrival rate λ was constant and independent of the number of units in the system. With a finite calling population, the arrival rate decreases as the number of units in the system increases because, with more units in the system, fewer units are in the population.

> The mean arrival rate λ is defined differently for the finite calling population model. Specifically, λ is defined in terms of the mean arrival rate for *each unit.*

The Operating Characteristics for the *M/M/*1 Model with a Finite Calling Population

The following formulas are used to determine the steady-state operating characteristics for an *M/M/*1 model with a finite calling population, where

$$\lambda = \text{the mean arrival rate for each unit}$$
$$\mu = \text{the mean service rate}$$
$$N = \text{the size of the population}$$

1. The probability that no units are in the system:

$$P_0 = \frac{1}{\displaystyle\sum_{n=0}^{N} \frac{N!}{(N-n)!} \left(\frac{\lambda}{\mu}\right)^n} \tag{15.33}$$

2. The average number of units in the waiting line:

$$L_q = N - \frac{\lambda + \mu}{\lambda}(1 - P_0) \tag{15.34}$$

3. The average number of units in the system:

$$L = L_q + (1 - P_0) \tag{15.35}$$

4. The average time a unit spends in the waiting line:

$$W_q = \frac{L_q}{(N - L)\lambda} \tag{15.36}$$

5. The average time a unit spends in the system:

$$W = W_q + \frac{1}{\mu} \tag{15.37}$$

6. The probability of n units in the system:

$$P_n = \frac{N!}{(N - n)!}\left(\frac{\lambda}{\mu}\right)^n P_0 \quad \text{for } n = 0, 1, \ldots, N \tag{15.38}$$

One of the primary applications of the $M/M/1$ model with a finite calling population is referred to as the *machine repair problem*. In this problem, a group of machines is considered to be the finite population of "customers" that may request repair service. Whenever a machine breaks down, an arrival occurs in the sense that a new repair request is initiated. If another machine breaks down before the repair work has been completed on the first machine, the second machine begins to form a "waiting line" for repair service. Additional breakdowns by other machines will add to the length of the waiting line. The assumption of first-come, first-served indicates that machines are repaired in the order they break down. The $M/M/1$ model shows that one person or one channel is available to perform the repair service. To return the machine to operation, each machine with a breakdown must be handled by the single-channel repair operation.

An Example   The Kolkmeyer Manufacturing Company has a group of six identical machines; each machine operates an average of 20 hours between breakdowns. Thus, the mean arrival rate or request for repair service for each individual machine is $\lambda = \frac{1}{20} = 0.05$ machine per hour. With randomly occurring breakdowns, the Poisson probability distribution is used to describe the machine breakdown arrival process. One person from the maintenance department provides the single-channel repair service for the six machines. The exponentially distributed service times have a mean of 2 hours per machine or a mean service rate of $\mu = \frac{1}{2} = 0.50$ machines per hour.

With $\lambda = 0.05$ and $\mu = 0.50$, we use equations (15.33) through (15.37) to compute the operating characteristics for this system. Note that the use of equation (15.33) makes the computations involved somewhat cumbersome. Confirm for yourself that equation (15.30) provides the value $P_0 = 0.4845$. The computations for the other operating characteristics are

$$L_q = 6 - \left(\frac{0.05 + 0.50}{0.05}\right)(1 - 0.4845) = 0.3295 \text{ machine}$$

$$L = 0.3295 + (1 - 0.4845) = 0.845 \text{ machine}$$

$$W_q = \frac{0.3295}{(6 - 0.845)0.05} = 1.28 \text{ hours}$$

$$W = 1.28 + \frac{1}{0.50} = 3.28 \text{ hours}$$

Operating characteristics of an M/M/1 waiting line with a finite calling population are considered in Problem 34.

Finally, equation (15.38) can be used to compute the probabilities of any number of machines being in the repair system.

As with other waiting line models, the operating characteristics provide the manager with information about the waiting line operation. Whether these operating characteristics suggest that better repair service is needed depends on the cost of the idle machine waiting time compared to the cost of assigning an additional person to make the repair operation either a two-channel system or a faster one-channel system.

Formulas for the operating characteristics of the single-channel waiting line with a finite calling population of size N are relatively easy to use. However, the complexity of the multiple-channel model makes a computer solution essential.

Computations for the multiple-channel finite calling population model are more complex than those for the single-channel model. A computer solution is virtually mandatory in this case. The Management Scientist software package that accompanies this text has the capability of analyzing the finite calling population model. The computer solution for the Kolkmeyer machine repair problem with a two-person, two-channel, repair system is shown in Figure 15.4. By considering the cost of machine waiting or down time and the cost of repair personnel, management can determine whether the two-channel system is cost effective.

Figure 15.4 THE MANAGEMENT SCIENTIST SOLUTION FOR THE KOLKMEYER TWO-CHANNEL MACHINE REPAIR PROBLEM

```
SUMMARY OF A 2-CHANNEL WAITING LINE FOR A POPULATION OF SIZE 6
****************************************************************
    MEAN NUMBER OF ARRIVALS = 0.05
    MEAN NUMBER OF SERVICES PER CHANNEL = 0.5


THE PROBABILITY OF NO UNITS IN THE SYSTEM               0.5602
THE AVERAGE NUMBER OF UNITS IN THE WAITING LINE         0.0227
THE AVERAGE NUMBER OF UNITS IN THE SYSTEM               0.5661
THE AVERAGE TIME A UNIT SPENDS IN THE WAITING LINE      0.0834
THE AVERAGE TIME A UNIT SPENDS IN THE SYSTEM            2.0834
THE PROBABILITY THAT AN ARRIVING UNIT HAS TO WAIT       0.1036


Number of Units in the System          Probability
*****************************          ***********
            0                              0.5602
            1                              0.3361
            2                              0.0840
            3                              0.0168
            4                              0.0025
            5                              0.0003
            6                              0.0000
```

SUMMARY

In this chapter we presented a variety of waiting line models that have been developed to help managers make better decisions concerning the operation of waiting lines. For each model, we presented formulas that could be used to develop operating characteristics for the system being studied. Some of the operating characteristics presented were the

1. probability that no units are in the system,
2. average number of units in the waiting line,
3. average number of units in the system,
4. average time a unit spends in the waiting line,
5. average time a unit spends in the system, and
6. probability that arriving units will have to wait for service.

We also showed how an economic analysis of the waiting line could be conducted by developing a total-cost model that includes the cost associated with units waiting for service and the cost required to operate the service facility.

As many of the examples in this chapter show, the most obvious applications of waiting line models are situations in which customers arrive for service such as at a grocery checkout counter, bank, or restaurant. However, with a little creativity, waiting line models can be applied to many different situations such as telephone calls waiting for connections, mail orders waiting for processing, machines waiting for repairs, manufacturing jobs waiting to be processed, and money waiting to be spent or invested. The Q.M. in Action article describes how a waiting line model provided the basis for improving productivity of a fire department in New Haven, Connecticut.

The complexity and diversity of waiting line systems found in practice often prevents an analyst from finding an existing waiting line model that fits the specific application being studied. Simulation, the topic discussed in Chapter 16, provides another approach to determining the operating characteristics of waiting line systems.

Q.M. IN ACTION

IMPROVING FIRE DEPARTMENT PRODUCTIVITY*

The New Haven, Connecticut, Fire Department implemented a reorganization plan with cross-trained fire and medical personnel responding to both fire and medical emergencies. A waiting line model provided the basis for the reorganization by demonstrating that substantial improvements in emergency medical response time could be achieved with only a small reduction in fire protection. Annual savings were reported to be $1.4 million.

The model was based on Poisson arrivals and exponential service times for both fire and medical emergencies. It was used to estimate the average time that a person placing a call would have to wait for the appropriate emergency unit to arrive at the location. Waiting times were estimated by the model's prediction of the average travel time to reach each of the city's 28 census tracts.

The model was first applied to the original system of 16 fire units and 4 emergency medical units that operated independently. It was then applied to the proposed reorganization plan that involved cross-trained department personnel qualified to respond to both fire and medical emergencies. Results from the model demonstrated that average travel times could be reduced under the reorganization plan. Various facility location alternatives also were evaluated. When implemented, the reorganization plan reduced operating cost and improved public safety services.

*Based on Sweeney, A. J., L. Goldring, and E. D. Geyer, "Improving Fire Department Productivity: Merging Fire and Emergency Medical Units in New Haven." *Interfaces*, vol. 23, no. 1, January–February 1993, pp. 109–129.

..../ /...........

GLOSSARY

Queue A waiting line.

Queuing theory The body of knowledge dealing with waiting lines.

Single channel waiting line A waiting line with only one service facility.

Poisson probability distribution The probability distribution used to describe the arrival pattern for some waiting line models.

Exponential probability distribution The probability distribution used to describe the service time for some waiting line models.

First-come, first-served (FCFS) The queue discipline that serves waiting units on a first-come, first-served basis.

Transient period The start-up period for a waiting line, occurring before the waiting line reaches a normal or steady-state operation.

Steady-state operation The normal operation of the waiting line after it has gone through a start-up or transient period. General operating characteristics of waiting lines are computed for steady-state conditions.

Mean arrival rate The average number of customers or units arriving in a given period.

Mean service rate The average number of customers or units that can be served by one service facility in a given period.

Multiple channel waiting line A waiting line with two or more parallel service facilities.

Blocked When arriving units cannot enter the waiting line because the system is full. Blocked units can occur when waiting lines are not allowed or when waiting lines have a finite capacity.

Infinite calling population The population of customers or units who may seek service has no specified upper limit.

Finite calling population The population of customers or units who may seek service has a fixed and finite value.

..../ /...........

PROBLEMS

1. Willow Brook National Bank operates a drive-up teller window that allows customers to complete bank transactions without getting out of their cars. On weekday mornings, arrivals to the drive-up teller window occur at random, with a mean arrival rate of 24 customers per hour or 0.4 customer per minute.
   a. What is the mean or expected number of customers that will arrive in a 5-minute period?
   b. Assume that the Poisson probability distribution can be used to describe the arrival process. Use the mean arrival rate in part (a) and compute the probabilities that exactly 0, 1, 2, and 3 customers will arrive during a 5-minute period.
   c. Delays are expected if more than 3 customers arrive during any 5-minute period. What is the probability that delay will occur?

2. In the Willow Brook National Bank waiting line system (see Problem 1), assume that the service times for the drive-up teller follow an exponential probability distribution with a mean

service rate of 36 customers per hour or 0.6 customer per minute. Use the exponential proba-bility distribution to answer the following questions.

   a.   What is the probability the service time is 1 minute or less?
   b.   What is the probability the service time is 2 minutes or less?
   c.   What is the probability the service time is more than 2 minutes?

3.   Use the single-channel drive-up bank teller operation referred to in Problems 1 and 2 to deter-mine the following operating characteristics for the system.

   a.   The probability of no customers in the system
   b.   The average number of customers waiting
   c.   The average number of customers in the system
   d.   The average time a customer spends waiting
   e.   The average time a customer spends in the system
   f.   The probability that arriving customers will have to wait for service

4.   Use the single-channel drive-up bank teller operation referred to in Problems 1–3 and find the probabilities of 0, 1, 2, and 3 customers in the system. What is the probability that more than 3 customers will be in the drive-up teller system at the same time?

SELF TEST

5.   The reference desk of a university library receives requests for assistance. Assume that a Pois-son probability distribution with a mean rate of 10 requests per hour can be used to describe the arrival pattern and that service times follow the exponential probability distribution with a mean service rate of 12 requests per hour.

   a.   What is the probability of no requests for assistance in the system?
   b.   What is the average number of requests that will be waiting for service?
   c.   What is the average waiting time in minutes before service begins?
   d.   What is the average time at the reference desk in minutes (waiting time plus service time)?
   e.   What is the probability that a new arrival has to wait for service?

6.   Trucks using a single-channel loading dock arrive according to the Poisson probability distrib-ution. The time required to load/unload follows the exponential probability distribution. The mean arrival rate is 12 trucks per day, and the mean service rate is 18 trucks per day.

   a.   What is the probability of no trucks in the system?
   b.   What is the average number of trucks waiting for service?
   c.   What is the average time a truck waits for the loading/unloading service to begin?
   d.   What is the probability that a new arrival will have to wait?

7.   A mail-order nursery specializes in European beech trees. New orders, which are processed by a single shipping clerk, have a mean arrival rate of 6 per day and a mean service rate of 8 per day. Assume that arrivals follow a Poisson probability distribution and that service times follow an exponential probability distribution.

   a.   What is the average number of orders in the system?
   b.   What is the average time that an order spends waiting before the clerk is available to be-gin service?
   c.   What is the average time an order spends in the system?

8.   For the Burger Dome single-channel waiting line in Section 15.2, assume that the arrival rate is increased to 1 customer per minute and the mean service rate is increased to 1.25 customers per minute. Compute the following operating characteristics for the new system: P_0, L_q, L, W_q, W, and P_w. Does this system provide better or poorer service compared to the original system? Dis-cuss any differences and the reason for these differences.

9.   Marty's Barber Shop has one barber. Customers arrive at the rate of 2.2 customers per hour, and haircuts are given at the average rate of 5 per hour. Use the Poisson arrivals and exponential ser-vice times model to answer the following questions.

   a.   What is the probability of no units in the system?
   b.   What is the probability that 1 customer is receiving a haircut and no one is waiting?
   c.   What is the probability that 1 customer is receiving a haircut and 1 customer is waiting?
   d.   What is the probability that 1 customer is receiving a haircut and 2 customers are waiting?

    e. What is the probability that more than 2 customers are waiting?

    f. What is the average time a customer waits for service?

10. Trosper Tire Company has decided to hire a new mechanic to handle all tire changes for customers ordering a new set of tires. Two mechanics have applied for the job. One mechanic has limited experience, can be hired for $14 per hour, and can service an average of 3 customers per hour. The other mechanic has several years of experience, can service an average of 4 customers per hour, but must be paid $20 per hour. Assume that customers arrive at the Trosper garage at the rate of 2 customers per hour.

    a. Compute the waiting line characteristics for each mechanic, assuming Poisson arrivals and exponential service times.

    b. If the company assigns a customer waiting cost of $30 per hour, which mechanic provides the lower operating cost?

SELF TEST

11. Agan Interior Design provides home and office decorating assistance to its customers. In normal operation, an average of 2.5 customers arrive each hour. One design consultant is available to answer customer questions and make product recommendations. The consultant averages 10 minutes with each customer.

    a. Compute the operating characteristics of the customer waiting line, assuming Poisson arrivals and exponential service times.

    b. Service goals dictate that an arriving customer should not wait for service more than an average of 5 minutes. Is this goal being met? If not, what action do you recommend?

    c. If the consultant can reduce the average time spent per customer to 8 minutes, what is the mean service rate? Will the service goal be met?

12. Pete's Market is a small local grocery store with only one checkout counter. Assume that shoppers arrive at the checkout lane according to the Poisson probability distribution, with a mean arrival rate of 15 customers per hour. The checkout service times follow an exponential probability distribution, with a mean service rate of 20 customers per hour.

    a. Compute the operating characteristics for this waiting line.

    b. If the manager's service goal is to limit the waiting time prior to beginning the checkout process to no more than 5 minutes, what recommendations would you provide regarding the current checkout system?

13. After reviewing the waiting line analysis of Problem 12, the manager of Pete's Market wants to consider one of the following alternatives for improving service. What alternative would you recommend? Justify your recommendation.

    a. Hire a second person to bag the groceries while the cash register operator is entering the cost data and collecting money from the customer. With this improved single-channel operation, the mean service rate could be increased to 30 customers per hour.

    b. Hire a second person to operate a second checkout counter. The two-channel operation would have a mean service rate of 20 customers per hour for each channel.

14. Keuka Park Savings and Loan currently has one drive-up teller window. The arrivals follow a Poisson probability distribution, with a mean arrival rate of 10 cars per hour. The service times follow an exponential probability distribution, with a mean service rate of 12 cars per hour.

    a. What is the probability that no customers are in the system?

    b. If you were to drive up to the facility, how many cars would you expect to see waiting and being served?

    c. What is the probability that at least one car will be waiting to be served?

    d. What is the average time in the queue waiting for service?

    e. As a potential customer of the system, would you be satisfied with the given waiting line characteristics? Why or why not?

15. To improve customer service, Keuka Park Savings and Loan (see Problem 14) managers want to investigate the effect of a second drive-up teller window. Assume a mean arrival rate of 10 cars per hour and a mean service rate of 12 cars per hour for each drive-up window. What effect would the addition of a new teller window have on the system? Does this system appear acceptable?

16. The new Fore and Aft Marina is to be located on the Ohio River near Madison, Indiana. Assume that Fore and Aft has decided to build a docking facility where one boat at a time can stop for gas and servicing. Assume that arrivals follow a Poisson probability distribution, with a mean of 5 boats per hour, and that service times follow an exponential probability distribution, with a mean of 10 boats per hour. Answer the following questions.
   a. What is the probability that no boats are in the system?
   b. What is the average number of boats that will be waiting for service?
   c. What is the average time a boat will spend waiting for service?
   d. What is the average time a boat will spend at the dock?
   e. If you were the manager of Fore and Aft Marina, would you be satisfied with the service level your system will be providing? Why or why not?

17. The manager of the Fore and Aft Marina in Problem 16 wants to investigate the possibility of enlarging the docking facility so that two boats can stop for gas and servicing simultaneously. Assume that the mean arrival rate is 5 boats per hour and that the mean service rate for each channel is 10 boats per hour.
   a. What is the probability that the boat dock will be idle?
   b. What is the average number of boats that will be waiting for service?
   c. What is the average time a boat will spend waiting for service?
   d. What is the average time a boat will spend at the dock?
   e. If you were the manager of Fore and Aft Marina, would you be satisfied with the service level your system will be providing? Why or why not?

18. The City Beverage Drive-Thru is considering a two-channel service system. Cars arrive according to the Poisson probability distribution, with a mean arrival rate of 6 cars per hour. The service times have an exponential probability distribution, with a mean service rate of 10 cars per hour for each channel.
   a. What is the probability that no cars are in the system?
   b. What is the average number of cars waiting for service?
   c. What is the average time waiting for service?
   d. What is the average time in the system?
   e. What is the probability that an arrival will have to wait for service?

SELF TEST

19. Consider a two-channel waiting line with Poisson arrivals and exponential service times. The mean arrival rate is 14 units per hour, and the mean service rate is 10 units per hour for each channel.
   a. What is the probability that no units are in the system?
   b. What is the average number of units in the system?
   c. What is the average time a unit waits for service?
   d. What is the average time a unit is in the system?
   e. What is the probability of having to wait for service?

20. Refer to Problem 19. Assume that the system is expanded to a three-channel operation.
   a. Compute the operating characteristics for this waiting line system.
   b. If the service goal is to provide sufficient capacity so that no more than 25% of the customers have to wait for service, is the two- or three-channel system preferred?

SELF TEST

21. Refer to the Agan Interior Design situation in Problem 11. Agan's management would like to evaluate two alternatives:
   • Use one consultant with an average service time of 8 minutes per customer.
   • Expand to two consultants, each of whom has an average service time of 10 minutes per customer.
   If the consultants are paid $16 per hour and the customer waiting time is valued at $25 per hour for waiting time prior to service, should Agan expand to the two-consultant system? Explain.

22. A fast-food franchise is considering operating a drive-up window food-service operation. Assume that customer arrivals follow a Poisson probability distribution, with a mean arrival rate

of 24 cars per hour, and that service times follow an exponential probability distribution. Arriving customers place orders at an intercom station at the back of the parking lot and then drive to the service window to pay for and receive their orders. The following three service alternatives are being considered.

- A single-channel operation in which one employee fills the order and takes the money from the customer. The average service time for this alternative is 2 minutes.
- A single-channel operation in which one employee fills the order while a second employee takes the money from the customer. The average service time for this alternative is 1.25 minutes.
- A two-channel operation with two service windows and two employees. The employee stationed at each window fills the order and takes the money for customers arriving at the window. The average service time for this alternative is 2 minutes for each channel.

Answer the following questions and recommend an alternative design for the fast-food franchise.

   a. What is the probability that no customers are in the system?
   b. What is the average number of cars waiting for service?
   c. What is the average time a car waits for service?
   d. What is the average time in the system?
   e. What is the average number of cars in the system?
   f. What is the probability an arriving car will have to wait for service?

23. The following cost information is available for the fast-food franchise in Problem 22.
- Customer waiting time is valued at $25 per hour to reflect the fact that waiting time is costly to the fast-food business.
- The cost of each employee is $6.50 per hour.
- To account for equipment and space, an additional cost of $20 per hour is attributable to each channel.

What is the lowest-cost design for the fast-food business?

24. Patients arrive at a dentist's office at a mean rate of 2.8 patients per hour. The dentist can treat patients at the mean rate of 3 patients per hour. A study of patient waiting times shows that, on average, a patient waits 30 minutes before seeing the dentist.

   a. What are the mean arrival and treatment rates in terms of patients per minute?
   b. What is the average number of patients in the waiting room?
   c. If a patient arrives at 10:10 A.M., at what time is the patient expected to leave the office?

SELF TEST

25. A study of the multichannel food-service operation at the Red Birds' baseball park shows that the average time between the arrival of a customer at the food-service counter and his or her departure with a filled order is 10 minutes. During the game, customers arrive at the average rate of 4 per minute. The food-service operation requires an average of 2 minutes per customer order.

   a. What is the mean service rate per channel in terms of customers per minute?
   b. What is the average waiting time in the line prior to placing an order?
   c. On average, how many customers are in the food-service system?

26. Manning Autos operates an automotive service counter. While completing the repair work, Manning mechanics arrive at the company's parts department counter at the mean rate of 4 per hour. The parts coordinator spends an average of 6 minutes with each mechanic, discussing the parts the mechanic needs and retrieving the parts from inventory.

   a. Currently, there is one parts coordinator. On average, each mechanic waits 4 minutes before the parts coordinator is available to answer questions and/or retrieve parts from inventory. Find L_q, W, and L for this single-channel parts operation.
   b. A trial period with a second parts coordinator showed that, on average, each mechanic waited only 1 minute before a parts coordinator was available. Find L_q, W, and L for this two-channel parts operation.
   c. If the cost of each mechanic is $20 per hour and the cost of each parts coordinator is $12 per hour, is the one-channel or the two-channel system more economical?

SELF TEST

27. Gubser Welding, Inc., operates a welding service for construction and automotive repair jobs. Assume that the arrival of jobs at the company's office can be described by a Poisson probability distribution with a mean arrival rate of 2 jobs per 8-hour day. The time required to complete the jobs follows a normal probability distribution with a mean time of 3.2 hours and a standard deviation of 2 hours. Answer the following questions, assuming that Gubser uses one welder to complete all jobs.

a. What is the mean arrival rate in jobs per hour?
b. What is the mean service rate in jobs per hour?
c. What is the average number of jobs waiting for service?
d. What is the average time a job waits before the welder can begin working on it?
e. What is the average number of hours between when a job is received and when it is completed?
f. What percentage of the time is Gubser's welder busy?

28. Jobs arrive randomly at a particular assembly plant; assume that the mean arrival rate is 5 jobs per hour. Service times (in minutes per job) do not follow the exponential probability distribution. Two proposed designs for the plant's assembly operation are shown.

| | | Service Time |
Design	Mean	Standard Deviation
A	6.0	3.0
B	6.25	0.6

a. What is the mean service rate in jobs per hour for each design?
b. For the mean service rates in part (a), what design appears to provide the best or fastest service rate?
c. What are the standard deviations of the service times in hours?
d. Use the $M/G/1$ model in Section 15.7 to compute the operating characteristics for each design.
e. Which design provides the best operating characteristics? Why?

29. The Robotics Manufacturing Company operates an equipment repair business where emergency jobs arrive randomly at the rate of 3 jobs per 8-hour day. The company's repair facility is a single-channel system operated by a repair technician. The service time varies with a mean repair time of 2 hours and a standard deviation of 1.5 hours. The company's cost of the repair operation is $28 per hour. In the economic analysis of the waiting line system, Robotics uses $35 per hour cost for customers waiting during the repair process.

a. What are the arrival rate and service rate in jobs per hour?
b. What is the hourly cost of the repair operation?
c. The company is considering purchasing a computer-based equipment repair system that would enable a constant repair time of 2 hours. For practical purposes, the standard deviation is 0. Because of the computer-based equipment, the company's cost of the new operation would be $32 per hour. The firm's director of operations has said no to the new equipment because the hourly cost is $4 higher and the mean repair time is the same 2 hours. Do you agree? What effect will the new system have on the waiting line characteristics of the repair service?
d. Does paying for the computer-based system to reduce the variation in service time make economic sense? How much will the new system save the company during a 40-hour work week?

SELF TEST

30. A large insurance company has a central computing system that contains a variety of information about customer accounts. Insurance agents in a six-state area use telephone lines to access the customer information database. Currently, the company's central computer system allows 3 users to access the central computer simultaneously. Agents who attempt to use the system

when it is full are denied access; no waiting is allowed. Management realizes that with its expanding business, more requests will be made to the central information system. Being denied access to the system is inefficient as well as annoying for agents. Access requests follow a Poisson probability distribution, with a mean of 42 calls per hour. The mean service rate per line is 20 calls per hour.

a. What is the probability that 0, 1, 2, and 3 access lines will be in use?

b. What is the probability that an agent will be denied access to the system?

c. What is the average number of access lines in use?

d. In planning for the future, management wants to be able to handle $\lambda = 50$ calls per hour; in addition, the probability that an agent will be denied access to the system should be no greater than your answer to part (b). How many access lines should this system have?

31. Mid-West Publishing Company publishes college textbooks. The company operates an 800 telephone number whereby potential adopters can ask questions about forthcoming texts, request examination copies of texts, and place orders. Currently, two extension lines are used, with two representatives handling the telephone inquiries. Calls occurring when both extension lines are being used receive a busy signal; no waiting is allowed. Each representative can accommodate an average of 12 calls per hour.

a. If the mean arrival rate is 20 calls per hour, what percentage of the calls receive a busy signal?

b. How many extensions should be used if the company wants to handle 90% of the calls immediately?

c. What is the average number of extensions that will be busy if your recommendation in part (b) is used?

32. City Cab, Inc., uses two dispatchers to handle requests for service and dispatch the cabs. The telephone calls that are made to City Cab use a common telephone number. When both dispatchers are busy, the caller hears a busy signal; no waiting is allowed. Callers who receive a busy signal can call back later or call another cab service. Assume that the arrival of calls follows a Poisson probability distribution, with a mean of 40 calls per hour, and that each dispatcher can handle a mean of 30 calls per hour.

a. What percentage of time are both dispatchers idle?

b. What percentage of time are both dispatchers busy?

c. What is the probability callers will receive a busy signal if 2, 3, or 4 dispatchers are used?

d. If management wants no more than 12% of the callers to receive a busy signal, how many dispatchers should be used?

33. Kolkmeyer Manufacturing Company (see Section 15.9) is considering adding 2 machines to its manufacturing operation. This addition will bring the number of machines to 8. Mr. Andrews, president of Kolkmeyer, has asked for a study of the need to add a second employee to the repair process. The mean arrival rate is 0.05 machine per hour for each machine, and the mean service rate for each individual assigned to the repair operation is 0.50 machine per hour.

a. Compute the following operating characteristics if the company retains the single-employee repair service.

• The probability that all machines are in operation and the repair person is idle

• The average number of machines waiting for repair

• The average number of machines down (those waiting plus those being serviced)

• The average waiting time before repair can begin

• The average down time (waiting time plus servicing time)

b. Use The Management Scientist software package to compute the same characteristics if a second employee is added to the machine repair operation.

c. Each employee assigned to the service operation is paid $20 per hour. Machine down time is valued at $80 per hour. From an economic point of view, should one or two employees handle the machine repair operation? Explain.

34. Five administrative assistants use an office copier. The average time between arrivals for each assistant is 40 minutes, which is equivalent to a mean arrival rate of $1/40 = 0.025$ arrivals per minute. The mean time each assistant spends at the copier is 5 minutes, which is equivalent to

a mean service rate of $^1/_5 = 0.20$ users per minute. Use the $M/M/1$ model with a finite calling population to determine the following:

a. The probability that the copier is idle
b. The average number of administrative assistants in the waiting line
c. The average number of administrative assistants at the copier
d. The average time an assistant spends waiting for the copier
e. The average time an assistant spends at the copier.
f. During an 8-hour day, how many minutes does an assistant spend at the copier? How much of this time is waiting time?
g. Should management consider purchasing a second copier? Explain.

Case Problem   AIRLINE RESERVATIONS

Regional Airlines is establishing a new telephone system for handling flight reservations. During the 10:00 A.M. to 11:00 A.M. time period, calls to the reservation agent occur randomly at an average of one call every 3.75 minutes. Historical service time data show that a reservation agent spends an average of 3 minutes with each customer. The waiting line model assumptions of Poisson arrivals and exponential service times appear reasonable for the telephone reservation system.

Regional Airlines' management believes that offering an efficient telephone reservation system is an important part of establishing an image as a service-oriented airline. If the system is properly implemented, Regional Airlines will establish good customer relations, which in the long run will increase business. However, if the telephone reservation system is frequently overloaded and customers have difficulty contacting an agent, a negative customer reaction may lead to an eventual loss of business. The cost of a ticket reservation agent is $20 per hour. Thus, management wants to provide good service, but does not want to incur the cost of overstaffing the telephone reservation operation by using more agents than necessary.

At a planning meeting, Regional's management team agreed that an acceptable customer service goal is to answer at least 85% of the incoming calls immediately. During the planning meeting, Regional's vice president of administration pointed out that the data show that the average service rate for an agent is faster than the average arrival rate of the telephone calls. The vice president's conclusion was that personnel costs could be minimized by using one agent and that the single agent should be able to handle the telephone reservations and still have some idle time. The vice president of marketing restated the importance of customer service and expressed support for at least two reservation agents.

The current telephone reservation system design does not allow callers to wait. Callers who attempt to reach a reservation agent when all agents are occupied receive a busy signal and are blocked from the system. A representative from the telephone company suggested that Regional Airlines consider an expanded system that accommodates waiting. In the expanded system, when a customer calls and all agents are busy, a recorded message tells the customer that the call is being held in the order received and that an agent will be available shortly. The customer can stay on the line and listen to background music while waiting for an agent. Regional's management will need more information before switching to the expanded system.

Managerial Report

Prepare a managerial report for Regional Airlines analyzing the telephone reservation system. Evaluate both the system that does not allow waiting and the expanded system that allows waiting. Include the following information in your report.

1. A detailed analysis of the operating characteristics of the reservation system with one agent as proposed by the vice president of administration. What is your recommendation concerning a single-agent system?
2. A detailed analysis of the operating characteristics of the reservation system based on your recommendation regarding the number of agents Regional should use and whether the system should allow customers to wait.
3. What appear to be the advantages or disadvantages of the expanded system? Discuss the number of waiting callers the expanded system would need to accommodate.
4. The telephone arrival data presented are for the 10:00 A.M. to 11:00 A.M. time period; however, the arrival rate of incoming calls is expected to change from hour to hour. Describe how your waiting line analysis could be used to develop a ticket agent staffing plan that would enable the company to provide different levels of staffing for the ticket reservation system at different times during the day. Indicate the information that you would need to develop this staffing plan.

Appendix 15.1 WAITING LINE MODELS WITH SPREADSHEETS

Spreadsheets provide a capability for quickly and easily evaluating waiting line formulas and determining the operating characteristics of a waiting line model. Figure 15.5 shows the formula spreadsheet for a single-channel waiting line with Poisson arrivals and exponential service times. You must input the mean arrival rate, λ, and the mean service rate, μ, in cells **B4** and **B6**, respectively. The input values shown with $\lambda = 0.75$ and $\mu = 1$ are the values used for the Burger Dome single-channel waiting line model presented in Section 15.2.

Equations (15.4) through (15.9) provide the operating characteristics for a single-channel waiting line model with Poisson arrivals and exponential service times. You can obtain a spreadsheet evaluation of this waiting line model by placing these equations (as formulas) in selected cells. In Figure 15.5 cell **B10** contains the formula = 1– B4/B6. With λ entered in cell **B4** and μ entered in cell **B6**, cell **B10** contains the probability of no units in the system, given by $1 - (\lambda/\mu)$ in equation (15.4). Verify that the formula in cell **B12** determines the average number of units in the waiting line as given by equation (15.5):

$$L_q = \frac{\lambda^2}{\mu(\mu - \lambda)}$$

Note that the average number of units in the system in cell **B14** is given by equation (15.6), where $L = L_q + (\lambda/\mu)$. Thus, **B14** contains the formula = B12 + B4/B6. As L_q has already been computed in cell **B12**, the formula in cell **B14** takes advantage of the computation made in cell **B12** in arriving at the average number of units in the system. Continuing with the formula spreadsheet, equations (15.7) through (15.9) for the single-channel model have been entered as the formulas for cells **B16**, **B18**, and **B20**, respectively.

For the mean arrival rate of 0.75 and the mean service rate of 1.00, the value spreadsheet in Figure 15.6 provides the operating characteristics for the Burger Dome single-channel waiting line model. Note that these are the same as those computed in Section 15.2.

Figure 15.5 FORMULA SPREADSHEET FOR A SINGLE-CHANNEL WAITING LINE MODEL

	A	B
1	SINGLE-CHANNEL WAITING LINE	
2		
3		
4	MEAN ARRIVAL RATE	0.75
5		
6	MEAN SERVICE RATE	1.00
7		
8		
9		
10	PROBABILITY OF NO UNITS	=1-B4/B6
11		
12	AVERAGE NUMBER IN WAITING LINE	=B4^2/(B6*(B6-B4))
13		
14	AVERAGE NUMBER IN SYSTEM	=B12+B4/B6
15		
16	AVERAGE TIME IN WAITING LINE	=B12/B4
17		
18	AVERAGE TIME IN SYSTEM	=B16+1/B6
19		
20	PROBABILITY OF WAITING	=B4/B6

Figure 15.6 VALUE SPREADSHEET RESULTS FOR THE BURGER DOME WAITING LINE MODEL

	A	B
1	SINGLE-CHANNEL WAITING LINE	
2		
3		
4	MEAN ARRIVAL RATE	0.75
5		
6	MEAN SERVICE RATE	1.00
7		
8		
9		
10	PROBABILITY OF NO UNITS	0.25
11		
12	AVERAGE NUMBER IN WAITING LINE	2.25
13		
14	AVERAGE NUMBER IN SYSTEM	3.00
15		
16	AVERAGE TIME IN WAITING LINE	3.00
17		
18	AVERAGE TIME IN SYSTEM	4.00
19		
20	PROBABILITY OF WAITING	0.75

After you have developed the spreadsheet, you can easily change input parameters and automatically adjust the operating characteristics throughout the spreadsheet. In Section 15.2 we discussed the design alternative of increasing the mean service rate at Burger Dome to $\mu = 1.25$ by using a combined order-taker, order-filler system. Thus, if you simply change the mean service rate to 1.25, the new operating characteristics, as previously shown in Table 15.3, will appear. Thus a spreadsheet enables you to ask "what-if" questions and immediately learn how changes in design will affect the operating characteristics of the system.

You will have to develop a similar, but slightly different, spreadsheet for each different waiting line model. For example, the multiple-channel waiting line model in Section 15.3 could be placed in a formula spreadsheet similar to that in Figure 15.5. In addition to the mean arrival rate and mean service rate, the multiple-channel spreadsheet would require a third input cell indicating the number of channels in the waiting line. The operating characteristic formulas of Figure 15.5 currently based on equations (15.4) through (15.9) would have to be modified to accommodate equations (15.11) through (15.16) for the multiple-channel model. Additional input cells for the cost of a service channel and the cost of waiting could be used to create another cell formula to compute the total cost of operating the waiting line system.

CITIBANK

LONG ISLAND CITY, NEW YORK

Citibank, a major subsidiary of Citicorp, makes available a wide range of financial services, including checking and savings accounts, loans and mortgages, insurance, and investment services, within the framework of a unique strategy for delivering those services called Citibanking. Citibanking entails a consistent brand identity all over the world, consistent product offerings, and a high level of customer service. Citibanking lets you manage your money anytime, anywhere, anyway you choose. Whether you need to save for the future or borrow for today, you can do it all at Citibank.

Citibanking's state-of-the-art automatic teller machines (ATMs) located in Citicard Banking Centers (CBCs), let customers do all their banking in one place with the touch of a finger, 24 hours a day, 7 days a week. More than 150 different banking functions from deposits to managing investments can be performed with ease. Citibanking ATMs are so much more than just cash machines that customers today use them for 80% of their transactions.

A Waiting Line Application

The New York franchise of U.S. Citibanking operates approximately 250 CBCs. Each CBC provides customers with one or more ATMs, called customer activated terminals (or CATs), which are capable of performing a variety of banking transactions. Approximately 70% of the CBCs are located in Manhattan, the Bronx, Brooklyn, Queens, and Staten Island. The remaining 30% are suburban CBCs located in Nassau, Suffolk, Orange, Rockland, and Westchester counties. Measuring performance

---

*The authors are indebted to Stacey Karter, Citibank, for providing this application.

and service capacity at each of the CBCs is an important part of Citibank's emphasis on providing superior access and convenience for its customers.

Each Citibank CBC operates as a waiting line system with randomly arriving customers seeking service at a CAT. Based on the use at each site, the number of CATs ranges from 1 to 20 with each site operating with a single queue. If 1 CAT is present, the system operates as a single-channel waiting line, with arriving customers waiting whenever the CAT is being used by another customer. At most of the CBC sites, multiple CATs provide a multiple-channel waiting line system.

A periodic CBC capacity study is used to determine the capacity needed at each center. The hardware supply at the center is measured in terms of the transactional volume the site is capable of supporting for a standard number of transactions per CAT per hour. The customer demand is measured in terms of the peak number of arrivals per hour at the site. Comparing supply and demand enables Citibank to classify each CBC as either

- Highly endangered—average peak hour waiting time exceeds 5 minutes.
- Borderline—average peak hour waiting time is 3–5 minutes.
- Sufficient—average peak hour waiting time is 3 minutes or less.

In a recent capacity study, demand data suggested approximately 6% of the CBCs should be classified as endangered and approximately 8% should be classified as borderline. In total, 34 sites were listed as candidates for possible capacity expansion with incremental CATs desired.

In order to make recommendations on the number of CATs to add at the selected sites, management needed additional information concerning the customer service levels at each site. Operating characteristics information provided by a waiting line model would be helpful in determining the number of CATs each center should have. Typical information provided by the model included:

- The average number of customers in the waiting line
- The average number of customers in the system
- The average time a customer spends in the waiting line
- The average time a customer spends in the system
- The probability that an arriving customer has to wait

In-house management information system (MIS) data on arrival rates and service times were collected to determine whether a multiple-channel waiting line model with Poisson arrivals and exponential service time could be used to model a CBC waiting line system. Customer arrivals were indeed random and adequately represented by a Poisson probability distribution. The mean arrival rate varied, depending on time of day and day of week. However, it was important for the operating characteristic information to be developed for the peak or high demand periods. An average of the top 10 hourly demands was used to determine the mean arrival rate for each CBC site. Observed service times showed that the exponential probability distribution provided a reasonable approximation of the service time distribution.

For example, one midtown Manhattan branch site was classified as an endangered center operating with 5 CATs. Onsite observations were conducted to verify the MIS data and the peak arrival rate of 172 customers per hour. From the observed session times of 2 minutes per customer, the mean service rate per CAT was estimated to be 30 per hour. Five CATs were insufficient to meet this peak demand. A multiple-channel waiting line model with an expansion to 6 CATs showed that 88% of the customers would still have to wait and that the average waiting time would be 6 to 7 minutes. Expansion to 6 CATs still provided an unacceptable level of service. Expansion to 7 CATs provided acceptable service levels with an average of 2.4 customers in the waiting line. Hence, expansion to 8 CATs was not necessary at that time.

Even though peak demand periods were not always long enough to reach the steady-state conditions projected by the waiting line model, the operating characteristics indicated by the model provided general guidelines for capacity decisions. Use of the observed mean arrival and service rates unique to each site enabled the waiting line model to provide useful information for making the incremental CAT decisions at each CBC location.

Questions

1. How did Citibank's CBCs operate as a waiting line system?
2. How did Citibank ensure appropriate arrival and service time rates for the CBC waiting line operation?
3. What information did the waiting line model provide? How was this information helpful in making the incremental CAT decisions for each site?

16

SIMULATION

Simulation is one of the most widely used quantitative approaches to decision making. It is a method for learning about a real system by experimenting with a model that represents the system. The simulation model contains the mathematical expressions and logical relationships that describe how to compute the value of the output given the values of the inputs. Any simulation model has two inputs: controllable inputs and probabilistic inputs. Figure 16.1 shows a conceptual diagram of a simulation model.

In conducting a **simulation experiment,** values for the **controllable inputs** are selected by the decision maker. Then, values for the **probabilistic inputs** are randomly generated. Based upon the values for the controllable and probabilistic inputs, the model is used to compute the value, or values, of the output. Simulation has been successfully applied in a wide variety of applications. The following examples are typical.

1. **New Product Introduction** The objective of this simulation is to determine the probability that a new product will be profitable. A model is developed relating profit (the output measure) to various probabilistic inputs such as demand, parts cost, and labor cost. The only controllable input is whether to introduce the product. A variety of possible values would be generated for the probabilistic inputs, and the resulting profit would be computed. We develop a simulation model for this type of application in Section 16.1.

2. **Airline Overbooking** The objective of this simulation is to determine the number of reservations the airline should accept for a particular flight. A model is developed relating profit for the flight to a probabilistic input, the number of passengers that show up to use their reservations, and a

Figure 16.1   DIAGRAM OF A SIMULATION MODEL

controllable input, the number of reservations made. For each choice of a value for the controllable input, a variety of possible values would be generated for the number of passengers that show up, and the resulting profit would be computed. Similar models are applicable for hotel and car rental reservation systems.

3. **Inventory Policy**   The objective of this simulation is to choose an inventory policy that will provide good customer service at a reasonable cost. A model is developed relating cost and service level (2 output measures) to probabilistic inputs, such as product demand and delivery lead time from vendors, and controllable inputs, such as the order quantity and the reorder point. For each setting of the controllable inputs, a variety of possible values would be generated for the probabilistic inputs, and the resulting cost and service levels would be computed.

4. **Traffic Flow**   The objective of this simulation is to determine the effect of installing a left turn signal on the flow of traffic through a busy intersection. A model is developed relating waiting time for vehicles to get through the intersection to probabilistic inputs, such as the number of vehicle arrivals and the fraction that want to make a left turn, and controllable inputs, such as the length of time the left turn signal is on. For each setting of the controllable inputs, values would be generated for the probabilistic inputs, and the resulting vehicle waiting times would be computed.

5. **Waiting Lines**   The objective of this simulation is to determine the waiting times for customers at a bank's automatic teller machine (ATM). A model is developed relating customer waiting times to probabilistic inputs, such as customer arrivals and service times, and a controllable input, the number of ATM machines installed. For each value of the controllable input (a number of ATM machines), a variety of values would be generated for the probabilistic inputs and the customer waiting times would be computed. We develop a simulation model for this type of application in Section 16.3.

Simulation is not an optimization technique. It is a method that can be used to describe or predict how a system will operate given certain choices for the controllable inputs and randomly generated values for the probabilistic inputs. Quantitative analysts often use simulation to determine values for the controllable inputs that are likely to lead to desirable system outputs. In this sense, simulation can be a very effective tool in designing a system to provide good performance.

In this chapter we begin by showing how simulation can be used for risk analysis; we use it to study the financial risks associated with a new product introduction. We continue with illustrations showing how simulation can be used to establish an effective inventory policy and how simulation can be used to design waiting line systems. Other issues such as verifying the simulation program, validating the model, and selecting a simulation software package are discussed in Section 16.4. All simulation models described in this chapter can be implemented on a spreadsheet. The chapter appendix shows how Excel can be used to obtain the simulation results shown.

16.1   RISK ANALYSIS

Risk analysis is the process of predicting the outcome of a decision in the face of uncertainty. In this section, we describe a problem that involves considerable uncertainty: the introduction of a new product. We first show how risk analysis can be conducted without using simulation; then, we show how a much more comprehensive risk analysis can be conducted with the aid of simulation.

The PortaCom Printer

PortaCom manufactures personal computers and related equipment. PortaCom's product design group has developed a prototype for a high-quality portable printer with a 30-sheet paper feeder. The new printer has an innovative design and the potential to capture a significant share of the market. Preliminary marketing and financial analyses have led to establishing a selling price and budget for first-year administrative and advertising costs.

$$\text{Selling price} = \$249 \text{ per unit}$$
$$\text{Administrative costs} = \$400,000$$
$$\text{Advertising costs} = \$600,000$$

In the simulation model that we develop for the PortaCom problem, these values are treated as constants and referred to as **parameters** of the model.

The cost of direct labor, the cost of parts, and the first-year demand for the printer are not known with certainty and are considered probabilistic inputs. At this stage of the planning process, PortaCom's best estimates of these inputs are $45 per unit for the direct labor cost, $90 per unit for the parts cost, and 15,000 units for the first-year demand. PortaCom would like an analysis of the first-year profit potential for the printer. Because of a tight cash flow situation, company management is particularly concerned about the potential for a loss.

The What-If Approach

One approach to risk analysis is called **what-if analysis.** A what-if analysis here involves generating values for the three probabilistic inputs (direct labor cost, parts cost, and first-year demand) and computing the resulting value for profit. With the selling price set at $249, administrative cost plus advertising cost set at $400,000 + $600,000 = $1,000,000, the PortaCom profit model is

$$\text{Profit} = (\$249 - \text{Direct labor cost per unit} - \text{Parts cost per unit})(\text{Demand}) - \$1,000,000$$

Letting

$$c_1 = \text{direct labor cost per unit}$$
$$c_2 = \text{parts cost per unit}$$

and

$$x = \text{first-year demand}$$

the profit model for the first year can be written as follows:

$$\text{Profit} = (249 - c_1 - c_2)x - 1,000,000 \qquad (16.1)$$

Recall that PortaCom's best estimates of the direct labor cost per unit, the parts cost per unit, and demand are $45, $90, and 15,000 units, respectively. These values constitute the **base-case scenario** for PortaCom. Substituting these values into equation (16.1) yields the following profit projection.

$$\text{Profit} = (249 - 45 - 90)(15,000) - 1,000,000 = 710,000$$

Thus, the base-case scenario leads to an anticipated profit of $710,000.

In risk analysis we are concerned with both the probability of a loss and the magnitude of the loss. Although the base-case scenario looks appealing, PortaCom might be interested in what happens if their estimates of the direct labor cost per unit, parts cost per unit, and first-year demand do not turn out to be as expected under the base-case scenario. For instance, suppose that PortaCom believes that direct labor costs could range from $43 to $47 per unit, parts cost could range from $80 to $100 per unit, and first-year demand could range from 1500 to 28,500 units. Using these ranges, what-if analysis can be used to evaluate a **worst-case scenario** and a **best-case scenario.**

The worst-case value for the direct labor cost is $47 (the highest value), the worst-case value for the parts cost is $100 (the highest value), and the worst-case value for demand is 1500 units (the lowest value). Thus, in the worst-case scenario, $c_1 = 47$, $c_2 = 100$, and $x = 1500$. Substituting these values into equation (16.1) leads to the following profit projection:

$$\text{Profit} = (249 - 47 - 100)(1500) - 1,000,000 = -847,000$$

So, the worst-case scenario leads to a projected loss of $847,000.

The best-case value for the direct labor cost is $c_1 = 43$ (the lowest value), the best-case value for the parts cost is 80 (the lowest value), and the best-case value for demand is 28,500 units (the highest value). Substituting these values into equation (16.1) leads to the following profit projection:

$$\text{Profit} = (249 - 43 - 80)(28,500) - 1,000,000 = 2,591,000$$

So, the best-case scenario leads to a projected profit of $2,591,000.

Problem 2 will give you practice with a what-if analysis application.

At this point the what-if analysis provides the conclusion that profits can range from a loss of $847,000 to a profit of $2,591,000 with a base-case scenario value of $710,000. The what-if analysis indicates that a substantial loss is possible, a substantial profit is possible, and the base-case profit of $710,000 is possible. Other scenarios that PortaCom might want to consider can also be evaluated. However, the difficulty with what-if analysis is that it does not tell us the likelihood of the various profit or loss values. In particular, we do not have any idea about the *probability* of a loss.

The Simulation Approach

The simulation approach to the PortaCom risk analysis problem is like playing out many what-if scenarios by randomly generating values for the probabilistic inputs. The advantage of the simulation approach is that it allows us to make an assessment of the probability of the possible profit and/or loss values. The PortaCom profit model can be depicted graphically as shown in Figure 16.2.

Using the what-if approach to risk analysis, we selected values for the probabilistic inputs [direct labor cost per unit (c_1), parts cost per unit (c_2), and first-year demand (x)], and then computed the resulting profit. The three sets of values we used were the base-, worst-, and best-case scenarios. Applying simulation to the PortaCom problem requires generating values for the probabilistic inputs that are representative of what we might observe in practice. To generate such values, we must know the probability distribution for each probabilistic input. Further analysis by PortaCom has led to the following probability distributions for the direct labor cost per unit, the parts cost per unit, and first-year demand:

One advantage of simulation is the ability to use probability distributions that are unique to the system being studied.

Direct Labor Cost: This cost ranges from $43 to $47 per unit and is described by the discrete probability distribution shown in Table 16.1. Thus, we see there is a 0.1 probability that the direct labor cost will be $43 per unit, a 0.2 probability that the direct labor cost will be $44, and so on. The highest probability of 0.4 is associated with a direct labor cost of $45 per unit.

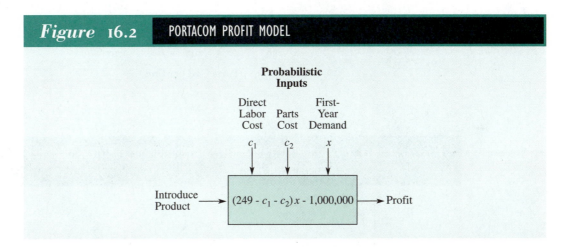

Figure 16.2   PORTACOM PROFIT MODEL

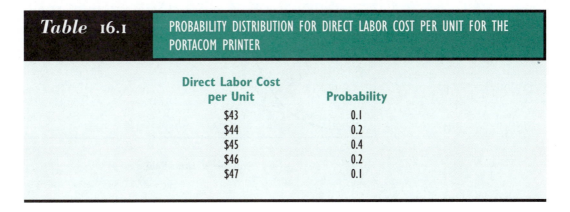

Table 16.1   PROBABILITY DISTRIBUTION FOR DIRECT LABOR COST PER UNIT FOR THE PORTACOM PRINTER

Direct Labor Cost per Unit	Probability
$43	0.1
$44	0.2
$45	0.4
$46	0.2
$47	0.1

Parts Cost: This cost depends upon the general economy, the overall demand for parts, and the pricing policy of PortaCom's parts suppliers. Parts cost ranges from $80 to $100 per unit and is described by the uniform probability distribution shown in Figure 16.3. Values from $80 to $100 are equally likely.

First-Year Demand: First-year demand is described by the normal probability distribution shown in Figure 16.4. The mean or expected value of first-year demand is 15,000 units. The standard deviation of 4500 units describes the variability in the first-year demand.

To simulate the PortaCom problem, we must generate values for the three probabilistic inputs, and compute the resulting profit. Then generate another set of values for the proba-

Figure 16.3 | UNIFORM PROBABILITY DISTRIBUTION FOR THE PARTS COST PER UNIT

Figure 16.4 | NORMAL PROBABILITY DISTRIBUTION OF FIRST-YEAR DEMAND FOR THE PORTACOM PRINTER

bilistic inputs, compute a second value for profit, and so on. We continue this process until we are satisfied that enough trials have been conducted to provide a good picture of the distribution of profit values. This process of generating probabilistic inputs and computing the value of the output is called *simulation*. The sequence of logical and mathematical operations required to conduct a simulation is often depicted as a flowchart. A flowchart for the PortaCom simulation is depicted in Figure 16.5.

A flowchart provides a graphical representation that helps describe the logic of the simulation model.

Following the logic described by the flowchart we see that the model parameters—selling price, administrative cost, and advertising cost—are set at their given values of $249, $400,000, and $600,000, respectively. These values will remain fixed throughout the simulation run.

The next three blocks depict the generation of values for the probabilistic inputs. First, a value for the direct labor cost (c_1) is generated. Then a value for the parts cost (c_2) is generated, followed by a value for the first-year demand (x). These probabilistic input values are combined using the profit model given by (16.1).

$$\text{Profit} = (249 - c_1 - c_2)x - 1{,}000{,}000$$

The computation of profit completes one trial of the simulation run. We then return to the block where we generated the direct labor cost and begin another trial. This process is repeated until a satisfactory number of trials have been generated.

At the end of the simulation, output measures of interest can be developed. For example, we will be interested in computing the average profit and the probability of a loss. It should be clear that for the output measures to be meaningful, the values of the probabilistic inputs must have been representative of what is likely to happen when the new printer is introduced into the market. An essential part of the simulation procedure is the ability to generate representative values for the probabilistic inputs. We now discuss how to generate these values.

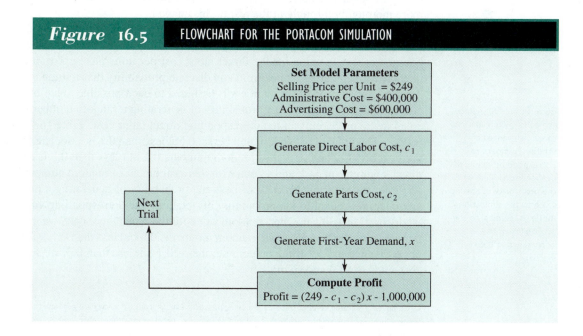

Figure 16.5   FLOWCHART FOR THE PORTACOM SIMULATION

Set Model Parameters
Selling Price per Unit = $249
Administrative Cost = $400,000
Advertising Cost = $600,000

Generate Direct Labor Cost, c_1

Generate Parts Cost, c_2

Generate First-Year Demand, x

Compute Profit
Profit = $(249 - c_1 - c_2)x - 1{,}000{,}000$

Next Trial

Random Numbers and Generating Probabilistic Input Values   In running the Porta-Com simulation, representative values must be generated for the direct labor cost per unit (c_1), the parts cost per unit (c_2), and the first-year demand (x). Random numbers and the probability distributions associated with each probabilistic input are used to generate representative values. To illustrate how to generate these values, we need to introduce the concept of *computer generated random numbers.*

Computer generated random numbers[1] are randomly selected over the interval from 0 up to, but not including, 1. Since each computer generated random number is equally likely, the computer generated random numbers are said to be uniformly distributed over the interval from 0 to 1. Computer generated random numbers can be obtained using built-in functions available in computer simulation packages and spreadsheets. For instance, placing =RAND() in a cell of an Excel spreadsheet will result in a random number between 0 and 1 being placed in that cell.

Table 16.2 contains 500 random numbers generated using Excel. These numbers can be viewed as a random sample of 500 values from a uniform probability distribution that takes on values over the interval from 0 to 1. A uniform probability distribution over the interval from 0 to 1 has a mean or expected value of 0.5; moreover, 10% of the values are between 0.0 and 0.1, 10% are between 0.1 and 0.2, and so on. Thus, for a sample of 500 observations selected at random, we should expect to see about 10% of the values, or 50 observations, in each interval of width 0.1.

Table 16.3 shows the frequency distribution for the 500 computer generated random numbers in Table 16.2 and a histogram is shown in Figure 16.6. The sample mean for the 500 random numbers is 0.5028. We should expect to see about 50 random numbers in each of the intervals of width 0.1. However, as you can see from the table, there is some variability about 50. Theoretically, the proportion in each interval will get closer and closer to 10%, and the sample mean will get closer and closer to the actual mean of 0.5 as more and more random numbers are generated. This same concept also applies in general to running any simulation. That is, the longer we run the simulation, the more likely the observed results will be representative of the system being simulated. We discuss these types of issues more thoroughly throughout the rest of this chapter.

Let us show how we use random numbers uniformly distributed over the interval from 0 to 1 to generate values for the PortaCom probability distributions. We begin by showing how to generate a value for the direct labor cost per unit. The approach described is applicable for generating values from any discrete probability distribution.

An interval of random numbers is assigned to each possible value of the direct labor cost in such a fashion that the probability of generating a random number in the interval is equal to the probability of the corresponding direct labor cost. Table 16.4 shows how this is done. The interval of random numbers 0.0 but less than 0.1 is associated with a direct labor cost of $43, the interval of random numbers 0.1 but less than 0.3 is associated with a direct labor cost of $44, and so on. With this assignment of random number intervals to the possible values of the direct labor cost, the probability of generating a random number in any interval is equal to the probability of obtaining the corresponding value for the direct labor cost. Thus, to generate a random value for the direct labor cost, we generate a random number between 0 and 1. If the random number is 0.0 but less than 0.1, we set the direct labor cost equal to $43. If the random number is 0.1 but less than 0.3, we set the direct labor cost equal to $44, and so on.

Because random numbers are equally likely, analysts can assign ranges of random numbers to corresponding values of probabilistic inputs so that the probability of any input value to the simulation model is identical to the probability of its occurrence in the real system.

---

1. Computer generated random numbers are called *pseudorandom numbers.* Since they are generated through the use of mathematical formulas, they are not technically random. The difference between random numbers and pseudorandom numbers is primarily philosophical and we shall use the term *random numbers* regardless of whether they are generated by a computer.

Table 16.2			500 COMPUTER GENERATED RANDOM NUMBERS						
0.6953	0.5247	0.1368	0.9850	0.7467	0.3813	0.5827	0.7893	0.7169	0.8166
0.0082	0.9925	0.6874	0.2122	0.6885	0.2159	0.4299	0.3467	0.2186	0.1033
0.6799	0.1241	0.3056	0.5590	0.0423	0.6515	0.2750	0.8156	0.2871	0.4680
0.8898	0.1514	0.1826	0.0004	0.5259	0.2425	0.8421	0.9248	0.9155	0.9518
0.6515	0.5027	0.9290	0.5177	0.3134	0.9177	0.2605	0.6668	0.1167	0.7870
0.3976	0.7790	0.0035	0.0064	0.0441	0.3437	0.1248	0.5442	0.9800	0.1857
0.0642	0.4086	0.6078	0.2044	0.0484	0.4691	0.7058	0.8552	0.5029	0.3288
0.0377	0.5250	0.7774	0.2390	0.9121	0.5345	0.8178	0.8443	0.4154	0.2526
0.5739	0.5181	0.0234	0.7305	0.0376	0.5169	0.5679	0.5495	0.7872	0.5321
0.5827	0.0341	0.7482	0.6351	0.9146	0.4700	0.7869	0.1337	0.0702	0.4219
0.0508	0.7905	0.2932	0.4971	0.0225	0.4466	0.5118	0.1200	0.0200	0.5445
0.4757	0.1399	0.5668	0.9569	0.7255	0.4650	0.4084	0.3701	0.9446	0.8064
0.6805	0.9931	0.4166	0.1091	0.7730	0.0691	0.9411	0.3468	0.0014	0.7379
0.2603	0.7507	0.6414	0.9907	0.2699	0.4571	0.9254	0.2371	0.8664	0.9553
0.8143	0.7625	0.1708	0.1900	0.2781	0.2830	0.6877	0.0488	0.8635	0.3155
0.5681	0.7854	0.5016	0.9403	0.1078	0.5255	0.8727	0.3815	0.5541	0.9833
0.1501	0.9363	0.3858	0.3545	0.5448	0.0643	0.3167	0.6732	0.6283	0.2631
0.8806	0.7989	0.7484	0.8083	0.2701	0.5039	0.9439	0.1027	0.9677	0.4597
0.4582	0.7590	0.4393	0.4704	0.6903	0.3732	0.6587	0.8675	0.2905	0.3058
0.0785	0.1467	0.3880	0.5274	0.8723	0.7517	0.9905	0.8904	0.8177	0.6660
0.1158	0.6635	0.4992	0.9070	0.2975	0.5686	0.8495	0.1652	0.2039	0.2553
0.2762	0.7018	0.6782	0.4013	0.2224	0.4672	0.5753	0.6219	0.6871	0.9255
0.9382	0.6411	0.7984	0.0608	0.5945	0.3977	0.4570	0.9924	0.8398	0.8361
0.5102	0.7021	0.4353	0.3398	0.8038	0.2260	0.1250	0.1884	0.3432	0.1192
0.2354	0.7410	0.7089	0.2579	0.1358	0.8446	0.1648	0.3889	0.5620	0.6555
0.9082	0.7906	0.7589	0.8870	0.1189	0.7125	0.6324	0.1096	0.5155	0.3449
0.6936	0.0702	0.9716	0.0374	0.0683	0.2397	0.7753	0.2029	0.1464	0.8000
0.4042	0.8158	0.3623	0.6614	0.7954	0.7516	0.6518	0.3638	0.3107	0.2718
0.9410	0.2201	0.6348	0.0367	0.0311	0.0688	0.2346	0.3927	0.7327	0.9994
0.0917	0.2504	0.2878	0.1735	0.3872	0.6816	0.2731	0.3846	0.6621	0.8983
0.8532	0.4869	0.2685	0.6349	0.9364	0.3451	0.4998	0.2842	0.0643	0.6656
0.8980	0.0455	0.8314	0.8189	0.6783	0.8086	0.1386	0.4442	0.9941	0.6812
0.8412	0.8792	0.2025	0.9320	0.7656	0.3815	0.5302	0.8744	0.4584	0.3585
0.5688	0.8633	0.5818	0.0692	0.2543	0.5453	0.9955	0.1237	0.7535	0.5993
0.5006	0.1215	0.8102	0.1026	0.9251	0.6851	0.1559	0.1214	0.2628	0.9374
0.5748	0.4164	0.3427	0.2809	0.8064	0.5855	0.2229	0.2805	0.9139	0.9013
0.1100	0.0873	0.9407	0.8747	0.0496	0.4380	0.5847	0.4183	0.5929	0.4863
0.5802	0.7747	0.1285	0.0074	0.6252	0.7747	0.0112	0.3958	0.3285	0.5389
0.1019	0.6628	0.8998	0.1334	0.2798	0.7351	0.7330	0.6723	0.6924	0.3963
0.9909	0.8991	0.2298	0.2603	0.6921	0.5573	0.8191	0.0384	0.2954	0.0636
0.6292	0.4923	0.0276	0.6734	0.6562	0.4231	0.1980	0.6551	0.3716	0.0507
0.9430	0.2579	0.7933	0.0945	0.3192	0.3195	0.7772	0.4672	0.7070	0.5925
0.9938	0.7098	0.7964	0.7952	0.8947	0.1214	0.8454	0.8294	0.5394	0.9413
0.4690	0.1395	0.0930	0.3189	0.6972	0.7291	0.8513	0.9256	0.7478	0.8124
0.2028	0.3774	0.0485	0.7718	0.9656	0.2444	0.0304	0.1395	0.1577	0.8625
0.6141	0.4131	0.2006	0.2329	0.6182	0.5151	0.6300	0.9311	0.3837	0.7828
0.2757	0.8479	0.7880	0.8492	0.6859	0.8947	0.6246	0.1574	0.4936	0.8077
0.0561	0.0126	0.6531	0.0378	0.4975	0.1133	0.3572	0.0071	0.4555	0.7563
0.1419	0.4308	0.8073	0.4681	0.0481	0.2918	0.2975	0.0685	0.6384	0.0812
0.3125	0.0053	0.9209	0.9768	0.3584	0.0390	0.2161	0.6333	0.4391	0.6991

Table 16.3	FREQUENCY DISTRIBUTION FOR 500 COMPUTER GENERATED RANDOM NUMBERS

Interval	Frequency
0.0 but less than 0.1	53
0.1 but less than 0.2	47
0.2 but less than 0.3	56
0.3 but less than 0.4	44
0.4 but less than 0.5	43
0.5 but less than 0.6	49
0.6 but less than 0.7	54
0.7 but less than 0.8	52
0.8 but less than 0.9	53
0.9 but less than 1.0	49
Total	500

Figure 16.6	HISTOGRAM OF 500 RANDOM NUMBERS

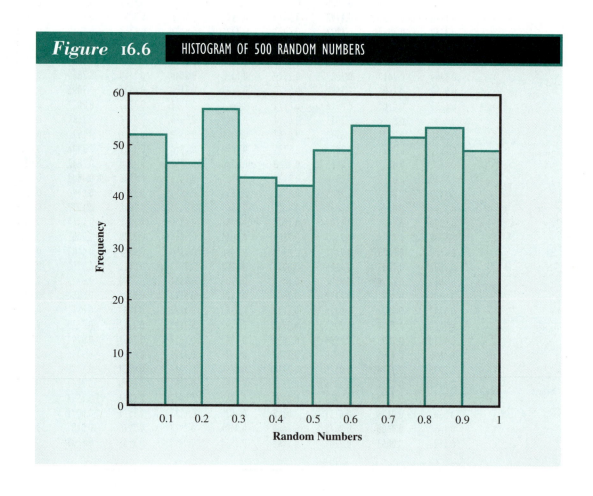

Table 16.4	RANDOM NUMBER INTERVALS FOR GENERATING VALUES OF DIRECT LABOR COST PER UNIT FOR THE PORTACOM PRINTER		

Direct Labor Cost per Unit	Probability	Interval of Random Numbers
$43	0.1	0.0 but less than 0.1
$44	0.2	0.1 but less than 0.3
$45	0.4	0.3 but less than 0.7
$46	0.2	0.7 but less than 0.9
$47	0.1	0.9 but less than 1.0

Problem 5 will give you the opportunity to establish intervals of random numbers and simulate demand from a discrete probability distribution.

Each trial of the simulation requires a value for the direct labor cost. Suppose that on the first trial the random number generated is 0.9109. From Table 16.4, we see that the simulated value for the direct labor cost is $47 per unit. Suppose that on the second trial the random number is 0.2841. Since this random number is in the second interval of Table 16.4, the simulated value for the direct labor cost is $44 per unit. Table 16.5 shows the results obtained for the first 10 simulation trials.

Each trial in the simulation run requires a value of direct labor cost, parts cost, and demand. Let us now turn to the issue of generating values for parts cost. The probability distribution for parts cost is the uniform distribution shown in Figure 16.3. Since this random variable has a different probability distribution than direct labor cost, we will use random numbers in a slightly different way to generate values for parts cost. With a uniform probability distribution, the following relationship between the random number and the associated value of the parts cost is used.

$$\text{Parts Cost} = a + r(b - a) \tag{16.2}$$

where

r = random number between 0 and 1

a = smallest value for parts cost

b = largest value for parts cost

Table 16.5	RANDOM GENERATION OF TEN VALUES FOR THE DIRECT LABOR COST PER UNIT	

Trial	Random Number	Direct Labor Cost ($)
1	0.9109	47
2	0.2841	44
3	0.6531	45
4	0.0367	43
5	0.3451	45
6	0.2757	44
7	0.6859	45
8	0.6246	45
9	0.4936	45
10	0.8077	46

For PortaCom, the smallest value for parts cost is \$80, and the largest value is \$100. Applying equation (16.2) with $a = 80$ and $b = 100$ leads to the following formula for generating parts cost given a random number, r.

$$\text{Parts Cost} = 80 + r(100 - 80) = 80 + 20r \qquad (16.3)$$

Let us use formula (16.3) to generate a value for parts cost. Suppose that a random number of 0.2680 is obtained. The value we would generate for the parts cost per unit is

$$\text{Parts Cost} = 80 + 20(0.2680) = 85.36 \text{ per unit}$$

Suppose that a random number of 0.5842 is generated on the next trial. The value we would generate for the parts cost is

$$\text{Parts Cost} = 80 + 20(0.5842) = 91.68 \text{ per unit}$$

With appropriate choices of a and b, formula (16.2) can be used to generate values for any uniform probability distribution. Table 16.6 shows the generation of ten values for parts cost.

Finally, we need a random number procedure for generating the first-year demand. Since first-year demand is normally distributed with a mean of 15,000 units and a standard deviation of 4500 units (see Figure 16.4), we need a procedure for generating random values from a normal probability distribution. Because of the mathematical complexity, a detailed discussion of the procedure for generating random values from a normal probability distribution is omitted. However, computer simulation packages and spreadsheets include a built-in function that provides randomly generated values from a normal probability distribution. In most cases the user only needs to provide the mean and standard deviation of the normal distribution. For example, using Excel the following formula can be placed in a cell to obtain a value for a probabilistic input that is normally distributed:

$$=\text{NORMINV}(\text{RAND}(),\text{Mean},\text{Standard Deviation})$$

Spreadsheet packages such as Excel have built-in functions that make simulations based on probability distributions such as the normal probability distribution relatively easy.

Since the mean for the first-year demand in the PortaCom problem is 15,000 and the standard deviation is 4500, the Excel statement

$$=\text{NORMINV}(\text{RAND}(),15000,4500) \qquad (16.4)$$

Table 16.6	RANDOM GENERATION OF TEN VALUES FOR THE PARTS COST PER UNIT	
Trial	**Random Number**	**Parts Cost ($)**
1	0.2680	85.36
2	0.5842	91.68
3	0.6675	93.35
4	0.9280	98.56
5	0.4180	88.36
6	0.7342	94.68
7	0.4325	88.65
8	0.1186	82.37
9	0.6944	93.89
10	0.7869	95.74

will provide a normally distributed value for demand. For example, if RAND() generates the random number 0.7005, the Excel function shown in equation (16.4) will generate a first-year demand of 17,366 units. If RAND() generates the random number 0.3204, a first-year demand of 12,900 is generated. Table 16.7 shows the results for the first ten randomly generated values for demand. Note that random numbers less than 0.5 generate first-year demand values below the mean, and random numbers greater than 0.5 generate first-year demand values greater than the mean. A random number of 0.5000 will generate a first-year demand value of 15,000 (the mean).

Running the Simulation Model Running the simulation model means implementing the sequence of logical and mathematical operations described in the flowchart in Figure 16.5. The model parameters are set at $249 per unit for the selling price, $400,000 for the administrative cost, and $600,000 for the advertising cost. Each trial in the simulation involves randomly generating values for the probabilistic inputs (direct labor cost, parts cost, and first-year demand) and computing profit. The simulation run is complete when a satisfactory number of trials have been conducted.

Let us compute the profit for one trial assuming the following values have been generated for the probabilistic inputs:

$$
\begin{aligned}
&\text{Direct Labor Cost:} & c_1 &= 47 \\
&\text{Parts Cost:} & c_2 &= 85.36 \\
&\text{First-Year Demand:} & x &= 17{,}366
\end{aligned}
$$

Referring to the flowchart in Figure 16.5, we see that the profit obtained is

$$\text{Profit} = (249 - c_1 - c_2)x - 1{,}000{,}000 = (249 - 47 - 85.36)17{,}366 - 1{,}000{,}000 = 1{,}025{,}570$$

The first row of Table 16.8 shows the result of this first trial of the PortaCom simulation.

The simulated profit for the PortaCom printer if the direct labor cost is $47 per unit, the parts cost is $85.36 per unit, and first year demand is 17,366 units is $1,025,570. This is the same profit value we would get from generating a what-if scenario with the given values for the probabilistic inputs. The difference is, with simulation, the values generated for the probabilistic inputs appear with the same likelihood they would be expected to occur in

Table 16.7	RANDOM GENERATION OF TEN VALUES FOR FIRST-YEAR DEMAND	
Trial	**Random Number**	**Demand**
1	0.7005	17,366
2	0.3204	12,900
3	0.8968	20,686
4	0.1804	10,888
5	0.4346	14,259
6	0.9605	22,904
7	0.5646	15,732
8	0.7334	17,804
9	0.0216	5,902
10	0.3218	12,918

Table 16.8	PORTACOM SIMULATION RESULTS FOR TEN TRIALS			
Trial	**Direct Labor Cost per Unit ($)**	**Parts Cost per Unit ($)**	**Units Sold**	**Profit ($)**
1	47	85.36	17,366	1,025,570
2	44	91.68	12,900	461,828
3	45	93.35	20,686	1,288,906
4	43	98.56	10,888	169,807
5	45	88.36	14,259	648,911
6	44	94.68	22,904	1,526,769
7	45	88.65	15,732	814,686
8	45	82.37	17,804	1,165,501
9	45	93.89	5,902	−350,131
10	46	95.74	12,918	385,585
Total	449	912.64	151,359	7,137,432
Average	44.90	91.26	15,136	713,743

practice. Of course, one simulation trial does not provide a complete understanding of the possible profit and loss levels. Since other values are possible for the probabilistic inputs, we can benefit from more simulation trials.

Suppose that on a second simulation trial random numbers of 0.2841, 0.5842, and 0.3204 are generated for the direct labor cost, the parts cost, and first year demand, respectively. These random numbers will generate values for the probabilistic inputs of $44 for the direct labor cost, $91.68 for the parts cost, and 12,900 for first year demand. These values provide a simulated profit of $461,828 on the second simulation trial (see the second row of Table 16.8).

Repetition of the simulation process with different values for the probabilistic inputs is an essential part of any simulation. Through the repeated trials, management will begin to understand what might happen when the product is introduced in the real world. We have shown the results of ten simulation trials in Table 16.8. For these 10 cases, we find a profit as high as $1,526,769 for the 6th trial and a loss of $350,131 for the 9th trial. Thus, we see both the possibility of a substantial profit and a substantial loss. Some summary statistics for the ten trials are presented at the bottom of the table. We see that the total profit is $7,137,432 and the average profit is $713,743. The probability of a loss is 0.10, since one of the ten trials (the 9th) resulted in a loss. We note also that the average values for labor cost, parts cost, and demand are fairly close to their population means.

In practice, analysts usually run simulations for a large number of trials to get a better picture of the distribution of output. Using an Excel spreadsheet, we simulated the Porta-Com new product project 500 times. (See Appendix 16.1 for details of the Excel spreadsheet.) A histogram of the profit values generated is shown in Figure 16.7 and some standard descriptive statistics are presented in Table 16.9. Interpretation of this information provides the risk analysis PortaCom management is seeking.

Running the simulation for a relatively large number of trials is recommended as a way of obtaining useful simulation results.

Interpretation of Simulation Results   The simulation run has provided us with much more information to use in conducting a risk analysis of the chances of PortaCom's new printer introduction being successful. The worst result obtained in a simulation of 500 tri-

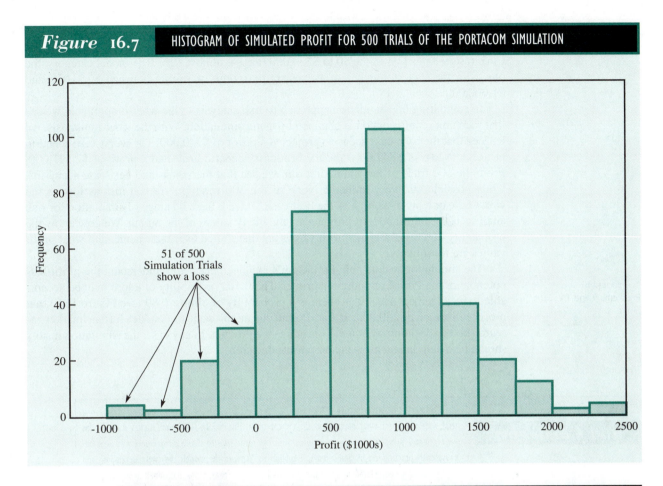

Figure 16.7 HISTOGRAM OF SIMULATED PROFIT FOR 500 TRIALS OF THE PORTACOM SIMULATION

Table 16.9 DESCRIPTIVE STATISTICS FOR 500 TRIALS OF THE PORTACOM SIMULATION

Statistic	Value
Sample Size	500
Mean Profit	$698,457
Median Profit	$709,695
Standard Deviation	$520,485
Minimum Profit	−$785,234
Maximum Profit	$2,367,058
Number of Losses	51
Probability of Loss	0.102

Simulation studies enable an objective estimate of the probability of a loss, which is an important aspect of risk analysis.

als is a loss of $785,234, and the best result is a profit of $2,367,058. The mean profit is $698,457, and the median profit is $709,695. Fifty-one of the trials resulted in a loss; the estimated probability of a loss is 51/500 = 0.102.

The histogram in Figure 16.7 shows the distribution of simulated profit values. We note that this distribution is fairly symmetric with a large number of values in the range of $250,000 to $1,250,000. The probability of a large loss or large gain is small. Only 3 trials resulted in a loss greater than $500,000, and only 3 trials resulted in a profit greater than $2,000,000. The probability of a small loss, however, is significant. Forty-eight of the 500 trials resulted in a loss in the $0 to $500,000 range—almost 10%. The modal category, the one with the largest number of values, is the range of profits between $750,000 and $1,000,000.

In comparing the simulation approach to risk analysis to the what-if approach, we see that much more information is obtained by using simulation. With the what-if anaylsis, we learned that the base-case scenario projected a profit of $710,000. The worst-case scenario projected a loss of $847,000, and the best-case scenario projected a profit of $2,591,000. From the 500 trials of the simulation run, we see that the worst- and best-case scenarios, while possible, are very unlikely. None of the 500 trials provided a loss as low as the worst-case or a profit as high as the best-case. Indeed, the advantage of simulation for risk analysis is the information it provides on the likely values of the output. We now know the probability of a loss, how the profit values are distributed over their range, and what profit values are most likely.

You should be able to work Problems 9 and 14 at this point.

The simulation results help PortaCom's management better understand the profit/loss potential of the PortaCom portable printer. The 0.102 probability of a loss may be acceptable to management given that there is a probability of almost 0.80 (see Figure 16.7) that profit will exceed $250,000. If not, PortaCom might want to conduct further market research before deciding whether to introduce the product. In any case, the simulation results should be a help in reaching an appropriate decision.

NOTES and Comments

1. The PortaCom simulation model is based on independent trials in which what happens during one trial does not affect what happens in subsequent trials. Historically, simulation studies such as this were referred to as *Monte Carlo simulations*. The term *Monte Carlo simulation* was used because early practitioners of simulation saw similarities between the models they were developing and the gambling games played in the casinos of Monte Carlo. Today, many individuals interpret Monte Carlo simulation as a term that refers to any simulation that involves randomly generating values for the probabilistic inputs.

2. The probability distribution used to generate values for probabilistic inputs in a simulation model is often developed using historical data. For instance, suppose that an analysis of daily sales at a new car dealership for the past 50 days showed: On 2 days no cars were sold; on 5 days 1 car was sold; on 9 days 2 cars were sold; on 24 days 3 cars were sold; on 7 days 4 cars were sold; and on 3 days 5 cars were sold. We can estimate the probability distribution of daily demand using the relative frequencies for the observed data. An estimate of the probability that no cars are sold on a given day is $2/50 = 0.04$, an estimate of the probability that 1 car is sold is $5/50 = 0.10$ and so on. The probability distribution of daily demand obtained is as follows:

Daily Sales	0	1	2	3	4	5
Probability	0.04	0.10	0.18	0.48	0.14	0.06

3. Spreadsheet add-in packages such as @RISK® and Crystal Ball® have been developed to make spreadsheet simulation easier. For instance, using Crystal Ball® we could simulate the PortaCom new product introduction by first entering the formulas showing the relationships between the probabilistic inputs and the output measure, profit. Then, a probability distribution type is selected for each probabilistic input from among a number of available choices. Crystal Ball will generate random values for each of the probabilistic inputs, compute the profit, and repeat the simulation for as many trials as specified. Graphical displays and a variety of descriptive statistics can be easily obtained.

..../ /............

16.2 AN INVENTORY SIMULATION

In this section we describe how simulation can be used to establish an inventory policy for a product that has an uncertain demand. The product is a home ventilation fan distributed by the Butler Electrical Supply Company. Each fan costs Butler $75 and sells for $125. Thus Butler realizes a gross profit of $125 − $75 = $50 for each fan sold. Monthly demand for the fan is described by a normal probability distribution with a mean of 100 units and a standard deviation of 20 units.

Butler receives monthly deliveries from its supplier and replenishes its inventory to a level of Q at the beginning of each month. This beginning inventory level is referred to as the replenishment level. If monthly demand is less than the replenishment level, an inventory holding cost of $15 is charged for each unit that is not sold. However, if monthly demand is greater than the replenishment level, a stockout occurs and a shortage cost is incurred. Since Butler assigns a goodwill cost of $30 for each customer turned away, a shortage cost of $30 is charged for each unit of demand that cannot be satisfied. Management would like to use a simulation model to determine the average monthly net profit resulting from using a particular replenishment level. Management would also like information on the percentage of total demand that will be satisfied. This percentage is referred to as the *service level*.

The controllable input to the Butler simulation model is the replenishment level, Q. The probabilistic input is the monthly demand, D. There are two output measures: the average monthly net profit and the service level. Computation of the service level requires that we keep track of the number of fans sold each month and the total demand for fans for each month. The service level will be computed at the end of the simulation run as the ratio of total units sold to total demand. A diagram showing the relationship between the inputs and the outputs is shown in Figure 16.8.

When demand is less than or equal to the replenishment level ($D \leq Q$), D units are sold, and an inventory holding cost of $15 is incurred for each of the $Q - D$ units that remain in inventory. Net profit for this case is computed as follows:

Case 1: $D \leq Q$

$$\text{Gross Profit} = \$50D$$
$$\text{Holding Cost} = \$15(Q - D)$$
$$\text{Net Profit} = \text{Gross Profit} - \text{Holding Cost} = \$50D - \$15(Q - D) \quad (16.5)$$

Figure **16.8**   Butler Inventory Simulation Model

When demand is greater than the replenishment level ($D > Q$), Q fans are sold, and a short-age cost of \$30 is imposed for each of the $D - Q$ units of demand not satisfied. Net profit for this case is computed as follows:

Case 2: D > Q

$$\text{Gross Profit} = \$50Q$$

$$\text{Shortage Cost} = \$30(D - Q)$$

$$\text{Net Profit} = \text{Gross Profit} - \text{Shortage Cost} = \$50Q - \$30(D - Q) \quad (16.6)$$

Figure 16.9 shows a flowchart that defines the sequence of logical and mathematical operations required to simulate the Butler inventory system. Each trial in the simulation rep-resents one month of operation. The simulation is run for 300 months using a given re-plenishment level, Q. Then, the average profit and service level output measures are computed. Let us describe the steps involved in the simulation by illustrating the results for the first two months of a simulation run using a replenishment level of $Q = 100$.

The first block of the flowchart in Figure 16.9 sets the values of the model parameters: gross profit = \$50 per unit, holding cost = \$15 per unit, and goodwill cost = \$30 per unit. The next block shows that a replenishment level of Q is selected; in our illustration, $Q = 100$. Then, a value for monthly demand is generated. Since monthly demand is nor-mally distributed with a mean of 100 units and a standard deviation of 20 units, we can use the Excel function = NORMINV(RAND(),100,20), as described in the previous section, to generate a value for monthly demand. Suppose that a value of $D = 79$ is generated on the first trial. This value of demand is then compared with the replenishment level, Q. With the replenishment level set at $Q = 100$, demand is less than the replenishment level, and the left branch of the flowchart is followed. Sales are set equal to demand (79), and then gross profit, holding cost, and net profit are computed as follows:

$$\text{Gross Profit} = 50D = 50(79) = 3950$$

$$\text{Holding Cost} = 15(Q - D) = 15(100 - 79) = 315$$

$$\text{Net Profit} = 50D - 15(Q - D) = 50(79) - 15(100 - 79) = 3635$$

The values of demand, sales, gross profit, holding cost, and net profit are recorded for the first month. The first row of Table 16.10 summarizes the information for this first trial.

For the second month, suppose that a value of 111 is generated for monthly demand. Since demand is greater than the replenishment level, the right branch of the flowchart is followed. Sales are set equal to the replenishment level (100), and then gross profit, short-age cost, and net profit are computed as follows:

$$\text{Gross Profit} = 50Q = 50(100) = 5000$$

$$\text{Shortage Cost} = 30(D - Q) = 30(111 - 100) = 330$$

$$\text{Net Profit} = 50Q - 30(D - Q) = 50(100) - 30(111 - 100) = 4670$$

The values of demand, sales, gross profit, holding cost, shortage cost, and net profit are recorded for the second month. The second row of Table 16.10 summarizes some of the in-formation generated in the second trial.

Results for the first 5 months of the simulation are shown in Table 16.10. The totals show that we have an accumulated total profit of \$22,310, which is an average monthly profit of \$22,310/5 = \$4462. Total unit sales are 472, and total demand is 501. Thus, the

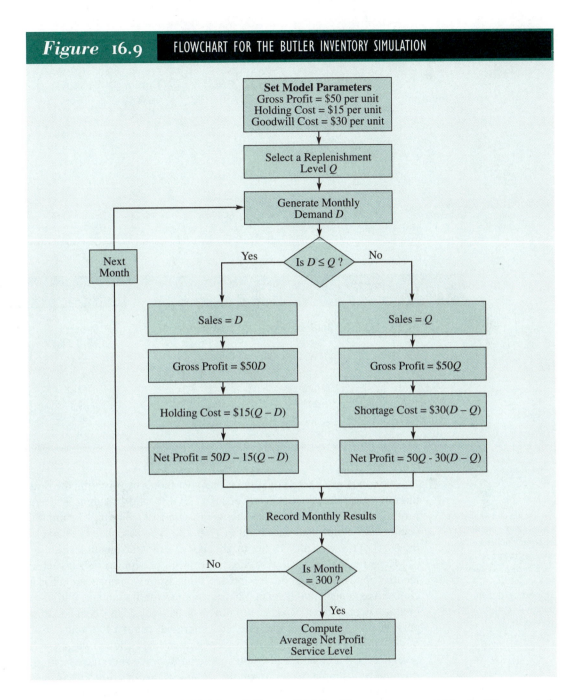

Figure 16.9   FLOWCHART FOR THE BUTLER INVENTORY SIMULATION

service level is $472/501 = .942$, or 94.2%. The average monthly holding cost is $\$420/5 = \$84$ and the average monthly shortage cost is $\$870/5 = \$174$.

We continued the Butler inventory simulation for a total of 300 trials. Row 1 of Table 16.11 represents a sample of 300 months of operations using an inventory replenishment level of 100 fans. The average net profit was $4293, and the service level was 0.925, indicating that 92.5% of customer demand was satisfied. We are now ready to use the simulation model to consider other replenishment levels that may improve the projected net profit and service level.

Table 16.10	BUTLER INVENTORY SIMULATION RESULTS FOR FIVE TRIALS WITH $Q = 100$					
Month	Demand	Sales	Gross Profit ($)	Holding Cost ($)	Shortage Cost ($)	Net Profit ($)
1	79	79	3950	315	0	3635
2	111	100	5000	0	330	4670
3	93	93	4650	105	0	4545
4	100	100	5000	0	0	5000
5	118	100	5000	0	540	4460
Totals	501	472	23,600	420	870	22,310
Average	100	94	$4,720	$ 84	$174	$4,462

Table 16.11	BUTLER INVENTORY SIMULATION RESULTS FOR 300 TRIALS	
Replenishment Level	Average Net Profit ($)	Service Level (%)
100	4293	92.5
110	4524	96.5
120	4575	98.6
130	4519	99.6
140	4399	99.9

Simulation allows the user to consider different operating policies and changes to model parameters and then to observe the impact of the changes on output measures such as profit or service level.

We conducted a series of simulation experiments by repeating the Butler inventory simulation with replenishment levels of 110, 120, 130, and 140 units. The average monthly net profits and the service levels are shown in Table 16.11. The highest monthly profit of $4575 occurs with a replenishment level of $Q = 120$. The associated service level is 98.6%. On the basis of these results, Butler might choose a replenishment level of $Q = 120$ fans.

Experimental simulation studies, such as this one for Butler's inventory policy, can help identify good operating policies and decisions. Butler's management has used simulation to choose a replenishment level of 120 for its home ventilation fan. With the simulation model in place, management can also explore the sensitivity of this decision to some of the model parameters. For instance, we assigned a shortage cost of $30 for any customer demand not met. With this shortage cost, the replenishment level chosen was $Q = 120$ with a service level of 98.6%. If management felt a more appropriate shortage cost might be $10 per unit, it would be a simple matter to run the simulation again using $10 as the shortage cost. We could expect then to see a lower value of Q yielding the best results.

We mentioned earlier that simulation is not an optimization technique. Even though we have used simulation to choose a replenishment level, we have no guarantee that our choice is optimal. All possible replenishment levels were not tested. Perhaps a manager would like to consider additional simulation runs with replenishment levels of $Q = 115$ and $Q = 125$ to search for an even better inventory policy. Also, we have no guarantee that with another set of 300 demand values generated the replenishment level with the highest profit would not change. However, with a large number of simulation trials, we should find a very good and, at least, near optimal solution.

..../ /...............

16.3   A WAITING LINE SIMULATION

The simulation models discussed thus far have been based on independent trials in which the results that occur on one trial do not affect what happens on subsequent trials. In this sense, the system being modeled does not change or evolve over time. These simulation models are referred to as **static simulation models.** In this section, we develop a simulation model of a waiting line system where the state of the system, including the number of individuals in the waiting line and whether the service facility is busy or idle, changes or evolves over time. To incorporate time into the simulation model, we use a simulation clock to record the time that each individual arrives for service as well as the time that each individual completes service. Whenever a simulation clock is used to keep track of the time that events occur in the system and the system changes or evolves over time, the simulation model is referred to as a **dynamic simulation model.** Since the arrivals and departures of individuals are *events* that occur at *discrete* points in time, the simulation model is also referred to as a **discrete-event simulation model.**

In Chapter 15, we presented formulas that could be used to compute the steady-state operating characteristics of a waiting line, including the average waiting time, the average number of individuals in the waiting line, the probability of waiting, and so on. In most cases, the waiting line formulas were based on specific assumptions about the probability distribution for arrivals, the probability distribution for service times, the queue discipline, and so on. Simulation is an alternative for studying waiting lines that is more flexible. In applications where the assumptions required by the waiting line formulas are not reasonable, simulation may be the only feasible approach to the study of the waiting line system. In this section we discuss the simulation of the waiting line for the Hammondsport Savings Bank automatic teller machine (ATM). In Appendix 16.1 we show the Excel spreadsheets that can be used to perform the simulation computations.

The Hammondsport Savings Bank ATM Waiting Line

Hammondsport Savings Bank will open several new branch banks during the coming year. Each new branch is designed to have one automatic teller machine (ATM). A concern is that during busy periods several customers may have to wait to use the ATM. This concern has led the bank to undertake a study of the ATM waiting line system. The bank's vice president wants to determine whether one ATM will be sufficient. The bank has published service guidelines for its ATM system stating that the average customer waiting time for an ATM should be one minute or less. Let us show how a simulation model can be used to study the ATM waiting line at a particular branch.

Customer Arrival Times

One probabilistic input to the ATM simulation model is the arrival times of customers who want to use the ATM. In waiting line simulations, the arrival times are determined by randomly generating time between two successive arrivals referred to as the *interarrival time.* For the branch bank being studied, the customer interarrival times are uniformly distributed between 0 and 5 minutes as shown in Figure 16.10. With r denoting a random number between 0 and 1, an interarrival time for two successive customers can be simulated using the formula presented in Section 16.1 for generating values from a uniform probability distribution.

$$\text{Interarrival Time} = a + r(b - a)$$

Figure 16.10 UNIFORM PROBABILITY DISTRIBUTION OF INTERARRIVAL TIMES FOR THE ATM WAITING LINE SYSTEM

where

$$r = \text{random number between 0 and 1}$$
$$a = \text{minimum interarrival time}$$
$$b = \text{maximum interarrival time}$$

A uniform probability distribution of interarrival times is used here to simplify the simulation computations. Actually, any interarrival time probability distribution can be assumed, and the logic of the waiting line simulation model will not change.

For the Hammondsport ATM system, the minimum interarrival time is $a = 0$ minutes, and the maximum interarrival time is $b = 5$ minutes; therefore, the formula for generating an interarrival time is

$$\text{Interarrival Time} = 0 + r(5 - 0) = 5r$$

Assume that the simulation run begins at time $= 0$. A random number of $r = 0.2804$ generates an interarrival time of $0.2804(5) = 1.4$ minutes for customer 1. Thus, customer 1 arrives 1.4 minutes after the simulation run begins. A second random number of $r = 0.2598$ generates an interarrival time of $0.2598(5) = 1.3$ minutes, indicating that customer 2 arrives 1.3 minutes after customer 1. Thus, customer 2 arrives $1.4 + 1.3 = 2.7$ minutes after the ATM simulation begins. Continuing, a third random number of $r = 0.9802$ indicates that customer 3 arrives 4.9 minutes after customer 2, which is 7.6 minutes after the ATM simulation begins.

Customer Service Times

Another probabilistic input in the ATM simulation model is the service time, which is the time a customer spends using the ATM machine. The service time does not include waiting time. Past data from similar ATMs indicates that a normal probability distribution with a mean of 2 minutes and a standard deviation of 0.5 minutes, as shown in Figure 16.11, can be used to describe service times. As discussed in the previous sections, values from a normal probability distribution with mean 2 and standard deviation 0.5 can be generated using the Excel function =NORMINV(RAND(),2,0.5). For example, the random number of 0.7257 generates a customer service time of 2.3 minutes.

Figure 16.11 NORMAL PROBABILITY DISTRIBUTION OF SERVICE TIMES FOR THE ATM WAITING LINE SYSTEM

Standard deviation
0.5 minutes

2

Service Time in Minutes

The Simulation Model

The probabilistic inputs to the Hammondsport Savings Bank ATM simulation model are the values of the interarrival time and the service time. The controllable input is the number of ATMs used. The output will consist of various operating characteristics (such as average waiting time, the probability of waiting and so on). We show a diagram of the ATM simulation model in Figure 16.12.

Figure 16.13 shows a flowchart that defines the sequence of logical and mathematical operations required to simulate the Hammondsport ATM system. The flowchart uses the following notation:

$$IAT = \text{Interarrival Time generated}$$
$$\text{Arrival Time } (i) = \text{Time at which customer } i \text{ arrives}$$
$$\text{Start Time } (i) = \text{Time at which customer } i \text{ starts service}$$
$$\text{Wait Time } (i) = \text{Waiting time for customer } i$$
$$ST = \text{Service Time generated}$$
$$\text{Completion Time } (i) = \text{Time at which customer } i \text{ completes service}$$
$$\text{System Time } (i) = \text{System time for customer } i \text{ (waiting time + service time)}$$

Figure 16.12 HAMMONDSPORT SAVINGS BANK ATM SIMULATION MODEL

Interarrival Time

Service Time

Number of ATMs

Model

Operating Characteristics

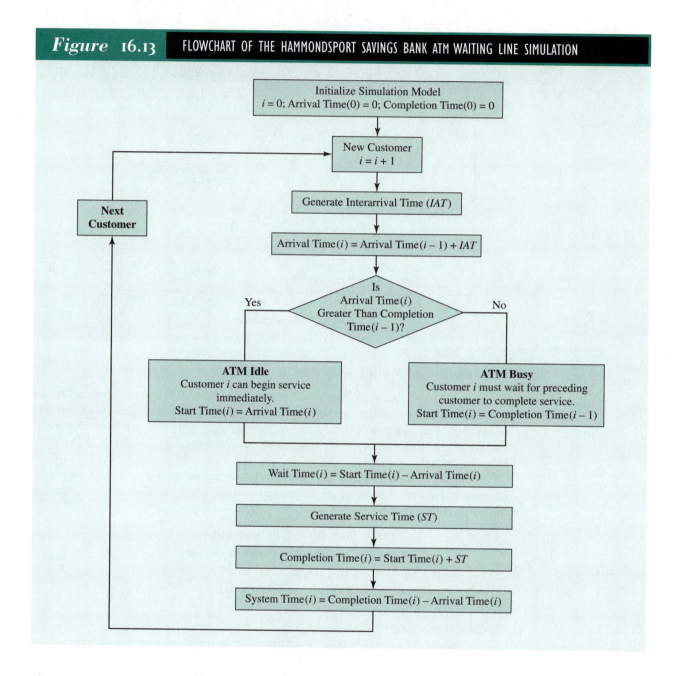

Figure 16.13   FLOWCHART OF THE HAMMONDSPORT SAVINGS BANK ATM WAITING LINE SIMULATION

Referring to Figure 16.13, we see that the simulation run is initialized in the first block of the flowchart. Then a new customer is created and arrives to use the ATM. An interarrival time is generated to represent the time since the preceding customer arrived. The arrival time for the new customer is then computed by adding the interarrival time to the arrival time of the preceding customer.

The arrival time for the new customer must be compared to the completion time of the preceding customer to determine whether the ATM is idle or busy. If the arrival time of the new customer is greater than the completion time of the preceding customer, the preceding customer will have finished service prior to the arrival of the new customer. In this case the

The decision rule for deciding whether the ATM is idle or busy is the most difficult aspect of the logic in a waiting line simulation model.

ATM will be idle, and the new customer can begin service immediately; in this case, the service starting time for the new customer is equal to the arrival time of the new customer. However, if the arrival time for the new customer is not greater than the completion time of the preceding customer, the new customer has arrived before the preceding customer has finished service. In this case, the ATM is busy; the new customer must wait to use the ATM until the preceding customer has completed service; therefore, the service starting time for the new customer is equal to the completion time of the preceding customer.

Note that the time the new customer has to wait to use the ATM is the difference between the customer's service starting time and the customer's arrival time. At this point, the customer is ready to use the ATM, and the simulation run continues with the generation of the customer's service time. The time at which the customer begins service plus the service time generated determine the customer's completion time. Finally, the total time the customer spends in the system is the difference between the customer's service completion time and the customer's arrival time. At this point, the computations are complete for the current customer, and the simulation run continues with the next customer. The simulation run is continued until a specified number of customers have been served by the ATM.

Simulation results for the first ten customers are shown in Table 16.12. We will discuss the computations for the first 3 customers to illustrate the logic of the simulation model and to show how the information in Table 16.12 was developed.

Customer 1

- An interarrival time of $IAT = 1.4$ minutes is generated.
- Since the simulation run begins at time 0, the arrival time for customer 1 is $0 + 1.4 = 1.4$ minutes.
- Customer 1 may begin service immediately with a start time of 1.4 minutes.
- The waiting time for customer 1 is the start time minus the arrival time: $1.4 - 1.4 = 0$ minutes.
- A service time of $ST = 2.3$ minutes is generated for customer 1.

Table 16.12	SIMULATION RESULTS FOR TEN ATM CUSTOMERS						
Customer	Interarrival Time	Arrival Time	Service Start Time	Waiting Time	Service Time	Completion Time	Time in System
1	1.4	1.4	1.4	0.0	2.3	3.7	2.3
2	1.3	2.7	3.7	1.0	1.5	5.2	2.5
3	4.9	7.6	7.6	0.0	2.2	9.8	2.2
4	3.5	11.1	11.1	0.0	2.5	13.6	2.5
5	0.7	11.8	13.6	1.8	1.8	15.4	3.6
6	2.8	14.6	15.4	0.8	2.4	17.8	3.2
7	2.1	16.7	17.8	1.1	2.1	19.9	3.2
8	0.6	17.3	19.9	2.6	1.8	21.7	4.4
9	2.5	19.8	21.7	1.9	2.0	23.7	3.9
10	1.9	21.7	23.7	2.0	2.3	26.0	4.3
Totals	21.7			11.2	20.9		32.1
Averages	2.17			1.12	2.09		3.21

- The completion time for customer 1 is the start time plus the service time: $1.4 + 2.3 = 3.7$ minutes.
- The time in the system for customer 1 is the completion time minus the arrival time: $3.7 - 1.4 = 2.3$ minutes.

Customer 2

- An interarrival time of $IAT = 1.3$ minutes is generated.
- Since the arrival time of customer 1 is 1.4, the arrival time for customer 2 is $1.4 + 1.3 = 2.7$ minutes.
- Since the completion time of customer 1 is 3.7 minutes, the arrival time of customer 2 is not greater than the completion time of customer 1; thus, the ATM is busy when customer 2 arrives.
- Customer 2 must wait for customer 1 to complete service before beginning service. Since customer 1 completes service at 3.7 minutes, the starting time for customer 2 is 3.7 minutes.
- The waiting time for customer 2 is the start time minus the arrival time: $3.7 - 2.7 = 1$ minute.
- A service time of $ST = 1.5$ minutes is generated for customer 2.
- The completion time for customer 2 is the start time plus the service time: $3.7 + 1.5 = 5.2$ minutes.
- The time in the system for customer 2 is the completion time minus the arrival time: $5.2 - 2.7 = 2.5$ minutes.

Customer 3

- An interarrival time of $IAT = 4.9$ minutes is generated.
- Since the arrival time of customer 2 was 2.7 minutes, the arrival time for customer 3 is $2.7 + 4.9 = 7.6$ minutes.
- The completion time of customer 2 is 5.2 minutes, so the arrival time for customer 3 is greater than the completion time of customer 2. Thus, the ATM is idle when customer 3 arrives.
- Customer 3 begins service immediately with a start time of 7.6 minutes.
- The waiting time for customer 3 is the start time minus the arrival time: $7.6 - 7.6 = 0$ minutes.
- A service time of $ST = 2.2$ minutes is generated for customer 3.
- The completion time for customer 3 is the start time plus the service time: $7.6 + 2.2 = 9.8$ minutes.
- The time in the system for customer 3 is the completion time minus the arrival time: $9.8 - 7.6 = 2.2$ minutes.

Using the totals in Table 16.12, we computed an average waiting time of $11.2/10 = 1.12$ minutes, and an average time in the system of $32.1/10 = 3.21$ minutes. Seven of the ten customers had to wait. We note that the average interarrival time for these ten customers is $21.7/10 = 2.17$ minutes, and the average service time is $20.9/10 = 2.09$ minutes. The total time for the ten-customer simulation is given by the completion time of the tenth customer: 26.0 minutes. However, at this point, we realize that a simulation run for ten customers is much too short a period to draw any firm conclusions about the operation of the waiting line.

Simulation Results with One ATM

Using an Excel spreadsheet, we continued the ATM simulation until a total of 1000 customers had completed service. The final spreadsheet contained 1000 rows of simulation data similar to that in Table 16.12. Before analyzing the data for the 1000 customers, let us point out that many simulation studies of dynamic systems focus on the operation of the system during its long-run, or steady-state operation. To ensure that the effect of startup conditions have worn off, a dynamic simulation model is usually run for a specified period without collecting any data about the operation of the system. The length of the startup period can vary depending on the application, but it is generally selected to be sufficient for the system to have stabilized at its long-run, or steady-state operation. For the Hammondsport Savings Bank ATM simulation, we treated the results for the first 100 customers as the startup period. This startup period required 274.5 minutes of simulated ATM operation.

Simulation data for the next 900 customers were then summarized. Figure 16.14 shows a histogram of the waiting times for these customers; 56.3% of the customers experienced waiting times of 1 minute or less. Thus, 43.7% of the customers experienced waiting times longer than 1 minute. Five percent of the customers experienced a waiting time of more than 6 minutes. The average waiting time for the 900 customers was 1.59 minutes.

> The mean arrival rate for the ATM system is 24 customers per hour, and the mean service rate is 30 customers per hour. As a result, the theoretical utilization of the ATM is 24//30 = 0.80 or 80%. The simulated utilization result of 78.6% suggests that the simulation model is accurately representing the waiting line system.

Excel functions can be used to summarize the simulation data and provide further insight into the performance of the waiting line system. We obtained a count of the number of customers with a waiting time of 0.0. Doing so showed that 351 of the 900 customers did not have to wait to use the ATM. Thus, 351/900 = 0.39, or 39%, of the customers did not wait; 549/900 = 0.61, or 61%, of the customers had to wait to use the ATM.

The simulation run for all 1000 customers ended with a completion time of 2536.4 minutes for the last customer. Since the 100-customer startup period ended at 274.5, we have a steady-state simulation period of 2536.4 − 274.5 = 2261.9 minutes. The total service time for all 900 customers was 1777.2 minutes; thus, the average service time was 1777.2/900 = 1.975 minutes. The utilization of the ATM was 1777.2/2261.9 = 0.786; the ATM was in use 78.6% of the time and idle 21.4% of the time.

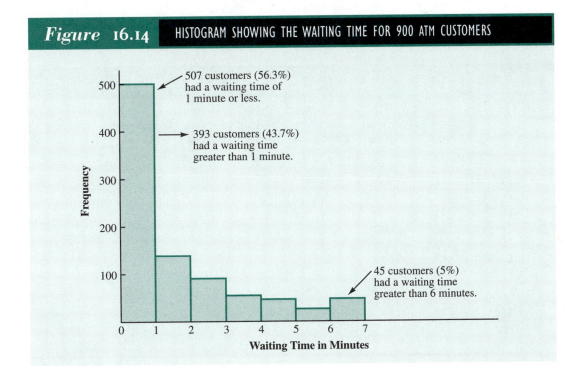

Figure 16.14 HISTOGRAM SHOWING THE WAITING TIME FOR 900 ATM CUSTOMERS

507 customers (56.3%) had a waiting time of 1 minute or less.

393 customers (43.7%) had a waiting time greater than 1 minute.

45 customers (5%) had a waiting time greater than 6 minutes.

This simulation run supports the conclusion that the branch will have a busy ATM system. With an average customer waiting time of 1.59 minutes, the branch does not satisfy the bank's customer service guideline. This branch is a good candidate for installation of a second ATM.

Simulation Results with Two ATMs

We extended the simulation model to the case of two ATMs. For the second ATM we also assume that the service time is normally distributed with a mean of 2 minutes and a standard deviation of 0.5 minutes. Table 16.13 shows the simulation results for the first ten customers. In comparing the two-ATM system results in Table 16.13 with the single ATM simulation results shown in Table 16.12, we see that 2 more columns are needed. These two columns show when each ATM becomes available for customer service. We assume that, when a new customer arrives, the customer will be served by the ATM that frees up first. When the simulation begins, the first customer is assigned to ATM 1.

Table 16.13 shows that customer 7 is the first customer that has to wait to use an ATM. We describe how customers 6, 7, and 8 are processed to show how the logic of the simulation run for two ATMs differs from that with a single ATM.

Customer 6

- An interarrival time of 1.3 minutes is generated, and customer 6 arrives 10.4 minutes into the simulation run.
- From the customer 5 row, we see that ATM 1 frees up at 5.8 minutes, and ATM 2 will free up at 11.3 minutes into the simulation run. Since ATM 1 is free, customer 6 does not wait and begins service on ATM 1 at the arrival time of 10.4 minutes.
- A service time of 1.6 minutes is generated for customer 6. So customer 6 has a system time of 1.6 minutes and a completion time of 12.0 minutes.
- The time ATM 1 will next become available is set at 12.0 minutes; the time available for ATM 2 remains 11.3 minutes.

Table 16.13   SIMULATION RESULTS FOR TEN CUSTOMERS FOR A TWO-ATM SYSTEM

Customer	Interarrival Time	Arrival Time	Service Start Time	Waiting Time	Service Time	Completion Time	Time in System	Time Available ATM 1	Time Available ATM 2
1	1.7	1.7	1.7	0.0	2.1	3.8	2.1	3.8	0.0
2	0.7	2.4	2.4	0.0	2.0	4.4	2.0	3.8	4.4
3	2.0	4.4	4.4	0.0	1.4	5.8	1.4	5.8	4.4
4	0.1	4.5	4.5	0.0	0.9	5.4	0.9	5.8	5.4
5	4.6	9.1	9.1	0.0	2.2	11.3	2.2	5.8	11.3
6	1.3	10.4	10.4	0.0	1.6	12.0	1.6	12.0	11.3
7	0.6	11.0	11.3	0.3	1.7	13.0	2.0	12.0	13.0
8	0.3	11.3	12.0	0.7	2.2	14.2	2.9	14.2	13.0
9	3.4	14.7	14.7	0.0	2.9	17.6	2.9	14.2	17.6
10	0.1	14.8	14.8	0.0	2.8	17.6	2.8	17.6	17.6
Totals	14.8			1.0	19.8		20.8		
Averages	1.48			0.1	1.98		2.08		

Customer 7

- An interarrival time of 0.6 minutes is generated, and customer 7 arrives 11.0 minutes into the simulation run.
- From the previous row, we see that ATM 1 will not be available until 12.0 minutes, and ATM 2 will not be available until 11.3 minutes. So customer 7 must wait to use an ATM. Since ATM 2 will free up first, customer 7 begins service on that machine at a start time of 11.3 minutes. With an arrival time of 11.0 and a service start time of 11.3, customer 7 experiences a waiting time of 0.3 minutes.
- A service time of 1.7 minutes is generated leading to a system time of 2.0 minutes and a completion time of 13.0 minutes.
- The time available for ATM 2 is updated to 13.0 minutes, and the time available for ATM 1 remains at 12.0 minutes.

Customer 8

- An interarrival time of 0.3 minutes is generated, and customer 8 arrives 11.3 minutes into the simulation run.
- From the previous row, we see that ATM 1 will be the first available. Thus, customer 8 starts service on ATM 1 at 12.0 minutes resulting in a waiting time of 0.7 minutes.
- A service time of 2.2 minutes is generated resulting in a completion time of 12.0 + 2.2 = 14.2 minutes and a system time of 0.7 + 2.2 = 2.9 minutes.
- The time available for ATM 1 is updated to 14.2 minutes, and the time available for ATM 2 remains at 13.0 minutes.

From the totals in Table 16.13, we see that the average waiting time for these ten customers is only $1.0/10 = 0.1$ minutes. Of course, a much longer run will be necessary before any conclusions can be drawn.

Once again we continued the simulation run until 1000 customers had completed service. Results for the first 100 customers were discarded to account for the startup period. Figure 16.15 shows a histogram of the waiting times for the next 900 customers. Using 2 ATMs, 98% of the customers experienced waiting times of 1 minute or less. Only two customers experienced a waiting time of more than 2 minutes. The average waiting time for the 900 customers was 0.0567 minutes or 3.4 seconds. Further analysis showed that only 75 customers (8.3%) had to wait.

Clearly the two-ATM system provides much better service and it satisfies the bank guideline that the average waiting time should be less than 1 minute. Management will now have to decide if the service improvements are sufficient to justify the added cost of a second ATM.

If necessary a straightforward extension of the two-ATM model can be developed to accommodate a waiting line system with more channels. Another column would have to be added to Table 16.13 for each additional ATM. Both simulation models presented in this section can be developed on a spreadsheet. We show the details in Appendix 16.1.

The ATM simulation model that we have developed can now be used to study the ATM operation at other branch banks. In each case, assumptions must be made about the appropriate customer interarrival time and customer service time probability distributions. However, once appropriate assumptions have been made, the same simulation model can be used to determine the operating characteristics of the ATM waiting line system. The Red Cross simulation model described in the Q.M. in Action possesses many of the same characteristics as the ATM simulation model.

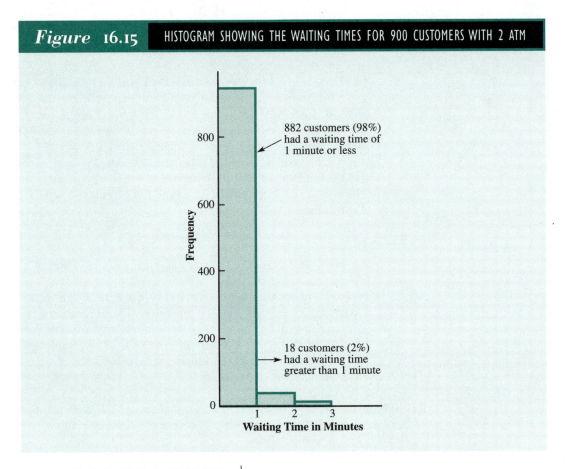

Figure 16.15 HISTOGRAM SHOWING THE WAITING TIMES FOR 900 CUSTOMERS WITH 2 ATM

882 customers (98%) had a waiting time of 1 minute or less

18 customers (2%) had a waiting time greater than 1 minute

Q.M. IN ACTION

RED CROSS USES SIMULATION TO IMPROVE BLOODMOBILE SERVICES*

The American Red Cross collects more than 6 million units of blood each year in the United States, making it the largest blood-product supplier in the country. Blood is collected daily at some 400 fixed and mobile sites.

The Red Cross relies heavily on repeat donations by the same group of individuals. A particular concern to the Red Cross was the length of the waiting times occurring at bloodmobile temporary sites sponsored by businesses, schools, and community groups. If bloodmobile waiting lines and times are excessive, blood donor dissatisfaction with the process could significantly decrease the number of future blood donations.

The Red Cross bloodmobile operation was simulated to study ways of reducing the waiting line and waiting times. Data were collected on the number of donor arrivals during 30-minute periods of time. The donors selected their own times to visit the bloodmobile, with these nonscheduled (random) visits described by a nonstationary Poisson probability distribution. Data on arrival rates and service times at the bloodmobile were based on the study of actual blood-

mobile operations in Atlanta, Georgia; Charlotte, North Carolina; and Washington, D.C.

The GPSS® computer simulation language was used to model the waiting line at the bloodmobile. After testing and validating the simulation model, the project team varied setup procedures, staff allocation, and work rules to determine how each change would affect the waiting line operating characteristics at the bloodmobile. Through a series of experiments with the simulation model, the project team developed recommendations for improved processing. Implementation of the recommendations markedly reduced waiting times. Improved blood donor satisfaction was noted, with the majority of donors reporting both less waiting time and less processing (service) time compared to previous visits.

*Based on Brennan, J. F., B. L. Golden, and H. K. Rappoport, "Go with the Flow: Improving Red Cross Bloodmobiles Using Simulation Analysis," *Interfaces*, vol. 22, no. 5, September–October 1992, pp. 1–13.

N O T E S
and Comments

I. The ATM waiting line model was based on uniformly distributed interarrival times and normally distributed service times. One advantage of simulation is its flexibility in accommodating a variety of different probability distributions. For instance, if we believe an exponential distribution is more appropriate for interarrival times, the ATM simulation could be repeated by simply changing the way the interarrival times are generated.

2. At the beginning of this section we defined *discrete-event simulation* as involving a dynamic system that evolves over time. The simulation computations focus on the sequence of events as they occur at discrete points in time. In the ATM waiting line example, customer arrivals and the customer service completions were the discrete events. Referring to the arrival times and completion times in Table 16.12, we see that the first 5 discrete events for the ATM waiting line simulation were as follows:

Event	Description	Time Event Occurred
1	Customer 1 arrives	1.4
2	Customer 2 arrives	2.7
3	Customer 1 completes service	3.7
4	Customer 2 completes service	5.2
5	Customer 3 arrives	7.6

3. We did not keep track of the number of customers in the ATM waiting line as we carried out the ATM simulation computations on a customer-by-customer basis. However, we can determine the average number of customers in the waiting line from other information in the simulation output. The following relationship is valid for any waiting line system:

(Mean Number in Waiting Line)(Length of Simulation Run) = Total Waiting Time

For the system with 1 ATM, the total length of the simulation run was 2261.9 minutes, and the average waiting time was determined to be 1.59 minutes. Since 900 customers were served during the simulation run, the total waiting time is 900(1.59) = 1431 minutes. Therefore, the mean number in the waiting line is

Mean Number in Waiting Line = 1431/2261.9 = 0.63

Therefore, the average number of customers waiting during the simulation run was 0.63.

16.4 OTHER SIMULATION ISSUES

Because simulation is one of the most widely used methods for quantitative analysis, a variety of software tools have been developed to help people implement a simulation model on a computer. In this section we comment on the software available and discuss some issues involved in verifying and validating a simulation model. We close the section with a discussion of some of the advantages and disadvantages of using simulation to study a real system.

Computer Implementation

In Appendix 16.1 we show how to develop an Excel spreadsheet for each simulation model developed in this chapter. The use of spreadsheets for simulation has grown rapidly in recent years, and third-party software vendors have developed spreadsheet add-ins that make building simulation models on a spreadsheet much easier. These add-in packages provide an easy facility for generating random values from a variety of probability distributions and provide a rich array of statistics describing the simulation output. Two popular spreadsheet add-ins are Crystal Ball® from Decisioneering and @RISK® from Palisade Corporation. Although spreadsheets can be a valuable tool for some simulation studies, they are generally limited to smaller, less complex systems.

With the growth of simulation applications, both users of simulation and software developers began to realize that computer simulations have many common features: model development, generating values from probability distributions, maintaining a record of what happens during the simulation run, and recording and summarizing the simulation output. A variety of special-purpose simulation packages are now available, including GPSS®, SIMSCRIPT®, SLAM®, and Arena®. These packages have built-in simulation clocks, simplified methods for generating probabilistic inputs, and procedures for collecting and summarizing the simulation output. Special-purpose simulation packages enable quantitative analysts to simplify the process of developing and implementing the simulation model.

Simulation models can also be developed using general-purpose computer programming languages such as BASIC, FORTRAN, PASCAL, C, and C++. The disadvantage of using these languages is that special simulation procedures are not built in. One command in a special-purpose simulation package often performs the computations and record-keeping tasks that would require several BASIC, FORTRAN, PASCAL, C, or C++ statements to duplicate. The advantage of using a general-purpose programming language is the greater flexibility in terms of being able to model more complex systems.

As part of a simulation application, an analyst will have to consider the relative merits of a spreadsheet, a special-purpose simulation package, and a general-purpose computer programming language to select a tool that is easy to use while still providing an adequate representation of the system being studied.

> The computational and record-keeping aspects of simulation models are assisted by special simulation software packages. The packages ease the tasks of developing a computer simulation model.

Verification and Validation

An important aspect of any simulation study involves confirming that the simulation model accurately describes the real system. Inaccurate models cannot be expected to provide worthwhile information. Thus, before using simulation results to draw conclusions about a real system, one must take steps to verify and validate the simulation model.

Verification is the process of determining that the computer procedure that performs the simulation calculations is logically correct. Verification is largely a debugging task to make sure that no errors are in the computer procedure that implements the simulation run. In some cases, an analyst may compare computer results for a limited number of events with independent hand calculations. In other cases, test runs may be performed to verify that the probabilistic inputs are being generated correctly and that the output from the simulation model seems reasonable. The verification step is not complete until the user has developed a high degree of confidence that the computer procedure is error free.

Validation is the process of ensuring that the simulation model provides an accurate representation of a real system. Validation requires an agreement among analysts and managers that the logic and the assumptions used in the design of the simulation model accurately reflect how the real system operates. The first phase of the validation process is done prior to, or in conjunction with, the development of the computer procedure for the simulation process. Validation continues after the computer program has been developed with the analyst reviewing the simulation output to see if the simulation results closely approximate the performance of the real system. If possible, the output of the simulation model is compared to the output of an existing real system to make sure that the simulation output closely approximates the performance of the real system. If this form of validation is not possible, an analyst can experiment with the simulation model and have one or more individuals experienced with the operation of the real system review the simulation output to determine whether it is a reasonable approximation to what would be obtained with the real system under similar conditions.

Verification and validation are not tasks to be taken lightly. They are key steps in any simulation study and are necessary to ensure that decisions and conclusions based on the simulation results are appropriate for the real system.

Advantages and Disadvantages of Using Simulation

The primary advantages of simulation are that it is easy to understand and that the methodology can be used to model and learn about the behavior of complex systems that would be difficult, if not impossible, to deal with analytically. Simulation models are flexible; they can be used to describe complex systems without requiring the simplifying assumptions, or approximations, that are often required by mathematical models. In general, the larger the number of probabilistic inputs a system has, the more likely it is that a simulation model will provide the best approach for studying the system. Another advantage of computer simulation is that a simulation model provides a convenient experimental laboratory for the real system. Changing assumptions or operating policies in the simulation model and rerunning it can provide results that help predict how such changes will affect the operation of the real system. Experimenting directly with a real system is often not feasible. The Q.M. in Action describes how simulation was used experimentally to select manufacturing configurations and to design new plants at Mexico's Vilpac Truck Company.

Using simulation, we can ask what-if questions and project how the real system will behave. The simulation does not guarantee optimality but will usually result in near-optimal solutions. In addition, simulation models often warn against poor decision strategies by projecting disastrous outcomes such as system failures, large financial losses, and so on.

Simulation is not without some disadvantages. For complex systems, the process of developing, verifying, and validating a simulation model can be time-consuming and expensive. In addition, each simulation run only provides a sample of how the real system will operate. As such, the summary of the simulation data only provides estimates or approximations about the real system. Consequently, computer simulation does not guarantee an optimal solution to a problem. Nonetheless, the danger of obtaining poor solutions is slight if the analyst exercises good judgment in developing the simulation model and if the simulation process is run long enough under a wide variety of conditions so that the analyst has sufficient data to predict how the real system will operate.

Q.M. IN ACTION

SIMULATION AT VILPAC TRUCK COMPANY*

Manufacturing has gone global, with U.S. firms joining diverse geographical and cultural partners in Western Europe, Asia, and Mexico to capitalize on each other's advantages and remain competitive in world markets. Mexico, the United States' third largest trading partner, offers a unique opportunity for integrating manufacturing operations. For example, Mexican and U.S. firms have been working together to turn the Mexican truck company, Vilpac, into a world-class manufacturing firm.

The selection of manufacturing configurations and the design of new plants at Vilpac is being guided by a simulation model of the firm's manufacturing operations. A network simulation language, SIMNET II, has been used to model the manufacturing system that comprises some 95 machines and 1900 parts. Various simulation runs were used to validate the model. When applied to a plant that was producing 20 trucks per day, the simulation model accurately predicted production at 19.8 trucks per day.

The three interrelated modules of the simulation model include operations, corrective maintenance, and preventive maintenance. Various components of the model include capabilities for handling changes in customer demand, manufacturing cost, capacity, and work-in-process and inventory levels. Experimentation with the model investigated capacity requirements, product-mix effects, new products, inventory policies, product flow, setup times, production planning and control strategies, plant expansion, and new plant design. Tangible benefits include an increase in production of 260%, a reduction in work-in-process of 70%, and an increase in market share.

*Based on Nuno, J. P., D. L. Shunk, J. M. Padillo, and B. Beltran, "Mexico's Vilpac Truck Company Uses a CIM Implementation to Become a World Class Manufacturer," *Interfaces,* vol. 23, no. 1, January–February 1993, pp. 59–75.

SUMMARY

Simulation is a method for learning about a real system by experimenting with a model that represents the system. Some of the reasons simulation is frequently used are:

1. It can be used for a wide variety of practical problems.
2. The simulation approach is relatively easy to explain and understand. As a result, management confidence is increased, and acceptance of the results is more easily obtained.
3. Spreadsheet packages now provide another alternative for model implementation, and third-party vendors have developed add-ins that expand the capabilities of the spreadsheet.
4. Computer software developers have produced simulation packages that make easier the development and implementation of simulation models for more complex problems.

We first showed how simulation can be used for risk analysis by analyzing a situation involving the introduction of a new product: the PortaCom printer. We then showed how simulation can be used to select an inventory replenishment level that would provide both a good profit and a good customer service level. Finally, we developed a simulation model for the Hammondsport Savings Bank ATM waiting line system. This model is an example of a dynamic simulation model in which the state of the system changes or evolves over time.

Our approach was to develop a simulation model that contained both controllable inputs and probabilistic inputs. Procedures were developed for randomly generating values for the probabilistic inputs, and a flowchart was developed to show the sequence of logical and mathematical operations that describe the steps of the simulation run. Simulation results were obtained by running the simulation for a suitable number of trials or length of time. Results were obtained and conclusions were drawn about the operation of the real system.

GLOSSARY

Simulation A method for learning about a real system by experimenting with a model that represents the system.

Controllable input A model input that is selected by the decision maker.

Probabilistic input A model input that is subject to uncertainty. In simulation models a probabilistic input is described by a probability distribution.

Simulation experiment The generation of a sample of values for the probabilistic inputs of a model and computing the resulting values of the model output. Conducting a simulation experiment is sometimes referred to as *running the simulation model.*

Risk analysis The process of predicting the outcome of a decision in the face of uncertainty.

Parameters Numerical values that appear in the mathematical relationships of a model. Parameters are considered known and remain constant over all trials of a simulation run.

What-if analysis A trial-and-error approach to learning about the range of possible outputs for a model. Trial values are chosen (these are the "what-ifs") for the model inputs and the value of the output(s) is computed.

Base-case scenario Determining the output given the most likely values for the probabilistic inputs of a model.

Best-case scenario Determining the output given the best values that can be expected for the probabilistic inputs of a model.

Worst-case scenario Determining the output given the worst values that can be expected for the probabilistic inputs of a model.

Static simulation model A simulation in which the state of the system at one point in time does not affect the state of the system at future points in time. Each trial in the simulation run is independent.

Dynamic simulation model A simulation in which the state of the system affects how the system changes or evolves over future points in time.

Event An instantaneous occurrence that changes the state of the system in a simulation model.

Discrete-event simulation model A simulation that describes how a system evolves over time by using events that occur at discrete points in time to update the state of the system.

Verification The process of determining that a computer program implements a simulation model as it is intended.

Validation The process of determining that a simulation model provides an accurate representation of a real system.

PROBLEMS

Note to Student: Problems 1–12 are designed to give you practice at setting up a simulation model and demonstrating how random numbers can be used to generate values for the probabilistic inputs. These problems, which ask you to provide a small number of simulation output trials, can be done with hand calculations. This approach should give you a good understanding of the simulation process, but the simulation results will not be sufficient for you to draw final conclusions or make decisions about the situation. Problems 13–24 are more realistic in that they ask you to generate simulation outputs for a large number of trials enabling you to draw conclusions about the behavior of the system being studied. These problems require the use of a computer to carry out the simulation computations. The ability to use Excel, or some other spreadsheet package, and a familiarity with the material in Appendix 16.1 will be helpful when you attempt problems 13–24.

1. Consider the PortaCom project discussed in Section 16.1
   a. An engineer on the product development team believes that first-year sales for the new printer will be 20,000 units. Using estimates of $45 per unit for the direct labor cost and $90 per unit for the parts cost, what is the first-year profit using the engineer's sales estimate?
   b. The financial analyst on the product development team is more conservative, indicating that parts cost may well be $100 per unit. In addition, the analyst suggests that a sales volume of 10,000 units is more realistic. Using the most likely value of $45 per unit for the direct labor cost, what is the first-year profit using the financial analyst's estimates?
   c. Why is the simulation approach to risk analysis preferable to generating a variety of what-if scenarios such as those suggested by the engineer and the financial analyst?

2. The management of Madeira Manufacturing Company is considering the introduction of a new product. The fixed cost to begin the production of the product is $30,000. The variable cost for the product is expected to be between $16 and $24 with a most likely value of $20 per unit. The

SELF TEST

product will sell for $50 per unit. Demand for the product is expected to range from 300 units to 2100 units, with 1200 units the most likely demand.

   a   Develop the profit model for this product.

   b. Provide the base-case, worst-case, and best-case analyses.

   c.   Discuss why a simulation risk analysis of the project would be desirable. Problem 14 asks you to develop a spreadsheet to conduct a risk analysis for the Madeira project.

3.   Use Table 16.4 and the random numbers 0.3753, 0.9218, 0.0336, 0.5145, 0.7000 to generate 5 simulated values for the PortaCom direct labor cost per unit.

4.   A retail store experiences the following probability distribution for sales of a product.

Sales (units)	0	1	2	3	4	5	6
Probability	0.08	0.12	0.28	0.24	0.14	0.10	0.04

   a.   Set up intervals of random numbers that can be used to simulate sales.

   b. Random numbers generated for the first 10 days of a simulation run are as follows: 0.4627, 0.8745, 0.4479, 0.6712, 0.4557, 0.8435, 0.2162, 0.1699, 0.1338, 0.2278. What is the sales value generated for each day?

   c.   What are the total sales over the 10-day period?

SELF TEST

5.   The price of a share of a particular stock listed on the New York Stock Exchange is currently $39. The following probability distribution shows how the price per share is expected to change over a three-month period.

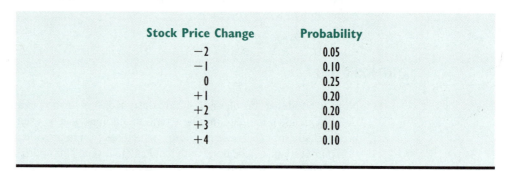

Stock Price Change	Probability
−2	0.05
−1	0.10
0	0.25
+1	0.20
+2	0.20
+3	0.10
+4	0.10

   a.   Set up intervals of random numbers that can be used to generate the change in stock price over a three-month period.

   b. With the current price of $39 per share and the random numbers 0.1091, 0.9407, 0.1941, and 0.8083, simulate the price per share for each on the next four 3-month periods. What is the ending simulated price per share?

6.   The Statewide Auto Insurance Company has the following probability distribution for automobile collision claims paid during the past year.

Payment ($)	Probability
0	0.83
500	0.06
1,000	0.05
2,000	0.02
5,000	0.02
8,000	0.01
10,000	0.01

a. Set up intervals of random numbers that can be used to generate automobile claim payments.

b. Using the first 20 random numbers in column 4 of Table 16.2, simulate the claims for 20 policyholders. How many claims are paid and what is the total amount paid to the policyholders?

7. A variety of routine maintenance checks are made on commercial airplanes prior to each take-off. A particular maintenance check of an airplane's landing gear requires between 10 and 18 minutes of a maintenance engineer's time. In fact, the exact time required is uniformly distributed over this interval. As part of a larger simulation model designed to determine total on-ground maintenance time for an airplane, we will need to simulate the actual time required to perform this maintenance check on the airplane's landing gear. Using random numbers of 0.1567, 0.9823, 0.3419, 0.5572, and 0.7758, compute the time required for each of five simulated maintenance checks of the airplane's landing gear.

8. Baseball's World Series is a maximum of 7 games, with the winner being the first team to win 4 games. Assume that the Atlanta Braves are in the World Series and that the first 2 games are to be played in Atlanta; the next 3 games at the opponent's ball park; and the last 2 games, if necessary, back in Atlanta. Taking into account the projected starting pitchers for each game and the homefield advantage, the probabilities of Atlanta winning each game are as follows:

Game	1	2	3	4	5	6	7
Probability of Win	0.60	0.55	0.48	0.45	0.48	0.55	0.50

a. Set up random number intervals that can be used to determine the winner of each game. Let the smaller random numbers indicate that Atlanta wins the game. For example, the random number interval "0.00 but less than 0.60" corresponds to Atlanta winning game 1.

b. Use the random numbers in column 6 of Table 16.2 beginning with 0.3813 to simulate the playing of the World Series. Do the Atlanta Braves win the series? How many games are played?

c. Discuss how repeated simulation trials could be used to estimate the overall probability of Atlanta winning the series as well as the most likely number of games in the series.

SELF TEST

9. A project has four activities (A, B, C, and D) that must be performed sequentially. The probability distributions for the time required to complete each of the activities are as follows:

Activity	Activity Time (weeks)	Probability
A	5	0.25
	6	0.35
	7	0.25
	8	0.15
B	3	0.20
	5	0.55
	7	0.25
C	10	0.10
	12	0.25
	14	0.40
	16	0.20
	18	0.05
D	8	0.60
	10	0.40

    a. Provide the base-case, the worst-case, and best-case calculations for the time to complete the project.

    b. Use the random numbers 0.1778, 0.9617, 0.6849, and 0.4503 to simulate the completion time of the project in weeks.

    c. Discuss how simulation could be used to estimate the probability the project can be completed in 35 weeks or less.

10. Larkin Corporation conducted a test designed to evaluate the effectiveness of a new television advertisement for one of its household products. The particular television advertisement was shown in a test market for a two-week period. In a follow-up study, randomly selected individuals were contacted by telephone and asked a series of questions to determine whether they could recall the message in the television advertisement and how likely they were to purchase the product. The test market study provided the following probabilities.

Individual could recall the message   0.40

Individual could not recall the message   0.60

Response to the question of how likely they were to purchase the product provided the following probabilities.

	Purchase		
If	Definitely No	Uncertain	Definitely Yes
Could recall message	0.30	0.30	0.40
Could not recall message	0.50	0.40	0.10

    a. Set up intervals of random numbers that can be used to determine whether a sampled individual could recall the message and then how the individual responded to the likelihood of purchase question.

    b. Use the following pairs of random numbers to simulate the results for three sampled individuals: individual 1 (0.5521, 0.6318), individual 2 (0.2189, 0.8432), individual 3 (0.3812, 0.1831). Which individual, if any, answered "definitely yes" to the likelihood to purchase question?

    c. Discuss how a large number of simulation trials could be used to estimate the overall probability of an individual answering "definitely yes" to the likelihood of purchase question.

11. A bowler has the following probability distribution for the number of pins knocked over on the first ball thrown.

Number of Pins	Probability
7	0.12
8	0.15
9	0.18
10	0.55

The probability distributions for the number of pins on the second ball are as follows:

	Second-Ball Pins			
First-Ball Pins	**0**	**1**	**2**	**3**
7	0.02	0.10	0.45	0.43
8	0.04	0.20	0.76	
9	0.06	0.94		

a. Set up intervals of random numbers that can be used to generate the number of pins on each ball.

b. The first two random numbers in column 6 of Table 16.2 are 0.3813 and 0.2159. Use these to simulate what the bowler did on the first two balls rolled?

c. Assume that the results in part (b) are for the first bowling frame. If you know how bowling scores are computed, continue to use the random numbers in Table 16.2 to compute the bowler's score for a full 10-frame game. The bowler's opponent rolled a 206 game. Did the simulated bowler beat the opponent?

12. The Brinkley Corporation is interested in using a simulation model that will help estimate the profit per unit for a new product. Probability distributions for the purchase cost, the labor cost, and the transportation cost are as follows:

Purchase Cost ($)	Probability	Labor Cost ($)	Probability	Transportation Cost ($)	Probability
10	0.25	20	0.10	3	0.75
11	0.45	22	0.25	5	0.25
12	0.30	24	0.35		
		25	0.30		

Assume that these are the only costs and that the selling price for the product will be $45 per unit.

a. Provide the base-case, worst-case, and best-case calculations for the profit per unit.

b. Set up intervals of random numbers that can be used to randomly generate the three cost components.

c. Using the random numbers 0.3726, 0.5839 and 0.8275, calculate the profit per unit.

d. Using the random numbers 0.1862, 0.7466, and 0.6171, calculate the profit per unit.

e. Management believes the project may not be profitable if the profit per unit is less than $5. Explain how simulation can be used to estimate the probability the profit per unit will be less than $5.

13. Using the formula spreadsheet in Figure 16.17, develop your own spreadsheet for the PortaCom simulation model.

a. Run your simulation for 300 trials. Compute the mean profit, the minimum profit, and the maximum profit.

b. What is your estimate of the probability of a loss?

SELF TEST

14. The management of Madeira Manufacturing Company is considering the introduction of a new product. The fixed cost to begin the production of the product is $30,000. The variable cost for the product is uniformly distributed between $16 and $24 per unit. The product will sell for $50 per unit. Demand for the product is best described by a normal probability distribution with a

mean of 1200 units and a standard deviation of 300 units. Use a spreadsheet simulation model similar to Figure 16.17. Use 500 simulation trials to answer the following questions.

a. What is the mean profit for the simulation?

b. What is the probability the project will result in a loss?

c. What is your recommendation concerning the introduction of the product?

15. Use a spreadsheet to simulate the rolling of dice. Use the VLOOKUP function as described in Appendix 16.1 to select the outcome for each die. Place the number for the first die in column A and the number for the second die in column B. Show the sum in column C. Repeat the simulation for 1000 rolls of the dice. What is your simulation estimate of the probability of rolling a 7?

16. Based on experience, the time required to complete a college statistics exam is normally distributed with a mean of 42 minutes and a standard deviation of 8 minutes. A class has 70 students. Use a spreadsheet to simulate the exam completion times for 70 students. How many students are still working when the professor stops the exam at 50 minutes?

17. Grear Tire Company has produced a new tire with an estimated mean lifetime mileage of 36,500 miles. Management also believes that the standard deviation is 5,000 miles and that tire mileage is normally distributed. Use a spreadsheet to simulate the miles obtained for a sample of 500 tires. Place the miles driven in cells A1 to A500 of your spreadsheet.

a. Use =COUNTIF(A1:A500,">40000") in any unused cell of the spreadsheet to count the number of tires that last longer than 40,000 miles. What is your estimate of the percentage of tires that will exceed 40,000 miles?

b. Use =COUNTIF(A1:A500,"<32000") to find the number of tires that obtain mileage less than 32,000 miles, then find the number with less than 30,000 miles and less than 28,000 miles.

c. If management would like to advertise a tire mileage guarantee such that roughly 10% of the tires would obtain mileage low enough to qualify for the guarantee, what tire mileage considered in part (b) would you recommend for the guarantee?

SELF TEST

18. A building contractor is preparing a bid on a new construction project. Two other contractors will be submitting bids for the same project. Based on past bidding practices, bids from the other contractors can be described by the following probability distributions:

Contractor	Probability Distribution of Bid
A	Uniform probability distribution between $600,000 and $800,000
B	Normal probability distribution with a mean bid of $700,000 and a standard deviation of $50,000

a. If the building contractor submits a bid of $750,000, what is the probability the building contractor will obtain the bid? Use a spreadsheet to simulate 1000 repeats of the contract bidding process.

b. The building contractor is also considering bids of $775,000 and $785,000. If the building contractor would like to bid such that the probability of winning the bid is about .80, what bid would you recommend? Repeat the simulation process with bids of $775,000 and $785,000 to justify your recommendation.

19. Using the formula spreadsheet in Figure 16.18, develop your own spreadsheet for the Butler inventory simulation model. Suppose that management prefers not to charge for loss of goodwill. Run the Butler inventory simulation model with replenishment levels of 110, 115, 120, and 125. What is your recommendation?

20. In preparing for the upcoming holiday season, Mandrell Toy Company has designated a new doll called Freddy. The fixed cost to produce the doll is $100,000. The variable cost including material, labor, and shipping costs is $34 per doll. During the holiday selling season, Mandrell will sell the dolls for $42 each. If Mandrell overproduces the dolls, the excess dolls will be sold

in January through a distributor who has agreed to pay Mandrell $10 per doll. Demand for new toys during the holiday selling season is extremely uncertain. Forecasts are for expected sales of 60,000 dolls with a standard deviation of 15,000. The normal probability distribution is assumed to be a good description of the demand.

a. Create a spreadsheet similar to the inventory model spreadsheet in Figure 16.18. Add a column to record when the demand exceeds the production volume and a stockout occurs. Use your spreadsheet to simulate the sales of the Freddy doll using a production quantity of 60,000. Using 500 simulation trials, what is your estimate of the mean profit associated with the production quantity of 60,000 dolls?

b. Before making a final decision on the production quantity, management has requested an analysis of a more aggressive 70,000 unit production quantity and a more conservative 50,000 unit production quantity. Run your simulation model with these two production quantities. What is the mean profit associated with each? What is your recommendation on the production of the Freddy doll?

c. Assuming that Mandrell's management adopts your recommendation, what is the probability of a stockout and a shortage of the Freddy dolls during the holiday season?

21. South Central Airlines operates a commuter flight between Atlanta and Charlotte. The plane holds 30 passengers, and the airline makes a $100 profit on each passenger on the flight. When South Central takes 30 reservations for the flight, experience has shown an average of 2 passengers do not show up. As a result, with 30 reservations, South Central is averaging 28 passengers with a profit of $28(100) = \$2,800$ per flight. The airline operations office has asked for an evaluation of an overbooking strategy where they would accept 32 reservations even though the airplane holds only 30 passengers. The probability distribution for the number of passengers showing up when 32 reservations are accepted is shown below.

Passengers Showing Up	Probability
28	0.05
29	0.25
30	0.50
31	0.15
32	0.05

The airline will receive a profit of $100 for each passenger on the flight up to the capacity of 30 passengers. The airline will incur a cost for any passenger denied seating on the flight. This cost covers added expenses of rescheduling the passenger as well as loss of goodwill, estimated to be $150 per passenger. Develop a spreadsheet model that will simulate the performance of the overbooking system. Simulate the number of passengers showing up for each of 500 flights by using the VLOOKUP function (see Figure 16.17). Use the results to compute the profit for each flight.

a. Does your simulation recommend the overbooking strategy? What is the mean profit per flight if overbooking is implemented?

b. Explain how your simulation model can be used to evaluate other overbooking levels such as 31, 33, 34 and ultimately recommending a best overbooking strategy.

22. Use the formula spreadsheets in Figures 16.19 and 16.20 to develop your own one-ATM and two-ATM waiting line simulation models for the Hammondsport Savings Bank problem. Assume that a new branch is expected to open with interarrival times uniformly distributed between 0 and 4 minutes. The service times at this branch are anticipated to be normal with a mean of 2 minutes and a standard deviation of 0.5 minutes.

a. Simulate the operation of this system for 600 customers using one ATM. What is your assessment of the ability to operate this branch with one ATM? What happens to the average waiting time for customers near the end of the simulation period?

b. Simulate the operation of this system for 600 customers using two ATMs. What is the average waiting time for customers? What is your recommendation for the ATM operation?

23. The Burger Dome waiting line model in Section 15.1 studies the waiting time of customers at its fast-food restaurant. Burger Dome's waiting line system has a mean of 0.75 arrivals per minute and a service rate of 1 customer per minute.

    a. Use a spreadsheet based on Figure 16.19 to simulate the operation of this waiting line. Assuming that customer arrivals follow a Poisson probability distribution, the interarrival times can be simulated with the cell formula $-(1/\lambda)*LN(RAND())$, where $\lambda = 0.75$. Assuming that the service time follows an exponential probability distribution, the service times can be simulated with the cell formula $-\mu*LN(RAND())$, where $\mu = 1$. Run the Burger Dome simulation for 500 customers. The analytical model in Chapter 15 indicates an average waiting time of 3 minutes per customer. What average waiting time does your simulation model show?

    b. One advantage of simulation is that a simulation model can be altered easily to reflect other assumptions about the probabilistic inputs. Assume that the service time is more accurately described by a normal probability distribution with a mean of 1 minute and a standard deviation of 0.2 minutes. This distribution has less service time variability than the exponential probability distribution used in part (a). What is the impact of this change on the average waiting time?

24. Telephone calls come into an airline reservations office randomly at the mean rate of 15 calls per hour. The time between calls follows an exponential distribution with a mean of 4 minutes. When the two reservations agents are busy, a telephone message tells the caller that the call is important and to please wait on the line until the next reservation agent becomes available. The service time for each reservation agent is normally distributed with a mean of 4 minutes and a standard deviation of 1 minute. Use a two-channel waiting line simulation model to evaluate this waiting line system. Use the spreadsheet design shown in Figure 16.20. The cell formula $=-4*LN(RAND())$ can be used to generate the interarrival times. Simulate the operation of the telephone reservation system for 600 customers. Discard the first 100 customers and collect data over the next 500 customers.

    a. Compute the mean interval arrival time and the mean service time. If your simulation model is operating correctly, both of these should have means of approximately 4 minutes.

    b. What is the mean customer waiting time for this system?

    c. Use the $=COUNTIF$ function to determine the number of customers who have to wait for a reservation agent. What percentage of the customers have to wait?

Case Problem   COUNTY BEVERAGE DRIVE-THRU

County Beverage Drive-Thru, Inc., operates a chain of beverage supply stores in Northern Illinois. Each store has a single service lane; cars enter at one end of the store and exit at the other end. Customers pick up soft drinks, beer, snacks, and party supplies without getting out of their cars. When a new customer arrives at the store, the customer waits until the preceding customer's order is complete and then drives into the store for service.

    Typically, three employees operate each store during peak periods; two clerks take and fill orders; and a third clerk serves as cashier and store supervisor. County Beverage is considering a revised store design in which computerized order-taking and payment are integrated with specialized warehousing equipment. Management hopes that the new design will permit operating each store with one clerk. To determine whether the new design is beneficial, management has decided to build a new store using the revised design.

    County Beverage's new store will be located near a major shopping center. Based on experience at other locations, management believes that during the peak late afternoon and evening hours, the time between arrivals follows an exponential probability distribution with a mean of 6 minutes. These peak hours are the most critical time period for the company; most of their profit is generated during these peak hours.

Most of County Beverage's business is generated from people stopping on the way home from work and picking up just a few items. However, occasionally a larger order is placed. An extensive study of times required to fill orders with a single clerk has led to the following probability distribution of service times.

Service Time (minutes)	Probability
2	0.24
3	0.20
4	0.15
5	0.14
6	0.12
7	0.08
8	0.05
9	0.02
Total	1.00

In case customer waiting times prove too long with just a single clerk, County Beverage's management is considering two alternatives: add a second clerk to help with bagging, taking orders, etc., or enlarge the drive-thru area so that two cars can be served at once (a two-channel system). With either of these options, two clerks will be needed. With the two-channel option, service times are expected to be the same for each channel. With the second clerk helping with a single channel, service times will be reduced. The following probability distribution describes service times given that option.

Service Time (minutes)	Probability
1	0.20
2	0.35
3	0.30
4	0.10
5	0.05
Total	1.00

County Beverage's management would like you to develop a spreadsheet simulation model of the new system and use it to compare the operation of the system using the following three designs:

Design

A   One channel, one clerk
B   One channel, two clerks
C   Two channels, each with one clerk

Management is especially concerned with how long customers have to wait for service. Research has shown that 30% of the customers will wait no longer than 6 minutes and that 90% will wait no longer than 10 minutes. As a guideline, management requires the average waiting time to be less than 1.5 minutes.

Managerial Report

Prepare a report that discusses the general development of the spreadsheet simulation model, and make any recommendations that you have regarding the best store design and staffing plan for County Beverage. One additional consideration is that the design allowing for a two-channel system will cost an additional $10,000 to build.

1. List the information the spreadsheet simulation model should generate so that a decision can be made on the store design and the desired number of clerks.
2. Run the simulation for 1000 customers for each alternative considered. You may want to consider making more than one run with each alternative. [*Note:* Values from an exponential probability distribution with mean μ can be generated in Excel using the following function: $= -\mu*LN(RAND())$]
3. Be sure to note the number of customers County Beverage is likely to lose due to long customer waiting times with each design alternative.

Appendix 16.1   SIMULATION WITH SPREADSHEETS

Spreadsheets enable small and moderate-sized simulation models to be implemented relatively easily and quickly. In this appendix we show the Excel spreadsheets for the three simulation models presented in the chapter.

The PortaCom Simulation Model

The probability distribution for the direct labor cost per unit in the PortaCom simulation model is shown in Table 16.14. In Section 16.1 we defined intervals of random numbers that could be used to simulate the direct labor cost per unit. These intervals are shown again in Table 16.15. Since there is a 0.10 probability of a random number in the interval of 0.0 but less than 0.1, there is a 0.1 probability that the direct labor cost will be $43 per unit. Similarly, since there is a 0.2 probability of a random number in the interval of 0.1 but less than 0.3, there is a 0.2 probability that the direct labor cost will be $44 per unit. Continuing in this fashion, we see that the random number intervals shown in Table 16.15 can be used to simulate the direct labor cost per unit consistent with its probability distribution.[1] Developing a table of random number intervals in the form shown here is necessary for Excel to simulate values from any tabular probability distribution.

Figure 16.16 shows the Excel spreadsheet with the first five trials of the PortaCom risk analysis simulation. Note that the random number intervals and their associated direct labor cost per unit appear in the upper left corner of the spreadsheet. Although this table can be placed anywhere in the spreadsheet, it will have to be referred to whenever the model requests a simulated value for the direct labor cost.

---

1. When Excel references the direct labor cost table, it will use random numbers of 0.0 *but less than* 0.1 for $43, 0.1 *but less than* 0.3 for $44, 0.3 *but less than* 0.7 for $45, and so on. Thus, there is no chance that the boundary random numbers of exactly 0.1, exactly 0.3, exactly 0.7, and so on will refer to two different direct labor costs.

Table 16.14	PROBABILITY DISTRIBUTION FOR DIRECT LABOR COST PER UNIT FOR PORTACOM

Direct Labor Cost per Unit	Probability
$43	0.1
$44	0.2
$45	0.4
$46	0.2
$47	0.1

Table 16.15	RANDOM NUMBER INTERVALS FOR THE SIMULATION OF THE DIRECT LABOR COST PER UNIT IN THE PORTACOM SIMULATION MODEL

Lower Random Number	Upper Random Number	Direct Labor Cost per Unit	Probability
0.0	0.1	$43	0.1
0.1	0.3	$44	0.2
0.3	0.7	$45	0.4
0.7	0.9	$46	0.2
0.9	1.0	$47	0.1

Figure 16.16	A PORTION OF THE EXCEL SPREADSHEET FOR THE PORTACOM SIMULATION MODEL

	A	B	C	D	E
1	Lower	Upper	Direct		
2	Random No.	Random No.	Labor Cost		
3	0.0	0.1	43		
4	0.1	0.3	44		
5	0.3	0.7	45		
6	0.7	0.9	46		
7	0.9	1.0	47		
8					
9		Direct Labor	Parts	Number of	
10	Trial	Cost Per Unit	Cost Per Unit	Units Sold	Profit
11	1	$47	$85.36	17,366	$1,025,570
12	2	$44	$91.68	12,900	$ 461,828
13	3	$45	$93.35	20,686	$1,288,906
14	4	$43	$98.56	10,888	$ 169,807
15	5	$45	$88.36	14,259	$ 649,911

Figure 16.17 shows the formula spreadsheet for the PortaCom simulation model. The function =VLOOKUP(RAND(),$A$3:$C$7,3) in column B is used to simulate values for the direct labor cost. The VLOOKUP function works as follows. The RAND() portion of the function instructs the computer to select a random number between 0.0 and 1.0. The $A$3:$C$7 entry tells the computer where the direct labor cost per unit table is located in the spreadsheet. For example, if the random number is 0.7308, the VLOOKUP function will determine that 0.7308 is in the interval of 0.7 but less than 0.9, corresponding to row 4 of the table. The 3 at the end of the function =VLOOKUP(RAND(),$A$3:$C$7,3) indicates that the corresponding direct labor cost per unit appears in the *third* column of the selected row. Thus, the random number 0.7308 provides the simulated direct labor cost of $46 per unit.

The parts cost per unit (column C) and number of units sold (column D) are generated by the functions for the uniform probability distribution and the normal probability distribution as discussed in Section 16.1. Finally, the profit is computed in column E.

Any number of simulation trials can be quickly carried out simply by selecting the first trial row of the spreadsheet and dragging the fill handle for as many rows or simulation trials as desired. When the fill handle is released, the simulation rows will be inserted in the spreadsheet automatically. Unless the simulation model is extremely complex, these simulation calculations should be completed fairly quickly.

The standard Excel spreadsheet functions can be used to compute summary statistics for the simulation results. In Table 16.9, we used the mean, median, standard deviation, and maximum and minimum values of the profit data in Column E to help evaluate the risk for the PortaCom project. In Figure 16.7, we provided a histogram of the profit data. Exactly how the simulation data are summarized depends upon the application. Generally, the user selects the summary measures that provide the best understanding of how the system operates.

Finally, the F9 key can be used to perform another complete simulation of PortaCom. In this case, the entire spreadsheet will be recalculated and a set of new simulation results will be provided. Any data summaries, measures, or functions that have been built into the spreadsheet earlier will be updated automatically.

The Butler Inventory Simulation Model

The formula spreadsheet for the Butler inventory simulation model from Section 16.2 is shown in Figure 16.18. Any replenishment level of interest can be entered in cell B1. Demand (column B) is generated by using the normal probability distribution function with a mean of 100 units and a standard deviation of 20 units. The statement =IF(B5<$B$1,B5,$B$1) in cell

Figure 16.17   FORMULA SPREADSHEET FOR THE PORTACOM SIMULATION MODEL

	A	B	C	D	E
1	Lower	Upper	Direct		
2	Random No.	Random No.	Labor Cost		
3	0	0.1	43		
4	0.1	0.3	44		
5	0.3	0.7	45		
6	0.7	0.9	46		
7	0.9	1	47		
8					
9		Direct Labor	Parts	Number of	
10	Trial	Cost Per Unit	Cost Per Unit	Units Sold	Profit
11	1	=VLOOKUP(RAND(),$A$3:$C$7,3)	=80+20*RAND()	=NORMINV(RAND(), 15000,4500)	=(249-B11-C11)*D11-1000000
12	2	=VLOOKUP(RAND(),$A$3:$C$7,3)	=80+20*RAND()	=NORMINV(RAND(), 15000,4500)	=(249-B12-C12)*D12-1000000
13	3	=VLOOKUP(RAND(),$A$3:$C$7,3)	=80+20*RAND()	=NORMINV(RAND(), 15000,4500)	=(249-B13-C13)*D13-1000000
14	4	=VLOOKUP(RAND(),$A$3:$C$7,3)	=80+20*RAND()	=NORMINV(RAND(), 15000,4500)	=(249-B14-C14)*D14-1000000
15	5	=VLOOKUP(RAND(),$A$3:$C$7,3)	=80+20*RAND()	=NORMINV(RAND(), 15000,4500)	=(249-B15-C15)*D15-1000000

Figure 16.18	FORMULA SPREADSHEET FOR THE BUTLER INVENTORY SIMULATION MODEL

	A		C	D	E	F	G
1	Quantity	= 100　　B					
2							
3				Gross	Holding	Shortage	Net
4	Month	Demand	Sales	Profit	Cost	Cost	Profit
5	1	=NORMINV(RAND(),100,20)	=IF(B5<$B$1,B5,$B$1)	=50*C5	=IF(B5<$B$1,15*($B$1−B5),0)	=IF(B5<$B$1,0,30*(B5−$B$1))	=D5−E5−F5
6	2	=NORMINV(RAND(),100,20)	=IF(B6<$B$1,B6,$B$1)	=50*C6	=IF(B6<$B$1,15*($B$1−B6),0)	=IF(B6<$B$1,0,30*(B6−$B$1))	=D6−E6−F6
7	3	=NORMINV(RAND(),100,20)	=IF(B7<$B$1,B7,$B$1)	=50*C7	=IF(B7<$B$1,15*($B$1−B7),0)	=IF(B7<$B$1,0,30*(B7−$B$1))	=D7−E7−F7
8	4	=NORMINV(RAND(),100,20)	=IF(B8<$B$1,B8,$B$1)	=50*C8	=IF(B8<$B$1,15*($B$1−B8),0)	=IF(B8<$B$1,0,30*(B8−$B$1))	=D8−E8−F8
9	5	=NORMINV(RAND(),100,20)	=IF(B9<$B$1,B9,$B$1)	=50*C9	=IF(B9<$B$1,15*($B$1−B9),0)	=IF(B9<$B$1,0,30*(B9−$B$1))	=D9−E9−F9

C5 shows that if the simulated demand in cell **B5** is less than the replenishment level entered in cell **B1**, sales will be equal to the simulated demand in cell **B5**. However, if the simulated demand in cell **B5** is not less than the replenishment level entered in cell **B1**, sales will be equal to the replenishment level in cell **B1**. Once the number of units sold has been determined, the gross profit (column D) is simply $50 times the number of units sold (column C). An IF function is used to compute the inventory holding cost (column E). The function =IF(B5<$B$1, 15*($B$1−B5),0) in cell **E5** checks to see if demand in cell **B5** is less than the replenishment level in cell **B1**. If it is, an inventory cost of $15 times the inventory surplus ($B$1−B5) is computed. If demand in cell **B5** is not less than the replenishment level in cell **B1**, there will be a stockout, and the inventory holding cost will be 0.

Another IF function is used to compute the shortage cost (column F). With =IF(B5<$B$1,0,30*(B5−$B$1)) in cell **F5**, we see that if demand in cell **B5** is less than the replenishment level in cell **B1**, there will not be a stockout, and the shortage cost will be 0. However, if this is not the case, a shortage cost of $30 times the number of units short (B5−$B$1) will be incurred. Finally, the net profit (column G) is computed from the spreadsheet commands that take the gross profit (column D) and subtract the holding cost (column E) and the shortage cost (column F). As we did for the PortaCom simulation model, the first simulation row or trial can be selected and dragged to create as many rows of simulation trials as desired.

Experimentation with the inventory simulation model can be carried out by changing the quantity appearing in cell **B1**. For each quantity considered, the user can press the F9 key and recalculate the spreadsheet. A corresponding revised set of simulation results will be provided. By comparing the outputs of the various simulation experiments, the user should be able to learn about the performance of the system and select a good beginning inventory quantity.

The Hammondsport ATM Waiting Line Simulation Model

The formula spreadsheet for the Hammondsport ATM waiting line simulation model from Section 16.3 is shown in Figure 16.19. This is for a single ATM. The rows correspond to the customers who arrive at the bank for the ATM service. The customer interarrival times are generated by the uniform probability distribution function =RAND()*5 in column B. Each customer arrival time in column C is computed by adding the interarrival time in column B to the arrival time of the preceding customer, which appears one row earlier in column C. The service start time is shown in column D. Using customer 2 (row 4) as an example, we see that the function =IF(C4>G3,C4,G3) appears in cell **D4**. Thus, if the arrival time of customer 2 in cell **C4** is greater than the completion time of the preceding customer 1 in cell **G3**, customer 1 has already completed service when customer 2 arrives. As a result, the start time for customer 2 is the customer's arrival time, which appears in cell **C4**. However, if **C4**>**G3** is not true, customer 1 has not completed service when customer 2 arrives. As a

Figure 16.19	FORMULA SPREADSHEET FOR THE ATM WAITING LINE SIMULATION MODEL WITH ONE ATM

	A	B	C	D	E	F	G	H
1		Interarrival	Arrival	Service	Waiting	Service	Completion	Time
2	Customer	Time	Time	Start Time	Time	Time	Time	in System
3	1	=RAND()*5	=B3	=C3	=D3–C3	=NORMINV(RAND(),2,0.5)	=D3+F3	=G3–C3
4	2	=RAND()*5	=C3+B4	=IF(C4>G3,C4,G3)	=D4–C4	=NORMINV(RAND(),2,0.5)	=D4+F4	=G4–C4
5	3	=RAND()*5	=C4+B5	=IF(C5>G4,C5,G4)	=D5–C5	=NORMINV(RAND(),2,0.5)	=D5+F5	=G5–C5
6	4	=RAND()*5	=C5+B6	=IF(C6>G5,C6,G5)	=D6–C6	=NORMINV(RAND(),2,0.5)	=D6+F6	=G6–C6
7	5	=RAND()*5	=C6+B7	=IF(C7>G6,C7,G6)	=D7–C7	=NORMINV(RAND(),2,0.5)	=D7+F7	=G7–C7

result, customer 2 cannot start service until customer 1 has completed service. Thus, the start time for customer 2 is set equal to the completion time for customer 1 shown in cell **G3**.

Waiting time (column E) is the difference between the service start time (column D) and the arrival time (column C). Service time (column F) is simulated by using the function for the normal probability distribution with a mean of 2 minutes and a standard deviation of 0.5 minutes. The completion time (column G) is the sum of the start time (column D) and the service time (column F). Finally, the time in the system (column H) is the difference between the completion time (column G) and the arrival time (column C).

In this spreadsheet, the simulation row for customer 2 can be selected and dragged to create as many rows of simulated customer arrivals as desired. As with the other simulation models, the F9 key can be used any time to recalculate the spreadsheet and provide a completely new set of simulation results.

The formula spreadsheet for the case of two ATMs is shown in Figure 16.20. Note that two new columns have been added. Columns I and J are needed to keep track of when each ATM is available; an ATM is unavailable if a customer is using it. Comparing row 3 in the 2-ATM case with row 3 in the 1-ATM case shows us that the only difference is the 2 additional columns needed in the 2-ATM case. The first customer is assumed to be served by ATM 1. The =G3 formula in cell **I3** shows that ATM 1 will not be available until after customer 1 completes service. The zero in cell **J3** shows that ATM 2 has been available since the beginning of the simulation run.

Looking below row 3, we see that the formulas in columns D, I, and J are different. Let us consider row 4 (Customer 2). The IF formula in cell **D4** is used to determine the service start time for customer 2. If the customer arrival time is less than or equal to the Time Available for both ATMs, then the customer waits and starts service at the time the first ATM frees up. If the customer arrival time is greater than the time when one ATM is available, then the customer does not wait and begins service at the time of the arrival.

Figure 16.20	FORMULA SPREADSHEET FOR THE ATM WAITING LINE SIMULATION MODEL WITH TWO ATMS

	A	B	C	D	E	F	G	H	I	J
1		Interarrival	Arrival	Service	Waiting	Service	Completion	Time	Time Available	
2	Customer	Time	Time	Start Time	Time	Time	Time	In System	ATM 1	ATM 2
3	1	=RAND()*5	=B3	=C3	=D3–C3	=NORMINV(RAND(),2,0.5)	=D3+F3	=G3–C3	=G3	0
4	2	=RAND()*5	=C3+B4	=IF(C4<=MIN(I3,J3),MIN(I3,J3),C4)	=D4–C4	=NORMINV(RAND(),2,0.5)	=D4+F4	=G4–C4	=IF(I3=MIN(I3,J3),G4,I3)	=IF(J3=MIN(I3,J3),G4,J3)
5	3	=RAND()*5	=C4+B5	=IF(C5<=MIN(I4,J4),MIN(I4,J4),C5)	=D5–C5	=NORMINV(RAND(),2,0.5)	=D5+F5	=G5–C5	=IF(I4=MIN(I4,J4),G5,I4)	=IF(J4=MIN(I4,J4),G5,J4)
6	4	=RAND()*5	=C5+B6	=IF(C6<=MIN(I5,J5),MIN(I5,J5),C6)	=D6–C6	=NORMINV(RAND(),2,0.5)	=D6+F6	=G6–C6	=IF(I5=MIN(I5,J5),G6,I5)	=IF(J5=MIN(I5,J5),G6,J5)
7	5	=RAND()*5	=C6+B7	=IF(C7<=MIN(I6,J6),MIN(I6,J6),C7)	=D7–C7	=NORMINV(RAND(),2,0.5)	=D7+F7	=G7–C7	=IF(I6=MIN(I6,J6),G7,I6)	=IF(J6=MIN(I6,J6),G7,J6)

THE UPJOHN COMPANY*
KALAMAZOO, MICHIGAN

The Upjohn Company is a worldwide supplier of high-quality, innovative pharmaceutical products. While its largest business is in prescription pharmaceutical products, Upjohn also operates related businesses in animal health care products, agronomic and vegetable seeds, and specialty chemical products. Founded in 1886, the company has approximately 19,000 employees worldwide, with major manufacturing facilities in Kalamazoo, Puerto Rico, and Belgium, and research laboratories in Kalamazoo, England, and Japan. Committed to total quality improvement—in service to its customers, its products, and its performance in the workplace—Upjohn is also dedicated to conducting businesses in an environmentally and socially responsible manner.

Quantitative Methods at Upjohn

The quantitative methods function at Upjohn is part of the Management Information and Office Services organization and offers a high-quality, professional problem-solving service to any part of the corporation. The mission of the group is to provide decision-making support for the company's customers, strategies, and priorities by using quantitative techniques to solve business problems and exploit business opportunities in a cost-effective manner. The primary areas of application are problem definition and analysis, modeling and simulation, capacity planning, resource allocation, scheduling, and project management.

*The authors are indebted to Dr. David B. Magerlein, Dr. James M. Magerlein, and Mr. Michael J. Goodrich of The Upjohn Company for providing this application.

A Computer Simulation Application

Demand for one of Upjohn's long-standing products had remained stable for several years at a level easily satisfied by the company's manufacturing facility. However, changes in market conditions caused an increase in demand to a level beyond the capacity of the current facility. In the discussion that follows, we describe a simulation study successfully undertaken to determine the most cost-effective means of increasing production to meet the new level of demand.

The production process is shown in Figure 16.21. It consists of three independent subprocesses: raw material processing, bulk processing, and spent material reprocessing. Raw material processing takes purchased material as input and transforms it into material that can be used in bulk processing. Bulk processing (shown within the dashed line in Figure 16.21), which involves initial processing, assay, and final processing, converts the raw materials into a finished product. The key step occurs when an assay of the initial bulk processing output or intermediate is performed to determine whether the lot is ready for final processing. If the assay is acceptable, the lot proceeds to final processing and completion. If the assay is not acceptable, the intermediate is returned to initial bulk processing and several steps are repeated. The new intermediate material, which is input during the repeat processing, is obtained by reprocessing one of the spent materials generated during a prior initial bulk processing.

Each time the initial bulk process is run, a quantity of spent material is generated for possible reprocessing. Although the primary use of the reprocessed material is as input for repeat bulk processing, it also can be used as a replacement for the original raw material at the start of

Figure 16.21   A PRODUCTION PROCESS AT UPJOHN

the bulk processing. Since the cost of the reprocessed material is significantly less than the cost of new raw material, using as much reprocessed material as possible is beneficial.

A simulation model of the production process was developed, and these questions were addressed:

1. What is the maximum throughput of the existing facility?
2. How can the production process be modified to increase the throughput of the existing facility?
3. How much equipment (tanks and centrifuges) must be added to the current facility to increase the capacity to meet the forecasted demand?
4. How should the reprocessed spent material be used to minimize the total production cost?
5. If a new facility is required, what is the optimal size and configuration?

The scope of the simulation model included the raw material, bulk- and spent-material processes already defined. The model was built in a modular flexible manner that allowed for the evaluation of resource levels within the facility, staffing levels and hours, changes in process times or equipment usage, changes in lot size, and/or yield changes. The logic of the process flow served as the core of the model and was developed in collaboration with the lead operators and supervisors of the production area. Since a good logical model is the key to good simulation results, a significant amount of time was spent defining the logic of the process flow. The model development process provided a secondary bene-

fit in that production personnel got to review and evaluate the process as they explained it.

The computer simulation model has been used on several occasions over the past two years. Simulation results have assisted management in addressing capacity, resource allocation, and operating policy issues. Each time a request to evaluate an issue is made, a detailed experimental design is developed that defines the alternatives to be evaluated. The appropriate simulation runs are made, the results are evaluated and presented to production management and personnel, and follow-up actions defined.

The computer simulation model was developed using the SLAMSYSTEM® Version 3.0 simulation language from the Pritsker Corporation. All simulation runs were made on a personal computer.

Benefits of the Simulation Model

The ongoing investigation of the production process using computer simulation has resulted in numerous benefits to the company, including the following:

1. Optimizing the use of reprocessed spent material to replace fresh raw material. Total material costs were reduced by approximately $3 million per year.
2. Demonstrating that the current facility, with some operating policy improvements, was large enough to satisfy the increased demand for the next several years. Expansion to a new facility was not necessary.

3. Determining the impact on facility throughput from alternative process changes. Numerous potential changes were investigated. The simulation model predicted how each change would affect total facility throughput. One change was identified that would increase throughput beyond what was needed for the 5-year forecasted demand.

4. Determining appropriate staffing levels within the facility. The model determined the number of operators that will be required as the production level increases in the future. This ensures that the proper number of operators will be trained by the time they are needed.

5. Determining the required size and configuration for a new facility. Although the current facility was found adequate to meet demand, the model still allowed management to determine the cost required to build a new facility.

The final actions taken based on the simulation results included alterations in policies for using reprocessed spent material, priority implementation of the process change that most impacted increasing facility throughput, establishment of appropriate staffing levels, and cost minimization because the expense of building a new or expanded facility was avoided.

Questions

1. Briefly describe the Upjohn production operation.
2. What is the primary reason Upjohn conducted a study of this operation?
3. Describe some of the factors that had to be included in the simulation model.
4. What were the advantages of computer simulation to Upjohn?

17

MARKOV PROCESSES

Markov process models are useful in studying the evolution of systems over repeated trials. The repeated trials are often successive time periods where the state of the system in any particular period cannot be determined with certainty. Rather, transition probabilities are used to describe the manner in which the system makes transitions from one period to the next. Hence, we are interested in the probability of the system being in a particular state at a given time period.

Markov process models have been used to describe the probability that a machine that is functioning in one period will continue to function or will break down in the next period. They have also been used to describe the probability that a consumer purchasing brand A in one period will purchase brand B in the next period. In this chapter we present a marketing application that involves an analysis of the store-switching behavior of supermarket customers. As a second illustration, we consider an accounting application that is concerned with the transitioning of accounts receivable dollars to different account-aging categories.

Since an in-depth treatment of Markov processes is beyond the scope of this text, the analysis in both illustrations is restricted to situations consisting of a finite number of states, the transition probabilities remain constant over time, and the probability of being in a particular state at any one time period depends only on the state in the immediately preceding time period. Such Markov processes are referred to as *Markov chains with stationary transition probabilities*.

··/ /··········

17.1   MARKET SHARE ANALYSIS

Suppose that we are interested in analyzing the market share and customer loyalty for Murphy's Foodliner and Ashley's Supermarket, the only two grocery stores in a small town. We focus on the sequence of shopping trips of one customer, and assume that the customer makes one shopping trip each week to either Murphy's Foodliner or Ashley's Supermarket, but not both.

Using the terminology of Markov processes, we refer to the weekly periods or shopping trips as the **trials of the process.** Thus, at each trial, the customer will shop at either Murphy's Foodliner or Ashley's Supermarket. The particular store selected in a given week is referred to as the **state of the system** in that period. Since the customer has two shopping alternatives at each trial, we say the system has two states, and since the number of states is finite, we can identify each state as follows:

State 1.   The customer shops at Murphy's Foodliner
State 2.   The customer shops at Ashley's Supermarket

If we say the system is in state 1 at trial 3, we are simply saying that the customer shops at Murphy's during the third weekly shopping period.

As we continue the shopping trip process into the future, we cannot say for certain where the customer will shop during a given week or trial. In fact, we realize that during any given week, the customer may be either a Murphy's customer or an Ashley's customer. However, using a Markov process model, we will be able to compute the probability that the customer shops at each store during any period. For example, we may find a 0.6 probability that the customer will shop at Murphy's during a particular week and a 0.4 probability that the customer will shop at Ashley's.

To determine the probabilities of the various states occurring at successive trials of the Markov process, we need information on the probability that a customer remains with the same store or switches to the competing store as the process continues from trial to trial or week to week.

Suppose that, as part of a market research study, we collect data from 100 shoppers over a 10-week period. Suppose further that these data show each customer's weekly shopping trip pattern in terms of the sequence of visits to Murphy's and Ashley's. To develop a Markov process model for the sequence of weekly shopping trips, we need to express the probability of selecting each store (state) in a given period solely in terms of the store (state) that was selected during the previous period. In reviewing the data, suppose that we find that of all customers who shopped at Murphy's in a given week, 90% shopped at Murphy's the following week while 10% switched to Ashley's. Suppose that similar data for the customers who shopped at Ashley's in a given week show that 80% shopped at Ashley's the following week while 20% switched to Murphy's. Probabilities based on these data are shown in Table 17.1. Since these are the probabilities that a customer moves, or makes a transition, from a state in a given period to each state in the following period, these probabilities are called **transition probabilities.**

An important property of the table of transition probabilities is that the sum of the probabilities in each row is 1; each row of the table provides a probability distribution. For example, a customer who shops at Murphy's one week must shop at either Murphy's or Ashley's the next week. The entries in row 1 give the probabilities associated with each of these events. The 0.9 and 0.8 probabilities in Table 17.1 can be interpreted as measures of store loyalty in that they indicate the probability of a repeat visit to the same store.

Table 17.1	TRANSITION PROBABILITIES FOR MURPHY'S AND ASHLEY'S GROCERY STORES	
Current Weekly Shopping Period	**Next Weekly Shopping Period**	
	Murphy's Foodliner	**Ashley's Supermarket**
Murphy's Foodliner	0.9	0.1
Ashley's Supermarket	0.2	0.8

Similarly, the 0.1 and 0.2 probabilities are measures of the store-switching characteristics of the customers.

In developing a Markov process model for this problem, we are assuming that the transition probabilities will be the same for any customer and that the transition probabilities will not change over time.

The chapter appendix contains a review of matrix notation and operations.

Note that Table 17.1 has one row and one column for each state of the system. We will use the symbol p_{ij} to represent the transition probabilities and the symbol P to represent the matrix of transition probabilities; that is,

$$p_{ij} = \text{probability of making a transition from state } i \text{ in a given period to state } j \text{ in the next period}$$

For the supermarket problem, we have

A quick check for a valid matrix of transition probabilities is to make sure the sum of the probabilities in each row equals 1.

$$P = \begin{bmatrix} p_{11} & p_{12} \\ p_{21} & p_{22} \end{bmatrix} = \begin{bmatrix} 0.9 & 0.1 \\ 0.2 & 0.8 \end{bmatrix}$$

Using the matrix of transition probabilities, we can now determine the probability that a customer will be a Murphy's customer or an Ashley's customer at some period in the future. Let us begin by assuming that we have a customer whose last weekly shopping trip was to Murphy's. What is the probability that this customer will shop at Murphy's on the next weekly shopping trip, period 1? In other words, what is the probability that the system will be in state 1 after the first transition? The matrix of transition probabilities indicates that this probability is $p_{11} = 0.9$.

Now let us consider the state of the system in period 2. A useful way of depicting what can happen on the second weekly shopping trip is to draw a tree diagram of the possible outcomes (see Figure 17.1). Using this tree diagram, we see that the probability that the customer shops at Murphy's during both the first and the second weeks is $(0.9)(0.9) = 0.81$. Also, note that the probability of the customer switching to Ashley's on the first trip and then switching back to Murphy's on the second trip is $(0.1)(0.2) = 0.02$. Since these are the only two ways that the customer can be in state 1 (shopping at Murphy's) during the second period, the probability of the system being in state 1 during the second period is $0.81 + 0.02 = 0.83$. Similarly, the probability of the system being in state 2 during the second period is $0.09 + 0.08 = 0.17$.

As desirable as the tree diagram approach may be from an intuitive point of view, this approach becomes cumbersome when we want to extend the analysis to three or more periods. Fortunately, we have an easier way to calculate the probabilities of the system being in state 1 or state 2 for any subsequent period. First, we introduce a notation that will allow us to represent these probabilities for any given period. Let

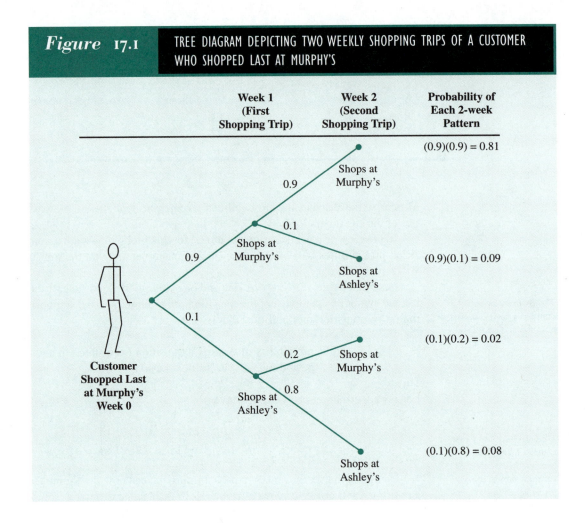

| | **Figure** 17.1 | TREE DIAGRAM DEPICTING TWO WEEKLY SHOPPING TRIPS OF A CUSTOMER WHO SHOPPED LAST AT MURPHY'S |

| | Week 1 (First Shopping Trip) | Week 2 (Second Shopping Trip) | Probability of Each 2-week Pattern |

$$[\pi_1(0) \quad \pi_2(0)] = [1 \quad 0]$$

$\pi_i(n)$ = probability that the system is in state i in period n

Index denotes the state

Denotes the time period or number of transitions

For example, $\pi_1(1)$ denotes the probability of the system being in state 1 in period 1, while $\pi_2(1)$ denotes the probability of the system being in state 2 in period 1. Since $\pi_i(n)$ is the probability that the system is in state i in period n, this probability is referred to as a **state probability.**

The terms $\pi_1(0)$ and $\pi_2(0)$ will denote the probability of the system being in state 1 or state 2 at some initial or starting period. Week 0 represents the most recent period, when we are beginning the analysis of a Markov process. If we set $\pi_1(0) = 1$ and $\pi_2(0) = 0$, we are saying that as an initial condition the customer shopped last week at Murphy's; alternatively, if we set $\pi_1(0) = 0$ and $\pi_2(0) = 1$, we would be starting the system with a customer who shopped last week at Ashley's. In the tree diagram of Figure 17.1, we consider the situation where the customer shopped last at Murphy's. Thus,

$$[\pi_1(0) \quad \pi_2(0)] = [1 \quad 0]$$

is a vector that represents the initial state probabilities of the system. In general, we use the notation

$$\Pi(n) = [\pi_1(n) \quad \pi_2(n)]$$

to denote the vector of state probabilities for the system in period n. In the example, $\Pi(1)$ is a vector representing the state probabilities for the first week, $\Pi(2)$ is a vector representing the state probabilities for the second week, and so on.

Using this notation, we can find the state probabilities for period $n + 1$ by simply multiplying the known state probabilities for period n by the transition probability matrix. Using the vector of state probabilities and the matrix of transition probabilities, the multiplication[1] can be expressed as follows:

$$\Pi(\text{next period}) = \Pi(\text{current period})P$$

or

$$\Pi(n + 1) = \Pi(n)P \tag{17.1}$$

Beginning with the system in state 1 at period 0, we have $\Pi(0) = [1 \ 0]$. We can compute the state probabilities for period 1 as follows:

$$\Pi(1) = \Pi(0)P$$

or

$$[\pi_1(1) \quad \pi_2(1)] = [\pi_1(0) \quad \pi_2(0)] \begin{bmatrix} p_{11} & p_{12} \\ p_{21} & p_{22} \end{bmatrix}$$

$$= [1 \quad 0] \begin{bmatrix} 0.9 & 0.1 \\ 0.2 & 0.8 \end{bmatrix}$$

$$= [0.9 \quad 0.1]$$

The state probabilities $\pi_1(1) = 0.9$ and $\pi_2(1) = 0.1$ are the probabilities that a customer who shopped at Murphy's during week 0 will shop at Murphy's or at Ashley's during week 1.

Using equation (17.1), we can compute the state probabilities for the second week as follows:

$$\Pi(2) = \Pi(1)P$$

or

$$[\pi_1(2) \quad \pi_2(2)] = [\pi_1(1) \quad \pi_2(1)] \begin{bmatrix} p_{11} & p_{12} \\ p_{21} & p_{22} \end{bmatrix}$$

$$= [0.9 \quad 0.1] \begin{bmatrix} 0.9 & 0.1 \\ 0.2 & 0.8 \end{bmatrix}$$

$$= [0.83 \quad 0.17]$$

---

1. Appendix 17.1 provides the step-by-step procedure for vector and matrix multiplication.

We see that the probability of shopping at Murphy's during the second week is 0.83, while the probability of shopping at Ashley's during the second week is 0.17. These same results were previously obtained using the tree diagram of Figure 17.1. By continuing to apply equation (17.1), we can compute the state probabilities for any future period; that is,

$$\Pi(3) = \Pi(2)P$$
$$\Pi(4) = \Pi(3)P$$
$$\vdots \qquad \vdots$$
$$\Pi(n + 1) = \Pi(n)P$$

Table 17.2 shows the result of carrying out these calculations for ten periods.

The vectors $\Pi(1)$, $\Pi(2)$, $\Pi(3)$, ... contain the probabilities that a customer who started out as a Murphy customer will be in state 1 or state 2 in the first period, the second period, the third period, and so on. In Table 17.2 we see that after a few periods these probabilities do not change much from one period to the next.

If we had started with 1000 Murphy customers—that is, 1000 consumers who last shopped at Murphy's—our analysis indicates that during the fifth weekly shopping period, 723 would be customers of Murphy's, and 277 would be customers of Ashley's. Moreover, during the tenth weekly shopping period, 676 would be customers of Murphy's, and 324 would be customers of Ashley's.

Now let us repeat the analysis, but this time we will begin the process with a customer who shopped last at Ashley's. Thus,

$$\Pi(0) = [\pi_1(0) \quad \pi_2(0)] = [0 \quad 1]$$

Using equation (17.1), the probability of the system being in state 1 or state 2 in period 1 is given by

$$\Pi(1) = \Pi(0)P$$

or

$$[\pi_1(1) \quad \pi_2(1)] = [\pi_1(0) \quad \pi_2(0)] \begin{bmatrix} p_{11} & p_{12} \\ p_{21} & p_{22} \end{bmatrix}$$

$$= [0 \quad 1] \begin{bmatrix} 0.9 & 0.1 \\ 0.2 & 0.8 \end{bmatrix}$$

$$= [0.2 \quad 0.8]$$

Table 17.2	STATE PROBABILITIES FOR FUTURE PERIODS BEGINNING INITIALLY WITH A MURPHY'S CUSTOMER										
State Probability						Period (n)					
	0	1	2	3	4	5	6	7	8	9	10
$\pi_1(n)$	1	0.9	0.83	0.781	0.747	0.723	0.706	0.694	0.686	0.680	0.676
$\pi_2(n)$	0	0.1	0.17	0.219	0.253	0.277	0.294	0.306	0.314	0.320	0.324

Proceeding as before, we can calculate subsequent state probabilities. Doing so, we obtain the results shown in Table 17.3.

In the fifth shopping period, the probability that the customer will be shopping at Murphy's is 0.555, and the probability that the customer will be shopping at Ashley's is 0.445. In the tenth period, the probability that a customer will be shopping at Murphy's is 0.648, and the probability that a customer will be shopping at Ashley's is 0.352.

As we continue the Markov process, we find that the probability of the system being in a particular state after a large number of periods is independent of the beginning state of the system. The probabilities that we approach after a large number of transitions are referred to as the **steady-state probabilities.** We shall denote the steady-state probability for state 1 with the symbol π_1 and the steady-state probability for state 2 with the symbol π_2. In other words, in the steady-state case, we simply omit the period designation from $\pi_i(n)$ because it is no longer necessary.

The analysis of Tables 17.2 and 17.3 indicates that as n gets larger, the difference between the state probabilities for the nth period and the $(n + 1)$th period becomes increasingly smaller. This analysis leads us to the conclusion that as n gets large, the state probabilities at the $(n + 1)$th period are very close to those at the nth period. This observation provides the basis of a simple method for computing the steady-state probabilities without having to actually carry out a large number of calculations.

In general, we know from equation (17.1) that

$$[\pi_1(n + 1) \quad \pi_2(n + 1)] = [\pi_1(n) \quad \pi_2(n)] \begin{bmatrix} p_{11} & p_{12} \\ p_{21} & p_{22} \end{bmatrix}$$

Since for sufficiently large n the difference between $\Pi(n + 1)$ and $\Pi(n)$ is negligible, we see that in the steady state $\pi_1(n + 1) = \pi_1(n) = \pi_1$, and $\pi_2(n + 1) = \pi_2(n) = \pi_2$. Thus, we have

$$[\pi_1 \quad \pi_2] = [\pi_1 \quad \pi_2] \begin{bmatrix} p_{11} & p_{12} \\ p_{21} & p_{22} \end{bmatrix}$$

$$= [\pi_1 \quad \pi_2] \begin{bmatrix} 0.9 & 0.1 \\ 0.2 & 0.8 \end{bmatrix}$$

After carrying out the multiplications, we obtain

$$\pi_1 = 0.9\pi_1 + 0.2\pi_2 \tag{17.2}$$

and

$$\pi_2 = 0.1\pi_1 + 0.8\pi_2 \tag{17.3}$$

Table 17.3	STATE PROBABILITIES FOR FUTURE PERIODS BEGINNING INITIALLY WITH AN ASHLEY'S CUSTOMER										
State						**Period (n)**					
Probability	**0**	**1**	**2**	**3**	**4**	**5**	**6**	**7**	**8**	**9**	**10**
$\pi_1(n)$	0	0.2	0.34	0.438	0.507	0.555	0.589	0.612	0.628	0.640	0.648
$\pi_2(n)$	1	0.8	0.66	0.562	0.493	0.445	0.411	0.388	0.372	0.360	0.352

However, we also know the steady-state probabilities must sum to 1 with

$$\pi_1 + \pi_2 = 1 \qquad (17.4)$$

Using equation (17.4) to solve for π_2 and substituting the result in equation (17.2), we obtain

$$\pi_1 = 0.9\pi_1 + 0.2(1 - \pi_1)$$
$$\pi_1 = 0.9\pi_1 + 0.2 - 0.2\pi_1$$
$$\pi_1 - 0.7\pi_1 = 0.2$$
$$0.3\pi_1 = 0.2$$
$$\pi_1 = \tfrac{2}{3}$$

Then, using equation (17.4), we can conclude that $\pi_2 = 1 - \pi_1 = \frac{1}{3}$. Thus, using equations (17.2) and (17.4), we can solve for the steady-state probabilities directly. You can check for yourself that we could have obtained the same result using equations (17.3) and (17.4).[2]

Thus, if we have 1000 customers in the system, the Markov process model tells us that in the long run, with steady-state probabilities $\pi_1 = \frac{2}{3}$ and $\pi_2 = \frac{1}{3}$, $\frac{2}{3}(1000) = 667$ customers will be Murphy's, and $\frac{1}{3}(1000) = 333$ customers will be Ashley's. The steady-state probabilities can be interpreted as the market shares for the two stores.

Market share information is often quite valuable in decision making. For example, suppose Ashley's Supermarket is contemplating an advertising campaign to attract more of Murphy's customers to its store. Let us suppose further that Ashley's believes this promotional strategy will increase the probability of a Murphy's customer switching to Ashley's from 0.10 to 0.15. The revised transition probabilities are given in Table 17.4.

Given the new transition probabilities, we can modify equations (17.2) and (17.4) to solve for the new steady-state probabilities or market shares. Thus, we obtain

$$\pi_1 = 0.85\pi_1 + 0.20\pi_2$$

Substituting $\pi_2 = 1 - \pi_1$ from equation (17.4), we have

$$\pi_1 = 0.85\pi_1 + 0.20(1 - \pi_1)$$
$$\pi_1 = 0.85\pi_1 + 0.20 - 0.20\pi_1$$
$$\pi_1 - 0.65\pi_1 = 0.20$$
$$0.35\pi_1 = 0.20$$
$$\pi_1 = 0.57$$

and

$$\pi_2 = 1 - 0.57 = 0.43$$

You should now be able to compute the steady-state probabilities for Markov processes with two states. Problem 3 provides an application.

We see that the proposed promotional strategy will increase Ashley's market share from $\pi_2 = 0.33$ to $\pi_2 = 0.43$. Suppose that the total market consists of 6000 customers per week. The new promotional strategy will increase the number of customers doing their weekly

---

2. Even though equations (17.2) and (17.3) provide two equations and two unknowns, we must include equation (17.4) when solving for π_1 and π_2 to ensure that the sum of steady-state probabilities will equal 1.

Table 17.4	REVISED TRANSITION PROBABILITIES FOR MURPHY'S AND ASHLEY'S GROCERY STORES	
Current Weekly Shopping Period	**Next Weekly Shopping Period**	
	Murphy's Foodliner	**Ashley's Supermarket**
Murphy's Foodliner	0.85	0.15
Ashley's Supermarket	0.20	0.80

With three states, the steady-state probabilities are found by solving three equations for the three unknown steady-state probabilities. Try Problem 7 as a slightly more difficult problem involving three states.

Other examples of Markov processes include the promotion of managers to various positions within an organization, the migration of people into and out of various regions of the country, and the progression of students through the years of college, including eventually dropping out or graduating.

shopping at Ashley's from 2000 to 2580. If the average weekly profit per customer is $10, the proposed promotional strategy can be expected to increase Ashley's profits by $5800 per week. If the cost of the promotional campaign is less than $5800 per week, Ashley should consider implementing the strategy.

This example is one illustration of how a Markov analysis of a firm's market share can be useful in decision making. Suppose that instead of trying to attract customers from Murphy's Foodliner, Ashley's directed a promotional effort at increasing the loyalty of its own customers. In this case, p_{22} would increase, and p_{21} would decrease. Once we knew the amount of the change, we could calculate new steady-state probabilities and compute the impact on profits.

NOTES and Comments

1. The Markov processes presented in this section have what is called the *memoryless property*: the current state of the system together with the transition probabilities contains all the information necessary to predict the future behavior of the system. The prior states of the system do not have to be considered. Such Markov processes are considered first-order Markov processes. Higher-order Markov processes are ones in which future states of the system depend on two or more previous states.

2. Analysis of a Markov process model is not intended to optimize any particular aspect of a system. Rather, the analysis predicts or describes the future and steady-state behavior of the system. For instance, in the grocery store example, the analysis of the steady-state behavior provided a forecast or prediction of the market shares for the two competitors. In other applications, quantitative analysts have extended the study of Markov processes to what are called *Markov decision processes*. In these models, decisions can be made at each period that affect the transition probabilities and hence influence the future behavior of the system. Markov decision processes have been used in analyzing machine breakdown and maintenance operations, planning the movement of patients in hospitals, developing inspection strategies, determining newspaper subscription duration, and analyzing equipment replacement.

17.2 ACCOUNTS RECEIVABLE ANALYSIS

An accounting application in which Markov processes have produced useful results involves the estimation of the allowance for doubtful accounts receivable. This allowance is an estimate of the amount of accounts receivable that will ultimately prove to be uncol-lectible (i.e., bad debts).

Let us consider the accounts receivable situation for Heidman's Department Store. Hei-dman's has two aging categories for its accounts receivable: (1) accounts that are classified as 0–30 days old and (2) accounts that are classified as 31–90 days old. If any portion of an account balance exceeds 90 days, that portion is written off as a bad debt. Heidman's fol-lows the procedure of aging the total balance in any customer's account according to the oldest unpaid bill. For example, suppose that one customer's account balance on Septem-ber 30 is as follows:

Date of Purchase	Amount Charged
August 15	$25
September 18	10
September 28	50
Total	$85

An aging of accounts receivable on September 30 would assign the total balance of $85 to the 31–90-day category because the oldest unpaid bill of August 15 is 46 days old. Let us assume that one week later, October 7, the customer pays the August 15 bill of $25. The remaining total balance of $60 would now be placed in the 0–30-day category since the old-est unpaid amount, corresponding to the September 18 purchase, is less than 31 days old. This method of aging accounts receivable is called the *total balance method* since the total account balance is placed in the age category corresponding to the oldest unpaid amount.

Note that under the total balance method of aging accounts receivable, dollars appear-ing in a 31–90-day category at one point in time may appear in a 0–30-day category at a later point in time. In the preceding example, this was true for $60 of September billings, which shifted from a 31–90-day to a 0–30-day category after the August bill had been paid.

Let us assume that on December 31 Heidman's shows a total of $3000 in its accounts receivable and that the firm's management would like an estimate of how much of the $3000 will eventually be collected and how much will eventually result in bad debts. The estimated amount of bad debts will appear as an allowance for doubtful accounts in the year-ending financial statements.

Let us see how we can view the accounts receivable operation as a Markov process. First, concentrate on what happens to *one* dollar currently in accounts receivable. As the firm continues to operate into the future, we can consider each week as a trial of a Markov process with a dollar existing in one of the following states of the system:

State 1.   Paid category
State 2.   Bad debt category
State 3.   0–30-day category
State 4   31–90-day category

Thus, we can track the week-by-week status of one dollar by using a Markov analysis to identify the state of the system at a particular week or period.

Using a Markov process model with the above states, we define the transition proba-bilities as follows:

p_{ij} = probability of a dollar in state i in one week moving to state j in the next week

Based on historical transitions of accounts receivable dollars, the following matrix of transition probabilities, P, has been developed for Heidman's Department Store:

$$P = \begin{bmatrix} p_{11} & p_{12} & p_{13} & p_{14} \\ p_{21} & p_{22} & p_{23} & p_{24} \\ p_{31} & p_{32} & p_{33} & p_{34} \\ p_{41} & p_{42} & p_{43} & p_{44} \end{bmatrix} = \begin{bmatrix} 1.0 & 0.0 & 0.0 & 0.0 \\ 0.0 & 1.0 & 0.0 & 0.0 \\ 0.4 & 0.0 & 0.3 & 0.3 \\ 0.4 & 0.2 & 0.3 & 0.1 \end{bmatrix}$$

Note that the probability of a dollar in the 0–30-day category (state 3) moving to the paid category (state 1) in the next period is 0.4. Also, there is a 0.3 probability that this dollar will remain in the 0–30-day category (state 3) one week later, while there is a 0.3 probability that it will be in the 31–90-day category (state 4) one week later. Note also that a dollar in a 0–30-day account cannot make the transition to a bad debt (state 2) in one week.

An important property of the Markov process model for Heidman's accounts receivable situation is the presence of *absorbing states*. For example, once a dollar makes a transition to state 1, the paid state, the probability of making a transition to any other state is zero. Similarly, once a dollar is in state 2, the bad debt state, the probability of a transition to any other state is zero. Thus, once a dollar reaches state 1 or state 2, the system will remain in this state indefinitely. We can conclude that all accounts receivable dollars will eventually be absorbed into either the paid or the bad debt state, and hence the name **absorbing state.**

When absorbing states are present, each row of the transition matrix corresponding to an absorbing state will have a single 1 and all other probabilities will be 0.

The Fundamental Matrix and Associated Calculations

Whenever a Markov process has absorbing states, we do not compute steady-state probabilities because each unit ultimately ends up in one of the absorbing states. With absorbing states present, we are interested in knowing the probability that a unit will end up in each of the absorbing states. For the Heidman's Department Store problem, we want to know the probability that a dollar currently in the 0–30-day age category will end up paid (absorbing state 1) as well as the probability that a dollar in this age category will end up a bad debt (absorbing state 2). We also want to know these absorbing-state probabilities for dollars currently in the 31–90-day age category.

The computation of the absorbing-state probabilities requires the determination and use of what is called a **fundamental matrix.** The mathematical logic underlying the fundamental matrix is beyond the scope of this text. However, as we show, the fundamental matrix is derived from the matrix of transition probabilities and is relatively easy to compute for Markov processes with a small number of states. In the following example, we show the computation of the fundamental matrix and the determination of the absorbing-state probabilities for Heidman's Department Store.

We begin the computations by partitioning the matrix of transition probabilities into the following four parts:

$$P = \begin{bmatrix} 1.0 & 0.0 & | & 0.0 & 0.0 \\ 0.0 & 1.0 & | & 0.0 & 0.0 \\ - & - & - & - & - & - & - \\ 0.4 & 0.0 & | & 0.3 & 0.3 \\ 0.4 & 0.2 & | & 0.3 & 0.1 \end{bmatrix} = \begin{bmatrix} 1.0 & 0.0 & | & 0.0 & 0.0 \\ 0.0 & 1.0 & | & 0.0 & 0.0 \\ - & - & - & - & - & - & - \\ & R & | & & Q \\ & & | & & \end{bmatrix}$$

where

$$R = \begin{bmatrix} 0.4 & 0.0 \\ 0.4 & 0.2 \end{bmatrix} \qquad Q = \begin{bmatrix} 0.3 & 0.3 \\ 0.3 & 0.1 \end{bmatrix}$$

A matrix N, called a *fundamental matrix,* can be calculated using the following formula:

$$N = (I - Q)^{-1} \tag{17.5}$$

where I is an identity matrix with 1s on the main diagonal and 0s elsewhere. The superscript -1 is used to indicate the inverse of the matrix $(I - Q)$. In Appendix 17.1 we present formulas for finding the inverse of a matrix with two rows and two columns.

Before proceeding, we note that to use equation (17.5), the identity matrix I must be chosen such that it has the *same size or dimensionality* as the matrix Q. In our example problem, Q has two rows and two columns, so we must choose

$$I = \begin{bmatrix} 1.0 & 0.0 \\ 0.0 & 1.0 \end{bmatrix}$$

Let us now continue with the example problem by computing the fundamental matrix.

$$I - Q = \begin{bmatrix} 1.0 & 0.0 \\ 0.0 & 1.0 \end{bmatrix} - \begin{bmatrix} 0.3 & 0.3 \\ 0.3 & 0.1 \end{bmatrix}$$

$$= \begin{bmatrix} 0.7 & -0.3 \\ -0.3 & 0.9 \end{bmatrix}$$

and (see Appendix 17.1)

$$N = (I - Q)^{-1} = \begin{bmatrix} 1.67 & 0.56 \\ 0.56 & 1.30 \end{bmatrix}$$

If we multiply the fundamental matrix N times the R portion of the P matrix, we obtain the probabilities that accounts receivable dollars initially in states 3 or 4 will eventually reach each of the absorbing states. The multiplication of N times R for the Heidman's Department Store problem provides the following results (again, see Appendix 17.1 for the steps of this matrix multiplication):

$$NR = \begin{bmatrix} 1.67 & 0.56 \\ 0.56 & 1.30 \end{bmatrix} \begin{bmatrix} 0.4 & 0.0 \\ 0.4 & 0.2 \end{bmatrix} = \begin{bmatrix} 0.89 & 0.11 \\ 0.74 & 0.26 \end{bmatrix}$$

The first row of the product NR is the probability that a dollar in the 0–30-day age category will end up in each absorbing state. Thus, we see that there is a 0.89 probability that a dollar in the 0–30-day category will eventually be paid and a 0.11 probability that it will become a bad debt. Similarly, the second row shows the probabilities associated with a dollar in the 31–90-day category; that is, a dollar in the 31–90-day category has a 0.74 probability of eventually being paid and a 0.26 probability of proving to be uncollectible. Using this information, we can predict the amount of money that will be paid and the amount that will be lost as bad debts.

Establishing the Allowance for Doubtful Accounts

Let B represent a two-element vector that contains the current accounts receivable balances in the 0–30-day and the 31–90-day age categories; that is,

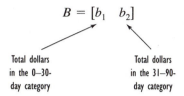

$$B = [b_1 \quad b_2]$$

Total dollars in the 0–30-day category

Total dollars in the 31–90-day category

Suppose that the December 31 balance of accounts receivable for Heidman's shows $1000 in the 0–30-day category (state 3) and $2000 in the 31–90-day category (state 4).

$$B = [1000 \quad 2000]$$

We can multiply B times NR to determine how much of the $3000 will be collected and how much will be lost. For example

$$BNR = [1000 \quad 2000] \begin{bmatrix} 0.89 & 0.11 \\ 0.74 & 0.26 \end{bmatrix}$$

$$= [2370 \quad 630]$$

Thus, we see that $2370 of the accounts receivable balances will be collected and $630 will be written off as a bad debt expense. Based on this analysis, the accounting department would set up an allowance for doubtful accounts of $630.

The matrix multiplication of BNR is simply a convenient way of computing the eventual collections and bad debts of the accounts receivable. Recall that the NR matrix showed a 0.89 probability of collecting dollars in the 0–30-day category and a 0.74 probability of collecting dollars in the 31–90-day category. Thus, as was shown by the BNR calculation, we expect to collect a total of $(1000)0.89 + (2000)0.74 = 890 + 1480 = \$2370$.

Suppose that on the basis of the previous analysis Heidman's would like to investigate the possibility of reducing the amount of bad debts. Recall that the analysis indicated that a 0.11 probability or 11% of the amount in the 0–30-day age category and 26% of the amount in the 31–90-day age category will prove to be uncollectible. Let us assume that Heidman's is considering instituting a new credit policy involving a discount for prompt payment.

Management believes that the policy under consideration will increase the probability of a transition from the 0–30-day age category to the paid category and decrease the probability of a transition from the 0–30-day to the 31–90-day age category. Let us assume that a careful study of the effects of this new policy leads management to conclude that the following transition matrix would be applicable:

$$P = \begin{bmatrix} 1.0 & 0.0 & | & 0.0 & 0.0 \\ 0.0 & 1.0 & | & 0.0 & 0.0 \\ - & - & - & - & - \\ 0.6 & 0.0 & | & 0.3 & 0.1 \\ 0.4 & 0.2 & | & 0.3 & 0.1 \end{bmatrix}$$

We see that the probability of a dollar in the 0–30-day age category making a transition to the paid category in the next period has increased to 0.6 and that the probability of a dollar in the 0–30-day age category making a transition to the 31–90-day category has decreased to 0.1. To determine the effect of these changes on bad debt expense, we must calculate N, NR, and BNR. We begin by using equation (17.5) to calculate the fundamental matrix N:

$$N = (I - Q)^{-1} = \left\{ \begin{bmatrix} 1.0 & 0.0 \\ 0.0 & 1.0 \end{bmatrix} - \begin{bmatrix} 0.3 & 0.1 \\ 0.3 & 0.1 \end{bmatrix} \right\}^{-1}$$

$$= \begin{bmatrix} 0.7 & -0.1 \\ -0.3 & 0.9 \end{bmatrix}^{-1}$$

$$= \begin{bmatrix} 1.5 & 0.17 \\ 0.5 & 1.17 \end{bmatrix}$$

By multiplying N times R, we obtain the new probabilities that the dollars in each age category will end up in the two absorbing states:

$$NR = \begin{bmatrix} 1.5 & 0.17 \\ 0.5 & 1.17 \end{bmatrix} \begin{bmatrix} 0.6 & 0.0 \\ 0.4 & 0.2 \end{bmatrix}$$

$$= \begin{bmatrix} 0.97 & 0.03 \\ 0.77 & 0.23 \end{bmatrix}$$

We see that with the new credit policy we would expect only 3% of the funds in the 0–30-day age category and 23% of the funds in the 31–90-day age category to prove to be uncollectible. If, as before, we assume a current balance of $1000 in the 0–30-day age category and $2000 in the 31–90-day age category, we can calculate the total amount of accounts receivable that will end up in the two absorbing states by multiplying B times NR. We obtain

$$BNR = \begin{bmatrix} 1000 & 2000 \end{bmatrix} \begin{bmatrix} 0.97 & 0.03 \\ 0.77 & 0.23 \end{bmatrix}$$

$$= \begin{bmatrix} 2510 & 490 \end{bmatrix}$$

Problem 11, which provides a variation of Heidman's Department Store problem, will give you practice in analyzing Markov processes with absorbing states.

Thus, the new credit policy shows a bad debt expense of $490. Under the previous credit policy, we found the bad debt expense to be $630. Thus, a savings of $630 − $490 = $140 could be expected as a result of the new credit policy. Given the total accounts receivable balance of $3000, this savings represents a 4.7% reduction in bad debt expense. After considering the costs involved, management can evaluate the economics of adopting the new credit policy. If the cost, including discounts, is less than 4.7% of the accounts receivable balance, we would expect the new policy to lead to increased profits for Heidman's Department Store.

SUMMARY

In this chapter we have presented Markov process models as well as examples of their application. We saw that a Markov analysis could provide helpful decision-making information about a situation that involves a sequence of repeated trials with a finite number of possible states on each trial. A primary objective is obtaining information about the probability of each state after a large number of transitions or time periods.

A market share application showed the computational procedure for determining the steady-state probabilities that could be interpreted as market shares for two competing supermarkets. In an accounts receivable application, we introduced the notion of absorbing states; for the two absorbing states, referred to as the paid and bad debt categories, we showed how to determine the percentage of an accounts receivable balance that would be absorbed in each of these states.

GLOSSARY

Trials of the process The events that trigger transitions of the system from one state to another. In many applications, successive time periods represent the trials of the process.

State of the system The condition of the system at any particular trial or time period.

Transition probability Given the system is in state i during one period, the transition probability p_{ij} is the probability that the system will be in state j during the next period.

State probability The probability that the system will be in any particular state. (That is, $\pi_i(n)$ is the probability of the system being in state i in period n.)

Steady-state probability The probability that the system will be in any particular state after a large number of transitions. Once steady state has been reached, the state probabilities do not change from period to period.

Absorbing state A state is said to be absorbing if the probability of making a transition out of that state is zero. Thus, once the system has made a transition into an absorbing state, it will remain there.

Fundamental matrix A matrix necessary for the computation of probabilities associated with absorbing states of a Markov process.

PROBLEMS

1. In the market share analysis of Section 17.1, suppose that we are considering the Markov process associated with the shopping trips of one customer, but we do not know where the customer shopped during the last week. Thus, we might assume a 0.5 probability that the customer shopped at Murphy's and a 0.5 probability that the customer shopped at Ashley's at period 0; that is, $\pi_1(0) = 0.5$ and $\pi_2(0) = 0.5$. Given these initial state probabilities, develop a table similar to Table 17.2 showing the probability of each state in future periods. What do you observe about the long-run probabilities of each state?

2. Management of the New Fangled Softdrink Company believes that the probability of a customer purchasing Red Pop or the company's major competition, Super Cola, is based on the customer's most recent purchase. Suppose that the following transition probabilities are appropriate:

	To	
From	**Red Pop**	**Super Cola**
Red Pop	0.9	0.1
Super Cola	0.1	0.9

a. Show the two-period tree diagram for a customer who last purchased Red Pop. What is the probability that this customer purchases Red Pop on the second purchase?

b. What is the long-run market share for each of these two products?

c. A Red Pop advertising campaign is being planned to increase the probability of attracting Super Cola customers. Management believes that the new campaign will increase to 0.15 the probability of a customer switching from Super Cola to Red Pop. What is the projected effect of the advertising campaign on the market shares?

SELF TEST

3. The computer center at Rockbottom University has been experiencing computer downtime. Let us assume that the trials of an associated Markov process are defined as one-hour periods and that the probability of the system being in a running state or a down state is based on the state of the system in the previous period. Historical data show the following transition probabilities:

	To	
From	**Running**	**Down**
Running	0.90	0.10
Down	0.30	0.70

a. If the system is initially running, what is the probability of the system being down in the next hour of operation?

b. What are the steady-state probabilities of the system being in the running state and in the down state?

4. One cause of the downtime in Problem 3 was traced to a specific piece of computer hardware. Management believes that switching to a different hardware component will result in the following transition probabilities:

	To	
From	**Running**	**Down**
Running	0.95	0.05
Down	0.60	0.40

a. What are the steady-state probabilities of the system being in the running and down states?

b. If the cost of the system being down for any period is estimated to be $500 (including lost profits for time down and maintenance), what is the breakeven cost for the new hardware component on a time-period basis?

5. A major traffic problem in the Greater Cincinnati area involves traffic attempting to cross the Ohio River from Cincinnati to Kentucky using Interstate I-75. Let us assume that the probability of no traffic delay in one period, given no traffic delay in the preceding period, is 0.85 and that the probability of finding a traffic delay in one period, given a delay in the preceding period, is 0.75. Traffic is classified as having either a delay or a no-delay state, and the period considered is 30 minutes.

a. Assume that you are a motorist entering the traffic system and receive a radio report of a traffic delay, what is the probability that for the next 60 minutes (two time periods) the system will be in the delay state? Note that this is the probability of being in the delay state for two consecutive periods.

b. What is the probability that in the long run the traffic will not be in the delay state?

c. An important assumption of the Markov process models presented in this chapter has been the constant or stationary transition probabilities as the system operates in the future. Do you believe this assumption should be questioned for this traffic problem? Explain.

6. Data collected from selected major metropolitan areas in the eastern United States show that 2% of individuals living within the city limits move to the suburbs during a 1-year period while 1% of individuals living in the suburbs move to the city during a 1-year period. Answer the following questions assuming that this process is modeled by a Markov process with two states: city and suburbs.

a. Prepare the matrix of transition probabilities.

b. Compute the steady-state probabilities.

c. In a particular metropolitan area, 40% of the population live in the city, and 60% of the population live in the suburbs. What population changes do your steady-state probabilities project for this metropolitan area?

SELF TEST

7. Assume that a third grocery store, Quick Stop Groceries, enters the market share and customer loyalty situation described in Section 17.1. Quick Stop Groceries is smaller than either Murphy's Foodliner or Ashley's Supermarket. However, Quick Stop's convenience with faster service and gasoline for automobiles can be expected to attract some customers who currently make weekly shopping visits to either Murphy's or Ashley's. Assume that the transition probabilities are as follows:

	To		
From	**Murphy's**	**Ashley's**	**Quick Stop**
Murphy's Foodliner	0.85	0.10	0.05
Ashley's Supermarket	0.20	0.75	0.05
Quick Stop Groceries	0.15	0.10	0.75

a. Compute the steady-state probabilities for this three-state Markov process.

b. What market share will Quick Stop obtain?

c. With 1000 customers, the original two-state Markov process in Section 17.1 projected 667 weekly customer trips to Murphy's Foodliner and 333 weekly customer trips to Ashley's Supermarket. What impact will Quick Stop have on the customer visits at Murphy's and Ashley's? Explain.

8. The purchase patterns for two brands of toothpaste can be expressed as a Markov process with the following transition probabilities:

	To	
From	**Special B**	**MDA**
Special B	0.90	0.10
MDA	0.05	0.95

a. Which brand appears to have the most loyal customers? Explain.

b. What are the projected market shares for the two brands?

9. Suppose that in Problem 8 a new toothpaste brand enters the market such that the following transition probabilities exist:

From	Special B	To MDA	T-White
Special B	0.80	0.10	0.10
MDA	0.05	0.75	0.20
T-White	0.40	0.30	0.30

What are the new long-run market shares? Which brand will suffer most from the introduction of the new brand of toothpaste?

10. Given the following transition matrix with states 1 and 2 as absorbing states, what is the probability that units in states 3 and 4 end up in each of the absorbing states?

$$P = \begin{bmatrix} 1.0 & 0.0 & 0.0 & 0.0 \\ 0.0 & 1.0 & 0.0 & 0.0 \\ 0.2 & 0.1 & 0.4 & 0.3 \\ 0.2 & 0.2 & 0.1 & 0.5 \end{bmatrix}$$

SELF TEST

11. In the Heidman's Department Store problem of Section 17.2, suppose that the following transition matrix is appropriate:

$$P = \begin{bmatrix} 1.0 & 0.0 & 0.0 & 0.0 \\ 0.0 & 1.0 & 0.0 & 0.0 \\ 0.5 & 0.0 & 0.25 & 0.25 \\ 0.5 & 0.2 & 0.05 & 0.25 \end{bmatrix}$$

If Heidman's has $4000 in the 0–30-day age category and $5000 in the 31–90-day age category, what is your estimate of the amount of bad debts the company will experience?

12. The KLM Christmas Tree Farm owns a plot of land with 5000 evergreen trees. Each year KLM allows retailers of Christmas trees to select and cut trees for sale to individual customers. KLM protects small trees (usually less than 4 feet tall) so that they will be available for sale in future years. Currently 1500 trees are classified as protected trees, while the remaining 3500 are available for cutting. However, even though a tree is available for cutting in a given year, it may not be selected for cutting until future years. While most trees not cut in a given year live until the next year, some diseased trees are lost every year.

In viewing the KLM Christmas tree operation as a Markov process with yearly periods, we define the following four states:

State 1.   Cut and sold
State 2.   Lost to disease
State 3.   Too small for cutting
State 4.   Available for cutting but not cut and sold

The following transition matrix is appropriate:

$$P = \begin{bmatrix} 1.0 & 0.0 & 0.0 & 0.0 \\ 0.0 & 1.0 & 0.0 & 0.0 \\ 0.1 & 0.2 & 0.5 & 0.2 \\ 0.4 & 0.1 & 0.0 & 0.5 \end{bmatrix}$$

How many of the farm's 5000 trees will be sold eventually, and how many will be lost?

13. A large corporation has collected data on the reasons both middle managers and senior managers leave the company. Some managers eventually retire, but others leave the company prior to retirement for personal reasons including more attractive positions with other firms. Assume that the following matrix of one-year transition probabilities applies with the four states of the Markov process being retirement, leaves prior to retirement for personal reasons, stays as a middle manager, stays as a senior manager.

	Retirement	Leaves— Personal	Middle Manager	Senior Manager
Retirement	1.00	0.00	0.00	0.00
Leaves—Personal	0.00	1.00	0.00	0.00
Middle Manager	0.03	0.07	0.80	0.10
Senior Manager	0.08	0.01	0.03	0.88

a. What states are considered absorbing states? Why?
b. Interpret the transition probabilities for the middle managers.
c. Interpret the transition probabilities for the senior managers.
d. What percentage of the current middle managers will eventually retire from the company? What percentage will leave the company for personal reasons?
e. The company currently has 920 managers: 640 middle managers and 280 senior managers. How many of these managers will eventually retire from the company? How many will leave the company for personal reasons?

14. Data for the progression of college students at a particular college are summarized in the following matrix of transition probabilities.

	Graduate	Dropout	Freshmen	Sophomore	Junior	Senior
Graduate	1.00	0.00	0.00	0.00	0.00	0.00
Dropout	0.00	1.00	0.00	0.00	0.00	0.00
Freshmen	0.00	0.20	0.15	0.65	0.00	0.00
Sophomore	0.00	0.15	0.00	0.10	0.75	0.00
Junior	0.00	0.10	0.00	0.00	0.05	0.85
Senior	0.90	0.05	0.00	0.00	0.00	0.05

a. What states are absorbing states?
b. Interpret the transition probabilities for a sophomore.
c. Use The Management Scientist software package to compute the probabilities that a sophomore will graduate and that a sophomore will drop out.
d. In an address to the incoming class of 600 freshmen, the dean asks the students to look around the auditorium and realize that about 50% of the freshmen present today will not make it to graduation day. Does your Markov process analysis support the dean's statement? Explain.
e. Currently, the college has 600 freshmen, 520 sophomores, 460 juniors, and 420 seniors. What percentage of the 2000 students attending the college will eventually graduate?

···/ /············

Appendix 17.1   MATRIX NOTATION AND OPERATIONS

Matrix Notation

A **matrix** is a rectangular arrangement of numbers. For example, consider the following matrix that we have named D:

$$D = \begin{bmatrix} 1 & 3 & 2 \\ 0 & 4 & 5 \end{bmatrix}$$

The matrix D is said to consist of six elements, where each element of D is a number. To identify a particular element of a matrix, we have to specify its location. Therefore, we introduce the concepts of rows and columns.

All elements across some horizontal line in a matrix are said to be in a row of the matrix. For example, elements 1, 3, and 2 in D are in the first row, and elements 0, 4, and 5 are in the second row. By convention, we refer to the top row as row 1, the second row from the top as row 2, and so on.

All elements along some vertical line are said to be in a column of the matrix. Elements 1 and 0 in D are elements in the first column, elements 3 and 4 are elements of the second column, and elements 2 and 5 are elements of the third column. By convention, we refer to the leftmost column as column 1, the next column to the right as column 2, and so on.

We can identify a particular element in a matrix by specifying its row and column position. For example, the element in row 1 and column 2 of D is the number 3. This is written as

$$d_{12} = 3$$

In general, we use the following notation to refer to specific elements of D:

$$d_{ij} = \text{element located in the } i\text{th row and } j\text{th column of } D$$

We always use capital letters for the names of matrices and the corresponding lowercase letters with two subscripts to denote the elements.

The *size* of a matrix is the number of rows and columns in the matrix and is written as the number of rows $\times$ the number of columns. Thus, the size of D is 2×3.

Frequently we will encounter matrices that have only one row or one column. For example,

$$G = \begin{bmatrix} 6 \\ 4 \\ 2 \\ 3 \end{bmatrix}$$

is a matrix that has only one column. Whenever a matrix has only one column, we call the matrix a *column vector*. In a similar manner, any matrix that has only one row is called a *row vector*. Using our previous notation for the elements of a matrix, we would refer to specific elements in G by writing g_{ij}. However, since G has only one column, the column position is unimportant, and we need only specify the row the element of interest is in. That is, instead of referring to elements in a vector using g_{ij}, we specify only one subscript, which denotes the position of the element in the vector. For example,

$$g_1 = 6 \qquad g_2 = 4 \qquad g_3 = 2 \qquad g_4 = 3$$

Matrix Operations

Matrix Transpose   The transpose of a matrix is formed by making the rows in the original matrix the columns in the transpose matrix, and by making the columns in the original matrix the rows in the transpose matrix. For example, the transpose of the matrix

$$D = \begin{bmatrix} 1 & 3 & 2 \\ 0 & 4 & 5 \end{bmatrix}$$

is

$$D^t = \begin{bmatrix} 1 & 0 \\ 3 & 4 \\ 2 & 5 \end{bmatrix}$$

Note that we use the superscript t to denote the transpose of a matrix.

Matrix Multiplication   We demonstrate how to perform two types of matrix multiplication: (1) multiplying two vectors and (2) multiplying a matrix times a matrix.

The product of a row vector of size $1 \times n$ times a column vector of size $n \times 1$ is the number obtained by multiplying the first element in the row vector times the first element in the column vector, the second element in the row vector times the second element in the column vector, and continuing on through the last element in the row vector times the last element in the column vector, and then summing the products. Suppose, for example, that we wanted to multiply the row vector H times the column vector G, where

$$H = \begin{bmatrix} 2 & 1 & 5 & 0 \end{bmatrix} \text{ and } G = \begin{bmatrix} 6 \\ 4 \\ 2 \\ 3 \end{bmatrix}$$

The product HG, referred to as a vector product, is given by

$$HG = 2(6) + 1(4) + 5(2) + 0(3) = 26$$

The product of a matrix of size $p \times n$ and a matrix of size $n \times m$ is a new matrix of size $p \times m$. The element in the ith row and jth column of the new matrix is given by the vector product of the ith row of the $p \times n$ matrix times the jth column of the $n \times m$ matrix. Suppose, for example, that we want to multiply D times A, where

$$D = \begin{bmatrix} 1 & 3 & 2 \\ 0 & 4 & 5 \end{bmatrix} \quad A = \begin{bmatrix} 1 & 3 & 5 \\ 2 & 0 & 4 \\ 1 & 5 & 2 \end{bmatrix}$$

Let $C = DA$ denote the product of D times A. The element in row 1 and column 1 of C is given by the vector product of the first row of D times the first column of A. Thus

$$c_{11} = \begin{bmatrix} 1 & 3 & 2 \end{bmatrix} \begin{bmatrix} 1 \\ 2 \\ 1 \end{bmatrix} = 1(1) + 3(2) + 2(1) = 9$$

The element in row 2 and column 1 of C is given by the vector product of the second row of D times the first column of A. Thus,

$$c_{21} = \begin{bmatrix} 0 & 4 & 5 \end{bmatrix} \begin{bmatrix} 1 \\ 2 \\ 1 \end{bmatrix} = 0(1) + 4(2) + 5(1) = 13$$

Calculating the remaining elements of C in a similar fashion, we obtain

$$C = \begin{bmatrix} 9 & 13 & 21 \\ 13 & 25 & 26 \end{bmatrix}$$

Clearly, the product of a matrix and a vector is just a special case of multiplying a matrix times a matrix. For example, the product of a matrix of size $m \times n$ and a vector of size $n \times 1$ is a new vector of size $m \times 1$. The element in the ith position of the new vector is given by the vector product of the ith row of the $m \times n$ matrix times the $n \times 1$ column vector. Suppose, for example, that we want to multiply D times K, where

$$D = \begin{bmatrix} 1 & 3 & 2 \\ 0 & 4 & 5 \end{bmatrix} \quad K = \begin{bmatrix} 1 \\ 4 \\ 2 \end{bmatrix}$$

The first element of DK is given by the vector product of the first row of D times K. Thus,

$$\begin{bmatrix} 1 & 3 & 2 \end{bmatrix} \begin{bmatrix} 1 \\ 4 \\ 2 \end{bmatrix} = 1(1) + 3(4) + 2(2) = 17$$

The second element of DK is given by the vector product of the second row of D and K. Thus,

$$\begin{bmatrix} 0 & 4 & 5 \end{bmatrix} \begin{bmatrix} 1 \\ 4 \\ 2 \end{bmatrix} = 0(1) + 4(4) + 5(2) = 26$$

Hence, we see that the product of the matrix D times the vector K is given by

$$DK = \begin{bmatrix} 1 & 3 & 2 \\ 0 & 4 & 5 \end{bmatrix} \begin{bmatrix} 1 \\ 4 \\ 2 \end{bmatrix} = \begin{bmatrix} 17 \\ 26 \end{bmatrix}$$

Can any two matrices be multiplied? The answer is no. To multiply two matrices, the number of the columns in the first matrix must equal the number of rows in the second. If this property is satisfied, the matrices are said to *conform for multiplication*. Thus, in our example, D and K could be multiplied because D had three columns and K had three rows.

Matrix Inverse   The inverse of a matrix A is another matrix, denoted A^{-1}, such that $A^{-1}A = I$ and $AA^{-1} = I$. The inverse of any square matrix A consisting of two rows and two columns is computed as follows:

$$A = \begin{bmatrix} a_{11} & a_{12} \\ a_{21} & a_{22} \end{bmatrix}$$

$$A^{-1} = \begin{bmatrix} a_{22}/d & -a_{12}/d \\ -a_{21}/d & a_{11}/d \end{bmatrix}$$

where $d = a_{11}a_{22} - a_{21}a_{12}$ is the determinant of the 2×2 matrix A. For example, if

$$A = \begin{bmatrix} 0.7 & -0.3 \\ -0.3 & 0.9 \end{bmatrix}$$

then

$$d = (0.7)(0.9) - (-0.3)(-0.3) = 0.54$$

and

$$A^{-1} = \begin{bmatrix} 0.9/0.54 & 0.3/0.54 \\ 0.3/0.54 & 0.7/0.54 \end{bmatrix} = \begin{bmatrix} 1.67 & 0.56 \\ 0.56 & 1.30 \end{bmatrix}$$

U.S. GENERAL ACCOUNTING OFFICE*

WASHINGTON, D.C.

The U.S. General Accounting Office (GAO) is an independent, nonpolitical audit organization in the legislative branch of the federal government. The GAO was created by the Budget and Accounting Act of 1921 and has three basic purposes:

1. To assist Congress, its committees, and its members in carrying out their legislative and oversight responsibilities, consistent with its role as an independent, nonpolitical agency.
2. To audit and evaluate the programs, activities, and financial operations of federal departments and agencies and to make recommendations toward more efficient and effective operations.
3. To carry out financial control and other functions with respect to federal government programs and operations including accounting, legal, and claims settlement work.

GAO evaluators, the main occupation in the GAO, determine the effectiveness of existing or proposed federal programs and the efficiency, economy, legality, and effectiveness with which federal agencies carry out their responsibilities. These evaluations culminate in reports to the Congress and to the heads of federal departments and agencies. Such reports typically include recommendations to Congress concerning the need for enabling or remedial legislation and suggestions to agencies concerning the need for changes in programs or operations to improve their economy, efficiency, and effectiveness.

GAO evaluators analyze policies and practices and the use of resources within and among federal programs,

identify problem areas and deficiencies in meeting program goals, develop and analyze alternative solutions to problems of program execution, and develop and recommend changes to enable the programs to better conform to congressional goals and legislative intent. To effectively carry out their duties, evaluators must be proficient in interviewing, data processing, records review, legislative research, quantitative methods, and statistical analysis techniques.

Impact of Services on the Well-being of Older People

GAO evaluators obtained data from a random sample of noninstitutionalized persons aged 65 and older living in Cleveland, Ohio. The health conditions of the sampled individuals in the 65- to 69-year-old groups were defined by the following three states:

- **Best.** Individual able to perform 13 identified activities of daily living without help.
- **Next best.** Individual able to perform the same 13 activities but required help for at least one activity.
- **Worst.** Individual unable to perform the same 13 activities even with help.

Using a 2-year period, GAO evaluators developed estimates of the year-to-year transition probabilities for individuals in the 65- to 69-year-old group. These estimates were then used to develop a transition probability matrix such as shown in the table below. Note that a death state has been added as an absorbing state.

Using the transition probabilities, a Markov process analysis can be used to determine the state probabilities for any number of periods (years) into the future. To ver-

---

*The authors are indebted to Bill Ammann, U.S. General Accounting Office, Washington, D.C., for providing this application.

Current Year Condition	Following Year Condition			
	Best	Next Best	Worst	Death
Best	p_{11}	p_{12}	p_{13}	p_{14}
Next Best	p_{21}	p_{22}	p_{23}	p_{24}
Worst	p_{31}	p_{32}	p_{33}	p_{34}
Death	0	0	0	1

ify the appropriateness of the Markov process model, GAO evaluators used the transition probabilities to determine the state probabilities for the 65- to 69-year-old age group 5 years into the future. The resulting state probabilities were compared with the health states of individuals in a known 70- to 74-year-old age group. No statistically significant difference occurred between the probabilities provided by the model and the actual state probabilities of the 70- to 74-year-old group.

Estimating the Likely Effects of Health Care Programs

The individuals in the original study were subdivided into two groups: those receiving appropriate health care and those not receiving appropriate health care. For the purpose of the study, a person was classified as receiving appropriate health care if the person was taking medication and/or treatment for each illness present and if the person was receiving help to perform each of the 13 activities of daily living as specifically needed. As a result, GAO evaluators developed two matrices of transition probabilities: one for individuals receiving appropriate health care and one for individuals not receiving appropriate health care.

For any individuals not receiving appropriate help, the kind of additional help needed was determined, and the cost of that help was estimated. Then those persons

were artificially aged using the transition probabilities to establish the likely benefits in terms of improved health states for the individuals. Over a 20-year period, a net savings occurred for the health care program provided all other factors remained equal. That is, the increased cost to provide sufficient appropriate help to all persons was eventually offset by individuals either improving their health state or by not spending as much time in a worse state. Although benefits of health care are often proclaimed theoretically, the Markov process model provided evidence that indicated benefits would be achieved with the health care program.

This type of Markov analysis was also conducted for economic, social, and life view status as well as for the health status. In some instances, the Markov model showed that additional help and/or programs did not result in net savings over time.

Questions

1. Suppose the transition probabilities in the table were as follows:

$$\begin{bmatrix} 0.80 & 0.10 & 0.06 & 0.04 \\ 0.05 & 0.75 & 0.15 & 0.05 \\ 0.00 & 0.05 & 0.75 & 0.20 \\ 0.00 & 0.00 & 0.00 & 1.00 \end{bmatrix}$$

   Assume that a particular city has 1000 individuals in the best state, 2000 in the next best state, and 500 in the worst state. Estimate how many of each of these individuals will be in each state 2 years from now.

2. How might health care programs affect the matrix of transition probabilities in question (1)? What effect would you expect to see in the distribution of individuals across the four states 2 years from now?

18

MULTICRITERIA DECISION PROBLEMS

In previous chapters we have shown how a variety of quantitative methods can help managers make better decisions. In each case, whenever we desired an optimal solution, we used a single criterion (e.g., maximize profit, minimize cost, or minimize expected cost). In this chapter we discuss techniques appropriate for situations in which the decision maker needs to consider multiple criteria in arriving at the overall best decision. For example, consider a company involved in selecting a location for a new manufacturing plant. The cost of land and construction may vary from location to location, so one criterion in selecting the best site could be the cost involved in building the plant. If cost were the sole criterion of interest, management would simply select the location that minimizes land cost plus construction cost. Before making any decision, however, management might also want to consider additional criteria such as the availability of transportation from the plant to the firm's distribution centers, the attractiveness of the proposed location in terms of hiring and retaining employees, energy costs at the proposed site, and state and local taxes. In such situations the complexity of the problem increases because one location may be more desirable in terms of one criterion and less desirable in terms of one or more of the other criteria.

To introduce the topic of multicriteria decision making, we first consider a technique referred to as **goal programming.** This technique was developed to handle multicriteria situations within the general framework of linear programming. The other approach we consider, referred to as the **analytic hierarchy process (AHP),** permits the inclusion of subjective factors in arriving at a decision. In this approach, the decision maker must make judgments about the relative importance of each criterion and then specify a preference for each alternative relative to each criterion. The output is a prioritized ranking indicating the overall preference for each decision alternative.

18.1   GOAL PROGRAMMING: FORMULATION AND GRAPHICAL SOLUTION

To illustrate the goal programming approach to multicriteria decision problems, let us consider a problem facing Nicolo Investment Advisors. A particular client has $80,000 to invest and, as an initial strategy, would like the investment portfolio restricted to two stocks:

Stock	Price/Share	Estimated Annual Return/Share	Risk Index/Share
U.S. Oil	$25	$3	0.50
Hub Properties	$50	$5	0.25

U.S. Oil, which has a return of $3 on a $25 share price, provides an annual rate of return of 12%, whereas Hub Properties provides an annual rate of return of 10%. The risk index per share, 0.50 for U.S. Oil and 0.25 for Hub Properties, is a rating Nicolo has assigned to measure the relative risk of the two investments. Higher risk index values imply greater risk; hence, Nicolo has judged U.S. Oil to be the riskier investment. By specifying a maximum portfolio risk index, Nicolo will avoid placing too much of the portfolio in high-risk investments.

To illustrate how to use the risk index per share to measure the total portfolio risk, suppose that Nicolo chooses a portfolio that invests all $80,000 in U.S. Oil, the higher risk, but higher return, investment. Nicolo could purchase $80,000/$25 = 3200 shares of U.S. Oil, and the portfolio would have a risk index of 3200(0.50) = 1600. Conversely, if Nicolo purchases no shares of either stock, there will be no risk, but also no return. Thus, the portfolio risk index will vary from 0 (least risk) to 1600 (most risk).

Nicolo's client would like to avoid a high-risk portfolio; thus, investing all funds in U.S. Oil would not be desirable. However, the client agreed that an acceptable level of risk would correspond to portfolios with a maximum total risk index of 700. Thus, considering only risk, one *goal* is to find a portfolio with a risk index of 700 or less.

Another goal of the client is to obtain an annual return of at least $9000. This goal can be achieved with a portfolio consisting of 2000 shares of U.S. Oil (at a cost of 2000($25) = $50,000) and 600 shares of Hub Properties (at a cost of 600($50) = $30,000); the annual return in this case would be 2000($3) + 600($5) = $9000. Note, however, that the portfolio risk index for this investment strategy would be 2000(0.50) + 600(0.25) = 1150; thus, this portfolio achieves the annual return goal but does not satisfy the portfolio risk index goal.

Thus, the portfolio selection problem is a multicriteria decision problem involving two conflicting goals: one dealing with risk and one dealing with annual return. The goal programming approach was developed precisely for this kind of problem. Goal programming can be used to identify a portfolio that comes closest to achieving both goals. Before applying the methodology, the client must determine which, if either, goal is more important.

Suppose that the client's top-priority goal is to restrict the risk; that is, keeping the portfolio risk index at 700 or less is so important that the client is not willing to trade the achievement of this goal for any amount of an increase in annual return. But, as long as the portfolio risk index does not exceed 700, the client seeks the best possible return. Based on this statement of priorities, the goals for the problem are as follows:

Primary Goal (Priority Level 1)

Goal 1:   Find a portfolio that has a risk index of 700 or less.

Secondary Goal (Priority Level 2)

Goal 2:   Find a portfolio that will provide an annual return of at least $9000.

The primary goal is called a *priority level 1 goal,* and the secondary goal is called a *priority level 2 goal.* In goal programming terminology, these are called **preemptive priorities** because the decision maker is not willing to sacrifice any amount of achievement of the priority level 1 goal for the lower priority goal. The portfolio risk index of 700 is the **target value** for the priority level 1 (primary) goal, and the annual return of $9000 is the target value for the priority level 2 (secondary) goal. The difficulty in finding a solution that will achieve these goals is that only $80,000 is available for investment.

In goal programming with preemptive priorities, we never permit trade offs between higher and lower level goals.

Developing the Constraints and the Goal Equations

We begin by defining the decision variables:

$$x_1 = \text{number of shares of U.S. Oil purchased}$$
$$x_2 = \text{number of shares of Hub Properties purchased}$$

Constraints for goal programming problems are handled in the same way as in an ordinary linear programming problem. In the Nicolo Investment Advisors problem, there is one constraint corresponding to the funds available. Since each share of U.S. Oil costs $25 and each share of Hub Properties costs $50, the constraint representing the funds available is

$$25x_1 + 50x_2 \leq 80,000$$

To complete the formulation of the model, we must develop a **goal equation** for each goal. Let us begin by writing the goal equation for the primary goal. Since each share of U.S. Oil has a risk index of 0.50 and each share of Hub Properties has a risk index of 0.25, the portfolio risk index is $0.50x_1 + 0.25x_2$. Depending on the values of x_1 and x_2, the portfolio risk index may be less than, equal to, or greater than the target value of 700. To represent these possibilities mathematically, we create the goal equation

$$0.50x_1 + 0.25x_2 = 700 + d_1^+ - d_1^-$$

where

$$d_1^+ = \text{the amount by which the portfolio risk index exceeds the target}$$
$$\text{value of 700}$$
$$d_1^- = \text{the amount by which the portfolio risk index is less than the target}$$
$$\text{value of 700}$$

To achieve a goal exactly, the two deviation variables must both equal zero.

In goal programming, d_1^+ and d_1^- are called **deviation variables.** The purpose of deviation variables is to allow for the possibility of not meeting the target value exactly. Consider, for example, a portfolio that consists of $x_1 = 2000$ shares of U.S. Oil and $x_2 = 0$

shares of Hub Properties. The portfolio risk index is $0.50(2000) + 0.25(0) = 1000$. In this case, $d_1^+ = 300$ reflects the fact that the portfolio risk index exceeds the target value by 300 units; note also that since d_1^+ is greater than zero, the value of d_1^- must be zero. For a portfolio consisting of $x_1 = 0$ shares of U.S. Oil and $x_2 = 1000$ shares of Hub Properties, the portfolio risk index would be $0.50(0) + 0.25(1000) = 250$. In this case, $d_1^- = 450$ and $d_1^+ = 0$, indicating that the solution provides a portfolio risk index of 450 less than the target value of 700.

In general, the letter d is used for deviation variables in a goal programming model. A superscript of plus $(+)$ or minus $(-)$ is used to indicate whether the variable corresponds to a positive or negative deviation from the target value. If we bring the deviation variables to the left-hand side, we can rewrite the goal equation for the primary goal as

$$0.50x_1 + 0.25x_2 - d_1^+ + d_1^- = 700$$

Note that the value on the right-hand side of the goal equation is the target value for the goal. The left-hand side of the goal equation consists of two parts:

1. a function that defines the amount of goal achievement in terms of the decision variables (e.g., $0.50x_1 + 0.25x_2$); and
2. deviation variables representing the difference between the target value for the goal and the level achieved.

To develop a goal equation for the secondary goal, we begin by writing a function representing the annual return for the investment:

$$\text{Annual return} = 3x_1 + 5x_2$$

Then we define two deviation variables that represent the amount of over- or under-achievement of the goal. Doing so, we obtain

$d_2^+ =$ the amount by which the annual return for the portfolio is greater than the target amount of \$9000

$d_1^- =$ the amount by which the annual return for the portfolio is less than the target value of \$9000

Using these two deviation variables, we write the goal equation for goal 2 as

$$3x_1 + 5x_2 = 9000 + d_2^+ - d_2^-$$

or

$$3x_1 + 5x_2 - d_2^+ + d_2^- = 9000$$

This step completes the development of the goal equations and the constraints for the Nicolo portfolio problem. We are now ready to develop an appropriate objective function for the problem.

Developing an Objective Function with Preemptive Priorities

The objective function in a goal programming model calls for minimizing a function of the deviation variables. In the portfolio selection problem, the most important goal, denoted P_1, is to find a portfolio with a risk index of 700 or less. This problem has only two goals, and the client is unwilling to incur a portfolio risk index greater than 700 to achieve the secondary annual return goal. Therefore, the secondary goal is denoted P_2. These goal priorities are referred to as preemptive priorities in goal programming terminology because the satisfaction of a higher level goal cannot be traded for the satisfaction of a lower level goal.

Goal programming problems with preemptive priorities are solved by treating priority level 1 goals (P_1) first in an objective function. The idea is to start by finding a solution that comes closest to satisfying the priority level 1 goals. This solution is then modified by solving a problem with an objective function involving only priority level 2 goals (P_2); however, revisions in the solution are permitted only if they do not hinder achievement of the P_1 goals. In general, solving a goal programming problem with preemptive priorities involves a sequence of linear programs with different objective functions; P_1 goals are considered first, P_2 goals second, P_3 goals third, and so on. At each stage of the procedure, a revision in the solution is permitted only if it causes no reduction in the achievement of a higher priority goal.

We must solve one linear program for each priority level.

The number of linear programs that we must solve in sequence to develop the solution to a goal programming problem is determined by the number of priority levels. One linear program must be solved for each priority level. We will call the first linear program solved the priority level 1 problem, the second linear program solved the priority level 2 problem, and so on. Each linear program is obtained from the one at the next higher level by changing the objective function and adding a constraint.

We first formulate the objective function for the priority level 1 problem. The client has stated that the portfolio risk index should not exceed 700. Is underachieving the target value of 700 a concern? Clearly, the answer is no because values of less than 700 correspond to less risk. Is overachieving the target value of 700 a concern? The answer is yes because portfolios with a risk index greater than 700 correspond to unacceptable levels of risk. Thus, the objective function corresponding to the priority level 1 linear program should minimize the value of d_1^+.

The goal equations and the funds available constraint have already been developed. Thus, the priority level 1 linear program can now be stated.

P_1 Problem

$$\text{Min} \qquad d_1^+$$

$$\text{s.t.}$$

$$
\begin{array}{rlcll}
25x_1 + 50x_2 & & \leq & 80{,}000 & \text{Funds available} \\
0.50x_1 + 0.25x_2 - d_1^+ + d_1^- & & = & 700 & P_1 \text{ goal} \\
3x_1 + 5x_2 & - d_2^+ + d_2^- & = & 9000 & P_2 \text{ goal} \\
\end{array}
$$

$$x_1, x_2, d_1^+, d_1^-, d_2^+, d_2^- \geq 0$$

The Graphical Solution Procedure

One approach that can often be used to solve a difficult problem is to break the problem into two or more smaller or easier problems. The linear programming procedure we use to solve the goal programming problem is based on this approach.

The graphical solution procedure for goal programming is similar to that for linear programming presented in Chapter 7. The only difference is that the procedure for goal programming involves a separate solution for each priority level. Recall that the linear programming graphical solution procedure uses a graph to display the values for the decision variables. Because the decision variables are nonnegative, we consider only that portion of the graph where $x_1 \geq 0$ and $x_2 \geq 0$. Recall also that every point on the graph is called a *solution point*.

We begin the graphical solution procedure for the Nicolo Investment problem by identifying all solution points that satisfy the available funds constraint:

$$25x_1 + 50x_2 \leq 80{,}000$$

The shaded region in Figure 18.1, feasible portfolios, consists of all points that satisfy this constraint—that is, values of x_1 and x_2 for which $25x_1 + 50x_2 \leq 80{,}000$.

The objective for the priority level 1 linear program is to minimize d_1^+, the amount by which the portfolio index exceeds the target value of 700. Recall that the P_1 goal equation is

$$0.50x_1 + 0.25x_2 - d_1^+ + d_1^- = 700$$

When the P_1 goal is met exactly, $d_1^+ = 0$ and $d_1^- = 0$; the goal equation then reduces to $0.50x_1 + 0.25x_2 = 700$. Figure 18.2 shows the graph of this equation; the shaded region identifies all solution points that satisfy the available funds constraint and also result in the value of $d_1^+ = 0$. Since any solution point for which $d_1^+ = 0$ will achieve the priority level 1 goal, the shaded region contains all the feasible solution points that correspond to portfolios with a risk index of 700 or less.

At this point, we have solved the priority level 1 problem. Note that there are alternative optimal solutions; in fact, all solution points in the shaded region in Figure 18.2 maintain a portfolio risk index of 700 or less, and hence $d_1^+ = 0$.

The priority level 2 goal for the Nicolo Investment problem is to find a portfolio that will provide an annual return of at least $9000. Is overachieving the target value of $9000 a concern? Clearly, the answer is no because portfolios with an annual return of more than $9000 correspond to higher returns. Is underachieving the target value of $9000 a concern?

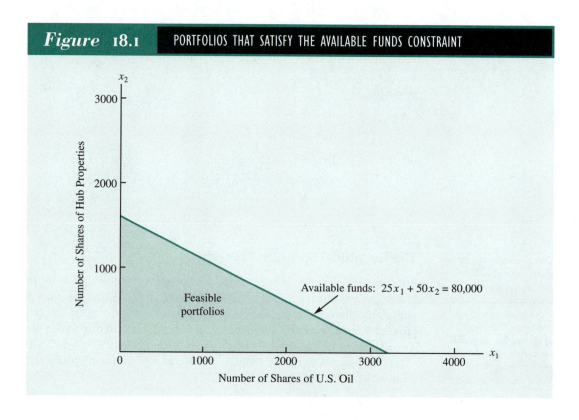

Figure **18.1**   PORTFOLIOS THAT SATISFY THE AVAILABLE FUNDS CONSTRAINT

Number of Shares of Hub Properties

Available funds: $25x_1 + 50x_2 = 80{,}000$

Feasible portfolios

Number of Shares of U.S. Oil

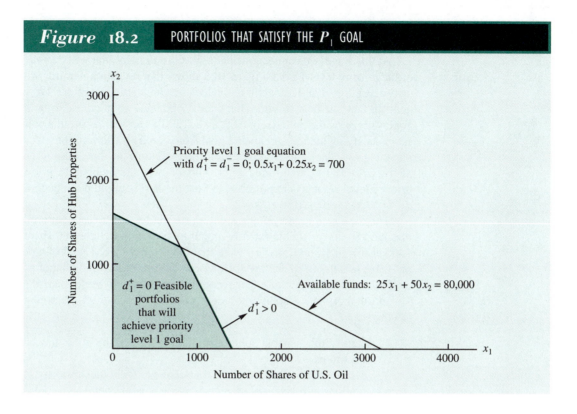

Figure 18.2 PORTFOLIOS THAT SATISFY THE P_1 GOAL

Priority level 1 goal equation
with $d_1^+ = d_1^- = 0$; $0.5x_1 + 0.25x_2 = 700$

$d_1^+ = 0$ Feasible
portfolios
that will
achieve priority
level 1 goal

Available funds: $25x_1 + 50x_2 = 80{,}000$

$d_1^+ > 0$

Number of Shares of Hub Properties

Number of Shares of U.S. Oil

The answer is yes because portfolios with an annual return of less than \$9000 are not acceptable to the client. Thus, the objective function corresponding to the priority level 2 linear program should minimize the value of d_2^-. However, since goal 2 is a secondary goal, the solution to the priority level 2 linear program must not degrade the optimal solution to the priority level 1 problem. Thus, the priority level 2 linear program can now be stated.

P_2 Problem

Min $\quad d_2^-$

s.t.

$$
\begin{aligned}
25x_1 + 50x_2 &\leq 80{,}000 && \text{Funds available} \\
0.50x_1 + 0.25x_2 - d_1^+ + d_1^- &= 700 && P_1 \text{ goal} \\
3x_1 + 5x_2 - d_2^+ + d_2^- &= 9000 && P_2 \text{ goal} \\
d_1^+ &= 0 && \text{Maintain achievement} \\
& && \text{of } P_1 \text{ goal}
\end{aligned}
$$

$$x_1, x_2, d_1^+, d_1^-, d_2^+, d_2^- \geq 0$$

Note that the priority level 2 linear program differs from the priority level 1 linear program in two ways. The objective function involves minimizing the amount by which the portfolio annual return underachieves the level 2 goal, and another constraint has been added to ensure that no amount of achievement of the priority level 1 goal is sacrificed.

Let us now continue the graphical solution procedure. The goal equation for the priority level 2 goal is

$$3x_1 + 5x_2 - d_2^+ + d_2^- = 9000$$

When both d_2^+ and d_2^- equal zero, this equation reduces to $3x_1 + 5x_2 = 9000$; we show the graph with this equation in Figure 18.3.

At this stage, we cannot consider any solution point that will degrade the achievement of the priority level 1 goal. Figure 18.3 shows that no solution points will achieve the priority level 2 goal and maintain the values we were able to achieve for the priority level 1 goal. In fact, the best solution that can be obtained when considering the priority level 2 goal is given by the point ($x_1 = 800$, $x_2 = 1200$); in other words, this point comes the closest to satisfying the priority level 2 goal from among those solutions satisfying the priority level 1 goal. Since the annual return corresponding to this solution point is $3(800) + \$5(1200) = \$8400$, identifying a portfolio that will satisfy both the priority level 1 and the priority level 2 goals is impossible. In fact, the best solution point underachieves goal 2 by $d_2^- = \$9000 - \$8400 = \$600$.

Thus, the goal programming solution for the Nicolo Investment problem recommends that the \$80,000 available for investment be used to purchase 800 shares of U.S. Oil and 1200 shares of Hub Properties. Note that the priority level 1 goal of a portfolio risk index of 700 or less has been achieved. However, the priority level 2 goal of at least a \$9000 annual return is not achievable. The recommended portfolio projects an \$8400 annual return.

In summary, the graphical solution procedure for goal programming involves the following steps.

1. Identify the feasible solution points; these are the ones that satisfy the problem constraints.
2. Identify all feasible solutions that achieve the highest-priority goal; if no feasible solutions will achieve the highest priority goal, identify the solution(s) that comes closest to achieving it.

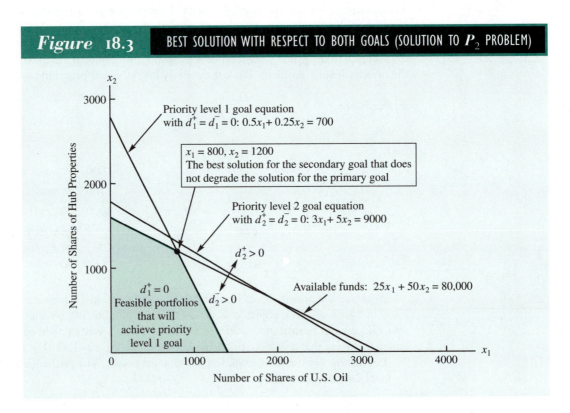

Figure 18.3   BEST SOLUTION WITH RESPECT TO BOTH GOALS (SOLUTION TO P_2 PROBLEM)

3. Move down one priority level, and determine the "best" solution possible without sacrificing any achievement of higher priority goals.
4. Repeat step 3 until all priority levels have been considered.

You should be able to formulate a goal programming model and use the graphical solution procedure to obtain a solution. Try Problem 2.

Although the graphical solution procedure is a convenient method for solving goal programming problems involving two decision variables, the solution of larger problems requires a computer-aided approach. In Section 18.2 we illustrate how to use a computer software package to solve more complex goal programming problems.

The Goal Programming Model

As we have stated, preemptive goal programming problems are solved as a sequence of linear programs; there is one linear program for each priority level. However, having a notation that permits writing a goal programming problem in one concise statement is helpful.

In writing the overall objective for the portfolio selection problem, we must write the objective function in a way that reminds us of the preemptive priorities. We can do so by writing the objective function as

$$\text{Min } P_1(d_1^+) + P_2(d_2^-)$$

The priority levels P_1 and P_2 are not numerical weights on the deviation variables, but simply labels that remind us of the priority levels for the goals.

We now write the complete goal programming model as

$$\text{Min} \quad P_1(d_1^+) + P_2(d_2^-)$$

s.t.

$$
\begin{aligned}
25x_1 + 50x_2 &\leq 80{,}000 \quad \text{Funds available} \\
0.50x_1 + 0.25x_2 - d_1^+ + d_1^- &= 700 \quad P_1 \text{ goal} \\
3x_1 + 5x_2 - d_2^+ + d_2^- &= 9000 \quad P_2 \text{ goal} \\
x_1, x_2, d_1^+, d_1^-, d_2^+, d_2^- &\geq 0
\end{aligned}
$$

With the exception of the P_1 and P_2 priority levels in the objective function, this model is a linear programming model. The solution of this linear program involves solving a sequence of linear programs involving goals at decreasing priority levels.

We now summarize the procedure used to develop a goal programming model.

1. Identify the goals and any constraints that reflect resource capacities or other restrictions that may prevent achievement of the goals.
2. Determine the priority level of each goal; goals with priority level P_1 are most important, those with priority level P_2 are next most important, and so on.
3. Define the decision variables.
4. Formulate the constraints in the usual linear programming fashion.
5. For each goal, develop a goal equation, with the right-hand side specifying the target value for the goal. Deviation variables d_i^+ and d_i^- are included in each goal equation to reflect the possible deviations above or below the target value.
6. Write the objective function in terms of minimizing a prioritized function of the deviation variables.

I. The constraints in the general goal programming model are of two types: goal equations and ordinary linear programming constraints. Some analysts call the goal equations *goal constraints* and the ordinary linear programming constraints *system constraints*.

2. You might think of the general goal programming model as having "hard" and "soft" constraints. The hard constraints are the ordinary linear programming constraints that cannot be violated. The soft constraints are the ones resulting from the goal equations. Soft constraints can be violated but with a penalty for doing so. The penalty is reflected by the coefficient of the deviation variable in the objective function. In Section 18.2 we illustrate this point with a problem that has a coefficient of 2 for one of the deviation variables.

3. Note that the constraint added in moving from the linear programming problem at one priority level to the linear programming problem at the next lower priority level becomes a hard constraint. No amount of achievement of a higher priority goal may be sacrificed to achieve a lower priority goal.

18.2 GOAL PROGRAMMING: SOLVING MORE COMPLEX PROBLEMS

In Section 18.1 we formulated and solved a goal programming model that involved one priority level 1 goal and one priority level 2 goal. In this section we show how to formulate and solve goal programming models that involve multiple goals within the same priority level. Although computer programs have been specially developed to solve goal programming models, these programs are not as readily available as general purpose linear programming software packages. Thus, the computer solution procedure outlined in this section develops a solution to a goal programming model by solving a sequence of linear programming models with a general purpose linear programming software package.

The Suncoast Office Supplies Problem

The management of Suncoast Office Supplies establishes monthly goals, or quotas, for the types of customers contacted. For the next 4 weeks, Suncoast's customer contact strategy calls for the sales force, which consists of four salespeople, to make 200 contacts with customers who have previously purchased supplies from the firm. In addition, the strategy calls for 120 contacts of new customers. The purpose of this latter goal is to ensure that the sales force is continuing to investigate new sources of sales.

Making allowances for travel and waiting time, as well as for demonstration and direct sales time, Suncoast has allocated 2 hours of sales force effort to each contact of a previous customer. New customer contacts tend to take longer and require 3 hours per contact. Normally, each salesperson works 40 hours per week, or 160 hours over the 4-week planning horizon; under a normal work schedule, the four salespeople will have $4(160) = 640$ hours of sales force time available for customer contacts.

Management is willing to use some overtime, if needed, but is also willing to accept a solution that uses less than the scheduled 640 hours available. However, management wants both overtime and underutilization of the work force limited to no more than 40 hours over the 4-week period. Thus, in terms of overtime, management's goal is to use no more than $640 + 40 = 680$ hours of sales force time, and in terms of labor utilization, management's goal is to use at least $640 - 40 = 600$ hours of sales force time.

In addition to the customer contact goals, Suncoast has established a goal regarding sales volume. Based on its experience, Suncoast estimates that each previous customer contacted will generate $250 of sales and that each new customer contacted will generate $125 of sales. Management wants to generate sales revenue of at least $70,000 for the next month.

Given Suncoast's small sales force and the short time frame involved, management has decided that the overtime goal and the labor utilization goal are both priority level 1 goals. Management also concluded that the $70,000 sales revenue goal should be a priority level 2 goal and that the two customer contact goals should be priority level 3 goals. Based on these priorities, we can now summarize the goals.

Priority Level I Goals

Goal 1:   Do not use any more than 680 hours of sales force time.
Goal 2:   Do not use any less than 600 hours of sales force time.

Priority Level 2 Goal

Goal 3:   Generate sales revenue of at least $70,000.

Priority Level 3 Goals

Goal 4:   Call on at least 200 previous customers.
Goal 5:   Call on at least 120 new customers.

Formulating the Goal Equations

Next, we must define the decision variables whose values will be used to determine whether we are able to achieve the goals. Let

$$x_1 = \text{the number of previous customers contacted}$$
$$x_2 = \text{the number of new customers contacted}$$

Using these decision variables and appropriate deviation variables, we can develop a goal equation for each goal. The procedure used parallels the approach introduced in the preceding section. A summary of the results obtained is shown for each goal.

Goal I

$$2x_1 + 3x_2 - d_1^+ + d_1^- = 680$$

where

$$d_1^+ = \text{the amount by which the number of hours used by the}$$
$$\text{sales force is greater than the target value of 680 hours}$$

$$d_1^- = \text{the amount by which the number of hours used by the}$$
$$\text{sales force is less than the target value of 680 hours}$$

Goal 2

$$2x_1 + 3x_2 - d_2^+ + d_2^- = 600$$

where

$$d_2^+ = \text{the amount by which the number of hours used by the}$$
$$\text{sales force is greater than the target value of 600 hours}$$

$$d_2^- = \text{the amount by which the number of hours used by the}$$
$$\text{sales force is less than the target value of 600 hours}$$

Goal 3

$$250x_1 + 125x_2 - d_3^+ + d_3^- = 70{,}000$$

where

$d_3^+ =$ the amount by which the sales revenue is greater than the target value of $70,000

$d_3^- =$ the amount by which the sales revenue is less than the target value of $70,000

Goal 4

$$x_1 - d_4^+ + d_4^- = 200$$

where

$d_4^+ =$ the amount by which the number of previous customer contacts is greater than the target value of 200 previous customer contacts

$d_4^- =$ the amount by which the number of previous customer contacts is less than the target value of 200 previous customer contacts

Goal 5

$$x_2 - d_5^+ + d_5^- = 120$$

where

$d_5^+ =$ the amount by which the number of new customer contacts is greater than the target value of 120 new customer contacts

$d_5^- =$ the amount by which the number of new customer contacts is less than the target value of 120 new customer contacts

Formulating the Objective Function

To develop the objective function for the Suncoast Office Supplies problem, we begin by considering the priority level 1 goals. When considering goal 1, if $d_1^+ = 0$, we will have found a solution that uses no more than 680 hours of sales force time. Since solutions for which d_1^+ is greater than zero represent overtime beyond the desired level, the objective function should minimize the value of d_1^+. When considering goal 2, if $d_2^- = 0$, we will have found a solution that uses *at least* 600 hours of sales force time. If d_2^- is greater than zero, however, labor utilization will not have reached the acceptable level. Thus, the objective function for the priority level 1 goals should minimize the value of d_2^-. Because both priority level 1 goals are equally important, the objective function for the priority level 1 problem is

$$\text{Min } d_1^+ + d_2^-$$

In considering the priority level 2 goal, we note that management wants to achieve sales revenues of at least \$70,000. If $d_3^- = 0$, Suncoast will achieve revenues of *at least* \$70,000, and if $d_3^- > 0$, revenues of less than \$70,000 will be obtained. Thus, the objective function for the priority level 2 problem is

$$\text{Min } d_3^-$$

Next, we consider what the objective function must be for the priority level 3 problem. When considering goal 4, if $d_4^- = 0$, we will have found a solution with *at least* 200 previous customer contacts; however, if $d_4^- > 0$, we will have underachieved the goal of contacting at least 200 previous customers. Thus, for goal 4 the objective is to minimize d_4^-. When considering goal 5, if $d_5^- = 0$, we will have found a solution with *at least* 120 new customer contacts; however, if $d_5^- > 0$, we will have underachieved the goal of contacting at least 120 new customers. Thus, for goal 5 the objective is to minimize d_5^-. If both goals 4 and 5 are equal in importance, the objective function for the priority level 3 problem would be

$$\text{Min } d_4^- + d_5^-$$

However, suppose that management believes that generating new customers is vital to the long-run success of the firm and that goal 5 should be weighted more than goal 4. If management believes that goal 5 is twice as important as goal 4, the objective function for the priority level 3 problem would be

$$\text{Min } d_4^- + 2d_5^-$$

Combining the objective functions for all three priority levels, we obtain the overall objective function for the Suncoast Office Supplies problem:

$$\text{Min } P_1(d_1^+) + P_1(d_2^-) + P_2(d_3^-) + P_3(d_4^-) + P_3(2d_5^-)$$

As we indicated previously, P_1, P_2, and P_3 are simply labels that remind us that goals 1 and 2 are the priority level 1 goals, goal 3 is the priority level 2 goal, and goals 4 and 5 are the priority level 3 goals. We can now write the complete goal programming model for the Suncoast Office Supplies problem as follows:

$$\text{Min } P_1(d_1^+) + P_1(d_2^-) + P_2(d_3^-) + P_3(d_4^-) + P_3(2d_5^-)$$

s.t.

$$
\begin{array}{llllll}
2x_1 + & 3x_2 - d_1^+ + d_1^- & & & = & 680 & \text{Goal 1} \\
2x_1 + & 3x_2 & - d_2^+ + d_2^- & & = & 600 & \text{Goal 2} \\
250x_1 + & 125x_2 & - d_3^+ + d_3^- & & = & 70{,}000 & \text{Goal 3} \\
x_1 & & - d_4^+ + d_4^- & & = & 200 & \text{Goal 4} \\
& x_2 & & - d_5^+ + d_5^- & = & 120 & \text{Goal 5}
\end{array}
$$

$$x_1, x_2, d_1^+, d_1^-, d_2^+, d_2^-, d_3^+, d_3^-, d_4^+, d_4^-, d_5^+, d_5^- \geq 0$$

Computer Solution

The following computer procedure develops a solution to a goal programming model by solving a sequence of linear programming problems. The first problem comprises all the constraints and all the goal equations for the complete goal programming model; however, the objective function for this problem involves only the P_1 priority level goals. Again, we refer to this problem as the P_1 problem.

Whatever the solution to the P_1 problem, a P_2 problem is formed by adding a constraint to the P_1 model that ensures that subsequent problems will not degrade the solution obtained for the P_1 problem. The objective function for the priority level 2 problem takes into consideration only the P_2 goals. We continue the process until we have considered all priority levels. We illustrate the procedure for the Suncoast Office Supplies problem using LINDO.

To solve the Suncoast Office Supplies problem, we begin by solving the P_1 problem:

$$\text{Min} \quad d_1^+ + d_2^-$$

s.t.

$$
\begin{array}{llll}
2x_1 + 3x_2 - d_1^+ + d_1^- & = & 680 & \text{Goal 1} \\
2x_1 + 3x_2 \quad\quad - d_2^+ + d_2^- & = & 600 & \text{Goal 2} \\
250x_1 + 125x_2 \quad\quad\quad - d_3^+ + d_3^- & = & 70{,}000 & \text{Goal 3} \\
x_1 \quad\quad\quad\quad\quad\quad - d_4^+ + d_4^- & = & 200 & \text{Goal 4} \\
x_2 \quad\quad\quad\quad\quad\quad - d_5^+ + d_5^- & = & 120 & \text{Goal 5}
\end{array}
$$

$$x_1, x_2, d_1^+, d_1^-, d_2^+, d_2^-, d_3^+, d_3^-, d_4^+, d_4^-, d_5^+, d_5^- \geq 0$$

In Figure 18.4 we show the LINDO solution for this linear program.[1] Note that D1MINUS refers to d_1^-, D1PLUS refers to d_1^+, D2MINUS refers to d_2^-, and so on. The solution consisting of $x_1 = 300$ previous customer contacts and $x_2 = 0$ new customer contacts achieves both goals 1 and 2 because D1PLUS and D2MINUS are equal to zero; alternatively, the objective function value of D1PLUS + D2MINUS = 0 also confirms that both priority level 1 goals have been achieved. Note that this solution also achieves the sales revenue goal since D3PLUS = $5000, achieves goal 4 since D4PLUS = 100, and underachieves goal 5 by D5MINUS = 100 new customers. Most importantly, however, we now know that a solution exists that achieves the priority level 1 and priority level 2 goals.

Since the solution to the P_1 problem also achieved the priority level 2 goal, we do not need to form a P_2 problem. Instead, we go directly to the formation of a P_3 problem. The model for the P_3 problem is formed by adding a constraint to the P_1 problem that ensures that subsequent solutions will not degrade the solution already obtained for the priority level 1 and priority level 2 goals. We can add a constraint by requiring that all future solutions satisfy the constraints $d_1^+ + d_2^- = 0$ and $d_3^- = 0$. Adding these constraints to the model and writing the objective function in terms of the priority level 3 goal, we obtain the linear program and LINDO solution shown in Figure 18.5.

The optimal solution to the P_3 problem is to contact $x_1 = 250$ previous customers and $x_2 = 60$ new customers. Although this solution overachieves the previous customer contact goal by D4PLUS = 50 previous customers, it underachieves the new customer contact goal by D5MINUS = 60 new customers.

All priority levels have been considered, so the solution procedure is finished. The optimal solution for Suncoast is to contact 250 previous customers and 60 new customers. Although this solution will not achieve management's goal of contacting at least 120 new customers, it does achieve each of the other goals specified. If management isn't happy with this solution, a different set of priorities could be considered. Management must keep in mind, however, that in any situation involving multiple goals at different priority levels, rarely will all the goals be achieved with existing resources.

---

1. The output shown was obtained using the Windows 95 version of LINDO.

Figure 18.4   THE LINDO SOLUTION OF THE P_1 PROBLEM

OBJECTIVE FUNCTION VALUE

1)   0.0000000

VARIABLE	VALUE	REDUCED COST
D1PLUS	0.000000	1.000000
D2MINUS	0.000000	1.000000
X1	300.000000	0.000000
X2	0.000000	0.000000
D1MINUS	80.000000	0.000000
D2PLUS	0.000000	0.000000
D3PLUS	5000.000000	0.000000
D3MINUS	0.000000	0.000000
D4PLUS	100.000000	0.000000
D4MINUS	0.000000	0.000000
D5PLUS	0.000000	0.000000
D5MINUS	100.000000	0.000000

Figure 18.5   THE LINDO SOLUTION OF THE P_3 PROBLEM

```
MIN     D4MINUS + 2D5MINUS
SUBJECT TO
2X1 + 3X2 - D1PLUS + D1MINUS = 680
2X1 + 3X2 + D2MINUS - D2PLUS = 600
250X1 + 125X2 - D3PLUS + D3MINUS = 70000
X1 - D4PLUS + D4MINUS = 200
X2 - D5PLUS + D5MINUS = 120
D1PLUS + D2MINUS = 0
D3MINUS = 0
END
```

OBJECTIVE FUNCTION VALUE

1)   120.0000

VARIABLE	VALUE	REDUCED COST
D1PLUS	0.000000	0.000000
D2MINUS	0.000000	1.000000
X1	250.000000	0.000000
X2	60.000000	0.000000
D1MINUS	0.000000	1.000000
D2PLUS	80.000000	0.000000
D3PLUS	0.000000	0.000000
D3MINUS	0.000000	0.000000
D4PLUS	50.000000	0.000000
D4MINUS	0.000000	1.000000
D5PLUS	0.000000	2.000000
D5MINUS	60.000000	0.000000

N O T E S	1. Not all goal programming problems involve multiple priority levels. For problems with one priority level, only one linear program needs to be solved to obtain the goal programming solution. The analyst simply minimizes the weighted deviations from the goals. Trade-offs are permitted among the goals because they are all at the same priority level.
and Comments	2. The goal programming approach can be used when the analyst is confronted with an infeasible solution to an ordinary linear program. Reformulating some constraints as goal equations with deviation variables allows a solution that minimizes the weighted sum of the deviation variables. Often, this approach will suggest a reasonable solution.
	3. The approach that we used to solve goal programming problems with multiple priority levels is to solve a sequence of linear programs. These linear programs are closely related so that complete reformulation and solution are not necessary. By changing the objective function and adding a constraint, we can go from one linear program to the next.

18.3   THE ANALYTIC HIERARCHY PROCESS

Most people prefer a problem-solving approach that is conceptually simple so that it can be understood. A strength of the analytic hierarchy process is that it is easy to understand and still robust enough to handle the complexities of real problems.

The analytic hierarchy process (AHP), developed by Thomas L. Saaty,[2] is designed to solve complex problems involving multiple criteria. The process requires the decision maker to provide judgments about the relative importance of each criterion and then specify a preference on each criterion for each decision alternative. The output of AHP is a prioritized ranking indicating the overall preference for each decision alternative. The Q.M. in Action: Using AHP and Goal Programming to Plan Facility Locations describes how the University of Missouri-Rolla used AHP and goal programming to allocate floor space in a new facility.

To introduce AHP, we consider the problem facing Diane Payne, who is planning to purchase a used car. After a preliminary analysis of the makes and models available, she has narrowed the list of decision alternatives to three cars, A, B, and C. Table 18.1 provides a summary of the information that she has collected regarding these cars.

Based on the information in Table 18.1—as well as her own personal feelings resulting from driving each car—Payne decided that she needed to consider several criteria in making the purchase decision. After some thought, she selected purchase price, miles per gallon (MPG), comfort, and style as the four criteria to consider. Quantitative data regarding the purchase price and MPG criteria are provided directly in Table 18.1. However, measures of comfort and style cannot be specified so easily. Payne will need to consider factors such as car interior, type of radio, ease of entry and exit, and seat-adjustment features to determine the comfort level of each car. The style criterion will need to be measured in terms of Payne's subjective evaluation of each car.

Even when we deal with a criterion as easily measured as purchase price, however, subjectivity becomes an issue whenever a particular decision maker indicates a personal preference. For instance, car A costs $3600 more than car C; this difference might represent a great deal of money to one person but not very much money to another person. Thus, whether car A is considered extremely more expensive than car C or only moderately more expensive is a subjective judgment that will depend primarily on the financial status of the person making the comparison. An advantage of AHP is that it is designed to handle situations such as this in which the subjective judgments of individuals constitute an important part of the decision process.

---

2. Saaty, T. L., *The Analytic Hierarchy Process*. New York: McGraw-Hill, 1980.

Q.M. IN ACTION

USING AHP AND GOAL PROGRAMMING TO PLAN FACILITY LOCATIONS*

The department of engineering management at the University of Missouri-Rolla needed to determine how 5072 square feet of floor space for a new computer-integrated manufacturing (CIM) laboratory should be allocated to best achieve the objectives of the university. An in-house planning team identified a list of 15 sections (e.g., production machines, physical simulation lab, robot system, etc.) to be located in the CIM laboratory. The floor space required for all 15 sections, however, totaled 6035 square feet. Thus, the team needed to find a method for allocating the available space among the sections.

The team identified five goals that reflected the teaching, research, and extension objectives of the university. Goal 1: increase student use of the new facilities; Goal 2: develop new courses; Goal 3: stimulate research; Goal 4: increase industry awareness of CIM concepts; and Goal 5:

enhance the university's image. The team used AHP to develop priority weights for each objective (teaching, research, and extension) and each goal. It incorporated the weights derived through the AHP analysis in a linear goal programming model that determined the fractions of the 5072 square feet of floor space to be allocated to each section.

The team found "the AHP methodology effective in eliciting judgment from the members of the facilities planning task force in a systematic and consistent manner. It helped obtain group consensus in a highly political environment in a timely manner for a fairly complex institutional planning problem."

*Based on Benjamin, C. O., I. C. Ehie, and Y. Omurtag, "Planning Facilities at the University of Missouri-Rolla." *Interfaces*, July–August 1992, pp. 95–105.

Table 18.1	INFORMATION FOR THE CAR-SELECTION PROBLEM		
Category	**Car A**	**Car B**	**Car C**
Price	$13,100	$11,200	$9500
MPG	18	23	29
Interior	Deluxe	Above average	Standard
Body	4-door midsize	2-door sport	2-door compact
Radio	AM/FM, tape	AM/FM	AM/FM
Engine	6-cylinder	4-cylinder turbo	4-cylinder

Developing the Hierarchy

The first step in AHP is to develop a graphical representation of the problem in terms of the *overall goal, criteria,* and *decision alternatives.* Such a graph depicts the **hierarchy** for the problem. Figure 18.6 shows the hierarchy for the car-selection problem. Note that the first level of the hierarchy shows that the overall goal is to select the best car. At the second level, the four criteria (purchase price, MPG, comfort, and style) will contribute to the achievement of the overall goal. Finally, at the third level, each decision alternative (car A, car B, and car C) contributes to each criterion in a unique way.

Using AHP, the decision maker specifies judgments about the relative importance of each criterion in terms of its contribution to the achievement of the overall goal. At the next level, the decision maker indicates a preference or priority for each decision alternative in terms of how it contributes to each criterion. For example, in the car-selection problem, Payne will need to specify her judgment about the relative importance of each of the four criteria. She will also need to indicate her preference for each of the three cars relative to each criterion. A mathematical process is used to synthesize the information on relative importance and preferences and provide a priority ranking of the three cars in terms of their overall preference.

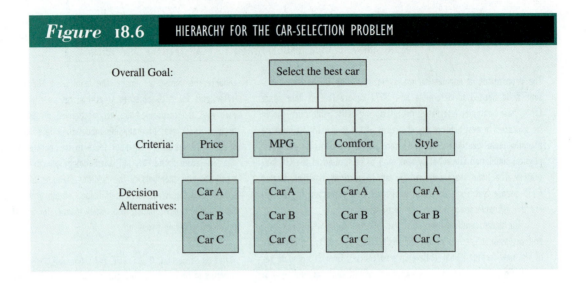

Figure 18.6 HIERARCHY FOR THE CAR-SELECTION PROBLEM

18.4 ESTABLISHING PRIORITIES USING AHP

In this section we show how AHP uses pairwise comparisons to establish priority measures for both the criteria and the decision alternatives. What needs to be determined in the car-selection problem are the priorities of

1. the four criteria in terms of the overall goal,
2. the three cars in terms of the purchase price criterion,
3. the three cars in terms of the MPG criterion,
4. the three cars in terms of the comfort criterion, and
5. the three cars in terms of the style criterion.

In the following discussion, we demonstrate how to establish priorities for the three cars in terms of the *comfort* criterion. The other sets of priorities can be determined similarly.

Pairwise Comparisons

Pairwise comparisons are fundamental building blocks of AHP. In establishing the priorities for the three cars in terms of comfort, we ask Diane Payne to state a preference for the comfort of the cars when the cars are considered two at a time (pairwise). That is, she must compare the comfort of car A to car B, car A to car C, and car B to car C in three separate comparisons.

AHP uses an underlying scale with values 1–9 to rate the relative preferences for two items. Table 18.2 provides the numerical ratings recommended for the verbal preferences expressed by the decision maker. Research and experience have confirmed the 9-unit scale as a reasonable basis for discriminating between the preferences for two items.

In the car-selection problem, suppose that Payne has compared the comfort of car A with the comfort of car B and is convinced that car A is more comfortable. She is then asked to state her preference for the comfort of car A compared to that of car B using one of the verbal descriptions shown in Table 18.2. If she *moderately* prefers car A to car B, a value of 3 is used in AHP; if she *strongly* perfers car A, a value of 5 is used; if she *very strongly*

Table 18.2	PAIRWISE COMPARISON SCALE FOR AHP PREFERENCES

Verbal Judgment of Preference	Numerical Rating
Extremely preferred	9
Very strongly to extremely	8
Very strongly preferred	7
Strongly to very strongly	6
Strongly preferred	5
Moderately to strongly	4
Moderately preferred	3
Equally to moderately	2
Equally preferred	1

prefers car A, a value of 7 is used; if she *extremely* prefers car A, a value of 9 is used. Values of 2, 4, 6, and 8 are the intermediate values for the preference scale. A value of 1 is reserved for the case in which the two items are judged to be *equally* preferred.

Suppose that when asked her preference between cars A and B with respect to the comfort criterion, Payne states that she prefers car A equally to moderately more than car B; the numerical measure that reflects this judgment is 2. She is then asked to state her preference between car A and car C. Suppose that in this case she states that she prefers car A very strongly to extremely more than car C; this corresponds to a numerical rating of 8. Finally, Payne is asked to state her preference for car B compared to car C. Suppose in this case that she indicates that she prefers car B strongly to very strongly to car C; AHP would assign a numerical rating of 6.

The Pairwise Comparison Matrix

To develop the priorities for the three cars in terms of the comfort criterion, we need to construct a matrix of the pairwise comparison ratings. Three cars are being considered, so the pairwise comparison matrix will consist of three rows and three columns. The following portion of the **pairwise comparison matrix** is based on the preferences that Diane Payne has specified.

		Comfort	
	Car A	Car B	Car C
Car A		2	8
Car B			6
Car C			

The value in the matrix that corresponds to comparing car A with car B is 2, comparing car A with car C is 8, and comparing car B with car C is 6.

To determine the remaining entries in the pairwise comparison matrix, first note that when we compare any car against itself, the judgment must be "equally preferred." Thus, based on the scale shown in Table 18.2, the rating of car A compared to car A, car B to car

B, and car C to car C must be 1. Hence, AHP assigns a 1 to all elements on the diagonal of the pairwise comparison matrix.

All that remains is to determine the rating for car B compared to car A, car C compared to car A, and car C compared to car B. Obviously, we could follow the same procedure and ask Payne to state her preferences for these pairwise comparisons. However, we already know that her rated preference for car A compared to car B is 2, so she does not need to make another pairwise comparison of these two cars. In fact, we will conclude that the preference rating for car B compared to car A is simply the reciprocal of the preference rating for car A compared to car B, or ½. Hence, AHP obtains the preference rating of car B compared to car A by computing the reciprocal of the rating of car A to car B. Using this inverse, or reciprocal, relationship, we find that the rating of car C compared to car A is ⅛ and the rating of car C to car B is ⅙. These numerical values of preference yield the complete pairwise comparison matrix for the comfort criterion, as shown in Table 18.3.

Synthesis

After we have developed the matrix of pairwise comparisons, we can calculate the *priority* of each of the elements being compared. For example, we now want to use the pairwise comparison information in Table 18.3 to estimate the relative priority for each car in terms of the comfort criterion. This part of AHP is referred to as **synthesization.**

The exact mathematical procedure required to perform this synthesization involves the computation of eigenvalues and eigenvectors and is beyond the scope of this text. However, the following three-step procedure provides a good approximation of the synthesized priorities.

Procedure for Synthesizing Judgments

Step 1. Sum the values in each column of the pairwise comparison matrix.
Step 2. Divide each element in the pairwise comparison matrix by its column total; the resulting matrix is referred to as the **normalized pairwise comparison matrix.**
Step 3. Compute the average of the elements in each row of the normalized matrix; these averages provide an estimate of the relative priorities of the elements being compared.

To show how the synthesization process works, we carry out the three-step procedure for the pairwise comparison matrix shown in Table 18.3.

Table 18.3	PAIRWISE COMPARISON MATRIX SHOWING PREFERENCES FOR THE THREE CARS IN TERMS OF COMFORT		
		Comfort	
	Car A	Car B	Car C
Car A	1	2	8
Car B	½	1	6
Car C	⅛	⅙	1

Step 1. Sum the values in each column.

	Comfort		
	Car A	**Car B**	**Car C**
Car A	1	2	8
Car B	½	1	6
Car C	⅛	⅙	1
Totals	13⅛	19⁄6	15

Step 2. Divide each element of the matrix by its column total.

	Comfort		
	Car A	**Car B**	**Car C**
Car A	8⁄13	12⁄19	8⁄15
Car B	4⁄13	6⁄19	6⁄15
Car C	1⁄13	1⁄19	1⁄15

Note: All columns in the normalized pairwise comparison matrix now have a sum of 1.

Step 3. Average the elements in each row. (The values in the normalized pairwise comparison matrix have been converted to decimal form.)

	Comfort			
	Car A	**Car B**	**Car C**	**Row Average**
Car A	0.615	0.632	0.533	0.593
Car B	0.308	0.316	0.400	0.341
Car C	0.077	0.053	0.067	0.066
				Total 1.000

This synthesis provides the relative priorities for the three cars with respect to the comfort criterion. Thus, considering comfort, the most preferred car is car A (with a priority of 0.593). Car B (with a priority of 0.341) is second, followed by car C (with a priority of 0.066). We write the priority vector showing the relative priorities of car A, car B, and car C with respect to the comfort criterion as

You should be able to set up the pairwise comparison matrix and determine priorities. Try Problem 12.

$$\begin{bmatrix} 0.593 \\ 0.341 \\ 0.066 \end{bmatrix}$$

Consistency

A key step in AHP is the establishment of priorities through the use of the pairwise comparison procedure just described. An important consideration in terms of the quality of the ultimate decision relates to the **consistency** of judgments that the decision maker demonstrated during the series of pairwise comparisons.

Realize that perfect consistency is difficult to achieve and that some lack of consistency is expected to exist in almost any set of pairwise comparisons. To handle the consistency question, AHP provides a method for measuring the degree of consistency among the pairwise judgments provided by the decision maker. If the degree of consistency is acceptable, the decision process can continue. However, if the degree of consistency is unacceptable, the decision maker should reconsider and possibly revise the pairwise comparison judgments before proceeding with the analysis.

AHP provides a measure of the consistency of pairwise comparison judgments by computing a **consistency ratio.** This ratio is designed in such a way that values of the ratio exceeding 0.10 are indicative of inconsistent judgments; in such cases, the decision maker would probably want to revise the original values in the pairwise comparison matrix. Values of the consistency ratio of 0.10 or less are considered to be a reasonable level of consistency in the pairwise comparisons.

Although the exact mathematical computation of the consistency ratio is beyond the scope of this text, an approximation of the ratio can be obtained. We will illustrate this computational procedure for the car-selection problem by considering Diane Payne's pairwise comparisons for the comfort criterion.

Estimating the Consistency Ratio

Step 1. Multiply each value in the first column of the pairwise comparison matrix by the relative priority of the first item considered; multiply each value in the second column of the matrix by the relative priority of the second item considered; multiply each value in the third column of the matrix by the relative priority of the third item considered. Sum the values across the rows to obtain a vector of values labeled "weighted sum." This computation for the car-selection problem is

$$0.593 \begin{bmatrix} 1 \\ \frac{1}{2} \\ \frac{1}{8} \end{bmatrix} + 0.341 \begin{bmatrix} 2 \\ 1 \\ \frac{1}{6} \end{bmatrix} + 0.066 \begin{bmatrix} 8 \\ 6 \\ 1 \end{bmatrix} = \begin{bmatrix} 0.593 \\ 0.297 \\ 0.074 \end{bmatrix} + \begin{bmatrix} 0.682 \\ 0.341 \\ 0.057 \end{bmatrix} + \begin{bmatrix} 0.528 \\ 0.396 \\ 0.066 \end{bmatrix}$$

$$= \begin{bmatrix} 1.803 \\ 1.034 \\ 0.197 \end{bmatrix} \quad \text{Weighted sum vector}$$

Step 2. Divide the elements of the vector of weighted sums obtained in step 1 by the corresponding priority value. For the car-selection problem, we obtain

$$\frac{1.803}{0.593} = 3.040$$

$$\frac{1.034}{0.341} = 3.032$$

$$\frac{0.197}{0.066} = 2.985$$

Step 3. Compute the average of the values found in step 2; this average is denoted λ_{max}. For the car-selection problem, we obtain

$$\lambda_{max} = \frac{3.040 + 3.032 + 2.985}{3} = 3.019$$

Step 4. Compute the consistency index (CI), which is defined as

$$CI = \frac{\lambda_{max} - n}{n - 1}$$

where

$$n = \text{the number of items being compared}$$

For the car-selection problem with $n = 3$, we obtain

$$CI = \frac{3.019 - 3}{2} = 0.010$$

Step 5. Compute the consistency ratio (CR), which is defined as

$$CR = \frac{CI}{RI}$$

where RI, the random index, is the consistency index of a randomly generated pairwise comparison matrix. The RI, which depends on the number of elements being compared, takes on the following values:

n	3	4	5	6	7	8
RI	0.58	0.90	1.12	1.24	1.32	1.41

Thus, for the car-selection problem with $n = 3$ and RI = 0.58, we obtain the following consistency ratio:

$$CR = \frac{0.01}{0.58} = 0.017$$

You should now be able to determine whether judgments are consistent. Try Problem 16.

As mentioned previously, a consistency ratio of 0.10 or less is considered acceptable. Our example shows a consistency ratio of 0.017, so the degree of consistency exhibited in the pairwise comparison matrix for comfort is acceptable.

Other Pairwise Comparisons for the Car-Selection Problem

Continuing with the AHP analysis of the car-selection problem, we need to use the pairwise comparison procedure to determine the priorities of the three cars in terms of the purchase price, MPG, and style criteria. Determining priorities requires that Diane Payne express pairwise comparison preferences for the cars, considering these criteria one at a time. Assume that she has done so and that her preferences are summarized in the pairwise comparison matrices shown in Table 18.4.

Table 18.4	PAIRWISE COMPARISON MATRICES FOR PRICE, MPG, AND STYLE IN THE CAR-SELECTION PROBLEM

Price

	Car A	Car B	Car C
Car A	1	1/3	1/4
Car B	3	1	1/2
Car C	4	2	1

MPG

	Car A	Car B	Car C
Car A	1	1/4	1/6
Car B	4	1	1/3
Car C	6	3	1

Style

	Car A	Car B	Car C
Car A	1	1/3	4
Car B	3	1	7
Car C	1/4	1/7	1

Following the same synthesis procedure that we used for the comfort criterion, we can compute the priority vectors for these criteria. Table 18.5 shows the result of this synthesis. Interpreting these priorities, we note that car C is the most preferable in terms of purchase price (0.557) and miles per gallon (0.639). Car B is the most preferable in terms of style (0.655). No car is the most preferred with respect to all the criteria. Thus, before a final decision can be made, we must assess the relative importance of the criteria.

In addition to the pairwise comparisons for the decision alternatives, we must use the same pairwise comparison procedure to set priorities for all four criteria in terms of the importance of each in contributing toward the overall goal of selecting the best car. To develop this final pairwise comparison matrix, Payne would have to specify the importance of each criterion compared to each of the other criteria. To do so, she has to make six pairwise judgments:

Table 18.5	PRIORITY VECTORS FOR PRICE, MPG, AND STYLE IN THE CAR-SELECTION PROBLEM

Price	MPG	Style
$\begin{bmatrix} 0.123 \\ 0.320 \\ 0.557 \end{bmatrix}$	$\begin{bmatrix} 0.087 \\ 0.274 \\ 0.639 \end{bmatrix}$	$\begin{bmatrix} 0.265 \\ 0.655 \\ 0.080 \end{bmatrix}$

| Table 18.6 | PAIRWISE COMPARISON MATRIX FOR THE FOUR CRITERIA IN THE CAR-SELECTION PROBLEM |

| | Criterion | | | |
	Price	MPG	Comfort	Style
Price	1	3	2	2
MPG	1/3	1	1/4	1/4
Comfort	1/2	4	1	1/2
Style	1/2	4	2	1

Purchase price compared to MPG
Purchase price compared to comfort
Purchase price compare to style

MPG compared to comfort
MPG compared to style

Comfort compared to style

For example, in the pairwise comparison of the purchase price and MPG, Payne indicates that purchase price is *moderately* more important than MPG. Using the AHP 9-point numerical rating scale (see Table 18.2), a value of 3 is recorded to show the higher importance of the purchase price criterion. Table 18.6 shows the summary of the pairwise comparison matrix preferences for the four criteria.

We can now use the synthesization process described earlier in this section to convert the pairwise comparison information into the priorities for the four criteria:

Priorities for the Four Criteria	
Price	0.398
MPG	0.085
Comfort	0.218
Style	0.299

The purchase price (0.398) is the highest priority, or most important, criterion in the car-selection decision. Style (0.299) and comfort (0.218) rank next in importance. Miles per gallon (0.085) is a relatively unimportant criterion in terms of the overall goal of selecting the best car. In the next section we show how AHP uses the priority information generated here to develop an overall priority ranking for the three cars.

18.5 USING AHP TO DEVELOP AN OVERALL PRIORITY RANKING

In the preceding section we showed how to use a pairwise comparison matrix to develop a prioritized ranking of the items being compared. Now we show how to combine the criterion priorities and the priorities of each decision alternative relative to each criterion to develop an overall priority ranking of the decision alternatives. Table 18.7 summarizes the

Table 18.7	THE PRIORITY MATRIX FOR THE CAR-SELECTION PROBLEM			
	Price	**MPG**	**Comfort**	**Style**
Car A	0.123	0.087	0.593	0.265
Car B	0.320	0.274	0.341	0.655
Car C	0.557	0.639	0.066	0.080

priorities for each car in terms of each criterion as computed in Section 18.4. We refer to this matrix as the **priority matrix.**

The procedure used to compute the overall priorities for each decision alternative can best be understood if we think of the priority for each criterion as a weight that reflects its importance. The overall priority for each decision alternative is obtained by summing the products of the criterion priority times the priority of its decision alternative. Recall that the criterion priorities were found to be 0.398 for purchase price, 0.085 for MPG, 0.218 for comfort, and 0.299 for style. Thus, the computation of the overall priority for car A is as follows:

$$\text{Overall car A priority} = 0.398(0.123) + 0.085(0.087) + 0.218(0.593) + 0.299(0.265)$$
$$= 0.265$$

Repeating this calculation for cars B and C provides their overall priorities:

$$\text{Overall car B priority} = 0.398(0.320) + 0.085(0.274) + 0.218(0.341) + 0.299(0.655)$$
$$= 0.421$$
$$\text{Overall car C priority} = 0.398(0.557) + 0.085(0.639) + 0.218(0.066) + 0.299(0.080)$$
$$= 0.314$$

Ranking these priority values, we have the AHP ranking of the decision alternatives:

You should be able to use AHP to determine overall priority ranking. Try Problem 20.

Alternative	Priority
Car A	0.265
Car B	0.421
Car C	0.314
Total	1.000

These results provide a basis for Diane Payne to make a decision regarding the purchase of a car. Based on the AHP priorities, she should select car B. Whether she actually decides to purchase car B based on the AHP analysis is still her decision to make. If Payne believes that the judgments she has made regarding the importance of the criteria and her preferences for the cars in terms of the criteria are valid, the AHP priorities show that car B is the preferred car. Whether Payne actually decides to purchase car B may not be as important as the additional understanding that she gained through the AHP analysis. That is, the process may be as helpful to her as the actual decision recommendation itself.

18.6 USING EXPERT CHOICE TO IMPLEMENT AHP

Expert Choice (EC), a software package marketed by Decision Support Software, provides a user-friendly procedure for implementing AHP on a microcomputer. In this section we provide an introduction to this software package by using it to compute the priorities for the car-selection problem.

Expert Choice enables the user to construct a graphical representation of the hierarchy easily. For example, to create the hierarchy for the car-selection problem, the user selects the option to develop a new application: what appears on the computer's monitor is a request to define the overall goal. After the user defines the overall goal—select the best car—a rectangular box, or node, appears on the screen with this goal description written directly above it. The user selects the **Edit** pull-down menu and then the **Insert** option; another rectangular box or node appears below the goal node, and the user now types the name of a criterion, such as price, which will be entered inside the box. This process continues until the user has specified all four criterion nodes, including MPG, comfort, and style. Figure 18.7 shows the partial hierarchy appearing on the computer screen after the four criteria have been entered.

Figure 18.7 shows that, in addition to the names of each criterion, the criterion nodes also contain the decimal value 0.250. This value represents the initial weight, or priority, given to each criterion at the start of the EC session. The user can now continue to use the Insert option to define the decision alternative nodes associated with each of the criterion nodes. Figure 18.8 shows the result of defining the decision alternative nodes of

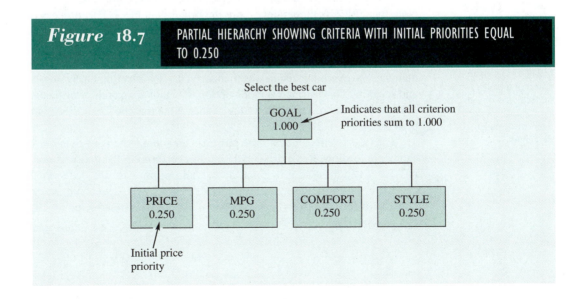

Figure 18.7 PARTIAL HIERARCHY SHOWING CRITERIA WITH INITIAL PRIORITIES EQUAL TO 0.250

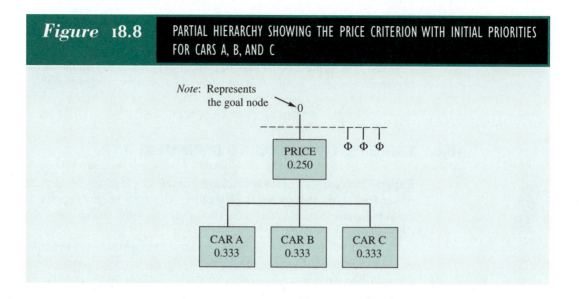

Figure 18.8   PARTIAL HIERARCHY SHOWING THE PRICE CRITERION WITH INITIAL PRIORITIES FOR CARS A, B, AND C

car A, car B, and car C for the price criterion; note that with three alternatives, the initial priorities are 0.333. Similar sets of decision alternatives are then identified for the other three criteria.

Now that the hierarchy has been input to EC, the user is ready to begin developing the pairwise comparisons needed to establish priorities for the decision alternatives. To illustrate the type of approach used, we moved back to the goal node and then selected the **Compare** pull-down menu. After selecting the option to make comparisons based on the importance of the decision criteria, the EC system begins to go through the pairwise comparison analysis.

First, EC asks the user if **PRICE** and **MPG** are equally important. A no response leads EC to ask if **PRICE** is more important than MPG; a yes response leads to a new screen on which the user specifies the comparative importance of **PRICE** and **MPG**, as shown in Figure 18.9. Note that **PRICE** is moderately more important than **MPG**. This process continues until all entries in the pairwise comparison matrix for criteria have been developed. Figure 18.10 shows the priorities that EC obtained after synthesization.[3]

Pairwise preferences for the cars relative to each criterion were entered in a similar manner. The overall decision was then arrived at by selecting the **Synthesis** pull-down menu and selecting the **Distributive Mode** option to obtain an overall prioritization of the decision alternatives. Figure 18.11 shows the results. Note that the final priority for car B, the most preferable, is 0.422.

The EC system is much more powerful and comprehensive than our brief introduction can begin to show. It is extremely helpful in performing the multicriteria decision analysis of AHP. In addition to providing the overall priorities for the decision alternatives, EC is capable of performing sensitivity analyses, whereby the decision maker can begin to learn how the overall priorities for the decision alternatives are affected by changes in the preference input data.

Practitioners in Japan originally viewed AHP as too complicated. However, in a 1985 symposium, Thomas L. Saaty, the founder of AHP showed the Japanese that the method is simple, is easy to use, and has a great potential to solve a variety of decision problems. Since then, a Japanese version of Expert Choice has been developed.

---

3. The priorities computed by EC differ slightly from those we obtained previously. The reason is that the method we used was an approximation to the EC synthesization procedure, which involves the computation of eigenvalues and eigenvectors.

Figure 18.9 — DETERMINING THE RATING FOR THE PRICE AND MPG PAIRWISE COMPARISON

```
           Goal:  Select the best car

                 with respect to

                  ┌─────────┐
                  │  GOAL   │
                  └─────────┘
```

PRICE
 is EQUAL to MODERATELY more IMPORTANT than
MPG:

```
┌────────────────────────────────────┐
│                                     │
│   EXTREME------------               │
│                                     │
│   VERY STRONG--------               │
│                                     │
│   STRONG-------------               │
│                                     │
│   MODERATE-----------               │
│                                     │
│   EQUAL--------------    <--        │
│                                     │
└────────────────────────────────────┘
```

> System initially positions pointer here because we said price and mileage are not equally important.

PRICE
 is MODERATELY more IMPORTANT than
MPG:

```
┌────────────────────────────────────┐
│                                     │
│   EXTREME------------               │
│                                     │
│   VERY STRONG--------               │
│                                     │
│   STRONG-------------               │
│                                     │
│   MODERATE-----------<-└            │
│                                     │
│   EQUAL--------------               │
│                                     │
└────────────────────────────────────┘
```

> User moves the arrow to the position that best describes the relationship.

Figure 18.10 — THE HIERARCHY SHOWING PRIORITIES FOR THE CRITERIA

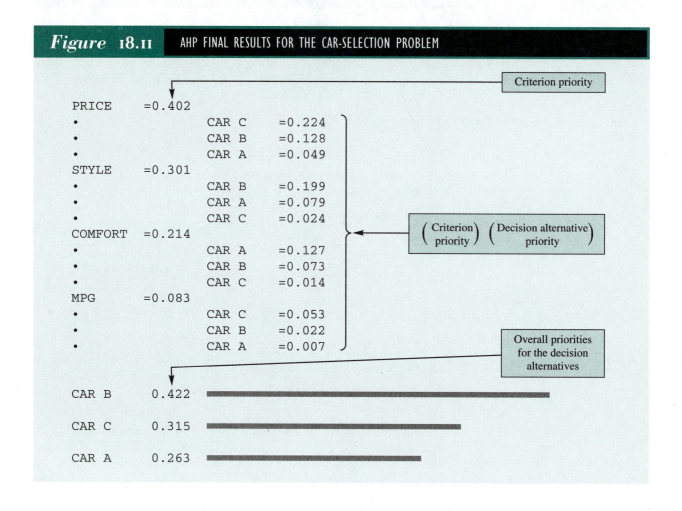

Figure 18.11 AHP FINAL RESULTS FOR THE CAR-SELECTION PROBLEM

SUMMARY

In this chapter we used goal programming to solve problems with multiple goals within the linear programming framework. We showed that the goal programming model contains one or more goal equations and an objective function designed to minimize deviations from the goals. In situations where resource capacities or other restrictions affect the achievement of the goals, the model will contain constraints that are formulated and treated in the same manner as constraints in an ordinary linear programming model.

In goal programming problems with preemptive priorities, priority level 1 goals are treated first in an objective function to identify a solution that will best satisfy these goals. This solution is then revised by considering an objective function involving only the priority level 2 goals; solution modifications are considered only if they do not degrade the solution obtained for the priority level 1 goals. This process continues until all priority levels have been considered.

We showed how a variation of the linear programming graphical solution procedure can be used to solve goal programming problems with two decision variables. Specialized goal programming computer packages are available for solving the general goal programming problem, but such computer codes are not as readily available as are general purpose linear programming computer packages. As a result, we showed how a general linear programming package such as LINDO can be used to solve a goal programming problem.

We presented an approach to multicriteria decision making called the analytic hierarchy process (AHP). We showed that a key part of AHP is the development of judgments concerning the relative importance of, or preference for, the elements being compared. A consistency ratio is computed to determine the degree of consistency exhibited by the decision maker in making the pairwise comparisons. Values of the consistency ratio less than or equal to 0.10 are considered acceptable.

Once the set of all pairwise comparisons has been developed, a process referred to as synthesization is used to determine the priorities for the elements being compared. The final step of the analytic hierarchy process is an overall synthesization, in which the priority levels established for the decision alternatives relative to each criterion are multiplied by the priority levels reflecting the importance of the criteria themselves; the sum of these products over all the criteria is the overall priority level for the decision alternative. We concluded the chapter with a brief introduction to Expert Choice, a software package designed to perform the computational steps of AHP.

GLOSSARY

Goal programming A linear programming approach to problems involving multicriteria whereby the objective function is designed to minimize the deviations from goals.

Preemptive priorities Priorities assigned to goals that ensure that the satisfaction of a higher level goal cannot be traded for the satisfaction of a lower level goal.

Target value A value specified in the statement of the goal. Based on the context of the problem, management will want the solution to the goal programming problem to result in a value for the goal that is less than, equal to, or greater than the target value.

Goal equation An equation whose right-hand side is the target value for the goal; the left-hand side of the goal equation consists of (1) a function representing the level of achievement and (2) deviation variables representing the difference between the target value for the goal and the level achieved.

Deviation variables Variables that are added to the goal equation to allow the solution to deviate from the goal's target value.

Analytic hierarchy process (AHP) An approach to multicriteria decision making based in part on pairwise comparisons for elements in a hierarchy.

Hierarchy A diagram that shows the levels of a problem in terms of the overall goal, the criteria, and the decision alternatives.

Pairwise comparison matrix A matrix that consists of the preference, or relative importance, ratings provided during a series of pairwise comparisons.

Synthesization A mathematical process that uses the preference or relative importance values in the pairwise comparison matrix to develop priorities.

Normalized pairwise comparison matrix The matrix obtained by dividing each element of the pairwise comparison matrix by its column total. This matrix is computed as an intermediate step in the synthesization of priorities.

Priority matrix A matrix that shows the priority of each decision alternative for each criterion.

Consistency A concept developed to assess the quality of the judgments made during a series of pairwise comparisons. It is a measure of the internal consistency of these comparisons.

Consistency ratio A numerical measure of the degree of consistency in a series of pairwise comparisons. Values less than or equal to 0.10 are considered acceptable.

Expert Choice (EC) A computer software package that performs the computations required by the analytic hierarchy process.

PROBLEMS

1. The RMC Corporation blends three raw materials to produce two products: a fuel additive and a solvent base. Each ton of fuel additive is a mixture of $2/5$ ton of material 1 and $3/5$ ton of material 3. A ton of solvent base is a mixture of $1/2$ ton of material 1, $1/5$ ton of material 2, and $3/10$ ton of material 3. RMC's production is constrained by a limited availability of the three raw materials. For the current production period, RMC has the following quantities of each raw material: material 1, 20 tons; material 2, 5 tons; material 3, 21 tons. Management wants to achieve the following P_1 priority level goals.

    Goal 1: Produce at least 30 tons of fuel additive.

    Goal 2: Produce at least 15 tons of solvent base.

    Assume no other goals.
    a. Can management achieve both P_1 level goals given the constraints on the amounts of each material available? Explain.
    b. Treating the amounts of each material available as constraints, formulate a goal programming model to determine the optimal product mix. Assume that both P_1 priority level goals are equally important to management.
    c. Use the graphical goal programming procedure to solve the model formulated in part (b).
    d. If goal 1 is twice as important as goal 2, what is the optimal product mix?

SELF TEST

2. DJS Investment Services must develop an investment portfolio for a new client. As an initial investment strategy, the new client would like to restrict the portfolio to a mix of two stocks:

Stock	Price/Share	Estimated Annual Return (%)
AGA Products	$ 50	6
Key Oil	100	10

The client has $50,000 to invest and has established the following two investment goals.

Priority Level 1 Goal

Goal 1: Obtain an annual return of at least 9%.

Priority Level 2 Goal

Goal 2: Limit the investment in Key Oil, the riskier investment, to no more than 60% of the total investment.

a. Formulate a goal programming model for the DJS Investment problem.
b. Use the graphical goal programming procedure to obtain a solution.

3. The L. Young & Sons Manufacturing Company produces two products that have the following profit and resource requirement characteristics.

Characteristic	Product 1	Product 2
Profit/unit	$4	$2
Dept. A hours/unit	1	1
Dept. B hours/unit	2	5

Last month's production schedule used 350 hours of labor in department A and 1000 hours of labor in department B.

Young's management has been experiencing work force morale and labor union problems during the past six months because of monthly departmental work load fluctuations. New hiring, layoffs, and interdepartmental transfers have been common because the firm has not attempted to stabilize work load requirements.

Management would like to develop a production schedule for the coming month that will achieve the following goals.

Goal 1: Use 350 hours of labor in department A.

Goal 2: Use 1000 hours of labor in department B.

Goal 3: Earn a profit of at least $1300.

a. Formulate a goal programming model for this problem, assuming that goals 1 and 2 are P_1 level goals and goal 3 is a P_2 level goal; assume that goals 1 and 2 are equally important.

b. Solve the model formulated in part (a) using the graphical goal programming procedure.

c. Suppose that the firm ignores the work load fluctuations and considers the 350 hours in department A and the 1000 hours in department B as the maximum available. Formulate and solve a linear programming problem to maximize profit subject to these constraints.

d. Compare the solutions obtained in parts (b) and (c). Discuss which approach you favor, and why.

e. Reconsider part (a), assuming that the priority level 1 goal is goal 3 and the priority level 2 goals are goals 1 and 2; as before, assume that goals 1 and 2 are equally important. Solve this revised problem using the graphical goal programming procedure and compare your solution to the one obtained for the original problem.

4. Industrial Chemicals produces two adhesives used in the manufacturing process for airplanes. The two adhesives, which have different bonding strengths, require different amounts of production time: the IC-100 adhesive requires 20 minutes of production time per gallon of finished product, and the IC-200 adhesive uses 30 minutes of production time per gallon. Both products use 1 pound of a highly perishable resin for each gallon of finished product. Currently, 300 pounds of the resin are in inventory, and more can be obtained if necessary. However, because of the shelf life of the material, any amount not used in the next 2 weeks will be discarded.

The firm has existing orders for 100 gallons of IC-100 and 120 gallons of IC-200. Under normal conditions, the production process operates 8 hours per day, 5 days per week. Management wants to schedule production for the next 2 weeks to achieve the following goals.

Priority Level 1 Goals

Goal 1: Avoid underutilization of the production process.

Goal 2: Avoid overtime in excess of 20 hours for the 2 weeks.

Priority Level 2 Goals

Goal 3: Satisfy existing orders for the IC-100 adhesive; that is, produce at least 100 gallons of IC-100.

Goal 4: Satisfy existing orders for the IC-200 adhesive; that is, produce at least 120 gallons of IC-200.

Priority Level 3 Goal

Goal 5: Use all available resin.

a. Formulate a goal programming model for the Industrial Chemicals problem. Assume both priority level 1 goals and both priority level 2 goals are equally important.
b. Use the graphical goal programming procedure to develop a solution for the model formulated in part (a).

5. Reconsider the RMC data presented in Problem 1. Assume that the two P_1 priority level goals remain the same and that both goals are equally important to management. Suppose that management has learned that additional amounts of material 3 can be obtained from another RMC plant. Although management wants to obtain a solution that satisfies their production goals using the 21 tons of material 3 currently available, it is willing to consider using additional amounts of material 3 from the other plant. With this new goal as a P_2 priority level goal, the problem goals can now be restated.

Priority Level 1 Goals

Goal 1: Produce at least 30 tons of fuel additive.
Goal 2: Produce at least 15 tons of solvent base.

Priority Level 2 Goal

Goal 3: Use no more than 21 tons of material 3.

a. Treat the amounts of materials 1 and 2 available as problem constraints and formulate a goal programming model for this problem.
b. Use the goal programming computer procedure illustrated in Section 18.2 to solve the model formulated in part (a).
c. How many tons of material 3 need to be obtained from RMC's other plant?

6. Michigan Motors Corporation (MMC) has just introduced a new luxury touring sedan. As part of its promotional campaign, the marketing department has decided to send personalized invitations to test drive the new sedan to two target groups: (1) current owners of an MMC luxury automobile and (2) owners of luxury cars manufactured by one of MMC's competitors. The cost of sending a personalized invitation to each customer is estimated to be $1 per letter. Based on experience with this type of advertising, MMC estimates that 25% of the customers contacted from group 1 and 10% of the customers contacted from group 2 will test drive the new sedan. As part of this campaign, MMC has set the following goals.

Goal 1: Get at least 10,000 customers from group 1 to test drive the new sedan.
Goal 2: Get at least 5000 customers from group 2 to test drive the new sedan.
Goal 3: Limit the expense of sending the invitations to $70,000.

Assume that goals 1 and 2 are P_1 priority level goals and that goal 3 is a P_2 priority level goal.
a. Suppose that goals 1 and 2 are equally important; formulate a goal programming model of the MMC problem.
b. Use the goal programming computer procedure illustrated in Section 18.2 to solve the model formulated in part (a).
c. If management believes that contacting customers from group 2 is twice as important as contacting customers from group 1, what should MMC do?

7. A committee in charge of promoting a Ladies Professional Golf Association tournament is trying to determine how best to advertise the event during the 2 weeks prior to the tournament. The committee obtained the following information about the three advertising media they are considering using.

Category	Audience Reached Per Advertisement	Cost Per Advertisement	Maximum Number of Advertisements
TV	200,000	$2500	10
Radio	50,000	$ 400	15
Newspaper	100,000	$ 500	20

The last column in this table shows the maximum number of advertisements that can be run during the next 2 weeks; these values should be treated as constraints. The committee has established the following goals for the campaign.

Priority Level 1 Goal

Goal 1: Reach at least 4 million people.

Priority Level 2 Goal

Goal 2: The number of television advertisements should be at least 30% of the total number of advertisements.

Priority Level 3 Goal

Goal 3: The number of radio advertisements should not exceed 20% of the total number of advertisements.

Priority Level 4 Goal

Goal 4: Limit the total amount spent for advertising to $20,000.

a. Formulate a goal programming model for this problem.

b. Use the goal programming computer procedure illustrated in Section 18.2 to solve the model formulated in part (a).

8. The shop manager of Morley Company wants to determine the best location for a new machine in an existing layout of three machines. The existing machines are located at the following x_1, x_2 coordinates on the shop floor.

$$\text{Machine 1:} \quad x_1 = 1, x_2 = 7$$
$$\text{Machine 2:} \quad x_1 = 5, x_2 = 9$$
$$\text{Machine 3:} \quad x_1 = 6, x_2 = 2$$

a. Develop a goal programming model that can be solved to minimize the total distance of the new machine from the three existing machines. The distance is to be measured rectangularly. For example, if the location of the new machine is $(x_1 = 3, x_2 = 5)$, it is considered to be a distance of $|3 - 1| + |5 - 7| = 2 + 2 = 4$ from machine 1. *Hint:* In the goal programming formulation, let

$$x_1 = \text{first coordinate of the new machine location}$$

$$x_2 = \text{second coordinate of the new machine location}$$

$d_i^+ = $ amount by which the x_1 coordinate of the new machine exceeds the x_1 coordinate of machine i ($i = 1, 2, 3$)

$d_i^- = $ amount by which the x_1 coordinate of machine i exceeds the x_1 coordinate of the new machine ($i = 1, 2, 3$)

$e_i^+ = $ amount by which the x_2 coordinate of the new machine exceeds the x_2 coordinate of machine i ($i = 1, 2, 3$)

$e_i^- = $ amount by which the x_2 coordinate of machine i exceeds the x_2 coordinate of the new machine ($i = 1, 2, 3$)

b. What is the optimal location for the new machine?

9. A fast-food chain is attempting to determine the best location of a new outlet. Management wants to determine the best location for drawing customers from three population centers. Letting (x_1, x_2) represent the map coordinates of the three population centers, we can show their locations as

$$\text{Population center 1: } x_1 = 2, x_2 = 8$$
$$\text{Population center 2: } x_1 = 6, x_2 = 6$$
$$\text{Population center 3: } x_1 = 1, x_2 = 1$$

If the new outlet were located at coordinates ($x_1 = 3, x_2 = 2$), it would be $|3 - 1| + |2 - 1| = 3$ miles from population center 3 (distance is measured as the sum of the east–west and north–south differences in coordinates).

a. Formulate and solve a goal programming model to determine the location for the new outlet that will minimize the total distance from the three population centers. (*Hint:* Let (x_1, x_2) represent the coordinates of the new location.)

b. Population center 1 is four times as large as center 3, and center 2 is twice as large as center 3. Management believes that the importance of locating near a population center is proportional to its population. Develop and solve a new goal programming model in which the weights for the deviation variables reflect this importance.

10. Use the pairwise comparison matrix for the price criterion shown in Table 18.4 to verify that the priorities after synthesization are 0.123, 0.320, and 0.557. Compute the consistency ratio and comment on its acceptability.

11. Use the pairwise comparison matrix for the MPG criterion shown in Table 18.4 to verify that the priorities after synthesization are 0.087, 0.274, and 0.639. Compute the consistency ratio and comment on its acceptability.

12. Use the pairwise comparison matrix for the style criterion as shown in Table 18.4 to verify that the priorities after synthesization are 0.265, 0.655, and 0.080. Compute the consistency ratio and comment on its acceptability.

SELF TEST

13. Dan Joseph was considering entering one of two graduate schools of business to pursue studies for an MBA degree. When asked how he compared the two schools with respect to reputation, he responded that he preferred school A strongly to very strongly to school B.

a. Set up the pairwise comparison matrix for this problem.

b. Determine the priorities for the two schools relative to this criterion.

14. An organization was investigating relocating its corporate headquarters to one of three possible cities. The following pairwise comparison matrix shows the president's judgments regarding the desirability for the three cities.

	City 1	City 2	City 3
City 1	1	5	7
City 2	1/5	1	3
City 3	1/7	1/3	1

a. Determine the priorities for the three cities.
b. Is the president consistent in terms of the judgments provided? Explain.

15. The following pairwise comparison matrix contains the judgments of an individual regarding the fairness of two proposed tax programs, A and B.

	A	B
A	1	3
B	1/3	1

a. Determine the priorities for the two programs.
b. Are the individual's judgments consistent? Explain.

SELF TEST

16. Asked to compare three soft drinks with respect to flavor, an individual stated that

> A is moderately more preferable than B,
> A is equally to moderately more preferable than C, and
> B is strongly more preferable than C.

a. Set up the pairwise comparison matrix for this problem.
b. Determine the priorities for the soft drinks with respect to the flavor criterion.
c. Compute the consistency ratio. Are the individual's judgments consistent? Explain.

17. Refer to Problem 16. Suppose that the individual had stated the following judgments instead of those given in Problem 16.

> A is strongly more preferable than C.
> B is equally to moderately more preferable than A.
> B is strongly more preferable than C.

Answer parts (a), (b), and (c) as stated in Problem 16.

18. The national sales director for Jones Office Supplies needs to determine the best location for the next national sales meeting. Three locations have been proposed: Dallas, San Francisco, and New York. One criterion considered important in the decision is the desirability of the location in terms of restaurants, entertainment, and so on. The national sales manager made the following judgments with regard to this criterion.

> New York is very strongly more preferred than Dallas.
> New York is moderately more preferred than San Francisco.
> San Francisco is moderately to strongly more preferred than Dallas.

a. Set up the pairwise comparison matrix for this problem.
b. Determine the priorities for the desirability criterion.
c. Compute the consistency ratio. Are the sales manager's judgments consistent? Explain.

19. A study comparing four personal computers resulted in the following pairwise comparison matrix for the performance criterion.

	1	2	3	4
1	1	3	7	1/3
2	1/3	1	4	1/4
3	1/7	1/4	1	1/6
4	3	4	6	1

    a. Determine the priorities for the four computers relative to the performance criterion.

    b. Compute the consistency ratio. Are the judgments regarding performance consistent? Explain.

SELF TEST

20. An individual was interested in determining which of two stocks to invest in, Central Computing Company (CCC) or Software Research, Inc. (SRI). The criteria thought to be most relevant in making the decision are the potential yield of the stock and the risk associated with the investment. The pairwise comparison matrices for this problem are

Criterion	Yield	Risk
Yield	1	2
Risk	1/2	1

Yield	CCC	SRI
CCC	1	3
SRI	1/3	1

Risk	CCC	SRI
CCC	1	1/2
SRI	2	1

    a. Draw the hierarchy for this problem.

    b. Compute the priorities for each pairwise comparison matrix.

    c. Determine the overall priority for the two investments.

21. The vice president of Harling Equipment needs to select a new director of marketing. The two possible candidates are Bill Jacobs and Sue Martin, and the criteria thought to be most relevant in the selection are leadership ability (L), personal skills (P), and administrative skills (A). The following pairwise comparison matrices were obtained.

Criterion	L	P	A
L	1	1/3	1/4
P	3	1	2
A	4	1/2	1

Leadership	Jacobs	Martin
Jacobs	1	4
Martin	1/4	1

Personal	Jacobs	Martin
Jacobs	1	1/3
Martin	3	1

Administrative	Jacobs	Martin
Jacobs	1	2
Martin	1/2	1

a. Draw the hierarchy for this problem.
b. Compute the priorities for each pairwise comparison matrix.
c. Determine an overall priority for each candidate.

22. A woman considering the purchase of a custom sound stereo system for her car looked at three different systems (A, B, and C) that varied in terms of price (P), sound quality (Q), and FM reception (FM). The following pairwise comparison matrices were developed.

Criterion	P	Q	FM
P	1	3	4
Q	1/3	1	3
FM	1/4	1/3	1

Price	A	B	C
A	1	4	2
B	1/4	1	1/3
C	1/2	3	1

Quality	A	B	C
A	1	1/2	1/4
B	2	1	1/3
C	4	3	1

FM Reception	A	B	C
A	1	4	2
B	1/4	1	1
C	1/2	1	1

a. Draw the hierarchy for this problem.
b. Compute the priorities for each pairwise comparison matrix.
c. Determine an overall priority for each system.

Case Problem   PRODUCTION SCHEDULING

EZ Trailers, Inc., manufactures a variety of general purpose trailers, including a complete line of boat trailers. Two of their best-selling boat trailers are the EZ-190 and the EZ-250. The EZ-190 is designed for boats up to 19 feet in length, and the EZ-250 can be used for boats up to 25 feet in length.

EZ Trailers would like to schedule production for the next two months for these two models. Each unit of the EZ-190 requires 4 hours of production time, and each unit of the EZ-250 uses 6 hours of production time. The following orders have been received for March and April.

Model	March	April
EZ-190	800	600
EZ-250	1100	1200

The ending inventory from February was 200 units of the EZ-190 and 300 units of the EZ-250. The total number of hours of production time used in February was 6300 hours.

The management of EZ Trailers is concerned about being able to satisfy existing orders for the EZ-250 for both March and April. In fact, it believes that this is the most important goal that a production schedule should meet. Next in importance is satisfying existing orders for the EZ-190. In addition, management doesn't want to implement any production schedule that would involve significant labor fluctuations from month to month. In this regard, its goal is to develop a production schedule that would limit fluctuations in labor hours used to a maximum of 1000 hours from one month to the next.

Managerial Report

Perform an analysis of EZ Trailers' production scheduling problem, and prepare a report for EZ's president that summarizes your findings. Include a discussion and analysis of the following items in your report.

1. The production schedule that best achieves the goals as specified by management.
2. Suppose that EZ Trailers' storage facilities would accommodate only a maximum of 300 trailers in any one month. What effect would this have on the production schedule?
3. Suppose that EZ Trailers can store only a maximum of 300 trailers in any one month. In addition, suppose management would like to have an ending inventory in April of at least 100 units of each model. What effect would both changes have on the production schedule?
4. What changes would occur in the production schedule if the labor fluctuation goal was the highest priority goal?

Entries in the following table give the probability of x successes in n trials of a binomial experiment, where p is the probability of a success on one trial. For example, with $n = 6$ trials and $p = 0.40$, the probability of $x = 2$ successes is 0.3110.

							p				
n	x	0.05	0.10	0.15	0.20	0.25	0.30	0.35	0.40	0.45	0.50
1	0	0.9500	0.9000	0.8500	0.8000	0.7500	0.7000	0.6500	0.6000	0.5500	0.5000
	1	0.0500	0.1000	0.1500	0.2000	0.2500	0.3000	0.3500	0.4000	0.4500	0.5000
2	0	0.9025	0.8100	0.7225	0.6400	0.5625	0.4900	0.4225	0.3600	0.3025	0.2500
	1	0.0950	0.1800	0.2550	0.3200	0.3750	0.4200	0.4550	0.4800	0.4950	0.5000
	2	0.0025	0.0100	0.0225	0.0400	0.0625	0.0900	0.1225	0.1600	0.2025	0.2500
3	0	0.8574	0.7290	0.6141	0.5120	0.4219	0.3430	0.2746	0.2160	0.1664	0.1250
	1	0.1354	0.2430	0.3251	0.3840	0.4219	0.4410	0.4436	0.4320	0.4084	0.3750
	2	0.0071	0.0270	0.0574	0.0960	0.1406	0.1890	0.2389	0.2880	0.3341	0.3750
	3	0.0001	0.0010	0.0034	0.0080	0.0156	0.0270	0.0429	0.0640	0.0911	0.1250
4	0	0.8145	0.6561	0.5220	0.4096	0.3164	0.2401	0.1785	0.1296	0.0915	0.0625
	1	0.1715	0.2916	0.3685	0.4096	0.4219	0.4116	0.3845	0.3456	0.2995	0.2500
	2	0.0135	0.0486	0.0975	0.1536	0.2109	0.2646	0.3105	0.3456	0.3675	0.3750
	3	0.0005	0.0036	0.0115	0.0256	0.0469	0.0756	0.1115	0.1536	0.2005	0.2500
	4	0.0000	0.0001	0.0005	0.0016	0.0039	0.0081	0.0150	0.0256	0.0410	0.0625
5	0	0.7738	0.5905	0.4437	0.3277	0.2373	0.1681	0.1160	0.0778	0.0503	0.0312
	1	0.2036	0.3280	0.3915	0.4096	0.3955	0.3602	0.3124	0.2592	0.2059	0.1562
	2	0.0214	0.0729	0.1382	0.2048	0.2637	0.3087	0.3364	0.3456	0.3369	0.3125
	3	0.0011	0.0081	0.0244	0.0512	0.0879	0.1323	0.1811	0.2304	0.2757	0.3125
	4	0.0000	0.0004	0.0022	0.0064	0.0146	0.0284	0.0488	0.0768	0.1128	0.1562
	5	0.0000	0.0000	0.0001	0.0003	0.0010	0.0024	0.0053	0.0102	0.0185	0.0312
6	0	0.7351	0.5314	0.3771	0.2621	0.1780	0.1176	0.0754	0.0467	0.0277	0.0156
	1	0.2321	0.3543	0.3993	0.3932	0.3560	0.3025	0.2437	0.1866	0.1359	0.0938
	2	0.0305	0.0984	0.1762	0.2458	0.2966	0.3241	0.3280	0.3110	0.2780	0.2344
	3	0.0021	0.0146	0.0415	0.0819	0.1318	0.1852	0.2355	0.2765	0.3032	0.3125
	4	0.0001	0.0012	0.0055	0.0154	0.0330	0.0595	0.0951	0.1382	0.1861	0.2344
	5	0.0000	0.0001	0.0004	0.0015	0.0044	0.0102	0.0205	0.0369	0.0609	0.0938
	6	0.0000	0.0000	0.0000	0.0001	0.0002	0.0007	0.0018	0.0041	0.0083	0.0156
7	0	0.6983	0.4783	0.3206	0.2097	0.1335	0.0824	0.0490	0.0280	0.0152	0.0078
	1	0.2573	0.3720	0.3960	0.3670	0.3115	0.2471	0.1848	0.1306	0.0872	0.0547
	2	0.0406	0.1240	0.2097	0.2753	0.3115	0.3177	0.2985	0.2613	0.2140	0.1641
	3	0.0036	0.0230	0.0617	0.1147	0.1730	0.2269	0.2679	0.2903	0.2918	0.2734
	4	0.0002	0.0026	0.0109	0.0287	0.0577	0.0972	0.1442	0.1935	0.2388	0.2734

Binomial Probabilities (*Continued*)

n	x	0.05	0.10	0.15	0.20	0.25	0.30	0.35	0.40	0.45	0.50
	5	0.0000	0.0002	0.0012	0.0043	0.0115	0.0250	0.0466	0.0774	0.1172	0.1641
	6	0.0000	0.0000	0.0001	0.0004	0.0013	0.0036	0.0084	0.0172	0.0320	0.0547
	7	0.0000	0.0000	0.0000	0.0000	0.0001	0.0002	0.0006	0.0016	0.0037	0.0078
8	0	0.6634	0.4305	0.2725	0.1678	0.1001	0.0576	0.0319	0.0168	0.0084	0.0039
	1	0.2793	0.3826	0.3847	0.3355	0.2670	0.1977	0.1373	0.0896	0.0548	0.0312
	2	0.0515	0.1488	0.2376	0.2936	0.3115	0.2965	0.2587	0.2090	0.1569	0.1094
	3	0.0054	0.0331	0.0839	0.1468	0.2076	0.2541	0.2786	0.2787	0.2568	0.2188
	4	0.0004	0.0046	0.0185	0.0459	0.0865	0.1361	0.1875	0.2322	0.2627	0.2734
	5	0.0000	0.0004	0.0026	0.0092	0.0231	0.0467	0.0808	0.1239	0.1719	0.2188
	6	0.0000	0.0000	0.0002	0.0011	0.0038	0.0100	0.0217	0.0413	0.0703	0.1094
	7	0.0000	0.0000	0.0000	0.0001	0.0004	0.0012	0.0033	0.0079	0.0164	0.0312
	8	0.0000	0.0000	0.0000	0.0000	0.0000	0.0001	0.0002	0.0007	0.0017	0.0039
9	0	0.6302	0.3874	0.2316	0.1342	0.0751	0.0404	0.0207	0.0101	0.0046	0.0020
	1	0.2985	0.3874	0.3679	0.3020	0.2253	0.1556	0.1004	0.0605	0.0339	0.0176
	2	0.0629	0.1722	0.2597	0.3020	0.3003	0.2668	0.2162	0.1612	0.1110	0.0703
	3	0.0077	0.0446	0.1069	0.1762	0.2336	0.2668	0.2716	0.2508	0.2119	0.1641
	4	0.0006	0.0074	0.0283	0.0661	0.1168	0.1715	0.2194	0.2508	0.2600	0.2461
	5	0.0000	0.0008	0.0050	0.0165	0.0389	0.0735	0.1181	0.1672	0.2128	0.2461
	6	0.0000	0.0001	0.0006	0.0028	0.0087	0.0210	0.0424	0.0743	0.1160	0.1641
	7	0.0000	0.0000	0.0000	0.0003	0.0012	0.0039	0.0098	0.0212	0.0407	0.0703
	8	0.0000	0.0000	0.0000	0.0000	0.0001	0.0004	0.0013	0.0035	0.0083	0.0176
	9	0.0000	0.0000	0.0000	0.0000	0.0000	0.0000	0.0001	0.0003	0.0008	0.0020
10	0	0.5987	0.3487	0.1969	0.1074	0.0563	0.0282	0.0135	0.0060	0.0025	0.0010
	1	0.3151	0.3874	0.3474	0.2684	0.1877	0.1211	0.0725	0.0403	0.0207	0.0098
	2	0.0746	0.1937	0.2759	0.3020	0.2816	0.2335	0.1757	0.1209	0.0763	0.0439
	3	0.0105	0.0574	0.1298	0.2013	0.2503	0.2668	0.2522	0.2150	0.1665	0.1172
	4	0.0010	0.0112	0.0401	0.0881	0.1460	0.2001	0.2377	0.2508	0.2384	0.2051
	5	0.0001	0.0015	0.0085	0.0264	0.0584	0.1029	0.1536	0.2007	0.2340	0.2461
	6	0.0000	0.0001	0.0012	0.0055	0.0162	0.0368	0.0689	0.1115	0.1596	0.2051
	7	0.0000	0.0000	0.0001	0.0008	0.0031	0.0090	0.0212	0.0425	0.0746	0.1172
	8	0.0000	0.0000	0.0000	0.0001	0.0004	0.0014	0.0043	0.0106	0.0229	0.0439
	9	0.0000	0.0000	0.0000	0.0000	0.0000	0.0001	0.0005	0.0016	0.0042	0.0098
	10	0.0000	0.0000	0.0000	0.0000	0.0000	0.0000	0.0000	0.0001	0.0003	0.0010
12	0	0.5404	0.2824	0.1422	0.0687	0.0317	0.0138	0.0057	0.0022	0.0008	0.0002
	1	0.3413	0.3766	0.3012	0.2062	0.1267	0.0712	0.0368	0.0174	0.0075	0.0029
	2	0.0988	0.2301	0.2924	0.2835	0.2323	0.1678	0.1088	0.0639	0.0339	0.0161
	3	0.0173	0.0853	0.1720	0.2362	0.2581	0.2397	0.1954	0.1419	0.0923	0.0537
	4	0.0021	0.0213	0.0683	0.1329	0.1936	0.2311	0.2367	0.2128	0.1700	0.1208
	5	0.0002	0.0038	0.0193	0.0532	0.1032	0.1585	0.2039	0.2270	0.2225	0.1934
	6	0.0000	0.0005	0.0040	0.0155	0.0401	0.0792	0.1281	0.1766	0.2124	0.2256
	7	0.0000	0.0000	0.0006	0.0033	0.0115	0.0291	0.0591	0.1009	0.1489	0.1934
	8	0.0000	0.0000	0.0001	0.0005	0.0024	0.0078	0.0199	0.0420	0.0762	0.1208
	9	0.0000	0.0000	0.0000	0.0001	0.0004	0.0015	0.0048	0.0125	0.0277	0.0537

Binomial Probabilities (*Continued*)

						p					
n	x	0.05	0.10	0.15	0.20	0.25	0.30	0.35	0.40	0.45	0.50
	10	0.0000	0.0000	0.0000	0.0000	0.0000	0.0002	0.0008	0.0025	0.0068	0.0161
	11	0.0000	0.0000	0.0000	0.0000	0.0000	0.0000	0.0001	0.0003	0.0010	0.0029
	12	0.0000	0.0000	0.0000	0.0000	0.0000	0.0000	0.0000	0.0000	0.0001	0.0002
15	0	0.4633	0.2059	0.0874	0.0352	0.0134	0.0047	0.0016	0.0005	0.0001	0.0000
	1	0.3658	0.3432	0.2312	0.1319	0.0668	0.0305	0.0126	0.0047	0.0016	0.0005
	2	0.1348	0.2669	0.2856	0.2309	0.1559	0.0916	0.0476	0.0219	0.0090	0.0032
	3	0.0307	0.1285	0.2184	0.2501	0.2252	0.1700	0.1110	0.0634	0.0318	0.0139
	4	0.0049	0.0428	0.1156	0.1876	0.2252	0.2186	0.1792	0.1268	0.0780	0.0417
	5	0.0006	0.0105	0.0449	0.1032	0.1651	0.2061	0.2123	0.1859	0.1404	0.0916
	6	0.0000	0.0019	0.0132	0.0430	0.0917	0.1472	0.1906	0.2066	0.1914	0.1527
	7	0.0000	0.0003	0.0030	0.0138	0.0393	0.0811	0.1319	0.1771	0.2013	0.1964
	8	0.0000	0.0000	0.0005	0.0035	0.0131	0.0348	0.0710	0.1181	0.1647	0.1964
	9	0.0000	0.0000	0.0001	0.0007	0.0034	0.0116	0.0298	0.0612	0.1048	0.1527
	10	0.0000	0.0000	0.0000	0.0001	0.0007	0.0030	0.0096	0.0245	0.0515	0.0916
	11	0.0000	0.0000	0.0000	0.0000	0.0001	0.0006	0.0024	0.0074	0.0191	0.0417
	12	0.0000	0.0000	0.0000	0.0000	0.0000	0.0001	0.0004	0.0016	0.0052	0.0139
	13	0.0000	0.0000	0.0000	0.0000	0.0000	0.0000	0.0001	0.0003	0.0010	0.0032
	14	0.0000	0.0000	0.0000	0.0000	0.0000	0.0000	0.0000	0.0000	0.0001	0.0005
	15	0.0000	0.0000	0.0000	0.0000	0.0000	0.0000	0.0000	0.0000	0.0000	0.0000
18	0	0.3972	0.1501	0.0536	0.0180	0.0056	0.0016	0.0004	0.0001	0.0000	0.0000
	1	0.3763	0.3002	0.1704	0.0811	0.0338	0.0126	0.0042	0.0012	0.0003	0.0001
	2	0.1683	0.2835	0.2556	0.1723	0.0958	0.0458	0.0190	0.0069	0.0022	0.0006
	3	0.0473	0.1680	0.2406	0.2297	0.1704	0.1046	0.0547	0.0246	0.0095	0.0031
	4	0.0093	0.0700	0.1592	0.2153	0.2130	0.1681	0.1104	0.0614	0.0291	0.0117
	5	0.0014	0.0218	0.0787	0.1507	0.1988	0.2017	0.1664	0.1146	0.0666	0.0327
	6	0.0002	0.0052	0.0301	0.0816	0.1436	0.1873	0.1941	0.1655	0.1181	0.0708
	7	0.0000	0.0010	0.0091	0.0350	0.0820	0.1376	0.1792	0.1892	0.1657	0.1214
	8	0.0000	0.0002	0.0022	0.0120	0.0376	0.0811	0.1327	0.1734	0.1864	0.1669
	9	0.0000	0.0000	0.0004	0.0033	0.0139	0.0386	0.0794	0.1284	0.1694	0.1855
	10	0.0000	0.0000	0.0001	0.0008	0.0042	0.0149	0.0385	0.0771	0.1248	0.1669
	11	0.0000	0.0000	0.0000	0.0001	0.0010	0.0046	0.0151	0.0374	0.0742	0.1214
	12	0.0000	0.0000	0.0000	0.0000	0.0002	0.0012	0.0047	0.0145	0.0354	0.0708
	13	0.0000	0.0000	0.0000	0.0000	0.0000	0.0002	0.0012	0.0045	0.0134	0.0327
	14	0.0000	0.0000	0.0000	0.0000	0.0000	0.0000	0.0002	0.0011	0.0039	0.0117
	15	0.0000	0.0000	0.0000	0.0000	0.0000	0.0000	0.0000	0.0002	0.0009	0.0031
	16	0.0000	0.0000	0.0000	0.0000	0.0000	0.0000	0.0000	0.0000	0.0001	0.0006
	17	0.0000	0.0000	0.0000	0.0000	0.0000	0.0000	0.0000	0.0000	0.0000	0.0001
	18	0.0000	0.0000	0.0000	0.0000	0.0000	0.0000	0.0000	0.0000	0.0000	0.0000
20	0	0.3585	0.1216	0.0388	0.0115	0.0032	0.0008	0.0002	0.0000	0.0000	0.0000
	1	0.3774	0.2702	0.1368	0.0576	0.0211	0.0068	0.0020	0.0005	0.0001	0.0000

Binomial Probabilities (*Continued*)

n	x	0.05	0.10	0.15	0.20	0.25	0.30	0.35	0.40	0.45	0.50
	2	0.1887	0.2852	0.2293	0.1369	0.0669	0.0278	0.0100	0.0031	0.0008	0.0002
	3	0.0596	0.1901	0.2428	0.2054	0.1339	0.0716	0.0323	0.0123	0.0040	0.0011
	4	0.0133	0.0898	0.1821	0.2182	0.1897	0.1304	0.0738	0.0350	0.0139	0.0046
	5	0.0022	0.0319	0.1028	0.1746	0.2023	0.1789	0.1272	0.0746	0.0365	0.0148
	6	0.0003	0.0089	0.0454	0.1091	0.1686	0.1916	0.1712	0.1244	0.0746	0.0370
	7	0.0000	0.0020	0.0160	0.0545	0.1124	0.1643	0.1844	0.1659	0.1221	0.0739
	8	0.0000	0.0004	0.0046	0.0222	0.0609	0.1144	0.1614	0.1797	0.1623	0.1201
	9	0.0000	0.0001	0.0011	0.0074	0.0271	0.0654	0.1158	0.1597	0.1771	0.1602
	10	0.0000	0.0000	0.0002	0.0020	0.0099	0.0308	0.0686	0.1171	0.1593	0.1762
	11	0.0000	0.0000	0.0000	0.0005	0.0030	0.0120	0.0336	0.0710	0.1185	0.1602
	12	0.0000	0.0000	0.0000	0.0001	0.0008	0.0039	0.0136	0.0355	0.0727	0.1201
	13	0.0000	0.0000	0.0000	0.0000	0.0002	0.0010	0.0045	0.0146	0.0366	0.0739
	14	0.0000	0.0000	0.0000	0.0000	0.0000	0.0002	0.0012	0.0049	0.0150	0.0370
	15	0.0000	0.0000	0.0000	0.0000	0.0000	0.0000	0.0003	0.0013	0.0049	0.0148
	16	0.0000	0.0000	0.0000	0.0000	0.0000	0.0000	0.0000	0.0003	0.0013	0.0046
	17	0.0000	0.0000	0.0000	0.0000	0.0000	0.0000	0.0000	0.0000	0.0002	0.0011
	18	0.0000	0.0000	0.0000	0.0000	0.0000	0.0000	0.0000	0.0000	0.0000	0.0002
	19	0.0000	0.0000	0.0000	0.0000	0.0000	0.0000	0.0000	0.0000	0.0000	0.0000
	20	0.0000	0.0000	0.0000	0.0000	0.0000	0.0000	0.0000	0.0000	0.0000	0.0000

Binomial Probabilities (*Continued*)

n	x	0.55	0.60	0.65	0.70	0.75	0.80	0.85	0.90	0.95
2	0	0.2025	0.1600	0.1225	0.0900	0.0625	0.0400	0.0225	0.0100	0.0025
	1	0.4950	0.4800	0.4550	0.4200	0.3750	0.3200	0.2550	0.1800	0.0950
	2	0.3025	0.3600	0.4225	0.4900	0.5625	0.6400	0.7225	0.8100	0.9025
3	0	0.0911	0.0640	0.0429	0.0270	0.0156	0.0080	0.0034	0.0010	0.0001
	1	0.3341	0.2880	0.2389	0.1890	0.1406	0.0960	0.0574	0.0270	0.0071
	2	0.4084	0.4320	0.4436	0.4410	0.4219	0.3840	0.3251	0.2430	0.1354
	3	0.1664	0.2160	0.2746	0.3430	0.4219	0.5120	0.6141	0.7290	0.8574
4	0	0.0410	0.0256	0.0150	0.0081	0.0039	0.0016	0.0005	0.0001	0.0000
	1	0.2005	0.1536	0.1115	0.0756	0.0469	0.0256	0.0115	0.0036	0.0005
	2	0.3675	0.3456	0.3105	0.2646	0.2109	0.1536	0.0975	0.0486	0.0135
	3	0.2995	0.3456	0.3845	0.4116	0.4219	0.4096	0.3685	0.2916	0.1715
	4	0.0915	0.1296	0.1785	0.2401	0.3164	0.4096	0.5220	0.6561	0.8145
5	0	0.0185	0.0102	0.0053	0.0024	0.0010	0.0003	0.0001	0.0000	0.0000
	1	0.1128	0.0768	0.0488	0.0284	0.0146	0.0064	0.0022	0.0005	0.0000
	2	0.2757	0.2304	0.1811	0.1323	0.0879	0.0512	0.0244	0.0081	0.0011
	3	0.3369	0.3456	0.3364	0.3087	0.2637	0.2048	0.1382	0.0729	0.0214
	4	0.2059	0.2592	0.3124	0.3601	0.3955	0.4096	0.3915	0.3281	0.2036
	5	0.0503	0.0778	0.1160	0.1681	0.2373	0.3277	0.4437	0.5905	0.7738
6	0	0.0083	0.0041	0.0018	0.0007	0.0002	0.0001	0.0000	0.0000	0.0000
	1	0.0609	0.0369	0.0205	0.0102	0.0044	0.0015	0.0004	0.0001	0.0000
	2	0.1861	0.1382	0.0951	0.0595	0.0330	0.0154	0.0055	0.0012	0.0001
	3	0.3032	0.2765	0.2355	0.1852	0.1318	0.0819	0.0415	0.0146	0.0021
	4	0.2780	0.3110	0.3280	0.3241	0.2966	0.2458	0.1762	0.0984	0.0305
	5	0.1359	0.1866	0.2437	0.3025	0.3560	0.3932	0.3993	0.3543	0.2321
	6	0.0277	0.0467	0.0754	0.1176	0.1780	0.2621	0.3771	0.5314	0.7351
7	0	0.0037	0.0016	0.0006	0.0002	0.0001	0.0000	0.0000	0.0000	0.0000
	1	0.0320	0.0172	0.0084	0.0036	0.0013	0.0004	0.0001	0.0000	0.0000
	2	0.1172	0.0774	0.0466	0.0250	0.0115	0.0043	0.0012	0.0002	0.0000
	3	0.2388	0.1935	0.1442	0.0972	0.0577	0.0287	0.0109	0.0026	0.0002
	4	0.2918	0.2903	0.2679	0.2269	0.1730	0.1147	0.0617	0.0230	0.0036
	5	0.2140	0.2613	0.2985	0.3177	0.3115	0.2753	0.2097	0.1240	0.0406
	6	0.0872	0.1306	0.1848	0.2471	0.3115	0.3670	0.3960	0.3720	0.2573
	7	0.0152	0.0280	0.0490	0.0824	0.1335	0.2097	0.3206	0.4783	0.6983
8	0	0.0017	0.0007	0.0002	0.0001	0.0000	0.0000	0.0000	0.0000	0.0000
	1	0.0164	0.0079	0.0033	0.0012	0.0004	0.0001	0.0000	0.0000	0.0000
	2	0.0703	0.0413	0.0217	0.0100	0.0038	0.0011	0.0002	0.0000	0.0000
	3	0.1719	0.1239	0.0808	0.0467	0.0231	0.0092	0.0026	0.0004	0.0000
	4	0.2627	0.2322	0.1875	0.1361	0.0865	0.0459	0.0185	0.0046	0.0004
	5	0.2568	0.2787	0.2786	0.2541	0.2076	0.1468	0.0839	0.0331	0.0054
	6	0.1569	0.2090	0.2587	0.2965	0.3115	0.2936	0.2376	0.1488	0.0515
	7	0.0548	0.0896	0.1373	0.1977	0.2670	0.3355	0.3847	0.3826	0.2793
	8	0.0084	0.0168	0.0319	0.0576	0.1001	0.1678	0.2725	0.4305	0.6634

Binomial Probabilities (*Continued*)

n	x	0.55	0.60	0.65	0.70	0.75	0.80	0.85	0.90	0.95
9	0	0.0008	0.0003	0.0001	0.0000	0.0000	0.0000	0.0000	0.0000	0.0000
	1	0.0083	0.0035	0.0013	0.0004	0.0001	0.0000	0.0000	0.0000	0.0000
	2	0.0407	0.0212	0.0098	0.0039	0.0012	0.0003	0.0000	0.0000	0.0000
	3	0.1160	0.0743	0.0424	0.0210	0.0087	0.0028	0.0006	0.0001	0.0000
	4	0.2128	0.1672	0.1181	0.0735	0.0389	0.0165	0.0050	0.0008	0.0000
	5	0.2600	0.2508	0.2194	0.1715	0.1168	0.0661	0.0283	0.0074	0.0006
	6	0.2119	0.2508	0.2716	0.2668	0.2336	0.1762	0.1069	0.0446	0.0077
	7	0.1110	0.1612	0.2162	0.2668	0.3003	0.3020	0.2597	0.1722	0.0629
	8	0.0339	0.0605	0.1004	0.1556	0.2253	0.3020	0.3679	0.3874	0.2985
	9	0.0046	0.0101	0.0207	0.0404	0.0751	0.1342	0.2316	0.3874	0.6302
10	0	0.0003	0.0001	0.0000	0.0000	0.0000	0.0000	0.0000	0.0000	0.0000
	1	0.0042	0.0016	0.0005	0.0001	0.0000	0.0000	0.0000	0.0000	0.0000
	2	0.0229	0.0106	0.0043	0.0014	0.0004	0.0001	0.0000	0.0000	0.0000
	3	0.0746	0.0425	0.0212	0.0090	0.0031	0.0008	0.0001	0.0000	0.0000
	4	0.1596	0.1115	0.0689	0.0368	0.0162	0.0055	0.0012	0.0001	0.0000
	5	0.2340	0.2007	0.1536	0.1029	0.0584	0.0264	0.0085	0.0015	0.0001
	6	0.2384	0.2508	0.2377	0.2001	0.1460	0.0881	0.0401	0.0112	0.0010
	7	0.1665	0.2150	0.2522	0.2668	0.2503	0.2013	0.1298	0.0574	0.0105
	8	0.0763	0.1209	0.1757	0.2335	0.2816	0.3020	0.2759	0.1937	0.0746
	9	0.0207	0.0403	0.0725	0.1211	0.1877	0.2684	0.3474	0.3874	0.3151
	10	0.0025	0.0060	0.0135	0.0282	0.0563	0.1074	0.1969	0.3487	0.5987
12	0	0.0001	0.0000	0.0000	0.0000	0.0000	0.0000	0.0000	0.0000	0.0000
	1	0.0010	0.0003	0.0001	0.0000	0.0000	0.0000	0.0000	0.0000	0.0000
	2	0.0068	0.0025	0.0008	0.0002	0.0000	0.0000	0.0000	0.0000	0.0000
	3	0.0277	0.0125	0.0048	0.0015	0.0004	0.0001	0.0000	0.0000	0.0000
	4	0.0762	0.0420	0.0199	0.0078	0.0024	0.0005	0.0001	0.0000	0.0000
	5	0.1489	0.1009	0.0591	0.0291	0.0115	0.0033	0.0006	0.0000	0.0000
	6	0.2124	0.1766	0.1281	0.0792	0.0401	0.0155	0.0040	0.0005	0.0000
	7	0.2225	0.2270	0.2039	0.1585	0.1032	0.0532	0.0193	0.0038	0.0002
	8	0.1700	0.2128	0.2367	0.2311	0.1936	0.1329	0.0683	0.0213	0.0021
	9	0.0923	0.1419	0.1954	0.2397	0.2581	0.2362	0.1720	0.0852	0.0173
	10	0.0339	0.0639	0.1088	0.1678	0.2323	0.2835	0.2924	0.2301	0.0988
	11	0.0075	0.0174	0.0368	0.0712	0.1267	0.2062	0.3012	0.3766	0.3413
	12	0.0008	0.0022	0.0057	0.0138	0.0317	0.0687	0.1422	0.2824	0.5404
15	0	0.0000	0.0000	0.0000	0.0000	0.0000	0.0000	0.0000	0.0000	0.0000
	1	0.0001	0.0000	0.0000	0.0000	0.0000	0.0000	0.0000	0.0000	0.0000
	2	0.0010	0.0003	0.0001	0.0000	0.0000	0.0000	0.0000	0.0000	0.0000
	3	0.0052	0.0016	0.0004	0.0001	0.0000	0.0000	0.0000	0.0000	0.0000
	4	0.0191	0.0074	0.0024	0.0006	0.0001	0.0000	0.0000	0.0000	0.0000
	5	0.0515	0.0245	0.0096	0.0030	0.0007	0.0001	0.0000	0.0000	0.0000
	6	0.1048	0.0612	0.0298	0.0116	0.0034	0.0007	0.0001	0.0000	0.0000
	7	0.1647	0.1181	0.0710	0.0348	0.0131	0.0035	0.0005	0.0000	0.0000
	8	0.2013	0.1771	0.1319	0.0811	0.0393	0.0138	0.0030	0.0003	0.0000
	9	0.1914	0.2066	0.1906	0.1472	0.0917	0.0430	0.0132	0.0019	0.0000
	10	0.1404	0.1859	0.2123	0.2061	0.1651	0.1032	0.0449	0.0105	0.0006

Binomial Probabilities (*Continued*)

n	x	0.55	0.60	0.65	0.70	0.75	0.80	0.85	0.90	0.95
						p				
	11	0.0780	0.1268	0.1792	0.2186	0.2252	0.1876	0.1156	0.0428	0.0049
	12	0.0318	0.0634	0.1110	0.1700	0.2252	0.2501	0.2184	0.1285	0.0307
	13	0.0090	0.0219	0.0476	0.0916	0.1559	0.2309	0.2856	0.2669	0.1348
	14	0.0016	0.0047	0.0126	0.0305	0.0668	0.1319	0.2312	0.3432	0.3658
	15	0.0001	0.0005	0.0016	0.0047	0.0134	0.0352	0.0874	0.2059	0.4633
18	0	0.0000	0.0000	0.0000	0.0000	0.0000	0.0000	0.0000	0.0000	0.0000
	1	0.0000	0.0000	0.0000	0.0000	0.0000	0.0000	0.0000	0.0000	0.0000
	2	0.0001	0.0000	0.0000	0.0000	0.0000	0.0000	0.0000	0.0000	0.0000
	3	0.0009	0.0002	0.0000	0.0000	0.0000	0.0000	0.0000	0.0000	0.0000
	4	0.0039	0.0011	0.0002	0.0000	0.0000	0.0000	0.0000	0.0000	0.0000
	5	0.0134	0.0045	0.0012	0.0002	0.0000	0.0000	0.0000	0.0000	0.0000
	6	0.0354	0.0145	0.0047	0.0012	0.0002	0.0000	0.0000	0.0000	0.0000
	7	0.0742	0.0374	0.0151	0.0046	0.0010	0.0001	0.0000	0.0000	0.0000
	8	0.1248	0.0771	0.0385	0.0149	0.0042	0.0008	0.0001	0.0000	0.0000
	9	0.1694	0.1284	0.0794	0.0386	0.0139	0.0033	0.0004	0.0000	0.0000
	10	0.1864	0.1734	0.1327	0.0811	0.0376	0.0120	0.0022	0.0002	0.0000
	11	0.1657	0.1892	0.1792	0.1376	0.0820	0.0350	0.0091	0.0010	0.0000
	12	0.1181	0.1655	0.1941	0.1873	0.1436	0.0816	0.0301	0.0052	0.0002
	13	0.0666	0.1146	0.1664	0.2017	0.1988	0.1507	0.0787	0.0218	0.0014
	14	0.0291	0.0614	0.1104	0.1681	0.2130	0.2153	0.1592	0.0700	0.0093
	15	0.0095	0.0246	0.0547	0.1046	0.1704	0.2297	0.2406	0.1680	0.0473
	16	0.0022	0.0069	0.0190	0.0458	0.0958	0.1723	0.2556	0.2835	0.1683
	17	0.0003	0.0012	0.0042	0.0126	0.0338	0.0811	0.1704	0.3002	0.3763
	18	0.0000	0.0001	0.0004	0.0016	0.0056	0.0180	0.0536	0.1501	0.3972
20	0	0.0000	0.0000	0.0000	0.0000	0.0000	0.0000	0.0000	0.0000	0.0000
	1	0.0000	0.0000	0.0000	0.0000	0.0000	0.0000	0.0000	0.0000	0.0000
	2	0.0000	0.0000	0.0000	0.0000	0.0000	0.0000	0.0000	0.0000	0.0000
	3	0.0002	0.0000	0.0000	0.0000	0.0000	0.0000	0.0000	0.0000	0.0000
	4	0.0013	0.0003	0.0000	0.0000	0.0000	0.0000	0.0000	0.0000	0.0000
	5	0.0049	0.0013	0.0003	0.0000	0.0000	0.0000	0.0000	0.0000	0.0000
	6	0.0150	0.0049	0.0012	0.0002	0.0000	0.0000	0.0000	0.0000	0.0000
	7	0.0366	0.0146	0.0045	0.0010	0.0002	0.0000	0.0000	0.0000	0.0000
	8	0.0727	0.0355	0.0136	0.0039	0.0008	0.0001	0.0000	0.0000	0.0000
	9	0.1185	0.0710	0.0336	0.0120	0.0030	0.0005	0.0000	0.0000	0.0000
	10	0.1593	0.1171	0.0686	0.0308	0.0099	0.0020	0.0002	0.0000	0.0000
	11	0.1771	0.1597	0.1158	0.0654	0.0271	0.0074	0.0011	0.0001	0.0000
	12	0.1623	0.1797	0.1614	0.1144	0.0609	0.0222	0.0046	0.0004	0.0000
	13	0.1221	0.1659	0.1844	0.1643	0.1124	0.0545	0.0160	0.0020	0.0000
	14	0.0746	0.1244	0.1712	0.1916	0.1686	0.1091	0.0454	0.0089	0.0003
	15	0.0365	0.0746	0.1272	0.1789	0.2023	0.1746	0.1028	0.0319	0.0022
	16	0.0139	0.0350	0.0738	0.1304	0.1897	0.2182	0.1821	0.0898	0.0133
	17	0.0040	0.0123	0.0323	0.0716	0.1339	0.2054	0.2428	0.1901	0.0596
	18	0.0008	0.0031	0.0100	0.0278	0.0669	0.1369	0.2293	0.2852	0.1887
	19	0.0001	0.0005	0.0020	0.0068	0.0211	0.0576	0.1368	0.2702	0.3774
	20	0.0000	0.0000	0.0002	0.0008	0.0032	0.0115	0.0388	0.1216	0.3585

Entries in the following table give the probability of x occurrences for a Poisson process with a mean λ. For example, when $\lambda = 2.5$, the probability of $x = 4$ occurrences is 0.1336.

	λ									
x	0.1	0.2	0.3	0.4	0.5	0.6	0.7	0.8	0.9	1.0
0	0.9048	0.8187	0.7408	0.6703	0.6065	0.5488	0.4966	0.4493	0.4066	0.3679
1	0.0905	0.1637	0.2222	0.2681	0.3033	0.3293	0.3476	0.3595	0.3659	0.3679
2	0.0045	0.0164	0.0333	0.0536	0.0758	0.0988	0.1217	0.1438	0.1647	0.1839
3	0.0002	0.0011	0.0033	0.0072	0.0126	0.0198	0.0284	0.0383	0.0494	0.0613
4	0.0000	0.0001	0.0002	0.0007	0.0016	0.0030	0.0050	0.0077	0.0111	0.0153
5	0.0000	0.0000	0.0000	0.0001	0.0002	0.0004	0.0007	0.0012	0.0020	0.0031
6	0.0000	0.0000	0.0000	0.0000	0.0000	0.0000	0.0001	0.0002	0.0003	0.0005
7	0.0000	0.0000	0.0000	0.0000	0.0000	0.0000	0.0000	0.0000	0.0000	0.0001

	λ									
x	1.1	1.2	1.3	1.4	1.5	1.6	1.7	1.8	1.9	2.0
0	0.3329	0.3012	0.2725	0.2466	0.2231	0.2019	0.1827	0.1653	0.1496	0.1353
1	0.3662	0.3614	0.3543	0.3452	0.3347	0.3230	0.3106	0.2975	0.2842	0.2707
2	0.2014	0.2169	0.2303	0.2417	0.2510	0.2584	0.2640	0.2678	0.2700	0.2707
3	0.0738	0.0867	0.0998	0.1128	0.1255	0.1378	0.1496	0.1607	0.1710	0.1804
4	0.0203	0.0260	0.0324	0.0395	0.0471	0.0551	0.0636	0.0723	0.0812	0.0902
5	0.0045	0.0062	0.0084	0.0111	0.0141	0.0176	0.0216	0.0260	0.0309	0.0361
6	0.0008	0.0012	0.0018	0.0026	0.0035	0.0047	0.0061	0.0078	0.0098	0.0120
7	0.0001	0.0002	0.0003	0.0005	0.0008	0.0011	0.0015	0.0020	0.0027	0.0034
8	0.0000	0.0000	0.0001	0.0001	0.0001	0.0002	0.0003	0.0005	0.0006	0.0009
9	0.0000	0.0000	0.0000	0.0000	0.0000	0.0000	0.0001	0.0001	0.0001	0.0002

	λ									
x	2.1	2.2	2.3	2.4	2.5	2.6	2.7	2.8	2.9	3.0
0	0.1225	0.1108	0.1003	0.0907	0.0821	0.0743	0.0672	0.0608	0.0550	0.0498
1	0.2572	0.2438	0.2306	0.2177	0.2052	0.1931	0.1815	0.1703	0.1596	0.1494
2	0.2700	0.2681	0.2652	0.2613	0.2565	0.2510	0.2450	0.2384	0.2314	0.2240
3	0.1890	0.1966	0.2033	0.2090	0.2138	0.2176	0.2205	0.2225	0.2237	0.2240
4	0.0992	0.1082	0.1169	0.1254	0.1336	0.1414	0.1488	0.1557	0.1622	0.1680
5	0.0417	0.0476	0.0538	0.0602	0.0668	0.0735	0.0804	0.0872	0.0940	0.1008
6	0.0146	0.0174	0.0206	0.0241	0.0278	0.0319	0.0362	0.0407	0.0455	0.0540
7	0.0044	0.0055	0.0068	0.0083	0.0099	0.0118	0.0139	0.0163	0.0188	0.0216

Poisson Probabilities (*Continued*)

					λ					
x	2.1	2.2	2.3	2.4	2.5	2.6	2.7	2.8	2.9	3.0
8	0.0011	0.0015	0.0019	0.0025	0.0031	0.0038	0.0047	0.0057	0.0068	0.0081
9	0.0003	0.0004	0.0005	0.0007	0.0009	0.0011	0.0014	0.0018	0.0022	0.0027
10	0.0001	0.0001	0.0001	0.0002	0.0002	0.0003	0.0004	0.0005	0.0006	0.0008
11	0.0000	0.0000	0.0000	0.0000	0.0000	0.0001	0.0001	0.0001	0.0002	0.0002
12	0.0000	0.0000	0.0000	0.0000	0.0000	0.0000	0.0000	0.0000	0.0000	0.0001

					λ					
x	3.1	3.2	3.3	3.4	3.5	3.6	3.7	3.8	3.9	4.0
0	0.0450	0.0408	0.0369	0.0344	0.0302	0.0273	0.0247	0.0224	0.0202	0.0183
1	0.1397	0.1304	0.1217	0.1135	0.1057	0.0984	0.0915	0.0850	0.0789	0.0733
2	0.2165	0.2087	0.2008	0.1929	0.1850	0.1771	0.1692	0.1615	0.1539	0.1465
3	0.2237	0.2226	0.2209	0.2186	0.2158	0.2125	0.2087	0.2046	0.2001	0.1954
4	0.1734	0.1781	0.1823	0.1858	0.1888	0.1912	0.1931	0.1944	0.1951	0.1954
5	0.1075	0.1140	0.1203	0.1264	0.1322	0.1377	0.1429	0.1477	0.1522	0.1563
6	0.0555	0.0608	0.0662	0.0716	0.0771	0.0826	0.0881	0.0936	0.0989	0.1042
7	0.0246	0.0278	0.0312	0.0348	0.0385	0.0425	0.0466	0.0508	0.0551	0.0595
8	0.0095	0.0111	0.0129	0.0148	0.0169	0.0191	0.0215	0.0241	0.0269	0.0298
9	0.0033	0.0040	0.0047	0.0056	0.0066	0.0076	0.0089	0.0102	0.0116	0.0132
10	0.0010	0.0013	0.0016	0.0019	0.0023	0.0028	0.0033	0.0039	0.0045	0.0053
11	0.0003	0.0004	0.0005	0.0006	0.0007	0.0009	0.0011	0.0013	0.0016	0.0019
12	0.0001	0.0001	0.0001	0.0002	0.0002	0.0003	0.0003	0.0004	0.0005	0.0006
13	0.0000	0.0000	0.0000	0.0000	0.0001	0.0001	0.0001	0.0001	0.0002	0.0002
14	0.0000	0.0000	0.0000	0.0000	0.0000	0.0000	0.0000	0.0000	0.0000	0.0001

					λ					
x	4.1	4.2	4.3	4.4	4.5	4.6	4.7	4.8	4.9	5.0
0	0.0166	0.0150	0.0136	0.0123	0.0111	0.0101	0.0091	0.0082	0.0074	0.0067
1	0.0679	0.0630	0.0583	0.0540	0.0500	0.0462	0.0427	0.0395	0.0365	0.0337
2	0.1393	0.1323	0.1254	0.1188	0.1125	0.1063	0.1005	0.0948	0.0894	0.0842
3	0.1904	0.1852	0.1798	0.1743	0.1687	0.1631	0.1574	0.1517	0.1460	0.1404
4	0.1951	0.1944	0.1933	0.1917	0.1898	0.1875	0.1849	0.1820	0.1789	0.1755
5	0.1600	0.1633	0.1662	0.1687	0.1708	0.1725	0.1738	0.1747	0.1753	0.1755
6	0.1093	0.1143	0.1191	0.1237	0.1281	0.1323	0.1362	0.1398	0.1432	0.1462
7	0.0640	0.0686	0.0732	0.0778	0.0824	0.0869	0.0914	0.0959	0.1002	0.1044
8	0.0328	0.0360	0.0393	0.0428	0.0463	0.0500	0.0537	0.0575	0.0614	0.0653
9	0.0150	0.0168	0.0188	0.0209	0.0232	0.0255	0.0280	0.0307	0.0334	0.0363
10	0.0061	0.0071	0.0081	0.0092	0.0104	0.0118	0.0132	0.0147	0.0164	0.0181
11	0.0023	0.0027	0.0032	0.0037	0.0043	0.0049	0.0056	0.0064	0.0073	0.0082
12	0.0008	0.0009	0.0011	0.0014	0.0016	0.0019	0.0022	0.0026	0.0030	0.0034

Binomial Probabilities (*Continued*)

					λ					
x	4.1	4.2	4.3	4.4	4.5	4.6	4.7	4.8	4.9	5.0
13	0.0002	0.0003	0.0004	0.0005	0.0006	0.0007	0.0008	0.0009	0.0011	0.0013
14	0.0001	0.0001	0.0001	0.0001	0.0002	0.0002	0.0003	0.0003	0.0004	0.0005
15	0.0000	0.0000	0.0000	0.0000	0.0001	0.0001	0.0001	0.0001	0.0001	0.0002

					λ					
x	5.1	5.2	5.3	5.4	5.5	5.6	5.7	5.8	5.9	6.0
0	0.0061	0.0055	0.0050	0.0045	0.0041	0.0037	0.0033	0.0030	0.0027	0.0025
1	0.0311	0.0287	0.0265	0.0244	0.0225	0.0207	0.0191	0.0176	0.0162	0.0149
2	0.0793	0.0746	0.0701	0.0659	0.0618	0.0580	0.0544	0.0509	0.0477	0.0446
3	0.1348	0.1293	0.1239	0.1185	0.1133	0.1082	0.1033	0.0985	0.0938	0.0892
4	0.1719	0.1681	0.1641	0.1600	0.1558	0.1515	0.1472	0.1428	0.1383	0.1339
5	0.1753	0.1748	0.1740	0.1728	0.1714	0.1697	0.1678	0.1656	0.1632	0.1606
6	0.1490	0.1515	0.1537	0.1555	0.1571	0.1587	0.1594	0.1601	0.1605	0.1606
7	0.1086	0.1125	0.1163	0.1200	0.1234	0.1267	0.1298	0.1326	0.1353	0.1377
8	0.0692	0.0731	0.0771	0.0810	0.0849	0.0887	0.0925	0.0962	0.0998	0.1033
9	0.0392	0.0423	0.0454	0.0486	0.0519	0.0552	0.0586	0.0620	0.0654	0.0688
10	0.0200	0.0220	0.0241	0.0262	0.0285	0.0309	0.0334	0.0359	0.0386	0.0413
11	0.0093	0.0104	0.0116	0.0129	0.0143	0.0157	0.0173	0.0190	0.0207	0.0225
12	0.0039	0.0045	0.0051	0.0058	0.0065	0.0073	0.0082	0.0092	0.0102	0.0113
13	0.0015	0.0018	0.0021	0.0024	0.0028	0.0032	0.0036	0.0041	0.0046	0.0052
14	0.0006	0.0007	0.0008	0.0009	0.0011	0.0013	0.0015	0.0017	0.0019	0.0022
15	0.0002	0.0002	0.0003	0.0003	0.0004	0.0005	0.0006	0.0007	0.0008	0.0009
16	0.0001	0.0001	0.0001	0.0001	0.0001	0.0002	0.0002	0.0002	0.0003	0.0003
17	0.0000	0.0000	0.0000	0.0000	0.0000	0.0001	0.0001	0.0001	0.0001	0.0001

					λ					
x	6.1	6.2	6.3	6.4	6.5	6.6	6.7	6.8	6.9	7.0
0	0.0022	0.0020	0.0018	0.0017	0.0015	0.0014	0.0012	0.0011	0.0010	0.0009
1	0.0137	0.0126	0.0116	0.0106	0.0098	0.0090	0.0082	0.0076	0.0070	0.0064
2	0.0417	0.0390	0.0364	0.0340	0.0318	0.0296	0.0276	0.0258	0.0240	0.0223
3	0.0848	0.0806	0.0765	0.0726	0.0688	0.0652	0.0617	0.0584	0.0552	0.0521
4	0.1294	0.1249	0.1205	0.1162	0.1118	0.1076	0.1034	0.0992	0.0952	0.0912
5	0.1579	0.1549	0.1519	0.1487	0.1454	0.1420	0.1385	0.1349	0.1314	0.1277
6	0.1605	0.1601	0.1595	0.1586	0.1575	0.1562	0.1546	0.1529	0.1511	0.1490
7	0.1399	0.1418	0.1435	0.1450	0.1462	0.1472	0.1480	0.1486	0.1489	0.1490
8	0.1066	0.1099	0.1130	0.1160	0.1188	0.1215	0.1240	0.1263	0.1284	0.1304
9	0.0723	0.0757	0.0791	0.0825	0.0858	0.0891	0.0923	0.0954	0.0985	0.1014
10	0.0441	0.0469	0.0498	0.0528	0.0558	0.0588	0.0618	0.0649	0.0679	0.0710
11	0.0245	0.0265	0.0285	0.0307	0.0330	0.0353	0.0377	0.0401	0.0426	0.0452

Poisson Probabilities (*Continued*)

λ

x	6.1	6.2	6.3	6.4	6.5	6.6	6.7	6.8	6.9	7.0
12	0.0124	0.0137	0.0150	0.0164	0.0179	0.0194	0.0210	0.0227	0.0245	0.0264
13	0.0058	0.0065	0.0073	0.0081	0.0089	0.0098	0.0108	0.0119	0.0130	0.0142
14	0.0025	0.0029	0.0033	0.0037	0.0041	0.0046	0.0052	0.0058	0.0064	0.0071
15	0.0010	0.0012	0.0014	0.0016	0.0018	0.0020	0.0023	0.0025	0.0029	0.0033
16	0.0004	0.0005	0.0005	0.0006	0.0007	0.0008	0.0010	0.0011	0.0013	0.0014
17	0.0001	0.0002	0.0002	0.0002	0.0003	0.0003	0.0004	0.0004	0.0005	0.0006
18	0.0000	0.0001	0.0001	0.0001	0.0001	0.0001	0.0001	0.0002	0.0002	0.0002
19	0.0000	0.0000	0.0000	0.0000	0.0000	0.0000	0.0000	0.0001	0.0001	0.0001

λ

x	7.1	7.2	7.3	7.4	7.5	7.6	7.7	7.8	7.9	8.0
0	0.0008	0.0007	0.0007	0.0006	0.0006	0.0005	0.0005	0.0004	0.0004	0.0003
1	0.0059	0.0054	0.0049	0.0045	0.0041	0.0038	0.0035	0.0032	0.0029	0.0027
2	0.0208	0.0194	0.0180	0.0167	0.0156	0.0145	0.0134	0.0125	0.0116	0.0107
3	0.0492	0.0464	0.0438	0.0413	0.0389	0.0366	0.0345	0.0324	0.0305	0.0286
4	0.0874	0.0836	0.0799	0.0764	0.0729	0.0696	0.0663	0.0632	0.0602	0.0573
5	0.1241	0.1204	0.1167	0.1130	0.1094	0.1057	0.1021	0.0986	0.0951	0.0916
6	0.1468	0.1445	0.1420	0.1394	0.1367	0.1339	0.1311	0.1282	0.1252	0.1221
7	0.1489	0.1486	0.1481	0.1474	0.1465	0.1454	0.1442	0.1428	0.1413	0.1396
8	0.1321	0.1337	0.1351	0.1363	0.1373	0.1382	0.1388	0.1392	0.1395	0.1396
9	0.1042	0.1070	0.1096	0.1121	0.1144	0.1167	0.1187	0.1207	0.1224	0.1241
10	0.0740	0.0770	0.0800	0.0829	0.0858	0.0887	0.0914	0.0941	0.0967	0.0993
11	0.0478	0.0504	0.0531	0.0558	0.0585	0.0613	0.0640	0.0667	0.0695	0.0722
12	0.0283	0.0303	0.0323	0.0344	0.0366	0.0388	0.0411	0.0434	0.0457	0.0481
13	0.0154	0.0168	0.0181	0.0196	0.0211	0.0227	0.0243	0.0260	0.0278	0.0296
14	0.0078	0.0086	0.0095	0.0104	0.0113	0.0123	0.0134	0.0145	0.0157	0.0169
15	0.0037	0.0041	0.0046	0.0051	0.0057	0.0062	0.0069	0.0075	0.0083	0.0090
16	0.0016	0.0019	0.0021	0.0024	0.0026	0.0030	0.0033	0.0037	0.0041	0.0045
17	0.0007	0.0008	0.0009	0.0010	0.0012	0.0013	0.0015	0.0017	0.0019	0.0021
18	0.0003	0.0003	0.0004	0.0004	0.0005	0.0006	0.0006	0.0007	0.0008	0.0009
19	0.0001	0.0001	0.0001	0.0002	0.0002	0.0002	0.0003	0.0003	0.0003	0.0004
20	0.0000	0.0000	0.0001	0.0001	0.0001	0.0001	0.0001	0.0001	0.0001	0.0002
21	0.0000	0.0000	0.0000	0.0000	0.0000	0.0000	0.0000	0.0000	0.0001	0.0001

λ

x	8.1	8.2	8.3	8.4	8.5	8.6	8.7	8.8	8.9	9.0
0	0.0003	0.0003	0.0002	0.0002	0.0002	0.0002	0.0002	0.0002	0.0001	0.0001
1	0.0025	0.0023	0.0021	0.0019	0.0017	0.0016	0.0014	0.0013	0.0012	0.0011
2	0.0100	0.0092	0.0086	0.0079	0.0074	0.0068	0.0063	0.0058	0.0054	0.0050

Poisson Probabilities (*Continued*)

| | | | | | λ | | | | | |
x	8.1	8.2	8.3	8.4	8.5	8.6	8.7	8.8	8.9	9.0
3	0.0269	0.0252	0.0237	0.0222	0.0208	0.0195	0.0183	0.0171	0.0160	0.0150
4	0.0544	0.0517	0.0491	0.0466	0.0443	0.0420	0.0398	0.0377	0.0357	0.0337
5	0.0882	0.0849	0.0816	0.0784	0.0752	0.0722	0.0692	0.0663	0.0635	0.0607
6	0.1191	0.1160	0.1128	0.1097	0.1066	0.1034	0.1003	0.0972	0.0941	0.0911
7	0.1378	0.1358	0.1338	0.1317	0.1294	0.1271	0.1247	0.1222	0.1197	0.1171
8	0.1395	0.1392	0.1388	0.1382	0.1375	0.1366	0.1356	0.1344	0.1332	0.1318
9	0.1256	0.1269	0.1280	0.1290	0.1299	0.1306	0.1311	0.1315	0.1317	0.1318
10	0.1017	0.1040	0.1063	0.1084	0.1104	0.1123	0.1140	0.1157	0.1172	0.1186
11	0.0749	0.0776	0.0802	0.0828	0.0853	0.0878	0.0902	0.0925	0.0948	0.0970
12	0.0505	0.0530	0.0555	0.0579	0.0604	0.0629	0.0654	0.0679	0.0703	0.0728
13	0.0315	0.0334	0.0354	0.0374	0.0395	0.0416	0.0438	0.0459	0.0481	0.0504
14	0.0182	0.0196	0.0210	0.0225	0.0240	0.0256	0.0272	0.0289	0.0306	0.0324
15	0.0098	0.0107	0.0116	0.0126	0.0136	0.0147	0.0158	0.0169	0.0182	0.1094
16	0.0050	0.0055	0.0060	0.0066	0.0072	0.0079	0.0086	0.0093	0.0101	0.0109
17	0.0024	0.0026	0.0029	0.0033	0.0036	0.0040	0.0044	0.0048	0.0053	0.0058
18	0.0011	0.0012	0.0014	0.0015	0.0017	0.0019	0.0021	0.0024	0.0026	0.0029
19	0.0005	0.0005	0.0006	0.0007	0.0008	0.0009	0.0010	0.0011	0.0012	0.0014
20	0.0002	0.0002	0.0002	0.0003	0.0003	0.0004	0.0004	0.0005	0.0005	0.0006
21	0.0001	0.0001	0.0001	0.0001	0.0001	0.0002	0.0002	0.0002	0.0002	0.0003
22	0.0000	0.0000	0.0000	0.0000	0.0001	0.0001	0.0001	0.0001	0.0001	0.0001

| | | | | | λ | | | | | |
x	9.1	9.2	9.3	9.4	9.5	9.6	9.7	9.8	9.9	10
0	0.0001	0.0001	0.0001	0.0001	0.0001	0.0001	0.0001	0.0001	0.0001	0.0000
1	0.0010	0.0009	0.0009	0.0008	0.0007	0.0007	0.0006	0.0005	0.0005	0.0005
2	0.0046	0.0043	0.0040	0.0037	0.0034	0.0031	0.0029	0.0027	0.0025	0.0023
3	0.0140	0.0131	0.0123	0.0115	0.0107	0.0100	0.0093	0.0087	0.0081	0.0076
4	0.0319	0.0302	0.0285	0.0269	0.0254	0.0240	0.0226	0.0213	0.0201	0.0189
5	0.0581	0.0555	0.0530	0.0506	0.0483	0.0460	0.0439	0.0418	0.0398	0.0378
6	0.0881	0.0851	0.0822	0.0793	0.0764	0.0736	0.0709	0.0682	0.0656	0.0631
7	0.1145	0.1118	0.1091	0.1064	0.1037	0.1010	0.0982	0.0955	0.0928	0.0901
8	0.1302	0.1286	0.1269	0.1251	0.1232	0.1212	0.1191	0.1170	0.1148	0.1126
9	0.1317	0.1315	0.1311	0.1306	0.1300	0.1293	0.1284	0.1274	0.1263	0.1251
10	0.1198	0.1210	0.1219	0.1228	0.1235	0.1241	0.1245	0.1249	0.1250	0.1251
11	0.0991	0.1012	0.1031	0.1049	0.1067	0.1083	0.1098	0.1112	0.1125	0.1137
12	0.0752	0.0776	0.0799	0.0822	0.0844	0.0866	0.0888	0.0908	0.0928	0.0948
13	0.0526	0.0549	0.0572	0.0594	0.0617	0.0640	0.0662	0.0685	0.0707	0.0729
14	0.0342	0.0361	0.0380	0.0399	0.0419	0.0439	0.0459	0.0479	0.0500	0.0521

Poisson Probabilities (*Continued*)

	λ									
x	9.1	9.2	9.3	9.4	9.5	9.6	9.7	9.8	9.9	10
15	0.0208	0.0221	0.0235	0.0250	0.0265	0.0281	0.0297	0.0313	0.0330	0.0347
16	0.0118	0.0127	0.0137	0.0147	0.0157	0.0168	0.0180	0.0192	0.0204	0.0217
17	0.0063	0.0069	0.0075	0.0081	0.0088	0.0095	0.0103	0.0111	0.0119	0.0128
18	0.0032	0.0035	0.0039	0.0042	0.0046	0.0051	0.0055	0.0060	0.0065	0.0071
19	0.0015	0.0017	0.0019	0.0021	0.0023	0.0026	0.0028	0.0031	0.0034	0.0027
20	0.0007	0.0008	0.0009	0.0010	0.0011	0.0012	0.0014	0.0015	0.0017	0.0019
21	0.0003	0.0003	0.0004	0.0004	0.0005	0.0006	0.0006	0.0007	0.0008	0.0009
22	0.0001	0.0001	0.0002	0.0002	0.0002	0.0002	0.0003	0.0003	0.0004	0.0004
23	0.0000	0.0001	0.0001	0.0001	0.0001	0.0001	0.0001	0.0001	0.0002	0.0002
24	0.0000	0.0000	0.0000	0.0000	0.0000	0.0000	0.0000	0.0001	0.0001	0.0001

	λ									
x	11	12	13	14	15	16	17	18	19	20
0	0.0000	0.0000	0.0000	0.0000	0.0000	0.0000	0.0000	0.0000	0.0000	0.0000
1	0.0002	0.0001	0.0000	0.0000	0.0000	0.0000	0.0000	0.0000	0.0000	0.0000
2	0.0010	0.0004	0.0002	0.0001	0.0000	0.0000	0.0000	0.0000	0.0000	0.0000
3	0.0037	0.0018	0.0008	0.0004	0.0002	0.0001	0.0000	0.0000	0.0000	0.0000
4	0.0102	0.0053	0.0027	0.0013	0.0006	0.0003	0.0001	0.0001	0.0000	0.0000
5	0.0224	0.0127	0.0070	0.0037	0.0019	0.0010	0.0005	0.0002	0.0001	0.0001
6	0.0411	0.0255	0.0152	0.0087	0.0048	0.0026	0.0014	0.0007	0.0004	0.0002
7	0.0646	0.0437	0.0281	0.0174	0.0104	0.0060	0.0034	0.0018	0.0010	0.0005
8	0.0888	0.0655	0.0457	0.0304	0.0194	0.0120	0.0072	0.0042	0.0024	0.0013
9	0.1085	0.0874	0.0661	0.0473	0.0324	0.0213	0.0135	0.0083	0.0050	0.0029
10	0.1194	0.1048	0.0859	0.0663	0.0486	0.0341	0.0230	0.0150	0.0095	0.0058
11	0.1194	0.1144	0.1015	0.0844	0.0663	0.0496	0.0355	0.0245	0.0164	0.0106
12	0.1094	0.1144	0.1099	0.0984	0.0829	0.0661	0.0504	0.0368	0.0259	0.0176
13	0.0926	0.1056	0.1099	0.1060	0.0956	0.0814	0.0658	0.0509	0.0378	0.0271
14	0.0728	0.0905	0.1021	0.1060	0.1024	0.0930	0.0800	0.0655	0.0514	0.0387
15	0.0534	0.0724	0.0885	0.0989	0.1024	0.0992	0.0906	0.0786	0.0650	0.0516
16	0.0367	0.0543	0.0719	0.0866	0.0960	0.0992	0.0963	0.0884	0.0772	0.0646
17	0.0237	0.0383	0.0550	0.0713	0.0847	0.0934	0.0963	0.0936	0.0863	0.0760
18	0.0145	0.0256	0.0397	0.0554	0.0706	0.0830	0.0909	0.0936	0.0911	0.0844
19	0.0084	0.0161	0.0272	0.0409	0.0557	0.0699	0.0814	0.0887	0.0911	0.0888
20	0.0046	0.0097	0.0177	0.0286	0.0418	0.0559	0.0692	0.0798	0.0866	0.0888
21	0.0024	0.0055	0.0109	0.0191	0.0299	0.0426	0.0560	0.0684	0.0783	0.0846
22	0.0012	0.0030	0.0065	0.0121	0.0204	0.0310	0.0433	0.0560	0.0676	0.0769
23	0.0006	0.0016	0.0037	0.0074	0.0133	0.0216	0.0320	0.0438	0.0559	0.0669
24	0.0003	0.0008	0.0020	0.0043	0.0083	0.0144	0.0226	0.0328	0.0442	0.0557

Poisson Probabilities (*Continued*)

	λ									
x	11	12	13	14	15	16	17	18	19	20
25	0.0001	0.0004	0.0010	0.0024	0.0050	0.0092	0.0154	0.0237	0.0336	0.0446
26	0.0000	0.0002	0.0005	0.0013	0.0029	0.0057	0.0101	0.0164	0.0246	0.0343
27	0.0000	0.0001	0.0002	0.0007	0.0016	0.0034	0.0063	0.0109	0.0173	0.0254
28	0.0000	0.0000	0.0001	0.0003	0.0009	0.0019	0.0038	0.0070	0.0117	0.0181
29	0.0000	0.0000	0.0001	0.0002	0.0004	0.0011	0.0023	0.0044	0.0077	0.0125
30	0.0000	0.0000	0.0000	0.0001	0.0002	0.0006	0.0013	0.0026	0.0049	0.0083
31	0.0000	0.0000	0.0000	0.0000	0.0001	0.0003	0.0007	0.0015	0.0030	0.0054
32	0.0000	0.0000	0.0000	0.0000	0.0001	0.0001	0.0004	0.0009	0.0018	0.0034
33	0.0000	0.0000	0.0000	0.0000	0.0000	0.0001	0.0002	0.0005	0.0010	0.0020
34	0.0000	0.0000	0.0000	0.0000	0.0000	0.0000	0.0001	0.0002	0.0006	0.0012
35	0.0000	0.0000	0.0000	0.0000	0.0000	0.0000	0.0000	0.0001	0.0003	0.0007
36	0.0000	0.0000	0.0000	0.0000	0.0000	0.0000	0.0000	0.0001	0.0002	0.0004
37	0.0000	0.0000	0.0000	0.0000	0.0000	0.0000	0.0000	0.0000	0.0001	0.0002
38	0.0000	0.0000	0.0000	0.0000	0.0000	0.0000	0.0000	0.0000	0.0000	0.0001
39	0.0000	0.0000	0.0000	0.0000	0.0000	0.0000	0.0000	0.0000	0.0000	0.0001

APPENDIX C: AREAS FOR THE STANDARD NORMAL DISTRIBUTION

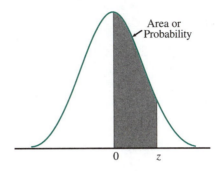

Entries in the following table give the area under the curve between the mean and z standard deviations above the mean. For example, for $z = 1.25$ the area under the curve between the mean and z is 0.3944.

z	0.00	0.01	0.02	0.03	0.04	0.05	0.06	0.07	0.08	0.09
0.0	0.0000	0.0040	0.0080	0.0120	0.0160	0.0199	0.0239	0.0279	0.0319	0.0359
0.1	0.0398	0.0438	0.0478	0.0517	0.0557	0.0596	0.0636	0.0675	0.0714	0.0753
0.2	0.0793	0.0832	0.0871	0.0910	0.0948	0.0987	0.1026	0.1064	0.1103	0.1141
0.3	0.1179	0.1217	0.1255	0.1293	0.1331	0.1368	0.1406	0.1443	0.1480	0.1517
0.4	0.1554	0.1591	0.1628	0.1664	0.1700	0.1736	0.1772	0.1808	0.1844	0.1879
0.5	0.1915	0.1950	0.1985	0.2019	0.2054	0.2088	0.2123	0.2157	0.2190	0.2224
0.6	0.2257	0.2291	0.2324	0.2357	0.2389	0.2422	0.2454	0.2486	0.2518	0.2549
0.7	0.2580	0.2612	0.2642	0.2673	0.2704	0.2734	0.2764	0.2794	0.2823	0.2852
0.8	0.2881	0.2910	0.2939	0.2967	0.2995	0.3023	0.3051	0.3078	0.3106	0.3133
0.9	0.3159	0.3186	0.3212	0.3238	0.3264	0.3289	0.3315	0.3340	0.3365	0.3389
1.0	0.3413	0.3438	0.3461	0.3485	0.3508	0.3531	0.3554	0.3577	0.3599	0.3621
1.1	0.3643	0.3665	0.3686	0.3708	0.3729	0.3749	0.3770	0.3790	0.3810	0.3830
1.2	0.3849	0.3869	0.3888	0.3907	0.3925	0.3944	0.3962	0.3980	0.3997	0.4015
1.3	0.4032	0.4049	0.4066	0.4082	0.4099	0.4115	0.4131	0.4147	0.4162	0.4177
1.4	0.4192	0.4207	0.4222	0.4236	0.4251	0.4265	0.4279	0.4292	0.4306	0.4319
1.5	0.4332	0.4345	0.4357	0.4370	0.4382	0.4394	0.4406	0.4418	0.4429	0.4441
1.6	0.4452	0.4463	0.4474	0.4484	0.4495	0.4505	0.4515	0.4525	0.4535	0.4545
1.7	0.4554	0.4564	0.4573	0.4582	0.4591	0.4599	0.4608	0.4616	0.4625	0.4633
1.8	0.4641	0.4649	0.4656	0.4664	0.4671	0.4678	0.4686	0.4693	0.4699	0.4706
1.9	0.4713	0.4719	0.4726	0.4732	0.4738	0.4744	0.4750	0.4756	0.4761	0.4767
2.0	0.4772	0.4778	0.4783	0.4788	0.4793	0.4798	0.4803	0.4808	0.4812	0.4817
2.1	0.4821	0.4826	0.4830	0.4834	0.4838	0.4842	0.4846	0.4850	0.4854	0.4857
2.2	0.4861	0.4864	0.4868	0.4871	0.4875	0.4878	0.4881	0.4884	0.4887	0.4890
2.3	0.4893	0.4896	0.4898	0.4901	0.4904	0.4906	0.4909	0.4911	0.4913	0.4916
2.4	0.4918	0.4920	0.4922	0.4925	0.4927	0.4929	0.4931	0.4932	0.4934	0.4936
2.5	0.4938	0.4940	0.4941	0.4943	0.4945	0.4946	0.4948	0.4949	0.4951	0.4952
2.6	0.4953	0.4955	0.4956	0.4957	0.4959	0.4960	0.4961	0.4962	0.4963	0.4964
2.7	0.4965	0.4966	0.4967	0.4968	0.4969	0.4970	0.4971	0.4972	0.4973	0.4974
2.8	0.4974	0.4975	0.4976	0.4977	0.4977	0.4978	0.4979	0.4979	0.4980	0.4981
2.9	0.4981	0.4982	0.4982	0.4983	0.4984	0.4984	0.4985	0.4985	0.4986	0.4986
3.0	0.4986	0.4987	0.4987	0.4988	0.4988	0.4989	0.4989	0.4989	0.4990	0.4990

λ	$e^{-\lambda}$	λ	$e^{-\lambda}$	λ	$e^{-\lambda}$
0.05	0.9512	2.05	0.1287	4.05	0.0174
0.10	0.9048	2.10	0.1225	4.10	0.0166
0.15	0.8607	2.15	0.1165	4.15	0.0158
0.20	0.8187	2.20	0.1108	4.20	0.0150
0.25	0.7788	2.25	0.1054	4.25	0.0143
0.30	0.7408	2.30	0.1003	4.30	0.0136
0.35	0.7047	2.35	0.0954	4.35	0.0129
0.40	0.6703	2.40	0.0907	4.40	0.0123
0.45	0.6376	2.45	0.0863	4.45	0.0117
0.50	0.6065	2.50	0.0821	4.50	0.0111
0.55	0.5769	2.55	0.0781	4.55	0.0106
0.60	0.5488	2.60	0.0743	4.60	0.0101
0.65	0.5220	2.65	0.0707	4.65	0.0096
0.70	0.4966	2.70	0.0672	4.70	0.0091
0.75	0.4724	2.75	0.0639	4.75	0.0087
0.80	0.4493	2.80	0.0608	4.80	0.0082
0.85	0.4274	2.85	0.0578	4.85	0.0078
0.90	0.4066	2.90	0.0550	4.90	0.0074
0.95	0.3867	2.95	0.0523	4.95	0.0071
1.00	0.3679	3.00	0.0498	5.00	0.0067
1.05	0.3499	3.05	0.0474	5.05	0.0064
1.10	0.3329	3.10	0.0450	5.10	0.0061
1.15	0.3166	3.15	0.0429	5.15	0.0058
1.20	0.3012	3.20	0.0408	5.20	0.0055
1.25	0.2865	3.25	0.0388	5.25	0.0052
1.30	0.2725	3.30	0.0369	5.30	0.0050
1.35	0.2592	3.35	0.0351	5.35	0.0047
1.40	0.2466	3.40	0.0334	5.40	0.0045
1.45	0.2346	3.45	0.0317	5.45	0.0043
1.50	0.2231	3.50	0.0302	5.50	0.0041
1.55	0.2122	3.55	0.0287	5.55	0.0039
1.60	0.2019	3.60	0.0273	5.60	0.0037
1.65	0.1920	3.65	0.0260	5.65	0.0035
1.70	0.1827	3.70	0.0247	5.70	0.0033
1.75	0.1738	3.75	0.0235	5.75	0.0032
1.80	0.1653	3.80	0.0224	5.80	0.0030
1.85	0.1572	3.85	0.0213	5.85	0.0029
1.90	0.1496	3.90	0.0202	5.90	0.0027
1.95	0.1423	3.95	0.0193	5.95	0.0026
2.00	0.1353	4.00	0.0183	6.00	0.0025
				7.00	0.0009
				8.00	0.000335
				9.00	0.000123
				10.00	0.000045

REFERENCES AND BIBLIOGRAPHY

Chapter 1   The Role and Nature of Quantitative Methods

Churchman, C. W., R. L. Ackoff, and E. L. Arnoff. *Introduction to Operations Research.* New York: John Wiley & Sons, 1957.

Forgionne, G. A. "Corporate Management Science Activities: An Update." *Interfaces* 13, 3 (1983): 20–23.

Hillier, F., and G. J., Lieberman. *Introduction to Operations Research,* 4th ed. San Francisco: Holden-Day, 1986.

Shannon, R. E., S. S. Long, and B. P. Buckles. "Operations Research Methodologies in Industrial Engineering: A Survey." *AIIE Transactions* 12, 4 (1980): 364–367.

Thomas, G., and J. DaCosta. "A Sample Survey of Corporate Operations Research." *Interfaces* (August 1979).

Thomas, G., and M. Mitchell. "OR in the U.S. Marine Corps: A Characterization." *Interfaces* (June 1983).

Chapters 2 and 3   Probability

Anderson, D. R., D. J. Sweeney, and T. A. Williams. *Statistics for Business and Economics.* 6th ed. Minneapolis/St. Paul: West Publishing, 1996.

Barr, D. R., and P. W. Zehna. *Probability: Modeling Uncertainty.* Reading, MA: Addison-Wesley, 1983.

Freund, J. E., and R. E. Walpole. *Mathematical Statistics.* 4th ed. Englewood Cliffs, NJ: Prentice-Hall, 1987.

Hogg, R. V., and Elliott A. Tanis. *Probability and Statistical Inference* 4th ed. New York: Macmillan, 1992.

Mendenhall, W., R. L. Scheaffer, and D. Wackerly. *Mathematical Statistics with Applications.* 4th ed. Boston: PWS-Kent, 1990.

Neter, J., W. Wasserman, and G. A. Whitmore. *Applied Statistics.* 4th ed. Boston: Allyn & Bacon, 1993.

Ross, S. M. *Introduction to Probability Models.* 5th ed. San Diego: Academic Press, 1993.

Chapters 4 and 5   Decision Analysis

Behn, R. D., and J. W. Vaupel. *Quick Analysis for Busy Decision Makers.* New York: Basic Books, 1982.

Berger, J. O. *Statistical Decision Theory and Bayesian Analysis.* 2d ed. New York: Springer-Verlag, 1985.

Bunn, D. *Applied Decision Analysis.* New York: McGraw-Hill, 1984.

Chernoff, H., and L. E. Moses. *Elementary Decision Theory.* New York: John Wiley & Sons, 1959.

Fishburn, P. C. "Foundations of Decision Analysis: Along the Way." *Management Science* 35, no. 4 (April 1989): 387–405.

French, S. *Decision Theory.* New York: John Wiley & Sons, 1986.

Keeney, R. L., and H. Raiffa. *Decisions with Multiple Objectives: Preferences and Value Trade Offs.* New York: John Wiley & Sons, 1976.

Raiffa, H. *Decision Analysis: Introductory Lectures on Choices Under Uncertainty.* Reading, Mass.: Addison-Wesley, 1968.

Samson, D. *Managerial Decision Analysis.* Homewood, Ill.: Richard D. Irwin, 1988.

Schlaifer, R. *Analysis of Decisions under Uncertainty.* New York: McGraw-Hill, 1969.

Winkler, R. L. *An Introduction to Bayesian Inference and Decision.* New York: Holt, Rinehart & Winston, 1972.

Winkler, R. L., and W. L. Hays. *Statistics: Probability, Inference and Decision.* 2d ed. New York: Holt, Rinehart & Winston, 1975.

Chapter 6   Forecasting

Bowerman, B. L., and R. T. O'Connell. *Time Series Forecasting,* 2nd ed. Boston: PWS-Kent, 1987.

Box, G. E. P., Jenkins, G. M., and Reinsel, G. C. *Time Series Analysis: Forecasting and Control.* 3rd ed. Englewood Cliffs, N.J.: Prentice-Hall, 1994.

Gilchrist, W. G. *Statistical Forecasting.* New York: John Wiley & Sons, 1976.

Hanke, J. E., and A. G. Reitsch. *Business Forecasting.* 2nd ed. Boston: Allyn & Bacon, 1986.

Makridakis, S., S. C. Wheelwright, and Victor E. McGee. *Forecasting: Methods and Applications.* 2nd ed. New York: John Wiley & Sons, 1983.

Nelson, C. R. *Applied Time Series Analysis.* San Francisco: Holden-Day, 1973.

Pankratz, A. *Forecasting with Univariate Box—Jenkins Models.* New York: John Wiley & Sons, 1983.

Sanders, N. R., and K. B. Manrodt. "Forecasting Practices in U.S. Corporations: Survey Results." *Interfaces* 24, no. 2 (1994): 92–100.

Thomopoulos, N. T. *Applied Forecasting Methods.* Englewood Cliffs, N.J.: Prentice-Hall, 1980.

Wheelwright, S. C., and S. Makridakis. *Forecasting Models for Management.* 4th ed. New York: John Wiley & Sons, 1985.

Wilson, J. H., and B. Keating. *Business Forecasting.* Homewood, Ill.: Richard D. Irwin, 1990.

Chapters 7 to 10 Linear Programming, Transportation, Assignment, and Transshipment Problems

Bazarra, M. S., and J. J. Jarvis, and H. D. Sherali. *Linear Programming and Network Flows*. 2nd ed. New York: John Wiley & Sons, 1990.

Bradley, S. P., A. C. Hax, and T. L. Magnanti. *Applied Mathematical Programming*. Reading, Mass.: Addison-Wesley, 1977.

Charnes, A., and W. W. Cooper, and E. Rhodes. "Measuring Efficiency of Decision Making Units." *European Journal of Operations Research* 2 (1978): 429–449.

Dantzig, G. B. *Linear Programming and Extensions*. Princeton, N.J.: Princeton University Press, 1963.

Greenberg, H. J. "How to Analyze the Results of Linear Programs—Part 1: Preliminaries." *Interfaces* 23, no. 4 (Jul–Aug 1993): 56–67.

Greenberg, H. J. "How to Analyze the Results of Linear Programs—Part 2: Price Interpretation." *Interfaces* 23, no. 5 (Sept–Oct 1993): 97–114.

Greenberg, H. J. "How to Analyze the Results of Linear Programs—Part 3: Infeasibility Diagnosis." *Interfaces* 23, no. 6 (Nov–Dec 1993): 120–139.

Hillier, F., and G. J. Lieberman. *Introduction to Operations Research*. 4th ed. San Francisco: Holden-Day, 1986.

Hooker, J. N. "Karmarkar's Linear Programming Algorithm." *Interfaces* 16, no. 4 (1986): 75–90.

Lewin, A. Y., and R. C. Morey. "Measuring the Relative Efficiency and Output Potential of Public Sector Organizations: An Application of Data Envelopment Analysis." *International Journal of Policy Analysis and Information Systems* 5, no. 4 (1981): 267–285.

Schrage, L. *LINDO: An Optimization Modeling System*. 4th ed. South San Francisco, Calif.: Scientific Press, 1986.

Schrage, L. *User's Manual for Linear, Integer, and Quadratic Programming with LINDO*. Redwood City, Calif.: Scientific Press, 1989.

Sherman, H. D. "Hospital Efficiency Measurement and Evaluation." *Medical Care* 22, no. 10 (October 1984): 922–938.

Winston, W. L. *Operations Research: Applications and Algorithms*. 3rd ed. Belmont, Calif.: Duxbury Press, 1994.

Chapter 11 Integer Linear Programming

Garfinkel, R. S., and G. L. Nemhause. *Integer Programming*. New York: John Wiley & Sons, 1972.

Nemhauser, G. L., and L. A. Wolsey. *Integer and Combinatorial Optimization*. New York: John Wiley & Sons, 1988.

Parker, G., and R. Rardin. *Discrete Optimization*. San Diego: Academic Press, 1988.

Salkin, H. M. *Integer Programming*. Reading, Mass.: Addison-Wesley, 1975.

Winston, W. L. *Operations Research: Applications and Algorithms*. 3rd ed. Belmont, Calif.: Duxbury Press, 1994.

Chapter 12 Project Scheduling: PERT/CPM

Evarts, H. F. *Introduction to PERT*. Boston: Allyn & Bacon, 1964.

Moder, J. J., and C. R. Phillips. *Project Management with CPM and PERT*. 2nd ed. New York: Van Nostrand, 1970.

Wasil, E. A., and A. A. Assad. "Project Management on the PC: Software, Applications, and Trends." *Interfaces* 18, no. 2 (March–April 1988): 75–84.

Wiest, J., and F. Levy. *Management Guide to PERT-CPM*. 2nd ed., Englewood Cliffs, N.J.: Prentice-Hall, 1977.

Chapters 13 and 14 Inventory Management

Buffa, E. S., and W. Taubert. *Production-Inventory Systems: Planning and Control*. 3rd ed. Homewood, Ill.: Richard D. Irwin, 1979.

Davis, E. W. *Case Studies in Material Requirements Planning*. Washington, D.C.: APICS, 1978.

Fogarty, D. W., J. H. Blackstone, Jr., and T. R. Hoffman. *Production and Inventory Management*. Cincinnati: South-Western Publishing Company, 1991.

Hadley, G., and T. M. Whitin. *Analysis of Inventory Systems*. Englewood Cliffs, N.J.: Prentice-Hall, 1963.

Hillier, F., and G. J. Lieberman. *Introduction to Operations Research*. 4th ed. San Francisco: Holden-Day, 1986.

Narasimhan, S., D. W. McLeavey, and P. Billington. *Production Planning and Inventory Control*. 2d ed. Englewood Cliffs, NJ.: Prentice-Hall, 1995.

Orlicky, J. *Material Requirements Planning*. New York: McGraw-Hill, 1975.

Plossl, G. W. *Manufacturing Control: The Last Frontier for Profits*. Reston, Va.: Reston, 1973.

Vollman, T. E., W. L. Berry, and D. C. Whybark. *Manufacturing Planning and Control Systems*. 3rd ed. Homewood, Ill.: Richard D. Irwin, 1992.

Chapter 15 Waiting Lines

Cooper, R. B. *Introduction to Queueing Theory*. 2d. ed. New York: North-Holland, 1981.

Cox, D. R., and W. L. Smith. *Queues*. New York: John Wiley & Sons, 1965.

Gross, D., and C. M. Harris. *Fundamentals of Queuing Theory*. 2d ed. New York: John Wiley & Sons, 1985.

Hall, R. *Queuing Methods for Service and Manufacturing*. Englewood Cliffs, N.J.: Prentice-Hall, 1991.

Hillier, F., and G. J. Lieberman. *Introduction to Operations Research*. 4th ed. San Francisco: Holden-Day, 1986.

Chapter 16   Simulation

Banks, J., and J. Carson. *Discrete-Event System Simulation.* Englewood Cliffs, N.J.: Prentice-Hall, 1984.

Christy, D. P., and H. J. Watson. "The Application of Simulation: A Survey of Industry Practice." *Interfaces* (October 1983).

Cochran, J. K., G. T. Mackulak, and Paul A. Savory. "Simulation Project Characteristics in Industrial Settings." *Interfaces* 25, no. 4 (July–August 1995): .

Fishman, George S. *Principles of Discrete Event Simulation.* New York: John Wiley & Sons, 1978.

Law, A. M., and W. D. Kelton. *Simulation Modeling and Analysis.* 2d ed. New York: McGraw-Hill, 1991.

Naylor, T. H. *Computer Simulation Experiments with Models of Economic Systems.* New York: John Wiley & Sons, 1971.

Naylor, T. H., J. L. Balintfy, D. S. Burdick, and K. Chu. *Computer Simulation Techniques.* New York: John Wiley & Sons, 1968.

Schmidt, J. W., and R. E. Taylor. *Simulation and Analysis of Industrial Systems.* Homewood, Ill.: Richard D. Irwin, 1970.

Thesen, A., and L. Travis. *Simulation for Decision Making.* St. Paul: West Publishing, 1992.

Winston, W. L., and S. C. Albright. *Practical Management Science.* Belmont, Calif.: Duxbury Press, 1997.

Chapter 17   Markov Processes

Bhat, N. *Elements of Applied Stochastic Processes.* 2d ed. New York: John Wiley & Sons, 1985.

Howard R. A. *Dynamic Programming and Markov Processes.* Cambridge, Mass.: M.I.T. Press, 1960.

Kemeny, J. G., and J. L. Snell, *Finite Markov Chains.* Englewood Cliffs, N.J.: Prentice-Hall, 1960.

Chapter 18   Multicriteria Decision Problems

Baird, B. F., *Managerial Decisions Under Uncertainty.* New York: John Wiley & Sons, 1989.

Bunn, D. W. *Analysis for Optimal Decisions.* New York: John Wiley & Sons, 1982.

Dyer, J. S. "A Clarification of Remarks on the Analytic Hierarchy Process." *Management Science* 36, no. 3 (March 1990): 274–275.

Dyer, J. S. "Remarks on the Analytic Hierarchy Process." *Management Science* 36, no. 3 (March 1990): 249–258.

Harker, P. T., and L. G. Vargas. "The Theory of Ratio Scale Estimation: Saaty's Analytic Hierarchy Process." *Management Science* 33, no. 11 (November 1987): 1383–1403.

Harker, P. T., and L. G. Vargas. "Reply to Remarks on the Analytic Hierarchy Process by J. S. Dyer." *Management Science* 36, no. 3 (March 1990): 269–273.

Ignizio, J. P. *Goal Programming and Extensions.* Lexington, Mass.: D. C. Health, 1976.

Keeney, R. L., and H. Raiffa. *Decisions with Multiple Objectives: Preferences and Value Tradeoffs.* New York: John Wiley & Sons, 1976.

Lee, S. M. *Goal Programming for Decision Analysis.* Philadelphia: Auerbach, 1972.

Saaty, T. *The Analytic Hierarchy Process.* Pittsburgh, Pa.: Publisher 1988.

Saaty, T. L. "An Exposition of the AHP in Reply to the Paper Remarks on the Analytic Hierarchy Process." *Management Science* 36, no. 3 (March 1990): 259–268.

Saaty, T. L. "How to Make a Decision: The Analytic Hierarchy Process." *Interfaces* 24, no. 6 (Nov–Dec 1994): 19–43.

Saaty, T. L. "Rank Generation, Preservation, and Reversal in the Analytic Hierarchy Decision Process." *Decision Sciences* 18, (1987): 157–177.

Weiss, E. N., and V. R. Rao. "AHP Design Issues for Large-Scale Systems." *Decision Sciences* 18 (1987): 43–61.

Winkler, R. L. "Decision Modeling and Rational Choice: AHP and Utlity Theory." *Management Science* 36, no. 3 (March 1990): 247–248.

Zahedi, F. "Analytic Hierarchy Process—A Survey of the Method and its Applications." *Interfaces* 16, no. 4 (August 1986): 96–108.

Chapter 1

2. Methodological developments based on research advances in computer technology

4. The problem is large, complex, important, new, and repetitive

6. Iconic—scale model of a new building
   Analog—barometer
   Mathematical—inventory cost equation

8. **a.** Max $10x + 5y$
   s.t.
   $$5x + 2y \geq 40$$
   $$x \geq 0, y \geq 0$$
   b. Controllable inputs: x and y
   Uncontrollable inputs: profit, labor hours per unit, and total labor hours available
   d. $x = 0, y = 20$, profit = $100

10. If $a = 3$, $x = 13\frac{1}{3}$ and profit = $133
    If $a = 4$, $x = 10$ and profit = $100
    If $a = 5$, $x = 8$ and profit = $80
    If $a = 6$, $x = 6\frac{2}{3}$ and profit = $67

12. A deterministic model with d = distance, m = miles per gallon, and c = cost per gallon, where total cost = $(2d/m)c$

14. Quicker to formulate, easier to solve, and/or more easily understood

16. **a.** 4706
    b. Loss $12,000
    c. $23
    d. $11,800

18. **a.** Max $6x + 4y$
    b. $50x + 30y \leq 80,000$
    $\quad 50x \quad\quad \leq 50,000$
    $\quad\quad\quad 30y \leq 45,000$

Chapter 2

2. $P(E_1) = .40$, $P(E_2) = .26$, $P(E_3) = .34$
   The relative frequency method was used.

4. **a.** Relative frequency
   b. P(Never married) = .5427
   P(married) = 0.4053
   P(other) = 0.0520

6. **a.** 0.31
   b. 0.69

8. No, not enough information to compute $P(A \cap B)$
   b. Yes; 0.45
   c. 0.80

10. P(part-time job or dean's list) = 0.50

12. **a.** $P(A \mid B) = 0.6667$
    b. $P(B \mid A) = 0.80$
    c. No; $P(A \mid B) \neq P(A)$

14. **a.**

		Do you own a U.S. car?		
		Yes	No	Total
Do you own a foreign car?	Yes	0.15	0.05	0.20
	No	0.75	0.05	0.80
Total		0.90	0.10	1.00

   b. 20% own a foreign car; 90% own a U.S. car
   c. 0.15
   d. 0.95
   e. 0.17
   f. 0.75
   g. No

16. **a.** 0.19
    b. 0.71
    c. 0.29

18. **a.** 0.25, 0.40, 0.10
    b. 0.25
    c. Independent; program does not help.

20. **a.** 0.10, 0.20, 0.09
    b. 0.51
    c. 0.26, 0.51, 0.23

22. **a.** 0.21
    b. Yes; Prob. of default > .20

24. **a.** 0.0625
    b. 0.0132
    c. Abandon after 3 consecutive dry wells.

26. **a.** $P(D_1 \mid S_1) = 0.2195$, $P(D_2 \mid S_1) = 0.7805$
    b. $P(D_1 \mid S_2) = 0.50$, $P(D_2 \mid S_2) = 0.50$
    c. $P(D_1 \mid S_3) = 0.8824$, $P(D_2 \mid S_3) = 0.1176$
    d. 0.1582 and 0.8418

Chapter 3

2. a. 0.05; probability of a $200,000 profit.
   b. 0.70
   c. 0.40

4. a. 6
   b. 4.50
   c. 2.12

6. a. 166
   b. −94; concern is to protect against the expense of a big accident

8. a. Medium 145; large 140; prefer Medium
   b. Medium 2725; large 12,400; prefer Medium

10. a. $f(0) = 0.3487$
   b. $f(2) = 0.1937$
   c. 0.9298
   d. 0.6513
   e. 1
   f. $\sigma^2 = 0.9000$, $\sigma = 0.9487$

12. a. Probability of a defective part must be 0.03 for each trial; trials must be independent
   b. 2
   c.

Number of defects	0	1	2
Probability	0.9409	0.0582	0.0009

14. a. $f(x) = \dfrac{2^x e^{-2}}{x!}$

   b. $\mu = 6$ for 3 time periods

   c. $f(x) = \dfrac{6^x e^{-6}}{x!}$

   d. $f(2) = \dfrac{2^2 e^{-2}}{2!} = \dfrac{4(0.1353)}{2} = 0.2706$

   e. $f(6) = \dfrac{6^6 e^{-6}}{6!} = 0.1606$

   f. $f(5) = \dfrac{4^5 e^{-4}}{5!} = 0.1563$

16. a. 0.0498
   b. 0.1465
   c. 0.3528
   d. 0.0009

18. a. $f(x)$

   b. 0
   c. 0.50
   d. 0.60

20. a. $f(x)$

   b. 0.50
   c. 0.30
   d. 0.40

22. a. 1.96
   b. 0.61
   c. 1.12
   d. 0.44

24. a. 0.3830
   b. 0.1056
   c. 0.0062
   d. 0.1603

26. a. 0.7745
   b. 36.32
   c. 19%

28. $\mu = 19.23$

30. a. 0.94
   b. 0.52

32. a. 50 hours
   b. 0.3935
   c. 0.1353

34. a. $\frac{1}{1.2} e^{-x/1.2}$
   b. 0.2246
   c. 0.4346

Chapter 4

2. a. Optimistic: d_1
   Conservative: d_3
   Minimax regret: d_3
   c. Optimistic: d_1
   Conservative: d_2 or d_3
   Minimax regret: d_{2F}

4. Optimistic: d_2
   Conservative: d_1
   Minimax regret: d_2

6. a. d_1 **b.** d_4

8. $p = 0.25$

10. a. If $p > 0.44$, location A; if $p < 0.44$, location C
   b. Location A because $0.65 > 0.44$

12. a. If s_1, then d_1; if s_2, then d_1 or d_2; if s_3, then d_2
   b. 192.5
   c. d_1; 182.5
   d. 10

14. 0.1905, 0.2381, 0.5714

16. a. 0.56, 0.44
   b. 0.57143, 0.42857, 0.18182, 0.81818
   c. If I_1, then d_2; if I_2, then d_1; EV = 292

18. b. Optimistic: d_3
      Conservative: d_1
      Minimax regret: d_2
   c. d_2
   d. 195
   e. If weak, then d_2; if average, then d_2; if strong, then d_3
   f. $38,500
   g. $195,000, 19.7%

20. b. $700, $0
   c. Yes
   e. Purchase blade attachment; $1250
   f. $2150
   g. Purchase snowplow; $4231
   h. Purchase blade attachment; $984

22. a. Accept St. Louis shipment
   b. $0 \le p < 0.67$, d_1; when $p = 0.67$, d_1 or d_2,
      $0.67 < p \le 1$, d_2
   c. $200
   d. If busy, then St. Louis
      If slow, then St. Louis
   e. 0.57
   f. 0%

24. a. Take expressway
   b. If $p < 0.75$, then d_2; if $p = 0.75$, d_1 or d_2; if $p > 0.75$, d_1
   c. Yes
   e. If clear, then expressway
      If overcast, then expressway
      If rain, then Queen City
   f. 60%

26. a. 0, 125, 250, 375
   b. Yes
   c. 0, 0.048, 0.092, 0.133
   e. 0, 0.159, 0.488, 0.353
   f. Yes
   g. $24.25

Chapter 5

2. a. d_2; EV(d_2) = $5,000
   b. p = probability of a 0$ cost
      $1 - p$ = probability of a $200,000 cost
   c. d_1; EV(d_1) = 9.9
   d. Expected utility approach; it avoids risk of large loss.

4. a. Route B; EV = 58.5
   b. p = probability of a 45-minute travel time
      $1 - p$ = probability of a 90-minute travel time
   c. Route A; EV = 7.6; risk-avoider

6. A − d_1; B − d_2; C − d_2

8. a.

	Win	Lose
Bet	350	−10
Do not bet	0	0

   b. d_2
   c. Risk takers
   d. Between 0 and 0.26

10. a. Western; EV = 26%
   b. p = probability of a 40% show
      $1 - p$ = probability of a 15% show
   c. Musical; risk taker

Chapter 6

2. a.

Week	4-Week	5-Week
10	19.00	18.80
11	20.00	19.20
12	18.75	19.00

   b. 9.65, 7.41
   c. 5-week

4. Weeks 10, 11, and 12: 18.48, 18.63, 18.27
   MSE = 9.25; $\alpha = 0.2$ is better

6. b. The more recent data receive the greater weight or importance in determining the forecast

8. a. 39.33
   b. 39.80
   c. 38.95
   d. Exponential smoothing; it has the smallest MSE (7.64)

10. a. Month 13: 106.4; MSE = 510.29
   b. Month 13: 104.62; MSE = 540.55
      Conclusion: A smoothing constant of 0.3 is better

12. 3117.01

14. $T_t = 20.7466 - 0.3514t$
   Enrollment appears to be decreasing by an average of 351 students per year

16. a. Linear trend appears to be reasonable
   b. $T_t = 19.993 + 1.774t$
      Average cost increase of $1.77 per unit per year

18. a. $T_t = 1997.6 + 397.545t$
   b. 6371; 6768

20. a. A linear trend appears to exist
   b. $T_t = -5 + 15t$
      Average increase in sales is 15 units per year

22. a. $T_t = 3.9049 + .0236t$

Personal income increasing at an average of 0.0236 per month

b. 4.21, 4.24, 4.26, 4.28, 4.31, 4.33

c. Actual 4.41 is above the forecast 4.33

24. a. Forecast for July is 236.97; forecast for August is 236.97

b. Forecast for July is 278.88; forecast for August is 297.33

c. Not fair; it does not account for upward trend in sales

26. 0.707, 0.777, 0.827, 0.966, 1.016, 1.305, 1.494, 1.225, 0.976, 0.986, 0.936, 0.787

28. a. Selected centered moving averages for $t = 5, 10, 15,$ and 20 are 11.125, 18.125, 22.875, and 27.000

b. 0.899, 1.362, 1.118, 0.621

d. Quarter 2, prior to summer boating season

30. a. $T_t = 6.329 + 1.055t$

b. 36.92, 37.98, 39.03, 40.09

c. 33.23, 51.65, 43.71, 24.86

32. a. Yes, there is a seasonal effect; seasonal indexes are 1.696, 1.458, 0.711, 0.326, 0.448, 1.362

b. Forecast for 12–4 is 166,761.13; forecast for 4–8 is 146,052.99

34. a. $T_t = 37.666 - 3.222t$

b. $3444

Chapter 7

6. $-\frac{7}{10}, -\frac{3}{2}, \frac{4}{7}$

10. $x_1 = 100, x_2 = 50, z = 750$

12. a. $x_1 = 3, x_2 = 1.5, z = 13.5$

b. $x_1 = 0, x_2 = 3, z = 18$

c. four: (0, 0), (4, 0), (3, 1.5), and (0.3)

14. a. Feasible region consists of a line segment

b. (5, 1) and (2, 4)

c. $x_1 = 2, x_2 = 4$

16. a. $x_1 = 300, x_2 = 420, z = 10,560$

b. $x_1 = 708, x_2 = 0, z = 14,160$

c. Sewing constraint is redundant; optimal solution is still $x_1 = 540, x_2 = 252$

20. b. $x_1 = \frac{20}{3}, x_2 = \frac{8}{3}, z = 30\frac{2}{3}$

c. $s_1 = \frac{28}{3}, s_2 = 0, s_3 = 0$

22. a. Max $5x_1 + 8x_2$

s.t.

$$1x_1 + \tfrac{3}{2}x_2 \le 900$$
$$\tfrac{1}{2}x_1 + \tfrac{1}{3}x_2 \le 300$$
$$\tfrac{1}{8}x_1 + \tfrac{1}{4}x_2 \le 100$$
$$x_1, x_2 \ge 0$$

b. $x_1 = 500, x_2 = 150$

c. $3700

d. 725, 300, 100

e. 175, 0, 0

24. a. Max $50x_1 + 80x_2$

s.t.

$$x_1 + x_2 = 1000$$
$$x_1 \ge 250$$
$$x_2 \ge 250$$
$$x_1 - 2x_2 \ge 0$$
$$x_1, x_2 \ge 0$$

b. $x_1 = 333.33, x_2 = 666.67, z = 70,000.10$

26. a. Max $1x_1 + 1.25x_2$

s.t.

$$5x_1 + 7x_2 \le 4480$$
$$3x_1 + 1x_2 \le 2080$$
$$2x_1 + 2x_2 \le 1600$$
$$x_1\, x_2 \ge 0$$

d. $x_1 = 560, x_2 = 240, z = 860$

28. b. $x_1 = 158\frac{1}{3}, x_2 = 25$, profit = 7583

c. $1x_2 \ge 1x_1$ or $-1x_1 + 1x_2 \ge 0$

d. $x_1 = 75, x_2 = 75$, profit = 6750

30.

Extreme Point	Slack/Surplus
(4000, 10,000)	0; 0; 7000
(9600, 3000)	420,000; 0; 0
(18,000, 3000)	0; 42,000; 0

32. b. (4, 1), $(2\frac{1}{4}, \frac{9}{4})$

c. $x_1 = 4, x_2 = 1$

34. 15 ounces of Bark Bits, $\frac{5}{2}$ ounces of Canine Chow, $z = 1.025$

36. a. Min $2.5A + 2B$

s.t.

$$2A + 1.5B \ge 1.7$$
$$2A + 3B \le 2.8$$
$$4A + 3B \le 3.6$$
$$A + B = 1$$
$$A, B \ge 0$$

b. A = 0.6, B = 0.4, z = $0.022

c. .1, .4, 0, 0

d. $0.176

38. $x_1 = 30, x_2 = 25$, cost = $55

40. Infeasibility

42. a. $x_1 = \frac{30}{16}, x_2 = \frac{30}{16}, z = \frac{60}{16}$

b. $x_1 = 0, x_2 = 3, z = 6$

c. Max $x_1 + \frac{5}{3}x_2$

44. a. 180, 20

b. Alternative optimal solutions

c. 120, 80

46. No feasible solution

48. a. No feasible region
  b. Need an additional 80 hours of cutting and dyeing, 32 hours of finishing, and 5 hours of inspection and packaging.

50. $6.3 \leq c_1 \leq 13.5$
  $6\frac{2}{3} \leq c_2 \leq 14\frac{2}{7}$

52. a. $x_1 = 3, x_2 = 7, z = 27$
  b. $1 \leq c_1 \leq 3$
  c. $2 \leq c_2 \leq 6$
  d. Same solution is optimal
  e. New solution has alternative optima solutions

54. a. $x_1 = 1, x_2 = 3, z = 4$
  b. $\frac{1}{2} \leq c_1 \leq 2$
  c. $\frac{1}{2} \leq c_2 \leq 2$
  d. Same solution is optimal
  e. New optimal solution is $x_1 = 0, x_2 = 5$

56. a. $x_1 = 7, x_2 = 7$
  b. $3 \leq c_1 \leq 10.5$
  c. $\frac{10}{3} \leq c_2 \leq \frac{35}{3}$
  d. New optimal solution is $x_1 = 0, x_2 = 10$; the value is 70
  e. Same solution is optimal

58. a. Optimal solution does not change
  b. $x_1 = 6, x_2 = 4, z = 26$

60. $x_1 = 65.45, x_2 = 261.82, z = \$45,818$

62. $x_1 = 384, x_2 = 80$

64. a. Max $\quad 160x_1 + 345x_2$
  s.t.

$$
\begin{aligned}
x_1 + \quad x_2 &\leq 15 \\
x_2 &\leq 10 \\
x_1 \quad\quad &\geq 5 \\
x_2 &\geq 5 \\
40x_1 + \quad 50x_2 &\leq 1000 \\
x_1, x_2 &\geq 0
\end{aligned}
$$

  b. $x_1 = 12.5, x_2 = 10$

Chapter 8

2. a. $4 \leq c_1 \leq 12 \quad 3.33 \leq c_2 \leq 10$

  c.

Min RHS	Max RHS
725	No upper limit
133.33	400
75	135

  d. $560

4. a. More than $7.00
  b. More than $3.50
  c. None

6. a. $x_1 = 30, x_2 = 25; \$55$
  b. $0.5 \leq c_1 <$ No upper limit
  $0.0 \leq c_2 \leq 2$
  c. $-0.50; -0.50; 0.0$
  d.

Min RHS	Max RHS
70.0	No upper limit
0.0	40.0
No lower limit	25.0

  e.

Min RHS	Max RHS
70	No upper limit
0	40
No lower limit	25

8. a. $x_1 = 0, x_2 = 25, x_3 = 125, x_4 = 0, z = 525$
  b. A and C
  c. B; 425 hours
  d. Yes

10. a. $x_1 = 7.30, x_2 = 0, x_3 = 1.89, z = 139.73$
  b. Two and three
  c. $0, -3.41,$ and -4.43
  d. Decrease the right-hand side of constraint 3 from 20 to 19

12. a. All Pro: 1000; College: 200; High School: 0
  b. Sewing and minimum All Pro production requirement
  c. 4000 minutes of unused cutting and dyeing time; all the sewing time is being used; 5200 minutes of unused inspection and packaging time; only the minimum number of All Pro models is being produced.
  d. No lower limit $< c_1 \leq 5$
  $5 \leq c_2 <$ No upper limit
  No lower limit $< c_3 \leq 4$

14. a. $x_1 = 25, x_2 = 0, x_3 = 25,$ profit $= 1250$
  b. Machine 1: 31.25, machine 2: 37.50
  c. $12.50
  d. $x_1 = 24, x_2 = 8, x_3 = 16,$ profit $= \$1440$

16. a. 333.3, 0, 833.3, 2500; risk $= 14,666.7$, return $= 18,000 \,(9\%)$
  b. 1000, 0, 0, 2500; risk $= 18,000$, return $= 22,000 \,(11\%)$
  c. $4000

18. b.

	San Diego	Tampa
Regular	20,000	18000
Stiff	75,000	0

20. a. Relevant
 b. $x_1 = 10,000$, $x_2 = 6000$, $x_3 = 4,000$, $z = \$29,000$
 c. \$2.90 is the maximum premium (over the normal price of \$1.00) that LaJolla Beverage Products should be willing to pay to obtain one additional gallon of wine.
 d. No
 e. Requiring 50% plus one gallon of white wine would reduce profit by \$2.40.
 f. Allowing the amount of fruit juice to exceed 20% by one gallon will increase profit by \$1.00.

22. a. $x_1 = 4181$, $x_2 = 41,806$, $x_3 = 30,000$
 c. Total cost will decrease by \$0.2210

Chapter 9

2. a. $x_1 = 77.89$, $x_2 = 63.16$, \$3284.21
 b. Department A \$15.79; department B \$47.37
 c. $x_1 = 87.21$, $x_2 = 65.12$, \$3341.34
  Department A 10 hours; department B 3.2 hours

4. a. $x_1 = 500$, $x_2 = 300$, $x_3 = 200$, \$550
 b. \$0.55
 c. Aroma 75; taste 84.4
 d. \$0.60

6. 50 units of product 1; 0 units of product 2; 300 hours department A; 600 hours department B

8. Schedule 19 officers as follows:
 3 begin at 8:00 A.M.; 3 begin at noon; 7 begin at 4:00 P.M.;
 4 begin at midnight, 2 begin at 4:00 A.M.

10.

Product	Modern Line	Old Line
1	500	0
2	300	400

Cost = \$3850

12. a. Purchase 5000 bases
 b. Same solution with objective function increased by \$80
 c. Yes; total cost = \$24,293.33; $FCP = 1333$ and $FCM = 1667$

14. b.

Quarter	Production	Ending Inventory
1	4000	2100
2	3000	1100
3	2000	100
4	1900	500

16. x_i = number of 10-inch rolls processed by cutting alternative i
 a. $x_1 = 0$, $x_2 = 125$, $x_3 = 500$, $x_4 = 1500$, $x_5 = 0$, $x_6 = 0$, $x_7 = 0$; 2125 rolls with waste of 750 inches
 b. 2500 rolls with no waste; however, 1½-inch size is overproduced by 3000 units

18. a. 5 super, 2 regular, and 3 econotankers
 b. Total cost \$583,000; monthly operating cost \$4650

20. Produce 10,250 units in March, 10,250 units in April, and 12,000 units in May

22. $x_1 = 48$, $x_2 = 96$, \$456
 Assembler times: 480, 480, and 456

24. Investment strategy: 45.8% of A and 100% of B
 Objective function = \$4340.40
 Savings/Loan Schedule

	Period			
	1	2	3	4
Savings	242.11	—	—	341.04
Funds from loan	—	200.00	127.58	—

26. b. Solution does not indicate that General Hospital is relatively inefficient.
 c. General Hospital

28. c. No; E = 1 indicates that the amount of resources used by Hospital E are required to produce the outputs of Hospital E.
 d. Hospital E

Chapter 10

2. a. Min $14x_{11} + 9x_{12} + 7x_{13} + 8x_{21} + 10x_{22} + 5x_{23}$
 s.t.

$$
\begin{aligned}
x_{11} + x_{12} + x_{13} &\le 30 \\
x_{21} + x_{22} + x_{23} &\le 20 \\
x_{11} \quad\quad + x_{21} &= 25 \\
x_{12} \quad\quad + x_{22} &= 15 \\
x_{13} \quad\quad + x_{23} &= 10 \\
x_{11}, x_{12}, x_{13}, x_{21}, x_{22}, x_{23} &\ge 0
\end{aligned}
$$

 b. $x_{11} = 5$, $x_{12} = 15$, $x_{13} = 10$, $x_{21} = 20$

4. b. $x_{12} = 300, x_{21} = 100, x_{22} = 100, x_{23} = 300, x_{31} = 100$
Cost $= 10,400$

6. b.

Seattle–Denver	4000;	Seattle–Los Angeles	5000;
Columbus–Mobile	4000;	New York–Pittsburgh	3000;
New York–Mobile	1000;	New York–Los Angeles	1000;
New York–Washington	3000		

Cost $= \$150,000$

c.

Seattle–Denver	4000;	Seattle–Los Angeles	5000;
Columbus–Mobile	5000;	New York–Pittsburgh	4000;
New York–Los Angeles	1000;	New York–Washington	3000

Cost actually decreases by $9000

8. Clifton Springs–D_2 4000;   Clifton Springs–D_4 1000;
Danville–D_1 2000;   Danville–D_4 1000;
Customer 2 has a shortfall of 1000; customer 3's demand is not satisfied.

10. 1–A 300; 1–C 1200; 2–A 1200; 3–A 500; 3–B 500

12. b. Jackson–2, Ellis–1, Smith–3 Total completion time $= 64$

14. b. Bostock–Southwest, Miller–Northwest

16. 1-B, 2-C, 3-A, 4-D; 74 hours required

18. A to MS, B to Ph.D., C to MBA, D to undergrad
Maximum total rating $= 3.3$

20. a.

			Supplier			
Division	1	2	3	4	5	6
1	614	660	534	680	590	630
2	603	639	702	693	693	630
3	865	830	775	850	900	930
4	532	553	511	581	595	553
5	720	648	684	693	657	747

b. Optimal Solution:

Supplier 1–Division 2	$ 603
Supplier 2–Division 5	648
Supplier 3–Division 3	775
Supplier 5–Division 1	590
Supplier 6–Division 4	553
Total	$3169

22. c. $x_{14} = 320, x_{25} = 600, x_{47} = 300, x_{49} = 20, x_{56} = 300,$
$x_{58} = 300, x_{39} = 380$
Cost $= \$11,220$

24. c. Note: Augusta: 1, Tupper Lake: 2, Albany: 3, Portsmouth: 4, Boston: 5, New York: 6 Philadelphia: 7

Variable	Value	Variable	Value
x_{13}	50;	x_{36}	0
x_{14}	250	x_{37}	150
x_{23}	100	x_{45}	150
x_{24}	0	x_{46}	100
x_{35}	0	x_{47}	0

26. Objective function $= 4300$

Optimal Solution	Units Shipped	Cost
Muncie–Cincinnati	1	6
Cincinnati–Concord	3	84
Brazil–Louisville	6	18
Louisville–Macon	2	88
Louisville–Greenwood	4	136
Xenia–Cincinnati	5	15
Cincinnati–Chatham	3	72
	Total	419

Two rail cars must be held at Muncie until a buyer is found

30. c. Regular-month 1: 275; overtime—month 1: 25; inventory—end of month 1: 150
Regular-month 2: 200; overtime—month 2: 50; inventory—end of month 2: 150
Regular-month 3: 100; overtime—month 3: 50; inventory—end of month 3: 0

Chapter 11

2. b. $x_1 = 1.43, x_2 = 4.29$; value $= 41.47$
Rounded: $x_1 = 1, x_2 = 4$; value $= 37$
c. $x_1 = 0, x_2 = 5$, value $= 40$
Not the same

4. a. $x_1 = 3.67, x_2 = 0$, value $= 36.7$
Rounded: $x_1 = 3, x_2 = 0$; value $= 30$
Lower bound $= 30$; upper bound $= 36.7$
b. $x_1 = 3, x_2 = 2$; value $= 36$
c. Alternative optimal solutions: $x_1 = 0, x_2 = 5$
$x_1 = 2, x_2 = 4$

6. b. $x_1 = 1.96, x_2 = 5.48$; value $= 7.44$
Rounded: $x_1 = 1.96, x_2 = 5$; value $= 6.96$
Lower bound $= 6.96$; upper bound $= 7.44$
c. $x_1 = 1.29, x_2 = 6$; value $= 7.29$

8. a. $x_3 = 1, x_4 = 1, x_6 = 1$; value = 17,500
   b. Add $x_1 + x_2 \le 1$
   c. Add $x_3 - x_4 = 0$

10. b. Choose locations B and E

12. a. $x_1 \le 15 + 15y_1$
      $x_2 \le 15 + 15y_2$
      $x_3 \le 15 + 15y_3$
      $y_1 + y_2 + y_3 \le 1$
   b. $x_1 = 15, x_2 = 15, x_3 = 30$
      $y_1 = 0, y_2 = 0, y_3 = 1$; value = 50

14. b. Modernize plants 1 and 3 or plants 4 and 5
   d. Modernize plants 1 and 3

16. b. Use all part-time employees
      Bring on as follows: 9:00 A.M.–6, 11:00 A.M.–2, 12:00 noon–6, 1:00 P.M.–1, 3:00 P.M.–6
      Cost = $672
   c. Same as in part (b)
   d. New solution is to bring on 1 full-time employee at 9:00 A.M., 4 more at 11:00 A.M., and part-time employees as follows:
      9:00 A.M.–5, 12:00 noon–5, and 3:00 P.M.–2

18. a. New objective function: Min $25x_1 + 40x_2 + 40x_3 + 40x_4 + 25x_5$
   b. $x_4 = x_5 = 1$; modernize the Ohio and California plants .
   c. Add the constraint $x_2 + x_3 = 1$
   d. $x_1 = x_3 = 1$

20. $x_1 + x_2 + x_3 = 3y_1 + 5y_2 + 7y_3$
      $y_1 + y_2 + y_3 = 1$

Chapter 12

2.

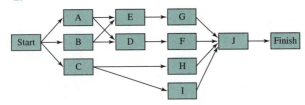

4. a. A–D–G
   b. No; time = 15 months

6. a. A–D–F–H
   b. 22 weeks
   c. No, it is a critical activity
   d. Yes, 2 weeks
   e. ES = 3, LS = 4, EF = 10, LF = 11

8. b. B–C–E–F–H
   d. Yes, time = 49 weeks

10. a.

Activity	Time	Variance
A	5.00	0.11
B	9.00	0.11
C	8.00	0.44
D	8.83	0.25
E	7.17	0.25
F	6.00	0.11

   b. 23.83, 0.47

12. a. A–D–H–I
   b. 25.66 days
   c. 0.2578

14. a. A–D–F–G
   b. 1.5 days
   c. 29.5, 2.36
   d. 0.6293

16. a.

E(T)	Variance
16	3.92
13	2.03
10	1.27

   b. 0.9783, approximately 1.00, approximately 1.00

18. c. A–B–D–G–H–I, 14.17 weeks
   d. 0.0951, yes

20. b. Crash B(1 week), D(2 weeks), E(1 week), F(1 week), G(1 week)
      Total cost = $2427
   c. All activities are critical

22. b. Crash C(1 day) and E(1 day)
   c. $9300

24. c. A–B–C–F, 31 weeks
   d. Crash A(2 weeks), B(2 weeks), C(1 week), D(1 week), E(1 week)
   e. All activities are critical
   f. $112,500

Chapter 13

2. $164.32 for each; total cost = $328.64

4. a. 1095.45
   b. 240
   c. 22.82 days
   d. $273.86 for each; total cost = $547.72

6. a. 15.95
   b. $2106

c. 15.04
d. 16.62 days

8. $Q^* = 11.73$, use 12
5 classes per year
$225,200

10. $Q^* = 1414.21$
$T = 28.28$ days
Production runs of 7.07 days

12. $Q^* = 1000$; total cost = $1200
Yes, the change saves $300 per year

14. New $Q^* = 4509$

16. 135.55; $r = dm - S$; less than

18. 64, 24.44

20. $Q^* = 100$; total cost = $3,601.50

22. $Q^* = 300$; savings = $480

24. a. 500
b. 580.4

26. a. 397
b. 0.70
c. 489, 0.35

28. a. 440
b. 0.60
c. 710
d. $c_u = 17

30. a. 13.68 (14)
b. 17.83 (18)
c. 2, $10; 6, $30

32. a. 31.62
b. 19.86 (20); 0.2108
c. 5, $15

34. a. 243
b. 93, $54.87
c. 613
d. 163, $96.17
e. Yes, added cost only $41.30 per year
f. Yes, added cost would be $4,130 per year

36. a. 40
b. 62.25; 7.9
c. 54
d. 36

Chapter 14

2. a. Projected balance—week 6: 70
Net requirement—week 4: 70
Planned order release—week 3: 400
b. Planned order release—week 1: 400
c. None

4. a. Projected balance—week 3: 250
Projected balance—week 6: 0
b. Projected balance—week 3: 370
Projected balance—week 6: 120
c. Projected balance—week 3: 550
Projected balance—week 6: 600
d. Lot size of 800

6. a. Net requirements—week 3: 250
b. Net requirements—week 3: 130
d. Lot-for-lot rule

8. a. Projected balance—week 5: 100
Net requirements—week 4: 150
b. Projected balance—week 5: 0
Net requirements—Week 4: 200
c. Fixed lot size has higher holding costs

10. a. Net requirements—week 24: 400
Planned order releases—week 21: 500
b. Net requirements—week 21: 450
Projected balance—week 23: 0

12. a. 800
b. Week 15, 800 units
c. Week 13, 800 units

14. 2000, 500, 200

Chapter 15

2. a. 0.4512
b. 0.6988
c. 0.3012

4. 0.3333, 0.2222, 0.1481, 0.0988, 0.1976

6. a. 0.3333
b. 1.3333
c. 0.1111 hours
d. 0.6667

8. 0.20, 3.2, 4, 3.2, 4, 0.80
Slightly poorer service

10. a. New: 1.3333, 2, 0.6667, 1, 0.6667
Experienced: 0.50, 1, 0.25, 0.50, 0.50
b. New $74; experienced $50; hire experienced

12. a. 0.25, 2.25, 3, 0.15 hours, 0.20 hours, 0.75
b. The service needs improvement

14. a. 0.1667
b. 5
c. 0.8333
d. 0.4167 hours
e. No; the service was poor

16. a. 0.50
b. 0.50
c. 0.10 hours
d. 0.20 hours
e. yes, unless $W_q = 0.10$ hours (6 minutes) is too long.

18. a. 0.5385
  b. 0.0593
  c. 0.0099 hours
  d. 0.1099 hours
  e. 0.1384

20. a. 0.2360, 0.1771, 1.5771, 0.0127 hours, 0.1127 hours
  b. $P(\text{wait}) = 0.2023$; prefer 3-channel system

22.

Characteristic		A	B	C
a.	P_0	0.2000	0.5000	0.4286
b.	L_q	3.2000	0.5000	0.1524
c.	L	4.0000	1.0000	0.9524
d.	W_q	0.1333	0.0200	0.0063
e.	W	0.1667	0.0417	0.0397
f.	P_w	0.8000	0.5000	0.2286

  System C provides the best service.

24. a. 0.0466, 0.05
  b. 1.4
  c. 11:00 A.M.

26. a. 0.2668, 10 minutes, 0.6667
  b. 0.0667, 7 minutes, 0.4669
  c. $25.33; $33.34; one-channel

28. a. 10, 9.6
  b. Design A with $\mu = 10$
  c. 0.05, 0.01
  d. A: 0.5, 0.3125, 0.8125, 0.0625, 0.1625, 0.5
     B: 0.4792, 0.2857, 0.8065, 0.0571, 0.1613, 0.5208
  e. Design B has slightly less waiting time.

30. a. 0.1460, 0.3066, 0.3220, 0.2254
  b. 0.2254
  c. 1.6267
  d. 4; 0.1499

32. a. 31.04%
  b. 27.58%
  c. 0.2758, 0.1092, 0.0351
  d. 3, 10.92%

34. a. 0.4790
  b. 0.3110
  c. 0.8320
  d. 2.9846 minutes
  e. 7.9846 minutes
  f. 95.8 minutes; 35.8 minutes
  g. Yes, assistants spend too much time waiting at the copier

Chapter 16

2. a. Profit $= (50 - c)x - 30,000$
  b. 6000, $-22,200$, 41,400
  c. Helps estimate probability of loss

4. a. 0.00–0.08, 0.08–0.20, 0.20–0.48, 0.48–0.72, 0.72–0.86, 0.86–0.96, 0.96–1.00

b. 2, 5, 2, 3, 3, 2, 4, 2, 1, 1, 2
  c. 24 units

6. a. 0.00–0.83, 0.83–0.89, 0.89–0.94, 0.94–0.96, 0.96–0.98, 0.98–0.99, 0.99–1.00
  b. 4 claims paid, total = $22,000

8. a. Atlanta wins each game if random number is in interval 0.00–0.60, 0.00–0.55, 0.00–0.48, 0.00–0.45, 0.00–0.48, 0.00–0.55, 0.00–0.50.
  b. Atlanta wins games 1, 2, 4, and 6
     Atlanta wins series 4 to 2
  c. Repeat many times; record % of Atlanta wins

10. a. 0.00–0.40 for Yes; 0.40–1.00 for No
     If Yes, 0.00–0.30, 0.30–0.60, 0.60–1.00
     If No, 0.00–0.50, 0.50–0.90, 0.90–1.00
  b. Uncertain, definitely yes, definitely no
  c. Repeat many times; record % of definitely yes

12. a. $7, $3, $12
  b. Purchase: 0.00–0.25, 0.25–0.70, 0.70–1.00
     Labor: 0.00–0.10, 0.10–0.35, 0.35–0.70, 0.70–1.00
     Transportation: 0.00–0.75, 0.75–1.00
  c. $5
  d. $7
  e. Provide probability profit less than $5/unit

14. a. Most simulations between $5500 and $6500
  b. Most simulations between 0.25 and 0.30
  c. Project is too risky

16. Most simulations between 6 and 16 still working; 11 is the expected number.

18. a. Most simulations between 0.60 and 0.65
  b. $775,000 roughly 0.82; $785,000 roughly 0.88
     Select $775,000

20. a. Results vary with each simulation run;
     Our results 50,000 provided $230,000
            60,000 provided $200,000
            70,000 less than $100,000
  b. Recommend 50,000 units
  c. Roughly 0.75; simulation results vary

22. a. Very poor operation; some customers wait 30 minutes or more.
  b. Average wait is from 0.10 to 0.13 minutes; 2 ATMs do a good job

24. a. Both should be approximately four minutes.
  b. Our simulation approximately 0.8 minutes; other simulations may vary slightly
  c. Most simulations between 150 and 170; roughly 30% to 35% wait

Chapter 17

2. a. probability = 0.82
  b. $\pi_1 = 0.5$, $\pi_2 = 0.5$
  c. $\pi_1 = 0.6$, $\pi_2 = 0.4$

4. a. $\pi_1 = 0.92, \pi_2 = 0.08$

   b. \$85

6. a.

	City	Suburbs
City	0.98	0.02
Suburbs	0.01	0.99

   b. $\pi_1 = 0.333, \pi_2 = 0.667$

   c. City will decrease from 40% to 33%; suburbs will increase from 60% to 67%

8. a. MDA

   b. $\pi = \frac{1}{3}, \pi_2 = \frac{2}{3}$

10. $3 - 1(0.59), 4 - 1(0.52)$

12. 3580 will be sold eventually; 1420 will be lost

14. a. Graduate and drop out

   b. P(Drop out) = 0.15, P(Sophomore) = 0.10, P(Junior) = 0.75

   c. 0.706, 0.294

   d. Yes; P(Graduate) = 0.54
            P(Drop out) = 0.46

   e. 1479 (74%) will graduate

Chapter 18

2. a. Min $\quad P_1(d_1^-) + P_2(d_2^+)$

   s.t.

$$50x_1 + 100x_2 \qquad\qquad\quad \leq 50,000$$
$$3x_1 + \;\; 10x_2 - d_1^+ + d_1^- = \quad 4500$$
$$x_2 - d_2^+ + d_2^- = \quad\; 300$$
$$x_1, x_2, d_1^+, d_1^-, d_2^+, d_2^- \geq 0$$

   b. $x_1 = 250, x_2 = 375$

4. a. Min $\quad P_1(d_1^-) + P_1(d_2^+) + P_2(d_3^-) + P_2(d_4^-) + P_5(d_5^-)$

   s.t.

$$20x_1 + 30x_2 - d_1^+ + d_1^- = 1800$$
$$20x_1 + 30x_2 - d_2^+ + d_2^- = 6000$$
$$x_1 \qquad\qquad - d_3^+ + d_3^- = \;\;100$$
$$x_2 - d_4^+ + d_4^- = \;\;120$$
$$x_1 + \quad x_2 - d_5^+ + d_5^- = \;\;300$$
$$x_1, x_2, \text{all deviation variables} \geq 0$$

   b. $x_1 = 120, x_2 = 120$

6. a. Let x_1 = number of letters mailed to group 1 customers
     x_2 = number of letters mailed to group 2 customers
     Min $\quad P_1(d_1^-) + P_1(d_2^-) + P_2(d_3^+)$

   s.t.

$$x_1 \qquad\quad - d_1^+ + d_1^- = 40,000$$
$$x_2 - d_2^+ + d_2^- = 50,000$$
$$x_1 + x_2 - d_3^+ + d_3^- = 70,000$$
$$x_1, x_2, \text{all deviation variables} \geq 0$$

   b. $x_1 = 40,000, x_2 = 50,000$

   c. Optimal solution does not change

8. a. Min $\quad d_1^- + d_1^+ + e_1^- + e_1^+ + d_2^- + d_2^+ + e_2^- +$
              $e_2^+ + d_3^- + d_3^+ + e_3^- + e_3^+$

   s.t.

$$x_1 \qquad\quad + d_1^- - d_1^+ = 1$$
$$x_2 + e_1^- - e_1^+ = 7$$
$$x_1 \qquad\quad + d_2^- - d_2^+ = 5$$
$$x_2 + e_2^- - e_2^+ = 9$$
$$x_1 \qquad\quad + d_3^- - d_3^+ = 6$$
$$x_2 + e_3^- - e_3^+ = 2$$
$$\text{all variables} \geq 0$$

   b. $x_1 = 5, x_2 = 7$

10. Since CR = 0.017 is less than 0.10, the degree of consistency exhibited in the pairwise comparison matrix is acceptable

12. Since CR = 0.029 is less than 0.10, the degree of consistency exhibited in the pairwise comparison matrix is acceptable

14. a. 0.723, 0.193, 0.083

   b. Yes; since CR = 0.055 is less than 0.10, the degree of consistency exhibited in the pairwise comparison matrix is acceptable

16. a.

	A	B	C
A	1	3	2
B	$\frac{1}{3}$	1	5
C	$\frac{1}{2}$	$\frac{1}{5}$	1

   b. 0.503, 0.348, 0.149

   c. Since CR = 0.417 is greater than 0.10, the individual's judgments are not consistent

18. a.

	D	S	N
D	1	$\frac{1}{4}$	$\frac{1}{7}$
S	4	1	$\frac{1}{3}$
N	7	3	1

   b. 0.080, 0.265, 0.655

   c. Since CR = 0.029 is less than 0.10, the manager's judgments are consistent

20. b. Criterion: 0.667, 0.333
       Yield: 0.75, 0.25
       Risk: 0.333, 0.667

   c. CCI: 0.611; SRI: 0.389

22. b. Criterion: 0.608, 0.272, 0.120
       Price: 0.557, 0.123, 0.320
       Quality: 0.137, 0.240, 0.623
       FM reception: 0.579, 0.187, 0.234

   c. A: 0.445, B: 0.163, C: 0.392

Chapter 1

4. A quantitative approach may be considered because
  a. the problem is large and complex
  b. the problem is very important
  c. the problem is new and no experience exists
  d. the problem is repetitive

8. a. Max $10x + 5y$
     s.t. $5x + 2y \le 40$
            $x \ge 0, y \ge 0$
  b. Controllable inputs: x and y
     Uncontrollable inputs: profit (10, 5), labor hours (5, 2), and labor hour availability (40)
  d. $x = 0, y = 20$; profit = \$100
     (Solution by trial-and-error)

15. a. $TC = 1000 + 30x$
  b. $P = 40x - (1000 + 30x) = 10x - 1000$
  c. Break even when $P = 0$
     Thus $10x - 1000 = 0$
           $10x = 1000$
             $x = 100$

Chapter 2

1. The sample points are major defect, minor defect, no defect; in set notation S = {major defect, minor defect, no defect}; each is an experimental outcome

2. $P(E_1) = 0.40$, $P(E_2) = 0.26$, $P(E_3) = 0.34$
  The relative frequency method was used

6. a. $P(A) = P(150\text{--}199) + P(200 \text{ and over})$
$$= \frac{26}{100} + \frac{5}{100}$$
$$= 0.31$$
  b. $P(B) = P(\text{less than } 50) + P(50\text{--}99) + P(100\text{--}149)$
$$= 0.13 + 0.22 + 0.34$$
$$= 0.69$$

7. a. $P(A) = 0.40$, $P(B) = 0.40$, $P(C) = 0.60$
  b. $P(A \cup B) = P(E_1, E_2, E_3, E_4) = 0.80$; yes,
     $P(A \cup B) = P(A) + P(B)$
  c. $A^c = \{E_3, E_4, E_5\}$; $C^c = \{E_1, E_4\}$ $P(A^c) = 0.60$;
     $P(C^c) = 0.40$
  d. $A \cup B^c = \{E_1, E_2, E_5\}$; $P(A \cup B^c) = 0.60$
  e. $P(B \cup C) = P(E_2, E_3, E_4, E_5) = 0.80$

12. a. $P(A \mid B) = \dfrac{P(A \cap B)}{P(B)} = \dfrac{0.40}{0.60} = 0.6667$
  b. $P(A \mid B) = \dfrac{P(A \cap B)}{P(A)} = \dfrac{0.40}{0.50} = 0.80$
  c. No, because $P(A \mid B) \neq P(A)$

13. a.

| | **Reason for Applying** | | | |
	Quality	Cost/ Convenience	Other	Total
Full Time	0.218	0.204	0.039	0.461
Part Time	0.208	0.307	0.024	0.539
Total	0.426	0.511	0.063	1.000

  b. A student will most likely cite cost or convenience as the first reason: probability = 0.511; school quality is the first reason cited by the second largest number of students: probability = 0.426
  c. $P(\text{Quality} \mid \text{full time}) = 0.218/0.461 = 0.473$
  d. $P(\text{Quality} \mid \text{part time}) = 0.208/0.539 = 0.386$
  e. $P(B) = 0.426$ and $P(B \mid A) = 0.473$
     Since $P(B) \neq P(B \mid A)$, the events are dependent

20. a. $P(B \cap A_1) = P(A_1)P(B \mid A_1) = (0.20)(0.50) = 0.10$
     $P(B \cap A_2) = P(A_2)P(B \mid A_2) = (0.50)(0.40) = 0.20$
     $P(B \cap A_3) = P(A_3)P(B \mid A_3) = (0.30)(0.30) = 0.09$
  b. $P(A_2 \mid B) = \dfrac{0.20}{0.10 + 0.20 + 0.09} = 0.51$
  c.

Events	$P(A_i)$	$P(B \mid A_i)$	$P(A_i \cap B)$	$P(A_i \mid B)$
A_1	0.20	0.50	0.10	0.26
A_2	0.50	0.40	0.20	0.51
A_3	0.30	0.30	0.09	0.23
	1.00		0.39	1.00

25.

Events	$P(A_i)$	$P(D \mid A_i)$	$P(A_i \cap D)$	$P(A_i \mid D)$
Supplier A	0.60	0.0025	0.0015	0.23
Supplier B	0.30	0.0100	0.0030	0.46
Supplier C	0.10	0.0200	0.0020	0.31
	1.00		$P(S) = 0.0065$	1.00

  a. $P(D) = 0.0065$
  b. B is the most likely supplier if a defect is found

Chapter 3

1. a. Values: 0,1,2, . . . ,20
    discrete
 b. Values: 0,1,2, . . .
    discrete
 c. Values: 0,1,2, . . . ,50
    discrete
 d. Values: $0 \leq x \leq 8$
    continuous
 e. Values: $x \geq 0$
    continuous

3. a.

x	$f(x)$
1	3/20 = 0.15
2	5/20 = 0.25
3	8/20 = 0.40
4	4/20 = 0.20
	Total 1.00

 b.

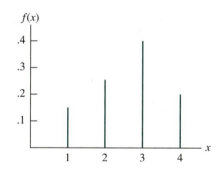

 c. $f(x) \geq 0$ for $x = 1, 2, 3, 4$
    $\Sigma f(x) = 1$

4. a.

x	$f(x)$	$xf(x)$
3	0.25	0.75
6	0.50	3.00
9	0.25	2.25
Totals	1.00	6.00

 $E(x) = \mu = 6.00$

 b.

x	$x - \mu$	$(x - \mu)^2$	$f(x)$	$(x - \mu)^2 f(x)$
3	-3	9	.25	2.25
6	0	0	.50	0.00
9	3	9	.25	2.25
				4.50

 Var $(x) = \sigma^2 = 4.50$
 c. $\sigma = \sqrt{4.50} = 2.12$

9. a. $f(1) = \binom{2}{1}(0.4)^1(0.6)^1 = \dfrac{2!}{1!1!}(0.4)(0.6) = 0.48$

 b. $f(0) = \binom{2}{0}(0.4)^0(0.6)^2 = \dfrac{2!}{0!2!}(1)(0.36) = 0.36$

 c. $f(2) = \binom{2}{2}(0.4)^2(0.6)^0 = \dfrac{2!}{2!0!}(0.16)(1) = 0.16$

 d. $P(x \geq 1) = f(1) + f(2) = 0.48 + 0.16 = 0.64$

 e. $E(x) = np = 2(0.4) = 0.8$
    $\text{Var}(x) = np(1 - p) = 2(0.4)(0.6) = 0.48$
    $\sigma = \sqrt{0.48} = 0.6928$

12. a. Probability of a defective part being produced must be 0.03 for each trial; trials must be independent
 b. Two outcomes result in exactly one defect
 c. $P(\text{no defects}) = (0.97)(0.97) = 0.9409$
    $P(1 \text{ defect}) = 2(0.03)(0.97) = 0.0582$
    $P(2 \text{ defects}) = (0.03)(0.03) = 0.0009$

14. a. $f(x) = \dfrac{2^x e^{-2}}{x!}$

 b. $\mu = 6$ for 3 time periods

 c. $f(x) = \dfrac{6^x e^{-6}}{x!}$

 d. $f(2) = \dfrac{2^2 e^{-2}}{2!} = \dfrac{4(0.1353)}{2} = 0.2706$

 e. $f(6) = \dfrac{6^x e^{-6}}{6!} = 0.1606$

 f. $f(5) = \dfrac{4^5 e^{-4}}{5!} = 0.1563$

18. a.

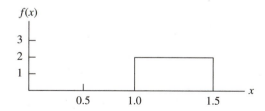

 b. $P(x = 1.25) = 0$; the probability of any single point is zero because the area under the curve above any single point is zero

c. $P(1.0 \le x \le 1.25) = 2(0.25) = 0.50$

d. $P(1.20 < x < 1.5) = 2(0.30) = 0.60$

21. a. 0.2967

b. 0.4418

c. $0.5000 - 0.1700 = 0.3300$

d. $0.0910 + 0.5000 = 0.5910$

e. $0.3849 + 0.5000 = 0.8849$

f. $0.5000 - 0.2612 = 0.2388$

23. a. Look in the table for an area of $0.5000 - 0.2119 = 0.2881$; the value we are seeking is below the mean, so the z value must be negative; thus, for an area of 0.2881, $z = -0.80$

b. Look in the table for an area of $0.9030/2 = 0.4515$; $z = 1.66$

c. Look in the table for an area of $0.2025/2 = 0.1026$; $z = 0.26$

d. Look in the table for an area of $0.9948 - 0.5000 = 0.4948$; $z = 2.56$

e. Look in the table for an area of $0.6915 - 0.5000 = 0.1915$; the value we are seeking is below the mean, so the z value must be negative; thus, $z = -0.50$

29. a. $P(x \le x_0) = 1 - e^{-x_0/3}$

b. $P(x \le 2) = 1 - e^{-2/3} = 1 - 0.5134 = 0.4866$

c. $P(x \ge 3) = 1 - P(x \le 3) = 1 - (1 - e^{-3/3}) = e^{-1} = 0.3679$

d. $P(x \le 5) = 1 - e^{-5/3} = 1 - 0.1889 = 0.8111$

e. $P(2 \le x \le 5) = P(x \le 5) - P(x \le 2) = 0.8111 - 0.4866 = 0.3245$

30. a. The mean time between fatalities is $\frac{1}{34}$ year, so for 1 month we have $\mu = \frac{12}{34}$ and
$$P(x \le 1) = 1 - e^{-1/(12/34)} = 1 - e^{-34/12} = 1 - e^{-2.833}$$
$$= 1 - 0.06 = 0.94$$
$P(\text{no fatalities in one month}) = P(x > 1) = 1 - 0.94 = 0.06$

b. $P(x \le 1 \text{ week}) = 1 - e^{-1/(52/34)} = 1 - e^{-34/52}$
$$= 1 - 0.52 = 0.48$$
Therefore, $P(x > 1 \text{ week}) = 0.52$

Chapter 4

1. a.

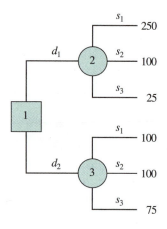

b.

Decision	Maximum Profit	Minimum Profit
d_1	250	25
d_2	100	75

Optimistic approach: Select d_1

Conservative approach: Select d_2

Regret or opportunity loss table:

Decision	s_1	s_2	s_3
d_1	0	0	50
d_2	150	0	0

Maximum regret: 50 for d_1 and 150 for d_2; select d_1

5. a. $EV(d_1) = 0.65(250) + 0.15(100) + 0.20(25) = 182.5$
$EV(d_2) = 0.65(100) + 0.15(100) + 0.20(75) = 95$
The optimal decision is d_1

8. $EV(d_1) = p(10) + (1 - p)(1) = 9p + 1$
$EV(d_2) = p(4) + (1 - p)(3) = 1p + 3$

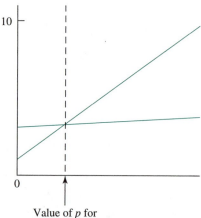

$9p + 1 = 1p + 3$ and hence $p = 0.25$

12. a. If s_1, then d_1; if s_2, then d_1 or d_2; if s_3, then d_2

b. $EVwPI = 0.65(250) + 0.15(100) + 0.20(75) = 192.5$

c. From the solution to Problem 5, we know that $EV(d_1) = 182.5$ and $EV(d_2) = 95$; thus, recommended decision is d_1; hence, $EVwoPI = 182.5$

d. $EVPI = EVwPI - EVwoPI = 192.5 - 182.5 = 10$

14.

State of Nature	$P(s_j)$	$P(I\|s_j)$	$P(I \cap s_j)$	$P(s_j\|I)$
s_1	0.2	0.10	0.020	0.1905
s_2	0.5	0.05	0.025	0.2381
s_3	0.3	0.20	0.060	0.5714
	1.0		$P(I) = 0.105$	1.0000

Chapter 5

1. a. $EV(d_1) = 0.40(100) + 0.30(25) + 0.30(0) = 47.5$
$EV(d_2) = 0.40(75) + 0.30(50) + 0.30(25) = 52.5 \; \}d_2$
$EV(d_3) = 0.40(50) + 0.30(50) + 0.30(50) = 50.0$

b. Using utilities

Decision Maker A	Decision Maker B
$EU(d_1) = 4.9$	$EU(d_1) = 4.45$ Best
$EU(d_2) = 5.9$	$EU(d_2) = 3.75$
$EU(d_3) = 6.0$ Best	$EU(d_3) = 3.00$

c. Difference in attitude toward risk; decision maker A tends to avoid risk, whereas decision maker B tends to take a risk for the opportunity of a large payoff

5. a.

b. A—risk avoider
B—risk taker
C—risk neutral

c. Risk-avoider A, at \$20 payoff $p = 0.70$
$\therefore$ EV(Lottery) $= 0.70(100) + 0.30(-100) = \$40$
$\therefore$ Will Pay $40 - 20 = \$20$
Risk-taker B, at \$20 payoff $p = 0.45$
$\therefore$ EV(Lottery) $= 0.45(100) + 0.55(-100) = -\$10$
$\therefore$ Will Pay $20 - (-10) = \$30$

Chapter 6

1. a.

Month	Time-Series Value	3-Month Moving Average Forecast	(Error)²	4-Month Moving Average Forecast	(Error)²
1	9.5				
2	9.3				
3	9.4				
4	9.6	9.40	0.04		
5	9.8	9.43	0.14	9.45	0.12
6	9.7	9.60	0.01	9.53	0.03
7	9.8	9.70	0.01	9.63	0.03
8	10.5	9.77	0.53	9.73	0.59
9	9.9	10.00	0.01	9.95	0.00
10	9.7	10.07	0.14	9.98	0.08
11	9.6	10.03	0.18	9.97	0.14
12	9.6	9.73	0.02	9.92	0.10
		Totals	1.08		1.09

MSE(3-month) = 1.08/9 = .12
MSE(4-month) = 1.09/8 = .14
Use a 3-month moving average.

b. Forecast = (9.7 + 9.6 + 9.6)/3 = 9.63

2. a.

Week	Time-Series Value	4-Week Moving Average Forecast	(Error)²	5-Week Moving Average Forecast	(Error)²
1	17				
2	21				
3	19				
4	23				
5	18	20.00	4.00		
6	16	20.25	18.06	19.60	12.96
7	20	19.00	1.00	19.40	0.36
8	18	19.25	1.56	19.20	1.44
9	22	18.00	16.00	19.00	9.00
10	20	19.00	1.00	18.80	1.44
11	15	20.00	25.00	19.20	17.64
12	22	18.75	10.56	19.00	9.00
		Totals	77.18		51.84

b. MSE(4-week) = 77.18/8 = 9.65
MSE(5-week) = 51.84/7 = 7.41

c. For the limited data provided, the 5-week moving average provides the smallest MSE

4.

Week	Time-Series Value	Forecast	Error	(Error)^2
1	17			
2	21	17.00	4.00	16.00
3	19	17.40	1.60	2.56
4	23	17.56	5.44	29.59
5	18	18.10	−0.10	0.01
6	16	18.09	−2.09	4.37
7	20	17.88	2.12	4.49
8	18	18.10	−0.10	0.01
9	22	18.09	3.91	15.29
10	20	18.48	1.52	2.31
11	15	18.63	−3.63	13.18
12	22	18.27	3.73	13.91
			Total	101.72

MSE = 101.72/11 = 9.25
$\alpha = 0.2$ provided a lower MSE; therefore $\alpha = 0.2$ is better than $\alpha = 0.1$

5. a.

Month	Y_t	3-Month Moving Averages Forecast	(Error)^2	$\alpha = 2$ Forecast	(Error)^2
1	80				
2	82			80.00	4.00
3	84			80.40	12.96
4	83	82.00	1.00	81.12	3.53
5	83	83.00	0.00	81.50	2.25
6	84	83.33	0.45	81.80	4.84
7	85	83.33	2.79	82.24	7.62
8	84	84.00	0.00	82.79	1.46
9	82	84.33	5.43	83.03	1.06
10	83	83.67	0.45	82.83	0.03
11	84	83.00	1.00	82.86	1.30
12	83	83.00	0.00	83.09	0.01
		Totals	11.12		39.06

MSE(3-month) = 11.12/9 = 1.24
MSE($\alpha = 0.2$) = 39.06/11 = 3.55
Use a 3-month moving average
b. (83 + 84 + 83)/3 = 83.3

14. $\Sigma t = 21; \Sigma t^2 = 91; \Sigma Y_t = 117.1;$
$\Sigma tY_t = 403.7; n = 6$
$$b_1 = \frac{\Sigma tY_t - (\Sigma t \Sigma Y_t)/n}{\Sigma t^2 - (\Sigma t)^2/n}$$

$$= \frac{403.7 - (21)(117.1)/6}{91 - (21)^2/6}$$
$$= -0.3514$$
$b_0 = \bar{Y} - b_1\bar{t} = 19.5167 - (-.3514)(3.5) = 20.7466$
$T_t = 20.7466 - 0.3514t$
Conclusion: Enrollment appears to be decreasing by an average of approximately 351 students per year

25. a. Four-quarter moving averages beginning with
(1690 + 940 + 2625 + 2500)/4 = 1938.75
Other moving averages are

1966.25	2002.50
1956.25	2052.50
2025.00	2060.00
1990.00	2123.75

b.

Quarter	Seasonal-Irregular Component Values		Seasonal Index	Adjusted Seasonal Index
1	0.904	0.900	0.9020	0.900
2	0.448	0.526	0.4970	0.486
3	1.344	1.453	1.3985	1.396
4	1.275	1.164	1.2195	1.217
			Total 4.0070	

c. The largest seasonal effect is in the third quarter which corresponds to the back-to-school demand during July, August, and September of each year.

33. Note: Adjustment for seasonal index = 4.000/4.007 = 0.9983

Restaurant (i)	x_i	y_i	x_iy_i	x_i^2
1	1	19	19	1
2	4	44	176	16
3	6	40	240	36
4	10	52	520	100
5	14	53	742	196
Totals	35	208	1697	349

$$\bar{x} = \frac{35}{5} = 7$$

$$\bar{y} = \frac{208}{5} = 41.6$$

$$b_1 = \frac{\Sigma x_iy_i - (\Sigma x_i \Sigma y_i)/n}{\Sigma x_i^2 - (\Sigma x_i)^2/n}$$

$$= \frac{1697 - (35)(208)/5}{349 - (35)^2/5}$$

$$= \frac{241}{104} = 2.317$$

$b_0 = \bar{y} - b_1\bar{x} = 41.6 - 2.317(7) = 25.381$

$\hat{y} = 25.381 + 2.317x$

b. $\hat{y} = 25.381 + 2.317(8) = 43.917$ or \$43,917

Chapter 7

1. Parts (a), (b), and (e) are acceptable linear programming relationships.

Part (c) is not acceptable because of $-2x_2^2$.

Part (d) is not acceptable because of $3\sqrt{x_1}$.

Part (f) is not acceptable because of $1x_1x_2$.

Parts (c), (d), and (f) could not be found in a linear programming model because they have the above nonlinear terms.

2. a.

b.

c.

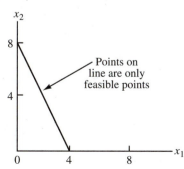

6. Slope of objective function: $-c_1/c_2$

For $z = 7x_1 + 10x_2$, slope $= -7/10$

For $z = 6x_1 + 4x_2$, slope $= -6/4 = -3/2$

For $z = -4x_1 + 7x_2$, slope $= -4/7$

7.

11.

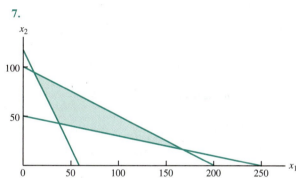

$$
\begin{aligned}
x_1 + 2x_2 &= 6 \quad (1)\\
5x_1 + 3x_2 &= 15 \quad (2)
\end{aligned}
$$

$(1) \times 5 \quad 5x_1 + 10x_2 = 30 \quad (3)$

$(2) - (3) \qquad\qquad -7x_2 = -15$

$\qquad\qquad\qquad\qquad x_2 = 15/7$

From (1) $\quad x_1 = 6 - 2(15/7)$

$\qquad\qquad\qquad = 6 - 30/7 = 12/7$

14. a.

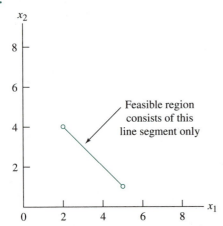

Feasible region consists of this line segment only

b. The extreme points are (5, 1) and (2, 4)

c.

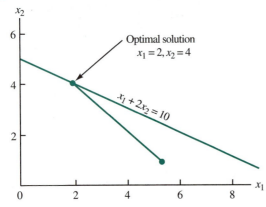

Optimal solution $x_1 = 2, x_2 = 4$

$x_1 + 2x_2 = 10$

18. Max $\quad 5x_1 + 2x_2 + 8x_3 + 0s_1 + 0s_2 + 0s_3$

s.t.

$$
\begin{aligned}
1x_1 - 2x_2 + \tfrac{1}{2}x_3 + 1s_1 &\qquad\qquad = 420\\
2x_1 + 3x_2 - 1x_3 \qquad + 1s_2 &\qquad = 610\\
6x_1 - 1x_2 + 3x_3 \qquad\qquad + 1s_3 &= 125\\
x_1, x_2, x_3, s_1, s_2, s_3 &\geq 0
\end{aligned}
$$

22. a. Let x_1 = number of units of regular model

$\qquad x_2$ = number of units of catcher's model

Max $\quad 5x_1 + 8x_2$

s.t.

$$
\begin{aligned}
1x_1 + \tfrac{3}{2}x_2 &\leq 900 \quad \text{Cutting and sewing}\\
\tfrac{1}{2}x_1 + \tfrac{1}{3}x_2 &\leq 300 \quad \text{Finishing}\\
\tfrac{1}{8}x_1 + \tfrac{1}{4}x_2 &\leq 100 \quad \text{Packaging and shipping}\\
x_1, x_2 &\geq 0
\end{aligned}
$$

b.

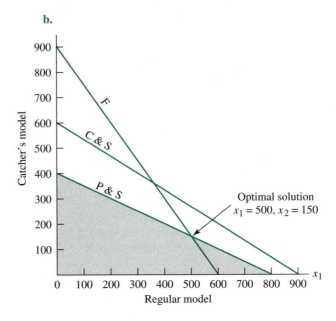

Optimal solution $x_1 = 500, x_2 = 150$

c. $5(500) + 8(150) = \$3700$

d. C & S $\qquad 1(500) + \tfrac{3}{2}(150) = 725$

F $\qquad\qquad \tfrac{1}{2}(500) + \tfrac{1}{3}(150) = 300$

P & S $\qquad \tfrac{1}{8}(500) + \tfrac{1}{4}(150) = 100$

e.

Department	Capacity	Usage	Slack
Cutting and sewing	900	725	175 hours
Finishing	300	300	0 hours
Packaging and shipping	100	100	0 hours

29.

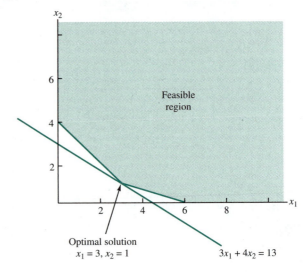

Feasible region

Optimal solution $x_1 = 3, x_2 = 1$

$3x_1 + 4x_2 = 13$

Objective function value = 13

32. a.

b. There are two extreme points

$x_1 = 4$ $x_1 = 21/4$
$x_2 = 1$ $x_2 = 9/4$

c. The optimal solution [see part (a)] is $x_1 = 4$, $x_2 = 1$

33. a. Min $6x_1 + 4x_2 + 0s_1 + 0s_2 + 0s_3$
     s.t.

$$2x_1 + 1x_2 - s_1 \qquad = 12$$
$$1x_1 + 1x_2 \qquad - s_2 \qquad = 10$$
$$1x_2 \qquad + s_3 = 4$$

$x_1, x_2, s_1, s_2, s_3 \geq 0$

b. The optimal solution is $x_1 = 6$, $x_2 = 4$

c. $s_1 = 4$, $s_2 = 0$, $s_3 = 0$

40.

41.

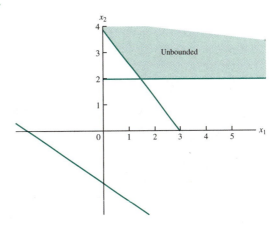

52. a. See figure below

b. Slope of line B $= -1$
Slope of line A $= -\frac{1}{3}$
$-1 \leq -c_1/3 \leq -\frac{1}{3}$
$1 \geq c_1/3 \quad c_1/3 \geq \frac{1}{3}$
$c_1 \leq 3 \quad c_1 \geq 1$
Range: $1 \leq c_1 \leq 3$

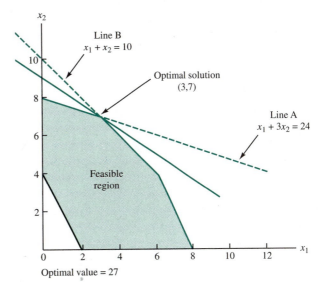

Optimal value = 27

c.
$-1 \leq -2/c_2 \leq -\frac{1}{3}$
$1 \geq 2/c_2 \quad 2/c_2 \geq \frac{1}{3}$
$c_2 \geq 2 \quad c_2 \leq 6$
Range: $2 \leq c_2 \leq 6$

d. Since this change leaves c_1 in its range of optimality, the same solution ($x_1 = 3$, $x_2 = 7$) is optimal

e. This change moves c_2 outside its range of optimality; the new optimal solution is shown below:

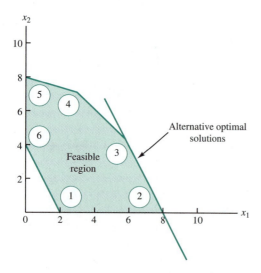

Alternative optimal solutions exist; extreme points 2 and 3 and all points on the line segment between them are optimal

53. By making a small increase in the right-hand side of constraint 1 and resolving, we find a dual price of 1.5 for the constraint; thus, the objective function will improve at the rate of 1.5 per unit increase in the right-hand side.
Since constraint 2 is not binding, its dual price is zero.
To determine the range over which these dual prices are applicable, you must obtain the range of feasibility.

Chapter 8

1. a. $x_1 = 500$; $x_2 = 150$; value = 3700
   b. The finishing, packaging, and shipping constraints are binding; there is no slack
   c. Cutting and sewing = 0
   Finishing = 3
   Packaging and shipping = 28
   Additional finishing time is worth \$3 per unit, and additional packaging and shipping time is worth \$28 per unit
   d. In the packaging and shipping department; each additional hour is worth \$28

2. a. $4 \leq c_1 \leq 12$
   $3.33 \leq c_2 \leq 10$
   b. As long as the profit contribution for the regular glove is between \$4.00 and \$12.00, the current solution is optimal. As long as the profit contribution for the catcher's mitt stays between \$3.33 and \$10.00, the current solution is optimal. The optimal solution is not sensitive to small changes in the profit contributions for the gloves.
   c. The dual prices for the resources are applicable over the following ranges.

Constraint	Min RHS	Max RHS
Cutting and Sewing	725	No upper limit
Finishing	133.33	400
Packaging and shipping	75	135

   d. Amount of increase = $(28)(20)$ = \$560

6. a. $x_1 = 30$, $x_2 = 25$, minimum production cost = \$55
   b. $0.5 \leq c_1 <$ No upper limit
   $0.0 \leq c_2 \leq 2$
   c. -0.50; -0.50; 0.0
   d.

Constraint	Min RHS	Max RHS
Raw material	70	No upper limit
Product 1 minimum	0.0	40.0
Product 2 minimum	No lower limit	25.0

8. a. $x_1 = 0$; $x_2 = 25$; $x_3 = 125$; $x_4 = 0$
   Value of solution = 525.0
   b. The constraints on machine A and machine C hours are binding
   c. Machine B has 425 hours of excess capacity
   d. Yes, the allowable increase is only 0.05

9. a. No lower limit $< c_1 \leq 4.05$
   $5.923 \leq c_2 \leq 9$
   $2 \leq c_3 \leq 12$
   No lower limit $< c_4 \leq 4.5$
   b. The allowance decrease for c_1 is ∞; thus, the percentage decrease is 0%
   $$\frac{1.5}{3.0} + \frac{1}{3.5} = 0.79$$
   The accumulated percentage of allowable increases and decreases is 79%; since this is less than 100%, the optimal solution will not change
   c.

Constraint	Min RHS	Max RHS
Machine A hours	133.33	800
Machine B hours	275	No upper limit
Machine C hours	137.5	825

   d. Yes, because that is outside the range of feasibility

Chapter 9

1. a. Let x_1 = number of television advertisements
   x_2 = number of radio advertisements
   x_3 = number of newspaper advertisements

Max $100,000x_1 + 18,000x_2 + 40,000x_3$

s.t.

$$2,000x_1 + 300x_2 + 600x_3 \leq 18,200 \text{ Budget}$$
$$x_1 \qquad\qquad\qquad \leq \quad 10 \text{ Max TV}$$
$$x_2 \qquad\qquad \leq \quad 20 \text{ Max radio}$$
$$x_3 \leq \quad 10 \text{ Max news}$$
$$-0.5x_1 + 0.5x_2 - 0.5x_3 \leq \quad 0 \text{ Max 50\% radio}$$
$$0.9x_1 - 0.1x_2 - 0.1x_3 \geq \quad 0 \text{ Min 10\% TV}$$
$$x_1, x_2, x_3, \geq 0$$

Solution:

		Budget $
$x_1 = 4$		$ 8,000
$x_2 = 14$		4,200
$x_3 = 10$		6,000
		$18,200 Audience = 1,052,000

b. The dual price for the budget constraint is 51.30. Thus, a $100 increase in the budget should provide an increase in audience coverage of approximately 5130. The range of feasibility for the right-hand side of the budget constraint will show that this interpretation is correct.

9. a. Decision variables A, P, M, H, and G represent the fraction or proportion of the total investment in each alternative.

Max $0.073A + 0.103P + 0.064M + 0.075H + 0.045G$

s.t.

$$A + P + M + H + G = 1$$
$$0.5A + 0.5P - 0.5M - 0.5H \leq 0$$
$$-0.5A - 0.5P + 0.5M + 0.5H \leq 0$$
$$- 0.25M - 0.25H + G \geq 0$$
$$-0.6A + 0.4P \leq 0$$
$$A, P, M, H, G \geq 0$$

Objective function $= 0.079$; $A = 0.178$; $P = 0.267$; $M = 0.000$; $H = 0.444$; $G = 0.111$

b. Multiplying A, P, M, H, and G by the $100,000 invested provides the following.

Atlantic Oil	$ 17,800
Pacific Oil	26,700
Huber Steel	44,400
Government Bonds	11,100
	$100,000

c. $0.079(\$100,000) = \$7900$

d. The marginal rate of return is 0.079.

12. a. The only change is in the objective function with the price per unit for the number of bases purchased (BP) lowered from 0.60 to 0.55. The solution for the new model provides an objective function value of $24,276.67, which is an overall savings of $166.66 compared to the previous solution. Janders will now purchase all 5000 bases from the supplier. In addition, Janders will increase the manufacturing of financial cartridges from 667 to 2333 units to take advantage of the manufacturing capacity freed by the fact that the company no longer needs to manufacture bases.

b. By referring to the computer solution in Figure 9.5, we can answer the question without modifying and re-solving the original problem. The range of optimality for the objective function coefficient for TTP is No Lower Limit to $0.875. Since the price increase to $0.82 is within the range, there will be no change in the manufacturing and purchasing plan. However, Janders purchases 2000 Technician tops. Thus, the price increase from $0.78 to $0.82 per unit will add $0.04(2000) = \$80$ to the total cost

c. The only change in the original problem is to reduce the objective function coefficient for overtime (OT) premium from $9 to $2 per hour. This change enables Janders to use all 50 hours of overtime for manufacturing. The total cost is further reduced to $24,293, but the company still needs purchases of 1333 financial cartridges (FCP), 3000 financial tops (FTP), and 2000 technician tops (TTP). The overtime is used to increase the manufacturing of financial cartridges (FCM) from 667 to 1667 units.

15. Let x_{11} = gallons of crude 1 used to produce regular
x_{12} = gallons of crude 1 used to produce high octane
x_{21} = gallons of crude 2 used to produce regular
x_{22} = gallons of crude 2 used to produce high octane

Min $0.10x_{11} + 0.10x_{12} + 0.15x_{21} + 0.15x_{22}$

s.t.

Each gallon of regular must have at least 40% A

$x_{11} + x_{21}$ = amount of regular produced
$0.4(x_{11} + x_{21})$ = amount of A required for regular
$0.2x_{11} + 0.50x_{21}$ = amount of A in $(x_{11} + x_{21})$ gallons of regular gas
$$\therefore 0.2x_{11} + 0.50x_{21} \geq 0.4x_{11} + 0.40x_{21}$$
$$\therefore -0.2x_{11} + 0.10x_{21} \geq 0$$

Each gallon of high octane can have at most 50% B

$x_{12} + x_{22}$ = amount high octane
$0.5(x_{12} + x_{22})$ = amount of B required for high octane
$0.60x_{12} + 0.30x_{22}$ = amount of B in $(x_{12} + x_{22})$ gallons of high octane
$$\therefore 0.60x_{12} + 0.30x_{22} \leq 0.5x_{12} + 0.5x_{22}$$
$$\therefore 0.1x_{12} - 0.2x_{22} \leq 0$$
$$x_{11} + x_{21} \geq 800,000$$
$$x_{12} + x_{22} \geq 500,000$$
$$x_{11}, x_{12}, x_{21}, x_{22} \geq 0$$

Optimal solution: $x_{11} = 266,667$, $x_{12} = 333,333$, $x_{21} = 533.333$, $x_{22} = 166,667$

Cost $= \$165,000$

19. a. Let x_{11} = amount of men's model in month 1
x_{21} = amount of women's model in month 1
x_{12} = amount of men's model in month 2
x_{22} = amount of women's model in month 2
s_{11} = inventory of men's model at end of month 1
s_{21} = inventory of women's model at end of month 1
s_{12} = inventory of men's model at end of month 2
s_{22} = inventory of women's model at end of month 2

Min $120x_{11} + 90x_{21} + 120x_{12} + 90x_{22} + 2.4s_{11} + 1.8s_{21} + 2.4s_{12} + 1.8s_{22}$
s.t.

$$
\left.\begin{array}{l}
x_{11} - \quad s_{11} = 130 \\
x_{21} - \quad s_{21} = 95 \\
s_{11} + x_{12} - s_{12} = 200 \\
s_{21} + x_{22} - s_{22} = 150
\end{array}\right\} \text{Satisfy demand}
$$

$$
\left.\begin{array}{l}
s_{12} \geq 25 \\
\\
s_{22} \geq 25
\end{array}\right\} \text{Ending inventory requirement}
$$

Labor hours: Men's $2.0 + 1.5 = 3.5$
Women's $1.6 + 1.0 = 2.6$

$$
\left.\begin{array}{l}
3.5x_{11} + 2.6x_{21} \geq 900 \\
3.5x_{11} + 2.6x_{21} \leq 1100 \\
3.5x_{11} + 2.6x_{21} - 3.5x_{21} - 2.6x_{22} \leq 100 \\
3.5x_{11} - 2.6x_{21} + 3.5x_{21} + 2.6x_{22} \leq 100
\end{array}\right\} \text{Labor smoothing}
$$

$x_{11}, x_{12}, x_{21}, x_{22}, s_{11}, s_{12}, s_{21}, s_{22} \geq 0$

Solution: $x_{11} = 193$; $x_{21} = 95$; $x_{12} = 162$; $x_{22} = 175$

Total cost = \$67,156

Inventory levels: $s_{11} = 63$; $s_{12} = 25$; $s_{21} = 0$; $s_{22} = 25$

Labor levels: Previous   1000 hours
              Month 1   922.25 hours
              Month 2   1022.25 hours

b. To accommodate the new policy, the right-hand sides of the four labor-smoothing constraints must be changed to 950, 1050, 50, and 50, respectively. The new total cost is \$67,175.

Chapter 10

1.

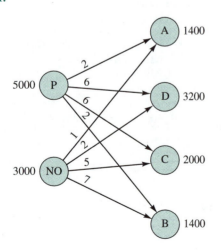

2. a. Let x_{11} = amount shipped from Jefferson City to Des Moines
x_{12} = amount shipped from Jefferson City to Kansas City
.
.
.
x_{23} = amount shipped from Omaha to St. Louis

Min $14x_{11} + 9x_{12} + 7x_{13} + 8x_{21} + 10x_{22} + 5x_{23}$
s.t.

$$
\begin{array}{rcl}
x_{11} + x_{12} + x_{13} & \leq & 30 \\
x_{21} + x_{22} + x_{23} & \leq & 20 \\
x_{11} \quad\quad\quad\quad + x_{21} & = & 25 \\
x_{12} \quad\quad\quad\quad + x_{22} & = & 15 \\
x_{13} \quad\quad\quad + x_{23} & = & 10
\end{array}
$$

$x_{11}, x_{12}, x_{13}, x_{21}, x_{22}, x_{23} \geq 0$

b.

Optimal Solution	Amount	Cost
Jefferson City–Des Moines	5	70
Jefferson City–Kansas City	15	135
Jefferson City–St. Louis	10	70
Omaha–Des Moines	20	160
	Total	435

8. The network model, in the linear programming formulation program and the optimal solution are shown. Note that the third constraint corresponds to the dummy origin; the variables x_{31},

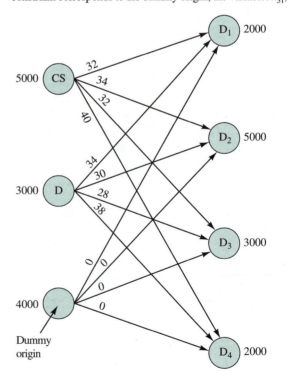

x_{32}, x_{33}, and x_{34} are the amounts shipped out of the dummy origin and do not appear in the objective function since they are given a coefficient of zero.

Max $32x_{11} + 34x_{12} + 32x_{13} + 40x_{14} + 34x_{21} + 30x_{22} + 28x_{23} + 38x_{24}$

s.t.

$$
\begin{array}{ll}
x_{11} + x_{12} + x_{13} + x_{14} & \leq 5000 \\
\quad x_{21} + x_{22} + x_{23} + x_{24} & \leq 3000 \\
\quad\quad x_{31} + x_{32} + x_{33} + x_{34} & \leq 4000 \\
x_{11} \quad + x_{21} \quad + x_{31} & = 2000 \\
\quad x_{12} \quad + x_{22} \quad + x_{32} & = 5000 \\
\quad\quad x_{13} \quad + x_{23} \quad + x_{33} & = 3000 \\
\quad\quad\quad x_{14} \quad + x_{24} \quad + x_{34} & = 2000 \\
\end{array}
$$

$x_{ij} \geq 0$ for all i, j

Optimal Solution	Units	Cost
Clifton Springs–D2	4,000	$136,000
Clifton Springs–D4	1,000	40,000
Danville–D1	2,000	68,000
Danville–D4	1,000	38,000
	Total	$282,000

Customer 2 demand has a shortfall of 1000; customer 3 demand of 3000 is not satisfied

12. a.

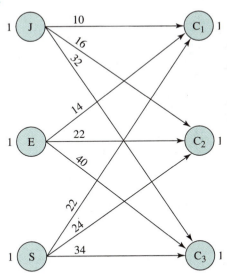

b.

Min $10x_{11} + 16x_{12} + 32x_{13} + 14x_{21} + 22x_{22} + 40x_{23} + 22x_{31} + 24x_{32} + 34x_{33}$

s.t.

$$
\begin{array}{ll}
x_{11} + x_{12} + x_{13} & \leq 1 \\
\quad x_{21} + x_{22} + x_{23} & \leq 1 \\
\quad\quad x_{31} + x_{32} + x_{33} & \leq 1 \\
x_{11} \quad + x_{21} \quad + x_{31} & = 1 \\
x_{12} \quad + x_{22} \quad + x_{32} & = 1 \\
x_{13} \quad + x_{23} \quad + x_{33} & = 1 \\
\end{array}
$$

$x_{ij} \geq 0$ for all i, j

Solution $x_{12} = 1, x_{21} = 1, x_{33} = 1$; total completion time = 64

21. a.

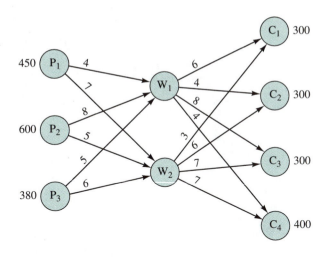

b.

Min $4x_{14} + 7x_{15} + 8x_{24} + 5x_{25} + 5x_{34} + 6x_{35} + 6x_{46} + 4x_{47} + 8x_{48} + 4x_{49} + 3x_{56} + 6x_{57} + 7x_{58} + 7x_{59}$

s.t.

$$
\begin{array}{ll}
x_{14} + x_{15} & \leq 450 \\
\quad x_{24} + x_{25} & \leq 600 \\
\quad\quad x_{34} + x_{35} & \leq 380 \\
-x_{14} \quad - x_{24} \quad - x_{34} \quad + x_{46} + x_{47} + x_{48} + x_{49} & = 0 \\
\quad - x_{15} \quad - x_{25} \quad - x_{35} \quad + x_{56} + x_{57} + x_{58} + x_{59} & = 0 \\
\quad\quad x_{46} \quad + x_{56} & = 300 \\
\quad\quad x_{47} \quad + x_{57} & = 300 \\
\quad\quad x_{48} \quad + x_{58} & = 300 \\
\quad\quad x_{49} \quad + x_{59} & = 400 \\
\end{array}
$$

c.

	Warehouse	
Plant	1	2
1	450	—
2	—	600
3	250	—

Total cost = $11,850

	Customer			
Warehouse	1	2	3	4
1	—	300	—	400
2	300	—	300	—

Chapter II

2. a.

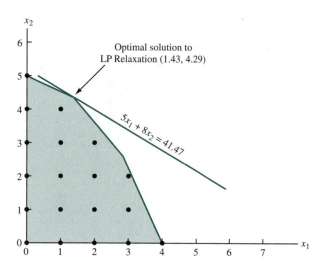

b. The optimal solution to the LP Relaxation is given by $x_1 = 1.43$, $x_2 = 4.29$ with an objective function value of 41.47. Rounding down gives the feasible integer solution $x_1 = 1$, $x_2 = 4$; its value is 37

c.

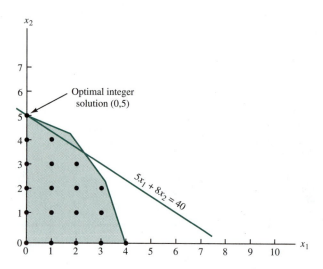

The optimal solution is given by $x_1 = 0$, $x_2 = 5$; its value is 40. This is not the same solution as found by rounding down; it provides a 3-unit increase in the value of the objective function

5. a. The feasible mixed-integer solutions are indicated by the boldface vertical lines in the graph

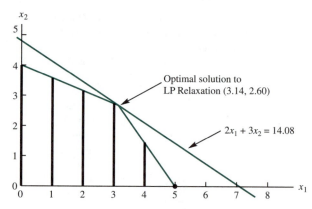

b. The optimal solution to the LP Relaxation is given by $x_1 = 3.14$, $x_2 = 2.60$; its value is 14.08
Rounding down the value of x_1 to find a feasible mixed-integer solution yields $x_1 = 3$, $x_2 = 2.60$ with a value of 13.8; this solution is clearly not optimal; with $x_1 = 3$, x_2 can be made larger without violating the constraints

c. The optimal solution to the MILP is given by $x_1 = 3$, $x_2 = 2.67$; its value is 14. See the figure below.

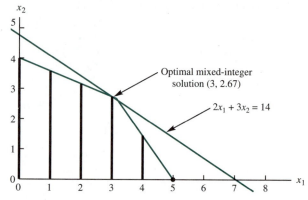

7. a. $x_1 + x_3 + x_5 + x_6 = 2$
b. $x_3 - x_5 = 0$
c. $x_1 + x_4 = 1$
d. $x_4 \leq x_1$
$x_4 \leq x_3$
e. $x_4 \leq x_1$
$x_4 \leq x_3$
$x_4 \geq x_1 + x_3 - 1$

13. a. Add the following multiple-choice constraint to the problem
$y_2 + y_2 = 1$
New optimal Solution: $y_1 = 1$, $y_3 = 1$, $x_{12} = 10$, $x_{31} = 30$, $x_{52} = 10$, $x_{53} = 20$
Value = 940

b. Since one plant is already located in St. Louis, it is only necessary to add the following constraint to the model

$y_3 + y_4 \leq 1$

New Optimal Solution: $y_4 = 1$, $x_{42} = 20$, $x_{43} = 20$, $x_{51} = 30$

Value = 860

Chapter 12

3.

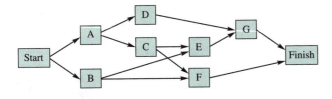

6. a. Critical path: A–D–F–H
b. 22 weeks
c. No, it is a critical activity
d. Yes, 2 weeks
e. Schedule for activity E:

Earliest start	3
Latest start	4
Earliest finish	10
Latest finish	11

10. a.

Activity	Optimistic	Most Probable	Pessimistic	Expected Times	Variance
A	4	5.0	6	5.00	0.11
B	8	9.0	10	9.00	0.11
C	7	7.5	11	8.00	0.44
D	7	9.0	10	8.83	0.25
E	6	7.0	9	7.17	0.25
F	5	6.0	7	6.00	0.11

b. Critical activities: B–D–F
Expected project completion time: 9.00 + 8.83 + 6.00 = 23.83
Variance of projection completion time: 0.11 + 0.25 + 0.11 = 0.47

13.

Activity	Expected Time	Variance
A	5	0.11
B	3	0.03
C	7	0.11
D	6	0.44
E	7	0.44
F	3	0.11
G	10	0.44
H	8	1.78

From Problem 6, A–D–F–H is the critical path, so

$E(T) = 5 + 6 + 3 + 8 = 22$

$\sigma^2 = 0.11 + 0.44 + 0.11 + 1.78 = 2.44$

$z = \dfrac{\text{Times} - E(T)}{\sigma} = \dfrac{\text{Time} - 22}{\sqrt{2.44}}$

a. Time = 21: $z = -0.64$ Area 0.2389
$P(21 \text{ weeks}) = 0.500 - 0.2389 = 0.2611$

b. Time = 22: $z = 0$ Area 0.0000
$P(22 \text{ weeks}) = 0.5000$

c. Time = 25: $z = +1.92$ Area 0.4726
$P(25 \text{ weeks}) = 0.5000 + 0.4726 = 0.9726$

21. a.

Activity	Earliest Start	Latest Start	Earliest Finish	Latest Finish	Slack	Critical Activity
A	0	0	3	3	0	Yes
B	0	1	2	3	1	
C	3	3	8	8	0	Yes
D	2	3	7	8	1	
E	8	8	14	14	0	Yes
F	8	10	10	12	2	
G	10	12	12	14	2	

Critical Path: A–C–E
Project completion time = $t_A + t_C + t_E = 3 + 5 + 6 = 14$ days
b. Total cost = $8400

22. a.

Activity	Max Crash Days	Crash Cost/Day
A	1	600
B	1	700
C	2	400
D	2	400
E	2	500
F	1	400
G	1	500

Min $600Y_A + 700Y_B + 400Y_C + 400Y_D + 500Y_E + 400Y_F + 400Y_G$

s.t.

$$X_A + \ Y_A \geq 3$$
$$X_B + \ Y_B \geq 2$$
$$-X_A + \ X_C + Y_C \geq 5$$
$$-X_B + \ X_D + Y_D \geq 5$$
$$-X_C + \ X_E + Y_E \geq 6$$
$$-X_D + \ X_E + Y_E \geq 6$$
$$-X_C + \ X_F + Y_F \geq 2$$
$$-X_D + \ X_F + Y_F \geq 2$$
$$-X_F + \ X_G + Y_G \geq 2$$
$$-X_E + X_{FIN} \geq 0$$
$$-X_G + X_{FIN} \geq 0$$
$$X_{FIN} \leq 12$$
$$Y_A \leq 1$$
$$Y_B \leq 1$$
$$Y_C \leq 2$$
$$Y_D \leq 2$$
$$Y_E \leq 2$$
$$Y_F \leq 1$$
$$Y_G \leq 1$$
$$\text{All } X, Y \geq 0$$

b. Solution of the linear programming model in part (a) shows

Activity	Crash	Crashing Cost
C	1 day	$400
E	1 day	500
	Total	$900

c. Total cost = Normal cost + Crashing cost
               = $8400 + $900 = $9300

Chapter 13

1. a. $Q^* = \sqrt{\dfrac{2DC_0}{C_h}} = \sqrt{\dfrac{2(3600)(20)}{0.25(3)}} = 438.18$

b. $r = dm = \dfrac{3600}{250}(5) = 72$

c. $T = \dfrac{250Q^*}{D} = \dfrac{250(438.18)}{3600} = 30.43$ days

d. $TC = \dfrac{1}{2}QC_h + \dfrac{D}{Q}C_0$

$$= \dfrac{1}{2}(438.18)(0.25)(3) + \dfrac{3600}{438.18}(20) = \$328.63$$

13. a. $Q^* = \sqrt{\dfrac{2DC_0}{(1 - D/P)C_h}}$

$$= \sqrt{\dfrac{2(7200)(150)}{(1 - 7200/25{,}000)(0.18)(14.50)}} = 1078.12$$

b. Number of production runs $= \dfrac{D}{Q^*} = \dfrac{7200}{1078.12} = 6.68$

c. $T = \dfrac{250Q}{D} = \dfrac{250(1078.12)}{7200} = 37.43$ days

d. Production run length $= \dfrac{Q}{P/250}$

$$= \dfrac{1078.12}{25{,}000/250} = 10.78 \text{ days}$$

e. Maximum inventory $= \left(1 - \dfrac{D}{P}\right)Q$

$$= \left(1 - \dfrac{7200}{25{,}000}\right)(1078.12)$$

$$= 767.62$$

f. Holding cost $= \dfrac{1}{2}\left(1 - \dfrac{D}{P}\right)QC_h$

$$= \dfrac{1}{2}\left(1 - \dfrac{7200}{25{,}000}\right)(1078.12)(0.18)(14.50)$$

$$= \$1001.74$$

Ordering cost $= \dfrac{D}{Q}C_0 = \dfrac{7200}{1078.12}(150) = \$1001.74$

Total cost $= \$2003.48$

g. $r = dm = \left(\dfrac{D}{250}\right)m = \dfrac{7200}{250}(15) = 432$

15. a. $Q^* = \sqrt{\dfrac{2DC_0}{C_h}\left(\dfrac{C_h + C_b}{C_b}\right)}$

$$= \sqrt{\dfrac{2(12{,}000)(25)}{0.50}\left(\dfrac{0.50 + 5}{0.50}\right)} = 1148.91$$

b. $S^* = Q^*\left(\dfrac{C_h}{C_h + C_b}\right) = 1148.91\left(\dfrac{0.50}{0.50 + 5}\right) = 104.45$

c. Max inventory $= Q^* - S^* = 1044.46$

d. $T = \dfrac{250Q^*}{D} = \dfrac{250(1148.91)}{12,000} = 23.94$ days

e. Holding $= \dfrac{(Q-S)^2}{2Q}C_h = \$237.38$

  Ordering $= \dfrac{D}{Q}C_0 = 261.12$

  Backorder $= \dfrac{S^2}{2Q}C_b = 23.74$

  Total cost $= \$522.24$

The total cost for the EOQ model in Problem 4 was $547.72; allowing backorders reduces the total cost

21. $Q = \sqrt{\dfrac{2DC_0}{C_h}}$

  $Q_1 = \sqrt{\dfrac{2(500)(40)}{0.20(10)}} = 141.42$

  $Q_2 = \sqrt{\dfrac{2(500)(40)}{0.20(9.7)}} = 143.59$

Since Q_1 is over its limit of 99 units, Q_1 cannot be optimal (see Problem 23); use $Q_2 = 143.59$ as the optimal order quantity

  Total cost $= \dfrac{1}{2}QC_h + \dfrac{D}{Q}C_0 + DC$

  $= 139.28 + 139.28 + 4850.00 = \$5128.56$

25. a.
  $c_o = 80 - 50 = 30$
  $c_u = 125 - 80 = 45$

  $P(D \le Q^*) = \dfrac{c_u}{c_u + c_o} = \dfrac{45}{45 + 30} = 0.60$

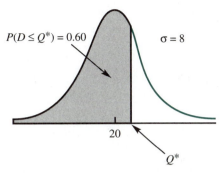

For an area of 0.60 below Q^*, $z = 0.25$
$Q^* = 20 + 0.25(8) = 22$
b. $P(\text{Sell all}) = P(D \ge Q^*) = 1 - 0.60 = 0.40$

29. a. $r = dm = (200/250)15 = 12$
b. $\dfrac{D}{Q} = \dfrac{200}{25} = 8$ orders/year

The limit of 1 stockout per year means that $P(\text{Stockout/cycle}) = 1/8 = 0.125$

For area in tail $= 0.125$, $z = 1.15$
$z = \dfrac{r - 12}{2.5} = 1.15$

or
$r = 12 + 1.15(2.5) = 14.875 \approx 15$
c. Safety stock $= 3$ units
  Added cost $= 3(\$5) = \$15$/year

33. a. $1/52 = 0.0192$
b. $M = \mu + z\sigma = 60 + 2.07(12) = 85$
c. $M = 35 + (0.9808)(85 - 35) = 84$

Chapter 14

1. a.

WHEEL SUBASSEMBLY	Lead Time: 2				Week			
Lot Size: 400	Safety Stock: 0		1	2	3	4	5	6
Gross requirements				250		300		260
Scheduled receipts				400				
Projected balance		80	80	230	230	330	330	70
Net requirements						70		
Planned order receipts						400		
Planned order releases				400				

b.

WHEEL SUBASSEMBLY	Lead Time: 2				Week			
Lot Size: 400	Safety Stock: 0		1	2	3	4	5	6
Gross requirements				250		300		260
Scheduled receipts				400				
Projected balance		180	180	330	330	30	30	170
Net requirements								230
Planned order receipts								400
Planned order releases						400		

c.

WHEEL SUBASSEMBLY	Lead Time: 2				Week			
Lot Size: 500	Safety Stock: 0		1	2	3	4	5	6
Gross requirements				250		300		260
Scheduled receipts				400				
Projected balance		80	80	230	230	430	430	170
Net requirements						70		
Planned order receipts						500		
Planned order releases				500				

3. a.

WHEEL SUBASSEMBLY	Lead Time: 2				Week			
Lot-for-Lot	Safety Stock: 0		1	2	3	4	5	6
Gross requirements				250		300		260
Scheduled receipts				400				
Projected balance		80	80	230	230	0	0	0
Net requirements						70		260
Planned order receipts						70		260
Planned order releases				70		260		

b.

WHEEL SUBASSEMBLY Lot-for-Lot	Lead Time: 2 Safety Stock: 0		1	2	3	4	5	6
				Week				
Gross requirements				250		300		260
Scheduled receipts				400				0
Projected balance		180	180	330	330	30	30	230
Net requirements								230
Planned order receipts								230
Planned order releases						230		

7. a.

DRAWER Lot size: 500	Lead Time: 1 Safety Stock: 30		1	2	3	4	5	6
					Week			
Gross requirements			450		300	250		500
Scheduled receipts			500					
Projected balance		0	50	50	250	500	500	500
Net requirements					280	30		30
Planned order receipts					500	500		500
Planned order releases				500	500		500	

The safety stock causes larger projected balances and therefore increases the inventory holding cost.

b.

DRAWER Lot size: 500	Lead Time: 1 Safety Stock: 100		1	2	3	4	5	6
					Week			
Gross requirements			450		300	250		500
Scheduled receipts			500					
Projected balance		120	170	170	370	120	120	120
Net requirements					230			480
Planned order receipts					500			500
Planned order releases				500			500	

The projected balances are the same as in part 4(b), so holding cost would not increase; however, over a longer planning period we could expect holding costs to be higher because the projected balance could not drop below 100.

10. a.

B Lot size: 500	Lead Time: 3 Safety Stock: 0		21	22	23	24	25	26
					Week			
Gross requirements				450		600		400
Scheduled receipts				500				
Projected balance		150	150	200	200	100	100	200
Net requirements						400		300
Planned order receipts						500		500
Planned order releases			500		500			

b.

D Lot-for-Lot	Lead Time: 1 Safety Stock: 0		Week			
			20	21	22	23
Gross requirements				500		500
Scheduled receipts						
Projected balance		50	50	0	0	0
Net requirements				450		500
Planned order receipts				450		500
Planned order releases			450		500	

Chapter 15

5. a. $P_0 = 1 - \dfrac{\lambda}{\mu} = 1 - \dfrac{10}{12} = 0.1667$

b. $L_q = \dfrac{\lambda^2}{\mu(\mu - \lambda)} = \dfrac{10^2}{12(12 - 10)} = 4.1667$

c. $W_q = \dfrac{L_q}{\lambda} = 0.4167$ hour (25 minutes)

d. $W = W_q + \dfrac{1}{\mu} = 0.5$ hour (30 minutes)

e. $P_w = \dfrac{\lambda}{\mu} = \dfrac{10}{12} = 0.8333$

11. a. $\lambda = 2.5;\quad \mu = \dfrac{60}{10} = 6$ customers per hour

$L_q = \dfrac{\lambda^2}{\mu(\mu - \lambda)} = \dfrac{(2.5)^2}{6(6 - 2.5)} = 0.2976$

$L = L_q + \dfrac{\lambda}{\mu} = 0.7143$

$W_q = \dfrac{L_q}{\lambda} = 0.1190$ hours (7.14 minutes)

$W = W_q + \dfrac{1}{\mu} = 0.2857$ hours

$P_w = \dfrac{\lambda}{\mu} = \dfrac{2.5}{6} = 0.4167$

b. No; $W_q = 7.14$ minutes; firm should increase the mean service rate (μ) for the consultant or hire a second consultant

c. $\mu = \dfrac{60}{8} = 7.5$ customers per hour

$L_q = \dfrac{\lambda^2}{\mu(\mu - \lambda)} = \dfrac{(2.5)^2}{7.5(7.5 - 2.5)} = 0.1667$

$W_q = \dfrac{L_q}{\lambda} = 0.0667$ hour (4 minutes)

The service goal is being met

19. a. $k = 2;\ \lambda/\mu = 14/10 = 1.4;\ P_0 = 0.1765$

b. $L_q = \dfrac{(\lambda/\mu)^2 \lambda \mu}{1!(2\mu - \lambda)^2} P_0 = \dfrac{(1.4)^2(14)(10)}{(20 - 14)^2}(0.1765)$

$\qquad = 1.3453$

$L = L_q + \dfrac{\lambda}{\mu} = 1.3453 + \dfrac{14}{10} = 2.7453$

c. $W_q = \dfrac{L_q}{\lambda} = \dfrac{1.3453}{14} = 0.961$ hours

d. $W = W_q + \dfrac{1}{\mu} = 0.0961 + \dfrac{1}{10} = 0.1961$ hours

e. $P_0 = 0.1765$

$P_1 = \dfrac{(\lambda/\mu)^1}{1!}P_0 = \dfrac{14}{10}(0.1765) = 0.2471$

$P(\text{wait}) = P(n \geq 2) = 1 - P(n \leq 1)$
$\qquad\qquad = 1 - 0.4236 = 0.5764$

21. From Problem 11, a service time of 8 minutes has $\mu = 60/8 = 7.5$

$L_q = \dfrac{\lambda^2}{\mu(\mu - \lambda)} = \dfrac{(2.5)^2}{7.5(7.5 - 2.5)} = 0.1667$

$L = L_q + \dfrac{\lambda}{\mu} = 0.50$

Total cost $= \$25L + \$16$
$\qquad\qquad = 25(0.50) + 16 = \$28.50$

Two channels: $\lambda = 2.5; \mu = 60/10 = 6$
Using equation (15.11) and $P_0 = 0.6552$, we get

$L_q = \dfrac{(\lambda/\mu)^2 \lambda \mu}{1!(2\mu - \lambda)^2} P_0 = 0.0189$

$L = L_q + \dfrac{\lambda}{\mu} = 0.4356$

Total cost $= 25(0.4356) + 2(16) = \$42.89$
Use one consultant with an 8-minute service time

25. $\lambda = 4, W = 10$ minutes
a. $\mu = \frac{1}{2} = 0.5$
b. $W_q = W - 1/\mu = 10 - 1/0.5 = 8$ minutes
c. $L = \lambda W = 4(10) = 40$

27. a. $\frac{2}{8}$ hours $= 0.25$ per hour
b. $1/3.2$ hours $= 0.3125$ per hour
c. $L_q = \dfrac{\lambda^2 \sigma^2 + (\lambda/\mu)^2}{2(1 - \lambda/\mu)}$

$\qquad = \dfrac{(0.25)^2(2)^2 + (0.25/0.3125)^2}{2(1 - 0.25/0.3125)} = 2.225$

d. $W_q = \dfrac{L_q}{\lambda} = \dfrac{2.225}{0.25} = 8.9$ hours

e. $W = W_q + \dfrac{1}{\mu} = 8.9 + \dfrac{1}{0.3125} = 12.1$ hours

f. Same as $P_w = \dfrac{\lambda}{\mu} = \dfrac{0.25}{0.3125} = 0.80$

80% of the time the welder is busy

30. a. $\lambda = 42; \mu = 20$

i	$(\lambda/\mu)^i/i!$
0	1.0000
1	2.1000
2	2.2050
3	1.5435
Total	6.8485

j	P_j	
0	1/6.8485	= 0.1460
1	2.1/6.8485	= 0.3066
2	2.2050/6.8485	= 0.3220
3	1.5435/6.8485	= 0.2254
		1.0000

b. 0.2254

c. $L = \lambda/\mu(1 - P_k) = 42/20(1 - 0.2254) = 1.6267$

d. Four lines will be necessary; the probability of denied access is 0.1499

34. $N = 5; \quad \lambda = 0.025; \quad \mu = 0.20; \quad \lambda/\mu = 0.125$

a.

n	$\dfrac{N!}{(N-n)!}\left(\dfrac{\lambda}{\mu}\right)^n$
0	1.0000
1	0.6250
2	0.3125
3	0.1172
4	0.0293
5	0.0037
Total	2.0877

$P_0 = 1/2.0877 = 0.4790$

b. $L_q = N - \left(\dfrac{\lambda + \mu}{\lambda}\right)(1 - P_0)$

$= 5 - \left(\dfrac{0.225}{0.025}\right)(1 - 0.4790) = 0.3110$

c. $L = L_q + (1 - P_0) = 0.3110 + (1 - 0.4790)$
$= 0.8320$

d. $W_q = \dfrac{L_q}{(N - L)\lambda} = \dfrac{0.3110}{(5 - 0.8320)(0.025)}$
$= 2.9846$ minutes

e. $W = W_q + \dfrac{1}{\mu} = 2.9846 + \dfrac{1}{0.20} = 7.9846$ minutes

f. Trips/day = (8 hours)(60 minutes/hour)(λ)
$= (8)(60)(0.025) = 12$ trips

Time at copier: $12 \times 7.9846 = 95.8$ minutes/day

Wait time at copier: $12 \times 2.9846 = 35.8$ minutes/day

g. Yes, five assistants $\times$ 35.8 = 179 minutes (3 hours/day), so 3 hours per day are lost to waiting
$(35.8/480)(100) = 7.5\%$ of each assistants day is spent waiting for the copier

Chapter 16

2. a. c = variable cost per unit
x = demand
Profit = $(50 - c)x - 30,000$

b. Base: Profit = $(50 - 20)1200 - 30,000 = 6,000$
Worst: Profit = $(50 - 24)300 - 30,000 = -22,200$
Best: Profit = $(50 - 16)2100 - 30,000 = 41,400$

c. Simulation will be helpful in estimating the probability of a loss

5. a.

Stock Price Change	Interval
-2	0.00 but less than 0.05
-1	0.05 but less than 0.15
0	0.15 but less than 0.40
$+1$	0.40 but less than 0.60
$+2$	0.60 but less than 0.80
$+3$	0.80 but less than 0.90
$+4$	0.90 but less than 1.00

b. Beginning price $39
0.1091 indicates -1 change; $38
0.9407 indicates $+4$ change; $42
0.1941 indicates 0 change; $42
0.8083 indicates $+3$ change; $45 (ending price)

9. a. Base case based on most likely;
Time = 6 + 5 + 14 + 8 = 33 weeks
Worst: Time = 8 + 7 + 18 + 10 = 43 weeks
Best: Time = 5 + 3 + 10 + 8 = 26 weeks

b. 0.1778 for A − 5 weeks
0.9617 for B − 7 weeks
0.6849 for C − 14 weeks
0.4503 for D − 8 weeks; Total = 24 weeks

c. Simulation will provide an estimate of the probability of 35 weeks or less.

14. a. Assume trial 1 is in row 5 of the spreadsheet
Cell A5 enter 1 (trial 1)
Cell B5 =16+RAND()*8 (Variable cost per unit)
Cell C5 =NORMINV(RAND)(),1200,300) (Units sold)
Cell D5 =(50 − B5)*C5 − 30000 (Profit)
Copy 500 rows to conduct 500 simulation trials
=AVERAGE(D5:D504) will provide the mean profit of $5500 to $6500 for most simulations

b. =COUNTIF(D5:D504," > 0") will count the number of times there was a loss; 125 to 150 for most simulations; thus, 0.25 to 0.30 is the probability of a loss.

c. Individual preference, but probability of a loss suggests project is too risky as it is currently defined.

18. a. *Note:* Data in 000's

Cell A1 =600+RAND()*200 (A's bid)

Cell B1 =NORMINV(RAND(),700,50) (B's bid)

Cell C1 =MAX(A1:B1)

Cell C1 contains the value of highest competitive bid.

Copy to 1000 rows to conduct 1000 simulation trials.

Cell D1 =COUNTIF(D1:D1000," < 750") will count the number of times the highest competitive bid is less than the Contractor's $750,000 bid. This formula counts the number of times the contractor wins.

Simulation results vary, but contractor wins roughly 60% to 65% of the time.

b. Cell D2 =COUNTIF(D1:D1000," < 775") and

Cell D3 =COUNTIF(D1:D1000," < 785") will count the wins for the $775,000 and $785,000 bids.

At $775,000 the contractor wins roughly 82%

At $785,000 the contractor wins roughly 88%

Bid $775,000 is recommended.

Chapter 17

3. a. 0.10 as given by the transition probability

b. $\pi_1 = 0.90\pi_1 + 0.30\pi_2$ (1)

$\pi_2 = 0.10\pi_1 + 0.70\pi_2$ (2)

$\pi_1 + \pi_2 = 1$ (3)

Using (1) and (3),

$$0.10\pi_1 - 0.30\pi_2 = 0$$
$$0.10\pi_1 - 0.30(1 - \pi_1) = 0$$
$$0.10\pi_1 - 0.30 + 0.30\pi_1 = 0$$
$$0.40\pi_1 = 0.30$$
$$\pi_1 = 0.75$$
$$\pi_2 = (1 - \pi_1) = 0.25$$

7. a. $\pi_1 = 0.85\pi_1 + 0.20\pi_2 + 0.15\pi_3$ (1)

$\pi_2 = 0.10\pi_1 + 0.75\pi_2 + 0.10\pi_3$ (2)

$\pi_3 = 0.05\pi_1 + 0.05\pi_2 + 0.75\pi_3$ (3)

$\pi_1 + \pi_2 + \pi_3 = 1$ (4)

Using (1), (2), and (4) provides three equations with three unknowns; solving provides $\pi_1 = 0.548$, $\pi_2 = 0.286$, and $\pi_3 = 0.166$

b. 16.6% as given by π_3

c. Quick Stop should take

$667 - 0.548(1000) = 119$ Murphy's customers

and $333 - 0.286(1000) = \underline{47}$ Ashley's customers

Total   166 Quick Stop customers

It will take customers from Murphy and Ashley.

11. $I = \begin{bmatrix} 1 & 0 \\ 0 & 1 \end{bmatrix}$ $Q = \begin{bmatrix} 0.25 & 0.25 \\ 0.25 & 0.25 \end{bmatrix}$

$(I - Q) = \begin{bmatrix} 0.75 & -0.25 \\ -0.05 & 0.75 \end{bmatrix}$

$N = (I - Q)^{-1} = \begin{bmatrix} 1.3636 & 0.4545 \\ 0.0909 & 1.3636 \end{bmatrix}$

$NR = \begin{bmatrix} 1.3636 & 0.4545 \\ 0.0909 & 1.3636 \end{bmatrix}\begin{bmatrix} 0.5 & 0.0 \\ 0.5 & 0.2 \end{bmatrix} = \begin{bmatrix} 0.909 & 0.091 \\ 0.727 & 0.273 \end{bmatrix}$

$BNR = \begin{bmatrix} 4000 & 5000 \end{bmatrix}\begin{bmatrix} 0.909 & 0.091 \\ 0.727 & 0.273 \end{bmatrix} = \begin{bmatrix} 7271 & 1729 \end{bmatrix}$

Estimate $1729 in bad debts

Chapter 18

2. a. Let x_1 = number of shares of AGA Products purchased

x_2 = number of shares of Key Oil purchased

To obtain an annual return of exactly 9%:

$0.06(50)x_1 + 0.10(100)x_2 = 0.09(50,000)$

$3x_1 + 10x_2 = 4500$

To have exactly 60% of the total investment in Key Oil:

$100x_2 = 0.60(50,000)$

$x_2 = 300$

Therefore, we can write the goal programming model as follows:

Min $P_1(d_1^-) + P_2(d_2^+)$

s.t.

$50x_1 + 100x_2 \leq 50,000$ Funds available

$3x_1 + 10x_2 - d_1^+ + d_1^- = 4,500$ P_1 goal

$x_2 - d_2^+ + d_2^- = 300$ P_2 goal

$x_1, x_2, d_1^+, d_1^-, d_2^+, d_2^- \geq 0$

b. In the graphical solution shown below, $x_1 = 250$ and $x_2 = 375$

12. *Synthesization*

Step 1: Column totals are $^{17}\!/_4$, $^{31}\!/_{21}$, and 12

Step 2:

		Style	
Style	**Car A**	**Car B**	**Car C**
Car A	$4/17$	$7/31$	$4/12$
Car B	$12/17$	$21/31$	$7/12$
Car C	$1/17$	$3/31$	$1/12$

Step 3:

		Style		Row
Style	**Car A**	**Car B**	**Car C**	**Average**
Car A	0.235	0.226	0.333	0.265
Car B	0.706	0.677	0.583	0.655
Car C	0.059	0.097	0.083	0.080

Consistency Ratio
Step 1:

$$0.265\begin{bmatrix} 1 \\ 3 \\ 1/4 \end{bmatrix} + 0.655\begin{bmatrix} 1/3 \\ 1 \\ 1/7 \end{bmatrix} + 0.080\begin{bmatrix} 4 \\ 7 \\ 1 \end{bmatrix}$$

Weighted Sum

$$\begin{bmatrix} 0.265 \\ 0.795 \\ 0.066 \end{bmatrix} + \begin{bmatrix} 0.218 \\ 0.655 \\ 0.094 \end{bmatrix} + \begin{bmatrix} 0.320 \\ 0.560 \\ 0.080 \end{bmatrix} = \begin{bmatrix} 0.803 \\ 2.010 \\ 0.240 \end{bmatrix}$$

Step 2: $0.803/0.265 = 3.030$
$2.010/0.655 = 3.069$
$0.240/0.080 = 3.000$
Step 3: $\lambda_{max} = (3.030 + 3.069 + 3.000)/3 = 3.033$
Step 4: $CI = (3.033 - 3)/2 = 0.017$
Step 5: $CR = 0.017/0.58 = 0.29$
Since $CR = 0.029$ is less than 0.10, the degree of consistency exhibited in the pairwise comparison matrix for style is acceptable

16. a.

		Flavor	
Flavor	**A**	**B**	**C**
A	1	3	2
B	$1/3$	1	5
C	$1/2$	$1/5$	1

b. Step 1: Column totals are $11/6$, $21/5$, and 8
Step 2:

		Flavor	
Flavor	**A**	**B**	**C**
A	$6/11$	$15/21$	$2/8$
B	$2/11$	$5/21$	$5/8$
C	$3/11$	$1/21$	$1/8$

Step 3:

		Flavor		
Flavor	**A**	**B**	**C**	**Row Average**
A	0.545	0.714	0.250	0.503
B	0.182	0.238	0.625	0.348
C	0.273	0.048	0.125	0.149

c. Step 1:

$$0.503\begin{bmatrix} 1 \\ 1/3 \\ 1/2 \end{bmatrix} + 0.348\begin{bmatrix} 3 \\ 1 \\ 1/5 \end{bmatrix} + 0.149\begin{bmatrix} 2 \\ 5 \\ 1 \end{bmatrix}$$

Weighted Sum

$$\begin{bmatrix} 0.503 \\ 0.168 \\ 0.252 \end{bmatrix} + \begin{bmatrix} 1.044 \\ 0.348 \\ 0.070 \end{bmatrix} + \begin{bmatrix} 0.298 \\ 0.745 \\ 0.149 \end{bmatrix} = \begin{bmatrix} 1.845 \\ 1.261 \\ 0.471 \end{bmatrix}$$

Step 2: $1.845/0.503 = 3.668$
$1.261/0.348 = 3.624$
$0.471/0.149 = 3.161$
Step 3: $\lambda_{max} = (3.668 + 3.624 + 3.161)/3 = 3.484$
Step 4: $CI = (3.484 - 3)/2 = 0.242$

Step 5: $CR = 0.242/0.58 = 0.417$

Since $CR = 0.417$ is greater than 0.10, the individual's judgments are not consistent.

20. a.

Overall Goal	Select the best investment
Criteria	Yield Risk
Decision Alternatives	CCI SRI CCI SRI

b.

Criterion		Yield		Risk	
Yield:	0.667	CCI:	0.750	CCI:	0.333
Risk:	0.333	SRI:	0.250	SRI:	0.667

c.

	Criterion	
Alternative	**Yield**	**Risk**
CCI	0.750	0.333
SRI	0.250	0.667

Overall priority for CCI:
$0.667(0.750) + 0.333(0.333) = 0.500 + 0.111 = 0.611$
Overall priority for SRI:
$0.667(0.250) + 0.333(0.667) + 0.167 + 0.222 = 0.389$

INDEX

*A page number followed by *n* indicates that the subject will be found in either a footnote, a side bar, or in the "Q. M. in Action" or "Notes and Comments" sections within the body of the text.

A

Absorbing states, 715, 719
Ackoff, R. L., 2
Activities, 489, 513*n,* 514
  critical, 492, 504, 514
activity times, 506*n*
  crashing, 509–511
  project scheduling
    with known, 490–500
    with uncertain, 500–508
Addition law, 34–38, 48
Additivity, in linear programming, 224*n*
AHP. *See* Analytic hierarchal process
Airline overbooking, 31, 653–654
All-integer linear programs, 447–454,
    466*n,* 470
  graphical and computer solution for,
    449–454
Allowable decrease, 283
Allowable increase, 283, 284
Alternative optimal solutions, 247–248, 261
American Airlines, 31, 190*n*
American Production and Inventory Control
    Society (APICA), 585
American Red Cross, 682*n*
Analog models, 6, 18
analytic hierarchy process, 16, 731, 746–761
  using to develop an overall priority rank-
    ing, 755–757
  developing hierarchy in, 747–748
  establishing priorities with, 748
    consistency in, 752
    estimating the consistency ratio,
      752–753
    pairwise comparison matrix, 753–755
    pairwise comparisons, 748–750
    pairwise comparisons for the car-
      selection problem, 753–755
    procedure for synthesizing judgments
      in, 750–751
    synthesis in, 750
    using Expert Choice to implement,
      757–760
Annual cost basis, 534
Annual ordering cost, 535
Annual percentage, 534
Apollo II, 5*n*
Arbitrary service times
  multiple-channel waiting line model with,
    632–634
  single-channel waiting line model with,
    630–632

B

Backorder, 545–548, 567
  costs, 547*n,* 548*n*
Backward pass, 495, 514
Bank location problem, 448, 463–466, 470
Base-case scenario, 656, 657, 687
BASIC, 684
Bayes, Reverend Thomas, 45*n*
Bayes' Theorem, 43–49, 116
Bayesian revision, 113, 123
Bellcore, 466
Bernoulli process, 66
Best-case scenario, 656, 657, 687
Beta probability distribution, 502, 515
Bill of materials (BOM), 588–589, 605–607
  explosion, 600, 607
Binary expansion, 466*n*
Binary variables, 447, 470
  See also 0–1 variables
Binomial distribution, 59, 65–69, 95
  expected value and variance for, 68–69
Binomial probabilities table, 771–777
Binomial probability distribution, 66–68, 88
Blending problems, linear programming ap-
    plications to, 362–367
Blocking, 627, 632, 633, 639
Branch(es)
  decision tree, 101, 123
  probabilities, computing, 116–117
Break-even analysis, 14, 22
Break-even point, 14, 18, 23
Bureau of Labor Statistics, 17
Business Week, 185
  Industry Outlook survey in, 198

Arborist, The, 122*n*
Arcs, 400, 407*n,* 408, 415, 423
Arcelik A. S., 604*n*
Area, as a measure of probability, 74, 77–79
Arena, 684
Arnoff, E. L., 2
Assignment problem, 399, 406–412, 423
  integer linear programming, 448*n,* 466*n*
  network model and a linear programming
    formulation, 406–410
    a general linear programming model
      of, 411
    multiple assignments, 411–412
    problem variations, 411
    spreadsheets, 440–444
Autoregressive models, 197, 200

C

C, 684
C++, 684
Capacitated transportation problem,
    406, 423
Capacitated transshipment problem, 416,
    419*n,* 422, 423
Capacity requirements planning, 603, 607
Capital budgeting, 448, 470
Capital, cost of, 533, 566
Causal forecasting, 164, 189, 196, 200
Centered moving average, 182
Central limit theorem, 506*n*
Churchman, C. W., 2
Cincinnati Gas & Electric Company,
    217–218
Citibank, 650–651
Classical method, of assigning probabilities,
    32–34, 38
Collectively exhaustive event, 46*n*
Comfort criterion, 748
Complement of an event, 34–35, 47*n,* 48
Computer-aided process planning
    (CAPP), 604*n*
Computer-generated random numbers, 660
Computer languages, 684
Computer simulation, 16, 664, 666,
    678–679, 683–686
Computer software, 110, 122*n,* 288*n,* 498*n,*
    668*n,* 684, 686
  Expert Choice, 757–762
  LINDO, 322–23, 447, 744, 761
  Lotus 1-2-3, 22
  Microsoft Excel, 22, 94, 280, 447, 660,
    664–666, 678, 683–684
  See also Computer solutions; Management
    Scientist; Spreadsheets
Computer solutions
  for integer linear programming, 447,
    453–454, 462, 465, 466, 470,
    481–484
  for linear programming, 280–328
    assignment problems, 410, 422
    blending problems, 366
    date envelopment analysis (DEA),
      373–374
    financial applications, 340–341,
      345–346
    goal-programming models, 743–745
    interpretation of computer output,
      280–283, 284–287
    marketing, 333–334, 337–338